ALSO BY JAMES L. KUGEL

The Ladder of Jacob

The God of Old:
Inside the Lost World of the Bible

The Great Poems of the Bible:
A Reader's Companion with New Translations

The Bible as It Was

Traditions of the Bible

On Being a Jew

In Potiphar's House:
The Interpretive Life of Biblical Texts

Early Biblical Interpretation

The Idea of Biblical Poetry:
Parallelism and Its History

HOW TO READ THE BIBLE

A Guide to Scripture,
Then and Now

JAMES L. KUGEL

FREE PRESS
New York   London   Toronto   Sydney

FREE PRESS
A Division of Simon & Schuster, Inc.
1230 Avenue of the Americas
New York, NY 10020

FREE PRESS and colophon are trademarks of Simon & Schuster, Inc.

For information about special discounts for bulk purchases,
please contact Simon & Schuster Special Sales at
1-800-456-6798 or business@simonandschuster.com

Manufactured in the United States of America

1   3   5   7   9   10   8   6   4   2

Library of Congress Cataloging-in-Publication Data
Kugel, James L.
How to read the Bible : a guide to scripture, then and now / James Kugel.
        p.   cm.
Includes index.
1. Bible. O.T.—Criticism, interpretation, etc. I. Title.
BS1171.3.K84 2007
221.6—dc22   2007023466
ISBN-13: 978-0-7432-3586-0
ISBN-10:   0-7432-3586-X

ACKNOWLEDGMENTS

Though it is a bit late in life for me to be thanking my teachers, I must nonetheless begin by acknowledging the great debt I owe to two former colleagues from whom I learned a great deal during our time together. Brevard Childs of Yale and Frank M. Cross of Harvard probably do not see eye-to-eye on many of the things discussed in this book, but each has, in different ways, left his mark on the pages that follow. Along with them I must mention my first teacher at Harvard and my colleague for many years after, Isadore Twersky of blessed memory.

I wish also to record my debt of gratitude to other teachers, friends, and colleagues (some no longer of this world) who, while not all directly involved in biblical scholarship, have helped me to understand some of the central issues connected to reading the Bible today: Professors Victor Erlich, Hans Frei, Claudio Guillen, Geoffrey Hartman, John Hollander, Michael Holquist, Lawrence Rhu, Tsvetan Todorov, and Michael Walton.

More directly involved in the writing of this book have been several colleagues who kindly agreed to read over large sections of it and offered suggestions for improvement. I am indebted in particular to Professors Gary Anderson, Ed Greenstein, Gary Knoppers, Bernard Levinson, Hindy Najman, and Baruch Schwartz. My thanks as well to Bruce Nichols of the Free Press for his meticulous reading and detailed comments on every part of the manuscript. Needless to say, any errors are my responsibility alone.

Sections of this book were worked out in lectures given at various institutions, in particular my Rudin Lecture at Auburn Theological Seminary in 2002 and, somewhat more extensively, in the 2007 Shier Lectures at the University of Toronto. I am grateful for having had the opportunity to test out some of my ideas in such lively intellectual communities. My thanks go as well to Dr. Tony Michael, Wade White, Gypsy da Silva, David Kugel, and Eva Mroczek for their help in bringing this book to completion, as well as to Ms. Jenny Jones of the University of Toronto's Department of Near and Middle Eastern Studies for her assistance with various technical matters.

Some of the translations of biblical texts in this book are my own; I have otherwise incorporated parts of two outstanding modern translations, those of the New Jewish Publication Society © 1985 and the New Revised Standard Version © 1989. My thanks to the publishers of both. In some spots, the numbering of biblical verses differs slightly in Jewish and Christian Bibles; in such cases I have usually noted both numbers, the second in parentheses.

For R.

יתיב רבי שמעון ובכה ואמר וי אי גלינא וי אי גלינא וי אי לא גלינא . . . פתח ר' שמעון ואמר: עת לעשות לה' הפרו

תורתך. אמאי עת לעשות לה' משום דהפרו תורתך.

CONTENTS

PRELIMINARIES

This book is intended as a guide to, and a tour through, the Hebrew Bible. In it, I've tried to write down most of what I know about the Bible, its past as well as its present. That makes it a little different from other books on the subject.

Its first aim is to acquaint readers with the contents of the Bible itself. By the end of this book readers will have met all the major figures of the Hebrew Bible—Abraham and Sarah; Moses, Miriam, and Aaron; Deborah, Samson, David, Solomon, and so forth. The book will also cover all the major events, from the story of Adam and Eve to the exodus from Egypt, and on to the conquest of the land, the rise of the United Monarchy, the fall of Jerusalem, the Babylonian exile, and Israel's eventual return to its homeland. Along with people and events, the Bible's major passages will themselves be examined—all the most important prophecies and psalms, laws, songs, and sayings.

In going through the Bible, however, this book will focus not only on what the text says but on the larger question of what a modern reader is to make of it, *how* it is to be read. This will mean examining two quite different ways of understanding the Bible, those of modern biblical scholars and of ancient interpreters.

By *modern biblical scholars* is meant a rather specific group of people (and not all modern people who study the Bible). Starting around 150 years ago, a major effort was launched in universities and divinity schools in different countries—principally in Germany and Scandinavia, Holland, England, and the United States—to understand the Bible afresh, reading it "scientifically" and without any presuppositions. A great deal of new information had just then begun to emerge that might shed light on the world of the Bible's creation. The fledgling science of archaeology had started to probe the distant past, first uncovering individual artifacts and treasures from ancient times, later whole towns and cities. Sometimes what the archaeologists found included bits of writing—inscriptions from here and there, indeed, whole libraries of documents written by ancient Egyptians, Babylonians, and other neighboring civilizations of biblical Israel. These texts were deciphered and translated. Using this new information, biblical scholars found themselves able to trace with new accuracy the whole history of the region and fill in many of the blanks left by the Bible itself. They also began to reflect on the nature of Israelite society and its institutions in the light of these neighboring civilizations. Most of all, they set themselves to analyzing the Bible itself in a new way, trying to fit its words to the emerging historical picture and to understand when and how and for what purpose different parts of it were written.

This effort to reinterpret the Bible has been carried on with increasing intensity ever since, and it has produced spectacular results. We are now able to piece together answers to some of the most basic questions about the Bible: Where did the people of Israel come from? How did they come to believe in the existence of only one God? How did they worship Him? What do we know about specific historical events—for example, when did Moses live, and who was the wicked pharaoh that would not let the Israelites leave Egypt? Moreover, what about the Bible itself—when were its various books written, and by whom?

All these questions, and their answers, belong under the heading "modern biblical scholarship." As this book proceeds through the different parts of the Bible, it will survey most of what modern scholars have discovered about the meaning of the text and its historical background. But that is only part of the material to be studied.

Along with modern biblical scholars, this book will examine another set of interpreters, who lived long before the archaeologists, historians, and linguists came along. These are the *ancient interpreters,* a largely anonymous group of scholars who flourished from around 300 BCE to 200 CE or so. By the time the ancient interpreters came along, most of the texts that make up our Bible had been around for quite a while—many for hundreds and hundreds of years, in fact. But this was still a very important moment in the Bible's development, and these ancient interpreters played a significant role. It was a time when, as never before, the Bible had become *the* central focus of Israel's religion. Reading Scripture, and doing what it said, was now the very essence of Judaism—and in its wake, Christianity. But what *did* Scripture mean, and what was it telling people to do? For various reasons, ordinary readers did not feel capable of deciding such things. It was up to the experts—the ancient interpreters—to explain the Bible to them.

As a result, the work of these ancient interpreters proved to be tremendously significant. As will be seen, they had a rather idiosyncratic, even quirky, way of interpreting the Bible. For example, they believed that the Bible did not always say openly what it meant; it was full of cryptic hints, and when these were carefully studied, all manner of hidden meanings could be revealed. In reading this way, ancient interpreters sometimes deduced the existence of whole incidents or teachings that the Bible had never mentioned—indeed, they often "found" here and there doctrines or ideas that came into existence only centuries after the biblical text in question had been written. Their interpretations soon became *what the Bible meant*. Their explanations of different stories and laws and prophecies were passed on for centuries afterward. Institutionalized by church and synagogue, preached and sung about, depicted in floor mosaics, stained-glass windows, paintings, and statues, endlessly talked about in monasteries and on village greens, echoed in poetry and philosophy and learned discourse of all kinds, this *interpreted Bible* (that is, the Bible as explained by the ancient interpreters) was *the* Bible all throughout the Middle Ages, the Renaissance, and to a large extent, even up to today.

One might well ask: now that modern biblical scholars have come to understand what biblical texts *really* meant when they were first written down, why should anyone bother with what a group of ancient interpreters thought the Bible meant centuries later, especially if their interpretations were sometimes a bit stretched? Part of the answer has already been given. For most of our history, what the Bible meant *was* what the ancient interpreters had said it meant. Even if what they said does not match the findings of modern scholars, this does not mean that their interpretations have not been, or are not still, significant. As a matter of fact, anyone who wants to understand European painting or sculpture, or the history of Western thought, or Dante or Milton or Shakespeare or almost any writer up to the present day, must know something about the Bible as it was understood by these ancient interpreters—since that *was* the Bible.

But there is an even more important reason for studying both ancient interpreters and modern biblical scholars. In a way that will be made clear throughout this book, the ancient interpreters are still with us. Despite the rise of archaeology and other sciences, the ancient interpreters' way of reading is directly tied to some of the most basic things we still think today about the Bible—its very standing as the Word of God, and its role as a guide to daily life—as well as to our understanding of some of its most important parts, from the Garden of Eden to the prophecies of Isaiah and Daniel.

Modern readers of the Bible are thus caught between two opposite ways of reading. On the one hand, the ancient interpreters' way is crucial for what most people still wish to believe about the Bible and its message. On the other hand, the way of modern scholars, which seems to make good, scientific sense, has undermined a great deal of what those ancient interpreters said. So what are we to do? If we adopt the modern scholars' way of reading, in a very real sense the whole Bible will be undone—much of its ethical instruction, its basic commandments, prophetic visions, and heartfelt prayers will turn out to be something other than what they have always seemed; indeed, the divine inspiration of all of Scripture will be seen to be undermined. But surely we cannot simply hide our heads in the sand and pretend that modern scholarship does not exist. And so an enormous question now poses itself to both Jews and Christians: How to read the Bible? That is the subject of this book.

WARNING: This book is intended for both the specialist and the general reader, those who already have great familiarity with the Bible and those who have never read a page of it. It is my hope that any reader will be able to learn a great deal from it. But there is one group of readers who must be cautioned about its contents. Precisely because this book deals with modern biblical scholarship, many of the things it discusses contradict the accepted teachings of Judaism and Christianity and may thus be disturbing to people of traditional faith. I should say that I count myself in this group, and some of the things I will relate have indeed been disturbing to me over the years. I hesitated for a long time before deciding to pursue modern biblical scholarship as my field of study, and I hesitated even longer before deciding to commit my thoughts on it to writing. If I nonetheless went ahead, it was because I felt that it was dishonest, and ultimately would prove impossible, to hide from the central question addressed by this book. Others, of course, may feel differently. It is up to them to decide whether or not to continue.

A word about the book's format: This book comes with two sets of notes. The first contain points of information intended for the general reader. These are marked with an asterisk (*) in the text and appear at the bottom of the page. The second set of notes—marked with numbers—is intended for specialists in the field; these notes consist mostly of references to scholarly articles or books, or are discussions of technical matters not intended for the general reader. They are found at the back of this book. A few further items are of such length that it was decided not to include them in the volume itself (since their inclusion would have added considerably to its cost), but instead to post them on a Web site where interested readers may consult them. These are: (1) an appendix to this volume, "Apologetics and Biblical Criticism Lite"; (2) a bibliography of the books and articles cited in the notes; and (3) an index of the writings of ancient biblical interpreters cited in the book, briefly describing their contents and date of composition. All these may be found on the Web site jameskugel.com. The same Web site contains links to other sites and will, I hope, eventually include questions and reactions from readers as well as some further words from me.

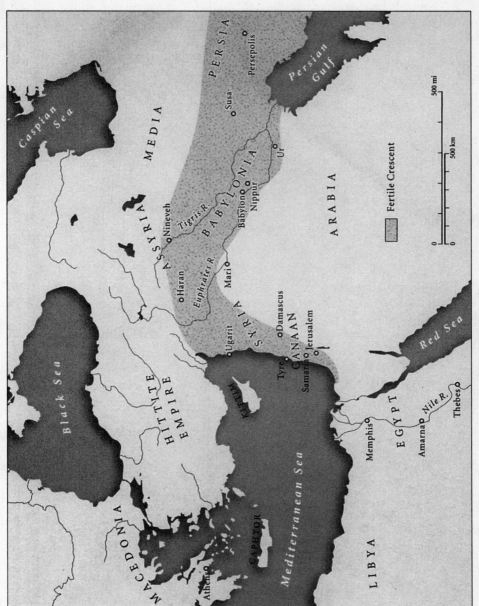

The Ancient Near East

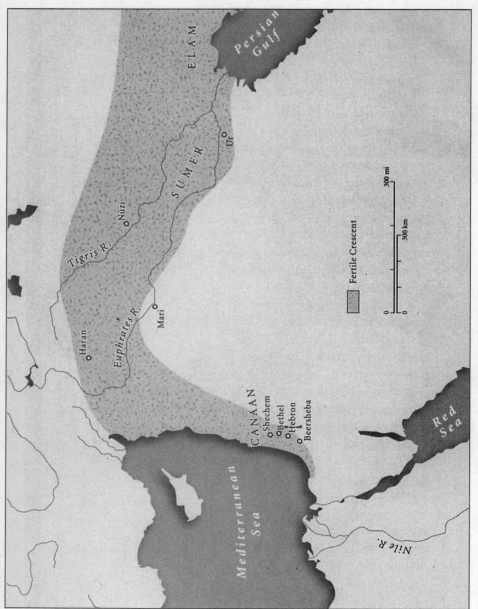

The World of the Patriarchs

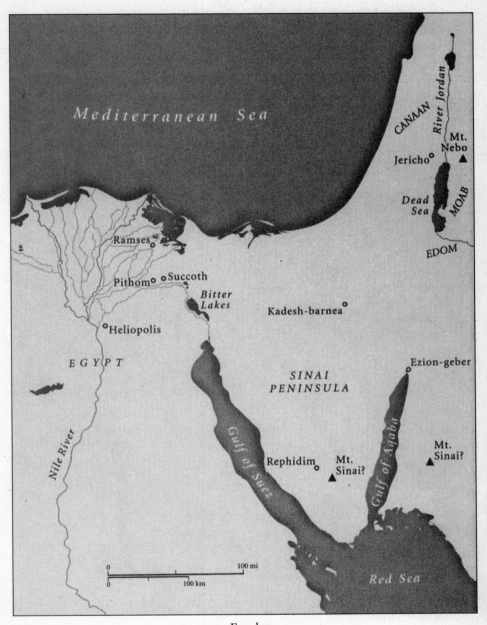

Exodus

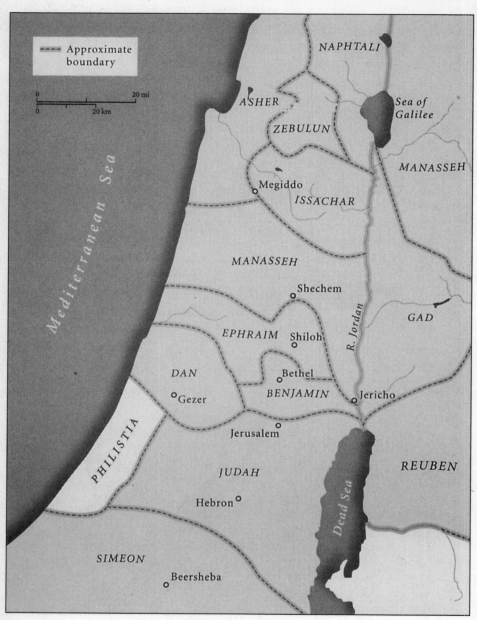

The Twelve Tribes of Israel

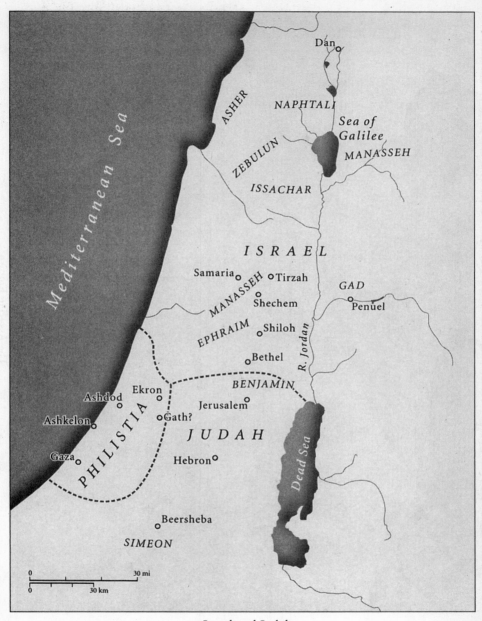

Israel and Judah

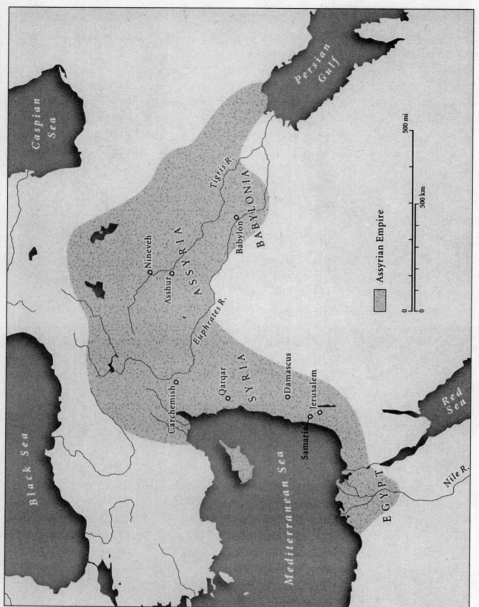

The Assyrian Empire

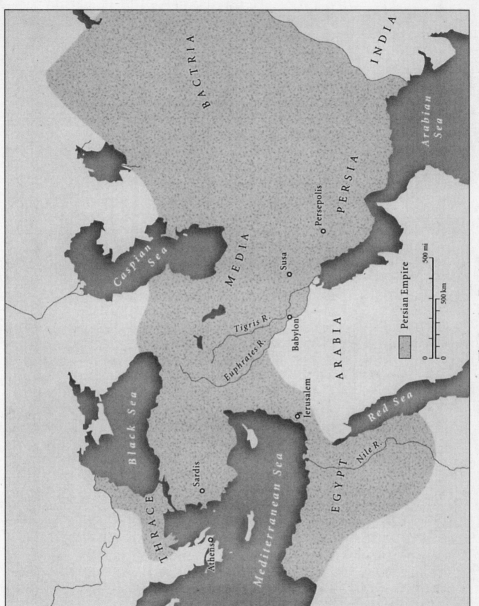

The Persian Empire

HOW TO READ
THE BIBLE

1

The Rise of Modern Biblical Scholarship

Prof. Charles Augustus Briggs, D.D., of New York.

This book is about understanding the Bible from two radically different points of view—that of the Bible's ancient interpreters and that of modern biblical scholars (see above, "Preliminaries"). But how did people go from reading the Bible one way to reading it in the other? This chapter tells that story.

On a warm May afternoon in 1893, a man stood on trial for heresy in Washington, D.C. This circumstance might in itself appear surprising. The defendant was being tried by the Presbyterian Church, which had always prided itself on its tradition of intellectualism and an educated clergy. While disagreements about church teachings were not rare in the denomination, going as far as putting a man on trial for his beliefs was certainly an extreme step.[1] Such a trial might also appear ill-suited to the end of the nineteenth century, a time of great openness to new ideas. Darwin's *Origin of Species* had been published a full three decades earlier, and Einstein's first writings on the theory of relativity were only twelve years away. America itself was a country of electric-powered machines and newfangled telephones, a rising economic and political center with its own burgeoning literary and intellectual avant-garde. Across the Atlantic, Sigmund Freud was working out his ideas on sexuality and the unconscious; Pablo Picasso was twelve years old, James Joyce was eleven, and D. H. Lawrence was eight. *Heresy?*

Still more surprising was the man in the dock; Charles Augustus Briggs hardly seemed fitted to the role of heretic. In his youth, he had been an altogether traditional Presbyterian, distinguished only by the fervor of his belief. In his sophomore year at the University of Virginia, he presented himself for formal membership at the First Presbyterian Church of Charlottesville, and thereafter he became a committed evangelical Christian.[2] The tone of his faith in those early years is well captured by a letter he wrote to his sister Millie:

> I trust you feel that you are a sinner. I trust that you know that Christ is your Savior, and I want to entreat you to go to him in prayer. I know by experience that Christ is precious, and that I would not give him up for the world. . . . Do you want to be separated from your brother and sister when they shall be with Jesus? Are you willing to be with the Devil in torment? You can decide the question in a moment.[3]

So great was Briggs's sense of calling that he soon abandoned plans to go into his father's highly prosperous business—Alanson Briggs, known as the "barrel king," owned and operated the largest barrel factory in the United States—in order to devote himself entirely to a life of Christian preaching and teaching.

Briggs proved to be a gifted student of biblical Hebrew and ancient history, and he was soon ordained a Presbyterian minister. After having served as pastor to a small congregation in New Jersey for a time, he accepted a teaching post at one of the mainline seminaries of his day, the Union Theological Seminary in New York, where he lectured on Hebrew grammar and various biblical themes. He became, by all accounts, a highly respected scholar, acclaimed at a relatively young age as already belonging to "the foremost rank among the scholars of his day." [4] Today, a century later, one of Briggs's books is still in print (a rare feat among academics!), a dictionary of biblical Hebrew that he coauthored with Francis Brown and S. R. Driver in 1906. Indeed, "BDB," as this dictionary is commonly known (for the initials of its three authors' last names), is still a required purchase for any graduate student undertaking serious work on the Hebrew Bible.

What, then, was this son of the Establishment, an expert in Hebrew lexicography and biblical theology, doing on trial? It all had to do with a speech he had made two years earlier, on the occasion of his being named to a prestigious new chair at Union Seminary. Briggs's inaugural address, delivered on the evening of January 20, 1891, went on for well more than an hour. It began innocently enough; as required of all such appointees at Presbyterian seminaries, he opened with a public declaration of his faith in the Bible and the church's system of governance:

> I believe the Scriptures of the Old and New Testaments to be the Word of God, the only infallible rule of faith and practice; and I do now, in the presence of God and the Directors of this Seminary, solemnly and sincerely receive and adopt the Westminster Confession of Faith [that is, the Presbyterian charter], as containing the system of doctrine taught in the Holy Scriptures. I do also, in like manner, approve of the Presbyterian Form of Government; and I do solemnly promise that I will not teach or inculcate anything which shall appear to me to be subversive of the said system of doctrines, or of the principles of said Form of Government, so long as I shall continue to be a Professor in the Seminary.

But as Briggs went on, he touched on some of the more controversial issues facing Presbyterians in his day, particularly those matters having to do with his specialty, the Hebrew Bible. What he had to say—new, disturbing ideas about how the Bible came to be written, and the nature of its authority, as well as its place in the life of the church—shocked some of his listeners. He said that, contrary to what was claimed by many of his coreligionists, the Bible was not *verbally inspired*—that is, there was no reason to think that each and every word of it came from God. In fact, he said, it was obvious that the Bible contained numerous errors.[5] What is more, he stated that it was now quite certain that the supposed authors of various books of the Bible—Moses and

David and Solomon and Ezra and the others—did not, in fact, write them; these books were the work of people whose true names would never be known.[6] He asserted that the things described as miracles in the Old and New Testaments could not actually have "violate[d] the laws of nature or disturb[ed] its harmonies"—thus they were not, at least in the usual sense, miracles at all. In particular, he suggested, the supposedly miraculous acts of healing recounted in the Old and New Testaments might merely have been the result of "mind cure,* or hypnotism, or [some] other occult power."[7] Finally, he pointed out that while the Bible's prophets frequently announced what God was to do in the future, many of their predictions had failed to come true; in fact, he said (a most surprising assertion for a Christian), most of the things predicted in the Old Testament about the coming of a Messiah had "not only never been fulfilled, but cannot now be fulfilled, for the reason that [their] own time has passed forever."[8]

What happened to Charles A. Briggs to cause him to say such things? The short answer is: he had become acquainted with modern biblical scholarship. Following his initial calling to the ministry, Briggs began to study the Bible in earnest, first in the United States and later in Germany, which was then the very center of modern biblical science. Once back in the United States, he had continued the line of his teachers' research with his own; during his years as a professor and scholar, he had published widely on various topics connected with the Hebrew Bible and biblical theology. Many of the things Briggs proclaimed out loud in his inaugural address were thus not altogether new—they had been building up over decades of intensive research and publication.

Still, that hardly made Briggs's assertions acceptable to everyone in the audience on that evening. Some of his listeners resented the confident, often aggressive tone of his remarks, and they liked even less his apparent endorsement of these new ideas. Despite the orthodox cast of his opening confession of faith, they found that most of his speech was anything but orthodox. Briggs seemed, they felt, out to undermine the Bible's place as the very heart of Protestant belief and practice.

The evening ended with handshakes and congratulations, but as news of Briggs's speech spread throughout the Presbyterian Church, his conservative opponents felt called upon to take action. They instituted formal proceedings within the church to have him suspended as a minister and removed from the academic chair to which he had just been appointed. No one who said such things could be considered a proper teacher for future Presbyterian ministers! The ensuing deliberations were long and complicated, moving from one judicial instance to the next. At first Briggs had been hopeful, believing that he could count on support from within the liberal wing of American Presby-

---

* The curing of a disease by the influence of the healer's mind on the patient's.

terians; but he had underestimated the strength and determination of his opponents. They pressed forward, and it was thus that Charles A. Briggs eventually found himself a defendant at the church's 1893 General Assembly in Washington, D.C., his future in the hands of the more than five hundred delegates gathered there.

The heresy trial was headline news across the country, closely followed by Americans of all faiths. (Indeed, according to one press report, a clergyman visiting India in 1892 was greeted with the query, "What is the latest phase of the Briggs case?")[9] Charles A. Briggs may have been the immediate defendant in the proceeding, but in a larger sense it was the Bible itself that stood accused. What was it, really? Was it a special book unlike any other, the very word of God? Or was it, as Briggs seemed to suggest, principally (though not exclusively) the product of human industry, indeed, the work of men who lived in a time and place far removed from our own? Are its stories really true? If they are, was not even questioning their accuracy a sacrilege—a heresy, as Briggs's accusers charged? Or was it perfectly proper for biblical scholars, like all other university-trained researchers, to pursue their theories untrammeled, looking deeply into every aspect of the Bible and letting the chips fall where they may?

As the delegates rose one by one to cast their votes at the General Assembly, many of them must have felt that they were taking a stand on the Bible's own future. What are we to believe about it from now on? And how had it happened that this basically decent man, a professing Protestant deeply committed to his church, ended up espousing beliefs that so profoundly clashed with traditional faith? The two questions are actually intertwined and a useful point of introduction to this book, since a full answer to both must begin with a look back to the time of the Bible's own origins, more than three thousand years earlier.

A Tour of the Bible

The Hebrew Bible* is actually not one book, but an anthology. No one can say for sure how old its oldest parts are; this—like so many of the things discussed by Charles Briggs that night—is a matter of dispute between religious traditionalists and modern, university-style scholars. Almost all would agree that the very oldest parts of the text go back very far, at least to some time in the tenth century BCE[§]—or considerably earlier. Its latest chapters are a little easier to date; they belong to the early second century BCE. As for the histor-

---

* "Hebrew Bible" refers to the "Old Testament" of Christianity. As mentioned, this was Charles Briggs's specialty and the focus of his speech, as it is the focus of this book. Unless otherwise indicated, the word "Bible" alone herein refers to the Hebrew Bible.

§ Before the Common Era (= BC)

ical circumstances in which its various books were written, and exactly how they came to us, this too is a matter of dispute. According to traditionalists, the first five books of the Bible (Genesis, Exodus, Leviticus, Numbers, and Deuteronomy—these books are collectively known as the *Torah* or the *Pentateuch*) were revealed by God to one man, Moses. Modern scholars are skeptical about the unity of the Pentateuch; according to them, as we shall see, these five books are actually the creation of at least four or five different authors from different periods in Israel's history.

Whichever is the case with regard to the Pentateuch, no one denies that the rest of the Bible comes from different authors—it is, and always has been, a collection of texts, a kind of literary miscellany. In fact, the word "Bible" itself indicates as much: our English term comes from what was originally a Greek plural, *ta biblía* ("the books")—this is how the Greek-speaking Jews of Alexandria in ancient times referred to Judaism's sacred library.

This library contains a range of different kinds of writings. The Pentateuch (Torah) is basically a **history** of Israel and its ancestors, starting with the very first human beings, Adam and Eve, and leading up to the time when the people of Israel were freed from slavery in Egypt and made their way to the border of the Promised Land. It is thus one long narrative, but interspersed with it are a great many **laws.** (The Ten Commandments are probably the most famous of these, but they are only one small part of the Pentateuch's legal codes.) In fact, it is principally these laws that gave the Pentateuch its special character among ancient Jews and, to a certain extent, early Christians as well. They saw in the Pentateuch a great divine guidebook, its laws constituting God's detailed set of do's and don'ts for every human life. The Pentateuch was thus read and studied more than other books of the Bible in ancient times. (For this reason, we will devote a good deal of attention to these first five books; they contain many of the best known parts of the Bible and have always occupied a special place in the hearts of its readers.)

The Pentateuch ends with the death of Moses. From there, the historical narrative follows the Israelites and their new leader, Joshua, into the land of Canaan; the conquest of that land is narrated in the book of Joshua. Other books—Judges, Samuel, Kings, Chronicles, and Ezra-Nehemiah—tell the story of Israel's subsequent history: the rise of Israel's mighty empire under David, and its subsequent split into two separate kingdoms; the conquest of the northern kingdom by the Assyrians and then of the southern kingdom by the Babylonians; the exile of the Jews to Babylon; and then the return from exile and subsequent reestablishment of their land, Judah,* under Persian rule.

---

* Judah (Hebrew: *yehuda*) is the name of the southern part of the land of Israel. The same territory was called *Judea* by ancient Greeks and Romans, and this name is also sometimes used nowadays. Its inhabitants were called *yehudim* in Hebrew, and this became the English word "Jews."

But historical narrative and laws are only two of the main categories of writing found in the Hebrew Bible. A third category consists of the pronouncements of various **prophets**—Isaiah, Jeremiah, Ezekiel, Amos, and others. Actually, prophetic speeches are themselves hardly of one sort; they include writings of different literary genres and styles. Sometimes prophets set out to reprove evildoers, and their words are full of biting sarcasm and social critique; at other times they seek to exhort the people to do what is right and warn of the dire consequences should they not. Sometimes the prophets report on their own visions or divine encounters. Words of comfort or coming judgment, reproaches aimed at Israel's neighbors or Israel's own officialdom, revelations of the future, glimpses of God's very being—all these are to be found in the writings of Israel's prophets.

In addition to these three main groupings is a fourth, fairly distinct group: the writings of Israel's **sages.** The word "sage" is intended to designate not so much a wise individual as a member of a certain class within Israel and an adherent to a certain specific outlook or set of views. The compositions of these sages are generally termed "wisdom writings," and they are to be found in the Hebrew Bible principally in three books, Proverbs, Job, and Ecclesiastes,[10] although traces of their influence have been detected elsewhere as well. The fifth and last main group of writings within the Bible consists of various **prayers and songs** of praise and thanksgiving, most notably those contained in the book of Psalms, but found elsewhere in the Bible as well. And beyond these five main groups are a number of other, minor categories—laments such as those found in the book of Lamentations, the love lyrics of the Song of Songs, the pastoral tale of Ruth, the court narrative of Esther, and yet others.

Within the Biblical Period

These writings had been transmitted from generation to generation, some of them doubtless orally for a time, but then eventually copied by hand onto parchment or papyrus. Even the most skeptical modern scholar would not deny that the oldest parts of the Bible go way back, so the fact that we possess these texts today indicates that well within the biblical period itself, they must have played some role in the life of the people—otherwise, why should anyone have bothered to remember them and keep copying them?*

In fact, scholars can make an educated guess as to who was responsible for

---

* Parchment and papyrus disintegrate fairly quickly under normal climatic conditions. Thus, in order to have survived, all but the latest parts of the Bible would have had to be recopied numerous times within the biblical period. If such effort was expended, it certainly must not have been done in vain—the texts must have had some role in society, in people's daily lives.

the preservation of these texts. Kings, no doubt, kept much of the historical material, not only for the sake of record keeping but, quite probably, for political reasons as well: the public reading of Israel's history might help maintain national unity and a sense of common identity, or rally people to this or that cause. Ordinary folk must likewise have taken pleasure in retelling by heart the tales of past heroes and significant events in history. Judges and other officials were certainly the guardians and preservers of laws. Priests had their own texts—instructions about performing this or that rite and other things of special concern to them. Some historical texts may also have been in the possession of priests, especially if the texts played a regular role in the celebration of Israel's religious festivals and other occasions at which priests officiated. The psalms were certainly recited as part of Israel's religious life, in temples and at other sacred sites; priests and other officials no doubt had charge of them too, though eventually the psalms may have moved to less formal settings, perhaps even to the homes of private individuals. The main concern of sages (some of whom were employees of the court) was mastering the wisdom of the past—they were thus most likely responsible for the survival of wisdom texts.

Not only did these texts survive in such different milieus, but they were no doubt also explained and commented upon there, supplemented now and again to bring them up to date or to make understandable a word or phrase or reference that had passed from common knowledge. In this sense, the Bible—or, rather, the books that were to become the Bible—had probably always been *interpreted* in some fashion. But there came a moment in history when interpretation of these texts suddenly became a great preoccupation in Israel, and a whole new kind of interpreter first emerged.

The Rise of the Ancient Interpreters

To understand why, at a certain point, the interpretation of these ancient texts became highly significant, it is necessary to mention a singularly important event in Israel's history: the Babylonian exile. In 586 BCE—long after the time of Israel's founders, Abraham and his descendants, and long after the time of some of the nation's greatest figures, Moses and Joshua and King David and King Solomon and all those who followed them—the city of Jerusalem fell into the hands of an invading army from Babylon. This was a cataclysmic event for the Jews: not only were they now a conquered people, but many of them, including the country's leadership, were forcibly relocated to Babylon (lest they regroup and rebel against the Babylonians). The exiles included, prominently, most of the country's political and intellectual leaders; for more than half a century they sat as virtual prisoners in a foreign land, powerless to return to Jerusalem.

When salvation came at last, it took the form of a new, upstart empire. The Persians, neighbors of Babylon, gathered their forces and, in surprisingly short order, overcame the Babylonian army. In so doing they took control not only of Babylon itself, but of its foreign holdings as well—including Jerusalem. Shortly thereafter, in 538 BCE, the Persian emperor Cyrus issued a decree allowing the Jews to return to their homeland. Many did so, and Jewish life started up again in its old setting.

But the period of exile had had a lasting effect on the people. To begin with, as with any such upheaval, the Babylonian episode had reshuffled the political deck. The returning exiles were not of one mind as to what should happen next: Who was to rule Judah—some member of the former royal family, or the priests who had controlled the (now-destroyed) temple, or yet some other group? And should the returnees—as the Persians expected—settle meekly into being a minor province in the Persian Empire, under the control of a distant regime? Or should they wait for the opportunity to gain a measure of political autonomy, even independence?

What is interesting is the role that Israel's ancient texts played in the debate over such questions. Perhaps it was the very fact of *returning* that brought people to evoke the past in trying to determine what to do in the future.[11] After all, some of the Jewish exiles had decided that returning to Zion was not for them; they stayed in Babylon. Those who made the long journey back to Judah were thus a self-selected group, eager, in one sense or another, to go back to what had been before—not just to the land itself, but to everything that living on that land had come to represent in their minds. In other words, returning to their homeland was, by the very nature of things, an attempt to resurrect the past. But what exactly *was* that past—how had things been arranged before? You could not pick up an old boulder and ask it about life before the exile; you could not interrogate the trees. It was Israel's own library of ancient texts that seemed to hold the answers to such questions—records of centuries of historical events as well as the weighty pronouncements of ancient prophets and sages. So different groups, even as they argued with one another as to the proper course to follow, used these ancient writings to bolster their positions.

We know this in particular from one biblical book that was composed at that time, the book of Chronicles. Essentially, Chronicles is a book about the glorious past—it retells in its own words many of the events recounted elsewhere in the Bible, especially in the books of Samuel and Kings. But in so doing, the author of Chronicles deliberately introduced changes in his sources, so that modern scholars have been able to find a whole political program hidden in his rewriting.[12] This author was, for example, in favor of a future union with Judah's neighbors to the north, and he dreamt of a time when the yoke of fealty to the Persians might be thrown off. He was also a firm supporter of the Davidic monarchy and looked forward to the day of its restoration to the throne. He also had his own ideas about theology and about the role of priests and others in the future state. Yet none of this was put forward as a political program as such; instead, he proposed what he proposed through a fictional retelling of things that happened long ago. The past, in other words, was to determine what would be in the future, and saying what had been was thus potentially an act of great political significance.[13]

For this same reason, the interpreters of Scripture became increasingly important figures in Israel after the Babylonian exile. Since ancient texts were being looked to for guidance about the future, part of the interpreter's job became specifically to trace a dotted line between past and present and say precisely what was to be concluded *for us* from this or that ancient text. It was not just Israel's historical books that were so scrutinized, but the entire library. Do the words of this ancient prophet or that ancient sage have any implications for our present situation?

It is difficult to overstate the importance of this change. From now on, the books in Israel's sacred library would have a new role: these books may have been written long ago, but they were not just about things that happened in the past. Carefully analyzed, the words of these ancient texts might reveal a message about how people ought to arrange their affairs now and in the future.

The Ancient Interpreters at Work

Who were the interpreters of these ancient writings?[14] For the most part, their names are unknown. From their writings and from their whole approach to interpreting Scripture, it would appear that most of them were teachers or professional sages of sorts;[15] some were probably independently wealthy men (and, possibly, women) who had the leisure to pursue their subject.[16] Indeed, we know that a few, like the second-century BCE sage Ben Sira, belonged to the ruling class and were close to the political leadership (Sir. 39:4; 50:1–24); such figures no doubt strengthened the connection between reading Scripture and determining how community affairs were to be run in their own day. Their ideas about how Scripture is to be interpreted have survived in a number of texts belonging to the end of the biblical period—texts like the Dead Sea Scrolls* and the biblical apocrypha and pseudepigrapha[§]— as well as in somewhat later writings such as those of early Christians and the founders of rabbinic Judaism.

---

* A trove of ancient manuscripts first discovered in 1948 near the shores of the Dead Sea. The manuscripts, many of which go back to the third and second centuries BCE, include numerous texts that interpret the Bible or otherwise reflect then-current interpretations.

§ Books written toward the end of the biblical period but ultimately excluded from the Jewish biblical canon. They include such works as the book of Judith, the Wisdom of Solomon, and the book of *Jubilees*.

The manner in which ancient interpreters read and explained Scripture is at first likely to strike modern readers as a bit strange. They did not go about the job of interpreting the way we do nowadays. Take, for example, the famous biblical story of how God ordered Abraham to sacrifice his son Isaac on an altar:

> And it came to pass, after these things, that God tested Abraham. He said to him, "Abraham!" and he answered, "Here I am." He said, "Take your son, your only son Isaac, whom you love, and go to the land of Moriah. Then sacrifice him there as a burnt offering on one of the mountains that I will show you." So Abraham got up early in the morning and saddled his donkey. He took two of his servants with him, along with his son Isaac; he cut the wood for the burnt offering and then set out for the place that God had told him about. On the third day, Abraham looked up and saw the place from afar. Abraham told his servants, "You stay here with the donkey while the boy and I go up there, so that we can worship and then come back to you."
>
> Abraham took the wood for the burnt offering and put it on his son Isaac; then he took the fire and the knife, and the two of them walked together. But Isaac said to his father Abraham, "Father?" and he said, "Here I am, my son." And he said, "Here is the fire and the wood, but where is the lamb for the burnt offering?" Abraham said, "God Himself will provide the lamb for the burnt offering, my son." And the two of them walked together.
>
> When they came to the place that God had told him about, Abraham built an altar and arranged the wood on it. He then tied up his son Isaac and put him on the altar on top of the wood. Abraham picked up the knife to kill his son. But an angel of the LORD called to him from heaven, and said, "Abraham, Abraham!" And he said, "Here I am." He said, "Do not harm the boy or do anything to him. For now I know that you fear God, since you have not withheld your son, your only son, from me." And Abraham looked up and saw a ram caught in a thicket by its horns. Abraham went and took the ram and sacrificed it as a burnt offering instead of his son.
>
> Gen. 22:1–13

The story itself is quite disturbing to modern readers—as it was to ancient readers. How could God, even as a test, order someone to kill his own son? And why would God ever *need* to test Abraham in this way? After all, God is supposed to know everything: presumably, He knew how the test would come out before it took place, and He certainly already knew that Abraham was one who "feared God," as the angel says after the test is over. Equally disturbing is the way Abraham deceives his son Isaac. He does not tell him what God has told him to do; Isaac is kept in the dark until the last minute. In fact, when Isaac asks the obvious question—I see all the accoutrements for the sacrifice, but where is the animal we're going to sacrifice?—Abraham gives him an evasive answer: "God Himself will provide the lamb for the burnt offering, my son." This actually turns out to be true; God does provide a sacrificial animal—but Abraham had no way of knowing it at the time.

Modern readers generally take these things at face value and then either wrestle with their implications or else just shrug their shoulders: "Well, I guess that's just the way things were back then." But ancient interpreters instead set out to give the text the most favorable reading they could and, in some cases, to try to get it to say what they thought it really meant to say, or at least ought to say. They did this by combining an extremely meticulous examination of its words with an interpretive freedom that sometimes bordered on the wildly inventive.

Thus, in the case at hand, they noticed that the first sentence began, "And it came to pass, after these things." Such phrases are often used in the Bible to mark a transition; they generally signal a break, "The previous story is over and now we are going on to something new." But the word "things" in Hebrew also means "words." So the transitional phrase here could equally well be understood as asserting that some *words* had been spoken, and that "it came to pass, *after these words,* that God tested Abraham." What words? The Bible did not say, but if some words had indeed been spoken, then interpreters felt free to try to figure out what the words in question might have been.

At this point, some ancient interpreter—we have no idea who—thought of another part of the Bible quite unrelated to Abraham, the book of Job. That book begins by reporting that Satan once challenged God to test His servant Job. Since the story of Abraham and Isaac is also a divine test, interpreters theorized that the *words* mentioned in the opening sentence of our passage might have been, as in the book of Job, a challenge spoken by Satan to God: "Put Abraham to the test and see whether he is indeed obedient enough even to sacrifice his own son." If one reads the opening sentence with this in mind, "And it came to pass, after these *words,* that God tested Abraham," then the problem of why God should have tested Abraham disappears. Of course God knew that Abraham would pass the test—but if He nevertheless went on to test Abraham, it was because some *words* had been spoken by Satan challenging God to prove Abraham's worthiness.

As for Abraham hiding his intentions from Isaac—well, again it all depends how you read the text. Ancient interpreters noticed that the passage contains a slight repetition:

Abraham took the wood for the burnt offering and put it on his son Isaac; then he took the fire and the knife, *and the two of them walked together.*

But Isaac said to his father Abraham, "Father?" and he said, "Here I am, my son." And he said, "Here is the fire and the wood, but where is the lamb for the burnt offering?" Abraham said, "God Himself will provide the lamb for the burnt offering, my son." *And the two of them walked together.*

Repetition is not necessarily a bad thing, but ancient interpreters generally felt that the Bible would not repeat itself without purpose. Between the two occurrences of "and the two of them walked together" is the brief exchange in which Abraham apparently hides his true intentions from Isaac. But Abraham's words were, at least potentially, ambiguous. Since biblical Hebrew was originally written without punctuation marks or even capital letters marking the beginnings of sentences, Abraham's answer to Isaac could actually be read as two sentences: "God Himself will provide. The lamb for the burnt offering [is]* my son." Read in this way, Abraham's answer to Isaac was not an evasion but the brutal truth: you're the sacrifice. If, following that, the text adds, "And the two of them walked together," this would not be a needless repetition at all: Abraham told Isaac that he was to be the sacrifice and Isaac *agreed;* then the two of them "walked together" in the sense that they were now of one mind to carry out God's fearsome command.

By interpreting the story in this fashion, ancient interpreters solved two of the major problems raised by this account, God's apparent ignorance of how the test would turn out and Abraham's apparent callousness and evasiveness vis-à-vis Isaac. But did these interpreters actually believe their own interpretations? Didn't they know they were playing fast and loose with the text's real meaning?

This is always a difficult question. I personally believe that, at least at first, ancient interpreters were sometimes quite well aware that they were distorting the straightforward meaning of the text. But with time, that awareness began to dim. Biblical interpretation soon became an institution in ancient Israel; one generation's interpretations were passed on to the next generation, and eventually they acquired the authority that time and tradition always grant. *Midrash,* as this body of interpretation came to be called,§ simply became what the text had always been intended to communicate. Along with the interpretations themselves, the interpreters' very modus operandi acquired its own authority: this was how the Bible was to be interpreted, period. Moreover, since the midrashic method of searching the text carefully for hidden implica-

---

* Hebrew has no verb "to be" in the present tense; thus, this sentence would be the same whether or not the word "is" is supplied in translation.

§ "Interpretation" is probably the best one-word translation of this Hebrew word, but *midrash* had a particular connotation: it was *non-obvious* interpretation. Any fool could tell you that God had tested Abraham; it took a skilled interpreter to show what words in the text hinted at why He had wanted to, as well as at Isaac's willing participation in the episode.

tions seemed to solve so many problems in the Bible that otherwise had no solution, this indicated that the interpreters were going about things correctly. As time went on, new interpretations were created on the model of older ones, until soon every chapter of the Bible came accompanied by a host of clever explanations that accounted for any perceived difficulty in its words.

The Four Assumptions

Readers always approach texts with certain assumptions, and the assumptions change depending on what they are reading; not every text is thought to *mean* in the same way. Thus, when we read a poem in which the poet says to his beloved, "I faint! I die!" we know he's not really dying; likewise, when he says he's wallowing in love in the same way that a cooked fish is wallowed in galantine sauce, well . . . we know this isn't really intended as an exact description of his emotional state. And it is not just poems. Novels and short stories, form letters and radio commercials and last wills and testaments—all sorts of different compositions come with their own conventions, and we as readers are aware of those conventions and interpret the texts accordingly. We expect to be amused by a stand-up comedian's recitation of his woes, and so we laugh in all the right places; yet if a somewhat similar monologue is spoken by a patient at his group therapy session, people will probably not laugh, in part because they bring an entirely different set of expectations to his "text." (Also, they don't want to hurt his feelings.)

It is a striking fact that all ancient interpreters seem to have shared very much the same set of expectations about the biblical text. No one ever sat down and formulated these assumptions for them—they were simply assumed, just like our present-day assumptions about how we are to understand texts uttered by poets and group-therapy patients. However, looking over the vast body of ancient interpretations of different parts of the Bible, we can gain a rather clear picture of what their authors were assuming about the biblical text—and what emerges is that, despite the geographic and cultural distance separating some of these interpreters from others, they all seem to have assumed the same four basic things about *how* the Bible was to be read:

1. They assumed that the Bible was a fundamentally cryptic text: that is, when it said A, often it might really mean B. Thus, when it said, "And it came to pass after these things," even though that might look like the familiar transitional phrase, what it might really mean was "after these *words*." Indeed, this text, they felt, was so cryptic that it did not even say what the words were—it had left it to the interpreters themselves to remember the book of Job and so figure out the rest. Similarly, when the Bible repeated "and the two of them walked together,"

the second occurrence of this phrase had a hidden meaning: Abraham and Isaac had agreed and now proceeded as if of one mind.

2. Interpreters also assumed that the Bible was a book of lessons directed to readers in their own day. It may seem to talk about the past, but it is not fundamentally history. It is instruction, telling us what to do: be obedient to God just as Abraham was and you will be rewarded, just as he was. Ancient interpreters assumed this not only about narratives like the Abraham story but about every part of the Bible. For example, Isaiah's prophecies about the Assyrian crisis contained, interpreters believed, a message for people in their own time (five or six centuries later). Likewise, when the book of Nahum had referred metaphorically to a "raging lion," the text was not talking about some enemy in Nahum's own day, but about Demetrius III, who was the king of Syria six hundred years later, in the time of the ancient interpreters.[17] Similarly, the Bible's laws were understood as being intended for people to obey in the interpreters' own time, even though they had been promulgated in a very different society many centuries earlier.

3. Interpreters also assumed that the Bible contained no contradictions or mistakes. It is perfectly harmonious, despite its being an anthology; in fact, they also believed that everything that the Bible says ought to be in accord with the interpreters' own religious beliefs and practices (since they believed these to have been ordained by God). Thus, if the Bible seemed to imply that God was not all-knowing or that Abraham had been callous and deceitful with his son, interpreters would not say that this story reflected beliefs about God or basic morality that had changed since ancient times. Instead, they stoutly insisted that there must be some way of understanding the Bible's words so as to remove any such implications: that cannot be what the Bible really intended! And of course the Bible ought not to contradict itself or even seem to repeat itself needlessly, so that if it said "and the two of them walked together" twice, the second occurrence cannot be merely repetitive; it must mean something different from the first. In short, the Bible, they felt, is an utterly consistent, seamless, perfect book.

4. Lastly,* they believed that the entire Bible is essentially a divinely given text, a book in which God speaks directly or through His prophets. There could be little doubt about those parts of the Bible that openly identify the speaker as God: "And the LORD spoke to Moses, say-

* I have mentioned this assumption last to avoid giving the impression that the other three are a natural by-product of the fourth. Actually, there is no reason to assume that a divinely given text ought to be *cryptic,* for example—on the contrary, would not God want His words to be easily understood by all? Moreover, while the first three assumptions are amply attested among the earliest of the ancient interpreters, that is not necessarily true of the fourth.

ing . . ." "Thus says the LORD, the God of Israel . . ." But interpreters believed that this was also true of the story of Abraham and the other stories in Genesis, even though the text itself never actually said there that God was the author of these stories. And it was held to be true of the rest of the Bible too—even of the book of Psalms, although the psalms themselves are prayers and songs addressed *to* God and thus ought logically not to have come *from* God. Nevertheless, most interpreters held the psalms to be in some sense of divine origin, written under divine inspiration or guidance or even directly dictated to David, their traditional author.[18]

How these assumptions came into existence is hard to say for sure, and in any case that question need not detain us here;[19] the fact is, they did come into existence, even before Israel's ancient library of sacred texts began to be called the Bible, in fact, even before its precise table of contents had been determined.

What are modern readers to make of these assumptions? Many readers will balk at the ancient interpretation of the Abraham and Isaac story given above, indeed, at many of the interpretations mentioned in this book. But it is simply in the nature of assumptions in general that they are *assumed,* not consciously adopted. Once biblical interpretation had started along the path of these Four Assumptions, it developed a logic, and a momentum, of its own. This was simply how the Bible was to be understood. The power and persuasiveness of these assumptions may be clearer if one considers that, to a remarkable degree, they continue to color the way people read the Bible right down to the present day (even if nowadays they may lead to somewhat different conclusions from those advanced by the ancient interpreters). Thus, many modern-day Jews and Christians continue to look to the Bible as a guidebook for daily life (Assumption 2); they do not read it as if it were just a relic from the ancient past. In fact, a significant number of contemporary Jews and Christians seek to act on a daily basis in accordance with the Bible's specific exhortations and laws, and many view the Bible's prophecies as being fulfilled in the events of today's world (another aspect of Assumption 2). Without quite saying so, quite a few readers also generally assume that the Bible has some sort of coherent message to communicate and that it does not contradict itself or contain mistakes (Assumption 3). Many also believe that the Bible's meaning is not always obvious (Assumption 1)—it even seems *deliberately* cryptic sometimes, they say. And the idea of divine inspiration, in fact, the conception of the Bible as a whole as the word of God (Assumption 4), is an article of faith in a great many denominations.

Thus, whatever one thinks of the Four Assumptions, there is no denying their staying power. What is more, some of the interpretations they gave rise to have demonstrated a comparable durability: to a degree not generally recognized, these interpretations are still with us and have actually succeeded in changing the meaning of quite a few biblical stories. As will be seen presently, the story of Adam and Eve only became "the Fall of Man" thanks to these ancient interpretive assumptions; the book of Genesis says nothing of the kind. The same is true of many other things that people have always believed the Bible says—that Abraham was the one who discovered that there is only one God, that David was a pious king who wrote the book of Psalms, or that the Song of Solomon speaks of God's love for His people. The Bible says these things only if it is read in accordance with the Four Assumptions. That is why, even today, trampling on these assumptions can get people's hackles up—Charles A. Briggs was neither the first nor the last modern scholar to learn that lesson.

Early Christian Interpreters

Jewish biblical interpretation has its own long and fascinating history. Starting from the Four Assumptions, it grew into the great body of rabbinic midrash in the early centuries of the common era, then developed further in the Middle Ages, branching off into philosophical, mystical, and other schools of interpreting Scripture. In another context it would be interesting to trace this evolution in some detail. But here our focus is on the rise of modern biblical scholarship. While Jews eventually came to play a role in that scholarship, it was at first mostly a Christian affair.

In its early stages, Christian biblical interpretation was not very different from Jewish interpretation. Since most of the first Christians were Jews, they not only read and studied the Bible in Hebrew but quite naturally adopted the interpretations and interpretive methods that Jews had been using for some time. About Abraham and Isaac, for example, Christians likewise maintained that God knew the outcome of the test before it began and that Isaac was well aware that he was to be the sacrificial victim. But gradually, Christianity acquired its own style of interpretation; building on elements in the Jewish approach to Scripture, its way of reading nonetheless became distinct.

One interpretive tactic that came to characterize Christian interpretation—reading the Bible allegorically—had originated with the Jews of Alexandria. Alexandria is a city on the Mediterranean coastline of Egypt, named after Alexander the Great, whose armies conquered Egypt (and the rest of the ancient Near East) in the late fourth century BCE. This is no insignificant detail: Alexandria became a magnificent Greek-style city, with Greek governmental institutions, Greek schools and theaters and gymnasia, and Greek as its official language. The Jews of Alexandria also came to be Hellenized; soon, they were thoroughly Greek in their education and outlook. Thus, when they read the books of the Bible, it was in Greek translation; most likely, many of them knew not a word of Hebrew. In seeking to interpret the Bible, they also went about things in a thoroughly Greek way. They allegorized it.

Allegorizing is the technique by which concrete details in a text—people, events, places in which things occur—are explained as representing abstract entities, ideas, or virtues or vices or philosophical doctrines. The practice of allegorizing seems to stem from the central part that the poetry of Homer came to play in Greek education: for Greeks, Homer was *the* text and constituted the average person's road to literacy and high culture. But as time went on, using the *Iliad* or the *Odyssey* as a primer for young minds came to be problematic: scenes of seduction or moral turpitude were especially troubling. Moreover, it bothered teachers that these central Greek writings did not contain any evidence of the things that later Greek civilization had come to believe essential—well-known teachings and philosophical doctrines and so forth. They therefore frequently resorted to "finding" such things in Homer even when they were not there, while at the same time eliminating parts that seemed objectionable by the same, allegorizing method: this concrete X or Y actually represents that abstract A or B.

Such an approach was of course tempting for Jews as well; their basic text, the Torah and other books of the Bible, presented a similar range of problems—not only biblical figures who seemed sometimes to act contrary to accepted norms, but laws that were no longer understood or seemed irrelevant in later times, as well as prophecies about nations that had long ago ceased to exist. Allegorizing offered a way of making such things seem relevant and up-to-date, indeed, true and noble and good.

This method of reading was followed—indeed, pursued at great length and with great panache—by the Jewish biblical commentator Philo of Alexandria (ca. 30 BCE–ca. 55 CE). A number of examples of Philo's allegorical way of reading the Bible will appear in the following chapters, but the essence of his approach can be summarized in just one example, the opening sentence of Philo's commentary on the story of Abraham's departure from his home town of Ur:

> The departure from home as depicted by the literal text of Scripture was made by a certain wise man [Abraham]; but according to the rules of allegory, [it is made] by the soul [of anyone] fond of virtue who is searching for the true God.

Here, Philo admits that the biblical story in Genesis is literally talking about an event from the past, the time when "a certain wise man," Abraham, left his home in Ur. But taken allegorically, the text is really not talking about Abraham at all, but about the human soul. Any soul in search of God, Philo goes on to say, must, like Abraham, leave its "home," the world of trusting only in the senses of sight, hearing, and so forth; such a soul must migrate to another "city," that is, to another way of perceiving. So, while the Bible literally means what it says about Abraham and other figures, it also has a deeper meaning, an "under-meaning" (*huponoia*), as Philo sometimes calls it, and it is this allegorical sense that is truly significant nowadays.

This same allegorical way of reading was picked up by early Christians. For example, Clement of Alexandria (ca. 150–ca. 215 CE), a careful reader of Philo, at one point comments on an agricultural law of the Bible that stipulates that the fruit of a newly planted tree is not to be eaten for the first three years (Lev. 19:23):

> This image of husbandry may [also] be taken as a kind of instruction, teaching that we ought to eradicate [destructive] sins and the barren weeds of the mind, which spring up alongside the productive fruit, until the shoot of faith has matured and grown strong.
>
> *Stromateis* 2.96.1

In other words, the newly planted fruit mentioned by the Bible really represents religious faith, which requires special nurturing in its first years, until it has become sufficiently strong for its owner to enjoy its fruits.[20]

Allegorical interpretations such as this one suited Christians not only because they helped make the Bible relevant (Christians eventually cared little about the Bible's agricultural laws, but a great deal about nurturing religious faith), but because allegorizing turned everything in the Bible that was particular and historical into something more general and immediately applicable. If you were a Greek-speaking convert to Christianity, even the name "Abraham" was foreign-sounding and hard to pronounce, and what this ancestor of the Jews did or did not do had no obvious connection to you and your life. But if Abraham represented any soul in search of God, then the passage was, in this sense, about you. On a more practical level, there also existed a great body of such allegorical interpretations that had been written in your own language, Greek, by an authoritative Jewish interpreter, Philo of Alexandria.[21] For both reasons, Philo's works were studied carefully by early Christians and his allegorical methods were adopted in the early church.

Connecting to the New Testament

Christianity differed from Judaism, of course, principally in its belief in Jesus and the events described in the gospels of the New Testament. From the very beginning, Christians had argued that these events had in fact been predicted by the Bible itself, in the prophecies of Isaiah and the psalms of David. (This, it will be recognized, was an application of the second of the Four

Assumptions, that the Bible is not merely about the past but is directed to readers in their own day.) Indeed, early Christians saw great importance in the uncovering of any hidden references to the life of Jesus in Old Testament texts; for them, such references were nothing less than proof of the veracity of their faith.

But soon, this search for biblical predictions spread from overt prophecy to biblical narratives and songs and even laws. These too, Christians felt, sometimes seemed to refer to events of the New Testament. For example, the same story of Abraham and Isaac soon came to be read as a cryptic foreshadowing, a divine prediction of the crucifixion hidden in ancient Scripture. After all, if Jesus was the son of God, then God must have known that His beloved son would be killed and yet did not intervene to spare him, just as Abraham had accepted that his son be killed and did not withhold him. In fact, some early Christians viewed the crucifixion not merely as an act of killing, but as a sacrifice of the "Lamb of God" to expiate sin once and for all. If so, God's order to offer up Isaac *as a sacrifice* thus seemed to suggest a closer parallel. Moreover, Isaac, as he proceeded to the designated place, carried the wood for the sacrifice (Gen. 22:6), just as Jesus was reported to have carried his own cross (John 19:17). Even the ram that Abraham eventually sacrificed in place of Isaac reminded interpreters of the crucifixion: Abraham had been able to sacrifice the ram because it was "caught in a [thorny] thicket by its horns" (Gen. 22:12), whereas Jesus had been mocked with a crown of thorns before he died. The early Christian interpreter Augustine of Hippo (354–430) summed up these connections. (He begins, however, by asserting—just as earlier Jewish interpreters had—that God had gone along with Abraham's test only to demonstrate *to others* that he was faithful.)

> Abraham was tested with the offering of his beloved son Isaac in order to prove his faithful obedience and so make it known to the world, not to God. . . . Comparing [Jesus to Isaac,] the apostle [Paul] says that [God] "did not *withhold* His own son . . ." [Rom. 8:32; the same word "withhold" is used by the angel in Gen. 22:12]. . . . For the same reason, Isaac himself carried to the place of the sacrifice the wood on which he was to be offered up, just as the Lord himself carried his own cross. Finally, since Isaac was not killed—for his father had been forbidden to kill him—who was that ram that was offered instead, by whose foreshadowing blood the sacrifice was accomplished? For when Abraham had caught sight of him, he was caught by the horns in a thicket. Who then did he represent but Jesus, who, before he was offered up, had been crowned with thorns?
>
> *City of God* 16:32

This way of reading Old Testament texts is usually described as *typological,* since it sees the people and events of the Old Testament as foreshadowings, or "types," of people or events in the New Testament. Eventually, almost any-one or anything became a potential foreshadowing: Adam, Abel, Isaac, Jacob, Moses, Joshua, and other figures from the Hebrew Bible were all thought in one way or another to represent Jesus, and numerous incidents besides the offering of Isaac were thought to prefigure the crucifixion. It was not just the New Testament per se that the Old Testament foreshadowed, but later Christian teachings and practices as well. For example, the idea of the Trinity (never actually presented as God's very nature in the New Testament, but adopted as Christian doctrine later on) was found to be foreshadowed in the "three men" who appear to Abraham in Gen. 18:2, or in the threefold repetition of the word "holy" in Isa. 6:3.

The typological and allegorical ways of reading Scripture obviously differ in their orientation. One might describe allegorizing as "vertical," moving up from the concrete to the abstract or from the physical to the spiritual, while the typological reading is "horizontal," moving from earlier things to later ones. But both approaches see the details of the Bible as representative of something else, and both fundamentally embody the same Four Assumptions of earlier interpreters: the Bible is cryptic, relevant, perfect, and divinely granted. Also shared with earlier interpreters was the overall idea that this way of reading was superior to taking the text at face value. The allegorical and typological approaches soon gained great prestige.[22] Together they came to be known as the "spiritual sense" of Scripture, as opposed to its mere "lit-eral sense."

The Letter and the Spirit

The first-century apostle Paul had unwittingly given an extra boost to the prestige of this spiritual sense. As one of Christianity's earliest and most dili-gent exponents, he had visited and corresponded with different Christian communities along the eastern Mediterranean; his letters became an impor-tant part of the New Testament. In these letters, he sometimes highlighted what he saw as the basic difference between the two faiths, the Judaism in which he had been raised and the new faith of Christianity. These were, he said, based on two different ways of relating to God, two covenants: the for-mer was a covenant based on keeping the laws of the Torah, the latter on divine grace. Here is how he put things succinctly in his second letter to the Corinthians: "God . . . has made us competent to be ministers of a new covenant, not of the letter but of the spirit; for the letter kills, but the Spirit gives life" (3:6). By "letter" Paul meant the laws that were written down in the Torah (in his Greek, *gramma* could mean both an individual letter of the alphabet and a whole written document, even a book). While following that written text was essential in the religion in which Paul had been raised, the new covenant of Christianity required only faith in God and His grace. Thus, this new covenant of Christianity was one "not of the letter but of the spirit."

But soon enough, Paul's words came to be misunderstood. They were taken to describe not two different ways of relating to God, two covenants, but two different ways of reading Scripture. Reading Scripture "according to the letter" meant taking it literally, in its plain sense. Since Paul had connected the "letter" with the old covenant of Judaism, Christians now began to associate Jews with reading literally. (In fact, however, the whole brief history we have been tracing says exactly the opposite. Midrash is anything but literal—it is often wildly imaginative.) Christianity, on the other hand, was understood as the religion of non-literalism—to find the spiritual sense, you had to look for some hidden allegorical or typological meaning, and preferring this spiritual meaning to the literal one now seemed to have Paul's official seal of approval. Such ideas were made explicit by the early Christian scholar Origen (ca. 185–254), who was a champion of allegorical interpretation; he passed on these ideas to later Christianity.

From the time of Origen on, this manifold spiritual sense was what commentators and interpreters pursued. Origen himself was eventually judged to have gone too far—much of his biblical interpretation was condemned and banned; some works were destroyed in their original Greek version and have only survived thanks to their Latin translations. But the allegorical and typological approaches championed by Origen and many others were too deeply embedded in the fabric of Christianity to be challenged—Christian interpreters like Augustine guaranteed that the pursuit of the multilayered "spiritual meaning" would continue for centuries afterward. Even with the Protestant Reformation, when so many of the earlier ideas of the Catholic Church (including ideas about interpretation) were challenged by the Reformers, the idea of the text's spiritual sense survived in the writings of the Reformation's early leaders; it played an important part, for example, in shaping the thought of Martin Luther about Scripture.[23]

Soon enough, Christians set out to systematize the spiritual sense of Scripture and broaden its implications. The allegorical and typological ways of reading both sought out hidden meanings, but they were different from each other. And even allegory was not just one way of reading—there were different possibilities for carrying out the abstract-for-concrete method: Abraham could represent the human soul, but he also could represent something on a different level of abstraction—a virtue, for example, or an approach to learning. Eventually, Christian thinkers sought to develop clearer definitions for the various spiritual senses of Scripture while at the same time exploring further the idea that any individual verse might have simultaneous, different senses. Soon enough, there emerged the notion of fourfold interpretation: every verse of the Hebrew Bible might actually have four different meanings simultaneously. These four senses were immortalized in a thirteenth-century Latin ditty:

> Littera gesta docet,
> Quid credas allegoria,
> Moralis quid agas,
> Quo tendas anagogia.

(The literal sense teaches the facts [or "deeds"]; the allegorical, what you should believe; the moral sense, what you should do; and the anagogical, where you are headed.)[24]

The standard example of the application of this fourfold reading of Scripture is that of the city of Jerusalem as it might appear in a biblical verse. According to the literal (or historical) sense, Jerusalem refers to an actual city, a place where the Jews dwelt in biblical times. According to the allegorical sense, however, Jerusalem refers to the church, so that when a biblical verse talks about "dwelling in Jerusalem," it might really mean "abiding in the Church." * Reading Scripture in this allegorical way teaches especially about the message of Christian doctrine; hence, it concerns what the Latin poem refers to as "what you should believe." The moral sense (sometimes also called the tropological sense) focuses more on the life of the individual soul—so that, in the moral reading, Jerusalem itself might be taken to represent a person's soul and therefore teach "what you [as an individual] should do." The anagogical, or eschatological, sense teaches about what is to be in the end-time—hence, Jerusalem here might represent the heavenly city of God that will be revealed in the fullness of time.

Modern readers might, at this point, be rolling their eyes: every verse means four different things? Not really. Even in medieval Europe, this fourfold approach was only a sometimes thing: it was hard to find many verses for which all four senses worked. But there were a few good examples. Psalm 114 begins, "When Israel went out from Egypt, the house of Jacob from a people of strange language . . ." One great champion of the fourfold reading, the Italian poet Dante Alighieri,[25] explained this verse's meaning as follows:

> Now if we look at the letter alone, what is signified to us is the departure of the sons of Israel from Egypt during the time of Moses; if at the allegory, what is signified to us is our redemption through Christ; if at the moral sense, what is signified to us is the conversion of the soul from the sorrow and misery of sin to the state of grace; if at the anagogical, what is signified

---

* This is not quite allegory in the way Philo used the term, concrete-for-abstract, but more in the way Paul used the term allegory in Gal. 4:24, where it is closer to typology, that is, the earlier refers to the later, or the Old Testament refers to the New.

to us is the departure of the sanctified soul from enslavement to the corruption of this world into the freedom of eternal glory. And although these mystical senses are called by various names, they may all be called allegorical, since they are all different from the literal or historical.

Letter to Can Grande[26]

Even if there were not many such verses, the very idea that Scripture had layers and layers of significance entered the popular imagination. In medieval Europe, the Bible became a vast, mysterious, and infinitely complicated world. The front and the back of this book were held together by hidden correspondences between Old and New; the most fundamental doctrines were nestled inside apparently innocent narratives, indeed, inside a single sentence made up of words that seemed to be talking about one thing but were authoritatively interpreted to be talking about something else entirely.

To enter the world of Scripture's mysteries was thus a matter for trained professionals; only a priest or a monk schooled in the ways of fourfold interpretation, and especially in the interpretations of his predecessors, could say for sure what this or that verse meant. It would never occur to ordinary people to try their hand at interpretation—to begin with, they did not own their own Bibles, and they could not read. No, the Bible was something that ordinary people experienced in other ways. It was read aloud in public, preached about at church or in open markets; its stories were illustrated on stained glass windows and mosaic floors and the carved capitals of columns; it was recounted in poems, sung in hymns, and retold in passion plays—in these ways the Bible was everywhere, and no one escaped its influence. But its interpretation was not up for discussion; that had been decided a long time ago.

There was a word in medieval Latin for what drove this attitude toward Scripture: *auctoritas*. This is our word "authority," but it had a special resonance in Latin. It was what the *auctores*—meaning both the "authors" and the "authorities"—had established long ago. Their wisdom—set down in the writings of the Church Fathers and later Christian teachers—could never be challenged, nor would anyone ever want to. (In fact, when, as sometimes happened, a later scholar had a new idea, he would usually seek to connect it to something that had been written by an earlier, authoritative figure—"This is what Augustine really meant when he said X or Y.") *Auctoritas* was all-powerful and unquestioned: the Bible meant what the authorities had always said it meant.

The Beginnings of Change

Here we must fast-forward through a host of interesting developments in medieval times[27] in order to arrive at the heady days of the Italian Renaissance and, more precisely, at the end of the fifteenth century. Even today, no one is quite sure why the Renaissance succeeded in overturning so many of the cherished ideas and sensibilities of the Middle Ages in such short order, but it did[28]—including medieval biblical interpretation. Suddenly, *auctoritas* began to look very rickety indeed. People now started to have their doubts about the long-entrenched idea of the fourfold meaning of Scripture. Was the Old Testament really a web of foreshadowings of the New? Were its stories really to be understood as allegorical representations of the inner life of the soul? What if Abraham was just Abraham, an actual person who lived long, long ago and was written about in the Bible? Why should he represent or correspond to anything other than himself?

One contributory factor in the breakdown of *auctoritas* was the rapidly spreading knowledge of the Hebrew language among Christians. Until the late Renaissance, an astonishingly small number of Christian scholars had any notion of this tongue (although they could easily have learned it from the Jews in their towns). Starting at this time, however, Christians began to learn biblical Hebrew (as well as Greek), soon aided by the availability of little primers on the language's grammar and vocabulary, written in Latin and printed on the recently invented printing press.[29] Throughout the Middle Ages, the great authority on Hebrew in the Christian world had been the fourth-century scholar Jerome, translator of the Hebrew Bible into Latin. His writings about the Hebrew language in general as well as about specific words were repeated unquestioningly. Now, at first tentatively and later with greater assurance, Christian scholars began to question his authority, until some finally dared utter the words, "Jerome was wrong."[30] Soon, everything was up for grabs. Careful scholars ought, of course, to consult the writings of their predecessors, but people no longer assumed that the proper understanding of the Bible lay in the translations and commentaries of the past. Now they could read the Bible's words for themselves and draw their own conclusions.

At this point, the scholarly reexamination of the Bible met up with another movement, the nascent Protestant Reformation. Well before the early 1500s, individual Christians had been expressing dissatisfaction with the ways of the church, and their dissatisfaction focused on a broad variety of issues. One of the things that bothered them was what they saw as corruption within its ranks—priests' sale of indulgences to their parishioners, for example, or the role of money in obtaining high office within the church hierarchy (called "simony"). Along with these, some Christians objected to the church's vast holdings of land and its evident concern for furthering its own wealth and political power (accompanied by a lack of concern for the poor): to many, the bishops and cardinals seemed more the servants of Mammon than of God.

In addition to these dissatisfactions, however, were others of a more theoretical and intellectual nature. The very idea of papal authority seemed illogical to some; how could a reasonable person accept a priori that the rulings of the altogether human leader of the church would always be correct? And why should a human institution like the church, even if its existence was divinely authorized, play such a crucial role as intermediary between God and the individual Christian? Lastly—but probably not last in importance— what about the Bible? Should the church have the unchallenged authority to say what the Bible means, especially when that meaning seemed to be derived not from the Bible's own words as much as from old doctrines and question- able methods of interpretation?

These trends advanced together. John Wyclif (1328–89), sometimes called the "first Protestant," not only attacked the church but took it upon himself to translate the Bible from Latin to English so that it might be available even to those without an education, to hear and consider on their own. Wyclif's ideas influenced other would-be reformers, including Jan Hus in Bohemia (ca. 1369–1415), who was excommunicated in 1412 for his public proclama- tions; three years later he was executed. Despite such stern measures, discon- tent with the church, and the new climate of intellectual inquiry that helped to fuel it, were unstoppable. In the fifteenth century, numerous scholars— some, like Erasmus, still well known today, many others now forgotten[31]— fed the move to reform with their researches into Scripture.

By Scripture Alone

In theory, the church was not the only potential authority in matters religious; there was also the Bible itself, the very word of God. It did not take the would- be Reformers long to understand that the Bible could become an important tool in opposing the power of the church. Wyclif, for example, had sought to promote the radical notion that the Bible should be the sole authority for church teaching, and his ideas influenced later figures. *Sola scriptura,* "by Scripture alone," eventually became a byword of the Protestant Reformation.[32] It was certainly a happy coincidence, or perhaps no coincidence at all, that the promotion of Scripture to the role of sole arbiter in matters of faith was being urged precisely at the time when Christian scholars were learning Hebrew and Greek and seeking to interpret Scripture anew, without the benefit of church- sponsored interpretations and church-approved translations.

We will be the ones to decide what Scripture really means, the Reformers now said, basing ourselves on the biblical text and everything that is being discovered about it; then we will seek to put its words into action. So Martin Luther, leader of the German Reformation, put the case clearly when, at the Diet of Worms in 1521, he was asked to recant his views:

Unless I be convinced by evidence of Scripture or by plain reason—for I do not accept the authority of the Pope or the councils alone, since it is demonstrated that they have often erred and contradicted themselves—I am bound by the Scriptures I have cited, and my conscience is captive to the Word of God. I cannot and will not recant anything, for it is neither safe nor right to go against conscience. God help me. Amen.

Here the "evidence of Scripture" is not subject to the "authority of the Pope" but opposed to it, and Scripture will, according to Luther, necessarily win any such contest. Elsewhere he bristled at the very idea that the church might

> assign to one man, the Roman Pontiff, the right of interpreting Sacred Scripture by the sole virtue of his exalted office and power against all intelligence and erudition. But Scripture is to be interpreted only by the Spirit through which Scripture was written, because the Spirit is never to be found more present and lively than in the sacred writings themselves.[33]

The church has no inherent right to say what Scripture means; it is up to the Spirit (Luther means the Holy Spirit of the Trinity) to guide the human interpreter, along with "all intelligence and erudition"—that is, the newfound knowledge of biblical Hebrew and Greek and everything scholars were discovering about the real meaning of Scripture. And so, the old, church-sponsored fourfold approach to meaning was, for Luther and his followers, on its way out: "Our first concern will be for the grammatical [literal] meaning," Luther wrote in his psalms commentary in 1519, "since this is the truly theological meaning."[34]

In its new, stripped-down state, no longer accompanied by centuries-old traditions of interpretation, Scripture could now become the heart and soul of the Protestant movement. And it did. The Bible was, in the words of a group of early British Protestants who sought temporary refuge in Geneva,

> the light to our paths, the keye to the kingdome of heaven, our comfort in affliction, our shielde and sworde against Satan, the school of all wisdome, the glasse [mirror] wherein we behold God's face, the testimonie of his favour, and the only foode and nourishment of our soules.[35]

But what exactly did Scripture mean? Was it always to be taken at face value, even when it commanded such things as capital punishment for someone who works on the sabbath (Exod. 31:14) or commits adultery (Lev. 20:10)? (Some reformers said yes.)[36] What about when it seemed to conflict with modern science or common sense—saying, for example, that Joshua had caused the sun to stop in the sky, or that Elijah had ascended into heaven on a chariot of fire? Did taking the Bible literally leave no room for metaphor or figurative speech or exaggeration?

For a time, at least in some circles, it was anybody's guess. So long as the Catholic Church had been the sole authority, it was able to control how the Bible was interpreted; after the Protestant Reformation, anyone could be an interpreter. The English poet John Dryden described a world in which biblical interpretation had been turned over to the common man:

> The book thus put in every vulgar hand,
> Which each presum'd he best could understand,
> The common rule was made the common prey,
> And at the mercy of the rabble lay.
> The tender page with horny fists was gall'd,
> And he was gifted most that loudest bawl'd:
> The spirit gave the doctoral degree,
> And every member of a company
> Was of his trade and of the Bible free.
> Plain truths enough for needful use they found,
> But men would still be itching to expound:
> Each was ambitious of th'obscurest place,
> No measure ta'en from knowledge, all from grace.
> Study and pains were now no more their care;
> Texts were explained by fasting and by prayer:
> This was the fruit the private spirit brought,
> Occasion'd by great zeal and little thought.[37]
> *Religio Laici* 822–38 (1682)

Some control had to be placed on the interpretive fancies of enthusiasts, and Dryden clearly alludes to what he, and many others, believed that control ought to be: the "doctoral degree," conferred by a proper school of divinity and not by "the spirit" alone; "study and pains," and not merely "fasting and prayer." Proper interpretation, in other words, had to be based on solid knowledge.

A Fateful Alliance

Thus was formed the great alliance between Protestantism and biblical scholarship. In a sense, it had been there almost from the very start. Although the questioning of *auctoritas* in interpretation had begun quite independently of the Reformation, it soon became one of the Reformers' favorite causes and helped lead to the break with Rome. Then, once the new Protestant denominations had been established on their own, they provided the framework, and the sponsorship, for the ongoing scholarly inquiry into Scripture's true meaning. This alliance proved to be crucial. It is no accident that, to this day, the great centers of modern biblical scholarship are to be found in largely Protestant countries—Germany and the Netherlands, Scandinavia and Great Britain, Canada and the United States.[38]

Here again we must pass quickly through a host of important events and trends. While all this was happening in the relatively limited domain of biblical interpretation, the sixteenth and seventeenth centuries watched the advance of scientific inquiry into the greatest questions of the natural order: Nicholas Copernicus (1473–1543) had argued that the earth rotated around the sun, and his ideas were soon taken up by others, notably Galileo Galilei (1564–1642) and Johannes Kepler (1571–1630). Once proven true, this idea sent shock waves through the whole of traditional belief. For centuries people had believed that the greatest source of knowledge about the world was divine revelation, specifically, the words of Holy Scripture. But Scripture contained not a hint about earth's orbiting the sun, indeed, its account of creation seemed to say just the opposite (Genesis 1), as did the words of King Solomon, allegedly the wisest man in history (Eccles. 1:5). So research was now suggesting that modern science was capable of unlocking life's secrets on its own, without the benefit of divine revelation—indeed, sometimes it even seemed to demonstrate that what was written in Scripture was false. In 1628 William Harvey announced his discovery of the workings of the circulatory system in the human body; this same period was marked by great advances in the study of anatomy, and surgery was becoming increasingly sophisticated. The newly perfected telescope gave scientists their first glimpse of the moons of Jupiter and the phases of Venus; soon, Isaac Newton (1642–1727) postulated his universal theory of gravitation. "Nature's book"—opened by science—was turning out to be more reliable than that other book, the Bible. At the same time, thinkers such as Francis Bacon (1561–1626) and René Descartes (1596–1650) were seeking to examine the very processes of human reasoning and, especially in the case of the latter, to proceed from a radical skepticism that took nothing for granted, including, prominently, the teachings of religion.

Did Moses Write the Torah?

With regard to the Bible, two important figures emerged in this period, the philosophers Thomas Hobbes (1588–1679) and Benedict Spinoza (1632–77). Among other things, both expressed their views on one of the touchiest items of traditional religious belief, the claim that Moses was the author of the Pentateuch.[39] This was a crucial item for both Jews and Christians (but probably even more for the former than the latter); if Moses, the greatest of the prophets, was not the Pentateuch's real author, then why should anyone believe its stories or bother to obey its commandments? Yet even in medieval times, a few Jewish scholars—including, prominently, Abraham ibn Ezra (ca. 1092–1167)—had pointed to a number of verses that seemed unlikely to have been written by Moses. For example, in describing Abraham's travels in the Promised Land, the book of Genesis said:

> Abram passed through the land to the place at Shechem, to the oak of Moreh. At that time the Canaanites were in the land.
>
> Gen. 12:6

By saying that the Canaanites were in the land "at that time," the text seems clearly to imply that when these words were being written, the Canaanites were no longer there. But if so, Moses was unlikely to be the author of this sentence—so long as he was alive, the Canaanites were indeed in the land.

Ibn Ezra pointed to other troubling instances. Why should the book of Deuteronomy, if it had been written by Moses, begin by saying that he had spoken to the Israelites "on the far side of the Jordan" (Deut. 1:1)? That expression implied that the person writing this was on the *near* side of the Jordan, which Moses never was, since he died before the entry into Canaan. And why should Gen. 22:14 contain the parenthetical observation, "as it is said today, 'On the mountain of the LORD He [*or* it] will be seen' "? The sense is not altogether clear, but to ibn Ezra this reference seemed to suggest a popular saying ("It is said today") that could not have existed until long after Moses' death, specifically, at a time after Solomon had built the Jerusalem temple on a mountain where "the LORD's face will be seen" (Deut. 16:16).[40]

Traditional interpretation had provided answers to these questions: as a prophet, Moses could have known that the Canaanites would be displaced (in fact, God had told him as much, Exod. 34:11); having likewise been told that the people of Israel would settle in Canaan, he wrote "on the far side of the Jordan" from their point of view, not his own, since he knew they were the ones who would be reading his words long after his death. (The same logic would explain "At that time the Canaanites were in the land.") As for "On the mountain of the LORD He [*or* it] will be seen," such a saying might have even existed since the time of Abraham and Isaac, so there was nothing unusual in Moses quoting it.

In raising these questions again, however, ibn Ezra seemed to suggest that these traditional answers were inadequate. Instead, he and other medieval writers implied that these verses were little exceptions: *most* of the Pentateuch was indeed written by Moses, he felt, but a few verses had been added in later by other writers.[41]

With the rise of the new approach to biblical interpretation, ibn Ezra's questions were asked anew—indeed, Hobbes, Spinoza, and others added some new questions.[42] How could Moses be the author of the Pentateuch if one of its verses noted: "Now the man Moses was very humble, more so than anyone else on the face of the earth" (Num. 12:3)? Surely, interpreters reasoned, a very humble man would not have said such a thing about himself. How could another verse assert, "These are the kings who reigned in the land of Edom, before any king reigned over the Israelites" (Gen. 36:31)? This verse seems to assume the knowledge that kings eventually did rule over Israel—a circumstance that did not exist until centuries after Moses, in the time of Saul and David. Indeed, how could the Pentateuch at one point quote from a source called the *Book of the Wars of the* LORD with regard to a battle that took place in Moses' time (Num. 21:14)? Such a book must have been written *after* the battle, perhaps long after—so how could Moses be quoting it as if it were an old, established historical source?

In raising these questions, Hobbes and Spinoza did not adopt the same course as ibn Ezra and suggest that these verses were merely later additions. Instead, they said that they were sufficient to call into question the whole idea that Moses had written the Pentateuch. As Hobbes summarized his argument, "It is therefore sufficiently evident that the five books of Moses [that is, the Pentateuch] were written after his time, though how long after it be not so manifest." [43] This was a shocking assertion.

While both these thinkers contributed significantly to the seventeenth century's wrestling with the Bible (and both dealt with far more than the authorship of the Pentateuch), it was Spinoza who ultimately had the greater influence on biblical scholars themselves. In a few pages of his remarkable little book the *Tractatus Theologo-Politicus* (1670), Spinoza outlined a new proposal for *how* the Bible was to be read, and this program became the marching orders of biblical scholars for the next three centuries. [44] Among Spinoza's main points:

1. Scripture is to be understood by Scripture alone. The time-honored traditions about what the Bible means (Spinoza had in mind rabbinic midrash as well as Christian typological and allegorical interpretations) often lead to "absurdities"; therefore only Scripture's own words are to be considered. "All knowledge of Scripture must be sought from Scripture alone." [45]

2. In order to understand Scripture, we must understand all the peculiarities of its language [46] and its world of ideas, and not impose on it our own, later conceptions. There is no reason to assume that what Scripture says conforms to our own values or our current knowledge—or even to logical thought. We should thus "take every precaution against the undue influence not only of our own prejudices, but of our faculty of reason." [47]

3. We should thus begin by assuming that Scripture means what Scripture says even when it disagrees with our own conceptions. For exam-

ple, when Moses* is said to have described God as a "[consuming] fire" (Deut. 4:24) or as a "jealous God" (Exod. 20:5), we have to take such things literally unless they can be shown to contradict some other saying of Moses, in which case they may be interpreted metaphorically.[48] In the first instance, the fact that Moses elsewhere is said to have asserted that God has no form or likeness (Spinoza's understanding of Exod. 20:4) proves that he could only have meant "fire" as a metaphorical description. The same cannot be said of "jealous God," however: since Moses nowhere denies that God has emotions,§ there is no reason to believe that he did not impute emotions to Him.

4. Someone who wishes to inquire into Scripture's meaning must likewise investigate how the books themselves were put together and the process of their transmission. The life of the reputed author must be studied, his personality traits as well as his historical context, in order to understand how he intended what he said to be understood—whether, for example, he intended something as an actual law or merely as moral instruction, and whether something was being put forward as eternally valid or merely as a short-term measure, "things of only temporary significance or directed only to the benefit of a few."[49]

5. Finally, in considering the words of prophets, one must recognize that they frequently contradict one another. Even on such essentials as "what God is [and] in what way He sees and provides for all things," Spinoza wrote, "we have clearly shown that the prophets themselves were not in agreement."[50] One must therefore concentrate on those few items on which all prophets do agree, "such as, for example, that there is one unique and omnipotent God and He alone is to be worshiped. . . ."

It is not difficult to see that the program outlined by Spinoza calls for the systematic dismantling of the Four Assumptions mentioned earlier. Scripture is cryptic and allusive? Not at all; Scripture should always be assumed to mean (unless clearly proven otherwise) exactly and literally what it says. Scripture has a lesson for us today? On the contrary, Scripture can be understood only in the context of its own time, and presumably some portion, perhaps most, of what it says was never intended as "eternally valid" but only applied to people living then (or even just *some* people living then, "a few"). Scripture

---

* Here Spinoza is assuming, for the sake of argument, that Moses is indeed the author of the entire Pentateuch.

§ An important point for Spinoza, since Maimonides and later Jewish thinkers specifically denied that the Torah attributes emotions to God, and that any mention of God being angry or pleased or the like is simply intended to make things comprehensible in human terms.

is perfectly harmonious and without error? Hardly. Prophets contradict one another and seem to agree only on a few essentials; moreover, some of the things the Bible says contradict our current understanding, including modern science. (In fact, Spinoza noted, some parts of Scripture were added in by later hands and cannot even be attributed to the prophets themselves.)[51] All of Scripture is divinely given or divinely inspired? Here, Spinoza is careful, but a close reading of his words will reveal his profound skepticism about the very nature of prophecy.[52] The prophets mostly saw images in their minds (Isa. 6:1–7; Num. 12:6), Spinoza says elsewhere;[53] their job consisted of translating these images into words, for which they relied on their imaginative faculty. Such a procedure is inherently unstable, Spinoza felt; their words can hardly be considered more reliable than the conclusions of solid science—the contradictions within Scripture demonstrate that. On the contrary, "prophets were not endowed with a more perfect mind [than other thinkers], but with a more vivid power of imagination."[54] The best one can say of the prophets, Spinoza ultimately claimed, is that they were concerned with what is "right and good";[55] they saw things or heard things and then their imagination turned these into words from God.

Spinoza was a controversial figure in his own day, blackballed by the Amsterdam Jewish community in which he had grown up and viewed with great suspicion by Christian divines. When his book was finally published, it was denounced as "harmful and vile," "most pernicious," "intolerably unrestrained," "subversive," "blasphemous," "diabolical," and "atheistic."[56] Yet people, especially biblical scholars, kept reading it and thinking about it.[57]

A Century of Lights

If Spinoza was ahead of his time, it was not by much; the eighteenth century introduced a host of new thinkers who set out to investigate the Bible in precisely the manner that he had advocated. This was the time known to Germans as the *Aufklärung* and to the English as the Enlightenment; in French it was the *siècle des lumières,* the "century of lights." By whatever name, it was a period of rationalism's triumph, a time of untrammeled scientific inquiry and a questioning of all received traditions. Catholicism and the various Protestant denominations continued their path, but alongside them sprang up a new faith altogether characteristic of the age: Deism. Deists defined themselves as those who "believe in the existence of a God or a Supreme Being but deny revealed religion, basing their belief instead on the light of nature and reason." The God revealed by reason may indeed be the world's Creator, but, Deists maintained, He is not a God who intervenes in human affairs, performs miracles, answers prayers, or does most of the other things reported about Him in Scripture. These are simply an illusion.

Deism was very popular among intellectuals on both sides of the Atlantic; among its American exponents were Thomas Jefferson and Benjamin Franklin. Few American schoolchildren who learn the opening sentences of the Declaration of Independence are told that its reference to "the Laws of Nature and Nature's God" is a passing reflection of Jefferson's deeply held Deism (and his profound skepticism about the God revealed in Scripture). In this new climate, the Bible was not always revered; indeed, some writers actually vilified it. The philosopher David Hume (1711–76), for example, asserted that the Pentateuch is

> a book presented to us by a barbarous and ignorant people [= the Jews], written in an age when they were still more barbarous, and in all probability long after the facts which it relates, corroborated by no concurring testimony, and resembling those fabulous accounts which every nation gives of its origin. Upon reading this book, we find it full of prodigies and miracles. It gives an account of a state of the world and of human nature entirely different from the present: Of our fall from that state: Of the age of man extended to near a thousand years: Of the destruction of the world by a deluge: Of the arbitrary choice of one people as the favourites of heaven: and that people the countrymen of the author: Of their deliverance from bondage by prodigies the most astonishing imaginable: I desire any one to lay his hand upon his heart, and after a serious consideration declare, whether he thinks the falsehood of such a book, supported by such testimony, would be more extraordinary and miraculous than all the miracles it relates; which is, however, necessary to make it be received.[58]

These sentiments were echoed by Voltaire—certainly no specialist on the Bible, but someone who knew well the arguments of those who were.[59] In his *Philosophical Dictionary* (1764), Voltaire wrote that the Pentateuch

> must appear to every polished people as singular as the [Jews'] conduct; if it were not divine, it would seem to be the law of savages beginning to assemble themselves into a nation; and being divine, one cannot understand how it is that it has not existed from all ages, for them and for all men.

About Moses, the Pentateuch's author, he wrote in the same work:

> Several learned men have finally doubted if there ever was a Moses, and whether this man was not an imaginary being, such as were Perseus, Bacchus, Atlas [et al.], and so many other heroes of romance whose lives and prowesses have been recorded. It is not very likely, say the incredulous, that a man ever existed whose life was a continual wonder. It is not very likely that he worked so many stupendous miracles in Egypt, Arabia, and Syria,

without their being known throughout the world. It is not likely, that no Egyptian or Greek writer should have transmitted these miracles to posterity. . . . According to these unbelievers, the books attributed to Moses were only written among the Babylonians during the captivity, or immediately afterward by Ezra.

Such ideas were considered radical in the eighteenth century; mainstream Christians continued to believe in the Bible's sanctity and in the truth of its words. There certainly was a Moses, they said, and he certainly did write the Pentateuch. But the acid pen of Hume and Voltaire and others challenged believing Christians to provide proof, or at least counterarguments, in the new spirit of rational inquiry.[60]

This put such believers in a difficult bind; in a sense, the minute one began to read Scripture with the same assumptions that one brought to the reading of humanly authored books, the argument was lost. How could one claim that such a book was holy or utterly unique? Nevertheless, many sincere Christians in the eighteenth century found themselves investigating Scripture's human side. One such man was Robert Lowth (1710–87). The son of a prominent theologian, Lowth served as professor of poetry at Oxford University for a time but resigned his post in 1752 and pursued service in the Anglican Church; he was ultimately named bishop of London and dean of the Chapel Royal. While still at Oxford, Lowth wrote an influential study of biblical poetry, *Lectures on the Sacred Poetry of the Hebrews* (published in 1753). The book is full of insights into the rules by which the Bible's songs and prayers were composed, but it raised a vexing question: did not his search for meter, rhyme, and other poetic features imply that the Bible's poems had been written in very much the same way as ordinary, human poems are composed? Lowth tried to justify his effort to his students in his opening lecture:

It would not be easy, indeed, to assign a reason why the writings of Homer, of Pindar, and of Horace should engross our attention and monopolise our praise, while those of Moses, of David, and Isaiah pass totally unregarded. Shall we suppose that the subject is not adapted to a seminary in which sacred literature has ever maintained a precedence? Shall we say that it is foreign to this assembly of promising youth, of whom the greater part have consecrated the best portion of their time and labour to the same department of learning? Or must we conclude that the writings of those men who have accomplished only as much as human genius and ability could accomplish should be reduced to method and theory; but that those which boast a much higher origin, and are justly attributed to the inspiration of the Holy Spirit, may be considered as indeed illustrious by their native force and beauty, but not as conformable to the principles of science nor to be circumscribed by any rules of art?

In other words, just because the Bible's words were inspired by the Holy Spirit does not mean they ought not to be analyzed in the same way as the writings of classical Greece or Rome. And if a committed Christian should succeed in discovering, as Lowth felt he had, the "principles of science" and "rules of art" that determined how biblical poetry had been composed, should he not go ahead and make these known to the world? Thus, although traditionalists and radicals disagreed sharply on what the Bible was and how it was to be read, they really were not far apart on matters of approach and method; even in the most orthodox circles, the words themselves (which were still called the "literal" or "grammatical" or "historical" sense of Scripture) were now primary, the starting point of any further discussion.[61]

Filling in the Blanks

But what exactly were those words? One interesting feature of the traditional Hebrew text has not been mentioned so far. Biblical Hebrew—like Arabic, Aramaic, and some other Semitic languages—often leaves the vowels inside words unexpressed. Such a system of writing wouldn't work at all in English. What would the following sentence mean?

I FND A BRD

Probably most people would guess that FND stands for "found" or "find." But it might also stand for "fined," "fanned," "foned" (that is, "phoned"), perhaps even "fond" or "fiend." As for BRD, that could represent "bird," "bread," "brad," "broad," "board," "bard," "bride," "buried," "beard," "braid," "by-road," and yet more. Thus, the little sentence above could be construed as saying, "I found a bird," "I find a bride," "I fined a bard," "I phoned abroad," "I fanned a beard," and all sorts of other combinations. Hebrew is less ambiguous than English: there are relatively few homonyms, and words are mostly built out of basic roots in predictable patterns. Still, this system of writing left plenty of room for ambiguity. (The consonants SPR, for example, will usually have some connection with the Hebrew root for "count" or "recount," but in various biblical verses these three letters can designate such diverse nouns as the words for "enumeration," "document," or "scribe," as well as different verbal forms meaning "he counted," "to count," "count!" "he told," "to tell," "tell!" and so forth. It all depends on what vowels one thinks ought to go between the three consonants.) What is more, as we have already seen in the case of Abraham and Isaac, the biblical text came without capital letters or commas or periods. That is what allowed interpreters to turn Abraham's vague words of assurance, "God Himself will provide the lamb for the burnt offering, my son," into the stark assertion, "God Himself will provide. The lamb for the burnt offering [is] my son."

Taken together, these two sources of ambiguity left plenty of room for different interpretations. Aware of this difficulty, Jewish scholars had developed a system of dots and other signs to represent the vowels of each Hebrew word as well as the basic punctuation of each sentence. Traditionalists maintained that this system was very old—some claimed it went back to Moses himself—but others, relying on the testimony of Renaissance Jewish scholarship, asserted that it went back only to the Middle Ages and therefore had no authority.[62] For such people, every word of the Hebrew Bible was now potentially suspect: perhaps the medieval vowel signs were wrong; perhaps the medieval punctuation was wrong; indeed, perhaps some scribe back in biblical times had made a mistake and had written the wrong letter. Given what they saw as the inherent unreliability of the traditional text, biblical scholars now proposed emendations freely; some even set out to create a whole new system for determining the text's vowels.[63]

"The German Science"

In short, by the end of the eighteenth century, every aspect of the Bible was found to be fair game for the probing, often skeptical, questions of scholars, and one by one the cherished interpretations of earlier Christians were being dismissed. Not only did most Protestant scholars now reject most of the typological foreshadowing of the New Testament in the Old (that is, the stories of Isaac, Joshua, and other figures were no longer accepted as containing hints about the life of Jesus), but even the application of actual prophecies to New Testament times came to be suspect. For example, the prophet Isaiah's prediction that "a virgin shall conceive and bear a son" (Isa. 7:14) could not, many maintained, possibly refer to Jesus: to begin with, they said, the word translated "virgin" really only means "young woman" in Hebrew, and in any case this was a prediction about the birth of a baby in the time of Isaiah himself, not of a baby to be born more than seven hundred years later.[64] Thus, if Isaiah's words had been cited in the gospel of Matthew in connection with Jesus' birth (1:23), this was "a simple, historical observation or an allusion." [65]

More generally, a rift now gradually developed between what the words of the Bible said and the historical events it purported to describe. In an earlier day, the Bible was primarily a book. People of course believed that the things it described were true, but, as we have glimpsed, throughout the Middle Ages and beyond, it was the *text* that was primary, since it contained all the secret meanings and doctrines and interrelationships that were the heart of the Bible's message. This did not change immediately with the Renaissance, but starting then, what earlier Christians had called the literal or "historical" sense of Scripture took on a new importance. Whatever else it was doing, the Bible was also talking about things that had happened in this world, and these events themselves took on a reality of their own. It is difficult to over-state the importance of this subtle shift, which became (and remains) a mainstay of the Protestant way of reading Scripture.[66] Gradually, the words of the text ceased to be primary, each verse the gateway to a host of hidden meanings. Instead, the text became important principally as an account of real events: it was the gateway to the actual things that had happened in the ancient past. By the end of the eighteenth century, however, the Bible's account of these things became increasingly suspect: Did the Red Sea really split in two? Was the Resurrection an actual event? The task, at least as some scholars saw it, was to come up with a plausible account of what might really have taken place. The *events* had become the real Bible for them, and the words of Scripture were increasingly seen as something other than a factual recitation—often something in need of apologetic explanation.[67]

Of course, scholarship is one thing and the real world another. Such thoughts may have appeared in learned tomes, but they were rarely repeated from the pulpit. Even today, ministers trained in liberal seminaries are taught all kinds of things about the Bible that their parishioners never hear about: there has always been an understandable tendency to soft-pedal the difficul-ties raised by scholarship and to accentuate the positive (without saying anything known to be untrue, of course). Thus, although scholars were pushing ahead with their own research, ordinary churchgoers did not neces-sarily confront its results on Sunday.

While biblical scholarship continued to be pursued in various countries, it now became the particular specialty of Germany.[68] German Protestant schol-ars investigated all manner of subjects connected with the Bible, both the Old Testament and the New; but they were particularly attracted to that same question that had puzzled biblical scholars during the Enlightenment, the authorship of the Pentateuch. If, as many now claimed, Moses was not its true author, who was?

The key to cracking this mystery, scholars came to feel, lay in the different words used by the Hebrew Bible to refer to God. Some parts of the Penta-teuch used the "generic" Hebrew word for God, *'elohim.** Other parts used the Tetragrammaton, that is, the ineffable "proper name" of God, consisting of the four Hebrew letters corresponding to our *Y, H, W,* and *H.*§ Why use

---

* This word is plural in form and is often used as a plural to refer to the deities of other nations, "foreign gods." When it is used of Israel's God it is construed as singular: " *'elo-him* says," " *'elohim* does," and so forth.

§ Since, even in biblical times, this name came to be considered too sacred to be uttered, its exact pronunciation has been lost; as with other words, scribes had no way of indicating the internal vowels when they wrote this name. For a time, Christian Hebraists believed the proper pronunciation was "Jehovah," since those vowels corresponded to the

two different names? In the same year that Lowth published his study of bib-lical poetry (1753), a French Protestant scholar, Jean Astruc, had suggested that Moses had combined two different sources in composing the Pentateuch, each of which used a different word for God. That would also explain why some of the stories that used one of these names sometimes overlapped with stories that used the other name—why, for example, there are two stories relating how Abraham made a covenant with God (Genesis 15 and 17), or two stories that explain how the city of Beer Sheba got its name (Gen. 21:22–31 and 26:28–33). In these cases, each of the paired stories uses one name for God while the other uses the other name.

In nineteenth-century Germany, many scholars accepted the idea that the Pentateuch had been written through a combination of different written sources. But that hardly answered all the questions. Was Moses the one who combined them (as Astruc had maintained), or was it some later figure? And were there just two sources? Scholars noticed that overlapping stories some-times used the *same* name for God: for example, there are two accounts of how Jacob's name was changed to Israel (Gen. 32:24–30 and 35:9–10), but both refer to God by the generic name *'elohim*. Perhaps there had thus been two different sources that used the name *'elohim*.[69]

At this point, a German doctoral student, W. M. L. de Wette (1780–1849), began working on the book of Deuteronomy, and he soon became con-vinced that the writer of Deuteronomy was different from *all* the other sources of the Pentateuch: his style was different, his laws differed in many particulars from earlier laws, and, most strikingly, de Wette argued, he had a completely different notion of the role played by the temple, particularly in connection with the sacrificing of animals. Not only did de Wette think that Deuteronomy came from a different hand, but he had a definite idea about *when* it was written. Its composition, he argued (on the basis of a certain pas-sage in 2 Kings 22), went back to the days of King Josiah, that is, to the end of the seventh century BCE. De Wette claimed that there was no evidence that anyone before Josiah had known of the laws contained in Deuteronomy—ever. If, for example, the prophet Samuel had known of the book of Deuteronomy, de Wette asked, why should he ever have expressed misgivings about the idea of anointing a king (1 Sam. 8:6–8), when Deuteronomy clearly called on people to do so (Deut. 17:14–20)? To this de Wette added many other examples.

For the German scholars, de Wette's work proved highly suggestive, since it gave them a fixed point in time from which to try to date the other sources

---

vowel dots that had been written in later by Jewish scholars. Eventually, however, it became clear that those vowel dots actually belonged to the Hebrew word for "My Lord" (*'adonay*) and had been written in to remind readers to substitute the word "My Lord" for this ineffable name.

they had identified. If the author of Deuteronomy lived, according to de Wette's theory, sometime in the seventh century (when Josiah was king), then before him must have been at least three other writers. The one who always used the Tetragrammaton, that is, the name for God spelled with the four Hebrew letters *Y-H-W-H*, the German scholars designated "J" (since the sound for *Y* is spelled in German with a *J*). The one who preferred *'elohim* they designated as "E." Both of these, they felt, had preceded the author of Deuteronomy ("D"), but in addition to them there must have been another source, a priestly writer ultimately designated "P." [70] Some scholars believed that P was the earliest writer of all, responsible for what they called the "basic text," the laws of priestly sacrifices and other ritual matters; to this "basic text" had been added J, E, and eventually D. It was a peculiarity of P that he avoided using the Tetragrammaton for any stories set before the time of Moses, since P maintained that this sacred name was first revealed to Moses and had been unknown in earlier times (Exod. 6:2–3). For those earlier stories, therefore, P consistently used the word *'elohim*. This would explain, the German scholars said, why there are duplicate stories in Genesis that both use this name: one would have been written by P and the other by E.

The Education of Charles Augustus Briggs

To learn more about such theories, Charles A. Briggs, who had begun his studies at Union Theological Seminary with some of the leading American scholars of the day, sailed to Germany in the summer of 1866, accompanied by his young wife, Julie. The place he had selected for further study was the University of Berlin, the same institution at which his teacher and close advisor at Union, Henry Boynton Smith, had pursued his doctoral studies.

At almost precisely the same moment, a young German divinity student, Julius Wellhausen, was beginning his studies at the University of Göttingen with one of the leading biblical scholars of the day, Heinrich Ewald (1802–75). Wellhausen and Briggs were thus close contemporaries (Briggs was three years older), and they were destined to play somewhat similar roles in their native lands. Both were eloquent spokesmen for the new, "historical" approach to understanding the Bible and its process of creation, and both succeeded in large measure in convincing their fellow scholars of the correctness of this approach (although neither managed to bring many of their conservative coreligionists to accept the new ideas). Both were also hailed as great scholars in their own right—indeed, in this respect, Julius Wellhausen was even more successful than Charles A. Briggs. Wellhausen is largely considered one of the founders—*the* founder, some would say—of contemporary biblical scholarship.

Wellhausen's reputation rests largely on his wide-ranging study *Prole-*

gomena to the History of Israel (1883).[71] Among the topics covered in this work was the puzzle of the Pentateuch. Building on the work of predecessors (notably K. H. Graf), Wellhausen put forward a fourfold *Documentary Hypothesis* to explain the authorship of the Pentateuch. According to his scheme, the Pentateuch had been composed in sequence. The priestly source (P), previously thought by some scholars to be the earliest source, was actually the latest, he said; before it came D, still earlier E, and before all of these, J. (The J source belonged, however, centuries after the time of the real Moses.) Wellhausen's claim was not only that these different sources existed, but that they in turn bore witness to the gradual evolution of Israel's religion.[72] At the time when the J texts were written, Wellhausen believed, Israel was still a naïve and unsophisticated people, not very different from its Canaanite neighbors. J thus demonstrates a rather "primitive," corporeal conception of God, and J's world is an altogether polytheistic (or even animistic) one. The E source, though also early, "breathes the air of the prophets" and bears witness to the first signs of a more advanced theology in Israel.[73] Nevertheless, the religion of both J and E is closely tied to the natural world and the agricultural cycle: to hear J and E tell it, the sole purpose of Israel's major festivals was to celebrate God's bounty at harvest time. Theirs is also an easygoing, spontaneous, and unencumbered faith; for example, there is as yet no fixed, hereditary priesthood. By the time D comes along, all this has changed. D's presentation of God is far more abstract, and his attention is turned from the natural world to that of law and history; the annual festivals have begun to be explained as celebrating events from Israel's past, and keeping God's more and more elaborate laws (including those of an established priesthood) becomes a central religious concern. Finally, in P, Israel's religion has become a thing of priestly ceremonies utterly divorced from the natural world and even from the common people, and the process of historicizing attested in D is far more pronounced.

Wellhausen's scheme, apart from the detailed support its author marshaled from every part of the Bible, appealed to his readers because the very idea of development—that more complex things evolve out of simpler forms—was much in vogue in Europe at the time. Today, we tend to take this idea for granted, but it had become a moving force and model for understanding history only in the nineteenth century. It was particularly characteristic of the Romantic movement in literature[74] and put its stamp on European thought particularly through the writings of the philosopher Georg W. F. Hegel (1770–1831). Israel's religious conceptions, in Wellhausen's view, could be shown to fit quite well with Hegel's ideas of historical development.

But is any of this true? Today, more than a century after Wellhausen wrote, many people of traditional religious faith—Christians and Jews—reject his claims and continue to maintain that Moses was the sole author of the Pentateuch. Any appearance of different documents or historical development is an illusion, they say. Indeed, a glance at the history recited above, they would point out, will show just how speculative the whole thing is: the theories keep changing—P is early, P is late; there are three sources; no, four; no, five; no, more! Thus, on the Internet today are numerous sites devoted to arguing against the Documentary Hypothesis: Wellhausen's theories are just that, they say, theories for which no absolute, scientific proof can ever exist. Indeed, a number of trained university scholars have endorsed some version of this position over the past century. But today, it must be conceded, the majority of biblical scholars in American and European universities are convinced by the idea of the Pentateuch's multiple authorship. Even if no absolute proof exists, they say, some theory of different authors is the most logical and parsimonious [75] way to make sense of the evidence. As will be seen on the following pages, some elements of Wellhausen's approach have been modified over time, [76] and of late a serious challenge has been mounted to its chronological ordering of things, [77] but the basic idea of the Documentary Hypothesis has nonetheless survived the sustained scrutiny of scholars over the last century.

The Documentary Hypothesis is only one issue among many in which current university scholarship is pitted against traditional religious belief. But at the end of the nineteenth century, it was a particularly emotional and symbolic one. Books and museums and Bibles themselves were full of pictures of the old, bearded Moses bringing God's sacred laws to the people of Israel. Could it be that this was all fiction, that in place of Moses stood four or more faceless figures who wrote at different times in Israel's history and whose overall ideas—about God as well as about the particulars of Israel's religion—were quite at odds with one another?

The Briggs Heresy

In Berlin, Briggs studied the ideas of Wellhausen's immediate predecessors and teachers, and they had an electric effect on the young evangelist's faith. He did not reject them—on the contrary, they came to Briggs (who had long been studying the Bible in Hebrew and knew it well) with the force of divine revelation. Describing his first six months of study at Berlin, Briggs wrote to his uncle Marvin in January of 1867:

> When a new light dawns from above, most men cling to the old and can't believe any new light possible. But the world needs new views of the truth. The old doctrines are good but insufficient. . . . Let us seek more light under the guidance of the Holy Spirit. I cannot doubt but that I have been blessed with a new divine light. I feel a different man from what I was a few months ago. The Bible is lit up with a new light. [78]

Briggs followed that "new light" with the enthusiasm of a proselyte. Back in the United States, he soon began his professional life of teaching and writing and made it his personal mission to promote the new biblical scholarship to his colleagues and students, all the while contributing mightily to it in his own research. What he was out to discover was nothing less than the truth, "what really happened," as German scholars like to put it.[79] Surely there could be nothing bad about the truth. It might jostle some long-held notions, Briggs felt, but in the end it *had* to be beneficial; indeed, it would reveal the unadulterated, pristine basis of Christian faith.

He did not pursue this mission unopposed; from the beginning, many of his coreligionists resisted the new ideas of German scholars and their American exponents. But when it came to these opponents—particularly old-guard ministers who were in the habit of using the Bible to support their own, dogmatic views—Briggs did not pull any punches:

> The real reason these men are battling us is because their kind of Bible is being attacked. Destroy their kind of Bible and you destroy them. The Dogmaticians must therefore do battle with Higher Criticism [that is, the efforts of Wellhausen and others to discover how Scripture came to be] because Higher Criticism is taking away their very bread and butter. For it is destroying their prooftexts, which is the very stuff of their sermons.[80]

Such combativeness, along with the substance of Briggs's ideas, are what ultimately got him in trouble with his denomination. In his famous inaugural address, Briggs denounced the "dead wood, dry and brittle stubble, and noxious weeds" of current teaching.[81] The old ways of thinking needed to go, not just with regard to biblical interpretation, but with fundamental matters of church teachings and its day-to-day policies. "Criticism is at work with knife and fire," he said that night. "Let us cut down everything that is dead and harmful, every kind of dead orthodoxy."[82]

In spite of his critics, Briggs forged ahead with his mission. Today, he is considered a hero of—and something of a martyr to—the cause of modern biblical scholarship. His trial did not turn out as he had hoped. When the votes were counted the next day in Washington, D.C., a hefty majority of the delegates were found to have voted against him. A formal statement was prepared following the vote, declaring that

> this General Assembly finds that Charles A. Briggs has uttered, taught and propagated views, doctrines and teachings as set forth in the said charges contrary to the essential doctrine of Holy Scripture and the Standards, and in violation of his ordination vow. . . . Wherefore this General Assembly does hereby suspend Charles A. Briggs, the said appellee, from the office of minister in the Presbyterian Church in the United States of America.

To be sure, unlike convicted heretics in an earlier age, Briggs was not burned at the stake. In fact, he was even able to stay on at Union Theological Seminary, which voted to sever its connection with the Presbyterian Church in order to keep Briggs in his new chair. (After a while, he also received a new ordination, this time as a priest of the Protestant Episcopal Church.) But he was certainly jarred, and scarred, by the trial.

Despite his tribulations, Briggs continued his mission to slash away the "dead wood" (a goal he pursued in connection with another of his long-standing causes, doctrinal reform and Christian unity). Indeed, in a particularly stirring passage from one of his later books, Briggs switched metaphors, comparing the modern scholar's work not to pruning and clearing an over-grown field but to the clearing done by a modern archaeologist digging down into an ancient site:

> Ancient Jerusalem lies buried beneath the rubbish of more than eighteen centuries. It is covered over by the blood-stained dust of myriads of warriors, who have battled heroically under its walls and in its towers and streets. Its valleys are filled with the débris of palaces, churches, and temples. But the Holy Place of three great religions is still there, and thither countless multitudes turn in holy reverence and pious pilgrimage. In recent times this rubbish has in a measure been explored; and by digging to the rock-bed and the ancient foundations bearing the marks of the Phoenician workmen, the ancient city of the holy times has been recovered, and may now be constructed in our minds by the artist and the historian with essential accuracy.
>
> Just so the Holy Scripture, as given by divine inspiration to holy prophets, lies buried beneath the rubbish of centuries. It is covered over with the débris of the traditional interpretations of the multitudinous schools and sects. . . . The valleys of biblical truth have been filled up with the débris of human dogmas, ecclesiastical institutions, liturgical formulas, priestly ceremonies, and casuistic practices. Historical criticism is digging through this mass of rubbish. Historical criticism is searching for the rock-bed of the Divine word, *in order to recover the real Bible*. Historical criticism is sifting all this rubbish. It will gather out every precious stone. Nothing will escape its keen eye.

This passage might, in some respects, be seen as prophetic. Written almost exactly a hundred years ago, it foretells the twentieth century's concerted effort to uncover some of the Bible's deepest secrets, as will be documented in the chapters that follow. Briggs could only sense some of the changes that the new century would inaugurate: the flowering of archaeology as a science, bringing with it a new accuracy in the dating of ancient sites and a wealth of information about how biblical Israelites lived and even what they really believed; the decipherment of literally thousands of ancient texts written by Israel's neighbors, which offer fresh insights into the history and culture of the ancient Near East; and a far more sophisticated understanding of the biblical text itself, shedding new light on the historical background of different biblical books as well as revealing the meaning of previously misunderstood words and verses and whole chapters. Yet along with its vision of the future, the above passage reveals Briggs's blind spot—one that he shared with the rest of his own and the next two or three generations of biblical critics. The "real Bible" he spoke of has proven to be a far more elusive item than he or they ever imagined. Indeed, as I hope to show, finding that real Bible may ultimately have something to do with all those traditional interpretations for which Briggs had only contempt—the "rubbish" or "débris" that he wished to sweep away in his search for the "rock-bed of the Divine word." The following chapters will attempt to tell that story too.

About the Author

This book is intended as a work of scholarship, albeit one addressed to a broad, general audience. In such circumstances, I would prefer that the author remain in the background. Yet I understand that some readers may justifiably want to know something about who I am and where I stand, the better to take the measure of what I have to say. So, if I owe them an account of myself, I would like it to be in the opening words of Sir Thomas Browne's *Religio Medici*:

> For my Religion, though there be several Circumstances that might perswade the World I have none at all, (as the general scandal of my Profession, the natural course of my Studies, the indifferency* of my Behaviour and Discourse in matters of Religion, neither violently Defending one, nor with that common ardour and contention Opposing another;) yet, in despight hereof, I dare without usurpation assume the honourable Stile of a Christian.

If you were to substitute for "Christian" in this sentence "Orthodox Jew," it would pretty well sum things up for me. For those requiring further precision I should add that, as such, I am a believer in the divine inspiration of Scripture and an inheritor of many of the traditions of ancient interpreters cited in this book, indeed, a keeper of the Jewish sabbath, dietary laws, and all the other traditional practices of Orthodox Judaism. But I am also someone who has spent most of his life studying and teaching modern biblical scholarship.

* In today's English: scientific objectivity.

That puts me right in the middle of the dilemma to which this book is devoted.

I am afraid some of this may be lost in the pages that follow. They have a relentless refrain: people used to think X about this or that biblical figure or story or law or prophecy, but now modern scholars claim that Y is actually the case. In reporting on this, I may seem like an advocate of Y. Yet as I hope to argue in greater detail presently, Y is not all there is to the Bible. Knowing about the discoveries of modern scholars may certainly cause many people (as it has me) to think about Scripture in a somewhat different way. But what Scripture is, and how it is to be read, cannot ultimately be separated from still larger questions, questions about our very way of thinking about God, and about ourselves in relation to Him.

There is no magic bullet at the end of this book that will make all of modern scholarship's disturbing conclusions simply disappear; the dilemma this book describes is very real. To say this, I know, will not satisfy all readers. Indeed, I am sure that quite a few (including some of my fellow Orthodox Jews) will, after sampling a few pages, wish only to forget what they have read and throw the book across the room. This is hardly a comforting thought for me. If I have nonetheless gone ahead and written what I have, it is because I know full well that the questions raised by modern biblical scholarship are not going to go away. No small part of my purpose in surveying this scholarship's scope and conclusions is to lead into some consideration of their implications for people such as myself. (I should add that many of the theologians who have addressed themselves to the problems raised by modern biblical scholarship have tended to do so in the abstract, far from the nitty-gritty of that scholarship; this all too often leads to nice, abstract solutions, which, however, suddenly look a bit naïve when confronted with the actual details.) What I would like to do, therefore, is to present a fairly representative, detailed sample of what ancient and modern scholars have had to say about the Bible, and then conclude by examining the questions that this survey raises, sketching out one or two of my own thoughts about how a person might go about honestly confronting modern scholarship and yet not lose sacred Scripture in the process. In the meantime, my advice to readers is: keep your eye on the ancient interpreters.

2

The Creation of the World—
and of Adam and Eve

GENESIS 1–3

Expulsion from the Garden by Gustave Doré.

A DAY OF A THOUSAND YEARS. IMMORTALITY CUT SHORT.
TWO ACCOUNTS THAT SEEM TO CONFLICT.

*The Bible begins with an account of how the world was created in six days
and what happened to the first two human beings to live in it, Adam and Eve.
In a sense, all of reality as we know it was set into motion by the events
addressed by these opening chapters.*

According to the first chapter of Genesis, God created the world in six days. On
each day, He created something new: light on the first day, the sky on the second, the earth on the third, the sun and the moon and stars on the fourth, fish
and birds on the fifth, reptiles and land animals and human beings on the sixth.
After these six days, God rested on the seventh day—the first sabbath rest in
history. Most people are so used to this account that they scarcely see the powerful assertion underlying it: our world is fundamentally God's world—
everything in it, including ourselves, was made by Him. To say this is more than
to report on the origin of things: it is to set out a whole way of perceiving.

Following this account of the creation comes the story of Adam and Eve in
Genesis 2–3. According to the Bible, God created the first human being,
Adam, and placed him in a marvelous garden:

> The LORD God took the man and put him in the Garden of Eden to plow it
> and guard it. And the LORD God commanded the man, "You may eat from
> any tree in the garden. But you shall not eat from the tree of knowing good
> and evil,* because on the day that you eat from it, you shall die."
>
> Gen. 2:15–17

The text then goes on to relate how Eve was created out of Adam's "rib" (or
"side") while he was asleep. These first two humans then went about living
a comfortable existence together in Eden, until a certain serpent appeared on
the scene:

> Now the serpent was cleverer than any other animal that the LORD God
> had made. He said to the woman, "Did God really say that you may not eat
> from any of the trees in the garden?" The woman answered the serpent,
> "We can eat the fruit of the *other* trees in the garden. But about the fruit of
> the tree right in the middle of the garden God said, 'You shall not eat of it,
> nor shall you touch it, or you will die.' " But the serpent said to the

---

* "Knowing good and evil" might also be translated as "knowing all things," that is,
the tree confers wisdom and knowledge.

woman, "You will not die; God knows that as soon as you eat of it, your eyes will be opened, and you will be like God [*or* the gods], knowing good and evil." When the woman understood that the tree was good for food, and that it was a delight to the eyes, and that the tree was desirable to contemplate, she took of its fruit and ate; and she also gave some to her husband, who was with her, and he ate.

Gen. 3:1–6

As a result of their disobedience, Adam and Eve were banished from the wonderful garden. Henceforth they would have to live life in the considerably harsher conditions outside its borders.

This story certainly seemed to be saying something unflattering about the first two human beings: God imposed only one restriction on them, yet they failed to observe it. The more that ancient readers read the story, however, the more some of its details seemed puzzling. For example, the very words quoted earlier were problematic. God told Adam he would die *on the day* that he ate the forbidden fruit, but that is not what happens. In fact, Adam and Eve go on to live exceptionally long lives: Adam does not die until the age of 930. (We do not know exactly how long Eve lived, but she apparently enjoyed a similarly long lifetime.) If so, why did God say that Adam would die on that very day? To many ancient readers this must have sounded a bit like the sort of empty threats that parents sometimes make to their children. But it seemed unlikely that God would have issued an empty threat— and even if that were true, there was little reason for the Bible to have reported it. Ancient scholars therefore cast about for some other explanation.

At a certain point (the date is unknown, but sometime before the second century BCE), someone thought of connecting this problem with a certain verse in the book of Psalms. There the Psalmist, contrasting God's eternal existence with the fleeting years that humans live, wrote:

For a thousand years in Your sight are as yesterday, the way it passes, or like a watch in the night.

Ps. 90:4

The point, clearly, is that God, being eternal, no doubt perceives time very differently—even a thousand years must pass quite quickly for Him.

For our anonymous ancient interpreter, however, this verse seemed to hold the key to the "day" mentioned by God in the Garden of Eden. For, if one day ("yesterday") in God's sight actually equals a thousand years, then the fact that Adam died at the age of 930 would put his demise sometime in the late afternoon of a single "day" of God's.

The idea of such a thousand-year day solved another problem as well. According to chapter 1 of Genesis, the world was created in six days. Yet the same chapter states that the sun, the moon, and the stars were all created on the fourth day. How could this be? The unit of time called a *day* is determined by the movement of the sun through the sky. If the sun was not created until the fourth day, how could the Bible say that there had been three "days" preceding the sun's creation? The answer suggested by Ps. 90:4 was that the days mentioned in the creation of the world were *days of God,* a thousand-year unit of time known to Him and quite independent of the sun. The world was thus really created over a period of six thousand years.

This idea is alluded to in a number of ancient texts: apparently, it simply became common knowledge that a "day of God" lasts a thousand years:

> But do not ignore this one fact, beloved, that with the Lord one day is as a thousand years, and a thousand years as one day.
>
> 2 Pet. 3:8

> . . . for with Him a "day" signifies a thousand years.
>
> *Letter of Barnabas* 15:4

And so, quite naturally, it was used to explain God's words to Adam:

> Adam died . . . and he lacked seventy years of one thousand years [that is, he died at the age of 930]. One thousand years are as a single day in the testimony of heaven; therefore it was written concerning the tree of knowledge, "On the day that you eat of it, you will die."
>
> *Jubilees* 4:29–30

> It was said to Adam that on the day in which he ate of the tree, on that day he would die. And indeed, we know that he did not quite fill up a thousand years. We thus understand the expression "a day of the Lord is a thousand years" as [clarifying] this.
>
> Justin Martyr, *Dialogue with Trypho,* 81:3

Loss of Immortality

The idea of the thousand-year day solved one problem, but it raised a new one. After all, what kind of a punishment was it for Adam to have to die at the age of 930? If God were really out to punish him, would He not have killed him right away?

In pondering this question, interpreters arrived at a startling conclusion. Adam and Eve must originally have been intended to be immortal. Only then could a lifetime of 930 years seem to be a punishment. Indeed, if, in addition to the "tree of knowing good and evil," there was a "tree of life" inside the garden (Gen. 2:9), perhaps its original purpose was to supply the couple with a special fruit every few hundred years that would keep them living on and on. However, God said to Adam, if you eat from the tree of knowing good and evil, your immortality will be taken away: on the day that you eat of it, you will "die," that is, you will become mortal (perhaps because you will be denied access to the "tree of life"). And so it happened, not only to Adam and Eve, but to all their children. Because of Adam and Eve's sin, ancient interpreters said, all human beings die.

> And You set one commandment on him [Adam], but he violated it. As a result you established death for him and his descendents.
>
> 4 Ezra 3:7

> Adam sinned, and death was decreed against those who were to be born.
>
> 2 Bar. 23:4

Of course, people were troubled by the idea that all subsequent human beings should have to die because of a misdeed done by Adam and Eve alone. On the face of things, this did not seem fair. But perhaps the point was not that the punishment of these first humans was being visited on subsequent generations, but that the very act of eating the forbidden fruit had changed things forever. In other words, theoretically human beings could have been immortal, sinless creatures, perfectly obedient to God's will. But what happened in the garden changed all that and determined the whole future course of the human race: henceforth, all human beings would be sinful and, consequently, all would die. The disobedience of Adam and Eve thus came to be thought of as the "Original Sin," from which all subsequent sins necessarily followed.

What happened in the Garden of Eden therefore seemed to ancient interpreters to be nothing less than what they called (as the book of Genesis did not) the "Fall of Man." Before the disobedience of Adam and Eve, human beings had the potential of living forever in a sinless existence inside the marvelous garden; after the transgression, all of humanity entered a new, fallen state. As for the serpent who caused such a calamity, interpreters concluded that he could not have been just an ordinary snake. Instead, they now identified him with Satan himself. Indeed, the struggle with Satan that began in the garden was to go on outside its walls ever after.

This, in short, is how the story of Adam and Eve was understood for centuries.[1] In fact, even today, most people think of it in these same terms, and they are surprised to learn that the phrase "Fall of Man" is not to be found in the Genesis story, nor is there any mention of sinless existence in Eden, nor is the serpent identified in the story as the devil (he is just a talking snake). All these familiar elements are actually the creation of ancient interpreters.[2] In their reading it became a profound lesson about human sinfulness and the reason for our death.

How Modern Scholars Understand Genesis 1–3

With the rise of modern biblical scholarship, however, the opening chapters of Genesis took on a new look. Many scholars, observing what seemed to be inconsistencies in the text, began to question whether the story of Adam and Eve in chapters 2 and 3 had even been written by the same hand that wrote chapter 1. The two accounts simply did not seem to fit together.

According to chapter 1, God made the first human beings sometime on the sixth day, creating at least two of them (although the text might also be understood to be referring to a whole group of people) in a single act: "male and female He created *them*" (Gen. 1:27). But then the next chapter goes on to describe how God creates Adam. Adam seems to be the first human in history, and he is, at first, very much alone—almost as if the creation recounted in chapter 1 had never happened. God puts Adam alone in the Garden of Eden to live, then creates all the animals and has Adam name them, and only after that goes on to create Eve.[3]

Not only do chapters 1 and 2 seem to differ in some of their details, but they also depict God's actions in quite different ways. In chapter 1, God is represented as a cosmic sovereign: He speaks, gives orders, and as a result things just come into existence. "And God said, 'Let there be light!' and there was light" (Gen. 1:3). In chapters 2 and 3, by contrast, He seems to be more of a divine craftsman. He Himself shapes Adam out of the fresh mud of the earth and then breathes air into his nostrils to start his life—this seems to be a more hands-on approach to creating. Later, God is said to "walk about" the garden very much like a human being (Gen. 3:8); when Adam and Eve hide from Him, He calls out, "Where are you?"—apparently, He Himself does not know. At the end, God makes "leather clothes" for the pair—another hands-on act that seems at odds with the cosmic deity portrayed in chapter 1.

These little differences were hardly overwhelming—indeed, ancient interpreters had come up with quite adequate explanations for all of them. Nevertheless, the slight dissonance between the two sections did not disappear, and with the rise of the Documentary Hypothesis,* a new way of viewing these chapters presented itself with brutal simplicity. God is referred to quite consistently in chapter 1 by the word "God" (*'elohim*) alone. But starting in Gen. 2:4, exactly where the story of Adam and Eve begins, He suddenly becomes "the LORD God," that is, the word "God" is now preceded by the Tetragrammaton (Y-H-W-H). This name is then used consistently from that

---

* See above, chapter 1.

point until the end of the story in chapter 3. To modern biblical scholars, this fact alone indicated that there were two different authors at work here. One writer referred to God in one way, the other in another way.

The other differences likewise seemed to fall into place. The writer who used the name "God" alone saw Him as a distant, cosmic deity, one who mostly spoke and gave orders; the writer who used the name "the LORD God" conceived of Him in more personal terms, as a divine humanoid who walked around and shaped things and made clothes and did not always know where human beings might be hiding (Gen. 3:8–9). If so, then there was nothing surprising about the fact that chapter 1 differed from chapter 2 in other particulars as well. The author of chapter 1 was apparently content to say that all of humanity, "male and female," was created on the sixth day, without going into further details. This author may have known nothing about two individuals named Adam and Eve (or else he did not care to talk about them); indeed, he did not even mention the Garden of Eden in his description of the earth's creation. By the same token, the author of chapters 2 and 3 did not seem to show any awareness of the creation account that was to precede his own: he begins his account (Gen. 2:4–7) as if he were starting to tell the story of creation from scratch:

> When the LORD God was making the earth and the heavens—but before any wild plant was yet on the earth, and before any wild grass had yet sprouted, since the LORD God had not yet caused the rain to fall, and there was no one to plow the ground [anyway]—a flow came up from the earth, and it watered the surface of the ground. Then the LORD God shaped a man from the mud. . . .
>
> Gen. 2:4b-7

Apart from the fact that these words seem to announce a wholly new beginning rather than a continuation of the preceding chapter, scholars noted one or two additional elements that appear to conflict with the description of the creation in chapter 1. Thus, this passage seems to say that man's creation was begun "before any wild plant was yet on the earth, and before any wild grass had yet sprouted"; but according to chapter 1, plant life was created on the third day, long before the creation of man on the sixth. A little later (Gen. 2:19), this same account reports that the animals and the birds were created *after* Adam himself was—here was another apparent conflict with chapter 1.

A Priestly Writer

For all these reasons, modern biblical scholars came to believe that the book of Genesis actually contains two different, quite independent, accounts of the creation written by two different hands.[4] Going further, they argued that the author of chapter 1 had strong affinities with the author of, specifically, those sections of the Pentateuch that deal with priests and their duties in the sanctuary (what scholars came to call the P source).[5] They pointed to the occurrence of certain words favored by this priestly source in Genesis 1 as well. For example, one word for "work"—*mel'akhah*—is used dozens of times in priestly texts, but not nearly so much elsewhere in the Bible. It was certainly striking that this word *mel'akhah* is used three times in the last two sentences of the first creation account (Gen. 2:2–3); this insistence on the word almost seemed like a kind of priestly "signature" at the end of this account. Priestly texts also demonstrate a great concern for numbers and order, and such a concern certainly characterizes this opening chapter of Genesis. Priestly texts do use the name "the LORD" for God, but only when talking about things that occurred after this name had been revealed to Moses in Exod. 6:2; before that, God is simply "God," just as here in Genesis 1. Priestly texts also avoid depicting God in human terms;[6] He is a great, cosmic deity. All these things in chapter 1 suggested a priestly connection; as one modern scholar put it:

> Anyone who expounds Genesis chapter 1 must understand one thing: this chapter is Priestly doctrine—indeed, it contains the essence of Priestly knowledge in a most concentrated form.[7]

Perhaps most striking of all for modern scholars was the whole matter of the sabbath.[8] The sabbath, they noted, was a subject dear to priests. True, it is mentioned outside of priestly texts as well, but in priestly writings the proper observance of the sabbath is stressed in a way not found elsewhere. When they considered Genesis 1 carefully, they concluded that the sabbath—and not the creation per se—was its true subject. This whole account of how the world was made, they said, had been set forth in this six-day scheme *so as to stress the importance of the seventh day, the sabbath.* From the very beginning of the world, this priestly author was saying, the sabbath has existed; indeed, God arranged the creation into six "days" so as to be able to rest on the seventh day, *and so should you.* That, rather than a simple recitation of the facts of the creation, seemed to modern scholars to be the whole point of chapter 1.[9]

Hunter-Gatherers and Farmers

What of the story of Adam and Eve? Modern scholars sought to connect this account with the source of texts designated as J. Not only did this story use the name "the LORD" just as J texts do throughout, but it also depicted God in the anthropomorphic (humanlike) fashion found elsewhere in texts attributed to the J source. They found that when the J source talked about the creation, it exhibited little interest in how other aspects of the world came into being—the earth and the sky, or the sun or stars or fish or birds—nor, of course, did it mention the sabbath.[10] What was important in this account, they said, were these first two humans and how the details of their creation related to later reality. And so, the story implies, later human beings are called "man" (*'adam* in Hebrew) because that was how the first created human was called, apparently because he was made out of the ground (*'adamah*). Likewise, people have to work for their food, the story says, and women have to suffer the pains of childbirth, because of something that happened long ago, when the first two human beings disobeyed God's orders. These past events, in other words, are recounted in part because their effects continue to be felt today.

Beyond these basic points, scholars were (and still are) divided about the original purpose of the story of Adam and Eve. One interesting theory to emerge of late is that this story seems to reflect on a particular moment in the development of civilization—not so much the time of humanity's creation per se, but a somewhat later moment, when people first learned the secret of agriculture and so ceased to live in what anthropologists call "hunter-gatherer" societies.[11] Figuring out that seeds can be collected and then deliberately planted in fields was a great step forward for humanity: thereafter, people no longer had to wander from place to place to find edible plants and game (and risk going hungry if they found nothing).[12] But agriculture also brought with it certain pains. To be a farmer meant working long hours under the sun, earning one's bread "by the sweat of your face" (Gen. 3:19). At approximately the same stage of development, people in some societies also begin to wear more—and more elaborate—clothing, and this, too, was not an unmixed blessing. Before that stage, "the man and his wife were both naked, and they were not ashamed" (Gen. 2:25). Modern scholars also know that the discovery of agriculture in some societies coincides roughly with another discovery, that childbirth, too, is preceded by an act of "planting" that takes place nine months earlier. Before human beings understood this, women just mysteriously became pregnant and had babies.[13] In such a world, a child's progenitor may not necessarily understand that he has any specific relationship to the children who are born to this or that woman. But once the reason for childbirth is discovered, children are understood to have *two* parents, and sometimes a new social organization results, with a new division of labor. The man "will cling to his wife and they shall be one flesh" (Gen. 2:24); he will toil in the fields for *his* wife and *his* children. Correspondingly, the story seems to be saying, the woman will toil for *her* harvest, delivering offspring in pain and suffering. Indeed, if the children she bears are to be exclusively hers and her husband's, then she will have to be his wife and no other's.

Of course, no biblicist would claim that the Genesis story itself is a direct reminiscence of such a societal change—for that to be true, the narrative would have to go back to an implausibly early date. Rather, according to this theory, the story of Adam and Eve would appear to be a kind of speculative reconstruction. Ancient Israelites were not modern anthropologists, of course, but that would not have stopped them from trying to consider how certain basic changes might have come about—specifically, how humans came to be farmers, learned the secret of childbirth, and came to fashion clothes for themselves. All of these elements may be rolled together into the account of events attributed by scholars to the J source.[14]

As for the serpent in the story, he is said to be "clever" (Gen. 3:1), and he also serves to convince Adam and Eve to *become* clever, that is, to eat from the knowledge-giving tree. His appearance in the story may have some connection with the worship of snakes attested elsewhere in the ancient Near East; such a divine or semidivine serpent might have been deemed an apt vehicle for transmitting the sacred knowledge of agriculture and the other things that go with it.[15] Or, the snake in the story may simply be an ordinary snake. After all, snakes were proverbially clever in the biblical world, and their lack of legs might indeed have looked like some sort of divine punishment: if so, this story explained their crime.

In short, for modern biblical scholarship, the opening chapters of Genesis combined two originally separate texts, each with its own agenda. The first set out in schematic fashion how the entire universe was created in six universal "days," the better to stress the importance of the sabbath on the seventh day. The second account was focused much more narrowly on Adam and Eve, whose way of life seemed to represent something like that of "hunter-gatherer" societies, at least at the beginning of the story. What happens next—the serpent, the fruit of "knowing good and evil," and all the rest—seeks to explain the transition from that sort of society to another, in which human beings cease to hunt, and have to work to eat, and wear clothes and live in families.

Scholars have also pointed out that this second account is full of what they call "folklore motifs." Thus, by eating from the tree of "knowing good and evil" (as noted, this expression can also mean "knowing all things" in Hebrew),[16] Adam and Eve not only found out about a lot of things—agriculture, childbirth, and so forth—but they became, in the process, a bit like God Himself. As God observes at the end of the story, "the man has become like one of us, knowing good and evil" (3:22). Yet there is a limit to how godlike humans can become, the story says. Like all creatures, humans still have to die, so they will never fully be like God; they will never be able to "take also from the tree of [eternal] life and eat and live forever" (ibid.). In this respect, scholars say, the story is reminiscent of Greek myths or other ancient folklore, explaining the basic facts of human nature or why life is the way it is. Folkloristic too is the presence of a talking snake or an object with special powers (in this case, a tree).

Two Sets of Interpretations

The two sets of interpretations of Genesis 1–3 pose squarely the question addressed by this book as a whole. How are we to read the Bible? The ancient interpreters' understanding of these chapters was uplifting, even sublime: in them, God explained the most basic facts of our existence—how the universe was created, why we must die, and why, despite our best efforts, we end up sinning. The concern with morality and obedience to God is central. These lessons were prized by ancient Jews and Christians, and they were no small part of the reason why these religions made the study of Scripture such an important activity. But according to modern biblical scholars, to understand these stories in such a way is largely wishful thinking. What they are *really* about has much more to do with the priestly promotion of sabbath observance, and with the discovery of agriculture and the resulting change in societal organization.

It would be nice to be able to read the way the ancient interpreters did. In fact, especially to some Christians, it may be vital: the New Testament understanding of the crucifixion and resurrection as God's remedy for the "Fall of Man" (see, for example, Rom. 5:12–19; 1 Cor. 15:20–22) depends on such a Fall actually having taken place. But modern scholars say that the idea of the Fall is not really there in the biblical text itself, only in the text as it was interpreted in ancient times. The story may be about a change in lifestyle—that is, in the way human beings make a living and dress and organize their society—but it is not about a change in the human beings' very nature.

What modern biblical scholars say about the Bible is often *not* sublime or uplifting. Indeed, if they are right and what the Bible is really about is different authors with their particular interests and programs, if it has to do only with contradictory details and hunter-gatherer societies and folkloristic motifs, then why bother with it at all? On the other hand, there is no denying that at least some of modern scholarship sounds persuasive—the pattern of different names used for God, and corresponding to it, the different agendas and characteristics of J and P, and so forth. Like it or not, it seems impossible simply to shut out modern scholarship entirely. What to do?

Having posed the question in these terms, I might now simply proceed to try to answer it, but I believe that would be unfair to both sides of this debate. To understand fully the achievement of modern biblical scholarship and its implications, it is necessary to look at the whole Bible and not just one story. Likewise, the true character of ancient biblical interpretation—and a real assessment of *its* achievements—will not emerge from examining the first three chapters of Genesis alone. From either standpoint, it is necessary to continue.

3

Cain and Abel

GENESIS 4:1–16

The Body of Abel Found by Adam and Eve by William Blake.

THE SON OF SATAN AND THE WORLD'S FIRST MURDERER.
HERMANN GUNKEL AND ANCIENT TALES. THE NOMADIC KENITES.

The story of Cain and Abel does not even fill a whole chapter, but it has long fascinated readers. How is it that Adam and Eve's first son turned out to be a murderer—and what does this imply about human nature?

Expelled from the Garden of Eden, Adam and Eve soon had their first children, Cain and Abel. The Bible recounts that these two sons chose different professions: Cain became a farmer and Abel a shepherd. When, one day, they decided to offer a sacrifice to God—Cain from his crops, Abel from his herds—God showed a preference for Abel's offering, and this infuriated his brother.

> So, when they were in the field, Cain rose up against his brother Abel and killed him. Then the LORD said to Cain, "Where is your brother Abel?" He said, "I do not know; am I my brother's keeper?"
>
> Gen. 4:8–9

Hearing this deceitful (and arrogant) answer, God sentenced Cain to leave his farmland and be a wanderer on the earth. When Cain objected that this would leave him exposed to attack, God reassured him: "Anyone who kills Cain will suffer vengeance sevenfold." He then gave Cain some sort of "sign"—what kind is not specified—to ward off any potential attackers. Chastened, Cain trudged off to the life of wandering to which he had been condemned.

Coming right at the beginning of human history, this story seemed to ancient interpreters to contain a lesson about our very nature. It was bad enough that Adam and Eve had been unable to keep the only commandment that God gave them, not to eat the forbidden fruit. Now, however, humanity in its second generation took a turn that was still worse: left to their own devices, this story seemed to say, some people will stop at nothing, not even murder. Yet the story had a positive message as well. Cain's crime did not go unpunished; there is a moral order in the universe. If he did not receive the death penalty for the crime of murder (as later biblical law would dictate, Exod. 21:12), Cain was nonetheless sentenced to walk the earth forever as a homeless wanderer. The unspecified "sign" given to him came to be understood as a mark of shame, the "brand of Cain."

A Tale of Good and Evil

All this, however, did not explain what had pushed Cain to murder his own brother. To ancient interpreters it seemed unlikely that a single little incident—Cain's anger over God's preference for Abel's sacrifice—could have led him to such a drastic step. There must have been more involved. And once again, a slight irregularity in the biblical story seemed to hold a clue. At the very beginning of the story, Cain's birth is announced in the following words:

> Now the man [Adam] knew his wife Eve, and she conceived and bore Cain, saying, "I have gotten a man with [the help of] the LORD."
>
> Gen. 4:1

It was odd, to begin with, for a mother to look at her newborn baby and refer to him as a "man." The Hebrew word 'ish is never used for a baby or even a young boy (there is nothing in Hebrew like the English hybrid "man-child," meaning a child of the male sex). The word 'ish means a grown man, and was sometimes even used as an honorific title, "sir." What is more, although most modern translations render the last phrase in Eve's words as "with the help of the LORD," the word "help" is not in the text. What the Bible literally says is: "I have gotten a man with the LORD." But what could Eve have meant by that?

Ancient interpreters did not contemplate these problems in isolation, of course; they knew full well that Cain had gone on to murder his brother, and so of course they tried to find a connection between these puzzling words and Cain's later sin. The conclusion that they reached was nonetheless surprising: Cain, they came to believe, was a half-human, half-angelic creature, the son of the devil.

The word 'ish, ancient interpreters knew, was sometimes also used to designate an angel (Gen. 18:2; 32:24, and so forth); thus, if Eve called her newborn son an 'ish, perhaps what she meant was that he was actually an angel, or part angel. If, in the next breath, she went on to say that she had gotten him "with the LORD," that might help explain how a female human ended up giving birth to an angelic being. Of course, she certainly did not mean to say that God Himself was the child's father! She must have been using "the LORD" elliptically, as a shorthand way of saying "an angel of the LORD." (This too, interpreters believed, was not altogether unique; a wicked angel is called simply "the LORD" in Exod. 4:24.) Given Cain's evil nature, it simply stood to reason that the angel involved was a wicked angel, indeed, none other than Satan himself.*

---

* In ancient times, Satan was often described as a wicked angel; indeed, he had different angel-type names (names with the suffix -el): Sammael, Gadriel, Satanel, and so forth.

The only problem with this theory was that the first part of the sentence cited above seemed to say unequivocally that Adam was the boy's father: "Now the man [Adam] knew his wife Eve, and she conceived and bore Cain." All modern readers of this text understand it to be using the biblical "know" euphemistically, as a reference to sexual relations. But perhaps not; perhaps what Adam in fact *knew* was that his wife had been made pregnant by someone else:

> And Adam *knew* that his wife Eve had conceived from the angel Sammael [= Satan], and she became pregnant and gave birth to Cain. He was like the angels and not like humans, so she said, "I have acquired a man, indeed, an angel of the LORD."[1]
>
> *Targum Pseudo-Jonathan,* translation of Gen. 4:1

This interpretation of the story circulated widely in late and postbiblical times. Cain simply came to be known as the son of the devil; that was why he killed Abel—he was evil from birth. Such an understanding is reflected, for example, in the New Testament:

> By this it may be seen who are the children of God and who are the children of the devil: whoever does not do right is not of God, nor he who does not love his brother. For this is the message that you have heard from the beginning,[2] that we should love one another, and not be like Cain *who was of the evil one* and murdered his brother. And why did he murder him? Because his own deeds were evil and his brother's righteous.
>
> 1 John 3:10–12

Similarly:

> Having been made pregnant by the seed of the devil . . . she brought forth a son.
>
> Tertullian, *On Patience* 5:15

The details thus fit together perfectly. The whole story of Cain and Abel turned out to be a classic struggle between good and evil. Cain, born of the devil, had been wicked from the start. How could God possibly have accepted a sacrifice from Satan's own offspring? But God's rejection of Cain's offering in favor of Abel's threw Cain into a murderous frenzy; nothing could stop him from shedding his brother's innocent blood. His punishment was altogether justified, and the story as a whole was intended to serve as a warning to later generations: anyone who allies himself with the devil will be condemned as Cain was, branded as an outcast from the civilized world.[3]

Cain and Abel in Modern Biblical Scholarship

One question often asked by modern scholars about the stories of Genesis is: why was this written down? Underlying this question is the notion that there is nothing in the biblical world that quite corresponds to our idea of "literature." Books were certainly not written for individual readers to purchase and read at their leisure; but even the idea of literature, of fictional worlds visited for a time and enjoyed, is a bit out of place in the biblical world. The same is true of our idea of "history," that is, the systematic narration of past events to give people a knowledge of what happened long ago. Stories set in the past were told, but it was usually with a specific purpose in mind, especially with texts purporting to talk about earliest times. That purpose was neither literary nor historical, at least not in our sense. The purpose was to explain the present.

The first scholar to pursue this understanding systematically with regard to the stories of Genesis was a great German biblicist, Hermann Gunkel (1862–1932).[4] Gunkel came of age at a time when the Documentary Hypothesis was all the rage in biblical studies, but he found its focus too narrow and confining. The very idea of constituent *documents* seemed to him misplaced. Many of the Bible's tales of Israel's remotest ancestors must have existed long before they became part of this or that "document," he believed. They must have been passed on orally, in some cases for generations or centuries—and in order to be preserved they must have served some purpose, and played some role, in the life of ordinary people.

Adopting a concept from the study of folklore and mythology, Gunkel suggested that many biblical narratives had an *etiological* character, that is, their basic purpose was to explain how things came to be the way they are now (at the time of the story's composition).[5] Thus, if the Bible relates that Abraham and Abimelech swore an oath while standing next to a certain well, that would explain why today the same place is known as Beer Sheba, since in Hebrew Beer Sheba means, or sounds like it might mean, "Well of the Oath." Other proper names too—place-names like Bethel and Babylon and Edom, or the names of people like Abraham and Jacob and Israel and many others—all have little narratives connected with them in the Bible; the stories explain these names via some incident, something that happened in the distant past, that resulted in a person or place being called in a certain way ever after.

Etiological stories, Gunkel noted, are not limited to names. Institutions in Israelite society, such as the hereditary priesthood or the existence of prophets or the division into twelve tribes, are likewise explained in the Bible as having come about because of this or that incident in the distant past. Thus: why are there prophets—why doesn't God speak directly to all of Israel instead of using individual chosen messengers? It all goes back to something that happened one day at Mount Sinai. So too with foreign relations: why is it that we Israelites do not get along with our neighbors the Edomites? It all goes back to the two founders of our respective nations, Jacob and Esau, and what happened when they were boys. Even the story of Adam and Eve was found to have a complex of etiological elements in it: it explained how human beings were first created, as well as why women give birth in pain and men must earn their bread through toil and snakes slither legless on the ground and there is enmity between snakes and humans—all because of some incident that took place in the distant past.

Gunkel's etiological approach to the stories of Genesis has proven to be remarkably influential. Many subsequent scholars have come to discern an etiological purpose behind various biblical stories—including the story of Cain and Abel.

An Etiological Tale

Cain's name in Hebrew is also the name of a tribe in the biblical world, the Kenites. (The two are spelled differently in English, but in Hebrew the spelling is the same, *qayin.*)* The Kenites were not part of Israel; they were a nomadic tribe that lived somewhat to the south of Israel's settled territory. They are mentioned in several places in the Bible—in the books of Genesis, Numbers, Judges, 1 Samuel, and 1 Chronicles. (They seem to have been closely associated with other nomadic peoples who also lived in the southland.)

According to the etiological approach of modern scholarship, a story about someone named Cain is likely to have something to do with the Kenites. Indeed, if, as is often the case with etiological tales, So-and-so is the founder and embodiment of the people or tribe or city named after him, then a story about Cain will most probably be out to explain the particular characteristics of the Kenites—what they are like (from an Israelite standpoint) and more precisely, *what happened in the past* to make them the way they are now.[6]

The story of Cain and Abel contains one piece of evidence in particular that offers some support for the idea that its overriding purpose was indeed etiological. After God sentences Cain to leave his farmland and wander

---

* The letter *q* in transcriptions of Hebrew (as well as Arabic and other Semitic languages) represents a sound similar to that of *k* in English, but articulated at the very back of the mouth (not on the roof of the mouth, like *k*).

about, Cain immediately objects that "anyone who finds me may kill me" (Gen. 4:14). God then replies:

> "Therefore, anyone who kills Cain will suffer vengeance sevenfold."
>
> Gen. 4:15

There are several ways of saying "anyone" in biblical Hebrew. Normally, "he who kills Cain" or "the man [or woman] who kills" would have done fine here. But this sentence passed up those phrases in favor of another way of saying "anyone" that envisages a whole potential class of people. What it literally says is "every killer of Cain." By using this phrase, one might argue, the text seems to have tipped its etiological hand. For, why speak of more than one killer? Surely Cain himself could be killed only once, nor was a whole group of attackers necessarily required to do the job. It would therefore seem, according to this theory, that what the text really had in mind was Cain as a representative of all subsequent Kenites. What God says, in effect, is that "every killer of a Kenite" or "anyone who ever kills a Kenite" will suffer seven times the usual revenge. Thus, "Cain" here—and, in fact, throughout the story—seems really to be an embodiment, or a representative, of the tribe that was to bear his name.*

What do scholars know about that tribe? By its location to the south of biblical Israel and its nomadic way of life, the tribe of Kenites was associated in particular with two nearby peoples, the Midianites and the Amalekites. We know a bit more about these—they both have a reputation in the Bible of being fierce fighters, and there is ample evidence that they were feared in Israel because of their brutality. The Amalekites cruelly attacked the weakened Israelites after the exodus from Egypt (Exod. 17:8–16), and God eventually commanded Israel to "wipe out" their name (Deut. 25:19). He likewise commanded Israel to assail the Midianites (Num. 25:16; 31:2) for their hostility. If the Kenites were the close neighbors of these two peoples and shared their way of life, they were probably also viewed with suspicion and fear by Israel. Indeed, a certain Lamech, mentioned at the end of Genesis 4, is said to have boasted of his own ferocity in these terms:

---

* As Gunkel and others have pointed out, this is true of numerous references to a group of descendants by the name of their founder or eponym. "Cursed be Canaan," Noah says of his grandson, "let him be the lowest of slaves to his brothers"—but these words apply not to Canaan, the young boy standing before him, but to the whole future Canaanite nation. So similarly, Balaam addresses "the Kenite" or "Cain" indiscriminately in Num. 24:21, but by either name this individual designates the whole nation of his descendants (Cain is by then long dead). The instructions in Leviticus that "Aaron" do this or that likewise refer to his descendants, the Aaronide priesthood, or, sometimes, to any future high priest. Examples could be multiplied.

Adah and Zillah, hear my voice! O women of Lamech, heed what I say!
I would kill a man to avenge a wound, or a boy for a mere bruise.
If Cain is avenged sevenfold, then Lamech seventy-seven!

Gen. 4:23–24

Lamech says this to scare off anyone tempted to attack him. But it is certainly significant that he can think of no better example of cruel, lopsided revenge than "Cain," that is, the Kenites. It must have been that, from a very early period, the Kenites already had a reputation for killing seven of your people if you killed one of theirs. (The normal arrangement in the ancient Near East—and elsewhere—was the so-called law of the talion: that is, if you kill one of our people then we have the right to kill one of yours.)[7]

If so, one scholar has argued, the true import of God's words to Cain cited earlier is now clear: "Anyone who kills Cain will suffer vengeance sevenfold" is the story's way of explaining why the Kenites are an apparent exception to the law of the talion. It was God who granted them the right to take sevenfold revenge. This right was given to the Kenites as a form of compensation for their having been turned into nomadic wanderers: since they would not have city walls to protect them, they would be given the special deterrent of sevenfold revenge.

The other etiological element identified by modern scholars in this story is a bit harder to pin down, but it concerns the odd association of Israel's God with the territory—and peoples—to its immediate southeast. Normally in the ancient Near East, gods were associated with this or that city or nation and would be located right there. That was true of Israel's God as well—he "dwelt" on Mount Zion in Jerusalem or in other sacred sites within the country. Yet some of the Bible's most ancient texts suggest that that had not always been the case—that His original locale was in Sinai, far to the south or southeast, or that He had "come from" Mount Seir or Mount Paran or Teman. The Kenites were in roughly this same area. If so, modern scholars reason, perhaps the Kenites had at one time worshiped the same God as the Israelites. Indeed, the Bible says that Moses married the daughter of a Kenite (Judg. 1:16), and it is while he was living with his father-in-law that Moses chanced upon the "mountain of God" and was summoned to His service (Exodus 3). To some modern scholars, this seemed a further indication that Israel's religion had actually originated in the region of the Kenites and was only "imported" at some later stage to the land where Israel came to dwell.[8]

Thus, according to this theory, an etiological story about the Kenites would have to reckon with what, for later Israelites, were this tribe's two outstanding characteristics, its ferocity and its odd association with Israel's God. And that is exactly what the story of Cain and Abel appears to do. It tells about the Kenites' eponym, Cain. He killed his own brother in a fit of jealousy—that certainly would explain why later Kenites are so fierce: they are all descended from a cruel murderer! What is more, when God exiled Cain and made him a wanderer for this crime, He allowed Cain to be an exception to the law of the talion and to take sevenfold revenge on his enemies. This further accounts for the Kenites' ferocity. As for their worshiping Israel's God, this too is explained by the story—naturally, from the standpoint of later Israelites. Cain, the story says, had once been a farmer—presumably he lived in the farmlands that Israel now inhabited. So of course he had worshiped the God who holds sway there. After Cain was exiled, he continued to worship this same God—which explains the Kenites' odd connection to "our" religion.*

One further observation followed from this analysis. If the story of Cain was an etiological tale about the Kenites, then it could not be that Cain was originally thought to be the son of Adam and Eve; the sentence that asserts this (Gen. 4:1) must have been added on later, when the story was incorporated into the Bible.[9] The reason is that biblical history relates that there was a great flood after the time of Cain, and it wiped out every human being except Noah and his immediate family. How could Cain be the ancestor of the Kenites, who lived long after the flood, if he were also the son of the first two humans and, consequently, lived before the flood? He and all his descendants would have perished in the flood, so there could be no Kenites later on. Therefore, according to this reasoning, the etiological tale of Cain must originally not have been located specifically before the flood; it must simply have taken place "sometime back there," in the distant past, but not necessarily at the beginning of human history.[10] Indeed, there are other indications within the story that its present location is artificial. For, if Cain is the eldest son of Adam and Eve and he has only one brother, whom he has just now killed, why does he complain to God that once he is exiled "anyone who finds me may kill me"? There is no "anyone" alive except his own mother and father.

The Sign of Cain

What about Cain's "sign"? In the light of modern biblical lexicography, it would appear that there was none. The word translated as "sign" here, 'ôt, can indeed mean that, as in "signs and wonders." But it also can mean "distinguishing mark" or even "pledge" or "oath"—and these seem far more appropriate in context. God says, "Anyone who kills Cain [= a Kenite] will suffer vengeance sevenfold"; the text then continues, "and He set it as a dis-

---

* If so, modern scholars would say, the tale of Cain actually reverses the historic reality—the religion of this God is said by the story to have moved from Israel's land southward, whereas the evidence, archaeological and biblical, suggests an opposite migration.

tinguishing mark [*or perhaps, a* pledge *or* oath] for Cain, to prevent any who might find him from slaying him." [11] In other words, Cain's "sign" or distinguishing mark was God's granting him the right to sevenfold vengeance.

Ancient interpreters, however, preferred to think that some actual *thing,* some physical sign, was given to Cain. Since this same word *'ôt* came to mean, in later Hebrew, a letter of the alphabet, *Targum Pseudo-Jonathan* and other texts suggest that God actually engraved a letter of the alphabet on Cain's forehead. Other ancient interpreters theorized that the sign consisted of a pair of ferocious-looking animal horns that might scare off any potential attacker. Still others proposed that God might have given Cain a dog to *signal* him at the approach of danger. Others said it was some kind of mark without entering into details; as already noted, this mark came in time to be thought of as a mark of shame, "the brand of Cain."

The Typological Cain

One of the favorite ways of early Christians to read biblical stories was *typologically,* that is, as foreshadowing the events of the New Testament. Since Abel was a shepherd who was murdered, this immediately suggested that he might be a foreshadowing of Jesus, who is called "the good shepherd" (John 10:11) and who was murdered as well, crucified by the Romans. A tradition thus developed of understanding the whole story as a hint of the crucifixion.

> But Cain took God's commandment [to avoid envy] heedlessly; indeed, as the sin of envy grew overpowering within him, he murdered his brother with malice aforethought. Such was the one who founded the earthly city. However, he also symbolized the Jews, by whom Christ, shepherd of the flocks of men, was killed. [It is Christ] whom Abel, shepherd of the flocks of sheep, prefigures.
>
> Augustine, *City of God* 15:7

It will be noticed that Augustine substituted the Jews for the Romans as the killers of Jesus. Modern historians know this to be untrue, but it served a useful purpose in Augustine's time (and was hardly Augustine's idea alone): after all, once Christians had begun to preach to, and try to convert, Romans to Christianity, it was expedient to shift the blame for the crucifixion away from the Roman governors of Palestine. Instead, Cain became, as Augustine says, a symbol of the Jews, and this biblical story, along with many others, was marshaled to the service of persecuting the Jews—in the Roman Empire and, unfortunately, long afterward.

Two Different Stories

Notwithstanding this sour note, it is striking to see again how differently our two sets of interpreters understand the Bible. It would not be an exaggeration to say that, in the light of the foregoing, the story of Cain and Abel actually turns out to be two very different stories.

For ancient interpreters, the story is all about crime and punishment, and about good and evil. Cain, as the offspring of Satan, was obviously destined for wickedness, whereas Abel was good. God's rejection of Cain's sacrifice was as inevitable as the subsequent shedding of his brother's innocent blood. Whatever Cain's sign was, it was some *thing* that was put on his body or given to him, the mark of a crime that would follow him all his days. Such was, by the Bible's account, the human race in its second generation. For some early Christians, the whole story was also understood as a foreshadowing of the crucifixion.

For modern biblical scholars this episode was originally an etiological tale intended to explain the nature of the Kenites by relating an incident connected with their putative founder and eponym, Cain. Cain's murder of his brother accounted for his descendants' legendary ferocity, as did God's special decree allowing them sevenfold vengeance. The fact that Cain was said to have been exiled from the settled farmland to live the life of a southern nomad also appears designed to explain a curious circumstance, namely, the connection of Israel's God to the Kenites' homeland. In the story's version of things, the worship of Israel's God must have traveled south with Cain and taken root in the desert wilderness. As for Cain's "sign," there actually was none—the word "sign" really refers to the distinguishing mark of the Kenites, namely, their sevenfold revenge.

If this story had only recently been dug out of the earth by modern-day archaeologists, it would no doubt be considered an interesting relic, an ancient Israelite reflection on the Kenites—but nothing more. As part of the Bible, however, the tale of Cain and Abel has always meant, and still seems to mean, so much more. Must that "so much more" be dismissed now that we know what modern scholars know? Or can we still hold on to the Cain and Abel of postbiblical interpreters, the story of good and evil locked in their eternal conflict?

4

The Great Flood

GENESIS 6–8

Going into the Ark by Philip James de Loutherbourg.

THE LUSTFUL ANGELS. NOAH AS A MORAL EXEMPLAR.
THE ANCIENT NEAR EASTERN FLOOD STORY. J AND P AGAIN.

*After the time of Cain and Abel, the Bible relates that Adam and Eve had
another son, Seth, and that humanity continued to grow in subsequent generations. But God eventually became displeased with human beings and
resolved to bring a great flood on the earth to destroy what He had made.
Only Noah and his family survived.*

The story of Noah and the great flood is one of those biblical narratives that
have caused many modern readers to denounce the God of the Hebrew Bible
as "wrathful." (This description is actually a leftover from an old Christian
argument against Judaism: the Old Testament God is wrathful, the New Testament God is loving.) Here is not the place for religious polemics, but it
ought to be observed that any view of God as *only* loving—a view which
hardly does justice to either testament—eventually runs aground of reality.
After all, we are just emerging from five or six decades of unprecedented
world tragedies, not only wars and slaughter and industrial-scale geno-
cide, but also several natural catastrophes, including at least one great
flood (the tsunami of 2004, whose victims in the Pacific and Southeast
Asia numbered more than a hundred thousand). It is fine to speak of God's
love for humanity, as both testaments do, but if that is all there is to God,
then who is responsible for all the suffering in the world? The biblical
story of the great flood presents a God who kills as well as keeps alive (see
also Deut. 32:39), who is—as the Bible says elsewhere—both "the maker of
good and the creator of ill" (Isa. 45:7), and such a description must, alas,
have some resonance for our own times. But there is also the positive element that total disaster was ultimately averted—a remnant, Noah and his
family, survived.

For ancient readers of the Bible, the story of the flood thus stood out first
as a model of God's power to destroy as well as to save. But the story itself was
not without difficulty. What concerned ancient interpreters in particular was
the reason for the flood: what was it that human beings had done that caused
God to wish to wipe them out? True, Cain had murdered his brother, but later
humanity seemed to have included a number of righteous individuals. In the
generation after Cain, for example, the Bible notes that people "began to call
on the name of the LORD" (Gen. 4:26), which certainly sounded like a good
thing to do;[1] somewhat later on came Enoch, who "walked with God" (Gen.
5:22, 24). In fact, Cain seemed to be the only truly *bad* person to have lived
in those ancient days. Why destroy all of humanity because of one rotten egg?

And even if one evil person was sufficient cause, why had God waited so many generations after Cain before actually bringing the flood?

For answers, the attention of ancient interpreters came to focus on the sentences that just precede the flood account:

> When people began to multiply on the face of the earth, and daughters were born to them, the sons of God saw that they were fair; and they took wives for themselves of all that they chose. Then the LORD said, "My spirit shall not abide in humanity forever, since they are flesh; their days shall be one hundred twenty years." The Nephilim were on the earth in those days—and also afterward—when the sons of God went in to the daughters of humans, who bore children to them. These were the heroes who were of old, men of renown. The LORD saw that the wickedness of humankind was great on the earth, and that every inclination of the thoughts of their hearts was only evil, continually. And the LORD was sorry that He had made humankind on the earth.
>
> Gen. 6:1–6

The passage was certainly puzzling. The phrase "sons of God" was generally understood to refer to the angels, and according to this passage their mating with human females apparently produced a race of superhumans, the Nephilim (the Hebrew term is obscure), "the heroes who were of old, men of renown." Was not this the proximate cause of the great catastrophe?[2] The idea of angels mating with humans certainly looked fishy; crossing divine lines for immoral purposes must indeed have been a serious offense. What is more, the angels seem to have done so for no more noble a reason than that they were attracted by the women's bodies ("the sons of God saw that they were fair"); surely *angels* ought to be above such tawdry lusts. For these reasons, ancient interpreters saw a direct connection between this paragraph and the flood that followed. The wicked angels were responsible:

> [Enoch said:] "In the generation of my father Jared, some from the height of heaven transgressed the word of the LORD. And behold, they *commit sin and transgress the law, and have been promiscuous with women and commit sin with them,* and have married some of them, and have begotten children by them. And there will be a great destruction over the whole earth, and there will be a deluge, and there will be great destruction for one year."
>
> 1 Enoch 106:13–15

Moreover, if the humans were going to be destroyed in the flood, it did not seem fair that angels or their hybrid offspring should be the only guilty ones. Perhaps the humans had been complicit in this great sin, as another ancient interpreter suggested:

> For thus they [the women] allured the Watchers [another name for this class of angels][3] before the flood; for as these [Watchers] continually beheld them, they lusted after them, and they conceived the act in their mind.
>
> *Testament of Reuben* 5:6

This same tradition of the alluring women was known to the English poet John Milton, who describes

> A Beavie of fair Women, richly gay
> In Gems and wanton dress; to th' Harp they sung
> Soft amorous Ditties, and in dance came on.
>
> *Paradise Lost,* 10:582–85

Noah the Preacher of Righteousness

At the same time, interpreters wondered about the figure of Noah. Why had *he* been saved? Although the Bible asserted that he was "a righteous man, blameless in his generation," it did not mention a single righteous act that he performed before the flood. Even after the flood, as a matter of fact, Noah does not appear to be particularly virtuous; at one point he becomes intoxicated and lies naked in his tent (Gen. 9:21).

Still, there was one little detail that seemed to argue in his favor. In the passage cited earlier, the text reads:

> Then the LORD said, "My spirit shall not abide in humanity forever, since they are flesh; their days shall be one hundred twenty years."
>
> Gen. 6:3

Interpreters felt that God could not have meant by this that from now on people would live only to the age of 120—after all, Noah himself went on to reach his 950th birthday, while his son Shem lived to the age of 600, his grandson Arpachshad to 438, and so forth. (It would not be until many centuries later that the righteous Moses would be limited to 120 years of life. On the other hand, how many humans now even come close to that age? If in Gen. 6:3 God was determining the life span of all humans henceforth, then logically each of us ought to live for exactly 120 years.) Interpreters therefore concluded that this verse was a warning to *that particular generation* that was then on earth: Shape up! If you people don't start behaving better soon, I will kill all of you exactly 120 years from now.

Such an understanding is reflected, for example, in the translation of this verse found in the Septuagint, a Greek rendering going back to the third century BCE:

And the Lord God said: "My spirit will not abide *with these men* forever, because they are flesh, but *their* days shall be one hundred and twenty years."

Septuagint, Gen. 6:3

But if these words were intended as a warning to that particular generation, then God must have passed the warning on to humanity in the same way that He did later on—through a human intermediary, a prophet. It thus seemed only natural that the words cited above, "My spirit shall not abide," were spoken *to someone* for the purpose of warning all of humanity. And if Noah is later singled out as being "a righteous man, blameless in his generation," then surely he must have been the one to whom God was speaking: like a prophet, he was sent by God to warn his contemporaries about the coming destruction, as well as to stress the power of *repentance* to save them:

Noah preached repentance, and those who obeyed were saved.

1 Clement 7:6 (also 9:1)

Noah preached repentance.

Clement of Alexandria, *Miscellanies* 1, 21

The righteous Noah used to warn them [his contemporaries] and say to them: Repent, for if you do not, God will bring a flood upon you.

b. *Sanhedrin* 108a

Here, then, was the full story of the flood as it was understood not only by ancient interpreters, but for centuries after them: God had warned humanity of its evildoing through the activity of the prophetlike Noah, who preached repentance to his contemporaries for 120 years. When, despite Noah's warnings, the other humans did not amend their ways, punishment was inevitable. As the waters rose and engulfed most living creatures, a small band—Noah and his family, along with a representative sampling of animals to ensure the survival of their species as well—escaped in the great container ship or "ark" that Noah had built. Could there be a more obvious warning than the one embodied in this narrative? Those who fail to heed God's words will be swept away, but those who obey will be saved, no matter how difficult the circumstances. This was how the story of Noah was understood for centuries and centuries.

A Startling Discovery

Then, late in the year 1872, the English Orientalist George Smith of the British Museum read a paper before the Society of Biblical Archaeology. The paper, "The Chaldean Account of the Deluge," created an immediate sensation among his listeners and, soon, in the general public as well: in his paper, Smith reported on the discovery—in the ruins of ancient Nineveh, now in Iraq—of a group of cuneiform tablets that contained a story very similar to the biblical account of the flood. Smith had access to only part of what was to be known as the *Epic of Gilgamesh,* but soon other parts were published, and evidence of similar accounts of a flood also appeared in other ancient sources, a somewhat fragmentary Sumerian version as well as a separate Babylonian (and Assyrian) text, the *Atrahasis Epic.* Suddenly it became clear that the story of a great flood had been known all over ancient Mesopotamia and even beyond its borders.[4]

The Mesopotamian accounts differ from the biblical story in some details, but the resemblances are nonetheless striking. Here are some excerpts from *Gilgamesh:*

> [*The gods say to Utnapishtim, wisest of men:*]
> "Wreck (your) house, build a boat!
> Forsake (your) possessions, seek (to save) life! . . .
> Take aboard the boat the seed of all living things."
> [*Utnapishtim obeys:*]
> What silver I had I loaded upon her,
> What gold I had I loaded upon her,
> What living creatures I had I loaded upon her,
> I sent up on board my family and kin,
> Beasts of the steppe, wild animals of the steppe,
> All types of skilled craftsmen I sent up on board.
> (The god) Shamash set for me the appointed time:
> "In the morning, cakes galore,
> In the evening, grains in rains,
> Go into your boat and caulk the door."
> I gazed upon the face of the storm,
> The weather was dreadful to behold!
> I went into the boat and caulked the door . . .
> Whatever was light was turned to darkness,
> [He flooded] the land, he smashed it like a [clay pot].
> For one day the storm wind [blew],
> Swiftly it blew, [the flood came forth],

It passed over the people like a battle,
No one could see the one next to him,
The people could not recognize one another in the downpour.
The gods became frightened of the deluge,
They shrank back, went up to Anu's highest heaven . . .
Six days and seven nights the wind continued,
the deluge and windstorm leveled the land.
When the seventh day arrived,
The windstorm and deluge left off their battle . . .
The sea grew calm, the tempest stilled, the deluge ceased . . .
The boat came to rest on Mount Nimush,
Mount Nimush held the boat fast, not letting it move . . .
When the seventh day arrived,
I brought out a dove and set it free.
The dove went off and returned,
No landing place came to its view, so it turned back.
I brought out a swallow and set it free,
The swallow went off and returned,
No landing place came to its view, so it turned back.
I brought out a raven and set it free,
The raven went off and saw the ebbing of the waters.
It ate, preened, left droppings, did not turn back.
I released all [the animals] to the four directions,
I brought out an offering and offered it to the four directions.
I set up an incense offering on the summit of the mountain . . .
The gods smelled the savor,
The gods smelled the sweet savor,
The gods crowded round the sacrificer like flies.[5]

The resemblance between *Gilgamesh* and the biblical flood story is certainly striking. In both texts we find the divine warning and commandment to build a ship; the further commandment to fill the ship with animals as well as the hero's family; the account of a great storm (abbreviated above) and then its abatement; the ship's landing atop a mountain; the trial release of birds to determine if the waters had receded; the offering of a sacrifice and libation on the mountain.

The discovery of the Mesopotamian flood texts proved troubling for traditional Christian and Jewish belief. The reason may not be immediately apparent. After all, if such a great flood had indeed taken place in ancient times, there ought to be nothing disturbing in the fact that some account of it survived outside of the Bible—on the contrary, the existence of other accounts would only seem to confirm the veracity of biblical history. But the fact that the biblical and Mesopotamian accounts agreed in so many details suggested to scholars that there was actually a *literary* connection between them: that is, the different accounts did not seem simply to agree on the events that had occurred, but on how those events should be retold, including things that could not have been based solely on historical observation. To mention one detail: why should the Bible have bothered to say that God "smelled the pleasing odor" of Noah's sacrifice (Gen. 8:21—this corresponds to the last three lines of *Gilgamesh* in the passage cited)? Certainly such a vivid anthropomorphism was a bit odd in the Bible, and the text could have as easily said that God "was pleased" with the sacrifice—or said nothing at all. More to the point, however: how could any on-site observer of the flood and its aftermath know that God/the gods had *smelled* anything (short of seeing Him/them breathe in deeply just above the altar's flames)? Surely this was not an observable event but an author's assertion; and the fact that the same assertion, indeed, *the very same expression,* is found in both *Gilgamesh* and the Bible seemed to suggest that one text was dependent on the other, or that both derived from a still earlier source. The problem was that even the friendliest dating eliminates any possibility that the Mesopotamian accounts derive from the biblical story; the oldest fragments go back to early in the second millennium BCE, perhaps even earlier—long before the time of Moses and the traditional setting for the giving of the Torah and *its* account of the flood. As a consequence, most modern scholars today see in the biblical flood story a direct dependence on the Mesopotamian literary tradition.

There was another, more concrete reason for believing that the Bible had borrowed a Mesopotamian story. Much of the land of Israel is mountainous, and rainfall there is sparse; the idea of a great flood wiping out all animals and humans would be little short of incredible in such a setting. And, in fact, as far as geologists can tell, no significant inundation has ever occurred there. It does not rain that much in Mesopotamia either, but the flat plain between the Tigris and the Euphrates in the southland could certainly have allowed whole cities there to be inundated. Geologists have indeed detected evidence of such floods in that area—nothing like the universal flood described in the texts, but at least enough to get such a story started.

It is not surprising, therefore, that not long after George Smith gave his paper, a distinctly apologetic tone crept into theologians' reckoning with the story of Noah and the flood. It was pointed out that, even if it was influenced by earlier accounts, "our" flood story had a tone and message quite different from that of the various Mesopotamian versions. In the Bible, the flood comes about as a result of human sinfulness (and not, as in *Gilgamesh,* because of human overpopulation and excess noisiness); Noah survives because he is virtuous, "a righteous man, blameless in his generation" (Gen. 6:9); God rewards him with continued life, but not with immortality, as was the case with Utnapishtim; the story ends in a solemn agreement or covenant between God and Noah's family, a characteristically biblical idea. All this is true—but it did not quite put to rest the uneasiness created by the similarities between the biblical account and the much earlier Mesopotamian one.

The Flood and the Documentary Hypothesis

In the meantime, the flood story also provided modern scholars with further evidence for the interweaving in the Bible of different sources or documents originating from within Israel itself. Scholars noted, for example, that when God instructs Noah about the coming flood, the text says:

> Then the LORD said to Noah, "Go into the ark, you and your whole household, for I have seen that you alone are righteous before Me in this generation. Take with you *seven pairs* of all clean animals, a male and its mate; and a pair of the animals that are not clean, a male and its mate."
>
> Gen. 7:2

The reason for taking seven pairs of clean animals is that God knows that Noah will want to offer Him sacrifices after the flood is over. It is a rule that only clean animals can be offered as sacrifices. (In biblical terminology, "clean" animals include, for example, cows and bulls and sheep and goats. Pigs and camels and lions and tigers are all examples of "unclean" animals.) Therefore, if Noah were to take only a single pair of sheep, for example, how would that species survive after Noah had killed one of the pair in order to make a sacrifice?

It is striking, however, that in the subsequent narrative, God's instructions about the seven pairs of clean animals seem to have been disregarded:

> And Noah with his sons and his wife and his sons' wives went into the ark to escape the waters of the flood. *Of clean animals,* and of animals that are not clean, and of birds, and of everything that creeps on the ground, *two and two,* male and female, went into the ark with Noah, as God had commanded Noah. And after seven days the waters of the flood came on the earth.
>
> Gen. 7:7–10

> On the very same day Noah with his sons, Shem and Ham and Japhet, and Noah's wife and the three wives of his sons, entered the ark; they and every wild animal of every kind, and all domestic animals of every kind, and every creeping thing that creeps on the earth, and every bird of every kind—every bird, every winged creature. They went into the ark with Noah, *two and two of all flesh in which there was the breath of life.*
>
> Gen. 7:13–15

Where are the seven pairs? Scholars noticed another interesting fact: the instruction about seven pairs of clean animals is introduced by the phrase "the LORD said to Noah" (Gen. 7:1), using the specific name "LORD" (written with the Hebrew consonants *Y, H, W,* and *H*) for God, whereas the above-cited passages use exclusively the general Hebrew term "God." This same divine name, LORD, then appears at the end of the story, in the account of Noah's sacrificing:

> Then Noah built an altar to the LORD, and took of every clean animal and of every clean bird, and offered burnt offerings on the altar. And when the LORD smelled the pleasing odor, the LORD said in His heart, "I will never again curse the ground because of humankind. . . ."
>
> Gen. 8:20–21

This suggested that underlying the biblical account were, in fact, two different versions of the events. The "LORD" version was identified as belonging to the source designated as J; according to it, Noah offered a sacrifice after the flood was over—that's why the "LORD" version also specified that Noah was to take seven pairs of "clean" animals. But, for one reason or another, this sacrifice was not part of the other version (identified by scholars as belonging to the priestly source, P); perhaps this priestly author was troubled by the idea of an untrained non-priest like Noah offering sacrifices, indeed, sacrifices that obey the laws of clean and unclean animals that are first specified later on, in the book of Leviticus. So this author said nothing about seven pairs. It was the combination of these two conflicting viewpoints, scholars said, that created this inconsistency within the biblical account itself.[6]

In short, for modern scholars the biblical story of Noah and the flood offers a glimpse at how the Bible was actually written, including some of the all-too-human mistakes that its authors had made along the way. This story was apparently incorporated into the Bible as part of an overall attempt to recount the world's history from earliest times.* In assembling that history, the biblical authors had turned to a number of ancient Mesopotamian traditions, including this one of a great, watery cataclysm that had struck the earth sometime in the distant past. (This tradition, to judge by the surviving texts, must have been quite well known in the region; its absence from the Genesis history would surely have made that history seem parochial and even incomplete.) The changes that were introduced into the Mesopotamian narrative—a single God instead of several gods; the flood as a punishment for sinfulness; survival, but not immortality, for the story's hero—helped to

---

* Chapters 1–11 of Genesis, known to scholars as the "Primeval History," appear to be a discrete unit designed as a preface to the more focused "Ancestral History" of Genesis 12–50.

make the story conform better to Israelite beliefs, but scholars have little doubt that the biblical narrative was ultimately based on one or another version of this Mesopotamian legend. What is more, the biblical narrative was found to contain significant duplications and contradictions, further evidence of its all-too-human character. But if so, can this be the word of God?[7]

"Wait a Minute!"

At this point I sense some readers may feel I have been unfair to modern scholars. "Wait a minute," they are saying. "Modern interpreters may be out to discover where biblical texts really come from, and this may indeed force them to part with long-held beliefs about the Mosaic authorship of the Pentateuch—perhaps even with their belief in the direct, divine inspiration of the Bible's every word. But they are not a bunch of amoral researchers. Most modern scholars believe that the Bible is still the Bible, and that the flood story, no matter where it came from, has important things to teach us—about God as the maker of all reality (including floods), about sin and punishment, and about God's going to any length to reward a good person. Certainly that's part of our Bible too, as much as Mesopotamia and J and P. Just listen for the word of God."

This is not a minor matter, and I have reserved the last chapter for a fuller discussion of it. In the meantime, however, I would point out a slight inconsistency in the preceding paragraph. "The Bible is still the Bible" is really a sentiment left over from the ancient interpreters. That is to say, the very idea that one should approach the Bible as a great book of divine instruction, and that the purpose of these stories in Genesis is therefore somehow to impart moral lessons or to provide ethical models for readers to imitate, is a creation of the ancient interpreters. This is not an idea that can be located in the words of the book of Genesis itself; and as modern scholars themselves have amply demonstrated, when read without blinders, the stories of Genesis sometimes seem rather lacking in ethical models. (Their purpose, scholars say, was to relate history—usually, history in the etiological sense.) So, despite the efforts of modern scholars to get at the truth of where the Bible came from and what it originally meant, many of them are still, in this most basic way, committed to a way of reading that comes from the ancient interpreters.

Indeed, the quandary in which modern scholars (and those who know their work) find themselves derives precisely from their straddling two positions at once. On the one hand, they feel they have to do away with all of ancient biblical interpretation, including its Four Assumptions (see chapter 1). These no longer seem axiomatically true, and besides, for reasons of simple intellectual honesty, such people are unwilling to hide from everything we now know about the historical circumstances of the Bible's composition and the true meaning of its words. On the other hand, they still wish to preserve the *idea* of the Bible and the traditional role it has played in their religion. The result is always an elaborate, and often quite eloquent, apologetic —but an apologetic nonetheless.

One can certainly sympathize with this predicament; it is, truly, the dilemma to which this book is devoted. But when all is said and done, apologetics are not the answer. Someone who reads the Babylonian flood story will likely find it interesting, or perhaps troubling (because of its clear connection to the Genesis account). But any question like "How are we to apply its lessons to our own lives?" would be greeted by such a reader with incomprehension, or derision. "*Lessons?* Why, it was written by a bunch of Mesopotamians four thousand years ago!" If that same person then reads what is essentially the same story in the book of Genesis but finds it full of all sorts of uplifting doctrines—well, such a person is either being dishonest or has simply failed to recognize a fundamental fact. What truly differentiates the two stories is not their content but their context. Reading something *in the Bible* has, since ancient times, brought with it certain assumptions, and these are, to an extent most people are unaware of, still with us.

5

The Tower of Babel

The Tower of Babel, 1604 by Abel Grimmer (1570–1619).

A TALE OF OVERREACHING. ZIGGURATS. DOWN WITH BIG CITIES.
THE FIRST LANGUAGE SPOKEN BY HUMANS.

After the flood, Noah's descendants continued to multiply; some reached the land of Shinar (Babylon). There they set out to build a great city with a huge tower, but God stopped them in the middle and scattered them all across the land.

The story of the tower of Babel occupies only a few verses in Genesis, but it seems to cover a great deal of territory.

> Everyone on earth used to speak the same language and the same words. As people migrated from the east, they came upon a plain in the land of Shinar and settled there. Then they said to one another, "Let us make bricks and harden them with fire"—since they used brick for stones, and bitumen for mortar—and they said, "Let us build a city for ourselves, with a tower that reaches to heaven, so that we can make a name for ourselves and will not be scattered all over the earth." But the LORD came down to inspect the city and tower that the people had built. Then the LORD said, "It is because they are one people and all speak the same language that they have been able to undertake this—in fact, nothing that they set out to do will be impossible for them. Let us go down and confuse their speech, so that they will not understand what they are saying to each other." Thus the LORD scattered them from there all over the earth, and the building of the city was stopped. That is why it is called Babel, because there the LORD confused [Hebrew *balal*] the speech of the whole land, and from there the LORD scattered them all over the earth.
>
> Gen. 11:1–9

At the story's beginning, all of humanity—descended from Noah and his family after the flood—is still a unified group; eight verses later, people are scattered all over the earth. With this scattering also comes the confusion, and profusion, of tongues; the one, universal human language is lost, ultimately to be replaced by thousands of different languages and dialects. Along with this, the human capacity for accomplishment undergoes a radical change: people go from unlimited potential—"nothing that they set out to do will be impossible for them"—to a state of disorder that prevents them even from finishing the city they had started to build. What went wrong?

A Problematic Tower

The more that ancient readers of the Bible contemplated this question, the more troubling it became. After all, what was so bad about a bunch of people seeking to build a city? Surely the reason the Bible gave for this project—the people's desire not to be "scattered all over the earth"—did not sound blameworthy in and of itself. Why, then, had God frustrated their plans and then sent them off in every different direction?

In seeking an answer, ancient readers eventually focused on the tower mentioned by the builders themselves: "Let us build a city for ourselves, with a *tower that reaches to heaven.*" Stipulating such a great height for the tower certainly sounded fishy. Perhaps, as so often, Scripture here was hinting in a word or two at some major point: the tower was the whole reason for God's displeasure. After all, God is in heaven and people are on earth. It just did not seem right that humans should try to reach the realm of the divine, perhaps even challenging God's heavenly rule in the process; the arrogance of this very idea must have been what caused God to frustrate their plans. Such a suspicion only seemed to be reinforced by the precise wording of the continuation of this text. The Bible said that God went down to earth "to inspect the city *and the tower*"; the latter specification seemed once again intended to indicate to readers that the tower itself had been the real sticking point.

As a consequence, ancient interpreters came to refer to this story not as the "City of Babel" but as the "Tower of Babel." In fact, interpreters came to believe that behind this building project stood still more nefarious, if unstated, aims: the builders actually wished to enter heaven itself or to challenge God's control of the supernal realm:

> For they [the descendants of Noah] had emigrated from the land of Ararat toward the east, to Shinar, and . . . they built a city and the tower, saying, *"Let us ascend on it into heaven."*
>
> *Jubilees* 10:19

> They were all of one language
> and they wanted to go up to starry heaven.
> *Sibylline Oracles* 3:99–100

> [An angel said to Baruch:] "These are the ones who built the tower of the *war against God,* and the Lord removed them."
>
> 3 Bar. 2:7

They said: Let us build a tower and climb up to the firmament and *strike it with hatchets until its waters flow forth.*

b. *Sanhedrin* 109a

Read in such a light, the story seemed no less than a parable of human arrogance in general. Human beings ought to know their place, it seemed to say. Ingenuity and teamwork are fine so long as they do not lead humans to think too much of themselves—and too little of God. The great half-built structure of Genesis 11 loomed ever afterward in people's minds as a model of what godless arrogance can lead to.

The Ziggurats of Mesopotamia

To modern scholars, the identity and significance of the tower are not all that mysterious. Almost as soon as archaeologists began to explore ancient Mesopotamia (modern Iraq), they came upon the ruins of various ancient structures, called ziggurats (more properly, ziqqurats), a kind of stepped pyramid that the Sumerians, Babylonians, and Assyrians built to honor their gods. Ziqqurats had become an essential feature of temple complexes in Mesopotamia as early as the end of the third millennium BCE. In all, archaeologists have uncovered the remains of some twenty-eight of them in Iraq and another four in Iran.

Since the area of the Tigris and Euphrates valleys did not feature large stone formations for people to quarry, the massive ziqqurats had to be built—just as the Bible reports—out of mud bricks (at first only sun-dried, but later fired in specially constructed kilns); the bricks were often stuck together with bitumen (a kind of asphaltlike substance). Because these materials are far less durable than actual stone, most of these ancient structures long ago collapsed into heaps of rubble—in fact, scholars believe that such collapses, especially of the ziqqurat façades, were probably not uncommon in ancient times. Thus, a biblical story about a great tower constructed in Mesopotamia—built out of baked mud bricks and bitumen, and perhaps one that was partially collapsed and subsequently abandoned—would certainly have rung true to any ancient Israelite who had traveled eastward to that great center of civilization.

At the same time, however, some modern scholars are skeptical about the emphasis placed on the tower by ancient interpreters.[1] The tower is certainly there in the story—no doubt about it. But it is hardly the whole point. If it were, there would have been no need to mention the building of a city at all—let the project be limited to the offending ziqqurat! In fact, it is remarkable that, after God's intervention, the text says, "and the building *of the city* was stopped." Not a word is said about the tower's fate; if it were so crucial, should not the text have mentioned its collapse or abandonment?

For such reasons, some scholars find the real point of this story to be neither the tower nor the universal "human overreaching" theme beloved by ancient interpreters. Rather, they say, the whole point is Babylon (*babel* in Hebrew). The thing that must have most characterized Babylon in the minds of ancient Israelites was its big cities with (for those days) their massive populations ("so that we will not be scattered all over the earth" was, it will be recalled, the builders' justification for their project). From the standpoint of ancient Israelites, who were sparsely settled in the Semitic hinterland, such teeming conglomerations and the complex urban culture they made possible—including Babylon's highly sophisticated religious practices, of which the ziqqurat was a fitting emblem—these things, the story seems to say, do not find favor with our God. In fact, long ago, He intervened and threw down one of those ancient towers of theirs just to show that all that pomp and filigree counts for nothing with Him. Precisely for that reason, the story adds, their country is known as Babel; this name does not derive, as one might suppose, from *bab ilu* ("gate of the god" in Akkadian), but from the Hebrew *balal,* since that is where God confused their speech to stop their urban building mania.[2]

Scholars differ about a possible dating of the story. Some say that an Israelite familiarity with Babylonian ziqqurats—and an Israelite interest in Babylon in general—is most appropriate to the period of the Babylonian exile in the sixth century; consistent with this date would be the depiction of Israel's God as being active far to the east of His usual sphere of influence in earlier times. Others hold that neither of these arguments is decisive. An ancient Israelite in almost any period would certainly have known about the massive cities of Mesopotamia and their ziqqurats. As for the depiction of the deity in the story, they point out that His urging, "Let us go down and confuse their speech," seems to bespeak the highly anthropomorphic God of earlier times, a God who moves from place to place and who is often surrounded by lesser members of His divine council ("Let *us* . . ."). Such a depiction appears inappropriate to the time of the Babylonian exile, when biblical texts tended to stress God's immensity and His sole control of reality. Beyond such considerations, it has been noted that ancient Israel ultimately developed its own sophisticated urban culture; if this story is indeed a polemic against the Babylonian metropolis, perhaps its origins are to be sought in a very early time, when Israel might still remember itself as primarily a people of the sparsely inhabited Canaanite highlands. This was also a time when, scholars say, Israelite religion actually forbade the use of even a simple metal tool to quarry or shape the stones of an altar (Exod. 20:25)—a law that seems virtually to thumb its nose at the architectural sophistication of the Babylonian temple and ziqqurat. "All that Babylonian stuff," this story seems to say, "is bunk."

The Original Language

As with the story of Cain and Abel, the Tower of Babel narrative has, for modern scholars, certain clearly etiological elements: not only its explanation for the name Babel, but also its accounting for the dispersion of peoples across the ancient Near East and the replacement of an originally single, common language by an array of different, mutually incomprehensible idioms. Behind this latter element, too, modern scholars see a message not about the world as a whole, but something rather more local and specific. Semitic languages all appeared to be related: any native speaker could tell that Babylonian and Assyrian and Aramaic and Hebrew all had common roots and expressions, but a speaker of one tongue would not necessarily understand much of what was being said in the others. It is this reality, rather than the existence of different languages per se, that the story seems out to explain: all the peoples of the ancient Near East *did,* it says, originally speak the same language, but that unity was destroyed quite intentionally by God. (Some scholars think that such an etiological tale may have at one time existed quite separate from its current Babylonian setting, but that it was eventually combined with an independent story of arrogant Babylonians and their tower; others say the two elements were probably from the beginning part of the same story.)[3]

What, according to the Bible, was that original language spoken by all of humanity? The story itself does not say, but ancient interpreters, Jewish and Christian, were almost unanimous in the belief that it was Hebrew. After all, the Bible quotes God speaking in Hebrew when He says, "Let there be light" and "Let us make man." (If He had been speaking Aramaic, the Bible surely would not have hesitated to quote His original words—there is plenty of Aramaic in other parts of the Bible.) To whom was He speaking when He said these words? Certainly not to the Israelites or any other people—no people had been created yet! Hebrew must thus be the primordial language, the language of God and the angels, and God must have taught this language to the first humans.[4] By the same logic, when the Bible says of Eve, "This one shall be called 'woman' [*'ishah*], since from a man [*'ish*] was she taken" (Gen. 2:23), this too seemed clear proof that the original language was Hebrew, since the words for "man" and "woman" were quite different in Aramaic, Akkadian, and other ancient languages. For such reasons Hebrew came to be known as "the holy tongue,"[5] and well into modern times most people believed that all other languages—Greek, Latin, German, and so forth—were corruptions of that original, universal speech, just as the Bible recounted.

This hypothesis has been largely rejected by modern scholars, and the ramifications of its rejection go well beyond the Tower of Babel narrative itself.

Scholars still do not have an absolutely clear picture of the actual origins and complex interrelationship of the various Semitic languages, but most hypothesize that all Semitic languages do indeed go back to an original ancestor. It was not Hebrew, however. Linguists call this grandfather tongue "Proto-Semitic." Proto-Semitic is still a theoretical entity; no actual text has ever been found to be written in it. But scholars do have a pretty good idea of what it must have looked like, and biblical Hebrew is quite a few developmental and chronological jumps away from it. Consider, for example, Hebrew's repertoire of significant sounds—its phonemes—which are the basic building blocks of any language. (Technically, a phoneme is defined as "the smallest unit of sound capable of distinguishing between two words in a given language."[6] A phoneme is quite different from a letter, which is merely a conventional sign used in writing.) As time goes on, languages sometimes lose phonemes or gain new ones: English used to have a phoneme *kh*, like the final sound of *loch* in Scotland, and it was indeed pronounced *kh* in words like "laugh" or "night"; now that sound has, in some cases, merged with *f*, while in others it has disappeared entirely. Hebrew, too, seems to have lost some of the phonemes that existed in Proto-Semitic. Thus, Proto-Semitic used to have two separate phonemes, corresponding to English *sh* and *th* (as in "thing"), which merged into *sh* in Hebrew.[7] Proto-Semitic had separate *z* and *ð* sounds (the latter corresponding to *th* in "this"), which merged into *z* in Hebrew; another three, originally distinct, phonemes of Proto-Semitic, represented by linguists as *ẓ*, *ḍ*, and *ṣ*, all merged into *ṣ* in biblical Hebrew (the same phoneme is realized as *ts* in modern Hebrew); and so forth. Vowels also changed: the "Canaanite shift" turned the formerly long *ā* sound into *ō* in Hebrew, hence Arabic *salām* versus Hebrew *shalōm*. (Something similar happened in English, when, for example, the long *ā* of Old English *stān* became *ō*, as in "stone.") In addition to such phonological shifts were many other changes—in morphology and grammar and syntax—and these too can be charted across the range of existing Semitic languages to situate Hebrew's place among them and, hence, its path from Proto-Semitic.

Quite apart from biblical Hebrew's relationship to Proto-Semitic and other languages, linguists have also studied how Hebrew itself changed over time. All spoken languages change—and rather more quickly than most people imagine. Therefore, by carefully studying the linguistic features of different biblical texts (and, sometimes, comparing these to Hebrew inscriptions found by archaeologists, as well as using data from other Semitic languages), scholars have been able to piece together a detailed picture of how biblical Hebrew evolved over a period of some centuries. At a very early stage, for example, Hebrew seems to have had grammatical case endings, like Latin, German, Russian, and other languages; but these for the most part died out, as they did in English too. Words themselves change: old words drop out of a language and new ones appear, and often a particular word will change its meaning, slightly or radically as the case may be. Linguists can track such changes and sometimes use them to situate a particular biblical text chronologically vis-à-vis other texts.[8] Finally, linguists have also distinguished different dialects of Hebrew in the Bible: the northern, or "Israelian," dialect is actually markedly different from the idiom of Jerusalem.[9]

All this has had great ramifications for the study of the Bible as a whole. Tradition may assign the Pentateuch to Moses, the whole book of Isaiah to the eighth-century prophet by that name, and so forth, but the linguistic evidence is simply not consistent with those traditions. Moses, linguists say, cannot have written the Pentateuch, at least not in the form in which we know it—virtually all of its Hebrew is later than that which putatively existed in the time of Moses. Nor, if they are right, can the Pentateuch, or the book of Isaiah, or Psalms, or almost any other biblical book be the work of a single author: the language of all these books apparently represents the Hebrew of at least two different periods and/or geographic areas.

And so in several ways, the Tower of Babel narrative confronts us with a now-familiar discordance. For centuries and centuries, this tale was read as a parable of human hubris and divine retribution: long ago, people had sought to overstep their bounds, and God quickly put them back in their place. This was, quite simply, what the story *meant*—and if its lesson was an obvious one, it was nonetheless worth taking to heart, as it is even (especially?) today. Such is not, however, the story's message for the modern scholar. Instead, this tale appears to be a deliberate jab at sophisticated Babylonian society, and along with that, an etiological explanation of the similarity-yet-distinctness of the Semitic languages. If, behind this etiology lies the belief that all Semitic languages were originally one, this belief could actually be historically accurate—but Proto-Semitic, not Hebrew, was the region's first language.

6

The Call of Abraham

GENESIS 12–15

Abraham Turns His Back on the Stars,
Dura Europas.

The departure from Ur. The man of faith. Religion
of the patriarchs. Abraham in history.
Ancient Near Eastern covenants.

Abraham is claimed by three great religions—Judaism, Christianity, and Islam—as their spiritual forefather. But who exactly was he—and did he exist at all? Opinions on the question are still divided.

After the Tower of Babel was abandoned, the now dispersed branches of humanity continued to grow unabated. While the earliest descendants of Adam and Eve had sometimes met with divine displeasure, that was not to be the case with those that followed. Notably, the genealogical line of Noah's son Shem led, eight generations later, to the birth of Abraham. Beloved by God, Abraham became the father of Isaac and grandfather of Jacob, the founder of the people of Israel.

Abraham is certainly one of the most significant figures in Genesis, perhaps in the whole of the Hebrew Bible. He is often thought of as the first monotheist, as well as an exemplar of religious faith; his was not an untroubled life, but throughout it all he maintained his trust in God. Some of these ideas are indeed rooted in the biblical text, but—as has been the case with other figures examined thus far—a good bit of what people associate with Abraham derives not so much from the words of the Bible itself as from the way in which those words were read by the Bible's earliest interpreters.

The Journey from Mesopotamia

Abraham truly steps onto the biblical stage in chapter 12 of Genesis (though his birth and other details are mentioned earlier, Gen. 11:26–31). His story is introduced in these terms:

> Now the LORD said to Abram,* "Go from your country and your kindred and your father's house to the land that I will show you. And I will make of you a great nation, and I will bless you and make your name great, so that it will be a blessing. I will bless those who bless you, and anyone who curses you I will curse; and by you will all the families of the earth be blessed."
>
> Gen. 12:1–3

* Abraham's original name, before God changed it; see Gen. 17:5.

Scripture does not tell us how Abraham reacted to this announcement, but it is clear how ancient interpreters reacted: with bewilderment. Their question here was rather similar to the one they asked about God's choice of Noah before the flood, only more so: why Abraham? To promise someone that he would become the ancestor of a great and mighty nation (in fact, as the Bible goes on to relate, several nations) and to grant him personally so many good things that his very name would turn into a blessing (that is, in the future people will say of their own child, "May he be like Abraham")—this was certainly heady stuff. What exactly had Abraham done at that point to deserve such things? As far as an ancient reader of Genesis was concerned, the answer was: nothing! Abraham had just now been introduced.

Not finding an adequate answer to this question in the book of Genesis, interpreters looked elsewhere, and eventually (we cannot know exactly when, but it was certainly before the start of the second century BCE) their gaze fell on a particular passage in the book of Joshua:

> And Joshua said to all the people, "Thus says the LORD, the God of Israel: Long ago, your ancestors—Terah and his sons Abraham and Nahor— lived on the other side of the Euphrates, and they worshiped other gods. Then I took your father Abraham from beyond the River and led him through all the land of Canaan and made his offspring many."
>
> Josh. 24:2–3

This passage seemed to be referring to the same moment in history as that just seen in Gen. 12:1–4, when Abraham still lived in Mesopotamia, "on the other side of the Euphrates," and God first told him to leave his homeland.

At first glance, the Joshua passage seems only to compound the problem of Abraham not having done much to deserve God's blessing: it says that Abraham, along with his father and brother, "worshiped other gods"—certainly a very bad thing to do in Israelite terms. But interpreters were intrigued by the apparent lack of any logical connection between this and the next sentence, "Then I took your father Abraham . . ." It seemed like a complete non sequitur. They also noticed that this sentence seemed to single Abraham out: "Then I took your father Abraham," God says, but, rather pointedly, *not* Terah and *not* Nahor. So . . . if worshiping other gods was a bad thing to do, and the next sentence says that God singled Abraham out and chose him to go to the land of Canaan and there receive the blessings of many offspring and mighty nationhood, then this sequence seemed to imply that Abraham must at some point have stopped worshiping other gods, while Terah and Nahor continued to do so. That was why God singled Abraham out from the rest of his family and rewarded him as He did. *"They,"* Terah and Nahor, "served other gods," but not Abraham.

True, such an interpretation seems to go against the plain sense of Josh. 24:2–3. As we have seen, however, one of the assumptions of ancient interpreters was that the Bible is perfectly harmonious and speaks with a single voice. Understanding these verses in Joshua as implying that Abraham did *not* serve other gods (or had stopped serving them at some point) fit well with everything else that was known about Abraham from elsewhere in the Bible. It not only explained why God chose Abraham to go to Canaan in Gen. 12:1–4, but it suited the rest of the Abraham stories in Genesis, which depict him as God's faithful servant, and it seemed to resonate with passages that come later in the Bible as well. At one point, for example, God is said to refer to Abraham as the one "who loved Me" (Isa. 41:8—some texts translate, "My friend"). Indeed, many times in the Pentateuch God is specifically described as "the God of Abraham, of Isaac, and of Jacob." In another place in Scripture, God says, apparently alluding to this same moment of Abraham's departure: "Consider Abraham your father, and Sarah who bore you: *him alone did I call,* and bless him and make him many" (Isa. 51:2). Singling out Abraham ("him alone") sounded exactly like what interpreters wished to say about Josh. 24:2–3—that God had singled Abraham out from the rest of his family because Abraham, uniquely, did *not* worship other gods. Considering all this, it seemed to interpreters only reasonable to suppose that Josh. 24:2–3 was also referring to Abraham in a positive sense: his other family members may have served other gods, but not Abraham, and that explains why Abraham alone was summoned to Canaan.

The First Monotheist

As a result, Abraham came to acquire a specific image among ancient interpreters, and one that has carried through even to the present day: he was thought of as the discoverer of monotheism, the first person to figure out that there is really only one God,[1] and that worshiping many gods and the *things* that they were identified with—the sun, the moon, and the stars, or statues or images of imagined powers—was useless, the practice of an illusion. This interpretation is very old; it is attested at the very beginning of the second century BCE:

> And he [Abraham] said to his father, "What help or advantage do we have from these idols, before which you worship and bow down? . . . Do not worship them. Worship the God of heaven."
>
> *Jubilees* 12:2–4

The fact that the Bible says that Abraham came from the land of the Chaldeans (Gen. 11:27, 31, etc.) fit perfectly with this line of interpretation.

For the Chaldeans were famous at the time of the ancient interpreters for one thing: their mastery of astronomy and astrology (the two pursuits were a single field in ancient times). So exact were their calculations concerning the sun, the moon, and the stars that the word "Chaldean" itself came to be a synonym for "astronomer" in Greek and Aramaic. If the Chaldeans pursued this science, it was not merely out of curiosity about the makeup of the universe: like many ancient peoples, they believed that the stars controlled human destiny, and that a careful study of astral movements might hold a clue to what was in store—indeed, by seeking the favor of this or that god identified with a certain celestial body, one might actually influence things for the good.

So, if Abraham was said to have left Chaldea, Astronomyland, for Canaan, interpreters saw this as a sign that he was turning his back on such foolish beliefs and devoting himself to God; indeed, perhaps it was precisely his training in this Chaldean science that led him, ultimately, to reject it:

> And he was sitting alone [in Chaldea] making observations [of the stars] when a voice came into his heart saying, "All the signs of the stars and the signs of the sun and the moon are under the Lord's control. Why am I seeking [them out]? If He wishes, He will make it rain morning and evening, and if He desires He will not make it fall, for everything is under His control."
>
> *Jubilees* 12:17–18

The same theme was taken up in the first century CE by another ancient interpreter, Philo of Alexandria. What he has to say is a good example of the **allegorizing** sort of interpretation that was popular with Alexandrian Jews and, later, early Christians:

> The departing from one's home as depicted by the literal text of Scripture was made by a certain wise man [Abraham]; but according to the rules of allegory, [it is made] by the soul [of anyone] fond of virtue who is searching for the true God. For the Chaldeans exercised themselves most especially with astronomy and attributed all things to the movements of the stars, believing that whatever is in the world is governed by forces encompassed in numbers and numerical proportions. They exalted the existence of what is visible, and took no thought for what is perceivable to the mind and [yet] invisible. But seeking out the numerical arrangement according to the cycles of the sun, moon, the planets and the fixed stars, as well as the changes of the yearly seasons and the overall connection of the things of heaven with what happens on earth, they supposed that the world itself was god, sacrilegiously making out that which is created to be like the One who had created it.
>
> He [Abraham] grew up with this idea and was a true Chaldean [i.e.,

astronomer] for some time, until, opening the soul's eye from the depth of sleep, he came to behold the pure ray in place of deep darkness, and he followed that light and perceived what he had not seen before, One who guides and steers the world, presiding over it and managing its affairs.

Philo, On Abraham 68–70

For Philo, the literal text of Scripture is true: there really was someone named Abraham who lived in Chaldea and left his home. But so what? The importance of this text (and of all of Scripture), he says, lies below the surface, in the hidden, allegorical meaning: Abraham here really symbolizes any soul looking for God. At first that soul is always a bit of a "Chaldean" in Philo's definition, since we all grow up using our senses of sight and hearing to perceive the world, and we all come to think that these senses are the only kind of perception that exists. But then at some point, Philo says, something happens: "opening [its] eye from the depth of sleep," the soul suddenly becomes aware of God's presence. At that point God will say to the soul, as He said to Abraham, "Leave Chaldea!"—that is, leave your old way of thinking, in which the human senses are considered to be the only form of perception, and proceed on to a new way of thinking and, ultimately, to the Promised Land of knowing God.

Another interesting version of Abraham's departure from Chaldea is found in the writings of the first-century historian Josephus:

He [Abraham] thus became the first person to argue that there is a single God who is the creator of all things, and that whatever any of these other things contribute to the good of the world, they are enabled to do so at His command, and not by any inherent force of their own. He was able to figure this out by the changes which land and sea undergo, and those that are connected with the sun and the moon, and from all those occurring in the skies. For if these bodies had any power over themselves, they would surely have arranged for themselves to be regularly ordered; but since this is not so, it is clear that they come together for our benefit not by any authority of their own, but by the power of One who commands, to whom alone it is proper to give honor and thanks. Because of these ideas the Chaldeans and the other people of Mesopotamia rose up against him, and having resolved, in keeping with God's will and with His help, to leave his home, he settled in the land of Canaan.

Josephus, Jewish Antiquities 1.154–57

Josephus's argument is as follows: as a good astronomer, Abraham knew that the length of the solar year is exactly 365¼ days. (We actually know that the Chaldeans had indeed calculated the length of the solar year with great accuracy, even in those ancient times.) But what kind of a number is 365¼? Certainly, if the sun were the supreme god, Josephus reasoned, it would have assigned itself a more handsome, rounder number—a hundred days, or a thousand days. The fact that the length of its cycle is this odd fraction proved to Abraham, according to Josephus, that the sun cannot be running things. Similarly with the moon: its annual cycle (that is, twelve full lunar months) comes out to 354 days. That's not much better. Moreover, the fact that neither the sun nor the moon can force the other to conform to *its* number and make its annual cycle the same shows that neither of them is in charge. Likewise for all the heavenly bodies and the cycles of tides and so forth—none of these seems to have arranged for itself to be what Josephus calls "regularly ordered," that is, having a cycle that comes out to some nice, round number. The conclusion was inescapable: some Higher Power had assigned all these insultingly odd numbers as a way of tipping off a sharp fellow like Abraham that there was indeed one Supreme Being, and one who was not to be identified with any observable body on earth or in the heavens.

The tradition of "Abraham the monotheist" is one of the oldest and best-known ideas about Abraham to this day. It of course passed from Judaism into early Christianity but also, somewhat later, became a central element in Islam.[2] Here, for example, is the Qur'an's description of Abraham's enlightenment:

And when Abraham said to his father Azar, "Takest thou idols for gods? I see thee, and thy people, in manifest error."

So We [God] were showing Abraham the kingdom of the heavens and earth, that he might be of those having sure faith.

When night outspread over him, he saw a star and said, "This is my Lord."

But when it set he said, "I love not setters."

When he saw the moon rising, he said, "This is my Lord." But when it set he said, "If my Lord does not guide me I shall surely be of the people gone astray."

When he saw the sun rising, he said, "This is my Lord—this is greater!" But when it set he said, "O my people, surely I am quit of that you associate. I have turned my face to Him who originated the heavens and the earth; [I am] a man of pure faith. I am not of the idolators."[3]

Qur'an 6:74–79 (trans. A. J. Arberry)

At the same time, these traditions about Abraham continued to be passed on by Jews and Christians and ultimately came to be part of the general culture. Here, for example, is how the poet John Milton introduced his readers to Abraham in *Paradise Lost*. God spied Abraham, he says,

> on this side Euphrates yet residing
> Bred up in Idol-worship; O that men
> (Canst thou believe?) should be so stupid grown,
> While yet the Patriark liv'd, who scap'd the Flood,*
> As to forsake the living God, and fall
> To worship thir own work in Wood and Stone
> For Gods! yet him God the most High voutsafes
> To call by Vision from his Fathers house . . .
> He leaves his Gods, his Friends, and native Soil
> Ur of *Chaldaea,* passing now the Ford
> To Haran.
>   XII:115–31

Thus, Abraham the monotheist, the one who rejected his father's idolatrous worship of the stars, has been part of Abraham's "image" in each of these three great monotheistic religions. But what do modern scholars know about Abraham and his religious beliefs?

Historicity's Zigzag

Modern biblical scholars like to ask the same questions again and again about different biblical texts: How reliable is this as history? Can we believe that this is what actually happened? This is sometimes referred to as the issue of the text's "historicity." In the case of Abraham, scholarship has performed something of a zigzag over the last hundred years or so.

In the late nineteenth century, when modern, critical scholarship was hitting its stride, scholars were often skeptical of the biblical account, particularly after the rise of the Documentary Hypothesis. They believed that someone (that is, J or E) who lived long after Abraham, indeed, long after the people of Israel had settled in Canaan, made up these stories in order to justify that settlement: the Abraham narrative, they said, was designed to claim that although Israel's illustrious ancestor had arrived in Canaan from a distant region, he was no mere squatter or land grabber; God Himself had granted the land to Abraham. In point of fact, scholars thought, this was no more than a retrospective fantasy (though they were kind enough not to use those words); nothing of the kind happened. In fact, Abraham may never have existed.

Then, early in the twentieth century, archaeologists began turning up evidence that seemed to confirm, or at least coincide with, elements of the Genesis narrative. Abraham's hometown, Ur, turned out to be an actual city that archaeologists rediscovered at the mouth of the Euphrates.[4] In its heyday it

---

* That is, Noah.

was a bustling metropolis of some twelve thousand people (that *was* bustling for those days!), with a magnificent ziqqurat and other urban niceties. Over the centuries the Persian Gulf coastline has moved drastically southward, but in Abraham's day it was not far from Ur, and ships could easily proceed up the Euphrates to this city to unload their wares.

Other excavations in the region turned up additional details connected with Abraham. Far to the north of Ur, archaeologists unearthed the ancient town of Nuzi, a provincial outpost in the land of the Hurrians (referred to in the Bible as the Horites or Hivites; the capital city of this kingdom today lies buried under the Iraqi city of Kirkuk). Nuzi was east of the Tigris and a few hundred miles from Haran, the place to which Abraham's family is said to travel after they leave Ur (Gen. 11:31). Particularly intriguing was Nuzi's collection of clay tablets, on which were recorded the day-to-day dealings of its citizens in the fifteenth and fourteenth centuries BCE. These texts seemed to reveal legal practices, customs, and a way of life that suited the Abraham narratives. Suddenly what had been altogether vague and hypothetical could be placed at actual excavation sites and in a social context that seemed to match the biblical accounts.

Another ancient site, Mari, was explored by French archaeologists starting in 1933. Mari sits nowadays on the border between Iraq and Syria, about 250 miles southwest of Nuzi; there archaeologists found a huge library of clay tablets—including diplomatic correspondence and royal archives, as well as numerous administrative and commercial documents. Here are mentioned, among other things, the names of cities in the neighborhood of nearby Haran. Thus, at one point, they refer to a city called Nahur; this is the same name as that of Abraham's brother, Nahor (Gen. 11:27), and "the city of Nahor" (Gen. 24:10) is where Abraham sends his servant to find a wife for Isaac. (Several of Abraham's ancestors similarly turn out to have the same name as places mentioned in other ancient tablets: Abraham's father, Terah, and his forebears Peleg [Gen. 11:18] and Serug [Gen. 11:22] all bear the names of actual sites.) The Mari tablets are quite ancient, extending from the mid–third millennium BCE to the early eighteenth century BCE. The lower date would do pretty well as the time of the historical Abraham, so any overlap between Genesis and the Mari texts seemed to support, if only indirectly, the historicity of the Bible's account of Abraham.

W. F. Albright

The connection of these archaeological finds with Genesis was highlighted by one of the central figures of biblical scholarship in the twentieth century, William Foxwell Albright. Born in 1891, Albright was the son of American Methodist missionaries working in Chile, where he spent his early years. (The family returned to the United States in 1903.) As the child of committed Christians, Albright had naturally been raised on the Bible and soon chose to make it the focus of his life; he studied at Johns Hopkins University with the great German biblicist Paul Haupt (1858–1926), completing his doctorate in Semitic languages. Albright traveled to Jerusalem to become the director of the American Schools of Oriental Research in 1920, a post he occupied until 1929 and then again from 1933 to 1936. His stay in the Holy Land allowed him to lead excavations at various sites, most notably at Tel Beit Mirsim; at the same time, he authored numerous studies on the whole gamut of subjects relating to the Bible and the ancient Near East. He also trained a good percentage of the entire next generation of American biblical scholars, all the while making a distinguished name for himself in a half-dozen different fields over the course of more than fifty years. Albright died in 1971.

This recital of the bare facts of his life will hardly suffice to explain Albright's great influence over the course of biblical studies in the twentieth century; much of his importance was tied up in the sort of man he was and the times in which he worked. Brought up a conservative Christian, Albright was inclined to believe in the basic historicity of the biblical record, but he was too much of a scholar to be a mere apologist or to waste his considerable talents on doctrinaire casuistry. Instead, he simply proceeded on the not unreasonable assumption that, although inaccuracies and anachronisms may occur here and there in the Bible, a great many biblical traditions probably go back to a period not long after the one they describe; what they have to say may thus contain a good deal of historically reliable material. Therefore, archaeology and the things that it unearths—walled cities and palaces and household artifacts and (sometimes) written texts—may prove to be a valuable independent source of information about some of the places and events mentioned in the biblical text. Under Albright's leadership, a whole school of American archaeologists set out to discover what they could about the history, particularly the political history (that is, wars and conquests, the rise of new centers of power and their eventual destruction) of the biblical period through excavations in the whole region of ancient Israel. This was the movement that came to call itself "biblical archaeology"—going out to do fieldwork "with the spade in one hand and the Bible in the other." [5]

The influence of this school of biblical archaeology was enormous. Apart from the specific discoveries and the new arguments it inspired, biblical archaeology breathed new life into a discipline that, for the preceding decades, had spent much of its energies on texts alone—analyzing the Bible in keeping with the Documentary Hypothesis or similar pursuits. Now, suddenly, the ground underfoot held the promise of new information, information that, in the course of things, might lead to solid new evidence about Abraham the man and the nations he founded. Although Albright's own training had been highly text-oriented—his teacher, Haupt, was a champion of the Documentary Hypothesis and close, philological analysis of the Bible—as time went on he became increasingly suspicious of what he considered the methodological fuzziness and subjectivity involved in such an approach. At the very least, Albright felt, textual work needed some outside correlative, some solid, objective, "scientific" basis for biblical studies—and archaeology seemed to hold the key.

Like any good archaeologist, W. F. Albright was a meticulous sorter. All human artifacts change over time; this is true of the design of automobiles and living-room chairs and can openers and ladies' jewelry and one-horse plows and ancient writing implements. Not only do such artifacts change, they *develop*, with this year's model being a modification of, but rarely a wholly new departure from, last year's. It was Albright who helped perfect the careful examination of pottery remains in order to trace the history and development of clay pots and jars and dishes over a long period. Pottery styles turned out to change fairly quickly, making them a rather accurate tool for dating things: once a particular style of pot could be connected with a specific date or period, the near and distant variants on that style could be put into chronological order and then used to date undated sites. Since pottery was also quite a common commodity, it could be used to fit almost any excavated site into an overall history of the region.

Albright handled such detailed work with great accuracy, both at home and in the field, but he hardly limited himself to archaeology alone: anything touching on the ancient Near East interested him, from the biblical text itself to comparative philology to the Hebrew onomasticon (the corpus of proper names) to the development of the alphabet and epigraphy (the decipherment of ancient writing) to the rise of Israelite religion and (after they were discovered in the late 1940s) the Dead Sea Scrolls. He made significant contributions to all these fields and wrote at a furious clip. Nor was he a particularly self-effacing figure. He had, a former student once observed, "a personality the size of a large lake." He was extremely generous to students and friends and possessed an undeniable magnetism, an unmistakable ego, and an intellect of sometimes breathtaking dimension.

It's Really True

Albright himself summarized in brief the zigzag in the scholarly consensus on the historicity of the Abraham narratives and the other stories of Israel's founders:

> Until recently it was the fashion among biblical historians to treat the patriarchal sagas of Genesis as though they were artificial creations of Israelite scribes of the Divided Monarchy or tales told by imaginative

rhapsodists around Israelite campfires during the centuries following the [Babylonian exile]. Eminent names among scholars can be cited for regarding every item of Gen. 11–50 as reflecting late invention, or at least retrojection of events and conditions under the Monarchy into the remote past, about which nothing was thought to have been really known to the writers of later days.

Archaeological discoveries since 1925 have changed all this. Aside from a few die-hards among older scholars, there is scarcely a single biblical historian who has not been impressed by the rapid accumulation of data supporting the substantial historicity of patriarchal tradition.[6]

Among the new bits of data Albright went on to mention was the very connection of Abraham's family to Ur; this, he said, bespoke a truly ancient element in the Genesis story, since the historical Ur was destroyed in the seventeenth century BCE and "disappears from history for centuries." If the text says that Abraham came from Ur, this assertion must come from the distant past—perhaps not long after the time when the historical Abraham himself was still alive, and of course well before the time when there even was a people of Israel.[7] As for the journey from Ur to Haran and thence to Canaan, the Mari archives gave ample testimony to the free movement of individuals throughout this Amorite-controlled area in the late eighteenth century BCE. Abraham, Albright suggested, was probably a wealthy "donkey caravaneer" who went west to Canaan and eventually made it his home.

Influenced by this approach, other scholars sought to bolster it with further evidence unearthed in Mesopotamia. One commentator thus pointed out that Abraham refers to his servant Eliezer as his legal heir in Gen. 15:2–3. Since Eliezer was apparently not a blood relative, he argued, Abraham must have legally adopted him; such adoptions of mature adults are to be found in various legal documents discovered among the Nuzi archives. Indeed, it was suggested that this adoption might have actually been a legal fiction through which Abraham had obtained a loan. That is, in a legal system where real estate could not be sold to an outsider, Abraham might have adopted the wealthy Eliezer as his heir and then willed to him some piece of property in order to secure a loan.[8] Another scholar pointed to the Bible's odd narration of how Abraham twice ran into trouble (in Genesis 12 and 20, as similarly did his son Isaac in Genesis 26) after a king thought that the beautiful Sarah was merely Abraham's sister and not his wife—and thus available for the king's own attentions. The confusion, it was claimed, derived from another sort of fictitious adoption documented in the Nuzi texts: according to an ancient Hurrian marriage custom, a wife could be "adopted" by her husband as his sister and thereby gain a status superior to that of an ordinary wife. Once again, a puzzling element in the Abraham narrative now appeared to be explained, and in a way that was utterly in keeping with Abraham's presumed geographic and chronological milieu.[9]

Was there an actual individual named Abraham? The very fact that his name is "changed" from Abram to Abraham (Gen. 17:5) suggested to some scholars that two sets of ancient traditions about the same person (one set referred to him as Abram, the other by what looks like a dialect variant of this name, Abraham) had been preserved and harmonized via the name-change story. While "Abraham" is quite unprecedented among the personal names preserved in ancient records, "Abram" might well be related to, or a variant of, the common name Abiram—which is indeed the name of a person, or several persons, within and outside the Bible.[10] Even if the existence of such an individual could not be proven conclusively, the story of Abraham's migration to Canaan might well have originated with a whole group of people who claimed him as an ancestor; he, or they, did indeed make the six-hundred-mile trek from Ur to Haran and, after a time, moved on to ancient Canaan, bringing with them their worship of their own God. As G. Ernest Wright, an archaeologist and Albright student, wrote, "We shall probably never be able to prove that Abram really existed, that he did this or that, said thus and so, but what we can prove is that his life and his times, as reflected in the stories about him, fit perfectly with the early second millennium, but imperfectly with any later period."[11]

Perhaps Not, After All

In more recent times, however, this whole approach to the historicity of the Abraham narratives has come to be questioned. Many of the stories have been found to contain elements reminiscent of a period long after the supposed time of Abraham. The Philistines, for example, are described as having dealings with Abraham and Isaac in Genesis 20 and 26, but nonbiblical sources suggest that the Philistine presence in the region began only hundreds of years after Abraham's supposed arrival, during the time of the Judges. Their mention in Genesis may thus be an anachronism (although some scholars have argued that these later Philistines were preceded by a quite distinct people that may have borne the same name).[12] As for the alleged overlap between ancient Mesopotamian laws and various elements in the Abraham narratives, scholars nowadays are quite skeptical. Just because a certain ancient law or custom is attested in a clay tablet from Mesopotamia in the second millennium does not mean that, centuries later, the same things were not still in practice, or at least not still known, either in Mesopotamia or in Israel itself.[13] What is more, when it comes down to cases, significant differences appear between the Nuzi texts and the biblical passages they supposedly explained. In the phony collateral scheme, for example, the transfer of land in the Nuzi documents is immediate and not contingent on the death of the adopting party; the purchaser really is not an heir at all. Further examination of the wife-sister adoption has thrown the validity of that explanation in doubt as well: in the Nuzi documents, the person who adopts the woman as his sister turns out usually *not* to be the woman's present or future husband.[14] Moreover, on reflection, the Nuzi law really did not explain these odd biblical tales anyway, which seemed designed to celebrate a certain deviousness or trickery on Abraham's part.[15]

Beyond all these points, scholars have noted the absence of any reference to Abraham in the writings of Israel's eighth- and seventh-century prophets. These prophets know, and refer to, *other* traditions about Israel's past—the destruction of Sodom and Gomorrah (Hos. 11:8; Amos 4:11; Isa. 1:9; Zeph. 2:9), the story of Jacob and Esau (Hos. 12:4–5, 13), and the exodus from Egypt and Israel's desert wanderings (Hos. 2:7; Amos 2:10; 3:1; Isa. 11:16; Mic. 6:4–5). But there is not a word about Abraham until we get to parts of the book of Isaiah that scholars generally date to the sixth century or later (Isa. 29:22; 41:8; 51:1–3; 63:16) and scattered references elsewhere, which scholars date to the same period (Mic. 7:20—all of this chapter is held to reflect the postexilic period—as well as Jer. 33:26 and Ezek. 33:24). This is most surprising for a figure who appears to be so central in Genesis. If he were well known as an ancestor of Israel in the eighth or seventh century, scholars now ask, would not one of these prophets have referred to him?

Perhaps the best one-word summary of the current state of research is: puzzled. The above considerations all argue against Albright's view of the Abraham stories in Genesis. But if these stories do not go back to authentic reminiscences of life in Mesopotamia in the second millennium, when were they written? Some scholars have gone over to the other extreme, claiming that the Abraham cycle is a late invention, one that was composed only in the postexilic period. Thus, one researcher has argued that if the Bible says that Abraham migrated from Babylon to Canaan, that is because Abraham's story was created to reflect the Jews' own "migration" from Babylon after having been exiled there in the sixth century, a millennium after the putative time of Abraham! *That* is why Abraham is never mentioned by the eighth-century prophets—he hadn't been invented yet.[16] Other scholars have built on this approach in order to claim more broadly that the whole history of ancient Israel as presented in the Hebrew Bible is altogether unreliable, much of it out-and-out invention and fantasy and political propaganda.[17]

Equally disturbing for contemporary scholars has been a new questioning of the validity of Wellhausen's understanding of the Pentateuch's composition and its sources.[18] In fact, some scholars are now arguing that the Documentary Hypothesis needs to be completely reconfigured. J and E, the two sources that Wellhausen and subsequent scholars had always considered the oldest, are actually not that old, they say—indeed, the source designated D, in the view of some, is the earliest Pentateuchal source. This view does not appear to have won instant acceptance—there are good arguments against it[19]—but it has scored enough points to leave many scholars hedging their bets.[20]

All this has had repercussions for the scholarly view of the stories about Abraham. These stories, most scholars would probably now concede, along with those of the other patriarchs and matriarchs, do seem to contain *some* very ancient material—probably nothing going back to the time when Abraham and company actually lived (if they did exist), but arguably going back to the tenth or eleventh century BCE, perhaps even earlier. The stories may have been transmitted orally for a time and/or been passed on in the form of story poems similar to the Song of the Sea (Exodus 15) or Deborah's Song (Judges 5). Then, at a certain point, they were transformed into their present, prose formulations—but when that actually happened remains the subject of debate. In short: how far back do the Abraham stories go, and how authentic are they? The pendulum seems to have swung one way, then another, and perhaps just now it is moving somewhere toward the middle.

One matter on which there is general agreement among modern scholars is that of Abraham the monotheist. Was Abraham truly an exponent of the belief that there is only one true God in the world? This idea, like the Fall of Man, Cain's satanic birth, and Noah the preacher, appears to have been wholly the creation of the ancient interpreters. When it comes down to cases, not a single verse in the book of Genesis actually says that Abraham believed in the existence of only one God. It is hard to see how he could have. If there even was an Abraham, a modern scholar would say, he lived and traveled about in a polytheistic world. There is nary a hint, even in the Bible's much later depiction of him, that Abraham's beliefs differed *in kind* from those of the people he encountered or even that this was ever a subject of discussion. He is presented as worshiping his own God (and perhaps as worshiping others as well),[21] but not as an exponent of monotheism.[22]

Covenants

One important biblical institution has, however, undeniably been illuminated by research into Abraham and the ancient Near East, and that is the institution of "covenant" (in Hebrew, *bĕrit*). "Covenant" is just a fancy English term for an agreement, and that is precisely what a *bĕrit* was: "treaty" or "charter" might likewise be appropriate translations. Normally, a *bĕrit* was concluded between two or more individuals, or between individuals representing their larger groups, as seems to be the case with the covenant between Abraham and Abimelech (Gen. 21:27). A *bĕrit* was different from modern-day agreements in one respect, however. Nowadays, when we make a solemn agreement with someone, it is usually followed by a particular act: a piece of paper with some writing on it is put in front of the agreeing parties, and each party then takes a pen (not a pencil!) and puts some squiggles on a blank line at the bottom of the document. People explain this ceremony by saying that it is required because, should some doubt later arise about the agreement's validity, an expert can be called in to make sure that the two signatures actually are those of the agreeing parties. This may, on rare occasions, happen. In my experience, however, disputes rarely arise about the validity of the signatures; usually, the dispute is about the meaning of the words that were printed on the page before either party signed it. Still, the signatures are deemed crucial—indeed, sometimes the signing has to be witnessed and even attested by a licensed notary. Why all this fuss? A cultural anthropologist would probably say that the real function of the signing ceremony is largely symbolic: it is a *ritual,* a ceremony designed to make the agreement official and put it into effect. After signing, both parties agree, there is no turning back.

In the ancient Near East they of course had documents—at first, as we have seen, clay tablets; these were inscribed with hatch marks from a wedge-shaped marker while the clay was still wet. (This is the writing system known as cuneiform, from the Latin *cuneus,* "wedge.") These clay tablets could be stored for future use and even authenticated in some fashion. But agreements were not generally solemnized and put into effect by being written down and authenticated (though they were often committed to writing at some point). Instead, there was a different sort of ceremony—or rather, a range of different sorts of ceremonies; one of the most common involved the killing and cutting up of an animal or animals, often leading to a festive meal. After the animals were slaughtered in the presence of the agreeing parties, the agreement was deemed to have gone into effect. Such covenants were known throughout the ancient Near East; they were called by different names, but the element of slaughtering an animal was basically the same. In Akkadian, "Let's go slaughter a donkey" was an idiom meaning, "Let us make an agreement."[23]

What the killing of the animal was meant to imply is difficult to say. Some texts unambiguously assert that the killing and dismemberment was intended to be a not-too-veiled threat. "Just as this calf is cut up, so may Matiel be cut up," says an Aramaic treaty of the eighth century BCE, implying that such is the penalty for breach of contract. Another document testifies: "Abba-AN swore to Yarim-lim the oath of the gods and cut the neck of a lamb, (saying): If I take back what I gave you. . . ."[24] Similarly: "If Mati'ilu violates the covenant and oath to the gods, then . . . as the head of this ram shall be struck off, so shall his head be struck off."[25] But such explanations may merely represent (as was the case with ordinary sacrifices) a later attempt to find a rationale for a long-established ritual whose original rationale lay shrouded in hoary antiquity. Whatever the true reason, the act of cutting up animals was apparently a big part of the original idea: in biblical Hebrew, covenants are usually "cut," and this seems to bespeak the centrality of this ritual act.[26]

"O Lord, Can I Get That in Writing?"

After Abraham has journeyed from Ur to Haran and from Haran on to Canaan, the Bible reports, God appeared to him in a vision, saying to him, "Do not be afraid, Abram, I am granting you a very great reward" (Gen. 15:1).[27] Abraham is skeptical—what good will it do to him to be rewarded if he has no heirs? God reassures him on this score: he will indeed have descendants, in fact, as numerous as the stars.

> Then He said to him: "I am the LORD who brought you from Ur of the Chaldeans, to give you this land to possess." But he said, "O LORD my Master, how can I know that I will possess it?" He said to him: "Bring me a heifer three years old, a female goat three years old, a ram three years old, a turtledove, and a young pigeon." He brought Him all of these and then cut them in two, laying each half over against the other. . . .
>
> Gen. 15:7–10

Until the twentieth century, this passage, like so many in the Bible, must have seemed somewhat mysterious. What was the point of cutting up these animals? Now, in the light of everything that is known about ancient Near Eastern covenants and treaties, scholars believe that Abraham's pious-sounding question, "O LORD my Master, how can I know that I will possess it?" might better be reworded: "O LORD, do you think I could have that in writing?" What Abraham is really asking is that God's promise to give him "this land to possess" be made official—and God obliges:

> When the sun had gone down and it was dark, a smoking fire pot and a flaming torch passed between these pieces [of animals]. On that day the Lord made a *covenant* with Abram, saying, "To your descendants I give this land."
>
> Gen. 15:17–18

The fire and torch, modern scholars say, are apparently intended to represent God's physical presence here, and by walking between the cut-up animal carcasses God was doing exactly what the text says He was doing (and what an ordinary human being would be doing by the same action), making a covenant with Abraham.[28] Henceforth, the land would belong to his descendants.

The idea of this covenant may thus, according to scholars, be altogether political in origin—a way for later Israelites to say, "This land was promised to us." Perhaps, some even assert, there never was an Abraham, and the existence of any such divine grant of the land to Israel was in any case the pipe dream of a later age. At the same time, however, the very idea of God as a maker of binding, legal agreements is not limited to this episode. It recurs elsewhere in the Bible—in fact, it seems to represent something basic about *how* Israel understood God and His way of interacting with them as a people.

7

Two Models of God
and the "God of Old"

Abraham Entertaining the Three Angels
by Rembrandt Harmensz van Rijn.

How the God depicted in Genesis and other parts of the Bible differs from later depictions.

Considered from a distance, the Bible actually seems to present two radically different ways of thinking about God.

Let us put aside the story of Abraham for a minute in order to consider a somewhat broader question: what is God *like* in the Genesis narratives—what sorts of things can He do and know, where is He to be found, and how does He interact with human beings? To ask these questions is to highlight an aspect of the Bible not often discussed, but one that is very important to understanding what the Bible is saying.

There were, in fact, two quite different ways of conceiving of God in biblical times. One way is familiar to us, because it is the later conception of God, the one that was, consequently, passed on to Judaism and Christianity at the end of the biblical period and has been with us in some form ever since. According to this model—and I mean "model" here in the same sense that today's physicists use the word, that is, a way of trying to conceptualize something that is not directly perceivable by the senses—God is everywhere all at once (that is, He is omnipresent) and, concomitantly, omniscient (He knows everything); indeed, He is also all-powerful (omnipotent). This is the later model; its beginnings are to be located in the sixth century BCE or so, though it does not appear fully until the end of the biblical period.

The earlier model, found in many of the narratives of Genesis and Exodus and Joshua and Judges, as well as in numerous psalms and prophecies and laws, might be defined as everything that the later model is *not*. That is, earlier biblical texts do not seem to presume that God is everywhere simultaneously. On the contrary, He often goes from one place to another. For example, in the brief narrative of the Tower of Babel examined earlier, God says about the tower builders, "Let us *go down* and confuse their speech" (Gen. 11:7). This implies that He is not "down" at the time He speaks these words—He is somewhere "up," presumably in heaven. Similarly, with regard to the wicked cities of Sodom and Gomorrah, God exclaims, "The outcry of Sodom and Gomorrah is so great, and their sin is so grievous! I *will go down and see* if they have indeed gone astray as their cry [indicates], and if not, then I will find that out, too" (Gen. 18:20–21). In fact, this sentence also implies that God is not omniscient either—He hears the sound, but has to go down and check in order to be sure what it means. In the Garden of Eden, Adam and Eve hear God "walking about in the garden at the time of the evening breeze" (Gen. 3:8). Walking is not something you do if you are omnipresent.

Even in heaven, according to some biblical texts, God needs a means of transportation: "Behold, the LORD is riding on a swift cloud" (Isa. 19:1); "He rode on a cherub and flew off, He was seen on the wings of the wind" (Ps. 22:11); "Make way for Him who rides upon the clouds" (Ps. 68:4 [5]).[1]

The Garden of Eden story also seems to presume that God does not necessarily know everything. Thus, as we have seen, after Adam and Eve hide among the trees and bushes of the garden, God calls out, "Where are you?" (Gen. 3:9); on the face of it, this question implies that He Himself does not know. Similarly, God asks Cain, "Where is your brother Abel?" It is only in the next sentence, when He presumably comes closer to Cain and hears "your brother's blood crying out to Me from the ground" (Gen. 4:10), that God discovers the horrible truth. Later on, God tests Abraham by telling him to sacrifice his beloved son; what would be the point of God conducting such a test if He were all-knowing and thus knew how the test would end before it took place? On the contrary: after it is over, God says to Abraham, "*Now* I know that you are someone who fears God" (Gen. 22:12)—presumably, before the test, He did not know.

What these texts all imply about God's finiteness is sometimes put in the most vivid terms: many of these early texts seem to maintain that God has an actual body, a discrete, physical being. True, people do not often see this body, but that is not because the human eye cannot perceive it, but for another reason entirely: to see it is dangerous. So when Moses requests to see God's "glory," His physical being, God answers: "No one can see Me and live." This is not the answer a later theologian might expect—"Sorry, Moses, I have no body for you to see," or, "You can never see Me because I am invisible—in fact, I am everywhere all at once." God does indeed have a body in these ancient texts—but because of the danger associated with catching sight of Him, He usually is said to appear surrounded by a protective cloud in order to shield human eyes from the danger. Frequently, He is also said to send a special kind of intermediary, an angel, to pass on His message to human beings.

Because, in this earlier model, God is deemed to have a body, it is no surprise that numerous passages refer to God's "face," "hand," "eyes," "ears," "arm," "fingers," and so forth. Interpreters have often asserted that these expressions are not to be taken literally, but there is no real basis for this assertion other than the fact that such human body parts did not go well with the interpreters' own conception of God as bodyless and omnipresent (that is, the second model). Indeed, God's body in these early texts is not only apparently similar to a human being's, it is also not much bigger. Thus, God speaks to Moses "face to face, as one man speaks to another" (Exod. 33:11; cf. Deut. 34:10) and "mouth to mouth" (Num. 12:8); at one point He "stands next to" Moses and then "passes in front of him" (Exod. 34:5–6). It is difficult to imagine a huge, cosmic deity—or even one significantly bigger than an ordinary man—doing such things.

These facts are nothing new: scholars and ordinary readers of the Bible have known about them for centuries. But for centuries their real significance was missed. People took such attributions of human traits to God as merely a poor or imperfect representation of what was called above the second, or later, "model" of God in the biblical period. In other words, people thought that if the Bible here and there represents God as finite or humanlike—saying that He has a body and walks, talks, grows angry, is pleased, and so forth—it did not really mean these things. It misrepresented the second model because omnipresence and omniscience were concepts too hard for ordinary people to grasp in biblical times, or because (a somewhat different argument) this was the only sort of language available to them to describe Him.[2] But when one considers the matter, this argument actually appears rather weak. Certainly there would be no difficulty in saying in biblical Hebrew, "God is in every place," "The eye of man cannot see Him," or the like—and it is hard to imagine that the ordinary biblical Israelite would find such an assertion particularly difficult to grasp. After all, parents who talk to their children about God nowadays usually say such things by the time the child is five or six or seven—with no apparent incomprehension on the child's part.

With the rise of modern biblical scholarship, an interesting variant on this argument has developed: it is not that biblical authors used anthropomorphisms to get their message across to simple people, but rather that the authors themselves were simple people. They did not have today's sophisticated understanding of God and so expressed themselves in the concrete, simple terms we know. Or—to put it a little more gently—God relied on the contemporary culture of His "penmen" when He inspired them to write, so that their way of putting things inevitably reflects their own culture's form of expression.[3] This, too, misses the fundamental point. The Bible's earlier way of representing God is not a poor version of the later way—*it is based on a completely different model,* a completely different way of conceiving of God's being, and one that could hardly be described (as many modern scholars imply) as unsophisticated. In some ways, in fact, it is more sophisticated than the later model that replaced it.

Unrecognized Angels

The key to understanding the essence of this earlier model comes from something just mentioned: the fact that, in various stories in Genesis and elsewhere, God sends angels to meet with various human beings. There are a great many such encounters—in the book of Genesis, for example, with Abraham and Sarah and Hagar and Jacob, and elsewhere in the Bible with Moses and Balaam and Joshua and so forth. What is striking in all these encounters is that *the angel never looks like an angel.* Unlike the angels represented in medieval paintings, these biblical angels never have flowing wings or haloes or light that radiates out of their garments—they look exactly like ordinary human beings, at least at first. That is why the biblical account of these meetings always goes to the trouble of narrating a "moment of confusion," during which the people in question think they are talking to some ordinary person. This confusion goes on for a while, and then somehow, it suddenly dawns on the humans that they are actually talking to an angel, at which time they fall to the ground in reverence. Here is one very brief example from the book of Joshua:

> And it came to pass, when Joshua was in Jericho, that he lifted up his eyes and saw, and behold! A man was standing across from him with his sword drawn in his hand. So Joshua went up to him and asked, "Are you one of us or one of our enemies?" And he answered, "Neither. But I am the chief of the LORD's army; I have just arrived." Then Joshua fell facedown to the ground in prostration and said to him, "What does my lord wish to say to his servant?" And the chief of the LORD's army said to Joshua, "Take your shoe from off your foot, for the place upon which you are standing is holy"—and Joshua did so.
>
> Josh. 5:13–15

When the "chief of the LORD's army" (an angel) first appears before Joshua, he looks altogether like an ordinary person—and this apparently makes Joshua a little nervous; after all, people with friendly intentions don't usually come at you with their swords drawn. On second thought, however, Joshua thinks this man may actually be one of his own troops or some allied fighter—hence his question, "Are you one of us or one of our enemies?" As soon as this angel tells Joshua who he really is, however, Joshua recognizes his mistake at once: he falls down in abject obeisance and waits for further instructions.

A somewhat longer "moment of confusion" occurs in the book of Judges:

> There was a certain man from Sore'ah, a Danite by the name of Manoah, whose wife was barren and had borne no children. Now, the angel of the LORD appeared to the woman and said to her: "Though you are barren and have not borne, yet you shall become pregnant and give birth to a son. But you must be careful not to drink wine or strong drink, nor may you eat anything impure. And after your pregnancy, when you give birth to a son, no razor shall touch his head, for the boy will be a nazirite[4] of God from the time of his birth . . ." Then the woman went and told her husband, "A man of God [that is, a prophet] came to me, but he looked very frightening, like an angel of God, so I did not ask him where he was from, and he did not tell me his name."

Then Manoah prayed to the LORD and said: "O my Lord! Let the man of God whom You sent come again to us and instruct us what to do for the boy to be born." God heeded Manoah's prayer and the angel of God returned to the woman while she was sitting outside, but her husband Manoah was not with her. So the woman quickly ran back and told her husband and said, "That same man is back who came to me the other time." Manoah went and followed his wife until he came to the man, and asked him, "Are you the man who spoke with my wife?" and he said, "Yes." Manoah said, "If what you said is true, then what are we supposed to do with the boy?" The angel of the LORD said to Manoah, "Let your wife be careful about everything I told her . . ." Manoah said to the angel of the LORD, "Permit us to detain you and kill a goat for you[r dinner]." The angel of the LORD said to Manoah, "Though you detain me I will not be able to eat your food; but if you wish to make a burnt offering to the LORD, then send it up"—because Manoah did not realize that he was an angel of the LORD. Then Manoah said to the angel of the LORD, "What is your name? For, when what you said comes true, we will want to honor you." The angel replied, "Why should you be asking about my name, since it cannot be known?" Then Manoah took the goat and the grain offering, and offered them up to the LORD on a rock, and something wondrous happened while Manoah and his wife were watching: As the flames were rising up from the altar toward the sky, the angel of the LORD rose up in the flames of the altar. When Manoah and his wife saw this, they fell on their faces to the ground.

The angel of the LORD never again appeared to Manoah and his wife; thus, Manoah understood that it was an angel of the LORD. And Manoah said to his wife, "We will surely die, because we have seen God." But his wife said to him, "If the LORD wanted to kill us, He certainly would not have accepted the burnt offering and grain offering, and He would not have shown us all these things; in fact, He would not let us be hearing this now." And the woman gave birth to a son and called him Samson.

Judg. 13:2–24

Here, it is not a *moment* of confusion but a considerably longer time, perhaps several days. At first, Manoah's wife (unnamed in the story) thinks her visitor is a "man of God": this is one of the terms used in the Bible for a prophet, and indeed, it is easy to understand her confusion. After all, she meets someone who appears altogether humanlike, and if he has announced that her barren womb will soon be opened and has further instructed her about preparing her future son to be a "nazirite to God," she draws the logical conclusion: the person to whom she was speaking must indeed have been some sort of prophet foretelling the future.

Her husband, Manoah, then asks God to send the "man of God" back again, and when he reappears, what Manoah's wife says only seems to underline the couple's confusion. "That same *man* is back who came to me the other time," she announces, and Manoah then asks him, "Are you the *man* who spoke with my wife?" Apparently, this God-sent messenger looks very much like an ordinary person (although we are meant to remember the first impression of Manoah's wife, namely, that the stranger appeared "very frightening, like an angel of God"—he is not altogether ordinary-looking). We, of course, appreciate the irony; the narrator has already said that this is actually an angel, and, as if to stress that fact, the narrator then repeats that it is "the angel of the LORD" whom Manoah invites to share a meal with his wife and himself. But they perceive nothing unusual. Now, it was apparently a well-known fact that angels do not eat or drink, so to the reader/listener, the angel's response to Manoah's invitation is altogether comprehensible: I cannot eat the animal you propose to serve me, so perhaps you should offer it as a sacrifice instead. Such a response ought to have tipped off the hospitable couple as well, but it does not. They seem to be in some sort of fog. Instead, they just go ahead as instructed and prepare a sacrifice.

By this point the narrative tension is almost unbearable: We know what is happening, but poor Manoah and his wife are still in the dark. When will they figure it out? Even the angel's cryptic response to their request to know his name—"Do not ask about my name, since it cannot be known"—does not seem to trigger any response in them; apparently still in a fog, they simply shrug it off and go on with their preparations for the sacrificial offering. It is only when the angel ascends to heaven on the flames of the altar that Manoah and his wife finally understand, and then their reaction is identical to that of Joshua above: they fall down on the ground in prostration.

This is reminiscent of yet another encounter with unrecognized angels, this one bringing us back to the book of Genesis and the story of Abraham. After he has journeyed to the land of Canaan, Abraham settles in Mamre, near Hebron.

The LORD appeared to him [Abraham] at the oak trees of Mamre, as he was sitting near the door of his tent during the hot part of the day. He looked up and saw three men standing near him. As soon as he saw them he ran from the tent door to meet them, and bowed to the ground. "Gentlemen," he said, "if you please, do not, I pray, just pass your servant by. Let a little water be brought so that you can wash your feet and rest underneath this tree. Then I will fetch a bit of bread so that you may satisfy your hunger before resuming your journey—after all, you have come this way to your servant's place." They replied, "Do just as you have said."

Then Abraham hurried into the tent to Sarah and said: "Quick! Knead three *seahs* of choice flour and make some loaves." Next, Abraham ran to the cattle and chose a calf, nice and tender, which he gave to the servant-boy to prepare quickly. After that, he took curds and milk, along with the calf that had been prepared, and set them out before them. Then he stood by under a tree while they ate.

They said to him, "Where is your wife Sarah?" and he answered, "In there, inside the tent." Then one said, "I will be back this time next year, and your wife Sarah will have a son." Sarah had been listening at the door of the tent, which was in back of him. Now Abraham and Sarah were old, well advanced in years; Sarah had stopped having the periods that women have. So Sarah laughed to herself, saying, "After I am all used up will I still have relations—not to mention that my husband is old too!" Then the LORD said to Abraham, "Why did Sarah laugh, saying, 'Can I really give birth, old as I am?' Is anything too much for the LORD? I will be back this time next year, and Sarah will have a son."

In this narrative—unlike the incident with Manoah and his wife—we are not told that Abraham ever really understood who his visitors were. The passage begins by asserting that "the LORD appeared" to Abraham—but this assertion seems to come from the narrator's point of view. What Abraham sees is "three men standing near him," and his exaggerated courtesy and zeal in preparing a meal for his unannounced guests seems intended simply to show what a generous host he is—it is no indication that Abraham has somehow figured out his visitors' secret identity.[5] Indeed, later interpreters of the story liked to stress that Abraham had no idea whom he was serving.[6]

In any event, just like Manoah and his wife, Abraham wishes to feed the visiting strangers, and they agree to eat (or at least to pretend to). Their gruff answer to Abraham's invitation—"Do just as you have said"—might have tipped Abraham off that these were no ordinary visitors, but he seems to notice nothing unusual. He tells Sarah and the servant boy to prepare the food without mentioning who these guests are—apparently, he himself has no idea. Even their question, "Where is your wife Sarah?"—but how do these strangers know his wife's name?—seems to arouse no curiosity in Abraham. Like Manoah and his wife, Abraham seems to be in some sort of fog. As in the previous example, the "moment of confusion" here is much more than a moment, it is apparently dragged out throughout the strangers' meal. But in the end, the truth does seem to have dawned on both of them, for when God* says to Abraham, "Why did Sarah laugh? . . . Is anything too much for the LORD?" Sarah immediately denies it "because she was frightened." If she is frightened, it would seem that she has figured out with whom she is speaking. But not much is made of this—the moment of recognition here (if that is what it is) certainly seems to receive less attention than the "moment of confusion" that precedes it.

---

* Note, "the LORD" and no longer the three men.

In a Fog

Apparently, there is something essential about these "moments of confusion"—otherwise there would be no reason to keep including them in all these narratives. In order to understand what that something is, it is necessary to observe another point about all these passages. While the "angel" is unrecognized at first—mistaken for an ordinary human being—after the recognition takes place, something equally striking occurs: usually, it is no longer an "angel" at all that is speaking, but God Himself. Thus, in the passage above about Abraham and the three men, these three effortlessly slide into being God at some point: "Then *the LORD said* to Abraham, 'Why did Sarah laugh?' " After the angel has ascended on the flames of the altar, Manoah and his wife are worried: "We will surely die," they say, "because *we have seen God*." "Go with these men," the angel says to Balaam in yet another moment of confusion (Num. 22:35), "but speak only what *I tell you* to speak."[7] These words may be "said" by the angel, but they are God's words: the "I" here refers to God and not some separate intermediary. (Note that God utters virtually the same sentence to Balaam—but without any intermediary—in a dream the night before [Num. 22:20].) In a sense, then, the angel is never *really* an angel—at first he looks like a man, but then he turns out to be God.

Here is another vivid example involving Abraham's grandson Jacob:

> And Jacob was left alone, and a man wrestled with him until the break of day. When he saw that he could not overcome him, he wrenched Jacob's hip in its socket, so that the socket of Jacob's hip was strained in the fight with him. Then he said, "Let go of me, since it is getting to be dawn." But Jacob said, "I will not let you go unless you bless me." He said, "What is your name?" and he answered, "Jacob." He said, "Your name will not be Jacob any longer, but Israel, since you have struggled with God and with men and have prevailed." Then Jacob said to him, "Please, now, tell me your name." He answered, "Why should you be asking for my name?" and he blessed him there. Jacob named the place Peniel, saying, "I have seen God face to face and yet my life has been spared."
>
> Gen. 32:24–29

At the beginning of the passage, Jacob's wrestling partner is a "man," and the fight lasts the whole night. But when the stranger is asked to bless Jacob, he obliges by giving him a new name and explaining that "you have struggled with God." In a similar vein, Jacob names the place Peniel because "I have seen God face to face." In other words, there really is no angel here at all, only an initial optical illusion, a "man," who actually turns out to be God.

What does all this mean?

These narratives are really predicated on the first model mentioned above. It presumes that God does indeed have some kind of physical existence, a body—why not?—but that, in this physical existence, He usually is simply *elsewhere,* in what one might call another dimension. He stands just behind the curtain of the everyday world. Normally, that is where He stays, but sometimes He crosses over to our side, and when He does, human beings are at first unaware of what they are perceiving; they are in a fog. Perhaps because we normally perceive things through our five senses, a person at first encountering God will, in this first model, think that those senses are what is doing the perceiving. The person thus "sees" another human or "hears" his voice. Then, after a while, the person suddenly understands that all this is an illusion—he is not seeing or hearing at all. At that point he falls to his knees in reverence, and from now on it is God Himself who addresses him.

In a way, the moment of confusion that accompanied this first model seems to have been analogous to dreaming. When people describe a dream they had, they say things like: "I saw this man coming toward me—he was wearing a blue suit and had a little pearl-handled revolver in his hand. Then, suddenly, I heard a scream, and I turned around. . . ." But of course, the dreamer did not actually *see* or *hear* anything: his eyes were closed the whole night, and his ears were similarly shut off to outside noise. Nevertheless, whatever it was that was going on inside his brain was being processed *as if* there were actual visual and auditory stimuli—in fact, sleep researchers have discovered that a dreamer's eyes will actually dart about needlessly behind his closed eyelids during a dream, as if he were actually seeing something. The biblical figures who encounter angels are not asleep, but what these texts seem to be saying is that their brains, like the brains of dreamers, initially processed the experience as if it were taking place "out there," with some actual person who looks a certain way and speaks certain words. Only later does it become clear that the "person" being seen and heard is an illusion: the person becomes God Himself, and He is not "out there" at all. At that point, the human being falls to the ground in reverence and God "speaks" to him directly.[8]

What caused this first model of God to be created? The question is really backwards, as we shall see. The question should really be: what caused the second model to be created? The repeated portrayal of someone in a fog, someone upon whom it suddenly dawns that he has been talking to an optical illusion and that he is actually addressing God—this all has the ring of truth. However conventionalized such portrayals may eventually have become, behind them seems to stand a lived reality. Thus, although these narratives are talking about figures from the past, they themselves sound a bit like *reports* of a world not unfamiliar to the writers, and listeners, of these texts. It is the second model that requires explanation: it represents a certain shift in perception, an ideological shift, and one that came about in a specific set of circumstances far later in the history of biblical Israel.

So what is God *like* in the Genesis narratives—what sorts of things can He do and know, where is He to be found, and how does He interact with human beings? God is in some ways like a human being, although, of course, He is *powerful*: indeed, the power to do and control things that humans cannot is actually what defines the crucial difference between God and us. However, rather than being omnipresent, God in Genesis is frequently said to move about from place to place, and He apparently does not automatically just *know* everything. (He can find things out, but that is not quite the same thing.) As for where He is: normally, He is simply *elsewhere,* behind the curtain of everyday reality, but from time to time He crosses into this world. When He does so and encounters human beings, He inevitably appears to them at first as having a human-sized and human-shaped body, so that the humans naturally think they are encountering an ordinary person. So locked are they into their usual ways of perception, sight and sound, that they miss even the most obvious clues as to His real identity—they are in a fog. But then, suddenly, the truth dawns on them, and they realize that God is right there in front of them. This is the true God of much of the book of Genesis—indeed, of much of the Bible as a whole.

To say this is once again to highlight the gap between what we now know about the Bible and what ancient interpreters thought. From the end of the biblical period on, people have always read the stories of Genesis in keeping with the second model. That is why they said that God's question to Adam and Eve, "Where are you?" was really no question at all but an expression of reproof or lament: "Where are you *now,* and from what good have you removed yourself, O man?" (Philo), or "How could you imagine it possible to hide from Me?" (*Targum Pseudo-Jonathan*).⁹ As for God's question to Cain, "Where is your brother Abel?" Josephus and other interpreters explained it as no real question at all but a mere interrogating tactic designed to get Cain to show his true colors. *Of course God knew,* these interpreters claimed; divine omniscience was the whole point of the story. The same was true of divine omnipresence; Abel's great virtue, Josephus says, is that he believed "that God was with him in all his actions." But this is the later model talking. During the earlier part of the biblical period, God does not dwell in the abstractions of omniscience and omnipresence; instead, He is right there, ready to *enter* and cross over into the human sphere, though unrecognized at first.

Even people of an abstract turn of mind may find themselves drawn, willy-nilly, to the God of Old. When the great French mathematician and philosopher Blaise Pascal (1623–62) died, his coat was discovered to contain a piece of paper sewn inside the lining. On it were written a few disjointed sentences, but they said much about what this extraordinary thinker carried, literally, closest to his heart. In part the paper read: "Fire. God of Abraham, God of Isaac, God of Jacob. Not the God of philosophers and scholars . . . The world has not known You, but I have known You. Joy! Joy! Joy! Tears of joy!"

8

The Trials of Abraham

GENESIS 12–22

The Sacrifice of Isaac (oil on copper)
by Jacopo Chimenti Empoli (1551–1640).

ABRAHAM THE TESTED. THE MAN OF FAITH. SARAH CAPTURED.
SODOM AND GOMORRAH. THE OFFERING OF ISAAC.

Abraham's life hardly went smoothly: from his youth on into old age, a series
of events brought him hardship and suffering. What had the Bible intended
by recounting Abraham's troubles?

The bare facts of Abraham's biblical biography are simple: From his native
Ur, he is said to have moved with his family to Haran in northern
Mesopotamia, and from there he continued on to Canaan. But life was not
easy for Abraham in his new home. At the time of his arrival, Canaan was in
the midst of a famine, so he and Sarah found themselves obliged to continue
on to Egypt in search of food. There the Egyptian king, believing Sarah to be
Abraham's sister, took her to the royal palace, presumably to be part of his
harem (Gen. 12:15). It was only after God "afflicted" him that the king
returned her to Abraham and they left Egypt for Canaan.

After the couple's return to Canaan, a major war broke out between the
kings of five Canaanite cities and the rulers of four foreign nations (Genesis
14), and Abraham's nephew Lot was caught up in the fray and taken prisoner. Abraham found himself obliged to enter the war with his own corps of
retainers, and he eventually succeeded in freeing Lot (Gen. 14:16). But his
troubles were far from over.

Abraham and Sarah had long been childless; at Sarah's urging, Abraham
sought to have a child with Sarah's servant Hagar, and in due time, Ishmael
was born. Afterward, however, tension developed between Sarah and her servant. Meanwhile, Sarah did at long last succeed in becoming pregnant, and
she bore a son, Isaac. Displeased with the behavior of Hagar and Ishmael,
Sarah now demanded that they be banished. Despite his own feelings for his
son, Abraham did as his wife had asked—Hagar and Ishmael were cast out.

Now Sarah and Abraham were left with their only son, Isaac. No sooner
was Isaac grown, however, than God confronted Abraham with what seemed
like his greatest challenge of all: He ordered him to take his beloved son to the
land of Moriah and offer him up as a sacrifice on an altar. Abraham set out
to do as he was told, but at the last minute God relented, and Abraham
offered a ram on the altar in place of his son.

Considering this sequence of events, ancient biblical interpreters could not
escape the impression that Abraham's life was itself intended as a kind of lesson. After all, it is not only the wicked who suffer in this world—often, adversity seems to befall those who least deserve it. This is not, of course, a
problem for biblical interpretation alone, but for the very belief in one God

(monotheism): for how can one maintain that all of reality is created by a single, benign God when so much of what happens in life seems unfair, bringing pain and heartbreak to the innocent, nay, to the unquestionably good? The story of Abraham did not provide an answer, but at least it provided a comforting proof that such things are indeed part of the divine plan. For here was a man who was quick to do whatever God demanded of him, yet his life's path was marked with hardship at every turn. Was this not confirmation enough that God sometimes imposes suffering even on those whom He loves most? At the same time, they noted that in old age Abraham at last found the peace and contentment that had eluded him earlier: "the LORD blessed Abraham in all things" (Gen. 24:1). He lived to see his children and grandchildren grow up, and he ended up becoming the ancestor of several mighty nations. Indeed, his name became a blessing among these many descendants—just as God had promised him at first (Gen. 12:1–3).

Abraham the Tested

If the end of Abraham's life was happy, why had it earlier been marked by so many difficulties? In seeking an answer to this question, ancient interpreters were drawn in particular to the last of these hardships, God's demand that Abraham offer up his own son Isaac as a sacrifice. The opening sentence of this episode describes it as a test: "And it came to pass, after these things, that God *tested* Abraham" (Gen. 22:1). The idea that God might be testing his chosen servants with adversity—to see, as it were, what they are made of and how well their devotion can survive under pressure—would certainly go far toward explaining suffering in the lives not only of biblical figures, but of ordinary humans as well. So it was that Abraham came to be thought of as "Abraham the tested." Indeed, since the sentence read, "And it came to pass, *after these things,* that God tested Abraham," interpreters were inclined to read the indicated phrase as a hint to the existence of previous tests in Abraham's life. In other words, if "*after* these things" God tested Abraham, perhaps this meant that the previous things in Abraham's life were also tests, that his leaving Ur and the famine in Canaan and his losing his wife and so forth were all part of one long series of divinely imposed trials:

> [Even before the offering of Isaac,] the Lord knew that Abraham was faithful in every affliction which He had told him of, *for He had tested him* with regard to [leaving his] country, and with famine, and had tested him with the wealth of kings, and had tested him again through his wife when she was taken forcibly, and with circumcision; and He had tested him through Ishmael and Hagar, his maid-servant, when he sent them away. And in everything in which He had tested him, he was found faithful; he

himself did not grow impatient, yet he was not slow to act; for he was faithful and one who loved the Lord.

Jubilees 17:17–18

Among *other things*—it would take too much time to mention all of them—Abraham was tested concerning the offering up of his beloved son Isaac, in order to prove his pious obedience and thereby make it known to the whole world (but not to God [since He already knew]). Not every test is a sign of disapproval—it may in fact be a sign of praiseworthiness, since it provides proof [of the person's virtue].

Augustine, *City of God* 16:32

The Man of Faith

But what exactly was being tested? Interpreters believed that it was not merely Abraham's ability to endure hardships, but his faithfulness to God, that was being proved by the difficulties that he encountered. The Bible in fact said as much—not in Genesis, but in a prayer of a much later figure, Ezra the scribe. Reviewing the events of Genesis, Ezra had praised God in these words: "You are the LORD, the God who chose Abraham and brought him out of Ur of the Chaldeans and gave him the name Abraham; and *You found his heart faithful* before You and made a covenant with him" (Neh. 9:7–8).

As a result, ancient interpreters came to think of Abraham's *faithfulness* as one of his outstanding characteristics:

He established His covenant in his flesh, and when tested he was found faithful.

Sir. 44:20

The Lord knew that Abraham was faithful in the midst of his afflictions . . . And in everything in which He had tested him he was found faithful, and his soul was not impatient, yet he was not slow to act, for he was faithful and a lover of God.

Jubilees 17:17–18

Abraham was found faithful to [G]o[d] for favor.

4Q226 *Pseudo-Jubilees b* fragment 7:1–2

There is certainly a difference between being a faithful servant of God—that is, one on whom God can rely—and having faith *in* God. In Greek, however, the word *pistos* can express both ideas. Thus, among Greek-speaking Jews and Christians (including New Testament writers), "Abraham the faithful" slid easily into "Abraham the man of faith." For this idea, too, there was biblical support: after all, when God had promised Abraham many descendants (despite his long-standing childlessness), the Bible observed: "And he had faith [*or* believed] in the LORD; and He reckoned it to him as righteousness" (Gen. 15:6). Abraham thus became the exemplar of trust in God:

> Thus "Abraham believed in God, and it was reckoned to him as righteousness." So you see that it is men of faith who are the sons of Abraham. And Scripture, foreseeing that God would justify the Gentiles by faith, preached the gospel beforehand to Abraham, saying, "In you shall all the nations be blessed" [Gen. 12:3]. So then, those who are men of faith are blessed with Abraham who had faith.
>
> Gal. 3:6–9

> For what does Scripture say? "Abraham believed God, and it was reckoned to him as righteousness." . . . That is why it depends on faith, in order that the promise may rest on grace and be guaranteed to all his descendants— not only to adherents of the law, but also to those who share the faith of Abraham, for he is the father of us all.[1]
>
> Rom. 4:3, 16

The Greatest Test

Surely the greatest test to Abraham's faith was God's demand that Isaac be offered up as a human sacrifice. Abraham's willingness to give up the son whom he had yearned for during all those years of Sarah's infertility, and in whom he had delighted since the day of the boy's birth, bespoke an uncommon devotion to God's will. Not only was Abraham prepared to carry out this most painful command, but the text even stressed Abraham's promptness in doing so: after receiving God's command, Abraham "rose early the next morning and saddled his donkey" (Gen. 22:3).

To some ancient interpreters, however, this very aspect of the story was troubling. The narrative gives not the slightest indication that Abraham felt sorrow (or anything else) at the prospect of having to slay his own son. He moves through the story like someone in a trance. Isaac seems to be a young man—old enough to carry the wood for the fire (Gen. 22:6), but young enough, or trusting enough, not to have the faintest idea of what is afoot. So, when Isaac says to his father, "The fire and the wood are both here, but where is the lamb for the sacrifice?" one might expect Abraham to take the occasion to inform his son of God's tragic commandment—but no. Apparently bent on keeping Isaac in the dark, Abraham hedges: "God will provide for Himself the lamb for the burnt offering, my son." (What he says actually turns out to be true—but Abraham presumably had no way of knowing this at the time.) In fact, after the altar is built, Abraham has to tie Isaac up in preparation for sacrificing him. There could scarcely have been any clearer indication in the text that Isaac was an altogether unwilling victim until the very end.

Certainly this picture of an apparently coldhearted father and his simple, trusting son was repellent; it was difficult for ancient interpreters to make their peace with it. It would be nice if, somehow, the text could have indicated that Abraham was pained at what was about to take place—indeed, that at some point he had actually confided in Isaac and explained his dilemma, thereby also telling his son what was being asked of him. Then, if they nevertheless went forward, it would mean that both parties had accepted God's decree. Far from a naïve victim, Isaac would be a willing martyr.

Apart from matters of sentiment, there was a more concrete reason for wishing that the story had unfolded in this way. Toward the middle of the second century BCE (that is, right at the time of the ancient interpreters), the Jews were seeking to rebel against their Syrian rulers, and not a few found themselves called upon to be martyrs and willingly give up their lives in the name of their religion. (This is recounted in 1 and 2 Maccabees, among the biblical apocrypha.) The line between martyrdom and suicide is not always clear, and some Jews must have wondered if the Bible even sanctions a person willingly giving up his own life. But there were no clear examples of martyrdom within the Hebrew Bible itself[2]—unless, of course, it could be argued that Isaac somehow knew that he was going to be sacrificed and nevertheless went along with it. Then he would indeed be a kind of martyr.

As was seen earlier, ancient interpreters did hit upon one anomalous detail in the biblical account:

And Abraham took the wood of the burnt offering and he put it on his son Isaac, and he took the fire and the knife, *and they walked the two of them together*. Then Isaac said to his father Abraham, "Father?" and he said, "Here I am, my son." And he said, "Here is the fire and the wood, but where is the lamb for the burnt offering?" Abraham said, "God will provide for Himself the lamb for the burnt offering, my son." *And they walked the two of them together*.

Gen. 22:6–8

Assumption 3 of the ancient interpreters—that the Bible contains no internal contradictions but is perfect in all its details and perfectly harmonious—eventually included within it the notion that every word of the Bible is significant. The Bible thus never repeats itself or says anything for emphasis, and when it seems to, there must be some additional, hidden meaning. Read with that in mind, the words indicated above seemed to be saying two different things. If the first *and they walked the two of them together* meant that Abraham and Isaac physically proceeded together along the same path, then the second use of this phrase must have been intended to communicate something else. Since the preceding sentence has Abraham saying, "God will provide for Himself the lamb for the burnt offering, my son," it did not seem too much of a stretch to conclude that this second appearance of the phrase meant that, in the intervening time, Abraham had somehow indicated to Isaac—through a gesture or otherwise—that *he* was to be the sacrifice, and despite this discomfiting bit of news, "they walked the two of them together."

Such a possibility seemed all the more likely in view of the ages of the two people involved. As mentioned, Isaac may still have been a boy, but he was old enough to carry the wood for the sacrifice—surely he was at least ten or twelve, perhaps even older.[3] As for Abraham, he was a hundred years old when Isaac was born (Gen. 21:5), so by the time of the sacrifice he would have to be, by the same logic, 110 or older. Even given the longevity of early biblical figures, it seemed unlikely that a man more than a hundred years old would be able to outrun a boy of ten or twelve, should the boy have chosen to flee. Still less likely did it seem that Abraham would have actually been able to tie his son up (Gen. 22:9) without the boy's assent.

On top of all this was the fact that, as we have already noted, the Hebrew text of the Bible contains a great potential for ambiguity. Not only are the vowels in a word usually left to be figured out by the reader, but the beginnings and ends of sentences are not marked: biblical Hebrew had neither capital letters nor periods at the ends of sentences. As a result, interpreters constantly had to decide between different ways of dividing up a sentence and construing the relationship of the various words within it. In this case, Abraham says to his son, "God will provide for Himself the lamb for the burnt offering, my son." But that sentence could, if forced a little, be read as two sentences: "God will provide for Himself. The lamb for the burnt offering [is] my son." (Note that Hebrew normally has no word for "is," so this second sentence is altogether grammatical.)

Thus developed the idea that Isaac was actually a willing victim, nay, a martyr to God:

> Going at the same pace—no less with regard to their thinking than with their bodies—down the straight path whose end is holiness, they came to the designated place.
>
> Philo, *Abraham* 172

> [Abraham said to Isaac:] The Lord will provide a lamb for Himself for the burnt offering, my son—and if not, you will be the lamb for the burnt offering. And the two of them walked together with firm intention.
>
> *Targum Neophyti* and *Fragment Targum* (Paris MS.), Gen. 22:8

Even without the specific connection to the phrase "and they walked the two of them together," the motif of Isaac the willing victim is widely attested:

> Remember what He [God] did with Abraham, and how *He tested Isaac* . . . For He has not tested us with fire, as He did *them*, to search their hearts.
>
> Jth. 8:26–27

> Remember . . . the father by whose hand Isaac would have submitted to being slain for the sake of religion.
>
> 4 Macc. 7:12–14

Given the basic clues of the text, some sources lovingly elaborated the full conversation that must have taken place between Abraham and Isaac on their way to the sacrifice:

> And as he was setting out, he said to his son, "Behold now, my son, I am offering you as a burnt offering and I am returning you into the hands of Him who gave you to me." But the son said to the father, "Hear me, father. If [ordinarily] a lamb of the flocks is accepted as a sacrifice to the Lord with a sweet savor, and if such flocks have been set aside for slaughter [in order to atone] for human iniquity, while man, on the contrary, has been designated to inherit this world—why should you be saying to me now, 'Come and inherit eternal life and time without measure'? Why if not that I was indeed born in this world *in order to* be offered as a sacrifice to Him who made me? Indeed, this [sacrifice] will be [the mark of] my blessedness over other men—for no such thing will ever be [again]—and in me the generations will be proclaimed and through me nations will understand how God made a human soul worthy for sacrifice." [4]
>
> Pseudo-Philo, *Biblical Antiquities* 32:2–3

The Foreshadowing of the Crucifixion

The typological approach to Scripture (see chapter 1) had some Jewish antecedents, but it was essentially a very Christian way of reading. According to this approach, early things foreshadow later ones; more specifically, Christians came to believe that things contained in the Old Testament are actually there as hints or allusions to events in the life of Jesus or to elements of Christian belief and practice (the Trinity, the Eucharist, baptism, and so forth). To put it another way: the Old Testament may not seem like a Christian book, but its stories and laws and prophecies all *correspond* to something in the New Testament or even in post–New Testament Christianity.

The roots of this idea are not hard to find: as we shall see, certain verses in the Psalms and the book of Isaiah were, from a very early stage of Christianity, taken as prophecies of the events of the Gospels. But after a while, the typologies began to suggest themselves at every turn: Adam, Abel, Jacob, Joseph, Moses, Joshua, and other figures were all read as foreshadowings or prefigurations (*figurae* they were called in Latin, "figures") of Jesus. So was Isaac. After all, his father offered him up to be killed as a sacrifice—certainly anyone who thought of Jesus as the son of God could see the parallel.

If God is for us, then who is against us? He who *did not spare** His own son but gave him up for us all, will He not also give us all things along with him?

Rom. 8:31–32

[Jesus was the fulfillment of] that which was foreshadowed in Isaac, who was offered upon the altar.

Letter of Barnabas 7:3

Eventually, other elements were found to suggest further correspondences between the story of Isaac and the crucifixion:

And on this account Isaac carried the wood on which he was to be offered up to the place of sacrifice, just as the Lord himself carried his own cross. Finally, since Isaac himself was not killed—for his father had been forbidden to kill him—who was that ram which was offered instead, and by whose foreshadowing blood the sacrifice was accomplished? For when Abraham had caught sight of him, he was caught by the horns in a thicket. Who then did he represent but Jesus, who, before he was offered up, had been crowned with thorns?

Augustine, *City of God* 16:32

Such, in short, is the portrait of Abraham that first emerged toward the end of the biblical period. Having been tested by God on multiple occasions, Abraham never lost his faith; even when God demanded he give up his beloved son, the biblical patriarch did not flinch. As for Isaac, he was a willing victim, a would-be martyr to his own trust in God. For Christians, the story of that great near-sacrifice was confirmation of the Old Testament's foreshadowing of the New—and hence, further proof that God had arranged all in advance and according to His own plan. These interpretations, created by the Bible's ancient interpreters, were then lovingly passed down from late

---

* An allusion to Gen. 22:12 and 17, both of which say that Abraham did not "spare" his only son.

antiquity through the Middle Ages and on to the present day. But modern scholars see a different picture.

All the Way to the Bank

To begin with, a modern scholar would hardly see the series of biblical narratives about Abraham as a unit. Different episodes in his life are attributed to different authors with different purposes, and while most of the stories are allocated to the source (or complex of sources) designated J, a number are connected with P and E.[5] Thus, the idea that these separate passages and incidents were all designed to transmit a single theme—"Abraham the tested" or "Abraham the man of faith"—would hardly seem self-evident to most modern scholars. Indeed, no such theme is actually evoked in some of the incidents mentioned. Take, for example, the episode of Sarah's being taken by Pharaoh against Abraham's wishes. On closer inspection, it hardly seems to be presented in Genesis as a test of Abraham's faith—or even as a hardship.

> Now there was a famine in the land. So Abram went down to Egypt to reside there as an alien, for the famine was severe in the land. When he was about to enter Egypt, he said to his wife Sarai, "Now I know that you are a beautiful woman, and when the Egyptians see you they will say, 'This is his wife'; then they may kill me and keep you alive [for themselves]. Say instead that you are my sister, so that it may go well with me because of you, and that my life will be spared on your account."
> When Abram entered Egypt, the Egyptians saw that the woman was indeed very beautiful. When the officials of Pharaoh saw her, they praised her to Pharaoh, and the woman was taken to Pharaoh's palace. He dealt generously with Abraham because of her, *and he had sheep, oxen, male donkeys, male and female slaves, female donkeys, and camels.* But the Lord afflicted Pharaoh and his house with great plagues because of Sarai, Abram's wife. So Pharaoh summoned Abram and said, "What is this you have done to me? Why did you not tell me that she was your wife? Why did you say, 'She is my sister,' so that I took her for my wife? Now then, here is your wife, take her and be gone."
>
> Gen. 12:10–19

If there is any victim here, it seems to be Pharaoh, not Abraham. Moreover, this episode hardly presents Abraham in heroic posture. He tells Sarah to say she is his sister in order to save his own life; then, as a consequence, he ends up surrendering her to Pharaoh—without a word of protest. This could hardly be considered a test of faith.

But then why, a modern biblical scholar might ask, was such a story ever told? There is still no scholarly consensus on this issue, but one thing is clear: the narrative highlights the fact that, as a result of Pharaoh's taking up with Sarah, Abraham became a rich man. All those sheep and oxen, donkeys, camels, and servants that Abraham ends up with—the ancient Near Eastern equivalent of a hefty investment portfolio—were apparently one of the perks of being the Egyptian king's brother-in-law.[6] Surely this was not an insignificant detail. Nor does the Bible say a word about any emotional hardship suffered by either Sarah or Abraham—for all we know, Abraham chuckled all the way to the bank. So . . . why was this story told? To some scholars it seems more a way of accounting for Abraham's great wealth than a divine test. After all, Abraham appears later on to be a wealthy man—at one point he is said to have had 318 retainers in his employ (Gen. 14:14), a detail no doubt reflecting his proverbial wealth. Indeed, mention of his wealth served to introduce the very next episode in Abraham's life, his separation from his nephew Lot. As the Bible remarks in introducing that episode, "Now Abram was very wealthy in livestock, in silver, and in gold . . . so that the land could not support both of them living together" (Gen. 13:2, 6). Some scholars say that accounting for Abraham's great riches may have been one reason for which the incident with Sarah and Pharaoh was told.

Lot and the Wicked Sodomites

The incident that follows Abraham's separation from Lot likewise has a different look for modern biblicists. Abraham decides to settle in the mountains of Hebron, while Lot chooses to settle in Jordan valley, in the ill-starred region of Sodom and Gomorrah. These two cities, along with others near them, were destroyed under unknown circumstances sometime early in the biblical period itself. Ever afterward, they were mentioned as an old ruin, a place that was wiped out and never rebuilt. For modern scholars, therefore, the whole tale of Lot and the people of Sodom (Genesis 19) looks like an etiological narrative, that is, the recounting of some incident from the distant past that serves to explain the way things are "now," at the time of the story's composition, when Sodom was a ghost town. The story thus relates that Lot settled in Sodom only to find that his fellow inhabitants were altogether wicked—that they quite literally sought to sodomize some visiting angels. The angels then tell Lot to leave the city with his family members, since it is to be destroyed; Lot does so, escaping as fire and brimstone rain down onto Sodom. For modern scholars, this narrative would appear designed to explain not only why the region had been wiped out (God could not tolerate the inhabitants' wickedness) but also why it had never been rebuilt and remained as an eyesore throughout biblical times (God intended it as a constant reminder about sinfulness and its consequences).

Indeed, the story's etiological interests go beyond merely accounting for the ruins of Sodom. Apparently among those ruins was a rock formation that bore a striking resemblance to the shape of a woman. Josephus, the first-century Jewish historian, attests that he had visited the area and seen such a formation (*Jewish Antiquities,* 203). Modern scholars thus see the story of Lot's wife being turned into a pillar of salt (Gen. 19:26) as another etiological element: "Why does that rock look like a turning woman? Well, it all goes back to something that happened to Lot's wife when she turned to get a last look at her hometown as they were escaping from Sodom." Once again, a story from the past serves to explain what "we" biblical Israelites see in the present.*

When Lot escapes with his two daughters (leaving his pillarized wife behind), they trick him into getting drunk and having sexual relations with them. Nine months later they give birth to two sons, respectively the ancestors of Israel's two neighbors the Ammonites and the Moabites. Modern scholars see this, too, as an etiological element—and a nasty swipe at these two nations. The story well accounts for the fact that the Ammonites and the Moabites speak a language similar to the Israelites' and are related to them in other ways: their ancestor (Lot) and the Israelites' forebear (Abraham) were from the same family. At the same time, the narrative describes these two neighbors of Israel as, quite literally, a bunch of bastards: both were engendered from an incestuous union of Lot with his own daughters. Indeed, the names of the two peoples are somewhat polemically explained in keeping with this tale of incest: Moab, eponym of the Moabites, is said to have been so named because of the phrase "From father" (*me'ab* in Hebrew), while the Ammonites are so called because of the phrase presumably spoken by Ammon's mother after his birth, "My dad's son" (*ben 'ammi*).[7]

An Etiological Sacrifice

Like these other narratives, the story of Abraham's near-sacrifice of his son Isaac seems to modern scholars to have had an etiological message for ancient Israelites. To understand it, one must be aware of a somewhat gruesome fact of life in the ancient Near East: apparently, various peoples in the region used to sacrifice their own children to their gods. Consider what the Moabite king Mesha did when it looked like he was about to lose a battle to Israel:

---

* Inhabitants of New England may recall the Old Man of the Mountain, a humanlike profile that used to be visible on a mountainside near Franconia Notch, New Hampshire. (It collapsed in 2003.) This rock formation also led to the making of a tale, Nathaniel Hawthorne's "The Great Stone Face."

When the king of Moab saw that the battle was going against him, he took with him seven hundred swordsmen to break through, opposite the king of Edom; but they could not. Then he took his firstborn son who was to succeed him, and offered him as a burnt offering on the wall. And great wrath came upon Israel, so they withdrew from him and returned to their own land.

> 2 Kings 3:26–27

According to this account, King Mesha sacrificed his own son in order to influence the outcome of the battle (presumably, to spur the Moabite god, Chemosh, into action). And it apparently worked: "great wrath" struck the Israelite side and they had to retreat.

It was not just among Israel's neighbors that child sacrifice was countenanced, but apparently within Israel itself. Why else would biblical law specifically forbid such things—and with such vehemence?

You shall not give any of your offspring to sacrifice them to Molech, and so profane the name of your God; I am the LORD. . . . Say further to the people of Israel: Any of the people of Israel, or any of the aliens who reside in Israel, who give any of their offspring to Molech shall be put to death: the people of the land shall stone them to death. I myself will set My face against them and will cut them off from their people, because they have given of their offspring to Molech, defiling My sanctuary and profaning My name.

> Lev. 18:21; 20:3

Do not inquire concerning their gods, saying "How did these nations worship their gods? I also want to do the same." You must not do the same for the LORD your God, because every abhorrent thing that the LORD hates they have done for their gods. They would even burn their sons and their daughters in the fire to their gods.

> Deut. 12:30–31

No one shall be found among you who makes a son or daughter pass through fire.

> Deut. 18:10

These and other texts have suggested to scholars that it was not just Israel's neighbors who contemplated offering their young to their deity but Israelites as well; the apparent purpose of these laws is to check that impulse.[8]

If so, then a story about Israel's distinguished ancestor Abraham, who showed himself willing to sacrifice his beloved son to God but, at the last moment, was told by God to offer a ram in his son's stead—such a story would seem to have a clear etiological message: our God does *not* demand that we sacrifice our children to Him. The one occasion on which He seemed to do so turned out to be only a "test"; ever afterward, we have sacrificed animals, like the ram in this story, as a substitute for our children. Once again, a story about something that happened in the distant past explains present-day reality, in this case, why the Israelites at some point ceased acting like their neighbors and no longer made such drastic demonstration of their loyalty to their God.[9]

In short, what looked to ancient interpreters like a series of tests seems to modern scholars more like a collection of independent narratives from different periods and of different purposes. The tale of Abraham and Sarah in Egypt may have been designed more to account for Abraham's fortune (and perhaps to celebrate a certain craftiness withal) than to praise his piety; the narratives of the destruction of Sodom and Gomorrah, the petrification of Lot's wife, and his scandalous unions with his daughters—all these appear connected to various etiological themes. Even the near-sacrifice of Isaac seems etiological in origin: its original purpose was less to commemorate Abraham's piety than to explain Israel's curious abstention from the practice of child sacrifice. That notwithstanding, scholars rightly point out that, whatever its origins, the biblical story is introduced as a divine test and not as a precedent for the prohibition of human sacrifice. The story of the binding of Isaac in its biblical form is now all about Abraham's willingness to carry out God's command in extremis, as well as God's unwillingness to let Abraham go through with it. In highlighting these two things, the biblical text and the postbiblical traditions are in rare agreement.

9

Jacob and Esau

GENESIS 25–28

Isaac Blessing Jacob by Govert Flinck.

Schematic narratives. An etiological rivalry.
Esau = Rome. Jacob's dream.

Abraham's grandsons Jacob and Esau never seemed to get along. One of them became the immediate ancestor of the people of Israel, the other the forefather of Israel's southern neighbor the Edomites.

By now, of course, it should be clear how different are the approaches of ancient and modern interpreters; I hope it is also becoming clear that my purpose in surveying both is not to favor one approach over the other, but to try to understand each on its own terms—and this, as already pointed out, is largely a matter of understanding the assumptions that each group brought to the act of reading the Bible. These assumptions have essentially created two different Bibles, the ancients' and the moderns'. The words of each Bible are exactly the same, but they turn out to mean something quite different.[1]

Everyone is aware of the role that assumptions sometimes play in the understanding of ordinary speech, though most people do not devote a great deal of thought to the matter. Yet even something as simple as the two-word greeting "Good morning" sometimes means quite different things—for example (1) "Hello," or (2) "Why are you just getting up now? I've been up for hours," or (3) "I beg your pardon, I don't believe we've ever met"—depending not so much on the tone of voice (though that can help) as the precise circumstances or context in which these two words are uttered. Meaning number 1, for example, will probably be automatically understood if the speaker of "Good morning" is an office secretary answering the telephone; number 2 might be inferred if these words are being spoken to someone in a bathrobe by a disgruntled spouse who has just returned from dropping the children off at school; number 3 might be understood if the words are spoken by a stranger at, say, some business breakfast. It is not the words alone that carry the meaning, but the situation in which they are spoken, a particular context that creates *expectations* on the part of the listener. No matter what the tone of voice, the person hearing the secretary answer the phone will probably never think of substituting meanings number 2 or number 3 for number 1. The same is true for the bathrobed spouse or the executive—the context will likewise create expectations that make substituting the wrong meaning impossible.

To say this much is to approach one of the great findings of modern philosophers and students of literature, namely, that *meaning is never inherent solely in the words of a text*. Rather, meaning derives from an interaction between text and reader, or speaker and listener; that is to say, the meaning of a text always depends in some measure on the set of assumptions about the text that a particular reader/listener carries with him or her.

If meaning were inherent solely in the written words, I would certainly be puzzled by a piece of paper I found in my university mailbox last week. It was a letter from the dean and began, "Dear Professor Kugel." "*Dear?*" I would say to myself, "but I hardly know you!" Still more puzzling would be the words just above his signature, "Sincerely yours." Actually, I could not identify a single word in the whole letter that could properly be described as heartfelt or sincere, and if he really meant that he was "mine," well, how about giving me a large raise next July? But of course I didn't misunderstand any of these things, because I know perfectly well the conventions of a business letter, and the assumptions I bring to the reading of such a letter will guide me in properly understanding it. It is never just a matter of the words themselves.

Literary scholars have remarked on the same phenomenon with larger units, even whole books. How do we know, for example, that Jonathan Swift was kidding when he wrote his famous 1729 pamphlet, *A Modest Proposal for Preventing the Children of Poor People in Ireland from Being a Burden to Their Parents or Country, and for Making Them Beneficial to the Public*? In it, Swift proposes to solve the problem of widespread hunger in Ireland, especially among the young, by taking a certain proportion of one-year-olds and turning them into food for the rest of the population, since (as he observes):

> A young healthy child well nursed is, at a year old, a most delicious, nourishing, and wholesome food, whether stewed, roasted, baked, or boiled; and I make no doubt that it will equally serve in a fricassee or a ragout.

We know he was not serious first of all because this is indeed sometimes an option in everyone's speech and writing, and second because most of us are acquainted with a certain literary genre called "satire." So it won't take a reader long—even if he doesn't know that Swift was himself a famous satirist, the author of *Gulliver's Travels*—to activate the assumptions that accompany the reading of a satire and properly understand this *Modest Proposal*. Beyond that, most readers would probably also be able to detect in Swift's words a not-too-subtle dig at English indifference and even cruelty (though certainly of a lesser order than that advocated by the pamphlet) in the face of Irish sufferings. But imagine, for a minute, some creature from Mars who has no notion of satire as an option. To such a person, these same words would necessarily appear to be the writings of a maniac.

In considering our two groups of interpreters, it is important to remember that *both* carry a set of assumptions about the biblical text. In saying this, I do not intend to reduce everything to some kind of mushy relativism: it is certainly not the case that one set of assumptions is just as good as the next. After all, people can sometimes be wrong in what they have assumed, and we are in any case never altogether free to choose our assumptions. But the point of juxtaposing ancient and modern interpretations is not to show that one way of reading is right and the other mistaken, or that one is scientific and the other fanciful. What truly separates these two groups of interpreters is the set of unwritten instructions that guide them in reading the biblical text. Accept the one's, and the other's interpretations appear irrelevant at best, at worst a willful and foolish hiding from the obvious. It is thanks to this crucial difference in assumptions that these two groups can read exactly the same words and perceive two quite different messages.

With regard to the stories of Genesis that we have been reading, readers thus far are likely to have concluded that the main contribution of the ancient interpreters consisted of their specific interpretive creations: "Original Sin," "Abraham the monotheist," and so forth. But these are only the surface manifestation of something much deeper, the assumptions that created the very approach of these interpreters in the first place—for example, their way of reading the Genesis narratives as stories about individual people, and stories with a lesson to impart. One need not read these narratives as either. Indeed, if modern scholars are to be believed, many of these tales were automatically understood by their original Israelite audience in the etiological sense, in which individual heroes really stand for whole nations and the purpose of the story is not to impart some moral lesson but to account for some aspect of present-day life. If this is so, then the transition from this original, corporate-and-etiological understanding of these texts to the individual, moral reading of them must be seen as an enormous change wrought by the Bible's earliest interpreters.

Jacob the Good

After Abraham, the story of Israel's ancestors continues with Abraham's son Isaac. Isaac married Rebekah, and in due time she gave birth to twins, Jacob and Esau. From the time they were in their mother's womb together, these two did not get along; in fact, their moving about within her was so violent that Rebekah sought out a divine oracle to explain what was happening. The answer she received was a portent of the future:

> Two [future] nations are in your womb, and two peoples will split off from inside you. But one will be stronger than the other—the older will end up serving the younger.
>
> Gen. 25:23

This prophecy proved to be true: Jacob and Esau did go on to found two different nations, Israel and Edom respectively—and ultimately, Esau's nation (though he had been the privileged brother at first) ended up in a position inferior to that of Jacob's.

Since Jacob was their people's immediate founder, Jewish interpreters were naturally interested in celebrating his virtues—and in stressing the faults of his rival, Esau. This approach was very much in keeping with the way ancient interpreters approached *all* the stories of Genesis. Believing that the purpose of biblical narratives was to present readers with moral exemplars and role models (either positive or negative), interpreters naturally had a tendency to exaggerate the virtues and vices of the people involved. As a result, readers soon came to expect biblical figures to come with a clear label: "altogether righteous" or "completely wicked." Anyone who has taken a very young child to the movies is acquainted with this phenomenon. Every time a new person appears on screen, the child has only one question, but a burning one: "Is he good, or bad?"

This was a difficult question to ask about Jacob and Esau, since at first glance, neither of them really seemed to fit these categories. Jacob, as the ancestor of the people of Israel, ought to have been good—but he did not seem so in some of the stories about his youth: he takes advantage and outmaneuvers, even lies and cheats. One of the jobs of ancient interpreters, therefore, was to look deeply into the biblical text itself, whose every detail might conceal some important, possibly mitigating, information. Their attention eventually fell upon one particular verse in Genesis, which seemed to contrast the two brothers:

> The two boys grew up, and Esau became a man skilled at hunting, an outdoorsman, while Jacob was a quiet fellow, staying in tents. Isaac loved Esau, because he liked eating game, but Rebekah loved Jacob.
>
> Gen. 25:27

At face value, the contrast seems to be between a rugged sportsman and a homebody, the former beloved by his father, the latter by his mother. This in itself hardly seemed to tip the scales in Jacob's favor. But one apparently insignificant detail caught the eye of ancient interpreters: Jacob is described as "staying [*or* dwelling] in tents." Why is "tents" in the plural—how many tents does one person need?[2] Obviously, only one. If, therefore, the text says "tents," it must be hinting at something unusual, something that is not being stated outright.

Of course, ancient interpretation was never merely a cold, objective search for the truth about the text: the interpreters had a stake in what the text would end up saying. If they had been out to sully Jacob's name, they might have used the mention of "tents" in the plural to suggest that he was a philanderer, going from tent to tent while the other menfolk were off hunting or shepherding. But of course they were not out to sully Jacob's name—quite the contrary; so instead, they immediately thought that something good was being hinted at in the plural "tents." Thus was born the figure of Jacob the scholar, the one who—while his brother was out killing animals for game—frequented someone else's tent, the home of an unidentified teacher who instructed him in reading and writing:

> And Rebekah bore to Isaac two sons, Jacob and Esau, and Jacob was a smooth and upright man, while Esau was fierce, a man of the field, and hairy; and Jacob dwelt in tents. And the youths grew, and Jacob *learned to write;* but Esau did not learn, for he was a man of the field, and a hunter, and he learned war, and all his deeds were fierce. And Abraham loved Jacob, but Isaac loved Esau.
>
> *Jubilees* 19:13–15

> And the two boys grew up, and Esau was a skilled hunter, a man who went out to the fields, but Jacob was a perfect man who frequented the schoolhouse.
>
> *Targum Onqelos,* Gen. 25:27

> And Jacob was a man perfect in good work, dwelling in schoolhouses.
>
> *Targum Neophyti,* Gen. 25:27

Esau the Wicked

The alert reader will notice that, in the *Jubilees* passage cited above, it is not only Jacob who has been transformed, but Esau as well. Here Esau has moved from being an apparently harmless outdoorsman to someone who was "fierce . . . and he learned war, and all his deeds were fierce." Part of Esau's reputation for violence among ancient interpreters derives (as usual) from their reading everything available on him in the Bible and not just the passage in question. For example, when the text describes the twins' birth, it does so in these terms:

> When [Rebekah's] time to give birth was at hand, it turned out that there were twins in her womb. The first came out red, *his whole body like a fur coat;* they named him Esau. Afterward his brother came out, with his hand grasping Esau's heel; he was named Jacob.
>
> Gen. 25:25–26

Apparently, the narrative mentions Esau's "furriness" in order to prepare us for a later detail in the story: Esau's hairy arms will ultimately help Jacob deceive his blind father. But in the *Jubilees* passage cited above, as well as in the writings of later interpreters, Esau's hairiness becomes symbolic of his animal nature; he is little better than a beast of prey himself.

Particularly significant for ancient interpreters was a certain verse in the book of Malachi, one of Israel's latest prophets:

> "I have loved you," says the LORD. But you [Israel] say, "How have you loved us?"
>
> "Is not Esau Jacob's brother?" says the LORD. "Yet I have loved Jacob, but I have hated Esau. I have laid waste his hill country and left his homeland to jackals of the desert."
>
> Mal. 1:2–3

If God is said to have "hated" Esau, this was a clear sign that the biblical description of his youth was not telling all. From his earliest youth, interpreters reasoned, Esau's life must have been a series of bad deeds, such as to bring down on him God's hatred:

> There were born two sons, Jacob and Esau. And God loved Jacob, but He hated Esau *because of his deeds.*
>
> Pseudo-Philo, *Biblical Antiquities* 32:5

Or perhaps Esau's wickedness was determined even before his birth, as part of God's master plan for Jacob and his descendants:

> When Rebekah had conceived children by one man, our ancestor Isaac—even before they had been born or had done anything good or bad (so that God's purpose of election might continue, not by works but by his call)—she was told, "The elder shall serve the younger." As it is written, "I have loved Jacob, but I have hated Esau."
>
> Rom. 9:10–13

Elsewhere in the Bible, Israel's ancient prophets seemed actually to have described some of Esau's bad deeds that were not mentioned in Genesis:

> Thus says the LORD: For three transgressions of Edom, nay, for four, I
>   will not revoke the punishment;
> He [Esau] chased after his brother with the sword, and he cast aside all pity;
> His anger ripped at his prey,[3] and his wrath stormed forever.
>
> Amos 1:11

> For the violence done to your brother Jacob, shame shall cover you
> [Esau], and you shall be cut off forever.[4]
>
> Obad. 1:10

If so, interpreters reasoned, there could be little doubt that Esau's relations with his brother had always been characterized by physical violence. He was a wicked man.

One final twist in Esau's reputation came about starting in the first century or so of the common era. Now Judea was ruled by the Roman Empire. The Romans were the dominant military power of the day: they had conquered peoples from the westernmost corners of Europe to the eastern Mediterranean and beyond, and the nations they had subdued writhed under the Roman boot. Executions (by crucifixion or equally cruel measures) and collective punishment were the rule of the day. Esau already had his reputation among ancient interpreters as a heartless warrior who took pleasure in killing animals and men; he was a hairy, bloodthirsty monster. It was not much of a stretch for interpreters now to identify such an Esau not simply as an evil individual, but one who had a great deal in common with the whole Roman military apparatus.[5] In describing Jacob's struggle with his brother in Genesis, the Bible might thus have been hinting as well about Rome's violent oppression of the Jews—and holding out the hope that, someday, the younger brother would succeed in overthrowing Rome's military might.

Jacob's Back Pages

Even to Jacob's most determined supporters, however, some of his early deeds must have seemed questionable. Prominent among these was his treatment of Esau with regard to the sale of his birthright.

As we have seen, Esau was the first to emerge from his mother's womb, and this circumstance automatically granted him the privileged status of firstborn son. To be the firstborn was no trifle: with this title came the *birthright* of the oldest son—a double portion of the father's estate (Deut. 21:17). Thus, Esau stood to inherit twice as much property as Jacob after Isaac's death. For Jacob, apparently, Esau's rank rankled, and one day he found the opportunity to wrest it from him:

> Once, when Jacob was cooking a stew, Esau came in from the field completely famished. Esau said to Jacob, "Give me a mouthful of that red stuff, since I am famished!" (Therefore he was called *Edom* [that is, "Red"]). Jacob said, "First sell me your birthright." Esau said, "Look, I am on the verge of death. What good is a birthright to me?" Jacob said, "Swear to me first." So he swore to him and sold his birthright to Jacob. Then Jacob gave

Esau bread and lentil stew, and he ate and drank, and got up and went his way. Thus it was that Esau thought little of his birthright.

Gen. 25:20–34

The passage did not seem to speak well of Jacob. After all, his brother (who presumably "came in from the field" because he had been hunting food for the whole family, including Jacob) was truly famished. "I am on the verge of death" might sound like an exaggeration on Esau's part, but perhaps it wasn't; sometimes tracking game may lead a hunter to stay out overnight and on into the next day, or perhaps even longer. Under these circumstances, Jacob's demand that the starving Esau sell his birthright seemed to many readers downright mean, an act of exploitation. True, the text ends by saying that Esau "thought little" of his birthright, and some interpreters seized upon this to justify Jacob's conduct: he knew all along that Esau could not care less about his birthright. Still, under the circumstances described, did Esau have any choice but to sell?

The Stolen Blessing

If interpreters were troubled by this incident, they were still more disturbed by the one that came two chapters later. Isaac, by now blind and infirm, tells Esau to go out and hunt some game for a festive meal, after which, Isaac says, he will give Esau his fatherly blessing. Rebekah overhears the conversation and decides to arrange things so that *her* favorite son, Jacob, will receive the fatherly blessing instead of Esau. First, she cooks up some goat meat taken from the nearby herds while Esau is still out hunting. Then she dresses Jacob up in his brother's pungent-smelling clothes and covers his arms and neck with goat skins to mimic his brother's hairy physique. So equipped, Jacob goes in to his blind father bearing the food:

[Jacob] went in to his father, and said, "My father"; and he said, "Here I am; who are you, my son?" Jacob said to his father, "I am Esau your first-born. I have done as you told me; now sit up and eat of my game, so that you may bless me." But Isaac said to his son, "How is it that you have found it [the animal] so quickly, my son?" He answered, "Because the LORD your God made it happen upon my way." Then Isaac said to Jacob, "Come near, that I may feel you, my son, to know whether you are really my son Esau or not." So Jacob went up to his father Isaac, who felt him and said, "The voice is Jacob's voice, but the hands are the hands of Esau." He did not recognize him, because his hands were hairy like his brother Esau's hands; so he blessed him. He said, "Are you really my son Esau?" He answered, "I am." Then he said, "Bring it to me, that I may eat of my son's game and bless you." So he brought it to him, and he ate; and he brought him wine, and he drank. Then his father Isaac said to him, "Come near and kiss me, my son." So he came near and kissed him; and he smelled the smell of his garments, and blessed him.

Gen. 27:18–27

If Rebekah was responsible for initiating this deception, Jacob himself comes off little better. After all, he tells an outright lie: "I am Esau your firstborn," he says. Then he tells another one, still more disturbing, explaining that he was able to find the game he was hunting so quickly "because the LORD your God made it happen upon my way." (This pious-sounding explanation was sure to soften Isaac up!) How pathetic is the picture of this blind old man desperately trying to rely on his other senses to figure out if it is Esau or not—and then being deceived precisely by the manipulation of those senses. Thus, Isaac *hears* the voice and recognizes it as Jacob's, but then he is confused by the apparently hairy hands and arms that go with that voice ("The voice is Jacob's voice, but the hands are the hands of Esau"). Apparently not persuaded by the conflicting data (sense of hearing versus sense of touch), Isaac asks again, "Are you really my son Esau?" Then he *smells* the characteristic smell of Esau's clothes, and this (perhaps along with the mind-dulling wine that Jacob has kindly also supplied) is enough to convince him to go ahead with the blessing.

If all this seemed to portray Jacob in a negative light, interpreters nevertheless found that the case against him was not absolutely watertight. The Hebrew Bible, it will be recalled, was transmitted for centuries without capital letters or punctuation. Where a sentence began and ended was thus often a matter of speculation. In this case, an interpreter sympathetic to Jacob might choose to understand Isaac's opening question, "Who are you, my son?" as if it were really two questions: "Who are you? My son?" Jacob's apparently lying answer, "I am Esau your firstborn," could then be analyzed as two quite separate, and truthful, statements. "I am," he says in answer to Isaac's second question, but then adds, as if reminding his addled father of another fact: "Esau is your firstborn." (Note that, in normal present-tense sentences, Hebrew has no equivalent of "is," so such an understanding is altogether grammatical.) It is hard to know how seriously to take such a reading of the text. Perhaps, as sometimes happened, it was offered a bit whimsically at first—but soon enough it came to be transmitted with a straight face:

He [Jacob] went in to his father and said, "*I am your son.* I have done as you told me; come and sit down and eat of what I have caught, father, so that you may bless me.". . . And Jacob went close to his father Isaac, and he [Isaac] felt him and said, "The voice is Jacob's but the hands are Esau's," and he did not recognize him, because there was an order from heaven to turn his mind astray . . . And he said, "Are you my son Esau?" and he said, *"I am your son."*

Jubilees 26:13–19

And Jacob said, "I am Esau your firstborn" [Gen. 27:19]. He stopped in the middle, [that is,] he said "I am," but "Esau is your firstborn."

Midrash Leqah Tov ad Gen. 27:19

It is to be noted that the *Jubilees* passage above offers a further explanation for the events, and this explanation constituted a more serious argument: "He did not recognize him, because there was an order from heaven to turn his mind astray." In other words, if Jacob succeeded in this shabby deception—despite the fact that his father was perfectly well aware that it was Jacob's voice and not Esau's—then it must be that God had wanted Jacob to succeed: He purposely led Isaac's mind astray and caused him to bless the younger son. If so, it followed that the deception itself was simply part of the divine plan: Rebekah, Jacob, and Isaac were all pawns on the divine chessboard, moved about in such a way as to get the desired result, Isaac's blessing Jacob.

The Etiological Twins

These same stories look quite different to biblicists nowadays. In fact, it was Gunkel's concept of the etiological tale that provided scholars in the twentieth century with a wholly new way of understanding the rivalry of these two brothers.

To begin with, the fact that Jacob and Esau are said to be the ancestors of two different nations—the peoples of Israel and Edom, respectively—effectively announces the etiological dimension of the stories right off the bat.[6] For modern biblicists, a narrative about Jacob and Esau will have been created in order to explain something having to do with Israel and Edom at the time of the story's composition, a kind of *projection of later reality* back to the "time of the founders." Indeed, it will probably do more than that—it will seek to say something about the national character (or national stereotype) of these two people in the way it portrays their eponyms.

In this etiological reading, the fact that Esau and Jacob were brothers, nay, twins, would appear to be an explanation of the close connection between Israel and its southern neighbor. In biblical times, these two peoples probably spoke two very similar dialects (archaeologists have not uncovered a great deal of Edomite writing, but from what has been found it seems clear that Hebrew and Edomite were closely related) and had deep cultural and even kinship ties; the reason, the Genesis narrative suggests, is that both peoples ultimately derive from ancestors who were themselves twins. At the same time, the off-and-on enmity between Israel and Edom that existed in the biblical period is also explained by the Jacob-Esau tales: these later nations did not get along because the original brothers did not get along; in fact, they even hated each other in utero.

As we have seen, Genesis actually relates three distinct stories about the brothers in their youth—the story of their birth (25:19–26), Esau's sale of his birthright to Jacob (25:29–34), and Jacob's acquiring a fatherly blessing intended for Esau (chapter 27). Each of these seems to embody a certain theme with regard to Israel and Edom—in fact, that theme is announced almost from the very beginning of the first story, in a verse already examined above:

> When [Rebekah's] time to give birth was at hand, it turned out that there were twins in her womb. The first came out *red,* his whole body like a *fur* coat; they named him Esau. Afterward his brother came out, with his hand grasping Esau's *heel;* he was named Jacob.
>
> Gen. 25:25–26

To a modern scholar, these verses contain some obviously etiological markers: Esau comes out *red* as a cue to readers, in case they did not already know, that he is the founder of Edom, a name which sounds like "red" (*'adom*) in Hebrew.[7] His furriness is mentioned not so much to prepare readers for the role that hairy arms will play in the "stolen blessing" story, but as a reference to the name of Edom's great mountain, Seir, which sounds as if it might mean "hairy" (*sa'ir*). "Esau," both these details seem to cry out, "is the Edomites." Similarly, on their way out of their mother's womb, Jacob tries to grab Esau's heel. This too is etiological: the word for heel, *'eqeb,* sounds as if it might be the root of the Hebrew for Jacob, *ya'aqob.* But beyond these points is the striking image of the younger brother trying to overtake his older sibling, as if, even on their way to being born, the younger one was saying, "I deserve to come before you!"

A similar message seems to underlie the story of the sale of Esau's birthright. Rightfully, the firstborn's portion belonged to Esau, but he gave it up in exchange for some stew: here again, the younger brother overtakes the older, ending up with what really should not have been his. Strikingly, the same theme is the basis of the third story as well, whereby Jacob masquerades as Esau and gets the blessing that rightly belonged to his older brother. To a modern scholar, the similar theme of all three stories can hardly be coincidental.

What *later reality* might have caused these three stories to be told? Some biblical scholars spotted a possible analogue in Israelite history. Esau's descendants, the Edomites, had, according to the Bible's own history, been a sovereign nation while the future Israel was still a collection of disparate, and sometimes warring, tribes (Gen. 36:31).[8] In this sense, Esau was definitely the "older brother." But then, in the tenth century BCE, David succeeded in unifying those tribes and, in short order, conquering Edom (2 Sam. 8:13–14; cf. 1 Kings 11:15–16 and the heading of Psalm 60; also 1 Chr. 18:12–13): Edom was now under Israel's thumb. That is the real reason, scholars believe, that the oracle given to Rebekah during her pregnancy had said that "the older will end up serving the younger." That prophecy (or as a modern scholar would say, that *vaticinium ex eventu,* a nice Latin phrase meaning a pseudoprophecy that was written *after* the event it predicts had already taken place) was carried out in the time of David.

If so, then the various stories of Jacob and Esau in their youth were actually created to reflect a political reality that came about only centuries later, in the time of David. In fact, the stories seemed to offer scholars a chronological clue as to the original date of these narratives, since Israel's rule over Edom was relatively short-lived. By the end of the reign of David's son Solomon, the Edomites had succeeded in throwing off their Israelite overlords. Thus, it would seem that these three stories about the kid brother overtaking the firstborn must have originated in the flush of Israel's subduing of Edom under the rule of David, that is, at the start of the tenth century BCE. It was precisely at that time that Israel in general, and the tribe of Judah in particular (since it was the one that bordered directly on the Edomites), might indeed feel like a little kid who had ended up with a prize that was not legitimately his.[9]

When Edom did subsequently manage to regain its independence, a new wrinkle was added, according to this same line of thought. The last Jacob-overcoming-Esau episode, the stolen blessing story, seems to have undergone a change (or perhaps was created out of whole cloth to reflect Edom's resurgence after a period of subservience). After all, while Israel still dominated Edom, the story ought to have ended with the words of blessing spoken by Isaac to Jacob:

> May God grant you the dew of heaven and the bounty of the earth, with much grain and wine. Let other peoples serve you and nations bow down to you. *Be lord over your brothers, and may your mother's sons bow down to you.* Cursed be everyone who curses you, and blessed be everyone who blesses you.
>
> Gen. 27:28

The indicated phrase appears to have been aimed specifically at the Edomites, descendants of Jacob's brother (here they are presented in the plural as Israel's "brothers" and "mother's sons"). This note of triumph would well fit Israel's ascendancy over its neighbor.

But, as scholars note, this is not where our present story ends. Instead, Esau shows up at his father's side after it is too late. "Haven't you saved some little blessing for me?" he plaintively asks Isaac (Gen. 27:36). The father does the best he can, concluding:

> By your sword you will live, and you will indeed serve your brother; but then it will happen that you will break loose and throw his yoke from off your neck.
>
> Gen. 27:40

It seems hardly conceivable to scholars that these lines could have been written during the time when Israel still dominated Edom. The original stories may indeed belong to the early tenth century, scholars say, but the stolen blessing narrative appears to have been reformulated (or perhaps created out of whole cloth) in the light of a new reality that developed half a century later: eventually, it says, Edom will indeed "break loose" and regain its independence.

Schematic Narratives

For modern scholars, Gunkel's notion of the etiological narrative thus appears to account for these Jacob-Esau narratives, as indeed for a great many stories in Genesis. These include not only the ones highlighted thus far—Adam and Eve, Cain and Abel, the Tower of Babel, Lot and the wicked Sodomites, the near-sacrifice of Isaac, Jacob and Esau, and so forth—but some that we have omitted or passed over lightly. For example, Abraham's second covenant with God (Genesis 17) explains a present-day reality (Israel's practice of infant circumcision) by narrating an event from the distant past.

At the same time, most scholars would agree that it is wrong to think of these stories as *merely* etiological. The Tower of Babel narrative, for example, appears to be as much an attempt to discredit the Babylonians as it is a way of explaining the name *Babel* or the dispersion of Semitic languages. As for the story of Abraham's covenant in Genesis 17, it is not merely an attempt to explain current reality—the practice of infant circumcision—but a legitimation of it: God ordered Abraham and his descendants to be circumcised as a sign of the eternal connection between him and Abraham's progeny, and so this is a wonderful thing and we must continue it forever.

Scholars thus find relatively few purely etiological narratives in Genesis. Nor, they add, should the etiological elements in these stories blind us to another of their salient characteristics. One of the most striking things researchers have noted about the stories we have been reading in Genesis is their spare, bare-bones quality. Indeed, one would not be wrong to highlight this quality in referring to them collectively as the Bible's *schematic narratives*.

A schematic narrative has a point to make, and the entire text is designed to make it. That is, every detail in this sort of spare little story is aimed at showing that this is what the Kenites are like, and how they got that way; or that God is not impressed by the sophistication of Babylonian civilization; or that there is a reason why child sacrifice is not practiced in Israel. In such narratives, according to this approach, the various people who are portrayed are often less than "characters," at least in the sense in which this term is used by literary critics. They have none of the complexity of a character in Shakespeare or Flaubert. In fact, very little is ever said about their thoughts or feelings; usually, they have no inner life at all. What was Abraham thinking on his way to sacrifice his son? How did Cain feel after he had murdered his own brother? Such questions, for a schematic narrative, are simply irrelevant. What matters is what the people did and the results of their actions, or the conclusions to which their actions led.

In a sense, according to this view, some of the Bible's schematic narratives might be compared to jokes or fairy tales in our own culture. No one cares what sort of people the three sailors in the bar were, or what Goldilocks had done before that fateful day; the priest, the minister, and the rabbi, if they have any traits of character at all, will turn out to be altogether stereotypical—which is just how we like it! The point is that not every narrative, just because it tells a story, is ipso facto literature, nor is every person in a tale necessarily a "character"; some may actually be more like stereotypes, or mere ciphers.[10]

At the same time, the schematic quality of these narratives can be misleading. Since they are pared down to relatively few sentences, every detail in them—even something that looks like an aside or a random observation—is likely to be significant. This is true not only of the events that are related, but of how the people themselves are presented. Precisely because Mr. X or Mrs. Y is the ancestor of an entire people and is thus expected to correspond perfectly to his descendants' stereotype, listeners or readers were expected to pick up on every slight detail in the narrative, every little wink of the text, and say: "Oh I see! Their ancestor was just as much of a skinflint [or numbskull, or whatever] as they themselves are." In schematic narratives, a little characterization goes a long way.

So it is, according to this approach, with the Jacob and Esau stories. The two brothers are not really "characters," at least not in the same way as the characters of later European or American literature. But there is no mistaking the somewhat obvious message that each brother seemed designed to embody; again, this is set forth at the very beginning of the Jacob-Esau narratives:

The two boys grew up, and Esau became a man skilled at hunting, an outdoorsman, while Jacob was a quiet fellow, staying in tents. Isaac loved Esau, because he liked eating game, but Rebekah loved Jacob.

Gen. 25:27

Throughout these narratives, Esau is a happy-go-lucky, not-too-intelligent sportsman—the proverbial "dumb jock." Jacob is just the opposite, a momma's boy who stays at home but who ends up outsmarting his more powerful sibling. A modern scholar would say that this is a reflection not merely of the political reality described above, but of a certain projection of national stereotypes (or would-be stereotypes) back to the time of the founders. Israel's Edomite neighbors are not dismissed—as the Ammonites and Moabites were—as a "bunch of bastards." But neither is the portrait of Esau altogether flattering: he is just not very smart, and certainly no match for his cleverer, sometimes scheming, younger brother, Jacob.[11]

We began this chapter by observing that the most significant contribution of the ancient interpreters consisted not of their specific interpretive creations ("Original Sin," "Abraham the monotheist," and so forth) but of their very approach to these texts—reading them as stories about individual people, and stories with a lesson to impart. We are now in a position to understand better at least one of the factors that helped to create this approach. The etiological side of these tales was not likely to interest ancient interpreters (if they spotted it at all). Their own historical circumstances were so distant from those of the stories' original audience that almost anything having to do with Israel's day-to-day reality in early biblical times—cruel Kenites and child sacrifice and Israel's first victory over Edom—would seem quite irrelevant to them. On the other hand, they deeply believed in the Bible's relevance. What was important was what it had to say to *them,* particularly any eternal teaching about proper behavior or God's ways with mankind or the special destiny of Israel. As a result, the etiological side of figures like Cain or Abraham or Jacob simply faded out; after a while, they were no longer thought of as representatives of later peoples. Instead, they were individuals in their own right, whose virtues and foibles, ancient interpreters believed, had been depicted in order to provide us later human beings with a lesson in how to behave.

A Ladder with Angels

Fleeing his brother's anger, Jacob sets out for his uncle Laban's house, but on the way he has his famous dream of a ladder reaching up to heaven (Gen. 28:10–22).[12] This episode was certainly an important turning point in Jacob's life: it marked the first time that God spoke to him directly and thus, in a sense, signaled the start of his career as a chosen servant of God. The actual words that were spoken seem no less meaningful. God tells the immediate ancestor of Israel, "I will be with you and will keep you wherever you go," and Jacob reciprocates by expressing his fealty and devotion: "You will be my God." Beyond all this was the vision itself—the eerie nighttime appearance of a great ladder with angels ascending and descending upon it has struck readers in every age as saying something profound about a reality beyond our everyday ken. Surely what Jacob saw was an image of the connection between heaven and earth, between the world that we know and all that is normally unseen but present nonetheless. Here is the passage in its entirety:

> Jacob left Beer-sheba and went on toward Haran. He chanced upon a certain place and spent the night there, because the sun had set. Taking one of the stones of the place, he put it under his head and lay down in the place. And he dreamed that there was a ladder stuck into the earth, whose top reached to heaven, and the angels of God were going up and down on it. The LORD stood over him and said, "I am the LORD, the God of Abraham your father and the God of Isaac; the land on which you are lying I will give to you and to your offspring; and your offspring will be like the dust of the earth, and you will spread out to the west and to the east and the north and the south; and all the families of the earth will be blessed in you and in your offspring. Know that I will be with you and will keep you wherever you go, and will bring you back to this land; for I will not leave you until I have done what I have promised you." Then Jacob woke from his sleep and said, "Surely the LORD is in this place—and I did not know it!" And he was afraid, and said, "How fearsome is this place! This is the very house of God and this is the gate of heaven." So Jacob rose early in the morning, and he took the stone that he had put under his head and set it up for a pillar and poured oil on the top of it. He called that place Bethel [that is, House of God], but the name of the city had earlier been Luz. Then Jacob made a vow, saying, "If God is with me, and preserves me on this journey I am on, and gives me bread to eat and clothing to wear, so that I return safely to my father's house, then the LORD will be my God, and this stone, which I have set up as a pillar, will become [part of] God's temple; and of everything that You give me I will give back one-tenth to You."

> Gen. 28:10–22

It is no wonder that this passage was lovingly explicated (in various ways) by ancient Jewish interpreters. To some, the ladder and angels embodied a message about the future of the Jewish people, specifically, their survival despite the domination of their homeland by foreign empires; to others, the ascending and descending angels were a mark of the special esteem in which Jacob was held on high; indeed, according to one ancient interpretive tradition, this passage hinted that Jacob's portrait was etched on God's heavenly throne.[13] This same passage was also alluded to, in passing, in the New Testament:

> Jesus answered, "Do you believe because I told you that I saw you under the fig tree? You will see greater things than these." And he said to him,

"Very truly, I tell you, you will see heaven opened and the angels of God ascending and descending upon the Son of Man."

John 1:50–51

To modern scholars, however, the passage in Genesis has, once again, a distinctly etiological ring. One of its apparent purposes is to explain how Bethel got its name: when he awakes, Jacob says, "How fearsome is this place! This is the very house of God." (The Hebrew phrase "house of God"—*beth 'elohim*—does indeed sound a bit like *beth 'el,* that is, Bethel.) The passage also explains how Bethel, which apparently had a long career as a sacred site (Gen. 35:7–8; Judg. 4:5; 1 Sam. 7:16, etc.) and ended up being chosen for one of two royal temples in the time of Jeroboam (1 Kings 12:29–33), first came to be considered holy.[14] It all goes back, the story seems to say, to our illustrious ancestor Jacob and the dream he had there.

But once again, this story of origins was found by modern scholars to have a less obvious side to it. Especially after archaeologists unearthed the epic Canaanite literature of Ugarit (in northern coastal Syria), starting in 1929, it became increasingly clear to biblicists that some uses of *'el* in the Bible are actually not intended in the generic sense of "deity" or of "[Israel's] God" (one meaning of *'el*), but rather are references to the proper name of the head of the Canaanite pantheon, *'El*. (See below, chapter 24, for a fuller account.) This discovery in turn seemed to suggest something about the real origin of the ancient site of Bethel and its sacredness: perhaps, long before its association with the God of Israel, Bethel had been a sacred place for the Canaanites,[15] a shrine to their god El. That, they said, is why it is called Bethel —house (*beth*) of El.[16]

Another interesting fact: the kind of stone pillar that Jacob sets up in the Genesis story, a *maṣṣebah,* is mentioned in the laws of the Torah, but always in a negative way:

You shall not make for yourselves any idols nor set up any statue or pillar (*maṣṣebah*); nor shall you place a carved stone in your land to bow down to it; for I am the LORD your God.

Lev. 26:1

You shall not plant for yourself any tree or sacred pole beside the altar that you make for the LORD your God, nor shall you set up any stone pillar (*maṣṣebah*) for yourself, since this is abhorrent to the LORD your God.

Deut. 16:21

The reason for this prohibition is that setting up a *maṣṣebah* was apparently deemed to be a form of worship associated with the Canaanites. Indeed, according to the Bible one of the first things the Israelites were instructed to do when they entered the land was to tear down all the Canaanite sanctuaries and objects of worship—including their *maṣṣebot:*

> [God said to the Israelites:] Carry out what I am commanding you today. For I am casting out the Amorites, the Canaanites, the Hittites, the Perizzites, the Hivites, and the Jebusites [to make room] for you. Be sure not to make a covenant with the inhabitants of the land to which you are going, lest it become a snare in your midst. [Instead,] you must tear down their altars, break their pillars (*maṣṣebot*), and cut down their sacred poles. You must not worship any other god, because the LORD, whose name is Jealous, is indeed a jealous God.
>
> Exod. 34:10–14

For modern scholars, the implications of all this are clear. Here is a story in Genesis that apparently goes to great lengths to deny the obvious—the connection of Bethel with "Canaanite" practices. Instead, it stresses that Jacob just happened to end up there one night; he "chanced upon a certain place" and had to sleep there because the sun was setting and it was getting dark. In other words, there was nothing special about this place until then, and it certainly was no well-known holy site; our ancestor just chanced to spend the night there and dreamt his dream. It was the dream itself, this story seeks to claim, that converted the place from ordinary to sacred. The next morning it was Jacob who set up the *maṣṣebah,* and no pagan Canaanites—and if that stone pillar is still there today, the story says, that is only because it is a relic, the stone on which our honored ancestor had once rested his head. It is certainly not an object of pagan worship! Finally, if the place is called Bethel, this does not mean that it was ever a shrine to El; on the contrary, before that fateful night, the name of the place was Luz (Gen. 28:19).[17] Rather, the name Bethel goes back to Jacob's exclamation upon awakening (even though he does not quite use the Hebrew word '*el* but the related term more commonly used of Israel's God): "How fearsome is this place! This is the very house of God [*beth 'elohim*]."

10

Jacob and the Angel

GENESIS 29–33

Jacob and Rachel by Caper Luyken.

TRICKY LABAN. FUTURE TRIBES. JACOB WRESTLES WITH AN ANGEL.

Jacob married two sisters and acquired their two servant women in the bargain. From these four wives came the ancestors of Israel's twelve tribes. But why did he end up wrestling with an angel until daybreak?

Jacob left Bethel and proceeded northward to Aram (present-day Syria), where he met up with his uncle Laban (Rebekah's brother). Laban had two daughters, Leah and Rachel. Jacob was immediately smitten with Rachel and agreed with Laban to acquire her as a wife in exchange for seven years' labor. On the night of their wedding, however, Laban switched brides, and the unknowing Jacob ended up sleeping with Leah instead. He had to work for Laban another seven years to get Rachel.

The person of Laban, Jacob's uncle, provides one of those rare instances in which ancient and modern interpreters have little to quibble about: everyone dislikes him. In the Bible, Laban is consistently presented as a hypocrite—nice enough on the outside, but deep inside a greedy and nasty fellow lacking in any moral scruple. This may well have been something of an Israelite stereotype of the Arameans; in keeping with the genre of the schematic narrative, this view is transmitted in a few deft, telling details. Take, for example, Laban's first appearance on the biblical scene, when Abraham has dispatched his servant to Aram to find a bride for Isaac (Genesis 24). The servant meets Rebekah at the well and immediately understands that she is the perfect candidate:

> When the camels had finished drinking, the man took a gold nose-ring weighing a half shekel, and two bracelets for her arms weighing ten gold shekels, and said, "Tell me whose daughter you are. Is there room in your father's house for us to spend the night?" She said to him, "I am the daughter of Bethuel son of Milcah, whom she bore to Nahor." She added, "We have plenty of straw and fodder and a place to spend the night." The man bowed his head and worshiped the LORD and said, "Blessed be the LORD, the God of my master Abraham, who has not forsaken his steadfast love and his faithfulness toward my master. As for me, the LORD has led me on the way to the house of my master's kin."
>
> Then the girl ran and told her mother's household about these things. Rebekah had a brother whose name was Laban; and Laban ran out to the man, to the spring. *When he saw the nose-ring, as well as the bracelets on his sister's arms,* and when he heard the words of his sister Rebekah, "Thus the man spoke to me," he went to the man; and there he was,

standing by the camels at the spring. He said, "Come in, O blessed of the
LORD. Why do you stand outside when I have prepared the house and a
place for the camels?"

Gen. 24:22–31

Surely we are meant to take the broad hint in this passage: it is when Laban
sees the generous gifts that this stranger has bestowed on his sister—"the
nose-ring, as well as the bracelets on his sister's arms"—that he puts out the
welcome mat. Indeed, he offers Abraham's servant his most pious, unctuous
greeting, "Come in, O blessed of the LORD. Why do you stand outside?"

One might compare this scene to Laban's behavior in the present context,
that is, just as Jacob has completed the same long journey northward and
found Laban's beautiful daughter Rachel at (presumably) the same well:

> While he was still speaking with [the men at the well], Rachel arrived
> with her father's sheep; for she was a shepherd. Now when Jacob saw
> Rachel, the daughter of his mother's brother Laban, and the sheep of his
> mother's brother Laban, Jacob went up and rolled the stone from the
> well's mouth, and watered the flock of his mother's brother Laban. Then
> Jacob kissed Rachel, and wept aloud. And Jacob told Rachel that he was
> her father's kinsman and that he was Rebekah's son; and she ran and told
> her father. When Laban heard the news about his sister's son Jacob, he ran
> to meet him; he embraced him and kissed him, and brought him to his
> house. Jacob told Laban all these things, and Laban said to him, "Surely
> you are my bone and my flesh!" And he stayed with him a month. Then
> Laban said to Jacob, "Just because you are my kinsman, should you serve
> me for nothing? Tell me, what shall your wages be?"

Gen. 29:10–13

Once again, it seems, we are meant to be struck by the contrast between
Laban's words and deeds. On the outside, Laban is the loving uncle: "Surely
you are my bone and my flesh!" he says, and kisses his young nephew. But
such sentiments do not, apparently, prevent him from taking advantage of the
new arrival: Laban puts him to work right away, without any discussion of
remuneration. Only after a month does he ask Jacob, as if the thought had
just now occurred to him, "Just because you are my kinsman, should you
serve me for nothing?"

But if the reader/listener is prepared to pick up on such traits, he or she is
probably not unfamiliar with Jacob and his own particular (and by now, well
known) set of stereotypical characteristics. So it is certainly no accident that
his attraction to Rachel is not presented in the above passage as altogether
romantic, the instantaneous marriage of true minds. What the text says
instead is: "When Jacob saw Rachel, the daughter of his mother's brother

Laban, *and the sheep of his mother's brother Laban."* Laban, apparently, is
not a poor man; he has a nice little flock of sheep, and Jacob, the text is telling
us, seems to have fixed on this right away. To put it in more modern terms, it
is as if Rachel has just driven up in the stylish little sports car her dad gave her
for graduation; the narrative seems to be hinting that this, as much as her
comely appearance, is what pushes Jacob to his exertions on her behalf. And
this too has a point. Though Laban is certainly nasty and Jacob is certainly
not, the two are nevertheless blood relatives—and when it comes to trickiness, they are not so terribly different from each other after all. Indeed, in the
end, Jacob will outfox his uncle.

The Switched Brides

Jacob's love for Rachel is frustrated: tricky Laban substitutes his less attractive, older daughter, Leah, for Rachel on their wedding night. Jacob wakes
up, "and in the morning, behold! It was Leah" (Gen. 29:25). The story of the
switched brides has been remembered, and puzzled over, by generations and
generations of Bible readers. How could Jacob not know who was in his bed
that night? Ancient interpreters offered several possibilities: Perhaps Jacob
had drunk a bit too much wine at the festivities. And no doubt, in keeping
with Oriental modesty, the bride must have been heavily veiled even after the
ceremony. Plus, it surely was quite dark in the bridal chamber. Still, one rabbinic text offered a further, pungent explanation:

> All night he kept calling her "Rachel" and she kept answering him, "Yes."
> But "in the morning, behold! It was Leah" [Gen. 29:25]. He said to her,
> "Liar and daughter-of-a-liar!" Leah answered: "Can there be a schoolmas-
> ter without any pupils? Was it not just this way that your father called out
> to you 'Esau' and you answered him [by saying 'Yes']? So when you called
> out [Rachel], I answered you the same way."
>
> *Genesis Rabba* 70:19

Apart from what switching the brides showed about Laban's trickiness, his
act had another important implication: although Jacob had to work another
seven years to pay for Rachel, he ended up with two wives—and as a bonus,
their two female servants (Bilhah and Zilpah) were ultimately given to him as
concubines. The result was a very large family indeed: Jacob and his four
mates produced twelve different sons (plus a daughter, Dinah), the future
twelve tribes of Israel.

Indeed, the story of Jacob's dealings with his uncle seemed to ancient interpreters to contain an overall message. After all, the Labans of this world are
numerous, and the path of a decent person is always beset with encounters

just like that of Jacob and his scheming, more powerful relative. The point, however, is that, try as they will, the Labans ultimately lose out. Jacob may have worked for his uncle for twenty years,* but he ended up with descendants who founded twelve tribes and, ultimately, a mighty nation. Moreover—through a maneuver (Gen. 31:37–43) that may have looked a bit tricky but, by ancient interpreters' lights, surely was not[1]—Jacob ended up taking possession of much of Laban's flocks. In short, this raw refugee who had arrived in Aram with the pack on his back left two decades later as a wealthy paterfamilias. Could there be a clearer demonstration of God's provident care for His servants—"The LORD watches over all those who love Him, but all the wicked He destroys" (Ps. 145:20)?

The final confrontation between the two—when Laban catches up with his departing nephew at the border between Aram and Canaan—seemed to sum up everything about their two characters:

> Laban said to Jacob, "What have you done? You tricked me and carried off my own daughters like captives in war! Why did you skulk off in secret and try to fool me and not tell me? Why, I would have sent you away with a party and songs, tambourines and lyres . . ."
>
> Then Jacob became angry, and argued with Laban. Jacob said to Laban, "What exactly is my crime? What wrong have I committed, that you should come chasing after me? . . . These twenty years that I've been with you, your ewes and your female goats never miscarried, and I have not eaten the rams from any of your flocks. If an animal was killed by wild beasts I never brought it to [show to] you. Instead, I bore the loss myself; you charged me for every one. I've been cheated day and night. I used to— why, during the day, the heat would consume me, and the cold by night; I never did get a good night's sleep. Of the twenty years I've been in your house, I worked for you for fourteen years for your two daughters, and then six more with your flock. You kept changing the terms of my wages, time and again. If the God of my father, the God of Abraham and the Kinsman of Isaac, had not been on my side, by now you would have sent me off empty-handed. But God saw my affliction and how I had labored, and He rebuked you last night."
>
> But Laban cried back at Jacob, "The daughters are my daughters, the sons are my sons, the flocks are my flocks, and all that you see belongs to me."
>
> Gen. 31:25–43

Throughout this exchange, Laban's true nature is apparent to all. If only you had told me you were going, the hypocrite says to Jacob, "I would have sent you away with a party and songs, tambourines and lyres. . . ." But surely no

---

* Fourteen years for the two brides, and then another six for payment (Gen. 30:28–34).

reader can believe that. Jacob then lays out in detail all the ways that Laban has tried to take advantage of him, adding what, for ancient interpreters, was the point of the whole story: God did watch out for Jacob's interests, and that is what ultimately allowed him to triumph. Yet, almost to the bitter end, Laban continued to deceive himself—and anyone else who would listen. Though Jacob had paid for his wives fair and square, Laban seems to have felt they still belonged to him—indeed, he even claims possession of Jacob's own sons and the flocks that Jacob has earned: "The daughters are my daughters, the sons are my sons, the flocks are my flocks, and all that you see belongs to me." Only in the last sentences of their story together does Laban propose to make his peace with God's chosen servant (Gen. 31:51–54).[2]

Brides and Tribes

Modern scholars have regarded with some skepticism the biblical account of the origins of the people of Israel—that the entire nation was descended from a single ancestor, Jacob/Israel. Apart from the fact that Israel's twelve tribes were dispersed over a wide geographic area and throughout most of their history seem to have shown rather little unity, scholarly skepticism derives from a number of anthropological studies that have been carried out in Africa and elsewhere with the purpose of investigating the role that genealogies, real or imagined, can play in a region's social and political organization. Native informants who are asked about the origin of this or that group of adjacent tribes or clans will often point to a common ancestor of all. The existence of such a common ancestor, anthropologists say, can serve a definite political or social function. It can unite all the groups as putative relatives—so that all members are deemed to be grandchildren, or great-great-great-great-grandchildren, of a single man or woman. Such a notion can be an important factor when unity is crucial—for example, it can persuade all members to accept a common leadership or to participate in warfare or some other common venture.

At the same time, the precise relationship of this or that group to a distinguished forebear may also function as an expression of rank: if group A are direct descendants of the forebear, whereas B are descendant from his brother or nephew or the like, then the genealogy will have placed A in a superior ranking to B. Ranking can also take place horizontally, as, for example, five sons of the same father. In many societies, the eldest son in such a situation will be understood to be the preferred one, and his descendants, therefore, the preferred group. If the father has children by different wives, *their* social rank will also reflect on that of their descendants. Finally, one of the most fascinating observations of anthropologists is that reported genealogies tend to change over time in order to take account of changes in the social or political pecking order. Group So-and-so, previously reported to be descended from the firstborn, may be replaced by a new "firstborn" in the reports of informants a generation or two later.[3]

The applicability of such studies to biblical material is not hard to spot. If, for example, Abraham had one "legitimate" wife, Sarah, and a concubine, Hagar, then Sarah's descendants (Isaac and his two sons, Jacob and Esau, along with their offspring) will surely be deemed to outrank the descendants of Hagar's son, Ishmael, and his offspring. Similarly, if Jacob has twelve sons, then the tribes descended from his "legitimate" wives, Leah and Rachel, will outrank those descended from his concubines, Bilhah and Zilpah. What is more, the fact that some tribes are said to be descended from the same mother as well as the same father will signal a greater level of kinship among them: the "Leah tribes" will be closer to one another than to the "Rachel tribes," for example.

In considering such matters, modern biblical scholars have also noticed the confluence of genealogy with geography. Of Leah's first four sons, three—Reuben, Simeon, and Judah—were said to have sired Israel's southernmost tribes (her fourth son, Levi, was, by the Bible's account, not given any territory to speak of). The descent of these three tribes from a common mother was thus paralleled by their geographical contiguity. To the north of them lay the great midland of Israel, and it was populated by the descendants of Rachel—the tribes of Benjamin and Ephraim and Manasseh. Here too, apparently, genetic closeness meant geographic proximity.

Which came first, geography or genealogy? To modern scholars, the answer seems to be geography. They theorize that the peoples who eventually became the nation of Israel had originally been separate, perhaps quite unrelated, groups. When they eventually did come together, their union was cemented by a tale of common descent—all came from the same father. This basic story of their interrelatedness was further refined by the existence of different mothers: the Rachel tribes were one subgroup, and the Leah tribes were a separate subgroup. The union of these two, history was to prove, was never perfect: brought together by the diplomacy (or was it power politics?) of David in the tenth century BCE, they parted company after only two generations, with the southern tribes becoming the Kingdom of Judah and the northern ones the Kingdom of Israel. Thus, the "fact" that they came from different mothers was an expression from the very beginning of the distinctness of these two groups. As for the tribes descended from the concubines Bilhah and Zilpah—no wonder that they were on the geographic outskirts of David's united kingdom! They were not thought of as total outsiders, since they had been included among Jacob's descendants, but they were, in ancestry as well as geographically, on the margins from the start.

The Change of Names

Throughout the Hebrew Bible are stories about how a person's name gets changed: Abram becomes Abraham, Sarai becomes Sarah, and, in the episode that follows his last confrontation with Laban, Jacob becomes Israel. (Nor is he the last biblical figure to have his name changed; a bit later, Moses' servant Hoshea will become Joshua [Num. 13:16], Gideon will become Jerubbaal [Judg. 6:28–32], and so forth.) In keeping with the biblical narratives themselves, ancient interpreters attached great significance to such changes: they seemed to mark important transition points in the life of the person involved, and the new name was often deemed to contain some special teaching. Indeed, Philo of Alexandria authored an entire treatise called "The Change of Names."

Modern scholars, however, see a different motive behind such narratives: their purpose was to harmonize what had originally been independent traditions about the same, or possibly different, figures. Thus, the variations Abram/Abraham and Sarai/Sarah may reflect dialect differences in the transmission of stories about this founding couple: certainly it is significant that both names are changed at the same time (Genesis 17)—almost as if a writer or editor were closing one book of traditions and opening another, one that had originated in a different locale and so had a slightly different version of the couple's names. Sometimes, scholars note, there is no such attempt to harmonize different traditions and the Bible offers no change-of-names story at all. Instead, a given person is simply identified with more than one name. Thus, Moses' father-in-law is known principally by the name Jethro (Exod. 3:1; 4:18, etc.), but he is also called Reuel (Exod. 2:18; Num. 10:29), Jether (Exod. 4:18),[4] and Hobab (Judg. 4:11; in Num. 10:29 Hobab is said to be Jethro's son). Here too it would seem that different traditions are simply being combined. Jacob's last son is named Ben-oni by his dying mother, Rachel, but Jacob calls him Benjamin (Gen. 35:18); perhaps these at one point were also competing names.

In the case of Esau, his "other name," Edom, seems to reflect the complex ethnic composition of the land associated with him. That territory was, according to the biblical account, originally an enclave of one people, the Horites (Hurrians), until the Edomites displaced them (Deut. 2:2). (Logically, eponymous "Edom" ought to have completely displaced the earlier founder figure, Esau—but as Genesis and other biblical books attest, Esau continued to be spoken of as the Edomites' legendary ancestor.) While some scholars are skeptical of the biblical account in Deut. 2:2, there seems no doubt that different ethnic groups at one point lived in proximity to one another in the area of Edom; it was not a homogeneous whole. Indeed, Egyptian records suggest that, for a while, Se'ir (the name of Edom's mountain) and Edom were considered to be different entities. So, one way or another, the figure of Esau/Edom probably represents the fusion of two originally distinct figures.

With Jacob and Israel the picture is, according to biblicists, rather similar. The name "Jacob-El" (presumably, "[the god] El protects") is actually known from a number of places in the ancient Near East even before the time of Jacob; it seems to modern scholars that our "Jacob" was thus an abbreviated form of this same name and belonged to a person, legendary or historical, who was held to be the founder of at least part of the future Israel.[5] "Israel" is also a plausible ancient Semitic name for a person (literally, "[the god] El rules" or "God rules"). This name is not attested nearly so early; it appears for the first time in an Egyptian stele* from the time of the exodus and apparently referred there to some kind of group or tribe. A patriarch named "Israel" may thus have originally been deemed the founder of such a group, which at some later point merged with the "Jacob-El" group, hence the necessity for Jacob's name to be changed to "Israel" at some point in his life. This name change is actually recounted twice (Gen. 32:27–28, in a passage attributed to the J source of texts, and 35:9–10, attributed to the E source). Despite this, Jacob continues to be the name by which this biblical figure is principally known.[6]

Jacob Fights an Angel

The longer version of Jacob's change of name, discussed briefly above (chapter 7), is one of the best known episodes in the whole Bible:

> That same night, Jacob got up and took his two wives, his two maidservants, and his eleven children, and crossed the ford of the Jabbok. After he took them across the stream, he sent all his possessions across as well. Then Jacob was left alone, and a man wrestled with him until the break of day. When he saw that he could not overcome him, he wrenched Jacob's hip in its socket, so that the socket of Jacob's hip was strained in the fight with him. Then he said, "Let go of me, since it is getting to be dawn." But Jacob said, "I will not let you go unless you bless me." He said, "What is your name?" and he answered, "Jacob." He said, "Your name will not be Jacob any longer, but Israel, since you have struggled with God and with men and have prevailed." Then Jacob said to him, "Please, now, tell me your name." He answered, "Why should you be asking for my name?" and he blessed him there. Jacob named the place Peniel, saying, "I have seen God face to face and yet my life has been spared."
>
> Gen. 32:24–30

* The Merneptah (or Merenptah) stele, dated to ca. 1207 BCE; see below, chapter 22.

For a modern scholar, every element in this schematic narrative has a point to it. Jacob's wrestling (*ye'abeq*) with the "man" is meant to connect with the name of the place, the Jabbok (*yabboq*) ford. The wound to Jacob's hip also has an etiological resonance, explained later on: "That is why the children of Israel to this day do not eat the thigh muscle that is on the socket of the hip, since Jacob's hip socket was wrenched at the thigh" (Gen. 32:32).* Then, as seen earlier (chapter 7), Jacob's change of name is connected to this same struggle. Instead of explaining his new name, Israel (*yisra'el*), as "God rules," the narrative suggests that it comes from a homonymous root meaning *struggle*: "You have struggled (*sarita*) with God and with men and have prevailed." Finally, the place itself was called Peniel/Penuel to commemorate this face-to-face (*panim*) combat with God (*'el*) that took place.

Indeed, for modern scholars there is something very suggestive about how these disparate elements have been combined into a single narrative line. Start off with the three basic proper names involved—*yabboq, yisra'el,* and *peni'el*—and throw them together; what do you get? Once *yabboq* has suggested *ye'abeq,* "he struggles," then some sort of combat is involved. *Yisra'el* may be then seen to reinforce the idea of struggle and refine it: his struggling (*yisra*) must have involved God (*'el*). Still more precisely, the struggle must have involved seeing God's face (*peni'el*). In a manner strangely reminiscent of Freud's explanation of how the unconscious creates dreams,[7] all these elements might be seen to have cooperated in the creation of the biblical combat narrative, to which a final etiological note—connecting Jacob's injury with Israel's later avoidance of the thigh muscle—has then been added.

And yet . . . To say this is hardly to say all. As we saw earlier, there is something quite eerie, and most evocative, about this combat—the "man" who is suddenly not a man at all but God Himself; the fight that turns out to have been something else entirely, carried on in the "fog" in which Jacob was plunged; perhaps most of all, a narrative that seems to bespeak a most real encounter that took place long, long ago. No wonder this brief episode begins with the mention of Jacob's sending everyone and everything to the other side of the stream; only thus could this fight ever take place, when the noise of voices in the tents had died down and night had fallen and Jacob found that he "was left alone."

To read this episode in Genesis is, once again, to brush up against the central question of this book. Which way of reading is the right one? Modern scholars certainly seem to have a lot of the truth—the etiological side of these narratives, their connection with Israelite history and geography, the process of composition and compilation that stands behind them. And yet . . . So

---

* To this day, the laws of kosher food require that sciatic nerve (that is, the "thigh muscle that is on the socket of the hip") be removed from the body of any animal other than a bird before it can be deemed fit for consumption.

many of these stories are about God and His interaction with human beings. This statement may sound obvious, but it has implications. To focus only on politics and history and national stereotypes is certainly to walk right past the most basic thing about these stories, their very vision of human reality as endlessly connected to, indeed, endlessly interacting with, God. Ancient interpreters may have gone off in their own direction—a highly idealistic and moralistic one, leading ultimately to a world in which "our guys" are altogether good and are usually paired off against such all-bad antitypes as Esau and Laban, a world in which the righteous inevitably triumph and everything works out for the best. But in so doing, they may have (though this remains to be explored) latched onto something else essential in these texts. Or is it the case that both readings are, in equal measure, distortions?

11

Dinah

GENESIS 34

Simeon and Levi Slew Hamor and Schechem
by Gerard Hoet.

THE PERILS OF INTERMARRIAGE. THE BROTHERS DIDN'T LIE.
A LATER ADDITION?

*Dinah was raped by Shechem; in return, her brothers killed Shechem and all
the men of his town. Was this the right thing to do?*

After crossing the Jabbok and meeting up with his brother, Esau (who, contrary to Jacob's expectations, bore no grudge against him), Jacob continued
on to the city of Shechem. There, his only daughter, Dinah, was seized and
raped by a certain Shechem (he had the same name as that of the city), the
son of the city's ruler, Hamor. Subsequently, young Shechem asked his father
to purchase Dinah as a bride for him, and Hamor approached Jacob with
that proposal; in fact, he suggested that this marriage might inaugurate a general intermarrying of the population of the city with Jacob and his family.

When Jacob's sons returned from their shepherding and heard the news of
the rape, they were outraged. Rather than simply turning down Shechem's
proposal, however, they devised a stratagem. If Shechem would agree to
have his son and all the other men of the city circumcised, they said, then
indeed Dinah could become Shechem's bride. The Shechemites cooperated
and organized a mass circumcision of all males. Then Jacob's sons went
into action:

> On the third day, when they [the Shechemites] were in great pain, two of
> Jacob's sons, Simeon and Levi, Dinah's brothers, took their swords and,
> entering the city unawares, killed all the males. They killed Hamor and his
> son Shechem at sword-point and took Dinah out of Shechem's house and
> left. Then the other sons of Jacob came upon the slain and plundered the
> city, because their sister had been defiled. They took their flocks and their
> herds, their donkeys, and whatever was in the city and in the field. All their
> wealth, all their little ones and their wives, everything that was in the
> houses, they captured and made their prey. Jacob said to Simeon and Levi,
> "You have brought trouble on me by making me odious to the inhabitants
> of the land, the Canaanites and the Perizzites; my numbers are few, and if
> they gather themselves against me and attack me, I will be wiped out, along
> with my whole household." But they said, "Should our sister be treated like
> a whore?"

> Gen. 34:25–31

For ancient readers, this violent tale was something of a mystery. As usual,
what interested them was the message the story was intended to convey—but

this was precisely what was most problematic about the Dinah episode. The story is told with a chilly neutrality, so that even at the end, there is no way to know whether the Bible is seeking to claim that the reaction of Simeon and Levi was justified or not. Jacob, of course, seems to think it was not, but we are never quite sure if he is right. Indeed, it is altogether appropriate that the story itself should end with a question mark—"Shall our sister be treated as a whore?" Along with this is the fact—quite surprising for the Bible—that God is nowhere mentioned in this narrative, almost as if the Dinah episode had somehow been exempted from the usual biblical concern with the divine will.

As ancient interpreters pored over this text, however, they found one indication, however slight, of what Scripture had really intended by relating this episode. That clue came in a brief passage describing the reaction of Dinah's brothers when they first heard the news of their sister's rape:

> Jacob heard that he [Shechem] had defiled his daughter Dinah. His sons were with his cattle in the field, so Jacob held his peace until they arrived . . . Jacob's sons came in from the field when they heard of it, and the men were indignant and very angry, because he [Shechem] had committed an outrage in Israel by lying with Jacob's daughter, *and such a thing ought not to be done.*
>
> Gen. 34:6–7

The indicated phrase appears to be what literary critics call "implied quotation." That is, the narrative does not say outright, "The brothers said, 'Such a thing ought not to be done' " (this is called *direct quotation,* asserting that these are precisely the words they spoke). Nor does it say, "The brothers said that such a thing ought not to be done" (*indirect quotation,* which gives the substance of what was said without actually quoting it). *Implied quotation* is one more step away; it simply says that the brothers were "indignant and very angry" and then juxtaposes some further words; the juxtaposition implies, without saying so outright, that these further words explain what precedes them and thus represent the brothers' point of view. They must have said to each other *words to the effect that* Shechem had committed an outrage and that such a thing ought not to be done.

Read in a somewhat different way, however, these same words can take on a different meaning. For if—in keeping with the last of the Four Assumptions—one believes that the entire text of the Bible is divinely inspired or in some other way comes from God, then it might appear that "such a thing ought not to be done" actually represents God's own judgment on what happened. After all, Genesis does not specifically attribute these words to the brothers; could they not be an editorial aside by the divine narrator? That is what ancient interpreters said:

You [God] gave a sword to take revenge on the strangers who had loosed the adornment of a virgin to defile her, and uncovered her thigh to put her to shame, and polluted her womb to disgrace her; for *You said,* "It shall not be thus"[1]—yet they did so.

Jth. 9:2

[The angel of *Jubilees* says]: And *let it not be done thus* henceforth again that a daughter of Israel shall be defiled.

Jubilees 30:5

A Tale of Intermarriage

One important issue throughout biblical times (and afterward) was that of intermarriage. Numerous texts in Genesis suggest that marriage with Canaanites, for example, was to be avoided: Abraham goes to great lengths to insure that Isaac will not marry a Canaanite woman (Gen. 24:1–4), and Isaac instructs his son Jacob, "You shall not marry one of the Canaanite women" (Gen. 28:1). Indeed, biblical law prohibits contracting marriages with the Canaanites and other people of the region:

> Do not intermarry with them, giving your daughters to their sons or taking their daughters for your sons, for that would turn away your children from following Me, to serve other gods . . . For you are a people holy to the LORD your God; the LORD your God has chosen you out of all the peoples on earth to be His people, His treasured possession.

Deut. 7:3–6

Concern with this issue did not diminish over time—quite the contrary. The Bible reports that long after the heyday of Israelite power—following the conquest of Judah by the Babylonians and the subsequent exile, and the return from exile—intermarriage was, perhaps more than ever, of great concern. When, in this postexilic period, Ezra discovered that some of his fellow Jews had taken wives from various foreign peoples (Ezra 9:1), he was sorely aggrieved; despite the emotional (and financial) cost involved, he urged his countrymen to divorce their foreign wives, and they did so:[2]

> [The men said to Ezra:] "We have broken faith with our God and have married foreign women from the peoples of the land, but even now there is hope for Israel in spite of this. So now let us make a covenant with our God to divorce all these wives and their children, according to the counsel of my lord and of those who tremble at the commandment of our God; and let it be done according to the law. Take action, for it is your duty, and we are

with you; be strong, and do it." Then Ezra stood up and made the leading priests, the Levites, and all Israel swear that they would do as had been said. So they swore.

Ezra 10:2–5

Against this background, the story of Dinah seemed to have an obvious lesson for ancient interpreters: don't intermarry! It was bad enough that Jacob's daughter had been raped. But the fact that the Bible then goes on to narrate Hamor's proposal that Jacob's family intermarry with the people of the city—that is, that Dinah's marriage to his son is to be only the first in a long series of marriages between the two peoples—certainly seemed to suggest to ancient interpreters that the rape itself was not the story's real subject. Intermarriage was.[3]

And let it not be done thus henceforth again that a daughter of Israel shall be defiled. For, the punishment had been decreed against them in heaven that they were to annihilate all the Shechemites with the sword, since they had committed an outrage in Israel . . . [Indeed,] if there is a man in Israel who wishes to give his daughter or his sister to any foreigner, he is to die. He is to be stoned because he has done something sinful and shameful within Israel. The woman is to be burned because she has defiled the reputation of her father's house; she is to be uprooted from Israel . . .

For this reason I have written for you in the words of the Torah everything that the Shechemites did to Dinah and how Jacob's sons said, "We will not give our daughters to a man who has a foreskin, because for us that would be a disgrace" [Gen. 34:14]. For it *is* a disgrace, for any Israelites who give [their own daughters to foreigners] or for any who take one of the foreign women [for their sons], because it is impure and despicable for Israel. Israel will never become cleansed of this impurity so long as it has one of the foreign women [in its midst] or so long as there is anyone who has given one of his daughters to any foreign man.

Jubilees 30:5–15

The Brothers Did Not Lie

In the above passage, the author of *Jubilees* makes a subtle argument. Why, he asks, should the Torah have bothered to narrate this whole story at such great length, when it could have summarized the whole thing much more quickly, and more delicately, in a sentence or two? (Shechem "outraged" Dinah, so her two brothers went and killed the whole town.) Certainly there was no reason to include all of Hamor's words about the benefits of intermarriage, first to Jacob and his sons (Gen. 34:9–10), and then to his own people

(Gen. 34:20–23), if the point of the story was the rape alone. And why should the Torah then go on to narrate the lie that the brothers told the Shechemites: "We're not allowed to marry our sister off to anyone who is not circumcised, so you'll all have to undergo circumcision"? They never intended to allow Shechem to marry Dinah.

Jubilees' answer to the first question is that the Torah's purpose was precisely to highlight the real point of the story, which was not the rape per se, but the subsequent proposal of marriage. "For this reason I have written for you in the words of the Torah" everything that happened. As for the second question, well, from *Jubilees'* point of view, the brothers did not lie. As far as this author was concerned, it is indeed a disgrace for any Israelite to marry his daughter to a non-Israelite, that is, "to a man who has a foreskin." The rest of what they said may have been a trick, but not that part: those words were meant for every subsequent Israelite to hear and obey.

Other ancient interpreters dealt with the Dinah story in different ways. Intermarriage was not so important to some of them, but the apparent lie of Jacob's sons was still a problem. One ancient interpretive approach therefore sought to claim that there had been a split in Jacob's family: ten of his sons actually wanted Shechem to marry Dinah—those were the ones who proposed the mass circumcision. But Simeon and Levi (who were full brothers of Dinah, related by their mother as well as their father) could not go along with this; the rape needed to be avenged. Consequently, they must have urged *against* the circumcision proposal—and even after they were overruled, they still went and killed the Shechemites anyway. Thus, no one lied: the proposal of circumcision was sincere, and Simeon and Levi were equally sincere in opposing it and then doing what they did. (This line of interpretation is found in two ancient texts, an old Greek poem by a certain Theodotus and the somewhat later *Testaments of the Twelve Patriarchs*.)[4]

Neither circumcision nor intermarriage was an issue in the later Christian church; medieval Christians therefore read the story allegorically. Nevertheless, Shechem and Hamor were understood as outstanding symbols of evil, indeed, of the devil himself. And meanwhile, what of poor Dinah? Ancient interpreters never liked loose ends—in keeping with their overall view of Scripture (and life!), everything had to work out for the best. One ancient tradition thus identified Dinah as the (otherwise anonymous) wife of the biblical sage Job (see *Testament of Job* 1:5–6)—in other words, she did get married after all. As for the rape, according to one tradition it did result in the birth of a child, Dinah's daughter, who was either given up for adoption or else magically transported to Egypt by an eagle. In either case, she ended up in the house of the Egyptian official Potiphera, who gave her the Egyptian name Asenath; some years later, she was married to none other than her long-lost uncle, Joseph (Gen. 41:45). Everything did indeed turn out for the best in the end.

A Puzzling Tale

For modern scholars, the purpose of the story of Dinah has always seemed somewhat mysterious.[5] It has no apparent etiological message, indeed, no long-term consequences at all. Dinah herself is not reported to have become pregnant as a result of the rape; in fact, she is never heard of again. The slaughter of the Shechemites did not bring about any act of reprisal. The incident appears to be referred to only once more in the Bible, when Jacob, near death, gathers his sons together to offer each his fatherly blessing. For Simeon and Levi, however, he has no blessing to give; all he can think of, apparently, is their cruel act of revenge years earlier. Here is what he says to them:

> Simeon and Levi are brothers; tools of violence are their stock-in-trade.
> May I never enter into their company, nor take pleasure in their
>   assembly.
> For in their anger they would kill a man, and in a good mood, hamstring
>   an ox!
> Cursed be their anger, how fierce! Their wrath is harsh indeed.
> I shall divide them in Jacob and scatter them in Israel.
>
> Gen. 49:5–7

The absence of any etiological point or any subsequent Canaanite revenge was not the only puzzling thing about this incident. According to the narrative, the city of Shechem is annihilated: all the males are killed, and the women and children and animals are carried off as captives. Shechem is left a ghost town. Yet later on, in the books of Joshua and Judges, the city is apparently again a thriving metropolis. Was it left to stand empty from the time of Jacob until after the exodus and then repopulated by Israelites in the time of Joshua (see Josh. 20:7; 21:21; 24:25)? There is no indication in the Bible that Shechem had been a ghost town, and such a hypothesis is in any case not supported by the archaeological record. But if not, then what *did* happen? These later books of Joshua and Judges speak about Shechem as if the slaughter had never happened.

The same apparent ignorance of the whole Dinah story is reflected—rather more surprisingly—in the words of Jacob himself. A little later in Genesis, Jacob says, in an oblique reference to the city of Shechem, that *he* conquered it "from the Amorites with my sword and with my bow" (Gen. 48:22). But in the Dinah story, Jacob quite explicitly has nothing to do with the conquest—he is opposed to it, which is why he condemns his sons' anger in the passage seen above, as well as in another passage immediately following the incident (Gen. 34:30). Why then should he be taking credit in Gen.

48:22 for a conquest that he elsewhere had nothing to do with and even repudiated? And why should he say that the people of Shechem were "Amorites" when the Dinah narrative itself identifies Hamor and his family as Hivites (Gen. 34:2) and the surrounding peoples in the area as "Canaanites and Perizzites" (Gen. 34:30)? It is almost as if these two texts in Genesis, the Dinah narrative in Genesis 34 and Jacob's words in Gen. 48:22, had never met.

Another problem for modern scholars is the identity of Hamor, father of the villain. As mentioned, Hamor and his son were both killed in the slaughter. Yet the same name, Hamor, appears hundreds of years later, in the book of Judges (Judg. 9:28)—and this Hamor, too, is also said to be the father of a son named Shechem and the ruler of the city of Shechem, just like the one in the Dinah story. Two people can, of course, have the same name, and they can also decide to give their sons the same name; they can even both have been rulers of the same city in different periods. Still, these two appearances of a "Hamor, the father of Shechem," chronologically separated by centuries, seemed a further complication in the puzzle. How did it all fit together?

A Late Addition

All such considerations have eventually led to one modern theory about the story of Dinah: it may not be nearly as ancient as the other parts of Genesis.[6] In fact, it may have been added in only at the latest stages of the editing of that book. That would explain why, in Gen. 48:22, Jacob can take credit for conquering Shechem: at the time those words were written, there was no tale of the rape of Dinah and the massacre led by Simeon and Levi. The same is true of the city of Shechem in the books of Joshua and Judges: these books know nothing of the sack of Shechem in Jacob's day, for the simple reason that the story that appears in Genesis did not yet exist.

According to this approach, such a hypothesis also explains another minor curiosity about Dinah, the precise way in which her own birth is announced. For all of Jacob's other children, Genesis is quite consistent: it always says, "And [name of the mother] conceived and bore a son." Then comes a sentence explaining the meaning of the name, "And she named him X, saying . . . ," or else, "And she said . . . and she called him X." In the case of Dinah, however, one finds none of this. After narrating how Leah gave birth to Zebulon and why he was given that name, the Bible adds the terse notice: "Afterwards, she bore a daughter and named her Dinah" (Gen. 30:21). No "and Leah conceived" and no "And she called her name Dinah, saying . . ." Some readers may see in this unequal treatment an instance of biblical sexism, but, quite apart from any sexism, the terseness of Dinah's birth notice would seem to fit well with the hypothesis that the whole Dinah story was a later addition.[7] Presumably, there was no mention of Dinah's birth in an earlier version of Genesis, but once the tale of Dinah's rape and revenge was inserted, by necessity there had to be some mention of Dinah being born. Whoever set out to meet this need did the absolute minimum—no mention was made of Dinah's mother conceiving, and no reason was thought up for the name she received.

Apart from Gen. 30:21 and the Dinah story itself, there is one other mention of Dinah in the Bible: it comes in Genesis 46, in a list of Jacob's descendants. There the Bible enumerates all the sons and grandsons Jacob had with Leah, his first wife. Dinah is not mentioned within the list itself, but only in the summary statement at the end: "These are the sons of Leah, whom she bore to Jacob in Paddan-Aram, *along with Dinah his daughter*; altogether his sons and daughters numbered thirty-three." It is odd that Dinah is not mentioned in the right place (after Zebulon, whose birth just preceded hers). Odder still is the fact that the numbers don't work out. The text says that there were thirty-three "sons and daughters" (in fact there was only one daughter, Dinah), but despite what the text says, Dinah has apparently not been included in the total. Thirty-three is actually the number of *sons* listed; if Dinah is added, the total is thirty-four. Could there be any clearer indication, according to this approach, that the mention of Dinah, here as in the birth announcement, was altogether an afterthought?

A Reason to Get Mad

But why would someone have inserted the Dinah story into the book of Genesis? According to this theory, the reason is not hard to discern: it lies precisely in the words cited above, Jacob's "blessing" of Simeon and Levi in Genesis 49.

These blessings of Jacob's, in the view of most modern scholars, are among the oldest passages in the Pentateuch. In each blessing, Jacob says something about the nature, and sometimes the future, of the son or sons in question. Thus, in the passage seen, Jacob does not simply condemn Simeon and Levi for their anger, but says what will happen to their tribes as a result:

> Cursed be their anger, how fierce! Their wrath is harsh indeed.
> I shall *divide them in Jacob and scatter them in Israel.*
>
> Gen. 49:7

Unlike the other tribes, Simeon and Levi will end up without their own home territory. And so, indeed, did it turn out: the Simeonites were eventually absorbed into the territory (and population) of Judah, while the Levites ended up being "divided" and "scattered" among different tribes, with only a few isolated cities to call their own. (Actually, most modern scholars see in these words attributed to Jacob not an actual prophecy that later came true, but another *vaticinium ex eventu,* a pseudoprediction of events that had already taken place.)

But imagine that there is as yet no story of Dinah in the book of Genesis. An ancient Israelite, reflecting on these words attributed to Jacob, would have had one obvious question: why are Simeon and Levi being described as angry and wrathful? *There is nothing else in all of Genesis to suggest such a thing.* Yet the passage is quite insistent: "Cursed be their anger, how fierce! Their wrath is harsh indeed." In fact, the sentence before this one asserts that these two are, if provoked, even capable of murder: "in their anger they would kill a man." I think I have correctly translated this as a hypothetical generalization, "*would* kill a man," but many translations render this as an actual statement of fact, "in their anger they *have killed* a man." Such an understanding of the words would only sharpen the question: What is Jacob talking about? Whom did Simeon and Levi ever murder?[8]

Thus, if the story of the rape of Dinah and her brothers' bloody revenge is a later addition to Genesis, this theory holds, its purpose is clear: it was an editor's attempt to provide some context for Jacob's words of reproof. Once the Dinah story had been inserted, ancient readers no longer had to guess why Jacob calls Simeon and Levi wrathful or whom the two brothers had killed—they killed the entire male population of Shechem! In other words, Jacob's excoriation now seemed to be an allusion to the bloody tale recounted in Genesis 34. But is it really? Let us take another look:

> Simeon and Levi are brothers; tools of violence are their stock-in-trade.
> May I never enter into their company, nor take pleasure in their
>   assembly.
> For in their anger they would kill a man, and in a good mood, hamstring
>   an ox!
> Cursed be their anger, how fierce! Their wrath is harsh indeed.
> I shall divide them in Jacob and scatter them in Israel.
>
> Gen. 49:7

There is no mention here of Shechem or Hamor, no reference to the rape or the phony circumcision proposal, nothing about the brutal collective punishment or the sacking of the city. The only line that *seems* to allude to the incident really does not: it speaks of killing "a man," whereas the story says that they killed a whole city. Moreover, there is absolutely nothing in the story about hamstringing an ox. On closer inspection, Jacob's words do not allude to the Dinah story at all; quite the contrary: the Dinah story has been inserted in an attempt to provide some context for Jacob's otherwise incomprehensible condemnation of his two sons.

Imported, Not Invented

Where did the Dinah story come from? According to this theory, it could not have been made up out of whole cloth, the ad hoc invention of some later editor. The same arguments just seen make that virtually impossible. For, if such an editor had set out to create a new story tailor-made to fit Jacob's actual words, surely that story would have had nothing to do with a rape or the destruction of an entire city. Instead, it should have told how some hapless stranger wandered into the *company* of Simeon and Levi (thus evoking Jacob's "May I never enter into their *company*"). The stranger would then unaccountably arouse the brothers' *anger* and end up being hacked to pieces by their *tools of violence*. The victim would certainly be one lone individual ("in their anger they would kill *a man*")—not a whole city!—and after doing away with him, the brothers would then go off and *hamstring his ox* for good measure. No, the Dinah story does not seem to have been a later invention; it must have been an already existing story, a story of rape and the unfair revenge that followed, which a later editor then took up and *adapted* (but only imperfectly) to fit the circumstances of Genesis.

The words of the Dinah story themselves provide modern scholars with further evidence supporting this hypothesis. In the original story, the Israelite group in question must have been a substantial population—otherwise, why would Hamor make it sound like he was proposing the merger of two *peoples*? "Make marriages with us: give your daughters to us, and take our daughters for yourselves; and the land shall be open to you, dwell in it and trade in it and get property in it" (Gen. 34:9). But Jacob and his sons were not yet a people, they were one single family—and at the time he did not have "daughters," but only Dinah. Elsewhere Hamor, seeking to persuade his countrymen to absorb Jacob and his sons, says, "for behold the land is large enough for them" (Gen. 34:21). Again, this would hardly be a worry for an entire city if only a single family were joining them; the words would be more appropriate if referring to a whole tribe or conglomeration. Perhaps the most striking evidence that the original story had to do with a much larger, and later, group of Israelites is what the text says about the rape itself: "For [Shechem] committed an outrage in Israel, to lie with a daughter of Jacob" (Gen. 34:7). But at the time there was no "Israel," only Jacob and his immediate family.

Modern scholars do not have any precise theory as to what the context of the original story might have been. Perhaps this story had first been told about the city of Shechem at some later time.[9] One thing seems clear, however: the approach outlined thus far would hold that the original story involved a somewhat larger group of Israelites going into the city and massacring all the males.

Circumcision may be painful, even incapacitating, but it strains credibility to assert that circumcision alone is what enabled two attackers to slay an entire urban population. More likely, in the original story the circumcision simply *helped* a doughty band of ten or twenty or fifty attackers overcome a larger number of opponents. But once the story was inserted in Genesis, that doughty band had to be reduced to two people, Simeon and Levi, *since they are the only ones* whom Jacob excoriates for the massacre.[10]

Who inserted the story in Genesis? A clue, according to this same approach, is to be found in the narrative's report of what happened to the Shechemites in the attack:

> Simeon and Levi, Dinah's brothers, took their swords and came against the city unawares, and killed all the males . . . And the other sons of Jacob came upon the slain, and plundered the city, because their sister had been defiled. They *took their flocks and their herds,* their donkeys, and whatever was in the city and in the field. All their wealth, *all their little ones and their wives,* all that was in the houses, they captured and made their prey.
>
> Gen. 34:25–29

In short: all the males were killed, but their wives, children, livestock, and possessions were given to the brothers as booty.

Those who think of the Old Testament as an unending series of cruelties may not be particularly struck by the specific character of the brothers' revenge, but it is actually at something of a halfway point between the biblical practice of *ḥerem* (total annihilation of everyone and everything) and the sparing and enslavement of a captured population. What the brothers do here is similar to what, for example, the Israelites do to the Midianites in Numbers 31: kill the men and spare the women and children and possessions. The same policy is reflected in a certain law in the book of Deuteronomy:

> When you draw near to a town to fight against it, offer it terms of peace. If it accepts your terms of peace and surrenders to you, then all the people in it shall serve you at forced labor. If it does not submit to you peacefully, but makes war against you, then you shall besiege it; and when the LORD your God gives it into your hand, you shall *put all its males to the sword. You may, however, take as your booty the women, the children, livestock, and everything else in the town, all its spoil.* You may enjoy the spoil of your enemies, which the LORD your God has given you.
>
> Deut. 20:10–14

This is precisely what Jacob's sons do in Genesis 34—almost as if they were obeying the above law even before it was given to Israel. Indeed, the telltale expression mentioned earlier, "For [Shechem] committed *an outrage in*

Israel," is found in four other places in the Bible; one of them is in the same book of Deuteronomy (22:21). This may not amount to proof positive, but it has suggested to some that the editor responsible for inserting the Dinah story might well have been someone particularly connected with Deuteronomy or at least familiar with its laws.

In conclusion, for some modern interpreters the entire story of Dinah is a late addition to the book of Genesis, inserted in order to account for Jacob's otherwise referentless allusion to the violent tempers of Simeon and Levi in Gen. 49:5–7. For this purpose, an editor imported and only slightly modified an originally unrelated tale, probably one that had been situated much later in the biblical period, during the time of the Judges. (Such a tale would fit well with the overall depiction of the lawlessness and civil disorder found in the book of Judges.) If this theory is correct, then the original version of this story had no connection with Israel's founding family: Jacob never had a daughter, and Simeon and Levi never massacred the Shechemites. If that is the case, then should we just forget about Dinah? Or does her story still have something to say to modern readers—about anger and revenge, about violence against women, perhaps even about the theme of intermarriage championed by ancient interpreters?

12

Joseph and His Brothers

GENESIS 37 AND 39–50

Potiphar and Wife from the Vienna Genesis (sixth century).

POTIPHAR'S WIFE. AN INDEPENDENT STORY. JOSEPH AND WISDOM.
THE HYKSOS. JOSEPH'S DOUBLE PORTION. JACOB BLESSES HIS SONS.

Jacob loved Joseph more than any of his other children. Joseph ended up pay-
ing dearly for his father's affection, although he eventually rose from the posi-
tion of household slave to second in command of all of Egypt.

The narratives of Genesis examined thus far have been relatively short and
relatively straightforward. The whole episode of the binding of Isaac occupies
nineteen biblical verses; Jacob's fight with the angel takes ten. The events of
Joseph's life, by contrast, stretch out over nine whole chapters and take up
more than three hundred verses. His story is a complicated series of interrelated events. Here, in brief, is what happens.

After Simeon and Levi had destroyed the city of Shechem, Jacob and his
family moved on to settle in Hebron, where Isaac and Abraham had lived.
Among Jacob's sons was Joseph, and he was the one whom Jacob loved the
most. Understandably, this made Joseph's brothers jealous. When Joseph
dreamt that he would someday rule over his brothers and they would bow
down to him, their jealousy only increased. One day, Jacob sent Joseph to
check on his brothers and their sheep, and when he reached them they took
hold of him and threw him into a nearby pit. At first they wanted to kill him,
but the oldest of the brothers, Reuben, intervened to save him. When another
brother, Judah, spotted an approaching caravan, he convinced his siblings to
sell Joseph as a slave instead. They then took Joseph's special garment—a gift
from Jacob—and dipped it in blood, leading their father to believe that
Joseph had been killed by a wild animal.

Joseph was transported to Egypt and sold as a slave to Potiphar, a high
Egyptian official. Joseph soon rose to the top of Potiphar's household staff.
But Potiphar's wife was attracted to Joseph, and although he rebuffed her
repeated advances, one day she nevertheless seized him and said, "Lie with
me!" Joseph fled, and Potiphar's wife, fearing that the matter would be discovered, told her husband that Joseph had tried to rape her. Joseph was
thrown into prison. There he met two jailed Egyptian officials, and one day
he correctly interpreted their dreams. In keeping with Joseph's interpretation,
the chief cupbearer was restored to his former post—but he forgot all about
the clever young man in prison.

When, two years later, the Egyptian king himself had a troubling dream,
the cupbearer remembered Joseph, and he was rushed from his cell to
Pharaoh's throne room. After hearing Pharaoh's dream, Joseph explained its

significance: Egypt would enjoy seven years of plenty, but these were to be followed by seven years of famine. To prepare for the lean years ahead, the king put Joseph in charge of storing up and distributing food. He was now a high official himself, second only to Pharaoh.

After famine hit the region, Joseph's brothers went down to Egypt to buy grain. They were brought before Joseph and bowed down before him, just as he had dreamt. He, of course, recognized them at once, but because of his Egyptian clothes and speech, they did not recognize him. Joseph accused them of being spies. "Not at all," they protested, "we are all brothers—in fact, we have one more brother, the youngest, whom we left in Canaan." Nevertheless, Joseph had them thrown into prison. After a short while he released all except Simeon; he would stay, Joseph said, until they brought this youngest brother, Benjamin, to Joseph to see.

Back in Canaan, Jacob was reluctant to release Benjamin to his sons' care, but with food running out, he had no choice. The brothers returned to Egypt with Benjamin. Joseph greeted them warmly but conspired to hide his precious goblet in Benjamin's grain sack before they left. On their way back to Canaan, the brothers were apprehended and the goblet was found in Benjamin's sack; Benjamin was charged with the theft. Judah, fearing that the news would kill their father, offered to go to prison in Benjamin's stead. At that point, Joseph could no longer restrain himself but burst into tears. "I am Joseph," he said to his startled brothers, "the one you sold as a slave."

Joseph made peace with his brothers and sent for his father to join him in Egypt. As a high official, Joseph was able to arrange for his father and brothers to settle in the rich area of Goshen. There Jacob lived in comfort and eventually died. His descendants stayed in the land of Goshen, where they grew to a mighty people.

Potiphar's Wife

The story of Joseph left little for ancient interpreters to explain or justify. Though lengthy, the biblical narrative presented none of the apparent difficulties that elements in the stories of Abraham or Jacob or Rachel had: Joseph seemed altogether good, sagacious, and moderate in his behavior. He put his trust in God, and everything worked out well in the end. Interpreters noted that, although Joseph had ample opportunity to take revenge on his brothers for their cruelty—all those years of slavery and imprisonment were their doing, after all—he did not. If he did throw a scare into them for a while, even that had a purpose. Joseph manipulated events, interpreters said, so that Judah—the same brother who had looked on unfeelingly as Joseph was sold into slavery—found himself potentially in the same position once again. This was the moment when Benjamin, Joseph's younger brother, was accused of theft and about to be jailed. But this time Judah did not stand idly by: he volunteered himself in Benjamin's place. For Joseph, this was proof positive that at least one brother had learned his lesson, and Joseph burst into tears.[1]

There was, however, one part of Joseph's story that particularly attracted the attention of ancient interpreters. As mentioned, the wife of Joseph's Egyptian master, Potiphar, at one point tried to seduce him. This was a relatively minor episode, occupying only a few verses (Gen. 39:6–20); it was important in the narrative principally because it was what landed Joseph in prison, where he then went on to meet the Egyptian cupbearer who would eventually bring him to Pharaoh's attention. Minor or not, however, the incident with Potiphar's wife seemed to hold a special importance for ancient interpreters:

> Now Joseph was handsome and good-looking. After these things, his master's wife cast her eyes on Joseph and said, "Lie with me." But he refused and said to his master's wife, "Look, having me, my master has no concern about anything in the house, since he has put me in charge of everything that he has. There is no one greater in this house than I am, nor has he kept back anything from me except yourself, because you are his wife. How then could I do this great wickedness, and sin against God?" And although she spoke to Joseph day after day, he would not consent to lie with her or be with her. On a certain day, however, when he went into the house to do his work, none of the members of the household was in the house. She caught him by his garment, saying, "Lie with me!" But he left his garment in her hand, and fled and ran outside. When she saw that he had left his garment in her hand and had fled outside, she called out to the members of her household and said to them, "See, this Hebrew man has been brought to us to 'sport' with us! He came in to lie with me, but I cried out with a loud voice; and when he heard me raise my voice and cry out, he left his garment beside me, and fled outside."

> Gen. 37:6–15

What was most significant to ancient interpreters was not this incident's role in the overall narrative, but Joseph's steadfast refusal to give in to the woman's solicitations. The reason was simple. Scarcely anyone else in the Hebrew Bible is ever confronted with sexual temptation. Adultery, of course, was forbidden, but steamy scenes between men and women were simply not a normal part of biblical narrative. The only biblical figure to be confronted by temptation besides Joseph was Samson, and he failed miserably; beautiful women repeatedly led him into sin (Judges 14–16). Interpreters were therefore curious to understand the reason for Joseph's stalwart resistance. Many seemed to chalk it up to his unusual character—indeed, in celebrating his virtue, they tended to exaggerate somewhat:

And she pleaded with him *for one year and [then] a second one,* but he refused to listen to her. She embraced him and held on to him in the house in order to compel him to lie with her, and *closed the doors of the house* and held on to him; but he left his garment in her hands and *broke the door* and ran away from her to the outside.

Jubilees 39:8–9

[Joseph recalled:] How often did the Egyptian woman threaten me with death! How often did she give me over to punishment, and then call me back and threaten me, and when I was unwilling to lie with her, she said to me: You will be my master, and [master] of everything that is in my house, if you will give yourself to me.

[Even after I was imprisoned,] she often sent to me saying: Consent to fulfill my desire and I will release you from the bonds and deliver you from the darkness. But not even in thought did I ever incline to her . . . When I was in her house, she used to bare her arms and breasts and legs, that I might go with her, and she was very beautiful, splendidly adorned to beguile me. But the Lord guarded me from her attempts.

Testament of Joseph 3:1–3; 9:1–2, 5

This was not true of all ancient interpreters, however. A close reading of the biblical text led some to believe that Joseph actually *had* been sorely tempted—it was only at the last minute that he changed his mind:

"On a certain day, however, when he went into the house to do his work . . ." [Gen. 39:11]: R. Yoḥanan said: This [verse] teaches that the two of them [Joseph and Potiphar's wife] had planned to sin together. "He went into the house to *do his work*": Rab and Samuel [had disagreed on this phrase]: one said it really means to do his work, the other said it [is a euphemism that] means "to satisfy his desires." He entered; [and then it says] "and none of the members of the household was in the house." But is it at all possible that no one else was present in the large house of this wicked man [Potiphar]? It was taught in the school of R. Ishmael: that particular day was a festival of theirs, and everyone else had gone to their idolatrous rites, but she told them that she was sick. She had said [to herself] that there was no day in which she might indulge herself with Joseph "like this day." [The biblical text continues:] "And she caught him by his garment . . ." At that moment the image of his father entered and appeared to him in the window.[2]

b. Talmud, *Sota* 36b

In this reading of the story, Joseph is not so innocent after all. If no one was in the house that day, the interpreter reasons, it must have been some kind of

holiday or festival, and everyone else had gone to the celebration. If, nevertheless, Potiphar's wife was at home that day, she probably had made up some
excuse, telling people she was not feeling well; she was certainly up to no
good. But what of Joseph? He is said to go to the house "to do his work," a
somewhat ambiguous phrase at best.[3] Surely he ought, under the circumstances, to have anticipated that she might be staying behind in the big,
empty house; if he nevertheless showed up at work as usual, did this not indicate that he was, at the very least, of two minds about the woman's oft-
repeated indecent proposal? Indeed, it seemed possible that he knew exactly
what was going to happen and had even arranged the whole thing with her.
It was only at the last minute, when his father's image[4] appeared to him
miraculously in the window, that Joseph changed his mind.

If the biblical narrative is interpreted in this fashion, Joseph acquires a
somewhat more human face. If, after all, Joseph had not been the slightest bit
interested in his master's wife (as the other interpreters above and, indeed, the
biblical text itself had maintained), well, perhaps that indicated that she
was not so beguiling after all—or that Joseph was some sort of superhuman,
unmoved by the desires to which all flesh is heir. Who could emulate such a
model? But if, to the contrary, Joseph had indeed been tempted but, aided by
his father's miraculous appearance (or, in an alternate scenario, by a sudden
attack of memory that brought back his "father's teachings"),[5] he had fled the
lady's beguilement, then he offered a ready lesson for later readers. Even the
greatest heroes, the story now suggested, are sometimes tempted to sin; their
greatness lies precisely in their ability to overcome that temptation. (As
Katharine Hepburn says to Humphrey Bogart in *The African Queen*,
"Nature, Mr. Allnut, is what we are put in this world to rise above.")

Too Good a Story

Modern interpreters have of course been struck by the contrast between the
story of Joseph and those of other figures in Genesis. Here, they point out, is
no schematic narrative at all, but a full-fledged tale of adventure, with a plot
that twists and turns and keeps the reader riveted until the climactic scene,
when Jacob reveals his true identity to his brothers. (Rightly did the Qur'an,
in retelling the biblical tale, call it "the most beautiful of stories.") But for
modern scholars, that is just the trouble; the story of Joseph reads more like
a work of fiction than anything having to do with history.[6] They suspect that
behind it may stand an altogether invented tale—Egyptian, or perhaps
Canaanite—that had enjoyed great popularity on its own before someone
came along and changed the main characters to Jacob and his twelve sons.[7]

According to this approach, the original story would have told of a family of brothers—not necessarily twelve, but at least four or five—in which the

youngest, because he *was* the youngest, was cherished and spoiled by their father. Of all the brothers, the least jealous in such a situation would likely be the oldest: he had, after all, his own privileged status, and he was also the furthest in age from the youngest and thus less prone to rivalry with him than the others. So it was the oldest who intervened to try to save his sibling when his other brothers threatened him. Nevertheless, the youngest was sold by these other brothers as a slave; then, through his cleverness as a dream interpreter, he ended up as the king's right-hand man. In this role he reencountered his brothers, who now failed to recognize him. There ensued all the back-and-forth maneuvering of the present story, since the youngest brother demanded that Brother X (perhaps his full brother and no half-brother, like the others) be brought before him as well, along with his mother and father. When this was finally done, the youngest revealed his true identity (or, possibly, Brother X recognized him). A tearful reunion ensued.

Scholars have pointed to various details in the biblical narrative of Joseph that indicate that it was indeed adapted from such a narrative. To begin with, Joseph is described in the Bible as if he were Jacob's youngest son: "Now Israel [= Jacob] loved Joseph more than any of his other children, because he was the son of his old age" (Gen. 37:3). But of course Joseph is not Jacob's youngest son; he certainly had been the youngest at some point, but even before the start of this story, Benjamin was born (Gen. 35:18). So why does it say "more than *any* of his other children"? Surely if being a "son of his old age" was the determining factor, Jacob ought to have loved Benjamin at least as much, or more.[8] Then there is the prophetic dream that Joseph has, in which "the sun, the moon, and eleven stars were bowing down to me" (Gen. 37:9). Clearly this refers to Joseph's father, mother, and eleven brothers. That is why Jacob, upon hearing the dream, asks Joseph, "Shall we indeed come, I *and your mother* and your brothers, and bow to the ground before you?" (Gen. 37:10). But in the book of Genesis, by the time Joseph has this dream, his mother, Rachel, has already died (Gen. 35:19). The adaptor may have adjusted the number of stars in the dream to fit the exact number of Joseph's brothers (including Benjamin), but interpreters suspect he forgot to omit the moon from the dream in his adaptation.

Finally, there is the role of the oldest son in the biblical story, Reuben. For the reasons already mentioned, he ought to be the brother who was not jealous and, hence, the hero—and that is indeed how Reuben starts out, boldly intervening to save Joseph (Gen. 37:21–22). He also speaks up later on, reproving his brothers for what they did (Gen. 42:22) and still later offering his own two sons as guarantors for Benjamin's safety (Gen. 42:37). So far, he is the only "good" brother besides Joseph. But at this point suddenly another brother, Judah, emerges. Now it is Judah who intervenes with Jacob to send Benjamin to Egypt, and unlike Reuben's offer of a guarantee, Judah's is accepted (Gen. 43:8–10). From this point on, Reuben disappears. It is "*Judah* and his brothers" who go to Joseph's house (Gen. 44:14), not "Reuben and his brothers," and it is Judah who acts as spokesman, as if he were indeed the oldest (Gen. 44:16). Judah is also the one who selflessly offers to take Benjamin's place in prison (Gen. 44:33–34). Scholars suppose that, in the adaptation of the story, Reuben was at first mechanically put in the role of the "oldest"—he was, after all, Jacob's oldest son. But whoever was doing the adapting knew full well that the tribe of Reuben had long ago virtually disappeared: his listeners would be principally descendants of the tribe of Judah—so Judah was, somewhat inconsistently, given the role of spokesman and hero at the end of the story.[9]

Joseph the Sage

Scholars noticed something else about the Joseph story. The story itself bears a particular "signature"; it seems to belong to the world of ancient Near Eastern wisdom literature.[10] As will be seen presently, wisdom was indeed a *world;* all over the ancient Near East were sages who pursued wisdom, and their writings have survived in Egyptian, Sumerian, Akkadian, Aramaic, and other ancient languages. One of the specialties of the ancient Near Eastern sage was advising the king—just as Joseph ends up doing. Indeed, sages were prominent in court as interpreters of dreams and other signs—just like Joseph. They also had a particular ideology, the "wisdom ideology": they maintained that underlying all of reality is a detailed, divinely established plan, so that everything that happens in this world unfolds in accordance with a preestablished pattern. This belief is precisely reflected in what Joseph says to his brothers (twice, in fact) as a kind of moral of the story: "Do not be distressed or angry with yourselves because you sold me here; for it was [really] God who sent me here ahead of you in order to keep [people] alive . . . You planned to do me harm, but God had planned it for the good" (Gen. 44:5; 50:20).

In short, to modern scholars, Joseph looks like the very model of the ancient Near Eastern sage. Indeed, he is the only one of Israel's ancestors who is called "wise" (Gen. 41:39—this is the same word as the noun "sage" in Hebrew), and throughout his whole story of ups and downs—first he is sold as a slave, then he rises to the top of Potiphar's staff, then back down to the darkest dungeon, then back up to Pharaoh's court and his ultimate vindication and triumph—Joseph reveals that cardinal sagely virtue of patience. An ancient Near Eastern sage was patient precisely because he believed that everything in this world happens according to the divine plan; things will always, therefore, turn out for the best, no matter how bad they may appear now. To scholars, the Joseph story thus looks like an altogether didactic tale designed not only to capture people's attention but to encapsulate, and inculcate, the basic ideology of wisdom. Such a story, they believe, may have circulated independently for a time, but it was eventually fitted to the circumstances of Jacob's family as a way of accounting for the fact that the Israelites ended up migrating en masse to Egypt and coming to be (as they are in the next biblical book, Exodus) enslaved to the Egyptian king.

The Hyksos

But if the Joseph story was, according to this line of argument, originally a work of fiction, it nonetheless intersected with a bit of historical reality. Ancient Egyptian records reveal that Semitic peoples from the area of Canaan did indeed frequently go down to Egypt in time of famine (as Abram and Sarai are reported to have done in Genesis 12). Egypt, after all, did not depend on the altogether undependable rainfall in Canaan to water its crops: it had the Nile, whose annual overflow made it the ideal source of irrigation. So, when there was a shortage of food in their own land, Canaanites could always make their way southward—they were probably not a strange sight to Egyptians.

Indeed, Egyptian records report on a period when some Western Semites, known as the Hyksos, actually took over control of Egypt for a century or so (approximately 1670–1570 BCE). These foreigners (*Hyksos* is actually the Greek form of an ancient Egyptian phrase meaning "rulers of foreign lands") appear to have gained control of a large area of Egypt and established their capital at Avaris, in the Nile delta; their rule extended to Memphis, Hermopolis, and other cities.[11] It would be tempting to identify Joseph and his family as part of this non-Egyptian, Western Semitic population, but that would require a leap of the imagination (and, probably, chronology); most scholars find it more prudent to suppose that the historical memory of such a period of Semitic rule in Egypt helped to shape either the original tale described above or its application in the Bible to Joseph and his brothers. In any case, the Hyksos were eventually expelled from Egypt, and many scholars believe that this historical circumstance may likewise have some relation to the Bible, namely, to the story of the mass exodus from Egypt under the leadership of Moses. (Again, while a straightforward identification of the two poses chronological and other difficulties, the role of these events in shaping historical memory can scarcely be discounted.) One thing is clear: a record of the period of Hyksos rule survived in Egypt long after the events themselves. A "reasonably accurate portrayal" of the Hyksos period was written up in Demotic script about a thousand years after the events,[12] and the memory of Hyksos rule is reflected even later in Greek and other writings. The events of the Joseph story, too, may reflect some memory of this historical reality.

Who, according to modern scholars, might be responsible for the adaptation of an originally fictional tale to Jacob and his family? On this subject there is scarcely any unity among modern scholars: some have tried to divide the story up among the traditional sources J and E, but with widely varying results. Estimates of the date of its composition also differ greatly from one another. There may be something of a clue to the biblical story's origin in the heroic role that Joseph plays. Joseph was, after all, the reputed ancestor of the two great northern tribes, Ephraim and Manasseh. The depiction of Joseph as the hero of the story, the one before whom his brothers bow, may thus betray an originally northern provenance for the story. (As we shall see, there are other reasons for associating the idea of an Israelite presence in Egypt specifically with these northern tribes.) If so, at some point the narrative must have made its way southward, to the Kingdom of Judah. The fact that Judah upstages Reuben as the de facto older brother can hardly be coincidental: this substitution argues the presence of a Judahite hand in the story's final version.

Joseph's Double Portion

After Joseph has revealed his true identity and settled his father and brothers in Egypt, the Bible reports an odd happening:

> After this Joseph was told, "Your father is ill." So he took with him his two sons, Manasseh and Ephraim. When Jacob was informed, "Your son Joseph has come to you," Israel [Jacob's other name] summoned his strength and sat up in bed. Then Jacob said to Joseph, "God Almighty appeared to me at Luz, in the land of Canaan, and He blessed me; He said to me, 'I will make you fruitful and increase your numbers. I will make of you a mass of peoples, and I will give this land to your offspring after you as a perpetual holding.' Now, those two sons of yours who were born to you in the land of Egypt before I came to you in Egypt—they are hereby mine. Ephraim and Manasseh will be mine, just as Reuben and Simeon are. But any children born to you after them will be yours; they will be recorded as heirs of their brothers [Ephraim and Manasseh] with regard to their inheritance."
>
> Gen. 48:1–6

What the aged Jacob does here is legally adopt Joseph's sons Ephraim and Manasseh as his own. Henceforth they will be considered coequal heirs with Jacob's other sons, Reuben, Simeon, Levi, and so forth. Thus, while Joseph formerly had one-twelfth of the inheritance coming to him, his single share will now be replaced by two shares, those of Ephraim and Manasseh. In effect, Joseph gets a double portion. (Any future sons of Joseph will, of course, be legally his own; at the same time, they will presumably have to be considered as sons of either Ephraim or Manasseh for purposes of inheritance.)

Modern scholars see behind this incident a midcourse correction in Israel's list of tribes. The idea that there were precisely twelve tribes seems to have become, at an early stage, a fixity; it could not be changed.[13] But, as we shall see presently, reality changed. At one point Levi was apparently a tribe like any other, and it may well have had its own tribal land. Later, however, this tribe became essentially landless; the Levites became a scattered people of priests and other religious functionaries, with only a few cities to call their own. Simeon, too, appears to have disappeared. So what was to become of the number twelve? To compensate for at least one of these absences, the territory elsewhere attributed to a single ancestor figure, Joseph—a territory that included the lands called "Ephraim" and "Manasseh"—was counted as two territories, each with its own ancestor figure. Joseph was said to have had two sons by those names, each of whom was a tribal founder on his own.[14] In that way, a tribal list could omit the Levites (like the list in Num. 26:1–51) or the Simeonites (as in Deuteronomy 33) and, by replacing "Joseph" with "Ephraim and Manasseh," still include the names of twelve tribes.

After adopting Ephraim and Manasseh, Jacob then asks to bless his two new sons—and here is another kind of midcourse correction:

> Joseph took them both, Ephraim in his right hand toward Israel's left, and Manasseh in his left hand toward Israel's right, and brought them near him. But Israel stretched out his right hand and laid it on the head of Ephraim, who was the younger, and his left hand on the head of Manasseh, crossing his hands, for Manasseh was the firstborn . . . When Joseph saw that his father laid his right hand on the head of Ephraim, it displeased him; so he took his father's hand, to remove it from Ephraim's head to Manasseh's head. Joseph said to his father, "Not so, my father! This one is the firstborn, put your right hand on his head." But his father refused, and said, "I know, my son, I know; he also will become a people, and he also will be great. Nevertheless his younger brother will be greater than he, and his offspring will become a multitude of nations."
>
> Gen. 48:13–20

Apparently—as in the case of Jacob and Esau—this patriarchal blessing portends the future dominance of the originally less powerful people. Perhaps indeed the land of Manasseh originally dominated Ephraim; in any case, we know that an Ephraimite, Jeroboam, eventually took control of the whole population of the north (1 Kings 11:26; 12:1–14:20), including Manasseh. That, modern scholars say, is really what is being enacted by Joseph's promotion of Ephraim to the status of firstborn.

To ancient interpreters, this whole incident was reminiscent of similar cases of the younger son displacing the older—Isaac supplanting Ishmael, and Jacob Esau. For some early Christians, however, the phrase "crossing his hands" seemed to hold added significance. They saw in it a reference to the cross itself, and thus to the ultimate triumph of their faith:

> And he [Joseph] brought Ephraim and Manasseh, intending that Manasseh, because he was the older, should be blessed, for he brought him to the right hand of his father Jacob. But Jacob saw in the Spirit [that is, prophetically] a symbol of the people to come [namely, Christianity]. For what does it say? "And Jacob crossed his hands . . ." Observe how, by these means, he has ordained this people [the Christians] should be first, and heir of the covenant.
>
> *Letter of Barnabas* 13:4–6

Jacob Blesses the Tribes

After these events, when Jacob knew he was soon to die, he summoned all his sons to his bedside to receive his final blessing. This certainly seemed a significant moment: by a common understanding, people who were on the brink of death already had one foot in the next world. Their last words were thus likely to contain extraordinary insight—and perhaps some clues as to what was to happen in times to come. (This is in fact stated explicitly in the present instance: in summoning his sons, Jacob says, "Gather around that I may tell you what will happen to you in days to come" [Gen. 49:1].)

Jacob starts off, however, by talking about the past. In blessing his first son, Reuben, he evokes the shameful incident of Reuben's sleeping with Jacob's concubine Bilhah (Gen. 35:21–22):

> Reuben, you are my firstborn, my strength and the first fruits of my
>   vigor, privileged in rank and in power.
> But wanton as water, you'll have privilege no more,
> For you went to your father's bed—and then defiled it. He went to my
>   bed!
>
> Gen. 49:3–4

The general sense of this text is clear enough: Reuben, as Jacob's firstborn, should have been entitled to the firstborn's special birthright (the same birthright that Esau sold to Jacob for some lentil stew). But because Reuben sinned with Bilhah, "you'll have privilege no more," Jacob says—in other words, I am awarding your birthright's double portion to Joseph (as explained above).

Bilhah's Innocence

If such is the general sense, however, interpreters were troubled by one phrase in Jacob's words: he says Reuben was "wanton as water." How can water be *wanton*? Water is just water. It has no character traits, and if it plays any role in human life, that role is undoubtedly a positive one: without water, we cannot survive. (Modern scholars are thus still puzzled by this phrase of Jacob's.)

Faced with this problem, some ancient interpreters proposed that Jacob was referring to something connected to the circumstances of Reuben's sin with Bilhah: perhaps what he was saying was that Reuben had been wanton *with* or *in* water. Eventually—thinking of a similar incident in the biblical story of David and Bathsheba—interpreters suggested that what Jacob meant was that Reuben had seen Bilhah *bathing in water,* and it was the sight of her nakedness there that led him into the subsequent wantonness:

> For, had I not seen Bilhah bathing in a covered place, I would never have fallen into this great iniquity. But my mind, clinging to the thought of the woman's nakedness, would not allow me to sleep until I had done the abomination.
>
> *Testament of Reuben* 3:11–15[15]

At the same time, Bilhah had not intended that Reuben see her: she was bathing "in a covered place."

Jacob's words to Reuben in Gen. 49:3–4 seemed to contain other clues as to the precise circumstances of Reuben's sin: "For you went to your father's bed," Jacob said. For ancient interpreters, this phrase[16] suggested that Bilhah was actually a passive participant in the whole affair. After all, Jacob did not speak of Reuben and Bilhah having arranged some tryst somewhere, nor even that they both entered the bed at the same time—otherwise, the text would have said, "For you *and Bilhah* went to your father's bed." Indeed, the very fact that it was Reuben's "father's bed" must have meant that Jacob was away at the time (otherwise, how could this all take place in *his* bed?). Interpreters therefore theorized that, in Jacob's absence, Bilhah had gone to bed alone; at some later point, Reuben "went to your father's bed" to commit his transgression when Bilhah was already asleep. She was thus altogether innocent.

A Narrative Anticlimax

In considering the full meaning of Jacob's words to Reuben, ancient interpreters naturally compared those words with the narrative account of this
same incident that appears somewhat earlier in Genesis. Even there, the
details are sparse; in fact, the episode is related in just a few words within the
surrounding passage:

> Israel [that is, Jacob] traveled on, and pitched his tent beyond Migdal-Eder.
> *Now, at the time when Israel was living in that land, Reuben went and lay
> with Bilhah his father's concubine; and Israel heard of it.*
>   Now, the sons of Jacob were twelve. The sons of Leah: Reuben, Jacob's
> firstborn, and Simeon, Levi, Judah, Issachar [and so forth].
>
> Gen. 35:21–23

Even these few words, however, raised questions for ancient interpreters. Particularly puzzling was the closing assertion, "and Israel heard of it." This
seemed terribly anticlimactic. Jacob *heard* about it? Surely something ought
to have been said about what happened as a result of his hearing of it—that
Jacob banished Reuben then and there, or that he punched him in the nose,
or at least that he resolved to disinherit him later on. (Indeed, the translators
of the Septuagint felt so strongly that something was missing that they added
the phrase "and he became very angry" after "and Israel heard of it.")
    Other interpreters, however, came up with another solution. They con-
nected the anticlimactic mention of Jacob's hearing about it to what comes in
the next sentence: "Now, the sons of Jacob were twelve . . ." At first this
could not have looked like a very promising tack; was not this just another
one of those tedious biblical genealogies? But on reflection, perhaps it could
indeed be related to the Reuben-Bilhah incident. After Jacob *heard of it*, he
said, "That's it! No more wives and concubines for me—they only bring trouble." In other words: "And Israel heard of it, [and as a result,] the sons of
Jacob were twelve" and no more.

> And Jacob was exceedingly angry with Reuben because he had lain with
> Bilhah . . . And Jacob did not approach her again because Reuben had
> defiled her.
>
> *Jubilees* 33:9

> And immediately an angel of God revealed to my father Jacob concerning my
> impiety, and when he came he mourned over me, and he touched her no more.
>
> *Testament of Reuben* 3:15

In short, from Jacob's blessing and the related narrative in Genesis 35, ancient interpreters were able to reconstruct a good deal of the circumstances of Reuben's sin. It all came about by accident, when Reuben saw Bilhah bathing in a covered place. Jacob was away at the time, so that night, after Bilhah had gone to bed alone, Reuben slipped into her room and committed his sin. Bilhah herself was quite innocent, but Jacob nonetheless refrained from further relations with her thereafter: there were to be only twelve sons of Jacob. As for Reuben, he was punished by losing the precious birthright.

The Scepter Will Not Depart

When Judah's turn comes to be blessed, Jacob waxes more positive:

> Judah are you, let your brothers praise* you.
> Your hand's on your enemies' neck, and even your brothers bow before
>   you.
> Judah is like a lion's cub—you arose, my son, from ravaging.
> Crouching and stalking like a lion, like the king of beasts[17] none dare
>   challenge.
>
> Gen. 49:8–9

Here, Jacob apparently praises Judah's physical strength and prowess in war. Although the Bible did not relate any specific instances of these, ancient interpreters assumed they must have taken place;[18] they thus understood Jacob's words as providing the justification for the next part of the blessing, in which Jacob predicts the future prominence of the tribe of Judah's descendants. In other words: Judah, since you have shown yourself to be so strong and brave that nowadays "even your brothers bow before you," it is only appropriate that in the future your tribe will be the one to dominate the others:

> The scepter shall not depart from Judah, nor the staff from between his
>   feet,
> Until he enters Shiloh—to him will nations pay homage.
>
> Gen. 49:10

The scepter and staff (symbols of kingly power) will never be transferred from the tribe of Judah to another; on the contrary, even foreign nations will pay Judah homage. And indeed, King David, Israel's greatest king, did come from the tribe of Judah.

---

* A play on the name Judah (*yehudah*), which sounds like "let them praise you" (*yodukha*).

For ancient interpreters, however, these very words seemed highly problematic. "The scepter shall not depart from Judah" means, quite unambiguously, that a Judahite king will rule over Israel forever. But that was not to be. After the heyday of David's reign and that of his son Solomon, the great empire that they had established split into two. David's grandson Rehoboam remained in power only in the southern part, the Kingdom of Judah, while the northern part, called the Kingdom of Israel, was taken over by an Ephraimite ruler. Then, in the sixth century, Davidic rule ceased even in the southern kingdom: Judah was conquered by the Babylonians, and thereby began a succession of foreign rulers, first Babylonians, then Medes and Persians, Greeks, Hellenized Egyptians, Hellenized Syrians, and Romans. Jacob's prediction, "The scepter shall not depart from Judah," must have appeared to later Jews as having fallen flat on its face.

Unless . . . Unless "the scepter shall not depart from Judah" did not really mean that a king from Judah would *always* rule over Israel. In the light of later events, interpreters reasoned, it couldn't have meant that. The scepter did depart. Perhaps, then, the meaning was that, although the scepter was to depart at some point, this condition was not final: what Jacob had meant was that the scepter will not depart *forever*. At some point, the tribe of Judah was to regain the kingship and then it would not only rule over Israel but foreign nations as well: "to him will nations pay homage."

Such thoughts in turn led interpreters to take a closer look at the beginning of the second line, "Until he enters Shiloh." Whatever else these words mean—as we shall see, they are somewhat difficult—the word "until" seemed to work well with the interpretation just given. What Jacob was saying was that, although the scepter would indeed depart from Judah for a time—the empire would split, then the Babylonians would invade, and so forth—that sorry state of affairs would last only *until* something else happened. Then God would return things to what they had been; indeed, foreign nations would now again pay homage to the Jewish king as they once had.

One ancient interpreter thus had Jacob's son Judah explain his father's prediction in somewhat different form:

> [Judah says:] The Lord will bring upon them factions, and there will be continuous wars in Israel, *and my rule shall be ended* by a foreign people, *until* the salvation of Israel comes, *until* the God of righteousness appears, so that Jacob may enjoy peace along with all the nations. [Then] He will guard the power of my kingdom forever. For with an oath the Lord swore to me that my kingship will not depart from my seed *all the days, forever.*
>
> *Testament of Judah* 22:1–3

Biblical interpretation never takes place in a vacuum, and it is no coincidence that this particular understanding of Jacob's words arose at a time when Jews

dreamt as never before of the possible restoration of Israel to political independence and military might. Indeed, they did not simply yearn in general
terms for an improvement in conditions; instead, their hopes focused on the
possibility of a specific new king coming to power. *He* would restore Israel's
fortunes. Such a king was sometimes referred to by the Hebrew word
mashiah, an elegant synonym for "king" that literally means "anointed
one." (This word came into Greek, and subsequently into English, as "messiah.")

As a consequence, some interpreters scrutinized Jacob's words for a reference to such a king. In this search, attention fell once again on the mysterious
word "Shiloh." Now a slightly different reading was proposed (remember,
vowels were often left unexpressed in the Hebrew writing system): *shello,*
"pertaining to him" or "of him." If the future king was not specifically
mentioned, was it not possible that Jacob had alluded to him in suggesting
that things would eventually change when *that which belongs to him* (the
future king) arrives? Then, even foreign nations would pay Israel homage:

> A ruler shall not be absent from Judah, nor a leader from his loins, until
> there come the things stored away *for him;* and he is the expectation of the
> nations.
>
> Septuagint, Gen. 49:10

> The ruler shall not depart from the house of Judah, nor the scribe from his
> children's children forever; until the Messiah comes, *to whom belongs* the
> kingdom, and to him shall the peoples be obedient.
>
> *Targum Onqelos* Gen. 49:10

And so, it turned out that, not only was Jacob's prediction not wrong, it was
actually a hint about the very thing that people were hoping for in the
ancient interpreters' own day. Jacob had subtly alluded to a time when a new
king would arise in Israel and bring it back to the glory days of David and
Solomon.

An Ancient Text

As usual, modern scholars have a somewhat different reading of these same
texts. To begin with, it should be recalled that this whole section of blessings
is considered by scholars to be among the oldest parts of the Bible. This conclusion is based in part on linguistic and stylistic considerations, but also on
the content of the blessings. Take, for example, the "blessing" of Simeon and
Levi already discussed in chapter 11:

Simeon and Levi are brothers; tools of violence are their stock-in-trade.
May I never enter into their company, nor take pleasure in their
    assembly.
For in their anger they would kill a man, and in a good mood, hamstring
    an ox!
Cursed be their anger, how fierce! Their wrath is harsh indeed.
I shall divide them in Jacob and scatter them in Israel.

Gen. 49:5–7

The last line "predicts" that the tribes of Simeon and Levi will be scattered among the other tribes. Even if this were written after the events, scholars theorize, the passage preserves a memory of the time when the Levites did indeed have their own land. Elsewhere, that memory is not preserved. It is simply axiomatic that the Levites are a priestly tribe and were never intended to have their own territory; "the LORD is their territory" (Deut. 10:9; 18:2). At the same time, there is nothing in Gen. 49:5–7 that even hints that its author had some awareness of the Levites' future role as priests; apparently, that had not happened yet.

For modern scholars, Jacob's "blessing" of Reuben provides another indication of the antiquity of this whole section. It also seems to have a quite different message from that seen earlier:

Reuben, you are my firstborn, my strength and the first fruits of my
    vigor, privileged in rank and in power.
But wanton as water, you'll have privilege no more,
For you went to your father's bed—and then defiled it. He went to my
    bed!

Gen. 49:3–4

What this passage implies for modern scholars is that although the tribe of Reuben had at first been Jacob's "firstborn," that is, it had been the most powerful and dominant tribe for a while, it subsequently lost this position and became a virtual nonentity. (The same conclusion, scholars say, is suggested by a number of passages elsewhere in the Bible.)[19] If so, these words would seem to reflect a relatively early stage of Israelite history. The replacement of Reuben by Judah as the dominant tribe in the south probably took place roughly around the time of King David, that is, at the start of the tenth century BCE, if not earlier. Of course, this "blessing" may well have been written after that time, but not long after, since it still feels the need to account for Reuben's demise. In fact, modern scholars say, that is what it is really talking about.

The reason it gives for the demise of the tribe of Reuben is one of the most stereotypical infractions in the ancient Near East: Reuben "went to [his] father's bed," a euphemism meaning he slept with his father's wife. (It should be noted that, in a polygamous society, sleeping with one's father's wife was not necessarily sleeping with one's own mother. More likely, the wife involved was the pretty young woman whom the father had recently acquired but who was actually closer, in age and perhaps in other ways, to the son.) This was not only a sexual infraction but a political one: he who slept with the king's wife was considered to have made a de facto claim to the throne (see 2 Sam. 16:21; 1 Kings 2:13–25), and no doubt, even when an actual king was not involved, this act was considered one of arrogant supersession. Perhaps for this reason does the prohibition of sleeping with one's father's wife appear no fewer than four times in the Pentateuch (Lev. 18:7; 20:11; Deut. 23:1; 27:20). So Reuben is asserted to have committed this act of lèse-majesté. Did any such thing ever happen? Of course not, a modern scholar would say. This ancient text is simply invoking a stereotypical sin to explain why the tribe of Reuben lost its homeland and disappeared.

The Overall Purpose of Jacob's Blessings

Taking a step backward, modern scholars surveying Jacob's blessings see one overall purpose in them. After all, they present Jacob as blessing each of his sons, the ancestors of Israel's twelve tribes; if so, and given the apparently early date of these blessings, their purpose appears to have been to put the official stamp, as it were, on their union. "Jacob had twelve sons," the text is saying, "and so it is only appropriate that the twelve tribes descended from them should be one kingdom." In political terms, this would again point to the time of David and Solomon, when such a union was first achieved. The blessing of Judah indicates an awareness that David, who came from Judah, would establish a royal dynasty. But nothing in that blessing or any of the others reveals any hint of the fact that the twelve tribes will split apart again soon after Solomon's reign; on the contrary, "the scepter shall not depart from Judah." Beyond these points, scholars also note that the blessings preserve the traditional order of the tribes (Reuben, Simeon, Levi, Judah, and so forth), an order that probably corresponds to an earlier ranking of size or power. But that ranking is now no longer valid: Judah is the big tribe of the south and the king's home territory. That is why the blessings take the three tribes that traditionally came before Judah and, in attributing some plausible sin to their founders (sleeping with one's father's wife, being violent hotheads), "predict" their eventual displacement.

In attributing to Simeon and Levi unbridled anger and violence, their blessing may have accounted for the ultimate disappearance of these tribes; as we have seen, however, scholars also believe that it created a problem. Later

Israelites, hearing or reading this passage, must have wondered: what violence? Nothing else in the Bible ever referred to these tribes as being violent. The question may have been pushed aside for a while, but eventually, as Scripture came to be thought of more and more as leaving no loose ends, some explanation seemed required. Out of this, scholars claim, came the insertion of the story of Dinah into the book of Genesis (see above, chapter 11).

By the same logic, this must also have occurred with Reuben's sin, "you went to your father's bed." When did *that* happen, later readers wondered, and who was the woman? It was to answer this question, scholars say, that the same editor who inserted the Dinah story also stuck a single sentence into chapter 35 of Genesis, a sentence that likewise sought to provide some context for Jacob's words:

> Israel [that is, Jacob] traveled on, and pitched his tent beyond Migdal-Eder. *Now, at the time when Israel was living in that land, Reuben went and lay with Bilhah his father's concubine; and Israel heard of it.*
> Now, the sons of Jacob were twelve. The sons of Leah: Reuben, Jacob's firstborn, and Simeon, Levi, Judah, Issachar [and so forth].
>
> Gen. 35:21–23

The insertion, indicated in italics, really has nothing to do with what precedes it or follows it; that alone, for modern scholars, might suggest that it is an insertion. Moreover, what it says betrays the same gingerly, minimalist approach that this editor displayed in an insertion seen earlier (Gen. 30:21). Here again, he includes the absolute minimum of required information: when and where the incident took place, and who the "wife" in question was. To these bare facts he adds only the observation "and Israel [that is, Jacob] heard of it." The reason for this is obvious: if Jacob is going to chew out his son for his crime in Gen. 49:3–5, he has to have heard about it from someone—and normally, the participants in an adulterous union are not eager to share that information with the woman's husband. But Jacob must have found out about it somehow, so, rather than speculate as to how, the editor simply said, "and Israel heard of it."

How often does it happen in the history of interpretation that an explanation designed to solve one problem in the Bible ends up creating another! So it turned out here as well. The assertion "and Israel heard of it" seemed terribly anticlimactic. It was this apparent anticlimax that produced the interpretive motif seen earlier (and others).[20]

Judah Rules

As for the blessing of Judah, modern scholars' understanding is likewise quite different from the ancient approach studied above.

> Judah are you, let your brothers praise you.
> Your hand's on your enemies' neck, and even your brothers bow before
>   you.
> Judah is like a lion's cub—you arose, my son, from ravaging.
> Crouching and stalking like a lion, like the king of beasts none dare chal-
>   lenge.
>
> Gen. 49:8–9

Here, for modern scholars, is a rather realistic portrait of this tribe's rise to power as epitomized in the career of King David (his tribe's eponym, Judah, really stands for him here). It was indeed David's abilities as a fighter—first as the leader of a small, vicious guerrilla band, and eventually as the commander of a regular army—that not only subdued Judah's out-and-out enemies ("Your hand's on your enemies' neck"), but likewise caused the other tribes ("your brothers") to submit to his authority. In putting these words in Jacob's mouth, the Bible was, according to most scholars, "predicting" what had probably already taken place, though not long before. (Elsewhere, in the books of 1 and 2 Samuel, the Bible recounts in greater detail the sometimes ruthless steps by which David and the Judahites gained the throne, quite literally rising up by ravaging.)

But then Jacob turns to the future of the kingdom that David had established:

> The scepter shall not depart from Judah, nor the staff from between his
>   feet,
> Until he enters Shiloh—to him will nations pay homage.
>
> Gen. 49:10

Unlike the previous lines, these two are, in the view of modern scholars, an actual prediction of the future. Judah will always rule, this text is saying. That is the general sense, but it must be admitted that the second line cited has always been mysterious to scholars, and still is today. The main problem is the word "Shiloh." Shiloh was an old city in the territory of Ephraim where the Ark of the LORD once rested. If so, the sense of the second line might be "until he [Judah] reaches Shiloh," that is, until Davidic power extends into Ephraim (and, by extension, the whole north). But the same letters might also spell out

Shelah, the name of one of the Judahite clans (see Gen. 38:5; Num. 26:20; 1 Chr. 2:3), perhaps one that was prominent when these lines were written. Along with these two possibilities, some modern scholars have maintained that the text has been corrupted in transmission, and that Shiloh/Shelah is really two words, *shai lo,* yielding "until a tribute is brought to him." Whichever reading is preferred, one further lexical point requires clarification: the word "until" does not mean that the scepter shall not depart *until* such-and-such happens—that, scholars say, would make no sense. Instead, it really means "to such an extent that" (as this phrase does elsewhere in the Bible: Gen. 26:13; 41:49; 2 Sam. 23:10): in other words, Judah will solidify its hold on power, *so much so that* tribute will be brought to him (or Shelah will come, or he will enter Shiloh) and the fealty of foreign nations will be his.

In short: for modern scholars, Jacob's blessings of his sons seem to go back to the time of David or Solomon. Although the tribe of Reuben had, in still earlier times, been dominant, his "blessing" demotes him to an inferior position. Simeon and Levi are likewise condemned to being scattered and dispersed, another *vaticinium ex eventu,* while Judah's blessing really refers to David's establishment of the royal dynasty, one that, as far as this passage is concerned, will last forever. History, however, was to tell a different tale.

13

Moses in Egypt

EXODUS 1:1–4:17

Moses Trampling Pharaoh's Crown by Enrico Tempestini.

MOSES IN PHARAOH'S COURT. EGYPTOLOGY. HISTORICITY OF THE EXODUS. THE 'APIRU. THE BURNING BUSH. THE GOD OF ISRAEL.

God appeared to Moses at the burning bush and instructed him to free the Israelites from slavery. But why are ancient Egyptian records silent on the subject?

Jacob's descendants remained in Egypt and grew numerous. Eventually, a new king arose who feared this foreign population; he set out to enslave them and to prevent them from further increase. At first, he ordered the Hebrew midwives to kill any newborn boy that they delivered. The midwives, however, made an excuse not to carry out this order, so Pharaoh instead issued a general decree to the entire population to cast any newborn boy into the Nile.

It was at this time that Moses was born. At first, his mother tried to hide him, but as he grew bigger she despaired of doing so; instead, she set out to obey the king's decree—but with a difference. She put Moses in the Nile inside a little basket. The basket floated down to where the king's daughter was bathing, and when the daughter saw the baby, she resolved to keep it as her own. Moses grew up in the king's court. Moses was thus raised in the very center of Egyptian royal power, the same power that he would later challenge as the leader of the Israelites.

An Evil Omen

What exactly happened in court when Pharaoh's daughter showed up with the new baby was a subject of speculation among ancient interpreters. After all, if she had adopted Moses, it seemed likely to interpreters that she had no children of her own at the time; in that case, Moses might well have been considered a potential heir to the throne. Certainly such an idea must not have been universally welcomed. Here, thus, is an incident from Moses' early childhood as recounted by Josephus, the first-century historian:

> On one occasion, she [Pharaoh's daughter] brought Moses to her father and showed him off and told [her father] that, having considered the royal succession—and if God did not will her to have a child of her own—then were this boy, of such godly appearance and nobility of mind, whom she had miraculously received through the grace of the river, brought up as her own, he might "eventually be made the successor to your own kingship." Saying these things, she gave the child into her father's hands, and he took

him and, as he embraced him, put his crown on the child's head as an act of affection toward his daughter. But Moses took it off and threw it to the ground and, as might befit a young child, stepped on it with his foot. Now this appeared to hold an evil omen for the kingdom. Seeing this, the sacred scribe who had foretold how his [Moses'] birth would bring low the Egyptian empire, rushed headlong to kill him, and crying out dreadfully, said: "This, O King, this is the child whom God had indicated must be killed for us to be out of danger! He bears witness to the prediction through this act of treading on your sovereignty and trampling your crown . . ." But Thermouthis [Pharaoh's daughter] snatched him away, and the king, having been so predisposed by God (whose care for Moses saved him), shrank back from killing him.

Josephus, *Jewish Antiquities* 2:232–36

As we have seen numerous times, when ancient interpreters add something to the biblical text, it is usually because they are seeking to explain something in the original, or sometimes, because of some problem. It would not be easy to guess what was on Josephus's mind (or rather, that of his source, since he merely transmitted this tale and did not invent it himself) if we did not have another version of it. The other version is basically similar, except for the ending. Instead of just letting Moses escape, Pharaoh's "sacred scribe" proposes a test to make sure that the child's gesture was meaningless:

He said to them, "[If] this child has no sense yet . . . you can verify [this] if you bring before him on a platter a piece of gold and a burning coal. If he puts his hand out for the burning coal, then he has no sense and he ought not to be condemned to death. But if he puts his hand out for the gold, then he does have sense and you should kill him." Whereupon they brought before him a piece of gold and a burning coal, and Moses put forth his hand to take the gold. But the angel Gabriel came and pushed his hand aside, so that his hand seized the coal and he put it to his mouth with the coal still in it; [thus] his tongue was injured, and from this he became "heavy of speech and heavy of tongue" [Exod. 4:10].

Exodus Rabba 1:26

As the last line of this passage indicates, the whole problem for ancient interpreters stems from something Moses says to God much later on, at Mount Horeb, when God seeks to enlist him to speak with Pharaoh on the Israelites' behalf. Moses at first refuses, saying, "I am heavy of speech and heavy of tongue." Presumably, what he meant was that he was not a particularly good speechmaker; as he puts it earlier in the same sentence, "I am not a man of words" (Exod. 4:10).[1] That might have been an acceptable thing for an ancient Israelite to say, but for later Jews like Josephus, or indeed for anyone in the Greco-Roman orbit, to say that you were not good at speaking was to confess that you had failed the most basic course, rhetoric, taught in the Greco-Roman educational system. It would be like a modern would-be politician saying, "I flunked out of school in fifth grade and never went back. But vote for me anyway."

To avoid giving such an impression about Moses, interpreters preferred to understand the phrase "heavy of speech and heavy of tongue" in some other way: what Moses must have meant was that he had some actual physical problem—a speech impediment. But would God have caused his future chosen servant to be *born* that way? Instead, ancient interpreters created the scenario with the burning coal to account for Moses' speech problem.

Other interpreters, while not citing this story, went out of their way to assert that Moses, far from a high school dropout, had actually had a wonderful Egyptian education:

> [Moses says:]
> Throughout my boyhood years the princess did,
> For princely rearing and instruction apt,
> Provide all things, as though I were her own.
> Ezekiel the Tragedian, *Exagoge* 36–38

> Arithmetic, geometry, the lore of meter, rhythm, and harmony, and the whole subject of music . . . were imparted to him by learned Egyptians. These further instructed him in the philosophy conveyed in symbols . . . He had Greeks to teach him the rest of the regular school course, and the inhabitants of the neighboring countries for Assyrian literature and the Chaldean science of the heavenly bodies.
> Philo, *Life of Moses* 1:23

> Pharaoh's daughter adopted him and brought him up as her own son, and Moses was educated in all the wisdom of Egypt, *and he was powerful in his words and actions.*
> Acts 7:21–22

The Birth of Egyptology

Thus began the life of the man who was to lead the Israelites from Egyptian slavery to freedom in their ancestral homeland of Canaan. The story of Moses' life frames not only the book of Exodus, but the next three books as well, Leviticus, Numbers, and Deuteronomy. In a sense, one might say, he is the most important figure not only of the Pentateuch but of the whole Hebrew Bible. Modern scholars have thus been eager to find out all they can about the person of Moses and the history of ancient Egypt in which his story unfolds.

The interest in ancient Egypt does not come from biblical scholars alone, however, nor is it solely a concern of modern investigators. Egypt has long been a subject of fascination to outsiders, ever since classical Greece and Rome. Indeed, Greek writers had often described Egypt as the font of ancient wisdom (the Greeks saw themselves as relative newcomers in this field); Greek and Latin historians were generally admirers of all things Egyptian. Later on, during the Renaissance, these classical writings served as a kind of countertradition to the mostly negative image of Egypt in the Bible. One thing that particularly attracted people to Egyptian lore was its association with the world of the occult and secret religious teachings—so much so that Renaissance scholars in Italy and elsewhere devoted themselves to trying to piece together what they could of ancient Egyptian religion from scattered Greek fragments (and later forgeries). In particular, the Egyptian writing system, dubbed "hieroglyphics" (Greek for "priestly carvings"), fascinated people, since it seemed to hold the key to this world of lost teachings. But no one could read those ancient signs.[2]

All this changed following Napoleon's expedition to Egypt at the end of the eighteenth century. A French officer with the expedition, Pierre Bouchard, discovered a large basalt stele inscribed, it turned out, with three parallel versions of the same text, a decree issued by Ptolemy V of Egypt written around 196 BCE. The three versions were written in Greek, Demotic,* and hieroglyphic script. This was the famous Rosetta Stone, and it at last offered the hope that hieroglyphics could be understood through direct comparison of those incomprehensible signs with the other two versions of the text.

The man who was to do much of the work—and who is often called the "father of Egyptology"—was a brilliant young Frenchman named Jean-François Champollion. Since his childhood, Champollion had been fascinated with the ancient Near East; he had a gift for learning languages and went on to study, among others, Hebrew, Arabic, Persian, Aramaic, Syriac (a form of Aramaic), and even Chinese. But his passion soon became Coptic, the language still spoken by a religious minority in Egypt. During his early studies at Grenoble, Champollion had made the acquaintance of a Syrian monk who had spent time in Egypt. The monk reported favorably the Copts' own claim that their language was actually a later form of the now-lost language of ancient Egypt; he urged Champollion to study that language as well. The young man followed this advice and soon authored a paper offering evidence in support of the Coptic-is-ancient-Egyptian hypothesis, which he submitted to the Academy of Grenoble in 1807. He was sixteen years old.

---

* The name of a somewhat later form of ancient Egyptian and the script used to write it, which came into use around 650 BCE.

Appointed a professor at Grenoble at the age of nineteen, he set himself to deciphering the ancient Egyptian writing system with the aid of the Rosetta Stone. It was no easy matter: while some of the symbols were, as people had long maintained, signs representing whole words, others seemed to be alphabetical. Champollion deduced this from the fact that some hieroglyphs were apparently used to represent proper names in the Greek version of the text. Eventually, he was able to show that 486 Greek words on the Rosetta Stone corresponded to 1,419 hieroglyphs—surely, these hieroglyphs functioned like letters and not whole words! But the writing system was difficult to crack, not only because of the mixture of whole-word symbols and individual-sound symbols, but because the same sound was sometimes represented by two different symbols. In addition, it turned out that vowel sounds were not fully represented in writing: the Greek *Ptolemaios* came out *Ptolmys,* for example.

Champollion was not the only one in pursuit of ancient Egyptian; notably, he had a British rival, Thomas Young, who published some of his discoveries even before Champollion and on which the young Frenchman built some of his own conclusions. But Champollion ultimately pulled ahead of his competitor. He not only expanded and refined his grasp of hieroglyphics, but he soon published studies of ancient Egyptian religion and the Egyptian pantheon; his work on a royal papyrus from the time of Rameses II led him to revise then-current ideas of Egyptian history and the arrangement of dynasties. His appointment in 1826 to head the Egyptian section of the Louvre Museum in Paris allowed him firsthand access to the treasures brought back from the Napoleonic expedition; then, in 1828, he traveled to Egypt itself, where he was able to study texts in situ. He returned a year and a half later with copious notes that would ultimately lead to the publication of his Egyptian grammar, an Egyptian dictionary, and his *Monuments of Egypt and Nubia.* But these were all posthumous publications; Champollion himself died in 1832, at the age of forty-one.

Nowadays, thanks to the pioneering work of Champollion and others, scholars have a detailed picture of ancient Egypt—not only its own history, including the names and dates of its kings, its religion, social and political organization, and daily life, but also what Egyptians reported in various periods about other nations in the region. In addition to actual texts, archaeologists have also uncovered some of the main cities of ancient Egypt, with their temples, palaces, and other monumental architecture. The study of all this material, Egyptology, is nowadays recognized as an important academic discipline in its own right—and, of course, it is important to the study of the biblical world as well.

When it comes to the events described in the book of Exodus, however, Egyptology seems to draw a blank. No ancient Egyptian text discovered so far describes anything like the ten plagues that are said to have afflicted Egypt in the biblical account, nor is there any mention of a mass exodus of foreign slaves at that time. It may be that no evidence has been found because these events were not deemed particularly flattering from an Egyptian standpoint; still, this total silence is troubling for those who wish to see in the Bible a report of actual, historical events.[3] And the doubts raised by this silence are not the only thing calling into question the historicity of the biblical account.

Historicity of the Exodus

Even in ancient times, some people wondered about the factual side of the Exodus story. The Jewish writer Josephus reports on "libels against us" spread by unsympathetic historians in connection with the exodus; their claim was that the Jews were not freed by God but expelled as undesirables by the Egyptian king, who saw to it that they were ushered out of the country in the company of some Egyptian lepers and other personae non gratae.[4] While it is true that such writings were doubtless motivated by openly anti-Jewish animus,[5] elements in the biblical account itself no doubt encouraged such writers to create their alternate version of the events. Josephus himself sounds just a touch skeptical about the miraculous dividing of the Red Sea:

> Each of the things I have recounted just as they are told in Sacred Scripture. And let no one wonder at the astonishing nature of this thing, that a road to safety was found through the sea itself—whether [this happened] by God's will or simply through happenstance—on behalf of an ancient people innocent of all wrongdoing. For indeed, it was but a short while ago that the Pamphilian Sea moved backwards for those who were accompanying Alexander, king of Macedonia, thus offering them a path through it when no other way out existed, and so [allowing them] to overcome, as was God's will, the Persian empire. All those who have written down Alexander's doings are in agreement on this. However, each person may decide on his own concerning such matters.
>
> Josephus, *Jewish Antiquities* 2:347–48

Quite apart from the miraculous events recounted—the ten plagues and the splitting of the Red Sea—people have wondered how six hundred thousand male Israelites, along with their wives, children, flocks, and herds, could have survived in the desert for forty years; the numbers seemed impossibly large for a group traveling together from tiny oasis to tiny oasis. In our own day, the silence of ancient Egyptian records has been compounded by the silence of archaeologists: many of the sites mentioned in the account of the Israelites' desert wanderings have been identified and excavated, but none of them has yielded anything that could be construed as attesting to the presence of such a mass of Israelites (or even of a considerably smaller group). What is more, as we shall see, the possibility of a subsequent mass entry of Israelites into Canaan is equally difficult to support, both with regard to the archaeological record and in view of some apparent contradictions within the Bible itself. On top of this, archaeologists have found no evidence of Egyptian influence in the earliest settlements in Canaan identified as Israelite: they are not laid out like Egyptian villages, and the Israelites who lived there did not use Egyptian-style tools or pottery or script—in short, there is nothing to indicate that the earliest Israelites had had any sustained, firsthand contact with life in Egypt.[6] Thus, as one popular survey recently noted, "The conclusion . . . that the exodus did not happen at the time and in the manner described in the Bible . . . seems irrefutable."[7] Another researcher's denial is even more sweeping: "Not only is there no archaeological evidence for an exodus, there is no need to posit such an event. We can account for Israelite origins, historically and archaeologically, without presuming any Egyptian background."[8]

But not so fast! Even if modern scholars have doubts about the numbers involved and other aspects of the biblical account, various details in the Exodus narrative do seem to many to have the ring of authenticity.

There is, to begin with, the matter of names. If some Israelite in a later day were making up this story out of whole cloth, it is difficult to understand why he would have given the story's great hero an Egyptian name. *Moses* is clearly that. Many Egyptian names combine the particle *-mose* ("is born") with the name of a god, thus: Thutmose ("Thut is born"), Ramose ("Ra is born"—this is the same name as Rameses in the Bible), and so forth. What is more, sometimes the divine name is dropped from such compounds, so that plain old *mose*, Moses, appears to be an altogether plausible Egyptian name.[9] Of course, the biblical narrative claims that Moses' name comes from a Hebrew word that means "drawn up [from water]" (Exod. 2:10), but this etymology is hardly credible to modern scholars. (Why would an Egyptian princess give her adopted son a newly minted Hebrew name—and how would she know enough Hebrew grammar to do so?)

Nor is Moses the only Egyptian name in the group. The name Phinehas (Exod. 6:25) is also of Egyptian origin ("southerner," hence also "dark-skinned one"), as perhaps are the names of Moses' brother and sister, Aaron and Miriam.[10] To be sure, I could make up a story about a group of Americans being led out of Mexico by Juan, José, and Maria; these names will all be found to be authentically Mexican, but that does not mean that my story is true, or even based on a firsthand knowledge of Mexico. But if my story claimed that these leaders were in fact Americans, why wouldn't I have simply called them John, Joe, and Mary Jane? In fact, why would I have said José was called José because his parents were fond of a patriotic American anthem that began, "José, can you see"? (This, a modern scholar would say, is roughly the equivalent of deriving the name Moses from "drawn up [from water].") One is thus left with the conclusion that the exodus tradition preserved in the Bible must have been connected from an early point with a group of indelible Egyptian names—despite the fact that that tradition had absolutely no interest in claiming that the people involved were anything but pure-blooded Israelites. Does this not suggest that there really was someone named Moses connected with some sort of exodus, and that, whatever else in the story may have been invented, his real name could not be suppressed later on because it was simply too well known?

Some of the Exodus place-names, too, bear the stamp of authenticity. Thus, the Israelite slaves are said to have built the cities of Pithom and Raamses (Exod. 1:11). The first of these represents the Egyptian city P(r) 'Atm, "House of [the god] Atum," while the second is P(r) R'mss, "House of Rameses," a city that was built by Rameses II (1290–1224 BCE). For this and other reasons, historians date the exodus to the time of this king, or possibly that of his son, Merneptah, that is, to the mid-to-late thirteenth century BCE, which fits fairly well with the overall chronology of this early period.[11] What is more, an ancient Greek historian, Diodorus Sicilus, reports the tradition that a certain king "Seoösis"[12] went out of his way to use foreign workers in his building projects rather than employing native Egyptians: "On these labors he used no Egyptians, but constructed them all by the hands of his captives alone."[13] This, too, fits with the Exodus account. Indeed, calling the Egyptian king at the time of the exodus by the title "Pharaoh" is another apparently authenticating detail. This word (pr'3) actually means "Big House" in Egyptian, namely, the royal palace; in the eighteenth dynasty, however, it came to be used as a way of referring to the king himself—somewhat similar to the way American press reports sometimes say, "The White House announced today . . ." Again, this would seem to put the Exodus account in the proper time frame.[14] And on top of this is the matter of the 'apiru.

The 'Apiru

It was said above that the Egyptian records do not speak of the Israelite slaves. One text, however, Papyrus Leiden 348, speaks of some 'apiru who were used for "hauling stones to the great pylon" of one of the public structures in the city of Rameses (that is, P(r) R'mss).[15] Who were the 'apiru? This has been the subject of much speculation among ancient Near Eastern scholars. The name appears in various forms in different languages, notably ḫabiru in Akkadian (also represented by the Sumerian ideogram SA.GAZ) and 'pr (='apiru) in Ugaritic (a northern brand of Canaanite); the 'apiru have also been found in Hittite texts. Because of the sound similarity, a case can be made that this word is none other than the Hebrew word 'ibri, "Hebrew."[16]

As scholars have come to understand, 'apiru itself cannot mean just

"Hebrew": there are too many texts (over 250) written over too broad a historical period and too wide a geographical area to make this even remotely plausible.[17] Most scholars nowadays identify 'apiru as designating a (low) social class, or possibly referring to a category of refugees or escapees from another country (the two ideas are not mutually exclusive). But the texts are hardly uniform in their use of the term: Old Babylonian texts refer to the 'apiru as mercenaries employed by the state, whereas the Mari texts and the El Amarna letters* seem to present the 'apiru as outlaws or highwaymen.

What is striking to scholars, however, is the possibility that later tradition still preserved the derogatory word 'apiru as how the Israelites (and perhaps others) were known to the Egyptians in the late second millennium. The evidence is in the Bible itself. Contrary to popular expectation, the word "Hebrew" actually does not appear very much in the Bible. What we call the Hebrew language, for example, is never called that in the Hebrew Bible; instead, it is called "Judean" or "Canaanite." Nor are the people of Israel generally called Hebrews. But here and there, thirty-four times in all, the word "Hebrew" does occur in this sense, and of these, fully twenty of the occurrences are found in the context of the story of the Exodus or the preceding narrative of Joseph. Thus, Pharaoh calls to the "Hebrew midwives" to do his bidding (Exod. 1:15), and when Pharaoh's daughter finds a little baby floating in the Nile she says, "This must be one of those Hebrew children" (Exod. 2:6). After he is grown, Moses sees "two Hebrew men fighting," and when he returns to Egypt he tells Pharaoh, "The God of the Hebrews appeared to us" (Exod. 5:3). All this may suggest that these ancient texts preserve the tradition that "Hebrew" is what the Egyptians themselves called the Israelites.[18] If so, the absence of direct reference to the Israelite slaves in Egyptian documents might be somewhat less troubling; indeed, the mention of the 'apiru in *Papyrus Leiden* 348 might actually seem to provide something like the smoking gun biblical scholars are looking for. True, this is only one text, and one robin doth not a springtime make; indeed, even this text may be talking about some *other* bunch of 'apiru quite unrelated to the biblical Israelites. But it does say that the 'apiru were used for building part of the city of Rameses, which is exactly what the Bible says of the Israelites in Exod. 1:11. Beyond this, it is to be noted that the 'apiru do not appear in firsthand reports in the ancient Near East after the end of the second millennium: if the book of Exodus uses this name for the Israelites in Egypt, it would seem to be basing itself on usage appropriate to the presumed time of the Exodus, or pretty close to it, in the late second millennium.

In short, the evidence that Egyptology provides is mixed. While there is no direct confirmation of the biblical account, a number of tantalizing details have led many otherwise hard-nosed modern scholars to conclude that there

* Below, chapter 22.

may be at least some historical basis to the biblical account of the Exodus—
even if, as we shall see, most such scholars believe it involved only a small
part of what was to become the nation of Israel. Beyond the onomastic
(that is, concerning proper names) and other linguistic evidence is an argument of somewhat larger dimension, namely, the nature of the overall message imparted by the Exodus narrative. For, as numerous writers have already
pointed out, this is not exactly the sort of story a people would be likely to
make up about itself out of whole cloth—"We were a bunch of low-class construction workers and domestic slaves for our neighbors to the south until,
after repeated negotiations, they allowed us to leave and come here." Usually,
myths of national origin try to strike a more heroic note—from Romulus and
Remus and *pius* Aeneas to Arthurian Britain and doughty Vercingetorix,
national myths tend to stress all that is positive and noble in their country's
founding.[19] The Exodus account is not exactly lacking in heroism, but it
seems to scholars more like the heroic recasting of a not particularly flattering set of facts than the sort of thing that would be simply invented.[20]

From the Bulrushes

This is not to say, of course, that nothing in the Exodus narrative appears to
modern scholars to have been invented. The story of Moses being found in
the bulrushes by the Egyptian princess has suggested various parallels in the
mythical literature of Egypt and Mesopotamia. Here, for example, is a (fictional) account of the birth of Sargon I of Agade (ca. 2371–2316 BCE) as
reconstructed from some much later cuneiform texts:

> [Sargon speaks:] I am the child of a priest and an unknown pilgrim from
> the mountains. Today, I rule an empire from the city of Agade.
>   Because my mother did not want anyone in the city of Asupiranu to
> know that she had given birth to a child, she left me on the bank of the
> Euphrates river in a basket woven from rushes and waterproofed with tar.
> The river carried my basket down to a canal, where Akki, the royal gar-
> dener, lifted me out of the water and reared me as his own. He trained me
> to care for the gardens of the great king.
>   With the help of Ishtar, divine patron of love and war, I became king of
> the black-headed people and have ruled for fifty-five years.[21]

The motif of a newborn child being exposed to the elements and left to fend
for itself is found in many places around the world (and no doubt had some
connection with gruesome reality—such exposure was usually, in effect, a
form of infanticide). Still, scholars have been struck by the similarity of the
Sargon legend with the biblical account of Moses' birth—the basket of reeds

waterproofed with tar (Exod. 2:3), a stratagem that enables the child to be saved by a member of the royal court and brought up there (Exod. 2:10). Once again, it looks to scholars as if the Bible has taken a leaf from the literature of its neighbors.

The Burning Bush

Growing up in Pharaoh's court, Moses apparently knew of his Israelite origins. At one point, Scripture recounts, He "went out to his people" (Exod. 2:11) and his heart was turned to the Israelites' suffering. On a certain occasion, he saw an Egyptian man beating a Hebrew; Moses came to the rescue and killed the Egyptian. When word of the deed spread, Moses feared for his life and fled to nearby Midian. There he met and married Zipporah, daughter of Jethro, the priest of Midian. He settled down to a life of comfortable tranquillity as a shepherd in Midian—until his fateful encounter with God.

> Moses was keeping the flocks of his father-in-law Jethro, the priest of Midian; he led his flock beyond the wilderness, and came to Horeb, the mountain of God. There the angel of the LORD appeared to him in a flame of fire out of a bush; he looked, and the bush was all ablaze, yet it was not being burned up. Then Moses said, "I must turn aside and get a look at this great sight, and see why the bush is not burned up." When the LORD saw that he had turned aside to see, God called to him out of the bush, "Moses, Moses!" And he said, "Here I am." Then he said, "Do not come any closer! Take your shoes from off your feet, for the place on which you are standing is holy ground." He said further, "I am the God of your father, the God of Abraham, the God of Isaac, and the God of Jacob." And Moses hid his face, for he was afraid to look at God.
>
> Then the LORD said, "I have seen the misery of my people who are in Egypt; I have heard how they cry out on account of their taskmasters; yes, I know about their sufferings. So I have come down to save them from the Egyptians, and to take them up out of that land to a good and broad land, a land flowing with milk and honey, to the country of the Canaanites, the Hittites, the Amorites, the Perizzites, the Hivites, and the Jebusites. In short, the cry of the Israelites has come to me and I have also seen how the Egyptians are oppressing them. So come now, I wish to send you to Pharaoh to take my people, the Israelites, out of Egypt." But Moses said to God, "Who am I that I should go to Pharaoh and take the Israelites out of Egypt?" He said, "I will be with you; and this is the guarantee that I am the one who is sending you: after you have brought the people out of Egypt, you will worship God on this mountain."

But Moses said to God, "Suppose I do go to the Israelites and say to them, 'The God of your fathers has sent me to you,' then they will say to me, 'What is His name?' What can I say to them then?" Then God said to Moses, "I am who I am." He said: "This is what you will tell the Israelites, '*I am* has sent me to you.' " Then God said further to Moses, "This is what you will tell the Israelites, 'The LORD, the God of your ancestors, the God of Abraham, the God of Isaac, and the God of Jacob, has sent me to you': This is My name forever, by this shall I be known for all generations."

                                                                  Exod. 3:1–15

In order to understand this passage, it is well to remember that its God is not the God of later biblical times, the omnipresent, omniscient deity; instead, this is the God of Old (above, chapter 7). Such a God dwells (when He is in the world at all) in a specific spot, what the first sentence calls "Horeb, the mountain of God." Apparently, Moses has never been to this mountain before—it must have been in a somewhat remote area. That is why the passage starts off by explaining the special circumstances that led him to this mountain at this time: he had led his flock "beyond the wilderness," some greater distance than usual, presumably in search of a good grazing site.

At this point he sees an odd sight, a desert shrub that has caught fire and continues to burn and burn. The fact of the fire itself is not surprising—bushes (if indeed that is what it was)[22] are proverbially dry in the Bible, and, set off by a spark or by lightning, they catch fire easily (see, for example, Judg. 9:15). But usually they burn out just as quickly—their spindly little branches cannot support any long-lasting flame (Eccles. 7:5–6). In this case, however, Moses has apparently seen the smoke from afar, and, as he draws closer, he is surprised to see that the flames are still flickering. So he decides to turn from the path he is on and take a closer look, a step that brings him to within the area of God's presence. The burning bush, in other words, was just a divine stratagem, a sort of "Yoo-hoo! Over here!" to bring Moses to that precise place. Once God sees that Moses is there, He can address him directly and tell him what is really happening. "Take off your shoes; this is holy ground," He says—in other words, you are not just anywhere anymore, Moses; you have entered My spot.

In keeping with what was said in chapter 7, it is interesting to note how the "angel of the LORD" slides effortlessly here into being simply "the LORD" in a matter of two sentences. At first, Moses is still in ordinary reality, but then, in a twinkling, he is in the midst of the extraordinary—and he is afraid. God then tells him, in the long and complicated middle paragraph above, how He wants Moses to go back to Egypt and take the Israelites from their suffering; but Moses is reluctant, despite God's assurances.[23] The text presents Moses as reluctant because, as we shall see, any ancient Israelite would expect him to be under the circumstances. When it comes to the

Bible's saying how a prophet became a prophet, the person's reluctance to take on the job is often mentioned; apparently, it was important for people to know that such a trusted figure had not been a self-promoter. This is true, as we shall see, of Samuel and Isaiah and Jeremiah, and it is true of Moses here: God tells him what He wants him to do, and Moses tries to say no. In fact, the exchange quoted above is just the beginning. Moses continues to defer and dither for the rest of the chapter, offering one excuse after another (including being "heavy of speech"), and God continues to insist. Finally, after much back-and-forth, Moses pleads: "O my Lord, just send someone else!" (Exod. 4:13).

In his initial casting about for an excuse, Moses hits upon the fact that he himself does not know the specific name of this God. God had introduced Himself by saying, "I am the God of your father, the God of Abraham, the God of Isaac, and the God of Jacob," but He had not said what His name was. Of course, Moses is curious about the name, but he is also playing for time; he is frightened, but also intrigued. Who *is* this God, and what is happening to me? So he presents his question not as a real question but as an objection: "If I tell the Israelites that You appeared to me, the first thing they will ask is: 'What was His name?' Since I do not know the answer to that, I cannot possibly accept this mission."

To this question God responds with a polite "None of your business": *I am who I am,* He says, and this is reminiscent of the answer that the angel gave to Jacob after their fight, "Why should you be asking my name?" (Gen. 32:29), and the answer that Manoah got from *his* angel, "Why should you be asking my name, since it is unknowable?" (Judg. 13:18). In this case, however (as almost every biblical commentator since ancient times has pointed out), God's refusal to answer—"I am who I am"—nevertheless contains a clue to the true answer anyway, since *I am* in Hebrew (*'ehyeh*) sounds something like God's name (YHWH). So, God tells Moses, you won't be far wrong if you tell the Israelites, " *'Ehyeh* has sent me to you." Moses is apparently still a bit confused, since, after a silence,[24] God then explains in the next sentence, "This is what you will tell the Israelites, 'The LORD [that is, YHWH] . . . has sent me to you.' " Moses thus does get the answer he is looking for, and eventually he even accepts the mission.

To say only this, however, is to miss something essential about this whole passage. After all, what it describes is nothing less than the moment when Moses' whole life changed. Up to this point, things had been going pretty well for him. True, he had had to flee his native Egypt, but now he was comfortably settled in Midian, married to the daughter of one of its most prominent citizens, with nothing more to do all day than take care of his father-in-law's substantial flocks. All the turmoil he had witnessed in Egypt was now far behind him; he was in new, far more tranquil surroundings. We do not know how old he was,[25] but presumably he was still a fairly young man, since this incident occurs just after his marriage and the birth of his sons (Exod. 2:21–22). So it is surely no accident that, when God summons him to return to Egypt, he answers the way he does: "Who am I that I should go to Pharaoh and take the Israelites out of Egypt?" *Who am I* is indeed the question of a still-young man, not at all sure of the course his life may take. And so, God answers him in kind: "You wish to know who you are? I will tell you: *I am.* 'I-am' is sending you to Egypt." Staring into the crackling flames, Moses suddenly has an answer to both the questions he asked, "Who am I?" and "Who are You?"—and in that glimmering moment, the two answers seem to have come together.

One might at this point take a step backward and consider *how* the Bible is telling its story. Clearly, this account of Moses and the burning bush is not what we have seen numerous times in the book of Genesis, a *schematic narrative*. It could have been. If the whole point were simply to evoke the standard theme of a prophet's initial refusal of his mission, then this text could have simply said, "God told Moses to go to Egypt. Moses wept and pleaded and said, 'Send someone else,' but God insisted and said, 'No, but I will send you,' and so Moses went." Instead, the narrative is apparently interested in taking its time and telling a more complicated story, inviting us, as it were, to participate in it and appreciate the full weight of this moment. But why? Or, to ask the modern scholar's question: Who is writing this, and for what purpose? Does the text say what it says because, at this stage of things, telling a story is no longer a matter of relating "just the facts, ma'am"? Or was there something special, something particularly deserving of weight, in this particular moment of the story?

Philo at the Burning Bush

For the most part, we have looked at ancient interpreters to see how different their approach to the biblical text is from that of modern interpreters, as well as to show how they reckoned with one or another problem they perceived in the text. But this is hardly all there is to say about ancient interpreters. Here is how Philo of Alexandria retells the same passage seen above:

> There was a bush, a thorny, puny sort of plant, which, without anyone setting it on fire, suddenly started burning and, although spouting flames from its roots to the tips of its branches, as if it were a mighty fountain, it nonetheless remained unharmed. So it did not burn up, indeed, it appeared rather invulnerable; and it did not serve as fuel for the fire, but seemed to use the fire as *its* fuel. Toward the very center of the flames was a form of extraordinary beauty, which was like nothing seen with the eye, a likeness of divine appearance whose light flashed forth more brightly than the fire,

and which one might suppose to have been an image of the One Who Is [God]. But let it rather be called an angel [that is, a herald], for, with a silence more eloquent than any sound, it heralded by means of a sublime vision things that were to happen later on. For the bush was a symbol of those who suffer the flames of injustice, just as the fire symbolized those responsible for it; but that which burned did not burn up, and those who suffered injustice were not to be destroyed by their oppressors.

Philo, *Life of Moses* 1:65–67

In the biblical narrative, as noted above, the burning bush serves as a way of attracting Moses' attention and so bringing him to the very foot of the "mountain of God," where God can address him. For Philo, however, such an interpretation was impossible. As far as he knew, God is everywhere; what need was there for Him to lead Moses to one spot or another? But then, if that was so, what *was* the purpose of this burning bush? Why did not God speak to Moses back in his own house, or in a dream at night, and tell him what He wanted? And so, for Philo and other interpreters, the whole story of the burning bush had to assume a different character.

For this purpose, Philo has stacked the deck a bit. He says that the bush was a "puny sort of plant," though there is nothing in the Bible to suggest this. Such puniness might make one think that the fire would make short work of this bush, but Philo says (again, going beyond the biblical description) that the bush "remained unharmed" and "appeared . . . invulnerable," indeed, "seemed to use the fire as *its* fuel." He says all this not particularly to aggrandize the miraculous nature of the sight, but in order to turn it into a symbolic message: the bush symbolizes the people of Israel, and the fire their Egyptian overlords. The fact that the bush keeps burning thus symbolizes for Philo the message that the Israelites will survive despite their oppression; indeed, they will triumph. That is why Philo says that the bush spoke to Moses "with a silence more eloquent than any sound." According to Philo's interpretation of the passage, Moses walks up to the bush, stares at it in silence for a minute or two, and then says, "Oh I get it! You want me to go back to Egypt and free the Israelites."

It is interesting how Philo enlists a little "flaw" in the biblical text to the service of this interpretation. We noted above how the text started off by saying that the "angel of the LORD" appeared to Moses, but then, two sentences later, it is no longer an angel but God Himself. That was fine for the early biblical period, the time of the God of Old, but by Philo's day, an angel was altogether different from the infinite and omnipresent God. Under other circumstances, perhaps, Philo might have simply said the angel was speaking *on behalf of* God and, for that reason, the text stopped saying "angel of the LORD" after the first mention and simply referred thereafter to God Himself. But the word "angel" in Greek, *angelos,* also means "announcer" or "herald." Such a meaning suited perfectly Philo's symbolic understanding of the burning bush: it was a visual announcement, a heralding of the fact that the Israelites would withstand their oppressors. Therefore, instead of saying that "God" or "LORD" in the rest of the passage is really a shorthand for "angel of the LORD," Philo says the exact opposite: this was actually a direct meeting between God and Moses, and if the Bible says that Moses saw an *angel,* it does not mean angel in the conventional sense, but only that Moses saw a sight—a bush that burned but did not burn up—that *announced* what would be in the future.

The Name of the Lord

Before we leave Mount Horeb, a word about the divine name hinted at in God's "I am who I am." The origin of the divine name YHWH, and its connection to the verb "to be" in Hebrew (*hwh* or *hyh*) has long fascinated biblical interpreters.[26] One rabbinic tradition understood "I am who I am" as if addressing the future: *I will be with Israel in this time of trouble just as I will be with them in later difficulties* (not very reassuring!). When the Greek-speaking Jews of Alexandria translated the passage of Moses and the burning bush, they rendered God's words "I am who I am" as "I am the One who is," or, "I am the Being One." This is of course not what the text says, but it pleased Hellenistic Jews of Neoplatonic sensibilities to suggest that the very essence of this God is His connection with existence itself. For Philo this translation became, as it were, canonical: he frequently refers to God simply as "the One who is." It was true of others in the same period:

> All men who were ignorant of God were thus foolish by nature; they could not perceive the *One who is* from the good things that are visible.
>
> Wisd. 13:1

> I am the *One who is,* but you consider in your heart.
> I am robed with heaven, draped around with sea,
> The earth is the support of My feet, around My body is poured
> The air, the entire chorus of stars revolves around Me.
>
> *Sibylline Oracles* 1:137–40

> Grace to you and peace from *Him who is* and who was and who is to come.
>
> Rev. 1:4

This understanding has survived into modern times; many people believe that at the heart of the biblical idea of God is His connection with *being* itself.

However, a number of scholars have proposed other theories about the meaning of this divine name. One of the issues is connected with the way biblical Hebrew was written: vowels, especially in the middle of words, were often left unexpressed. Since the pronunciation of this name was considered sacred, even within biblical times there was a tendency to avoid saying it, or even to substitute another respectful word for it—which is how various words meaning "lord" came to be a substitute for this name, first in Hebrew (*adonai*), then Greek (*kurios*), Latin (*dominus*), and in other languages. When the name YHWH itself was the subject of discussion, it was sometimes called in Greek the Tetragrammaton (four-letter name) rather than said or spelled out, and scholars still use this word today.

After a while, since Jews had ceased to pronounce the name in Hebrew, the vowels that go between the consonants were no longer known—and that, of course, has something to do with our ignorance today of what the name might mean (if anything). On the basis of bits of evidence from here and there, many modern scholars have concluded that the original pronunciation of God's name must have been something like *yah-weh*—but this is not absolutely certain; besides, there are indications that an apocopated (shortened) form of the name was sometimes used, perhaps as a way of avoiding full pronunciation, perhaps not. In any case, if scholars are right in their restoration of the original vowels, then the name might seem to be in the causal form of the verb "to be," that is, "He causes to be" (although the causative form of this verb appears nowhere else in the Bible). This too has a kind of Neoplatonic ring, and that leaves some scholars skeptical: it is difficult to understand how a deity such as the God of Old—who was not specifically associated in the earliest stages with causing all things to be—could have received such an appellation, though it is certainly not impossible. One contemporary scholar, Frank M. Cross, has connected the origin of this name with a fuller title that sometimes appears in the Bible, *YHWH Seba'ot* (usually translated as "the LORD of Hosts"). "Hosts" here means the hosts (or armies) of heaven, that is, the stars (sometimes identified as deities themselves). This full name would thus mean "He brings the armies of heaven into being," suggesting that this deity is responsible for the creation of all other gods.[27] However, this is highly speculative and lacking in solid evidence.

But perhaps the most striking thing about the name YHWH for modern scholars is connected to the passage just examined, Moses' dialogue with God at the burning bush. According to what Moses says there, he apparently does not know God's name—otherwise, why would he ask? Of course, one might suppose that long years of life in Egypt had caused all the Israelites to forget the name of their old deity; alternately, it might be that His name had heretofore been a divine secret, just like the names of the angels who appeared to Jacob and Manoah. Modern scholars, however, point to the fact that the burning bush episode seems to be the work of the text source designated E, a source that, up until this point, had been careful never to use the name YHWH. Behind these E texts, scholars believe, was a tradition to the effect that, before the time of Moses, the name YHWH was not known. Something similar appears a bit later, in a passage attributed to the source P. There God says to Moses, "I am YHWH. I appeared to Abraham, Isaac, and Jacob as *El Shaddai* [sometimes rendered as 'God Almighty'], but I was not known to them by my name YHWH" (Exod. 6:2–3). Both sources thus seem to agree that God's name somehow changed at the time of Moses (in contrast to texts from the J source, which use the name YHWH to refer to God long before the time of Moses—for example, in the story of Cain and Abel or in the J version of the flood story).

But why would God's name suddenly change? Some scholars have suggested that the text is not talking just about a new name, but about an entirely new deity. After all, Moses is in Midian at the time that he encounters this God, in a place called, appropriately, "the mountain of God" (or possibly, "the mountain of the gods"). If this was Israel's longtime God, "the God of Abraham, Isaac, and Jacob," what was He doing stationed at what seems to be His permanent home *in Midian*? Midian was, like its neighbor Edom, to the south and east of biblical Israel, a rugged land populated by rough-and-tumble desert nomads. Israel's God, the God of Abraham, Isaac, and Jacob, ought to be somewhere to the north and west, in the land of Canaan proper. (It should be remembered that we are talking about the God of Old, who is *not* everywhere all at once. A deity that can promise the land of Canaan to Abraham ought to be the deity *of that land*, and the "mountain of God" on which He dwells ought likewise to be there and not in Midian.) Thus, despite the text's insistence that YHWH is none other than "the God of Abraham, Isaac, and Jacob," some scholars nowadays entertain a different hypothesis: the God known as YHWH was not originally associated with the land of Canaan at all but arrived there only at a certain point, from elsewhere—specifically from the barren wastes of Edom and Midian, far to the south and east of the Israelite homeland (see Deut. 33:2; Judg. 5:4; and Hab. 3:3, 7, all of which suggest that YHWH came to Canaan from the southeast). The circumstances of this divine invasion remain to be seen a few chapters hence (and it must be conceded from the start that the evidence for this hypothesis is sparse and the scholarship rather speculative). If modern scholars are right, however, what the Bible seems to be saying here (perhaps in spite of itself) is that, at this moment on Mount Horeb, a new God walked into Israel's life, one who ultimately changed the world's thinking about divinity.

14

The Exodus

EXODUS 4:18–15:21

Moses Commanding the Return of the Red Sea
by Philip James de Loutherbourg.

GROOM AT THE INN. MIRACLES. THE TEN PLAGUES. SYMBOLISM
OF THE RED SEA. THE SONG OF MOSES AND MIRIAM.

*The story of the Israelites' struggle for freedom is studded with miracles—the
ten plagues that strike Egypt, the parting of the Red Sea, the Israelites' safe
passage through it, and the drowning of the Egyptian army. But how did it
really happen?*

No sooner had Moses accepted his mission to speak with the Egyptians on
behalf of the Israelites than he was almost killed. He and his family started on
the long journey back to Egypt when suddenly, God attacked Moses. It was
only the quick thinking of his wife Zipporah that saved him:

> On the way, at a place where they spent the night, the LORD met him
> [Moses] and tried to kill him. But Zipporah took a flint and cut off her
> son's foreskin, and touched his feet with it, and said, "Truly you are a bride-
> groom of blood to me!" So He let him alone. It was then she said a "bride-
> groom of blood" for circumcision.
>
> Exod. 4:24–26

This attack on Moses seems quite inexplicable. After all, God had just commissioned him to go back to Egypt, and now, without explaining why, the
text says that "the LORD met him and tried to kill him." Just as mysterious is
Zipporah's response: she hurriedly circumcises her son, then touches "his"
(apparently, Moses') feet with the bloody foreskin and declares, "Truly you
are a bridegroom of blood to me!" With that, the attack on Moses ceases.

Considering these facts, ancient interpreters sought to proceed logically. If
God had tried to kill Moses but then stopped after this bit of emergency surgery, it must be that it was some failure to circumcise the child earlier that
was the reason for the divine attack. In other words, Moses must, for some
reason or other, have delayed circumcising one or both of his sons in Midian,
and although God had selected him for an important mission, even Moses
was not spared the divine wrath for his negligence. Perhaps, then, the point
of this brief passage was to teach how important circumcision was: no one
was exempt from carrying out this divine commandment:

> Great indeed is [the commandment of] circumcision, for not the slightest
> delay was granted [even] to the righteous Moses in regard to it.
>
> Mishnah, *Nedarim* 3:11

Such an interpretation seemed not only warranted but appropriate; since Hellenistic times, Jews had in various periods been pressured to neglect the rite of circumcision. It was thus encouraging for religious authorities to find a biblical story that taught that even a slight delay in circumcising would meet with the sternest divine disapproval.

But why should Moses, a paragon of virtue and devotion, have delayed? Here interpreters' attention was directed to the fact that Zipporah's father was a pagan, indeed, a "priest of Midian" (Exod. 2:16). Surely, they reasoned, such a person, a worshiper of many gods, would not have gladly accepted the fact that his daughter was marrying someone who believed in the existence of one God alone—and the God of Israel at that! The father-in-law must therefore have insisted that Moses raise his children to worship his *father-in-law's* gods, bow down to *his* idols—or at least that his first grandchild be so raised:

> At the time that Moses had said to Jethro, "Give me Zipporah your daughter as a wife," Jethro said to him, "Accept this one condition that I will tell you and I will give her to you as a wife." He said: "What is it?" Jethro said to him: "The son that is born to you first will be given over to idolatry [and hence will not be circumcised]; those born thereafter can be given to the worship of [your] God." He accepted this condition . . . For that reason did the angel* seek to kill Moses at the inn, whereupon "Zipporah took a flint and cut the foreskin of her son."
>
> *Mekhilta deR. Ishmael, Jethro; Amalek*

According to this interpretation, it must have been all right for Moses to stick to this agreement while he was still under his father-in-law's watchful eye: he had no choice. But the minute that he and Zipporah were on their way out of Midian, there was no longer any reason for Moses to put off performing the circumcision. Yet apparently he had; he was already "on the way, at a place where they spent the night" (this phrase was actually understood by interpreters, in keeping with a later stage of Hebrew, as "on the way, *at the inn*"). Here thus were Moses and Zipporah, after at least one day of traveling, settling down for the night at some inn—and they still had not bothered to circumcise their one uncircumcised son. No wonder that God became impatient and dispatched his angel! Fortunately, the couple immediately understood what was wrong, and before Moses could be harmed, the circumcision was performed and all was set aright.[1]

---

* Here, in common with other ancient sources, it is not God who "tried to kill" Moses—since, if He had tried, He surely would have succeeded—but an angel.

"That Was When . . ."

For modern scholars, as usual, this same passage seems to have a rather different interpretation.[2] The key to understanding this episode, according to one theory, lies in the little Hebrew word 'az. Literally, 'az means "then," but often it should really be rendered as "that was when." What's the difference? "That was when" more clearly implies that the reader or listener has already heard something of the matter being discussed; the narrative comes to specify when exactly it was that this already-known thing took place or got started.[3] So, for example, Gen. 4:26 mentions the birth of Adam's grandson Enosh, adding that "that was when" humanity first began to be called by this name ('enosh is indeed a general term for humanity in biblical Hebrew).[4] Similarly, when a hymn like that of Exodus 15 is introduced (or the Song of the Well in Num. 21:17, or of Moses in Deuteronomy 32), the narrative says "that was when" this well-known song was first sung. So here too, the narrative says, "*That was when* [the expression] 'bridegroom of blood' was first used in connection with circumcision."

Why was it important for ancient Israelites to know the original context of the expression "bridegroom of blood"? The Torah is quite insistent that circumcision is to be performed *on infants,* indeed, on the eighth day after an infant's birth. But this was a specifically Israelite practice; anthropologists know that, in many cultures, circumcision is instead a rite of puberty, performed not long before (sometimes only a month or two) the boy is to be married.[5] Apparently, "bloody bridegroom" was a term in circulation at the time this episode was written—perhaps indeed, the Midianites or even some of Israel's own ancestors performed circumcision as a prenuptial rite[6] and referred to the newly circumcised young man as a "bloody bridegroom."

If so, then this little story is out to deny the potential implications of this expression, "bloody bridegroom." What it seeks to say is that one should *not* understand the use of this term to mean that it is proper to circumcise a boy in anticipation of his marriage (that is, at puberty or thereafter). No, the story contends; this term was originally coined to refer not to the circumcisee but to Moses, Zipporah's bridegroom, when she touched him with the bloody foreskin of their newborn son and so saved his life. (She apparently did so as an apotropaic act, to ward off evil—and it worked!) "*That was when* [the expression] 'bridegroom of blood' was first used in connection with circumcision," the story concludes. So this expression does not mean—and never did!—that future bridegrooms should be circumcised at puberty or a few months before the wedding.

Like so many *schematic narratives,* this one is short and utterly self-contained. Modern scholars believe that it may have circulated independently for some time. But later, they theorize, an editor or compiler of Moses' life story had to decide where to put it, and this was no easy task. Obviously, it had to take place after Moses was married and had become a father, but not long after (since he has to still be able to be referred to as a "bridegroom")—hence, sometime when he was in Midian, presumably just after his first son is born. The story could thus conceivably have been put right after the mention of Gershom's birth in Exod. 2:22. But that would have located it *before* Moses' long conversation with God at the burning bush, and such a location would have been quite awkward: the whole point of the story of the burning bush is that this is the first time that Moses had actually met the God YHWH, whereas the "bridegroom of blood" story has this same God meeting Moses face-to-face and trying to kill him. Therefore, scholars suppose, the editor in question decided to locate this episode just *after* the burning bush episode, adding, on his own initiative, that the incident occurred at some vague location "on the way, at a place where they spent the night." Inadvertently, however, this placement created a problem for later interpreters: why, if God had recently commissioned Moses to return to Egypt, did He now try to kill him just as he was performing that very task? Moreover (since ancient interpreters were not likely to think of circumcision as an apotropaic act but simply as a divine commandment), why should circumcising the child cause God to cease trying to kill Moses and "let him alone"? These considerations, as we have seen, brought ancient interpreters to an entirely different understanding of the story.

Miracles

Not long ago, I saw a book for sale that purported to tell what it called "the real story of the exodus." Written by an eminent British scientist, it provided logical explanations for the various biblical miracles involved, thus demonstrating, apparently, the veracity of the biblical account. I quote from a summary of the book's main points as listed on its back cover:

- *The Burning Bush:* Caused by a volcanic vent that opened up under the bush.
- *Crossing the Red Sea:* The water was pushed back by a very strong wind blowing all night. This is a known physical phenomenon called wind setdown. The details given in the Bible mean we can pinpoint where the Red Sea crossing occurred.
- *Drowning Pharaoh's Army:* When the very strong wind suddenly stopped blowing, the water rushed back in the form of a rapidly returning "bore" wave, sweeping Pharaoh's army into the sea.
- *Mount Sinai:* The real Mount Sinai is in present-day Arabia, not the Sinai Desert as is generally assumed.[7]

I suppose one ought to be sympathetic to such books, but I confess that whenever I start reading one (this was hardly the first),[8] I find that I myself am engulfed by "a rapidly returning 'bore' wave." Why is it that, when the Bible reports on something miraculous—something that, it is at pains to claim, was the result of God's direct intervention into our world, a changing of the natural order—there are always people who try to say, often explicitly in "defense" of the Bible, that what happened really has a perfectly logical explanation? The answer, obviously, is that such people don't believe in miracles. Instead, they hold that this world is a basically orderly place with its own immutable rules of operation, and that if something appears to have happened that contradicts those rules, then the people observing it must have simply failed to discern its real, natural cause, or they must have been the victim of some sort of mass delusion or clever trick or fata morgana. But if that is so, then there is a real problem here: If what the Israelites *perceived* as God's mighty intervention into human affairs was really just an unusual manifestation of the natural order, then is not their (and the Bible's) whole notion of God based on illusion? Isn't some notion of the miraculous necessary to the belief in a God who actually does things—answers prayers, speaks to prophets, and intervenes in human history?[9]

The point I wish ultimately to make, however, is that the realistic and totally unrealistic approaches to biblical miracles seem to have coexisted side by side since the time of the Bible itself.[10] Careful readers of chapters 14 and 15 of Exodus will observe that the Bible evidences two (in fact, as we shall see, perhaps three) different approaches to the splitting of the Red Sea. At first, God instructs Moses simply to "lift up your staff and stretch out your hand over the sea and divide it, so that the Israelites may enter the sea on dry ground" (Exod. 14:15). This sounds like it is going to be an altogether instantaneous, mind-mauling miracle. But later, after Moses does lift up his hand, the text adds: "The LORD drove the sea back by a strong east wind all night, and turned the sea into dry land; and the waters were divided. The Israelites went into the sea on dry ground" (Exod. 14:21–22). So what was it, a miracle or just a particularly strong, wind-induced low tide? And why, after both these options were, so to speak, on the table, should anyone opt for the utterly miraculous one? Yet—this is such an interesting point!—people did. Long after the book of Exodus was written, the book of Nehemiah summed up these same events without any mention of the strong east wind; it simply asserted, "You split the sea before them and they crossed over in the midst of the sea on dry ground" (Neh. 9:11). Indeed, later on in our same Exodus account, the pendulum seems to swing back to the miraculous side: "The Israelites walked on dry ground through the sea, and the water was like a wall for them, to their right and to their left" (Exod. 14:29). In other words, what might appear to be the more primitive, unrealistic approach was never successfully swept aside by the realists: both existed in parallel.

The same is true in postbiblical times. On the one hand, a rational fellow like the Greek-speaking author of the Wisdom of Solomon (late first century BCE) has this to say about Moses and the miracles of the Exodus:

> A holy people and blameless race
> Wisdom delivered from a nation of oppressors.
> She entered the soul of a servant of the Lord,
> and withstood dread kings with wonders and signs.
> She gave to holy people the reward of their labors;
> she guided them along a marvelous way,
> and became a shelter to them by day,
> and a starry flame through the night.
> She brought them over the Red Sea,
> and led them through deep waters;
> but she drowned their enemies,
> and cast them up from the depth of the sea.
>   Wisd. 10:15–19

Throughout the Wisdom of Solomon, God does very little; His desires on earth are generally carried out by a female figure called Wisdom (*Sophia*). She is a purposely ambiguous figure. At times she seems to be what scholars call a hypostasis of God, an actual being or entity, a sort of God-in-action-on-earth; at other times the author seems to be using this same word *sophia* as the common noun meaning ordinary human wisdom, of the sort said to be possessed by mothers and ex-presidents. So when he says above that Wisdom "entered the soul of a servant of the Lord," we are not sure if he is talking about God actually entering the soul of Moses (he is the "servant of the Lord" in question), or whether it simply means that Moses suddenly became wise.

One thing is clear, however: this sentence, which alludes to Moses' encounter with God on Mount Horeb, makes no mention of a miraculously burning bush or an angel speaking from its midst. Obviously, this author does not like miracles. So the ten plagues here are summed up in a single, throwaway phrase: Moses used "wonders and signs" to wear down Pharaoh's resistance. No detailing of blood, frogs, or killing of the firstborn—apparently, these vivid facts are purposely eschewed. As for the miraculous pillars of cloud and fire that guided the Israelites on their journey (Exod. 13:21–22), these turn out to be, in this author's phrasing, Wisdom herself, who "became a shelter to them by day, and a starry flame through the night." Again, this is ambiguous: it might mean that Wisdom-the-hypostasis physically sheltered the Israelites by day, or it might simply be that, protected by wisdom, the Israelites proceeded safely on their journey. But in the "*starry* flame" at the end of this sentence the author appears to have tipped his hand: he seems to be suggesting that there really was no pillar of fire at all, only the stars at night that enabled these travelers to navigate in the dark.[11]

At roughly the same period of time, other interpreters were pulling in the opposite direction. Here is another Greek-writing commentator on the burning bush:

> Moses prayed to God that the people might be delivered from their sufferings. While he was thus supplicating, fire suddenly appeared *up out of the ground . . .* and it burned, *although there was no firewood nor other wooden substance* in that place. Moses was frightened by what happened and he fled. But a divine voice told him to make war against Egypt and to save the Jews and lead them to their ancient homeland.
>
>   Artapanus, cited in Eusebius, *Praeparatio Evangelica* 9.27.21

The same tendency to aggrandize biblical miracles is at times apparent among rabbinic writers as well, who claimed that not one but "ten miracles were performed on Israel's behalf at the Sea"[12] or that, after the ten plagues inside Egypt, the Egyptians were afflicted with fifty more plagues at the Red Sea.[13] Indeed, one ancient tradition held that, at the moment when the sea divided, a fish happened to be swimming precisely along the dividing line: it too was split in half, with its head going with the waters on one side of dry land and its tail with the waters on the other.

The Ten Plagues

Once back in Egypt, Moses went before Pharaoh to demand that he release the Israelites. But Pharaoh refused and even increased the Israelites' labor, withholding straw for the brickmaking. Discouraged, Moses turned to God, who told him to perform the miraculous acts He had showed him on Mount Horeb. Accordingly, Moses and his brother Aaron returned to Pharaoh and Aaron cast his staff on the ground; it turned into a snake. Pharaoh's sorcerers did the same, and their staffs were also transformed into snakes, but Aaron's snake swallowed up the others. Still, Pharaoh was unimpressed and refused to let the people go.

As a consequence, God brought upon the Egyptians the ten plagues, a series of apparently miraculous events designed to cause Israel's oppressors suffering and misfortune. According to the Exodus account, Moses first lifted up his staff and the Nile was turned to blood, killing all the fish in it; then, frogs swarmed all over the land, infesting the Egyptians' houses; next, gnats or mosquitoes attacked the Egyptians, and after these, flies; a plague struck the Egyptians' livestock, and the Egyptians themselves were afflicted with boils on their bodies. A crushing hail then hit Egypt, striking people and livestock, trees and crops; following this, a plague of locusts arrived, devastating the remaining crops. Then a dense darkness fell on Egypt—but where the Israelites lived there was light. In the last plague, all the firstborn of the Egyptians were killed, from the firstborn of Pharaoh himself to the firstborn of the lowliest servant—but God passed over the houses of the Israelites and did not afflict them. At last Pharaoh relented and begged the Israelites to leave.

Seeking a natural explanation for these events as well, some people in the anti-miracles camp have suggested that Moses did not so much turn the Nile to blood (Exod. 7:17–20) as benefit from the multiplication of certain species of red algae in its waters, which gave the Nile a bloodlike appearance. The same choking algae then caused the water to be undrinkable and the fish in the Nile to die (Exod. 7:21). As a consequence, the frogs that normally live in the Nile were forced to abandon their habitat and seek shelter on dry land; some of them entered the houses of Egyptians, where *they* died (Exod. 8:1–6). The corpses of the dead frogs (Exod. 8:14) then brought on an infestation of gnats (Exod. 8:16–19) and swarms of flies (Exod. 8:20–24). And so forth.[14] All of this may please the sensibilities of some—but such a reconstruction is, of course, no more verifiable than the biblical account itself.[15]

More interesting to biblicists is the fact that the Bible itself is not particularly consistent with regard to the ten plagues. Apart from the Exodus account, the plagues are listed in two other places in the Bible, in Ps. 78:43–51 and 105:27–36. Psalm 78, however, fails to mention the third plague (*kinnim*, usually understood as lice or gnats), the sixth (boils), or the ninth (darkness), whereas Psalm 105 omits boils as well as the fifth plague, the pestilence on livestock. Moreover, both these psalms present the plagues in an order that is different from the plagues in the book of Exodus. It is difficult to know what to make of this; even postbiblical sources sometimes fail to list all the plagues or put them in the same order as Exodus.[16] Perhaps, scholars say, the differences between the Exodus account and these two psalms indicate that both are dependent on earlier, orally transmitted accounts that were committed to writing only somewhat later on—and somewhat inconsistently.[17]

How Did They Know the Words?

After the Egyptians were struck with the last plague and Pharaoh had given in, the Israelites set out at once to leave Egypt. No sooner had they departed, however, than Pharaoh had second thoughts. He dispatched his army to overtake the fleeing Israelites. The army caught up with them at the Red Sea,[18] trapping them at the water's edge—but then God miraculously divided the sea and the Israelites walked across on dry land. When the Egyptians tried to pursue them, the waters returned to their former state and the Egyptians drowned. Safe on the other side, the Israelites sang a great song of praise to God for saving them, the lengthy hymn now found in Exodus 15.

This hymn, sometimes known as the Song of the Sea, is justly famous and found an honored place in early Jewish and Christian liturgies. The most interesting exegetical problem that ancient interpreters found in the song began from what was, relatively speaking, a minor question. The song is introduced by the words "Then Moses and the Israelites sang this song . . ." Moses, of course, was a prophet, so there was hardly any wonder at his breaking spontaneously into song about events that had just then concluded: he was divinely inspired. But how could the other Israelites sing along with him—how did they know the words? One possibility was that they didn't: Moses sang the first line on his own, "I will sing of the LORD, how greatly He has triumphed—horse and rider He has cast into the sea," and then the Israelites simply repeated the last words as a refrain throughout the rest of the song.[19] (Alternately, they might have repeated the concluding words of each verse right after Moses had sung them.)

Another possibility occurred to ancient interpreters, however: not only Moses, but *all* the Israelites were divinely inspired at that moment, and thus all of them were able simultaneously, and in unison,[20] to sing the same song. The song, after all, is more than a hymn of thanksgiving for what had already happened. It also speaks prophetically of events to come, foreseeing the terrified reaction of other peoples as Israel marches through the wilderness, and even Israel's founding a "sanctuary of the LORD" in the land of Canaan after their arrival (verses 13–18). Surely, then, this was not so much an act of singing as a collective prophetic vision of the future (the only one recorded in the Bible).

Further support for this hypothesis came from the second line of the song, "This is my God and I will glorify Him, the God of my father and I will exalt Him" (Exod. 15:2). The word "this" (*zeh*) can be used in various ways in Hebrew; a modern scholar would say that here *zeh* means something like "such" in English—that is, the description in the previous line of a gloriously triumphant deity is altogether true, "such is indeed my God."[21] But *zeh* is also a demonstrative in Hebrew, and ancient interpreters preferred to understand it here in this demonstrative sense: the Israelites, having just been saved from mortal danger, actually caught sight at that moment of God's very being, shimmering right there in front of them. Then they all exclaimed, *"This* is my God." Such a direct vision of God indicated that each and every Israelite was at that moment like a prophet; indeed, it put them ahead of later prophets, who only heard God's words or saw figurative visions of Him:

Rabbi Eliezer said: [from the word *this* we know] that the lowliest servant-girl at the Red Sea perceived what the prophets Isaiah and Ezekiel had not.
Mekhilta deR. Ishmael, Shirtah 3

The same verse posed a further difficulty, however. Granted, the Israelites were actually like prophets at that moment and, seeing God, exclaimed, "This is my God and I will glorify Him." But how could they know that this God appearing before them at that moment was the same God who had appeared to Abraham, Isaac, and Jacob—that is, how could they utter the second half of this verse, ". . . the God of my father and I will exalt Him"? Surely the God they saw carried no sign identifying Himself as the God of Abraham, Isaac, and Jacob! Considering the problem, ancient interpreters came up with an ingenious solution: the two halves of this verse were not necessarily sung by the same people. The Israelite fathers could have sung, "This is my God and I will glorify Him"; then, hearing their fathers utter these words, the children might have chimed in, "the God of my father and I will exalt Him":

> They sang hymns, O Lord, to Your holy name, and praised with one accord Your defending hand; because Wisdom opened the mouth of the dumb,[22] and *made the tongues of babes speak clearly.*
>
> Wisd. 10:20–21

> Said R. Yose the Galilean: when Israel came up from the Sea and saw their enemies were now corpses stretched out on the shore, they all praised God. Even the newborn on his mother's knees and the suckling at his mother's breast . . . sang forth and said, "This is my God and I will praise Him [my father's God and I will exalt Him]."
>
> *Tosefta Sotah 6:4*

The Song of the Sea

This same hymn has attracted the attention of modern scholars, but for a different reason. Its style, vocabulary, morphology, and orthography all indicate that it is in a very old form of Hebrew. For example, scholars have established that none of the Semitic languages originally had a definite article (corresponding to "the" in English). Like Russian today or classical Latin, ancient Semitic tongues simply did without one for a while; later, however, most developed some way of indicating definiteness, the prefix *ha-* in Hebrew or *al-* in Arabic, the suffixes *-a'* and *-ta'* in Aramaic, and so forth.[23] In most parts of the Bible, the prefix *ha-* is found in abundance; in this song, however, it is not found even once.[24] That—along with a host of apparently ancient morphological and lexical features—would indicate to modern scholars that it has been preserved from a very early stage of the Hebrew language and thus may be one of the oldest parts of the Bible.[25]

Two of W. F. Albright's students, Frank M. Cross and David N. Freedman, noticed an interesting thing about this hymn: it never mentions the sea being split apart.[26] The closest it comes is in two verses toward the beginning of the song:

> In the greatness of Your majesty You overthrew Your adversaries;
> You unleashed your fury, it consumed them like stubble.
> At the blast of Your nostrils the waters piled up, the floods stood up in a
>   heap; the deeps congealed in the heart of the sea.

Exod. 15:6–7

If you read these verses in the light of the surrounding narrative, they certainly appear to be talking about the same act of splitting the sea that is described in Exodus 14: "the waters piled up," "the floods stood up in a heap." However, Cross and Freedman argued, if you imagine for a minute that the account in Exodus 14 is actually a later text and then try to read this one on its own terms, no mention of the sea being divided or the Israelites walking on dry land will be found. Indeed, the passage just cited would seem instead to be talking about some great storm at sea. Presumably, the Egyptian soldiers, loaded onto boats or barges, had been in hot pursuit of the Israelites—but then suddenly the wind picked up: "At the blast of Your nostrils the waters piled up, the floods stood up in a heap; the deeps congealed in the heart of the sea."[27] Particularly revealing is this last phrase, "the heart of the sea," since it usually indicates a spot somewhere out in the midst of deep waters, far offshore.

It is no accident, according to this same way of understanding, that these lines occur where they do. Just before them, the song says, "In the greatness of Your majesty You overthrew Your adversaries; You unleashed Your fury, it consumed them like stubble." The song then goes on to tell *how* that was done: "At the blast of Your nostrils the waters piled up. . . ." Far from being a description of what saved the Israelites and allowed them to cross the sea on dry land, Cross and Freedman observed, these words describe what finished the Egyptians off. As a matter of fact, we are never really told in the song where the Israelites were when the Egyptians were drowned or how they got there. Apparently, however, there was nothing miraculous involved, *or else it would surely be mentioned;* the sole miracle described here is the drowning of the Egyptians. Other elements in the song seemed to the young scholars to point in the same direction. Thus, the Egyptians are described as going "down into the depths like a stone" (Exod. 15:5) and sinking "like lead in the mighty waters" (15:10). But if the Egyptians had been pursuing the Israelites on a dry path in the midst of the waters, then there was nowhere for them to "go down" and "sink" to—they were already walking on the bottom of the seabed.

How did these conflicting accounts come to be created? Cross and Freedman theorized that the narrative account in Exodus 14 is actually based on a misunderstanding of the (much older) hymn in Exodus 15. After all, someone in the pro-miracles camp would have no difficulty in reading a line like "At the blast of Your nostrils the waters piled up, the floods stood up in a heap" and imagining that it was talking about *walls* of water being held in place by the mighty gusts of God's own breath. With the water piled up in that way, the Israelites were free to walk right next to this watery "heap" and stay quite dry. Under such circumstances, it is not hard to imagine what the pursuing Egyptian army would do: seeing the walls of water, they would naturally follow the Israelites into this miraculous patch of dry land and continue their pursuit. How could they know that it would all collapse as soon as the last Israelite was safely on the other side?

Cross elsewhere[28] noted another brief reference to these same events in the book of Joshua, one that has some links to (while apparently being independent of) the hymn of Exodus 15:

> When I brought your fathers out of Egypt, you came to the sea; and the Egyptians pursued your fathers with chariots and horsemen to the Red Sea. When they cried out to the LORD, He put darkness between you and the Egyptians, and made the sea come over them and cover them; and your eyes saw what I did to Egypt. Afterwards you lived in the wilderness a long time.
>
> Josh. 24:6–7

Note that here too, there is no mention of the sea splitting, nothing at all miraculous about the Israelites' own crossing of the sea (if they crossed at all!); the whole miracle consists of the fortuitous arrival of darkness, under cover of which the Israelites presumably made their escape, and then the sea's "coming over" the Egyptians and drowning them. This reference may indeed constitute something like the "missing link" between Exodus 15 and 14.

A Clue about Composition

In one sense, as modern scholars see it, the song in Exodus 15 is actually *later* than the surrounding narrative. That is, many scholars believe that, while it was composed long before, the song itself was inserted into our current text only after the prose account had already been written. This is hardly a rare phenomenon in the Bible: for various reasons, scholars have argued that many songs found amidst prose narratives were later insertions—the Song of Deborah in Judges 5, Hannah's hymn in 1 Samuel 2, David's song in 2 Samuel 22, and Jonah's prayer from the belly of the whale are commonly cited examples.[29] So, too, with the Song of the Sea. Indeed, although the text begins by asserting that "then [*or rather*, that was when] Moses and the Israelites sang," like many inserted songs, this one, scholars say, really does not fit the historical context to which it was assigned. The reason is that (as already noted) after describing the miraculous drowning of the Egyptians, the song goes on to speak of later events:

> In Your love You led the people whom You redeemed; You guided them
>   by your strength to Your holy abode.
> When the peoples heard, they were panicked; trembling seized the
>   inhabitants of Philistia.
> Then the chiefs of Edom were dismayed; fear shook the leaders of Moab;
>   all the inhabitants of Canaan were aghast.
> Terror and dread fell upon them; by the might of Your arm, they became
>   still as a stone—
> Till Your people, O LORD, passed through, till the people whom You
>   ransomed passed through.
> You brought them in and planted them at the mountain of Your territory,
>   the place, O LORD, that You made Your abode,
> The sanctuary, O LORD, that Your hands established.
> The LORD will reign forever and ever.
>
> Exod. 15:13–18

All the events in this latter part of the song take place after the Egyptians have drowned. The Philistines and Edomites and Moabites could hardly have known anything about the Israelites at the time they were supposed to be singing this song. It was only long after, when the Israelites were actually crossing through these other peoples' lands on their way to Canaan, that the nations might be said to "tremble" and be "aghast" at the Israelites. Indeed, the song refers to an even later event, God's settling the Israelites "at the mountain of Your territory," that is, at some "sanctuary, O LORD, that Your hands have established." Cross and Freedman thus theorized that this song was originally a hymn connected to a particular temple somewhere in ancient Israel (there were several) and that it had been intended to be sung at the occasion of a festival, perhaps that of Passover (which celebrates the exodus) and/or that of the particular sanctuary's founding.[30] It was thus an altogether independent text to start with. Since, however, to a later way of thinking, the Israelites were obliged to offer *some* words of thanksgiving to God after being saved, the hymn was eventually inserted where it was: *that was when*, the introductory line says, this well-known hymn was first sung, as a way of thanking God.

But if the insertion was done at a relatively late point, that hardly means that this was the first point of contact between the song and the prose narrative. In Cross and Freedman's reconstruction, the very idea that the sea split in two and formed a wall of water on either side of the dry land may have been suggested by the ambiguous phrasing of "at the blast of Your nostrils the waters piled up, the floods stood up in a heap." If this is correct, then it would seem to indicate that this hymn had provided the raw material out of which the prose narrative was later shaped. People heard the song and misunderstood it: thus were born the walls of water and the dry path through the sea. If so, this would not be the only such case of alleged misprision: as we shall see, scholars have found the same to be true of the Song of Deborah (Judges 5), which provided the basis for the (somewhat different) prose narrative in the chapter that precedes that song.

To modern scholars, the comparison of parallel prose (chapter 14) and poetic (chapter 15) accounts has suggested a more general conclusion about the prose narratives of the Pentateuch and other historical parts of the Bible. They were not (or not all of them) simply written down on the basis of vague, orally transmitted traditions. Instead, some were prose rewritings of an ancient cycle of songs, an anthology that may have been put together in David's time, perhaps even a lengthy poetic epic. This theory is difficult to assess, since it depends on a wholly unverifiable hypothesis, and one that is redolent of ideas about the priority of poetry to prose that are part of the baggage of German Romanticism of the nineteenth century. But it does have in its favor the evidence from ancient Israel's northern neighbor Ugarit, whose clay tablets preserve a large quantity of narrative material written in poetic style (and no historical narratives in prose). What is more, the Bible itself refers to various now-lost historical sources, including the *Book of the Wars of the Lord* (Num. 21:14) and *The Book of Yashar** (2 Sam. 1:18). Perhaps, scholars say, these lost books contained hymns such as that of Exodus 15, hymns that had been assembled from here and there for the purpose of uniting the northern and southern parts of David's kingdom. After that kingdom split in two, the theory goes, this same national songbook served as the raw material for two different prose rewritings of early Israelite history, one in the north and the other in the south—namely, the collections of texts known as J and E.[31]

Piecing It All Together

What, then, do modern historians make of the various matters discussed in the present and the previous chapter? Can they be pieced together into some plausible historical event? About this there is no general agreement. Some scholars still feel the whole story of the exodus is an invention—but, for reasons already discussed (the improbability of anyone making up such a

---

* Or, according to the variant reading of the Old Greek translation of the Bible, *The Book of Song* (that is, not *y-sh-r,* but *sh-y-r*).

national myth, the presence of authenticating names and other details here and there), many others reject this idea. To them it seems more likely that there is a kernel of historical truth in the exodus account. It may be that the story was originally much more localized and involved far fewer people—perhaps only a small band of escapees from Egyptian servitude. Scholars have long noted that the exodus theme is especially prominent in northern (non-Judahite) texts. For that reason, some have supposed that the whole exodus tradition was originally found only among some of the northern tribes, most likely, the Rachel tribes of Ephraim and Manasseh. After David succeeded in uniting the twelve tribes under one flag, this formerly local bit of history would have become part of the common heritage of all tribes.[32]

Certainly such a turn of events would not be unparalleled. After all, Americans of my generation were taught in school about "our Pilgrim fathers" who came over on the *Mayflower* or "our Founding Fathers," the signers of the Declaration of Independence and drafters of the Constitution—whereas the overwhelming majority of Americans could hardly be said to be descended from this idealized ancestor group. Perhaps the American analogy is apposite to the biblical case in an even more exact sense, since even back in the seventeenth and eighteenth centuries, only a small portion of the population of the thirteen colonies might ever have been described as Pilgrims or Puritans; certainly many of those who settled in the south did so principally for material reasons that had little to do with religion, and this was true of quite a few northerners as well. Yet schoolchildren today are regularly taught that "freedom to worship as they pleased" was a main motivation in the colonies' founding. It is not hard to imagine, scholars say, that a similarly pious theme—God's miraculous intervention to save the Israelites from Egyptian slavery—came to be transferred from the experience of a few to the foundation myth of an entire nation.

15

A Covenant with God

EXODUS 17–20

Moses, Aaron, and Hur
miniature from Hebrew Pentateuch
before 1300, artist unknown.

UPRAISED ARMS AT REPHIDIM. MANNA AND THE TRAVELING WELL.
AN AGREEMENT WITH GOD. HITTITE TREATIES.

*From Egypt the Israelites made their way to Mount Sinai, where God made
a solemn pact with them. But why did He do it the way that He did?*

After the Israelites had crossed the Red Sea to safety, they began the long trek
toward their promised homeland, Canaan. God preceded them, as before, in
a pillar of cloud that sheltered them during the day, and in a pillar of fire at
night that lit their way—allowing them to travel both day and night (Exod.
13:21–22). Despite this divine presence, however, they ran into trouble
almost immediately. At a place called Rephidim, they were attacked by the
forces of the Amalekites, a desert-dwelling people.

> Then Amalek came and fought against Israel at Rephidim. Moses said to
> Joshua, "Choose some men for us and go out and fight against Amalek
> tomorrow. I will stand on the top of the hill with the staff of God in my
> hand." So Joshua did as Moses told him and fought against Amalek, while
> Moses, Aaron, and Hur went up to the top of the hill. Whenever Moses
> held up his hands, Israel prevailed; but whenever he lowered his hands,
> Amalek prevailed. Now Moses' hands grew weary; so they took a stone
> and put it under him, and he sat on it. Aaron and Hur held up his hands,
> one on one side and the other on the other side; so his hands were steady
> until the sun set. Thus Joshua defeated Amalek and his people with the
> sword.
>
> Exod. 17:8–13

This incident is quite puzzling; in fact, it seems potentially blasphemous. It
implies that Moses' hands had some sort of magical power. But most ancient
interpreters could not believe the Bible was suggesting that this had indeed
been magic (and that it had worked!). Elsewhere in the Pentateuch, working
magic is strictly forbidden. On reflection, it seemed far more likely that
Moses' upraised hands were meant to communicate some symbolic message:

> [Moses' hands] became by turns very light and very heavy, and whenever
> they were in the former condition and rose aloft, [Israel] was strong and
> distinguished itself by its valor; but whenever his hands were weighed
> down, the enemy prevailed. Thus, by symbols, God showed that the earth
> and the lowest regions of the universe were the portion assigned to the one
> party, and the ethereal, the holiest region, to the other; and that, just as

heaven holds kingship in the universe and is superior to earth, so this nation would be victorious over its opponents in war.

Philo, *Moses* 1:217

But did Moses' hands actually make Israel win, and was it they that crushed Amalek? Rather [this text means that] when Moses lifted his hands toward heaven, Israel would look upon him and put their trust in Him who ordered Moses to do so; then God would perform miracles and wonders for them.

Mekhilta deR. Ishmael, Amaleq 1
(see also m. *Rosh ha-Shanah* 3:5)

And it happened that, whenever Moses would raise his hands in prayer, the Israelites would prevail and be victorious, but when he would withhold his hands from prayer, the Amalekites prevailed.

Targum Neophyti Exod. 17:11

The same general approach to this passage was passed on to Christian interpreters, but they soon saw in Moses' upraised hands another sort of symbolic message:

The Spirit, speaking to the heart of Moses, [tells him] to make a representation of the cross and of him who was to suffer upon it. . . . So Moses . . . kept stretching out his hands, and Israel again began to be victorious; then, whenever he let them drop, they began to perish. Why? So that they might know that they cannot be saved if they do not hope in Him.

Letter of Barnabas 12:2–3

Moses prefigured him [Christ], stretching out his holy arms,
Conquering Amalek by faith so that the people might know
That he is elect and precious with God his father.

Sibylline Oracles 8:251–53

For early Christians this brief incident became particularly significant, since it was a striking demonstration that, as the Latin saying had it, *quod in vetere latet in novo patet* (what is hidden in the Old [Testament] is made explicit in the New). As they saw it, Moses' hands in the form of the cross were only part of the hidden message. Surely it was not without significance that Moses himself stood to the side while his heretofore unmentioned assistant, Joshua, actually led the battle. The name Joshua in its Greek form is Jesus. Any early Christian who read the Bible in Greek simply knew that there were two biblical figures named Jesus, one in the Old Testament and one in the New. To the typologically minded, there could thus scarcely be any doubt that the Old

Testament Jesus, taking Moses' place in the lead, was a foreshadowing of the one in the New whose religion would replace that of Moses—*quod in vetere latet in novo patet*. What is more, Amalek scarcely seemed like an ordinary, human enemy. If he were, why should God, here and later on, single him out as Israel's archenemy, commanding Israel to "blot out the name of Amalek from off the earth—do not forget!" (Deut. 25:19)? Amalek, Christians concluded, must symbolize the devil. Thus the fact that this Old Testament Jesus made his first appearance here, fighting the devil, while Moses stood to the side and made the sign of the cross, virtually clinched the case:

> Wherever the Lord fought against the devil [that is, Amalek], the form of the cross was necessary—the cross by which Jesus was to win victory.
>
> Tertullian, *Against Marcion* 3:18

The question typically asked by modern scholars—why was this story told?—receives, as so often, an etiological answer in the case of this episode. The name of the place where the battle took place, Rephidim, sounds as if it might be derived from the Hebrew root *r-p-d*, which means both "spread out" and "prop up." What is more, when this place-name itself is uttered, it sounds a bit like the short phrase *raphu yadayim*, "the hands grew weak." To scholars this suggests that, just as in the case of Jacob's struggle with the angel at the Jabbok ford, a number of word associations have come together here to create the narrative: Moses *spread out* his hands, but then *the hands grew weak*, so then Aaron and Hur had to *prop them up*. The actual site of Rephidim is unknown today, but scholars speculate that there probably was a hill there with a large stone on it—a stone that gave rise to the element of Moses *sitting* as he watched the battle.[1]

No Water, No Food

Setting out into the wilderness, the Israelites' main worry was food and water—both scarce in the rugged terrain. The Bible recounts that, during their forty years of wandering, the Israelites received a regular supply of a special food called *manna*:

> Then the LORD said to Moses, "I am going to rain bread from heaven for you, and each day the people shall go out and gather enough for that day . . ."
>
> In the morning there was a layer of dew around the camp. When the layer of dew lifted, there on the surface of the wilderness was a fine flaky substance, as fine as frost on the ground. When the Israelites saw it, they said to one another, "What is it? [*man hu'*, suggesting the name *manna*]."

They did not know what it was. Moses said to them, "This is the food that the LORD has given you to eat."

The house of Israel called it manna; it was like coriander seed, white, and the taste of it was like wafers made with honey . . . The Israelites ate manna forty years, until they came to a habitable land; they ate manna, until they came to the border of the land of Canaan.

Exod. 16:4, 13–15, 31, 35

Most modern scholars do not doubt that this description corresponds to something in the natural world. Some have identified manna with an edible substance used by today's desert Bedouin as a sweetener: this wilderness "honeydew" is excreted by insects and plant lice after ingesting the sap of tamarisk trees. But for ancient interpreters, manna was altogether miraculous: its supernatural quality was confirmed by the fact that it came in a double portion on Fridays, obviating the need to collect manna on the sabbath (Exod. 16:22–26). It thus became, for both Christians and Jews, one of the principal elements in the Exodus narrative, lovingly embellished in ancient retellings of the story.[2]

Water was no less of a challenge. From the time they left Egypt, the Israelites found drinking water in short supply, and almost immediately God had to intervene to provide miraculously for their needs (Exod. 15:22–25). Then, at Rephidim (before the Amalekite attack), the people found themselves without water a second time:

They camped at Rephidim, but there was no water for the people to drink. The people quarreled with Moses, and said, "Give us water to drink." Moses said to them, "Do not quarrel with me, and do not test the LORD!" But the people thirsted there for water; and the people complained against Moses and said, "Why did you bring us out of Egypt, to kill us and our children and livestock with thirst?" So Moses cried out to the LORD, "What shall I do with this people? Any more and they will stone me!" The LORD said to Moses, "Pass in front of the people and take some of the elders of Israel with you; and when you go, take in your hand the staff with which you struck the Nile. I will be standing there in front of you on the rock at Horeb. Then you will strike the rock, and water will come out of it, so that the people may drink." Moses did so, in the sight of the elders of Israel. *The place was then called Massah* ["test"] *and Meribah* ["quarrel"], because the Israelites quarreled and tested the LORD, saying, "Is the LORD among us or not?"

Exod. 17:1–7

This was certainly an extraordinary happening—causing water to flow forth from a rock—but, as it turned out, it was not an entirely unique occurrence.

Sometime later (the Bible does not say when, but arguably toward the end of the Israelites' forty years of wandering), the people come to a new place, Kadesh, and something rather similar happens:

> Now there was no water for the congregation; so they complained against Moses and against Aaron. The people quarreled with Moses and said, "Would that we had died when our kindred died before the LORD! Why have you brought the assembly of the LORD into this wilderness for us and our livestock to die here? Why have you brought us up out of Egypt, to bring us to this wretched place? This is not the place of grain and figs and vines and pomegranates [you told us about]; there is not even any water to drink!" Then Moses and Aaron went away from the assembly to the entrance of the tent of meeting and they fell on their faces; then the glory of the LORD appeared to them.
>
> The LORD spoke to Moses, saying: Take the staff, and assemble the congregation, you and your brother Aaron, and command the rock before their eyes to yield its water. Thus you shall bring water out of the rock for them and provide drink for the congregation and their livestock.
>
> So Moses took the staff from before the LORD, as He had commanded him. Moses and Aaron gathered the assembly together before the rock, and he said to them, "Listen, you rebels, shall we bring water for you out of this rock?" Then Moses lifted up his hand and struck the rock twice with his staff; water came out abundantly, and the congregation and their livestock drank . . . These are the waters of Meribah ["quarrel"], because the people of Israel quarreled with the LORD, and then He showed his holiness by means of them [the waters].
>
> Num. 20:2–13

At first glance this might simply appear to be a second occurrence of the same sort of miracle; again there was a rock handy, and again Moses was ordered to extract water from it. If a similar miracle occurred twice, that was apparently because the same set of circumstances (the people complaining about the lack of water) had come up again. But if so, why did Scripture now say that "these are the waters of Meribah"; weren't the waters of Meribah back in Rephidim, many miles to the west? Interpreters noticed another thing as well: from the time when Moses had struck the rock at Rephidim, in the book of Exodus, to this moment at Kadesh, in the book of Numbers, there had not been a word about the Israelites lacking water. At the same time, Scripture did not report on their reaching any new oasis or digging any new wells.

Rock Around the Flock

The more interpreters considered the matter, the more what must at first have seemed an unlikely explanation now recommended itself. If, in the time that separated the incidents at Rephidim and Kadesh, the Israelites had not lacked for water—neither they nor their considerable livestock—it must have been that they continued to have their needs supplied by that very same rock that Moses had struck. *This* was their source of drinking water for a full forty years. And if Scripture said that the "waters of Meribah," which had been located at Rephidim, were now found at Kadesh, that must mean that the rock that provided those waters had somehow moved (or been transported) from Rephidim to their present location, so as to be constantly in proximity of the Israelites and their flocks.

Thus was born the tradition of the traveling rock that followed Israel in its desert wanderings for forty years:

> Now He led His people out into the wilderness; for forty years He rained down for them bread from heaven [manna], and brought quail to them from the sea, and brought forth a well of water to follow them.
>
> And it [the water] followed them in the wilderness forty years and went up to the mountains with them and went down into the plains.
>
> Pseudo-Philo, *Book of Biblical Antiquities* 10:7; 11:15

> I want you to know, brethren, that our fathers were all under the cloud, and all passed through the sea, and all . . . drank the same spiritual drink. For they drank from the supernatural Rock which followed them, and the rock was Christ.
>
> 1 Cor. 10:1–4

> And so, the well that was with Israel in the desert was like a rock the size of a large container, gushing upwards as if from a narrow-neck flask, going up with them to the mountains and going down with them to the valleys.
>
> *Tosefta Sukkah* 3:11

Interpreters noticed another thing about this traveling rock. Its waters seem to have given out right after the death of Miriam, Moses' sister (Num. 20:1); the very next verse begins the account of the lack of water seen above (Num. 20:2), and this shortage apparently occurred again (Num. 20:19) and again (Num. 21:5). *Post hoc propter hoc:* it seemed from the juxtaposition of Miriam's death and the suddenly renewed water shortage that the rock had yielded its abundant supply of water only thanks to Miriam. When she died, the waters stopped. This traveling rock thus came to be known to some ancient interpreters as "the well of Miriam." It was Miriam's virtuous nature, interpreters reasoned, that had caused God to give the Israelites the traveling rock in the first place—a rock went far toward explaining how the Israelites managed to survive all those years in the barren wastes.

Modern scholars have no such recourse to a theoretically mobile rock, however. They note that, while the account of Moses striking the rock at Rephidim occurs in a section of the book of Exodus attributed to either J or E, the similar narrative in Numbers that locates the event at Kadesh is attributed to the source known as P. It would thus appear to scholars that this is another *narrative doublet,* comparable to the two versions of the flood story, attributed to J and P, or the two accounts of how Jacob's name came to be changed to Israel, attributed to E and P. Here again, it would seem, a similar story was known to these two different sources, but in slightly different versions—E's was associated with one geographic location and P's with another.[3] In the final editing of the Pentateuch, scholars say, both versions were allowed to survive; perhaps the fact that one came in the middle of Exodus while the other occurred two books later was enough to allow them to coexist in harmony . . . until the ancient interpreters came along. They were the ones who noticed that the "waters of Meribah" were said to be located in two different places, Rephidim and Kadesh—and then came up with the explanation we have seen.

The Covenant at Mount Sinai

After a period of wandering about, the Israelites at last reached the wilderness of Sinai, the same place where God had first revealed Himself to Moses. (The mountain there is known in the Bible both as Mount Sinai and Mount Horeb.)[4] Now God called out to Moses from the mountain once again and told him to transmit to the Israelites a surprising offer:

> On the [day that] the third new moon [appeared] after the Israelites had gone out of the land of Egypt—on that very day, they entered the wilderness of Sinai. They had traveled from Rephidim and entered the wilderness of Sinai, camping in the wilderness; Israel camped there in front of the mountain. Then Moses went up to God; and the LORD called to him from the mountain, saying, "Thus you shall say to the house of Jacob, and tell the Israelites: 'You have seen what I did to the Egyptians, and how I bore you on eagles' wings and brought you to Myself. Now therefore, if you obey My voice and keep My covenant, you will be My treasured possession from among all peoples—for all the land is Mine. But you shall be for Me a king-

dom of priests and a holy nation.' These are the words that you shall
speak to the Israelites."

Exod. 19:1–6

Thus begins the event that, in ancient times, was considered by many to be
the most important in the whole Hebrew Bible. God's offer is that, in
exchange for Israel agreeing to keep the laws that He is about to give them
(that is, "if you obey My voice and keep My covenant"), He will make
Israel "My treasured possession from among all peoples." The point of the
observation that follows this promise, "for all the land is Mine," seems to be
that, since this God possesses the entire land, He rules over other peoples as
well. But by agreeing to observe the laws that God is about to promulgate,
Israel will somehow be singled out from among these other peoples and attain
to a unique status: "You shall be for Me a kingdom of priests and a holy
nation." [5]

What are the laws that Israel has to agree to keep? They start with the Ten
Commandments in Exod. 20:1–17 and then continue on into chapters
21–23—dozens of other laws dealing with all manner of things, not only governing relations between God and man (not worshiping other gods, keeping
the sabbath, and so forth) but all sorts of civil and criminal legislation: torts,
damages, and felonies of various kinds. Indeed, God's laws do not end with
Exodus 23. The next three books—Leviticus, Numbers, and Deuteronomy—
are themselves packed full of laws, some having to do specifically with
priests (*kohanim*) and the offering of sacrifices, others concerning the people
as a whole and their religious obligations, still others touching on matters not
normally found in any law code: the prohibition of hating one's fellow, for
example, or the allied injunction to "love your neighbor as yourself." It
would be no exaggeration to say that, from this point in the Pentateuch
onward, God's laws move to front and center; indeed, in a more general
sense, the religion outlined in the Pentateuch as a whole is a *religion of
divine laws*. (The point bears emphasis because, as we shall see, nascent
Christianity sought—for reasons of its own—to diminish the importance of
these laws. The result has been that, in actual Christian teaching and worship,
the legal parts of the Pentateuch have often been marginalized or even
skipped over entirely.)

A religion of laws might sound like a rather unattractive package. Aren't
most religions about being good, doing the right thing *without laws*—and,
along with this, perhaps, about arriving at some heightened consciousness of
God, and of the world as God's creation?

A fair answer would probably be: no. The truth is, religions vary greatly all
over the world (some do not even have anything corresponding to the belief
in God), and one people's religious beliefs and practices often strike other

people as superstitious or wrong or absolutely horrible. But the question about the very essence of the above-cited proposal—"Keep My laws and you will become My special people"—is nevertheless an important one to ask, since it highlights not only what is rather unique about the religion of Moses (or, a modern scholar might say, what the Bible presents as the religion of Moses), but how that religion is different from what preceded it. Up until the time of Moses, it will be noticed, God had not spelled out very many demands for Israel to follow (apart from circumcision and a few other matters). There really weren't any divine laws. At the same time, God's very presence in the world had been, as we have seen, a rather intermittent and fleeting thing. He spoke to different figures now and again—Noah and Abraham and Jacob and so forth—but then disappeared as if He had never been; indeed, intermittence might be said to be God's principal characteristic in the book of Genesis.

But now, with God's offer to the people of Israel at Mount Sinai comes the promise of some steadier, more defined interaction. "You," God says to Israel, "will be My treasured possession from among all peoples . . . a kingdom of priests and a holy nation." To understand the second half of this promise, it is essential to know that throughout the ancient Near East, the priests of any given people were the ones who were uniquely privileged to be in touch with their gods. The priests' job consisted of caring for the god's house (that is, his temple), offering sacrifices in front of his image, and in general serving him in the place where he was deemed to reside. By saying that Israel would become a *kingdom of priests,* God seemed to be bypassing this common arrangement. He was saying, in effect: You will *all* be My intimates—just keep these simple rules that make up My covenant with you.

This may still seem a less unusual idea than it actually was in its original context. It is not only that an established group of professional priests within society seems to have been a staple elsewhere in the ancient Near East; there was also the matter of a covenant consisting of divinely given laws. Gods in the ancient world did not issue laws; men did. Thus we have law codes from earliest times in ancient Mesopotamia—the laws of Ur-Namma of Ur (who ruled from 2112 to 2095 BCE), Lipit-Ishtar (ca. 1930 BCE), Eshnunna (ca. 1770 BCE), Hammurabi (ca. 1750 BCE), and other kings. These ancient codes often begin by mentioning that the gods X and Y established the king on his throne;[6] in some cases, the king even claims to be of partially divine ancestry. But the laws themselves are created by the king or his own legists and are thus a matter between human beings. So, for example, if someone in Hammurabi's kingdom stole a sheep, he committed a crime and had to make restitution to the sheep's owner (HL ¶8). In ancient Israel, too, he had to make restitution (Exod. 22:1), but he had done much more than commit a crime; he had violated one of God's laws, that is, he had *sinned.* By the same token, an ancient Babylonian who obeyed Hammurabi's laws and never got into trouble was, well, a good citizen. An ancient Israelite who kept God's laws was more than just a good citizen; he was doing God's bidding. It is, of course, hard to know how much this difference counted in the minds of ordinary Israelites: a thief is a thief, after all. What is more, the kings of other nations claimed to rule by divine right and sometimes even identified themselves with a god (or, in Egypt, claimed to be divine incarnations themselves); the laws issued in their name thus had some sort of godly backing. Still, there is a categorical difference here, and it is this difference that seems to underlie God's promise that if Israel keeps His laws it will attain a special, unique status among nations. Indeed, observing all the do's and don'ts promulgated by God came to be seen, at least at some point in Israel's history, as a form of divine service—more and more so, in fact, as time went on. This simple fact, as we shall see, determined the whole future of both Judaism and Christianity.

No Other Gods

The very first explicit commandment of the Ten Commandments[7] is also one of the strangest: the Israelites are to "have no other gods before [or besides] Me" (Exod. 20:3). Many people mistake this as referring to monotheism, the belief that there is only one God in the world. But that is not what it says. On the contrary, the very formulation "no other gods before [or besides] Me" seems to concede some reality to these other gods: they do exist, and they may even make things happen in the world, but you are not to worship them before, or along with, Me. This view is not what is traditionally called monotheism but *monolatry* ("worshiping one"), the devotion to a single deity while at the same time accepting the existence of other deities.

When one considers the matter from a distance, monolatry seems an odd practice. After all, different gods and goddesses were usually conceived to exercise different functions in the world—this one was in charge of fertility, that one could bring success in war, a third might preside over the life-giving rains. What good did it do for a whole nation to devote itself exclusively to the worship of the war god, say, when everyone knew full well that drought might strike at any time, necessitating help from the rain god? There is thus something inherently limiting, and ultimately unstable, about monolatry. Where did this commandment come from?

Modern scholars found a possible clue to the answer in the civilization of the ancient Hittites, whose capital, Hattuša (now located in the town of Bogazköy, in north central Turkey), was excavated starting in 1906. In the Late Bronze Age, the Hittites ruled over a vast empire that stretched deep into the territory of present-day Syria, and the library of its capital was found to contain some ten thousand inscribed clay tablets, many of them dealing with international relations and other matters of state. Starting in the 1930s, a number of Hittite treaties were published, and it was not long before these attracted the attention of biblical scholars.[8]

What interested biblicists in particular was the *form* these treaties took. As has already been observed, all sorts of documents—business letters, wedding invitations, U.N. resolutions—come to acquire a standard form; the conventions that they obey help readers to identify them immediately and understand their words, both the boilerplate and what is unique in them. So was it with the treaties concluded between the Hittite emperor and his various vassal states. These agreements—conventionally known as *suzerain treaties* or *vassal treaties*, since in them the dominant party (suzerain) spells out his demands to the vassal—turn out to have a relatively standardized form. There is, of course, some variety from treaty to treaty, but most of them contain a mixture of the following basic elements:

1. *Self-identification of the speaker* (that is, the suzerain): "These are the words of the Sun-god [i.e., the king], Mursilis the great king, the king of the Hatti-land, the valiant, the favorite of the storm god, the son of Suppiluliumas, the great king, the king of the Hatti-land, the valiant."

2. *Historical prologue* reviewing relations between the suzerain and the vassal: Having thus introduced himself, the king would then proceed to narrate all that he had done for the lowly vassal state. Actually, what the king had usually done was conquer the vassal, but, accentuating the positive, the prologue might instead mention that the great king had installed the present (puppet) ruler of the vassal state on his throne, or the present ruler's grandfather, and that ever since he had acted justly toward the vassal.[9]

3. *Treaty stipulations:* Next came the heart of the matter, the demands imposed on the vassal by the great king. Two concerns were prominent among these: money and loyalty. The first scarcely needs explanation; one of the perquisites of conquering a vassal state was demanding a certain percentage of its gross annual income, payable, it was sometimes stipulated, in pure gold. Loyalty was just as important, however. After all, the very essence of an ancient empire was the radiation of power and influence from one central city or conglomeration of cities outward to more distant cities and towns. The farther these outposts were from the center, the weaker the great king's influence was likely to be—not only because lines of supply were longer and more difficult, but also because, as one moved farther away from the sphere of influence of one suzerain, one often moved closer to the sphere of influence of a rival suzerain. What was crucial for the suzerain, therefore, was preventing the farthest vassal states in his empire from falling into his rival's hands. This might, of course,

necessitate the stationing of troops on the outskirts of the empire, but the vassal king himself needed to be warned in the strictest terms not to have any secret contact or negotiations with a rival empire. The vassal had to swear absolute loyalty to his suzerain and his allies. As Mursilis put it succinctly with one vassal: "With my friend you shall be a friend, and with my enemy you shall be an enemy." Further stipulations might involve the obligation to muster troops on behalf of the suzerain, to hand over escaped deportees of the suzerain, to report any seditious speech to the suzerain, and so forth.

4. *Provisions for placing the text of the treaty* in a public place and for regular public reading: these were necessary lest anyone claim ignorance of the treaty contents.

5. *Mention of the gods* who acted as witnesses (and guarantors) of the vassal's acceptance of the treaty.

6. *Blessings and curses* invoked on those who did, or did not, uphold the treaty's provisions.

As noted, not all treaties contained all six of these elements, and there were certainly other elements involved in making the treaty official—such as the sacrifice of animals or some ratifying meal or the like—that are not mentioned above. But these are the written essentials.

What captured the attention of biblicists, starting in the 1950s, was the similarity of the form of these treaties to the form of various presentations of God's covenant with Israel, including, prominently, the narrative of Exodus 19–20 culminating in the proclamation of the Ten Commandments.

The text of the Ten Commandments itself (Exod. 20:1–17; also Deut. 5:6–21) is relatively brief, but it does start off with God's self-identification ("I am the LORD your God") and a short allusion to His previous relations with Israel ("who took you out of the land of Egypt, the house of bondage"). It then proceeds to a list of stipulations. The first of these looks strikingly like the suzerain's demand for exclusive loyalty, "You shall have no other gods before [or besides] Me." These words, it appeared to scholars, must have carried a definite connotation when they were first uttered: God was approaching the people of Israel like a foreign conqueror and setting out His conditions, the first of which, at least, was altogether standard.

That was not all. Scholars likewise noted that, after listing the rest of the Ten Commandments and the other laws that follow (Exodus 21–23), the text concludes with the typical acts that served to seal a covenant in the human sphere elsewhere in the ancient Near East:

Moses came and told the people all the words of the LORD and all the ordinances; and all the people answered with one voice, and said, "All the words that the LORD has spoken we will do." And Moses wrote down all the words of the LORD. Then he rose early in the morning and built an altar at the foot of the mountain, and set up twelve pillars, corresponding to the twelve tribes of Israel. He sent young men of the people of Israel, who offered burnt offerings and sacrificed oxen as offerings of well-being to the LORD. Moses took half of the blood and put it in basins, and half of the blood he threw against the altar. Then he took the document of the covenant and read it aloud to the people. They said, "Everything that the LORD has spoken we will do, and we will be obedient." Then Moses took the blood and threw it over the people, and said, "This is the blood of the covenant that the LORD has made with you in accordance with all these words."

Then Moses and Aaron, Nadab, and Abihu, and seventy of the elders of Israel went up, and they saw the God of Israel. Under His feet there was something like a pavement of sapphire stone, like the very heavens for brightness. And He did not lay his hand on the chief men of the people of Israel, but they beheld God, and they ate and drank.

Exod. 24:3–11

To many scholars, this actually looks as if two different ceremonies of conclusion have been edited together. In the first paragraph, the people, who are standing at the foot of the mountain, formally accept the terms of the covenant by saying that they will do everything that God has stipulated. This acceptance is then sealed by the offering of sacrifices and the sprinkling of the sacrificial blood. In the second paragraph, scholars see an alternate ceremony: Moses and the other notables actually go up the mountain to meet the Great King—apparently a dangerous and potentially suicidal act, but one that God permits in this instance; then they "ate and drank" in a covenant-concluding meal, and the deal was completed.

The other characteristic elements of a Hittite treaty—the mention of storing the treaty text in some public place, the list of blessings and curses, and so forth—are not found in the immediate environment of the Ten Commandments, but to scholars the whole atmosphere of an ancient Near Eastern treaty was nonetheless unmistakable. Indeed, it was explicitly presented as such: God Himself, it will be recalled, had said He was proposing a *běrit*, a covenant or solemn agreement, between Himself and the people of Israel (Exod. 19:5). What could be more natural than the use of the standard form and language of a *běrit*, such as might be concluded between human beings? Indeed, elsewhere in the Bible, *all* of the other elements of the Hittite treaty do appear. Scholars thus pointed to the provision that the Ten Commandments be placed in the Ark of the Covenant (Deut. 10:2), as well as to the lengthy list of blessings and curses that conclude the legal corpora of Leviticus (chapter 26) and Deuteronomy (chapter 28, in addition to the public recitation of curses prescribed in Deut. 27:11–26). What, they asked, could these long lists of curses mean apart from the conventions of an ancient treaty?

Indeed, scholars also saw in the overall form of the book of Deuteronomy something similar to the basic treaty pattern: that book starts with a very lengthy historical introduction reviewing relations between God and Israel (chapters 1–11); then moves to the insistence on exclusive loyalty and, consequently, the avoidance of anything connected with the worship of other gods (chapters 12–13); other laws (14–26); blessings and curses (27–28); provision for public reading of the stipulations (31:9–13); provision for deposit of the text in the Ark of the Covenant (31:24–29).

One more biblical text, Joshua 24, also seemed to combine most of the elements of an ancient treaty. This chapter includes the self-presentation of the suzerain (24:2); a historical prologue (24:2–13); insistence on exclusive loyalty (24:14–21); mention of witnesses (there could be no divine witnesses, of course, so "You are witnesses against yourselves, that you have chosen the LORD to serve Him," 24:22); and placement of the text at a public site (24:26–27). All these instances, scholars said, could leave little doubt: God's covenant with Israel followed a standardized treaty form, and his demand of exclusive loyalty, that is, monolatry, was nothing more than the translation into the divine sphere of a demand that any ancient emperor might have made of his vassal.

The Dust Settles

As with many proposed insights of modern scholars, the initial enthusiasm that greeted these ideas was followed by a period of reconsideration and second thoughts. Most of these hesitations concerned the connection of the various treaty elements with, specifically, the Hittites. After all, it was argued, the Hittite empire had essentially gone out of business by the end of the second millennium, even before Israel's rise as a great nation under David. How could the characteristically Hittite form of treaty have played such an important role in texts dated by many scholars to a much later period? Certainly there were other, later treaties—notably those of various neo-Assyrian emperors, who dominated Israel precisely in the period when, scholars thought, some of the biblical texts involved might actually have been written.[10] True, the Assyrian treaties had a somewhat different form—they may have lacked a historical prologue,[11] and they certainly had more elaborate demands and penalties—but these, some argued, might actually be more likely than the Hittite treaties to have inspired the biblical models.[12] The issue was not merely one of dates but of theology: those who wished to claim that the whole idea of a covenant of divine *laws* was a relatively late element in the religion of

Israel tended to reject the close Hittite comparison.[13] Covenant, some said, was a favorite theme of the law code of Deuteronomy (which, as we shall see, they dated to the seventh century BCE—or even later);[14] the passages in Exodus 19–24, they argued, must therefore belong to the same period. Other scholars, while not arguing that the traditions reflected in these chapters went all the way back to Hittite times, nonetheless felt that they must be very old. After all, the idea of a divine suzerain concluding a pact with all of Israel, the "nation of priests," would hardly be conceivable after the time when Israel had an actual king ruling over it; any covenant after that point should presumably be concluded between God and the king.[15] Nor would an entrenched priesthood be particularly happy about a text that proclaimed that all Israelites were priests. For these reasons, some scholars argue, the idea of a divine covenant must have been a fundamental of Israelite religion even before the time of David, in the tenth century.[16]

This is a complicated, ongoing debate and not given to easy summary. Some scholars have pointed to a verse in the eighth-century prophet Hosea as a telling piece of evidence:

> Hear the word of the LORD, O people of Israel; for the LORD has a legal
>   case against the inhabitants of the land.
> There is no *faithfulness or loyalty,* and no *obedience to God* in the land.
> *False swearing,* and *murder,* and *stealing,* and *adultery* break out; blood-
>   shed follows bloodshed.
> Therefore the land mourns, and all who live in it languish.
>
> Hos. 4:1–3

The connection to the Ten Commandments is clear enough; if these are indeed the words of an eighth-century prophet (and most scholars agree that they are), then that would put the Ten Commandments back at least that far—in fact, somewhat earlier, since God here is presented as saying He has a "legal case" (*rib*) against Israel. In order for Him to indict Israel on these grounds, Israel would have to be presumed to have sworn at some earlier point that it would uphold the provisions that it was now being charged with violating. In other words, Israel's acceptance of the Ten Commandments would have to have been something of an established fact at the time these words were uttered. (To be sure, this passage does not use the word "covenant" in presenting its charge; perhaps, as some scholars have claimed, this reflects the fact that the theological centrality of the covenant concept emerged only later.[17] At the same time, "covenant" does specifically appear later on in the book: see Hos. 8:1.)

This would certainly seem to be a strong point in favor of the antiquity of the Ten Commandments. What is more, however old the actual text of the Ten Commandments might be, the idea that God had established His sovereignty over Israel through the issuance of a set of laws might be still older.[18] True, opponents of this idea point to the relative paucity of allusions elsewhere in the Bible to these supposedly early laws. Indeed, it is really only in the books written just before and then after the Babylonian exile of the sixth century, these scholars say, that law itself seems to become a central focus of the religion of Israel. Still (for reasons to be explored in chapter 23), other scholars associate the promulgation of a list of ten simple commandments—the last six of which seem specifically designed to extend kinship obligations to a broader group of unrelated tribes—to the period of Israel's first emergence as a nation. Only later did these laws come to be conceived as the stipulations of a covenant as such; still later, according to this approach, the original covenant stipulations were modified and augmented by the great set of laws found currently in Exodus 21–23.

Somewhat lost in this debate, however, has been the very conception of God underlying the passages we have been reading. Whether it was influenced more by Hittite or by Assyrian treaty models, the account of God's conduct with Israel at this point—that is, His sudden appearance as a divine suzerain who announces to this tiny nation His offer of a treaty—seems, on consideration, a very odd way for God to have presented Himself to any group of human beings. What exactly this meant at the time will require further clarification.

16

The Ten Commandments

EXODUS 20 AND 34:10–26; DEUTERONOMY 5:6–21

Moses Holding the Ten Commandments by Jan Gossaert.

THE ORIGIN OF PROPHECY. GOD SPOKE TWO AT MOUNT SINAI.
WHY TWO TABLETS? HONOR YOUR FATHER AND MOTHER.
A "RITUAL DECALOGUE"? NO GRAVEN IMAGES.

The Ten Commandments are probably the most famous bit of legislation in the world. Modern scholars are not sure, however, where exactly the Ten Commandments are, nor what they really mean.

The Ten Commandments were the beginning of God's great gift of the Torah to Israel, the means of Israel's becoming a "kingdom of priests and a holy nation" (Exod. 19:6). Theoretically, Israel ought to have been eager to be so singled out—yet the Bible seemed to say that, at the time, they were actually rather reluctant:

> When all the people saw the thunder and lightning and the sound of the trumpet [*shofar*] and the mountain smoking, they were afraid and trembled and stood at a distance. They said to Moses, "You be the one to speak to us, and we will obey; but let not God speak to us [directly] or we will die." Moses said to the people, "Do not be afraid! The reason why God has come is to test you, and in order that the fear of Him will be upon you—so that you will not sin." But the people still stood at a distance, so Moses drew near to the thick darkness where God was.
>
> Exod. 20:18–21

Apparently, the very process of hearing the divine voice was absolutely terrifying—not only the voice itself, but all that accompanied it, the thunder and lightning and smoke and something that resembled the blast of trumpets. That is why the people say to Moses, "You be the one to speak to us." But it is not altogether clear from the text at what point God stopped speaking directly to Israel and began to use Moses as a go-between. The above-cited passage is found right after the recitation of the Ten Commandments (Exod. 20:1–17). That might indicate that the people heard the Ten Commandments directly from God and all the rest from Moses—indeed, this might explain why the Ten Commandments are separated off from the rest of God's laws, a problem that troubled some ancient interpreters. (Certain "heretics" had fixed on this fact to suggest that all that God had really demanded of Israel were these Ten Commandments and that the rest had been the creation of Moses himself.)[1]

As they pondered this question, however, ancient interpreters came upon a curious fact. The opening part of the Ten Commandments is written as a direct address by God to the people: God speaks of Himself as "I" and calls the people "you":

> I am the LORD your God, who took you out of the land of Egypt, the house of bondage. You shall have no other gods before [or besides] Me. You shall not make for yourself any statue or image [of anything] in the heavens above or the earth below or in the waters beneath the earth—you shall not bow down before them or worship them, since I the LORD your God am a jealous God, visiting the guilt of the fathers on the children, to the third and fourth generations of those who reject Me, but showing kindness to the thousandth generation of those who love Me and keep My commandments.
>
> Exod. 20:2–6

After these first two commandments, however, the form suddenly changes. The people of Israel continue to be addressed as "you," but God is now always spoken of in the third person, "He" or "Him":

> You shall not make wrongful use of the name of the LORD your God, for the LORD will not acquit anyone who misuses His name.
>   Remember the sabbath day and keep it holy. Six days you shall labor and do all your work. But the seventh day is a sabbath to the LORD your God . . . For in six days the LORD made the heavens and the earth and the sea and all that is in them, but He rested on the seventh day.
>
> Exod. 20:7–11

This third-person form is maintained throughout the rest of the Ten Commandments. It thus seemed to interpreters that God must have spoken only the first two commandments to Israel directly—all the rest was mediated through Moses.

In support of this hypothesis, interpreters brought two further proofs. First was a verse from the book of Psalms:

> One thing [or one time] God has spoken, two things have I heard:
> Might is indeed God's, yet Yours as well is kindness, Lord;
> You do indeed pay a man in keeping with his deeds.
>
> Ps. 62:12–13

Certainly God had spoken more than once and had said more than one or two things! If the psalm nonetheless says what it says, it must be alluding to those first two commandments that Israel heard at Mount Sinai directly from God (that is, on *one occasion* God *spoke* directly to Israel, and it was then that "I" [Israel] *heard two things* straight from God's mouth).

The other proof came from a verse at the end of the book of Deuteronomy. Alluding to the great revelation at Mount Sinai, the text said:

> The Torah was commanded to us by Moses as an inheritance [to be passed on] to the people of Jacob.
>
> Deut. 33:4

Normally one would think it more appropriate to say that *God* had commanded the Torah, not Moses; if the text said "Moses," it seemed to be highlighting his role as a go-between in the Torah's transmission. More than that, however, was the word "Torah" itself, appearing emphatically as the first word of this sentence in Hebrew. In the time of the ancient interpreters, Jews and Christians did not have our present set of special symbols to represent numbers (1, 2, 3, and so forth); instead, they simply used letters of the alphabet. One common system thus used *A* for 1, *B* for 2, and so on up to ten (*J* in the Hebrew alphabet); after that, *JA* was used to represent 11, *JB* for 12, and so forth; next, *K* could stand for 20, *KA* for 21, etc.; then *L* for 30, and so on until the last letter of the Hebrew alphabet, *tav*, which represented 400. Using this system, the word *Torah* itself was found to equal exactly 611. This might seem to be too bad, since, by the traditional count, the Torah was said to contain 613 commandments. Unless . . . that was precisely the point! God Himself had spoken the first two commandments directly to Israel, and then Moses took over: "*Torah* [that is, 611] were commanded to us by Moses as an inheritance [to be passed on] to the people of Jacob."[2]

The Etiology of Prophecy

In contemplating the above-cited passage, in which the Israelites ask Moses to act as a go-between (Exod. 20:18–21), modern scholars noticed that the same moment was discussed again later on, in the book of Deuteronomy. There Moses strictly warns the people against consulting soothsayers or sorcerers or the like; instead, he says:

> The LORD your God will raise up for you a prophet like me from among your own people; you shall do what he says. This is [after all] what you requested of the LORD your God at Horeb on the day of the assembly, when you said: "Let me not hear the voice of the LORD my God any more or see this great fire, lest I die." Then the LORD said to me: "It is good that they have said what they said: [in the future as well,] I will raise up for them a prophet like you from among their own people. Then I will put My words in his mouth, so that he can tell them everything that I have commanded

him. And I myself will hold accountable anyone who does not heed the
words that the prophet speaks in My name."

Deut. 18:15–19

To modern scholars, both this passage and the earlier one (Exod. 20:18–21)
seemed to be designed to answer the same question: why do we have
prophets at all? Ancient Israelites must have often wondered why, if God had
a message to deliver to them, He did not do so directly, with the divine voice
booming forth out of heaven so that everyone could hear it and make no mistake about its source. The answer given by both passages is the same: God
tried this once, at Mount Sinai/Horeb, but it did not work. People found the
act of listening directly to God so frightening that *they* demanded that God
use human intermediaries to carry His words; ever since then, we have had
prophets.

As we will see in a later chapter, modern scholars have earnestly studied
the institution of prophecy in biblical times, seeking to connect the office of
biblical prophet with earlier social niches that existed in Israelite society
(sage, priest, professional curser) as well as with prophetlike figures from elsewhere in the ancient Near East. Few would probably take the Bible's etiological explanation here (that prophecy originated by popular request at Sinai)
at its word. Most scholars would probably prefer to see in the biblical
prophet an Israelite representative of a much broader, perhaps universal, phenomenon, the "religious genius" whose ear is especially attuned to the realm
of the divine—the mediums, diviners, shamans, and others known from
many different cultures and civilizations. If so, the Deuteronomy passage can
be seen to have a dual role. On the one hand, it legitimates the institution of
prophecy: I Myself created it, God says, in response to your terror at Sinai. At
the same time, however, this passage establishes certain limits: prophets are
the *only* legitimate intermediaries in the supernatural realm—no soothsayers
or sorcerers or those who can communicate with the dead are to be permitted (Deut. 18:10–14). What is more, even the prophet may not "speak in the
name of other gods" or "presume to speak in My name something I have not
commanded"; anyone who does so is to be condemned to death (Deut.
18:19–20).

Five and Five

When Moses came down from Mount Sinai, he had in his hand two stone
tablets (Exod. 31:18; 32:15–16). It might seem, in context, that these tablets
contained *all* the laws that God had passed on to Moses on Mount Sinai, but
elsewhere the Pentateuch makes it clear that the tablets contained the Ten
Commandments alone:

He was there with the LORD forty days and forty nights; he neither ate bread nor drank water. And he wrote on the tablets the words of the covenant, the Ten Commandments.

Exod. 34:28

[Later, Moses recalls:] Then the LORD spoke to you out of the fire. You heard the sound of words but saw no form; there was only a voice. He declared to you his covenant, which He charged you to observe, that is, the Ten Commandments; and He wrote them on two stone tablets.

Deut. 4:13

There was something a bit troubling about all this. Ancient interpreters knew full well that the Ten Commandments could easily fit on a single stone tablet. (Indeed, modern-day archaeologists have unearthed inscriptions with far more writing than this on a single tablet.) If, nevertheless, the Torah says that there were *two* tablets, there must have been a reason. Perhaps, interpreters reasoned, God had intended to highlight some fundamental division within the Ten Commandments by separating them into two groups. And indeed, one such separation seemed clear enough: while the opening commandments have to do with relations between God and man (not worshiping other gods; not making divine images; not misusing God's name; keeping the sabbath), the last five were clearly about relations among human beings (no murder,[3] adultery, theft, false testimony, or coveting). To many it thus seemed obvious that the two tablets had been intended to stress this division:

> Further, the ten words on them . . . are divided equally into two sets of five, the former comprising duties to God, and the other duties to men.
>
> Philo, *Who Is Heir* 168

There was only one problem with this. The fifth commandment—which should have been the last of the between-God-and-man laws—dealt instead with relations between children and their parents: "Honor your father and your mother, so that you may live long in the land that the LORD your God is giving you" (Exod. 20:12). This was indeed troubling. One could, of course, claim that the first tablet contained four commandments and the second six, but such asymmetry would have seemed an imperfection. Instead, ancient interpreters sought to claim that honoring one's parents was, in a sense, like honoring God:

> After giving the commandment concerning the seventh day, he gives a fifth commandment concerning the honoring of parents, putting it on the borderline between the two sets of five. For it is the last of the first set, in which laws of the sacred are given, and yet it is connected as well to the second

set, which deals with the duties of man to man. I believe the reason to be this: the very nature of parenthood places it on the borderline between the immortal and the mortal, the mortal because they [that is, parents] belong to [the class of] men and other animals through the perishability of the body; the immortal because the act of generation assimilates them to God, the parent of all.

Philo, Decalogue 106–7

Honor your father [even] in your poverty and your mother [even] in your difficulties. For as God is to a man, so is his father [to him], and as a lord is to a person, so is his mother [to him]; for they are the smelting pot of your conception. [Moreover,] He is the one who gave them dominion over you and formed . . . the spirit; serve* them therefore.

4Q416 *Instruction,* fragment 2 column 3

The Torah ranks the honoring of parents second only to that of God . . . It requires respect to be paid by the young to all their elders because God is the most ancient of all.

Josephus, *Against Apion* 2:206

It says "Honor your father and mother," whereas elsewhere it says "Honor the LORD . . ." [Prov. 3:9]. Honoring one's father [and mother] is thus to be equated with honoring God.

Mekhilta deR. Shimon b. Yohai, p. 152

Why These Ten?

There was still one unanswered question: why had God singled out these ten commandments in particular? It was not that they were necessarily the most important commandments of the Torah, since other obviously important ones (for example, "You shall love the LORD your God with your whole heart and your whole soul and your whole might" [Deut. 6:5] and "You shall love your neighbor like yourself" [Lev. 19:18]) had not been included in these ten. Some ancient interpreters therefore concluded that the Ten Commandments had been created for mnemonic purposes, to help people remember *all* the commandments of the Torah. Each one of the ten was thus a "general heading": the commandment to keep the sabbath, for example, might sug-

---

* The word translated as "serve" here ('*abad*) is the same as that regularly used for "worship." The implication is thus that, since God is ultimately responsible for having placed parents over a person, serving them is thus a form of respecting God's will, indeed, of worshiping Him.

gest all the other commandments concerning holy days and festivals, and the prohibition of false oaths might bring to mind all the other commandments concerning courts and courtroom behavior.[4] Indeed, the prohibitions of worshiping other gods and of swearing falsely against one's neighbor might have been intended to suggest, among others, precisely the two important commandments mentioned above, loving God "with your whole heart" (that is, not dividing that love between God and some other deity) and loving one's neighbor (since the prohibition of false oaths mentioned one's "neighbor").

If so, then the picture was now complete. Moses had gone up to Mount Sinai and stayed there with God for forty days and forty nights, during which time God taught him all the laws of the Torah. He then inscribed on two tablets ten of those laws, each of which was intended to help Moses— and the people of Israel—to recall all the other laws.

> Then Moses turned and went down from the mountain, carrying the two tablets of the covenant in his hands . . . The tablets were the work of God, and the writing was the writing of God, engraved upon the tablets.
>
> Exod. 32:15–16

If only the people could keep these Ten Commandments constantly in mind, they would be able to remember the rest and thus would always have a sure guide to lead them wherever they should go.

The Ten Commandments in Modern Scholarship

One of the remarkable things about the Ten Commandments is their scope. If, as modern scholars believe, these commandments are basically presented as the covenant stipulations of a suzerainlike God, then it is certainly striking that this divine suzerain is not interested only in relations between Himself and his subjects. He cares about what they do to one another—which is why He prohibits such things as murder, adultery, and theft. In fact, in this respect God's covenant really stretches the implied analogy to human covenants between suzerains and vassals; it is much, much broader.

Since the rise of the Documentary Hypothesis, modern scholars have carefully studied the wording of the Decalogue (as the Ten Commandments are sometimes known in modern scholarship)—or rather, the *wordings* of the Decalogue, since there are actually two versions in the Bible, one in Exodus (20:2–17) and the other in Deuteronomy (5:6–21). Considering these two, many have concluded that they both represent the end product of a long process of transmission. Some scholars postulate that the earliest written source to contain these commandments was that group of texts designated as

E, but that the present version in Exodus shows signs of the text having been augmented by a priestly editor. On the other hand, the Deuteronomy version of the Decalogue features parallel modifications indicative (not surprisingly) of D's favorite themes and turns of phrase. For example, the two texts differ greatly in what they say about the sabbath:

> Remember the sabbath day, and keep it holy. Six days you shall labor and do all your work. But the seventh day is a sabbath to the LORD your God; you shall not do any work—you, your son or your daughter, your male or female slave, your livestock, or the alien resident in your towns. For in six days the LORD made heaven and earth, the sea, and all that is in them, but rested the seventh day; therefore the LORD blessed the sabbath day and consecrated it.
>
> Exod. 20:8–11

> Observe the sabbath day and keep it holy, as the LORD your God commanded you. Six days you shall labor and do all your work. But the seventh day is a sabbath to the LORD your God; you shall not do any work—you, or your son or your daughter, or your male or female slave, or your ox or your donkey, or any of your livestock, or the resident alien in your towns, so that your male and female slave may rest as well as you. Remember that you were a slave in the land of Egypt, and the LORD your God brought you out from there with a mighty hand and an outstretched arm; therefore the LORD your God commanded you to keep the sabbath day.
>
> Deut. 5:12–15

While the two versions have some formal features in common, they differ markedly as to *why* people should rest on the sabbath: Exodus says our resting is in imitation of God's rest after the creation of the world, while Deuteronomy says it comes in memory of the period of slavery in Egypt. Scholars suggest either that one of these versions is a free rewriting of the other or that the original commandment was much shorter, a simple prohibition of working on the seventh day, and that this simple law was subsequently expanded in different ways by both sources.

No Idols

The Decalogue's prohibition of making idols has also been the subject of debate. Some time ago, scholars noted that in the present form of the Decalogue this prohibition appears as an intrusion in an otherwise smooth-running text:

I am the LORD your God, who took you out of the land of Egypt, the house of bondage. You shall have no other gods before [or besides] Me. *You shall not make for yourself any statue or image [of anything] in the heavens above or the earth below or in the waters beneath the earth*—you shall not bow down before them or worship them, since I the LORD your God am a jealous God, visiting the guilt of the fathers on the children, to the third and fourth generations of those who reject Me, but showing kindness to the thousandth generation of those who love Me and keep My commandments.

Exod. 20:3–6

If one eliminates the highlighted portion, this entire paragraph has only one theme: Israel is not to worship other gods. The highlighted words, by contrast, prohibit making any kind of statue or image, *even one of Israel's God.* Such a ban on image making, scholars point out, is an entirely different matter from a prohibition of worshiping other deities. Someone, this theory goes, must at some point have inserted this further prohibition.[5] This is not to say that such a ban was not in existence from a very early period—indeed, archaeologists have yet to find a single, undisputedly cultic, representation of Israel's God.[6] But if scholars are right, the prohibition of image-making did not originally have any place in the traditional Decalogue.*

In short, modern scholarship has not been kind to traditional religious views of the Ten Commandments. Their very form now appears to most scholars to assimilate them to the covenant stipulations found in old Hittite and other ancient Near Eastern treaties. This fact itself raises disturbing questions about the divine origin of these laws. For why should God, in this crucial act of binding the people of Israel to Himself, have chosen to rely on an utterly human set of conventions instead of going about things in some very different, divine sort of way? Moreover, doubt hovers over the content of the Ten Commandments: the Exodus and Deuteronomy versions have striking divergences from each other. As a result, most modern scholars are unable to say with certainty what the original Ten Commandments might have been, or when or where the various texts preserved in our Bible might have originated.

---

* If this is so, however, then according to the numbering followed by most Christians, one would be left with nine commandments. To get back to the original figure of ten, Christians would either have to consider the prologue ("I am the LORD your God, who took you out of the land of Egypt, the house of bondage") as an actual commandment, in keeping with the Jewish view, or subdivide the last commandment, not to covet a neighbor's wife or house or other possessions, into two separate prohibitions.

17

A Religion of Laws

EXODUS 21–23

Moses Expounding the Law of Unclean Beasts,
Master Hugo.

APPLYING BIBLICAL LAWS. FOUR KINDS OF GUARDIANS.
IS ABORTION FORBIDDEN? LAW IN THE ANCIENT NEAR EAST.
THE COVENANT CODE. WHAT THE TORAH DOESN'T COVER.
CHRISTIANITY AND "THE LAW."

The Bible contains a great many laws, and finding their precise application was the task of generations of ancient interpreters. But what would those interpreters have made of the resemblances between the Bible's laws and those of ancient Mesopotamia?

As time went on, keeping God's laws became an increasingly central concern in Israel. The Pentateuch itself came to be known as *the* Torah, the divine guidebook that told people in intricate detail what to do every day. This was the genius of a religion of laws. In all the little encounters of daily life— between children and parents, customers and shopkeepers, beggars and almsgivers, natives and foreigners—the Pentateuch set out the precise form of behavior that God had prescribed. Do what it said and you were serving God; fail to do so and you were committing a sin. Some of its commandments had the broadest scope (Lev. 19:17–18): others told you what to do when you chanced upon a bird's nest in the road (Deut. 22:6) or specified that you had to put a safety railing on the roof of your house (Deut. 22:8). There were rules about vows to God that you might utter in a moment of panic; what God had ordered you to do in case you contracted a then-common skin disease; rules about festivals and pilgrimages and fasting, menstruation and seminal emissions, rules and rules and rules, until it seemed like there was no area of life about which the Torah did not have *something* to say—and that, for later Judaism, was the beauty of it. In doing each thing according to the way that God had prescribed, a person could, as it were, turn life itself into a constant act of reaching out to God. Nothing was done for its own sake; everything was done to serve God. And so, without having to retreat to a monastery or a mountaintop, one could live each minute in a state of holiness and sanctity, creating a living, vibrant connection between one's little life on earth and God in heaven.

Of course, the Bible did not always spell out all its laws in detail. To mention the most commonly cited case: the Pentateuch said that a person had to refrain from working on the sabbath, but nowhere did it say what constituted "work." It seemed likely that people were not supposed to practice their regular profession on the sabbath—but could they practice someone else's? That is, if you were a farmer, could you go up on your roof on the sabbath to fix a leak? And if you were a roofer, could you use the sabbath to tend your garden? A modern reader might think that such decisions should best be left up to the individual, but this was not the mentality of ancient times: the rules needed to be spelled out in detail, if only because the Pentateuch itself required that violators of the sabbath be punished (Exod. 31:14). From ancient times, therefore, traditions had been passed on from generation to generation specifying exactly what constituted a violation of the sabbath.

Indeed, an important factor in the rise of ancient biblical interpreters in the first place had been the need of officials and ordinary people to know exactly what the laws of the Bible required of them. Authoritative interpreters could tell them. In fact, it seems likely that interpreters first developed their close but imaginative style of interpreting precisely because the Bible itself had left a considerable number of gaps specifically *in its laws*. An interpreter who paid careful attention to every detail in a particular law could use the very words of the text to justify his interpretation. "I'm not just giving you my own opinion," the interpreter would say. "The fact that this law contains this unusual word, or repeats itself needlessly here, proves that it was hinting at just my way of explaining things." At the same time, such an approach was quite liberating. Since the slightest detail in the Bible's way of expressing itself might carry some hidden message, interpreters felt authorized to give their imaginations free rein. At the end of the day, people absolutely *needed* to know how to apply a biblical law to their daily lives; such close reading plus imagination provided the means.

Often, these interpreters also sought to make biblical laws as down-to-earth as possible. For example, a certain biblical law forbids people from "taking revenge or holding a grudge" (Lev. 19:18). Stated in this form, the law might seem to be prohibiting the sort of smoldering hatred that characterized the bloody Hatfield-McCoy feud, which raged along the border of Kentucky and West Virginia in the late nineteenth century. But such situations are rare. Instead of understanding the law in those terms, rabbinic interpreters understood it in a much homier, everyday sense. Suppose, they said, you should ask to borrow your neighbor's scythe and he refuses. Then, a week later, his scythe breaks and he comes to you to borrow yours. If you should say, "No, you cheapskate, you wouldn't lend me yours, why should I lend you mine?" then, according to these interpreters, you would have violated the biblical injunction against taking revenge. In other words, *revenge* doesn't necessarily involve killing or violence of any kind; it could mean something as simple as mistreating someone to pay him or her back for earlier mistreatment. But if so, these same interpreters asked, what did the Torah intend by further prohibiting the holding of a grudge? Ah, that refers to the case in which you do agree to lend your scythe to your nasty neighbor, but then you add, as you go to fetch it, "You see, I'm not a cheapskate like you." Even doing that, they said, is forbidden by the Torah.

Guarding Someone Else's Property

Some of the Bible's laws seemed utterly impossible to understand. Take, for example, what the Bible says about guarding a piece of property given to you by someone else:

> When a man gives his neighbor money or goods for safekeeping, and they are stolen from the neighbor's house, if the thief is caught, he shall pay double. If the thief is not caught, then the owner of the house shall draw near to God[1] [and swear] that he himself did not appropriate his neighbor's property. In any criminal accusation, whether it involves an ox, a donkey, a sheep, clothing, or any other loss, if one party says that this is [what occurred], then the case of both parties shall come before God; the one whom God finds guilty shall pay double to the other.[2]
>
> Exod. 22:7–9

So far, the matter seems clear enough. A gives B his rare coin collection to keep while he is on vacation in Florida. When he comes back, B tells him that the coins were stolen. B then has to "draw near to God" (the precise locale is not specified) and swear that he didn't pawn the collection and pocket the cash. If he so swears, he is off the hook—unless, of course, it later turns out that he was lying.

Immediately after this, however, comes a slightly different law:

> When a man gives his neighbor a donkey, ox, sheep, or any other animal for safekeeping, and it dies or is injured or is carried off, without anyone having seen it, an oath before the LORD shall decide between the two of them that the one has not appropriated the property of the other; the owner must acquiesce and no restitution shall be made. *But if it was stolen, he must make restitution to the owner.* If it was mangled by beasts, he shall bring it as evidence; he need not replace what has been mangled by beasts.
>
> Exod. 22:10–13

Here, A has given B his cow to take care of while he is in Florida. When he comes back, the cow is gone. If B says, "Sorry, it died as soon as you left," then B has to take an oath to the effect that this is in fact what happened, and A has to take his word for it. If, however, B says, "Sorry, it was stolen one day while I was out shopping," that is not a sufficient excuse. B has to pay A the value of the cow; he cannot get off by taking an oath.

But wait! Didn't previous law say that in the case of theft he *could* take an oath? "If the thief is not caught, then the owner of the house shall draw near to God [and swear] that he himself did not appropriate his neighbor's property." Now, one might say that this applied in the case of rare coins but not for a cow: after all, the first law starts, "When a man gives his neighbor *money or goods* for safekeeping," while the second begins, "When a man gives his neighbor *a donkey, ox, sheep, or any other animal* for safekeeping." You can take an oath for money or goods, but not for an animal. This would be a fine distinction, except that the first law, although it begins by talking about money or goods, then adds that the oath option exists in any case of theft "whether it involves an ox, a donkey, a sheep, clothing, or any other loss." In other words, law #1 says that if a cow is stolen, the person guarding it can take an oath and avoid paying, while law #2 says he cannot.

No doubt ancient interpreters pondered this matter long and hard. How could the Bible so obviously contradict itself—and in two adjacent laws? After a great deal of thought, however, they found a clue to resolving the problem in the very next words of the text:

> When a man borrows [an animal] from his neighbor and it dies or is injured, if the owner was not with it [at the time], he must make restitution. If the owner was with it, no restitution shall be made; if it was rented, the rental fee is due.
>
> Exod. 22:14

Here, B *borrows* A's cow and the cow dies. So long as the cow dies after A has dropped it off at B's house, B has to pay. If it dies before B actually takes possession (even though A and B have already made arrangements for the borrowing), then B has no liability. On the other hand if, instead of borrowing the cow, B had agreed to *rent* it from A for a period of time, then if the cow dies B bears no responsibility—in fact, he can recover the rental fee.

How might this new case help resolve the contradiction between the previous two? Interpreters noticed that the new case focused on the matter of B's *status*. That is, in the new case, B was either a borrower or a renter; in the previous two cases, the Bible had simply said that A had "given" his goods to B for safekeeping—B was neither borrowing them nor renting them, he was just keeping them for A. Still, as interpreters came to see, "just keeping" A's property might actually involve one of two different things. A might have said to B, "Keep these things for me; I'll be back from Florida in a week," or he might have said, "Keep these things for me; I'll be back from Florida in a week and pay you ten dollars for your trouble." In the first case, B would have been doing A a favor; in the second case, B would have been watching A's property as a paid guardian.

What interpreters concluded was that the Bible—without quite saying so—had intended to distinguish between these two different scenarios. Law #1 involved a guardian for free, law #2 a guardian for hire. Since the latter was being paid to guard, he of course had a greater level of responsibility than the guardian for free—if the goods were stolen, the guardian for hire had to pay. That was, after all, what he had been hired to avoid. Since the guardian for free was just doing the owner a favor, he had a lesser level of responsibility: he just had to swear that it was not his fault.

But how was a person supposed to figure out that law #1 was talking about a guardian for free? The answer: this was hinted at in the opening words, "When a man gives his neighbor money or goods for safekeeping." After all, money or goods do not usually require a great deal of effort to guard; I can put your rare coin collection in a corner of my attic and forget about it. Law #2, by contrast, begins by saying, "When a man gives his neighbor a donkey, ox, sheep, or any other animal for safekeeping." If I am going to guard your donkey or ox, I will have to feed it every day, and also let it out into the field in the morning and get it back in the barn before night—in short, guarding it will require some effort and expense on my part. So I probably won't do all that for free; in most cases, I will be a guardian for hire. But if you're my friend I *might* do it for free; for that reason, law #1 had taken the trouble to say that its provisions could apply to any sort of a guardian for free, even if the person were guarding an animal ("whether it involves an ox, a donkey, a sheep, clothing, or any other loss"). In other words, law #1 and law #2 had been deliberately worded the way they were to challenge the interpreters. It was up to them to figure out that the distinction between *money or goods* on the one hand and *a donkey, ox, sheep, or any other animal* on the other was not really a distinction between the type of things being guarded, but between two types of guardians:

> Scripture is distinguishing between one kind of guardian and another kind.
> *Mekhilta deR. Ishmael, Neziqin* 15

Once interpreters had figured this out, everything made sense—but what's more, this biblical law now seemed to hold a larger lesson. The Bible as a whole makes sense. It does not contradict itself, and when it seems to, it is up to human interpreters to look deeply into the text and find that hidden something that will make everything work out.

Is a Fetus a Human Being?

Biblical interpretation was sometimes a matter of life and death, hotly debated by opposing sides. A number of sources report on the existence of different groups in the late biblical period, each of which followed its own biblical interpreters. The New Testament mentions two such groups, the Pharisees and the Sadducees; Josephus speaks of these two as well as a third group, the

Essenes. Rabbinic sources such as the Babylonian Talmud mention the Pharisees, the Sadducees, and the Boethusians. Scholars are still divided as to the precise relationship and affiliations of these groups, but one thing is clear: the disagreements of these groups about biblical interpretation were at the center of what was often a highly charged rivalry, even enmity, among them.

Their disagreements extended over a range of different biblical topics, but among them was one that remains a very controversial subject in our own day: is the fetus in its mother's womb to be considered a human life? Nowadays, this question has direct implications for the matter of abortion. In ancient times it was connected to abortion as well, but, as we shall see, it influenced other matters of law too.

The Bible does not contain a specific ruling on abortion per se, but it does have one law that seemed to shed light on the question:

> When men are fighting and one of them strikes a pregnant woman so that her offspring comes out, and there is no mishap, he [the one responsible] shall be fined in accordance with what her husband shall impose upon him, and it will be given over to adjudication. But if there is a mishap, then you shall give a life for a life [*literally* a soul for a soul], an eye for an eye, a tooth for a tooth, a hand for a hand, a foot for a foot, a burn for a burn, a wound for a wound, a bruise for a bruise.
>
> Exod. 21:22–25

What happened here? The Bible seems to be describing two possible outcomes of an accident in which a man who was fighting with someone else ended up striking a pregnant woman by mistake. The first possible outcome—that the woman gives birth but "there is no mishap"—results in the man being fined; the second, where "there is a mishap," imposes the death penalty on the man.

At first glance it might seem that "there is no mishap" means that mother and baby are fine. But no ancient interpreter read this passage that way. The reason was simple. Normally, in the case of an accident, if no harm resulted, then no fine would be due; if both mother and baby emerged without a scratch, why should the fighter be punished? He meant no harm to her and no harm had been caused. So *something* bad must have happened. Here is how this passage was translated in the third century BCE by the Jewish makers of the Septuagint, the earliest Greek translation of the Pentateuch:

> If two men are fighting and a pregnant woman is struck in her belly, and her child comes out *not fully formed,* he shall pay a fine. As the woman's husband shall impose, he shall pay it with a valuation. But if *it is fully formed,* he shall give a soul for a soul. An eye for an eye, a tooth for a

tooth, a hand for a hand, a foot for a foot, a burning for a burning, a wound for a wound, a stripe for a stripe.

Septuagint, Exod. 21:22–25

This translation assumes that, no matter what, the accident described resulted in the death of the fetus. Then what could the Bible have meant by distinguishing between a case in which "there is no mishap" and the one in which there is? It was referring, these translators concluded, to the state of development of the unborn child. That is, if such an accident and subsequent miscarriage should occur early in the woman's pregnancy, at a time when the fetus is "not fully formed," then the man cannot truly be deemed to have killed another human being.[3] He did cause a spontaneous abortion and thereby killed a *potential* human being, so he should definitely be fined—but he is not guilty of murder. If, on the other hand, the accident occurred late in the pregnancy, even though the fetus was still in its mother's womb, it was deemed to be in every sense a human being, since it was already fully formed. Having thus taken another human's life, the man was subject to the death penalty.[4]

It would follow from this that the Bible deems a fully formed fetus to be in every sense a human being. The law does not define exactly how "fully formed" the fetus has to be, but certainly it would seem that, according to this passage, late-term abortions are nothing less than a form of murder.

However, there was an entirely different way of understanding this same passage. Here is how Jerome translated it in the Vulgate, which was to become the approved translation of the Roman Catholic Church:

If men were fighting and someone struck a pregnant woman and she miscarried but she herself lived, he will be subject to a fine, as much as the woman's husband shall request and as the judges decree. If, however, her death shall follow, let him pay a soul for a soul, an eye for an eye, a tooth for a tooth, a hand for a hand, a foot for a foot, a burning for a burning, a wound for a wound, a bruise for a bruise.

Vulgate, Exod. 21:22–25

According to this understanding, the "mishap" is the death of the mother. That is, in either scenario the fetus dies—apparently it does not matter in Jerome's interpretation whether the accident occurred in the first or the ninth month of pregnancy. The only thing that matters is whether or not the mother survives. Underlying this interpretation, therefore, must be the belief that, so long as a fetus is inside its mother, it is not a separate human being. Instead, the fetus is, as rabbinic interpreters (who had espoused the same approach as that adopted in the above translation) explained, a "limb of the mother" until its head emerges from the womb.

This difference in interpretation had the most serious consequences for daily life—and not just with regard to abortion. A common occurrence in the ancient world was that of a woman who had difficulty in giving birth—even after hours of protracted labor, her child would not emerge from the womb. Unless something could be done, the result might be the death of the mother in labor; this is in fact what happened to Jacob's wife Rachel (Gen. 35:17–19). In some cases, killing the child inside the womb might save the mother's life—but was that lawful? According to interpretation #1 (the interpretation reflected in the Septuagint), the answer would appear to be no, since the fetus was usually "fully formed" at the time of labor; according to interpretation #2 (reflected in the Vulgate), yes, since even a fully formed fetus was still a "limb of the mother" until its head emerged.[5]

The same basic disagreement over the status of a fetus carried over into other matters. The Dead Sea Scrolls community, which followed interpretation #1 above, outlawed killing a pregnant animal for a sacrifice, since that would violate another biblical law that forbade offering a "bull or a sheep along with its offspring in a single day" (Lev. 22:28). Since interpretation #1 held that a cow and the calf in its womb were (or could be) two separate animals, the Dead Sea Scrolls said that slaughtering the mother would thus violate this law. Followers of interpretation #2 said, "No such thing!" So long as the calf is in its mother's womb, they are a single animal. By the same token, interpretation #1 would consider the mother of a stillborn child to have been in a state of ritual impurity sometime before the child's birth, since she was "touching" a dead human's body (an act that normally imparts impurity); according to interpretation #2, she was not impure in the slightest, since the dead fetus was a "limb of the mother" and no separate human being.[6]

An Eye for an Eye

Perhaps no phrase in the popular imagination sums up biblical justice more than the one that concludes this law, "an eye for an eye, a tooth for a tooth, a hand for a hand, a foot for a foot, a burn for a burn, a wound for a wound, a bruise for a bruise." It is therefore noteworthy that some ancient biblical interpreters explained this phrase in exactly the opposite sense of its apparent meaning. It means *not an eye* for an eye.

> A person who injures someone shall undergo the same [injury], being deprived of the same limb of which he deprived the other, unless indeed the injured party is willing to accept money [instead]. *For the law permits the victim to establish damages for the incident,* unless he wishes to be particularly severe.
>
> Josephus, *Jewish Antiquities* 4:278–80

Does not Scripture say an eye for an eye? Why not take this literally to mean the [offender's] eye [is to recompense the victim's]? Let this not even enter your mind! . . . Rabbi Dosthai b. Yehudah said: "An eye for an eye" means monetary compensation [for an eye]. But could not actual retaliation be meant? What then would you say if the eye of one was big and the eye of the other was little[7]—how in such a case will an [actual] eye for an eye [be just]? . . . Rabbi Simeon b. Yohai said: . . . What can you say in the case of a blind man who put out the eye of someone, or of a maimed person [without arms] who caused someone else's hand to be cut off, or of a lame person [without legs] who caused someone else's leg to be broken? How can I uphold the principle of an eye for an eye in such cases?

b. Talmud Baba Qama 83b-84a

Thus, one of the Bible's most famous laws turned out to mean, by careful interpretation, quite the opposite of what it seemed to mean.

Nowadays, many people are likely to consider such matters picayune hairsplitting, but in ancient times they were crucial. After all, the laws of the Bible came from God; what could be more important than establishing precisely what He had meant us to do—in regard to abortion, the law of guardians, the rules of the sabbath, and everything else covered in the laws of the Pentateuch. Legal interpretation was, for various reasons, less of a preoccupation for Christians than for Jews—although the Decalogue and certain other biblical laws were nonetheless an important source in the establishment of the church's canon law. But among Jews, studying and applying biblical laws to daily life was itself nothing less than a way of serving God. As a consequence, a great literature of legal interpretation soon arose. The Babylonian Talmud, much of which is concerned with the interpretation of biblical laws, runs to some twenty folio-sized volumes, but it is only one source of interpretation. An adequate library of Jewish legal rulings today would contain the Talmud plus many more volumes, indeed, shelves and shelves of the writings of later interpreters. Although they were the product of human authors, these books were all founded on, and so constituted a natural extension of, God's own words in the Bible; it was all one sacred corpus.

Yet, in the early twentieth century, a discovery was made that was to throw into question the whole concept of divinely given laws in the Bible. In southwestern Iran, archaeologists unearthed a law code written in the second millennium that seemed to show striking similarities to the laws of Exodus. Had the Bible copied some of its regulations from the ancient Babylonians? And what did this say about the divine origin of Scripture?

Hammurabi and the Bible

In 1901, a team of French archaeologists led by M. J. de Morgan found three fragments of what had once been a single inscription carved into black igneous rock (diorite). Reassembled, the mammoth stele was found to stand some eight feet high; it is now part of the permanent collection of the Louvre Museum in Paris.

The archaeologists had been excavating the acropolis of the ancient Elamite city of Susa. To their surprise, however, the inscribed black rock that they found turned out to have originated not in Susa, but in Mesopotamia, to the west. Apparently, this huge inscription had been captured by the Elamites and brought home as booty.[8] It did not take long for the text to be deciphered and published.[9] It turned out to be a collection of some 282 laws promulgated by Hammurabi (Hammurapi), a great king who had ruled Babylon in the first part of the second millennium. Subsequent archaeological finds within the area of Mesopotamia itself have yielded further copies and fragments of these same laws.

Because of uncertainties surrounding the dating system, scholars are still not sure exactly when Hammurabi's forty-three-year reign began; they believe that the year in question was 1848 BCE, 1792 BCE, or 1736 BCE. Even using the lowest date, however, it is clear that Hammurabi's collection of laws easily antedates those of the Hebrew Bible by quite a few centuries. The laws promulgated by Hammurabi are not, of course, exactly the same as those in the Torah (in fact, one striking difference is that sometimes different punishments are stipulated depending on the social class of the offender).[10] But very often they describe the same, very specific, situations—the runaway slave who seeks refuge in a freeman's house (LH ¶16; Deut. 23:16), the goring ox whose owner has been warned that his animal is a public danger (LH ¶251; Exod. 21:28–32), the slave whose belonging to his master is symbolized by his master inflicting an injury to the slave's ear (LH ¶282; Exod. 21:5–6). It seemed hardly plausible to modern scholars that these specific legal situations—fourteen in all[11]—should have been devised by Hammurabi and then, several centuries later, transmitted quite independently to the divine amanuensis. Indeed, some of the very laws examined above turn out to be strikingly paralleled in Hammurabi's collection. Here, for example, is Hammurabi's law of guardians:[12]

If a man gives his property for safekeeping and his property together with the householder's property is lost either by [theft achieved through] a breach or by scaling over a wall, the householder who was careless shall make restitution and shall restore to the owner of the property that which was given to him for safekeeping and which he allowed to be lost; the householder shall continue to search for his own lost property, and he shall take it from the one who stole it from him.

LH ¶125

Here, it is true, there is no mention of the guardian taking an oath, as in Exod. 22:7–8. Such a provision does appear, however, in yet another Mesopotamian collection, the Laws of Eshnunna (ca. 1770 BCE):

> If the man's house has been burglarized, and the owner of the house incurs a loss along with the goods which the depositor gave him [for safekeeping], the owner of the house shall swear an oath to satisfy him at the gate of [the temple of] the god Tishpak: "My goods have been lost along with your goods; I have not committed a fraud or misdeed"; thus shall he swear an oath to satisfy him and he will have no claim against him.

LE ¶37

Not only is the legal ruling similar to the biblical law,[13] but the wording here bears a striking resemblance to the Bible's as well. Thus, the guardian of the item in question is not actually called a "guardian" (though that might be the most logical way of referring to him); instead he is called by exactly the same term as is used in Exodus and Hammurabi, translated above as "the house-holder" or "the owner of the house" (that is, Hebrew *ba'al habbayit* and its Akkadian cognate *bēl bītim*). What is more, it was noted above that one sentence in the Exodus version seemed a bit problematic:[14] "If the thief is not caught, then the owner of the house shall *draw near to God*." Where is "near to God"? In the light of the Eshnunna version of this law, the Hebrew expression would seem likewise to refer to the gate of the temple.[15]

As for the other situation examined earlier, in which a pregnant woman is struck and miscarries as a result:

> If an *awīlu** strikes a woman of the *awīlu* class and thereby causes her to miscarry her fetus, he shall weigh and deliver 10 shekels of silver for her fetus. If that woman dies, they shall kill his daughter. If he should cause a woman of the commoner class to miscarry her fetus by the beating, he shall weigh and deliver 5 shekels of silver. If that woman should die, he shall weigh and deliver 30 shekels of silver.

LH ¶209

This is certainly not the same law as Exod. 21:22–23, but it is nearly the same situation, and it presents the same two possible outcomes (at least according

---

* That is, a free person, whether man, woman, or child, as opposed to members of the two lower classes, commoners and slaves.

to rabbinic sources and the Vulgate): the death of the fetus but no harm to the mother, and the death of the fetus and the death of the mother.[16] But Hammurabi cannot take credit for conceiving this (come to think of it) somewhat unlikely scenario—it is actually all over ancient Mesopotamian law codes. Here is a fragment from the Laws of Lipit-Ishtar (ca. 1930 BCE):

¶d If [a . . .] strikes the daughter of a man and causes her to lose her fetus, he shall weigh and deliver 30 shekels of silver.
¶e If she dies, that male shall be killed.

Similarly:

¶1 If he jostles the daughter of a man and causes her to miscarry her fetus, he shall weigh and deliver 10 shekels of silver.
¶2 If he strikes the daughter of a man and causes her to miscarry her fetus, he shall weigh and deliver 20 shekels of silver.
                    Sumerian Laws Exercise Tablet, ca. 1800 BCE

Similarly:

¶50 [If a man] strikes [another man's wife thereby causing her to abort her fetus, . . .] a man's wife [. . .] and they shall treat him as he treated her; he shall make full payment of a life for her fetus. And if that woman dies, they shall kill that man; he shall make full payment of a life for her fetus.
                    Middle Assyrian Laws, ca. 1076 BCE

Indeed, even the end of this biblical law, "an eye for an eye," has its equivalent in laws from elsewhere in the ancient Near East:

If an *awīlu* should blind the eye of another *awīlu,* they shall blind his eye. If he should break the bone of another *awīlu,* they shall break his bone . . . If an *awīlu* should knock out the tooth of another *awīlu* of his own rank, they shall knock out his tooth.
                    LH ¶196, 197, 200

In addition, it should be noted that the idea of payment instead of inflicting the same injury was not exactly an innovation of the Bible's ancient interpreters:

If anyone blinds a free person or knocks out his tooth, they used to pay 40 shekels of silver. But now he shall pay 20 shekels of silver. He shall look to his house for it.[17]
                    Hittite Laws ¶7

The Covenant Code

If these resemblances were not disturbing enough, scholars were also struck by the fact that they were all concentrated in the group of laws that immediately follows the Ten Commandments, that is, the legal corpus found in chapters 21, 22, and 23 of Exodus. The Bible implies that this corpus, no less than the Ten Commandments, was part of God's original covenant with Israel. Indeed, this group of further laws is often referred to as the *Covenant Code* (on the basis of Exod. 24:7).[18] But was it really part of the original covenant? We have already glimpsed a number of passages that seem to imply that the only stipulations in God's covenant were the laws of the Decalogue—after all, they were, by various accounts, the only laws inscribed on the two tablets. Most scholars therefore believe that the laws of the Covenant Code could not originally have been part of the deal; instead, these laws must have existed in some other form and functioned as a quite independent legal corpus in use in biblical times.[19] Then, at some point, they came to be inserted into the Sinai narrative as if they had been a set of further "covenant stipulations" (thereby swelling those stipulations to well beyond the limits of what, according to these scholars, might be found in a human-to-human covenant of normal proportions).[20]

In keeping with this view, scholars have noted that, while the simplicity of the Decalogue might well have suited Israel at an early stage of its existence, the laws of chapters 21–23 seem to presume a more established society, one with a jurisprudential apparatus in place (23:1–3, 6–8) to interpret laws and enforce its own rulings. The society itself does not seem to consist of small, family-based settlements: there are resident aliens (22:21; 23:9, 12), loans to the poor secured by property (22:25), thieves who tunnel into houses (22:2), and other telltale signs of a fairly complex and variegated community.

Combining this observation with the many resemblances observed between the Covenant Code and Hammurabi's laws, scholars soon came up with an explanation of diabolical simplicity: God's original covenant with Israel consisted only of the Ten Commandments, as the biblical text itself repeatedly implies.[21] After these ten laws were promulgated in chapter 20 of Exodus, the text then would have jumped to chapter 24, which recounts how the people agreed to accept this covenant of ten laws and solemnized it ceremonially. At some later point, however, someone inserted chapters 21–23. Perhaps these other ordinances, largely copied from a version or versions of Hammurabi's code, had been the law of the land for some time; the editor who stuck them in after the Ten Commandments simply wished to give them a divine pedigree. But all the evidence, these scholars say, indicates that these chapters are a foreign import.

Theologians have struggled mightily with the implications of all this for the doctrine of the Bible's divine inspiration. At the very least, some have asserted, the resemblance of the Covenant Code to legal material from Mesopotamia shows that the Bible's laws were not created in a heavenly vacuum. However the divine inspiration or divine origin of the Torah might have worked, it apparently did not involve starting with an absolutely clean slate. [22] The best one might say is that

> Moses did know these things [that is, Hammurabi's laws], but in such a way that, guided by God, he used them so far as they were in accordance with Divine revelation; independently indeed as exercising his own discretion in selecting them, but dependently in so far as they had found out already, by man's wisdom or the light of nature, that which was good and of good report.[23]

This may well be a theologically acceptable maneuver to account for the common material. Nevertheless, for some modern scholars and ordinary readers, the discovery of these ancient Near Eastern laws, like the discovery of various Mesopotamian versions of the flood narrative, raised the most troubling questions about the divine origin of Scripture.

Keeping Things New

There is a potential problem with any written code of laws: eventually, it grows old. Civilization continues to develop and change, but the words of the old laws remain the same. Remaining the same is not all bad, of course; stability and tradition are also a great source of strength. "These are the laws our ancestors followed," people say. "What was valid for them is still valid today." Indeed, those who first created the laws—"Solon the Wise," "our Founding Fathers"—are often revered figures from the distant past whose authority, therefore, makes the laws unshakeable. But after a while, the fact that the laws remain the same also becomes a burden. People's way of life changes from herding to farming, or from farming to heavy industry, from heavy industry to high-tech; populations shift, and with them social mores and standards of behavior. It becomes harder to stick to the old ways, and new situations arise that do not seem to be covered by any of the old laws.

Such problems have been dealt with in a variety of ways. One obvious solution is *interpretation:* the aging laws can be interpreted so as to apply to new situations. This happened with the Bible in the matter of intermarriage, for example. The Torah contained no absolute prohibition of intermarriage; when intermarriage came to be a pressing issue,[24] the author of the *Book of Jubilees* "discovered" an implicit prohibition of intermarriage in the story of

Dinah. This act of interpretation departed completely from what modern scholars understand to have been the original sense and purpose of the story, but no matter; now the Torah had a blanket condemnation of intermarriage. Indeed, many ancient interpreters (including the author of *Jubilees*) also chose to understand a certain verse in Leviticus—

> You shall not give any of your offspring to be passed to Molech, and you shall not profane the name of your God; I am the LORD.
>
> Lev. 18:21

—as if it, too, were a prohibition of intermarriage, although on the face of it the verse refers to worshiping the pagan god Molech through child sacrifice.[25] Here, in the clearest fashion, an old law has been interpreted in a new way to cover a new social reality.

In any legal system, however, new interpretations of old laws may be controversial. It is rare that a broad consensus is found for one particular reinterpretation; people everywhere tend to follow their own interests, and when interests differ, interpretations do as well. To work, therefore, an interpretation usually has to be perceived as *authoritative* in order to be widely accepted. Often, it must be endorsed and promulgated by some institution whose authority is beyond question.

In the case of the Bible and its ancient interpreters, various institutions (the temple priesthood, the leadership of different groups) did promulgate interpretations and bring them into common use. But human institutions and the ordinary human wisdom that stood behind them were often not enough.[26] Sometimes, therefore, the source of the interpretation was said to be God Himself—as with the teachings of the "True Teacher" of the Dead Sea Scrolls community:

> This refers to the True Teacher, to whom God has made known all the secrets of the words of his servants, the prophets.
>
> 1Q *Pesher Habakkuk* 7:4–5

In rabbinic texts, authoritative interpretation was sometimes directly connected to Moses and the divine revelation at Mount Sinai:

> Moses received the Torah [that is, the text *and* its proper interpretation] and passed it on [orally] to Joshua and Joshua to the elders and the elders to the prophets and the prophets passed it on to the men of the Great Assembly.
>
> m. *Abot* 1:1

Laws Outside of the Bible

Quite apart from interpretation, however, the old laws can also be modernized by *supplementary material.* Here, it is not that the old laws themselves are understood or applied in new ways, but that a group of entirely different laws or some other new material comes into force. The new material can then cover situations not covered by the earlier laws or take cognizance of societal or other changes. Indeed, many modern legal systems have in place provisions for the constant generation of new legislation (as well as the repeal of old legislation), popular amendment of a constitution, and so forth.

Once again, however, authority is a potential problem. In modern democracies, the authority to create new laws rests ultimately with the electorate. With any group seeking to be governed by biblical laws, however, the problem is somewhat thornier. Who, after all, has the right to add to (or repeal) what is written in the Bible? One answer was: people from within the Bible itself. That is why so many of the Jewish writings from the third century BCE onward are pseudepigrapha, that is, writings falsely attributed to one or another figure from the ancient past: the *Book of Enoch,* the *Testament of Abraham,* the *Fourth Book of Ezra,* the *Letter of Jeremiah,* and so forth. Scholars are quite sure that the *Book of Jubilees* was written sometime near the beginning of the second century BCE; the book itself, however, claims to have been written down by Moses a millennium earlier, in fact, to have been dictated to Moses by the "angel of the presence" at Mount Sinai.

It is noteworthy that this problem of authority for supplementary material was *not* dealt with in any particularly convincing way by the founders of rabbinic Judaism. (This may be an indication that, at least for a time, the authority for their supplementary laws and traditions was simply not an issue.) The earliest datable texts simply say that their additional laws and rules go back not to some biblical figure but merely to a vague group of predecessors known as the "fathers" or the "elders":

> For the Pharisees, and all the Jews, do not eat unless they wash their hands, observing the tradition of the elders; and when they come from the market place, they do not eat unless they purify themselves; and there are many other traditions which they observe, the washing of cups and pots and vessels of bronze.
>
> Mark 7:4–5

The Pharisees had passed on to the people certain ordinances handed down by the fathers and not written in the laws of Moses, for which reason they are rejected by the sect of the Sadducees, who hold that only those ordinances should be considered valid which were written down, and those which had been handed down by the fathers need not be observed.

Josephus, *Jewish Antiquities* 13:297

Eventually, however, it became a matter of rabbinic teaching that these other laws, along with the proper interpretation of the laws written in the Torah, originated with Moses on Mount Sinai. In effect, there were two Torahs, a written one (the Pentateuch) and a complementary "Oral Torah" passed on by word of mouth from generation to generation, until it was finally committed to writing starting at the end of the second century CE in the Mishnah (a basic legal code of Judaism) and other books:

It happened that someone stood before Shammai and said to him, "Rabbi, how many *torahs* do you have?" He said, "Two; one that is written and one that is oral."

Abot deR. Natan (A) 15

Christianity and the Laws of the Bible

And what of Christianity? The relationship of early Christians to the laws of the Torah is a complicated, and much discussed, subject.[27] It is clear, however, that Paul—and consequently, Christianity after his time—ultimately saw no significant role for the laws of the Torah in Christian practice. The old laws had served for a while, guarding the Jews in the same way that a *paidagogos* (a Greek slave in charge of the household's children) might look after his charges, sometimes disciplining them with a stern hand—but that time was now past.[28] Indeed, Paul said, trying to live by the written code (the "letter") of the Torah ultimately condemned people to death, whereas the new covenant of Christianity ("the spirit") gave life (2 Cor. 3:6). Similarly:

For the law brings wrath, but where there is no law there is no transgression. Sin indeed was in the world before the law was given [at Mount Sinai], but sin is not counted where there is no law.

Rom. 4:15; 5:13

The authority for such an enormous change in outlook derived from the very events on which Christianity was founded; the crucifixion and resurrection, Paul said, had made the old laws obsolete. One might think that such a stance would make the Hebrew Bible as a whole—replete, as we have seen briefly, with all sorts of laws—basically irrelevant to the new religion of grace. What reason was there to keep *any* of its material? Just as no one should need the now-outdated rules and regulations of the Torah, there could be little purpose for Christianity's new, universal message to be accompanied by the historical and other writings of one small, particular people. And indeed, some early Christians did endorse the idea of scrapping Hebrew Scripture entirely.

Instead of throwing out the Old Testament, however, most Christians wished to preserve it, in fact, to highlight its ties to their new faith. For as we have seen, a particularly Christian approach to Hebrew Scripture was to read it as a foreshadowing of the events of the Gospels. From Christianity's very beginning, the prophecies of Isaiah, certain psalms, and narratives like the offering of Isaac were all seen as precious hints in Jewish Scripture of things that were to come to pass centuries later. It would have seemed foolish, especially in the years when Christianity was first establishing itself, to give up these proofs of the new faith's legitimacy. On the contrary, as the list of such biblical foreshadowings increased—soon including the "three men" who visited Abraham in Genesis 18, Moses' outstretched hands leading to Joshua's victory in Exodus 17, and many more—the place of the Old Testament in Christianity became only more secure.

But it was not as a book of laws. On the contrary, what was valuable was precisely the non-legal material: the stories, which, apart from their typological relationship to the New Testament,[29] might teach this or that lesson by example; the prophecies, which, in addition to their direct relationship to the New Testament and later Christian history and practice, also contained valuable teaching and preaching; the psalms and canticles (songs found in the midst of narratives), which were incorporated into Christian worship; and the wise sayings of Solomon and others, which might serve as a guide in daily affairs. Indeed, even the laws themselves were sometimes read typologically, as mini-prophecies: the laws of Passover (Exod. 12:1–28) were thus interpreted as referring to the crucifixion (John 19:33–36; 1 Cor. 5:7–8; 1 Pet. 1:13, 18–19),[30] or a certain law about oxen (Deut. 25:4) was applied to the role of pastors and elders in the church (1 Cor. 9:3–11; 1 Tim. 5:17).[31]

So the Hebrew Bible did not disappear from Christianity, but it did change its character. It was no longer a book of rules, a detailed set of do's and don'ts by which people could steer their course in life. Instead, it became a great *grimoire,* an infinitely rich, infinitely textured fabric of divine teachings, including allusions to the New Testament and to Christian doctrines, as well as a weave of symbolic representations of all that can happen deep within a person's soul. Unrolled and examined from end to end, this same multicolored bolt revealed a pattern of cryptic, intermittent assurances about the final salvation that was certain to come. This was the great Bible of medieval Christianity. In it, the narratives of Adam or Abraham or David turned from history into heraldry, unfolding in slow motion time and again before readers or congregants in church; these stories, it turned out, were actually a combination of various discrete, representative elements, each of which had its own hidden significance, and which could have been brought together into the complex machinery of biblical narrative only by the Supreme Narrator Himself. It is difficult to stress sufficiently the importance for Christians of this change in the Hebrew Bible's character. This transformation not only marked a significant event in the history of biblical interpretation; it is also one of great meaning today, when Christians as well as Jews (but in a rather different fashion) are seeking a response to the question of *how to read the Bible* that is this book's subject.

18

Worship on the Road

Exodus 32 and Leviticus 10, 16, 19, 23

Moses Breaking the Tables of the Law
by Gustave Doré.

AARON'S GREAT MISTAKE. ANCIENT NEAR EASTERN TEMPLES.
NADAB AND ABIHU. LOVING YOUR NEIGHBOR.

Moses' brother Aaron was the first priest, the founder of the priestly dynasty. Yet he led the people into their great sin, the worship of the Golden Calf. Did the Bible regard him as a hero or a villain?

Moses stayed on Mount Sinai for forty days and forty nights while God was giving him the laws that went with His covenant. Moses was some eighty years old at the time, and as the period of his absence grew longer and longer, some of the Israelites camped at the foot of the mountain drew the natural conclusion. They thought their old leader must simply have died:

> When the people saw that Moses was taking a long time to come down from the mountain, the people reproved Aaron and said to him, "Come, make us some gods to lead us;* for this fellow Moses, who took us up out of the land of Egypt—no one knows what may have become of him." Aaron said to them, "Strip off the gold rings that are on the ears of your wives, your sons, and your daughters, and bring them to me." So all the people stripped off the gold rings from their ears and brought them to Aaron. He took the gold from them, formed it in a mold, and made it into a molten calf. Then they proclaimed, "These are your gods, O Israel, who brought you up out of the land of Egypt!" When Aaron saw this, he built an altar before it; and Aaron announced, "Tomorrow will be a festival to the LORD." So they rose early the next day and offered burnt offerings and brought sacrifices of well-being. Then the people sat down to eat and drink, and rose up to revel.
>
> Exod. 32:1–6

This whole incident was extremely troubling. Only three months had passed since God had freed the Israelites from slavery, afflicting the Egyptians in the process with the ten plagues. When the Egyptians nonetheless pursued the departing Israelites, God had miraculously divided the Red Sea, saving the Israelites and drowning their Egyptian pursuers. Nor did the supernatural events cease there: the pillars of cloud and fire, the water drawn from the rock at Rephidim, and the miraculous victory over the Amalekites were soon followed by the great divine revelation at Mount Sinai, when God's very words were heard by every Israelite man, woman, and child. And now, only

---

* Literally, "to go before us."

a month or so later and with the Ten Commandments still ringing in their ears, the Israelites went and did precisely what those commandments had forbidden, making a molten metal image, the Golden Calf, and bowing down before it. If this were not incredible enough, the Bible even related that Aaron, Moses' trusted older brother, was the one responsible for this perfidious act.

In considering these events, ancient readers of the Bible assumed some lesson must be intended. But what could it be? That even a righteous man like Aaron can make a mistake? Even if this were true, it was hardly the sort of thing that needed to be communicated to potential sinners, especially since, after Moses returned from the mountain and confronted his brother with his wrongdoing, Aaron seemed only to dodge the blame in the most cowardly fashion, without showing the slightest sign of personal remorse:

> Moses said to Aaron, "What did this people do to you to [make you] bring this great sin upon them?" And Aaron said, "Do not let my lord be too angry; you know this people, how they are bent on evil. They said to me, 'Make us gods to lead us; for this fellow Moses, who took us up out of the land of Egypt—no one knows what may have become of him.' So I said to them, 'Whoever has gold, strip it off'; then they gave it to me, and I threw it into the fire, and out came this calf!"
>
> Exod. 32:21–24

What a lame excuse! What, then, could this story be intended to impart?

As they further considered the matter, interpreters noticed something odd: Aaron's colleague Hur had disappeared. Just before Moses and Joshua went up the mountain, Moses had left Aaron and Hur in charge, saying to the elders, "Wait here for us, until we come to you again. Aaron and Hur are with you; whoever has a dispute may go to them" (Exod. 24:14). That was the last thing said about Hur in the Bible—when Moses came back down, Aaron was apparently the only one in charge. Of course, Hur might have died in the interim. But surely the death of such a leader of Israel, the one who, together with Aaron, had supported Moses' tired arms at Rephidim, would not have passed without mention. The more interpreters thought about it, the more it seemed that Hur's sudden absence was one of those little hints that the Torah dropped from time to time, preferring to relate by indirection events that were too troubling to narrate openly. So it was that interpreters came to the conclusion that Hur had indeed died, but not as a result of natural causes.

A righteous man and a responsible leader, he must have been against the whole Golden Calf project from the start, publicly opposing it and urging Aaron in the strongest terms not to cooperate. If so, then what was an enraged mob likely to have done? Hur's unexplained disappearance must represent the Bible's delicate way of pointing to an ugly truth: the mob rose up against Hur and killed him for his opposition to the Golden Calf. Then Aaron, fearing that any further provocation might put his own life in danger (and so bring down yet another sin on the people of Israel), reluctantly complied with their wishes:

> When the people of Israel started to do that deed [of the Golden Calf], they first went to Hur and said to him, "Come make a god for us."[1] When he did not do as they said, they went and killed him . . . Afterward they went to Aaron and said to him, "Come, you make us a god." When Aaron heard he took fright, as it is said, "And Aaron was afraid and he built an altar in front of it" [variant reading of Exod. 32:5].
>
> *Leviticus Rabba* 10:3

Seen in this light, Aaron's action seemed not only reasonable, but almost heroic. Wishing to spare the Israelites further sin, he cooperated with their plan; then, when Moses came down from the mountain, Aaron told him nothing of Hur's murder and the Israelites' threats against him, instead pretending that no one was really responsible: "I threw it into the fire, and out came this calf!" Indeed, Aaron's willingness to preserve harmony at almost any cost may have contributed to his postbiblical reputation as a peacemaker:

> Hillel said: "Be of the disciples of Aaron, loving peace and pursuing peace, loving other people and leading them to the Torah."
>
> m. *Abot* 1:12

Broken Tablets

Moses was of a somewhat less irenic constitution. When he learned what the Israelites had done, he took the two stone tablets that he had carried down from the mountain, tablets that had been inscribed by God's own hand, and threw them to the ground, shattering them to bits. (Ever after, these bits of broken stone were preserved in the sacred Ark of the Covenant, a precious memorial.)

In breaking God's own handiwork, it seemed as if Moses might have gone too far, giving in to the emotion of the moment—though interpreters labored to find some explanation for his act.[2] In any event, after the Golden Calf incident, Moses and his fellow Levites also killed three thousand of the sinners, and God further afflicted the Israelites with a plague (Exod. 32:25–35). God then announced that He would be sending Moses and the Israelites off to Canaan alone. They were too sinful for God Himself to accompany them—He would remain at Mount Sinai and send along an angel instead (Exod. 33:1–3).

But Moses went again to intercede with God, and presently He agreed to accompany the Israelites into Canaan: "I will do the very thing that you have asked; for you have found favor in my sight, and I know you by name" (Exod. 33:17). God then told Moses to make a new pair of stone tablets so that He might write out the commandments once again. Moses did so and went back up Mount Sinai, once again asking God to forgive His people's sinfulness. What Moses received was more than he had asked for. God revealed to him His own essence: He is a God who is not indifferent, but fundamentally kind and merciful:

> Moses carved out two stone tablets like the first ones and rose early in the morning to go up on Mount Sinai as the LORD had commanded him, taking the two stone tablets in his hand. Then the LORD came down in a cloud and stood with him there, and proclaimed the name "LORD." [That is,] the LORD passed before him and proclaimed, "The LORD, the LORD, a God merciful and compassionate, slow to anger, and abounding in kindness and faithfulness, extending kindness to the thousandth generation, forgiving iniquity and transgression and sin; yet He does not give up punishment completely, but [sometimes] visits the iniquity of the parents upon the children and the children's children, to the third and the fourth generation." Then Moses quickly dropped to the ground and bowed low.[3]
>
> Exod. 34:4–8

Temples and the Gods

The incident of the Golden Calf was a horrible apostasy. Ironically, the narration of those events is sandwiched in the midst of God's instructions to Moses concerning the building of a special structure, the tabernacle, which was to serve as a kind of mobile temple or sanctuary during the Israelites' desert wanderings on their way to Canaan.

What was the purpose of such a mobile temple? Scholars have learned a great deal about temples in the ancient Near East over the past century. One thing is clear: the temple was not (as the word might seem to indicate to many people today) principally a place where the faithful assembled to pray or read Scripture. This is the main purpose of a synagogue or church, but not of an ancient temple. A temple in the ancient Near East was essentially the *house of the deity.* The god or goddess was actually deemed to take up residence inside the temple. Temples were therefore lavishly appointed, so as to provide truly royal surroundings in which the deity might abide in splendor. This same general conception of the temple is reflected in God's instructions to the Israelites to build the tabernacle:

The LORD said to Moses: Tell the Israelites to bring Me an offering; from everyone whose heart so moves him shall you receive the offering for Me. This is the offering that you shall receive from them: gold, silver, and copper; blue dye and purple, with crimson yarns, fine linen, and goats' hair; tanned rams' skins, fine leather, and acacia wood; oil for lighting, spices for the anointing oil and for the fragrant incense; onyx stones and gems to be set in the ephod and for the breast-piece. *And have them make Me a sanctuary, so that I may dwell among them.* Exactly as I shall show you—the plan of the tabernacle and of all its furnishings—so you shall make it.

Exod. 25:1–9

Of course, in the ancient Near East, the deity was not thought to exist just in that one place: he or she might also be somewhere else in the natural world or in the sky, or simultaneously in another temple (though how this was done was not explained). But the presence of the deity inside the temple meant that there would always be a spot within human reach where the deity could be approached and served, where people might go to offer gifts that would bring favor on them or to present their heartfelt requests for help.

Temples in the ancient Near East were a very, very old institution. The oldest surviving Mesopotamian remains of temples go back to the early fifth millennium BCE—long before there were written records of any kind—but it is quite likely that temples existed even before then, perhaps built out of perishable materials that have left no trace. As with any very ancient institution, trying to understand the place of temples and gods in the life of ordinary people is no simple task; once such an institution is established, most people soon stop speculating about why it exists or how it works. So is it also, for example, with prayer nowadays. Many Jews and Christians and Muslims pray to God regularly. But how many of them think consciously about what occurs when they pray? Does God "hear" them wherever they are—and can He hear and respond to millions of prayers simultaneously? Is it enough merely to *think* a prayer for God to hear it, or does a person actually have to whisper the words or speak them aloud? Is a prayer spoken by a hundred people simultaneously more likely to be answered than one spoken by a single individual? Different answers have been offered to all these questions by philosophers and theologians, but for the most part, ordinary people just don't think about them: prayer simply *exists,* it is how one speaks to God—the mechanics are not that important (and perhaps unknowable).

So was it with temples in the ancient Near East. They had always been there and, as far as anyone knew, always would be. The temple was where the god lived, in a special niche, embodied in a spindly little statue of wood overlaid with precious metals and cloth. The statue was not a *representation* of the god; the god was believed to have actually entered its wood and metal or stone, so that now this *was* the god—he was actually right over there.[4] "Go before Enki," people would say, or, "Offer this to Marduk." The statue may have been small, but the god inside it radiated power. After all, the gods controlled all that was beyond human controlling, and humans fell before them in abject deference. People invoked the gods, implored the gods, named their own children after gods ("Marduk-Have-Mercy-on-Me," "Ishtar-Is-Heaven's-Queen," "Guard-Me-Shamash"), and even when people were not consciously thinking about the gods, they nonetheless lived every minute of their lives in the gods' shadow.

Animal Sacrifices

Inside the temple was a special coterie of the god's servants. These were the priests, who in many ways were comparable to the slaves or household staff of a high official or king. Their job was to do all that was possible to insure that the god was properly served and so was able to look to the prosperity and success of the city in which his temple stood. This involved, among other things, offering animal sacrifices to the god—and this, like the idea of the temple itself and the divine statues, is so far from the experience of most of us that it requires a willful act of imagination to recapture its essence.

Why did peoples of the ancient Near East (and elsewhere) pile the altars of their gods with the still-warm carcasses of sheep or bulls? Ancient texts themselves offer a host of explanations: this was the deity's food (indeed, in the Bible itself God refers to "My sacrifice, the food of My offerings by fire" [Num. 28:2]); the life of the slaughtered animal was offered as a substitute for the offerer's life (that is, "better it than me"); the animal was a costly possession given up as a sign of fealty or in the hope of receiving still more generous compensation from the deity.[5] To these traditional explanations have been added more recent ones that see the sacrifice as establishing a tangible connection between the sacrificer and the deity.[6] Others have sought to stress the connection of the sacred with violence or see the function of religion overall as defusing violence that would otherwise be directed at other human beings.[7]

Even if it were possible to recapture the original idea behind animal sacrifices—and it isn't—the search for such an original idea can tell us little about the function of sacrifices in Israel during the biblical period (or in any other ancient society). As one scholar has recently argued, that would be like trying to understand the meaning of a word by searching for its etymology: the word "silly" is an adjective originally derived from *sele,* a Middle English noun that meant happiness or bliss, and "silly" itself used to mean "spiritually blessed" or even "holy"—but that does not mean that the word nowadays has any such associations in the minds of English speakers. Similarly, the function of sacrifice—or any ritual act—cannot be understood by trying to reconstruct the original circumstances that gave rise to it.[8]

Moreover, such thinking betrays a fundamental misunderstanding of religious ritual. The ritual act itself is what is important, not its symbolism or purported meaning. To a certain way of thinking, ritual *does* something. (As the American writer Flannery O'Connor, a devout Roman Catholic, once said about the Eucharist: "If it's a symbol, the hell with it.")[9] Animal sacrifices in Israel were conceived to be the principal channel of communication between the people and God. In prayers, of course, people spoke to God, but for all that, prayer was not primary. The sacrifice—the passage of a small, palpable, breathing animal from life to death and from the world of the living upward through the flickering flames of the altar—spoke louder than any prayer. As Platonis Sallustius, a fourth-century philosopher and author of *On the Gods and the World,* observed, "Prayer without sacrifice is just words."[10]

Such was worship in biblical Israel and elsewhere in the ancient Near East. It is to be stressed that the temple itself was a world apart; the house in which the god lived was not conceived to be continuous with the world outside. It was separate, sealed off; and it radiated holiness. One interesting piece of testimony to this fact is the temple recently excavated at 'Ein Dara', in modern Syria.[11] The temple resembles others excavated from that part of the world (as well, incidentally, as Solomon's temple, according to its biblical description)—save for one striking feature. On the steps leading up to this temple's doorway, the builders carved a set of huge footprints, symbolically representing the god's entrance into his sanctuary. The footprints are sunk into the temple steps in the same way that human footprints might be sunk into mud or wet concrete—but the feet themselves are many times bigger than human feet, and the length of the stride they mark off is far greater than a human's stride. Archaeologists estimate that, on the basis of this stride, the god or goddess of that temple would have to have been some sixty-five feet tall! How could such a huge deity ever make its way through the rather normal-sized entrance of the temple? This, apparently, did not trouble the temple's otherwise careful planners. Why not? Because they knew that the inside of this temple, of every temple, was a world apart, a little condensed, time-stopped bit of eternity that was discontinuous with the everyday world that surrounded it, a world in which a spindly little statue could indeed *be* the same god that stood sixty-five feet high on the outside.

The Tabernacle and Modern Scholarship

Modern scholars note that the religion of Israel was a relatively late development in the ancient Near East. Long, long before there had even been an

Israel, the gods had been worshiped in temples that dotted the landscape of ancient Canaan and environs. Israel's own religion ended up being, in some respects, strikingly different from those of its neighbors; but modern scholars are equally attuned to the similarities. Thus, Solomon's temple as described in the book of Kings seems to have a floor plan altogether typical of West Semitic temples such as the ones excavated at 'Ein Dara' or Tel Ta'yinat in Syria; the different classes of sacrifices offered in Israelite temples used some of the same names found in ancient Canaanite texts; the priests were designated by the same word; and so forth. Indeed, even Israel's way of referring to its God parallels phrases and appellations used for Canaanite gods in texts discovered in northern Syria.

It is therefore not surprising that, like Solomon's temple, which eventually replaced it, the desert tabernacle that God commanded the Israelites to build (Exodus 25–27) should—in its dimensions, appurtenances, and the sacrifices that were to be offered within its precincts—resemble the sanctuaries found at neighboring sites in the ancient Near East and the worship conducted within them. About this tabernacle, however, modern scholarly opinion continues to fluctuate. To Julius Wellhausen and other late-nineteenth- and early-twentieth-century scholars, it seemed obvious that the tabernacle was simply a literary fiction. There never was a tabernacle. Long after the people of Israel had emerged—indeed, long after it had been decided that, instead of multiple holy sites dotting the landscape, there was to be a single, centralized temple in Jerusalem—some priest or scribe, in seeking to imagine the Israelites' desert wanderings after the exodus from Egypt, naturally supposed that they too had had a central shrine. But how could they if they were wandering all the time? It must have been a *portable* shrine, he supposed, a tent that could be packed up and moved from place to place. Thus was created, according to Wellhausen and others, yet another biblical fiction: the whole account of the desert tabernacle was a wholesale retrojection of the much later reality of temple worship in Judah.

More recently, some scholars have taken issue with this view. In particular, F. M. Cross has suggested that the whole idea of a tent shrine is actually borrowed from an ancient Canaanite notion, according to which the supreme god El dwells in a tent; the Israelite cherubim throne, the planks (*qerashim*), and other appurtenances, Cross and others have argued, are likewise borrowed motifs attested in the ancient writings of Ugarit.[12] This may not necessarily authenticate the biblical picture of a portable shrine, but it certainly could make the idea of such a shrine far older than Wellhausen supposed. Similarly, other scholars have suggested that, while such a tent shrine may not go back to the period of desert wanderings, the idea may have been based on an actual tent shrine in David's day or possibly on a tent sanctuary at Shiloh; its dimensions, others have noted, seem to match those of an ancient temple unearthed at Arad.[13]

When it comes to the actual details of how the Israelites built the desert tabernacle, most modern readers feel their eyes closing. The instructions given by God (Exodus 25–31) are themselves somewhat repetitious, and the account of these instructions subsequently being carried out (chapters 35–40) is, for pages and pages, virtually a verbatim recapitulation of the instructions themselves. Why all this verbiage, when the whole thing could have been summed up in a sentence or two? But for ancient Israelites, the tabernacle itself was highly significant, and the detailed account of its construction must have held a certain fascination. Here were the precise specifications of the structure that allowed God to take up residence once again in the midst of humankind—the first time He had done so since the Garden of Eden.

A Mysterious Death

With the tabernacle complete, the Bible next turns to what is supposed to go on inside it—laws governing the offering of different kinds of sacrifices and what the priests are to do to prepare them. All this occupies the first seven chapters of the book of Leviticus. (The book's name, incidentally, derives from the fact that priests and other temple officials were all said to descend from a single tribe, Levi.) Once those instructions have been imparted, the Israelites can begin their sacrificial worship of God. The tabernacle is made ready and anointed; the priests—Aaron and his sons—are given their special priestly vestments and consecrated; and then . . . the unthinkable happens.

> Now Aaron's sons, Nadab and Abihu, each took his censer, put fire in it, and laid incense on it; and they offered unholy fire before the LORD, such as He had not commanded them. And fire came out from the presence of the LORD and consumed them, and they died before the LORD. Then Moses said to Aaron, "This is what the LORD meant when He said, 'Through those who are near Me I will be kept holy, and [thus] by all the people I will be honored.' " And Aaron was silent.
>
> Lev. 10:1–3

On what ought to have been one of the happiest days in Israel's history—the inauguration of the tabernacle service—two of Aaron's sons slip up somehow in priestly procedure and immediately die as a result. But was God really so severe as to kill two novices simply because they made a mistake on their first day on the job?

The text did offer some clues as to what went wrong. To begin with, Nadab and Abihu are said to have brought "unholy fire" right before God. The word "unholy" here (*zarah*) actually means something closer to "foreign" or "strange," but in the context of the tabernacle, it designates anyone or anything that is not authorized to be there (see Num. 1:51; 3:10, 38; 18:7). Apparently, Aaron's sons had willfully used incense coals from somewhere outside of the sanctuary—a grave infraction. Perhaps, too, that was the sense of God's words cited by Moses immediately following the incident, "Through those who are near Me I will be kept holy, and [thus] by all the people I will be honored." [14] *Those who are near Me* are the priests, the ones who get to enter directly before the place of God's presence. These words might thus be reworded more directly as: "Only if you priests respect My holiness will I be honored by the rest of the people, so don't take liberties or get sloppy." Perhaps it was important that this matter be straightened out on the tabernacle's very first day—even if it did mean the death of two of Aaron's sons.

On the other hand, immediately following the incident came a divine instruction that offered another clue:

> And the LORD spoke to Aaron: Drink no wine or strong drink, neither you nor your sons, when you enter the tent of meeting, lest you die; it is a statute forever throughout your generations. You are to distinguish between the holy and the ordinary, and between the unclean and the clean; and you are to teach the people of Israel all the statutes that the LORD has spoken to them through Moses.
>
> Lev. 10:8–9

If, following his sons' death, the first thing that Aaron is told is, "Drink no wine or strong drink, neither you *nor your sons,* when you enter the tent of meeting, *lest you die,*" then it would seem that the cause of their death might well have been drunkenness. Indeed, this may have been the full story behind the incident: Nadab and Abihu had become intoxicated, and that is what led them to bring the "unholy fire" into the sanctuary. Drunkenness might indeed cause a person to fail to (in God's words just cited) "distinguish between the holy and the ordinary, and between the unclean and the clean." If so, this certainly was a grave error. After all, distinguishing between the holy and the ordinary is precisely what being a priest is all about, as Moses had intended to say in citing God's words "Through those who are near Me I will be kept holy, and [thus] by all the people I will be honored." It was a hard lesson to have to learn on the sanctuary's first day, but one that would forever echo in the ears of the temple staff. [15]

The Holy People

While much of Leviticus is thus taken up with priestly matters, there are nonetheless more than a few items that pertain to all of Israel. Particularly striking is a large section of instructions from Leviticus 17–26, whose main theme is that of holiness. For that reason, these chapters are known to scholars as the Holiness Code.[16]

What exactly does "holiness" mean? The Bible never defines it. Perhaps the reason is that no definition was necessary. *Holy* just is; it is an unmistakable state of being. In biblical Israel, this adjective belongs, first and foremost, to God: He is *holy* beyond any other trait. The seraphim who praise Him in heaven have, according to Isaiah, only one thing to say about Him: "Holy, holy, holy is the LORD of Hosts." He is, time and again, "Israel's Holy One." *Holy* is that which most characterizes God.[17]

God's holiness rubs off, however, on whatever is close to Him or belongs to Him. Thus heaven is His "holy dwelling" and the earthly tabernacle or temple in which He dwells is likewise the "holy place," or even "the holy place of holiness" (*miqdash ha-qodesh*). Indeed, the place inside it set off for Him is called the *"most* holy place" (literally, the "holy of holies"). The furnishings of the sanctuary are also holy, as are the priests who serve before Him and the sacrifices that they offer. The day that God set aside for rest— God's day, as it were—is also holy (Exod. 16:23; 20:8; 31:14–15; 35:2; Deut. 5:12; Isa. 58:13–14, etc.). The fact that Israel is the people chosen by God to receive His covenant makes them holy too; they are to be, according to the formulation already seen, a "kingdom of priests and a holy nation" (Exod. 19:6). It thus seems that God's holiness is not only His salient characteristic, but one that radiates out and sticks in various degrees to everything that is His or is near Him.

The surprising thing about the laws of Leviticus 17–26 is the extent to which Israel's holiness is stressed there. Repeatedly the text urges people to *be holy:* "Act holy and be holy; for I am the LORD. Keep My statutes and observe them; I the LORD have made you holy" (Lev. 20:8). But what does it mean to be commanded to *be holy?*

If the laws accompanying this exhortation are any guide, being holy involves things connected with sacrifices and the tabernacle and ritual purity (which was maintained by keeping oneself from eating unclean animals and from forbidden sexual relations, contact with dead bodies, and so forth); but it also includes certain moral and ethical strictures. To put it another way: the Holiness Code brings together the "vertical" and "horizontal" dimensions of religion, matters between humans and God on the one hand and matters that are between humans and their fellow creatures on the other.[18] These two types of laws are lumped together in a way that can only seem intentional—as if the Bible were saying, "Your being holy involves this as much as that." Thus, for example:

> The LORD spoke to Moses, saying: Speak to all the congregation of the people of Israel and say to them: You shall be holy, for I the LORD your God am

holy. You shall each respect your mother and father, and you shall keep My sabbaths: I am the LORD your God. Do not turn to idols or make cast images for yourselves: I am the LORD your God.

When you offer a sacrifice of well-being to the LORD, offer it in such a way that reflects well on you. It shall be eaten on the same day you offer it, or on the next day; and anything left over until the third day shall be consumed in fire. If it is eaten on the third day, this is a perversion; it cannot be accepted. All who eat it shall be subject to punishment, because they have profaned what is holy to the LORD; and any such person shall be cut off from the people.

When you reap the harvest of your land, you shall not reap to the very edges of your field, or gather the gleanings of your harvest. You shall not strip your vineyard bare, or gather the fallen grapes of your vineyard; you shall leave them for the poor and the alien: I am the LORD your God.

You shall not steal; you shall not deal deceitfully or falsely with one another. And you shall not swear falsely by My name, profaning the name of your God: I am the LORD.

You shall not defraud your neighbor; you shall not rob; and you shall not keep for yourself the wages of a laborer until morning. You shall not curse the deaf or put a stumbling block before the blind; you shall fear your God: I am the LORD.

Lev. 19:1–14

This assemblage begins with the exhortation to "respect your mother and father"—certainly an interhuman concern. But then in the next breath it commands people to keep the sabbath, a matter between man and God. In the latter category as well are the next matters treated, avoiding idol worship and acting properly with regard to sacrifices. But then come more interhuman matters: Always leave a little of your grain harvest behind in the fields, the text says, so that poor people and foreigners can glean some of it for themselves. The same goes for your vineyard. Outlawed as well are shady business practices: "You shall not steal; you shall not deal deceitfully or falsely with one another." It is even forbidden to withhold a day laborer's wages until the next day: payment must be made that very day. All this, the text says, is part of being holy.

A great many of these laws are completely unenforceable. After all, what is involved in "respecting" your mother and father—and who is going to determine that you have violated such a stricture? If I leave behind a single stalk of wheat in the corner of my field, will I be deemed to have kept the requirement of leaving some food for the gleaners? Probably not. But then, how much is enough? The Bible doesn't say. How about avoiding deceitful business practices—am I still allowed to "forget" exactly how old is the horse I've brought to market, and can I imply, without quite saying so, that the house I'm selling has never had any structural problems? Since none of these things is spelled out, what actually violates the law is always going to be a matter of opinion. That is perhaps true most of all of the last commandment, "You shall fear your God." "Fear of God" in biblical Hebrew actually has nothing to do with God directly; this is an old idiom meaning something like "common decency" in English.[19] How can you *order* someone to have common decency? That seems to be the reason why the text keeps coming back to its main point, being holy. "You know what it means to be holy," it seems to say. "So there is no reason to try to specify everything involved. Just don't do anything that is not appropriate to someone who is holy."

Loving Your Neighbor

Precisely because they seemed to cover so much—and to cover things that no other law code would ever dare include, dependent as they are on the individual's own heart and judgment—these laws drew the attention of the ancient interpreters, whose job, after all, was to determine exactly how biblical laws were to be applied to daily life. Particularly significant for them was the series of brief laws that appears somewhat later in this same chapter:

> You shall not hate your brother in your heart; you shall reprove your neighbor, and you shall incur no guilt because of him. You shall not take revenge or bear a grudge against any of your people, but you shall love your neighbor as yourself: I am the LORD.
>
> Lev. 19:17–18

Hatred "in the heart," interpreters concluded, was hidden hatred, resentment that simmered inside a person but never expressed itself openly. (It was "in the heart" but not in the mouth.) The antidote to such hatred they found in the next clause, "You shall reprove your neighbor." That is, if A finds out that B has insulted him behind his back, B must not simply be quiet about it. He should go right up to A and *reprove* him, "I heard what you said and I don't like it one bit." Here is how one ancient interpreter, Ben Sira, explained this law in the early second century BCE:

> Reprove a friend so that he not do it—and if he did, that he not do it again.[20]
> Reprove a neighbor so that he not say it—and if he did, that he not repeat it.
> Reprove a friend, since often it [what you heard] is slander—so don't believe everything [you hear].

It also happens that someone errs without meaning to—and who has not
    sinned with his speech?
Reprove your friend before you grow angry—and give place to the
    Almighty's Torah.

Sir. 19:13–17

Ben Sira's account is sensitive to the ways (and wiles) of the human heart.
Even if the harm has already been done, he says, it is always worthwhile for
you to reprove the offender, at least to prevent a repetition. And who knows?
Perhaps the whole thing will turn out to have been untrue, the invention of
someone who wanted to stir up trouble between you and B. Even if it is true,
Ben Sira suggests, perhaps B did not mean it; only by openly confronting the
offender will such things come out. Finally, if B proves to have intended every
word, the reproof will at least serve to defuse the situation "before you
grow angry." After all, there are legal remedies for such offenses, so "give
place to the Almighty's Torah."

The next verse went on to forbid revenge and bearing a grudge—and to
this too ancient interpreters gave a down-to-earth application in everyday
life.* But what about the very last part of this passage, the commandment to
"love your neighbor as yourself"? These words were both an inspiration and
a puzzle.[21] Did they mean that if, for example, I win a million dollars in the
lottery, I have to distribute half that sum to my neighbor? Or, if my life and
my neighbor's are both in danger, is the Bible telling me that I cannot give my
own life preference? This seemed like a tall order, virtually inhuman—but
some ancient interpreters nonetheless took that route:

> Be loving of your brothers as a man loves himself, with each man seeking
> for his brother what is good for him, and acting in concert on the earth, and
> *loving each other as themselves.*

Jubilees 36:4

> You shall not hate any man, but some you shall reprove, others you shall
> pray for, and *others you shall love more than your own life.*[22]

Didache 2:7

> You shall love your neighbor even above your own soul [life].

Letter of Barnabas 19:5

To other ancient interpreters, however, the Bible seemed to be saying something rather different. To love your neighbor "as yourself" did not mean to
love him *as much as yourself,* but rather *as you would wish him to love you.*

---

* See above, opening section of chapter 17.

(Technically speaking, this interpretation takes "yourself" as the direct object not of your loving, but of his: "You shall love your neighbor as [he should love] yourself.") Thus:

> The way of life is this: First, you shall love the Lord your Maker, and secondly, your neighbor as yourself. And whatever you do not want to be done to you, you shall not do to anyone else.[23]
>
> *Didache* 3:1–2

> Do not take revenge and do not hold on to hatred, and love your neighbor; for what is hateful to you yourself, do not do it him; I am the LORD.
>
> *Targum Pseudo-Jonathan* Lev. 19:18

As such, this one commandment seemed to sum up everything the Torah had to say about the "horizontal" dimension of biblical law, interhuman relations.[24] It was often cited in precisely this sense:

> But among the vast number of particular truths and principles studied, two, one might almost say, stand out higher than all the rest, that of [relating] to God through piety and holiness, and that of [relating] to fellow men through a love of mankind and of righteousness.
>
> Philo, *Special Laws* 2:63

> The commandments are summed up in this one sentence, "You shall love your neighbor as yourself."
>
> Rom. 13:9

> "And you shall love your neighbor as yourself"—R. Akiba said: This is the great general principle in the Torah.
>
> *Sifra Qedoshim* 4

In short, while much of Leviticus was taken up with technical matters connected to the tabernacle (sacrifices, laws of purity and impurity), the great section of laws that began in chapter 19 seemed to strike a different note. Here God told His people that their unique status as a "holy nation" imposed on them duties well beyond anything any human legislator might impose. Being holy meant always trying to do the right thing, to walk about in the halo of purity that befits those chosen to receive God's commandments.

19

P and D

LEVITE.   HIGH PRIEST.   PRIEST.

Levite, High Priest, Priest from *The Story of the Bible.*

The Documentary Hypothesis. Meet the Cohens.
The theology of P. The Deuteronomic core.
Deuteronomy and wisdom. Who's a priest?

The Documentary Hypothesis was one of the early results of modern biblical scholarship. If anything, its sting has only grown sharper with the years.

Certainly one of the most disturbing aspects of modern biblical scholarship has been the Documentary Hypothesis—the belief that the Pentateuch, rather than being a single, unified text dictated by God to Moses, is actually a collage made up of four or five (or more) different documents, put together rather clumsily by the book's final editor or editors.

In principle, the idea that the Pentateuch might have come from different hands ought not to have been too troubling in itself. After all, if, according to the Bible, a prophet is simply a conduit for God's words, what difference did it make if there had been one conduit for the Pentateuch or four? Wine from the same spigot can be poured into four different bottles, after all. And who could say that J, E, P, and D (the four authorial sources identified by Wellhausen and others) were not prophets of equal standing with Moses? Indeed, perhaps behind these anonymous initials were real figures known to us from elsewhere in the Bible—say, Micah, Hosea, Ezekiel, and Jeremiah—who, for reasons unknown, had decided (or had been ordered) to present their texts as if transmitted through Moses?*

But the Documentary Hypothesis was much more than a theory of who wrote what. Underlying it was a whole picture of how Israel's religion had developed. Wellhausen and others had thought that Israel at first had polytheistic, or animistic, beliefs, close to nature and the natural world; with time, their beliefs had evolved into a devotion to a single God, YHWH, and from there Israel eventually soared into the "ethical monotheism" preached by its great prophets. Its religion had then further morphed into a thing of laws and priestly ceremonies—a definite downturn, from Wellhausen's point of view.

The different sources of the Pentateuch were fitted to this developmental picture. J and E, it was thought, represented a relatively early period—they belonged to the time shortly after David and Solomon's great kingdom had split in two (and some of their material was arguably far earlier than that). J had been an inhabitant of the southern kingdom, Judah, while E lived in the

---

* In point of fact, Deuteronomy is the only book that appears to be attributed almost entirely to the authorship of Moses (Deut. 1:1; 31:9); Exodus, Leviticus, and Numbers quote God's words to Moses but say nothing about the overall authorship of the book.

northern kingdom, Israel. At some later point, it was argued, the writings of J and E had been combined into a single text, JE, but this text remained faithful to the worldview of its two underlying components. Thus, the ideas found in either J or E (or JE) would be significantly different from those found in the later sources, D and P. The God described in J and E, for example, was very much the God of Old, human-sized and possessed of human traits. In the Bible's most ancient texts, this God was principally a divine warrior fighting Israel's enemies (and its enemies' gods), a wise counselor and a champion of justice, and in general the deity associated with one particular people, Israel. He was worshiped in different temples and sacred spots that dotted Israel's land. People often offered sacrifices to Him spontaneously, as the spirit moved. His festivals were altogether focused on the cycles of nature and the gratitude people felt for God's bounty: the springtime barley harvest and (somewhat later) the wheat harvest, then the fall ingathering of crops.

Wellhausen and other scholars found D and P to be quite different from J and E. Thus, D (the Deuteronomic source) was thought to have been composed in the seventh century BCE,[1] at a time when the old, spontaneous, close-to-nature side of Israel's religion was beginning to harden into doctrines and laws, as well as to become more theoretical. The difference between D and the earlier authors was evident not only in D's different literary style and vocabulary, but also in what this author had to say. D, according to scholars, insisted on an absolute separation between Israel's devotion to its own God and the practices of Israel's neighbors or predecessors. Worshiping any other deity was, in the book of Deuteronomy, the gravest of sins, and it commanded that every effort be made to root out any vestige of Canaanite religion from Israel's midst. The God of Deuteronomy was also more abstract and distant than that of J and E: He did not even really "dwell" on earth—His abode was heaven, and His temple (there was now to be only one) was merely the place where He "caused His name to dwell."[2] When the Israelites encountered God at Mount Sinai, Moses later reminds them, "You heard the sound of words but saw no form; there was only a voice" (Deut. 4:12). D was also a champion of strict morality. J's and E's Abraham and Jacob might have sometimes lied and cheated, but D would have none of that. Indeed, Deuteronomy's laws showed an overriding concern for the welfare of the powerless, "the stranger, the widow, and the orphan."

Then came P, so named because this is the first letter of the word "priest" in German (and other languages); P, Wellhausen believed, belonged to the period *after* the exile of the Jews to Babylon in the sixth century BCE. When the Jews were allowed to return to their homeland in 539 BCE after more than half a century in Babylon, they suddenly found themselves living in markedly changed circumstances (no king of their own; no national sovereignty; a politically powerful priesthood). It was these changes, Wellhausen felt, that caused P to strike a decidedly different note from that of his predecessors. D had been at least half in the real world, but P was almost utterly divorced from it; the outside world must have seemed, in national and historical terms, a depressing place. So he dwelt in a reality of priestly ceremony and cultic abstractions: sin and guilt, products of the exile, loomed large in his mind. P also believed in pinning everything down in rules and laws; spontaneity was gone, Wellhausen felt.[3] It was P who wrote the tedious priestly rules and procedures found in the books of Leviticus and Numbers, and he also changed or edited significant other portions of what was now the Pentateuch, modifying them to suit his own priestly concerns and particular cast of mind.[4] It was this Pentateuch that then gradually became the central focus of Judaism, and the study of its laws and institutions eventually turned into a form of religious devotion. The great religion of Israel was on its way down, Wellhausen thought.

This view of things, as we will see, has been substantially modified by subsequent scholars. Nevertheless, the basic, underlying idea of multiple authorship for the Pentateuch has survived these modifications; virtually all modern scholars hold by it[5]—and so it still sticks in the throat of many traditionally religious people. The reason is that accepting the Documentary Hypothesis in any form means retreating substantially from the most basic idea of Scripture itself, that the Bible represents words given by God to man. If God had something to say to different writers in different periods, He ought nonetheless to be basically the same God and say basically the same things: however many "bottles" there were, they ought still to contain the same wine. Then why should He say to one prophet that He is essentially a divine humanoid while saying to another that He is an abstract, distant deity who dwells in heaven?[6] Why should God imply, in telling the prophets J or E (or whoever) what to write about Abraham or Jacob, that sometimes it is all right to lie, and yet say specifically in dictating His legislation to a later, priestly writer, "You shall not deal deceitfully or falsely with one another" (Lev. 19:11)? Indeed, why should the laws that God gives to two different prophets contradict each other, saying to one that the Passover sacrifice must be a sheep or a goat (Exod. 12:5) and that it cannot be boiled (Exod. 12:8), while saying to another that the Passover sacrifice can also be a cow or a steer (Deut. 16:2) and is indeed to be boiled (Deut. 16:7)? Should a servant woman's release be exactly the same as a male's (Deut. 15:12), or completely different (Exod. 21:7)? So long as people could hold that the Torah had been given to Moses on Mount Sinai, ingenious answers could be (and were) found for such apparent contradictions. This was part of the great achievement of the ancient interpreters: they were able to solve all such problems, so that the Bible never failed to conform to the Four Assumptions (in this case, Assumption 3, that of perfect harmony between the Bible's various parts). The Documentary Hypothesis made all such ingenious answers unnecessary: the contradictions, it said, are real, and they arose from the combination of originally different sources. But in so saying modern scholarship also undermined the basic idea of Scripture.

As his thoughts developed on these matters, Wellhausen himself became increasingly agitated. Finally, he resolved to quit his job preparing future ministers at a Protestant theological faculty. In his letter of resignation he explained:

> I became a theologian because I was interested in the scientific study of the Bible. It has only gradually dawned on me that a professor of theology also has the practical task of preparing his students to serve in the Evangelical Church, and that I was not performing this practical task, but rather, in spite of all restraint on my part, I was actually incapacitating my listeners for their position.[7]

It may have helped Wellhausen's conscience to get a different job, but it scarcely did anything for the rest of the faculty back at his seminary; they still had to train future ministers. And now they were stuck with his ideas about J, E, D, and P. What could they do?

This is a question that, more than a century later, still haunts Christians and Jews. Many simply hide from it; others, as we shall see, seek some apologetic route around the problem. Still others, while mentioning its existence, simply reject it on principle: the Documentary Hypothesis must be wrong; therefore it is. The chief rabbi of the British Empire wrote on the first page of his Torah commentary (published in 1936): "My conviction that the criticism of the Pentateuch associated with the name of Wellhausen is a perversion of history and a desecration of religion is unshaken; likewise, my refusal to eliminate the Divine either from history or from human life."[8] Brave words! But are they a sufficient answer to the doubts raised by modern biblical scholarship? As I have already mentioned, a fuller discussion of this issue has been left for the last chapter. For now, however, it will be important to cover some of the subsequent developments and modifications of Wellhausen's Documentary Hypothesis, specifically those aspects of it having to do with P and D. In some ways, more recent scholarship has only made matters worse.

Meet the Cohens

A wag once observed that P is the only hypothetical author of the Documentary Hypothesis whose last name we know for sure—Cohen. (This common Jewish last name is actually the Hebrew word for "priest.") The problem, a modern scholar might add, is that no one knows P's *first* name. And why is that a problem? Because it is certainly possible that two texts, both demonstrating an interest in things priestly, could have been written by two completely different Cohens living in different times and having radically different views. This, in fact, turned out to be what most modern scholars have concluded about the various parts of Leviticus (and more than Leviticus).

The priestly parts of the Pentateuch comprise, according to most scholars, a hefty percentage of the total.[9] Traces of P have long been identified here and there in the books of Genesis and Exodus: thus, the account of creation in Genesis 1 is, as we have seen, attributed by scholars to P, and P is also said to be the author of a version of the flood story that was combined with (but somewhat contradicted) J's. Priestly fingerprints were found as well in parts of the stories of Abraham (like his covenant of circumcision in Genesis 17) and here and there in the narratives of Jacob and Moses and the exodus and the lawgiving at Sinai. But the greatest stretch of uninterrupted priestly authorship was found to begin with the section about building the desert tabernacle in the latter part of Exodus, and then to carry through to include all of Leviticus as well as a good chunk of the next book, Numbers—a not insubstantial part of the entire Pentateuch.[10]

Were all these parts authored by the same person? In assigning Leviticus and other parts of the Pentateuch to P, scholars did not base themselves solely on the fact that many of the passages involved subjects of interest to priests, but on certain characteristic traits of language and style. The priestly writer, scholars found, liked giving detailed descriptions of things and did not shy away from repetitions. Thus, it seemed plausible that the priestly pen that had written the formulaically repetitive account of the building of the tabernacle was also responsible for the creation narrative in Genesis 1, not only because of that chapter's priestly vocabulary and priestly concern with the sabbath, but because of the six occurrences of "And it was evening and it was morning" and the other formulaic repetitions ("And God saw that it was good")[11] in that chapter. This same author seemed likewise to be responsible for the verbatim repetition—twelve times!—of the details of the princely sacrifices in Numbers 7. After all, such repetitions were also found to characterize the heartland of P, the sacrificial instructions in Leviticus 1–7.

Priestly passages also demonstrated certain linguistic tics, scholars found: these passages liked to refer to the people of Israel as a "congregation" ('edah); they called a tribe a maṭṭeh, whose leader was its "chief" (naśi); people's hearts sometimes "lifted them up" (naśa' libbam 'otam) to do things voluntarily; and when people "fell on their faces" in priestly texts, it was in shock or in prayer, and not as a sign of obeisance in front of a king or an angel.[12] To "spill blood" was a priestly way of saying to murder; the sabbath was a favorite topic of priestly writings, a time when no professional work (mel'ekhet 'abodah) was done. In general, scholars found that God's earthly presence in priestly passages was spoken of as His "glory" (kabod).[13] Priestly writings were also found to have a very noticeable interest in numbers and chronology—they liked to give the dimensions of things (Noah's ark, the tabernacle) and to say exactly when something occurred and how long it lasted; they also liked giving people's exact ages at the time of an event. Priestly passages were also said to structure larger units according to certain architectonic patterns.[14] Since many of these elements were found in the great priestly composition that extended from the tabernacle construction to the end of Leviticus, scholars felt some reinforcement when they found one or more of them in the passages outside of this block that, for other reasons, had been attributed to a priestly writer. Indeed, it seemed reasonable to attribute passages with a concentration of these linguistic tics and other traits to a *single individual priest.* After all, linguistic tics and literary style tend to be highly personal; their presence in a wide variety of texts seemed to suggest that these texts were not just "of priestly authorship" but were written by the very same man.

To this generalization there was one glaring exception. Even before Wellhausen's *Prolegomena,* scholars had noted that the complex of laws from Leviticus 17 to 26 (the Holiness Code discussed in the previous chapter) seemed to be different from the surrounding priestly texts. It too had its linguistic tics, but they were different; perhaps the most prominent of them was the frequent assertion "I am the LORD" following a law. That did not occur elsewhere. The whole stress on a person's holiness, which gave this unit its name, was also a distinguishing characteristic. The nature of the laws in this section was also found to be somewhat unique: despite the exclusive focus on priests and their doings that characterized the preceding chapters, some of the laws here were addressed to "the whole congregation of Israel" and had to do, as we have seen, with relations between ordinary people. Even in talking about the tabernacle and its sacrifices, this code's attention seemed less exclusively focused on the priesthood per se and to leave more room for nonpriestly Israelites. All this suggested to scholars another priestly source besides P, and they called it "H" (for "holiness"). Scholars had initially concluded that H was earlier than P, which suited Wellhausen's developmental scheme just fine. There had been J and E, then D, then a slight dip down into H, who, while priestly, still had some contact with the natural world and real, nonpriestly Israelites; and then finally P.

Whence P and H?

Over the last few decades, however, ideas about the dating of P and H have changed. To begin with, many scholars, including a prominent group of researchers at the Hebrew University of Jerusalem (starting in the 1930s with Yehezkel Kaufmann),[15] have argued forcefully for an early date for P.[16] Among their points: ample evidence of priests and priesthoods exists in other parts of the ancient Near East from a very early period; indeed, some of the technical terms and concepts of these other nations are precisely paralleled in Israelite priestly texts.[17] There is no reason to think that the Kingdoms of Israel and Judah would *not* have had a developed priesthood from an early time—the Bible certainly says they did—and the rules of sacrifices and other procedures detailed in Leviticus 1–16 therefore might arguably go back to practices rooted in very early times (though certainly changes might have been introduced later). In keeping with this, the technical terms used by P have been shown on linguistic grounds to antedate the similar technical vocabulary of the priest Ezekiel, who lived at the start of the Babylonian exile.[18] That would put P clearly in the pre-exilic period, these scholars said. Indeed, it has been argued that a number of P's linguistic tics cited earlier (*'edah, matteh, 'elef,* and *naśi*) fell out of use after the ninth century;[19] if so, the formulations found in P would have to go back more than two centuries before the Babylonian exile. (On the other hand, critics of this approach say, that does not mean that P itself goes back that far—liturgical formulae often contain lexical elements that have otherwise disappeared from the language or changed their meaning.)*

Scholars have recently argued that Wellhausen's idea of a postexilic P does not work for other reasons as well. Ezekiel and Jeremiah, who prophesied just before the Babylonian exile, seem to show a detailed awareness of some of the laws in P; again, this would suggest a pre-exilic date for P. (Moreover, quite apart from actual texts, the whole Wellhausian notion of a concern for the priesthood as an exilic and postexilic degeneration simply cannot be reconciled with the evident importance of the priesthood far earlier—not just in Ezekiel and Jeremiah, but in the eighth-century prophets as well.) Intermarriage was apparently a hot issue in postexilic times (see Ezra 9), but P did not apparently have any objection *in principle* to the Israelites taking unmarried Midianite females for themselves (Num. 31:18). Intermarriage must not have been such an important subject in his own time.[20] In addition to these arguments is another that has been much debated of late: D may have known P and based some of his laws on laws that existed earlier in P.[21] If so, this would suggest that P—or at least *some* priestly code of procedures—did *not* come after D, as Wellhausen had thought.[22] The last word has certainly not been written on this subject, but in general a number of contemporary scholars now seem to hold that the

---

* The English word "man" used to mean, among other things, "husband" (like its German cognate *Mann*). This meaning basically died out long ago, but it did survive in the liturgical formula, "I now pronounce you man and wife." ("Wife" [*wif*], incidentally, has also changed: in Old English it also meant "woman." This meaning, too, has been lost, save for a few frozen expressions ["old wives' tale"] and some compounds [fishwife, midwife]. "I now pronounce you man and wife" thus originally had a double symmetry about it.)

priestly rules and regulations of Leviticus are indeed quite ancient.[23] They say that P was not written after—and in the shadow of—D, as Wellhausen claimed; rather, both these authors lived well before the Babylonian exile. They differed not so much in time as in viewpoint.

And what of H? As noted, H had always been assumed to be earlier than P. But most modern scholars now accept the idea that the two Cohens, P and H, are actually representatives of two opposing schools of priests, who differed on some of the most basic issues of religious belief. These two schools, and the texts that they produced, seem to go back to roughly the same period, and although it is impossible to assign them precise dates, both of them apparently wrote most of what they wrote well before the Babylonian exile took place, the P school coming first and then H a bit later.[24] And H (that is, some member of the H school) apparently had the final word, since it was a member of the H school who seems to have edited their combined texts.[25]

The H school, as Israel Knohl, Jacob Milgrom, and others have argued, was quite different in outlook from that of P. H sought to "interweave and blend the priestly elements of belief and ritual with popular traditions and customs," while P "maintained a basic separation between priestly and popular cultic spheres."[26] For example, H cared about, and related to, the stories and other traditions that scholars connect with the sources J and E; P cared much less for this popular material.[27] Perhaps more strikingly: for the H school, holiness itself "includes all areas of life and applies to the entire community of Israel and the land that they inhabit."[28] H was thus a priestly-popular movement with a concern for social issues and social reform; P was a priesthood-only school whose idea of holiness ended at the outer gates of the temple precincts.

These recent conclusions about the ideas and dating of P and H have only intensified the distress caused by the Documentary Hypothesis. True, most scholars had long ago accepted that there were four documentary sources, indeed, five. But now, if the argument for a pre-exilic dating of both P and H is accepted, the disagreements found in the sources of the Pentateuch do not fit very well into the evolutionary scheme proposed by Wellhausen. In particular, evolution will not explain the great differences between P, H, and D if they all belong to roughly the same time period. Instead, one would have to conclude that these rough contemporaries simply held widely differing views on some very basic issues: it is *their opinions,* not God's word as revealed to His prophets over many centuries, that the Bible contains. With regard to P in particular, perhaps the most basic issue of all is that of God's very nature. P's understanding of God, scholars have recently argued, utterly contradicts that of other biblical writers, including his fellow priest H.[29]

A Cold and Indifferent God

In the view of many scholars, P seems to have been possessed of the most chilling conception of the deity. It was already noticed that the God of Genesis 2–3 had a more "hands-on" approach to creating the world than the God of chapter 1, attributed by scholars to P. In chapter 1, God simply speaks and things happen—suddenly there is light, suddenly there is a firmament, and so forth. One would not be wrong to characterize this God as somewhat more impersonal. But even this depiction is more personal than the God revealed in later portions of the priestly text, according to scholars. Recent analysis has in fact highlighted the difference between the way God is depicted in the priestly parts of Genesis and the way He is depicted after that. In P's part of Leviticus, for example, God does not even speak in the first person, "I will do this" or "I have ordered that"—not even to Moses. It is as if P seeks to deny that God can even be thought of as a personlike Being, one who can say "I." So too, P's God does not personally punish people; punishment just somehow falls on wrongdoers and they are "cut off" (in the passive voice) or otherwise disciplined (P doesn't say how). Nor does He personally forgive; instead, "it is forgiven" to the sinner who makes good his infraction. P's version of the giving of the Torah at Mount Sinai is consistent with this picture; Moses *enters the cloud* and hears a voice, but the people outside hear nothing at all. All this seems to correspond to something profound in P's theology.

Perhaps the most striking thing to scholars about the God of P is that people do not pray to Him. The book of Psalms is full of prayers and songs of praise to God, many of them quite ancient, and scholars have established that the majority of these psalms were composed to be recited in God's "house," the temple where He was deemed to be present. But a reader of the words of P would never guess that that was so. P describes in great detail the offering of sacrifices in the temple, but he never says a word about prayers or songs being recited there. In fact, in P people never pray; what good would it do? P's God is an almost utterly impersonal force. So, too, the ancient festive hymns praising Him are never mentioned in P either; they existed, but, as far as P was concerned, such hymns were an embarrassing bit of human weakness that had no practical effect.[30] Even sacrifices in P are not connected with bringing well-being, or victory in time of war, or with satisfying human needs.[31] They are just part of the autonomous life of the temple.

In our own, modern society, such a vision of God might actually appear comforting to some. After all, without quite putting the thought into words, we live in a world that is based on ruling out a role for the divine in daily life. That would suit P just fine—keep supporting the temple, he would say, and we'll keep offering the sacrifices. Meanwhile, political upheavals, natural catastrophes, the suffering of the righteous—these are not problems for P's theology: God is enthroned in splendid isolation. He has no interest in your prayers or thank-yous, so save your breath.

Whatever one may think of it, this modern understanding of P's religion stands in jarring contrast to that of the rest of the Pentateuch. And so, as scholars have found themselves obliged to modify Wellhausen's original conclusions and push their own research further, they have only succeeded in widening the gap between P's views and those of the other sources, while at the same time foreshortening the chronological distance between them. The main consequence, already mentioned, is that it has become more and more difficult to claim that God changed his message from D to H to P in order to suit Israel's slowly evolving religious consciousness. The sources seem now to be grouped too closely together to support this evolutionary view.

The Ways of D

What of that other writer identified by scholars, D? The book of Deuteronomy takes the form of a series of three long discourses pronounced by Moses as he looked out across the Jordan River onto the land of Canaan in the last days of his life. He begins by reviewing the history of the Israelites' wanderings in the wilderness for the previous forty years, and then turns to various laws that Israelites are to keep after they are settled in Canaan. The very first of these (Deut. 12:1–32) focus on the centralization of sacrifices. People will not be able to go to some local altar, Moses says, in order to offer up their sheep or goats. All such local altars and "high places" (which would probably strike onlookers today as large barbecue pits)[32] are to be destroyed—they belonged, Moses says, to the Canaanites. Instead, sacrificial animals will be offered at only one central shrine as soon as it is established:

> You shall seek the place that the LORD your God will choose out of all your tribes as His habitation, to put His name there. You shall go there, bringing there your burnt offerings and your sacrifices, your tithes and your donations, your votive gifts, your freewill offerings, and the firstlings of your herds and flocks. And you shall eat there in the presence of the LORD your God, you and your households together, rejoicing in all the undertakings in which the LORD your God has blessed you.
>
> Deut. 12:5–7

Did that mean that the only place where one could eat a fine meal of lamb or beef was at this future central shrine? For many people, this would have meant a long trek from wherever they lived—a definite hardship. But in the next breath Deuteronomy provided a solution:

Yet whenever you desire you may slaughter and eat meat within any of your towns, according to the blessing that the LORD your God has given you; the impure and the pure may eat of it, as they would of gazelle or deer. The blood, however, you must not eat; you shall pour it out on the ground like water.

Deut. 12:15–16

A person was, according to Deuteronomy, authorized to kill and eat animals in his own backyard, outside of the central shrine: "secular slaughter" within one's own city gates was altogether permitted for sacrificial animals like sheep and cattle just as it was for game animals like gazelles or deer. In fact, one did not even need to be in a state of ritual purity in order to eat such meat: the only provision was that blood not be eaten but poured out onto the ground.

The nineteenth-century German scholar W. M. L. de Wette was the first to use this law as a way of dating Deuteronomy's composition. De Wette argued that no real evidence of this central sanctuary or "secular slaughter" can be found in the Bible before the time of King Josiah, late in the seventh century BCE (just before the Babylonian exile). On the contrary, de Wette noted, not only the book of Genesis but books like Judges, Samuel, and Kings (which describe a period long after Moses) unhesitatingly and without criticism report on various biblical figures offering up sacrifices wherever they liked. As Wellhausen went on to observe: "In the early days, worship arose out of the midst of ordinary life, and was in most intimate and manifold connection with it. A sacrifice was a meal, a fact showing how remote was the idea of antithesis between spiritual earnestness and secular pleasure." [33] The prophet Elijah thus builds (or, rather, rebuilds) an improvised altar on Mount Carmel for the purpose of sacrificing (1 Kings 18:31–32); that was in the ninth century BCE, long after the time of Moses and even David. It was only when King Josiah was shown an ancient "book of the law" found in the Jerusalem temple that he realized that nobody had been obeying this important provision about a central sanctuary:

> The high priest Hilkiah said to Shaphan the secretary, "I have found a book of the law in the house of the LORD." When Hilkiah gave the book to Shaphan, he read it. Then Shaphan the secretary came to the king [Josiah], and reported to the king . . . "The priest Hilkiah has given me this book." Shaphan then read it aloud to the king. When the king heard the words of the book of the law, he tore his clothes [as a sign of grief]. Then the king commanded [his servants], saying, "Go, entreat the LORD on my behalf, on behalf of the people and of all Judah, concerning the words of this book that has been found. For great must be the LORD's anger against us, since our ancestors did not heed the things in this book or act in accordance with what is written here."

2 Kings 22:8–13

Josiah, frightened at the prospect of having violated God's will in such an important matter, set out to change things at once, destroying the local altars and "high places" and limiting all sacrifices to the Jerusalem temple. This momentous move is known as "Josiah's reform."

De Wette theorized that the "book of the law" that Josiah was shown was none other than the book of Deuteronomy. Someone—the shadowy author known as D—had, for his own reasons, written up his own Mosaic history and his own collection of laws and then passed them off as an ancient text. Some of these laws (like the centralization of sacrifices) were entirely D's own idea. Who D was remained a mystery, but he might well have been the very man who "discovered" this book in the temple, Hilkiah (2 Kings 22:8). In any event, D's book won immediate acceptance; not only were his laws put into effect, but the book itself was incorporated into Israel's library of ancient Scripture, eventually becoming the fifth and last book of the Pentateuch.

Modern scholars have accepted de Wette's basic identification of D as a separate source—like P, it too has a distinctive style, and they found that D also frequently contradicts what is said in other parts of the Pentateuch. But, for various reasons, they have backed off from some of de Wette's other conclusions. To begin with, scholars do not think that all of Deuteronomy is of one piece. For example, the book begins with an introductory paragraph (Deut. 1:1–5), after which Moses reviews recent events (Deut. 1:6–4:40). But then comes a *second* introductory paragraph (Deut. 4:44–5:1), almost as if the preceding four chapters did not exist. This, scholars believe, reflects what actually happened: the first introduction and the material that follows it are, it seems, a later addition, the work of a later author, in fact, two authors.[34] As for the law code at the heart of Deuteronomy (chapters 12–28), it was, scholars believe, originally an independent collection of laws. This code is introduced by a review of the Ten Commandments (chapter 5) and some further exhortations of the people (chapters 6–11). As for the code itself, it is a great body of "statutes and ordinances" (Deut. 12:1), some of which parallel the laws given in Exodus–Numbers, while others are altogether new. Following this legal code come other items, such as Moses' farewell song (Deuteronomy 32) and his blessing of the tribes (Deuteronomy 33), both of which, scholars say, are of different, arguably quite ancient, provenance, but which an editor must have tacked on to round out the book.

To this day no modern scholar has put forward a compelling case for the identity or affiliation of the original D. De Wette had supposed that Deuteronomy was composed ad hoc to provide the legal basis for Josiah's reform—that it was, in other words, a pious fraud. Modern scholars find this unlikely. To begin with, Deuteronomy does not match Josiah's reform in all details.[35] What is more, Josiah was not the first person to think of centralizing worship in Jerusalem: his grandfather Hezekiah had apparently undertaken a similar, but less successful, program (see 2 Kings 18:4; 22) at the end of the eighth century. Ideas don't just spring up out of nowhere. If Deuteronomy ordained that the provincial sacrificial sites (the "high places") be torn down and that worship be centralized in one place, it seems to scholars that the roots of Deuteronomy may go back at least to the time of Hezekiah, perhaps earlier. They note that the prophet Hosea, speaking at the start of the eighth century, had already had some sharp words to say about the multiplication of altars in the north (Hos. 8:11; 10:1–2, 8). Whoever D was, scholars say, he may well have lived some time before Josiah, perhaps even before Hezekiah.

And what would D's profession have been? Scholars think it unlikely that he was a priest. After all, D's laws hardly served the interests of priests; some of their provisions appear even to have harmed the priesthood. (Centralizing worship in one sanctuary would certainly have thrown quite a few priests out of work.) On the other hand, no other plausible affiliation has been proposed for D. He seems unlikely to have been an agent of the king— the king's powers are limited by D's code (Deut. 17:15–20), and his very role is presented as a concession to Israel's desire to be like its neighbors (Deut. 17:14). Nor have scholars been able to connect the laws of Deuteronomy with any one place or time period. True, Deuteronomy does single out a particular locale in the northern kingdom of Israel for a covenant ceremony (Deut. 11:26–32; 27): it is to take place at two mountains outside the northern city of Shechem. This, scholars say, is something that a southern author would hardly have come up with. Moreover, the great stress in Deuteronomy on the person of Moses and his central role is, scholars say, more characteristic of northern than southern writers. Thus, even though the law code ended up being discovered in the Jerusalem temple (in the south), most think it probably originated in the north. Perhaps it was then brought south by priests fleeing the Assyrian conquerors of the northern kingdom in 723 BCE. This time period might also suit the laws in another way as well. The one hundred years between 740 and 640 BCE were a time when Assyria dominated the whole region, introducing its own culture, including its gods and temple architecture and forms of worship.[36] Deuteronomy's vehement struggle against worshiping "other gods" might have been launched, scholars say, in the face of large-scale defections to the Assyrian gods or the syncretistic adoption of some of their practices.

Yet scholars have also noted that the laws of Deuteronomy seem in some ways *not* to fit in such a time frame. Many of these laws seem to presuppose a decentralized population of farmers—people dwelling in villages and towns rather than a place of major urban agglomerations. There are, for example, laws about how to plant a vineyard (22:9) or plow a field (22:10); there are laws about runaway oxen or sheep or donkeys (22:1–3). But there are no laws governing business contracts, or the activities of various sorts of artisans, or relations between landlords and tenants, or other typically urban concerns. Similarly, the only financial dealings that are spoken of are not investments (these do appear elsewhere in the Bible)[37] but short-term, interest-free loans to farmers to tide them over until the harvest (23:20; 24:10)—essentially a form of charity. In short, the odor of fresh-mown hay wafts through Deuteronomy's laws.

Many of the laws also seem to bespeak a rough-and-tumble society, in which the long arm of the law is not particularly long. A wayfarer gets killed on his way from one town to the next (21:1); a woman gets raped outside her village (22:25); an accidental killer's only hope is to make his way to a special "city of refuge" before the victim's family finds him (19:1–13). This does not seem to be a particularly settled, orderly society. Men are mustered to go to war, but there does not seem to be any standing army. The monarchy is mentioned only once, and there is no hint of a great royal bureaucracy or life at the king's court; logically, such things ought to play a central role in a legal code originally composed in a monarchy. For these reasons, some scholars suppose that a fair number of Deuteronomy's laws existed as a kind of rural common law far back in Israel's history; in any case, the code as is seems for the most part better suited to life in Israel before the time of Assyrian domination.

Is there some way to fit these contradictory data together? Perhaps, some scholars say, even the legal code of Deuteronomy is not of one piece. Its roots may go back to the ninth century or even earlier; it may then have been recast in the face of Assyrian cultural pressure, with new laws added to stress the gravity of worshiping other gods. This revised law code might then have been brought south to Jerusalem after the northern kingdom fell; bruited about a bit during the reign of Hezekiah,* the laws could then have gone underground during the reign of his son Manasseh, who is said to have rebuilt the shrines that Hezekiah destroyed and in other ways to have embraced foreign worship (2 Kings 21:2–7). During this time, D's text might indeed have been hidden by priests in Jerusalem; the laws were then "discovered" (accidentally or on purpose) and put into effect during the reign of Josiah.

Deuteronomy and Wisdom

If D's identity still remains mysterious for modern scholars, one aspect of his intellectual makeup has been highlighted by recent research: he appears to be closely connected to the world of wisdom. Wisdom was an international pur-

---

* Hezekiah, Josiah's grandfather, had made some moves in the direction of centralizing worship in Jerusalem, destroying the "high places" at which animals were sacrificed (see 2 Kings 18:4; 22)—but apparently these were ineffective or subsequently overthrown.

suit in the ancient Near East, carried on by sages in different countries. Indeed, wisdom was something like scientific research nowadays, and like scientists, wisdom writers had their own characteristic vocabulary and themes. The word "wise" itself was almost a code word (and certainly more specific than "wise" sounds in English); like "scientist," "wise" meant someone who pursued a certain way of knowledge.

Many of these wisdom elements have been found to be present in Deuteronomy.[38] Thus, God's commandments, statutes, and ordinances, as well as "this book of law [or Torah]," are spoken of in Deuteronomy in much the same way that wisdom is spoken of in the biblical book of Proverbs and other wisdom texts: people are urged to "cling" to the Torah, to "guard" it, to "bind it as a sign," and so forth.[39] Those who administer the laws—judges and other officials—ought themselves to be "wise" (16:19), and the country's leaders should likewise be "individuals who are wise, discerning, and reputable" (1:13). Similarly important is the central wisdom theme of reward and punishment and, therefore, the connection of Israel's survival and material prosperity to its adherence to God's laws. All these elements seem to whisper: "wisdom." Indeed, at one point Deuteronomy suggests that its laws are themselves the equivalent of collections of wise sayings elsewhere:

> You must observe them diligently, for this will show your *wisdom and discernment* to the peoples, who, when they hear all these statutes, will say, "Surely this great nation is a wise and discerning people!"
>
> Deut. 4:5

This wisdom perspective has also left its mark on Deuteronomy's view of history, scholars say. History is not—as it was in the etiological narratives of J and E—a way of understanding how present reality came to be what it is (that is, explaining why Beer Sheba is so named, or why Israel does not practice child sacrifice, or why there are prophets in Israel). Instead, history is the repository of eternal truths, lessons that never grow old. For that reason, Deuteronomy constantly urges its readers to *remember*: "Remember that you were a slave in the land of Egypt" (5:15; 15:15, etc.); "Remember what the LORD your God did to Pharaoh" (7:18); "Remember the long journey on which the LORD your God has led you these forty years" (8:2); "Remember—do not forget!—how you provoked the LORD your God to wrath in the wilderness" (9:7); "Remember what Amalek did to you" (25:17), "Remember what the LORD your God did to Miriam" (28:9).

Perhaps its wisdom connection is responsible for what scholars see as another of Deuteronomy's outstanding traits, its broad, one might even say *internationalist,* perspective. Wisdom was an international pursuit, and sages trained in Egypt or Mesopotamia did not differ markedly in education or orientation from those in Israel. These sages were themselves aware of this fact, and they generally presented their wisdom in non-nationalistic, universal terms. (There is not a single allusion to Israel's history or land or leadership in any of the biblical wisdom books of Proverbs, Job, and Ecclesiastes—not one!) Such a global outlook may have left its mark on D, scholars say, if this author had been educated in the ways of wisdom. Deuteronomy may preach vehemently against the worship of other gods, but this fact in itself attests to its awareness that those other gods are indeed being worshiped elsewhere. Unlike P, Deuteronomy mentions other nations—Egypt, Edom, Ammon, and Moab. It seeks to explain why the great and powerful God chose tiny Israel as His own (7:7) and why He did not impose His worship on other peoples (4:19–20). In all these respects, scholars say, Deuteronomy seems to be observing Israel as part of a much larger environment. Indeed, the very abstract quality of God in Deuteronomy—He lives in heaven and merely causes His name to dwell in his earthly temple; He controls all of reality and has no true heavenly rival—seems to be part and parcel of this same outlook.

Deuteronomy also shares with wisdom writings certain other favorite themes. For example, one should never "add to or subtract from" God's words (this injunction is found only in Deut. 4:2; 13:1; and in Prov. 30:5–6). Boundary marks are not to be moved (Deut. 19:14; 27:17); this very specific sort of offense is also mentioned as well in Prov. 22:28; 23:10, as well as in ancient Egyptian wisdom texts. (It is also found in Hos. 5:10, significant because of the other resemblances found between Hosea and Deuteronomy.) Using false weights and measures is another wisdom theme (Prov. 11:1; 20:10, 23) also present in Deuteronomy (25:13–16).

One contemporary student of Deuteronomy's wisdom connection, Moshe Weinfeld, has stressed how different D's views are from those expressed in P.[40] True, P's God was impersonal, a great force or incorporeal *kabod*—but as far as P was concerned, God was nonetheless right there, present in His temple. The holiest object of the temple, the ark, was the place where, God tells Moses, "I will meet with you, and from which . . . I will deliver to you all My commandments to the Israelites" (Exod. 25:22). For P, scholars observe, this divine presentness was the only reality that counted, and his priestly gaze never contemplated anything beyond the temple precincts and their immediate environs; even the rest of the land of Israel existed only insofar as it supplied tithes and produce and pilgrims to the temple. As for other nations, they did not play any significant role in P's thinking. For D, Weinfeld and others have argued, things were quite the reverse. The temple was *not* God's dwelling: nowhere does Deuteronomy (or any of the subsequent biblical writings of D's school) ever speak of God *dwelling* in the temple or of people building a "house" for God; at best, the temple was some sort of symbolic presence for God's "name."[41] The holy ark has no cover or cherubim on whose extended wings the deity might appear; it is really only a storage chest for keeping the Ten Commandments—hence D's name for it, the "Ark of the

LORD's Covenant" (Deut. 31:9).[42] By the same token, the temple sacrifices are never called (as they are in P) God's "food," whose burning on the altar makes a "pleasing odor" before God. In fact, Deuteronomy has almost nothing to say about the sacrifices per se. It does, however, mention that, in the case of sacrifices that can be eaten by the person bringing the offering, the meat is to be shared with "foreigners, orphans, and widows" (16:11, 14). This, according to Weinfeld, is their real importance for D: they are an instrument of public charity. Thus P and D are, to a certain extent, opposites: if P is altogether priestly, D is in some respects close to "secular." Of course, D believes in God and in God's historic intervention in the affairs of men. But this seems to be more of a doctrine in D than a lived reality. Social justice is of great concern to D, but, significantly, it is first up to human beings, those charged with creating "justice and righteousness," to bring it about.[43]

It should be recalled here that a major tenet of D's religion is the central-ization of sacrificial worship at a single locale (Deut. 12:1–32). This law says a great deal about D's whole theology—but perhaps "centralization" glosses over the main effect of this new provision. What it meant in practice was that that "central" locale, wherever it was to be, would in fact always be far away from most of the country's villages and towns—a day's journey or more.[44] As a result, sacrificial worship would necessarily be rather remote from most people's daily lives. What then was to bind them to their God? In its stead, Deuteronomy offers . . . *all those laws*. Deuteronomy urges that people "cling" to them, "bind" them, "guard" them, and so forth, and it endlessly asserts that by so doing they will "serve" and "love" God with their whole hearts. In short, keeping these divinely given laws was a kind of surrogate for the now-remote service of God through sacrifices in the temple. (Indeed, Deuteronomy uses the phrase that was commonly associated with sacrifices, "to serve ['*abod*] God," to refer instead to the keeping of God's laws [Deut. 10:12; 11:13, and many more].) By the same token, the temple's remoteness was really of no great consequence to D precisely because, as we have seen, God really did not dwell there anyway; He was in heaven.

Who's a Priest?

Another subject on which P and D disagree is more down-to-earth: the priesthood. When P speaks about priests, scholars note, he calls them "the priests, Aaron's sons." This is because, as far as P was concerned, the only legitimate priests were descended from the priestly line of Aaron. P does speak of another group of hereditary temple officials, the Levites. But the Levites had a different status: although they were from the same tribe as Aaron's sons, the tribe of Levi, they were not part of Aaron's line, so, in P's view, they could not offer sacrifices or perform the other crucial jobs assigned to priests. In fact, their main job was to serve Aaron's descendants as helpers:

> Then the LORD spoke to Moses, saying: "Bring the tribe of Levi near, and put them in attendance before Aaron the priest, so that they may assist him. They shall perform duties for him and for the whole congregation in front of the tent of meeting, doing service at the tabernacle; they shall be in charge of all the furnishings of the tent of meeting, and attend to the duties for the Israelites as they do service at the tabernacle. You shall give the Levites to Aaron and his descendants; they are altogether given to him from among the Israelites. But you shall make a register of Aaron and his descendants; it is they who shall attend to the priesthood, and any outsider who comes near shall be put to death."
>
> Num. 3:5–10

D, on the other hand, never talks about Aaron's descendants as special. His phrase is "the Levitical priests." Many modern scholars have interpreted this to mean that D believed that *any* Levite was ipso facto a proper priest and could offer sacrifices and perform other priestly tasks. This may indeed have been the case for some time in Israel, scholars say. When Moses blesses the tribe of Levi at the end of his life, he says:

> Let them teach to Jacob Your ordinances, and to Israel Your laws;
> may they place incense before You, and whole burnt offerings on Your
>   altar.
>
> Deut. 33:10

Placing incense and whole burnt offerings before God were the priestly functions par excellence. This text, which many scholars claim had been inherited from a far earlier era, may thus indicate that *all* Levites had been considered fit priests from a very early time.

The question "Who's a priest?" was not limited to this apparent disagreement between P and D. A still more restrictive view of the priesthood appears in the closing chapters of Ezekiel; there, only the descendants of Zadok (himself said to be a descendant of Aaron) can function fully as priests; other descendants of Aaron are in a different category (as are Levites as well). Such disagreements were rarely just armchair disputes in biblical times; they must have been bitterly fought. Indeed, modern scholars believe that some of the best-known narratives of the Pentateuch center precisely on the ongoing claims of different groups to the priesthood.

Golden Calf Bis

One of these narratives has already been discussed, the story of the Golden Calf. Scholars have long connected the actual origin of the story with an incident recounted much later in the Bible. After David and his son Solomon had united the twelve tribes of Israel and ruled over this mighty empire for a time, a split occurred: a certain Jeroboam led the northern component of this empire to secede and form an independent kingdom of their own. Naturally, Jeroboam believed that his citizens ought not to continue to frequent the great temple established by Solomon in the southern capital of Jerusalem. Instead, the Bible recounts, he created two new shrines within his own territory:

> So the king [Jeroboam] took counsel, and made two golden calves. He said to the people, "You have gone up to Jerusalem long enough. These are your gods, O Israel, who brought you up out of the land of Egypt." He set one in Bethel, and the other he put in Dan.
>
> 1 Kings 12:28

Aaron is said to have uttered precisely the same sentence when he built *his* Golden Calf, "These are your gods, O Israel, who brought you up out of the land of Egypt" (Exod. 32:8). Clearly, scholars say, this incident in Exodus was actually a later writer's projection of Jeroboam's sin back to the time of Moses and Aaron.

But why, these scholars ask, was such a tale created? Some argue that it was not aimed at Jeroboam so much as at the Aaronid priesthood, using Jeroboam's famous sin as a way of getting at the descendants of Aaron.[45] After all, if the purpose were simply to criticize the actions of Jeroboam by creating a shameful precedent for them centuries earlier, there would have been no need to assign Aaron such a central role in the incident: let the Golden Calf be manufactured by the crazed mob *against* Aaron's wishes, or by some easily recognized prototype of Jeroboam, say, the mad metallurgist Beroboam. Instead, it is Aaron who is front and center, altogether eager to cooperate with the mob's evil desires. Once the Golden Calf is built, Aaron even has the effrontery to proclaim, "Tomorrow will be a festival to the LORD" (Exod. 32:5), and the next day, stirred by this prospect, the people get up to "sport" (perhaps a euphemism for sexual license). Later on, reproved by Moses, Aaron merely sputters; the only explanation he can come up with: "I said to them, 'Whoever has gold, strip it off'; then they gave it to me, and I threw it into the fire, and out came this calf!" (Exod. 32:24). Surely, scholars say, none of this is attributable to chance: the Aaronids are being pilloried here by someone, perhaps a non-Aaronid Levite with a bone to pick.

Behind this narrative may thus stand another aspect of the P-versus-D dispute.

In any event, the disagreement between P and D about who is a priest is yet one more bit of sorrow brought on by the Documentary Hypothesis. J, E, P, H, and D disagree, scholars say, about so *many* ideas—not just who is a priest, but who God is and how He is to be served. And they disagree as well about dozens of practical issues, including individual laws and their precise wording. They have sharply contrasting views on the giving of the Torah— not only on the name of the mountain (Sinai or Horeb), but on what the people saw or did not see, heard or did not hear.[46] This, therefore, is the central question raised by the Documentary Hypothesis today: can *any* of this be thought to be Scripture, when so much of it reflects human disputes between different writers and their schools? Where is the word of God in a book that contradicts itself on so many different, and fundamental, items?

20

On the Way to Canaan

Leviticus 16; 23 and Numbers 11–14; 16–17; 28–29

Death of Korah, Dathan, and Abiram
by Gustave Doré.

HOLIDAYS AND FEASTS. THE DAY OF ATONEMENT.
NADAB AND ABIHU AGAIN. MURMURINGS. KORAH'S REVOLT.

*The books of Leviticus and Numbers contain further laws and narratives,
including the account of a full-scale revolt against Moses. Why did the rebels
mind having to put tassels on their clothes?*

God did not only direct Israel to worship Him at the desert tabernacle, He
also established a series of fixed festivals that the people might celebrate with
joy and festivity. These festivals are explained in various places in the Torah,
in particular in two inclusive lists, one in the book of Leviticus (chapter 23)
and the second in the book of Numbers (chapters 28–29).

The most prominent festival in the Pentateuch is Passover, also called the
Festival of Unleavened Bread, which occurred in the spring and commemorated the Exodus from Egypt. It was celebrated in an unusual way: every family in Israel was commanded to make an all-night feast of a roasted sacrificial
lamb or goat, called the *pesah,* and every last bit of its meat had to be finished
before dawn. No bone in the animal's body could be broken during the eating. That night, and for the next seven days, no regular bread could be
eaten—in fact, all such bread and leavening needed to be removed earlier from
every house. The only kind of bread that was allowed was *matzah,* unleavened
bread prepared without any yeast and cooked quickly enough to prevent it
from rising. (Today, matzah mostly comes in very flat, dry wafers, but the biblical kind was probably thicker and spongier, more like today's Middle Eastern pita bread. Unlike pita bread, however, matzah purposely had no
leavening, so it would lose its sponginess in a matter of hours and become
hard as rock by the next day.) The Bible explained why specifically these two
foods—the roasted *pesah,* and the unleavened bread—were to be eaten on a
festival commemorating the Exodus:

> And when your children ask you, "What does this observance mean to
> you?" you shall say, "It is the Passover [*pesah*] sacrifice to the LORD, for He
> passed over [*pasah*] the houses of the Israelites in Egypt, when He struck
> down the Egyptians but spared our houses."
>
> Exod. 12:27

The Egyptians urged the people to hasten their departure from the land, for
they said, "We shall all be dead." So the people took their dough before it
was leavened . . . They baked unleavened cakes of the dough that they
had brought out of Egypt; it was not leavened, because they were driven

out of Egypt and could not wait, nor had they prepared any provisions for themselves.

Exod. 12:33–34, 39

The *pesaḥ* sacrifice was so called, in other words, because it sounded like the verb meaning "pass over": God had *passed over* the Israelite houses at the time of the last plague. Unleavened bread was eaten to commemorate the fact that, as the Israelites were rushing to leave Egypt, they had no time to let their bread rise.

The above-cited passage, Exod. 12:27, said that parents were to instruct their children about the meaning of the Passover offering. Apparently, this was a very important matter, because the Torah went on to repeat the commandment three more times:

> You shall *tell your child* on that day, "It is because of what the LORD did for me when I came out of Egypt."
>
> Exod. 13:8

> When in the future your child asks you, "What does this mean?" *you shall answer,* "By strength of hand the LORD brought us out of Egypt, from the house of slavery."
>
> Exod. 13:14

> When your children ask you in time to come, "What is the meaning of the decrees and the statutes and the ordinances that the LORD our God has commanded you?" then *you shall say to your children,* "We were Pharaoh's slaves in Egypt, but the LORD brought us out of Egypt with a mighty hand."
>
> Deut. 6:20–21

The Passover festival apparently only grew in importance as time went on. In the era of the ancient interpreters, a fixed rite began to develop whereby parents carried out the above commandments: on the night of the Passover feast, passages from the Bible and other lore would be recited, telling children about the exodus, and these eventually crystallized into the Passover "narration" (*haggadah*), the main feature of the *seder* celebrated by Jews to this day.

Interpreters did have one, somewhat whimsical, question about the Bible's commandments to recount the events of the exodus: why was the commandment repeated four times in the Pentateuch? This would seem to contradict the third of the interpreters' Four Assumptions, namely, that Scripture is perfect and, therefore, never contradicts itself or even needlessly repeats itself. They therefore concluded that, if the commandment to teach one's children about the Exodus appears four times, it must be that each time something different was being imparted. It seemed possible that the Bible was in fact hinting about four different *ways* of telling one's children, each way particularly suited to one of four different types of children:

> [From the four appearances of this commandment] you must conclude that there are four [different types of] children: the wise, the wicked, the simple-minded, and the type that does not [yet] know how to ask. What does the wise sort ask? "What is the meaning of the decrees and the statutes and the ordinances that the LORD our God has commanded you?"[1] (Deut. 6:20). Discuss with him, therefore, *all* the laws of Passover [as outlined in the Mishnah]. What does the wicked sort ask? "What does this observance mean to you?"(Exod. 12:33). "To *you*," he says, but not to himself! So, since [by his question] he has heretically excluded himself, you should answer him in kind and say, "It is because of what the LORD did *for me* when *I* came out of Egypt" (Exod. 13:8). *For me* but not for him; had he been there, he would not have been among those saved. What does the simple-minded sort ask? "What does this mean?" (Exod. 13:14). So to him say [simply:] "By strength of hand the LORD brought us out of Egypt, from the house of slavery" (Exod. 13:14). With the sort of child that does not know how to ask you ought to take the initiative, as it says, "You shall *tell your child* on that day" [without having mentioned earlier that the child asked any question] (Exod. 13:8).
>
> *Mekhilta deR. Ishmael, "Bo' " 18*

For Christians, too, the Passover meal held particular significance. The Last Supper fell, apparently,[2] on Passover, so that the holiday of Easter came itself to be intertwined with the biblical feast. (The connection is somewhat obscured in English, but in many languages the very word for Easter is a form of the Hebrew *pesaḥ* or its Aramaic equivalent *pasḥa—Pâques, Pascua, Πасха,* and so forth. Indeed, after a time church law came to arrange the ritual calendar to make sure that Easter never fell on the first day of the Jewish holiday of Passover, so as to make clear the distinctness of the two.)

If Passover and the crucifixion and resurrection were thus typologically linked, it stood to reason that some of the laws prescribed for the holiday were also typological hints to the events of the Gospels:

> But when they [the Roman soldiers] came to Jesus and saw that he was already dead, they did not break his legs. Instead, one of the soldiers pierced his side with a spear, and at once blood and water came out . . . These things occurred so that the scripture might be fulfilled, "None of his bones shall be broken" [≈ Exod. 12:46].
>
> John 19:33–36

For our paschal lamb, Christ, has been sacrificed. Therefore, let us celebrate the festival, not with the old yeast, the yeast of malice and evil, but with the unleavened bread of sincerity and truth.

1 Cor. 5:7–8

In addition to Passover, there were two other annual festivals, those of Weeks (*Shavuot* or Pentecost) and Booths (*Sukkot*). These two were eventually connected to events that took place after the Exodus itself. The Festival of Weeks was timed to occur in the third month, the same month when the Israelites, having left Egypt, arrived at Mount Sinai to receive the Torah (Exod. 19:1). The Festival of Booths was also connected with the period of wilderness wanderings that took place after the Exodus. In commemoration thereof, later Israelites were ordered to dwell in specially constructed harvest booths outside of their houses for a period of seven days, "so that your generations may know that I made the people of Israel live in booths when I brought them out of the land of Egypt" (Lev. 23:43).

A Day of Atonement

Quite different was the spirit of another holy day, the Day of Atonement. The people of Israel were ordered to spend the entire day in self-affliction, abstaining from all food or drink from sunset to sunset. Yet, while it had its somber side, the day was also one of great spiritual significance.

This shall be a statute to you forever: In the seventh month, on the tenth day of the month, you shall afflict yourselves [by fasting] and shall do no work, neither the citizen nor the alien who resides among you. For on this day atonement shall be made for you, *to purify you from all your sins*; you shall become purified before the LORD.

Lev. 16:29–30

In some ways, this text seemed too good to be true. All the wickedest sinner had to do was make it to the Day of Atonement alive and then, by fasting (and thanks to certain other rituals performed in the temple), he or she would be purified of all previous misdeeds and be able to start the new year with, as it were, a clean slate.

Although that was what the Torah seemed to be saying, ancient interpreters were quick to stress that it was not giving sinners a blank check:[3]

And about the Israelites it has been written and ordained [that, on the Day of Atonement] if they *repent* in righteousness, He will forgive all their transgressions and pardon all their sins.

Jubilees 5:17

One who says, "I will sin and then I will repent, I will sin and I will repent," it will not be given to such a person to repent. [If he says,] "I will sin and the Day of Atonement will atone [for me]," the Day of Atonement will not atone . . . The Day of Atonement may atone for the sins of a man toward God, but not for sins committed against one's fellow; [in the latter instance] the Day of Atonement will not atone until the person himself seeks to assuage his fellow.

m. Yoma 8:9

Such limitations notwithstanding, the Day of Atonement still seemed to be an extraordinary act of mercy on God's part—and a token of His great love:

It has been written and ordained that He will have *mercy* on all who turn from their errors once each year.

Jubilees 5:17

But You, our God, are good and true, slow to anger, and governing all with *mercy. For even if we sin, we are yours,* since we are cognizant of your might; but knowing that we are reckoned yours, we will not sin.

Wisd. 15:1–2

[God said:] "A fast of *mercy* you will fast for me [on the Day of Atonement] for your own souls [that is, to save your own lives] so that the promises [of long life] made to our fathers [in Gen. 6:3] may be fulfilled."

Pseudo-Philo, Biblical Antiquities 13:8

In short: this regular cycle of holy days, spaced throughout the year, seemed perfectly designed to keep Israel constantly mindful of God. In addition to their weekly sabbath observance and their monthly marking of the new moon (observed in the temple with special sacrifices and ceremonies), Israelites from throughout the land went on regular pilgrimages to Jerusalem to observe the festivals of Passover, Weeks, and Booths. In addition, the Day of Atonement, coming on the heels of the fall "Day of Trumpet Blasts" celebration, was a time of reflection and repentance, when all of Israel's sins were forgiven and the people could start again spiritually purified and refreshed.

The Calendar and Modern Scholarship

Wellhausen conceived of Israel's religion in its earliest period to be close to nature and the annual cycle. "Year after year, the return of the grape-harvest, the grain harvest, and sheep-shearing brought together the members of the household to eat and to drink in the presence of the Lord."[4] The fact that Scripture connects Israel's various festivals to historical events like the exodus from Egypt was, he believed, something of an afterthought. In this matter subsequent scholars have generally agreed with him: all three of Israel's festivals—Passover, Weeks, and Booths—were, they say, originally celebrations arising out of the annual harvest cycle, and similar festivals were probably observed outside of Israel in much the same basic manner.[5]

About the first of these, scholars long ago observed that there actually appear to have been two originally quite separate holidays. One involved the sacrificing and eating of an animal from the flock, the *pesaḥ* sacrifice. Such an annual rite, scholars believe, must have sprung up among shepherds, not farmers. Presumably, the animal was sacrificed as a way of bringing divine favor on the rest of the flock; perhaps, scholars have suggested, pastoral nomads performed this rite in the spring to help guarantee a safe and prosperous time for their animals in the blazing summer months that followed.[6] "Do not break a single bone," the rite prescribed, lest this betoken evil for the flock from which the sacrifice came. The slaughter of the animal and subsequent meal were apparently performed at home, since the rite also stipulated that some of the animal's blood be daubed on the doorposts and lintel of the house (Exod. 12:7), apparently as an apotropaic act—a way of warding off evil.[7] The faint outlines of such a festival can still be seen, scholars say, in elements of Exodus 12–13. From these chapters it would appear that the holiday was held sometime in the month of Abib (Exod. 13:4), perhaps indeed on, specifically, the evening of the fourteenth day (Exod. 12:6), that is, in the light of the full moon of the month that marked the vernal equinox and the end of winter. As for the name *pesaḥ*, scholars note that the verb from which it seems to derive means not so much "pass over" as "hop" or "limp" (1 Kings 18:21, 26; cf. 2 Sam. 4:4) or possibly, "protect."[8] Some scholars thus theorize that the slaughter of the animal in this holiday may originally have involved some sort of ritual "hopping" or "limping" (this is how the verb *pasaḥ* is used in 1 Kings 18). Only much later, scholars say, was the holiday connected to the Exodus story. That was when it began to be said that God had "hopped over" the houses of the Israelites when he was afflicting the Egyptians with the last of the Ten Plagues (Exod. 12:13, 27).

This same time of year, scholars say, was marked by farmers with an entirely different holiday, the Festival of Unleavened Bread. The Bible specifies (Lev. 23:6) that this festival was to take place on the fifteenth of the month, one day after the date given for the eating of the *pesaḥ*, but the fixing of this precise date, scholars say, may have been a later innovation. Originally, the festival may have taken place when the winter's barley crop had reached maturity and was ready to be harvested: farmers would mark the event by eating unleavened barley bread for seven days. Whatever its origins, the Festival of Unleavened Bread was at first a holiday entirely separate from Passover.* It was rooted in an entirely different population—the farmers, not the shepherds—and included an obligatory trip to a local sanctuary (Exod. 23:17; 34:23) rather than being marked strictly in the home, like Passover. Why *unleavened* bread? Though the point is still debated, most scholars believe that the absence of yeast in the bread was felt to be a mark of purity. After all, it says elsewhere in the Bible (quite unconnected to this particular holiday), "No grain offering that you bring to the LORD shall be made with leaven" (Lev. 2:11).

The Bible itself has provided scholars with evidence that the Passover (*pesaḥ*) holiday was, at least for a while, quite separate from the Festival of Unleavened Bread. Here, for example, is one (apparently early) list of Israel's three annual festivals:

> Three times in the year you shall hold a festival for Me. You shall observe the festival of unleavened bread; as I commanded you, you shall eat unleavened bread for seven days at the appointed time in the month of Abib, for in it you came out of Egypt. No one shall appear before Me empty-handed. You shall [also] observe the festival of harvest, of the first fruits of your labor [Feast of Weeks], of what you sow in the field. You shall observe the festival of ingathering at the end of the year, when you gather in from the field the fruit of your labor [Feast of Booths]. Three times in the year all your males shall appear before the Lord GOD.
>
> Exod. 23:14–17

Where is Passover? Apparently, it was never part of this list, scholars say; certainly there is no hint of it being part of the Festival of Unleavened Bread. Similarly:

> You shall keep the festival of unleavened bread. Seven days you shall eat unleavened bread, as I commanded you, at the time appointed in the month of Abib; for in the month of Abib you came out from Egypt . . . You shall observe the festival of weeks, the first fruits of the wheat harvest, and the festival of ingathering at the turn of the year. Three times in the year all your males shall appear before the LORD God, the God of Israel.
>
> Exod. 34:18–23

Here again, there are three festivals, but nothing about Passover.[9] Somewhat later on, however, the farmers' Festival of Unleavened Bread and the shepherds' Passover began to be merged into a single festival. Passover also

---

* And indeed, the two holidays are treated quite separately, seriatim, in Exod. 12:1–13, 14–20, 21–28, 40–51; see also Lev. 23:5, 6–8 and Num. 28:16, 17–23.

moved from the home to the temple, and each aspect of the combined festival came to be explicitly connected to history, namely, the Exodus:

> Observe the month of Abib and prepare the Passover sacrifice for the LORD your God, for in the month of Abib the LORD your God brought you out of Egypt by night. You shall offer the passover sacrifice to the LORD your God, from the flock and the herd, at the place that the LORD will choose as a dwelling for his name. You must not eat with it anything leavened. For seven days you shall eat unleavened bread with it—the bread of affliction—because you came out of the land of Egypt in great haste, so that all the days of your life you may remember the day of your departure from the land of Egypt. No leaven shall be seen with you in all your land for seven days; and none of the meat of what you slaughter on the evening of the first day shall remain until morning.[10]
>
> Deut. 16:1–4

As for the other two major festivals, Booths and Weeks, scholars believe that they too underwent a similar process of historicization. With regard to the former, its earlier name seems to have been "Festival of Ingathering" (*'asif*, Exod. 34:22); it is called "Booths" in Leviticus and Deuteronomy.[11] Agricultural in origin, scholars say, Ingathering/Booths came to be connected only later with the Exodus narrative: "I caused the Israelites to dwell in booths on their way out of Egypt" (Lev. 23:43). But the Exodus narrative itself doesn't say a word about the people "dwelling in booths"! Scholars thus see this as another example of what Wellhausen called the "hardening" of originally natural, spontaneous expressions of joy into religious doctrine. "It is in Deuteronomy," he wrote, "that one detects the first very perceptible traces of a historical dress being given to the religion and the worship."[12] Indeed, the third festival, Weeks, has no explicit connection whatsoever to the Exodus narrative in the Bible itself. However, since it was to take place in the third month, the same month as the Sinai revelation (Exod. 19:1), the connection was eventually made (*Jubilees* 6:17–19).[13]

Purifying the Temple

As for the Day of Atonement, scholars have noted that this holiday exists only in what they identify as priestly writings. It is never mentioned in the book of Exodus or in the calendar of holidays in Deut. 16:1–17; as far as these books are concerned there was no such holiday. There is a reason for that, scholars say. Originally, the Day of Atonement was not an all-Israelite holy day devoted to atoning for one's sins. Rather, it was at first a strictly priestly observance, a procedure by which priests purged the sanctuary after it had been defiled.

Similar procedures for purging a sanctuary are attested elsewhere in the ancient Near East. Particularly striking is the description of one such ceremony from ancient Babylon. There, the procedure calls for a priest to wash himself and then put on a special linen garment, in which he is to enter the temple:

> The priest shall arise and bathe . . . he shall put on a linen robe in front of the god Bel and the goddess Beltiya. When the purification of the temple is completed, he shall enter the temple . . . He shall call the slaughterer to decapitate a ram, the body of which the *mašmašu* priest shall use in performing the purgation (*kuppuru*) ritual for the temple . . . He shall then go out into the open country. The slaughterer shall do the same with the ram's head [and not return for a week].[14]

Scholars have been struck by the similarities of this procedure with that of the Day of Atonement, which also involved the priest bathing and putting on a linen robe (Lev. 16:4) and entering the sanctuary/temple (Lev. 16:3). There followed the slaughtering of an animal in the sanctuary (Lev. 16:15) and the escorting of another animal, the scapegoat, out into the open country ("the wilderness," Lev. 16:21–22).

The purpose of both ceremonies was the atonement, or more properly, the purgation of the sanctuary: "Thus he [the priest] shall make atonement *for the sanctuary,*" it says in Lev. 16:16. Indeed, the same word used for atonement/purgation in the Bible (*kippurim*) is used in the Babylonian text (*kuppuru*). So, if modern scholars are right, then the Day of Atonement originally had nothing to do with God forgiving people their sins once a year. Indeed, that subject of forgiveness comes up only at the very end of the chapter, 16:29–34—a section that, according to some, may represent the school of H turning P's priestly ceremony into a holiday that (in typical H fashion) involved the common people more directly in the life of the temple.[15] Moreover, some scholars have suggested that the original ritual was not even an annual event occurring on a specific date, but an ad hoc rite performed whenever the sanctuary had been profaned. It was only later that it became a yearly ceremony that followed the fall "Trumpet Blasts" festival, and still later that it became a nationwide fast. (These thoughts can be of little comfort to anyone who has spent a hot September day abstaining from food and drink for twenty-five hours.) This reconstruction, one theory holds, may solve another biblical mystery: the death of Nadab and Abihu.

Once Again: Nadab and Abihu

Many modern scholars remain puzzled about the death of Aaron's two sons. Different ideas about the incident abound. One connection that has suggested itself is with Jeroboam, who ruled the northern tribes after their secession from the once united kingdom of David and Solomon. Jeroboam had two sons, whose names were suspiciously similar to Nadab and Abihu: Nadab and Abijah. (In fact, these are essentially the same names, Abijah being simply a variant pronunciation of Abihu.) What is more, both of Jeroboam's sons died unnatural deaths, just as Aaron's sons did (see 1 Kings 14:1–17; 15:25–28). This could not be a coincidence. Still, what was the point of giving Aaron's two sons the same names as Jeroboam's and having them die prematurely in the sanctuary?

If they died for having brought before God an "unholy fire," coals from outside of the sanctuary, then, some scholars suggest, perhaps indeed the point was to drive home the great sanctity of the temple and the need for constant care therein. Or perhaps, more polemically, the story was a warning against offering incense in "private, idolatrous cults" [16] or, in fact, anywhere outside of the central sanctuary. Alternately, the story might be understood as reflecting some aspect of the battle over "Who's a priest?" seen earlier.

One intriguing theory, however, connects the story specifically with the laws concerning the Day of Atonement.[17] These actually begin by evoking the death of Nadab and Abihu:

> The LORD spoke to Moses *after the death of the two sons of Aaron, when they drew near before the LORD and died.* The LORD said to Moses: Tell your brother Aaron not to come just at any time into the sanctuary inside the curtain before the mercy seat that is upon the ark, or he will die; for I appear in the cloud upon the mercy seat. Thus shall Aaron come into the holy place: with a young bull for a sin offering and a ram for a burnt offering.
>
> Lev. 16:1–3

It has seemed odd to scholars that God should speak to Moses "after the death of the two sons of Aaron" in chapter 16, when their death was actually narrated six chapters earlier. Perhaps, some have suggested, those intervening chapters, which all concern various rules of impurity, were added later, and chapter 16 was meant to follow immediately after chapter 10.[18]

That in itself does not explain the deaths of Nadab and Abihu, of course. But if, as scholars believe, the original purpose of the Day of Atonement was the purgation of the sanctuary after defilement, then a possible answer does suggest itself. After all, the tabernacle had just now been set up in accordance with God's specifications, and the priests had been instructed about how to offer sacrifices. If, as this line of argument goes, P's next pedagogical job was to outline the procedure for purging the sanctuary after defilement, then the sanctuary needed somehow to be defiled in the narrative. But how could it be—it had just been set up! Enter Nadab and Abihu. According to this theory,

P invented these two sons of Aaron, giving them the names of the discredited Jeroboam's two sons, in order to have them die in the sanctuary and so defile it in the severest way (corpse defilement imparted the highest level of impurity). Once that had happened, God could then instruct Aaron about how to purify the sanctuary: "Thus shall Aaron come into the holy place [to perform the purification]" (Lev. 16:3).[19] In other words, there is no intended *lesson* in the death of Aaron's sons: they do not die as a warning about foreign incense cults or a reminder of the necessity of great care in the sanctuary or as a polemical snipe at the Zadokite priesthood or an injunction against priestly drunkenness or any of the other solutions that have been proposed. Aaron's sons die, according to this theory, simply to provide a source of corpse defilement for the tabernacle and thus introduce the procedure for purging it.

Presumably, this theory holds, such a procedure had originally been used any time during the year that it was necessary. Therefore, there was great logic in having the sanctuary contaminated in the narrative (chapter 10) and then immediately purged (chapter 16). But eventually, sanctuary purgation became an annual rite every fall. That is why the text no longer says explicitly that the things done in chapter 16 were done as a way of restoring the sanctuary's purity. In fact, that may also be why the intervening chapters 11–15 were made to intervene: now the procedures of chapter 16 were no longer an ad hoc remedy but a yearly ritual—so there was no longer any point in having them follow on the heels of chapter 10. (Instead, the text now went on to list other potential sources of impurity that might require the sanctuary to be purged.) The only remaining hint of P's original design is the (otherwise inexplicable) opening verse of chapter 16, "The LORD spoke to Moses after the death of the two sons of Aaron."

Supporters of this approach point to another episode in the priestly writings, the death of Miriam (Num. 20:1). As ancient interpreters long ago pointed out, it can be no accident that her death is narrated just after Moses and Aaron have received instructions about how people are to be purified after contact with a dead body (Num. 19:1–22). In that case, the instructions *precede* the narrative to which they apply, whereas with Nadab and Abihu they follow the narrative, but in both cases the purpose would have been the same, to provide a narrative "anchor" for P's priestly instructions.

Complaints

Having camped out at Mount Sinai for nearly a year, Israel at last received the sign that it was time to move on. They packed up their things, including the tabernacle and all its appurtenances, and set out on their journey for the land of Canaan (Numbers 10).

One might think that, having seen all of God's miraculous interventions on their behalf—including the very manna that they ate each day, and the pillars of cloud and fire that accompanied them on their travels—the people would have departed for Canaan full of confidence and hope. But, as the prophet Jeremiah was to observe in another context, "Oh, the mind has more twists than anything and is so intractable—who can figure it out?" (Jer. 17:9). So it was that Israel's journey to Canaan was marked by a series of complaints. They complained about God: "Is God in our midst or not?" (Exod. 17:7), they asked. They complained about the lack of meat in their diet (Num. 11:4) and about the taste of manna (Num. 11:6; 21:5). Their minds invented great meals that they had never had: "We remember the fish we used to eat in Egypt for free, the cucumbers, melons, leeks, onions, and garlic" (Num. 11:5). Later, Moses' two siblings Miriam and Aaron became jealous of their brother and complained about *him:* "Has the LORD spoken only through Moses? Has he not spoken through us also?" (Num. 12:2). For readers of the Bible, these stories seemed to share a common point: human beings, it seems, often overlook God's gifts and focus only on their hardships.

One of the most serious incidents occurred when Moses sent out a party of scouts to investigate the land of Canaan (Numbers 13). Their report on the fierce inhabitants frightened the Israelites, and they complained bitterly. All they wanted to do, they said, was to go back to being slaves in Egypt:

> And all the Israelites complained against Moses and Aaron; the whole congregation said to them, "If only we had died in the land of Egypt! Or if only we could die in this wilderness! Why is the LORD bringing us into this land to fall by the sword? Our wives and our little ones will become booty—would we not be better off if we went back to Egypt?" So they said to one another, "Let us choose a leader and go back to Egypt . . ." But Joshua son of Nun and Caleb son of Jephunneh, who were among those who had spied out the land, tore their clothes and said to all the congregation of the Israelites, "The land that we went through as spies is an exceedingly good land . . . Do not rebel against the LORD, and do not be afraid of the people of the land—they are ours! Their protection is gone, and the LORD is with us; do not be afraid of them." But the whole congregation threatened to stone them.
>
> Num. 14:2–9

God was so angry at the people's cowardly response that He told Moses He would strike them all down with a plague and start to build the nation over again with Moses' own descendants (Num. 14:12). It was only because of Moses' earnest intervention that God agreed to let the Israelites live. But He also made Moses a chilling promise: the cowardly spies, along with their fainthearted countrymen, would never be allowed to enter the land of Canaan. Instead, they would have to wander about the wilderness for the next forty years, until the last of their generation was dead (Num. 14:34). The only people exempted from this harsh sentence were Joshua and Caleb, since they had not lost heart like the other spies. They would be allowed to survive the forty years and then enter Canaan and settle there.

Korah's Revolt

Another incident occurred on the way that caused the people great harm. Korah, Moses' own first cousin, led a revolt against him. In fact, he managed to attract numerous followers to his cause and might have succeeded in overthrowing Moses' leadership. In the end, however, God intervened, and Korah was swallowed up in what seems to have been an earthquake (Num. 16:32). Nevertheless, the revolt that he started continued for a time and ultimately resulted in the death of thousands of people.

This incident, like so many in the Bible, contains a number of puzzling elements, for which there are now two sets of answers—those of the ancient interpreters and those of modern scholars. Both of these groups began by focusing on the basic fact of the story, the rebellion itself. What might have caused it? The issue, the Bible seems to say, was Moses himself:

> Now Korah son of Izhar son of Kohath son of Levi, along with Dathan and Abiram sons of Eliab, and On son of Peleth—descendants of Reuben—took two hundred fifty Israelite men, leaders of the congregation, chosen from the assembly, well-known men, and they confronted Moses. They complained against Moses and against Aaron, and said to them, "Now you have gone too far! Everyone in the congregation [of Levites] is holy, and the LORD is in their midst. So why then *do you exalt yourselves* above the assembly of the LORD?"
>
> Num. 16:1–3

According to this opening paragraph of the story, it was the fact that Moses "exalted himself" that led to the revolt. But for ancient readers of the Bible, this claim sounded completely out of keeping with Moses' character. Had not the text just observed: "Now this man Moses was extremely humble, more than any man on the face of the earth" (Num. 12:3)? No, the rebels must have been motivated by something else.

The real reason for Korah's discontent was, in fact, alluded to later on in the story. He and the other Levites had certain duties in the tabernacle—to burn incense and the like—but since they were not direct descendants of Aaron, they were not allowed to be priests. They could not offer sacrifices in the tabernacle or receive the considerable material benefits reserved for priests. *That* was what was really on their minds. As Moses goes on to say to

Korah and the other Levites: "Yet you seek the priesthood as well" (Num. 16:10). He therefore challenges them to take their incense holders and go before God the next day; then they would see if God approves of their being considered priests. The result was inevitable. The next day, "the earth opened its mouth and swallowed them up, along with their households—everyone who belonged to Korah and all their goods" (Num. 16:32).

Still, as the introductory paragraph cited above attests, Korah was not alone. He had, in addition to his own Levite allies, a group of Reubenites led by Dathan and Abiram. Their complaint could not have been about their exclusion from the priesthood—they were not from the tribe of Levi, but from Reuben. Instead, they seemed to have been bothered by their being put in a subservient position by Moses' leadership:

> Moses sent for Dathan and Abiram sons of Eliab; but they said, "We will not come! Is it too little that you have brought us up out of a land flowing with milk and honey to kill us in the wilderness, that *you must also lord it over us?*"
>
> Num. 16:12–14

Why should two members of the tribe of Reuben object to Moses' "lording it over" them? Perhaps it was precisely their tribal origin. Reuben, after all, was Jacob's firstborn; by rights, his tribe ought to be the leaders. Even though he personally had been discredited because of his sin with his father's concubine (Gen. 35:22), that was no reason—Dathan and Abiram seemed to be implying—for Reuben's descendants to lose out. Moses should never have become the head of the people. That role should have been granted to someone from the tribe of Reuben.

It is not clear from the text how Dathan, Abiram, and their allies died—apparently they too went down in the earthquake—but however it happened, their death did not end the destruction. The next day "the whole congregation of Israelites" revolted against Moses and Aaron (Num. 16:41), and God struck the people with a plague. "Those who died by the plague were fourteen thousand seven hundred, besides those who died in the affair of Korah" (Num. 16:49).

The Tassels Did It

Such were the basic facts of the story, but they still left a lot of questions unanswered. For example: how was it that Korah managed to convince people to join him in revolt?

One tactic ancient interpreters often employed in trying to fill out the details of a story was to examine the connection between it and whatever just preceded it in the narrative. (They did this, for example, with the biblical account of Moses' birth.) [20] In the case of Korah's rebellion, this might at first have seemed a rather unpromising course. What immediately precedes this story is no particular incident, but a law requiring Israelites to wear a special blue tassel or fringe on their clothing:

> The LORD said to Moses: Speak to the Israelites, and tell them to make tassels on the corners of their garments throughout their generations, and to put a blue thread on the tassel at each corner. In that way it will catch your eye* and, when you see it, you will remember all the commandments of the LORD and do them, and not act according to your own ideas or your own desires.
>
> Num. 15:37–39

On reflection, interpreters saw in the juxtaposition of this law with the beginning of the Korah narrative a subtle hint as to how Korah might have enlisted his followers. Forcing people to put a special blue tassel on their clothes, Korah must have said, was an intolerable intrusion into their lives. This time Moses had gone too far!

> In that time He commanded that man [Moses] about the tassels. And then Korah and two hundred men with him rebelled and said, "Why is an unbearable law imposed upon us?"
>
> Pseudo-Philo, *Biblical Antiquities* 16:1

Later interpreters took a more subtle approach:

> What did Korah do [after hearing the law of tassels]? He went and made some garments that were completely dyed blue. Then he went to Moses and said: Moses our teacher, is a garment that is already completely blue nonetheless obliged to have the [blue corner] tassel? He said: It is ... Whereupon Korah said: the Torah is not of divine origin, and Moses is not a prophet and Aaron is not a high priest.
>
> j. *Sanhedrin* 10:1

Korah's question seems straightforward enough: why, if someone's whole garment is already dyed blue, does that person need to add an extra blue thread to the corner tassel? But this question, ancient interpreters meant to imply, was really a metaphorical version of Korah's complaint in the Bible: "Everyone in the congregation [of Levites] is holy, and the LORD is in their midst. So why then do you exalt yourselves above the assembly of the LORD?" In

---

* Literally, "it will be for you as a tassel." But we already knew that! Apparently, a pun is intended, connecting the word for tassel (ṣiṣit) with the root for "peep" or "peer" (ṣuṣ).

other words, we are all part of the same garment and we are all blue. What makes you think you are special just because you are the corner thread?[21]

In saying this, of course, Korah set a pattern to be followed endlessly in later history. How many times has a would-be revolutionary sought to bring down the ruling powers with the familiar taunt *What makes you better than the rest of us*? It seemed clear to ancient interpreters that Korah was not really interested in changing the system, merely in taking it over. He was thus a dangerous demagogue, an example of how easily power can be usurped by those without scruples. Here, clearly, was a lesson for the ages.

Korah's Rebellion in Modern Scholarship

Modern scholars suspect that the narrative of Korah's rebellion is really a composite of different texts. A clue to this, they say, may be found in the book of Deuteronomy. There a report of the rebellion is found, but Korah is nowhere to be seen:

> You shall love the LORD your God, therefore, and keep his charge, his decrees, his ordinances, and his commandments always. Remember . . . what He did to Dathan and Abiram, sons of Eliab son of Reuben, how in the midst of all Israel the earth opened its mouth and swallowed them up, along with their households, their tents, and every living being in their company; for it is your own eyes that have seen every great deed that the LORD did.
>
> Deut. 11:1–7

Nowhere in this paragraph—or, in fact, all of Deuteronomy—is there any mention of Korah. As far as Deuteronomy is concerned, the famous rebellion was the work of Dathan and Abiram alone. The same thing is true of the book of Psalms:

> They were jealous of Moses in the camp, and of Aaron, the holy one of the LORD.
> The earth opened and swallowed up Dathan, and covered the faction of Abiram.
> Fire also broke out in their company, the flame burned up the wicked.
>
> Ps. 106:16–18

Once again: no Korah. For this reason (as well as because of internal inconsistencies and repetitions within Numbers 16),[22] many scholars believe that the Korah element of the story in Numbers 16 was actually grafted onto an original rebellion narrative associated with the Reubenites alone, Dathan and

Abiram. Such a story might, scholars believe, reflect a relatively early stage in Israelite history, a time when the formerly dominant tribe of Reuben was still struggling to regain its earlier rank.[23] Their complaint, quite naturally, was indeed that the new leadership was "lording it over" people like themselves.

The Korah element, scholars say, was added in later by a priestly writer; it was another salvo in the "Who's a priest?" battle that we have already seen. According to the view that held *all* Levites to be fit for the priesthood, Korah would indeed have been right to say that "everyone in the congregation [of Levites] is holy, and the LORD is in their midst." In other words: we're all Levites, and any Levite can be a priest. But the purported priestly author of this revised version of the episode did not hold that view; he believed that only Aaronids could be priests. Indeed, this is the great lesson, according to scholars, that the Korah episode in its final form was designed to impart: Be content with what you have, Levites! God has made it clear that the priesthood belongs only to Aaron and his sons (a lesson reinforced in the next chapter, Numbers 17), and if you try to usurp their priestly duties, you are in danger of ending up like Korah.

21

Moses' Last Words

NUMBERS 22–24 AND

DEUTERONOMY 5:6–21; 6:4–9; 27–28; 32–34

The Death of Moses, 1851 (oil on canvas)
by Alexandre Cabanel (1823–89).

A PROPHET FOR SALE. "HEAR, O ISRAEL!" GUARDING THE SABBATH.
ISRAEL'S LAST WARNINGS. ESARHADDON AND THE LOVE OF GOD.
DEATH OF MOSES.

The Israelites wandered the desert for forty years. Finally, as they approached
Canaan, Moses gave them their final instructions. He himself was not to enter
Canaan, however; God had ordered him to die on the brink of his mission's
completion.

After Korah's rebellion, the people continued on their slow march to Canaan.
They tried at first to enter via Edom, to the southeast of their future homeland, but the Edomites refused them passage (Num. 20:18). So they turned
north instead and ultimately circled around Edom, scoring victories on the
way over the Amorite king, Sihon, and Og, king of Bashan. Soon they were
on the doorstep of Moab, directly east of Canaan. It was then that the
famous confrontation with Balaam occurred. It happened like this:

The Moabite king, Balak, was clearly worried at the progress of this new
people in the region. He therefore appealed to a renowned soothsayer, Balaam son of Beor, to help rid him of the Israelites. Balaam had a reputation as
a curser, someone who was capable of harming people through his imprecations. Balak therefore offered Balaam a hefty sum to travel from Aram to
Moab and curse the Israelites, and after some hesitation, Balaam agreed.
Before his departure, however, Balaam received a divine warning: "Do only
what I tell you to do" (Num. 22:20).

On his way to Moab, Balaam ran into the snag: his donkey, spotting an
angel in front of them, shied from the road and ran into a nearby field, refusing to budge. Balaam at first saw nothing and, furious at his donkey, beat the
poor animal mercilessly. It was only when she protested (actually speaking to
her master in human words) that he finally spotted the angel himself and
understood why she would not move. The angel then told Balaam that he
could continue his journey but cautioned him again in God's name: "You can
say nothing other than what I [God] tell you" (Num. 22:35).

Arrived in Moab, Balaam tried to cooperate with the king's wishes. But
every time he opened his mouth to curse Israel, all that came out were
blessings. Some of them were worded in the elegant language of biblical
poetry:

From the top of these crags I see them, as I gaze from the mountain
    heights:
A people that dwells apart and is not reckoned among the nations!

Who can count the dust of Jacob, or number Israel's dust-clouds?
Let me die the death of the righteous* that my offspring may be like him!

How lovely are your tents, O Jacob; O Israel, your encampments!
Like softly swaying palm groves, or gardens beside a river,
Like aloes the LORD has planted, and cedars on watery banks.
Water shall flow from his buckets, and his seed shall have mighty
        streams.

A star will come forth from Jacob, and from Israel rise up a scepter.
It will crush the Moabites' brow, and the forehead of all of Seth.
Edom will be its possession, and Seir will fall to its spoil:
Yes, Israel will triumph!

Num. 23:9–10; 24:5–7, 17–18

Needless to say, these words did not find favor with Balaam's employer, King Balak. He dismissed Balaam without the promised emolument, and the professional curser returned to his homeland.

One would think, given this bare recital, that Balaam would have been one of Israel's cherished heroes, a foreign soothsayer who blessed Israel instead of cursing. But his reputation among ancient interpreters was quite the opposite: he was Balaam the Wicked. Part of the reason lay in the story itself. After all, he *tried* to curse Israel; it was only that God would not let him. More than that, however, was the role that money played in the story. When Balak's envoys approached Balaam with their offer, they said in the king's name: "I will surely do you great honor, and whatever you say to me I will do; come, curse this people for me" (Num. 22:17). Much of this was diplomatic code language. "Great honor" is an elegant way of saying "a lot of money," and "whatever you say to me I will do" meant: name your price. Balaam took the hint, replying, "Even if Balak were to give me his palace full of silver and gold, I could not go beyond the command of the LORD my God." Nice words—but what they really meant, interpreters felt, was, "This could really cost you."

> Woe to them [ungodly men]! For they . . . abandon themselves to Balaam's error for the sake of gain.
>
> Jude 11

Whence do we know that Balaam had a large appetite [for money]? From his saying, "Even if Balak were to give me his whole palace full of silver and

---

* In other words, let me be judged to have led a righteous life, so that, as a reward, I will have offspring as numerous as Israel is now. The word for "righteous" (*yesharim*) may be an allusion to Israel's poetic name, Jeshurun.

gold, I could not go beyond the command of the LORD my God." [That is, he would not have mentioned silver or gold if that were not what was really on his mind.]

Abot deR. Natan (B) ch. 45

At first he was a holy man and a prophet of God, but afterward, through disobedience and the desire for lucre, when he tried to curse Israel, he was called by the Holy Writ a "soothsayer" [Josh. 13:22].

Jerome, Questions in Genesis 22:22

In short, Balaam the Wicked was one of the great villains of the Hebrew Bible, taking his place next to the diabolical fratricidal Cain and the seditious Korah in the rogues' gallery of ancient Israel. "Don't be like these," Scripture was saying.

Balaam and Modern Scholarship

In 1967, an Arab worker at an excavation site at Deir 'Alla', in Jordan, discovered a piece of plaster with writing on it. It turned out to be part of an inscription dating back deep into biblical times, perhaps belonging to the late eighth or early seventh century BCE.[1] It was written in a dialect that seemed to be some sort of mixture of Aramaic and Hebrew. The inscription was full of lacunae, but it clearly reported on someone named Balaam son of Beor,

who was a seer of the gods. The gods came to him in the night, and he saw a vision like an oracle of [the god] El. Then they said to [Balaa]m son of Beor: Thus he will do [   ] hereafter, which [   ]. And Balaam arose the next day . . .[2]

The inscription went on to tell a (very fragmentary) story different from the one in the Bible, but it nevertheless delivered a shock to scholars. After all, there could hardly be a story in the Bible that seemed more fictional than Balaam's—a professional curser and his talking donkey! Yet here was a certifiably ancient inscription that spoke of precisely such a man, and described him just the way the Bible did, as a seer who communicated with the divine at night. Indeed, the fact that the inscription spoke of "the gods" in the plural and named the Canaanite god El in particular only added to its historical cachet: apparently such a man, or at least the legend of such a man, existed outside of the biblical orbit. In the Bible, Balaam obeys "the LORD," but in the inscription he belonged to the world of those who still spoke of "the gods" and El. Did this mean that behind the biblical narrative stood some real, historical figure?[3]

This point of contact between the Bible and an excavated text has not, however, stopped scholars from asking the usual questions about the biblical story as it now exists: Is it all of one piece? Why was it written? And by whom? On all these questions opinion is still somewhat divided.[4] One thing on which most scholars agree, however, is the episode of Balaam and the talking donkey: they believe that this is an insertion into an earlier story. The reason is that this episode seems intended to portray Balaam in a negative light: the great seer cannot even perceive what his donkey can! Take that incident out, scholars say, and you have a smoothly running narrative that presents Balaam altogether positively, as someone who, from the beginning, knew that Israel was blessed by God (Num. 22:12). Although he went to Moab as Balak requested, Balaam nevertheless warned the king time and again that he could say only what God allowed (Num. 22:38; 23:12, 26; 24:12).

The fact that, without the donkey incident, the story portrays Balaam altogether positively does not mean, however, that this positive portrayal is itself all the work of a single author. After all, scholars note, the prose framework seems at variance with the blessings spoken by Balaam in some of its details.[5] Moreover, because of their language and orthography (spelling), the blessings appear to be quite ancient. Albright in particular highlighted some of their archaic features.[6] But even the blessings may not be of one piece. One theory holds that the first two blessings (Num. 23:7–10 and 18–24), which refer to the basic situation described in the story, may have been composed to go with the frame narrative: in them Balaam keeps saying why he cannot curse Israel. But the latter two blessings (24:3–9 and 15–24) seem disconnected from the frame story. Cut away their (nearly identical) opening verses, this approach claims, and these passages could well be two (or more) ancient prophetic oracles originally attributed to someone else entirely, or to no one in particular.[7] In them, the speaker "predicts" the conquest of Edom by David but knows nothing of Edom's subsequent resurgence. He mentions among the enemies of Israel the "Sethites" (24:17); this seems to be a memory from the distant past. All this makes these last two blessings sound particularly old. The surrounding prose, scholars say, does not. It is written in standard biblical Hebrew, of the sort spoken in the middle of the pre-exilic period. Still, the basic prose narrative, with its positive portrayal of Balaam, is probably earlier than the talking donkey incident, which seeks to denigrate Balaam. Indeed, the positive portrayal of Balaam would certainly fit well with the positive assessment of Balaam found in the words of the eighth-century prophet Micah:

O my people, remember what King Balak of Moab plotted, and what Balaam son of Beor answered him, and what happened from Shittim to Gilgal—so that you may know the saving acts of the LORD.

Mic. 6:5

Though it is not entirely clear, this passage as well might seem to be present-ing Balaam as a positive figure: he *answers* the wicked Balak, presumably by blessing Israel rather than cursing, and by that answer he apparently gives proof of the "saving acts" of God.[8]

Putting all this together: it seems to some scholars that Balaam's last two blessings may go back to the time of David's kingdom, if not earlier. These only later came to be attributed to Balaam, a legendary soothsayer, and the first two blessings added to them. At that time or possibly still later on, a sur-rounding narrative was created to contain them, one that presented Balaam as an altogether positive figure. Then—perhaps at a time when the very idea of a pagan prophet being addressed by Israel's God had become anathema—the talking donkey was introduced, and with it, the presentation of Balaam as a buffoon. This negative assessment of Balaam may well have been the work of a priestly writer, scholars say, since such an assessment is reflected elsewhere in priestly writings. (Thus, Balaam is blamed for the Israelites' sin at Baal Peor in Num. 31:16; Balaam's well-deserved death by the sword is reported in Num. 31:8, cf. Josh. 13:22.) This negative portrayal was then picked up and carried forward by the ancient interpreters. Thus was born "Balaam the Wicked."[9]

Moses' Farewell

The book of Deuteronomy, as noted, contains a series of three discourses pro-nounced by Moses before his death. Addressing the people as they stood in Moab on the brink of their entry into Canaan, Moses reviewed for them the events of their recent history and all that God had done on their behalf. He stressed how important it was for Israel to keep the provisions of God's covenant and observe all the laws that He had given them. The larger part of the book is then devoted to a detailed presentation of God's laws—some of them basically the same as those presented elsewhere in the Torah, others quite new. The name of the book, Deuteronomy, means "second law" in Greek, a reflection of its Hebrew name in postbiblical sources, *mishneh torah*. This phrase, which appears in Deut. 17:18, was understood as mean-ing a "repetition of the law" and thus came to be used as the title of the whole book.*

In urging the people to remain faithful to God's covenant with them, Moses stressed the central duty to recognize that God is the only deity in the universe: "Realize [this] today and turn it over in your mind: the LORD is indeed God, in heaven above and on the earth below; there is no other" (Deut. 4:39). This teaching is stressed repeatedly, but perhaps it is best

---

* As is frequently observed, *mishneh torah* in Deut. 17:18 actually means a "version" or "copy" of the Torah; "repetition of the law" is probably thus a willful distortion.

known from a paragraph that came to play a central part in the teachings of Judaism and Christianity:

> Hear, O Israel: The LORD is our God, the LORD alone. You shall love the LORD your God with all your heart, and with all your soul, and with all your might. Take to heart these words that I am commanding you today. Teach them to your children and speak about them when you are at home and when you are away, when you lie down and when you get up. Bind them as a sign on your hand, fix them as a frontlet on your forehead, and write them on the doorposts of your house and on your gates.
>
> Deut. 6:4–9

This paragraph came to be known as the "Shema" because of its opening word, "Hear!" (Hebrew, shĕmaʻ). As with the rest of the Torah, ancient readers did not see this paragraph as mere oratory or good advice, but as a *commandment,* one that God intended people to carry out scrupulously. But—come to think of it—how is someone supposed to do that? That is, what does the text mean by telling people to love God "with all your heart," and how is that different from loving Him with all your soul and all your might?[10] Moreover, when it says to take "these words" to heart and teach them to one's children and speak about them, which words precisely are meant? And how much speaking about them is enough? As for binding them "as a sign on your hand and . . . a frontlet on your forehead"—surely God did not intend people to go around wearing "these words" on their arms and heads. But if not, what did He mean?

A modern reader would probably say that the basic import of this paragraph is: love God deeply and think about everything I (Moses) have been telling you—in fact, think about it all the time. While that might indeed be the overall meaning, ancient interpreters were eager to pin down anything in the Torah that might appear vague or general. This was their approach to "You shall not hate your brother in your heart" and to "You shall not take revenge or bear a grudge" (Lev. 19:17–19), and it was their approach to the Shema as well.

What, then, did it mean to love God "with all your heart"?

> "With all your heart" means with your two inclinations, the inclination to do good and the inclination to do evil . . . and with all your soul, even should He demand your soul [that is, your death] . . .
>
> Rabbi Akiba said: If the verse says "with all your soul," then certainly this must include "all your might" too—why, then, should these words ["all your might," bekhol me'odekha] be added? They mean: with whatever measuring-cup He measures out to you, whether good measure or ill, be thankful [modeh] to Him for all.
>
> *Sifrei Deuteronomy 32*

To the ancient interpreters' way of thinking, the human heart is divided between two inclinations, the one to good and the other to evil.[11] It is not enough, therefore, to love God with one's good inclination, since that will leave it still at war with the evil inclination; rather, one must work to convert the evil inclination to love God as well. Rabbi Akiba, finding the phrase "with all your might" somewhat anticlimactic after "with all your soul," suggested that it be understood (because of the similar sound of the words meaning "your might" and "thankful") as "for *all* things [I] thank You," that is, that one ought to express gratitude to God no matter whether one's portion is good or bad.[12]

As for "these words," the phrase might indeed be taken to refer to anything or everything that Moses had said in his discourse thus far. Since, however, teaching them and speaking of them constantly seemed a potentially limitless task, ancient interpreters preferred to see in this phrase a reference to *the words just spoken by Moses,* starting with "Hear, O Israel." A person was required to teach these words in particular to his or her children, and to recite them regularly. How regularly? The passage specified two particular moments in the day, "when you lie down and when you get up." It therefore became customary to say the Shema twice a day, in the morning and at night.

> He commands us that "on going to bed and rising," men should meditate on the ordinances of God.[13]
>
> *Letter of Aristeas* 160

> With the entrance of day and of night, I shall enter into the covenant of God, and with the going out of evening and of morning, I shall speak His laws.
>
> (1QS) *Community Rule* 10:10

> Two times each day, at dawn and when it is time to go to sleep, let all acknowledge to God the gifts that He has bestowed upon them.
>
> Josephus, *Jewish Antiquities* 4:212–13

This practice is maintained to this day in Judaism: day and night, the verses of the Shema are recited by religious Jews. Christians as well accord Deut. 6:5 special attention, since it was singled out in the Gospels as the "first commandment":

> One of the scribes . . . asked him [Jesus], "Which commandment is the first of all?" Jesus answered, "The first is, 'Hear O Israel: the Lord our God, the Lord is one; you shall love the Lord your God with all your heart, and with all your soul, and with all your mind, and with all your strength.'"
>
> Mark 12:28–30 (also Matt. 22:35–38; Luke 10:25–28)

Some ancient interpreters took as metaphorical the commandment to "bind them as a sign on your hand, fix them as a frontlet on your forehead, and write them on the doorposts of your house and on your gates." After all, elsewhere in the Bible (Song 8:6), a woman says to her beloved, "Set me as a seal upon your heart, as a seal upon your arm." Surely she did not mean this literally, but only as a way of saying, "Don't forget me! Think of me always!" Other interpreters, however—in keeping with the tendency to translate potentially vague or general commandments into the specific and concrete— took these words quite literally: what the Torah meant was indeed that people ought to attach *these words* to their frontlets (leather bands that, in the ancient world, held the hair in place, often topped with jewels or lockets), and that they ought similarly to bind *these words* on their arms, indeed, enclose them in little cases to be fastened to the doorposts and gates of their houses. This interpretation, attested in (among other things) the *tefillin* found among the Dead Sea Scrolls,[14] is still the normative practice in today's Judaism.

"Remember" and "Keep"

In reviewing the Ten Commandments (Deut. 5:6–21), Moses presented them in a wording somewhat different from that which appeared in the book of Exodus (20:1–17). For example, the fifth commandment in the Exodus version had said: "Remember the sabbath day," but in Deuteronomy it began, "Keep [or guard] the sabbath day." To be sure, even this minor difference was a problem for ancient interpreters: if the Torah was perfect in all its details (Assumption 3), then the two versions ought to match each other perfectly. Of course, it was possible to claim that, in reviewing things, Moses (or God speaking to Moses) had purposely changed a few things to drive home a new message. Still, why would it say "remember" first and "keep" second—logically, the Torah ought to have told people to *keep* the sabbath in Exodus and then *reminded* them in Deuteronomy.

Considering, however, the extraordinary circumstances that accompanied the giving of the Torah—a great divine voice speaking to all of Israel simultaneously—it occurred to some interpreters that the apparent conflict between "remember" and "keep" might not be an inconsistency at all, but a hint as to the extraordinary thing that went on that day (and was never repeated): in addressing the people directly, God had actually uttered both words simultaneously, and they had somehow absorbed both—something that is certainly impossible in normal, human-to-human communication:

"Remember" and "keep"—these two words were said [by God] in a single word.

Mekhilta deR. Ishmael, Yitro 7

That still begged the question of why. To some interpreters it seemed that, if the word "keep" was understood in its other sense of "guard," then the Torah might actually be adding some specific teaching by its use of that word: not only was one to "remember" the sabbath and observe all its rules during the twenty-four hours it was in effect, but one ought as well to cease weekday activities a little before the sabbath, in effect, *guarding* its beginning lest any forbidden work be done inadvertently after the start of the sabbath:

> No one shall do work on Friday from the time when the sphere of the sun is distant from the gate [by] its [the sun's] full size, for this is why it is said, "Guard the sabbath day to sanctify it" [Deut. 5:12].
>
> *Damascus Document* 10:14–17

Other interpreters extended this idea, suggesting that a little time be added to the sabbath at both ends, fore and aft:

> "Remember" and "guard"—*remember* before [the sabbath starts] and *guard* it after [the sabbath is over]. From this it was deduced that one is to add [time] from the profane [that is, from the rest of the week] to the sacred [that is, the sabbath].
>
> *Mekhilta deR. Ishmael, Yitro* 7

Modern scholars, of course, are inclined to chalk up such differences between the Exodus and Deuteronomy versions of the Ten Commandments to human beings.[15] As already mentioned, they note that the two sabbath laws in Exodus and Deuteronomy are actually quite different in what follows their first words:

> Remember the sabbath day, and keep it holy. Six days you shall labor and do all your work. But the seventh day is a sabbath to the LORD your God; you shall not do any work—you, your son or your daughter, your male or female slave, your livestock, or the alien resident in your towns. *For in six days the LORD made heaven and earth, the sea, and all that is in them, but rested the seventh day; therefore the LORD blessed the sabbath day and consecrated it.*
>
> Exod. 20:8–11

> Observe the sabbath day and keep it holy, as the LORD your God commanded you. Six days you shall labor and do all your work. But the seventh day is a sabbath to the LORD your God; you shall not do any work—you, or your son or your daughter, or your male or female slave, or your ox or your donkey, or any of your livestock, or the resident alien in your towns, so that your male and female slave may rest as well as you. *Remember that*

you were a slave in the land of Egypt, and the LORD *your God brought you*
out from there with a mighty hand and an outstretched arm; therefore the
LORD *your God commanded you to keep the sabbath day.*

Deut. 5:12–15

Neither of these versions, scholars feel, can correspond to the "original" sabbath commandment. The original text must have been much shorter: "You
shall not do any work on the sabbath day," or the like.[16] The current versions
therefore reveal something about their final editors. The text in Exodus 20,
scholars say, shows the influence of a priestly editor, who has added his justification for the sabbath, namely, God's having rested on the seventh day—
the same justification that is found in the priestly version of the creation in
Genesis 1. The Deuteronomy version, by contrast, says nothing at all about
God resting. Instead, scholars point out, it is strictly a day of *human* rest and,
in keeping with the overall "humanitarian" quality of that book, the text says
twice that "your male and female slave" are to be given a day off as well. The
justification for this, the Deuteronomy text adds, is the whole story of the
Exodus, a favorite theme of that book: you know what it means to be a slave,
so let your slaves rest with you.

Dire Consequences

After giving Israel a great body of laws (Deuteronomy 12–26), Moses told the
people what they were to do when they arrived in the land of Canaan: in the
area of Shechem, a ceremony was to mark their reacceptance of God's
covenant, with half the tribes standing on Mount Gerizim and half on Mount
Ebal (Deuteronomy 27). He then warned the Israelites to observe scrupulously the conditions of this covenant: should they do so, God would bless
them and provide for all their needs; but should they fail to do so, they would
suffer a series of disasters. This section—similar to chapter 26 of Leviticus—
is graphic in the extreme:

> But if you will not obey the LORD your God by diligently observing all his
> commandments and decrees, which I am commanding you today, then all
> these curses shall come upon you and overtake you:
>   Cursed shall you be in the city, and cursed shall you be in the field.
> Cursed shall be your basket and your kneading bowl. Cursed shall be the
> fruit of your womb, the fruit of your ground, the increase of your cattle and
> the issue of your flock. Cursed shall you be when you come in, and cursed
> shall you be when you go out.
>   The LORD will send upon you disaster, panic, and frustration in every-
> thing you attempt to do, until you are destroyed and perish quickly, on

account of the evil of your deeds, because you have forsaken Me. The LORD will make the pestilence cling to you until it has consumed you off the land that you are entering to possess. The LORD will afflict you with consumption, fever, inflammation, with fiery heat and drought, and with blight and mildew; they shall pursue you until you perish. The sky over your head shall be bronze, and the earth under you iron. The LORD will change the rain of your land into powder, and only dust shall come down upon you from the sky until you are destroyed.

Deut. 28:15–24

This might seem enough, but this list of the dire consequences of disobedience goes on and on, for another forty-four verses. (This on top of the similar list of warnings in Lev. 26:14–43!) For ancient readers of the Bible, however, none of this could seem particularly surprising. God was certainly right to have warned Israel at length, and in the strictest terms—after all, no one, according to biblical jurisprudence, could be punished without having received prior warning,[17] and Israel was indeed punished severely for not keeping God's commandments. In the eighth century BCE, God allowed the northern kingdom of Israel to fall victim to the invading Assyrian army as punishment for their disobedience, and when, still not chastened, the southern kingdom of Judah continued its heedlessness, it too fell to a foreign army, the Babylonian, in the sixth century BCE. Indeed, at one point this passage of curses in Deuteronomy seemed to allude specifically to such a foreign invasion:

The LORD will bring a nation from far away, from the end of the earth, to swoop down on you like an eagle, a nation whose language you do not understand, a grim-faced nation showing no respect to the old or favor to the young. It shall consume the fruit of your livestock and the fruit of your ground until you are destroyed, leaving you neither grain, wine, and oil, nor the increase of your cattle and the issue of your flock, until it has made you perish. It shall besiege you in all your towns until your high and fortified walls, in which you trusted, come down throughout your land; it shall besiege you in all your towns throughout the land that the LORD your God has given you. In the desperate straits to which the enemy siege reduces you, you will eat the fruit of your womb, the flesh of your own sons and daughters whom the LORD your God has given you. Even the most refined and gentle of men among you will begrudge food to his own brother, to the wife whom he embraces, and to the last of his remaining children, giving to none of them any of the flesh of his children whom he is eating, because nothing else remains to him, in the desperate straits to which the enemy siege will reduce you in all your towns. She who is the most refined and gentle among you, so gentle and refined that she does not venture to set the sole of her foot on the ground, will begrudge food to the husband whom she embraces, to her own son, and to her own daughter, begrudging even the afterbirth that comes out from between her thighs, and the children that she bears, because she will eat them in secret for lack of anything else, in the desperate straits to which the enemy siege will reduce you in your towns . . .

The LORD will scatter you among all peoples, from one end of the earth to the other; and there you shall serve other gods, of wood and stone, which neither you nor your ancestors have known. Among those nations you shall find no ease, no resting place for the sole of your foot. There the LORD will give you a trembling heart, failing eyes, and a languishing spirit. Your life shall hang in doubt before you; night and day you shall be in dread, with no assurance of your life. In the morning you shall say, "If only it were evening!" and at evening you shall say, "If only it were morning!"— because of the dread that your heart shall feel and the sights that your eyes shall see. The LORD will bring you back in ships to Egypt, by a route that I promised you would never see again; and there you shall offer yourselves for sale to your enemies as male and female slaves, but there will be no buyer.

Deut. 28:49–57, 64–68

This picture of a foreign invader—not a neighboring kingdom, but one "from the end of the earth . . . a nation whose language you do not understand"—certainly matched the historical circumstances that eventually overtook Israel, and the description of unbearable suffering under foreign siege corresponded, alas, to the gruesome details of cannibalism and other horrors catalogued elsewhere in the Bible (Lam. 2:20–21; 4:8–10). Yet even if Israel disobeyed and suffered all these dire consequences, the people knew that that would not spell the end to their existence. The Torah had already given them such assurance in the earlier set of warnings (Lev. 26:44–45), and now Moses reiterated the promise more explicitly:

When all these things have happened to you, the blessings and the curses that I have set before you, if you call them to mind among all the nations where the LORD your God has driven you, and return to the LORD your God, and you and your children obey Him with all your heart and with all your soul, just as I am commanding you today, then the LORD your God will restore your fortunes and have compassion on you, gathering you again from all the peoples among whom the LORD your God has scattered you. Even if you are exiled to the ends of the world, from there the LORD your God will gather you, and from there He will bring you back. The LORD your God will bring you into the land that your ancestors possessed, and you will possess it; He will make you more prosperous and numerous than your ancestors.

Deut. 30:1–5

This prediction came true as well, at least for the Kingdom of Judah. Although its citizens were sent into exile into Babylon, eventually the exile ended and, just as He had rescued the Israelite slaves from Egypt, God led the exiles back from Babylon into their ancestral homeland. In this respect, the Torah's words were indeed carried out to the letter.

Deuteronomy and Ancient Near Eastern Treaties

As already observed, some modern scholars see in the very form of the book of Deuteronomy a structure reminiscent of that of ancient suzerainty treaties: historical prologue (1–4); insistence on exclusive loyalty to the suzerain (12–13, preceded here by the general exhortations of chapters 5–11); further covenant stipulations (14–26); provisions for deposit of the text (27:3–8; 31:9) and its public recitation (31:11–13); blessings and curses (27:15–28:68); and even a kind of covenant "witness" (31:19, 28; 32:1) in place of the usual gods who were mentioned as witnesses in human-to-human treaties. The match is not perfect: the elements appear in a slightly different order and form, and Deuteronomy as a whole is much longer than any extant suzerainty treaty. Still, the presence of the same basic six elements has convinced many scholars that the resemblance cannot be a matter of chance.

That supposition has been bolstered by a number of close verbal ties between, specifically, the words of warning in Leviticus and Deuteronomy and similar warnings appended to a number of ancient Near Eastern treaties. For example:

> The sky over your head shall be copper, and the earth under you iron.
>
> Deut. 28:23

> I will make your skies like iron and your earth like copper.
>
> Lev. 26:19

> May all the gods . . . turn your ground into iron, so that no one may plow it. Just as rain does not fall from a bronze sky, so may rain and dew not come upon your fields and meadows.
>
> Vassal Treaty of Esarhaddon 528–31[18]

Similarly:

> The LORD will afflict you with madness, blindness, and confusion of mind; you shall grope about at noon as blind people grope in darkness, but you shall be unable to find your way.
>
> Deut. 28:28–29

May Shamash . . . deprive you of the sight of your eyes, so that they will wander about in darkness.

Vassal Treaty of Esarhaddon 422–24

You shall become engaged to a woman, but another man shall lie with her. You shall build a house, but not live in it. You shall plant a vineyard, but not enjoy its fruit . . . Your sons and daughters shall be given to another people, while you look on.

Deut. 28:30–32

May [the deity of the star Venus], the brightest of stars, make your wives lie in your enemy's lap while your eyes look on. . . . May your sons not be masters of your house. May a foreign enemy divide all your goods.

Vassal Treaty of Esarhaddon 428–30

She who is the most refined and gentle among you . . . will begrudge food . . . *to her own daughter,* begrudging even the afterbirth that comes out from between her thighs, and the children that she bears, because she is eating them *in secret* for lack of anything else, in the desperate straits to which the enemy siege will reduce you in your towns . . .

Deut. 28:56–57

A mother will lock her door against her daughter. In your hunger, eat the flesh of your sons! In the famine and want, may one man eat the flesh of another.

Vassal Treaty of Esarhaddon 448–50

Nor do these exhaust the ancient Near Eastern parallels. A ninth-century inscription from Tell Fakhariyeh warned of the penalties for removing the king's name from its monument:

One hundred women will bake bread in a single oven and not fill it.[19]

Similarly:

When I break your staff of bread, ten women shall bake your bread in a single oven, and they shall dole out your bread by weight; and though you eat, you shall not be satisfied.

Lev. 26:26

All these resemblances suggest to scholars that the imprecations at the end of Leviticus and Deuteronomy were themselves rooted in the standard treaty curses of the ancient Near East—not only the general idea of such curses, but the specific things that the treaties invoked. What is more, the specific resemblances between Deuteronomy and the vassal treaty of the Assyrian king Esarhaddon, who ruled from around 681 to 669 BCE, would support the connection some scholars have made between other elements of Deuteronomy and the influence of Assyrian culture in the region (particularly strong during the years 740–640 BCE).

Renewing the Covenant

If so, then what Deuteronomy essentially describes is a great covenant between God and Israel—not the one at Mount Sinai, but another one concluded in the plains of Moab just before Moses' death.[20] Thus, having spelled out the covenant's conditions of exclusive loyalty and all the other stipulations, and having then concluded with the covenant's "teeth" (that is, the list of calamities that will befall Israel if they do not obey), Moses makes explicit what is going on:

> You are standing today, all of you, before the LORD your God—your chiefs and leaders, your elders and your officials, every notable in Israel; [moreover] your children, your women, and the aliens who are in your camp, from those who cut your wood to those who draw your water—*as you enter into the covenant of the LORD your God,* sworn by an oath, which the LORD your God *is making with you today;* in order that He may establish you today as His people, and that He may be your God, as He promised you and as He swore to your ancestors, to Abraham, to Isaac, and to Jacob.
>
> Deut. 29:10–13

Moses stresses that this covenant is to cover not only those who are physically present, but future generations as well:

> I am making this covenant, sworn by an oath, not only with you who stand here with us today before the LORD our God, but also with those who are not here with us today . . .
>
> Deut. 29:14–15

He then presents the acceptance of this agreement between God and Israel in the starkest terms:

> Surely, this commandment that I am commanding you today is not too hard for you, nor is it too far away. It is not in heaven, that you should say, "Who will go up to heaven for us, and get it and tell it to us, so that we can observe it?" Nor is it beyond the sea, so that someone should say, "Who

will cross to the other side of the sea for us, and get it and tell it to us, so that we can observe it?" No, the word is very near to you; it is in your mouth and in your heart for you to observe.

See, I have set before you today life and well-being, death and adversity. If you obey the commandments of the LORD your God[21] that I am commanding you today—loving the LORD your God, walking in His ways and keeping His commandments, decrees, and ordinances—then you will live and grow greater, and the LORD your God will bless you in the land that you are entering to possess. But if your heart turns away and you do not obey, but are led astray to bow down to other gods and serve them, then I declare to you today that you shall surely perish; you shall not live long in the land that you are crossing the Jordan to enter and possess.

I call heaven and earth to witness against you today that I have set before you life and death, a blessing and a curse. Choose life—so that you and your descendants may live, loving the LORD your God, obeying Him, and holding fast to Him; for that means life to you and length of days, so that you may live in the land that the LORD swore to give to your ancestors, to Abraham, to Isaac, and to Jacob.

Deut. 30:11–20

The Life of Torah

These words resounded in the ears of later generations of Jews and Christians. If God demanded all-out devotion, they were prepared to give it. Pledging themselves to God, they felt, was not merely a matter of accepting God's existence and dominion, but of expressing that acceptance in concrete terms, in their own lives. In a sense, all aspects of Jewish and Christian devotion—attendance at religious services, but also individual prayers; the study of Scripture, whether in a public place or at home; and dozens of other little acts intended as a carrying out of God's will—find at least part of their origin and inspiration in these words of Deuteronomy. The starkness of the choice described here—between good and ill, a blessing and a curse—bespeaks the pure, unambiguous world of the soul.[22] Implicit in such a choice, therefore, is always the possibility of asceticism; after all, how much devotion can ever be enough? So it was that, from biblical times onward, certain individuals chose to give their lives over to God. The vow of the biblical nazirite (Numbers 6) was succeeded by other forms of self-denial and self-affliction, as represented by the (probably) monastic Jewish community at Qumran and the ascetic Thereputae described by Philo of Alexandria (*De Vita Contemplativa*), as well as by later, indisputably monastic communities of Christian men and women—not to speak of the numerous celibates, cave dwellers, pillar sitters, and other ascetics, and beyond these the actual martyrs

(Jews and Christians at first, and then Jews in large numbers) who have preferred death to breaking with their devotion to God.

In less drastic form, devotion to God has found expression in the lives of
countless ordinary individuals who, turning from the material pleasures of
this world, set for themselves a regimen of divine service. For Jews of postbiblical times, the words of the Mishnah have carried forward Deuteronomy's
central theme:

> This is the path of Torah: Bread and salt shall you eat, and drink water by
> measure; you shall sleep upon the ground, and live a life of privation, and
> in the Torah shall be your work. And if you do thus, "You shall be happy,
> and it will be well with you" (Ps. 128:2)—"happy" refers to this world, and
> "well" to the world to come.
>
> The Torah is supreme, for it gives life to those who perform it[s com-
> mandments] in this world and in the world to come, as it is said, "It is a tree
> of life to those who hold on to it, and all who maintain it are blessed"
> (Prov. 3:18).
>
> m. *Abot* 6:4, 7

Telling, too, is the well-known Talmudic anecdote concerning Rabbi Akiba
(second century CE):

> Once, the wicked regime [Rome] decreed that Jews be forbidden to study
> the Torah. Papos son of Judah subsequently found Rabbi Akiba nonetheless
> convening groups in public for the study of Torah. "Akiba," he said, "are
> you not afraid of the regime?" He said, "Let me answer you with a compar-
> ison. It is like a fox that was walking along the riverbank when he saw some
> fish moving in groups from place to place. He said to them: 'What are you
> fleeing from?' They said to him: 'From the nets that the human beings cast
> over us.' He said to them: 'Wouldn't you like to climb up onto the dry land
> so that you and I might live together as your ancestors and mine once did?'
> They said: 'Are you indeed the one who is alleged to be the cleverest of ani-
> mals? You are not clever but foolish! For if there is danger in the place where
> we do live [that is, our natural environment], is it not all the more so in the
> place where we must die?' So it is with us now: for we sit and study Torah,
> about which it is said, 'For it is your life and your length of days' (Deut.
> 30:20); were we to abandon it, we would be in far greater danger."
>
> b. *Berakhot* 61b

Loving God

The meaning of "loving" God in the various passages cited from Deuteronomy may seem self-evident; but is it really? In 1963, an American Jesuit teaching in Rome published an article that, in its own way, gave the world of biblical scholarship another jolt.[23] William L. Moran was part of that vanguard of Roman Catholic scholars who emerged after the encyclical *Divino Afflante Spiritu* (1943), the first papal document that encouraged Catholics to become thoroughly trained in the ways of modern biblical research. Moran studied with W. F. Albright at Johns Hopkins and ultimately specialized in ancient Akkadian texts and their relationship to the world of the Bible.[24]

While teaching at the Pontifical Biblical Institute at Rome, Moran was struck by something in the same Vassal Treaty of Esarhaddon mentioned above. Esarhaddon had apparently been eager to insure that his vassals would continue to be loyal to his successor, Assurbanipal. At one point in his treaty, therefore, he commanded his vassals: "You shall love Assurbanipal as yourselves." This struck Moran as an odd choice of language: *love?* Surely the vassals were not being told to become enamored of the future king's winning personality! It seemed to Moran as if *love* here must have less to do with emotion than with loyalty, political loyalty. Although the Akkadian word for love came from a different Semitic root, Moran set out to investigate the various ways in which the Hebrew word for love, *'ahab,* was used in the Bible.

What he found was that *'ahab* was indeed sometimes used for emotion: Jacob *loves* Rachel and so goes to work for her father for seven years (Gen. 29:18). At other times, however, people in the Bible seem to love more in the Esarhaddon way. This seemed especially true of the book of Deuteronomy, where loving God is often directly juxtaposed to serving God and keeping his commandments:

So now, O Israel, what does the LORD your God require of you? Only to fear the LORD your God, to walk in all His ways, to *love* Him, to serve the LORD your God with all your heart and with all your soul, and to keep the commandments of the LORD your God and His decrees that I am commanding you today, for your own well-being.

Deut. 10:12

You shall *love* the LORD your God, therefore, and keep His charge, His decrees, His ordinances, and His commandments always.

Deut. 11:1

If you will only heed His every commandment that I am commanding you today—*loving* the LORD your God, and serving Him with all your heart and with all your soul . . .

Deut. 11:13

If you will diligently observe this entire commandment that I am commanding you, *loving* the LORD your God, walking in all His ways, and holding fast to Him . . .

Deut. 11:22

Choose life so that you and your descendants may live, *loving* the LORD your God, obeying Him, and holding fast to Him . . .

Deut. 30:19–20

Remarkably, Moran found, although Deuteronomy sometimes compared the relationship of God to Israel to that of a father to his son (Deut. 8:5; 14:1), the word for love was *not* invoked there, where one would expect some expression of emotional attachment. Instead, Israel was commanded to love God only in the ways seen above, where love is virtually a synonym of "fear," "obey," "serve," and the like. And come to think of it, how can you *command* someone to love someone else? If the word means anything like "love" in our sense, that would seem to be impossible.

Esarhaddon was not the only ancient Near Eastern potentate to demand "love" from his servants. A Canaanite vassal of Pharaoh writes in one of the El-Amarna letters: "My lord, just as I love the king my lord, so [does] the king of Nuhašše [love him, and] the king of Ni'i . . .—all these kings are *servants* of my lord." Here, apparently, to love is to be a servant. Another ancient king described a civil war in these terms: "Behold the city! Half of it loves the sons of 'Abd-Aširta, half of it [loves] my lord."

Thus, the peoples of the ancient Near East would probably have been puzzled by the observation attributed to Talleyrand, "Nations do not have friends; they have interests." National interests in the ancient Near East were often presented precisely in terms of friendship (that is, love). Thus, Hiram of Tyre is called David's "friend" (1 Kings 5:1—from the same root, *'ahab*), but they were really only political allies. In 2 Sam. 19:6–7, Joab accuses David of "loving those who hate you and hating those who love you," that is, crying over the death of Absalom, his political opponent; David's "friends" are referred to in the next verse as "your servants." "All Israel and Judah loved David," it says in 1 Sam. 18:16, but this was not a matter of love so much as of political support, and the rest of the sentence goes on to make clear why: "for it was he who went out and came in" ("going out and coming in" is a biblical idiom meaning "to lead," often, as here, to lead the army).

In short, Moran's article suggested that when the Shema said, "You shall love the LORD your God with all your heart," it had in mind nothing like the all-out, deep-in-the-heart devotion understood by later interpreters, loving God with one's inclination to evil as well as to good, or loving God so profoundly as to feel gratitude to Him no matter which "measuring cup" He uses to measure out one's portion. And it certainly had nothing to do with the *unio mystica* of medieval adepts, nor yet with Spinoza's *amor Dei intellectualis*. All the verse meant was to do God's bidding. The point is made clear time and again in Deuteronomy: "And so, if you carefully heed My commandments, which I am commanding you today—to love the LORD your God and to serve Him with all your heart and with all your soul . . ." (Deut. 11:13). Here too, loving and serving are said in the same breath because they are essentially the same thing.

This concept of love as service, Moran felt, may have been a fundamental theme in Deuteronomy, but, he asserted, it was older than that. Noting its presence in both versions of the Ten Commandments—

> . . . for I the LORD your God am a jealous God, punishing children for the iniquity of parents, to the third and the fourth generation of those who reject Me, but showing kindness to the thousandth generation of *those who love Me and keep My commandments.*
>
> Exod. 20:6; Deut. 5:10

—Moran concluded that the idea of *loving* God went back to the very beginning of the idea of a covenant, a treatylike agreement, between God and Israel. "The Deuteronomic love of service is older [than the writings of the prophet Hosea]," he wrote, "probably as old, or almost as old, as the covenant itself."[25]

The Song of Moses

Having concluded his solemn charge to the people of Israel, Moses made his last preparations to bid them farewell. God had repeatedly told him that he could not enter Canaan himself but would have to die on the far side of the Jordan (Num. 27:12–14; Deut. 1:37; 3:27; 31:2, 32:49–50; 34:4). He knew he would have to submit to God's decree.[26] Before taking his final leave, however, Moses recited for the people a prophetic song that might serve as a warning to future generations (the "Song of Moses," Deuteronomy 32), and then he blessed each of the tribes in turn (Deuteronomy 33).

On the basis of their archaic language and other features, both these chapters have been judged by modern scholars to be older than the rest of Deuteronomy. The precise referents of some parts of the Song of Moses are in dispute among different scholars, but they note in particular its way of accounting for Israel's privileged place in the world:

> Remember the days of old, consider the years long past;
> Ask your father, and he will inform you; your elders, and they will tell
>   you.
> When the Most High established nations and split up the sons of men,
> He fixed the boundaries of peoples according to the number of gods.[27]
> But the LORD's own portion is His people, Jacob His allotted share.
> Deut. 32:7–9

What is striking to scholars about this passage is, first of all, the divine names. The "Most High" (Hebrew, 'Elyon) was actually how the ancient Canaanites referred to the highest of the gods in their pantheon. Scholars note that this name also appears in the Bible a few times in reference to the God of Israel, though it is not clear to them at what point the names 'Elyon and YHWH might have become synonymous in Israel. (In Gen. 14:18–21, the Canaanite Melchizedek seems to mention 'El 'Elyon as his own deity, but Abraham then apparently identifies this god—perhaps syncretistically—with the God of Israel.) In the passage just cited (Deut. 32:7–9), it seems clear that Israel's God is meant, but, scholars say, by using the name 'Elyon this passage may be invoking an ancient (perhaps pre-Israelite) creation motif. In addition to this, the original text of this passage also referred to the "sons of El" or "the sons of God" (verse 8; the traditional Hebrew text apparently amended this to "sons of Israel" to avoid the polytheistic implications). Again, it is difficult to know how this appellation was intended to be understood, but in the context of the song, scholars say, it is part of an explanation of how the world ended up the way it did. The song says that when the "Most High" was dividing up the human population into different nations and granting each its national territory, He did so on the basis of the total number of the "sons of God" (or "sons of El"). That is, things were arranged so that each of these lesser deities would have his own nation to look after. But God kept Israel for Himself: "the LORD's own portion is His people, Jacob His allotted share." It is certainly significant that there is no hint here of monotheism, the belief that only one God exists—indeed, the opposite seems to be just the point. Nor is any reason offered for God's choice of Israel—it was apparently simply Israel's good fortune that things turned out that way. This contrasts somewhat with the rest of Deuteronomy, which stresses God's love of Israel's ancestors Abraham, Isaac, and Jacob as the reason for Israel's privileged position. (The Song of Moses makes no mention of these ancestors—in fact, it seems to suggest that Israel first encountered God in the wilderness after the exodus [verse 10], a theme echoed in Hos. 2:14–15 and Jer. 2:2.)

Scholars have pointed to what they consider a later passage in Deuteronomy that says something rather similar. There Moses warns the Israelites:

> And when you look up to the heavens and see the sun, the moon, and the stars, all the host of heaven, do not be led astray and bow down to them and serve them, things that the LORD your God has allotted to all the peoples everywhere under heaven.

Deut. 4:19

Here too, God has assigned the sun, the moon, and the stars—astral deities worshiped by the Assyrians and others—to all other peoples except Israel. Apparently, the idea that God Himself was responsible for the polytheism in other nations became an accepted explanation for polytheism's continued existence.

Moses Blesses the People

When, next, Moses turns to bless the different tribes of Israel, he seems to be following the same pattern as Jacob, who had blessed each of his twelve sons just before his death (Genesis 49). Modern scholars, however, have noticed significant differences between these two sets of blessings and have relied on them to support some ideas (somewhat speculative, they concede) about Israel at a very early period in its history.

Thus, about the tribe of Reuben, Moses says: "Let Reuben live and not die" (Deut. 33:6). Scholars see in this a reflection of Reuben's endangered existence as an independent entity. Even at the time of Genesis 49, they say, the tribe of Reuben was apparently not flourishing; that is why, they believe, Jacob is presented as rebuking his son Reuben for his alleged sin with his father's concubine (Gen. 49:3–4). "You'll have privilege no more," Jacob tells him, thereby "predicting" this tribe's precipitous fall from first place. Now, in Deut. 33:6, that fall seems to be bordering on extinction: Reuben (that is, the tribe) is on the brink of "death." Not long after these lines were written, some scholars hold, the tribe of Reuben did, in fact, disappear forever. Originally located on the far side of the Jordan, it may have begun to be absorbed by its neighbors as early as the eleventh century BCE, perhaps amalgamating with the neighboring tribe of Gad or becoming part of nearby Moab.[28] In any case, according to one scholar, "in the time of David . . . Reuben as a tribal entity with a fixed territory has disappeared."[29]

Simeon may have suffered a similar fate, at least to judge by this same set of blessings in Deuteronomy: Moses does not even mention Simeon. The Simeonites had been located south of Judah, so it may be, scholars believe, that at some early point the tribe simply came to be absorbed by the more powerful Judah. As for the fourth tribe, Levi, it too seems to have undergone a change—but not extinction:

> And of Levi he [Moses] said [to God]:
> Give to Levi Your Thummim,* and Your Urim to Your loyal one,
> whom You tested at Massah, with whom You contended at the waters of
>   Meribah . . .[30]
> May they teach Jacob Your ordinances, and Israel Your law;
> Let them place incense before You, and whole burnt offerings on Your
>   altar.
> Bless, O LORD, his substance, and accept the work of his hands;
> crush the loins of his adversaries, of those that hate him, so that they do
>   not rise again.
>
>   Deut. 33:8, 10–11

In Jacob's joint blessing of Simeon and Levi (Gen. 49:5–7), the two tribes had seemed destined to share the same fate: "I will divide them in Jacob and scatter them in Israel." And indeed, the tribe of Levi does seem to have lost any concentrated tribal territory it once had, being allocated instead a number of separate cities in different parts of the country (according to Josh. 21:1–40, forty-eight in all).[31] The Levites thus lost out on a large tribal homeland. But in Moses' blessing they have clearly gotten a consolation prize: the Levites have become the priestly tribe par excellence. Moses declares that the Levites are to receive the Urim and Thummim and to be assigned the (priestly) job of instructing the nation in God's law as well as offering incense and sacrifices in the temple. While the association of the Levites with the priesthood is certainly quite ancient, scholars note that, at a very early time, there may not have been a fixed, hereditary priesthood associated with one tribe. After all, Cain and Abel and Noah and Abraham are all represented as offering sacrifices to God, and none of them is described as a Levite or trained in the priestly arts. Indeed, a certain wealthy man in the book of Judges, having hired a Levite for his household, asserts: "Now I know that the LORD will be good to me, since the Levite has become my priest" (Judg. 17:13). Apparently a non-Levite would not have been as sure a bet, but the text may be implying that such a person was not beyond consideration for the job.[32]

---

* The Urim and Thummim were a priestly instrument of divination (Exod. 28:30; Lev. 8:8; Num. 27:21; 1 Sam. 14:41–42, and so forth).

The Death of Moses

When at last Moses passes into the next world, the Torah is unstinting in its eulogy. Its words form a fit conclusion to the Five Books of Moses:

> Moses was one hundred twenty years old when he died. His eyes had not dimmed nor had his vigor diminished. The Israelites wept for Moses in the plains of Moab thirty days; then the period of mourning for Moses was ended . . . Never since has there arisen a prophet in Israel like Moses, whom the LORD knew face to face, with all the signs and wonders that the LORD sent him to perform in the land of Egypt, against Pharaoh and all his servants and his entire land, and all the great might and fearsome power that Moses performed before all of Israel.
>
> Deut. 34:7–12

For readers ever after, Moses has always stood as the model of the Hebrew Bible's greatest prophet. In late antiquity and the Middle Ages, commentators and philosophers sought to elaborate on the above passage, asserting that no other prophet had ever attained to Moses' status. Indeed, even in more recent times, Moses has exercised a special hold on the very image of prophecy. In the famous prologue of *Paradise Lost,* the English poet John Milton called upon Moses' source of divine inspiration to guide him in his own writing:

> Sing, Heav'nly Muse, that on the secret top
> Of Oreb* ³³ or of Sinai, didst inspire
> That Shepherd, who first taught the chosen Seed,
> In the Beginning how the Heav'ns and Earth
> Rose out of Chaos . . .

In still later times, Moses became the model of the Romantic poet, leaving the noisy throng of humanity behind as he ascended to Sinai/Parnassus, where true inspiration is to be found:

---

* **Oreb** is Mount Horeb; its top is "secret" because its precise location is unknown. **Sinai,** as we have seen, is apparently another name for God's mountain. **That Shepherd** is Moses, who was caring for Jethro's flock when he met God at the burning bush; he taught **in the Beginning** (the first words of the Pentateuch, as well as the rabbinic name for the book of Genesis) about the creation of **the Heav'ns and Earth.**

Prophète centenaire environné d'honneur,
Moïse était parti pour trouver le Seigneur.*

Alfred de Vigny, *Moïse*

An Obvious Gap

Here ends the Pentateuch. The preceding pages are not given to simple summary, but, as far as the composition of the Bible's first five books is concerned, one obvious conclusion emerges: a great gap separates the traditional view of the Pentateuch in Judaism and Christianity from the various reconstructions of modern scholars.

The traditional view, of course, sees the entire Pentateuch as the word of God, passed on to Israel through a single prophet, Moses. Moses began his writing by describing how the world was created in six days (obviously, no human could know such a thing unless it had been communicated to him by God) and went on to chronicle the first generations of humanity, from Adam and Eve to the great flood and on to Abraham and Sarah, Isaac and Rebekah, and Jacob and his four wives—the immediate ancestors of the people of Israel. The story of Joseph explained how Israel's ancestors then came to dwell for a time in Egypt, where they were eventually enslaved by a wicked pharaoh. The Israelites managed to weather their extended captivity, finally escaping Egypt under the leadership of Moses. After their miraculous crossing of the Red Sea, they made their way to Sinai, where God adopted them as His special people, a "kingdom of priests and a holy nation" bound to Him by the conditions of His great covenant. The detailed laws that followed—not only the ones presented in Exodus 21–23, but the many other laws contained in the next three books—were offered to Israel as a divine guide to daily life. This was the greatest of gifts, and these laws were, as we have seen, lovingly interpreted in all their details.

The forty years of Israel's wanderings in the wilderness were not easy; military confrontations, internal strife, and the day-to-day difficulties of life on the move all took their toll. But in the end, Israel emerged strong and ready to proceed with their final entrance into the land that God had promised them. The divine presence, accompanying them in the tabernacle that they had constructed, was their greatest source of strength. Although Moses would no longer be with them, his former servant Joshua had inherited his mantle. It was he who would take the lead as the Israelites crossed the Jordan into Canaan.

Modern scholars find most of the foregoing quite incompatible with the

---

* "Hundred-year-old prophet, surrounded with honor, Moses had gone off to find the Lord."

truth as they know it. Moses cannot, they assert, have been the author of the Pentateuch—indeed, no one person could be, since the text contains so many internal inconsistencies and contradictions. The events recounted in the Pentateuch are likewise seen as largely ahistorical. The stories of Adam and Eve, Cain and Abel, Abraham and Isaac and Jacob are generally viewed as etiological narratives composed in an age far distant from the events they describe; their real purpose was not to record past history, but to explain various aspects of then-current reality through reference to one or another invented ancestor. Other parts of the Pentateuch, while they may have some historical basis, are viewed as greatly exaggerated. If there was an Exodus, scholars say, it can have involved only a tiny part of the future Israel, perhaps a few hundred souls at most. The number and nature of the plagues that may have struck Egypt, and what really happened at the Red Sea will, scholars say, probably never be known—but again, the Pentateuch's version seems unlikely and is, in any case, contradicted by the evidence of archaeology, Egyptology, and even the biblical text itself. For similar reasons, the Israelites' forty years in the wilderness, their construction of the elaborate tabernacle that accompanied them, and their ultimate entry into, and conquest of, Canaan raise numerous difficulties in the minds of scholars. Very little of this, they say, will square with evidence assembled from elsewhere.

As for modern scholars' views on how the Pentateuch came into existence, there is currently little consensus. For many scholars, the Pentateuch began with orally transmitted traditions going back to before the time of David—etiological tales connected with one or another sacred site or eponymous founder, schematic narratives reflecting early relations with neighboring countries or tribes, and other faint recollections of events from the distant past. With the passage of time, these individual traditions may have been grouped around the figures of different ancestors—Abram/Abraham, Jacob/Israel, and so forth—or around specific themes such as the Exodus from Egypt.[34] But how those ancient traditions may have led to the collections of texts currently identified as J and E, and when and under what circumstances priestly texts and priestly editors came to intervene in the creation of the Pentateuch's final form, is the subject of fierce debate. Likewise, while the legal code that stands at the heart of Deuteronomy is generally dated to the time before Josiah and its original composition located in the north, the circumstances of the creation of the current book of Deuteronomy as well as the role of a Deuteronomy-influenced writer or editor in the Pentateuch's final shape are also in dispute.

What modern scholars certainly do agree on is that the Pentateuch in its current form represents the writings of a number of disparate people and schools, and that it came together through a series of different recensions. Its diverse origins are attested even in its earliest stages. Thus, while it used to be maintained that J and E were the creation of individual historians, many scholars today find this unlikely. There are too many internal contradictions within the J complex of texts to support the idea that they were the work of one person; moreover, it seems unlikely that the E texts that we possess could in themselves have been an integrated, sequential history. How, or even if, these two collections of texts came later to be combined into a single history (the hypothetical text scholars call JE) also remains unclear, though one hypothesis is that, with the fall of the northern kingdom of Israel, refugees fleeing south brought with them some of the E texts, and these were subsequently woven into a new version of national history.

The intervention of different authors and editorial hands did not end there. If scholars are correct in identifying P and H as pre-exilic sources, then the creation and integration of at least some priestly material into the non-priestly history may go back to pre-exilic times. As for Deuteronomy, scholars believe that the law code that stands at its heart was once an independent document that was later combined with the surrounding historical framework; even this framework, however, was not the creation of a single author. The hand of a Deuteronomic editor has been detected here and there in Genesis–Numbers as well. Many current scholars identify a member of the H school as the Pentateuch's very last editor; his activity would have taken place shortly after Israel's return from the Babylonian exile, according to some,[35] though others would prefer to speak of a more diffuse and prolonged process, extending well into the Persian period.

The oldest traditions of interpretation in connection with the Pentateuch go back long before this final editing. Scholars since the nineteenth century have observed how Deuteronomy, for example, seems to have recast older laws in Exodus on the basis of this or that interpretation of their precise wording; similarly, later narrative traditions sometimes appear to be interpreting older versions of the same events, just as later prophecies, as we shall see, sometimes rework earlier ones. But the interpretation of Scripture appears to have become a major, recognizable activity—an academic specialty, as it were—only in the postexilic period. Those given charge of Scripture and its interpretation were by and large part of the emerging cadre of teachers and sages influenced by the great wisdom traditions of the ancient Near East. These sages sought to put their own "spin" on the Pentateuch in particular.[36] The Pentateuch was now viewed, as Ben Sira and other sages attest (Sir. 24:23; Bar. 3:36–41), as nothing less than divine wisdom in written form, one great book of legal and ethical instruction. As a result, the Pentateuch as a whole came to be radically transformed: its etiological narratives now became moral exempla, and its ancient laws became an up-to-date guide for daily life today. Rather than a record of the past, the Pentateuch became, like all wisdom writings, a set of instructions for the present. Indeed, other characteristics of wisdom writing now also clung to the Pentateuch.[37]

The transformations wrought by ancient biblical interpretation belong in any account of the Pentateuch's origins. Much more, in fact, than the anonymous redactors of the hypothetical documents scholars call JE, JEP, or JEPD, the anonymous interpreters of the third and second and first centuries BCE changed utterly the whole character of the Pentateuch, as we have observed all along. No less formidable, however, has been the activity of modern biblical scholars over the last two centuries. They have succeeded, at least for those attentive to their arguments, in utterly undoing the work of those ancient interpreters and returning the Pentateuch to the disparate fragments and *disiecta membra* from which, by their account, it started. Has this been a good thing? Certainly not, at least not from the standpoint of those who wish to see in the Pentateuch a divinely given guidebook, a sacred and timeless text that is free of contradiction and error and speaks to people today. But good or not, modern biblical scholarship is—no less than the activity of previous interpreters and editors and authors—a fact of the Bible's history. The question that remains is: in the light of all this, how is one to read the Pentateuch, and the rest of the Bible, today? Some elements of an answer to this question have already been introduced; I hope to present others in the chapters that follow.

22

Joshua and the Conquest
of Canaan

JOSHUA 1–24

Joshua Spares Rahab by Gustave Doré.

A SECOND MOSES. RAHAB'S HELP. THE DEUTERONOMISTIC HISTORY.
WHERE DID THE ISRAELITES REALLY COME FROM? EL AMARNA.

*Although the Bible relates that Joshua led the people into the Promised
Land and triumphed over the native Canaanites, archaeologists and biblical
scholars read the story somewhat differently.*

The book of Joshua opens with God's assurance that, although Moses has
died, He will help his successor, Joshua, to conquer the whole land promised
to Israel's ancestors:

> After the death of Moses, the servant of the LORD, the LORD spoke to
> Joshua son of Nun, Moses' assistant, saying, "My servant Moses is dead.
> Now proceed to cross the Jordan, you and all this people, into the land that
> I am giving to them, to the Israelites. Every place that the sole of your foot
> will tread upon I am giving to you, as I promised to Moses. From the
> wilderness and the Lebanon as far as the great river, the river Euphrates, all
> the land of the Hittites, to the Great Sea in the west shall be your territory.
> No one shall be able to stand against you all the days of your life. As I was
> with Moses, so I will be with you; I will not fail you or forsake you."
>
> Josh. 1:1–5

This is indeed how things turned out. Joshua was very much the same kind of
leader as Moses—in fact, strikingly so. Like Moses, Joshua sent out spies to
scout the land (chapter 2), and like Moses, he led the people on a miraculous
crossing, causing the waters of the Jordan River to stand still, "while all of
Israel crossed over on dry land" (Josh. 3:17). Later, Joshua encountered the
"captain of the LORD's army" (above, chapter 7), who said to Joshua exactly
what God had said to Moses at the burning bush: "Take your shoes from off
your feet, for the place that you are standing on is holy ground" (Exod. 3:5;
Josh. 5:15).

Like Moses, Joshua was also capable of working miracles. In the course of
a battle against the Amorites, he prayed to God for more daylight—apparently so that he and his forces might triumph:

> On the day when the LORD gave the Amorites over to the Israelites, Joshua
> spoke to the LORD; and he said in the presence of Israel: "O sun, stand still
> at Gibeon, and you, O moon, in the Ayalon valley." Then the sun stood still
> and the moon was stopped, until the nation could overcome its enemies. (Is
> this not written in the Book of Jashar? The sun stopped halfway in the sky,

and did not hurry to set for about a whole day. There has been no day like it before or since, when the LORD heeded a human voice; for the LORD fought for Israel.)

                                                                    Josh. 10:12–14

This briefly noted but impressive feat came to be celebrated in songs and pictures;[1] it offered vivid proof of God's support for this new leader of Israel.

Why had God chosen Joshua to succeed Moses? It was not only that, as Moses' assistant, he had come to know firsthand what was involved in leading the people. In addition, Joshua had already proven his courage. He and Caleb had been the only two spies not to lose heart at the sight of the Canaanite fortifications; indeed, they had tried to persuade their reluctant countrymen to go ahead with God's plan. He was thus the perfect candidate to stand at the head of the Israelite forces now, forty years later, as they at last were finally ready to enter the land of Canaan. The events that followed—marked not only by Joshua's military success but by miraculous events such as the sun's stopping for him in midsky—demonstrated that Joshua was in all respects a second Moses. Clearly, despite His beloved prophet's death, God was still with the people of Israel.

For ancient interpreters, Joshua's position as the heir to Moses' leadership role was thus his outstanding characteristic. For early Christians this circumstance took on special significance, since as we have seen, the name Joshua, for anyone who read the Bible in Greek, was indistinguishable from the name Jesus. The fact that this "Old Testament Jesus" took over for Moses was understood to symbolize Christianity's taking over for the religion of Moses, its "new covenant" mediated by Jesus replacing the old covenant that had been mediated through Moses at Mount Sinai. This was, for ancient Christians, one of those extremely significant ties between Old and New: it not only said something about Jesus, it also showed something profound about the Bible itself, a book brimming with hidden meanings and half-concealed correspondences. Indeed, thanks in part to this equation of Joshua and Jesus, the new church came to think of itself as *verus Israel,* the "true Israel" (as opposed to the Jews, who were the people of Israel only in the genetic, "fleshly" sense—see 1 Cor. 10:18; Rom. 2:28–29; Phil. 3:3).

Rahab the Harlot

This is not to say, of course, that under Joshua's leadership things always turned out as they had under Moses. When Joshua dispatched spies to scout out the land, the incident ended in a way quite different from that of the cowardly spies sent by Moses. To begin with, Joshua sent out only two spies (their names are not given in the Bible), and for some reason, as soon as they crossed the Jordan they headed straight for the house of a prostitute. Perhaps they were looking for an unobtrusive place to spend the night:

> So they went off, and came to the house of a certain prostitute, whose name was Rahab, and spent the night there. The king of Jericho was told, "Some men have come here this very night—some of the Israelites—to scout out the land." So the king of Jericho sent a message to Rahab, "Throw out those men who came to you, the ones who came to your house. They are here to scout out the whole land!" But instead, the woman took the two men and hid them. Then she said, "True, some men did come to me, but I did not know where they were from. And when it was time for the gate to close at dark, the men went out—I have no idea where they went. If you hurry after them, however, you may catch up with them." Meanwhile, she had brought them up to the roof and hidden them in some stalks of flax that she had laid out on the roof. So the men chased after them along the Jordan as far as the fords . . .
>
> Before they went to sleep, she came up to them on the roof and said to the men: "I know that the LORD is giving you this land, and all of us are afraid of you . . . For we have heard how the LORD [has helped you] . . . The LORD your God is indeed God in heaven above and on earth below. Now then, since I have dealt kindly with you, swear to me by the LORD that you will deal kindly with my family in return. Pledge to me in good faith that you will spare my father and mother, my brothers and sisters, and everyone else who belongs to them, and save us from death." The men said to her, "Our lives for yours! If you do not mention this business of ours, then we will treat you kindly and faithfully when the LORD gives us the land."
>
> Then she let them down by a rope through the window, since her house was on the outer side of the city wall and she lived right along the wall . . . The men said to her, "We will be released from this oath that you have made us swear to you [unless], when we invade this country, you tie this piece of crimson cord to the same window through which you let us down . . ." She said, "Let it be just as you say." She sent them away and they departed. Then she tied the piece of crimson cord to the window.
>
> Josh. 2:2–22

A puzzling incident, to be sure; at first it must have seemed somewhat mystifying that the Bible should have presented a prostitute in a heroic light at all. Still, Scripture often spoke cryptically, and this story seemed full of hints—especially to early Christians who thought of Joshua as a foreshadowing of Jesus. That this Jesus should have established contact, through his emissaries, with the very model of a sinner seemed to say much about the church itself:

Her name is Rahab. Now Rahab means "breadth" [in Hebrew]. What breadth is this if not the Church of Christ, composed of sinners and harlots? It is this breadth that accepts the spies of Jesus.

Origen, Third Homily

And then there was the crimson cord: surely the fact that it was crimson could not be devoid of typological significance:

They went on to give her a sign, telling her to hang a crimson thread from her house, foreshadowing thereby the redemption which all who believe and trust in God will find through the Lord's blood. Be aware, dear friends, how in this woman there was not only faith, but prophecy as well![2]

First Epistle of Clement 12:7–8

Indeed, Rahab even figured in the genealogy of Jesus:

And Salmon the father of Boaz *by Rahab,* and Boaz the father of Obed by Ruth, and Obed the father of Jesse, and Jesse the father of King David.

Matt. 1:5–6

Rabbinic interpreters also held Rahab in high esteem:

It is said that Rahab the harlot was ten years old when the Israelites went forth from Egypt, and during all the forty years that Israel was in the desert she was a harlot. At the age of fifty, *she became a convert* and prayed, "Master of the Universe, just as I have sinned with three things,[3] bring about my forgiveness with three things, a rope, a window, and a wall," as it is said: "Then she let them down by a rope through the window, since her house was on the outer side of the city wall and she lived right along the wall."

Mekhilta deR. Ishmael, Yitro 1

Eight priests and eight prophets came forth from Rahab the harlot, and they are these: Jeremiah, Hilkiah, Sariah, Mahsiah, Baruch, Neriah, Hanamel, and Shallum. Rabbi Judah added: Likewise Huldah the prophetess was among Rahab's descendants . . . Because she brought herself near [to the worship of God], so too did God bring her near.

Sifrei Numbers 78

The Deuteronomistic History

As modern scholars studied the book of Joshua, they noticed that it sometimes sounded surprisingly like the previous book, Deuteronomy. This resemblance is apparent even in the few passages seen above. For example, when God tells Joshua—

> Every place that the sole of your foot will tread upon I am giving to you, as I promised to Moses. From the wilderness and the Lebanon as far as the great river, the river Euphrates, all the land of the Hittites, to the Great Sea in the west shall be your territory.
>
> Josh. 1:3

—this sounds remarkably like a verse in Deuteronomy:

> Every place on which you set foot shall be yours; your territory shall extend from the wilderness to the Lebanon and from the River, the river Euphrates, to the Western Sea.
>
> Deut. 11:24

True, in the Joshua passage God does add the words "as I promised to Moses," so He might simply be repeating what had been said earlier (although, to be technical about it, Deut. 11:24 is *not* presented as God's promise, but Moses'). Still, scholars noted, this was not just reiteration but near-exact quotation—almost as if whoever was writing down the words in Joshua had a copy of Deuteronomy in front of him.

They found other reminiscences of Deuteronomy in Joshua. For example, Rahab tells the Israelite spies: "The LORD your God is indeed God, in heaven above and on earth below." Scholars had noted that such unabashed assertions of monotheism are rare in the Pentateuch; in fact, they are found only in a few places in one book: Deuteronomy. Indeed, Rahab's formulation sounded remarkably like a word-for-word quotation from Deuteronomy: "Realize [this] today and turn it over in your mind: the LORD is indeed God, in heaven above and on the earth below; there is no other" (Deut. 4:39). (And come to think of it, why should Rahab be holding forth about theology anyway? All she needed to tell the spies was that she knew Israel was going to conquer the land.)

The book of Joshua was not the only one found to contain such little flashbacks to Deuteronomy. For example, the book of 1 Samuel included a long speech (1 Samuel 12) that was full of phrases known elsewhere only or principally from Deuteronomy:

> [Samuel says:] If you will *fear the LORD and serve Him* and *heed his voice* and *not rebel* against *the commandment of the LORD*, and if both you and the king who reigns over you will follow the LORD your God, it will be well; but if you will not *heed the voice of the LORD*, but *rebel* against *the commandment of the LORD*, then the *hand of the LORD will be against* you and

your king. Now therefore *take your stand* and see this *great thing* that the LORD will *do before your eyes.*

1 Sam. 12:14

Each of the italicized phrases in this passage is characteristic of the style of Deuteronomy. The resemblances may be more striking in Hebrew, but they carry through in translation for anyone familiar with Deuteronomy's rhetoric.[4]

Nor was it just a matter of literary style. From the time of de Wette on, scholars had noticed that one of the dominant issues of Deuteronomy's laws was the centralization of worship. It seemed to de Wette that this idea must be an innovation going back to the time of Josiah. In earlier times, worshiping at the "high places" and other noncentralized sites was generally described without any indication that it might have been wrong. This is *generally* true—but here and there in the books that come after Deuteronomy, a king's career is sometimes summed up in terms like these:

Jehoash did what was right in the sight of the LORD all his days, because the priest Jehoiada instructed him. Nevertheless *the high places were not taken away; the people continued to sacrifice and make offerings on the high places.*

2 Kings 12:2

In the second year . . . King Amaziah son of Joash of Judah, began to reign. He was twenty-five years old when he began to reign . . . He did what was right in the sight of the LORD, yet not like his ancestor David; in all things he did as his father Joash had done. *But the high places were not removed; the people still sacrificed and made offerings on the high places.*

2 Kings 14:1–4

In the twenty-seventh year . . . King Azariah son of Amaziah of Judah began to reign. He was sixteen years old when he began to reign . . . He did what was right in the sight of the LORD, just as his father Amaziah had done. *Nevertheless the high places were not taken away; the people still sacrificed and made offerings on the high places.*

2 Kings 15:1–4

Such remarks seemed to suggest that whoever was writing these little summaries was intimately familiar with Josiah's campaign to centralize worship in Jerusalem; in fact, this person was judging Josiah's predecessors on the basis of this one issue.

A number of scholars had noticed such resemblances, notably Yehezkel Kaufmann, who wrote about them in modern Hebrew. (Most biblical scholars in Europe and America do not read modern Hebrew easily, so Kaufmann's insights did not reach them until a highly abridged version of his mul-tivolume work appeared in English in 1960.)[5] Meanwhile, in 1943, a German biblical scholar, Martin Noth, worked out on his own a new hypothesis con-cerning the relationship between Deuteronomy and the subsequent historical books (Joshua, Judges, 1 and 2 Samuel, and 1 and 2 Kings), and his account-ing of things won immediate acceptance among Western scholars.[6]

Noth believed that the group of laws and exhortations that form the cen-ter of Deuteronomy (4:44–30:20)[7] constituted, with a few adjustments, the "original" book of Deuteronomy, the one that had been found in the Jerusalem temple in Josiah's time. That book was thus essentially a law code, many of whose provisions embodied D's characteristic ideology—rad-ical devotion to Israel's God, fervent opposition to anything smacking of "Canaanite" worship, along with an evident concern for the downtrodden ("the stranger, the widow, and the orphan"), a rather abstract conception of God, and a broad perspective on the surrounding world.

Noth thought that someone—the "Deuteronomistic historian"—had taken this law code and used it as the starting point for composing a long his-tory of Israel, from the time of Moses to the Babylonian exile.[8] This writer was someone who was steeped in the ideology of Deuteronomy, but he must have lived long afterward; since this history ended with the Babylonian exile, Noth concluded, he must have composed his work sometime in the sixth century BCE.

How did this historian proceed? First, Noth believed, he composed the opening four chapters of Deuteronomy, in which Moses reviews the people's desert wanderings. This would serve as an introduction to the old law code, the "original" Deuteronomy. The same historian then ended the book with an account of Moses' death. To this he then added the bulk of his work—a thor-ough-going history of Israel, starting with Joshua and the conquest of the land, then on to the period of the Judges, David's rise to power, the United Monarchy, and so forth down to the fall of Jerusalem and the Babylonian exile. This whole history thus stretched from the beginning of Deuteronomy to the end of 2 Kings.

That would be a prodigious amount of research and writing even for a modern, professional historian. Noth did not think that the historian in question had actually *authored* every word of these books—not only because of the amount of material involved, but also because of the numerous inter-nal contradictions he and other scholars had found within these books. No, the Deuteronomistic historian was a collector. He (or she, or perhaps most likely, *they*) had simply gathered things from here and there—old legends, royal archives, perhaps earlier histories—and had arranged and edited the material into one fairly smooth-flowing account. It was only *fairly* smooth because the historian(s) involved did not even try to eliminate all contradic-tions—all that was desired was an account that could be read as one continuous story: first this happened, then that happened. Only here and there was entirely new material added: in transitions from one episode to the next or in places where a major figure might make a speech, the editor or editors felt free to propagandize. These passages include some that we have already seen—the opening of the book of Joshua and Rahab's theological affirmations—as well as others to be examined presently, such as Samuel's speech in 1 Samuel 12 and Solomon's speech at the dedication of the Jerusalem temple (1 Kings 8). For Noth, all these additions bespoke the ideology of the book of Deuteronomy (indeed, they often quoted that book): hence, the "*Deuteronomistic* historian."[9]

Noth's idea has survived the subsequent half-century of scholarly scrutiny fairly well, although just now some aspects are being seriously reexamined.[10] Perhaps the least disputed of proposed modifications has been the suggestion that the present history was actually composed in stages.[11] The exact stages are still the subject of controversy, but one suggestion is that the original history was scheduled to end with the glorious reign of King Josiah. That might explain why the subject of Josiah's reform and the book of Deuteronomy itself figured so prominently within it—the Deuteronomistic historian was a member of Josiah's own court. Only later, after the Babylonians had conquered Jerusalem, was this historical anthology updated—and in ways that bespoke a different editor or editors and a different mentality.[12]

The story of Rahab might serve as a good example of how various modern scholars conceive of the Deuteronomistic historian's work habits. At the very base of this story, they believe, is yet another etiological narrative. No one knows who the "sons of Rahab" were in ancient Israel, but whoever they were, this theory holds, they were not held to be part of the people of Israel. They were a foreign body in Israel's midst, living somewhere in or around Jericho. The story thus seeks to account for this unusual circumstance. In fact, a later passage says as much. In reporting how Joshua and his men destroyed Jericho, it says:

> They burned down the city and everything in it . . . But Rahab the prostitute, with her family and all who belonged to her, Joshua spared. She [that is, the Rahab clan] has lived in the midst of Israel *to this day*.
>
> Josh. 6:24–25

It is the persistence of the Rahab clan "in the midst of Israel to this very day," this theory holds, that this etiological tale seeks to explain.[13]

The explanation offered by the story is characteristically unflattering to these non-Israelites, indeed, it is somewhat reminiscent of the etiological explanation of the origin of the Ammonites and Moabites ("a bunch of bastards") seen earlier. The sons of Rahab,[14] the story says, are all descended from a prostitute. But their ancestress was spared because of her charitable action at the time the land was conquered, so they have survived here ever since. Indeed, supporters of this theory point out, the original etiological tale had been careful to specify Rahab's request that her whole family be spared. "Pledge to me in good faith that you will spare my father and mother, my brothers and sisters, and everyone else who belong to them." That is why this whole clan persists in our midst "to this day."

The Deuteronomistic historian heard this tale or found it written somewhere and incorporated it where he felt it belonged, in the account of the Israelites' battle for Jericho at the beginning of the conquest of the land. It might well be that the original story had the spies sparing Rahab and her family because she hid them that fateful night, or perhaps, somewhat more cynically, because they offered to allow her family to survive in lieu of payment for her services. Whatever the original story, the Deuteronomistic historian had a better idea: let's make her some kind of righteous person who *knows* that there is only one God, the God of Israel, and who therefore understands that Canaanite Jericho is doomed. Thus was born the somewhat paradoxical figure of a prostitute passing on theological verities to her clients.[15] Still later, in the time of the ancient interpreters, this paradox grated somewhat. Surely she couldn't have known what she knew about God and continued to be a prostitute! Rahab therefore must have *reformed* at some point, married, and become the mother of prophets and priests, indeed, the ancestress of David and Jesus; or else she was an altogether symbolic figure, an embodiment of the future church of sinners, with her crimson cord foreshadowing the blood of the crucifixion.

The Walls of Jericho

Modern historians have a problem with what follows: the account of the conquest of the mighty Canaanite city of Jericho. According to archaeologists, it didn't happen. Of course archaeology is, by the most generous account, only an approximate science; by definition it must be based on things that have been found, not on things that have not. Still, one sort of find that archaeologists have little difficulty identifying is destruction: when city walls have been breached to allow in an invading army, the evidence of devastation, burning, and pillaging is not difficult to spot. In the case of Jericho, it turns out, no such evidence can be found anytime near the purported Israelite invasion.

Much of the credit for the present understanding of Jericho's ancient history belongs to the British archaeologist Kathleen Kenyon. Along with her colleague Sir Mortimer Wheeler, Kenyon significantly improved the way archaeologists go about exploring a site and determining its chronological levels. Although Jericho had been examined by earlier archaeologists, Kenyon felt their results were inaccurate; she was eager to reexamine the evidence with her new methodology. She therefore set out to take another look, leading extensive excavations at Jericho between 1952 and 1958.

Everyone has heard of the story of how Joshua and the Israelites conquered Jericho. When they approached the city, they found it "shut up inside and out because of the [threatening] Israelites; no one came out or went in" (Josh. 6:1). God therefore instructed Joshua to have his men circle the city once each day for six days, and on the seventh day:

> "You shall march around the city seven times, the priests blowing the trumpets. When they make a long blast with the ram's horn, as soon as you hear the sound of the trumpet, then all the people shall shout with a great shout; and the wall of the city will fall down flat . . ."
>
> On the seventh day they rose early, at dawn, and marched around the city in the same manner seven times . . . And at the seventh time, when the priests had blown the trumpets, Joshua said to the people, "Shout! For the LORD has given you the city . . ." So the people shouted, and the trumpets were blown. As soon as the people heard the sound of the trumpets, they raised a great shout, and the wall fell down flat; so the people charged straight ahead into the city and captured it.
>
> Josh. 6:4–5, 15–20

What Kenyon found was that, while the city of Jericho had been an important center at an earlier point in its history, by the Late Bronze age (ca. 1200 BCE, the approximate time of this reported event), Jericho was a poor, and poorly defended, little settlement.[16] No archaeological data, scholars have subsequently concluded, can support the idea that a walled town even existed at Jericho during this whole period. Indeed, archaeologists say that Jericho may have already been abandoned by the time this incident was said to take place; the site was not resettled until the seventh century BCE, six hundred years after the purported time of Joshua, in fact, not long before the Babylonian exile. Then, once again, Jericho briefly became a fortified city. Perhaps it was this later reality, scholars say, that inspired the picture of Jericho's mighty walls as reported in the Deuteronomistic history.

Was Canaan Ever Conquered?

Jericho is only one piece of evidence in the larger puzzle presented by the book of Joshua. What actually *did* happen when the Israelites crossed the Jordan into the land God had promised them? The book of Joshua says that the Israelites swept across the whole land in a series of three separate campaigns (chapters 6–8, 9–10, and 11).[17] Nothing stood in their way. The various Canaanite "kings" (we would more properly call them mayors or governors, that is, rulers of individual cities and the surrounding countryside) were all mercilessly put to the sword: a list of thirty-one executed kings (identified by place, however, not by name) appears in Josh. 12:9–24. The Israelites overcame all opposition "from Baal-gad in the valley of Lebanon to Mount Halak, that rises toward Seir" (Josh. 12:7), that is, from the far north to the far south. Then they proceeded to divide up the land among different Israelite tribes (chapters 13–21).

This record of conquest cannot, however, be confirmed by archaeologists.[18] Not only Jericho, but other allegedly defeated Canaanite cities turn out to have been either undefended or unoccupied sites in the Late Bronze period (including Ai, Jericho's close neighbor—"destroyed" in Joshua 8).[19] Indeed, of more than a dozen sites that archaeologists have identified with the various cities reported conquered by Joshua and the Israelites, only two—Lachish and Hazor—have yielded signs of destruction in the appropriate period.[20] To make matters worse, what the book of Joshua says does not even seem to match what is said elsewhere in the Bible. If Joshua conquered everything in sight, scholars ask, then why does the next biblical book, Judges, present a picture so contradictory to this claim? The Canaanites, supposedly annihilated or exiled by the Israelite invasion in Joshua's time, are everywhere in evidence. Indeed, the very first sentence of Judges says: "After the death of Joshua, the Israelites inquired of the LORD, 'Who shall go up first for us against the Canaanites to fight against them?' " (Judg. 1:1). This seems to imply that the Canaanites had not been routed by Joshua, as reported in the previous book.[21] Moreover, as modern scholars have examined the book of Joshua, they have determined that, although it presents the picture of a Canaan-wide conquest in general terms, when it comes down to specifics, the incidents reported include only a very small swath of territory. The great Canaanite city of Shechem, for example, is never mentioned among Joshua's conquests; wouldn't that be the first place to which a mighty invading army would march?[22] (The area of Shechem is mentioned in Josh. 8:30–35, but there is no indication of any conflict, indeed, of any enemy presence whatsoever. Shechem then reappears in Judges 9, now somehow the province of a reportedly Israelite ruler named Abimelech. It thus seems to scholars that Shechem's Canaanite population at one point—perhaps then or perhaps much later—simply "became" Israelite without a drop of blood being spilled.) In fact, the most detailed part of the story of Joshua's conquest (Joshua 5–8) centers on a tiny area—Jericho, Ai, and Gilgal are all within a few miles of one another. To many scholars it thus seems that the Deuteronomistic History adopted a few stories connected specifically to the Jericho region and the territory of the tribe of Benjamin, then used them to add detail and, thus, the air of authenticity to its overall picture of a great Assyrian-style conquest of the land.

Indeed, even the figure of Joshua, these scholars say, may be at least partly fictitious. They note that the Bible reports, in an apparent aside, that Joshua's original name had been Hoshea, but that Moses for some reason changed it to Joshua (Num. 13:16). These scholars believe that this change-of-names story was a late editor's invention, for the very good reason that any ancient Israelite would have readily identified the "Jo-" part of Joshua's name as part of the Tetragrammaton (YHWH). Having a contemporary of Moses who was *born* with such a name ran counter to the biblical claim that the Tetragrammaton was revealed to Moses only when he was already an old man (Exod. 6:2). Therefore the text reports that it was Moses himself who gave Joshua the name by which he is known everywhere else, changing it when Joshua was already a grown man.

But if this change of names is an invention, who was the "real" Joshua and when did he live? Some scholars suppose that he started off as a hero of, specifically, the tribe of Ephraim sometime during the period of the Judges or later. (In this case, Joshua could have been his name from birth—he *never* was Hoshea.) Perhaps this Joshua played a leading role in the battle of Beth-horon, which was in the territory of Ephraim (the battle is reported in Josh. 10:1–15, but it may actually have occurred in a later period).[23] In any case, these scholars hold, the original Joshua was indeed held to be a brilliant fighter and tactician, the stuff of local legends. It was the Deuteronomistic historian who, needing a successor to Moses and a mighty conquistador, seized on these legends and elevated Joshua to his current central role. In so doing the historian was also careful to attribute to him actions highly reminiscent of Moses' own deeds: sending out spies, crossing the Jordan on dry land as Moses had crossed the Red Sea, and so on. The same scholarly argument holds that someone else—apparently the Pentateuch's final editor—then went even further, mentioning Joshua in various narratives in the Pentateuch so as to make him Moses' constant sidekick and apprentice, and even inserting him as a second hero (to stand beside Caleb) in the cowardly spies episode—an episode in which, these scholars say, Joshua originally had no part.[*][24]

But if so, then what really did happen? How did the land of Canaan turn into the land of Israel?

Whence the People of Israel?

There is probably no issue more debated by today's biblical scholars than that of Israel's origins.[25] The biblical account of where Israel came from, as we have seen repeatedly, raises troubling questions for each of the periods cov-

---

* Many scholars believe that the sole hero of the original version was Caleb. Note thus Num. 14:24, where Caleb alone is mentioned as having a "different spirit." Deut. 1:36 asserts that Caleb alone of his whole generation will see the land of Canaan.

ered. Historians tend to discount the material relating to Israel's remotest ancestors, Abraham and Sarah, Isaac and Rebekah, Jacob and his wives and concubines, as etiological projections from a later period; there is little if anything here, they say, on which to base a history. By the same token, the whole account of the exodus, even if it contains some sort of historical kernel, cannot, in the current view, have involved anything like the numbers of people alleged in the biblical account; at best, this is a tribal legend relating to one small segment of the future population of Israel. The exodus became a myth of national origins only at the time of King David (at the earliest). If the great conquest account of the book of Joshua is likewise in doubt, lacking support from either the archaeological record or the rest of the Bible, then how *did* the Israelites end up in a land that was not originally theirs, Canaan?

For a time, despite its difficulties, the Bible's own conquest account was supported by some modern scholars, particularly those influenced by the work and approach of W. F. Albright. Albright felt that the evidence of Bethel—apparently destroyed by fire in the late thirteenth century—and Hazor, which met the same fate at the same time, provided at least some support for the Bible's conquest narrative. So too, he believed, did his own excavations at Tell Beit Mirsim (south of Hebron), which he identified as the biblical city of Debir. True, the archaeological evidence of Jericho, Ai, and other sites was troubling, but perhaps these could be explained in time.[26] Today, however, the idea of a Canaan-wide conquest is supported by very few scholars. Some, as we shall see, nonetheless maintain that part of the future Israel was indeed created out of an ethnic group or groups originally foreign to Canaan—people who entered Canaan from the east or southeast and, through armed conflict or otherwise, ended up settling in the Canaanite highlands and from there extending their influence to other parts of the country.[27] In the meantime, however, other approaches to the question of Israel's emergence in Canaan have been advanced.

One rival explanation goes back to the 1920s and 1930s, when it was put forward most prominently by the German biblicist Albrecht Alt (Martin Noth's teacher). Alt had spent some time in Palestine and studied, among other things, the movements of modern-day desert nomads (the Bedouin). They live principally off their flocks of sheep and goats, Alt observed, and during the rainy winter, when vegetation is relatively lush, they lead these flocks into the rugged, uninhabited areas close to the desert, where they can graze freely. Later, however, after the farmers have finished harvesting their crops, the Bedouin move into the settled land. There their animals can feed on the stubble left over after the harvest, and the farmers don't mind (the manure the flocks leave behind enriches their soil). During the hottest part of the summer, when even the stubble has given out, the Bedouin move up into the cooler highlands with their flocks, seeking out whatever patches of green still exist and waiting for the heat to give way to the first winter rains. A visitor to Jerusalem today can still sometimes see Bedouin flocks at the height of summer, munching tranquilly on the grass of a traffic island in the midst of a busy city street.

Surveying this pattern, repeated year after year, Alt concluded that there are very few "pure" nomads in the region. Most spend only part of the year wandering from place to place in the wilderness; the rest of the year they are camped in or near one of the green, settled areas. Indeed, Alt observed that the Bedouin themselves sometimes take up farming, cultivating a little farm patch in one spot while grazing their flocks in another. They are thus best described as *semi-nomads*. True, the Bedouin are not enthusiastic farmers. "When a plow crosses the threshold," an old saying has it, "manhood departs." But the bigger their little farm patches became, the less the Bedouin would find themselves in need of the local farmers to get grain and other staples. For Alt, this provided a model of what might have happened in ancient times. The Israelites, semi-nomadic grazers, moved in and out of settled Canaan for a long while and then, gradually and at first peacefully, began to settle down themselves, leaving the first traces of their habitation in the sparsely populated mountain highlands. They went there, Alt said, precisely because these areas were underpopulated; they could move in and start farming on their own without ruffling anyone's feathers. Only later did they begin encroaching into the valleys and such urban centers as Shechem. At that point their infiltration may have ceased to be unopposed—after all, signs of conflict and conquest *were* found at Hazor, Bethel, and elsewhere. But if there was no evidence of a countrywide conquest, and if places like Jericho and most other sites had never been put to the sword, that was because the conquest was basically a later invention: Israel's real origins were in the desert wastes.

Alt's explanation had much to recommend it and survives today, in modified form, in the ideas of various contemporary scholars.[28] It is not, however, the only alternative model to the Bible's conquest account that has been put forward to explain Israel's origins. In particular one piece of somewhat more tangible evidence has provided the basis for a rather different reconstruction of the events.

The El Amarna Letters

In 1887 a group of clay tablets was discovered a little more than a hundred miles south of Cairo, Egypt, at the site of what had once been the magnificent palace of the Egyptian pharaoh Akhenaten (otherwise known as Amenhotep IV, ca. 1350–1334 BCE). The tablets eventually made their way to local antiquities dealers and thence to various European museums and private collectors. Scholars soon identified the tablets as letters, most of them written by various Canaanite vassals to Akhenaten or his father, Amenhotep III. Although the Egyptians generally used hieroglyphic writing for their own language, these foreign ministry letters were in Akkadian, the language of international diplomacy; the writing system used was thus cuneiform, the wedge marks sunk into wet clay tablets.

It is difficult to overstate the importance of the El Amarna letters to historians looking for the origins of ancient Israel. The letters present a picture of the land of Canaan more or less in the same period in which the Israelites were supposed to be invading it. (As a side note, they also tell us something about the Canaanite language at the time. The reason is that, although the Canaanite scribes of the letters were writing in a form of Akkadian, the language itself was somewhat different from other forms, one profoundly influenced by the West Semitic idiom. In addition, the scribes sometimes glossed an Akkadian word with the Canaanite equivalent.[29] As a result, the letters provide some very early evidence of the language that was later to be spoken by the people of Israel, biblical Hebrew.)

How do you address a mighty Egyptian emperor when you yourself are a lowly vassal, the ruler of a little Canaanite city? The El Amarna letters usually begin with what was then the florid Near Eastern equivalent of "Dear Mr. President":

> To the king, my lord, my god, my Sun, the Sun from heaven; thus says Yabni-ilu, the ruler of Lachish, your servant, the dust under your feet, the groom of your horses. At the feet of the king, my lord, my god, my Sun, the Sun from heaven, I have fallen seven and seven times, on the belly and on the back.
>
> EA 328

Or:

> To the king, my lord, my Sun; Message of Abi-Milku, your servant: I fall at the feet of the king, my lord, seven times and seven times. I am the dirt under the feet and sandals of the king, my lord. You are the Eternal Sun; the sweet breath of life belongs to my lord, my Sun.
>
> EA 146

With such preliminaries out of the way, the letters go on to paint a detailed picture of the political situation in which their writers lived. In particular, the vassals frequently complain about a group of marauders—apparently scattered all across the land of Canaan—who raid the Canaanite cities and wreak havoc among the urban population. Interestingly, the letters refer to these marauders by the same name that may have been used of the underlings in Egypt, the 'apiru or ḫabiru (above, chapter 12).

May the king, my lord, know that [the city of] Gubla,[30] the maidservant of the king from ancient times, is safe and sound. The war, however, of the 'apiru against me is severe. . . . The 'apiru killed Aduna, the king of Irqata, but there was no one who said anything to Abdi-Ashirta, so they go on taking territory for themselves . . . I am afraid . . .

And again:

Speak to your lord so he will send you at the head of the archers to drive off the 'apiru from the mayors. If this year no archers come out, then all the lands will be joined to the 'apiru. If the king, my lord, is negligent, and there are no archers, then let a ship fetch the men of Gubla, your men, and the gods, to bring them all the way to you so I can abandon Gubla. Look, I am afraid the peasantry will strike me down.

Later:

Listen to me! Why are you negligent so that your land is being taken? Let it not be said in the days of the commissioners, "The 'apiru have taken the entire country."

EA 75, 77, 83

These are only three of many references to the 'apiru in the El Amarna letters.

Out of these letters developed a third theory of where Israel came from.[31] The Israelites were neither outside conquerors nor peaceful semi-nomads who gradually infiltrated from the desert. Instead, they were Canaanite revolutionaries. Dissatisfied with the Egyptian hegemony that operated in Canaan through a network of puppets and vassals, the 'apiru and other disgruntled elements eventually overthrew these entrenched powers and took over. The letters frequently mention the danger of people being "joined to the 'apiru," suggesting that there was some sort of grassroots movement afoot. In one of the passages cited above, the trembling ruler confesses: "Look, I am afraid the peasantry will strike me down." This too might suggest some sort of popular revolt.

As we have seen, 'apiru/ḫabiru was a term used throughout the ancient Near East, and its appearance in the El Amarna letters may have nothing to do with the putative 'apiru-Hebrew connection in the exodus narrative. After all, the El Amarna letters themselves are dated approximately a century before the usual dating of the exodus. Nevertheless, it is not impossible to imagine a group of 'apiru escaping from Egypt making common cause with a group of 'apiru malcontents who had been opposing the local regime in Canaan for a century or more. (A modern analogue might be the Muslim

Brotherhood, founded in 1928, which continues to this day to operate illegally or in the margins of various regimes in the modern Middle East, threatening their stability.) Both groups had been derided as 'apiru by their social betters, and the name now became, briefly, a badge of honor. The escaping slaves proved to be the spark that set the discontented Canaanite "tinder" on fire.[32] The oppressed peasantry outside the urban centers rose up as one man. Their new religion, centered on a God previously unknown in the region, may have had no small role in joining the disparate elements into an effective revolutionary movement.

The Canaanites Are Us

Most scholars today would probably admit (some grudgingly) that we will probably never know exactly where the people of Israel came from or how they got started on their separate existence. There is some merit to all of the theories mentioned, they say, but none of them alone can decisively account for all of the biblical and extrabiblical data. One thing is clear, however: *something* must have happened. The name "Israel" had not always been associated with the region that Israel eventually occupied. The El Amarna letters mention no such name, for example, nor do numerous and detailed earlier documents dealing with the region.

But to what period can one assign the appearance of the name "Israel," and what does that appearance signal? As a matter of fact, the first recorded use of the name "Israel" known to us is found (in passing) on a victory stele attributed to the Egyptian king Merneptah (or Merenptaḥ) in the late thirteenth century—the same time as that given for the exodus.[33] Scholars at first seized on this as evidence suggesting that "Israel" had only begun to emerge in the land of Canaan at that time: the new name came about as a direct result of the exodus. But such a conclusion is hardly inevitable. Indeed, others have since argued that the Merneptah stele indicates exactly the opposite, that the entity designated "Israel" must have already existed before the time that the exodus is alleged to have taken place, and what is more, that this entity could have had no particular association with any exodus in the mind of Egyptians.[34] Moreover, the appearance of a new name does not necessarily mean the appearance of a new people. (Persia became "Iran" in 1935 for ideological reasons,[35] not because of any shift in its population; like other African nations, today's Republic of Zaire has had other names over the last hundred years.)

As contemporary scholars have wrestled with earlier theories, as well as with new archaeological data, most of them have come to agree on one point: at least a good part of what was to become the future nation of Israel had probably always been there—or, to put it somewhat sharply, "We have met the Canaanites and they are us." There may indeed have been a mini-exodus from Egypt, and there may likewise have been a further infiltration from the east or southeast at some point, but from the standpoint of the over-all population, these movements were minor; most of what was to become Israel's population was most likely there from the start.

To be sure, an earlier generation of archaeologists, relying on the Bible's repeated assertions that the Israelites had come into ancient Canaan from elsewhere, fixed on what looked like peculiarly Israelite features of the material culture (the collared-rim jar discovered at many sites deemed to be early Israelite,[36] as well as the characteristic Israelite four-room house)[37] as confirmation of their non-Canaanite origins. Surely the conquering Israelites had brought their unique pottery and architectural styles with them from wherever they had come. Nowadays, the same evidence is read differently: these allegedly Israelite features are not limited to areas supposedly settled by the early Israelites, and archaeologists in any case stress the similarity of these items to the Canaanite material culture.[38] It seems unlikely that any massive influx of outsiders could have been responsible for the evidence found at the earliest Israelite settlements.[39]

Such a hypothesis, scholars point out, is supported not only by the absence of evidence for conquest and destruction by outside invaders, but by the rather murky events that would have followed such a conquest. The book of Joshua relates that the Israelites replaced the native Canaanites, but it presents no clear picture of what happened to that earlier population. There are no reports of massive emigration at the time of the emergence of Israel (and no evidence of such emigration elsewhere); there is little reason, scholars say, to believe that the native populations were simply slaughtered and buried somewhere. Indeed, the book of Judges itself mentions the numerous places in Canaan where "the Canaanites continued to live" among the Israelites or—equally surprising—where the Israelites lived "in the midst of the Canaanites" (Judg. 1:27–35; 3:5–6). To this point most archaeologists add that during the whole period when Israel might conceivably have emerged (that is, between 1300 and 1000 BCE), there is in fact no evidence of *any* sizeable influx of people into the region, save for that of the coast-dwelling Philistines.

It is for these reasons that most modern scholars reject the Bible's own picture of a great exchange of populations—more than a million Israelites* entering Canaan and displacing the native population. Instead they suppose that, in one way or another, the people of Israel ended up incorporating significant elements of the locals.[40] (Indeed, in the revolution model, the future Israelites are in every sense Canaanites themselves, massing just outside the walled cities—peasants, brigands, and *'apiru*. If anyone is an outsider in

---

* That is to say, 600,000 adult males plus their wives and children.

this third model, it is really the ruling bureaucracy, lackeys of a distant Egyptian overlord.)

The Flight to the Highlands

Over the past few decades, archaeologists have shifted their focus somewhat. Instead of concentrating on the great mounds of ruined cities, they have looked instead at the remains of smaller villages that existed between the big cities, studying how these rural populations made a living and organized themselves. This research has led to a surprising finding, one that, for some at least, only strengthens the idea that "the Canaanites are us."

Archaeologists have found that the central highlands of Canaan were settled relatively sparsely in the Late Bronze Age. Thereafter, however, the region experienced a sudden boost in population: starting around 1200 BCE, the number and density of permanent settlements in the Canaanite highlands increased dramatically. In just a generation or two, a network of roughly 250 highland settlements sprang up. Settlements continued to increase for a time thereafter.[41] Interestingly, this spurt in highland settlements seems to have accompanied the depopulation of previously thriving Canaanite urban centers; just as suddenly, it seems, the cities in this same period dropped to less than half the number of their former inhabitants.[42]

One obvious possibility arising from these data was that the new settlers in the highlands were none other than the old city dwellers.[43] That is, starting at the end of the Late Bronze period, for some reason, groups of Canaanites moved from elsewhere in the land up to the mountaintop ridges. Perhaps, some scholars suggest, people left the cities because this was a time of political chaos—the weakening of Egyptian power (previously sovereign in Canaan);[44] the breakup of the Hittite empire in present-day Turkey and northern Syria; the settling of the Sea Peoples* in coastal Canaan. Whatever the precise combination of factors, such a reconstruction of events would see the first Israelites as refugees from the Canaanite cities.

Some scholars have suggested that this internal migration was also connected to two or three new technological developments. The first was terrace farming. By this technique, the natural slope of a hill was reshaped into a series of steplike terraces, so that farmers could plant and harvest their crops on a series of flat surfaces running down the hill's flank. This not only made farming easier, but it also helped prevent erosion of the soil and made better use of rainwater. The vertical retaining walls that connected one terrace to another were made of dry-laid stones, easily identified by today's archaeologists. Scholars thus suppose that the introduction of such terraces in the early Iron Age is

* See next chapter.

one thing that made possible the proliferation of the highland settlements.[45] (This has also led some scholars to suggest that farming was indeed the basic profession of the first highland settlers—they simply moved their operations from the lowlands up to the hills.) Another bit of technology that may also have encouraged settlements in the highlands was the availability of iron tools. Thanks to these, heavily wooded hilltop areas could be cleared and made suitable for farming, and iron-tipped plows could then make farming them more productive. What is more, iron tools could be used to hew out large cisterns for water storage, and—another handy bit of technology—the introduction of a new type of waterproof plaster to line these cisterns allowed rainwater to be collected and preserved far more efficiently.[46] Before these innovations, permanent settlements had been located mostly in places of abundant water; now, a village could survive solely on rainwater collected in the new cisterns. All of these changes may have encouraged the move up to the hills.

Contemporary scholars do not all buy into this reconstruction, however. If the founders of these highland villages were former city dwellers, they say, it is certainly noteworthy that their settlements did not bear any sign of their earlier way of life—for example, they did not include any public buildings of the sort that existed in the cities below them. Instead, people seem to have settled down in a wholly new pattern of living, forming themselves into little family-based groups and adopting a deliberately simple, rude existence. Such a radical break with their past seems possible, but puzzling. Moreover, along with the terraces on which the settlers grew their crops, archaeologists have found evidence of animal flocks—something the exurbanites would have had no experience with. For both these reasons (as well as because of certain ancient biblical texts, to be discussed presently) these other scholars prefer to connect the burgeoning hilltop settlements with semi-nomads (much as Alt did). Where such semi-nomads may have come from remains the subject of debate. They may have always been inhabitants of the region, who suddenly switched their way of life at some point from semi-nomadism to settled farming. Alternately, they may have been shepherds and herdsmen who had come from the fringes of Canaan or who entered Canaan from the territory of Seir/Edom and Midian. Whatever their origins, according to this school of thought, these people eventually settled down and began to farm the then-unoccupied central highlands.[47]

No Pork upon Thy Fork

The idea that the settlers were *not* exurbanites is supported by other discontinuities between their way of life and that of the Canaanite city dwellers (as well as, for that matter, the way of life of highland settlers from far earlier periods). One of these discontinuities is most intriguing. The archaeologist

Israel Finkelstein has pointed to the absence of pig bones in hilltop sites starting in the Iron I period (roughly 1200–1000 BCE) and continuing through
Iron II; before that, in Bronze Age sites, pig bones abound.[48] Some have
questioned Finkelstein's data, but if correct, they suggest that the new hilltop
residents were fundamentally different from both their predecessors in the
highlands and the city Canaanites—either because they were a different ethnic group, or because they had adopted (for ideological or other reasons) a
different way of life.[49] Still more important, his findings imply that these highlanders shared something in addition to their common pattern of settlement: if all of them abstained from eating bacon or pork (like modern-day
Jews and Muslims), perhaps they did so for a similar reason—that is, they
must have shared some ideology (if only a food taboo).

There is a further objection to be made to the "Canaanite exurbanite"
model: the archaeological record seems to indicate that the central highland
settlements sprang up east to west.[50] If the first settlers had been emigrants
from the Canaanite cities, one would expect the earliest settlements to be closest to those cities. If the reverse is true (though the evidence is not unequivocal), that might suggest that the hilltop settlers came from outside Canaan,
settling gingerly in the highlands closest to their point of entry and then gradually making their way to more remote hilltops.

In short: whether the settlers were exurbanites or fringe-area pastoralists
(and if the latter, from where?) remains an open question; there are good
arguments on both sides. Whichever reconstruction they adopt, however,
most contemporary scholars agree that the bulk of the future population of
Israel would have consisted overwhelmingly of people from within Canaan.
There was, they say, no murderous invasion of conquerors and no massive
influx of foreigners and exchange of populations. Rather, a distinct highland
population would have developed on its own for a time, gradually expanded
in size, and then spread out to the low-lying cities, sometimes peacefully,
sometimes not. Eventually, scholars believe, the distinct identity and self-
understanding of these mountain dwellers came to be adopted by, or imposed
upon, much of the land. The fruitful valleys, along with old Canaanite
strongholds such as Shechem, just suddenly *were* Israelite. As time went on,
this people of "Israelites" insisted ever more vehemently on the great gap separating themselves from the "Canaanites," who were now simply, mysteriously, but oh so completely, gone. The new nation never tired of repeating
that they were utterly distinct from the land's former inhabitants, enshrining
this belief in their laws and stories, even suggesting that their own ancestors—
who, they said, had come from elsewhere—had gone to the greatest lengths
to avoid intermarriage with the Canaanites and had banned any religious
observance that smacked of Canaanite influence. But the Bible's dark secret,
these scholars say, is that the people of Israel really weren't outsiders at all;
most of them had been in Canaan since time immemorial.[51]

23

Judges and Chiefs

JUDGES 1–21 AND THE BOOK OF RUTH

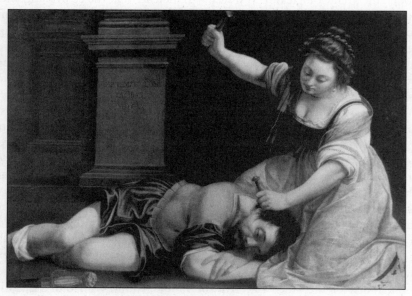

Jael and Sisera by Artemisia Gentileschi.

CHARISMATIC LEADERSHIP. GIDEON. THE SONG OF DEBORAH.
WOMEN IN THE BIBLE. SAMSON'S STORY. THE SEA PEOPLES.
MOUNTAIN DWELLERS AND THE ORIGINS OF MONOLATRY.

The book of Judges recounts the history of Israel's tribes during the early years of their settlement in the land of Canaan. A series of outstanding, God-inspired leaders directed the people's affairs in those days—Ehud, Deborah, Gideon, Jephthah, Samson, and others. These leaders are called *shofetim* in the Bible, usually translated as "judges." This translation is actually somewhat misleading. True, in later times, the word *shofet* came to mean specifically a judge or magistrate, but at an earlier stage of Hebrew it designated any sort of rough-and-tumble leader or chief. (Of course, any leader might be called upon to mediate disputes and act as a judge, but this was a minor part of the *shofet*'s functions.) It would thus not be inappropriate to translate the term differently and think of the biblical book that comes after Joshua as the *Book of Chiefs.*

This book begins by describing the circumstances under which the Israelites' various chiefs arose. In those early days, the Bible says:

> The Israelites used to do what was evil in the sight of the LORD and worship the Baals. They would abandon the LORD, the God of their ancestors, who had brought them out of the land of Egypt, and follow other gods from among the gods of the peoples who were all around them, bowing down to them . . . The LORD would grow angry with Israel, and He would give them over to plunderers who plundered them and sell them out to enemies all around . . .
>
> Then the LORD would raise up chiefs to save them from those who had plundered them . . . Whenever the LORD would raise up a chief for them, the LORD would be with the chief, and He would save them from their enemies all the time that the chief was alive . . . But whenever the chief died, they would relapse and behave worse than their ancestors, following other gods, worshiping them and bowing down to them. They would not drop any of their practices or their stubborn ways.
>
> Judg. 2:11–19

The book of Judges thus presents a series of intermittent leaders, each rising to prominence for a time to save Israel from its enemies and lead the people on the right path. No sooner would the leader die, however, than the people would revert to their sinful ways and sink back into the old cycle of apostasy and oppression.

Charismatic Leaders

Sociologists have studied the Bible from the standpoint of their own academic specialty, and one of the subjects on which they have focused is the various forms of leadership evidenced in the Bible. Leadership is an issue in all societies: who, if anyone, will have the authority to govern and make decisions affecting everyone? Different societies have answered this question in different ways. The world has thus known clan councils and tribal chiefs, emperors, dictators and oligarchs, kings and queens, constitutional monarchies, and parliamentary or presidential democracies.

Whatever the system of rule, one of the trickiest problems is that of succession. Especially when a single leader is empowered to make most of the decisions, his or her death can touch off a crisis. Who will be the next leader? Unless this question has a clear answer that has been accepted in advance by all members of the society, the old leader's death can lead to a protracted power struggle, bringing with it the gravest consequences: civil war, economic collapse, or conquest by outsiders. That is why so many societies develop fixed, unalterable systems for the automatic replacement of the old leader. Perhaps the commonest of these in the past was kingship. The essence of kingship is that power passes *automatically* to the next heir to the throne. There is no test of fitness, nor any scrutiny of the heir by an outside body; as the old saying has it, "The king is dead; long live the king!" So dangerous is the chaos that might result from *not* having an established process of succession that, all over the world, people have been willing on principle to accept the king's son or daughter as their new ruler even without proof that the new ruler will be any good at the job, indeed, without any guarantee that he or she will not be profligate or utterly decadent (often a hazard with kings and queens) or even a congenital idiot; almost anything is better than chaos.

Yet Israel in the book of Judges was a society without a king. The individual tribes had their own "elders," but there was no satisfactory, ongoing coordination among tribes. Instead, they seem to have had a succession of temporary, ad hoc leaders, the "judges" or chiefs on which the book of Judges centers. These leaders all shared one striking trait: none of them had any prior claim to rule. They did not come from a dominant family or rise up through the ranks to take over. Instead, their rise to power was created by a crisis; something occurred that required someone to take over, and the person in question suddenly emerged. He or she was then put into power by general acclamation—"This is just the leader we need!" The sociologist Max Weber (who wrote extensively about the Bible) referred to this phenomenon as "charismatic leadership."[1]

It is striking that the book of Judges seems to stress precisely this aspect of its various chiefs: they are anything but natural candidates for the job. Scholars point, for example, to the case of Gideon, whose rise to power is described in these terms:

> Now the angel of the LORD came and sat beneath the oak-tree in Ophrah, which belonged to Joash the Abiezrite, as his son Gideon was beating out wheat in the wine press to keep it safe from the Midianites. The angel of the LORD appeared to him and said to him, "The LORD is with you, you mighty warrior." Gideon said to him, "Excuse me, sir, but if the LORD is with us, why are we having all this trouble? Where are all the miracles that our ancestors recorded for us, saying, 'Truly, the LORD took us up out of Egypt'? But now the LORD has abandoned us and left us in the power of the Midianites." Then the LORD turned to him and said, "Go in this strength of yours and save Israel yourself from the Midianites; am I not the one who is sending you?" But he said, "Please, sir, how should I be the one to save Israel? My clan is the poorest in Manasseh, and I am the least in my family."
>
> Judg. 6:11–15

Here once again is a human who encounters an angel and does not recognize him at first—but this belongs to an earlier discussion (above, chapter 7). What is relevant in the present context is the angel's commissioning of Gideon to lead the people. One could hardly imagine a less qualified candidate. The scene opens with Gideon so intimidated by the raiding Midianites that he has to hide his spare grains of wheat inside a winepress. What a pathetic figure! The angel's opening words to him—"The LORD is with you, you mighty warrior"—seem almost a joke in view of his timorousness. Nor is Gideon presented as a particularly pious individual. To the angel's assertion that God is with him Gideon replies tartly: Oh yeah? If the LORD is with us, why are we having all this trouble? Most important, the passage spells out Gideon's political unfitness to become a leader: he comes from a not particularly powerful tribe, Manasseh, in fact, from "the poorest clan" in that tribe, and he himself is "the least in my family."

Yet it is precisely this unlikely candidate who ends up in charge, at least for a while, leading his troops to victory twice against Midian (Judges 7–8). Scholars also note that the biblical text was careful to specify, a few verses after the passage cited, that "the spirit of the LORD took possession of Gideon"; it is this that completes his transformation into a worthy chieftain (Judg. 6:34). But such a transformation occurs against the background of what sociologists see as a somewhat amorphous population, one in which an external crisis (Midianite depredations) can bring to the fore someone with no obvious claim to the top spot. So it is, in fact, with the other judges: these include the illegitimate son of a prostitute who supports himself as a highwayman (Jephthah, Judges 11–12); an impulsively violent man who marries a daughter of the enemy Philistines for a time, consorts with prostitutes, and ultimately surrenders to the sexual blackmail of Delilah (Samson, Judges 14–16); and a woman—not usually the stuff of leadership in ancient Israel, but in this case she actually goes on to lead a four-star general into battle (Deborah, Judges 4–5). Deborah seems already to have been a prophet (Judg. 4:4), but the others, just like Gideon, undergo a divine transformation: the "spirit of the LORD" comes over them and they are suddenly capable of great feats (Judg. 11:29; 14:6, 19; 15:14). They are the very model of charismatic leadership.

Since these leaders have no ongoing, statutory claim to power, they are unable to pass power on to their descendants—to become kings, in other words. In the biblical version of events, this circumstance is given a theological justification:

> Then the Israelites said to Gideon, "Rule over us, you and your son and your grandson also; since you have saved us from the Midianites." But Gideon said to them, "I will not rule over you, and my son will not rule over you; the LORD will rule over you."
>
> Judg. 8:22–23

This, many scholars think, is putting the best face on what was actually a rather different reality. The political situation was such that neither Gideon nor any of the other judges was *able* to establish a royal dynasty or to unify the various tribes under one rule (if such a thought even occurred at the time).

A Woman Warrior

One of the most striking figures in the book of Judges is Deborah. The crisis that brings her to the fore is similar to that of Gideon's time. In her case, "King Jabin of Canaan, who reigned in Hazor" (Judg. 4:2) was oppressing the Israelites, and they cried out to God for help.

Deborah was a prophet of sorts. "She used to sit," the Bible says, "under the palm of Deborah between Ramah and Bethel in the hill country of Ephraim" (Judg. 4:3). This, scholars say, is not merely a geographical note. The ability to encounter or converse with God was apparently sometimes associated specifically with certain trees or groves; thus, the angel seen earlier appeared to Gideon at the "oak tree in Ophrah," and a group of angels is said to have appeared to Abraham at the "oak trees of Mamre" (Gen. 18:1). Other trees as well may be associated with prophecy.[2] That Deborah used to station herself under a certain palm tree may thus indicate that she was in regular communication with the divine; in any case, when Israel's situation worsened, she acted exactly in the role of a prophet, speaking on God's behalf:

She sent a message to Barak son of Abinoam, [who was] from Kedesh in Naphtali, saying, "The LORD, the God of Israel, has issued you an order: 'Go, take up your position at Mount Tabor, and take with you ten thousand troops from the tribe of Naphtali and the tribe of Zebulun. Then I [God] will draw out Sisera, the general of Jabin's army, to meet you by Wadi Kishon with his chariots and his infantry; and I will hand him over to you [to defeat].' " Barak said to her, "If you go with me, I will go; but if not, I will not go." And she said, "All right, I will go with you; but there will be no glory for you in the course that you are following, since now the LORD will be handing over Sisera to a woman." Then Deborah got up and went with Barak to Kedesh.

Judg. 4:6–9

The ancient Near Eastern equivalent of the modern tank was the war chariot. It could mow through an army of foot soldiers with ease, its whirring wheels and snorting horses sowing panic through the ranks. Sisera, the enemy general, had nine hundred such chariots, each made out of impenetrable iron (Judg. 4:3, 12). How could he lose? Still, Deborah *was* in communication with God. When she spoke with the Israelite general, Barak, she was quite unequivocal: God says that this is the moment to take the offensive. And so Barak did. Although hesitant at first ("If you go with me," Barak tells Deborah, "I will go"), the Israelite general proceeded to Mount Tabor, accompanied by a massive force of ten thousand soldiers. When the enemy Canaanites suddenly saw this huge army sweeping down on them, they were the ones who panicked. Even their general, Sisera, abandoned his chariot and left the battlefield on foot (Judg. 4:16). The Israelites won a stunning victory.

Sisera's own death was ignominious. Fleeing the scene, he frantically searched for someplace in which to hide; it was then that he encountered Jael, wife of Heber the Kenite.

Jael came out to meet Sisera, and said to him, "Turn aside, my lord, turn aside to me; have no fear." So he turned aside to her into the tent, and she covered him with a coverlet. Then he said to her, "Please give me a little water to drink; for I am thirsty." So she opened a skin of milk and gave him a drink and covered him. He said to her, "Stand at the entrance of the tent, and if anybody comes and asks you, 'Is anyone here?' say, 'No.' " But Jael wife of Heber took a tent peg, and took a hammer in her hand, and went softly to him and drove the peg into his temple, until it went down into the ground—he was lying fast asleep from weariness—and he died.

Judg. 4:18–21

This was the end of the fearsome Sisera, outsmarted by one woman and then put to death by another.

The Song of Deborah

After narrating these events in chapter 4 of Judges, the Bible presents in chapter 5 a stirring hymn of praise, known as the "Song of Deborah," that basically recounts the same events in poetic style. This hymn, distinguished by its vivid language and thumping rhythm, has been of particular interest to modern scholars. The reason is that it seems to them to afford a rare glimpse of a biblical historian at work.

We saw above (chapter 13) that the Song of the Sea in Exodus 15 was, according to a hypothesis first put forward by Frank M. Cross and D. N. Freedman, the ultimate source of the narrative account of the splitting of the Red Sea that precedes it (Exodus 14). But according to Cross and Freedman, the author of the prose narrative did not understand fully the words of the ancient song; its mention of the waters standing up "in a heap" was taken to refer to the creation of a dry path in the midst of the sea, whereas all the Song of the Sea meant to say by this phrase was that the waves at sea were so high that they capsized the Egyptians' boats and drowned them. Scholars see a similar error in the prose retelling of Sisera's death (Judg. 4:17–21).[3] According to the prose version, Jael gives Sisera some milk to drink and puts him to bed, then sneaks up on him while he is asleep and drives a tent spike into his head. On close examination, however, the Song of Deborah seems to be telling a slightly different story:

> Most blessed of women be Jael, the wife of Heber the Kenite, of tent-
> dwelling women most blessed.
> He asked for water and she gave him milk, she brought him curds in a
> lordly bowl.
> She put her hand to the tent peg [and] her right hand to a workman's
> mallet;
> she struck Sisera a blow, she crushed his head, she shattered and pierced
> his temple.
> He sank, he fell, he lay still at her feet;
> at her feet he sank, he fell; where he sank, there he fell dead.
>   Judg. 5:24–27

If one reads these words without preconception, they seem clearly to describe a different sort of death scene. There is nothing here about Jael covering Sisera with a coverlet and him then dozing off or even lying down. On the contrary, Sisera *falls*, and so he must have been standing when Jael delivered the fatal blow. In order to understand how someone knowing this song's version could have produced the very different prose account, it is necessary to know something about the workings of biblical poetry.

Biblical poetry does not have rhyme or even a fixed meter. Its basic feature is a short, two- or three-part sentence. The parts, called *clauses,* are usually only three or four words apiece, and they are separated by a brief syntactic pause, of the sort usually represented in English by a comma. The poetic line is always end-stopped, that is, it always ends in a major pause (period or semicolon).

_____ ,	_____ .
Clause A	Clause B

Writing poetry according to this formula is not very challenging (it is certainly easier than writing rhyming iambic pentameter, as classical English poets once did!). Still, ancient listeners or readers had to be informed in some way that clause B was the *continuation* of clause A and not some wholly new beginning—otherwise they might mistake B for the start of a whole new line. So it was that Hebrew poets developed various ways of signaling to people that B was A's continuation. They could make B somehow dependent on A by omitting a verb or other essential word. Thus:

> He subdues peoples beneath us, and nations beneath our feet.
>
> Ps. 47:4

The clause "and nations beneath our feet" cannot stand on its own; it needs to borrow a subject ("He") and a verb ("subdues") from the previous clause. Such omissions serve to bind B back to A and identify it as A's continuation rather than a whole new start.

Another way of accomplishing the same thing is repetition: the same phrase that occurs in A occurs again in B, binding the two together. The Song of Deborah has many such repetitions; for example:

> *In the days of* Shamgar son of Anath, *in the days of* Jael, caravans ceased . . .
>
> Judg. 5:6

> *Up, up,* O Deborah! *Up, up* and sing it out!
>
> Judg. 5:12

> *The torrent Kishon* swept them away, the onrushing torrent, *the torrent Kishon.*
>
> Judg. 5:21

A third alternative is taking commonly paired items and putting one of them in clause A and the other in clause B:

An *ox* knows its owner, and an *ass* its master's trough.

Isa. 1:2

By day the LORD sends forth His love, and *at night* His song is with me.

Ps. 42:8

Finally, it is not uncommon for clause A to say one thing and clause B to say something similar:

Let me exalt You, O God my king, and let me bless Your name forever and ever.

Ps. 145:1

Like repetition or commonly paired terms, such paralleling serves to cement the connection between A and B, identifying B as A's continuation rather than a new beginning.

Just because they contain parallel actions or ideas, however, does not mean that A and B are saying the same thing. Usually B adds something quite new; sometimes, in fact, the whole point seems to be that clause B tops clause A and goes it one better. (In the last example, exalting God and blessing His name are fairly similar, but clause B has added something new, the element "forever and ever," which extends and intensifies what was said in A.)

But having clause B go beyond A inevitably creates a potential ambiguity. What does the line as a whole now mean? Is B intended simply to supplement A (that is, "Let me exalt You, O God my king, and *in addition to that,* let me bless Your name forever and ever")? Or are they to be mentally recombined into one assertion (that is, "Let me both exalt You and bless Your name forever and ever, O God my king")? Or is the apparent distinction between A and B merely what English stylists used to call "elegant variation"—that is, it makes no real difference whether either or both are true ("Let me exalt You and/or bless Your name—*it really doesn't matter which*")? Or is B actually intended to correct or replace A (that is, "Let me exalt You, O God my king—*no, that isn't enough; instead,* let me bless Your name forever and ever")? This last possibility may seem a bit stretched for Ps. 145:1, but it actually occurs a great deal in biblical poetry. This is especially true when numbers are involved:

Three things are too wondrous for me, and four I do not know . . .

Prov. 30:18

For three things the earth groans, and for four it cannot endure . . .

Prov. 30:21

In both these cases, the "four" in B is actually intended to cancel out the "three" in A. (We know this because in each case the text goes on to list four things, not seven.) We might thus reword each as "three, nay four," or "three, and as a matter of fact, four."

The "replacement" option may be clear in these cases involving numbers, but in other lines one cannot say for sure if the writer meant to assert that both A and B are separately true, or that A and B are to be mentally recombined into a single assertion, or that B is intended to replace A, or that the difference between them is insignificant. Thus, an ancient Canaanite poet once wrote:

My house I built of silver, my mansion of gold.

CTA 4 VI 36–38

Did he mean: "I built my house out of silver, and then I built a separate building (my mansion) out of gold"? Probably not; in this case, the separate-and-simultaneously-true option is unlikely. But any of the other three is indeed possible: "I built my house/mansion out of silver *and* gold" or "I built my house/mansion out of silver—as a matter of fact, *not* silver but gold" or "I built my house/mansion out of precious metal, silver or gold, it doesn't matter." Usually one can tell from the context, but often, as in this case, one cannot quite be sure.

So what did Jael do to Sisera? The song says:

She put her hand to the tent peg, [and] her right hand to a workman's mallet.

Judg. 5:26

But this line is actually much more ambiguous in Hebrew than it is in English. The word translated above (by the NRSV) as "tent peg" can certainly mean that, but it can also designate a digging tool (Deut. 23:13) and perhaps other things. "Stick" would probably be a better translation (because it is less specific). The phrase translated "workman's mallet" is likewise overly specific in English. The "workman" part is pretty clear, but the word rendered as "mallet" probably only means something like "club" or "smasher." In other words: "She put her hand to a stick, [and] her right hand to a workman's club." In such a version, it is altogether unclear whether this poetic line is describing two separate actions—first she took A, then she took B—or simply describing the same action via the "replacement" strategy: she grabbed an

A; as a matter of fact, not an A but a B (or even, possibly, stick or club, it doesn't really matter).

What follows, however, makes it pretty clear that Jael picked up only one implement.[4] The reason is that, as we have seen, Sisera is standing when Jael strikes him—he had to be if he subsequently fell at her feet. It is very difficult to imagine her holding a tent peg in one hand and a mallet in the other, approaching the standing Sisera, and saying, "Hold still a minute while I line this up with your temple." Much more imaginable is that Jael, having grabbed an appropriate implement—a stick, nay, a mighty club—then approached the drinking Sisera and, whirling around with all her might, smashed him with it on the side of his head. That, it seems likely, is what the song was trying to describe.

Years, perhaps centuries, later, songs that tell stories were no longer in fashion; their words now had to be "translated" into continuous, historical-sounding prose narratives. Whoever sought to render Sisera's death in prose read the same crucial line differently. "She put her hand to a stick, [and] her right hand to a workman's club" seemed to him to refer to two different implements, so that is how he reworded it in prose: "a tent-peg . . . and a hammer" (Judg. 4:21). Perhaps, indeed, he liked the overall picture of a more ladylike Jael, who maternally tucks Sisera into bed, gives him some warm milk, and waits for him to doze off—rather than confronting him head-to-head. So the prose writer created these other elements: there is no coverlet in the song, Sisera is standing, and so she of course does not drive a tent peg through his head and *into the ground,* as the prose narrative says.

If, for modern scholars, this process of rendering story poems into prose occurred in the case of the Song of Deborah and the Song of the Sea, then perhaps it happened as well for other prose narratives in the Bible, narratives whose original song versions have been lost. That, scholars say, would explain why the southern stories of the J source and the northern ones of E had so much material in common—they independently put into prose a collection of narrative traditions that had once been transmitted in hymns or story poems. If so, this might suggest that the *raw material* used by the J and E sources were considerably older than J and E themselves, perhaps going back to the time of King David or even earlier.

Samson

Perhaps the most unforgettable of all of the judges is Samson. His parents, as we have seen earlier (chapter 7), had long been childless—until the visit of a certain angel (Judges 13). The angel announced that they would at last have a child and instructed the future mother to abstain from wine and strong drink during her pregnancy and to follow other rules, since her son was destined to be "a nazirite to God from birth" (Judg. 13:5). (A nazirite was a kind of Israelite ascetic. Elsewhere, nazirites took their vow themselves, as adults; their self-affliction included not consuming wine or other grape products and not cutting their hair; see Num. 6:1–21.) After Samson was born, he—like any nazirite—was also forbidden to cut his hair, indeed, to allow any razor ever to come in contact with his head (Judg. 13:5).

Samson observed these requirements, and he grew into an extraordinary adult, a man of superhuman strength and courage. He also led an active social life. (The anti–Vietnam War slogan of the 1960s, "Make love, not war," would have quite puzzled Samson, who seems to have gone at both activities with equal zeal.) Chapter 14 of Judges finds him smitten with a young woman from the enemy side, the Philistines. His parents naturally objected to the union, but Samson insisted: "Get her for me, because she pleases me" (Judg. 14:3). On their way down to Timna, where she lived, Samson and his parents suddenly encountered a roaring lion. The "spirit of the LORD" came mightily over Samson, and he tore the lion apart with his bare hands. Later, during the wedding feast, he killed thirty men from Ashkelon in order to use their clothing to pay off a bet. After that, he set fire to the Philistines' fields in an act of revenge, and then killed a thousand more Philistines when they tried to capture him. One night, after consorting with a prostitute in Philistine Gaza, he pulled up the city gates with his bare hands and dragged them all the way to Hebron (forty miles, as the crow flies). Decidedly, here was a divine servant of a kind rarely seen.

"You Can Tell the Truth When You Hear It"

At this point in his life, however, Samson met his match: he fell in love with the ravishing Delilah. As soon as they learned of her involvement with Samson, the Philistines approached Delilah with an offer: if you can get Samson to reveal the source of his strength and how he can be overcome, we will give you eleven hundred pieces of silver. Delilah agreed.

> So Delilah said to Samson, "Tell me, what makes you so strong? And what would you have to be tied up with so that someone could overcome you?" Samson said to her, "If they were to tie me with seven fresh tendons that had not been dried, then I would become as weak as an ordinary person." So the Philistine chiefs brought her seven fresh tendons that had not been dried, and she tied him with them while an ambush was waiting in her room. Then she called out to him, "Samson, the Philistines are after you!" But he snapped the tendons as a strand of fiber snaps when it touches the fire. So the secret of his strength remained unknown.
>
> Judg. 16:6–9

Delilah did not give up. In fact, surprisingly, she acted as if *she* were the injured party: "You deceived me! You lied to me! Now come on—tell me what you have to be tied up with" (Judg. 16:10). Samson gave her another, somewhat similar answer (new ropes, never used) and the same thing happened: the Philistines entered and he snapped the ropes with ease. She tried a third time, and his answer this time was a little different: "If you weave the seven locks of my head with the web and make it tight with the pin, then I shall become as weak as an ordinary person." So Delilah tried a third time, but once again Samson escaped harm.

Now Delilah was truly upset. "How can you say you love me," she asked, "when you do not confide in me? That makes three times that you have deceived me and have not told me what makes you so strong."

> Finally, after she had nagged him day after day and pestered him, he was tired to death. So he confided the whole thing to her and said to her, "A razor has never come upon my head; for I have been a nazirite to God from my mother's womb. If my head were ever shaved, then my strength would leave me; I would become as weak as an ordinary person." When Delilah realized that he had confided everything to her, she sent a message to the Philistine chiefs, saying, "This time come up; he has confided everything to me."
>
> Judg. 16:16–18

The end was inevitable. Once Samson's hair was snipped, all his strength disappeared. The Philistines captured him with ease and, having gouged out his eyes for good measure, took him in chains back to Gaza, where he was put to work as a mill slave. But Samson's hair began to grow back, and with it, apparently, some of his old strength. Brought to the temple of Dagon, Samson prayed to God for one last burst of power, and seizing the temple pillars in his arms, he pulled them down on himself and the assembled Philistines, killing more of the enemy in that one blind act than he had killed before in all the days of his strength. Thus ended the life of this toughest of judges.

About all this rabbinic interpreters had one main question. How did Delilah know, after Samson had given her three wrong answers, that he was finally telling the truth? The text is quite clear: "Delilah *realized* that he had confided everything to her," it says, and she was so sure that this time she knew his secret that she at once sent a message to that effect to the Philistines. But how did she know for sure? The Talmud's answer (b. *Sota* 9b) is a curt three words: *nikkarin dibrei emet,* or in a contemporary idiom: "You can tell the truth when you hear it."

Who Were the Philistines?

The Bible reports that five cities in the region of Israel belonged to the Philistines: Gaza, Ashkelon, Ashdod, Ekron, and Gath. (The first three are ports on the Mediterranean coast, the other two slightly inland.) This coastal constellation made them a mighty power in biblical times. For a while, they managed to guard jealously the secret of forging and sharpening iron (1 Sam. 13:19–21), which gave them a profound strategic advantage;[5] at times their power stretched far from the coast into the hill country of the Israelite tribes. But who exactly *were* the Philistines? Modern scholars know that they were not originally a Semitic people. They seem to have arrived in Canaan from somewhere in the Aegean region. Their ultimate origin may have been as far north as the southern Balkans, or else in the Greek islands, or nearby Crete or Cyprus. It is also possible that they came from Anatolia (what is today Turkey, north of Syria). Wherever they came from, however, to understand the Philistines it is necessary to speak of another group of whom they were apparently a part, the Sea Peoples.[6]

The term "Sea Peoples" refers to different seafaring nations who tried to attack the Egyptian coast during the reigns of Merenptah and his successor, Rameses III—that is, at the end of the thirteenth and start of the twelfth centuries BCE. The Egyptian texts name nine different peoples, one of whom, represented as P-r-š-t-w, seems to be the same name as "Philistine." Hittite records, from the area of modern Turkey, as well as the El Amarna letters, also mention some of these peoples. The Egyptians succeeded in holding off the attack on their own shores, but they were less successful in defending the shoreline of the eastern Mediterranean. The Sea Peoples (or some subdivision thereof) may have worked their way overland down the coast of Canaan and/or arrived by sea; in addition to the Philistine cities mentioned, other Sea Peoples appear to have established settlements at Joppa (today's Yafo), Dor, and other sites. One witness thereto is the temple excavated at Tel Qasile near Joppa, built in the style of a typical Mycenean temple, which is radically different from that of a Canaanite temple.[7] Interestingly, Greek mythology tells that the heroic Perseus married Andromeda, daughter of the king of Joppa, after saving her from being eaten by a sea monster. The two stayed for a time in Joppa before moving on. The ancient geographer Strabo makes cautious mention of this myth in his brief survey of the area:

> Then [comes] Joppa, where the coastline of Egypt—which at first stretches towards the east—makes a remarkable bend towards the north. In this place, according to some writers, Andromeda was exposed to the sea monster. It is sufficiently elevated, it is said, to command a view of Jerusalem,

the capital of the Jews, who, when they descended to the sea, used this place
as a naval arsenal.

                                        Strabo, *Geography* 16:2.28

Perhaps, scholars say, this myth hides a faded historical memory of Aegean
interlopers who came to settle at Joppa and mixed with the locals.

If no one is exactly sure of the Philistines' ultimate origin or of the route
that they followed to Canaan, one thing is clear: in terms of their material culture they were quite similar to the Greeks, at least for a while. Their mono-
chrome pottery is like that of Greece and unlike Canaanite pottery. With
time, they settled in and adopted many elements of Canaanite civilization,
although, as we shall see, they were still perceived as foreigners in King
David's time—and his sworn enemy once his throne was established.

In the light of the Philistines' apparent Aegean connection, the story of
Samson takes on a somewhat different look for modern scholars. Examined
in his broad perspective, Samson emerges as the only biblical hero who even
remotely resembles the heroes of Greek myths. It is not only that he has the
superhuman strength of the Greek Heracles (Hercules), and the impetuous-
ness and fits of anger that go with it. In addition to this, scholars point out,
he is truly the only biblical hero to suffer from "woman trouble." [8] Elsewhere
in the Bible, what goes on between men and women is basically nobody's
business but theirs. There really are no biblical love stories. Rebekah, the
Bible reports, replaced Isaac's *mother* in his affections (Gen. 24:67)—not
exactly the stuff of high romance. Jacob falls in love with the beautiful
Rachel in a single verse (Gen. 29:20). The Hebrew Bible features no protracted courtships, no face that launched a thousand ships, no men whose
love for fair maidens leads them to deeds of derring-do or dastardly disgrace[9]—except Samson. Samson gets entangled with—if the archaeologists
are to be believed—Aegean women, not once, in fact, but three times (his
Philistine wife from Timna, a prostitute from Philistine Gaza, and Delilah,
ally of the Philistines and probably, though not explicitly, a Philistine herself).

And these women are all quite similar—so beautiful, so treacherous!
Samson's first wife coaxes and wheedles and weeps to get Samson to reveal
the answer to a riddle—and then betrays the secret to her townsmen (Judg.
14:15–18). That's exactly what Delilah does too—coaxes and wheedles him
almost to death (Judg. 16:16), then turns the information over to the enemy.
Such females are not found elsewhere in the Bible—and certainly not in the
book of Judges. Scholars also point out that Samson himself does not really
fit with the other leaders of the book of Judges. He does not *lead* anyone; no
crisis brings him to prominence, and he does not save any tribe of Israel from
its enemies.[10] The part of his saga that does sound authentically Israelite—his
mother's infertility and the subsequent visit of an angel (Judges 13)—is completely separate from the story of Samson himself (Judges 14–16); the

Deuteronomistic historian has apparently not even gone to the trouble of composing a transitional sentence to bridge the gap between these two. This editorial shrug may offer proof of the hero story's distinct origins, scholars say. Even Samson's name sounds fishy, as if it were derived from the word for "sun"—a deity worshiped by other peoples, but not, as far as the Deuteronomistic historian is concerned, Israel.[11]

Some scholars, therefore, see Samson's saga as a typical "border story," born on the Philistine side but then imported to the neighboring Israelite tribe of Dan (Samson's tribe).[12] Some of the details remained the same, scholars say, but the originally Aegean protagonist was now an Israelite superhero who, for some reason, has a fatal attraction to Philistine females. One might look back at the question that Samson's parents asked when he first announced to them that he wanted to marry a Philistine woman: "Is there not a woman among your kin, or among all our people, that you must go to take a wife from the uncircumcised Philistines?" (Judg. 14:3). The real answer, scholars suspect, is that Samson himself—culturally if not genetically—was born from the same stock.

The Book of Ruth

Apart from leaders like Deborah and Gideon and Samson, there is another important figure associated with the period of the book of Judges, Ruth. She is said to have lived "in the time when the chiefs/judges (*shofetim*) were ruling" (Ruth 1:1); for that reason, the book of Ruth is located in Christian Bibles just after the book of Judges. (In Jewish Bibles it is placed toward the end, after the Torah and the prophetic books.)

The book of Ruth is a pastoral story, set at the time of the spring grain harvest. Its heroes are two women, Naomi and her Moabite daughter-in-law, Ruth. Some years earlier, Naomi had left Bethlehem to settle in Moab with her two sons. Both then took Moabite brides. But when Naomi's husband and the two sons suddenly die, she is left with no means of support and so resolves to return to Bethlehem. "Stay here with your parents," she advises her widowed daughters-in-law—after all, what hope can Naomi offer of finding new husbands for these Moabite women in Bethlehem? But Ruth refuses to abandon her mother-in-law: "Wherever you go, I will go, and wherever you stay, I will stay: your people will be my people, and your God will be my God." So Ruth and Naomi travel back from Moab to Bethlehem together.

When they arrive, Bethlehem is in the midst of the busy harvest—and this ultimately will cause Ruth to meet Boaz, a relative of Naomi's and one of Bethlehem's leading citizens. While Boaz is a wealthy householder, Ruth now finds herself at the other end of the social scale—she joins in with the gleaners, paupers who scurry around in back of the harvesters in the hope of picking up a stray stalk or two of grain. Boaz notices her and, having heard of her noble behavior with Naomi, makes sure she gets ample grain. One thing leads to another, and it is not long before she finds herself, at midnight, next to Boaz, who has fallen asleep on the threshing floor. The scene is handled with great delicacy—and indeed, with a touch of humor:

> After Boaz had eaten and drunk and was in a merry mood, he went to lie down next to a pile of grain. Then she entered discreetly and, lifting the cover from his feet, lay down. In the middle of the night the man gave a start and jumped back—a woman was lying at his feet! "Who are you?" he said. She answered, "I am your handmaiden Ruth. Spread your cloak over your handmaiden, for you have the right to reclaim me."* He said, "May you be blessed by the LORD, my daughter; this latest instance of your loyalty is even better than the first; you have not gone after young men, whether poor or rich. And now, my daughter, do not be afraid, I will do for you all that you ask, for all the assembly of my people know that you are a worthy woman."
>
> Ruth 3:7–11

What should have been a scene of great tenderness gets off to a bad start, with the old man suddenly jumping up in panic at finding a young woman in his bed. But Boaz recovers his composure and, in his own, highly elevated (if not pompous) idiom, agrees to take her on as his wife—indeed, he goes on to tell her to stay the rest of the night, which Ruth does (being careful to leave before daylight to avoid a scandal). Then, having taken care of the legal requirements (4:1–12), Boaz and Ruth are duly married. The story ends with a genealogy: Ruth and Boaz have a son, Obed, whose son Jesse is none other than the father of David, king of Israel.

The story of Ruth has been cherished by Christians and Jews alike. For the latter it has been important principally because Ruth is a model of the ideal convert. Her words to Naomi, "Your God will be my God," were taken as the affirmation of one who has understood the truth of Israel's faith and embraced it as her own. To this day, it is customary for women converts to Judaism to adopt "Ruth" as their new name.[13] The story did pose one exegetical difficulty for ancient interpreters. A certain law in Deuteronomy had been quite specific: "No Ammonite or Moabite shall enter into the congregation of the LORD—not even in the tenth generation, they shall not enter into the congregation of the LORD" (Deut. 23:4). How then could the Moabite Ruth have been accepted as Boaz's bride? The answer exegetes gave depended on a tech-

---

* "Spread your cloak" is a bit of a pun, since it also means "protect me." As a relative of Naomi's, Boaz has the right to "redeem" or reclaim Ruth and take her as his wife.

nicality: the word "Moabite" in this verse is in the masculine form, hence, "A Moabite [is forbidden], but not a Moabitess" (b. *Yebamot* 69a).

Modern scholarship has not always been kind to the book of Ruth. While the text claims to record events from the time "when the chiefs [*or* judges] were ruling," many scholars believe the book was written long, long after the time of the book of Judges. Its unconscious use of Aramaisms and, on the other hand, its deliberate effort (not always successful) to have the characters speak in highly inflated, ancient-sounding language point to a late date, they say—probably to the period after the Babylonian exile. That would also explain why the redemption ceremony that precedes the marriage is described as "the custom in former times in Israel" (4:7)—such wording indicates the narrator's own chronological remove from the time of the story.

The story itself has a fablelike quality. Naomi's two sons, who die almost as soon as they are introduced, have emblematic names: Mahlon means something like "Sickling," and Chilion "Bound-to-Go." It seems doubtful that either was ever anyone's real name. As for Ruth's profession of faith, "Your God will be my God," this seems to modern scholars less the words of a convert (actually, there is no evidence of the existence of such a concept in biblical times) than a simple statement of Ruth's desire to return with Naomi to Judah and, in the process, to take on a fully Judahite identity.

Why was the story written? The key, scholars say, seems to be the genealogy at the end. As noted earlier, intermarriage was a very sensitive subject in the postexilic period: Ezra took a strong stand against it, ordering the men of Judah to divorce their non-Judahite wives. Now here comes a story in which an upstanding citizen, Boaz, not only marries a non-Judahite, but a Moabite—the sort of marriage partner explicitly forbidden by Deut. 23:4. Not only did such a marriage take place, the story affirms, but Ruth turns out to be none other than the great-grandmother of David, founder of the royal dynasty and, hence, possessor of the bluest blood of all of Israel's bluebloods! To assert such a thing in postexilic Judah would have been as shocking as saying today that a member of Britain's royal family actually has a goodly portion of Pakistani or Indian (or Jewish) blood in his or her veins. Seen in this light, the polemical purpose of the story would appear unmistakable: mixed marriages, it says, are perfectly acceptable. No wonder, scholars assert, that the author went to the trouble of trying to get his characters to speak in archaic-sounding Hebrew and having them greet each other with such pious exchanges as "The LORD be with you," followed by "May the LORD bless you" (2:4). It was crucial to give readers the impression that all this took place long, long ago (thus "grandfathering" intermarriage to the time of David) and among people whose devotion to God was beyond question.

Women in the Book of Judges

The biblical account of the period of the Judges contains some striking female figures, but considered together, they present a conflicting picture of women's lives.[14] On the one hand are the portraits of Deborah and Jael, which suggest that women may have played an active leadership role in ancient Israel—these two, in any case, are strong, take-charge heroes. Ruth and Naomi are closer to traditional women's roles; indeed, the way in which they maneuver Boaz comes close to suggesting some of the usual clichés about female guile; but in the end we are made to feel that they are quite admirable people, and the attention lavished on their thoughts and feelings in the narrative bespeaks an evident sympathy and respect for them as women. On the other hand, there is Delilah, a temptress straight out of Hollywood B-movies, who nags and wheedles and lies unashamedly until she finally succeeds in betraying her man. Finally, there are female victims. The anonymous daughter of Jephthah the Gileadite ends up being sacrificed like a barnyard animal because of a rash vow that her father had made on the eve of an important battle (Judg. 11:29–40). At least Jephthah expresses some regret, tearing his clothes because "I cannot take back my vow" (11:35), but the text hardly censures him for having brought about his daughter's demise. Wasn't her death itself important? And as will be seen presently, the book of Judges concludes with the story of a brutal rape, in which the most horrifying element is that the narrative does not even afford the victim a voice: she says not one word. She seems to be more of a prop, or a casus belli, than a real person. So what *were* women in biblical times—powerful leaders; or men's equal but quite opposite halves; or perfidious temptresses, morally and in all other ways men's inferiors; or simply less important than men, often the victims, sometimes mourned, sometimes virtual nonentities?

These questions became particularly important with the rise of feminism in the latter part of the twentieth century.[15] Biblical scholars began to reexamine some of the most basic issues connected with women, as well as the effect that Scripture may have played in determining women's social roles in Western society. Many feminist scholars highlighted the inferior status of women in biblical laws: most obviously, women were given *to men* in marriage in exchange for a bride price; they did not normally inherit property or manage their own affairs (for the daughters of Zelophehad, see Num. 27:8–11; 36:1–11); their vows to God could be annulled by their husbands or fathers (Num. 30:1–15). Women could not serve as priests; only men were required to carry out the pilgrimages associated with the three festivals (Exod. 23:17; 34:23; Deut. 16:16). These and similar practices certainly bespeak a fundamental presumption of inequality, one that carried over into later times.[16]

Feminists also pointed to the extraordinary number of anonymous female figures as symptomatic. We know the names of Noah and Lot and Manoah, but not those of their wives (although the wives of the latter two certainly played important roles).[17] The story of the rape of Dinah goes on in great detail about the revenge exacted by her brothers, but of Dinah's fate we hear not a word. Such omissions have seemed to many scholars to betray an obvious undervaluing of women that is woven into the very fabric of biblical narrative. Indeed, that supernal moment of divine revelation at Mount Sinai is preceded by Moses' blunt instructions: "And he [Moses] said to the people, 'Prepare for the third day [when God will appear to you]: do not go near a woman' " (Exod. 19:15). Certainly, "Let men and women stay separated for three days" (apparently, for reasons of ritual purity) might have had a more even-handed sound, but "And he said *to the people*" grated as much on feminist ears: don't you mean *half the people*?[18] And what about poor Eve, to whom God says, "Your desire shall be for your husband, and he shall rule over you"? Did not this officialize women's inferiority sub specie aeternitatis, giving it nothing less than God's own seal of approval?

Considering such matters, many feminist critics have responded by denouncing what they see as the Bible's dyed-in-the-wool sexism, unremitting from beginning to end.[19] Indeed, some have gone so far as to suggest that biblical monotheism is itself a form of sexism on high, in that it essentially replaced the earlier constellation of gods *and goddesses* with a single, all-powerful, and unmistakably masculine deity—one who, whatever the extra-biblical evidence, is presented in the Bible as not even having a divine consort beside Him.[20] The society out of which such a view of things could have emerged, such scholars say, must have been one that, by nature, relegated women to second-class status, a hypothesis only confirmed by biblical laws and biblical narrative. But they point out that things may not have always been thus. Going back as far as the Old Stone Age (30,000 BCE!), ample evidence has been found for the worship of a Great Mother goddess, whose naked, big-breasted, and broad-hipped representations have turned up at numerous sites in the ancient Near East. In Canaan in particular, archaeologists have found many statuettes from the Middle Bronze Age IIB (ca. 1800–1550 BCE) of a

> Naked Goddess, represented as Mistress of the Plants . . . The goddess also appeared as Mistress of the Animals. Goddesses are especially dominant. Their physical gender characteristics are often given special emphasis.[21]

The prominence of such a deity in the religious sphere has suggested to some scholars a parallel female prominence in everyday life; women, they argue, must have once exercised a highly diverse and altogether "primary" role in the economic and physical survival of primitive, agricultural villages in ancient Palestine.[22]

Why did things ever change? Perhaps, it is argued, a combination of plagues, wars, and famines in the late Bronze Age caused women's previously diverse social roles to become focused almost exclusively on childbearing and child rearing; rebuilding the population was a vital concern. Later, this societal focus became ingrained and institutionalized, even after it was no longer so vital.[23] Alternatively, the organizational change from a decentralized village economy to a larger-scale national or regional economy "created hierarchical relationships and robbed females of their customary equality and interdependence with men."[24] However it came about, such scholars believe, women's subordination persisted through the rest of the biblical period and has continued from then into modern times.

If so, then dynamic female leaders like Moses' sister, Miriam, along with Deborah and Jael and the prophet Hulda, may represent the last gasp of an ancient gender equality, "dynamic remnants" of a time when women were an integral part of the power structure.[25] Of course, female dynamism and gender equality would not have disappeared with a snap of the fingers; indeed, some New Testament scholars see the reflection of these trends carrying on into the period of Jesus and the early church, as evidenced in Jesus' nonpatriarchal relations with Mary Magdalene and other female figures, as well as in ancient synagogue inscriptions and other material finds that attest to the early prominence of women in the religious establishment.[26] Gnostic Christianity notably celebrated the female. But such instances of gender equality were later reversed by the benighted forces of patriarchy, which also sought to destroy any traces of it in the church's canonical literature.

This is a multifaceted and convoluted topic, certainly not one that can be discussed meaningfully in a few paragraphs. It should be stated, however, that, precisely because of feminism's centrality in the latter part of the twentieth century, biblical scholars have sometimes tended to the extremes of apologetics or denunciation. Often, neither seems appropriate. For example, there seems little likelihood that the biblical laws reflecting women's socially inferior status were a relatively new, or even particularly Israelite, development: as we have seen, they are paralleled by Mesopotamian legal codes going back to the third millennium BCE. The social roles played by women in biblical times are altogether comparable to those found in many traditional societies all across the globe; to claim that they came about by some social cataclysm unique to biblical Israel is wishful thinking. Many societies have worshiped a Great Mother goddess; it seems risky to jump from this religious way of conceptualizing fertility to any conclusions about social organization or gender-determined roles. As for the God of Israel's masculinity, a number of feminist scholars have pointed to biblical passages in which God is portrayed in decidedly feminine terms. One passage entertains the hypothesis that God might have "given birth" to Israel (Num. 11:12); others make Him metaphorically Israel's mother:

> Could a woman forget her own baby? Could she disown the child of her
>   womb?
> Even if she could, I will not forget you . . .
> As a mother comforts her child, so I will comfort you;
> you shall be comforted in Jerusalem.
>
> Isa. 49:11; 66:13

God may often be presented in masculine terms, but passages such as these seem to imply that such an assignment of gender characteristics sometimes has a highly metaphorical quality, one that can, therefore, be contradicted by metaphors from the opposite gender.

It is true that Deborah displays uncommon courage in leading the forces of Barak against Sisera; she *is* a hero. Yet the same biblical text that presents her as such has her remark to Barak, "There will be no glory for you in the course that you are following, since now the LORD will be handing over Sisera to a woman" (Judg. 4:8). Apparently, everyone knew that being defeated or killed by a woman was an ignominious death.[27] The terms in which Jael is praised, "most blessed of women in tents,"* are revealing; in ordinary village life, women rarely strayed far from home unaccompanied. The proud boast of a certain Cilician king of the eighth century BCE was that "in my days, a woman might go alone [in 'dangerous' places] with her spindles, thanks to Baal and the gods," that is, she could actually walk around anywhere in broad daylight unescorted without having to worry about being raped or kidnapped or killed.[28] The perils facing a lone woman outside her village are attested not only in Cilicia but in biblical Israel. According to biblical law, if a woman claimed to have been raped within the confines of her town, both she and the rapist were to be killed, because if she had in fact "cried out" at any point, surely someone in that densely inhabited space would have heard her. But if, on the contrary, she claimed that the rape took place beyond the confines of the village, "in the field," then the man alone was to be killed (Deut. 22:23–24). Quite simply, outside the village was a dangerous place for women.

A number of biblical narratives seem to highlight this vulnerability of women—"texts of terror" they are called by the pioneering feminist scholar Phyllis Trible. The biblical accounts of Abraham's expulsion of Hagar, Amnon's rape of Tamar, the gang rape at Gibeah, and Jephthah's sacrifice of

---

* Some translations of this verse read, "*more* blessed than women in tents." But this apparent comparative is (as often in Hebrew) actually a superlative (cf. Deut. 33:24—the same grammatical construction—translated as "Most blessed of sons be Asher"). The point is certainly not to imply that Jael is something other than a "woman in tents," since in the story that is clearly what she is.

his daughter all turn on the relative helplessness of females in biblical society. What is one to learn from these sad episodes? Trible writes:

> Misogyny belongs to every age, including our own. Violence and vengeance are not just characteristics of a distant, pre-Christian past; they infect the community of the elect to this day. Woman as object is still captured, betrayed, raped, tortured, murdered, dismembered, and scattered. To take to heart this ancient story, then, is to confess its present reality . . . Beyond confession, we must take counsel to say, "Never again." Yet this counsel is itself ineffectual unless we direct our hearts to that most uncompromising of all biblical commands, speaking the words not to others but to ourselves: Repent. Repent.[29]

She is right, of course, and few readers familiar with the day-to-day reality of violence against women can remain unmoved by her words. Yet this passage, and indeed much of feminist scholarship of the Bible, seems to me noteworthy for an entirely unrelated reason. One can hear in it loud and clear the same assumptions first adopted by the Bible's ancient interpreters. That is: the Bible is addressed to us today; it contains lessons for us to apply in our own lives ("Misogyny belongs to every age, including our own"). In regard to other parts of the Bible, modern scholars—and Trible is certainly that—are generally rather skeptical about such a stance (save perhaps within the creative context of a Sunday sermon). Truthfully, what "lessons" could the etiological tales of Cain and Abel or Jacob and Esau hold for such scholars? Indeed, what sense do these narratives make outside of their original historical context? Isn't that why so much of modern scholarship is devoted to reconstructing the historical reality of biblical Israel, the better to understand the *original* meaning of this or that biblical law or narrative or prophetic speech—before people started reading them on the basis of the Four Assumptions? Yet this stance is not maintained with utter consistency: nowadays certain elements in the Bible—particularly things having to do with woman's unequal legal or social status, or violence against women—cannot be distanced the way other things can, with a "That was then, this is now." They must, in one way or another, be presented as containing a message (positive or negative) for us today, hence: "Repent. Repent." (Surely no modern scholar would claim that such is the *original meaning* of these narratives!)

Seen in this light, a good bit of feminist biblical scholarship does not appear to be very different from the activity of the Bible's ancient interpreters. In both cases, the aim is to get the biblical text to contain a lesson for us, and that lesson must fit with the interpreter's own beliefs and practices. Often, the only way to accomplish this is by claiming that, although the text seems to be saying X (women were of unequal status, exploited and even abused; that's just the way it was, no value judgment intended), what it really means is Y (Repent. Repent). Only in such a way can the bumps in Scripture be smoothed away, allowing it to continue to be, at least in some sense, a book with a message for today.

"In the Mountains, There You Feel Free"

The oft-repeated theme of the book of Judges is that "there was no king in Israel" (Judg. 17:6; 18:1; 19:1; 21:25). This was, from that book's standpoint, unequivocally a bad thing: the absence of a king meant that there was no social order, and people could just go around doing whatever they saw fit. For modern scholars, this assertion betrays a certain viewpoint, that of the Deuteronomistic historian. There *ought* to have been a king in Israel, this author believed; after all, there was one at the time that he wrote, and he must have thought that kingship was the ideal form of governance, the form that God eventually designated for Israel for all times (2 Sam. 7:13). In fact, scholars believe that such thoughts are what led the Deuteronomistic historian to compile the stories of the various judges in this book and present them in sequence: they provided at least something close to kingship.[30] So, scouring various oral traditions and, perhaps, some written records, this historian came up with a series of ad hoc leaders, a broken chain of inspired men and women who could at least be said to have provided some sort of divinely chosen leadership now and again. But even the picture of this broken chain, most scholars say, is a distortion. The reality is that there was no king in Israel because there was no Israel; in fact, at an early enough period, there was not even any recognition among the disparate tribes that they might someday come together to form a unified nation.

Part of the reason for this has to do with the topography of the land of Israel. According to archaeologists, what was later to become the distinct "Israel group" in Canaan is first attested in little, undefended settlements on the mountaintops of the central highlands. There is a reason why they were undefended: conquerors are generally not interested in mountaintop settlements. In terms of real estate, mountaintops are not nearly as valuable as the fruited plain below. On the fruited plain, grain can be grown in broad, swaying fields; a little brook or mighty stream, fed with water that flows down from the mountains, provides sustenance for the crops as well as drinking water for animals and people. To capture that land, with its relatively dense population and its other riches, is to win a prize. By contrast, the sloping, rocky terrain of the mountains is not particularly easy to farm and is not thickly settled. Even when—as happened in this period in Canaan—the technology of terraced farming is invented, it is no economic match for the agricultural potential of the land below. The fruited plain thrives; the mountaintop survives.

If mountaintops are poorer, they are also more difficult to subdue. Any conqueror will have, quite literally, an uphill battle if he tries to take possession of a mountain; the mountain dwellers will have the advantage of shooting down on the attackers, whether with rifles or bow and arrow or spears or simply rocks. If the conqueror persists and does get to the top, slaughtering everyone he encounters, what will he have accomplished? He is now the proud owner of some very second-rate real estate. (The only thing a high perch can offer him—and this is true of only some mountaintops—is strategic domination of a highway or other sensitive point below.) So, as a rule, the conqueror leaves the mountain dwellers alone. This is especially true when a sizeable group of mountains is involved. If he and his troops could conquer the first and then somehow fly from that mountaintop to the next, then they might be able to subdue the whole range in one movement; but they cannot. All they can do is leave some men on the first conquered mountain to secure it, and then walk all the way down again and start up the next mountain. Even marching *through* a mountain range to the other side is a potentially dangerous maneuver, since the mountain dwellers may come swooping down at any time.

It is for all these reasons that conquerors notoriously leave mountain people alone. If you hold a relief map of the world in your hands, chances are that one or another of the little elevated bumps your fingers touch will be found to be the home of some doughty little mountain people utterly disconnected from the valley dwellers below—and often the place will prove to be one of the world's "trouble spots." In the Pyrenees (between Spain and France), for example, are the Basques, who speak a language totally unrelated to any other known language in the world. This fact alone should say something about the extent of their involvement with the people down below! Where they came from no one knows, but once settled in those mountains, they pursued a fiercely independent course: conquerors came and went (Visigoths, Romans, Moors, and Christians), the Basques remained unchanged. Even today, many of them refuse to accept Spanish rule—despite the enormous disparity in force between themselves and the Spanish militia. The result has often been violence on a major scale. The next big mountain range eastward, the Alps, is not a trouble spot, but rather one enormous modus vivendi: this cluster of mountains is home to the Swiss, one nation with four official languages and many different, rather doggedly self-governing cantons. The unity of Switzerland is, to put it kindly, more formal than actual. Equally important for our point, however, is Switzerland's lack of integration with the valley nations around it. As of this writing, this mountain stronghold has not displayed the slightest interest in joining the European Union, to which belong all of its neighbors in any direction; while everywhere around it the euro is legal tender, the Swiss franc has so far turned up its nose to this convenient means of exchange and continued to go it alone. This is altogether mountain people behavior. (It may also be no accident that both of the mountain ranges mentioned, the Pyrenees and the Alps, are today home to two notorious tax havens, Andorra and Liechtenstein respectively.) Farther east are the Balkans, where different mountain peoples have been fighting one another since time immemorial; the people in the fruited plain have been by and large unsuccessful at imposing any long-term central government on them. In fact, there are so many different little groups up there that a witty French chef of the eighteenth century began calling his new salad, composed of lots of different types of chopped-up tidbits, a "Macedonia" of fruits or vegetables (*macédoine de fruits/légumes*). Of course, the violence that regularly flares up among those fiercely independent mountain people and their neighbors can be sickeningly brutal. Taking the long view, however, an unwillingness to compromise, or even sometimes to cooperate, seems simply to be part of the mountain heritage. Moving eastward, the mountain Christians in the otherwise Muslim Levant, the Kurds holed up in the peaks of Kurdistan, the bandit chieftains of highland Afghanistan, and so on and so forth all bear witness to a single mentality. The state motto of New Hampshire, "Live free or die," would be more striking if it belonged to Texas or Nebraska; amid the snowy peaks of northern New England, it has a somewhat inevitable quality ("Sure—who cares?").

The central highlands of the land of Israel are not as high as any of these other mountain ranges, but they are high enough, scholars theorize, to have led to a somewhat comparable state of fierce autonomy in the twelfth or eleventh century BCE. The people up in the mountains soon grew used to being left alone (that's why they settled there, according to the various contemporary scenarios outlined earlier); scholars do not imagine that they were particularly enthusiastic about any grand reamalgamation of themselves with the valley dwellers, or even with other mountaintop tribes. True, they had some things in common with one or both groups (language, culture—and perhaps religion); still, was that any reason to make common cause with them and voluntarily submit to the rule of a single king? Kings only took away your wealth in taxes and your children in the military draft or in forced work brigades. Indeed, elsewhere in the ancient Near East, kings were often all-powerful despots. The Egyptian kings were sometimes proclaimed to be incarnations of this or that god; they could do with their subjects whatever they wished.[31] Mesopotamian kings, while not called gods themselves, ruled by the gods' decree; who dare oppose them? In such an atmosphere, kingship was viewed with deep suspicion. Jotham's fable (Judg. 9:7–15)—which tells how the trees seek to name a king and end up with a thornbush as their monarch—captures the mountaintop spirit: only worthless, low, power-hungry scoundrels are interested in ruling.[32]

The Dangers of Disunity

On the other hand, there were times when united action seemed warranted. Even if no conquistador sought to subdue the mountain people, plenty of others seemed bent on taking whatever they could steal; the lower elevations were particularly vulnerable. In His anger against the people during this period, God "gave them over to plunderers who plundered them" (Judg. 2:14). Gideon, it will be recalled, was from the tribe of Manasseh; he was hiding wheat in his winepress when the angel appeared to him. Midianites, Moabites, Ammonites, and Canaanites seem to have taken turns oppressing God's people in the book of Judges (see especially Judg. 6:2–5). Although the battle fought by Barak against Sisera ended in victory, Deborah's song berates those tribes that did not answer the call to arms:

> Among the clans of Reuben, there were great searchings of heart.
> Why did you tarry among the sheepfolds, to hear the piping for the
> flocks?
> Among the clans of Reuben, there were great searchings of heart.
> Gilead stayed beyond the Jordan; and Dan, why did he abide with the
> ships?
> Asher sat still at the coast of the sea, settling down by his landings . . .
> Curse Meroz, says the angel of the LORD, curse bitterly its inhabitants,
> Because they did not come to the aid of the LORD, to the aid of the LORD
> against the mighty.
>
> Judg. 5:15–17, 23

Just as striking as the disunity reflected in this passage is its failure even to mention the southern tribes of Simeon and Judah: apparently, they were not yet even potential allies of the northern tribes!

Nor was the problem limited to military disunity. Even in those fractious times, the absence of any central rule had an impact on everyday life. Henri Frankfort may have exaggerated somewhat in saying that "the ancient Near East considered kingship the very basis of civilization. Only savages could live without a king." [33] Still, even in the mountains, the absence of some commonly agreed, and enforced, code of laws meant that civil order ended at one's own village gate. Beyond the domain of a person's immediate kin lay a frightening no-man's-land. Perhaps the most chilling story in the book of Judges is that of a certain Levite and his concubine. Traveling late in the afternoon, they enter the Benjaminite town of Gibeah in search of shelter for the night. After finding the townspeople remarkably inhospitable, the Levite and his concubine are at last taken in by an old man. But the townsmen, in an episode suspiciously reminiscent of Lot and the Sodomites (Genesis 19), surround the house and demand that the old man surrender his guest "so that we may have intercourse with him" (Judg. 19:22). The host tries to calm the crowd, but they do not listen until the Levite traveler himself offers them his own concubine:

> They wantonly raped her and abused her all through the night until the morning. And as the dawn began to break, they let her go. As morning appeared, the woman came and fell down at the door of the man's house where her master was, until it was light. In the morning her master got up, opened the doors of the house, and when he went out to go on his way, there was his concubine lying at the door of the house, with her hands on the threshold. "Get up," he said to her, "we are going." But there was no answer. Then he put her on the donkey; and the man set out for his home. When he had entered his house, he took a knife and, grasping his concubine, he cut her into twelve pieces, limb by limb, and sent her throughout all the territory of Israel. Then he commanded the men whom he sent, saying, "Thus shall you say to all the Israelites, 'Has such a thing ever happened since the day that the Israelites came up from the land of Egypt until this day? Consider it, take counsel, and speak out.' "
>
> Judg. 19:25–30

The callousness of the narrative is clearly intentional, the better to underscore its message. These are the kind of things that happen when there is no agreed minimum of civility; this is what happens when there is no king.

"The Lord Is King"

Some scholars suggest that such domestic disorder, along with military disunity, created the real-life situation that led to the fiercely independent tribes' adoption of the God YHWH as their "king." [34] He would call them to battle when needed, and He would promulgate a minimal set of laws that would essentially extend kinship obligations to a much broader group; that would keep people in line.

In the biblical account of what happened at Mount Sinai (Exodus 20), God approaches Israel as a great suzerain or emperor, proposing to take Israel on as His "special people" if they keep the conditions of His covenant. The first of those conditions is that they have "no other god before [or beside] Me." [35] From a theological standpoint, such exclusive devotion to one deity while recognizing the efficacy of other gods—monolatry, as this is called—is rather odd. If other gods exist and really do make things happen—the rain, the harvest, reproductive fertility, and so forth—why should Israel be told to (as it were) put all their eggs in one divine basket? [36] Why, for that matter, even conceive of God as some ancient Near Eastern potentate, presenting His covenant stipulations in a form altogether reminiscent of treaties between human suzerains and the vassal states?

The answer may be: this was the only kind of king that the disparate tribes of Israel could put up with at this point. As Gideon is represented as saying: "I will not rule over you, and my son will not rule over you; the LORD will rule over you" (Judg. 8:23). Any ordinary king might actually interfere in the internal affairs of the tribes, supplanting such system of rules and decision making as they had, taxing their material wealth and their manpower; soon, there would be no stopping him. A divine king, one who came to them like a victorious suzerain, was a different matter. Even in those ancient days, proclaiming Him as king might best be understood as establishing a loosely federalist, almost libertarian form of government: "True, we are now all united under one divine ruler, and this binds us together and obligates us, but only in certain minimal ways." Under such a king, tribal rule could remain very much as before. It may therefore be significant that, in keeping with this theory, a certain verse toward the end of the Pentateuch (regarded by scholars as quite ancient) implies that God became Israel's king at Sinai as a result of a collective decision *of the existing tribal leadership*: "There [thus] came to be a [divine] king in Jeshurun [Israel], when the heads of people gathered together, all the chiefs[37] of Israel" (Deut. 33:5).

If, in practical terms, a divine king's powers were somewhat limited, what *could* He do? Scholars have long noted that, in what they believe to be the most ancient stratum of biblical texts, God is consistently presented as a divine warrior:

> The LORD is a warrior, the LORD is His name!
> He has thrown Pharaoh's chariots and army into the deep; the best of his
>   troops drowned in the Red Sea . . .
> Your right hand, O LORD, so glorious in power, Your right hand, O
>   LORD, shatters the enemy.
>
> Exod. 15:3–6

> There is none like the God of Jeshurun, riding the heavens to save you, and
> who triumphs on high.
>
> Deut. 33:26

> LORD, when You went out from Seir, when You marched from the fields
>   of Edom,
> The earth trembled, and even the heavens poured forth, yes, the clouds
>   poured out water . . .
> The stars fought from heaven, from their courses they fought against
>   Sisera . . .

Curse Meroz, says the angel of the LORD, curse bitterly its inhabitants,
Because they did not come to the aid of the LORD, to the aid of the LORD
    against the mighty.
Judg. 5:4, 20, 23

When You drive Your horses, Your chariots to victory,
You wield Your naked bow . . .
Sun and moon stand still on high as Your arrows fly by in a flash, in the
    brightness of Your lightning spears.
You march across earth in anger, in fury You crush the nations;
You have gone out to save Your people, to save Your anointed one.
Hab. 3:11–13

O God, when You went at the head of Your army,[38] when You marched
    through the desert,
the earth trembled, the heavens dripped rain,
for fear of[39] the One from Sinai, by God, the God of Israel.
Ps. 68:8–9 (7–8)

It may be no accident, scholars say, that God is depicted as a warrior in these ancient texts.[40] This was His nature as a deity, and it was thus primarily in military matters that His kingship, such as it was, expressed itself. In the book of Judges, as we have seen, the function of divinely chosen leaders is to lead *in battle* (Judg. 3:28–30; 4:10; 5:15; 7:19–23); they constitute the first step down in the chain of command from the divine warrior-king Himself. For the same reason, more than once we glimpse these leaders announcing, prophet-like, that God has determined that this is the moment to attack (Judg. 3:28; 4:14; 5:12;[41] 7:15; 11:33; 20:28): the General has passed the order down to His subordinates. As God's spokesman, the prophetess Deborah also excoriates those who failed to join the ranks—that is, to answer the divine call to arms. All this has suggested to scholars that, at this early stage, God's principal function was to fight for Israel on high while summoning His subjects to fight on earth below. Those who did not join in were deemed to have rebelled against the divine king's orders. (It is also worth recalling that the Pentateuch itself cites an ancient source called the "Book of the Wars of the LORD" [Num. 21:14]. The title itself may say much about this God's early function.)

    The divine suzerain of Exodus 19–20 is, scholars say, quite consciously modeled on a human suzerain: a conqueror and holder of territories. As such He will have the duty, and the authority, to muster troops to protect His vassal—that is what suzerains do, after all. But human suzerains also have other covenant stipulations, and what is interesting in the case of the Sinai covenant is precisely that the *rest* of its stipulations are so different from those of ordinary suzerains. Which human suzerain ever cared if his far-off vassals

committed adultery or stole or swore false oaths? This divine suzerain, however, promulgated just such a set of covenant stipulations: His demands turn
out to be a supremely simple set of ten laws that all His subjects must agree
to obey so that, even in the wilds of the Canaanite highlands, a certain minimum of human decency could be enforced. In other words, some scholars
believe, the proclamation of this God as king, and the laws that went with
His kingship, were precisely what living conditions in premonarchic Canaan
called for. The scene may be set at Mount Sinai, some scholars say, but the
real acceptance of God's kingship took place in the Canaanite highlands.

If this (admittedly somewhat speculative) reconstruction is correct, then
what can be said about the true chronology of the hero stories in the book of
Judges? Some scholars still speak of the "period of the judges" as if it were a
definable band of time, sandwiched in between the time of the exodus on the
one hand and the emergence of the Israelite nation on the other. But to others—especially those who see the emergence of Israel as a principally inter-
Canaanite phenomenon—no such specific period ever really existed. Instead,
they say, what underlies the stories in the book of Judges is a fluid and fractious political situation involving many different groups, mountain dwellers
and valley dwellers, Egyptian overlords who sometimes cared and sometimes
did not, Canaanite city-states plus marauding Midianites, Moabites, Hivites,
Benjaminites,[42] and other discrete groups, all moving in and out of ever-
shifting coalitions and political alignments. This situation may have gone on
for centuries; no one involved even thought of independent nationhood as a
possibility. Then, at first slowly but soon with increasing strength, the idea of
some sort of loose federation or common bond began to emerge. It is precisely
in such a context that Deborah's words of expostulation to the nonparticipat-
ing tribes could make sense. Some vague feeling of obligation existed: they
really ought to have done their share, but they did not. At the same time, no
mechanism seems to have been in place to force these tribes' cooperation or
to punish their indifference; no group, except the somewhat murky "Meroz,"
is actually cursed for nonparticipation.[43] Indeed, the roster of tribes does not
even correspond to the later, fairly standardized list of Israel's twelve.

Perhaps, some scholars say, sometime not much before the composition of
this song—under circumstances to be explored next—a new God appeared in
Canaan, a deity previously unknown, whose principal association was with
warfare. At first some, and then more and more, of the various groups in that
land adopted Him as their warrior-king, the sovereign under whose rule
they were prepared to come together and whose simple rules of conduct all
were prepared to accept.

24

The Other Gods of Canaan

*The Storm-god Baal with
a Thunderbolt*
from Ugarit (Ras Shamra)
c. 1350–1250 BCE (sandstone).

THE BELIEF IN GOD. ANCIENT UGARIT. EL AND BAʿAL.
THE ONOMASTICON DOES NOT LIE. THE SOUTHERN CONNECTION.

When most people speak about God nowadays, they mean the Supreme Being, the Master of the Universe, the one "than Whom none greater can be conceived." [1] And, quite naturally, they assume that this is who God has always been. But we have already glimpsed that this is not really the God of much of the Hebrew Bible. He is not necessarily supremely powerful or omniscient or omnipresent. He is a specific, definite, being; He has a name, YHWH,* which, like all other personal names, apparently distinguishes Him from other, potentially similar, beings. Indeed, especially in earlier books and passages of the Bible, He is explicitly a God among other gods; "Who is like You among the gods, O LORD?" is, apparently, a flattering question in the hymn of Exod. 15:11. In the same book, Moses' father-in-law declares in evident admiration, "Now I know that the LORD is greater than all the gods" (Exod. 18:11). Similarly, Ps. 135:5 asserts, "For I know that the LORD is great, greater indeed than all the gods." Ps. 95:3 echoes these sentiments: "For the LORD is a great God, and a great King above all gods." Ps. 89:6 asks: "For who in the skies can be compared to the LORD, or who among the heavenly beings§ is like the LORD? A God feared in the council of the holy ones, great and awesome above all that are around Him. O LORD God of hosts, who is as mighty as You, O LORD?"

This, of course, is not a happy subject for believing Jews and Christians. It is disquieting, to say the least, to think that God has not always been understood to be what He is now—and far worse than disquieting to think that the evidence for that assertion is to be found in God's own holy book. Still, among the many subjects that modern biblical scholars have studied, one of the most prominent has been Israel's God Himself: At what point in their history did the people of Israel come to believe in and worship Him? What was His nature in those early days? And at what point can Israel's religion be described as true monotheism?

---

* As explained earlier, these are the consonants of this deity's proper name; fitting in the vowels is still something of a guess.

§ For modern scholars, these "heavenly beings" are the lesser gods of the divine council, the same "council of the holy ones" mentioned in the next clause. See below, chapter 30.

The Divine

Belief in—or, some would prefer to say, an awareness of—the divine is older than any religion, older than any talk about God or the gods. Some contemporary neuroscientists have concluded that this belief/awareness is hardwired into the human brain, or at least into *some* human brains—an ancient genetic flaw or a now-fading superior consciousness, depending on one's viewpoint. Whatever its cause, this general turn of mind must have existed for millennia, eons, before anything resembling an actual religion or specific form of worship first appeared. As far as human history is concerned, the elusive or illusory divine was simply part of human consciousness from the very beginning.

At a certain point, however, this general dimension of human consciousness begins to take a specific form: belief in the existence of gods. This too is very ancient; no one can even guess, for example, when a belief in the gods first appeared in the ancient Near East. The very oldest texts from that region simply *assume* that the gods exist and always have. Indeed, long before writing was invented, Near Eastern peoples built sanctuaries and shrines to their gods, and the eerie remains of these most ancient structures offer mute testimony to the gods' hold on people's thought at that time. Stretching still farther back are burial and other practices that likewise seem to bespeak a belief in some sort of spiritual realm. Some scholars, working from such remains as well as from the most ancient texts we possess, have attempted to compile a developmental history of, for example, Mesopotamian religion, tracing broad lines of change; but others have found even this sort of broad history to exceed the possibilities offered by the available data.[2] The most we can say for certain is that gods of various sorts seem to have been part of Semitic culture for a very long time.

The ancient conception of the gods is not particularly difficult to grasp: the gods were, to give a concise definition, the unseen causers just behind ordinary reality, the divine beings responsible for all the different things that seem to just happen in the world. Thus, the ripening of fruits on the trees and of grains in the field, the fertility (or lack thereof) of one's flocks and herds, the coming of the rains, the movement of the sun through the sky and the regular changes of moon and stars and seasons, weal and woe, war and peace—none of these things, to a certain way of thinking, could possibly happen on their own. They must have been caused—caused by *someone*. After all, I know that if I throw a rock into a stream or build a new house, I am the evident cause of the subsequent plop in the water or the rickety dwelling on the hill. So similarly, even when the cause is not immediately apparent, if the crops start to ripen but are then consumed by drought, or if, instead, lightning comes shooting out of the sky to herald the life-bringing rains, these things must also have been caused. I may not see the authors of such actions, but causality itself can hardly be questioned; in this case, the cause is simply hidden—or, to put it in more Near Eastern terms, the *causer* is simply hidden. Enter the discrete, divine beings: it is the gods who are the hidden causers.

People did not, of course, usually encounter the gods themselves on the street; their ongoing presence on earth was to be found, as we have seen, in houses specially constructed for them (temples), where they dwelt in concentrated form inside little figurines. This compressed form of existence notwithstanding, the same gods who lived in temples also acted in the world and *interacted* with other gods and goddesses. These deities thus led something of a double life. The real world apparently had some sort of upper shelf or dark backdrop; the gods were present—up there, or back there—as much as in their temples, and they manipulated like puppeteers the things that make up our ordinary existence. These powerful beings were, quite naturally, on everyone's mind. Parents gave their children names that invoked a goddess or god; people spoke of the gods' interventions in their ordinary conversation. Bards sang the mighty deeds that the gods perform, and sages charted the movements of the stars or peered into the intestines of a slaughtered animal in order to discover what the gods had decreed for the future. Certainly, no one ever questioned the gods' existence; one might as well question reality itself. Anything that happened in the world whose cause was not apparent was obviously their doing. Nowadays most people believe that matter is made up of molecules and atoms, even though they have had no direct experience of these invisible entities in their own lives, and even though this belief is scarcely more than a century old. How, then, could anyone doubt the gods' existence when it was evident in all the happenings of everyday life, from the sunrise and sunset to the phases of the moon and changes in the weather, famine or feast, war or peace? And how could anyone question a way of seeing the world that had been part of people's understanding not for a century or two, but for millennia, stretching back into the unremembered beginnings of time?

The Gods of Canaan

Israel at its start was, according to modern scholars, like other ancient peoples in this respect: there were, as far as Israelites knew, many gods and goddesses in the world, and these deities together were responsible for reality. At a certain point, however, Israelites began to assert that their God was the only deity in the world, and that the existence of other gods was in fact an illusion. How did this belief—which has had the greatest impact on human life, being espoused today by more than half the world's population, including (apart from the relatively small number of Jews in the world) approximately 2 billion Christians and 1 billion Muslims—ever get started?

About this subject there is scarcely any agreement among today's biblical scholars. Some few seek to claim that Israelite monotheism began very early: it was part of the "Mosaic revolution" that occurred at the very start of Israel's existence as a people. Others assert that it was quite late—that even in the time of the Babylonian exile and the restoration that followed it, many Jews still entertained polytheistic beliefs, and that to speak of any sort of monotheism before that time is wishful thinking. If the advent of true monotheism is thus in dispute, one aspect of the question does at present seem to be building to something like a consensus. Just as a growing number of scholars have begun to see the emergence of the people of Israel as a result principally of internal developments within the native population of Canaan, so have a growing number come to see the earliest stages of Israelite religion to be virtually indistinguishable from that of their Canaanite neighbors.

In a sense, such scholars say, the evidence was always there. After all, as we have seen, God is said to have revealed his particular name (YHWH) to Moses on Mount Horeb/Sinai. The Pentateuchal sources E and P both seem to report that, until the time of Moses, the name of this deity was unknown; up until then, a passage attributed to P asserts, God was worshiped under the name "El Shaddai" (Exod. 6:2–3). Scholars doubt, however, that it was merely God's *name* that changed. The sudden appearance of a new name, they say, really indicates that this deity had been unknown in Israel up to that point.[3] Once Israelites started worshiping this deity, they eventually came to believe that, in fact, He had always been their God, under some other name.

If this God was a new arrival, what deity had the Israelites worshiped before? A number of references, including the verse just cited, suggest that Israel's God had previously been known by the name *'el* in some combination—*'el shaddai* (Exod. 6:2–3; cf. Gen. 49:25; Num. 24:16), *'el 'elyon* (Gen. 14:22; cf. Num. 24:16; Deut. 32:8–9; Ps. 73:11; 107:11, etc.), *'el 'olam* (Gen. 21:33), *'el 'elohei yisra'el* (Gen. 33:20), and so forth. The word *'el*, it has been pointed out, is simply a general term for "deity" and exists in many Semitic languages, including Hebrew. Indeed, we have seen that the word *'elohim,* which seems to be the plural of *'el,* is regularly used in the Hebrew Bible as a synonym for YHWH.[4] For that reason, ancient readers of the Bible assumed that these various references to *'el,* like the word *'elohim,* were simply another way of referring to the one true God; they were elegant epithets for Israel's God and were translated accordingly: "God Almighty," "God Eternal," and so forth.

As modern scholarship progressed, however, the suspicion grew (in part because *'el* was recognized to be a common Semitic word) that *'el* in the Bible might sometimes refer not to Israel's God but to someone else's. Perhaps the use of this name was connected somehow with Canaanite worship, which may not have been utterly eradicated by the Israelites, at least at first.[5] In a famous essay published in 1929, Albrecht Alt suggested that the various *'el* combinations ("El Elyon," "El Shaddai," and so forth) referred to little local deities or spirits (*numina*) associated with this or that place encountered by the Israelites.[6]

The Discovery of Ugarit

The same year that Alt published his essay marked the beginning of the excavation of a site on the coast of northern Syria, Ras Shamra, not far from Latakia (where the famous pipe tobacco comes from). As with so many great archaeological finds, the ruins underneath Ras Shamra were discovered quite by accident: a farmer's plow, according to the story, bumped against a hard, unmovable object that, upon examination, turned out to be part of an ancient burial site. French archaeologists soon moved in (Syria still being, at the time, a French protectorate), and over the course of many seasons of careful excavations, they slowly revealed an undreamed-of treasure: a major city under the earth, complete with acropolis, temples, royal palaces, residential areas, and—perhaps most precious—an entire library of texts, most of which were written in a strange, unknown language. The ancient name of the site, it turned out, was Ugarit.

The script in which the strange texts were written consisted, like ancient Akkadian,* of little hatch marks sunk into wet clay (cuneiform). But at first, no Akkadian expert could make any sense of them. It was noticed after a while that the exact same configurations of wedge marks kept recurring far more frequently than in normal cuneiform, and it dawned on two scholars—the German Hans Bauer and the Frenchman Edouard Dhorme—that those configurations might in fact represent letters rather than syllables. (Having signs for syllables means you need quite a few—separate ones for *bi, ba,* and *bu; ti, ta,* and *tu,* and so forth. Akkadian thus regularly uses a roster of three hundred or more signs. The new texts, on inspection, turned out to have only thirty signs. The signs thus seemed to be functioning more like the letters of an alphabet.)[7] Both scholars succeeded in deciphering more than half the signs, and the results of each scholar's decipherments complemented the other's. Once the writing system had been cracked, there began the massive task of translating and studying the great cache of texts found at Ugarit. The language itself—which scholars termed *Ugaritic*—turned out to be quite close to biblical Hebrew. (Nowadays, a student who has studied biblical Hebrew can usually acquire a pretty good reading knowledge of Ugaritic in a semester.) The Ugaritic texts were of all sorts: there were letters, inventories, legal documents, commercial and diplomatic records telling of the city's day-to-day affairs, but also tales of gods and heroes and other religious

---

* The general name for the language of Babylon, Assyria, and other regions.

texts. The texts were found to go back to the fourteenth century BCE, a time even before that assigned to Moses and the exodus. It is from these writings that modern scholars have been able to learn much about the religious beliefs of the Canaanites in ancient times, from whose midst, as we have seen, many hold the people of Israel to have come.

At the head of the Ugaritic pantheon stood El. El was his actual name, even though the same word also means "a deity" in Hebrew and other Semitic languages.* El was the supreme Canaanite deity and the father of other gods, sometimes referred to collectively as the "sons of El." He is generally depicted as an old, wise, kindly, paternal figure; he created the earth and humanity itself. El had a lady friend named Athirat, mother of the gods. Although El must at one time have been the most active of the gods, at Ugarit he had begun to be supplanted by a more youthful and vigorous figure, Baal. Baal (ba'al means "master" and was apparently at first only an epithet for the god Hadad) controlled the storm clouds and the life-giving rain; he was the "cloud rider" whose arrival was heralded by peals of thunder and flashes of lightning. He dwelt on Mount Sapan (in today's Arabic, jabl al-Aqra', the highest mountain in Syria) with his consort, the bloodthirsty 'Anat—although other Ugaritic texts identify Baal's consort with another goddess, 'Ashtorte/Astarte.

As details of the Ugaritic pantheon unfolded, what was striking to scholars was how much the gods of Ugarit seemed to overlap with various representations of Israel's God in the Bible. Of course, God in the Bible is depicted in many different ways—and in any case, some overlap of general characteristics would seem almost inevitable between two central deities. Still, the very fact that, as we have seen, God is sometimes called by the name El in various combinations was certainly suspicious. If the Canaanites next door called their supreme god El, oughtn't the Israelites to have bent over backward to avoid the appearance of worshiping the same deity? Indeed, the fact that Israel's God was, like El, a fatherly figure (Exod. 4:22; Deut. 14:1), beneficent and kindly (Exod. 34:6 and frequently thereafter), and was frequently referred to by the same name has suggested to some scholars just the opposite, that Israel's God was actually a development of, or had taken on the characteristics of, the old head of the Canaanite pantheon. At the same time, Israel's God was also a bit like Baal. The same epithet used of Baal, the "cloud rider" (rkb 'rpt), is echoed (and perhaps deliberately distorted) in the epithet of God the "desert rider" (rkb b'rbt) in Ps. 68:4. Baal's dwelling on Mount Sapan seems likewise to be echoed in the praise of Zion in Ps. 48, "joy of all the earth, Mount Zion, *summit of Saphon,* the city of the great King"

---

* Compare with English, where "God" (capital G) refers to a specific deity, our Supreme Being, while "god" can refer to any deity—the Roman gods, the god of war, and so forth.

(Ps. 48:2). Another hymn, Ps. 29, seemed so much like a Ugaritic paean to Baal that more than one scholar suggested that the word "Baal" had actually been erased by an ancient scribe and "YHWH" scrawled in its place.[8] Some scholars even argued that an inscription found in the southland of biblical Israel spoke of God having a consort, a certain *Asherah,* this being the Hebrew equivalent of El's consort Athirat.[9]

And yet, the Hebrew God was not principally known as El; He may be called that here and there, but, as we have seen, He is far more frequently known by the name YHWH. Where did *this* name come from?

The Midianite Hypothesis

It is striking that a number of biblical texts—some of them, according to scholars, going back to the very oldest layers of the Hebrew Bible—connect the home of Israel's God with various sites to the southeast of Israel, the land once inhabited by Kenites and Midianites and Edomites. Thus, for example:

> The LORD came from *Sinai,* and dawned from *Seir* [the mountain of
>   Edom] upon them;
> He shone forth from Mount *Paran* [precise location unknown, but gener-
>   ally south of Israel and west of Edom].
>
>   Deut. 33:2

> LORD, when You went out from *Seir,* when You marched from the fields
>   of *Edom,*
> The earth trembled, and even the heavens poured forth, yes, the clouds
>   poured out water.
> The mountains quaked for fear of the LORD, the One from *Sinai,* for fear
>   of the LORD, the God of Israel.
>
>   Judg. 5:4–5

> God came from *Teman* [literally, "the south," sometimes a synonym for
>   Edom], the Holy One from Mount *Paran. Selah*
> His glory covered the heavens, and the earth was full of His praise.
>
>   Hab. 3:3

> O God, when You went at the head of Your army, when You marched
>   through the desert,
> the earth trembled, the heavens dripped rain,
> for fear of *the One from Sinai,* of God, the God of Israel.
>
>   Ps. 68:8–9

These very ancient texts all seem to say fairly clearly that "the LORD" was not native to the land of Israel but arrived there from somewhere else. Although the location of Sinai is today unknown, there can be little doubt that it, too, belongs to the same general area as Seir, Teman, and Paran, that is, to the southeast of biblical Israel's territory. It is therefore certainly significant that, according to the Exodus narrative as well, Israel's God is said specifically to dwell on "Horeb, the mountain of God" (Exod. 3:1) or on Sinai. Indeed, Moses was living with his father-in-law, Jethro, "priest of Midian," when he happened upon this "mountain of God" and was first addressed by the deity named YHWH. Why, modern scholars ask, should the Bible report that the God of Israel was originally located far from His people, permanently settled, it would appear, on a mountain in the southeastern wasteland? The simplest answer would appear to be: because that was the truth as Israelites knew it. All these biblical texts seem to be saying the same thing, that originally Israel's God did not live in the land of Canaan but took up residence there only after a time.

These things are hardly obscure, and it did not take modern scholars long to come up with a hypothesis to fit them: if Jethro, Moses' father-in-law, was a "priest of Midian" and he himself dwelt not far from the "mountain of God," then he must have been the one to introduce Moses to the worship of a deity who was in fact *his* God, a Midianite deity named YHWH. Moses then brought this new deity to the Israelites, claiming (à la Exod. 3:15, 6:2–3, and 15:2) that He was none other than the God worshiped by their ancestors. Jethro's central role in this transformation of Israel's faith was, these scholars said, deliberately obscured by the biblical narrative, but not quite successfully. After all, the book of Exodus has Jethro exclaim, "Now I know that the LORD is greater than all the gods" (Exod. 18:10), which seems to imply that, while Jethro may not have realized this deity's great power until that moment, he certainly had known of His existence previously. (This is not true of other biblical non-Israelites: Pharaoh, for example, had never heard of this God [Exod. 5:2].) The Bible also reports that it was Jethro who advised Moses how to set up a judicial system (Exod. 18:11–24); thereafter, however, Jethro disappears and the Israelites move on alone to Mount Sinai and, ultimately, Canaan. Nevertheless, this hypothesis maintained, the religion that they brought with them was originally foreign to Canaan—it belonged to the wastelands to the south and east of fruitful Canaan, which is why it was associated with the Midianites, Kenites,[10] or Amalekites,[11] all nomadic or semi-nomadic peoples in that region.

This reconstruction, presented by F. W. Ghillany, B. Stade, and others in the nineteenth century,[12] came to be known as the Midianite (or Kenite) hypothesis. It was then taken up by a number of outstanding scholars, including Hugo Gressmann, Eduard Meyer, and Hermann Gunkel,[13] and more recently (and in somewhat different form) by Manfred Weippert, F. M. Cross, and others.[14] As first presented, this hypothesis had no hard evidence outside the Bible to support it. More recently, some archaeological finds have been offered as partial outside confirmation. Thus, two Nubian temple inscriptions from the second half of the second millennium refer to nomads in the region of Seir as the "Shasu [*š3śu*, that is, Bedouins] of YHWH" (though this reading is not quite uncontested).[15] An inscription found at Kuntillet Ajrud, an eighth-century BCE settlement in the northern Sinai, refers to "YHWH of Teman," or "YHWH of the south," which could also indicate some sort of primary association with that region. (On the other hand, another inscription found at the same site refers to "YHWH of Samaria," so perhaps both references should be taken as reflecting the location of shrines associated with this deity.)

Even if this extrabiblical evidence is something short of unequivocal, modern advocates of the Midianite/Kenite hypothesis say that the biblical evidence itself is as sound as ever—and persuasive. After all (to take up an earlier question), what purpose would have been served by biblical writers saying that the "mountain of God" had *ever* been Sinai—if they were free to invent history, they ought to have said that His mountain had always been Zion, in the heartland of Judah! (Even if this Zion-based God had wished to meet the Israelites during their desert wanderings and accompany them to Canaan, that hardly would have necessitated His ever having *resided* outside of His homeland).[16] If the most ancient biblical poetry, along with the Exodus narrative, locates the first appearance of this God in the southeast wasteland—and if no pre-Israelite Canaanite text ever mentions such a divine name—then these data ought to be the starting point of any attempt to understand where this God came from and how He came to be Israel's.

To this might be added another point. If one takes seriously the connection between the suzerainty treaty form and its various reflections in the Bible (Exodus 20; Joshua 24; the book of Deuteronomy), then one must return to a question asked earlier: why should ancient Israel have been content to think of their God as a suzerainlike figure, a conqueror come from elsewhere? Why not their own native king? The obvious answer is: because, as far as Israel knew, He *did* come from elsewhere. That is to say, the entire gestalt of a great suzerain who approaches a certain people and, announcing that "all the land is Mine" (Exod. 19:5), proposes that they now come under His wing makes sense only if the suzerain is known to dwell at some great distance from the people in question. At the time this image or metaphor was put forward, therefore, it would seem that Israel was in Canaan but its God was not—at least, not yet. He still dwelled far to the southeast, at the "mountain of God."

Some scholars connect this putative southeastern location of God's home mountain with their own scenario for the emergence of the people of Israel. If indeed those early Israelite hilltop settlements were the result of seminomads occupying the uninhabited highlands, perhaps these settlers (or at least some of them) had come in from the grazing lands of the southeast, where YHWH (according to this hypothesis) was worshiped. Trying to flesh out some of the details of this scenario, F. M. Cross has pointed to the existence of a caravan route connecting Midian with Egypt during the thirteenth and twelfth centuries; travelers on that axis might have regularly moved farther north on routes controlled by Midian and ultimately made their way to the region of Canaan.* [17] If a group connected with the future Israel had followed such a path in search of lands for grazing and small-time farming, they would likely have settled first in the near-vacant steppes on the far side of the Jordan, the land that was, for a while, the home territory of the tribe of Reuben, at the southeastern corner of the future Israel's territory. It therefore seems highly significant, Cross said, that Reuben consistently appears in the Bible as Jacob's "firstborn." Not Judah, which was to become the dominant tribe in the south in monarchic times, and not Joseph, progenitor of the mighty tribes of Ephraim and Manasseh, but Reuben. Presumably Reuben was said to be Jacob's first son because the segment of biblical Israel he represented had been, at a very early point, the powerful, vanguard tribe whose land was the staging area for future Israel's spread to the west and north. Later, even though other tribes became more powerful and Reuben's tribe underwent a precipitous decline (reflected, inter alia, in Gen. 49:2–5), the title of firstborn was "frozen" and remained his. All this, Cross has argued, suggests that the first Israelites were seminomadic pastoralists who came from, or through, the territory of Reuben into the western and northern parts of Canaan. They brought with them the worship of a God who had been theirs down south, a deity shared by the Midianites or Kenites or Amalekites.

Indeed, some scholars have sought to connect this same itinerary with the account of the Israelite exodus from Egypt. Although few modern historians credit the tradition of a great national exodus of twelve whole tribes, most (as we have seen) nonetheless attribute some historicity to the exodus tradition. If a group of western Semites had at one point left Egypt and made their way—possibly over a period of generations—into Canaan via this same route, perhaps it was they who at some point met up with settlers of the Canaanite highlands; they brought with them the worship of their God, YHWH. Then, as they and their ideology gradually took root in the lowlands as well, this God became the deity of the inchoate group of tribes that would be Israel.[18] Their God, like their exodus tradition, became "nationalized." If so, then the etiological understanding of the story of Cain would actually be

---

* Note that the book of Judges reports on such an apparent migration: "The descendants of Hobab the Kenite, Moses' father-in-law, went up with the people of Judah from the city of palms [Jericho] into the wilderness of Judah, which lies in the Negeb near Arad" (Judg. 1:16).

a great reversal of the historical facts (see chapter 3): it was not that the Kenites' eponym was originally a farmer who was exiled from the Canaanite land of YHWH to become a wandering nomad, bringing the worship of his old God with him to the rugged steppes; rather, a group of Kenite-influenced nomads entered the land of Canaan in days of old and, bringing the worship of their God with them to their new home, settled down and eventually made that God the common deity of most of Canaan.

Named for God

"The biblical onomasticon does not lie."* The meaning of this scholarly maxim is that, while the tellers of tales may sometimes stretch the truth or even make things up out of whole cloth, they usually fail to notice the proper names in the stories they tell. Those names—to the extent that they can shed light on the ancient past—may thus provide a far more reliable, unbiased witness as to what really happened. How does this apply to Israelite religion?

As we have already seen, many personal names in the Bible, and a few biblical toponyms, contain a *theophoric* element—the name of a deity. The various deities evoked in ancient Israelite names can be most significant in telling us about the development of Israelite religion. It is striking that the name YHWH appears regularly in the biblical onomasticon, starting with the names of people alleged to have lived in the tenth century BCE or so, at the time of the rise of David's mighty empire.[19] It is then that one finds an abundance of such names—David's friend *J*onathan (a name meaning "YHWH has given"), David's army chief *J*oab ("YHWH is [my] father"),[20] and so forth. From that time on, such names come to predominate in the Israelite onomasticon. Before that time, however, the theophoric particle is much more frequently '*el*: Abraham's son Ishma*el,* his servant *Eli*'ezer, or, for that matter, Isra*el*. There are even some Baal names, like Gideon's "other" name, Jerubaal (Judg. 6:32).

Completing these data is the evidence for place-names (also called *toponyms*). Here, the facts are even more striking: a few toponyms contain the particle '*el*—Bethel, for example, or Peniel or Elaleh. There is, however, not even one toponym formed from the name YHWH.[21] By contrast, there are some place-names invoking Baal or other deities, nearly forty by one recent count: Baal-perazim (2 Sam. 5:20), Baal-hermon (Judg. 3:3), Anathoth (Jer. 1:1, etc., apparently named after the goddess Anath), and so forth.[22]

What is one to make of these facts? The obvious conclusion would seem to be that, up to the time of David or so, people named their children by invok-

---

* "Onomasticon" is a scholars' word for a corpus of names—in our case, all the proper names found in the Bible.

ing El or Baal, but not YHWH. That would seem to say that the religion of YHWH really did not catch on until the tenth century or so.

Not so fast, however. To begin with, the theophoric particle *'el* is altogether noncommittal: it could refer to El, but it could also be simply the generic Semitic word for a god, in this case, the God of Israel. (Plenty of biblical texts use this word to refer to YHWH.) That Israelites preferred to incorporate this theophoric particle into names up to a certain point hardly proves that they were El worshipers, or even that the name YHWH was unknown to them; in fact, *'el* names continue to be used throughout the biblical period and thereafter. (It could also be, as some have suggested, that at a certain point the identities of El and YHWH were merged into one deity; see below.) The same opacity may accompany names formed with *ba'al*. While Baal was indeed the name of a Canaanite god, there are some indications that *ba'al* was also used at times as an epithet for YHWH (see Hos. 2:16; Isa. 1:3).²³ So this name, too, appears inconclusive.

Beyond these considerations, it is necessary to factor in the conservatism that surrounds proper names in most civilizations: they have great staying power. Indeed, toponyms tend to be the most conservative element in a language. I lived for quite a few years in a place called Massachusetts. I still have no idea what the name means, but one thing is clear: this was a Native American name that somehow survived in New England despite the foreign origin and strong Christian faith of the first British settlers of the region, both of which led them regularly to confer English or biblical toponyms on the towns they founded (Boston, New Bedford, Salem, and so forth). Nor is "Massachusetts" the sole Native American survivor—in fact, the state is full of such names: Natick, Saugus, Neponset, Titicut, Nantucket, Mattapan, Nonantum, and so on and so forth. If so many native toponyms can survive the invasion of an utterly foreign people and culture, it is not difficult to understand that, in a relatively undisturbed and homogeneous population, toponyms just seem to stay on forever. Once biblical sites had been named with *'el* or *ba'al* names, they tended to stay that way no matter how people's loyalties or beliefs subsequently changed.

Personal names are not far behind toponyms in their conservatism. Many Americans named John or Mary, William or Elizabeth or Frederick, have no idea what their names actually mean or where they originally came from; for all they know, they could be Greek or Hebrew for "frog's head" or "eternal wallflower." It does not matter; these people were named after their lamented uncle Fred or great-grandmother Mary, or simply because the name pleased one or both of their parents—and this is altogether typical of how people's names are chosen in many different societies. (Even when modern-day parents look up names in one of those *What Shall We Name the Baby?* books, they are choosing from among established names rather than creating a new one; what's more, they are rarely even interested in the etymology given for the name they choose—a good thing, since many of the etymologies supplied in such books are wrong.) Thus, personal names tend to be almost as conservative as toponyms.

For this reason, one ought not to be too quick to assign dates for the spread of the worship of Israel's God on the basis of the onomasticon. Nevertheless, the relative frequency of 'el in personal names at the early end of Israel's history, and the relative frequency of YHWH among figures from the tenth century and later, does seem to dovetail with the other factors already seen. At an early point, scholars suppose, the future territory of Israel was simply part of the great Canaanite cultural continuum; the inhabitants worshiped El and Baal and the other gods and goddesses known from Ugarit and elsewhere. At some later point, "Israel" began to emerge on the Canaanite hilltops. If (as some scholars believe) those first Israelites included pastoralists who had originated in or had passed through the rugged steppes around Sinai/Seir/Edom/Paran/Teman, they may have brought with them the worship of the God who resided there, YHWH, "the one of Sinai." This worship they passed on to others—other mountaintop settlers, and eventually Canaanites elsewhere in the land. Not long after that, they proclaimed this God their king, who, like a conquering suzerain residing at some distance from them, could nevertheless call up their troops to muster and could issue laws to be obeyed.

This notwithstanding, devotees of this new deity were hardly likely to have thrown off their old gods and old religious practices. Why should they have? Even if the somewhat ambiguous wording of the Ten Commandments ("You shall have no other gods before Me [or beside Me]") is interpreted to mean that no other gods were henceforth to be worshiped at all, and even if this commandment is associated with the time of Israel's first emergence in the Canaanite highlands (and both these contentions are doubted by some scholars), that would hardly guarantee that the new Israelites would have made a clean break with their religious past. History is full of examples of the exact opposite. New gods arrive and are worshiped alongside old gods, or are sometimes identified with old gods (so that Zeus equals Jupiter, Mars equals Ares, and so forth), or old forms of worship are adapted to the newly arrived faith. Along the lines of the latter: many religious Christians today buy a Christmas tree for their houses, put up mistletoe in their doorways, and sit around the yule log on Christmas Eve—and they fully believe that, in so doing, they are observing this Christian holiday. But of course all of these customs are actually pre-Christian, "pagan" practices that were taken over by Christianity. For that matter, some American Jews have recently taken to purchasing an annual "Hanukkah bush"—an obvious attempt to create a parallel to the Christmas tree in their own religion. All these are examples of what scholars of religion call religious *syncretism*.[24]

Something similar, scholars say, may well have happened in ancient Canaan. Whenever it was that the worship of YHWH reached them, many

Canaanites must have understood this new deity to be something like the equivalent of El and Baal. That is why they referred to Him by some of the same epithets and depicted Him like El, as a kindly father figure, or like Baal, as a powerful and sometimes violent deity, accompanied by the accouterments of storm clouds, lightning, and thunder; and that is why they sometimes set up a Canaanite-style sacred pillar (*maṣṣebah*) to Him or planted a sacred grove (*asherah*) as part of their worship.[25] Indeed, in the minds of ordinary people, the distinction between this deity YHWH on the one hand and El and Baal on the other may have been quite blurry. (Some scholars have gone so far as to suggest that the name YHWH itself was originally an epithet for El and only gradually developed into the name of a separate deity). Worshipers of the new deity may have sometimes converted sites that had been sacred to these other gods into sites dedicated to Him,[26] as well as building new temples that followed the same plan as temples built elsewhere to the gods of Canaan. But it also seems possible that this God was worshiped *alongside* other gods and goddesses for quite some time; the Ten Commandments notwithstanding, the historical reality—as evidenced in the Bible itself as well as by archaeological finds—was apparently rather different.[27]

How much polytheism existed in Israel, and for how long, is still hotly debated among scholars. Since biblical texts themselves may have been out to prove a point at the time they were written or may reflect the religious prejudices of much later authors or editors, scholars tend to give greater weight to evidence from outside the Bible—inscriptions and other archaeological finds. But such evidence itself is open to different interpretations. For example, does a profusion of little palm-sized statuettes of naked goddesses found at various Israelite sites say something profound about the state of the owners' religious beliefs, or did such objects have approximately the same significance as a rabbit's foot key chain in our own day?[28] Some scholars have claimed—on the basis of biblical and extrabiblical evidence—that Baal was not only worshiped alongside YHWH by some northern Israelites (1 Kings 18:20), but that these two deities were considered coequal partners whose combined worship was something like the official religion of the northern kingdom.[29] On the other hand, in a ninth-century Moabite inscription (the Mesha stele, on which see below, chapter 29), the Moabite king boasts of pillaging objects sacred to YHWH; no other god or goddess is mentioned. This is certainly significant.[30]

One scenario for the development of Israel's religion posits the coexistence of different groups or parties among the people, most of whom were syncretists of one sort or another.[31] Starting as early as the eighth or ninth century BCE, however, a more exclusivist form of Israel's religion would have begun to emerge. This take-no-prisoners faith, which may have been inspired by early prophetic circles, had little tolerance for Baal worship or other cults; it sought to root out anything that smacked of pagan ceremonies in order to draw the clearest distinction between the worship of YHWH and that of other gods. At first, not everyone subscribed to this "extremist" position; the worship of other gods and goddesses may well have continued in other circles. Ultimately, however, the exclusive devotion to Israel's God came to be enshrined in the laws of Deuteronomy and led to Josiah's great religious reform in the seventh century. That may not have meant the instant disappearance of polytheism, but it certainly changed the religious landscape. The distance is not far from such an exclusivist faith to the affirmation that other gods are not only unworthy of worship, but utterly powerless or even nonexistent, an illusion: "The LORD is God in the heavens above and on the earth below; there is no other" (Deut. 4:39). This is true monotheism. Yet even in later times, according to scholars, there is evidence that some Jews continued to worship other deities alongside of Israel's God.[32] When one considers the matter in the abstract, it should hardly seem surprising that people were reluctant to abandon the basic notion that many different gods and goddesses are responsible for the multifaceted reality of our lives. But the monotheistic idea did eventually triumph. The author of the book of Judith (third or second century BCE) was probably describing quite accurately his or her own era by having that book's heroine proclaim,

> "For never in our generation nor in these present days has there been any tribe or family of people or city of ours which worshiped gods made by [human] hands, as was done in days gone by; for that was why our fathers were handed over to the sword, and to be plundered, so that they suffered a great catastrophe before our enemies. But we know no other God but Him."
>
> Jth. 8:18–20

Although the path to true monotheism was long, it was eventually adopted by all Jews. Moreover, the triumph of this way of thinking in biblical times was reenacted subsequently throughout much of the world: in Europe, Africa, Asia, Australia, and the Americas, the monotheistic understanding of reality has been taken over by the most diverse populations. Today, it may truly be said to characterize the thinking of much of humanity overall.

A Simple Faith

Before we leave those early mountaintop settlements, one further aspect of life there needs to be stressed: its simplicity. To be sure, since the Industrial Revolution, rustic simplicity has been the subject of much nostalgia and not a little romanticizing; modern-day historians are still sometimes wont to find simplicity where it wasn't really, as well as to equate the simple with the good.

That notwithstanding, archaeologists are certainly correct in highlighting the apparent ethos of simplicity embodied in various aspects of those early highland villages.[33] The people who lived there dwelt in small, unadorned houses of three or four rooms, which were apparently occupied by a father, mother(s), and their children (and perhaps, if there was room, other immediate relatives as well). There was nothing elegant about these houses—in fact, the family members shared their living quarters with some of the family's livestock, who lived on the bottom floor during at least part of the year and whose pungent odor filled the air. (Keeping a donkey or a cow or two inside the house itself not only gave these valuable animals safe shelter but also provided additional warmth for the family during the chilly months of winter.)

Such individual houses were grouped together, and sometimes walled off, in ways that make sense only if one assumes that these areas constituted larger family compounds, presided over by the aging paterfamilias, who lived in one of the houses.[34] Indeed, it seems altogether possible that nearly *all* the inhabitants of a hilltop village were linked by kinship ties of one degree or another.[35] Thus the villagers—brothers and uncles, cousins and in-laws—lived together and eked out a meager living by farming the terraces that had been laid out along the sloping hillsides (these are the "elevated fields" of Judg. 5:18 and 2 Sam. 1:21),[36] as well as by keeping sheep and goats and other animals. (Eventually, of course, there would not be enough farmland or grazing land available for the increasing population, so younger sons or other relatives had to be split off from these ancestral villages.)[37] The rainy season, from mid-October through March, provided the moisture needed to grow crops as well as for drinking water, stored in cisterns lined with waterproof lime plaster.[38] The dry period lasted from April or May through September; it was certainly cooler in the highland villages than in the valleys, but still quite hot (and dry) in summer. The changing seasons, whose regular rhythm is preserved in a Hebrew inscription of the late tenth century (the Gezer Calendar),[39] left their imprint on the villagers' way of life and way of thought; the crops they grew and ate, like the animals they raised and bred, kept them altogether tied to the cycles of nature.

The religious practices of these people were quite in keeping with the other aspects of their life, archaeologists say; here too, simplicity reigned. It is not possible to know for sure which deity or deities the villagers worshiped (or when they worshiped them); it may well be that a variety of gods and goddesses were at first honored in the highlands. The archaeological remains suggest, in any case, a rather uncomplicated religious regime, practiced in individual homes or villagewide, in "cult rooms" and local shrines ("high places"), or in open-air, hilltop areas like the twelfth-century "Bull Site" discovered in northern Samaria,[40] as well as at a few actual temples of widely differing design.

Among others, the God YHWH was worshiped in those hills. Particularly fascinating about this particular deity must have been the apparent absence of cultic images representing Him. The biblical prohibition of worshiping such images, scholars have suggested, may be relatively late,[41] but judging by the evidence, such a prohibition was apparently in effect from earliest times.[42] It is difficult to say for sure what this evidence means, but it certainly suggests that, for the adherents of this God, He must have somehow seemed—despite other similarities and even syncretisms—different from other deities. He did not (as we have seen to be the case with the gods and goddesses of Mesopotamia) dwell inside a statue set off in a magnificent house (that is, a temple) constructed for Him. Instead, He was worshiped at what appear to be deliberately crude installations: perhaps He might infuse or appear above a standing stone (*maṣṣebah*) or in a sacred grove (*asherah*) for a time, or else reveal Himself to a chosen servant at an oak tree or other outdoor site; then He disappeared. His presence, in any case, was not captured by the skilled work of human hands. This practice may be said to reflect a similar aesthetic of religious simplicity, perhaps a historic descendant of the outlook of those early hilltop settlers. Under this same rubric of simplicity one might list the blunt laws of the Ten Commandments—"Do this!" and "Don't do that" (so different from the complicated case law of Mesopotamian legal codes)[43]—which, it has been suggested, may owe their origin to this same period of early highland villages. In keeping with this same aesthetic of religious simplicity is the Bible's commandment to build only plain, dirt altars or, if stones were to be used, then only unhewn stones (Exod. 20:24–25). It is certainly tempting for some scholars to see in all this a single cultural continuum. Where else in the Bible does this same mentality show itself?

It is, scholars say, dangerous to look to the narratives of Genesis for a reliable source of information about ancient times: the time of the composition of these narratives is widely disputed, and as we have seen, many scholars in any case believe them to be etiological tales quite unrelated to the persons or times they describe. Still, one cannot but be struck by the great gap separating the life of the patriarchs, including their religious practices, from those of later Israelites. Abraham, Isaac, and Jacob wander about Canaan, building here and there a rude altar to their God. No professional clergy exists in their world, nor any complicated rules of purity and impurity such as already held sway in Mesopotamian temples and would eventually take root in the rules governing Israel's priests. Instead, the patriarchs themselves slaughter and sacrifice animals to God at their homemade altars, spontaneously turning to God in prayer and acknowledgment, wherever they might happen to be. God sometimes appears to them in the guise of a fellow human being, at least for a time—then they recognize the truth and fall to the ground in worship. It is difficult to imagine how a later Israelite, raised on the notion of temples staffed by cadres of cultic specialists—priests schooled in the rules of proper slaughter and the avoidance of any cultic impurity, who alone were authorized to come close to the place where the God of Israel Himself dwelt, enthroned in man-made splendor—could have thought that some other reality was even possible. For that reason, among others, some scholars cling to the idea that behind these stories stand traditions that are indeed quite old.[44] The traditions do not go back, these scholars theorize, to patriarchal times, as Albright and others once thought; instead, the picture of life reflected in them seems to belong to the period of those hilltop settlements, when a paterfamilias presided over his extended family of farmers and shepherds, perhaps splitting off a branch of the family "because the land could not support both of them living together, since their possessions were so great that they could not live together" (Gen. 13:6), building altars and "calling on the name of the LORD." That God was none other than the "One of Sinai" who was, increasingly, the focus of the highlanders' piety.

25

Samuel and Saul

1 SAMUEL 1–3; 8–11; 15–17

Eli and Samuel by John Opie.

PROPHECY AND KINGSHIP. THE BIRTH AND CALL OF SAMUEL.
THE RISE OF SAUL. MILITARY CAMPAIGNS. ḤEREM OF
THE AMALEKITES. SAUL'S YOUNG RIVAL.

The period of time covered by the books of 1 and 2 Samuel is short—only a few decades. But these decades marked an enormous change. At their start, the future Israelite kingdom was still a group of scattered and persecuted tribes. By the end, these tribes had not only united to form a kingdom; together they had turned into a mighty empire, holding sway from Egypt to deep into Syria. Or had they?

Three men stand out in the period that follows that of the book of Judges. Not surprisingly, two of them are kings—Saul and David. But the first, no less an important figure, is the prophet Samuel. Indeed, the story of this period begins with a detailed account of Samuel's birth and how he came to be a servant of God.

Hannah, Samuel's mother, had been childless for some years; like Sarah and Rebekah (and Samson's unnamed mother) before her, this "barren wife" was destined to give birth to one of Israel's heroes. Her husband, Elkanah, who had another wife, tried to comfort her over her childlessness, but Hannah's only wish was for a baby of her own. After some years, she went in desperation to the temple at Shiloh:

> She was deeply distressed and prayed to the LORD, and wept bitterly. She made this vow: "O LORD of hosts, if only You will look on the misery of Your servant, and remember me, and not forget Your servant, but will give to Your servant a male child, then I will put him before You as a nazirite until the day of his death. He shall drink neither wine nor intoxicants, and no razor shall touch his head."
>
> 1 Sam. 1:10–12

God heard Hannah's prayer and answered: she soon became pregnant and gave birth to a little boy. In keeping with her vow, she prepared Samuel as a nazirite:* as soon as he was of age, Samuel was brought to Eli, the priest of Shiloh, to serve before God. On that occasion Hannah sang a hymn of thanksgiving (1 Sam. 2:1–10).

---

* See above, chapter 23, "Samson."

The Call of Samuel

Samuel was thus indentured as a boy to Eli, serving as an apprentice priest at Shiloh. Now, "the word of the LORD was rare in those days; visions were not widespread" (1 Sam. 3:1). Nevertheless, it happened one night that God called to Samuel:

> At that time Eli was lying down in his usual place; his eyesight had begun to grow weak, so that he could not see well. The lamp of God had not yet burnt out, and Samuel was lying down in the temple of the LORD, where the ark of God was. Then the LORD called to Samuel. He cried out "Here I am!" and ran to Eli. He said, "Here I am; you called me?" But he said, "I did not call you; go back to bed." So he went and lay down. The LORD called again, "Samuel!" Samuel got up and went to Eli, and said, "Here I am; you called me?" But he said, "I did not call, my son; go back to bed." Now Samuel did not yet know the LORD; the word of the LORD had not yet been revealed to him. Then the LORD called to Samuel again, a third time. And he got up and went to Eli, and said, "Here I am; you called me?" Then Eli understood that the LORD was calling the boy. Therefore Eli said to Samuel, "Go, lie down; and if He calls you, say, 'Speak, LORD, for Your servant is listening.' " So Samuel went and lay down in his place. Now the LORD entered and stood there, and He called as before, "Samuel! Samuel!" And Samuel said, "Speak, for Your servant is listening."
>
> 1 Sam. 3:2–10

This was a signal event not only in Samuel's life, but in the life of the people of Israel. If, until then, "the word of the LORD was rare," it was not to be rare any longer. Soon, everyone was aware that a true prophet had come: "All Israel from Dan [in the far north] to Beer-sheba [in the far south] knew that Samuel was a trustworthy prophet of the LORD" (1 Sam. 3:20).

In fact, scholars note, from the time of Samuel onward, the Deuteronomistic History maintains that prophecy was a fixture in Israel's collective life. This had not been so earlier. True, Moses is sometimes presented as a prophet in the books from Exodus to Deuteronomy (Num. 12:6–8; Deut. 18:15–19; 34:10), but many modern scholars would say that the prophetic portrayal of Moses in these books has been influenced by the succession of prophets long after his time; what Moses was really like (or even if he ever existed) is, they say, something that had been lost in the sands of time long before these books were written. In any case, the Deuteronomistic History scarcely mentions prophecy from the time of Moses until that of Samuel. True, some of the judges seem to have prophetlike abilities (announcing when the time is right to attack, for example), and Deborah is at one point called a "prophetess" (Judg. 4:4), but the other judges are not described as prophets, and their prophetic traits may in any case—as scholars allege about Moses' portrayal—likewise be a retrojection from later times.

From the time of Samuel on, however, prophecy is presented as an established institution in Israel. Following Samuel come narratives about Nathan, the prophet of David's time, and after him, Elijah and Elisha in the ninth century. The Bible then includes the actual writings attributed to various prophets: the books of Amos and Hosea and Isaiah and Micah from the eighth century BCE, Nahum and Habakkuk and Zephaniah in the seventh century, along with Jeremiah and Ezekiel in the late seventh and early sixth—and the writings of still later prophets. Indeed, the books of the three "major"* prophets Isaiah, Jeremiah, and Ezekiel (so called not because of their importance, but because of the bulk of writings attributed to them) actually account for about 20 percent of the whole Hebrew Bible. Add to these three the books of the twelve "minor" prophets, as well as the historical narratives that center on various prophets and their doings, and a still greater part of Hebrew Scripture turns out to be tied up with these central religious figures. What was prophecy all about, and why were these figures deemed so important?

Prophets in Modern Scholarship

A straightforward definition of the prophet might be: a messenger sent by God to speak on His behalf. The need for such a go-between, as we have seen, was taken for granted in biblical times: direct contact between God and ordinary humans was deemed to be too dangerous (Gen. 32:30; Exod. 33:20; Judg. 13:22), or too frightening and painful (Exod. 20:18–21; Deut. 18:16–18) for people to bear. Therefore, when God had a message to be delivered to someone or some group (such as the king or some other individual; the royal house; foreign kings and their nations; or the people of Israel as a whole), He would send a messenger. Not a *mere* messenger, of course; apart from speaking on God's behalf, prophets were also holy men and women. Indeed, some of them are reported to have performed miraculous deeds or to have acted as intercessors with God on Israel's behalf (such things seem particularly characteristic of prophets from the north).[1] But their role as divine messengers is central to the biblical portrayal of most prophets. Accordingly, one of the most characteristic features of prophetic speech is the opening phrase "Thus says the LORD." Scholars long ago noticed that this same *messenger formula,* "Thus says X," was also regularly used by envoys who had

---

* Daniel is usually classified as a fourth "major" prophet in Christian Bibles.

been sent by human kings or even just ordinary individuals (Gen. 32:5; 45:9; Exod. 5:10; Num. 20:14; 22:16, and many more). Its standard use by prophets thus makes clear that they were presenting themselves to their listeners essentially as messengers sent by God.[2]

This is an important point, since many people today associate prophecy with predicting the future. It is true that the messages that prophets carried often did bear on things about to happen, but to think of their messages as predictions is to distort their character. Rather, what prophets typically did was announce God's verdict or judgment, to be carried out or acted upon soon, if not right away.[3] Indeed, one of the most characteristic sorts of message that prophets brought had an altogether legal ring to it, in which first the offending party's sin was announced and then God's punishment: "Because you have done such-and-such, therefore I will do thus-and-so."[4] The punishment had yet to be carried out, but the prophet was not a forecaster; he was reporting on a decision that had already been made, announcing the sentence just passed on high.

Many societies, ancient and modern, prominently include prophetlike figures, even if they do not precisely fit the portrait of biblical prophets—sibyls and oracles and soothsayers of various kinds are found across the globe.[5] Modern scholars have therefore been eager to discover what, if anything, biblical prophets had in common with such other figures, perhaps with an eye to understanding how the regular institution of prophecy got started.

At one point the Bible itself seems to suggest that, despite the existence of potentially similar figures elsewhere, the Israelite prophet was altogether unique. His uniqueness was in fact a token of the great gap separating Israel's religion from that of its neighbors:

> [Moses tells the Israelites:] When you come into the land that the LORD your God is giving you, you must not learn to imitate the abhorrent practices of those nations. No one shall be found among you who makes a son or daughter pass through fire, or who practices divination, or is a soothsayer, or an augur, or a sorcerer, or one who casts spells, or who consults ghosts or spirits, or who seeks oracles from the dead. For whoever does these things is abhorrent to the LORD; it is because of such abhorrent practices that the LORD your God is driving them out before you . . . [Instead,] the LORD your God will raise up for you a prophet like me from among your own people; he is the one whom you shall heed.
>
> Deut. 18:9–15

In other words: other nations may have various sorts of people who provide oracles or auguries, but God will give you prophets instead.

Despite the claim of this passage, scholars have pointed to various ancient texts that suggest that the Israelite prophet was not God's ad hoc creation to make consulting oracles and mediums unnecessary. There was, these scholars say, an organic connection between the biblical prophet and figures known from elsewhere in the ancient Near East. To begin with, a number of prophet-like functionaries have been identified in the writings of Israel's neighbors, particularly in texts from Mari (eighteenth century BCE)[6] and in neo-Assyrian writings (seventh century BCE).[7] These people have different titles and, judging by their titles, different roles: *āpilu/āpiltu* ("answerer"), *muḫḫu/muḫḫutu* ("ecstatic"), *raggimu/raggimtu* ("proclaimer"), and others.[8] Indeed, the most common biblical word for prophet, *nabi'*, has been found to exist in its Akkadian cognate in the Mari texts (*nabû*); an Akkadian text from Emar, on the middle Euphrates, dated to around 1300 BCE, refers to a female figure with titles apparently derived from this same root, *anabbi'ātu* and *munabbi'ātu*.[9] Sometimes these figures are said specifically to advise the king or other official, as biblical prophets also did. The texts also indicate at times that the source of these figures' prophecy was a dream (as with biblical prophets, Num. 12:6) or a revelation in a temple (such as Samuel's, described above), or an ecstatic trance (Num. 11:26; 1 Sam. 10:5); several texts also refer to a god "sending" the messenger or the message. All this suggests that the idea of prophecy—indeed, the very terminology used (*nabi'*)—did not originate in Israel and was not utterly distinct from prophecy elsewhere in the region. Indeed, the Canaanite god Baal is said in several places to have had prophets (*nebi'im*) (1 Kings 18:19, 22, 40; 2 Kings 10:19), as did the goddess Asherah (1 Kings 18:19). Likewise, the Deir 'Allā inscription (above, chapter 21) speaks of the non-Israelite Balaam as having had a vision of the god El. Apparently, then, the idea of Israel's God sending His own agents or messengers was, despite the implications of Deut. 18:15, not altogether unique. Here, it might seem, was yet another blow to traditional religious belief.

At the same time, scholars have found nothing elsewhere that is truly comparable to the actual social niche occupied by the prophet in Israel, nor anything comparable to the writings of Israel's great "writing prophets";* if Israelite prophecy's origins share something with prophecy elsewhere, the institution soon developed its own unique characteristics.[10] With regard to the prophet's social role, it is striking that Israelite prophets do not just advise the king, but often reproach him on God's behalf (as Nathan reproaches David, for example). Sometimes the prophet was actually the enemy of the king; Ahab calls Elijah "you troublemaker" (1 Kings 18:17). Nor, more generally, are Mesopotamian prophets spoken of as champions of justice or moral reformers; there is nothing reported of them that might correspond to "Let justice roll down like waters, and righteousness like an ever-flowing

---

* This term is used of prophets whose words are recorded in biblical books—Isaiah, Jeremiah, and so forth—as opposed to prophets like Elijah and Elisha, whose words were never set down in separate collections.

stream" (Amos 5:24). Moreover, there is nothing from Mesopotamia corresponding to the great collections of prophetic writings found in the Hebrew Bible. In the end, then, most scholars concede that while the Israelite office of prophet has formal analogues elsewhere, those who exercised this function soon became, to judge by the (admittedly) incomplete comparative evidence, a unique phenomenon in the ancient Near East.

This observation ought to be connected to another made by scholars: as a regular *institution* in Israel, prophecy was basically coterminous with kingship.[11] That is, the prophet Samuel appeared precisely at the moment when Israel was about to appoint its first king. Thereafter, for more than four centuries, prophets and kings continued to coexist (often, not on the friendliest of terms). But then kingship died: the Babylonians conquered the kingdom of Judah in 586 BCE, took the king captive, killed his sons, and exiled much of Judah's population to Babylon, where it remained for half a century. After the Persians conquered the Babylonians and allowed the Jews to return to their old homeland, there was some brief hope that a Davidic heir might also be restored to the throne (even if only as a puppet). But that hope was never to be realized. Interestingly, it is at the point that this bit of bad news began to sink in that prophecy seems to have died out too, or at least to have lost its former place in society and in the public's confidence. The last canonical prophets, Haggai, Zechariah, and Malachi, belong to the period just after the Jews' return from exile.

Why should prophecy have begun at the same time as kingship and then ceased to function after kingship was gone? Perhaps, some scholars believe, the two offices had been joined at the hip from birth. That is, the particular role that prophets came to play during the early years of the monarchy (at least, to judge by the historical sources at scholars' disposal) had something to do with the Israelite tribes' early and ongoing suspicion of kingship. Even after these disparate tribes had been united into a single kingdom, the population remained fearful of the power a king might wield; how far would he go? Under the circumstances, people were only too happy to have in their midst holy men and women who, speaking as God's messengers, could approach the king and say, "To do that would be going too far," or, "What you are doing is wrong." And indeed, prophets did often rebuke kings in just these terms. As already mentioned, Nathan rebukes David (2 Sam. 12), as does the prophet Gad (2 Sam. 24:10–14); Ahijah of Shiloh speaks out against Solomon (1 Kings 11:11–13), and later against Jeroboam (1 Kings 14); the prophet Shemaiah condemns Rehoboam (1 Kings 12:21–24); Elijah and Elisha, as mentioned, are constant critics of the northern rulers; Isaiah strongly warns King Ahaz (Isaiah 7); and so forth. Such an arrangement may fall short of a modern government's system of checks and balances, but it at least held out the hope that kingship might, in Israel, be less of an absolute dictatorship than it was elsewhere in the ancient Near East.

"We Want a King!"

Samuel soon took his place among the leaders of his people, serving as a judge at various locations in his home territory of Benjamin (1 Sam. 7:15–17). During this time, he seems to have functioned a bit like the leaders who preceded him in the book of Judges, aiding the people in their struggles against the Philistines (1 Sam. 7:7–14). He was thus already an old man when the people approached Samuel with a request: "Give us a king to rule over us!" (1 Sam. 8:6). Up until then, the Bible says, God had been their only king, and this request was thus a tacit throwing off of God's direct authority. As God says to Samuel, "They are rejecting Me as their king" (1 Sam. 8:7). The prophet therefore did his best to discourage the people:

> He said, "This is how a king will be when he rules over you: he will take your sons and make them his charioteers and his cavalry, and have them run before his own chariot. He will make some of them commanders of thousands and commanders of fifties, and use others to plow his lands and bring in his harvest, and to make his weaponry and tackle for his horses. He will take your daughters to be perfumers and cooks and bakers. Then he will take over the best of your fields and vineyards and olive orchards and give them to the men of his court. He will take a tenth of your grain and of your vineyards and give it to his officials and court personnel. He will take your male and female slaves, and the best of your cattle and donkeys, and put them to work for him. He will take a tenth of your flocks. Eventually you yourselves will become his servants. And in that day you will cry out because of this king of yours, whom you chose; but the LORD will not answer you in that day."
>
> Nevertheless, the people refused to heed Samuel. They said, "No! We will have a king over us, so that we can be like any other nation, and so that our king may govern us and lead us in battle."
>
> 1 Sam. 8:11–20

Samuel ultimately gave in to the will of the people. He anointed a man from the tribe of Benjamin, Saul the son of Kish, to be king.[12] At least Saul had all the physical requirements for leadership: he was "a handsome man; in fact, there was not a man among the people of Israel more handsome than he; he stood a head taller than everyone else" (1 Sam. 9:2).

Saul's Rise(s) to the Throne

Since the beginning of modern scholarship, the story of how Saul came to be king has seemed to scholars a patchwork composed of originally separate strands.

The first strand is found in 1 Sam. 9:1–10:16, which relates a somewhat comical story. Saul's father, Kish, has lost some donkeys; he dispatches the young Saul, along with a servant, to go find them. They look all over Saul's home territory of Benjamin and are about to give up when the servant suddenly mentions that a certain "seer" lives in a nearby town. (What exactly is a "seer"? The narrative adds parenthetically that "the person who is nowadays called a prophet used to be called a seer," 1 Sam. 9:9.) Presumably, such a seer might be able to locate the missing donkeys by supernatural means. However, being a seer is apparently a paying job, and this worries Saul, since he does not have anything on him to offer as an emolument. By chance, however, the servant has a quarter-shekel of silver, so off they go.

The seer is, of course, Samuel, and God has already told him of Saul's imminent arrival. As soon as Saul appears, God says to Samuel: "This is the man I told you about. He is the one who will rule over my people" (1 Sam. 9:17). Samuel therefore tells Saul and the servant that they must eat with him and also spend the night. "And don't worry about the donkeys that got lost three days ago," Samuel adds. "They've been found."

Early the next morning, Samuel wakes Saul up and says that it is time to leave. As they reach the edge of town, however, Samuel says to Saul, "Tell the servant to walk ahead of us, while you stop here." He then pulls out a flask of oil and pours it on Saul's head. "Your Majesty," [13] he says, "The LORD hereby names you to lead His people." Saul is apparently somewhat flabbergasted, but Samuel goes on to predict a number of signs that will prove that Saul is indeed God's choice. All the signs predicted by Samuel then come to pass.

But Saul apparently still does not feel like a king. He runs into his uncle, who asks him what he is doing there. "We came looking for the donkeys," he answers, "but when we saw that they weren't around, we went to consult Samuel." "And what did Samuel say to you?" Surely this was the occasion for Saul to relate the extraordinary events that had occurred, leading up to his being anointed king and all the signs that followed. "He said the donkeys had already been found," is all Saul answers.

To biblical scholars, this narrative sounds—despite its present location—like something straight out of the book of Judges. Like Israel's other charismatic leaders in that book, Saul does not feel he has any claim to rule: "I am only a Benjaminite," he says, "from the smallest of Israel's tribes, and my family is the humblest of all the families of the tribe of Benjamin" (1 Sam. 9:21). This sounds suspiciously like what Gideon says to the angel in Judg. 6:15, "My clan is the weakest in Manasseh, and I am the least in my family." And just as happens again and again with the heroes of the book of Judges (Judg. 6:34; 11:29; 14:6, 19; 15:14), the "spirit of the LORD" comes over Saul and he undergoes a complete transformation (1 Sam. 10:6, 10).*

But then there is a second, apparently quite separate, account of how Saul becomes king. It starts right after the first account.

> Samuel summoned the people to the LORD at Mizpah and said to them, "Thus says the LORD, the God of Israel, 'I brought up Israel out of Egypt, and I rescued you from Egyptians and from all the kingdoms that were oppressing you.' But today you have rejected your God, who saves you from all your calamities and your troubles, and you have said, 'No! but set a king over us.' Now therefore present yourselves before the LORD by your tribes and by your clans."
>
> Then Samuel brought forward all the tribes of Israel, and the tribe of Benjamin was chosen by lot. He brought the tribe of Benjamin forward by families, and the family of the Matrites was chosen by lot. Finally he brought the family of the Matrites near, [naming] one man at a time, and Saul the son of Kish was chosen by lot. But when they looked for him, he was nowhere to be found. So they inquired again of the LORD, "Did the man come here?" and the LORD said, "Look! There he is, hiding among the baggage." Then they ran and brought him out. When he stood up among the people, he was a head taller than any of them. Samuel said to all the people, "Do you see the one whom the LORD has chosen? There is no one like him among all the people." And all the people shouted, "Long live the king!"
>
> 1 Sam. 10:17–24

This passage seems to show no awareness of the narrative that just precedes it. Here, Saul is chosen by lots—almost as if his previous selection by God somehow did not count. In fact, he is introduced here by his full name, "Saul the son of Kish," as if for the first time—even though this introduction had been made earlier (9:1–2). And here we are told once again that Saul is a head taller than any other Israelite—just as in 9:2. The conclusion seems inevitable: these two were originally quite independent accounts of how Saul came to rule Israel.

Scholars have noted other differences between the two accounts. In the first story, "Kish's Lost Donkeys," there is not the slightest hint that God

---

* Indeed, Saul is specifically said to have acted as a "judge" in Israel in 1 Sam. 7:6, 15 and to have appointed his sons as judges after him (1Sam. 8:1–3).

objects to naming a king. On the contrary, He tells Samuel, "Tomorrow about this time I will send to you a man from the land of Benjamin, and you shall anoint him to be ruler over my people Israel. *He shall save my people* from the hand of the Philistines; for I have seen the suffering of my people, because their outcry has come to me" (1 Sam. 9:16). Thus, the new leader is to be nothing less than the instrument of God's salvation. The other story, "Saul Chosen by Lot," starts off with Samuel again berating the people for having rejected God's kingship in favor of a human ruler—as if this story were meant to be a direct continuation of Samuel's long speech about the evils of kings in 1 Sam. 8:11–20. Here, kingship is definitely bad.

The image of Samuel is also quite different in the two accounts. In "Kish's Lost Donkeys," Samuel is a very local figure; Saul lives in the same geographic area as Samuel but is apparently quite unaware of his existence until his servant mentions him. And despite the narrative's parenthetic equation of "seer" with "prophet," Samuel does not seem very much like a prophet in this story. Instead, he is presented as a small-time operator, the kind of fortune-teller or medium you can turn to and, after paying a fee, have your donkey handed to you. In "Saul Chosen by Lot," by contrast, Samuel is a national leader: he *summons* the people to Mizpah and speaks as a prophet; "Thus says the LORD, the God of Israel . . ."

What can these differences tell us about where the two versions came from? Scholars have argued about this for more than a century.[14] Wellhausen and others saw the "antimonarchic source" as a late addition, reflecting disillusionment with kingship after the fall of Judah to the Babylonian conquerors. The "kingship is bad" passages certainly must have been written later than Deuteronomy, Wellhausen reasoned, since that book clearly views kingship as a natural, and altogether permissible, institution (Deut. 17:14–20). But others have pointed to the antimonarchic strains of the eighth-century prophet Hosea:

[God says to Israel:]
"Where is your king? Where is your champion?
[Where are] all those princes and officers of yours, back when you said,
    'Give me a king and rulers'?
Well, I gave you a king in My anger, and in My wrath I took him away."
Hos. 13:10–11

The last line, according to these scholars, is actually an allusion to an old tradition about Saul: he ascended the throne against God's wishes, "in My anger," which is pretty much what 1 Sam. 10:18–19 says.[15] So, even if the antimonarchic material has been reworked by later editors, it may well repose on ancient tradition.

These chapters of 1 Samuel open a window onto the modus operandi of the Deuteronomistic historian(s). As one recent scholar has highlighted, there was something quite scholarly and detached about this whole project of writing a history of Israel.[16] Eliminating all contradictions was not part of the plan. To be sure, seams were sometimes smoothed over, and editorializing additions are sometimes found. Still, nothing would have been easier for a historian than to cut out one version or another, or harmonize them by slashing here and there. But the Deuteronomistic historian(s) had too much respect for ancient traditions and texts to do that. Instead, the two different versions we have seen were fitted together and preserved.

Indeed, it appears that, in addition to these two stories explaining Saul's rise, yet a third has been included in the Deuteronomistic History, the brief account of Saul's victory against the Ammonites in 1 Samuel 11. This narrative, some scholars say, may have started out as another, quite independent version of how Saul became king; it is striking that here, even more than elsewhere, Saul is presented as a figure out of the book of Judges. Thus, like Gideon or Samson, Saul is leading an ordinary life until "the spirit of God" seizes him (11:6). He then cuts up a pair of oxen and sends them with a message to the neighboring tribes: "This is what will happen to your cattle," Saul says, "if you don't follow Samuel and me into battle" (1 Sam. 11:7). Saul then musters a huge army and handily defeats the Ammonites; as a result, he is made king by acclamation (11:15).[17]

That these various stories about Saul's rise to power *could* be read as sequential rather than contradictory is clear from the fact that, for centuries and centuries, no one seemed to notice the apparent overlaps and inconsistencies. In other words, the Deuteronomistic History was composed as a plausible recitation of the past. Of course, reading that history as a single, harmonious, and perfect account was, for centuries, a natural result of the assumptions with which readers approached the text (in this case, the third of our Four Assumptions). As soon as those assumptions melted away, however, the tensions between the various versions were suddenly obvious, and the composite nature of the biblical text was plain for scholars to see.

Good King Saul

The period of Saul's rise to power was a unique one in the ancient Near East. Throughout most of its recorded history, the little strip of territory between the Jordan River and the Mediterranean Sea had been dominated by its larger, more powerful neighbors. In biblical times, these neighbors included Egypt to the south, Babylon and Assyria to the east, Aram/Syria to the north, and still farther north, the Hittites (who ruled part of the territory now occupied by Turkey and Syria).

But the time of Saul and David was one in which *all* these traditional centers of imperial power were consumed with their own internal problems. This gave the coalescing tribes of Israel a unique opportunity, not only to cast off foreign domination, but to form a mini-empire of their own in the process. In fact, historians theorize, this historic opportunity may have a lot to do with the real reason for Saul's rise to power: the tribes looked to him principally as a warrior and army organizer. It is no surprise, therefore, that much of the Bible's account of Saul's reign is taken up with his military successes: Moabites, Ammonites, Edomites, Philistines, Amalekites, and other foreign powers are said to have fallen to his sword. (An account of some of these battles is found in 1 Samuel 11; 13–14; 15; 17; 28–31.) Modern scholars suspect that some of these victories may be an exaggeration, but there is little skepticism about the overall character of Saul's rule. If he was the leader around whom most of the tribes coalesced (there is actually no indication that the mighty southern tribe of Judah was ever part of his kingdom—see 2 Sam. 2:9–10), he must have had, from the start, the makings of a great general.

Ḥerem of the Amalekites

The Amalekites were one of Israel's fiercest enemies. They were the ones who, according to the biblical account (Exod. 17:8–16), attacked the ragtag Israelites shortly after the exodus, at a time when "you were tired and weary; they [the Amalekites] came from behind and picked off all the stragglers behind you—they had no common decency" (Deut. 25:18). No wonder that God had commanded Israel to "wipe out the name of Amalek" when the time was ripe (Deut. 25:19). Now that Israel had suddenly become a regional power, that time seemed to have arrived.

> Samuel said to Saul, "I am the one that the LORD sent to make you king over His people Israel. Heed, therefore, what the LORD has said [to me]. Thus says the LORD of hosts, 'Now I will punish the Amalekites for what they did in opposing the Israelites when they came up out of Egypt. Go attack Amalek, and utterly destroy everything that they have; do not spare them, but kill both men and women, children and little babies, oxen and sheep, camels and donkeys.' "
>
> 1 Sam. 15:1–3

God's commandment to kill everything in sight—men, women, and little babies, as well as dumb beasts—has, for centuries, stuck in the throats of Bible readers. How could a God who is supposedly "merciful and compassionate" even allow such a thing to happen—never mind actually *order* it to happen. Indeed, this passage and similar ones have been disowned by many modern theologians ("This is no God that I know," declared Martin Buber), and more than one modern commentator has sought to explain away such passages as an "anachronistic literary formulation" that could not actually have taken place.[18]

Anachronism or not, the practice of putting the entire enemy population to death (that is, putting them under the "ban," as the Hebrew word *herem* is usually translated) has to be seen in the broader context of ancient Near Eastern warfare. War in that orbit was, by all accounts, unbelievably brutal. Although the circumstances and precise measures varied, captured enemies, whether combatants or not, were regularly taken as booty. Men were turned into slave laborers, women were raped and then taken as concubines or domestic slaves, and frightened young children were handed over to whoever wanted them. As for the domestic animals and other material possessions of the defeated party, these were likewise divided up by the victorious army. Under such circumstances, warfare was actually a most profitable enterprise. One good reason for besieging a foreign city was to get rich—and biblical law seems to approve of the practice (Deut. 20:10–15; 21:10–14).

It is against this background that one must view the peculiar biblical institution of the "ban." It might best be described as "not-for-profit warfare." Under this system, instead of the spoils of war going to the conquerors, they were to be utterly destroyed. Having been offered to God as *His* spoils (indeed, perhaps as a way of ensuring His help in the conquest), the booty could not then be used for the conquerors' own gain. To do so would be the equivalent of taking anything else that belonged to God—the firstborn of the flocks and herds, or the first fruits of the harvest—and keeping them for one's own use. That was the gravest of sins.

So, that is what Samuel instructs Saul to do—enforce the "ban" on the Amalekites. Saul agrees. Fortified with this holy mission, Saul then defeats the Amalekites utterly, "from Havilah as far as Shur, which is east of Egypt" (1 Sam. 15:7). Surveying the captured goods, however, he cannot bring himself to put everything to the torch. Instead, "Saul and the people spared [the Amalekite king] Agag, and the best of the sheep and of the cattle and of the fatlings and the lambs, and all that was valuable. They did not implement the ban [*herem*]; only that which was despised and worthless did they destroy" (1 Sam. 15:9).

The next morning, Samuel, who has learned of Saul's disobedience, goes off to find him. The encounter between these two men—the tall, tergiflexuous, rule-stretching Saul and the shorter, aged, but unbending prophet who anointed him—presents a stark contrast in character:

> Samuel got up early in the morning to meet Saul. But someone told Samuel, "Saul had to go to Carmel to set up a monument, and on the way back he went down to Gilgal." So Samuel went to see Saul. Saul said to him, "May you be blessed by the LORD—I have carried out what the LORD said."

Samuel said, "Oh yes? Then what is that bleating sound I hear? And what is that mooing of cows in my ears?" Saul said, "Those . . . they brought them from the Amalekites—the soldiers did, so as to spare the best of the sheep and the cattle, to sacrifice to the LORD your God. But the rest we have completely destroyed."

Then Samuel said to Saul, "That's enough! Let me tell you what the LORD said to me last night." He said, "Go on." Samuel said, "You may be small in your own eyes, but are you not still the head of Israel's tribes? The LORD made you king over Israel. Then the LORD sent you on a journey and said, 'Go and utterly destroy those evildoers, the Amalekites. Fight them until none of them is left.' Why then did you not obey the LORD's words? Why instead did you swoop down on the spoils, and do what was evil in the sight of the LORD?"

Saul said to Samuel, "I did do what the LORD said to do. I traveled to where the LORD sent me, and I brought back Agag, the Amalekite king— and I utterly destroyed the Amalekites. It is just that the troops took some sheep and cattle from the spoils—the best of the things that were to be destroyed—in order to sacrifice them to the LORD your God in Gilgal."

1 Sam. 15:12–21

It is certainly a telling detail that Saul was off setting up a monument to his own glory (one of those victory steles that archaeologists have turned up here and there on the eastern Mediterranean coast) when Samuel first came look-ing for him. How different this Saul is from the shy young man whom Samuel had proclaimed king some years earlier! Noteworthy as well is the fact that the normally taciturn Saul is suddenly all talk. "May the LORD bless you," he says to the prophet, hoping that this pious greeting may help deflect Samuel's wrath—and then he adds, even before Samuel gets to respond, "I've carried out what the LORD told me to do." Surely a guilty conscience sounds the same in any language. But Samuel is not buying: "Then what are all these sheep and goats and cattle doing here?" he asks. To this question Saul twice gives the same excuse: It's not my fault—you know how soldiers are— and besides, they saved those animals only in order to offer them as sacrifices.

But Samuel said, "What does the LORD prefer—burnt offerings and sacri-fices, or obedience to what the LORD says? 'Surely, to obey is better than sacrifice, and to heed than the fat of rams. Rebellion is as much a sin as div-ination, and stubbornness is like the wickedness of idol-worship.'* There-fore, since you have rejected the word of the LORD, He hereby rejects you as king."

---

* Samuel may be quoting some well-known oracle or proverb, or perhaps propounding one of his own.

Then Saul said to Samuel, "All right, I made a mistake. I did transgress the LORD's commandment and your words—but it was because I was afraid of the soldiers and did what they said. So please: forgive my mistake and come back with me, so that I can worship the LORD." But Samuel said to Saul, "I will not return with you. Since you have rejected the word of the LORD, the LORD has rejected you as king over Israel."

1 Sam. 15:22–26

As far as Samuel is concerned, Saul is finished as king—and indeed, he will soon meet his tragic end.[19]

Some readers would no doubt be happier if that were the end of the story of the Amalekite *ḥerem,* but it is not. Samuel is still determined that the death sentence pronounced by God on Israel's archenemy be carried out—even if he has to do it himself:

Then Samuel said, "Bring Agag king of the Amalekites here to me." And Agag came to him hesitatingly. Agag said, "Surely this is the bitterness of death." Samuel said: "As your sword has made women childless, so your mother shall be childless among women." And Samuel hacked Agag to pieces before the LORD in Gilgal. Then Samuel went to Ramah; and Saul went up to his house in Gibeah of Saul. Samuel did not see Saul again until the day of his death, but Samuel grieved over Saul. And the LORD was sorry that he had made Saul king over Israel.

1 Sam. 15:32–35

Saul's Rival, David

Just as scholars have identified conflicting, originally independent accounts of how Saul became king, so have they done with regard to the biblical account of the rise of Saul's successor, David. Here too there seem to be three independent stories.

According to the first (1 Samuel 16), God dispatches the aging Samuel to Bethlehem to choose a new king (since Saul has been rejected). It will be one of Jesse's sons, God says to Samuel. When the prophet arrives at Jesse's house, he is convinced that the oldest son, Eliab, is the one whom God had designated—apparently on the same grounds that Saul had been chosen years earlier: Eliab is tall and handsome. But God says that Eliab is not His choice. He then tries the next, and the next, and the next—seven sons in all— but God rejects each in turn. "Is that all?" Samuel asks. "There is one more," Jesse says, "the youngest—but he is off with the sheep" (not a very honored occupation).[20] "Send for him," Samuel says, "because I cannot leave until he comes here." When David arrives, God at once tells Samuel to anoint him, and, as with Israel's chiefs/judges, "the spirit of the LORD came mightily over David" (1 Sam. 16:13). He is now ready to lead.

This account of David's rise to power is immediately followed by two more. In the first, King Saul is suffering from bouts of insanity (in the biblical phrase, an "evil spirit from the LORD tormented him," 1 Sam. 16:14). Music was believed at times to be an effective palliative for insanity, so Saul's courtiers advise him to hire a musician. But who?

> One of the young men answered, "I have seen a son of Jesse the Bethlehemite who is skillful in playing, a man of valor, a warrior, prudent in speech, and a man of good presence; and the LORD is with him." So Saul sent messengers to Jesse and said, "Send me your son David who is with the sheep." . . . So David came to Saul, and entered his service. Saul loved him greatly, and he became his armor-bearer . . . And whenever the evil spirit from God came upon Saul, David took the lyre and played it with his hand, and Saul would be relieved and feel better, and the evil spirit would depart from him.
>
> 1 Sam. 16:18–23

Here, David comes to court not as Saul's already-anointed successor but as a musician and singer. It is this position that will allow him to walk freely in the corridors of power and, eventually, take over from his employer.

The third account (1 Samuel 17) is the best known: a great Philistine bully, Goliath, is threatening and taunting the Israelites. According to the traditional Hebrew text, Goliath is some nine feet tall—a giant—and he keeps challenging the Israelites to send forth their best man to fight him *mano a mano*. The Israelites are terrified. Finally, after forty days of such taunts, David, the youngest of Jesse's eight sons, appears and persuades King Saul to send him out against Goliath. He is so young and small that he cannot wear the traditional armor or bear the arms that usually go with it; instead, he takes only his slingshot and five smooth stones. With a single shot he fells the arrogant Philistine, then finishes him off with his own sword.[21]

> When Saul first saw David go out against the Philistine, he asked Abner, the commander of the army, "Abner, whose son is that boy?" Abner said, "By your life, your Majesty, I do not know." The king said, "Then find out whose son that young fellow is." So, when David had come back from killing the Philistine, Abner took him and brought him before Saul, with the head of the Philistine in his hand. Saul said to him, "Whose son are you, young fellow?" And David answered, "I am the son of your servant Jesse the Bethlehemite."
>
> 1 Sam. 17:55–58

David the Anointed

It is simply a coincidence, but these three accounts happen to highlight the three (in fact, four) main aspects of David's "image" among ancient interpreters. Taken together, they encapsulate much of what David meant to readers of the Bible for centuries and centuries.[22]

In the first account, Samuel chooses David from among his seven brothers and immediately anoints him king. But what did it mean to anoint someone? Quite literally, "anoint" means to pour or rub oil on the person's head. To us, this is likely to sound rather messy and unpleasant, but that is because we tend to think of the gooey sort of oils used for salad dressing and frying. The oils used for anointing were highly refined. More important, they were perfumed—that was their whole purpose, in fact. In the ancient world, people enjoyed rubbing their bodies with the most wonderful scents they could obtain, surrounding themselves with a world of olfactory sensation. The Bible gives ample evidence that spice merchants traveled long distances with their products—from Arabia and points still farther away—and the anointing oils produced from their wares were clearly a luxury item.[23] Thus, when Amos denounces the selfish upper classes of Israel, he mentions specifically those who "drink wine from fancy bowls and anoint themselves with the finest oils" (Amos 6:6). So willing were people to pay hefty prices for scented oils that the precise processes for manufacturing certain spices were sometimes kept secret.[24] Abstaining from anointing oneself even for a single day was felt to be a form of self-affliction, comparable to fasting.[25]

To pour anointing oil on someone was thus a nice thing to do, in fact, an honorific gesture, and in Israel it became the symbolic act by which a person was granted exalted office: kings were anointed, and so, at a certain point, were high priests.[26] So much was anointing associated with the office of king that the word *mashiah*, "anointed one," became an elegant synonym for king in biblical Hebrew.

It may have taken some time for David to become king after Samuel had anointed him (and if so, this was quite atypical, since anointing usually symbolized the actual assumption of the new office), but eventually he did take the throne; indeed, he was, by the Bible's own account, Israel's dynastic founder and greatest king. And so, many centuries later, when the nation's heyday was only a distant memory and what was left of the Jewish people now suffered under foreign domination, hope was kindled that sometime in the future things might somehow return to what they had once been: Israel would regain its former glory through the restoration of a Davidic king, a *mashiah*, to the throne. This hope has never been abandoned in Judaism; indeed, long ago it became an established item of Jewish faith: three times a day, pious Jews turn in prayer toward Jerusalem to ask for (among other things) the restoration of the Davidic king, since this will inaugurate a return to the way things were when Israel held sway. As the ancestor of this future king, David thus acquired a particular coloring among ancient interpreters: he was, despite whatever missteps he might have taken in his life, the very model of the royal ideal.

In Christianity the theme of David the *mashiah* acquired, if possible, even greater significance. The first Christians held that Jesus was indeed the long-awaited *mashiah* and so referred to him as the Messiah (from the Greek transliteration of the Hebrew word) as well as the *christos* (Greek for "anointed one"). As a consequence, David was seen as a forerunner, and a foreshadowing, of Christ: the story of his struggles with enemies and his ulti-mate victory were understood by Christians to presage the suffering and final triumph of Jesus. His being anointed by Samuel and becoming the *christos* were therefore a highly significant part of the biblical saga—and yet another proof that "what is hidden in the Old lies open in the New."

Sweet Singer of Israel

That David came to Saul's court as a musician and singer was connected to another part of David's image among ancient (and modern) Bible readers, David the musician and singer. Relatively few political leaders are remembered as talented musicians; their gifts usually lie in other, less aesthetic areas. This alone marked David as unusual—and indeed, his accomplishments as a singer and player seem to have accompanied him throughout his days. When Saul and his sons died in battle, David is said to have composed a moving elegy (2 Sam. 1:19–27); later in life, free from the cares of warfare, he is credited with authoring a hymn of praise (2 Samuel 22). Indeed, David is referred to in 2 Sam. 23:1 as *ne'im zemirot yisra'el,* traditionally translated as the "sweet singer of Israel." And quite apart from the narrative in 1 and 2 Samuel, David's talents as a musician are highlighted at various other spots in the Bible. Thus, the book of Chronicles credits David with having arranged the Levites' singing and playing in the temple (1 Chron. 15:16; 16:4) and even with designing the musical instruments used there for praising God (1 Chron. 23:6; 2 Chron. 7:6); long before, the prophet Amos seemed to have said as much (Amos 6:5).

In view of these many references, ancient interpreters came to think of David—despite his standing as Israel's king—primarily as a composer of songs and prayers. For reasons to be explored presently, David was thought to be the author of the book of Psalms—150 chapters of divine praise, thanksgiving, and petition. But for some ancient readers, that was hardly enough! A text found among the Dead Sea Scrolls actually credits David with more than four thousand works:

And David the son of Jesse was wise, and radiant[27] as the light of the sun, and a sage—wise and unblemished in all his ways before God and men. And the LORD gave him a discerning and radiant spirit, and he wrote three thousand six hundred psalms; and songs to sing each and every day before the altar over the *tamid* sacrifice—for all the days of the year, three hundred and sixty-four; and for the sabbath sacrifices, fifty-two songs; and for the sacrifices of the New Moon and for all the festival days and for the Day of Atonement, thirty songs. Thus, all the songs that he composed were four hundred and forty-six; and songs to be performed against evil spirits, four. Thus, the grand total was four thousand and fifty. All these he composed through prophecy which was given to him by the Most High.

11QPs.[a] ("David's Compositions")

David the Prophet

David was not merely a musician; by singing and playing on the lyre (a small harp) he was able to drive away the "evil spirit from the LORD" that afflicted Saul. This suggested to ancient interpreters that David's singing itself must have had God's backing; and since the lyre was frequently used by prophets to bring on their prophecy (1 Sam. 10:5; 2 Kings 3:14–16), it did not seem too much of a stretch to suppose that David himself might have been, in some sense, a prophet—that is, God's emissary and a transmitter of His words. Indeed, at the end of his life, David pronounced what is clearly described as a prophetic oracle (2 Sam. 23:1), in which he introduces himself in these terms:

> The spirit of the LORD speaks through me, His word is upon my tongue;
> the God of Israel has spoken, the Rock of Israel has said to me . . .

2 Sam. 23:2

From such considerations arose a further refinement of the biblical picture of David and his lyre: David the prophet.[28] This theme is already adumbrated in the Dead Sea Scrolls passage cited earlier, in which David is said to have composed his four-thousand-plus compositions "through prophecy which was given to him by the Most High." At roughly the same time that these words were being written, Philo of Alexandria was referring to David as "a certain prophetic fellow" (*Who Is Heir* 290). If these two sources seem hesitant to call David a prophet outright (saying only that he spoke "through prophecy" or was "prophetic"), that hesitation soon disappeared. Early Christian and rabbinic texts frequently refer to David as a prophet plain and simple.

Indeed, David's status as a regular prophet was particularly crucial to Christians since, among other texts, verses from the psalms were marshaled to demonstrate that the events of the Gospels had been prophetically foretold

(Mk. 12:10–11, 35–37 and parallels; Matt. 4:6; 13:34; etc.). David must therefore have spoken "in the Holy Spirit" (Mk. 12:36). The book of Acts asserts that the Holy Spirit "spoke beforehand by the mouth of David" (Acts 1:16) and that God "spoke by the mouth of our father David His servant" (4:25). Elsewhere in that book, Peter addresses the crowd with these words:

> "Fellow countrymen, we all know[29] that the patriarch David died and was buried, indeed, his tomb is in our midst to this day. *Since he was a prophet,* however, he knew that God had sworn with an oath to him that He would put one of his descendants on his throne [2 Sam. 12:7–13; Ps. 132:11]. Foreseeing this, he [David] spoke of the coming[30] of the Messiah, saying that he [David] 'was not abandoned to Hades, nor did his flesh experience corruption'" [cf. Septuagint translation of Ps. 15 (MT 16):10.][31]
>
> Acts 2:29–31

David the Warrior

The story of David and Goliath was often understood in the light of the former themes, "David the prophet" and "David the singer." On the face of it, the biblical story seems intended to celebrate David's gifts as a warrior—even at a young age he proved himself on the field of battle against the fiercest of enemies. But for later generations it was the fact that David went out to meet Goliath essentially unarmed and invoked God's name (1 Sam. 17:46–47) that was important—this is how an unarmed prophet makes war:

> In his youth, did he not kill a giant, and take away the people's disgrace,
>   when he whirled the stone in the sling and struck down the boasting
>   Goliath?
> *For he called on the* LORD, *the Most High,* and He gave strength to his
>   right arm
> to strike down a mighty warrior, and to exalt the power of his people.
>
> Sir. 47:4–5

> Saul admired the lad's daring and courage, but could not place full confidence in him by reason of his years, because of which, he said, he was too weak to fight with a skilled warrior. "The promises," replied David, "I make with the assurance that God is with me, for I have already had proof of aid."
>
> Josephus, *Jewish Antiquities* 6:181

Such was the David of the Bible as it was read for centuries—anointed forerunner of the Messiah, sweet singer and prophet, God's warrior who had no need of weapons. If you were to ask anyone from the closing centuries BCE to the nineteenth century CE who David was, this is the David you would get. Particularly by dint of his authorship of the book of Psalms, David's was a towering presence in the Hebrew Bible: he was one of God's chosen ones, an example for generations of Jews and Christians. But the truth that modern scholars present is, as usual, somewhat different.

26

The Psalms of David

THE BOOK OF PSALMS

David Playing the Lyre, from the Paris Psalter.

"To David." Psalms and cultic worship. Gunkel's categories. Ugarit and the Psalms. Despiritualization.

Why were the Psalms written—and who wrote them? Here is another subject on which ancient and modern commentators disagree.

The book of Psalms is the Bible's book of the soul. In psalm after psalm, the human being turns directly to God, expressing his or her deepest thoughts and fears, asking for help or forgiveness, offering thanks for help already given. And so, for centuries and centuries, people have opened the book of Psalms in order to let its words speak on their behalf: "O God, You know my foolishness; the things I have done wrong are not hidden from You" (69:5). "O God, you are my God; I long for You, my soul thirsts for You" (63:1). "I thank the LORD with my whole heart; let me tell of all the wonderful things that You have done" (Ps. 9:1). "Why, O LORD, do You stand far off? Why should You hide Yourself in time of trouble?" (10:1). These psalms—in fact, all the Psalms—open a direct line of communication between us and God. No wonder, then, that the pages of the book of Psalms tend to be the most worn and ragged in any worshiping family's Bible. And even Americans who know nothing else of Scripture often know Psalm 23 in the majestic language of the King James Version:[1]

> The LORD is my shepherd; I shall not want.
> He maketh me to lie down in green pastures: he leadeth me beside the
>   still waters.
> He restoreth my soul: he leadeth me in the paths of righteousness for his
>   name's sake.
> Yea, though I walk through the valley of the shadow of death, I will fear
>   no evil:
> for thou art with me; thy rod and thy staff they comfort me.
> Thou preparest a table before me in the presence of mine enemies: thou
>   anointest my head with oil; my cup runneth over.
> Surely goodness and mercy shall follow me all the days of my life: and I
>   will dwell in the house of the LORD for ever.

Where did the book of Psalms come from? Tradition assigns its authorship to King David. The reason is obvious enough: roughly half of the Psalms (73 out of a total of 150) have the phrase "to [*or* of] David" (*ledawid*) in their title or heading, for example, "A Psalm of David" (Psalm 15), "A Prayer of David" (Psalm 17), "To the leader. Of David" (Psalm 11), and so forth. Some of these headings actually spell out the circumstances that led David to compose the psalm in question: "A psalm of David, when he fled from his son Absalom" (Ps. 3:1); "Of David, when he feigned madness before Abimelech, so that he drove him out and he went away" (Ps. 34:1), and the like. Although quite a few psalms do not have a heading (and a few have headings that mention other biblical figures), it soon became traditional to think of David as having written all of them.[2]

Modern biblical scholars inherited the tradition of David's authorship, and at first they raised no questions about it. True, some psalms seemed, on the face of things, to speak of a time long after David's death. For example, the well-known opening verses of Psalm 137 read:

> By the rivers of Babylon—there we sat down and wept as we remem-
> bered Zion.
> On the willows in its midst we hung up our harps.
> For there our captors demanded we sing songs, and our tormentors
> called for entertainment, "Sing us one of those songs of Zion!"
> How could we sing a song of the LORD's in a foreign land?
>
> Ps. 137:1–4

The setting is obviously Babylon—apparently at the time of the Babylonian exile (for when else did the Jews have Babylonian "captors" and "tormen-tors"?). That was fully four centuries after David's death. As we have seen, however, David was widely understood to have been not only a singer, but a prophet. Perhaps, people reasoned, David had foreseen in the tenth century BCE what God had in store for Israel in the sixth; he wrote this song so that his people might have it in their darkest hour. The fact that the psalm also mentioned the Edomites only strengthened this hypothesis:

> Repay, O LORD, the Edomites, for the day Jerusalem fell—
> how they kept saying, "Strip her down! Strip her down to the
> foundations!"
>
> Ps. 137:7

By the time of the ancient interpreters, *Edom* was becoming a symbolic name; it did not only designate the actual kingdom to the south of Judea, but was understood to be an oblique way of referring to Rome.[3] If so, interpreters said, Psalm 137 was not only David's prophecy of Jerusalem's destruction by the Babylonians; it also contained a hint that the Holy City would be destroyed a second time, by the Romans of the first century CE.[4]

Not David

By the middle of the nineteenth century, however, scholars began to have their doubts. To begin with, they realized that the expression *ledawid* could mean many things: "for David," "about David," or "belonging to David" are equally acceptable understandings. Perhaps someone else wrote these psalms about David or on David's behalf. Moreover, the Bible sometimes uses personal names to refer to an office—"Aaron" to mean any high priest, for example. So *ledawid* could actually refer to any Davidic king:* this psalm might have been written for the Davidic king Josiah, that one for some other Davidic descendant.[5] Perhaps *ledawid* was a simple fraud, added in by editors to help legitimate the role that psalmody came to play in later times.[6] To these was added yet another possibility: since *ledawid* was found specifically in the psalm's *heading*, it seemed reasonable that this might originally have been some sort of scribal note indicating where the psalm had come from, that is, it belonged *ledawid*, to the Davidic (or royal) collection of psalms, as opposed to some other source or collection.[7]

Considering all these possibilities, there no longer seemed to be any good reason to understand the phrase *ledawid* as an indication of authorship.[8] For a time, scholars still accepted the idea that David might have written those psalms that specifically mentioned circumstances in his life (like "A psalm of David, when he fled from his son Absalom" in the heading of Ps. 3:1). Eventually, however, the authenticity of these headings came to be doubted as well. Scholars nowadays believe that such headings are actually the work of much later scribes who—perhaps no longer understanding the original meaning of the phrase *ledawid*—sought to flesh out the circumstances under which David might have written the psalm in question. Being quite familiar with David's biography as narrated in 1 and 2 Samuel, these scribes simply chose some incident in David's life as having been the occasion for his writing this particular psalm and stuck a reference to it in the heading (often quoting directly a phrase from 1 or 2 Samuel).[9]

In addition to the new understanding of *ledawid*, there were other indications that seemed to rule out Davidic authorship. Apart from Psalm 137 and its reference to the Babylonian exiles, a number of psalms contained what looked like obvious clues that David could not be their author. Many, for example, refer to worshiping God in Jerusalem or Zion or on God's "holy mountain" *as if this were a long-established practice*. But the Jerusalem temple was, according to the account in 1 Kings, built only in the time of

---

* So, for example, the Davidic king Rehoboam is called "O David" in 1 Kings 12:6.

David's son Solomon. And beyond this specific anachronism, there was the whole matter of the psalms' language.

Every language changes over time—in fact, in a remarkably short time. This lesson was brought home to me once when I was reading *The Wonderful Wizard of Oz* to one of my children. It starts off with Dorothy's house being swept up by a cyclone and carried off to parts unknown. "What's a cyclone?" my son asked, and I answered immediately, "a tornado." *That* word he knew. The book had been written only seventy-five years earlier, but in that time the previously disdained "tornado" had come back to replace "cyclone" in normal American usage.[10] Words also vary from place to place. Depending on where you were born in America, you refer to what I call "pancakes" as "griddle cakes," "hotcakes," "flapjacks," or yet something else. Traveling around the country, I have noticed that local TV reporters in some regions refer to what New Englanders call an "accident" on Route 91 as a "crash." Of course, both words exist for all speakers; it is just a matter of local preferences.

The same thing happened with biblical Hebrew—it varied from place to place and also changed over time. When scholars looked closely at the Psalter, they began to realize that its language was not all of one piece. Some psalms, like Psalm 1 or 119 or 145, used terms or expressions that were simply not found in the earlier parts of the Bible but that existed in abundance in its latest datable books. It seemed unlikely that David, even if he were a prophet, would have used a word that his own contemporaries had never heard of. Other words actually changed their meanings. To David, the word *shalal* meant "spoils of war, booty" (2 Sam. 3:22); this meaning persisted into later times, but then a new meaning developed, "wealth" or "treasure" (as in, for example, Prov. 31:11, "Her husband's heart relies on her, and *wealth* will not be lacking [in the household]"). Why would David have used the word in the latter sense ("I rejoice in Your words as someone who has found great *shalal*," Ps. 119:162) when his contemporaries would have misunderstood him to be comparing God's words not to precious treasure but to plundered goods?[11]

What's more, David was a southerner, born and bred in Judah. But a number of psalms are written in a distinctly northern Hebrew—for example, they say *mah* to mean "don't," an altogether northern way of speaking (Song 5:8; 7:1; 8:4 [cf. 2:7]). When scholars find this *mah*, along with other northernisms and even evocations of northern geographic sites,[12] clustered together in Psalm 42, it seems to them that the author of this psalm must have come not from Judah but some northern location. In short, the great chronological and geographical span indicated by the Psalms' language ruled out a single author or even a single period: the Psalms were written in different places and over a long span of time.

The Cultic Connection

But if David did not write the Psalms, who did? For a time, biblical scholars looked to later figures—Ezra, for example—as the potential authors of some of the Psalms. But then, along came the great German critic Hermann Gunkel, and scholars' ideas about the Psalms changed radically.

Throughout his research, Gunkel had sought to understand *why* biblical texts had been composed; to his mind, writing *literature* or seeking some form of self-expression was a later pursuit, and it would be anachronistic to attribute such a purpose to biblical authors. Instead, what they composed must have had some practical purpose—they must have intended their works to fit into the life of the community somehow and to be used in a certain way or on certain occasions. He therefore sought to uncover what he called a text's *Sitz im Leben,* its setting in daily life.

What was the *Sitz im Leben* of the psalms? Since many of them referred to "coming before" God's presence, entering "Your house," bowing down in "Your holy place," walking around "Your altar," making "free will offerings," offering "sacrifices in His tent," and similar things, it seemed to Gunkel that a great many psalms must have been composed to be recited in a temple or sanctuary of some sort. Certainly communal offerings, as well as festivals and other special occasions, might likely call for special choirs to sing hymns at a temple.[13] That seemed to be the case elsewhere in the ancient Near East: by the time Gunkel had begun his investigations, scholars were aware of numerous Egyptian and Mesopotamian hymns and prayers whose connection with temples and sanctuaries was quite explicit. So perhaps that was where at least some of the Psalter's songs had originated.

Quite apart from festivals and communal occasions, individual worshipers coming to the temple might have chanted (or had chanted for them) the words of one or more of the psalms. It is true, of course, that in ancient worship, the sacrifice itself was the "main event"; words apparently played a lesser role. Still, we know of a few specific instances in which, when individuals brought an offering to a temple, that act was accompanied by certain words. For example, when ordinary farmers arrived in Jerusalem with their obligatory annual "firstfruits" offerings, they would have to accompany this gesture with some words. In this instance, the words were completely standardized: every Israelite bringing his firstfruits had to declaim exactly the same formula (Deut. 26:5–10). But what about other offerings—a voluntary sacrifice, for example, or the payment of a vow? It would seem only reasonable that worshipers who brought these offerings would have said something as well; the same logic presumably applied to people who came to the temple to ask for God's help. Yet the Bible is quite silent about all these cases;

apparently, no standard formula existed for them. What does exist is a biblical book containing 150 psalms, some of which ask for help while others offer thanks. It has thus seemed plausible to many scholars that worshipers in such circumstances may have had recourse to one or more of these psalms. Indeed, temple officials may have routinely sought to match such people up with the particular psalm that most suited their specific circumstances. And so, "What's this for?" the priest might have inquired. "Recovery from illness," the visitor would reply. "Okay," the priest would say, and, after he had signaled the choir or perhaps a lone singer, the opening strains of Psalm 30 would soon fill the air:

> I will exalt You, O LORD, since you have drawn me up, and have not let
>   my foes rejoice over me.
> O LORD my God, I cried out to You for help and *You healed me.*
> O LORD, You brought up my soul from Sheol, restored me to life from
>   among those gone down to the Pit.
>
> Ps. 30:1–3

Such a hypothesis, scholars noticed, seemed to fit well with a rather striking feature of the Psalms, their lack of specificity.[14] For example, a great many psalms (including the one just cited) speak of "my enemies" or "my foes," but they rarely say anything more specific. Personally, if I had my own thirty seconds to stand directly before God and discuss my enemies, I would not beat around the bush: "Punish N———," I would say to Him, mentioning by name a certain prolific but misguided student of rabbinic Judaism; or "Squash W———," I would urge, referring to someone who has had the temerity to disagree with some of my ideas about biblical poetry. But the Psalms never mention names. On the contrary, they are full of metaphors that could apply to almost anyone—"roaring lions" threaten the Psalmist or "bulls of Bashan" surround him; he overcomes snakes and panthers, jumps over traps that have been dug for him, and escapes snares that have been spread out for him. And it is not just a matter of enemies. The psalmist begs to be saved from the underworld, Sheol, the gates of death, and so forth—but he almost never gets around to saying what's wrong with him or even what makes him think such danger is imminent. It seems to scholars, therefore, that the great variety of psalms in the Psalter on the one hand, and their somewhat vague language on the other, derive from the balancing of two contrary tendencies. A psalm had to be somewhat individualized, reflecting the specific occasion that had brought a person to the temple; so there had to be a lot of them. On the other hand, such psalms could not be overly specific, since they had to be used again and again for a multitude of different worshipers, each of whose circumstances would be somewhat different.

To Gunkel, and even more to those who followed in his footsteps, the temple thus seemed to be the main institution for which psalms were written. It now appeared almost impossible that David had ever had anything to do with their composition—nor was there any reason to assume that the Psalms had been written by Solomon or Ezra or any other known individual. Instead it now seemed most likely that the authors of most of the Psalms were people directly connected with the temple setting—priests or Levites who worked there.

Types of Psalms

One striking feature of the book of Psalms is the great variety of material in it: some psalms are happy, some are sad; some seem to be tied to a particular occasion or time of year, others are altogether general and might be recited by anyone at any time. To better understand what each particular psalm was saying and why it had been written, Gunkel embarked on that great Germanic occupation: classifying.[15] He set out to organize the different psalms into different groups according to their apparent purpose and/or occasion, as well as to determine on whose behalf they seemed to speak. In this effort of classification, Gunkel was followed by his (Scandinavian) student Sigmund Mowinckel and still more recent scholars.

Though much has been made of the different psalm types that have been identified, the results have, if truth be told, rarely gone beyond the obvious. Some psalms are written in the first person singular and seem therefore to have been intended to be recited by individuals (though this turns out to be true of only some first-person psalms);[16] others are to be spoken by, or on behalf of, the collectivity. A great many psalms are requests for something (Gunkel and other German scholars called them *Klagen,* "laments"—but they are really petitions for help by the psalmist, who, in the course of asking, usually also bewails the dire circumstances in which he finds himself). Others are hymns or songs that praise God; these are distinct from psalms of thanksgiving, which express gratitude for some particular act of divine beneficence. Apart from these are certain narrower, more specific types: psalms that celebrate God's kingship, psalms of Zion, pilgrim psalms, festival psalms, psalms of the king, wisdom psalms, and so forth.

Having identified these various types, Gunkel and other scholars also sought to find in them a standard form. The idea is that, just as a business letter has certain essential elements (date at the top; then name and address of intended recipient; "Dear Sir," and so forth), so each of the different types of psalms must have developed its own standardized content. Thus, psalms of praise often have a standard opening, in which the psalmist exhorts himself or some group of people to pay tribute to God: "I will give thanks to the LORD with my whole heart" (Psalm 9); "Bless the LORD, O my soul" (Psalm 103); "Sing aloud to God our strength" (Psalm 81); "Sing to the LORD another song" (Psalm 96). Prayers (petitions), on the other hand, never have this kind of opening. Instead, they tend to begin with a blunt cry for help, followed immediately with a "for" clause to support their plea: "Protect me, O God, for in You I take refuge" (Psalm 16); "Vindicate me, O LORD, for I have walked in my integrity" (Psalm 26); "Be gracious to me, O God, for people trample on me" (Psalm 56).

Beyond their opening words, psalms also demonstrate certain standard, conventional elements.[17] For example, prayers that ask for help often describe the psalmist as "poor," "downtrodden," or "indigent." For a time, scholars thought that these psalms were meant to be recited by Israel's underclass, people too poor to bring sacrifices. Now it seems that, on the contrary, *any* suppliant, even a king, would describe himself as poor before God—this was just standard petitionary language. Elsewhere in the Bible, when people suffer or get sick, the details are usually sketchy. When King Hezekiah is sick to the point of death, the narrative says nothing more than that: we never learn the nature of his illness or his symptoms. But in the book of Psalms, the text sometimes goes on and on about personal suffering, since presumably on hearing such things, a merciful God will be forced to act:[18]

I am poured out like water, and all my bones are coming apart.
My heart is like a piece of wax, melting inside my chest.
The roof of my mouth is as dry as a potsherd, and my tongue sticks to
    my palate;
You can consign me to the dust of death.
Dogs surround me; a gang of evildoers is closing in.
My hands and feet ache; I can count all my bones.
People stare and gloat over me; they divide my clothes among themselves,
and cast lots for pieces of clothing.
                                        Ps. 22:14–19

For my days pass away like smoke, and my bones burn like a furnace.
My heart is beaten down and withered like grass; I am too wasted to eat
    my bread.
Whenever I cry out in pain, my bones press up through my skin.
I am like an owl of the steppes, or a little owl perched in the ruins.
While I lie awake, I am like a lonely bird on a rooftop.
All day long my enemies taunt me; those who deride me use my name for
    a curse.
Ashes are my bread, and I mix tears with my drink, fleeing Your
    indignation and wrath.
For You have picked me up and thrown me away.
My days are like an evening shadow; I am withering like grass.
                                        Ps. 102:3–11

Quite unique as well is another standard element in prayers for help. They often feature a curious vow, in which the psalmist promises (or at least implies) that, if he is saved, he will devote himself to praising God forever more:

> Have compassion on me, O LORD; consider my unbearable affliction and
>   lift me up from the gates of death,
> so that I may recount all Your praises; at Zion's gates I will exult in Your
>   salvation.
>
> Ps. 9:13–14

> What is to be gained from my being silenced,[19] my going down into the
>   Pit?
> Can dust praise You? Can it proclaim Your faithfulness?
> Hear, O LORD, and have mercy on me . . .
> So that I may sing Your praises and not be silenced, O LORD my God I
>   will extol you forever.
>
> Ps. 30:10–12

> Free me from my shackles, so that I may praise Your name—
> Indeed, the righteous shall glory in it, if only You deal graciously with me.
>
> Ps. 142:8

These are not immutable requirements, as the classifiers sometimes imply.[20] Nevertheless, the lesson is clear: the Psalms were not composed spontaneously, their authors having been moved by this or that event. Instead, they were apparently written to fit certain established categories, just as, in ancient Greece or Rome, poets wrote lyrics and epics and elegies and so forth. Not only were the different types of psalms and their basic forms standardized, but what they actually had to say, and how they went about saying it, was likewise the product of age-old conventions.

The Psalms and Ugaritic

If all this was fairly disturbing news for the traditional image of the Psalms, the twentieth-century discovery of a cache of texts from ancient Ugarit (above, chapter 24) was still more upsetting.

No collection of prayers or hymns was found in the library at Ugarit, but the texts that were discovered there nevertheless contained a great deal of material reminiscent of lines from the Psalms. It was not just a word or two, such as the already-mentioned appellation of Baal as the "cloud-rider" (*rkb b'rpt*), echoed in the epithet of Israel's God (*rkb 'rbt*). Rather, the whole religious vocabulary of Ugarit, the way the denizens of this ancient city spoke of their gods and depicted their interaction, turned out to be strikingly reminiscent of elements in Israel's own religion. As at Ugarit, so in the Psalms God was said to preside over a certain "assembly" of divine beings, angels or lesser deities—indeed, that assembly was called by the identical name (*'dt 'il[m]*) in the Psalms and Ugaritic (see Ps. 82:1).[21] The divine mercy so often appealed to in the Psalter turned out to be a standard characteristic of the god El at Ugarit. The sacrifices spoken of in the Psalms, and the temples that Gunkel and Mowinckel had hypothesized were the Psalms' *Sitz im Leben*—these too had ready parallels at Ugarit.

Beyond these, the very style of Ugaritic poetry strikingly resembled that of the biblical Psalms. The same basic system of adjoining clauses (seen earlier in the Song of Deborah; chapter 23) was found to characterize Ugaritic prosody:

_____, _____.

Clause A   Clause B

Moreover, the ways in which the connection between the clauses was established—omission of an essential word in clause B; repetition of the same word or phrase in A and B; the use of commonly paired words in A and B ("By day . . . by night")—all were found in Ugaritic poetry; in fact, Ugaritic often featured the very same words that sealed the connection between adjacent clauses.[22] One difference between Ugaritic poetry and most of that in the Psalter is that the Ugaritic poetic line does not nearly so regularly consist of only two clauses: often there are three or even more. In this feature it seems to share something with the Song of Deborah—not surprising, since, scholars say, that song is closer to Ugarit than most other biblical poems, both in time and in place of composition.

There are a few biblical psalms in particular that have an unmistakably Ugaritic sound. For example:

The voice of the LORD is over the waters; the God of glory thunders, the
    LORD, over mighty waters.
The voice of the LORD is powerful; the voice of the LORD is full of
    majesty.
The voice of the LORD breaks the cedars; the LORD breaks the cedars of
    Lebanon.

                                                    Ps. 29:3–5

These lines reminded researchers of what was said of Baal in an Ugaritic epic:

Baal gives forth his holy voice, Baal repeats the utterance of his lips.
His holy voice [shatters] the earth.

[At his roar] the mountains quake, afar [   ] before Sea,
the high places of the earth shake.

One of the most significant contributions of the Ugaritic texts (along with
some literary texts from Mesopotamia) had to do with the meaning of specific
words. Some of the things that people had always believed about words in the
Bible—including, prominently, verses in the Psalms—turned out to be wrong.
For example, the most common Hebrew word for soul, *nefesh,* means something a little less spiritual elsewhere in the Semitic world: throat or neck (as
well as the desire connected with that part of the body, "appetite"). Thus,
when the Psalmist cries out (to quote the old King James translation), "Save
me, O God; for the waters are come in unto my soul" (Ps. 69:2), it turns out
what he really meant was: the water is up to my neck! (Similarly, when the
Israelites complain about the manna they got in the desert—"For there is no
bread, neither is there any water; and our soul loatheth this light bread,"
Num. 21:5 [KJV]—what they really meant was, "There is no bread and there
is no water and our throats/appetites are sick of this miserable food.") In other
places, *nefesh* meant a person, oneself, so that "Bless the LORD, O my soul"
might probably be translated more accurately as, "I will bless the LORD." (Of
course, *nefesh* sometimes does mean soul; indeed, sometimes, as in Ps. 42:1,
the interplay between "soul" and "throat" is precisely the point.)

Another example: the Psalms are full of references to God's "goodness," or
so scholars used to think. At least in some cases now, the word previously
translated as "goodness" (*ṭob*) ought probably to be understood more specifically—in keeping with a certain Ugaritic use of the cognate *ṭb*—as "[agricul-
tural] plenty," the result of ample rainfall; indeed, sometimes *ṭb* itself appears
to be a kind of code word for "rain." So, for example, a verse that had once
been translated as:

Yea, the LORD shall give *that which is good*; and our land shall yield her
increase.

Ps. 85:13 (King James Version)

rather seems to mean that God "will give *rain* and our land shall yield her
increase." Similarly, since Psalm 84 describes the fate of the blessed in terms
of plentiful water—"As they go through the valley of Baca they make it a
place of springs; the early rain also covers it with pools" (Ps. 84:7)—it is not
surprising that it should end by asserting:

The LORD will not withhold abundance [*ṭob*] from those who walk
uprightly.

Ps. 84:12

Indeed, precisely the same expression, to "withhold/deprive *ṭob*," appears when Jeremiah denounces his fellow Judahites:

> They do not say in their hearts, "Let us fear the LORD our God, who
>> gives the rain in its season,
> the autumn rain and the spring rain, and keeps for us the weeks
>> appointed for the harvest."
> It is your iniquities that have turned these away, and your sins have
>> deprived you of *ṭob*.
>
> Jer. 5:24–25[23]

Psalms Outside the Temple

An interesting thing happened within the biblical period: as time went on, the Psalms' connection with the temple and the offering of sacrifices gradually weakened. They still had their place in the Jerusalem temple, of course, right down to the day in 70 CE when that temple was destroyed by the Romans. But long before, it appears, the Psalms had begun to take on a different role. Individuals, or perhaps groups of people, began to recite them outside of that cultic setting. Perhaps, some scholars theorize, this began as early as Josiah's reform: once the Jerusalem temple became the only legitimate place for animal sacrifices, the other, provincial temples may nonetheless not have ceased to function; people might still have continued to go there to worship in some form—and to recite psalms.[24] Whether that is true or not, certainly during the Babylonian exile (when there was no temple), reciting psalms may have functioned as the Jews' main form of worship. Some of the latest psalms in the Psalter give every indication that they were never connected to cultic worship—they make no allusion to the accouterments of the temple, but instead speak of praising God "at all times" (Ps. 34:2) and "continually" (Ps. 145:1). A number of these late psalms are alphabetical acrostics (Psalms 34, 37, 111, 112, 119, 145), that is, each line or half-line or stanza starts with a succeeding letter of the alphabet. This arrangement seems to have been designed to help the individual worshiper remember the words—again, something that might suggest an intended setting outside the world of the temple and its professional choirs. The evidence is not altogether unambiguous, but it is difficult in any case to think of a long and repetitive psalm like Psalm 119 (176 verses) as having been intended for singing in the temple. Instead, this psalm appears to be a kind of litany in which repetition was the whole point. The individual worshiper may have gone through its great length as an act of piety, an offering made of words themselves.[25]

Eventually, of course, the connection with the Jerusalem temple was severed entirely. With that building in ruins after 70 CE, the Psalms became the exclusive property of the synagogue and the church—places where the faithful might gather and, without sacrificing animals on sacred altars, nonetheless offer praise and thanksgiving and prayers to God. Interestingly, these early liturgies did not limit themselves to psalms that were apparently composed for recitation outside the temple. Instead, the old temple psalms—with their evocation of coming "before God" and bowing down in "Your holy place"— were also recited. With time, apparently, their words had taken on a new meaning: one might come before God anywhere, and old prayers and thanksgiving might be uttered quite apart from their original context and meaning.

This historical fact is of great significance to the larger theme of this book, how we are to read the Bible today. For the case of the Psalms is, in miniature, the case of the whole Bible. We know now, better than ever before, what the Psalms *originally* meant and why they were written. But is that original meaning to be decisive? If, even within the biblical period, the Psalms came to mean something else—if people prayed the same words in a setting different from the intended one and with a different meaning, and if they have continued to do so for more than twenty centuries since—does it really matter that the original authors did not mean for their words to be used and understood in the way that we use and understand them?

This is not a question to be answered glibly. The insights of modern scholarship certainly have changed some things for worshipers, and probably will continue to do so. For example, despite the beauty of the old King James translation of Psalm 23, many modern Bibles have found themselves obliged to abandon its key elements: the basic understanding of the psalm as embodied in that seventeenth-century translation is no longer acceptable to modern scholars. Consider, for example, the psalm's last line in the King James Version:

> Surely goodness and mercy shall follow me all the days of my life: and I will dwell in the house of the LORD for ever.

At some point in this psalm's history,[26] the phrase "dwell in the house of the LORD for ever" came to be understood as a reference to life after death. This was in part because of the psalm's earlier reference to walking "through the valley of the shadow of death"—that shadow extends over all the words that follow. (And if one walks *through* that valley, getting to its other side, this implies that one arrives at what lies beyond death.) Moreover, the psalm's reference to dwelling "in the house of the LORD *for ever*" suggests an unlimited length of time, going on even after "all the days of my life" (mentioned in the previous clause) are over. So it was that Psalm 23 came to be taken as *the* psalm in the Psalter that holds out the clear hope for life after death; among other functions, it became a staple of funeral services.

Most contemporary scholars reject this understanding. To begin with, the "valley of the shadow of death" seems to be a misreading (and misdivision) of the original Hebrew text: "a very dark valley" or "valley of darkness" is closer to what the psalm really says.[27] And it does not say "through" that valley; the Hebrew preposition means only "in." As for the psalm's last verse, the words translated as "for ever" really only mean "for a length of days" or "for a long time." It seems more like a reaffirmation, rather than an extension, of "all the days of my life." (That is why most modern translations render this phrase not as "forever" but "my whole life long" or the like.) As for "the house of the LORD," everywhere else in the Hebrew Bible this means the temple. One certainly could not be buried in the temple and so *dwell* there after death: such corpse defilement would render the temple utterly unfit for God's presence. Putting all this together, it seems that what the psalm originally meant was:

> [Although things may at times be frightening, and] even though I might sometime be walking in a very dark valley, I will not be afraid . . . My only pursuers will be abundance and [divine] generosity my whole life long; and I will stay[28] in God's temple for a long time.

Which is the real Psalm 23?[29] The one that talks about life after death, or the other one? And in a broader sense, what are we to think of the Psalms today, now that we know that, far from being the personal lyrics of King David, scribbled down by a prophetlike servant of God in time of trouble or celebration, they are mostly cultic pieces penned by anonymous temple functionaries, studded with conventional phrases and themes and worded in a one-size-fits-all vocabulary that was designed to give worshipers the feeling of specificity while equipping them for multiple reuse?

The answer to this question rests, to a surprising degree, with the person reading the Psalms and the context in which that reading takes place. Few modern readers will wish to put their hands over their ears and drone out the scholars in Göttingen and New Haven. "The truth as best we can know it" has a claim on every human heart, and in the case of the Psalter, it has changed forever the meaning of many of its words. At the same time, as some scholars have noted, the basic *gesture* of the psalms—as an offering of words parallel (if subordinate) to the offering of sacrifices—still survives today.[30] People who recite the Psalms are still, in unmistakable fashion, offering up their time and their energy to God, subordinating themselves to Him in a concrete act of devotion and faithfulness. Even within the biblical period, this basic gesture survived the transition from the Israelite temple to other sites untroubled, and it continues to survive today.

Beyond this point, however, is another peculiarity of the Psalms. When someone reads the words of a psalm as an act of worship, he or she takes over, in a sense, the psalm's authorship. It may have been written by an ancient Levite, but at the moment of its recitation, its words become the worshiper's own: they speak on his or her behalf to God. There are few other cases I can think of in which such a total adoption of a text takes place. Even an ardent lover, reciting someone else's poem (or singing someone else's song) to the woman of his dreams never becomes the words' new author in quite the same way; he *identifies* with the text, but both he and she are aware that what he is uttering is not his own composition, and this slight distance between himself and the author never quite disappears. Perhaps the only analogous case in the secular world is the taking of an oath: someone being sworn into the army speaks the words composed by someone else not as an act of quotation or even identification, but as if they were fully his own. So is it, too, with the Psalms. This seems to me a remarkable phenomenon, precisely because what is crucial are not the words themselves, but the mind of the worshiper who utters them. The very attitude of prayer pushes to the background the historical circumstances of the psalm's composition. The true author is now the worshiper himself.[31]

27

David the King

1 Samuel 18 through 2 Samuel 12

King David in Prayer by Pieter de Grebber.

CAN A CHRISTIAN STUDY LITERATURE? SAUL'S LAST STAND.
THE MOVE TO JERUSALEM. DANCING BEFORE THE ARK.
THE PROMISE OF A HOUSE. DAVID'S AFFAIR WITH BATHSHEBA.
NATHAN'S REPROACH.

Modern scholars are divided about David. Some see him as a ruthless guerrilla who strong-armed his way to a powerful empire, killing and pillaging in the process; others believe the real David (if he existed at all) was a small-time politician whose military exploits and mighty empire were the creation of a later age. Which is worse?

Somehow, in all the talk about specific interpretations of this or that biblical passage, the larger profile of the Bible throughout most of its history gets lost. It may therefore be appropriate here (for reasons which will become clear presently) to take a quick step backwards and consider the larger picture: what was the overall profile of the Bible in Europe from antiquity through the Middle Ages and beyond?

The Bible was, quite simply, *the* book. It was the one book that counted, the one book (if any) that people studied and quoted, the only book anyone ever needed to know about. So much was this the case that the phrase "as it is written," in Greek or Latin (as earlier in Hebrew and Aramaic), meant—*it went without saying*—as it is written in the Bible. Its stories were everyone's stories, depicted in illuminated manuscripts and church capitals and stained-glass windows and delicate oil paintings. People analyzed the doings of their own kings and officials, the plagues that sometimes struck their duchies and fiefdoms, and the wars and political intrigues of their own day in terms of biblical models. Indeed, the Bible's own wording, its examples, metaphors, comparisons, and odd turns of phrase, became, with the Christianization of Europe, part of the everyday speech of millions. Soon, people referred to "the writing on the wall" and "the sweat of your brow" and "the salt of the earth" and "a drop in the bucket" and hundreds of other things without even being aware that they were quoting Scripture; these expressions were (and still are) part of the language. Quite simply, the Bible had no peer; there was nothing even remotely similar to it, and its shadow spread across an entire civilization.

One question that came up early in the history of the Western church was: is it proper for a Christian to study books other than the Bible?[1] The fact that such a question was even asked is remarkable. After all, the Europeans who accepted Christianity had not exactly been illiterate savages before their conversion. They had read Homer and Hesiod and Virgil and Ovid, philosophers and playwrights and historians. Yet once the Bible came along, it cleared the deck: every other piece of writing was now, from a Christian standpoint, irrelevant.

This is all the more remarkable when you consider that the earliest Latin translation of the Bible (the Vetus Latina) was a rather botched job that generally struck ordinary Latin readers as the work of someone who "no speaka da language too good." Augustine describes his first encounter with Scripture in these respectful yet telltale terms:

> So I made up my mind to examine the Holy Scriptures and see what kind of books they were. I discovered something that was at once beyond the understanding of the proud and hidden from the eyes of children. Its gait was humble, but the heights it reached were sublime. It was enfolded in mysteries, and I was not the kind of man to enter into it or bow my head to follow where it led. But these were not the feelings I had when I first read the Scriptures. To me they seemed quite unworthy of comparison with the stately prose of Cicero, because I had too much conceit to accept their simplicity and not enough insight to penetrate their depths.
>
> *Confessions 3:5*

Early Christians were therefore in something of a quandary. On the one hand, the Bible was true and vital to one's salvation, whereas the writings of pagans like Cicero or Virgil were simply "lies" (*mendacia*) and might actually stand in salvation's way. On the other hand, the Bible's style was clumsy, and these other works were so beautiful—and besides, in more practical terms, such secular writings had long served as the primary texts for education in grammar and rhetoric in Roman schools (a role that, obviously, the Vetus Latina could not fill). So was it acceptable for Christians to send their children to school if they were to be exposed there to the classics, with their scenes of gods and goddesses, sexual license, and ways of thought and speech that were wholly unconnected with the Christian message?[2] Even after Christianity gained the support of the Roman Empire and could determine the curriculum, the question remained a live one: should all of secular literature, with its beautiful Latin style, be junked in favor of the exclusive use of the Bible?

As with any other question, the Bible itself was appealed to for an answer in this debate. One of the specific passages invoked was not one that a person would normally think had any light to shed on the question. It had to do with King Saul—specifically, with his preparations for a certain battle against the Philistines:

> Now there was no smith to be found throughout all the land of Israel; for the Philistines said, "The Hebrews must not make swords or spears for themselves"; so all the Israelites went down to the Philistines to sharpen

their plowshares, mattocks, axes, or sickles. The cost was two-thirds of a shekel for the plowshares and for the mattocks, and one-third of a shekel for sharpening the axes and for setting the goads. So on the day of this battle, neither sword nor spear was to be found in the possession of any of the soldiers with Saul and Jonathan; but Saul and his son Jonathan had them.

1 Sam. 13:19–22

The technology involved in extracting iron ore and hardening it to make weapons and tools was still a relatively new thing. Apparently, the Philistines had a monopoly on this knowledge and did not share it with their Israelite neighbors (although, for a fee, they would sell and sharpen agricultural tools). Consequently, on the day in question, only Saul and his son had the prized weapons.

Centuries later, in Christian Europe, such a situation must have seemed quite incomprehensible. By then, of course, iron implements were plentiful, a blacksmith was an ordinary sight, and the idea that his "technology" might have been an industrial secret in biblical times must have seemed utterly ludicrous to most people. Besides, how could it be that God's people would ever have been deprived of any knowledge? And so, as with so many biblical passages, this one was assumed to have some hidden teaching quite unrelated to its overt subject. Here is how Gregory the Great (ca. 540–604) explains the verse:

What is the meaning of the verse "An ironsmith was not to be found in Israel," if not that we are made ready for spiritual battles not through secular literature, but through divine? So indeed, an ironsmith is *not* to be found in Israel—because God's faithful do not do battle against evil spirits with the art of secular learning . . .

Yet the erudition of secular books, even if it is of itself of no use for the spiritual battle of the holy, will, if it is combined with sacred Scripture, allow the lessons of that same Scripture to be taught even better. Precisely for this reason are the liberal arts to be studied, so that, through their instruction, divine pronouncements may be more properly understood . . .

Hence even Moses . . . did not first study divine things but, so that he might well understand or express the divine things, educated his unseasoned soul with all the learning of the Egyptians [Acts 7:22]. Likewise, Isaiah outshone all the other prophets in eloquence, for he was not like Jeremiah of the [rustic village of] Anathoth or Amos the herdsman, but a city dweller and nobly educated.

Commentary on First Reigns (Migne, *Patrologia Latina* 79:355)

Jerome's Dream

One of the most famous dreams in Western European history was dreamt by Jerome, the great Christian biblical translator and commentator. He describes it in a letter written in 384 CE. Jerome prefaces his account by recalling how, as a youth—despite his having become a monk and devoting himself utterly to sacred things—he found himself unable to kick the secular literature habit. Try as he would, he could not bring himself to get rid of his (expensive) collection of Latin classics:

> And so I, poor fellow, would fast and then read my Cicero; after nights of successive vigils, and after the tears that the recollection of my past sins would wrench from my innermost breast, there, back in my hands again, would be Plautus . . .

Things apparently went on seesawing like that for some time, until one day Jerome found himself ill with a fever. His condition thereafter deteriorated rapidly.

> Arrangements were made for my funeral, and through my chill body the warmth of the breath of life now pulsed only in my lukewarm chest.
> Suddenly, I found myself seized up in the spirit and handed over to the divine tribunal. There was such light, and so great was the splendor emanating from those standing about, that I, cast down upon the ground, did not dare look up around me. I was asked what my status was. But when I answered that I was a Christian, the One in charge replied, "You lie. You are a Ciceronian, not a Christian. For 'where your treasure is, there shall your heart be also' [Matt. 6:21]."
> At once I fell silent, and in between blows of the whip—for He had ordered that I be flogged—I was tormented even more by the fires of conscience, and I kept repeating to myself that little verse, "In the world of the dead, who can confess to Thee?" [Ps. 6:5] . . . Finally . . . taking an oath, I called upon His name and said, "O Lord, if ever again I own secular books, if I read them, I will have denied You."
>
> Jerome, *Letter 22, to Eustochium*

One might think this would have clinched the case against secular literature forever. But as Gregory the Great argued (above), reading the classics might still be justified as a way of honing one's interpretive skills for the Bible—or, for that matter, to help one write better commentaries in Latin. Various manuals of good style were written by medieval Christians, and although the

Bible might here and there serve as a model, even churchmen like the Venerable Bede (672–735) found it necessary to use classical texts to help impart a command of tropes and figures.[3]

Still, a good Christian ought not to make a practice of reading outside the sacred realm, certainly not after reaching a mature age. At best, such things might be forgiven if done by an impetuous young man who repented thereafter. And so it was the pleasure of certain pious medieval scholars to allude to the wild literary oats that they had sown in their youth. Here, for example, is Gregory of Tours (ca. 530–83), sternly warning against the reading of secular literature, all the while winking at the reader about his own profligate past:

> The priest Jerome, best teacher of the church after the apostle Paul, says that he was led bound before the judgment seat of the eternal Judge and was tied up and lashed severely as a punishment, because too often he had read the clever arguments of Cicero and the false tales of Virgil . . .
>
> Since I fear this, and since I long to disclose some of the miracles of the saints which still lie hidden, I am most eager not to be conquered or trapped by these snares. So I shall not mention in this work the flight of Saturn, the wrath of Juno, the adulteries of Jupiter, the wrongdoing of Neptune, the scepters of Aeolus, the wars, shipwreck, and contests of Aeneas. I will be silent about the mission of Cupid, the cherishing of Ascanius, the marriage, tears, and savage death of Dido, the dreary antechamber of Pluto, the criminal seizure of Proserpina, the three-headed Cerberus. I will not repeat the speeches of Anchises, the ingenuity of the Ithacan, the shrewdness of Achilles, the deception of Sinon. I will not reveal the counsels of Laocoon, the strength of the son of Amphitryon, the battle, fight, and death of Cacus. I will describe neither the appearance of the Eumenides and various monsters, nor the other fabulous stories which this author [Virgil] mendaciously invented or depicted in heroic verse. Having glanced at these events built on sand and soon to perish, let us rather return to the divine miracles of the Gospel.
>
> *The Glory of the Blessed Martyrs,* Introduction

By contrast, it might be interesting to observe briefly the situation among medieval Jews.[4] For them, the Bible was indeed the source of basic education, and, in this "culture of literacy," learning to read and write was accomplished through studying the Bible, along with the biblical targum (Aramaic translation) and, in later times, Rashi's Torah commentary. Basic literacy was the expected norm for at least all young boys (this was not the case in medieval Christendom). But "higher education"—that is, anything beyond the Torah and basic literacy—soon led to other texts: the Mishnah, the Babylonian Talmud, and various collections of midrash, as well as (depending on the time and place) legal codes and novellae, philosophical texts, Kabbalistic writings, and even didactic poetry—all in Hebrew or Aramaic. These other texts had a way of squeezing the Bible out. The complaint was thus occasionally made that literate Jews neglected the study of the Bible in favor of the Talmud, and this was (and still is) no doubt largely true;[5] indeed, it is not an unimportant circumstance for the overall theme of this book, which will be taken up in the last chapter. In the meantime, however, let us return to the struggles of King Saul with his younger rival.

Saul versus David

After Samuel's rebuke of Saul over the Amalekite *herem,* Saul continued on as king, but he soon encountered rocky times. David, according to the biblical account, was a fixture in Saul's court, and it was not long before the king became jealous of the younger man's popularity, as well as suspicious of his military prowess (1 Samuel 18). After killing Goliath, David is said to have scored military victories against the hated Philistines; the common people sang of his feats. Although he was now Saul's son-in-law (he had married Saul's daughter Michal) and the close friend and ally of Saul's son Jonathan, the king's suspicion of David and hatred for him—depicted in the text as the result of Saul's mental illness (1 Sam. 18:10)—would not let him rest. Eventually, Saul plotted against his life, and David escaped in the nick of time (1 Samuel 19–21).

It is not easy to guess the degree of historical accuracy to be attributed to these accounts or for what purpose they were first put together.[6] Nevertheless, some scholars say, one can here and there glimpse flashes of what seems to be a rather common situation in national politics. After all, David was from the powerful tribe of Judah; Saul was from the relatively weak* neighboring tribe of Benjamin (by biblical genealogy, a Rachel tribe and hence tied to the tribes of Ephraim and Manasseh to its north). According to the biblical account, Saul was anointed king of the northern tribes, but his kingdom apparently did not include the hill country of Judah (2 Sam. 2:9). If one strips away the nice stories about David's lyre playing and his divinely inspired selection as Saul's successor, scholars say, one is left with the picture of a once-successful leader (Saul) ultimately being pushed aside by a younger, more powerful upstart (David). Whether David ever set foot in Saul's court—as singer, son-in-law, military champion, friend of Jonathan, or yet something else—will, historians say, probably never be known for sure. One thing rings true, however, and that is Saul's reported distress at David's increasing promi-

---

* Indeed, historians say, that may be why he was chosen—less chance of the king's tribe becoming all-powerful.

nence. The biblical narrative recounts that, upon David's return from battle, the women sang of him:

> Saul has killed by the thousands, but David by the tens of thousands.
>
> 1 Sam. 18:7

A king and military leader, seeing another military figure from a more powerful tribe garnering more and more power and prominence, would likely be (just as the Bible reports, 1 Sam. 18:8–9) quite edgy about such a slogan getting around.

Whatever he may eventually have become, many scholars believe that David was, at the start of his political career, little more than a ruthless gang leader. He went around extorting money and goods at swordpoint from his fellow citizens (such as Nabal, 1 Samuel 25) in order to pay for his increasingly large entourage of fighters. Sometimes he and his men battled against the Philistines, but sometimes he also fought as a Philistine mercenary against his fellow Judahites (1 Samuel 27); apparently, whoever paid the piper called the tune. Eventually David's guerrilla band became so powerful that it threatened Saul's very hold over his own kingdom. *That,* scholars say, may be what lies behind the "evil spirit from the LORD" that afflicted Saul—not paranoid delusions but a well-founded fear of being pushed aside.

Saul's Death

On the eve of yet another battle with the Philistines, Saul sensed that his end might be near. David, after all, was his enemy; perhaps David's forces would join in the Philistine attack against Saul's army (1 Sam. 28:1–2). Saul would have liked to ask a prophet what was in store, but Samuel, the truth-telling seer who had anointed him, was now dead (1 Sam. 25:1). No other suitable prophet was on the horizon. In desperation, therefore, the king put on a disguise (since he was about to do something illegal) and went off to consult a medium, the "witch of Endor," in the hope that she might be able to summon Samuel up from the grave (1 Sam. 28:3–24).[7] She succeeded, although at first Samuel was upset at having been roused from the dead:

> Samuel said to Saul, "Why did you bother me and make me come up?" Saul said, "I am in great difficulty: for the Philistines are fighting against me, and God has left me and will not answer me any more, even by prophets or by dreams. That is why I called you to tell me what to do." Samuel said, "Why then do you ask me, since the LORD has already turned away from you and become your enemy? The LORD has done to you just what He said

he would, through me; the LORD has torn the kingdom out of your hand, and given it to your fellow, David. Since you did not obey the LORD and carry out his fierce wrath against Amalek, therefore the LORD has done this thing to you today. So now the LORD is handing Israel, and you along with them, over to the Philistines. By tomorrow, you and your sons will be here with me."

1 Sam. 28:15–19

As Samuel predicted, so did it occur. Saul's sons were killed by the Philistines, and he fell on his sword, a suicide (1 Sam. 31:2–6).

David Takes Over

After Saul's death, David might have exulted at his enemy's demise, but according to the biblical narrative, he did not. On the contrary, he grieved over the old king's downfall and composed a moving elegy, whose opening lines strike a note of simplicity and straight-from-the-shoulder emotion that are unmistakable, even at a distance of three millennia:

> Is Israel's glory slain, a corpse upon your high places? Oh, how the
>   mighty have fallen!
> Do not tell of it in Gath, nor bring news of it to the streets of Ashkelon,
> lest the Philistine women cheer, lest the heathens' daughters stamp and
>   shout.
> O mountains in Gilboa—no dew. No rain upon you, terraced fields,
> For there the mighty shield was profaned; there the shield of Saul—the
>   chosen king—gave way . . .[8]

2 Sam. 1:19–21

Now the leader of a potent military force, David was a natural candidate to follow Saul on the throne, but he chose to act with deliberation. First he was anointed king of his own tribe of Judah, chosen by popular acclaim (2 Sam. 2:1–4). There followed a period of struggle over Saul's succession between David's supporters and those of Saul's son Ishboshet,* that is, "between the house of Saul and the house of David" (2 Sam. 3:1). During this uncertain period, Abner, Saul's general, and Ishboshet were killed in separate incidents. Now, with no one else around to fill Saul's shoes, the "elders of Israel" (that is, the northern tribes) came to David at his capital, Hebron, with a request:

---

* Also known as Ishbaal. The latter name contains the divine name "Baal" and may thus have been replaced by Ishboshet as a euphemism (cf. Saul's other son, Mephiboshet, 2 Sam. 21:8–9), though this is not certain.

Then all the tribes of Israel came to David at Hebron, and said, "Look, we are your bone and flesh. For some time, while Saul was king over us, it was you who led out Israel and brought it in [that is, you were the military leader]. The LORD said to you: It is you who shall be shepherd of My people Israel, you who shall be ruler over Israel." Thus all the elders of Israel came to the king at Hebron; and King David made a covenant with them at Hebron before the LORD, and they anointed David king over Israel. David was thirty years old when he began to reign, and he reigned forty years. At Hebron he reigned over Judah seven years and six months; and at Jerusalem he reigned over all Israel and Judah thirty-three years.

2 Sam. 5:1–5

As noted previously, some historians are skeptical about this whole narrative concerning David's rise to power.[9] To begin with, the narrative reports two very similar incidents in which David could have killed Saul but piously refrained from doing so, even though he was standing fully armed over the helpless monarch (1 Sam. 24:5–8; 26:10–12). Later, Saul dies in a battle with the Philistines that David is said to have had nothing to do with, although he had been fighting in their army as a mercenary just before; for some reason, the Philistines had ordered him to depart on the eve of the fateful battle (1 Samuel 29). Was this what really happened, or was it just a cover for some undisclosed role David might have played in bringing about Saul's demise? Then, following Saul's death, David is selected by "the people of Judah" as their king. The Bible is candid enough to report that this move was preceded by David's sharing a large stash of booty with his "friends" (that is, allies) among the elders of Judah (1 Sam. 30:26–31). His selection as king thus looks somewhat less spontaneous and merit-based than the narrative implies. Rather, it seems that it was David's largesse that persuaded the elders to proclaim him their king, or a combination of largesse and the threat of a military takeover. As for the northern tribes' subsequent plea to David to become their king, this seems to historians even less likely to have happened as reported. The entrenched powers of the north no doubt would have preferred to be ruled by one of their own, someone with extensive ties of kinship and common concerns.* After all, why trust your fate to someone from down south who may prove to care nothing for what happens to you? So what was it that precipitated their alleged turning to David? Somehow, both Saul's son Ishboshet and the military leader Abner (two potential successors to Saul) were assassinated under circumstances in which David, the narrative seeks to assert, had no role whatsoever. Uh-huh.[10]

---

* Indeed, the first words out of the northerners' mouths were, "Look, we are your bone and flesh." But this, scholars say, only highlights the incongruity of their request: their own "bone and flesh" was precisely what David was *not*—he was from a different tribe in a different region with very different strategic interests.

In short, all this appears to some modern scholars to be a case of protesting too much. What really happened, they say, is not hard to glimpse between the lines. David was the head of what was now basically a full-fledged guerrilla army. He and his men, fighting for the Philistines, probably were directly involved in Saul's death. David then forced and bribed his way into power in Judah. Later, with Ishboshet and Abner conveniently dead (and after a period of some intense fighting alluded to in 2 Sam. 3:1), David essentially took over Saul's leaderless kingdom to the north by force. There may have been some ceremonial niceties afterward, but what really occurred was a military coup. In view of all this, the moving elegy that David is said to have composed upon Saul's death is now eyed with as much suspicion as the rest. It too, modern scholars say, is simply part of the Bible's massive cover-up of a brutal takeover.

The Minimal David

However unflattering this picture of David may seem to traditional readers of the Bible, a new portrait has emerged among "minimalist" historians over the last two decades, and it is, if possible, even less flattering. The biblical portrait of David, they say, is an invention almost from start to finish. He never created the mighty kingdom the Bible attributes to him, nor, for that matter, did his son Solomon inherit and expand such an empire. In fact, there may never have been a David, and if there was, he was altogether small potatoes, the head of a tiny outpost in the Judean hills whose alleged reign hardly left a trace in the territories he is said to have ruled or conquered.

In support of this position, historians point to the fact that neither David nor Solomon is mentioned in any ancient Egyptian or Mesopotamian text— somewhat surprising if, as the biblical account claims, their empire bestrode the region like a colossus. As far as archaeologists can tell, Jerusalem, the supposed capital of this mighty empire, remained a relative backwater:[11] they have yet to find David's palace or other structures befitting a great kingdom (although, as of this writing, a new site just outside of the old city walls has been proposed as his palace—it was, in any case, a large public building dated to the tenth century BCE).[12] Some new construction has been identified elsewhere in what would have been the Kingdom of Israel, and it has been dated to the end of Solomon's kingship—a promising sign, but the dating itself is still disputed. So is it all a pipedream?[13]

It is not my purpose to take sides in this debate, but mention should be made of a few of the arguments put forth to counter the minimalist view. To begin with, David may have been a great military leader, but that does not necessarily mean that he undertook a lot of building projects; those may indeed have been left to later generations. As for the other arguments from silence, they have precisely that weakness: just because evidence has not been found does not mean that it does not exist or never existed. Indeed, in 1993 a new item suddenly turned up, the Tel Dan inscription, in which the phrase "house of David" appears in apparent reference to the king of Judah. The inscription is dated to the ninth century—a short while after Solomon's death—and was found close to what must have been Israel's northern border. Its meaning and significance are still disputed, but if the text is correct as originally deciphered, then it seems most unlikely that David's reign was a fabrication, or even just a little local blip unknown outside of the Judean hills.[14] One scholar has recently claimed that another inscription, the Mesha stone (see chapter 29), might also contain a reference to the "house of David," making it a second ninth-century witness to Davidic rule—but the restoration is somewhat speculative.[15] Beyond all such arguments, however, is the biblical account itself and what other scholars have found in it. If lurking behind the air-brushed portrayal of David's accession to the throne is a rather unflattering picture of striking verisimilitude, then it seems altogether likely that that unflattering picture corresponds to some actual lived reality. There indeed was a tough military chief named David, and he did strong-arm his way to power, first gaining control of his native Judah and then, when the opportunity presented itself, succeeding Saul as ruler of the north (though it is to be admitted that the extent of Saul's kingdom remains undetermined).

The Capture of Jerusalem

David's first move after taking over all of Israel was to go off and conquer a small hilltop town, Jerusalem. The town was located at the edge of the Judean desert, but it was not officially part of Judah; in fact, it was inhabited by a distinct people, the Jebusites. The Jebusites were no match for David's army, and, despite Jerusalem's natural defenses, he apparently took over the town in short order (2 Sam. 5:6–10). Then he made it the capital of his kingdom.

In every respect this was a brilliant move.[16] To begin with, Jerusalem, while not altogether a natural fortress, nevertheless offered a number of strategic advantages. The terrain around it was rugged and not easy for an enemy to negotiate. Armies attacking from below had a steep climb in front of them; defenders of the city could shoot down on them with ease. What is more, Jerusalem had its own water supply gushing within the city walls—an important advantage in the case of a prolonged siege.

The Bible does not say what happened to the Jebusite inhabitants after the city was conquered. It is certainly possible that, as with other conquered cities, the inhabitants were distributed among the troops as slaves or were murdered outright. But a canny conqueror like David probably took at least some of the Jebusite army—their best fighters—and incorporated them into his own forces.[17] Soldiers who no longer had any hope of resisting had to face a new reality in any case; staying in their old town and serving David would not have been a bad fate. For his part, David would have gained thereby a corps of veteran fighters who owed everything to him. Any ruler, especially a new one, has to worry first about his own hold on power. Having a Praetorian Guard with no ties to any of his potential rivals was all someone like David could ask for. If this was indeed what happened to the Jebusite army, then moving against Jerusalem was doubly clever.

But the biggest advantage Jerusalem offered David was its location. Not far from his hometown of Bethlehem, it was nonetheless perched on the border between Judah and the northern tribes. Making it his capital was thus a clear statement: this town, and my whole administration, belong neither to the north or the south, but to both. Three millennia later, faced with a similar situation (and perhaps inspired by the biblical model), the founders of the American republic carved out a piece of territory between north and south and called it the District of Columbia, in which they built the capital city of Washington. In both cases the result was the creation of a new center of power, one that could inspire the loyalties of all the country's inhabitants in equal measure.

David Dances

Once Jerusalem was his, David also saw to it that the "ark of God" was moved there (2 Samuel 26). The ark—a great wooden chest overlaid with gold—was Israel's most sacred object. According to the Bible, it had been fashioned for the desert tabernacle as a kind of platform (or perhaps footstool) above which the divine presence might appear (Exod. 25:10–22; 37:1–2). After Israel's entry into the land, the ark had moved about a great deal, crossing the Jordan with Joshua's troops, then apparently residing at Gilgal, Bethel, and Shiloh (where it was housed in the temple in which Eli, and later Samuel, served God). Captured by the Philistines for a time, the ark was returned after a plague broke out among them (1 Samuel 5–6); it subsequently resided at Kiryat Yearim. After establishing himself in Jerusalem, David personally escorted the ark to his new capital; on the way, he and the people around him "danced before the LORD with all their might, with songs and lyres and harps and tambourines and sistrums and cymbals" (2 Sam. 6:5). Apparently, however, this did not sit well with his aristocratic wife:

> As the ark of the LORD came into the city of David, Michal daughter of Saul looked out of the window, and saw King David leaping and dancing before the LORD; and she despised him in her heart . . . [Later she said to him:] "The king of Israel has certainly done himself proud today, uncovering him-

self right in front of his retainers' slave girls, just as any common vulgarian might do!" David said to Michal, "It was before the LORD, who chose me over your father and his whole family and appointed me as ruler over the LORD's people Israel, that I have been dancing. [If I feel like it], I may make even more of a fool of myself, so that even I am ashamed (although the slave girls you mentioned will surely only respect me the more)." And Michal the daughter of Saul had no child to the day of her death.

2 Sam. 6:16–23

Thus it was that the ark arrived in Jerusalem. There was no temple yet in which to put it: instead, as of old, the ark was kept in a sacred tent.

The moving of the ark to Jerusalem was also a highly symbolic gesture. Although, according to scholars, the idea of a single, exclusive shrine in Jerusalem was still centuries away, moving the ark to Jerusalem certainly put that city on the sacred map, so to speak: it became a "temple city"—an old idea in the ancient Near East[18]—a political capital and central shrine. What is more, scholars point out that Gilgal, Bethel, and Shiloh were all within the territory of the powerful northern tribe of Ephraim; this suggests that the ark had been particularly associated with the north, perhaps even serving as a unifying symbol during Saul's reign. Moving it to Jerusalem was thus another way for David to assert his intention to be equally a king of all the tribes.

God's Promise to David

Having settled in Jerusalem, David set about building his royal palace. After it was done, he had in mind to build another structure, a great temple to house the ark. Nathan, the resident prophet of David's court, at first gave his okay, but that night God spoke to Nathan and told him to instruct the king to hold off. Instead of his building a house for Me, God told Nathan, I will build a house for him:

> [God told Nathan to say to David:] When your life is over and you lie down with your fathers, I will raise up your offspring after you, one who comes from your own loins, and I will establish his kingdom. He shall build a house for My name, and I will establish the throne of his kingdom forever. I will be a father to him, and he shall be a son to Me. Should he do something wrong, I will [of course] punish him with a rod such as men use, with the blows inflicted by human beings. But I will never withdraw My support from him as I did with Saul, whom I rejected in favor of you. Your dynasty and your kingdom will always stand firm before Me; your throne is established forever.

2 Sam. 7:12–16

What Nathan's oracle essentially promised was that a single dynasty, the house of David, would rule over Israel forever. Forever is a long time, of course, and things did not turn out that way; but as we shall see, the house of David did rule in Judah for some four centuries, certainly an impressive record.

In view of modern scholarship's overall skepticism about early dates—as well as everything we have seen specifically about the Deuteronomistic history and its sources—it would appear unlikely that such an oracle was ever delivered in David's own time. Instead, it seems to scholars to be a typical prediction after the fact, a pseudo-oracle composed sometime after (perhaps *long* after) the Davidic dynasty was an established reality. When exactly it might have been written is hard for them to say. The sentence about Solomon's building a temple ("He shall build a house for My name, and I will establish the throne of his kingdom forever") seems to interrupt the flow of the paragraph; take it out and you have one continuous theme, that God is establishing the Davidic dynasty forever. Since this interruptive sentence is very much in the style of Deuteronomy—Deuteronomy is the book where the temple is consistently described as a place for God's "name" to dwell—scholars feel that this insertion must be the work of the compilers or subsequent editors of the Deuteronomistic history; they stuck this sentence into an already-existing text. Thus, this original oracle might arguably go back sometime before the mid–seventh century—but how far back is anyone's guess.[19]

A Roof with a View

One day, after his midday nap, David got up and decided to go for a stroll on the flat roof of his palace.

> He saw from the roof a woman bathing; the woman was very beautiful. David sent someone to inquire about the woman. It was reported, "She is Bathsheba daughter of Eliam, the wife of Uriah the Hittite." So David sent messengers to get her, and she came to him, and he lay with her. (Now she had been purifying herself after her period.)* Then she returned to her house. The woman became pregnant, so she sent a message to David: "I am pregnant." David then sent word to Joab, "Send me Uriah the Hittite." And Joab dispatched Uriah to David.
>
> 2 Sam. 11:2–6

---

* This detail is added to imply that not only was Bathsheba in a state of ritual purity when she slept with David, but also that the child born of this union was indeed David's and not Uriah's.

What happened next is not very pretty. David first issued Uriah a furlough in the hope that he would go home and have relations with Bathsheba—that way, Uriah might believe that the child was his. But Uriah did not go home; perhaps he thought the king was testing his soldierly devotion.* In any case, the next day David invited him back to the palace and plied him with wine, but Uriah still did not go home. So David sent a message to Uriah's commander the following morning, telling him to arrange for Uriah to be killed "accidentally" in battle—which he was. With Bathsheba now a widow, David was free to take her on as one of his wives—which he did.

God was not happy with this turn of events, however, and He dispatched the prophet Nathan to speak with David. Nathan did not start off by accusing David of wrongdoing. Instead, he pretended to be bringing a legal case to David, who, as king, might regularly be asked to give his ruling in a lawsuit.

[Nathan] came to him, and said to him, "Two men were in the same city, one of them rich and the other poor. The rich man had very many flocks and herds; but the poor man had nothing but one little ewe lamb, which he had bought. He fed it and it grew up with him and with his children; it used to eat of his meager fare, and drink from his cup, and nestle in his bosom— it was like a daughter to him. Now there came a traveler to the rich man, and he [the rich man] did not want to take one of his own flock or herd to prepare for the visitor who had come to him, so instead he seized the poor man's lamb and he slaughtered it for the guest who had come to him." Then David became quite angry at the man and he said to Nathan, "As the LORD lives, the man who did this deserves to die. Let him [at least] pay for the lamb four times over, insofar as he did this thing and showed no pity."

Nathan said to David, "The man is you. Thus says the LORD, the God of Israel: I anointed you king over Israel, and I saved you from Saul. Then I gave you your master's house and your master's wives as your own, and I gave you the house of Israel and of Judah; and if that had not been enough, I would have added this, that, and the other. Why, then, have you flouted the LORD's commandment and done what is evil in His sight, having Uriah the Hittite killed in battle and then taking his wife to be your wife—in fact, you had him killed in a battle with the Ammonites . . .

David said to Nathan, "I stand guilty before the LORD." Nathan said to David, "Indeed. The LORD is putting away your sin [that is, reducing your sentence]; you shall not die. Nevertheless, because by this deed you have shown no respect for the LORD, the child that is to be born to you shall die." Then Nathan went to his house.

2 Sam. 12:1–15

* Soldiers on a sacred mission were expected to refrain from sexual contact; see 1 Sam. 21:5.

Now David was desperate. He begged God to spare the baby's life, he fasted and cried, he lay on the ground and would not move, but nothing availed. After seven days of illness, the child did indeed die.

Though it was customary after such an event to afflict oneself as a sign of grief, David decided to skip the traditional mourning period:

> David got up from the ground and put on anointing oil and changed his clothes and went into the temple of the LORD to bow down. Then he went home and, at his request, food was brought to him and he ate. His servants said to him, "Why are you doing this? While the baby was still alive, you fasted and wept. Now that the baby is dead, you get up and eat food?" He said, "While the baby was alive, I fasted and wept because I thought, 'Perhaps the LORD will take pity on me and let the baby live.' But now that it is dead, why should I fast? Can I bring it back to life? I will go to join it—it will not come back to me." And David comforted his wife Bathsheba, and went to her, and lay with her and she gave birth to a son. He called him Solomon, and this one the LORD loved.
>
> 2 Sam. 12:20–24

Thus was born the man who would eventually inherit David's kingdom.

David's sin with Bathsheba posed a challenge to ancient interpreters. Normally, these interpreters sought to accentuate the positive or the negative: figures like Abraham or Jacob had to be all good (even when they sometimes did not seem so), whereas others, like Esau or Balaam, usually came out all bad. David, too, was generally in the "good" camp—but how could that be squared with the painfully detailed story of his adulterous union? Perhaps the earliest "reckoning" known to us is that of the biblical book of Chronicles: it simply sweeps the entire episode under the rug. Although Chronicles painstakingly duplicates 1 and 2 Samuel in other matters of David's life, the incident with Bathsheba has been entirely air-brushed out of its account; as far as the author of this book is concerned, there was no sin.[20]

It was not long, however, before another motif developed: David the Penitent. This motif is rooted in the biblical narrative itself, but it soon came to be elaborated: now the point of the story of David and Bathsheba was that even a great man can sin. What the story shows is that, while God punishes, He is also merciful. Not long after the book of Chronicles was written, scholars say, an anonymous scribe wrote a new heading to an old psalm that asked for divine forgiveness, Psalm 51. The heading he inserted read: "To the leader. A Psalm of David, when the prophet Nathan came to him, after he had gone in to Bathsheba." Ever after, this psalm has been connected with the theme of David's repentance and desperate plea for purification after his terrible sin:[21]

Wash me clean of my misdeed, purify me of my sin.
For I know I did wrong. My sin is always on my mind.

David's sin and repentance became such a common theme that, eventually, some interpreters came to suggest that there were a few things that were even worse than adultery. A somewhat witty passage in the Babylonian Talmud presents David not only as a king but, apparently in his spare moments, a somewhat harried teacher of rabbinic law as well. All he wishes to do is to teach his students the complicated rules of biblical purity, but they keep bringing up his sin with Bathsheba in an attempt to embarrass him:

> He who publicly shames his fellow, it is as if he had actually killed him. [Commented Rabbi Nahman ben Isaac:] A good comparison! For I have noticed [with people who are embarrassed in public] that the[ir] red-facedness soon departs, and a pallor sets in [as if they were dead].
>   Raba expounded the verse [attributed to King David]: "When I stumbled they rejoiced and gathered together . . . they tore at me and did not cease [lo' damu]" (Ps. 35:15). David said to God: "Master of the Universe, you know full well that if they were actually to tear at my flesh, no blood would come out of me [that is, lo' dami, "no blood of mine," because I have been shamed so many times because of my sin with Bathsheba that my blood has departed]. And what's more, even as I am teaching them the laws of ritual purity, [when it comes time for questions] they say to me, 'David, by the way—what is the penalty for an adulterer?' But then I answer them: 'He is punished by death [if proven guilty], yet he still will not have forfeited his place in the World to Come. But he who shames his fellow in public does indeed forfeit his place in the World to Come.'"
>
> b. Talmud, *Baba Metzi'a* 48b–49a

The Biography of David

Much of 1 and 2 Samuel is taken up with incidents from David's biography, not just political and military events like his conquest of Jerusalem or his war against the Ammonites, but personal matters such as Michal's complaint about his dancing or his affair with Bathsheba and subsequent rebuke by the prophet Nathan, as well as events yet to be seen—the rape of Tamar and Absalom's rebellion, and the behind-the-scenes maneuvering by Bathsheba and others that led to Solomon's appointment as David's successor. All of this makes for a hefty quantity of material about David's life, and—especially in view of the personal nature of much of it—scholars have always wondered why all this was written and by whom.

In the past, biblicists have seen a good chunk of this material as one continuous history, the "Succession Narrative," whose purpose, they supposed, was to legitimate Solomon's succession of David and, hence, the whole Davidic line that was to follow. According to this hypothesis, this narrative would have been composed early in Solomon's reign by someone—perhaps a court sage or advisor—with access to inside information.[22] Indeed, some scholars saw this narrative as the product of the "Solomonic Enlightenment," which led to the first real history writing in the ancient Near East.[23] In more recent scholarship, the separateness and purpose of this narrative have been contested. Few critics today maintain that there ever was a "Succession Narrative" distinct from the rest of David's biography.[24] As for the date of this material, the jury is still out. Some scholars have observed that there is no hint in the account of David and Solomon's rise that their United Monarchy would soon fall apart; that might argue that this account must have been penned not long after the events themselves. Likewise, there is no mention in it of the Ten Commandments or any other biblical laws—this too might seem to suggest an early date. But arguments from silence are notoriously weak. Perhaps the strongest argument for the account's closeness to the historical David (though the argument is hardly unequivocal) is a literary one. The biblical portrait of David seems uncannily consistent: nearly everything that he is said to have done seems to fit pretty well with everything else. The David who emerges from this narrative is striking in another way as well: it would be no exaggeration, I think, to describe him as the most vigorous, realistic, and in some ways the most *human* of all the Bible's heroes. If Moses and Isaiah and Jeremiah scale the vertical axis of human existence, the one that leads from earth to heaven, David, by contrast, spans a good part of the horizontal one. The Bible certainly does not idealize him, but he is all the more appealing for that. No bit of human hope and despair, bravura and foolishness and bitter melancholy, smoldering hatred and deepest love, is foreign to him. True, a great novelist or playwright could create such a person out of whole cloth, but one might find it appealing to turn that argument on its head. David may be the Bible's best character because he is no *character* at all.

28

Solomon's Wisdom

2 Samuel 13 through 1 Kings 4

Feast of the Dedication of the Temple by Matthys Pool.

THE RAPE OF TAMAR AND ABSALOM'S REBELLION.
ABISHAG THE SHUNAMMITE. SOLOMON MADE KING.
SOLOMON'S WISDOM. ANCIENT NEAR EASTERN WISDOM.
SOLOMON'S THREE BOOKS.

Solomon, David's son, eventually succeeded him. God blessed him with wisdom surpassing that of any man. But if he was so wise, why did he make such a mess of his kingdom?

The oldest of David's sons was Amnon, and he was thus slated to succeed David on the throne. But it did not turn out that way. Things started to unravel, the Bible reports, because of a beautiful girl, Tamar, who was Amnon's half sister. (She was the full sister of Amnon's younger brother Absalom.) Amnon could not stop thinking about Tamar. One day, his friend Jonadab told Amnon he was worried about him:

> "Why do you look so bad, prince, morning after morning? Do you want to tell me about it?" Amnon said to him, "I am in love with Tamar, my brother Absalom's sister." Jonadab said to him, "Lie down on your bed, and pretend to be sick; then, when your father comes to see you, say to him, 'Let my sister Tamar come and give me something to eat. Let her make the food herself, right here, so that I can see and then she can feed me.' "

It is not clear what exactly Jonadab's plan was intended to lead to. As Amnon's half sister, Tamar would not normally be required to avoid casual contact with him; they might even share a sibling embrace—so long as it was in public (Song 8:1). Her going unescorted into his bedroom would presumably be another matter, however, one that required a good excuse, which is why Amnon had to claim to be ill.

> So Amnon lay down, and pretended to be sick; and when the king came to see him, Amnon said to the king, "Please have my sister Tamar come and make some cakes, right here, so that she can then feed them to me." So David sent word to Tamar, saying, "Go to your brother Amnon's house, and make some food for him." Tamar went to her brother Amnon's house, where he was in bed. She took dough, kneaded it, made cakes in front of him, and baked the cakes. Then she took the pan and set them out before him, but he did not eat. [Instead,] Amnon said, "Get everyone out of here." So everyone left. Then Amnon said to Tamar, "Bring the food in here so that you can feed it to me." So Tamar took the cakes she had made, and

brought them into her brother Amnon's room. But when she began to serve them to him, he grabbed hold of her and said to her, "Come, lie with me, my sister." She said him, "No, my brother, no! Don't force me! People don't do that in Israel. Don't do something so wrong! Where could I hide my shame? And you—you would be considered a common criminal in Israel. Talk to the king, I beg you; he won't prevent you from [marrying] me." But he would not listen to her; and since he was stronger than her, he took her by force and lay with her.

But then Amnon was seized with a great loathing for her; indeed, his loathing was even greater than the love he had felt for her before. Amnon said to her, "Get out!" But she said to him, "No, my brother! Sending me away now—that would be even worse than the other thing you did to me." But he would not listen to her. He called his young servant and said, "Get her out of here, and lock the door after her." (Now she was wearing an ornamented robe, since that was what the king's virgin daughters used to wear as cloaks.) So his servant put her out, and locked the door after her. Then Tamar put ashes on her head and tore the ornamented robe* that she was wearing; she put her hand on her head,§ and walked about, crying as she went.

2 Sam. 13:4–19

When Absalom heard that his sister had been raped by Amnon, he said nothing to him about it, but secretly he was already planning his revenge. The opportunity came two years later. Amnon, by then suspecting nothing, accompanied Absalom to a sheep shearing (a festive event marked by eating and drinking). After Amnon had consumed a certain quantity of alcohol and was "merry with wine," Absalom had his servants murder him. He then fled to the land of Geshur.

Absalom's Rebellion

Fearing David's wrath, Absalom stayed in exile in Geshur (his mother's homeland) for three years. Eventually, with the help of a court insider (Joab, David's nephew and general) and a certain "wise woman of Tekoa," Absalom persuaded David to allow him to return to Jerusalem. But David was still angry at his son. It took two more years before the king even allowed Absa-

---

* The point is that such ornamented robes (the phrase is the same used of Joseph's "coat of many colors" in Gen. 37:3) were quite costly; ripping hers—as a conventional sign of grief, as well as perhaps a sign that she was no longer one of the "king's virgin daughters"—was no casual act.

§ Another sign of grief, along with putting ashes on the head.

lom to come to court to see him. But then David forgave him (2 Sam. 14:33).

What was on Absalom's mind during his exile in Geshur? Apparently, the long wait there, along with David's (temporary) blackballing of him after he returned, had started Absalom thinking. After all, he *was* David's son, a potential heir to the throne. His good looks were legendary (2 Sam. 14:25), and, as we have seen, physical appearance certainly counted in the selection of a king (1 Sam. 9:2; 16:12). Part of Absalom's beauty he owed to his long, flowing hair—so long and flowing that, when he got his annual haircut, the hair cut off would weigh two hundred shekels (about twice the weight of the wool produced by an average sheep at shearing!). And Absalom was in an excellent political position to succeed David. As the son of a Geshurite mother, he had some potential appeal to the northern tribes (since Geshur was on the far side of the Jordan right next to the eastern half of the tribe of Manasseh); as David's son, he could also count on the southerners' support. So why wait for David to decide on his successor? Absalom began winning allies for himself. He would buttonhole people who had come to the capital for a lawsuit and talk with each one personally: "Where are you from? What's your case about?" Then he would seem to sympathize with their cause. "Too bad I am not the country's judge! Then anyone who had a lawsuit would be able to come to me, and I would make sure he got justice" (2 Sam. 15:4). The person would usually start to bow down to him, but Absalom would grab him by the hand instead and embrace him.

After a time, Absalom invented a pretext that would allow him to travel to Hebron with two hundred of his supporters. When he got there he had himself proclaimed king, just as his father had done years earlier. Among those who joined Absalom's cause was one of David's top advisors, Ahitophel. This was a great coup on Absalom's part; soon, people "throughout all the tribes of Israel" were backing him (2 Sam. 15:10). Absalom was now on his way. So great was the groundswell for this usurping son that David had to flee his own capital of Jerusalem, taking everyone except ten of his concubines, whom he left to look after the palace. Absalom moved right in and, on Ahitophel's advice, set up a very visible tent on the palace roof, in which he had relations with David's concubines—a demonstration that he was the de facto new king.

But David and his forces regrouped on the far side of the Jordan. On the brink of the confrontation between his army and his son's, David seemed more worried about the fate of Absalom than the outcome of the fight: "Deal gently with my boy Absalom," he warned his generals. Perhaps it was already obvious who would win. Although Absalom had ample men, apparently swelled by northern recruits, they were soon overcome by David's seasoned soldiers. In all, twenty thousand men perished that day. As for Absalom, his long, flowing hair proved his undoing:

Absalom was riding on his mule, and the mule went under the thick branches of a great oak. His head caught fast in the oak, and he was left hanging between heaven and earth, while the mule that was under him went on. A man saw it, and told Joab [David's general], "I saw Absalom hanging in an oak."... [Joab] took three spears in his hand, and thrust them into Absalom's heart while he was still alive in the oak. Then ten young men, Joab's armor-bearers, surrounded Absalom and struck him, and killed him.

2 Sam. 18:9–15

It did not take long for the news to reach David:

Then Joab said to a Cushite, "Go, tell the king what you have seen." The Cushite bowed before Joab, and ran... Now David was sitting between the two gates. The sentinel went up to the roof of the gate by the wall, and when he looked up, he saw a man running alone... Then the Cushite came; and the Cushite said, "Good news for my lord the king! The LORD has taken your side today against all your enemies." The king said to the Cushite, "Is my boy Absalom safe?" The Cushite answered, "May the enemies of my lord the king, and all who rise up to do you harm, end up like that boy."... The king was shaken. He went up to the chamber over the gate, and as he went, he said, "Oh, Absalom my son! My son, my son Absalom! If only I could have died instead of you, Absalom. My son, my son!"

2 Sam. 18:21–33

Measure for Measure

The details of Absalom's rebellion once again cause scholars to wonder where this account came from. On the one hand, it has the hallmarks of a contemporaneous account. The portrait of a headstrong young man, perhaps resentful of his older half-brother from the start, and certainly even more so after the reported rape of Tamar (if indeed that was what happened and not an excuse invented after Amnon's murder), a potential heir to the throne kept in exile by a king as wary of his son as he was angry at him—all this seems altogether plausible. So too is Absalom's conduct prior to the open rebellion, slowly building a power base where David was weakest, with the northern tribes, then winning Ahitophel to his cause; this was truly a classic palace revolt.[1] On the other hand, it is so well written and so engaging that at times it seems more like the work of an ancient writer of fiction—"a novel," in the words of one scholar.[2] In particular, the tension over Absalom's fate in battle, the brutal description of his death, and then the pathetic picture of his father's grief—all these have seemed to scholars to show a creative flair that

is different from the cold, dispassionate recital of facts characteristic elsewhere of biblical historiography.

Needless to say, either judgment would be quite out of place in the period
when the Bible was first becoming *the* Bible. The earliest interpreters of
Scripture viewed the account of David's struggles as they viewed everything
else in the Bible. These stories, they felt, were certainly true recitations of the
facts, but if they were included in God's holy book it was because they contained some lesson applicable to their own—and our—daily lives. In this case,
it did not require much scrutiny for interpreters to understand that God had
arranged the events to convey the great principle of "measure for measure"—that is, God punishes or rewards people in keeping with their deeds,
often designing the punishment or reward in such a way as to suggest a direct
connection to its specific cause.

> By the same measuring cup that a person measures out with, so is it meas-
> ured back to him [by God] . . . Samson went after his own eyes [that is, fol-
> lowed his carnal desires], therefore Philistines plucked out his eyes, as it is
> said, "And the Philistines seized him and plucked out his eyes" (Judg.
> 16:21). Absalom was overly proud about his hair, therefore he got caught
> up by his hair. And since he had relations with his father's ten concubines,
> therefore ten javelins were plunged into him, as it says, "ten young men,
> Joab's armor-bearers, surrounded Absalom [and struck him, and killed
> him]" (2 Sam. 18:15). And since he deceived three different parties—his
> father, the courts,* and all of Israel, [this last] because it is written, "And
> Absalom deceived the men of Israel" (2 Sam. 15:6)—therefore three spears
> pierced him, as it says, "He took three spears in his hand, and thrust them
> into the heart of Absalom" (2 Sam. 18:4).
>
> m. *Sotah,* 1:7–8

A Warm Shunammite

After Absalom's death, David still faced some rocky times—notably, a new
revolt led by Sheba son of Bichri, from the tribe of Benjamin (which, however,
David suppressed handily, 2 Samuel 20). But after that a new David emerged,
one whose hold on power was unshakable. No one else rose up to challenge
his rule, and his chief concern now was designating his successor, since
David himself was growing old and weary.

---

* Not, as one might have supposed, because he was buttonholing people outside of
court, but because his planned revolt is said to have won the approval of Ahitophel, who
then convinced the "elders of Israel"—understood as meaning specifically the judges of the
court. "The advice pleased Absalom and all the elders of Israel" (2 Sam. 17:4).

It is at this point that the Bible reports on a troublesome physical problem faced by the king:

> Now King David was old and advanced in years; and although they covered him with blankets, he could not get warm. So his servants said to him, "Let a young virgin be sought for His Majesty the king, and let her serve the king, and be his attendant; let her lie right next to you, so that my lord the king may be warm." So they searched for a beautiful girl throughout all the territory of Israel, and found Abishag the Shunammite, and brought her to the king. The girl was very beautiful and she became the king's attendant and served him, but the king was not intimate with her.
>
> 1 Kings 1:1–4

Here, certainly, was a creative solution to the problem of poor circulation caused by clogged arteries—though why exactly David's bed warmer had to be a young and beautiful virgin is not explained. These qualities were to prove significant, however, for what happened next.

Adonijah was David's oldest surviving son, and quite possibly considered his heir apparent. Like his late older brother Absalom, Adonijah was quite handsome (1 Kings 1:6) and eager to take over; he won a number of powerful supporters to his side. The prophet Nathan was not one of them, however, and when he learned that Adonijah had his eye on the throne, he persuaded Bathsheba to take the matter up with her husband, David. In fact, Nathan looks at this point to be a bit of a shady dealer. He tells Bathsheba to go to the king and "remind" him of a solemn oath that David had taken promising that Solomon, Bathsheba's son with David, would be the next king. (The text seems to imply that there never was such an oath.) Nathan arranges to then enter the throne room and spontaneously confirm the existence of this oath. The plan works: David—probably addled by old age—is convinced that Solomon was indeed his promised heir, and he therefore has the priest Zadok anoint him as king (1 Kings 1:32–40). Shortly thereafter, David dies quietly in bed.[3]

So it was that Adonijah lost the kingship. He did, however, have one minor request of the new king. It was apparently a delicate matter, and so, rather than approach Solomon directly, Adonijah went to see Solomon's mother, Bathsheba:

> "There is something I wish to tell you," he said. She said, "Go ahead." He said, "You know that the kingship was supposed to be mine, and that all Israel had turned to me to be king. But the kingship has instead become my brother's; it became his by the LORD's will. What I want now is just one thing—do not refuse me." She said to him, "Go ahead." He said, "Please ask King Solomon—he will never refuse you—to give me Abishag the

> Shunammite as my wife." Bathsheba said, "Very well; I will speak to the
> king about this."
>
> 1 Kings 2:14–18

Adonijah's request was ambiguous. It seems quite possible that all he really
wanted was to marry Abishag. After all, she *was* young and beautiful; perhaps he had been smitten with her since the day she first came to the royal
court. At the time, Adonijah probably expected to inherit her as soon as he
became king—indeed, perhaps the two had even acted on this expectation
during those times when she was not busy serving David or warming his bed.
On the other hand, it may have been that, when he made this request for
Abishag, Adonijah had not yet given up all hope of overthrowing Solomon.
In ancient Israel, as we have seen, sleeping with the king's wife or concubine
was a de facto claim to the throne. (That is why Absalom had earlier made a
point of sleeping with his father's ten concubines.) If Adonijah could indeed
end up with Abishag as his wife, he might at some later point claim that
David himself had willed her to him—and hence that the kingship had really
been promised to him.

Solomon chose to interpret his half-brother's request in the latter sense.
When Bathsheba told him what Adonijah was asking for, he exploded:

> King Solomon said to his mother, "And why are you requesting only
> Abishag the Shunammite for Adonijah? You might as well ask for the
> kingship for him too! After all, he is my *older* brother—and he and the
> priest Abiathar and Joab son of Zeruiah [are in league together]."* Then
> King Solomon swore by the LORD, "So may God do to me, and more so [if
> I don't carry out this oath:] Adonijah will pay with his life for raising this
> matter! As the LORD lives, who has established me and placed me on the
> throne of my father David, and who has given him a dynasty as he prom-
> ised, Adonijah will be executed this very day." So King Solomon sent
> Benaiah son of Jehoiada; he struck him [Adonijah] down, and he died.
>
> 1 Kings 3:22–25

The Real Shunammite

With such brutality did the new king secure his place as David's uncontested
successor. Centuries later, however, interpreters had difficulty believing that
God's book had intended to instruct them in all the seamy dealings of

---

* The fact that Adonijah is older might make him the heir presumptive to the throne.
The rest of this sentence seems to have been garbled in transmission—the bracketed
phrase is not in the received text.

Solomon's first days on the throne. Surely, there must be a hidden message here too! Jerome had no difficulty discovering it.

> In the seventieth year of his life, David, who had theretofore been a man of war, now was unable to keep warm because of the chills of old age. Therefore, a girl was sought throughout the land of Israel who might sleep with the king and warm his aged body: Abishag the Shunammite. Now, if you were to take Scripture literally, wouldn't this seem to you to have been invented as some kind of farce, one of those Atellan comedies? The freezing old man is wrapped round and round with bedclothes but cannot be warmed except by the embrace of some young girl! Bathsheba was still around at the time, as were Abigail and the rest of his wives and concubines mentioned by Scripture, but all were apparently rejected as lacking heat: the old man could be warmed by the embrace of one girl alone. Abraham was much older than David, yet so long as Sarah was alive he didn't go looking for another wife. Isaac was twice as old as David, but he never grew cold with Rebekah, even when she was old. I will not even mention those earlier men from before the Flood, whose limbs, I should say, were, after nine hundred years, not merely aged but almost decomposing—yet they did not seek out the embrace of young women. And certainly Moses, the leader of the people of Israel, was one hundred and twenty years old and never changed from his Sephora.
>
> So who is this Shunammite, both a wife and a virgin, so fervid as to warm up a cold man, yet so holy as to not provoke a warmed one to lust?* [She is a symbol of] Wisdom. "Get wisdom, and above all your possessions, get understanding . . ." [Prov. 4:7]. Even the name *Abishag* in its secret significance refers to wisdom, which is greater among the aged.§
>
> Jerome, *Letter 52* 2–3

For Jerome, the whole story of Abishag is, like the rest of Scripture, fraught with symbolic meaning. In truth, David's difficulties in getting warm were quite beside the point. What the Bible was saying in its own cryptic way was that, having spent his life as a fighter and a man of war, David in his last years sought to embrace wisdom and pursue the sorts of insights that are available only to those who have reached old age.

Solomon's Dream

Shortly after he succeeded his father on the throne, Solomon was blessed with an extraordinary dream vision:

---

* Because 1 Kings 1:4 had specified that "the king was not intimate with her."

§ Jerome is interpreting the name as "my father increased [wisdom]."

At Gibeon, the LORD appeared to Solomon in a dream by night; and God said, "Make a request—what can I give you?" And Solomon said, "You have been so kind with my father, Your servant David, because he acted faithfully toward You, in righteousness and integrity of heart. Moreover, You have maintained that great kindness to this day by granting him a son to sit on his throne. So it is, O LORD my God, that you have made me, Your servant, king in place of my father David. But I am a raw youth; I know nothing about being a leader. And Your servant finds himself in the midst of a people who, since You have chosen them, are so great and numerous that they cannot even be numbered or counted. Give Your servant therefore an understanding mind to rule over Your people; [make me] able to decide what is right and what is wrong. For who can govern this great people?"

It pleased the LORD that Solomon had asked for this. God said to him, "Because you requested this—you did not ask for long life or riches for yourself, or for the life of your enemies, but you asked for understanding to discern what is right—I hereby grant you what you have asked. I hereby give you a wise and discerning mind, such as no one like you before has had and no one who comes after you will. I am also granting you what you did not ask for, both wealth and glory your whole life long, such as no other king has had. I will also grant you a long life, if you walk in My ways and keep My laws and My commandments, as your father David did." Then Solomon awoke; it had been a dream.

1 Kings 3:5–15

So it was that, in one night, Solomon became the wisest of kings.

This is one of those passages in the Deuteronomistic history in which modern scholars find the heavy hand of the editor; the vocabulary, as well as the idealization of wisdom, smack of Deuteronomy.[4] Yet it seems unlikely to most scholars that Solomon's association with wisdom was an invention of the Deuteronomistic historians.[5] A passage usually thought to be somewhat older[6] is similarly unstinting in its praise of Solomon's wisdom:

God gave Solomon wisdom—knowledge in great measure and breadth of mind as vast as the sand on the seashore. Solomon's wisdom was greater than that of all the peoples of the east and all the wisdom of Egypt. He grew wiser than anyone—wiser than Ethan the Ezrahite, and Heman, Calcol, and Darda, the sons of Mahol; his fame spread throughout all the surrounding nations. He spoke three thousand proverbs, and his songs numbered a thousand and five. He could speak of trees, from the cedar that is in the Lebanon to the hyssop that grows out of the wall; he could speak about animals, birds, reptiles, and fish. People came from all the nations to hear Solomon's wisdom; they came from all the kings of the earth who had heard of his wisdom.

1 Kings 4:29–34 (Hebrew, 5:9–14)

It is in part on the basis of these two passages that tradition came to assign Solomon a crucial role. He was held to be the author of three of the Bible's books: Proverbs, Ecclesiastes, and the Song of Songs. Indeed, this belief is still espoused today by many Jews and Christians, although modern scholars have advanced reasons for skepticism.

But if Solomon was indeed so wise, how did he end up making such a mess of things? Shortly after his son Rehoboam took over the throne, the northern tribes seceded from the great United Monarchy that David had cobbled together. We have seen how careful David himself had been to try to cultivate the favor of the northerners, establishing his capital at a midpoint between north and south and moving the (northern-associated) ark and its tent shrine to Jerusalem. How, then, did the the country's unity collapse so quickly? To modern historians, it seems unlikely that poor Rehoboam should bear all the blame for the secession that occurred shortly after the beginning of his reign; surely his father Solomon was at least partly at fault.[7]

And, in fact, at the time they seceded, the northerners were not coy about the reason for their discontent: Solomon had taxed them nearly to death, they said. "Your father made our yoke too heavy. Lighten the hard work imposed by your father and his heavy yoke" (1 Kings 12:4). There was some obvious justice to this complaint: the biblical record reports that Solomon was a spendthrift of almost unbelievable proportions. He began by assembling a huge bureaucracy; then he kept his bloated payroll of civil servants happy with lavish banquets à la Louis XIV. *Every day,* the Bible says, he and his people consumed "thirty cors of choice flour, and sixty cors of meal, ten fat oxen, and twenty pasture-fed cattle, one hundred sheep, besides deer, gazelles, roebucks, and fatted fowl" (1 Kings 4:22–23). He also maintained a huge standing army, with "forty thousand stalls of horses for his chariots, and twelve thousand horsemen" (1 Kings 4:26); he also had fourteen hundred chariots, each of which was worth six hundred shekels of silver (1 Kings 10:26). By comparison, fifteen shekels in biblical times would buy you an ox or approximately two tons of grain; a ram sold for two shekels (Lev. 5:15).

Solomon was equally well stocked with wives; he is said to have married "the daughter of Pharaoh, [and] Moabite, Ammonite, Edomite, Sidonian, and Hittite women" in addition to his native-born wives and concubines, including "seven hundred princesses and three hundred concubines" (1 Kings 11:1, 3). Even allowing for a certain amount of exaggeration, this was an impressive harem. Inside Solomon's palace:

The king also made a great ivory throne, and overlaid it with the finest gold. The throne had six steps. The top of the throne was rounded in the back, and on each side of the seat were arm rests and two lions standing beside the arm rests, while twelve lions were standing, one on each end of a step on the six steps. Nothing like it was ever made in any kingdom. All King Solomon's drinking vessels were of gold, and all the vessels of the House of the Forest of Lebanon were of pure gold; none was of silver—it was not considered as anything in the days of Solomon. For the king had a fleet of ships of Tarshish at sea with the fleet of Hiram. Once every three years the fleet of ships of Tarshish used to come bringing gold, silver, ivory, apes, and peacocks.

1 Kings 10:16–22

It is sometimes said that Solomon greatly expanded trade and that that is what is responsible for both his lavish expenditures and his ability to pay for them. But that does not sit well with the biblical report of the northerners' complaint. If there is any truth to the biblical account of Solomon's wealth, it seems obvious that he overspent and overtaxed—breaking the most elementary rule in the book of political leadership. So why doesn't the Bible remember him as a fool rather than the wisest of kings? Whence this great, and apparently ancient, reputation for wisdom?

To some modern scholars it appears more likely that Solomon's connection to wisdom—if it has any historical basis—reflects the fact that he might have been a *patron of wisdom* rather than a particularly wise man himself.[8] That is, in the course of his endless spending, he no doubt surrounded himself with advisors, both native and foreign-born sages who might help steer the ship of state. After all, such was simply expected of a great king. Just as today, government offices in Washington and Paris and London typically include legions of economic advisors, military attachés, foreign policy analysts, agronomists, environmentalists, sociologists, demographers, statisticians, and bean counters of all varieties, so too in ancient Egypt and Mesopotamia, a host of sages and counselors flocked to court to help guide the decisions of the king. So it was, according to some scholars, that Solomon first brought wisdom—in the persons of a group of sage advisors—to the former backwater of the Jerusalem hills. If so, scholars say, later tradition might naturally have come to associate him personally with the pursuit of wisdom. But as a political leader, Solomon did little to merit his "wise" label; on the contrary, he may have been one of the most foolish rulers of biblical times.

Two Prostitutes and a Baby

One specific incident attributed to Solomon does, however, bespeak a certain wisdom on the king's part. According to the biblical account, two prostitutes at one point approached Solomon in a legal dispute. (As king, he had the authority to rule in such cases.) The two were roommates, and they had each given birth to a son a few days apart. Then, one of the babies died in the middle of the night. Each woman claimed that the living baby was hers.

Solomon considered the two women carefully and then summarized the facts as they had presented them:

> "The one says, 'My son is the one that is alive, and your son is dead'; while the other says, 'Not so! Your son is dead, and my son is the living one.'" Then the king said "Fetch me a sword," so they brought the king a sword. The king said, "Divide the live baby in two and give half to the one, and half to the other." But the woman whose son was alive said to the king— because she was overcome with feelings for her son—"Please, my lord, let her have the live baby; don't kill him!" The other woman said, "Let it be neither mine nor yours; divide it." Then the king responded: "Give the first woman the live baby; do not kill it. She is his mother." When all Israel heard of the verdict that the king had rendered, they stood in awe of the king, because they saw that he had divine wisdom in carrying out justice.
>
> 1 Kings 3:23–28

Modern readers usually think this story is pretty silly—who could be stupid enough to believe the king would actually "divide" the baby in two, killing it in the process? What is not mentioned in the text, however, is the legal principle according to which disputed property for which there is no clear record of ownership—a field, for example, or an unoccupied house—would most likely be divided equally among the disputants.[9] No doubt Solomon uttered some legal mumbo-jumbo to that effect, enough at least to convince the two women under those stressful circumstances that he actually intended to apply that principle to this case. The other point worthy of mention is that Solomon does not actually pronounce on who is the baby's *real*, biological, mother. In ancient Israel, as in more modern times, people were not always sane and certainly did not always react logically under pressure. No doubt it would have taken considerably more investigation to determine with certainty who the true mother really was. But it did not matter. Solomon does not say, "She is the *true* mother," or the like, only, "She is the mother." Whatever the biological relationship, this woman is the only one of the two fit to be given the responsibility for the child henceforth.

Wisdom in the Ancient Near East

The word "wisdom" is generally used in the Bible in a somewhat different sense from the one it has in English. In English it is used for the most part to describe a quality of mind—good judgment, discernment, sagacity, and the like. It sometimes had this meaning in Hebrew too, but for the most part "wisdom" referred to *things known,* knowledge.[10] So, in the passage cited earlier, the assertion that Solomon was the wisest of men is immediately followed by the "proof" thereof: he knew a huge number of proverbs and could "speak of trees, from the cedar that is in the Lebanon to the hyssop that grows out of the wall; he could speak about animals, birds, reptiles, and fish" (1 Kings 4:33).

We tend to think of knowledge as an ever-growing body of information: each day, scientists discover new things about the universe and about ourselves. But to a denizen of the ancient world, knowledge was a fixed, utterly static set of facts, the unchanging rules that underlie all of reality as we know it. Those rules had been established since the world had been created; indeed, when the Bible asserts that God had created the world "with wisdom" (Prov. 3:19; Ps. 92:6–7; 104:24), what it means is that He had established it according to certain immutable patterns. Possessing *wisdom* thus meant knowing those rules, not only the rules that governed the natural world (Solomon's knowledge of trees and animals, birds, reptiles, and fish), but the rules that governed the way people, both the righteous and the wicked, behaved and the way God treated them in consequence. God had created these rules and immutable patterns, but He did not publicize them; on the contrary, they often lay hidden beneath the surface of things. It was the job of sages to try to discover them and to pass their findings on to later generations. Not everything, of course, could be known; some things were too well hidden. But with dogged perseverance and after centuries of observation, much of the underlying set of rules that govern reality had indeed been discovered. To possess wisdom was therefore to master all that had been discovered of life's underlying pattern.

This had been an ongoing, international effort.[11] By the time biblical Israel came along, wisdom had already been pursued for centuries and centuries in ancient Egypt and Mesopotamia; indeed, if the same above-cited passage says of Solomon's wisdom that it was greater than that of "all the peoples of the east and all the wisdom of Egypt," it is because these easterners and Egyptians were, at the time, the gold standard of wisdom, the patrons of individual sages and the wisdom academies wherein they taught. A good part of the ancient Near Eastern texts excavated in Egypt and Mesopotamia consists of the writings of such sages. But what form did they adopt to publish their findings?

Someone who makes a discovery in the "hard sciences" today usually writes it up in an article and prints it in a scientific journal or on the Internet. Other sorts of modern sages—social scientists or scholars of the humanities—tend to put their ideas into still longer treatises, hefty tomes that are published by university presses. But in the ancient Near East, if you discovered something about how the world works, you had to package your insight in a form in which it could travel. So it was that the standard form of ancient wisdom was a simple, two-part sentence—the same two-part sentence that was seen earlier to be the basic unit of biblical poetry:

$$\rule{2in}{0.4pt}, \rule{2in}{0.4pt}.$$
$$\quad\quad\quad\text{A}\quad\quad\quad\quad\quad\quad\quad\quad\quad\text{B}$$

This two-part wisdom sentence was called in Hebrew a *mashal* (usually translated as "proverb").[12] Part of the skill involved in being a sage was the ability to take a complex idea and stick it into the six or seven words that the *mashal* typically comprised. The sense might not be immediately apparent, but if not, so much the better! After all, learning wisdom meant knowing how to look deeply into the words of a *mashal*, examining it and turning it over and over until its full sense had revealed itself. Only then could a person be said to have mastered it. Thus, when it says of Solomon that he "spoke three thousand proverbs, and his songs numbered a thousand and five," what the Bible means was that he had mastered a huge number of *meshalim* (the plural of *mashal*) and thus possessed much of what humanity had been able to discover about the underlying rules that govern reality as we know it.

The Book of Proverbs

The first of the three books that Solomon is said to have written is the biblical book of Proverbs, and this name well describes its contents: thirty-one chapters of brief, two-part sentences that explain the underlying principles of the world. Many of these *meshalim* take the form of a comparison: Part A presents an image of some kind, and Part B presents the thing in life that the image explains. So, for example—to return to the theme of how a proverb has to be *mastered* before someone can truly be said to possess it—consider the following:

A thorn got stuck in a drunkard's hand, and a proverb in the mouth of a fool.
Prov. 26:9

It seems obvious that some sort of unfavorable comparison is being made here—but what exactly is the point? Modern drunkards may frequently be said to "feel no pain" or exhibit their bad temper or drive too fast (and indeed, many actually manage to do all three at the same time), but in ancient Israel drunkards were known mostly for their inability to keep their balance: they "stagger" and fall to the ground (Isa. 19:14; 24:20; Ps. 107:27; Job 12:25). So it is that in this *mashal* the drunkard in question has fallen to the ground and, groping about on all fours, has gotten a thorn or thistle stuck in his hand. This image sets up the comparison for Part B. In similar fashion—that is, quite by accident and through no personal virtue—a *mashal* may end up in the mouth of a fool, but the fact that he has acquired it, as it were, does not mean that he has actually learned its truth and internalized it. It just ended up with him by chance, with no more effort or conscious intention than that of the mindless drunkard. So just because you hear someone spouting words of ancient wisdom, this proverb asserts, don't think that the person in question really understands what he is saying, and certainly not that he has taken that wisdom to heart. (The comparison of the proverb to a thorn in this verse is particularly apt, since a *mashal* in ancient Israel was often imagined to be something sharp or pointed that could guide people on the proper path, in the same way that a goad or pointed stick was used to guide an animal.)*

Here is another proverb that requires some contemplation before its full sense is revealed:

> One who grabs a dog by the ears, a passerby who meddles in a dispute not his own.
>
> Prov. 26:17

Someone who grabs a dog by the ears is, in the biblical world of unfailingly nasty dogs, in trouble. He should have just let the dog go by. Now, as soon as he lets go, the dog will bite *him*; in fact, if he lets go of just one ear, the dog will surely try to wheel around and bite the hand that is still holding the other ear. So is it with the person who meddles in someone else's quarrel. At first he was in no danger, but as soon as he butted in, he became a party to the dispute. Now he cannot extricate himself, and he certainly cannot side with one of the disputants without the other turning to attack him. Beside this point, the proverbist probably intended us to understand that although such meddling begins with the disputants' ears—that is, the meddler seeks to be *heard* by them—in the end, he is going to get it from their mouths.

Of such proverbs is the book of Proverbs made. But did Solomon write them? The book actually refers to Solomon as the author in three different places (Prov. 1:1; 10:1; 25:1), but modern scholars believe these three verses are later, editorial additions. Like the book of Psalms, they say, Proverbs is

---

* Thus proverbs are like goads or nails in Eccles. 12:11; see also Deut. 28:37; 1 Kings 9:7.

actually a collection of smaller collections. The first of these, chapters 1–9, is a self-contained unit, which concludes with the assertion that personified Wisdom has now "built her house, she has hewn her seven pillars" (Prov. 9:1), perhaps corresponding to seven* basic subunits in the preceding text.[13] Other apparent subunits are 10:1–22:16; 22:17–24:34; chapters 25–29; chapters 30–31 (these last two chapters are actually openly attributed to sages other than Solomon). The fact that Proverbs is a collection of collections does not, of course, prove that Solomon did not write one or all of them. But the "all" option seems to scholars quite unlikely on linguistic and stylistic grounds; the mixture of different dialects and phases of Hebrew suggests different authors, most of them connected with periods and/or geographic areas other than Solomon's. What is more, at least one section of Proverbs seems to be a translation or paraphrase of an older Egyptian text.[14] Perhaps most telling of all is the anthological character of wisdom texts in general, including those of ancient Egypt or Mesopotamia.[15] To be a sage was to know, not to compose. In a sense, wisdom's true author was God or the gods; after all, the "ways of the world" that were wisdom's bailiwick had been divinely established at the beginning of time and then merely *discovered* by different human beings. The sage's job was thus to collect and transmit the received wisdom to those eager to study it; even if he wrote a book, it was for the most part a rewording of truths discovered long ago. And indeed, the apparent intention of the Bible's mention of Solomon *speaking* "three thousand proverbs" is not that he composed them (although this is how the verse is sometimes mistranslated) but that he had mastered them.

Orthodox Wisdom

The two proverbs cited above have to do with the way humans behave—how some spout proverbs without understanding them, and how many people tend to meddle needlessly in the affairs of others. These are indeed the sorts of insights that one might arrive at through ordinary observation—they do not seem to betray any particular ideology. In fact, on the basis of everything that has been said so far, one would probably conclude that the pursuit of wisdom consisted mostly of such observed truths.

But this is not so. The world of wisdom was highly ideological (and idealistic). One element of the wisdom ideology has already been glimpsed: all sages believed in the existence of an underlying body of rules that determined reality. In other words, things do not just happen in this world; they happen according

---

* Although the text is today divided into nine chapters, this division, like all chapter divisions, was made long after the text itself was written. Proponents of this analysis see seven blocks of text here.

to certain set, eternal patterns, and in a sense, even God is subject to their rules. That is not the view one usually finds in the Bible. Elsewhere God reacts, *decides* to do one thing or another as a consequence of this or that event; sometimes He grows angry at what happens or is pleased or even changes His mind. Such ideas are foreign to the world of wisdom. In that world, certain things are simply inevitable. Thus, justice must always prevail in the end: the righteous must always be rewarded and the wicked must always be punished:

> The house of the wicked will be destroyed, but the tent of the upright will flourish.
>
> Prov. 14:11

Along with this is the related notion that self-restraint and humility are destined to win out in the end. Thus, in the above proverb, it is no accident that the wicked live in a *house* while the upright live in a flimsy tent. But it doesn't matter: despite their wealth, the wicked will end up badly, while the humble dwelling of the upright will ultimately prevail.

Indeed, one of the most telling features of Israelite wisdom is its consistent division of humanity into two opposite categories, the wicked versus the righteous (or, above, the "upright").[16] Proverb after proverb contrasts the way these two groups behave, and the way in which they are rewarded or punished by God. But surely this is ideology talking. In the real world, there are very few people who could be described as altogether righteous or altogether wicked; most of us are somewhere in the middle. That middle ground is never mentioned in orthodox wisdom: deep inside the soul, we must make absolute choices, and these ultimately stamp us as allying ourselves with one camp or another. Indeed, it is striking that this "wicked versus righteous" contrast is sometimes presented in terms of another set of opposites, the foolish versus the wise. Neither of these latter terms is used to describe a person's mental capacities but rather the way of life that he or she chooses:

> The heart of the wise seeks out knowledge, the mouth of the fool seeks out foolishness.*
>
> Prov. 15:14

The *wise* person is someone who treads the path of wisdom, learning its simple lesson of following the strait and narrow and seeking to live life in accordance with it; the fool, by contrast, may actually be a diabolical genius,

---

* The contrast here is not simply between the wise and the foolish, but between "heart" and "mouth." In the world of wisdom literature, the search for true knowledge is always internal, deep inside a person, whereas the pursuit of foolishness (unrestrained excess) is always flashy and superficial.

but by having rejected wisdom's lessons from his own life, he has allied himself with anti-wisdom ("foolishness"), immoral excess, and all of human vice.

The Book of Ecclesiastes

This brings us to the second biblical book attributed to Solomon. If the book of Proverbs is chock full of "orthodox wisdom," the book of Ecclesiastes is in some ways its opposite.[17] The speaker of the book is obviously someone learned in the ways of wisdom, but he is too down-to-earth to buy into some of wisdom's lofty idealism:

> The sayings of Koheleth, son of David, king in Jerusalem:
> "So futile," says Koheleth, "everything is so futile!"
> What does a person ever net from all the effort he expends in this world?
> One generation goes out and another comes in, but the earth stays the
>   same forever.
> The sun rises and the sun sets; then rushing back to its place, it rises
>   again.
> The wind blows to the south and then turns to the north,
> it turns and turns as it goes—the wind—and goes back again by its
>   turning.
> All the rivers flow to the sea, but the sea is never full,
> [because] to the source of the rivers' flowing, there they flow back
>   again . . .
> There is no remembrance of former things, just as, with regard to the
>   later things that will be,
> they will have no remembrance either with those who will be after them.
>   Eccles. 1:1–11

Where orthodox wisdom sees virtues and vices, people getting ahead by dint of hard effort and modest self-restraint, the author of Ecclesiastes sees only futility—or, as his book's opening words are sometimes translated, "vanity of vanities."* Orthodox wisdom holds that the righteous are ultimately rewarded and the wicked are punished, but this writer asserts the contrary:

---

* The term *hebel* was translated into Latin as *vanitas* and from there to English as "vanity." But *hebel* does not mean "emptiness" (the meaning of *vanitas*) and certainly not vainglory or narcissism (that is, our "vanity"). In Ecclesiastes *hebel* (which elsewhere means "vapor" or "breath") actually has a wide range of meanings. Sometimes it designates something fleeting or elusive (like a breath), sometimes "futility," sometimes a thing of baffling unfairness or injustice.

I have seen everything in my fleeting days:
A righteous man may die despite his righteousness, while a wicked one
  lives on despite his wickedness.
So do not be too righteous or act too much the sage, lest you be
  destroyed.
(But do not be overly wicked or play the fool, lest you die before your
  time.)

Boorishness is exalted to great heights, while the worthy are set low.
I have watched slaves riding by on horseback, and princes walking on the
  ground like slaves.

Eccles. 7:15–17; 10:6–7

The book of Ecclesiastes might best be described as a lover's quarrel with orthodox wisdom. The author wishes things were indeed the way traditional sages claimed—he is truly a student of (and a lover of) ancient proverbs and their ideology. But somehow, he says, reality rarely seems to match wisdom's claims.

This is not to say, however, that the entire book is one long protest against the wisdom ideology (as is, for example, the book of Job).[18] Ecclesiastes accepts many of wisdom's lessons: wisdom is better than folly (2:13), self-restraint better than self-indulgence. Indeed, this author is capable of wording a *mashal* as cleverly as the best of ancient sages:

A name is better than scented oil, and the day of death better than the day
  of one's birth.

Eccles. 7:1

Part A is certainly undeniable. A person's *name*—here the author means not only a person's reputation, but the sum total of everything he or she does in life—is more precious than any material possession, even the $100–an-ounce anointing oil described above (chapter 26). But how can Part B be true? The day of a person's death is almost always an occasion for sadness, and birth an occasion for rejoicing; in what way is death "better"?

As with every *mashal*, Parts A and B are related. So here, the point throughout is indeed the person's name. When a baby is born, Ecclesiastes is saying, it has no name—quite literally—and even after it has been given one name or another, that name is essentially meaningless until the person has actually grown and begun to do things in life. Little by little, he or she becomes a person, first doing this, then that, until slowly that "name" begins to mean something, for good or for ill. Eventually, it is full of rich detail and nuance—as detailed and nuanced as the person's own life. And like any nonmaterial thing, it is impervious to change; no one can steal someone else's name, and it will not erode or wash away. Meanwhile, that same person's physical existence has started down the long path of decline that is the lot of all humans. In a physical sense, we are all like the precious anointing oil of Part A: what was very valuable at first begins to lose its savor, and sooner or later the whole vial will be used up or go bad and have to be disposed of. That day, the day of a person's death, is certainly a sad day, but it is no less a day of great significance, since it marks the completion of the process of building a name. One can now take a step backward and contemplate (as one could not before) the whole person. In the end, each of us becomes our name; this is all that survives the dissolution of our "precious oil," our physical selves. But, says Ecclesiastes, since you agree with Part A—a name is indeed better than precious oil—then you must also agree with Part B.

Did Solomon write any of this? Here too modern critics are skeptical. To begin with, the book contains two words that were not originally Hebrew but Persian: *pardes* (an enclosed orchard or garden, Eccles. 2:5) and *pitgam* (a royal decree, Eccles. 8:11). Loan words enter a language when two different civilizations have some ongoing, sustained contact. It was only after the British colonized India in the nineteenth century that Indian words like *pundit, shampoo, jungle,* and *juggernaut* entered the English language. A period of sustained contact between Persia and ancient Israel did not occur until long after Solomon's time: in the late sixth century BCE, four hundred years after his death, Persia began to rule over Israel's remnant, the inhabitants of Judah, and it continued to rule over them for the next three centuries. That is the period when these and other Persian words first entered the language. One could of course say that Solomon, being the wisest of kings, had studied Persian on his own. But why would he use a word that no one else in his kingdom would understand for the next four hundred years? If King Henry VIII had suddenly started talking about pundits and shampoos, who in six-teenth-century England would have known what he was saying? Quite apart from these loan words, however, the whole dialect in which Ecclesiastes is written is markedly different from the classical Hebrew of earlier times—no serious student of Hebrew could confuse the two.[19]

In fact, the author of Ecclesiastes does tell us his name (or nickname): Koheleth (more properly transcribed as Qohelet). It probably comes from a late meaning of the root *qhl,* "argue" or "reprove."[20] He is thus the Arguer. His full name—Koheleth son of David—probably indicates that he was a descendant (though not literally the *son*) of David, a fact of which he was no doubt justly proud. That may also have something to do with the office that he says he occupied: he describes himself as "king" over Israel in Jerusalem (1:1, 12). Perhaps this is in fact how he presented himself (or was known) to his own people, but we would more likely describe him as a governor, since any Judean ruler at the time would have been altogether subject to the Persian authorities.

Long after the book was written, this mention of "Koheleth son of David" (like the phrase "to David" in the Psalms headings) took on a different look. If the author of the book described himself as the *son* of David who ruled over Israel in Jerusalem, well, that could only mean that he was literally David's son and successor, King Solomon. Perhaps indeed, people theorized, Solomon had decided for one reason or other to refer to himself in this book by the name Koheleth.[21] This attribution to Solomon ultimately proved highly significant. Certainly, from the standpoint of the ideas it contains, Ecclesiastes borders on the heretical. How was a religious Jew or Christian to understand bits of advice like "Do not be too righteous"? Moreover, ancient readers were troubled by the frequent contradictions and about-faces in the book.[22] But if Ecclesiastes was indeed written by Solomon, the man to whom God granted greater wisdom than any other mortal, then surely every word of it was precious; its place in the canon was secure.

The Song of Songs

The third book attributed to Solomon's authorship, the Song of Songs (also called the Song of Solomon or Canticles), seems even less likely to have been written by him. At times its Hebrew seems as late as that of Ecclesiastes, with Persian and perhaps even Greek borrowings (although it has also been suggested that different parts of the work date to different periods). Solomon may be named as the author in the editorial title, but the mythic king also appears twice in the body of the Song (3:9, 11; 8:12) as a third-person character, neither time presented in a particularly sympathetic light.

Moreover, the Song does not, at first glance, have anything to do with the world of wisdom. It seems to be all about love—and not love in the ethereal abstract, but love between a certain young man and a specific young woman, who are desperately, messily, deliriously, taken with each other. That is all the Song talks about. "Let him give me some of his kisses to drink,"[23] the woman begins dreamily, "since love is sweeter than wine!" (Song 1:2). Speaking in a decidedly northern dialect (whether real or imitation),[24] these two main figures stand in stark contrast to the sophisticated "Jerusalem girls" who appear here and there in the Song. *Those* young women—pale city dwellers from the distant south—are the polar opposite of the beautiful, tanned mountain girl of the Song. So it is probably no accident that, in one of their appearances, the Jerusalem girls are dazzled by the arrival of King Solomon in all his royal pomp (Song 3:11). How wrong it is for people to care about such things, the Song seems to say (cf. 8:7, 11–12); money and fancy possessions are meaningless. Love is the only thing in life that matters.

> You are so beautiful, my love, your eyes like doves behind a veil—
> and the way your hair hangs down, like herds come down from Gilead,

with your teeth as white as ewes freshly washed in a brook . . .
Your lips are like a crimson thread, and your mouth is so sweet,
your face like ripened fruit behind your veil,
your neck like David's tower, fashioned to perfection,
with a thousand shields hung around it, the bucklers soldiers carry.
Your two breasts are like two fawns, twins grazing in the lilies.
Before the day drifts off and the shadows flee,
I'll find my way to Spice Mountain, the fragrant hill.
Everything about you is beautiful, there's not one thing that's not.

Modern scholars see the Song as part of the great ancient Near Eastern tradition of love poetry, with its conventional descriptions of the lovers' physical beauty and its frank exaltation of eroticism. Indeed, if we read through its light veil of metaphor, the Song is sometimes shockingly graphic in its description of the couple's embraces. Perhaps, like certain similar ancient Mesopotamian or Egyptian poems, this one was created to be sung at wedding celebrations (although the Song contains not a word about the couple's recent or upcoming marriage), containing equal measures of encouragement and instruction. Its refrain is "Give me your word, Jerusalem girls, and don't start up, don't get started with love until it's time" (2:7; 3:5; 8:4). The Song certainly came to be associated with weddings in later days;[25] however, the original purpose of its composition remains the subject of debate.[26]

What is this Song doing in the Bible? From early times, apparently, it came to be read as an allegory of the love between God and His people.[27] After all, its lush language *was* often highly metaphorical; why not read the metaphors a little differently, as if they referred to the yearnings, the consummations and frustrations, of the love that joins human beings with the divine? Frustration plays no small part in the Song: "I called to him, but he did not answer" is a frequent theme (Song 5:6; cf. 1:7; 3:1; 6:1). Is this so different from the Psalmist's frustration: "I've called out with all my heart—answer me, O LORD" (Ps. 119:145)? And if the Song raises love itself to the very summit of human existence—

Keep me as a locket on your heart, a signet on your arm.
For love is as strong as death, and as harsh as Sheol.
Its flames burn like a fire, a holy conflagration.
Deep waters can't put it out, and rivers will not drown it.
If a man gave all his family's wealth for love, would anybody blame him?
                                                    Song 8:6–7

—then perhaps it really is just one long metaphor, its real subject the love between man and God.

• • •

Once, a bearded sage heard an old American song:

> *She'll be comin' round the mountain when she comes.*
> *She'll be comin' round the mountain when she comes.*
> *She'll be comin' round the mountain, she'll be comin' round the mountain,*
> *She'll be comin' round the mountain when she comes.*

> *She'll be drivin' six white horses when she comes.*
> *She'll be drivin' six white horses when she comes.*
> *She'll be drivin' six white horses, she'll be drivin' six white horses,*
> *She'll be drivin' six white horses when she comes.*

> *Oh, we'll all come out to meet her when she comes . . .*

> *We will kill the old red rooster when she comes . . .*

> *Oh, we'll all have chicken and dumplings when she comes . . .*

> *We'll all be shoutin' Hallelujah when she comes . . .*

"Do you think," he asked, "that this song is talking about a real woman? Why should one person need six white horses? No, it is talking about the messianic age, when God's earthly presence—always referred to as she[28]—will once again reappear, rounding the corner of Mount Zion. The six white horses are a token of the Messiah's colt, mentioned by the prophet [Zech. 9:9], and if the song speaks of six it is because all this will come to pass in sixty years. Then everyone will be gathered from the earth's four corners to welcome the event. As for the old red rooster, this is the rooster Ziz [Ps. 50:11], companion of Leviathan, symbol of evil; both will be killed in the end of days to make the messianic meal—these are the chicken and dumplings—as tradition long ago foretold.[29] Then Hallelujah will ring from every quarter."

That is what he said, and soon everyone was singing the old song—but now, its meaning was completely different. The words had not changed in the slightest, but what they meant had been transformed utterly. Henceforth no one could think of the old song the same way.

• • •

In one way, the Song of Songs is the most important biblical book to be dealt with in the present volume, since it poses most squarely the question of original meaning. If biblical texts mean only what they meant when they were first composed, then why should we still include the Song of Songs in the Bible? According to modern scholars, its words originally had nothing to do with God; they are no different from the love lyrics of ancient Egypt. True, people were misled for a while. Rabbi Akiba of the second century CE declared that "the whole world altogether is not as worthy as the day on which the Song of Songs was given to Israel,"[30] and Christian interpretations—from the homilies and commentary written on the Song by the early exegete Origen (ca. 185–254 CE) to the eighty-six (!) sermons on it by Bernard of Clairvaux (1090–1153) and beyond—show the extent to which their authors exhausted themselves in attributing to it all sorts of hidden meanings. But now that we know what the Song is really talking about, we ought to have no further use for it; indeed, we ought to protect the delicate minds of children from exposure to its sometimes too easily deciphered metaphors.

Unless . . . Unless a text's original meaning is not necessarily its meaning for ever and ever. This is a disturbing idea, of course; the whole point of writing something down is to put it into fixed form that will last—presumably unchanged. But sometimes things happen that do change the meaning of a text, or of any artifact. A photograph of the World Trade Center in New York came to mean something very different after September 11, 2001. The photographer who took it probably thought little about what he was doing at the time. For him it was a big building; that is why, shooting it from a certain angle, he sought to emphasize its great height and the sweep of its lines. But who can look at his photograph today and see what he saw, just another New York skyscraper? For most people nowadays, the photograph instantly stirs up memories. Peering into the picture's details, some people must now, willynilly, see a deeper meaning—in fact, more than one. To some, the picture may embody the frailty of orderly civilization in the face of terrorism; to others, it has became a symbol of an earlier era, a time of self-confidence and peaceful ease; to still others, it now stands for America's intolerable arrogance, justly struck down by God's holy martyrs. But whatever the photograph now means, that meaning is quite different from the one originally intended by the photographer. All he thought he was doing was taking a picture of a tall building (which he was).

Someone like the bearded sage a few paragraphs ago heard in the Song of Songs a message that had probably not been intended by its original author. In a sense, one might think of him as the Song's *second author*. He did not change a word, but he utterly transformed what the Song meant. "Listen to it my way," he said, "and it's not about a man and a woman at all." He probably never claimed that this was what the Song had been composed to mean, only that one *could* understand it that way; and people agreed. Soon they were singing it and winking to each other—"Get it?" This was how the Song of Songs became part of Holy Scripture. Then, after a while, the winking stopped: the religious meaning became the only meaning.

In a sense, what happened with the Song of Songs is what happened with all of Scripture. Psalms that had been meant to be recited in the temple as an accompaniment to sacrifices came to be recited at home or in synagogue or church. In the process, the Psalmist's "I bow down before You" changed its meaning. It no longer denoted a cultic act, "I bow down before the Holy of Holies where You, O God, are said to be enthroned," but was now a non-cultic turning to the omnipresent deity, "I acknowledge You to be everywhere." At roughly the same time, the story of Abraham also changed. "Read it my way," a clever exegete must have said, "and it will be seen to recount the life of a sorely tried model of virtue, the world's first monotheist. That is what I interpret Josh. 24:3 to mean, and this will explain its otherwise troubling non sequitur, 'So I took Abraham . . .' " In this same period, a story about the transition from a hunter-gatherer society to an agricultural one also came to be interpreted differently; it now might be understood to contain a hidden message, an explanation for human mortality and sinfulness, indeed, the "Fall of Man." Soon it was found that Jacob did not actually lie to his father; you just had to put in the right punctuation. Not long after, David's Shunammite bed warmer became a symbol of wisdom and Rahab stood for the church of reformed sinners. Some of these changes may have been accompanied by a little wink, but soon the winks disappeared.

Without these changes, would there ever have been a Bible? That seems most unlikely. Why should anyone seeking to worship God devote himself or herself to reading the etiological narratives and political self-puffery of a civilization long dead, the guerrilla tactics and court shenanigans of various ancient kings, law codes endorsing *ḥerem* and the stoning of a rebellious child, or statutes forbidding Molech worship and similarly outdated concerns, psalms specifically designed to accompany the sacrificing of animals at a cultic site, or erotic love poetry? All of these texts underwent a radical change in meaning when they began to be interpreted in the somewhat quirky, highly creative, and altogether God-centered approach of ancient scholars in the late biblical period. The original meaning of these texts disappeared. In a sense, ancient interpreters *rewrote* every one of them, even though they did not change a word.

The question that poses itself to today's readers is: can we still read the Bible with the approach and assumptions that these ancient interpreters brought to it, even though modern biblical scholarship has now convinced many people that this way of reading is quite out of keeping with the original meaning of the text? Or (to refine the question a bit), if you and I now know a little too much to espouse that old way of reading naïvely and unquestioningly, can we somehow nevertheless manage to espouse it as what *the Bible* (as distinguished from its original, constituent parts) means? Indeed, can we hold both old and new together in our heads, perhaps recalling a hypothetical "Read it my way . . ." and a wink?

29

North and South

1 KINGS 5–12; 17–19; 21 AND 2 KINGS 2–4

AND PSALM 29

Elijah Going Up into Heaven
by Philip James de Loutherbourg.

SOLOMON'S TEMPLE. THE GREAT SCHISM AND THE GOLDEN CALVES.
ELIJAH AT MOUNT CARMEL. GOD VERSUS BAAL. PSALM 29.
ELIJAH THE ETERNAL. THE MESHA STONE.

*Solomon built the great Jerusalem temple, but his empire collapsed shortly
after his son took the throne. Now there were two kingdoms, Israel in the
north and Judah in the south.*

One of Solomon's great achievements was the building of a magnificent temple in Jerusalem to house, as it were, God's presence on earth. Once he had
resolved to do so, he set out to purchase the finest materials. He sent a message to his father's old ally Hiram of Tyre, asking for the wood from the
cedars from Lebanon to fashion the future temple's furnishings (1 Kings
5:3–6). Hiram agreed. As for where in Jerusalem the temple was to stand,
Solomon chose what might seem an unlikely locale, a threshing floor that had
belonged to a Jebusite man, Arauna (it is to be recalled that Jerusalem was,
until the time of David, a Jebusite city). The site had actually been bought
from Arauna by Solomon's father, David, who had used it to build an altar to
God in time of distress (2 Sam. 24:15–25). Having fixed on this site, Solomon
took the costly materials he had assembled and ordered the building of the
temple to begin.

Construction took seven years to complete. The Jerusalem temple was similar to, but far bigger than, the traveling tent sanctuary that had served
Israel since the time of its desert wanderings. The building consisted of three
sections of increasing holiness: the innermost part, called the Holy of Holies
(the equivalent of the superlative in Hebrew, hence, "holiest place"), was
designed to house the Ark of the Covenant, above which God was said to be
enthroned. When at last the construction had been completed,

> the priests brought the ark of the covenant of the LORD to its place, in the
> inner sanctuary of the temple—the Holy of Holies—underneath the wings
> of the cherubim . . . There was nothing in the ark except the two tablets of
> stone that Moses had placed there at Horeb, where the LORD made a
> covenant with the Israelites, when they came out of the land of Egypt. And
> when the priests came out of the holy place, a cloud filled the house of the
> LORD, so that the priests could not stand and serve there because of the
> cloud; for the glory of the LORD filled the house of the LORD. Then Solomon
> said, "The LORD had said that He would dwell in a thick cloud. But now I
> have built You a lofty house, a place where You may dwell forever."
>
> 1 Kings 8:6–13

The Jerusalem temple was to remain the focus of Israel's worship for a thousand years. This is, when one considers it, an extraordinary fact. Seemingly endless generations of hereditary priests (*kohanim*) and Levites served there; kings, prophets, and ordinary people trooped to its precincts for century after century to demonstrate their fealty to God. There was one interruption. Destroyed by the Babylonians in 586 BCE, Jerusalem's rugged old sanctuary lay in ruins as its people went into exile; it was rebuilt, however, almost exactly seventy years later by the Jews who returned to their land after the Babylonian Empire fell. This rebuilt structure then survived for many centuries more, until it too was destroyed by a foreign army, that of the Romans, in 70 CE. Ever since, and even today, Jews have prayed at the foot of the Temple Mount, hoping for the time when the great Jerusalem sanctuary will once again rise on or near its original spot.

Although the Temple Mount on which it was built has not been excavated by archaeologists (principally because of Muslim objections to any digging on the site, since it currently houses the al-Aqsa mosque and the Dome of the Rock), scholars have little doubt about the accuracy of the temple's overall plan as outlined in 1 Kings 6. Actually, it is rather like a number of ancient temples that *have* been excavated elsewhere in the ancient Near East, particularly the temple at 'Ein Dara' in Syria.[1] But this very resemblance once again raises the question—disturbing for traditional Jews and Christians—of just how different Israel's religion was from that of its neighbors. Certainly the layout of the Jerusalem temple and the nature (and even the names) of the types of sacrifices offered there have parallels elsewhere in greater Canaan and beyond; so do the priestly officials, the laws of temple purity, temple hymns and prayers, and other details from the Bible.

Indeed, some scholars have suggested that the Bible's account of *where* the temple was built conceals another such connection. Saying the site had been a threshing floor before David bought it sounds rather odd. True, a threshing floor was a public space[2] that would certainly be large enough to house a temple. But as everyone in biblical times knew, a threshing floor had little to suggest its aptness for such a use; it was generally considered a public nuisance, since the chaff scattered by the process of threshing grain would blow all over.[3] Asserting that *that* is what the site had been used for before David bought it may thus have been intended to scotch any rumor that it had ever served as a sacred spot before (cf. Jacob's "chancing" upon Bethel, Gen. 28:11). The truth, some scholars suspect, may have been quite the opposite: Solomon's temple was built quite intentionally on a site that had always been considered sacred, one that had been used by the Jebusites for worshiping their gods before David conquered their city.[4]

David's Kingdom Falls Apart

If Solomon's building projects and other grandiose schemes sorely taxed the public treasury, his son Rehoboam was apparently not clever enough to try to make things better. In the manner of many rulers new to the throne, he mistakenly thought the best answer to any sign of discontent among his subjects was to act tough. Thus, when Jeroboam, leader of the northern tribes, came to Rehoboam with a complaint, the young king chose the wrong course of action:

> Jeroboam and all the assembly of Israel came and said to Rehoboam, "Your father made our yoke hard. Lighten this hard labor of your father's and the heavy yoke that he set on us; then we will serve you." He said to them, "Go away for three days and come back to me." So the people went away.
>
> King Rehoboam then sought the advice of the elders who had personally served his father, Solomon, while he was still alive, saying, "What is your advice for me to answer these people?" They answered him, "If, for now, you give in to these people and bow to their will, responding positively to their request and exempting them [from the duty of forced labor] when you speak with them,[5] then they will bow to your will ever afterwards." But he disregarded the advice that the elders gave him, and sought instead the advice of the young men who had grown up with him and were now his personal attendants. He asked them, "What do you advise that we answer the people who are saying to me, 'Lighten the yoke that your father set on us'?" The young men who had grown up with him said to him, "This is what you should say to the people who said to you, 'Your father made our yoke heavy, but you must lighten it for us'; you should say to them, 'My little finger is thicker than my father's loins. My father put a heavy yoke on you? I will make your yoke even heavier. My father punished you with whips? I will punish you with scorpions.' "
>
> Jeroboam and all the people came to Rehoboam on the third day, since the king had said, "Come back to me on the third day." The king answered the people harshly, disregarding the advice that the elders had given him, and answered them instead with the words that the young men had advised: "My father put a heavy yoke on you? I will make your yoke even heavier. My father punished you with whips? I will punish you with scorpions." . . .
>
> When all of Israel realized that the king would not listen to them, the people said to the king, "What share do we have in David? We have no

inheritance in the son of Jesse. To your tents,* O Israel! Look now to your own house, O David."

So Israel went away to their tents.

1 Kings 12:3–16

Thus, it would appear, the great empire put together by Rehoboam's grandfather David split in two because of one faulty bit of advice. The bigger, northern part became the Kingdom of Israel, ruled by Jeroboam, while the southern part became the Kingdom of Judah.

As we have seen, however, modern scholars are somewhat skeptical about just how united the United Monarchy was, even at the very height of its success. If David had, as many scholars suppose, taken over rule of the northern tribes by force, their cooperation with him and his son Solomon could have been only an iffy thing at best. So long as it served their interest to remain in league with the south, they did so. Once it became clear that the high taxes and other costs would continue without any noticeable improvement in their lot, their course became clear. "You can do what you want with your kingdom," they said to Rehoboam; "we're going to rule ourselves." Still, however rickety their union may have been to begin with, the open split between Israel and Judah weakened both and ultimately left them exposed to the depredations of outsiders.[56]

The Sin of Jeroboam

The Bible sometimes refers to the "sin of Jeroboam" (1 Kings 13:34; 14:16; and frequently thereafter), but, interestingly, this phrase does not refer to the northerners' secession that he led. Instead, it refers to one of his first acts as king. Surveying his new kingdom,

> Jeroboam said to himself, "This kingdom might still go back to the house of David [that is, rejoin Rehoboam's southern kingdom]. For, if people keep

---

* That is, "O northern tribes [= Israel], return home [to rule yourselves]"—withdraw from your union with the south.

§ Indeed, the Kingdom of Judah was almost immediately attacked. 1 Kings 14:25–27 reports on an invasion by the Egyptian king Shishak (Shoshenq): "In the fifth year of King Rehoboam, King Shishak of Egypt came up against Jerusalem. He took away the treasury of the LORD's temple and the treasury of the king's palace; [in fact,] he took everything. He even took away all the golden shields that Solomon had amassed, so King Rehoboam had shields of bronze made in place of them." This report is actually paralleled by that of an ancient Egyptian account of the same events discovered in a temple at Karnak (Thebes). Cf. 2 Chr. 12:2–10.

going up to offer sacrifices in the house of the LORD at Jerusalem, the people's hearts may turn again to their [former] master, King Rehoboam of Judah; then they will kill me and return to King Rehoboam of Judah." So, after consultations, the king made two golden calves. He said to them [the people], "You have gone up to Jerusalem long enough. These are your gods, O Israel, who brought you up out of the land of Egypt." He set up one of them in Bethel, and the other he put in Dan. And this thing became a sin, for the people went to worship before the one at Bethel and before the other as far as Dan.

1 Kings 12: 26–30

The great "sin of Jeroboam," according to the Bible, was his commissioning these two golden calves as cultic objects for the temples at Dan and Bethel. Surely, bowing down to a golden calf is just what got Israel into trouble at Mount Sinai (Exodus 32)—and yet here they were, doing it again! So the prophet Hosea intoned against the "calf of Samaria" (Hos. 8:5–6) as a cause of God's anger against the northerners: "For it is from Israel, an artisan made it; it is not God" (8:6). And indeed, the sins of Jeroboam were, according to the Deuteronomistic History, what ultimately led God to have Assyria conquer the Kingdom of Israel and send its people into exile forever (2 Kings 17:21–23).

Once again, however, modern scholars see a somewhat different reality underlying the Bible's words. To begin with, there could have been no problem with the northern kingdom boycotting the Jerusalem temple in favor of temples at Dan and Bethel; according to scholars since de Wette, the idea of having one single, central temple in Jerusalem to serve the whole country did not exist until the time of Josiah, more than two centuries after Jeroboam. Before that, all Israelites worshiped at a host of local temples and "high places," and no one saw anything wrong with this practice. Indeed, both Dan (Judges 18) and Bethel (Genesis 28; Judg. 20:26–28) appear to have been centers of worship with their own temples long before Jeroboam came along.

As for the golden calves, many scholars have argued that there was nothing more idolatrous about them than the cherubim that Solomon is said to have installed on either side of the Ark of the Covenant (1 Kings 6:23–28). (Indeed, God Himself is said to have instructed Moses to make such cherubim for the desert tabernacle, Exod. 25:17–20.) These great, winged, mythic creatures dominated the Holy of Holies: God was said to be enthroned on their outstretched wings above the ark, from which spot He would be in contact with Israel (Exod. 25:22; Psalm 80:1; etc.). Thus, scholars say, all that Jeroboam did was substitute one type of iconographic throne for another, the golden calves for the cherubim. In so doing, Jeroboam probably was not even inventing some entirely new iconography; both types of divine thrones had probably been in existence at different sites in the country prior to the secession of the northern tribes.[7]

As we have also seen, scholars are skeptical about the account of Aaron's sin in making the Golden Calf (Exodus 32); the words he is reported to have said, "These are your gods, O Israel, who brought you up out of the land of Egypt," turn out to be the very words spoken by Jeroboam in the passage just cited. The whole narrative of Exodus 32 is thus, these scholars say, a polemic designed to retroject the sin of Jeroboam back to the time of Aaron. What really happened, they say, is this: first came the secession and Jeroboam's endorsement of the golden bull iconography, a perfectly normal sort of divine throne; then came the Deuteronomistic historian's misrepresentation of this throne iconography as an actual object of worship ("These are your gods, O Israel"); last of all, these same words and deeds came to be attributed to Aaron in Exodus 32.

Whether these scholarly hypotheses are right or not, it is interesting to observe how the northern secession and the "sin of Jeroboam" have been used since the Reformation in Protestant-Catholic polemics. One of the Reformers' early claims was that the Catholic Church was guilty of falling back "from the living God to dumme and dead idoles"[8]—that is to say, bowing down to statues of Mary, Jesus, and other figures. This was, they said, a violation of the second of the Ten Commandments and a return to the golden calf and the sin of Jeroboam. Roman Catholics countered that the real Jeroboam was Martin Luther—that the Protestant withdrawal from the church was a secession every bit as grave as the northern Israelites' and that the results would be equally disastrous. Catholics cited with approval the words of Irenaeus, "Those who rend the unity of the Church receive the Divine chastisement awarded to Jeroboam; they must all be avoided" (*Against the Heresies* iv, 26). "Not at all," retorted the Protestants: "the 'sin of Jeroboam' was not secession but bowing down to statues—and that's one of the reasons why we left the church in the first place."

Nowadays, such polemics have largely ceased. Yet one might not be wrong to hear, in today's scholarly insistence that Jeroboam's secession was only natural and that even his golden calves were not *really* idolatrous, the faint echo of the early Protestant apologetic. If so, this may serve somewhat obliquely as another example of the persistence of the Four Assumptions among even the most hardheaded modern researchers—specifically Assumption 2, the belief that Scripture's account of the ancient past contains a lesson for today.

Elijah the Prophet

After recounting the split that separated the kingdoms of Judah and Israel, the Bible's focus does not (as one might have expected) turn exclusively to events in the south. The books of 1 and 2 Kings recount subsequent events in the north, starting with the power struggles that followed Jeroboam's death (1 Kings 14:20; 15:16–16:14) and continuing with the rise of Omri to the throne of Israel and the succession of Omri's son Ahab. This was a particularly significant moment—not because of Ahab but because of the man who caused him so much trouble, Elijah the Tishbite.[9]

Elijah was a prophet and a miracle worker, feeding the hungry and bringing a dead child back to life (1 Kings 17). One would think that such a man would be universally revered, and yet King Ahab saw him as an enemy of the state, since Elijah led a campaign against the (royally sanctioned) "prophets of Baal," who urged the people to worship this deity alongside of, or instead of, the LORD. No wonder, then, that Ahab did not extend a friendly greeting to Elijah when he ran into him:

> When Ahab saw Elijah, Ahab said to him, "Is it you, you troublemaker of Israel?" He answered, "I am not the one who has troubled Israel—it is you, you and your father's house, because you have forsaken the commandments of the LORD and followed the Baals."
>
> 1 Kings 18:17–18

Baal is written in the plural here (*ha-beʿalim*, "the Baals"), probably in reference to different local cults of the great Canaanite storm god.* As far as Ahab was concerned—and, if numerous archaeologists and biblical scholars are right, a great many ordinary Israelites as well—there was nothing wrong with worshiping Baal. Some scholars have even suggested that Baal and the God YHWH were worshiped together, in tandem or syncretistically, as the northern kingdom's divine patron(s).[10] But Elijah would have none of that. As he later says of himself, he is "exceedingly zealous" (some translations read "jealous") on the LORD's behalf (1 Kings 19:14)—in other words, he will not tolerate anyone worshiping Baal alongside of the LORD. He therefore issues a challenge to Ahab:

> "Summon all of Israel to join me at Mount Carmel, along with the four hundred fifty prophets of Baal and the four hundred prophets of [the goddess] Asherah, who eat at [Queen] Jezebel's table." So Ahab sent word to all the Israelites and assembled the prophets at Mount Carmel. Elijah then approached all the people and said, "How long will you keep hopping [like birds] from one bough to the other? If the LORD is God, then follow Him. But if it is Baal, then follow him." The people did not answer him a word. Then Elijah said to the people, "I am the only prophet of the LORD left;[§] but

---

* On Baal and the Canaanite pantheon, see above, chapter 24.

§ Most of the others had been killed by Jezebel, though Elijah may be exaggerating a little; see 1 Kings 18:4.

Baal's prophets number four hundred fifty. Let two bulls be brought to us and let them choose one bull for themselves and cut it into pieces and lay it on the wood—but do not let it be set on fire. Meanwhile, I will prepare the other bull and lay it on the wood without setting it on fire. Then you call on the name of your god and I will call on the name of the LORD, and the god who answers by fire is indeed God." All the people cried out, "Very good!"

1 Kings 18:19–24

Elijah had challenged the prophets of Baal on, as it were, their own home court. After all, as the storm god, Baal was in charge of lightning—indeed, a lightning bolt was one of his iconographic weapons.[11] Who better than Baal could send fire down from heaven to set his prophets' bull ablaze?

So they [the prophets of Baal] took the bull that was given to them and prepared it and called on the name of Baal from morning until noon, shouting, "O Baal, answer us!" But there was not a sound, and no one answered. They kept hopping around the altar that they had made. When it got to be noon, Elijah made fun of them, saying, "Yell louder! He may be a god, but still . . . Perhaps he's in conference, or maybe he has gone off to relieve himself somewhere—or else he might be on a trip, or fast asleep. Maybe he needs to be woken up." They kept calling out loud and, as was their custom, they cut themselves with swords and lances until the blood gushed out over them. Even after noon had passed, they kept gyrating like [ecstatic] prophets until it was time for the [afternoon] meal offering, but still there was not a sound; no one answered or heeded [them].

Elijah said to all the people, "Come forward," and all the people came forward. Then he fixed the altar of the LORD that had been damaged: Elijah took twelve stones—corresponding to the number of the tribes of the sons of Jacob, to whom the word of the LORD had come, saying, "Israel shall be your name"—and with the stones he built an altar in the name of the LORD. Then he made a trench around the altar, large enough to contain two measures of seed. He arranged the wood [on the altar] and cut the bull into pieces and laid it on top of the wood. Then he said, "Fill four jars with water and pour them out onto the burnt offering and onto the wood." Then he said, "Do it again," and they did it a second time. "Do it again," he said, and they did it a third time, so that the water ran all around the altar and also filled the trench with water.

When it was time for the meal offering, the prophet Elijah came forward and said, "O LORD, God of Abraham, Isaac, and Israel, let it be known this day that You are God in Israel, that I am Your servant, and that I have done all these things at Your bidding. Answer me, O LORD, answer me, so that this people may know that You, O LORD, are God, and that You have turned their hearts back." Then the fire of the LORD came down and consumed the burnt offering, the wood, the stones, and the dust, and even licked up the water that was in the trench. When all the people saw it, they fell on their faces and said, "The LORD is God; the LORD is God."

1 Kings 18:25–39

The people's answer was no doubt clear at the time, but nowadays it seems somewhat ambiguous. Some scholars think it should be rendered "The LORD is *the* God"—that is, the only deity that counts, or our only deity henceforth; [12] it might even be rendered (remembering that the word 'elohim is formally a plural) "The LORD is the gods," that is, He covers all the functions normally fulfilled by El, Baal, Astarte, and the other gods of Canaan. [13]

However understood, this narrative presents scholars with an important snapshot in the development of Israel's religion. Presumably, ancient Israelites had continued for some time to worship many gods, whether or not that practice was officially sanctioned. To be sure, worshiping the God uniquely connected to the people of Israel must have enjoyed some prestige in both north and south. After all, He was uniquely "ours," while the other gods were also worshiped by non-Israelites; as time went on, such gods must increasingly have been seen as "theirs." Still, did that require worshiping the LORD to the exclusion of all other gods? If scholars are right, Israel's God, at least at the beginning, had no association with fertility or the life-giving rains; He seems (as we have seen) to have been connected more to the waging of war. So, in time of drought, when rain might mean the difference between life and death, what sense did it make to worship the LORD alone? Who would forbear to heap Baal's altar high with offerings in the hope of steering some storm clouds toward the parched fields? Yet this is precisely Elijah's message: either Baal or the LORD, but not both. Indeed, the name Elijah means in Hebrew "My God is the LORD."

And so, in this important confrontation at Mount Carmel, Israel is portrayed as ultimately taking its stand for the exclusive devotion to its one God (monolatry). In order for such a position to make any sense at all, one must be convinced that that one God will be able to help out in a drought just as effectively as Baal—hence the significance of Elijah bringing down the fire from heaven. The real import of "The LORD is God; the LORD is God" is that worshiping any other god is unnecessary: the LORD can bring the rain and ripen the grain and protect His people in every other way. Soon, He will be the only God in town.

Psalm 29

Scholars see a similar mentality underlying one of the Bible's most famous psalms:

Give the LORD, O sons of the mighty, give the LORD glory and strength.

Give the LORD His own name's glory, bow down to the LORD in holy splendor.

Listen![14] The LORD is over the waters; the glorious God is thundering, the LORD is over the deep.

Listen! The LORD is in strength! Listen! The LORD is in splendor!

Listen! The LORD is shattering cedars, the LORD shatters the cedars of Lebanon.

He makes Lebanon skip like a calf, Sirion like a young wild ox.

Listen! The LORD shoots forth sparks. Listen! The LORD makes the wilderness shake, the LORD shakes the wilderness of Kadesh.

Listen! The LORD makes the oak trees quiver as He strips the forest bare; and in His temple all say, "Glory!"

The LORD is enthroned above the flood, and the LORD will continue, forever king.

May the LORD give strength to His people, may the LORD bless His people with peace.

Psalm 29

The psalm seems to describe God's arrival amidst a storm coming in off the sea. First He is "over the waters," "thundering . . . over the deep"; then the storm hits land, "shattering the cedars" and making the whole earth tremble. Certainly this is a fearsome spectacle; "sparks" (lightning) shoot forth from the clouds as He arrives, and the storm's ferocious winds strip the forest bare. But with His arrival comes the precious rain of which Canaan never seems to have enough.

After scholars came to know the literature of biblical Israel's northern neighbor Ugarit, this psalm took on a new look. To put it bluntly, Psalm 29 seemed to many like a cheap knockoff of an originally northern Canaanite hymn, in which the name of Baal had simply been scratched out and replaced with the name of Israel's national deity.[15] Thus, the psalm opens with a summons to the "sons of the mighty" (*benei 'elim*) to praise the LORD. But to scholars, the phrase *benei 'elim* suggested the cognate phrase (*bn 'ilm*) found at Ugarit; there, the "sons of the mighty" are other, minor gods less powerful than Baal. If this is what these same words mean in Hebrew, then the opening lines of this psalm would seem to be calling on the lesser gods to give glory to the chief or most powerful deity, the LORD. Needless to say, such an opening would not sit very well with later Israelite monotheism, but it might indeed be the sort of thing that ninth-century Israelites could unreflectively take over from a hymn originally composed to honor Baal.[16] The geographic location evoked in the mention of the mountain range "Lebanon" as well as of "Sirion" (Mount Hermon) places us squarely in northern Canaan. To be sure, this is not nearly as far north as Ugarit, but it is on the very northern

edge of the Kingdom of Israel—by all accounts, Baal country in the ninth century (1 Kings 18–19). Given this background, the psalm's whole presentation
of Israel's God thundering forth out of rain clouds and making the wilderness
tremble was likewise seen by scholars as strikingly reminiscent of the descriptions of Baal in Ugaritic poetry:

> So now may Baal enrich with his rain, may he enrich with rich water in a
>   downpour.
> And may he give forth his voice in the clouds, may he flash lightning-
>   bolts to the earth . . .
> Baal opens a break in the clouds, Baal gives forth his holy voice;
> Baal gives forth the utte[rance?] of his [li?]ps, his ho[ly?] voice
>   conv[ulses?] the earth . . .
> The high places of the Ear[th] shake.[17]

Other scholars read the same evidence slightly differently, however. They
believe it would be more accurate to view this psalm not as a bowdlerized
Baal hymn, but as a northern Israelite polemic, and one that fits rather well
with the story of Elijah on Mount Carmel. In both cases, the God of Israel is
being pointedly portrayed in Baal's traditional garb—rain clouds, lightning
shooting down from the sky, supernal power. Wasn't the point of Psalm 29 to
say to northern Israelites—just as Elijah had in his challenge on Mount
Carmel—"You don't need Baal anymore"?

The Still, Small Voice

The same message seems to be embodied in the episode that follows Elijah's
defeat of Baal's prophets. Actually, he not only defeated them on Mount
Carmel, he also had them killed: "Elijah said to [the people], 'Seize the prophets
of Baal; do not let one of them escape.' So they seized them, and Elijah brought
them down to the River Kishon, where he killed them" (1 Kings 18:40).

Not surprisingly, this did not sit well with the royal family, and particularly
not with Jezebel, King Ahab's wife. She was a patron of Baal and Asherah
worship and an out-and-out enemy of prophets who advocated worshiping
the LORD (18:4), including, of course, Elijah. When she heard that Elijah had
killed off the prophets of Baal, she considerately sent him a message inform-
ing him that she intended to do the same to him (19:2). Elijah immediately
fled to the south.

> He got up, and ate and drank; then he went in the strength of that food
> forty days and forty nights to Horeb, the mountain of God. At that place he
> came to a cave, and spent the night there.

Then the word of the LORD came to him, saying, "What are you doing here, Elijah?" He answered, "I have been very zealous for the LORD, the God of hosts; for the Israelites have forsaken your covenant, thrown down your altars, and killed your prophets with the sword. I alone am left, and they are seeking my life, to take it away." He said, "Go out and stand on the mountain before the LORD."

And behold, the LORD passed by and a great, strong wind split the mountains and broke rocks into pieces before the LORD. The LORD was [or is] not in the wind. And after the wind a shaking; the LORD was [or is] not in the shaking. And after the shaking a fire; the LORD was [or is] not in the fire. And after the fire was *the sound of the thinnest stillness.* When Elijah heard it, he wrapped his face in his mantle and went out and stood at the entrance of the cave. Then there came a voice to him that said, "What are you doing here, Elijah?"

1 Kings 19:8–13

The phrase rendered above as "the sound of the thinnest stillness" was translated in the King James Version as "a still, small voice," and as such it has enjoyed a rich afterlife in the English language. The poet John Greenleaf Whittier (1807–92) composed a famous hymn, "Dear Lord and Father of Mankind," which concludes:

> Breathe through the heats of our desire
> Thy coolness and Thy balm;
> let sense be dumb, let flesh retire;
> speak through the earthquake, wind, and fire,
> O still, small voice of calm.

Perhaps emblematic of the transition from the nineteenth century in America to the mid-twentieth is the somewhat pantheistic use of the same phrase in a song performed to wide approval by the pop artist Perry Como:

> A still small voice will speak to you one day.
> A still small voice will call to you and say,
> "I am the earth, the sky, the brightest star on high,
> the tallest tree, the smallest drop of dew."
> A still small voice one day will say to you![18]

Endless sermons and devotional tracts have also been entitled "The Still, Small Voice." Rather early on, this phrase became identified with the promptings of a person's own conscience, and it is principally in that sense that it is used today—hence the 1918 film *And a Still, Small Voice,* directed by Bert Bracken, a "tale of crime and redemption" in which the criminal, tormented by conscience, gives himself up, reforms, and ends up marrying the girl of his dreams. But it may also be relevant to observe that "the still, small voice" has served of late as the name of a guide to Buddhist meditation techniques; a technological innovation in the telecommunications industry; an editorial about tax alternatives in the Eugene (Oregon) *Register Guard*; a biography of the novelist Zona Gale; two collections of poetry; a CD album by the guitarist Paul Jackson Jr.; four or five novels; "a psychic's guide to awakening intuition"; and an article on the difficulties attendant to the identification of WIMPs, weakly interacting massive particles, which have been drifting around the universe ever since the Big Bang.

Needless to say, none of these is quite the sense in which the phrase was used in 1 Kings. In fact, scholars connect its use in the passage cited to the theme already seen, Baal's displacement by the God of Israel, save that here, the very idea of the deity's immanence in the natural world is challenged. Thus, the LORD is not in the great, strong wind (like Baal), nor, like Baal, is He immanent in the storm winds that shake the earth or the fire that comes down from heaven. What this passage seems to reject is the deity's identification with any of the pyrotechnics of the natural world (including, perhaps pointedly, those that were said to have accompanied the first great revelation of the LORD at Sinai/Horeb).[19] Instead, the true God's voice is beyond the natural world, it is "the sound of the thinnest stillness."[20]

Elijah the Immortal

Elijah is a classically northern (Israelite) sort of prophet. A Moses-like worker of miracles, he splits the Jordan in two (2 Kings 2:8; cf. Exod. 14:21) and makes abundant food and drink from a short supply (1 Kings 17:10–16; cf. Exod. 16:4–18). Also like Moses, he survives for forty days and forty nights without food or drink (1 Kings 19:8; cf. Deut. 9:9). He can also make it rain or make it stop (1 Kings 17:1) and bring a dead boy back to life (17:17–24); he is fed by the ravens (17:6) or by angels (19:5). An outsider, he is for the most part an out-and-out enemy of the king (Ahab in fact calls him "my enemy" in 1 Kings 21:20) whose duties include reprimanding royal improprieties[21] (such as in the case of Naboth, who was executed on a trumped up charge so that the royal family could take possession of Naboth's vineyard, 1 Kings 21).

Such things, scholars say, were altogether typical of the expected repertoire of prophets in the north,[22] so it is no accident that some of the same things were done by Elijah's equally northern understudy, Elisha. Elisha, who is also an enemy of the king (2 Kings 2:13–14), provides abundant potable water from a single bowl of salt water (2:19–22; cf. Exod. 15:25) and abundant oil from a single cruse (4:1–7). Like Elijah, Elisha also knows how to revive a boy from the dead (4:18–37).[23] He also feeds a hundred people with a small number of barley cakes (4:42–44), cures an Aramean leper (2 Kings 5; cf. Exod. 4:6–7; Num. 12:10–16), and levitates an axe handle from the Jordan (6:1–7). Some of these items are likewise reminiscent of the things related of a later Galilean, Jesus of Nazareth.[24] As we will see, they stand somewhat in contrast to the actions of the prophets of the southern kingdom, Judah, who are less given to working miracles and more focused on prophetic visions and lengthy speeches.

According to the biblical account, Elijah's string of miracles was not brought to an end by his death; in fact, he did not die. Instead, the prophet ascended bodily into heaven:

> When they had crossed [the Jordan], Elijah said to Elisha, "Tell me what I may do for you, before I am taken from you." Elisha said, "Please let me inherit a double share of your spirit." He responded, "You have asked a hard thing; yet, if you see me as I am being taken from you, it will be granted you; if not, it will not." As they continued walking and talking, a chariot of fire and horses of fire separated the two of them, and Elijah ascended in a whirlwind into heaven. Elisha kept watching and crying out, "Father, father! The chariots of Israel and its horsemen!" But when he [Elisha] could no longer see him, he grasped his own clothes and tore them in two pieces.
>
> 2 Kings 2:1–12

Modern scholars tend to shrug their shoulders at the accounts of such miracles or, putting on them the best face possible, describe them as "hagiography."[25] But for ancient readers the story of Elijah's heavenly ascent was extremely important. If he went up to heaven and was not heard from again, it certainly seemed possible to them that he was still up there, waiting to be ordered back down to earth.

Thus developed the motif of "Elijah the Immortal." Its earliest reflex is to be found within the Hebrew Bible itself at the very end of the book of Malachi. There, this late biblical prophet announces in God's name:

> Remember the teaching of My servant Moses, the statutes and ordinances that I commanded him at Horeb for all Israel. *For I will send you the prophet Elijah before the arrival of the great and terrible day of the LORD.* He will turn the hearts of fathers to their children and the hearts of children to their fathers, so that when I come I will not strike the land with destruction.
>
> 1 Mal. 4:4–5 (Hebrew, 3:23–24)

According to Malachi, Elijah not only had been spared death but was waiting around in heaven so as to be able to fulfill this important mission before the events of the end-time. Ben Sira, the second-century BCE Jewish sage, described Elijah in these terms:

> You were taken on high by a whirlwind, by fiery legions to heaven.
> Ready, it is written, for the time to put [divine] wrath to rest, before the
>   day of the LORD,
> to turn back the hearts of fathers to their children and to reestablish the
>   tribes of Israel.
>
> Sir. 48:9–11

Ben Sira basically restates what Malachi had said, although he does go beyond the prophet's words in two particulars. According to Ben Sira (but not Malachi), Elijah will actually stave off disaster *in general,* putting the divine wrath to rest, whereas all Malachi seemed to say was that Elijah would prevent the coming destruction from "striking the land." Beyond this, it is noteworthy that, according to Ben Sira, Elijah's return will inaugurate the restoration of the long-lost ten tribes.[26]

Elijah was still eagerly awaited two centuries later, in the time of Jesus. Quite naturally, some people thought that John the Baptist might be Elijah:

> This is the testimony given by John [the Baptist. They asked him:] "Who are you?" He confessed and did not deny it, but confessed, "I am not the Messiah." And they asked him, "What then? Are you Elijah?" He said, "I am not."
>
> John 1:20–21

The same was apparently thought of Jesus:

> Jesus went on with his disciples to the villages of Caesarea Philippi; and on the way he asked his disciples, "Who do people say that I am?" And they answered him, "John the Baptist [who had been killed]; and others, Elijah; and still others, one of the prophets."
>
> Mark 8:27–28 (cf. 6:15; 9:11–13; 15:35–36)

Part of Elijah's biblical afterlife, so to speak, derived from his identification with Phinehas, the zealous priest who lived in the time of Moses and had been among the Israelites during their desert wanderings. Phinehas therefore seemed to ancient readers to have had an extraordinarily long existence—he is mentioned long after the exodus and the entry into Canaan, at the end of the period of the Judges (Judg. 20:28). In fact, the Bible contains no mention of his death,[27] a surprising circumstance for such a distinguished and aged person. Out of this developed the supposition that Phinehas never did die: he and Elijah were one and the same person. On consideration, their identification did not seem so far-fetched: after all, both Elijah and Phinehas were described in the Bible (twice each) as being "very zealous/jealous" for God—the only two biblical figures so described (Num. 25:11, 13; 1 Kings 19:10, 14). Surely this had been intended as a clue. It thus seemed possible to ancient interpreters that, having last been glimpsed in the period of the Judges, the zealous/jealous (and immortal) Phinehas simply lay low for a few hundred years, only to reappear as the ninth-century prophet. When he did reappear, the Bible curiously never said who Elijah's father was, he was just "Elijah the Tishbite" from Gilead. This would be the equivalent nowadays of introducing a historical figure by his first name only, "Then Tom came to Washington from Virginia." Was this not further confirmation that "Elijah" (meaning "My God is the LORD") was actually a kind of *nom de guerre* for the embattled, immortal zealot? Little wonder, then, that Elijah, having fought against the forces of Baal in the ninth century, had ascended into heaven to wait for his next appearance—or that people in later times might think that John the Baptist, or even Jesus, was really Elijah returned to earth.[28]

Such, in short, was Elijah's image for generations and centuries of Bible readers—he was Ahab's enemy, the man who challenged the prophets of Baal and miraculously caused the fire to come down from heaven, the one to whom God revealed Himself in the "still, small voice," the prophet who ascended bodily into heaven and who is there still, waiting for the day to come when he will announce the arrival (or return) of the Messiah.

The Mesha Stone

Many of the archaeological finds of the last century have seemed to disagree with one or another detail of the biblical record, casting doubt on the historicity of (among other things) the story of the exodus, the forty-year period of desert wanderings, or the conquest narrative. But sometimes archaeologists turn up things that startlingly confirm the biblical record.

Chapter 3 of 2 Kings recounts a horrific event that ended a battle in which the combined forces of the Kingdoms of Israel and Judah had been pitted against Moab, their neighbor across the Jordan River. Until that time, Moab had been a compliant vassal of Israel:

> Now King Mesha of Moab was a sheep breeder, who used to deliver to the king of Israel [as tribute] one hundred thousand lambs and the wool of one hundred thousand rams. But when Ahab died, the king of Moab rebelled against the king of Israel. So King Jehoram marched out of Samaria [the Israelite capital] at that time and mustered all Israel. As he went he sent word to King Jehoshaphat of Judah, "The king of Moab has rebelled

against me; will you go with me to battle against Moab?" He answered, "I will; I am with you, my people are your people, my horses are your horses."

2 Kings 3:4–7

Having concluded this alliance with his erstwhile countrymen, the Kingdom of Judah, Jehoram decides to consult the prophet Elisha to make sure that victory will indeed be his. But Elisha is no great fan of Jehoram; Jehoram's father was none other than Ahab, the sworn enemy of Elisha's master, Elijah. So at first Elisha refuses to predict the battle's outcome: "What do I have to do with you?" he says to the king. "Go to your father's prophets or to your mother's," that is, the prophets of Baal. But Jehoram insists ("No; it is the LORD who has summoned us," he says), so Elisha agrees to give an oracle: victory will indeed be Jehoram's.

In the course of the battle, however, King Mesha makes a desperate move:

When the king of Moab saw that the battle was going against him, he took with him seven hundred swordsmen to break through, opposite the king of Edom; but they could not. Then he took his firstborn son who was to succeed him, and offered him as a burnt offering on the wall. And great wrath came upon Israel, so they withdrew from him and returned to their own land.

2 Kings 3:26–27

Repugnant as it may seem to us, this human sacrifice seems to have saved the day:[29] Israel retreated and Moab was left an independent country.

Excavating in what is now Jordan in the summer of 1868, a German missionary stationed in Jerusalem, F. A. Klein, came upon a large rectangular basalt stone, rounded at the top, that had been inscribed with what looked like Hebrew words. This was not the alphabet used for Hebrew today, but was quite similar to the paleo-Hebrew script used in biblical times. Anyone trained in that script would have no difficulty in reading what the clearly incised letters were saying:

I am Mesha, son of Chemosh[yat?][30] King of Moab, the Dibonite. My father was king over Moab for thirty years and I was king after my father. I made this high place for Chemosh* in Qarḥoh, . . . for he saved me from all the kings, and he allowed me to see the downfall of all my foes.

Amazingly enough, the inscription turned out to be a first-person account by the very same Mesha mentioned in 2 Kings 3, and in the inscription he

---

* A Moabite god.

reviewed the history of his country's relations with Israel as well as recounting his victorious campaign.[31]

> Omri [was] the king of Israel and he oppressed Moab for many days, for Chemosh was angry with his land. And his son* succeeded him, and he said: I too shall oppress Moab. In my time he said this; but I got to see his downfall and that of his house, and Israel was lost forever.

The inscription then goes on to describe at length some of Mesha's other victories and building projects.

Apart from its mention of some of the names and other details found in the biblical account, the inscription is noteworthy for its presentation of Chemosh, a god whose "anger" with his land results in oppression by foreigners. Chemosh also tells Mesha when the time is right to attack ("And Chemosh said to me: 'Go take Nebo against Israel,' " line 14). These same two things were said of Israel's God here and there in the Bible and feature as prominent motifs in the book of Judges.

---

* Omri's son was Ahab. According to the biblical account, however, Mesha rebelled only *after* Ahab's death (2 Kings 1:1; 3:5). It is possible that the inscription intends "son" in the sense of *descendant*, since according to the biblical account it was against Omri's grandson Jehoram that Mesha rebelled.

30

The Book of Isaiah(s)

ISAIAH 1–66

Isaiah by Gustave Doré.

Major and minor prophets. The call of Isaiah. The Syro-Ephraimite crisis. "A virgin shall conceive." A vision of peace. A second Isaiah and the return to Zion. What a mess!

Isaiah's words are among the best known, and most stirring, of the Hebrew Bible. Since the very start of the Christian movement, his book has been taken as a foretelling of the events recounted in the Gospels and, hence, as confirmation of the truth of the Christian message. For Jews, his prediction of a great ingathering of their scattered remnant back to its historical homeland served as a guiding vision through their more than twenty centuries of exile. But scholars have raised a troubling question: how many Isaiahs were there?

The books of 1 and 2 Kings highlight the doings of two ninth-century prophets, Elijah and Elisha. While their words are quoted here and there, they did not leave behind any collection of their writings; the phenomenon of "writing prophets" begins only in the next century, the eighth, with the books of Hosea, Amos, Isaiah, and Micah. Of these four, only Isaiah was privileged, as it were, to have a volume all his own, the book of Isaiah. The writings of the other three are all included in what is called in Aramaic "[the scroll of] the twelve" or, in English, the "twelve minor prophets."

The reason for this distinction is altogether mechanical. In ancient times, biblical texts were preserved not in books with pages, but in scrolls.[1] A group of specially prepared animal hides would be cut to a uniform width and then sown together to make one long scroll. The text would then be written on the scroll in separate columns (roughly the size of a page in a large book today); as the reader finished reading one column of writing, he would unroll the scroll further to reveal the next column of text. To keep the scrolls orderly, one end would usually be attached to a stick of wood and the scroll rolled up around it; sometimes there would be a stick at both ends, so that, as the scroll was unrolled from the stick on one side, it would be rolled up around the stick on the other side. But what did you do with a precious text that was only a few columns long? Rolling it up around a stick seemed impractical, and letting it just lie around as a single piece of parchment was like leaving a single photocopied page in your office today—sooner or later it would end up lost or crumpled. In such cases, therefore, ancient scribes preferred to combine two or more short texts to make a single, long scroll. Thus, while the lengthy book of Isaiah could have its own scroll, the shorter collections of prophetic sayings by Hosea, Amos, and the others ended up being joined together on a single scroll, the "scroll of the twelve." (The name "twelve *minor* prophets" is thus not a judgment of their importance but goes back to the Latin, where *minor* also means smaller in length.) There are, in fact, three prophets who got their own books, Isaiah, Jeremiah, and Ezekiel—and a fourth, Daniel, who is counted as a prophet in the Christian canon but not in the Jewish one. In this book, we will survey each of these "major" prophets in turn, as well as examining some of the "minor" prophets.

Holy, Holy, Holy

Isaiah the son of Amoz had a prophetic vision, he reports, in the year that King Uzziah died, probably 742 BCE.[2] Isaiah does not tell us much about the particulars of his life at that time: was he a priest connected to the Jerusalem temple,[3] or a wealthy landowner in or around that city, or perhaps a counselor in the king's court? Whatever the case, he does offer a detailed description of what he saw in his vision:

> In the year that King Uzziah died, I saw my Lord seated high up on a lofty throne and His skirts filled the Temple.[4] Seraphim hovered above Him. Each had six wings: with two of them each would cover his face, and with two others he would cover his feet, and with the two others he would fly. And one would call to another and say, "Holy, holy, holy is the LORD of hosts; His glory fills the whole earth." The supports of the threshold began to shake from the sound of the calling, and the Temple began to fill with smoke. And I said, "Woe is me! I am as good as dead. For I am of impure lips, and I live among a people of impure lips—yet my eyes behold the king, the LORD of hosts!" But then one of the seraphim flew toward me carrying a coal, which he had picked up with tongs from off of the altar, and he touched it to my mouth and said, "Now that this has touched your lips, your sin is gone and your wrongdoing has been done away with." Then I heard the voice of my Lord saying, "Who can I send? And who will go for us?" And I said, "I am here. Send me!"
>
> Isa. 6:1–8

What Isaiah seems to be describing is nothing less than his transformation into a prophet—how an ordinary man was made fit to answer the call and carry God's word.

One point may require clarification, however. We have seen that biblical law forbade people to enter the sanctuary if they were impure. Impurity could be contracted in various ways, but one way was simple carelessness—walking along and bumping by accident into someone else who bore corpse impurity (Num. 19:22), or stepping by accident onto the carcass of a dead mouse or lizard by the side of the road (Lev. 11:29–31). Isaiah, when he realizes he is in the presence of God Himself, thinks he is doomed because he is "of impure lips." But there is no such concept as "impure lips" in biblical law. Interpreters have thus long debated precisely what he meant. Perhaps, some have said, the prophet was using the language of cultic impurity in a different sense: I have spoken in a way analogous to that careless, ordinary way of walking that can lead to physical impurity—in fact, I live among a people who are also, in this sense, "of impure lips," and I have been in constant contact with them. By what right can I now behold God's very being?

If this is what he was saying, Isaiah was not showing some sort of false modesty. He felt that he was in mortal danger, and the danger would not go away by his just standing there. He needed to be purified, and so he was. What the seraphim—usually understood as some sort of angel, but the word literally seems to mean "burners," "burning ones"—did was to cleanse his lips with a burning coal. Once so purified, he could go on and stand before God, indeed, bear God's message on his own lips.

This passage was extremely significant to ancient readers—not so much for what it said about Isaiah as for what it taught about heaven. The night sky is full of stars and planets, meteors and comets, and for ancient peoples these had great significance. Many people identified these heavenly bodies with gods and goddesses; their path through the heavens was seen as containing clues as to what these deities were planning for people down below. Ancient Israelites, too, were heir to the same belief, but as they came to see their own God as the most significant or powerful—and eventually as the only—deity, they naturally wondered what the role of those stars and planets could be. This passage from Isaiah reflected one answer: they were actually *seraphim,* "burners," who lit up the sky but whose principal function was to praise God, calling out, "Holy, holy, holy" to the Creator. Partly with reference to this passage, a fundamental theme emerged during the later biblical period and afterward to the effect that God not only sits enthroned in heaven but resides in a *heavenly sanctuary,* a temple above the clouds where He is praised and served by His angelic attendants.[5]

This idea had consequences for people down below. When ancient Jews sought to praise God in their prayers, they naturally saw themselves as the earthly equivalent of the angels serving and praising God on high. What words should they say to praise Him? One obvious answer lay in the words that the seraphim were, according to Isaiah, uttering around the heavenly throne: "Holy, holy, holy is the LORD of hosts; His glory fills the whole earth." For that reason, it soon became standard practice in Jewish prayer to recite these same words:[6]

And holy seraphim, together with six-winged cherubim, singing to You the triumphal song, cry out with never-silent voices, "Holy, holy, holy, Lord Sabaoth, the heaven and the earth are full of Your glory."[7]

An ancient prayer incorporated into
the *Apostolic Constitutions* 7.35.9–10

Let us sanctify Your Name in the world in the same manner as it is sanctified in highest heaven, as was written by Your prophet, "And each called to the other and said: Holy, holy, holy is the LORD of Hosts, the whole earth is full of His glory."

Kedushah (Jewish daily prayer)

The same practice was adopted by the early church, and it continues in modern Christian worship:

And now with angels and archangels, with thrones and dominions, and with all the soldiery of the heavenly army, let us sing the hymn of Your glory, uttering ceaselessly, "*Sanctus, sanctus, sanctus*—Holy, holy, holy is the Lord God Sabaoth, the heavens and the earth are full of Your glory."

The *Sanctus* (or *Tersanctus*), preface to
the Eucharistic Prayer in the Roman Catholic mass

Therefore with Angels and Archangels, and with all the company of heaven, we laud and magnify thy glorious Name; evermore praising thee, and saying,

Holy, holy, holy, Lord God of Hosts: Heaven and earth are full of thy glory.

Glory be to thee, O Lord Most High.

Book of Common Prayer (Episcopal Church)

Why Three?

Isaiah's vision was not without its exegetical difficulties, however. Why, for example, did the seraphim say "holy" three times? If, according to Assumption 3, the Bible was an altogether perfect book without needless repetition, then each of these three *holy*s must have a different meaning:

Around the throne, and on each side of the throne, are four living creatures, full of eyes in front and behind: the first living creature like a lion, the second living creature like an ox, the third living creature with a face like a human face, and the fourth living creature like a flying eagle.* And the four living creatures, each of them with six wings, are full of eyes all around and inside. Day and night without ceasing they sing, "Holy, holy, holy, the Lord God the Almighty, *who was and is and is to come.*"

Rev. 4:6–8

Holy attendants stand on high before Him, each with six wings; with two he covers his face, that he not see; with two he covers his body, that he not be seen; and with two he serves. And they receive one from another and say, "Holy *in the highest part of heaven,* the place of His presence; holy *on earth,* the work of His mighty power; holy *forever and for eternity* is the Lord of Hosts. The whole earth is full of the splendor of His glory."

Targum Jonathan to Isa. 6:2–3

According to the first passage, the three "holy's" refer to three different time periods, holy in the past, present, and future; according to the second, they refer to heaven, earth, and eternity.

A modern-day Christian might well ask why the book of Revelation, part of the New Testament, did not associate the three "holy's" with the Trinity. At the time that book was written, however, the Trinity was not yet part of the teachings of the church. It did not take long, however, for that interpretation to be put forward:

This hymn is not alone praise, but also a prophecy of the good things slated for the world, and an accurate rendition of right teachings. For why is it that, having spoken once [the word "holy"], they did not grow silent, or having said it twice they did not desist, but said it yet a third time? Is it not clear that they wished to cause the hymn to refer to the Trinity?

John Chrysostom (ca. 347–407) *Commentary on Isaiah* vi 3

Another exegetical question that came up was: why were the seraphim saying "holy" to one another? (And *one would call to another* and say, "Holy, holy, holy is the LORD of hosts.") Oughtn't they to be directing their words to God? Ancient interpreters thus interpreted the passage as implying that the seraphim were not so much saying "holy" to one another as coordinating their praise so that they might say the words in perfect unison. This may be implied in the passage cited from the *Jonathan Targum* above:

---

* These creatures derive from a different biblical vision of God's throne, that found in chapter 1 of Ezekiel; see below, chapter 32.

And they *receive** one from another and say, "Holy in the highest part of heaven, the place of His presence; holy on earth, the work of His mighty power; holy forever and for eternity is the Lord of Hosts. The whole earth is full of the splendor of His glory."

This idea of "receiving one from another" was elaborated elsewhere:

All His heavenly servants stand in the eternal heights and together, in unison, respectfully utter the words of the living God and eternal king . . . All of them open their mouths in holiness and purity . . . and *accept upon themselves* the yoke of heaven, *one from another,* and *give permission one to another* to sanctify their Creator. . . .

> *Yotser 'Or,* Jewish morning prayer

And whence do we know that they [the angels] are respectful of one another and do honor to one another and are more modest than human beings? Because when they open their mouths to offer praise, each says to his fellow, "You begin, for you are greater than me," and the other says, "No, you begin, for you are greater than me"—not as human beings do— (while others say that the angels are organized into groups, and one group says to the other, "You begin for you are greater than us"). This is why it is said, "And one called to another and said . . ."

> The Tractate *Abot* According to R. Nathan, version A, chapter 12

Jerome cleverly associated the same phrase with the Christian idea that the Old Testament is a foreshadowing of the New:

"And one called to the other . . ." Well said, "one to the other"!§ For whatever we may read in the Old Testament we will find as well in the Gospel; and what has been composed in the Gospel is drawn from the authority of the Old Testament: there is nothing unharmonious or divergent. And so it says, "Holy, holy, holy is the Lord of Hosts"—the Trinity is announced in both Testaments.

> *Letter to Pope Damasus*

---

* The root *qbl,* meaning to "face" or to "receive," seems to imply some act of coordination or harmony.

§ The text does not say "one seraph to another," but simply "one to another." Jerome interprets this as meaning one *testament* to the other, the Old to the New and the New to the Old.

The Divine Council

For modern scholars this scene of Isaiah's prophetic commission has a rather different point of interest, the apparently insignificant use of the plural in God's question at the end, "Who can I send? Who will go for *us*?" This is probably not an instance of the "royal we"—rare to nonexistent in biblical Hebrew—but a reference to those six-winged seraphim surrounding God's throne. To scholars, the seraphim in Isaiah's vision seem to constitute something parallel to the "divine council" known from elsewhere in the ancient world.

The idea that the different deities in the pantheon get together in some sort of council is widely attested in the literature of ancient Israel's neighbors, in particular in Mesopotamian texts and, closer to biblical Israel, in Phoenician inscriptions and in the library of ancient Ugarit. There this divine council is called, among other things, the *'dt 'ilm* or *pḫr 'ilm* (assembly/council of the gods, or, possibly, of El, the chief god). It is striking, scholars say, that the cognate phrase *'adat 'el* is found in Psalm 82, which depicts God standing amidst the assembly of the gods and rebuking them for their failure to practice justice.[8] Apparently, some biblical writers saw no harm in invoking this ancient concept, even though it eventually rubbed against biblical monotheism. True, in Psalm 82 the lesser gods of the council are mentioned quite intentionally, according to scholars: the purpose of this psalm is to account for the fact that Israel's God is now "in charge of all the nations," having gotten rid of the other gods because of their incompetence or corruption. But elsewhere, their appearance may simply reflect an old habit of mind that died slowly:

> For who in the skies can be compared to the LORD, or who among the
>   heavenly beings is like the LORD?
> a God feared *in the council of the holy ones*, great and awesome above
>   all that are around Him? O LORD God of hosts, who is as mighty
>   as You, O LORD?
>
> Ps. 89:6–8

For who [among the false prophets] has ever stood in *the council of the LORD*, so as to see and to hear His word? Who has given heed to His word so as to announce it? Look, the LORD's storm of wrath is coming, a whirling storm that will swirl down on the heads of the wicked. The LORD's anger will not turn back until it has done and carried out His mind's plans. In time to come you will understand this clearly. [God says:] "I did not send the prophets, yet they ran; I did not speak to them, yet they prophesied. But if they *had stood in My council,* then they would have proclaimed My words to My people, and they would have turned them from their evil way, and from the evil of their doings."

Jer. 23:18–22

In this latter passage, Jeremiah's words reflect another tradition associated with the divine council at Ugarit and elsewhere. Since the purpose of the council was to issue decisions, a messenger was naturally needed to carry the council's decrees to human beings. The Ugaritic texts do indeed depict the gods dispatching such messengers. Evoking these traditional conceptions, Jeremiah says that this is in fact what a true prophet is, a messenger who has actually "stood in My council" and has been dispatched to "proclaim My words to My people." The prophets that Jeremiah is denouncing are, he says, frauds; they never were actually summoned on high to the divine council.

In the light of all this, Isaiah's report on a vision of the seraphim looks somewhat different to modern scholars. The "temple" to which he is called is really another version of the divine council, save that, in place of the lesser gods, there are only the seraphim, whose job it is to wait on the one true God and praise Him. For Isaiah, as later for Jeremiah, a prophet is thus someone who has been summoned on high and enlisted to carry back to humankind the decrees of the divine council. "Who can I send?" this God asks in the Isaiah passage, using the first person singular. Then, perhaps with a glance at the surrounding six-winged creatures thronging about His throne, He adds, "And who will go *for us*?" [9]

As for Isaiah's "impure lips," scholars have suggested an ancient Near Eastern precedent for that phrase as well. For some time, Assyriologists have known of a certain ceremony known as *mīs-pî,* or "cleansing of the mouth," whereby Mesopotamian cultic functionaries (among others) were purified. In particular, the *baru* priest, whose job description included delivering sacred oracles, had to have his mouth cleansed in a *mīs-pî* ritual, in which he would put cedar resin to his lips and intone: "I am placing upon my mouth pure cedar." This step symbolized "complete purification." [10] Against such a background, the action of the seraphim takes on a different aspect: the burning coal put to Isaiah's lips was apparently meant to suggest that, like a *baru* priest, Isaiah was now fit to transmit divine oracles.

The Syro-Ephraimite War

Things were not bad in Isaiah's native Judah at the time God first summoned him, but they were not particularly good either. A great power had, in recent times,*[11] come back to dominate the region: Assyria. Located at some distance from Judah (its great city, Nineveh, was nearly seven hundred miles to the northeast, on the spot in northern Iraq currently occupied by the Kurdish city of Mosul), Assyria nonetheless maintained an aggressive political and military presence in the lands to its west, particularly during the hundred-year period from 740 to 640 BCE.[12] Its army was terrifying; it seemed to be made up of supermen.[13] Isaiah described the Assyrian troops in these terms:

> Here they come in a rush!
> None of them is tired, not one gives out—they do not sleep or doze.
> Not a single belt is loosed; no one's bootlaces are undone.
> And their arrows are razor-sharp; their bows are drawn back all the way.
> The hooves of their horses are as sharp as flint, and their chariot-wheels
> 　　　are a whirlwind.
> Their roar is like a lion's, they roar by like a beast of prey.
> [The beast] growls as it grabs its food, then trots off. No one can stop it.
> 　　　　　　　　　　　　　　　　　　　　　　　　　　Isa. 5:26–30

Faced with this powerful threat, the little Kingdom of Judah nonetheless tried to hold on to its nominal independence, but ultimately managed to do so only in the same way as the weaker neighbors of Germany and Russia did in Europe during most of the twentieth century: by cooperating and submitting, sometimes being exploited, and always keeping a low profile. Judah's northern neighbor, the Kingdom of Israel, was not so fortunate. Conquered by

---

* Assyria's regional ascendancy might properly be said to go back to the time of Elijah and Ahab (Ahab ascended the throne of Israel in 872 BCE). The Assyrian king at this time, Assurnasirpal II (884–859 BCE), was a skilled fighter who stomped through the neighboring kingdoms of northern Mesopotamia and then, by his own account, "seized the entire extent of the Lebanon mountain and reached the Great Sea [the Mediterranean] of the Amurru country. [Then] I washed my weapons in the deep sea and performed sheep-offerings to [all] the gods." His son, Shalmaneser III (859–824 BCE), fought a series of campaigns in Syria, where he encountered a coalition of armies to oppose him, including troops contributed by Ahab. While Shalmaneser's success was not total—he apparently failed to conquer Damascus—he did receive tribute from other nations, including Israel (then ruled by King Jehu), thus establishing Assyria as the preeminent power in the region. Assyrian power then waned for a period of about forty years, until the rise of King Tiglath-pileser III in 744 BCE, the period of Isaiah's prophesying.

Assyria in 723–722 BCE, it was essentially wiped off the map. Assyria forcibly deported much of Israel's population to other parts of its empire,[14] meanwhile settling its own citizens in the vacated Israelite houses or filling the land with the citizens of other conquered nations (2 Kings 17:24–31). So it was that many of the northern inhabitants of the once-mighty kingdom of David and Solomon—members of the tribes of Ephraim and Manasseh, Dan and Issachar and the others—were forced from their homeland and soon disappeared, melting into the native populations of the countries to which they were deported.

Prophecy and politics are more closely allied than many people would like. It is certainly no accident that this same period of Assyrian threats and conquests saw a flurry of prophetic activity, and, in the view of many scholars, the emergence of prophecy in its classical form. From the eighth century we have the written records of four different prophets, Hosea, Amos, Isaiah, and Micah. It would seem that it was the turbulent political situation confronting the people of Israel and Judah that called forth these prophets—to warn of impending disaster and to transmit to those in power God's words of advice or reproach.

In the case of Isaiah, that advice first concerned a threat not from Assyria but from Judah's own kinsmen to the north, the Kingdom of Israel, along with Israel's still more northern ally, Damascus (capital of Aram). The historical details are still a bit foggy,[15] but it seems that the Kingdom of Judah was caught in a political bind. Its northern neighbors were eager to build a coalition to stand up to the Assyrians; if Judah joined with them they would certainly be that much stronger—but if the mighty Assyrian army nonetheless prevailed, disaster would surely befall all of them. On the other hand, if Judah refused to join, that too might lead to disaster: Israel and Damascus might (and, in fact, did) try to invade Judah preemptively and install a puppet regime more favorable to their cause (Isa. 7:1, 5–6; cf. 2 Kings 16:5). What to do? Judah's king, Ahaz, was young and new to the job. When he heard that Israel and Damascus were indeed forming such an alliance, "his heart . . . shook as the trees of the forest shake before the wind" (Isa. 7:2).

It was at this point that the prophet Isaiah was summoned by God to give some advice to the young king:

> Then the LORD said to Isaiah, "Go and meet Ahaz, you and your son Shear-jashub, at the far end of the ditch from the upper pool, along the highway leading to the Fuller's Field. Say to him: Be careful and be calm. Do not be afraid or lose your nerve because of those two smoking bonfire sticks, [that is,] Rezin of Aram [Damascus] and the son of Remaliah,* how-

---

* Pekah, son of Remaliah; omitting his first name ("son of Remaliah") was considered a sign of disrespect.

ever much they smolder. For, since Aram has been plotting against you
with . . . the son of Remaliah, saying, 'Let us invade Judah and cut it off and
conquer it, and then install the son of Tabeel as king in it,' therefore has my
Lord GOD decreed:

It will not work; it will not even come to pass.
For Aram's head* is Damascus, and [at] the head of Damascus is
    [merely] Rezin . . .
And [Israel's] head is Samaria, and [at] the head of Samaria is [merely]
    the son of Remaliah.
If you don't stand tall, you won't stand at all.

Isa. 7:3–9

In other words: Ahaz, you have nothing to fear but fear itself. Those two
kings who frighten you so much are merely "two smoking bonfire sticks";
lifted out of the fire, they do make a lot of smoke, but they have no power to
harm you and will eventually sputter out.[16]

To reinforce the point, Isaiah offered Ahaz God's further assurance:[17]

Suppose a certain young woman gets pregnant and gives birth to a son; she
should give him the name "God-amidst-us" [Hebrew: *'Immanu-'el*]. For, by
the time he knows how to feed himself,§ he will be eating curds and honey,
since even before the child knows how to feed himself, the land whose two
kings you so dread will lie deserted.[18]

Isa. 7:14–16

All little babies tend to pick up whatever they find and put it in their mouths;
it takes a vigilant parent to make sure they don't end up swallowing pebbles
or pennies or other harmful items. But in a very few years, that is, by the time
this hypothetical baby reaches the age when it can distinguish between the
edible and inedible (literally, "refuse the bad and choose the good"), it will be
dining on royal fare, "curds and honey," because the military threat (presumably, a siege) that has you, King Ahaz, quaking in your boots will have
evaporated, and the good times will have returned. Indeed, such a baby
should really be named "God-amidst-us," since that is the reason everything is sure to turn out all right. God's own residence, his temple, sits in the
midst of our capital of Jerusalem; surely He will not allow it to be conquered
or harmed in any way.

All this was good advice, but the young king failed to heed it. Instead, he

---

* Capital.
§ The Hebrew idiom means literally, "by the time he knows to reject the bad and choose
the good."

went running to Assyria for help, which then exacted a heavy price for its protective services. The account in 2 Kings sums up the events in a few sentences:

> Then King Rezin of Aram and King Pekah son of Remaliah of Israel came up to wage war on Jerusalem; they besieged Ahaz but could not conquer him. . . . Ahaz then sent messengers to King Tiglath-pileser of Assyria, saying, "I am your servant and your son.[19] Come up and save me from the king of Aram and the king of Israel, who are attacking me." Ahaz also took the silver and gold found in the house of the LORD and in the royal treasury, and sent a "gift" to the king of Assyria. The king of Assyria heeded his request; the king of Assyria marched up against Damascus and captured it, deporting its inhabitants to Kir; then he killed Rezin.
>
> 2 Kings 16:5–9

The "gift" was only part of Ahaz's submission. He later traveled to Damascus in person to pay homage to the victorious Tiglath-pileser III, and remained his loyal vassal thereafter.[20]

Immanuel

The exact identity and nature of the "certain young woman" who gets pregnant in Isaiah's above-cited oracle is somewhat controversial: was she a real person, or merely hypothetical? To begin with, it is unclear whether the first word of Isa. 7:14 is to be translated as "Behold," "Look," and the like, or (as I have done) "Suppose . . ." The latter is indeed sometimes a meaning of the Hebrew *hinneh* (for example, in Exod. 3:13, "Suppose I do go to the Israelites . . .") and would seem to fit the context better, since in those pre-amniocentesis days one would probably not say, "Behold! This woman is pregnant and is going to give birth to a son."* The next word, *ha-'almah*, translated as "a certain young woman," might also be rendered simply as "the young woman." Some scholars have in fact suggested that the definite article here implies a known individual—perhaps Ahaz's own wife, or Isaiah's. (The woman in Prov. 7:19 says, "The husband is not in his house," but what she really means is *my husband*.) However, biblical Hebrew sometimes also uses definite articles and even demonstratives in an indefinite sense,[21] in the same way that an English speaker might say, "This guy came up to me and started talking French," where "this guy" really means "an undefined person, someone I never met before." Considering this ambiguity, "*a certain* young woman" seems to preserve better the vagueness of the Hebrew: she might be known or

---

* True, a prophet might know in advance that the child would be a boy, but why would he say "Behold!" unless he were talking to another prophet?

might not be. As for "young woman," that is how *'almah* is usually translated nowadays; the word does not necessarily tell us whether she is married or not.[22]

It is interesting, however, that when the Bible was translated into Greek, starting in the third century BCE, Isaiah's "young woman" was translated as *parthenos,* which probably did mean "virgin" to the translators. (It seems unlikely, however, that in so translating they meant to imply an actual parthenogenesis or virgin birth; more likely, they simply meant that a virgin would get married, become pregnant in the usual way, and then give birth.) Since, at least in Greek, the Bible now specified that the young woman was a virgin, this verse was cited by the Gospel of Matthew in connection with its account of the virgin birth of Jesus:

> When his mother Mary had been engaged to Joseph, but before they lived together, she was found to be pregnant from the Holy Spirit. Her husband Joseph, being a righteous man and unwilling to expose her to public disgrace, planned to divorce her quietly. But just when he had decided to do this, an angel of the Lord appeared to him in a dream and said, "Joseph, son of David, do not be afraid to take Mary as your wife, for the child conceived in her is from the Holy Spirit. She will bear a son, and you are to name him Jesus, for he will save his people from their sins." All this took place to fulfill what had been spoken by the Lord through the prophet: "Look, the virgin shall conceive and bear a son, and they shall name him Immanuel," which means, "God is with us." When Joseph awoke from sleep, he did as the angel of the Lord commanded him; he took her as his wife, but had no marital relations with her until she had borne a son, and he named him Jesus.
>
> Matt. 1:18–25

The name to be given to this child thus came to acquire a new meaning: "God-amidst-us" referred not to God's presence in the Jerusalem temple, but to God's presence in the midst of Israel in the person of Jesus. Once again, the Old Testament seemed to early Christians to have predicted the events of the New. For that reason, the precise meaning of Isaiah's words apparently became a much-discussed item in the early debates between Jews and Christians:

> Also the words "Behold, the virgin shall conceive and bear a son" were spoken in advance of him [Jesus] . . . But you [Justin's Jewish interlocutor Trypho] dare to pervert the translations which your own elders [the translators of the Septuagint] made at the court of King Ptolemy of Egypt and say that the text does not have the meaning as they translated it but "Behold, the *young woman* shall conceive"—as if something of importance were being signified by a young woman giving birth after human inter-

course, which all young women do, save for the infertile, and even these God can, if He will, cause to give birth.

Justin Martyr, Dialogue with Trypho 84

"The Wolf Shall Dwell with the Lamb"

As mentioned, some scholars today believe that Isaiah's reference to a "certain young woman" becoming pregnant referred specifically to the much-anticipated birth of an heir to King Ahaz. After all, for people who had long waited for peace and prosperity, Ahaz himself had turned out to be something of a disappointment; he was not a great king. They therefore pinned their hopes on his successor, and it was apparently the birth of the next heir to the throne that caused Isaiah in a later passage to burst forth with enthusiasm:

> A boy has been born to us! We have been given a son, and majesty is set
>   on his shoulders!
> He has been named "Mighty-God-counsels-wondrous-things," "Eternal-
>   father-is-a-peaceful-ruler."
> There will be no end to the greatness of majesty or to peace, on David's
>   throne and over his kingdom,
> setting it firm and sustaining it, in justice and righteousness from now
>   henceforward. The LORD of Hosts will zealously see to it!
>
> Isa. 9:5–6

A second, more extended reference to the birth of an anticipated royal heir comes in Isaiah's remarkable vision of the future, a great new day dawning in Judah.[23]

> Then a shoot will spring up from the tree trunk of Jesse,* and a sprout
>   will rise from its roots.
> The spirit of the LORD will rest upon him, the spirit of wisdom and insight;
> the spirit of counsel and courage, the spirit of knowledge and fear of the
>   LORD.
> Yes, he will be guided by the fear of the LORD, not to judge by the way
>   things appear, nor decide by hearsay or rumor.
> He will judge the needy with righteousness, and bring fairness to the
>   poor of the earth.
> He will punish the proud at his word, put the guilty to death at his lips'
>   decree.
> Justice will be his everyday clothing, and firmness his regular dress.

* That is, a member of the royal line of David, whose father was Jesse.

Then the wolf will dwell with the lamb, and a leopard lie near a small
 goat; the calf and the lion will pasture together, with a small boy to
 lead them.
The cow will feed with the bear, and their young will graze in one field;
 the lion will eat hay like an ox.
A baby will play near the viper's hole, and a toddler will touch the
 snake's lair.
On My whole holy mountain no evil will come, for the land will be
 brimming with devotion to the LORD, like the waters that cover the
 sea.

Isa. 11:1–9

One matter should be explained about both this and the previous passage. In
the ancient world, it went without saying that a new golden age could be
brought about only by a new golden ruler. To that old way of thinking, it was
not that conditions would somehow change on their own—the economy
would not simply pick up or the international situation suddenly turn by itself
from hostility to peace. Rather, life worked from the top down. Only a great
new ruler could change things, but if such a ruler did arrive, he might indeed
cause *everything* to be different: righteousness and justice and peace would all
come about as a result of his rule.

If one reads Isaiah's vision of the peaceful animals in the context of his
own times—and keeping in mind that change moves from the top down—it
is not hard to understand what he meant. Certainly no inhabitant of Judah
could have failed to see who the "lamb," the "small goat," or the "baby"
were; they represented the Kingdom of Judah itself, scattered in the rugged
Judean hills and endlessly subject to foreign domination by wolves, leopards,
and lions, the great powers to its south, east, and north. If only the right ruler
came along, Isaiah was saying, then someday all that might change. Those
great carnivorous neighbors would be turned into harmless vegetarians, and
peace and justice and righteousness would become the hallmark of the new
king's internal rule. Even today, it is difficult to read these words without feeling that same surge of hope that the ancient inhabitants of Judah must have
felt, although such enthusiasm might well be tempered by Woody Allen's cau-
tionary rewording of Isaiah: "The lion and the calf shall lie down together,
but the calf won't get much sleep." [24]

Hezekiah the King

The much awaited new king, Hezekiah, earns high marks in the Deuteronomistic History: He "did what was right in the sight of the LORD" (2 Kings
18:3), apparently undertaking a religious reform that in some ways antici-

pated that of his grandson Josiah (2 Kings 18:4–6; cf. 2 Chronicles 29–31). Three full chapters of the Deuteronomistic History (2 Kings 18–20) are devoted to his story—a rare tribute![25] In terms of foreign policy, however, he appears to have made a grave error, seeking to throw off the Assyrian yoke at a moment when its power seemed to be waning. The Assyrian response was not long in coming: Sennacherib, the new Assyrian king, invaded Judah in 701 BCE. Here scholars are fortunate enough to be able to read Sennacherib's own account of the invasion:

> Because Hezekiah of Judah did not submit to my yoke, I laid siege to forty-six of his fortified cities, walled forts, and to the countless villages in their vicinity. I conquered them using earthen ramps and battering rams. These siege engines were supported by infantrymen who tunneled under the walls. I took 200,150 prisoners of war, young and old, male and female, from these places. I also plundered more horses, mules, donkeys, camels, large and small cattle than we could count. I imprisoned Hezekiah in Jerusalem like a bird in a cage.
>
> Sennacherib Prism iii 20–40[26]

In characteristic fashion, this account gives the impression of an all-out victory for the Assyrians. Scholars have noted, however, that it fails to mention any actual conquest of Jerusalem itself, and this indeed matches the biblical account.[27] According to chapters 36–37 of Isaiah, King Hezekiah was attacked by Assyria and—with his back to the wall, so to speak—prayed to God for help. His prayer was answered. Apparently some sort of plague suddenly broke out among the Assyrian troops: "Then the angel of the LORD set out and struck down one hundred eighty-five thousand in the camp of the Assyrians; when morning dawned, they were all dead bodies. Then King Sennacherib of Assyria left, went home, and lived at Nineveh" (Isa. 37:36–37; cf. 2 Kings 19:35–36; 2 Chronicles 32).[28]

The events of 701 were nevertheless a debacle. Hezekiah was forced to pay a heavy tribute to the Assyrians—according to Sennacherib's account, thirty talents (420 pounds) of gold, eight hundred talents of silver, precious stones, valuable furniture, and other possessions, plus the king's "daughters, concubines, and male and female musicians. He sent his personal messenger to deliver this tribute and bow down to me."[29] It would seem that Hezekiah too, despite his good press in the Bible, fell far short of the ideal king foreseen by Isaiah.

In any event, the yearning for that ideal king was renewed in the time of the Bible's ancient interpreters. The remnant of the people of Judah was, in late biblical times, once again subject to foreign domination—by the armies of Ptolemaic Egypt and Seleucid Syria, and later by the dreaded Roman Empire. If Isaiah's prophecy of the coming king had not been fulfilled back then, perhaps that was because (in keeping with Assumption 2) his words were really talking about the interpreters' own era. So it was that the passages cited above, along with others to be seen shortly, came to be understood as predictions of a *messiah,* a new king in the interpreters' own day, one who would set everything aright.

The Suffering "Servant of the Lord"

When a branch of this messianic movement came to focus its faith on Jesus of Nazareth, Isaiah's words were eagerly cited as proof that all the events of the Gospels had indeed been foretold by biblical prophets. For who else could Isaiah have been talking about when he said, "A boy has been born to us! We have been given a son, and majesty is set on his shoulders!"? And when Isaiah likewise spoke of a descendant of Jesse arising sometime in the future and inaugurating a new age, surely he must likewise have intended this as a reference to the Christian messiah: "The root of Jesse shall come, the one who rises to rule the nations; in him the nations shall hope" (Rom. 15:12).

But perhaps the most evocative element in the book of Isaiah for early Christians was the frequent mention of a certain "servant of the LORD." These references are clustered in chapters 42 through 53, and although this servant is not the main subject of these chapters, references to him keep coming back now and again:

> [God says:] Here is My servant, whom I uphold, My chosen one, whom I
>   view with favor;
> I have set My spirit upon him, so that he may bring forth justice to the
>   nations.
> He will not cry out or lift up his voice, or make it heard in the street;
> He will not break a bruised reed, or even put out a wick grown dim; but
>   he will faithfully bring forth justice.
> And he himself will not grow dim or be bruised until he has established
>   justice in the earth, and the coastlands long for his teaching.
> Isa. 42:1–4

The idea of someone being a "servant of the LORD" is not all that uncommon in the Bible: Moses is frequently so described (Deut. 34:5; Josh. 1:1; etc.), as are Joshua (Josh. 24:29), David (1 Kings 8:66), and other figures. But what was striking to early Christians in these references was the implication that this "servant of the LORD" was one who *suffered.* If Isaiah said that this servant "will not cry out or lift up his voice," certainly the implication was that pain would be inflicted upon him *and yet* he would not cry out; and if the prophet asserted that the servant "will not grow dim or be bruised," that too might be interpreted as an indication that others would try to bruise him or make him grow dim.

This element of suffering was made more explicit later in the book:

> [The servant says:] The Lord GOD has opened my ear, and I was not
>   rebellious, I did not turn backward.
> I gave my back to those who struck me, and my cheeks to those who
>   pulled out the beard; I did not hide my face from insult and
>   spitting.
> The Lord GOD helps me; therefore I have not been disgraced;
> therefore I have set my face like flint, and I know that I shall not be put
>   to shame.
>
>   Isa. 50:5–7

Perhaps most important, in one particular passage this "servant of the LORD" was said to have suffered *on behalf of other people*.

> He was despised and rejected by others; a man of suffering and
>   acquainted with infirmity;
> and as one from whom others hide their faces he was despised, and we
>   held him of no account.
> Surely he has borne our infirmities and carried our diseases;
> yet we accounted *him* stricken, struck down by God, and afflicted.
> But he was wounded for our transgressions, crushed for our iniquities;
> upon him was the punishment that made us whole, and by his bruises we
>   are healed.
> All we like sheep have gone astray; we have all turned to our own way,
>   and the LORD has laid on him the iniquity of us all.
>
> He was oppressed, and he was afflicted, yet he did not open his mouth;
> like a lamb that is led to the slaughter, and like a sheep that before its
>   shearers is silent, so he did not open his mouth.
>
>   Isa. 52:13–53:7

Some of the early followers of Jesus had expected him to become king—after all, that is what the word "Messiah" meant—and thereafter to take over, kicking out the Romans and restoring the Jewish people to the prominence and prosperity that had once been theirs. When, instead, he was killed—and not just killed, but executed by the Romans in their characteristically cruel and humiliating manner, being nailed to a cross and left to die in public view—many of his followers shrugged their shoulders and went home: "I guess we were wrong." For others, however, the passages in Isaiah about the "servant of the LORD" seemed to offer a different interpretation of those same events. Jesus was indeed the long-anticipated Messiah people had spoken of, but way back in the time of Isaiah his role had been defined differently. The man whom Isaiah had described was not a king who would take the throne, but an apparently lowly citizen who was destined to suffer and be humiliated, in fact, to die on behalf of other people. Far from being contradicted by Scripture, then, the life of Jesus seemed to correspond exactly to Isaiah's description of the servant and his life (Matt. 8:17; 12:15–21; Luke 22:37; John 12:38; Acts 8:32–35; Rom. 15:21).[30]

For that reason, these passages from Isaiah, along with others from the Psalms and other biblical books, became exhibit A in the early days of the Christian movement. Only a purblind obscurantist, adherents argued, could fail to see that these passages confirmed the truth of Christianity. This argument, in turn, had a crucial effect on the place of Hebrew Scripture within the new faith. For it did not take long after Christianity's establishment for a few members of the new religion to wonder out loud why they were still reading the Bible of the Jews—were not its laws completely irrelevant to Christian belief and practice?* Such a view might indeed have won the day, were it not for such passages from Isaiah. How could Christianity ever part with such precious confirmation of its message? Indeed, the passages about the "servant of the LORD" opened the way for a deeper understanding of the entire relationship between the Old and New Testaments: what is stated openly in the New will always have been hinted at somewhere in the Old (*quod in vetere latet in novo patet*). For that reason, Hebrew Scripture was absolutely vital for Christians.

Today, as with so many other matters, modern scholars are somewhat skeptical about the identification of these references to the "servant of the LORD" with Jesus.[31] To begin with, there are really only four passages that discourse on the servant as an individual figure (42:1–4; 49:1–6; 50:4–9; 52:13–53:12); elsewhere in Isaiah, it is Israel itself that is consistently described as God's "servant." Indeed, in one of these four, it is difficult to tell whether the servant is an actual person or rather a sort of metaphorical representation of collective Israel:

[The servant says:] Listen, O coastlands, to me, and you faraway nations, give ear!
The LORD called me before I was born; while I was still in my mother's womb, He named me, and He made my mouth as sharp as a sword.
He sheltered me in the shadow of his hand, and He turned me into a polished arrow, hiding me in His quiver.

* This was the position of, for example, the Christian Marcion of Sinope (ca. 110–160 CE), ultimately condemned as a heretic and excommunicated in 144 CE.

Then He said to me, *"You are my servant, Israel,* in whom I will be
glorified."

Isa. 49:1–3

The issue of Isaiah's suffering servant is thus one that, like so many in this
book, divides today's readers of the Bible. If you believe that the Bible is often
cryptic, and that some words spoken in one historical context can actually be
understood to refer to another, much later time, then Isaiah may indeed be
referring to Jesus. But if not, then the "suffering servant" is just one more illusion of ancient interpreters that must be abandoned in the cold light of
modern scholarship.

More Than One Isaiah?

The book of Isaiah is long—sixty-six chapters in all. But no serious reader can
mistake a certain change in tone and content that occurs at the start of the
fortieth chapter. Much of the previous thirty-nine chapters could properly be
described as words of condemnation and reproach. Chapters 13–23 in particular are focused on various enemies of Israel—Babylonians, Assyrians and
Philistines, Moabites, Syrians, and Egyptians, Nubians, Edomites, and Tyri-
ans. Isaiah announces God's judgment against these nations—such "oracles
against the nations" were a standard sort of prophetic speech.[32] Isaiah also
has some scathing words for his fellow Judahites, as well as for the Israelites
to his north (chapters 28–29). Starting in chapter 40, however, all this harsh-
ness is forgotten. The tone is one of comfort and reconciliation—in fact, those
are the very first notes sounded in that chapter: "Comfort, O comfort my
people, says your God" (Isa. 40:1).

In stylistic terms, too, there is a noticeable change. From chapter 40
onward, Isaiah has an eerie quality not heard before, at once simple and
starkly visionary:[33]

A voice was saying, "Speak up!" but I said, "What can I say?
Humanity is only grass, and all its glories are like a little wildflower.
Grass dries up and the flower withers, for the breath of the LORD blows
   over them."
[*The voice replies:*] Yes, the people are grass, and the grass will dry and
   the flower will wither. But the word of our God will prevail forever.

Climb up the highest hill, you sentinel of Jerusalem, and shout, don't be
   afraid!
Tell the townships of Judah, "Look! Look over there! Your God is coming!"

Look, the LORD your God is coming in strength, with His powerful arm
    triumphant!
Look! He is bringing His bounty; the reward even goes before Him.
And He will guard His flock like a shepherd, in His own arms He will
    pick up the lambs,
and carry them next to His breast as He leads their mothers beside Him.

Isa. 40:6–11

Styles sometimes change in a single writer, depending on his mood or his message. But long ago (starting as far back as Abraham ibn Ezra, ca. 1092–1167),
scholars pointed to other, more easily pinpointed differences between the material found before chapter 40 and after it that might also explain this change in
style. Thus, the latter part of the book repeatedly refers to the people of Judah
having been exiled and now returning to their homeland—indeed, that is its
great theme, hinted at even in the passage cited above, where God is depicted as
going back with His "flock" to the townships of Judah.[34] This theme is not
found in the earlier part of the book, nor, frankly, should one expect it to be.
Although Assyria conquered and exiled the northern kingdom, Judah remained
secure during Isaiah's time. Why then, from chapter 40 onward, are the people
of Judah time and again said to be returning to their homeland?

Scholars knew perfectly well that there *was* a time when the inhabitants of
Judah had been exiled from their land: the time following the Babylonian
destruction of Jerusalem in 586 BCE. The exiles had been forced to remain in
Babylon until that country fell to the Persian army and Cyrus, the Persian
king, issued his famous edict (538 BCE) allowing the Jews to go back to
their old homeland. Now, the striking thing about the later chapters of Isaiah
is that they actually mention Cyrus by name—twice, in fact:

I am the LORD, who made all things, who alone stretched out the
    heavens,
who by Myself spread out the earth . . .
who says of Jerusalem, "It shall be inhabited," and of the cities of Judah,
    "They shall be rebuilt—I will raise up their ruins";
who says to the deep, "Be dry—I will dry up your rivers";
who says of Cyrus, "He is My shepherd, and he shall carry out all My
    purpose";
and who says of Jerusalem, "It shall be rebuilt," and of the temple,
    "Your foundation shall be laid."

Isa. 44:24–28

Thus says the LORD *to His anointed, to Cyrus,*
whose right hand I have grasped to subdue nations before him

and strip kings of their robes,
to open doors before him—and the gates shall not be closed . . .

Isa. 45:1

Of course, a prophet might theoretically foresee events centuries before they happen. Still, what sense did it make for Isaiah in the eighth century to be telling his contemporaries about a king who would not come along until two hundred years later—and to be telling them about him without ever explaining who this "Cyrus" might be, apparently assuming that people would just recognize the name?

Along with this, scholars observed another difference in chapters 40–66: their striking monotheism. As we have seen, Israel had not always believed that only one God exists: even in the ninth century, according to the prophet Elijah, people were "hopping from branch to branch" like birds, from the Baal branch to the God branch and back again. The same theme is continued explicitly into the eighth century in the writings of Hosea (3:1; 13:1; etc.) and others—nor were rival deities merely a problem in the north (on King Manasseh's polytheistic practices, see 2 Kings 21). What is more, even those prophets who urged exclusive loyalty to Israel's God were, when one examines their words carefully, preaching monolatry, not true monotheism.

All this changes in the later chapters of Isaiah. Here, in unmistakable terms, there is only one God—a huge, cosmic deity who bestrides the whole universe:

Who [like Him] has measured the oceans in the palm of his hand, or
    checked the heavens with his yardstick?
Who has held the earth's soil in his bushel, or weighed mountains on his
    scale, or the hills in a merchant's balance? . . .
The nations are a drop from the bucket, they weigh less than the dust on
    a scale; He brushes off islands like specks.
All of Lebanon won't do for kindling, nor its wildlife suffice on His altar.
All nations together are nothing for Him, insignificant, worth less than
    zero.
So to whom will you compare God? . . .

I am the LORD, and there is no other; there are no gods but Me.
I surround you, yet you do not know Me.
But let everyone know, from where the sun rises
to where it grows dark, that there is none but Me.
I am the LORD and no other exists—the maker of light and creator of
    darkness,
the bringer of weal and creator of woe—I, the LORD, make all these.

Isa. 40:12, 15–18; 45:5–7

Considering all such differences, many scholars began to consider the possibility that chapters 40–66 had actually been written some two hundred years *after* the eighth-century Isaiah—they must have been written by an anonymous Jew who lived precisely in the time of Cyrus, when the Babylonian exile was just coming to a close and when Israel's religion was fast becoming one of unequivocal monotheism. Of course, this idea was found to be disturbing to traditional Christian belief, since, as we have seen, passages from those chapters had played a crucial role in the New Testament and other early Christian writings; they seemed to offer no less than a way of interpreting Jesus' life and crucifixion as the fulfillment of a divine plan. If the author of chapters 40–66 was not the real Isaiah, the one who had been called on high to God's heavenly throne, but some unknown writer two centuries later whose prophetic credentials were thus a matter of speculation, what authority did his words have?

The question of the unity of the book of Isaiah was thus fought among scholars with a tenacity surpassed only by that accompanying the debate over the Pentateuch.[35] Although the case for more than one author was argued forcefully by the eminent eighteenth-century German critic J. G. Eichhorn, it was not until the latter part of the nineteenth century that this claim began to gain widespread acceptance (Charles A. Briggs, among others, supported it). By that time, the unknown author of chapters 40–66 had been given a scholarly name: Deutero-Isaiah (the "second Isaiah").

Indeed, scholars soon argued that there were more than merely two Isaiahs. The German critic Bernhard Duhm (1847–1928), Wellhausen's disciple and comrade in arms, published a highly influential commentary on the book of Isaiah in 1892. In it, he claimed that chapters 40–66 were actually the work of two different authors, Deutero-Isaiah, who lived during the Babylonian exile, and Trito-Isaiah, who was among those who returned to Zion after the exile was over. What is more, Duhm wrote, even chapters 1–39 were not the work of a single man, but the work of many different hands over the course of quite a few centuries.

A century of further research has modified some of these conclusions. Although the idea of a Trito-Isaiah won acceptance for a time, some skepticism about it had been expressed from the start, and a number of recent studies have strongly argued that the whole notion ought to be abandoned: Trito-Isaiah, they say, is probably just Deutero-Isaiah at a later stage of his life.[36] On the other hand, chapters 1–39 of Isaiah are now largely viewed as a complicated patchwork of material from different periods, with several clear subunits. The already mentioned section of oracles against foreign nations (chapters 13–23) seems to come from different periods after that of the Assyrian ascendancy. Chapters 24–27 are widely recognized as a separate unit, "the Isaiah apocalypse," whose date of composition is also uncertain but may tentatively be identified with the period of the Babylonian exile or that immediately following it. The focus of chapters 28–33 belongs, in the opinion of many scholars, back in the eighth century, but then things seesaw to a prophetic condemnation of Edom (chapters 34–35) which, scholars believe, might again best be dated to some time during or following the Babylonian exile. As for the closing chapters of First Isaiah, 36–39, these parallel the historical material presented in 2 Kings 18:13–20:19. Some scholars (though hardly all) believe that this historical summary was added to serve as a conclusion for an original book of Isaiah (which did not include chapters 40–66). What a mess!

Stages of Composition

As biblical criticism advanced in the twentieth century, scholars began looking at this situation afresh and asking themselves *why* the book of Isaiah was such a mess. If modern readers can see clearly that the last third of the book did not come from the original, eighth-century Isaiah, then surely the editor who first attached these later chapters to the earlier ones must have known this; so why did he do it? And if a modern scholar could identify chapter 6 as Isaiah's "call narrative"—a specific literary form, like the call of Moses on Mount Sinai (Exodus 3–4) or that of Samuel in the temple (1 Samuel 3), in which it is related how the prophet was first called to that office[37]—an ancient editor could scarcely be thought to have missed the same point. Why, then, is this narrative in chapter 6 and not at the very start of the book, where, from a chronological standpoint, it would seem to belong? In fact, how smart do you have to be to see that the earlier part of the book of Isaiah jumps from one chronological setting to another and then back to the first again?

As scholars considered the matter, they began focusing more and more on the anonymous editors or redactors who had arranged the material in the way they had. Surely, they must have been trying to make some point in chronologically mis-ordering things as well as in putting writings from the eighth and the sixth centuries under the same roof. In fact, even before turning to Isaiah, twentieth-century scholars had asked a similar set of questions about the Pentateuch: why is it arranged the way it is, and why does it contain all that it contains? Hermann Gunkel had argued that the earliest stages of what is now the Pentateuch included a number of short, originally independent stories that revolved around Israel's ancestors, stories that were probably passed on orally from generation to generation before being written down. Most of these, as we have seen, were less concerned with the actual people involved than with how this or that tribe or nation or place got its name, or with other etiological concerns. If so, critics now pointed out, when these little stories were eventually combined with others centering on the same ancestral figure, they became little life histories of the people involved and so acquired a certain "spin" that they had not necessarily had before. One story or incident was now read in the light of the others. In the next stage, these biographies of Abraham, Jacob, and other figures were joined into a continuous historical narrative and fitted into an overall chronological framework that further changed their meaning; the resultant text was later combined with yet other material and reedited, until finally the whole thing became the Pentateuch as we know it. At each stage in this process, the meaning of the individual components changed; each editor had a particular message or set of themes he was trying to get across. It is thus crucial, these scholars said, to try to trace the *stages of development* of books like the Pentateuch, isolating each phase in a book's composition, since the meaning of the text was not one thing, but the sum of everything it had meant on the way to acquiring its final form. The point was made by the German theologian Gerhard von Rad (1901–71):

> There is no doubt that the present Hexateuch [the Pentateuch plus Joshua] in its final form makes great demands on the understanding of every reader. Many ages, many men, many traditions and theologies, have constructed this massive work. Only someone who does not look superficially at the Hexateuch but reads it with a knowledge of its deep dimension will arrive at true understanding. Such a person will know that revelations and religious experiences of many ages are speaking from it. For no stage in this work's long period of growth is really obsolete; something of each phase has been conserved and passed on as enduring until the Hexateuch attained its final form.[38]

The same argument was made about the book of Isaiah.[39] Like the Pentateuch, the composition of the various parts of Isaiah covered a huge period. As we have seen, the earliest material went back to the 740s BCE, when the Assyrian king Tiglath-pileser III was preparing his rampage of conquest and the young Judean king Ahaz was trembling in his sandals. The next chronological swath belongs to the events of the Syro-Ephraimite crisis (734–732 BCE?), followed by the fall of the northern kingdom to Assyria (722 BCE) and, still later, Sennacherib's siege of Jerusalem and the disaster of 701. After this comes material from still later times—some from the seventh century, some from the Babylonian exile, some from the return of the exiles in the late sixth century, and some still later material, perhaps, scholars said, extending even to the third century BCE.

The older model of biblical scholarship would have sought to isolate the "authentic" words of Isaiah from everything else—this is essentially what the aforementioned Bernard Duhm did in his famous commentary of 1892. But various twentieth-century scholars have argued that the subsequent stages in the book's development are equally significant. After all, if the original Isaiah's words were preserved, these scholars argue, they were probably first saved by the prophet's own inner circle—disciples of some sort, perhaps even fellow prophets. Their decisions about how to edit and arrange his pronouncements ought not simply to be dismissed. Even if they added to their master's words here and there or preserved them in some order other than the strictly chronological, perhaps this was because they were seeking to transmit a particular message that they felt the prophet had intended for the coming generations. As for the still later material, some of it may have originated from people who were actually prophets themselves, recognized as such by their contemporaries, but whose words came to be incorporated, for one reason or another, in a book named for the prophet Isaiah.

This line of argument has been adopted in various forms by different contemporary scholars, including, notably, Yale's Brevard Childs.[40] The book of Isaiah, Childs notes, starts out with five chapters that, from a historian's point of view, probably postdate Isaiah's call in chapter 6.[41] Why not present things in chronological order? Chapter 1 is, according to Childs, a "theological summary of the message of the entire Isaianic corpus . . . using material from several periods of Isaiah's ministry." Much of it may have originated as late as the time of the Assyrian invasion of 701. If so, then, according to this approach, an editor must have intentionally moved this later material to the front of the book in order to open with a strong (and not particularly time-connected) message. The chapters that follow are likewise from diverse periods, but would have been assembled by the same editor to present a picture of chaos and sinfulness in Judah, setting the stage for Isaiah's plaint, "I am of impure lips, and I live among a people of impure lips." This same editor, according to this analysis, wished to present Isaiah's encounter with the seraphim not as his *initiation* as a prophet, but as a prophetic vision that led immediately into his warning to Ahaz in chapter 7 to avoid any entangling alliances, "If you don't stand tall, you won't stand at all."[42] Indeed, this argument, scholars say, applies as well to chapters 40–66. Deutero-Isaiah was not just tacked on to First Isaiah, but was tacked on because of an intricate web of correspondences between the two works.[43]

Perhaps. From our point of view, in any case, the argument is interesting because it raises once again the question of original meaning and what, consequently, "the text" really is. Is the meaning of the text always precisely what the person who originally wrote it intended it to mean? Doesn't the meaning sometimes change—not just because, as we saw with the Song of Songs, someone came up with a whole new way of interpreting the text, but sometimes because, at some later point, an editor came along and actually rearranged the words, now juxtaposing this original saying of Isaiah to that one in a new way, or adding to the original text some entirely new material that changed the sense of Isaiah's authentic words? This seems quite indisputable. But then, is it our job as readers to accept the text as it is now, or to restore it to some earlier, more pristine condition?

With regard to this question, Childs and his followers have stressed the importance of the final, "canonical shape" of the book. *The Bible,* after all, is not an abstract concept: it is a specific group of texts, canonized by ancient Jews and Christians and placed at the center of their religions. Modern readers, Childs and others assert, should thus pay special attention to this final form of the text; indeed, they should seek to interpret Isaiah in the light of all the other biblical books around it (including, for Christians, the New Testament as well). This does not mean, for Childs, forgetting everything scholars have discovered about how the text began or what stages of editing it went through; these too must be factored into any attempt to understand a text's meaning. But any such reckoning must ultimately consider the final form of the text in the light of the whole canon.

Other scholars prefer to deny the canonical form and surroundings of the book any special status. Instead, they say something similar to what von Rad said above in regard to the Pentateuch. What Isaiah *means* is neither what the earliest hypothetical form of the book meant (Isaiah's words as he uttered them), nor what the last, canonical form of the book seems to mean, but these and everything in between them. Such critics thus seek to read Isaiah, and most books of the Bible, in the same way an architect might look at an old New England house: "Oh I see! This central section was built in the 1780s, then someone added on that alcove in the middle of the nineteenth century; someone else put up those second-floor bedrooms still later, moving the kitchen to one of the old bedrooms; then the driveway was moved from the left to the right side of the lot, and the present garage was added about sixty years ago." Each stage of the text, in other words, was once a real building in which real people lived, and each stage thus must have had its own rationale and internal logic. Why should one pay special attention to the earliest recoverable form of the text—or, for that matter, to its final, canonical form? The book's message for us today, such critics argue, is nothing less than the sum total of all these earlier meanings.[44]

None of these approaches is without problems, however. If, for example, you set out after the "original meaning" of the eighth-century prophet Isaiah, then you have to start by separating his authentic words from everything else. (Here you will be dealing with a *very* small group of verses: most modern scholars agree that only a tiny fraction of the book of Isaiah could conceivably have been uttered by the original prophet himself.) In keeping with the "original meaning" approach, these authentic words ought also to be rearranged into their putative chronological order, since it was presumably some later editor, and not Isaiah, who changed their order and, in some measure, their meaning. But then what of all the surrounding, non-Isaiah texts? After all, it was an editor's decision to insert this foreign material into Isaiah's book—if you don't accept his *reordering* of the authentic parts, how can you accept his adding sentences or even whole chapters that were not Isaiah's own words? Throw them out!

But such a stance soon runs into trouble. Whether you are a Christian or a Jew, chapters 40–66 of Isaiah are highly significant for you. In them are numerous passages that describe God's undying love and care for Israel, as well as some possible references to messianic times, a detailed foretelling of the ingathering of Israel's exiles, and the Bible's most striking depictions of God as the master of all reality, the only God who exists. Who would say that these chapters ought to be thrown out? Still, they are evidently not the authentic words of the prophet Isaiah—in fact, we know nothing about their author, save that for centuries people erroneously believed he *was* Isaiah. Apparently, then, these chapters were included in the Bible under false pretenses.

So how, in the end, ought you to act with regard to chapters 40–66? Keeping them means declaring unimportant the true identity of their author—and thereby, it would appear, dismissing the whole matter of whether or not this author was a divinely inspired prophet. Instead, you seem to be agreeing to put your trust in what was essentially an editorial decision made by an unknown editor or editors. That certainly sounds bad. On the other hand, once you start questioning editorial decisions about Isaiah, all of Scripture is in jeopardy. After all, who decided what the Bible should consist of? Not Moses, not Isaiah—not anyone we know by name, in fact. The very idea of a Bible, along with its present table of contents, is essentially an editorial decision.[45] If you accept *that* decision as valid, then should you not also accept all of its particulars as valid—the arrangement and full contents of Isaiah, the borders of the Pentateuch, the inclusion of the Song of Songs, and so forth? Somehow, the very idea of the Bible seems to mean accepting the decisions of those who first came up with the idea.

When it comes down to cases, however, accepting the Bible as is sometimes requires us actually to *prefer* an editor's decision as to what the text should mean over and above what the original Isaiah himself had intended to say.[46] This is not a very comforting thought. As already noted, at least one or two of the book's editors would seem to have been out to deceive the public, since they apparently sought to pass off the words of Deutero-Isaiah and other writers as if they were the authentic words of the real Isaiah. Should such people really be granted more of a say in determining what a text means than the divinely inspired prophet? And so the argument goes, back and forth and back again.

Perhaps the best thing that exponents of the Bible-as-it-is can say is that the Bible's authority—and, consequently, its role in our lives today—does not derive strictly from the fact that its original authors were divinely guided prophets and sages, nor yet from the authority of its (perhaps divinely guided) editors, but from those ancient Jews and Christians who first accepted it as the guidebook of their faiths. Forget about "original meaning" and earlier stages! The book of Isaiah that they accepted and canonized is the present book of Isaiah. Any other, earlier form of the book is a hypothesis—who says it ever would have been part of anyone's Bible?

This approach dovetails somewhat with an argument that the philosopher Thomas Hobbes made a long time ago. He said that the phrase "the word of God" really has two different meanings as a description of the Bible: it means words spoken *by* God and (somewhat more broadly) words spoken *about* God. Thus, the Ten Commandments begin with the words "I am the LORD your God . . . ," and these words were presumably spoken by God Himself. But the sentence that precedes this, "Then God spoke all these words . . . ," are not, Hobbes said, God's own words but those of a human author, "him that wrote the holy History."[47] So why should anyone bother with anything but the "word of God" in the first, narrower sense? What authority do anonymous history writers, editors, and other mere humans have when it comes to Scripture?

Hobbes's answer was surprising. When people ask, "From whence [do] the Scriptures derive their authority?" he said, they are making a mistake if they think that this question addresses the divine origin of every word. "The question truly stated," Hobbes said, "is, *By what authority* [are] *they* [the words of Scripture] *made law?*"[48] In other words, it is not the divine origin of each and every word that gives Scripture its authority, but the fact that the Bible as we know it was at one point put forth as the law of the land (by Ezra, Hobbes believed) and accepted as such by Jews and, later, by Christians. Undoubtedly, it did contain some "words of God" in Hobbes's narrow sense, but that is not the source of Scripture's authority. Its authority derives from its having been accepted in its present form—words *of* and words *about* God all together—and given the status of Scripture, the great book of divine teaching.

The question that Hobbes did not address was how this book is to be read now. If, in our case, the decisive moment was not the one in which the historic Isaiah said this or Deutero-Isaiah said that, but the one in which the completed book of Isaiah was adopted as Scripture, then are we free to ignore what the book actually meant back then to those who adopted it? As one recent study has stressed, Jews and Christians in the late- and postbiblical period generally interpreted biblical prophecy in a way quite out of keeping with what modern scholars suppose to have been the original purpose and setting of the prophets themselves.[49] Thus, for ancient readers, chapters 6 and 7 of Isaiah were prized not so much for their legitimation of Isaiah as a prophet and of the advice he subsequently gave to Ahaz as for what they revealed about God and the ways of heaven—that, for example, God resides in a heavenly temple, where He is served and praised by the seraphim who say, "Holy, holy, holy." Indeed, the practical lesson imparted to those early readers by chapter 6 was, as we have seen, that people down here on earth ought to use these same words, "Holy, holy, holy," in praising Him in their own assemblies. By the same token, to these same readers the book's picture of a great ingathering of exiles was not taken as a reference to the immediate aftermath of the Babylonian exile (which, for them, was past history, and which in any case had failed to match the rhapsodic picture of Isaiah 60—city gates left open day and night for lack of marauders, nations and kings bringing their wealth and falling down before Jerusalem in abject servitude, Isa. 60:3, 6–7, 11–12, 18).[50] Instead, this and other chapters of Isaiah were understood as predicting some great redemption still in the future—an understanding amply documented by the writings of the ancient interpreters. As for the ideal king described by Isaiah, he must certainly have been connected to this future ingathering, so he too was understood as a prediction: a great Messiah would someday come and preside over the total reversal of Israel's ill-fortune.[51] If that was what the Bible was saying to those who adopted it as Scripture, are we really free to read it today in a way utterly out of keeping with what it meant at the decisive moment of its adoption? We may still call it the Bible, but if we accept the conclusions of modern biblical scholarship, it is not at all the same book! Or, to return to the issue of the Four Assumptions: if those same people who created the very *idea* of a Bible and determined its contents also read the book of Isaiah according to certain assumptions about *how* it means, then isn't there something a bit paradoxical about scholars who, while endorsing the present "canonical shape" of the book of Isaiah, reject utterly the unwritten set of instructions that, in the canonizers' view, came with it?

31

Jeremiah

JEREMIAH 1–2; 7; 15; 22; 25–26; 29; 31–32

AND 2 KINGS 24–25 AND LAMENTATIONS 1–5

Jeremiah Lamenting the Destruction of the Temple
by Rembrandt Harmensz van Rijn.

As with Isaiah, scholars are not sure how much of the book of Jeremiah was written by Jeremiah. Many think it is a matter of poetry and prose.

We have already examined some of the issues connected with that most mysterious figure, the biblical prophet. According to modern scholars, people somewhat analogous to biblical prophets seem to have existed elsewhere in the ancient Near East.[1] Nevertheless, a large gap still separates them from the great Israelite prophets of the eighth century on: for one reason or another, no attestations of any Mesopotamian Isaiah or Jeremiah have yet been discovered.[2] Scholars thus believe that prophecy developed in its own, fairly unique way in biblical Israel and—in part for the political reasons discussed earlier— became an important institution of society, at least to hear biblical authors tell it. But who *were* these men (and, apparently, women)? What made someone suddenly conceive of himself or herself as God's messenger?

People have sought to answer this question from biblical times on. In recent years, research has suggested that the prophet's own society had a definite role to play: its support was vital to the prophet.[3] That is probably why prophecy is not much of a factor today in most of the Western world: the office of prophet is largely discredited among us. A few people may still be spotted in Lafayette Park with signs saying, "The World Is Coming to an End," but very few of their fellow Washingtonians pay them any mind. Elsewhere on the globe, however, prophets are still a reality, expected and supported by their communities, and this support is crucial. The established niche of prophet in their societies has to be occupied by someone, so in each generation certain individuals arise to fill it.

Still, who decides who will be a prophet? For biblical Israel, there does not appear to have been one uniform answer to this question. In fact, in some ways, the Israelite prophet's situation might be compared to that of the poet. Nowadays, poets just start writing and hope that other people will like what they write. Nevertheless, we know that in far earlier times, being a poet was a profession mastered like any other—indeed sometimes a bard would learn his craft from his father or by being apprenticed, just as a carpenter or a cobbler might. Similarly, biblical prophets at some stage seem to have belonged to "bands" or guilds of prophets (see 1 Sam. 10:5–11; 19:20; 1 Kings 18:4; 19:1; 20:35; etc.), presumably learning their craft from older members; one rabbinic tradition, on the basis of 1 Sam. 10:13 and Amos 7:14, even suggests that the office was sometimes hereditary. At other times, however, it seems that prophets became prophets by being called—perhaps in this way they were a bit more analogous to poets in our own day. (Indeed, there is some evidence that the principal word for prophet in biblical Hebrew, *nabi'*, means "one who is called.")[4] Their being called to their task was not quite as diffuse as a modern poet's, however:[5] as we have seen, the heavenly voice that called Samuel was so real that he mistook it three times for the voice of his human employer, Eli. Similarly, Isaiah was called in the sense that he was, by his account, transported to God's heavenly sanctuary and purified there by the seraphim.* Elsewhere, however, biblical prophets do sometimes sound a bit more like poets as they reflect on their calling: "The Lord GOD has given me a skilled tongue, so that I might know how to sustain the weary with a word" (Isa. 50:4). Indeed, God complains to Ezekiel that people go to listen to him as if he were some sort of entertainer or poet:

> My people come and sit down before you to hear the things you have to say, but they do not *do* them. Their mouths may speak sweetly, but their minds are only on money. You—you are for them like a singer of love songs, with a beautiful voice and skilled at playing. They hear what you say, but they do not do it.
>
> Ezek. 33:31–32

Other things further strengthen this connection between prophets and poets. For example, prophets are sometimes said to have accompanied their prophecies with music, just like ancient Greek or Anglo-Saxon bards. Thus, 1 Sam. 10:5 mentions a "band of prophets coming down from the high place with harp, tambourine, flute, and lyre, prophesying." Similarly, the prophet Elisha summons a musician, "And when the musician played, the power of the LORD came upon him and he said, 'Thus says the LORD' " (2 Kings 3:16). Ancient Greek and Latin poets were, from their side of things, rather prophetic at times. The sibyls (female oracles) uttered prophecies in verse.

---

* Biblical books often stress that the prophet did not seek out the office. Thus, Moses is said to have offered one lame excuse after the next in trying to refuse God's summons, finally murmuring, "Please, Lord, send someone else!" (Exod. 4:13). Similarly, as just mentioned, Samuel was so little seeking the job that he mistook God's voice for Eli's. Isaiah thought his "impure lips" made him unfit. Apparently these "call narratives" all stressed the prophet's reluctance because no ancient Israelite would have wanted a self-promoter for the job. In this sense, the summons to be a prophet was not very different from the summons to be a *shofet* in the period of the Judges—witness in particular the "call" of Gideon (Judg. 6:11–22)—whereby an utterly unlikely candidate is transformed by the "spirit of the LORD" into a divine representative. (Or, as a modern scholar might prefer to say, the very idea of the *shofet* was a Deuteronomistic retrojection of the divinely selected leader—both prophet and king—back to the days before either of these offices was a fixture in Israelite society.)

What is more, even the ordinary classical poet's invocation of his muse announces his quasi-prophetic standing. The muse may have become conventional after a while, but at first she seems to have been a real divine being who was said to transmit her words to the poet: "Sing, goddess, of the wrath of Peleus' son Achilles . . ." Was poetic inspiration, especially back then, terribly different from prophetic inspiration? [6]

Considering all these matters together, many scholars have indeed come to think of Israel's prophets as poets, albeit of a very special variety. Biblical society had a ready-made niche for them, and in each generation new prophets arose to fill that niche just as poets do (or did) in ours: unlike poets, however, they did not seek to entertain or even make things up on their own, but to transmit to their listeners words that, however artfully arranged, had come to them from God.

Poetry and Prose

In fact, the similarity of prophets and poets was an idea that had been pursued at various earlier stages in the history of biblical interpretation. Particularly in the Renaissance, biblical prophets-as-poets were sometimes called to witness in defense of poetry against its critics. It was often said that prophets wrote their words in poetic meters, although the precise meters they used stubbornly resisted discovery.[7] In the seventeenth century, the English poet John Donne evoked this theme in one section of his well-known poem "The Litanie":

> The Eagle-sighted Prophets too,
> Which were the churches Organs, and did sound
>   That harmony, which made of two
> One law, and did unite, but not confound;
>   Those heavenly poëts which did see
>   Thy will, and it expresse
> In rhythmique feet, in common pray for mee,
> That I by them excuse not my excesse
> In seeking secrets, or Poëtiquenesse.*

The idea that biblical prophets were "heavenly poëts" seemed to acquire scientific confirmation in the research of one eighteenth-century scholar in par-

---

* **the churches Organs:** the prophets were the church's instruments, both in the musical sense and as the means (instruments) by which the church propagated its teachings; **which made of two** . . . that is, their prophecies united the Old and New Testaments without, however, confusing (**confound**ing) them; **in rhythmique feet,** without using a precise, classical-style meter.

ticular, Robert Lowth (1710–87). Lowth's aim was finally to demonstrate scientifically that Isaiah, Jeremiah, and other prophets wrote their words in meter, just like Homer or Virgil or Milton. True, Lowth said, given our ignorance of poetic practice in biblical times and the lamentable state of the biblical text itself (which, he felt, had been corrupted beyond repair over centuries of transmission), we will never be able to reconstruct the actual meters used by the ancient Israelites. Still, he remarked, there is one feature of biblical verse that might nonetheless prove that such meters existed. Poetic lines in Hebrew, he pointed out, consist largely of two brief, interrelated clauses of roughly equal length—and in this, as we have seen, he was right.[8]

_____, _____.
         Clause A   Clause B

This basic line form is found, for example, throughout the book of Proverbs as well as in the songs and prayers of the book of Psalms—the Bible's poetry par excellence. Thus, even if we do not know the precise meter, we can still use the presence of this two-part line to distinguish poetry from prose. (Scholars were later to conclude that there is no "precise meter," but Lowth did not know that.) Looking over the Bible as a whole, Lowth pointed out that this sentence form was as common in biblical prophecy as it was in the Psalms. Stylistically, he concluded, the prophets *were* poets; they wrote in verse.

He had a point. Even in English, it is easy to see how the lines from Isaiah cited in the last chapter are different from ordinary prose. They break into little, two-part sentences:

A voice was saying, "Speak up!" | but I said, "What can I say? ||
Humanity is only grass, | and all its glories are like a little wildflower.||
Grass dries up and the flower withers, | for the breath of the LORD blows over them." ||

Isa. 40:6–8

The same is true of Isaiah's sharp advice to King Ahaz and his court:

If you don't stand tall | you won't stand at all.||

(In Hebrew, Isaiah's two-part line is also strikingly assonantal: *'im lo' ta'aminu, ki lo' te'amenu.*) And it was not just a matter of formal devices like meter or assonance; the speech of prophets was often strikingly metaphorical:

Hear, O heavens, and listen, earth | for the LORD is speaking: ||
"I raised sons, brought them up | and they rebelled against Me.||

An ox knows [that is, obeys] its master | and an ass its owner's trough. ||
Israel does not know | My people does not begin to understand!" ||
Ah, sinful nation | people laden with wickedness ||
Offspring of evildoers | depraved children ||
They have left the LORD | spurned Israel's Holy One || and turned away. |||

Isa. 1:2–4

The people of Israel are like ungrateful sons; God "raised" them in two senses—not only as a father raises his children, but also in the sense that He "exalted" them (another sense of "raised" in Hebrew) and made them great ("made great" is, more literally, the verb translated above as "brought up"). Despite this, they have refused His authority. Isaiah then provides an insulting, and rather telling, analogy. Oxen and asses are frequently paired in biblical Hebrew, but the two animals are quite different in one respect, obedience. An ox *knows* his master in the sense that he generally obeys, lowering his neck to take on his master's yoke; an ass, on the other hand, is frequently disobedient, sometimes kicking or even lying down in the middle of the road and refusing to budge. When it comes to mealtime, however, even an ass heeds its owner's call, that is, it knows "its owner's trough." But Israel is worse even than an ass; it does not "know" God even in this second sense—that is, it does not realize Who supplies its food. In fact, it does not even begin to understand this fundamental truth.*

It was for such clever conceits, as well as because of Isaiah's strikingly consistent use of the two-part line seen above (especially in chapters 40–66), that Robert Lowth declared Isaiah "the most perfect model" of a poetic prophet, "at once elegant and sublime, forcible and ornamented." [9] But what of the biblical book that follows that of Isaiah, that of the prophet Jeremiah?

The Man from Anathoth

With the book of Jeremiah, the historical scene shifts to the early sixth century BCE, the last days of the southern kingdom's independence. The northern kingdom, Israel, was long gone, swept away by the Assyrians in the late eighth century BCE. But now a new foe arose to threaten the little kingdom of Judah: the Babylonians.

Babylon, the southern part of Mesopotamia (stretching roughly from today's Baghdad southward to the Persian Gulf), had previously been dominated by the Assyrians to their north, but in the late seventh century the southerners succeeded in driving out their oppressors. The Babylonians then

---

* The point is made even more sharply in Hebrew, where both "master" and "owner" can be used to refer to God.

pressed forward into Assyrian territory; the city of Asshur fell to them in 614 BCE and Nineveh in 612. Egypt, alarmed at Babylon's growing strength, had begun sending troops to reinforce the Assyrians in 616—to little avail. In 610 or 609,[10] the Babylonians defeated the combined Assyrian and Egyptian garrison at Harran and chased their armies into Syria. Finally, at the decisive battle of Carchemish in 605, the Babylonians routed the Egyptian forces. The Babylonian giant now shook itself off, stood up, and looked around; after that battle, it was the only great power left in the region.[11] The general who had led the Babylonians to success at Carchemish, Nebuchadnezzar, was crowned king in 604. He was to reign for the next four decades.

Like the other inhabitants of Judah, Jeremiah would watch these events to the east with growing alarm. But when, according to Jer. 1:1–10, he began his career as a prophet, life must have appeared far more tranquil. Born in Anathoth, a few miles from Jerusalem, Jeremiah was a priest by birth, perhaps a descendant of the famous Abiathar, who had served as David's high priest for a time before being exiled to Anathoth (1 Kings 2:26). No doubt a bright and promising young man, Jeremiah may have studied in his early years in Jerusalem itself; at any rate, he was never far from the capital and the corridors of power. Judah's ruler at the time was King Josiah, a decisive and powerful monarch who, as we have seen, ushered in an age of religious reform. Josiah's Reform was founded on the exclusive devotion to Israel's God, the centralization of all sacrifices in the Jerusalem temple, and the rooting out of anything that smacked of the worship of other gods. Under such a king, a man like Jeremiah, equally devoted to the same causes, could scarcely have anticipated a difficult future. Nevertheless, he reports that, at the time when he was summoned to be a prophet, he was—just like Isaiah, Samuel, and Moses before him—reluctant to take on the job.

> Now the word of the LORD came to me saying, "Before I formed you in the womb I knew you, and before you came out of your mother, I had consecrated you. I hereby appoint you to be a prophet to the nations." But I said, "Oh no, Lord GOD! I do not know how to make speeches—I am too young." But the LORD said to me, "Do not say, 'I am too young.' You will go wherever I send you, and you will say whatever I tell you to say. Do not be afraid of anyone; I will be with you to save you, says the LORD."
>
> Then the LORD put out His hand and touched my mouth; and the LORD said to me, "I hereby put My words in your mouth. See, I am appointing you today over nations and over kingdoms, to pluck up and to pull down, to destroy and to overthrow, to build and to plant."
>
> Jer. 1:3–10

The simplicity and directness of Jeremiah's call have long made it a favorite subject of writers and artists. God had assigned Jeremiah his mission even before he was born. To be told this in so many words was no doubt reassuring, but also troubling; now it was up to the young man to begin to carry out his divinely assigned task. According to God's words, two-thirds of Jeremiah's mission was to be negative, "to pluck up and to pull down, to destroy and to overthrow"—this would not be a happy time. But the last two verbs, "to build and to plant," at least held out some hope for the distant future.

Inspiring as it may be, some modern scholars are reluctant to attribute this passage (and, indeed, a good deal more in the book) to Jeremiah himself.[12] As noted earlier, "call narratives" eventually came to be conventional; people simply expected to be told that the prophet in question had not been a self-promoter, that, in fact, he had at first resisted God's call. More than one scholar has been struck by the similarities between this account of Jeremiah's call and other call narratives already seen. Thus, like Moses on Mount Horeb, Jeremiah objects to God's summons on the grounds that he is not a particularly good orator; Moses had told God that he was "heavy of speech," while Jeremiah here protests that he does not "know how to make speeches." Still more strikingly, the central gesture in Isaiah's call narrative, whereby one of the seraphim *touches his mouth* with a burning coal, is paralleled here by God's gesture: He "put out His hand and *touched my mouth*." These resemblances do not prove that the account of Jeremiah's call is inauthentic—indeed, God may have purposely touched Jeremiah's mouth precisely in order to make vivid his resemblance to his prophetic predecessor. But some modern scholars are suspicious, especially in view of the broader backdrop of current theories about the book as a whole.

Speaking in Prose

Almost as soon as modern scholars began to analyze the book of Jeremiah in detail, they became aware of a certain unevenness in the work. Sometimes the prophet spoke in the short, two-part sentences that are the mark of biblical poetry. At other times, however, his sentences were longer and syntactically more complicated—he sounded more like Moses in the book of Deuteronomy, addressing the people in highly rhetorical prose. Still other parts of the book make no pretense to being Jeremiah's own writings: they speak of him in the third person, and some of the things he is quoted as saying parallel Jeremiah's own words elsewhere in the book—almost as if someone who knew him was summarizing the highlights of Jeremiah's career. So how much of the book did he himself actually write?

Many scholars believed (and some still do) that poetry is an older form of expression than prose. This belief was largely an inheritance of nineteenth-century German Romanticism, in particular as articulated by the philosopher Johann Gottfried Herder (1744–1803), teacher of the great poet Goethe and himself the author of an influential book about the Bible, *The Spirit of Hebrew Poetry* (1782–83). Herder felt that poetry went back to "humanity's infancy" and was thus naturally emotional, sincere, a bit flighty at times, and frequently unrestrained. Prose, by contrast, was a more mature and sober form of expression; it represented a later stage of human development but lacked the vitality and energy of poetry. These generalizations seem somewhat silly today, but they exercised great influence on Herder's countrymen throughout the nineteenth century, especially German biblical scholars. The idea that the only authentic part of the book of Jeremiah consisted of its poetic oracles achieved its definitive form in another influential book by the commentator Bernhard Duhm, *Das Buch Jeremia* (1901).

Duhm divided the book into three classes of material: poetic prophecies, presumably going back to Jeremiah himself; sermonic first-person prose that at times resembles the style of Deuteronomy (and thus, presumably, not Jeremiah's own words, though perhaps based on some things he once said); and third-person narratives about Jeremiah, perhaps originally composed by Jeremiah's scribe, Baruch son of Neriah (mentioned in Jer. 32:12, 13, 16, and so forth). Surprisingly, this analysis of the material is still espoused by many scholarly treatments today,[13] although it is far from clear why the poetic passages have any more claim to authenticity than the prose. (Were later editors and interpolators incapable of writing Hebrew verse? Is the looser, semipoetic style of much of the "prose" an indication that Jeremiah could *not* have been its author?)[14] Before considering these questions, let us consider an example of each of the three kinds of writing identified by Duhm.

Jeremiah the Poet

> The word of the LORD came to me, saying: Go announce this to Jerusalem:
> Thus says the LORD:
> I remember [to your credit] your devotion, your love as a bride—
> how you followed Me into the wilderness, in a land not sown.
> Israel is holy to the LORD, the first fruits of His harvest.
> All who consume of it will be guilty; "Evil will find them!" says the LORD.
>
> Jer. 2:1–3

This is indeed a good example of the pithy, compressed style of Hebrew verse—a great deal is said in very few words. God begins by mentioning the period following the exodus, the time when He and Israel were first "married." "You were a devoted bride," He recalls, "following Me into the sandy wasteland after crossing the Red Sea. How did you know where your next meal would come from? Yet you followed Me." Thinking of this now, God says, "I chalk it up to your credit [more literally, it says, "I recall *for you* the devotion of your youth," but the "for you" really means "for your benefit now"].[15] Your youthful devotion to Me will stand you in good stead in time to come."

The next two lines are even more compressed (though Jeremiah's own listeners would certainly have understood them right away). As we have seen, the people of Israel were conventionally described as *holy* in the sense that they belonged to God. Indeed, as God's "firstborn" (Exod. 4:22), Israel was holy more precisely in the sense that the firstfruits of the harvest were holy—whatever is born first or harvested first was automatically God's property. But what, this passage asks, will this mean for Israel in practical terms? According to biblical law, someone who eats the firstfruits is essentially stealing from God (Exod. 23:19); even eating the tiniest bit of them was punished most severely. So, since Israel is holy in the same way, attacking her or taking even the slightest piece of her territory is also considered "eating" what is God's—God will surely punish anyone who tries!*

This is the poetic style at its best—clever, compact, easily remembered. One can imagine these lines being passed on by word of mouth throughout Judah: "Did you hear what the prophet said? Everything is going to be all right." It is difficult to guess when exactly Jeremiah might have uttered these reassuring words, but apparently they did not remain his message for long. As the Babylonian threat became increasingly palpable, what he had to say turned more and more somber.

Perhaps the best-known example of Jeremiah's "prose" is his so-called Temple Sermon, in which he denounces those who are still saying everything will be all right:

> The word that came to Jeremiah from the LORD: Stand at the gate of the LORD's house [that is, the Jerusalem temple] and declare there the following: Say, Hear the word of the LORD, all you people of Judah, you that enter these gates to bow down to the LORD. Thus says the LORD of hosts, the God of Israel: Mend your ways and your doings, and I will dwell with you in this place. But do not trust those lying words, 'The temple of the LORD, the temple of the LORD, the temple of the LORD is here.'[16]
>
> For if you indeed mend your ways and your doings, and if you indeed treat one another justly; if you do not oppress the foreigner, the orphan, and the widow, or shed innocent blood in this place; and if you do not follow other gods (which will only hurt you), then I will stay with you in this place, in the land that I gave to your fathers of old, forever and ever.

---

* Most modern translations of this passage read "Israel *was* holy to the LORD, the first-fruits of His harvest," and they likewise construe the other verbs in the past tense. In so doing, these translations seek to understand Jeremiah's words in the context of the somewhat gloomy passage that follows. But there is no reason, grammatical or otherwise, to read these as past-tense verbs: what Jeremiah is saying here is an altogether positive prophecy (and apparently intended to contrast with the next passage in the book).

But instead, you put your trust in lying words—and to no avail! Will you steal, murder, commit adultery, swear falsely, sacrifice to Baal, and go after other gods that you never paid mind to in the past—and then come and stand before Me in this house, which is called by My name, and say, "We are safe!" so as to keep on doing all these abominations? Has this house, which is called by My name, become a robbers' hangout for you? I too have been watching, says the LORD.

Just go to My place at Shiloh, where I once had established My name, and see what I did to it because of the wickedness of "My people," Israel. So now, since you have done all these things, says the LORD, and even though I have spoken to you time and again, you have not listened, and even though I have called you, you have not answered. Therefore I will do to the house that is called by My name, in which you trust, and to the place that I gave to you and to your fathers, exactly what I did to Shiloh. And then I will get rid of you, just as I got rid of all your brethren, the whole people of Ephraim.

Jer. 7:1–15

What Jeremiah says is rather the opposite of what Isaiah had said to his countrymen during the Syro-Ephraimite crisis. God is with us (that is, 'Immanu-El), Isaiah had said, dwelling in His temple in Jerusalem; He will not let it be captured by foreigners. This had apparently become the common wisdom among Jeremiah's contemporaries, and the drumbeat refrain that he cites— "The temple of the LORD, the temple of the LORD, the temple of the LORD is here"—had apparently put many people's minds at ease. But, Jeremiah tells them, the northern kingdom ("Ephraim") also had a temple of the LORD at Shiloh—and look at what happened to it, and to them! The same thing will happen to you if you do not start acting completely differently.

Even if the words are not arranged into pithy, two-part sentences, they are certainly quite memorable, and given the parallel account (to be examined presently) in Jeremiah 26, it is difficult to believe that the prophet himself did not say something very much like these things one day at the gates of the Jerusalem temple. Nevertheless, scholars point out that certain phrases—"the foreigner, the orphan, and the widow," [17] "follow other gods," "the land that I gave to your fathers of old," and "I establish[ed] My name"—are stereotypical expressions found frequently in the book of Deuteronomy and the Deuteronomistic history.* Unless Jeremiah was consciously alluding to Deuteronomy (but why just to Deuteronomy?) or had himself been particu-

* See, among many others in Deuteronomy alone, "the foreigner, the orphan, and the widow," Deut. 14:29; 16:11, 14; 24:19, 20, 21; etc.; "follow other gods," Deut. 11:28; 28:14; "the land that I gave to your fathers," Deut. 1:35; 7:8; 19:8 (and many more with "swore to/swore to give to your fathers"); "establish[ed] My name," Deut. 12:11; 14:23; 16:2, 6, 11; etc.

larly immersed in that book—perhaps as one of the Deuteronomistic historians—it is difficult to avoid the hypothesis, these scholars say, that his original
message was at some early point recast in the idiom of Deuteronomy.[18] If so,
then one has to regard this passage, for all its force, as something other than
the very words Jeremiah uttered, something other than what scholars sometimes call the prophet's *ipsissima verba.*[19]

In any case, the message that the real Jeremiah delivered could scarcely
have been less shocking than its Deuteronomistic reworking, at least judging
by the reaction of the temple officials and others who stood by while Jeremiah
spoke. That reaction is catalogued in the third sort of text distinguished by
scholars, the third-person narratives about Jeremiah.

> At the beginning of the reign of King Jehoiakim son of Josiah of Judah, this
> word came from the LORD: Thus says the LORD: Stand in the court of the
> LORD's house, and say everything I tell you to say; [say it] to everyone from
> the cities of Judah who comes to bow down in the house of the LORD; do
> not hold back a word. Perhaps they will listen and each will turn away
> from his wrongdoing; then I may change My mind about the punishment
> that I am planning to do to them because of their wickedness. So say to
> them: Thus says the LORD: "If you do not listen to Me and follow the teach-
> ings that I have given you, and listen to the words of my servants the
> prophets whom I send to you time and again—but you have not listened!—
> then I will make this house like Shiloh, and I will make this city a curse for
> all the nations of the earth."
>
> The priests and the prophets and all the people heard Jeremiah speaking
> these words in the house of the LORD. And when Jeremiah had finished
> speaking all that the LORD had commanded him to speak to all the people,
> then the priests and the prophets and all the people laid hold of him, saying,
> "You shall die! Why have you prophesied in the name of the LORD, saying,
> 'This house shall be like Shiloh, and this city shall be desolate, without
> inhabitant'?" And all the people gathered around Jeremiah in the house of
> the LORD.
>
> When the officials of Judah heard about this, they went up from the
> king's palace to the house of the LORD and sat in judgment at the entrance
> of the New Gate of the house of the LORD. The priests and the prophets
> said to the officials and to all the people, "This man deserves the sentence
> of death because he has prophesied against this city, as you heard with your
> own ears."
>
> Then Jeremiah spoke to all the officials and all the people, saying, "It was
> the LORD who sent me to prophesy against this house and this city [and say]
> all the words you heard. Now therefore mend your ways and your doings,
> and listen to the LORD your God, so that the LORD may change His mind
> about the punishment that He has decreed against you. As for me, I am in

your hands. Do to me whatever seems right and proper to you. But know that if you put me to death, you will bring [the crime of shedding] innocent blood upon yourselves and upon this city and its inhabitants, for in truth the LORD sent me to you to speak all these words to you."

Jer. 26:1–15

What shines through this account is the personal courage of the prophet. Anyone can prognosticate about the future, but saying *in the name of the LORD* that, unless things change, Jerusalem and its temple would be destroyed was considered to be an actual offense against the city and its inhabitants. Words spoken in God's name have consequences, as Jeremiah knew well. Surrounded by an angry mob, he nonetheless held his ground—and history would soon prove that his prophecy was correct.

As noted earlier, Duhm and later scholars have supposed that Baruch, Jeremiah's faithful secretary, was the one who composed such third-person accounts of Jeremiah's life. Lately, however, this contention has been questioned by scholars. Truly, there is no way to know for sure who wrote this or other biographical passages, or even if all were composed by the same person.[20] In this case, however, the description has a firsthand, eyewitness quality that is difficult to chalk up to fictional hagiography. It is also noteworthy that the brief summary of Jeremiah's address in this passage contains none of the expressions characteristic of Deuteronomy that were identified in Jeremiah 7. This may not prove anything, but it would certainly accord with the scholarly hypothesis that Jeremiah 7 is a reworking of the prophet's words.[21]

So what, according to most contemporary scholars, does the book of Jeremiah contain? Without necessarily endorsing Duhm's prose-versus-poetry analysis, most scholars agree that the book contains some passages that might credibly be identified as Jeremiah's own words, some other speeches attributed to him but quite possibly the product of Deuteronomistic revision, the third-person biographical material just seen, and, toward the end of the book, a number of twenty-twenty hindsight prophecies that skeptical scholars prefer to associate with the period of the return from Babylonian exile. In the scholarly consensus, then, the book of Jeremiah is a composite not terribly different from the book of Isaiah, although the material originated in a far more concentrated period of time.

The Real Jeremiah

This is not to say that the actual man Jeremiah and the events recounted in his book have altogether disappeared into a haze of scholarly skepticism. As a matter of fact, thanks to the work of archaeologists and ancient Near

Eastern historians, there is probably no period in biblical history better known or better documented than that of Jeremiah's own lifetime. Jeremiah's actual authorship of this or that passage may be in doubt, and some may even question his existence or importance, but, as we will see, a number of the historical events and incidental details included in the biblical account have been confirmed precisely by Babylonian records and other archaeological finds.

Jeremiah was still a young man when, according to the account in 2 Kings 22, the "scroll of the law" (consisting, modern scholars say, of the legal code of Deuteronomy) was found in the Jerusalem temple and brought to King Josiah. Jeremiah must have been as excited by this discovery as the king himself was*—and indeed, it may be that the prophet was thinking back to that day when he said later:

> When Your words were found, I devoured them, and Your words were a
>   joy to me—
> It delighted my heart to be called by Your name,§ O LORD God of Hosts.
>   Jer. 15:16

The sweeping nature of Josiah's reform and the decisiveness and heroism displayed by that charismatic king no doubt also filled Jeremiah with excitement. And yet, danger was never far from the Judean hills. In an apparently early prophecy, Jeremiah had a vision of "a bubbling cauldron whose front is tipped back from the north" (Jer. 1:13), ready at any moment to spill its contents southward. God then explained this vision to the prophet: "From the north will the evil burst forth, over all the land's inhabitants." (This prophecy may have referred to Babylon, even though it lay to Judah's east, not north. Directly between them was a formidable desert, so that would-be invaders from Mesopotamia would have to first go north and then swoop down southward.)²²

Of all the books attributed to biblical prophets, none tells the reader more about the prophet's own life, including his inner religious life, than Jeremiah. The first twenty chapters of the book are dotted with Jeremiah's own reflections on his experiences, particularly the pain and loneliness he sometimes felt because of his mission as God's messenger:

> I have not sat around and enjoyed life with the revelers. For fear of Your
> power, I have sat by myself; indignation is what You filled me with. But

---

* The priest who is said to have discovered the scroll was Hilkiah (2 Kings 22:8). It is not clear if this is the same Hilkiah who is listed as Jeremiah's own father (Jer. 1:1).

§ That is, as a member of the people of Israel, Jeremiah belongs to God (a frequent theme in Deuteronomy). For this expression, see Isa. 4:1.

why should my pain go on forever? Mortally stricken, my wound will not heal. You have been a failing spring for me, a source of water that ceases to flow.*

Jer. 15:17–18

Elsewhere he complains:

You tricked me, O LORD, and I was taken in; You really got the better of me.
So now I've become a joke; all day long, everyone laughs about me,
because every time I speak I end up railing; "Thieves! Robbers!" I yell.
Yes, "the word of the LORD has come to me"—for shame and embarrassment all day long.
But if I say, "I won't mention Him, I won't speak anymore in His name,"
then a fire burns in my heart, it rages inside my bones,
and I am too tired to hold it in; I just can't.

Jer. 20:7–9

These passages, taken from what are known as Jeremiah's "confessions," present the most vivid picture we have of what it felt like to be a biblical prophet.[23] They show Jeremiah at his most human—and his most vulnerable.

Jeremiah's prophetic activity continued and intensified as the political situation of his country became more and more precarious. Sandwiched between Egypt and Babylon, little Judah was buffeted by a series of upsets that followed the collapse of Assyrian military power and the subsequent rise of Babylon. The first big shock delivered to Judah was the sudden death of its beloved ruler: King Josiah was apparently killed in a battle against the Egyptian king Necho.[24] (According to the biblical account, Necho was on his way to fight on the side of the Assyrians against the Babylonians at Carchemish, 2 Kings 23:29–30). Jeremiah is said to have composed laments for Josiah's death (2 Chron. 35:25).

There followed a period of anxious waiting as the new Babylonian king, Nebuchadnezzar, sought to extend his power to the lands to his west. From his standpoint, Judah was just another ripe fruit waiting to be picked. He began, however, with Judah's northern neighbor Syria, which fell to the Babylonians in the last years of the seventh century BCE. Next came Ashkelon, on the Mediterranean coast to the west of Judah. Outflanked, Judah's king Jehoiakim had no choice but to bow his head and become a reluctant vassal of Nebuchadnezzar.

---

* Perhaps a "failing spring" (*akzab*) in the sense that what God has told Jeremiah did not always prove to be the truth but was a lie or disappointment (*kazab*); sometimes, indeed, no words flowed at all.

After three years, however, Jehoiakim made a tactical error. The Babylonian army failed in its campaign to subdue Egypt in 601 BCE, and this debacle seriously weakened Nebuchadnezzar; it took him two full years to rebuild his army.[25] In this situation of instability, serious political disturbances broke out within the Babylonian Empire, and these apparently emboldened Jehoiakim to declare Judah's independence from its Babylonian overlords and cast his lot instead with Egypt. At first the Babylonians ordered their proxies— Arameans, Moabites, Ammonites—to initiate raids into Judah (2 Kings 24:2). In 598 BCE, however, the now-reconstituted Babylonian army undertook a full-scale invasion of Judah.

The picture of Nebuchadnezzar that emerges from the various accounts of this and other invasions is of a brutal and pitiless tyrant. One precious record that has survived from his kingdom is the *Babylonian Chronicle,* which gives a terse account of the king's various conquests, frequently studded with boasting reports of his own rapacity and cruelty.[26] For example, the previously mentioned conquest of Ashkelon is narrated in these terms: "He marched on Ashkelon; he took it in the month of Kislev [November/December], seized its king, pillaged and [plu]ndered it. He reduced the city to a heap of rubble." [27] Similarly, about Nebuchadnezzar's invasion of Judah in 598 the *Babylonian Chronicle* writes:

> The seventh year, in the month of Kislev [=November/December], the king of Akkad [Nebuchadnezzar] mustered his troops, marched on the Hatti,* and set up his quarters facing the city of Yehud [Jerusalem]. In the month of Adar [March], the second day, he took the city and captured the king [Jehoiachin].§ He installed there a king of his choice [Zedekiah]. He colle[cted] its massive tribute and went back to Babylon.[28]

Included in this first shipment of spoils were, according to the biblical account, all the funds accumulated in the king's treasury as well as the monies of the temple and its golden ornaments and other valuables, plus "all the noble men, seven thousand of them, and a thousand craftsmen and smiths—all of them warriors and fighters" (2 Kings 24:16).

Zedekiah, newly installed as king by Nebuchadnezzar, at first had little choice but to do Babylon's bidding—and so he did. He was only slightly older than the previous monarch—twenty-one at the time of his accession—and, in addition to his own lack of experience, he suffered from a lack of competent advisors and administrators: most of them had been deported to Babylon. In

---

* A general name for Syria-Palestine.

§ King Jehoiakim had died (was assassinated?) before the Babylonians' reentry into the region, and his son, the eighteen-year-old Jehoiachin, took his place. Nebuchadnezzar then replaced Jehoiachin with the young king's uncle, Zedekiah.

any case, Zedekiah did his best to remain a faithful Babylonian vassal for some time. But then, heartened by troubles elsewhere in the Babylonian Empire (and probably egged on by Egypt), he revolted, apparently believing that Nebuchadnezzar's army would be unable to intervene with full force against him. This was a second, and still more disastrous, blunder for the Kingdom of Judah. Babylonian troops marched back into Judah in 588 BCE and prepared to take Jerusalem in what was to be a prolonged, and cruel, siege.

The Lachish Ostraca

In 1932, a team of British archaeologists began excavating the ancient city of Lachish (Tell ed-Duweir), southwest of Jerusalem. Today Lachish is a pile of stones, but in biblical times it was a fortified city of some importance. Among the things that the archaeologists discovered there was a cache of ostraca—pieces of broken pottery used for jotting down brief messages (potsherds provided a cheap and convenient writing surface). The ostraca were inscribed in biblical Hebrew, and a few of them appeared to be brief notes sent by a subordinate to "my lord Yaosh," who may have been the military commander at Lachish.[29] Although fragmentary and often hard to decipher, these ostraca seem in several places to refer to the progress of Nebuchadnezzar's invasion. Thus, at one point Letter 4 reports: "And may [my lord] know that we are watching for the signals of Lachish according to all the signs which my lord gave. For we do not see Azekah." Azekah was another fortress town about ten miles north of Lachish. What is interesting in this is that the book of Jeremiah itself reports that the prophet had spoken to King Zedekiah "when the army of the king of Babylon was fighting against Jerusalem and against all the cities of Judah that were left, *Lachish and Azekah*; for these were the only fortified cities of Judah that remained" (Jer. 34:7). It seems quite possible that Letter 4 was written at very much the same moment: the letter writer, at some remove from Lachish, was nervously waiting to see some sign of life from there. If he could no longer see anything coming from Azekah, perhaps that was because the Babylonians had already conquered it.[30]

Jerusalem was, inevitably, the Babylonians' main target. The Babylonians' tactics with regard to Judah's capital were altogether standard—they proceeded as any army would in attacking a well-stocked, walled town.[31] In such cases the attackers would begin by surrounding the town's outside walls, perhaps trying to smash through them, or the (often more vulnerable) main gates, with battering rams. Sometimes they would also seek to scale the walls with ladders, or else to dig their way into the city underneath the walls. But such tactics would not work with a city that was well defended and well prepared. Some cities, including Jerusalem, were protected by an inner as well as an outer wall; these were not easily breached.[32] The attackers would therefore concentrate on the main part of the conflict, the maintenance of a strict siege that would seal the city off from any contact with the outside world. Those behind the city walls might periodically try to attack the enemy soldiers from atop the city walls or through sorties, inflicting individual casualties. Apart from this, however, they had no choice but to stay where they were, surviving on stores of grain and other edibles that had been put aside beforehand. The war was thus basically a waiting game. The attackers were waiting until the city's food or water gave out, while the citizens hoped that the attackers' supply lines, or patience, would be exhausted first. Sometimes it went one way, sometimes the other.

A graphic picture of the Babylonians' siege of Jerusalem emerges from another biblical book, Lamentations. Although the book is traditionally ascribed to Jeremiah, modern scholars believe it may be the work of different hands. Its first four chapters describe life under the siege itself, while the fifth seems to reflect what happened immediately after the fall of the city. They present a striking picture of human suffering:

> My eyes have no more tears and my insides are like clay.
> My feelings are numb at my people's catastrophe,
> as little babies, infants, lie helpless in the streets.
> They whine to their mothers, "I'm hungry!" "Something to drink!"
> but they're left like the helpless corpses in the city streets,
> as they languish in their mothers' arms . . .
>
> Even jackals offer the breast to suckle their young,
> but not my people; they have turned crueler than an ostrich in the desert.
> From thirst, a baby's tongue is stuck to the roof of its mouth,
> and little children beg for bread, but no one gives them a crumb.
> People who once fed on dainties are wasting in the streets,
> and those who dressed in purple sift through garbage.
> This nation's sin must be greater than Sodom's,
> which was crushed in a flash, untouched by human hands.
> Her [Jerusalem's] rulers were purer than snow and whiter than milk,
> with limbs that were ruddy as coral, frames of sapphire.
> Now they are blacker than soot, unrecognized in the streets;
> their skin lies shriveled on their bones, dried up like wood.
> The ones killed in battle fared better than those killed by hunger:
> at least they oozed [blood] from wounds and not from [lack of] grain.
> Tenderhearted women boiled their children with their own hands.
> Then they ate them as food. [This] is my people's catastrophe.[33]
>
> Lam. 2:11–12; 4:2–10

The siege went into its second year and still the Jews held out. But finally hunger, thirst, and the crushing summer heat overcame them. Jerusalem's walls were at last breached; the end was now in sight. King Zedekiah and his troops took flight by night through the broken walls, hoping to find safety in the desert or, perhaps, on the far side of the Jordan.

> But the Babylonian army went after the king in pursuit and caught up with him at the plains of Jericho; all his troops scattered and left him. They seized the king and brought him to the king of Babylon at Ribla; there they put him on trial. Then they slaughtered Zedekiah's children in front of him, and they put out Zedekiah's eyes and bound him in bronze chains and took him to Babylon.
>
> 2 Kings 25:5–7

Back in Jerusalem, the Babylonians inflicted similar revenge on the city itself, burning down the great temple as well as the private houses in the city, then tearing apart sections of the city walls stone by stone so that no one could dwell there in safety again. Those inhabitants who had not been killed were dragged off as prisoners and marched across the desert to Babylon.

The Burnt Bullae

Among the victims of the Babylonian attack was a small building in Jerusalem that had been used for (among other things) the storing of official documents.[34] When the Babylonians put the building to the torch, all the documents went up in smoke. But the fire actually did some good, at least from the standpoint of biblical scholars.

In Jeremiah's day, a set procedure existed for handling property deeds and other official documents written on papyrus or parchment. The document would be signed by the relevant parties; then it would be rolled up and tightly bound with twine. Next, a wet lump of clay, shaped into a small, almost flat cylinder, would be stuck onto the twine. One or more officials would then sink his seal or signet into the wet clay. The seal usually consisted of the official's first and last names. After the clay had dried, the text could not be reopened or tampered with without breaking or severing the lump of clay and the seals it bore. In this way, the authenticity of a document could be guaranteed for a long period of time. (The book of Jeremiah contains a description of just this procedure, Jer. 32:9–12.)

Archaeologists have often found such clay seals, or *bullae,* but because the dried clay is easily damaged, many of them have proven to be unreadable. That was not the case with the bullae in the Jerusalem house, however. The same fire that burned up the documents themselves also fired the dry clay that sealed them, just as if a potter had put them in a hot oven to harden. When archaeologists excavating the City of David in the 1980s dug down to the level of the Babylonian destruction and began to sift through the rubble, they discovered more than fifty little round seals, most of them perfectly preserved thanks to the attackers' inferno. What a find! Almost exactly 2,500 years earlier, the temple officials of Jeremiah's day had affixed their seals to documents and deposited them in this house—and now here were their first and last names for all to see. It was as if the archaeologists had discovered Jeremiah's personal address book.

One seal in particular caught the archaeologists' eye. It bore the name Gemaryahu ben Shaphan. Readers familiar with the book of Jeremiah knew that name—it belonged to a high official (called "the secretary") in Jeremiah's time.

> In the fifth year of King Jehoiakim son of Josiah of Judah, in the ninth month, all the people in Jerusalem and all the people who came from the towns of Judah to Jerusalem proclaimed a fast before the LORD. Then, in the hearing of all the people, Baruch read the words of Jeremiah from the scroll, in the house of the LORD, in the chamber of *Gemariah* * *son of Shaphan* the secretary, which was in the upper court, at the entry of the New Gate of the LORD's house. When Micaiah, son of *Gemariah son of Shaphan,* heard all the words of the LORD from the scroll, he went down to the king's house, into the secretary's chamber; and all the officials were sitting there: Elishama the secretary, Delaiah son of Shemaiah, Elnathan son of Achbor, *Gemariah son of Shaphan,* Zedekiah son of Hananiah, and all the officials . . .
>
> Jer. 36:9–12

Some of the other bullae were also connected with names known from elsewhere in the Bible—there was even one seal that the archaeologists first believed to be that of Baruch, Jeremiah's own secretary—but these identifications have subsequently been disputed.[35] Whatever the case with Baruch, finding Gemaryahu's seal had an electric effect on scholars; it was a solid point of connection between a biblical text preserved for more than two millennia and a piece of clay dug out of the ruins of Jerusalem in the late twentieth century.

Seventy Years

Jeremiah lived through his people's most traumatic hour. From the heyday of Josiah's reform and the heady feeling of new possibilities that accompanied it,

---

* Many Bible translations use the abbreviated form *Gemariah* for *Gemaryahu,* but the latter is what actually appears in the Hebrew Bible—and on the seal.

he witnessed his country's rapid spiral into disaster. Josiah died; his son Jehoiakim simply could not fill his shoes. Jeremiah openly reproved all the country's officials for their blundering policies, he but saved his sharpest words for the king himself:

> Woe to him who builds his up lodgings through unrighteousness, and his
>   upper rooms through injustice;
> who makes a worker work for free or does not give him proper wages;
> who says, "Let me make myself a fancy palace, with wide rooms at the
>   top,"
> with windows and cedar paneling, and painted all vermilion.
>
> Are you king because you're the best at cedar paneling?
> Didn't your father [merely] eat and drink, and then "make merry" by
>   acting justly and fairly?
> He would take up the cause of the poor and the downtrodden—*that* was
>   what made him merry.
> Is that not how to obey Me, says the LORD?
> But you—all you care about is money,
> and shedding innocent blood, and oppression and violence.
> Therefore, thus says the LORD concerning King Jehoiakim son of Josiah
>   of Judah:
> No one will mourn him—"Too bad, O brother, O sister!"
> No one will mourn him—"Too bad, your lordship, your honor!"
> He'll be buried like a donkey, dragged away and thrown out past the
>   gates of Jerusalem.[36]
>
> Jer. 22:13–19

But if most of Jeremiah's prophetic mission was to denounce unrighteousness and people's blind faith that, despite their sins, Jerusalem would survive, he also struck a more positive note, especially as the end came closer. In the year that Nebuchadnezzar ascended the throne, Jeremiah is said to have foreseen not only the fall of Jerusalem, but the fall of Babylon seventy years later—at which time the people would return to Judah:

> Therefore thus says the LORD of hosts: Because you have not obeyed My words, I am going to send for and fetch all the peoples of the north, says the LORD, including My servant, King Nebuchadrezzar of Babylon, and I will have them attack this land and its inhabitants and all these nations around it; I will wipe them out, and make them into a ruin and a thing of dread, an everlasting desolation. And I will banish from them the cries of celebration and shouts of gladness, the voice of the bridegroom and the voice of the bride, the grinding of the millstones and the light of the lamp. This whole

land will become a desolate ruin, and these nations will serve the king of Babylon seventy years.

But after seventy years are over, I will punish the king of Babylon and that nation, the land of the Chaldeans, for their sin, says the LORD. I will make it into an everlasting waste. I will bring down upon that land everything that I have decreed for it, everything that is written in this book, which Jeremiah prophesied against all the nations.

Jer. 25:8–13

The number seventy is something of a conventional number in Hebrew and other Semitic languages, a bit like one hundred in English: it means "a lot." Thus, Jeremiah probably did not intend to make an accurate prediction of the duration of Babylonian ascendancy—if he even said something like the above (which some scholars doubt).[37] Indeed, he may have been influenced by external traditions; scholars have long noted a temple inscription of the Assyrian king Esarhaddon (681–669 BCE) that speaks of "seventy years as the duration of its [Babylon's] desolation [that is, punishment]."[38] Whatever the case, however, "seventy years" was not far off the mark: Nebuchadnezzar began his depredations in 605 BCE and the Babylonian empire fell sixty-six years later, in 539 BCE.

Indeed, the same prediction of seventy years appears a bit later. After they had reduced Jerusalem to a smoldering ruin, the Babylonians rounded up most of the city's inhabitants and deported them back to Babylon. Jeremiah (who, by the biblical account, escaped to Egypt) is then said to have addressed a letter to the Jewish exiles in Babylon, urging them to hunker down and wait out their punishment, whose end, he said, was seventy years off. (Again, scholars doubt that Jeremiah himself wrote this part of the book—many believe it was composed toward the end of the exile or later.)

Thus says the LORD of hosts, the God of Israel, to all the exiles whom I have sent into exile from Jerusalem to Babylon: Build houses and live in them; plant gardens and eat what they produce. Take wives and have sons and daughters; take wives for your sons, and give your daughters in marriage, that they may bear sons and daughters; multiply there, and do not decrease . . .

For thus says the LORD: Only when Babylon's seventy years are completed will I visit you, and I will fulfill for you My promise and bring you back to this place. For surely I know the plans I have for you, says the LORD, plans for your welfare and not for harm, to give you a future with hope. Then when you call upon Me and come and pray to Me, I will hear you. When you search for Me, you will find Me; if you seek Me with all your heart, I will let you find me, says the LORD, and I will restore your fortunes and gather you from all the nations and all the places where I have driven

you, says the LORD, and I will bring you back to the place from which I sent
you into exile.

                                                                    Jer. 29:4–14

Whenever it was written, this passage seems to sum up well the combination
of resignation and hopefulness that must have characterized the Jews' experience of exile in Babylon. For more or less seventy years they survived
there, doing their best to pursue everyday life in a foreign and unfriendly environment, all the while waiting for the day when their fortunes might change.
That day came in 539 BCE. The Babylonian Empire collapsed, surrendering to
the leader of the victorious Persian forces, Cyrus the Great. Cyrus subsequently issued a decree allowing the Jews to return to their homeland of
Judah (Ezra 1:2–4; 6:3–5), which, however, was not to regain its former status as an independent kingdom. Instead, it would henceforth be a (largely
insignificant) western province in the vast Persian Empire.[39]

The New Covenant

Looking back on all that had happened to them in less than a century, many
Jews must have struggled to understand how they could have fallen so far so
fast, from the optimism of Josiah's reign to the vassalage of his successors,
and then on to conquest and exile. Some, no doubt, understood these events
simply in terms of realpolitik: the great empires were simply stronger than
any opposition the Judeans could muster. But those who finished off the
Deuteronomistic History sought to explain the same events theologically:
after all, God had made an agreement, a covenant, with the people of Israel
way back at Mount Sinai. If, in the eighth century BCE, the northern tribes
had been punished because of the sin of Jeroboam (his establishment of the
golden bull statues at Dan and Bethel), a corresponding violation of the
covenant must have been responsible for Judah's downfall in the sixth century. It was not hard to find. While Josiah had been an exemplary king, the
same could hardly be said of his father, Manasseh. Manasseh reigned for an
extraordinarily long period, fifty-five years, and from the standpoint of the
Deuteronomistic history, this had been a horrible period: Manasseh built
altars to Baal and put an image of Asherah in the Jerusalem temple, as well as
indulging in child sacrifice, magical divinations, and other forbidden practices
(2 Kings 21:3–9). As a result, according to the biblical account, God resolved
to punish Judah: "I will cast off the remnant of My possession and hand them
over to their enemies" (2 Kings 21:14). Even all of Josiah's subsequent good
deeds were not sufficient to reverse this divine decree. In short, it was the sin
of Manasseh, his violation of the stipulations of God's original covenant, that
brought about Judah's downfall.

Once an agreement is broken, is it over forever? To this question the book of Jeremiah provides a memorable answer.

> The days are coming, says the LORD, when I will make a new covenant with the house of Israel and the house of Judah. It will not be like the covenant that I made with their fathers when I took them by the hand to lead them out of the land of Egypt—they broke that covenant, so I rejected them, says the LORD. But such is the covenant that I will make with the house of Israel after that time, says the LORD: I will put my Torah* inside them, I will write it on their very hearts: I will be their God, and they will be My people. No longer will they need to teach one another or say one to the other, "Be obedient to the LORD," for they shall all be obedient to Me, from the least of them to the greatest, says the LORD; then I will forgive their iniquity, and remember their sin no more.[40]
>
> Jer. 31:31–34

In these simple words, God promised that His pact with His people was not over after all. Israel had been severely punished with destruction and with exile. But indeed, after the predicted seventy years were over, the people were to return to their ancient homeland, Jerusalem and environs, and resume life as before. In terms of actual *content,* the new covenant God promised here does not seem to be any different from the old one; the difference lies in its observance.[41] In time to come, God promises, obedience to God's laws will not be externally imposed, and no one will have to ask his or her neighbor what the Torah calls upon people to do. Instead, each person will know the laws and seek to do them, since the Torah will be written "on their very hearts."

This passage bespeaks one of the most characteristic features of the religion of Judaism. The idea that it is incumbent on the whole society to learn and obey the Torah's ordinances—that indeed, the renewal of God's covenant and His future protection of Israel would depend on the people scrupulously obeying God's laws—meant that attention would henceforth be focused as never before on the proper interpretation and inculcation of those laws within the general population. Still more important, seeking to carry out God's ordinances in all their particulars was to become something like a form of worship in itself. Of course, this is not the only, or the earliest, biblical evidence of such a turn. All the exhortations of Deuteronomy to keep "this Torah" or "these laws and statutes," indeed, all the detailed legislation of that book as well as that found in Numbers, Leviticus, and Exodus, pointed in the

---

* "Torah" here does not, most scholars would point out, refer to the completed Pentateuch, but is a general term for divine instruction, as well as, more specifically, for the legal core of the book of Deuteronomy.

same direction. What this God demanded in particular was to live according to all the details of His law.

But that was not the only way of understanding the phrase "new covenant." When, four centuries after Jeremiah, the Jewish people found themselves divided into different groups and schools, one of these—the founders of the Dead Sea Scrolls community—saw Jeremiah's "new covenant" as a prophetic reference to their own group: since they alone had the proper understanding of God's laws, it was to them alone that the new covenant had been given:

> None of those who have been initiated into the covenant shall enter the Temple to light His altar in vain . . . They shall separate themselves from the "sons of the Pit" [that is, any Jews who were not members of the Dead Sea Scrolls community] and seal themselves off from the impure wealth of the wicked . . . [Instead, they shall] keep the sabbath day according to its [proper] interpretation, and the festivals and the fast day [that is, the Day of Atonement], according to the practices of those who entered the New Covenant in the land of Damascus.
>
> *Damascus Document* 6:11–19

Perhaps influenced by such thinking, the early Christians, too, came to see their new faith as the fulfillment of Jeremiah's words about a new covenant. This, as we have already glimpsed, was a great theme of Paul's letters: the old covenant, based on the observance of God's laws, was supplanted by a new covenant of divine grace. (For the phrase "new covenant," see 1 Cor. 11:25.) The same theme is taken up elsewhere:

> For if that first covenant had been faultless, there would have been no need to look for a second one. Yet He is finding fault with them when He says: "The days are surely coming, says the LORD, when I will establish a new covenant with the house of Israel and with the house of Judah . . ." In speaking of "a new covenant," He has made the first one obsolete. And what is obsolete and growing old will soon disappear.
>
> Heb. 8:7–13

Indeed, the canonical collections of Gospels and various epistles soon came to be called the New Testament, that is, the new covenant (the Greek word for a covenant or property agreement, *diathēkē,* also means "testament").

Textual Criticism

The Hebrew Bible was translated into Greek even before the end of the biblical period—first the Torah, in the third century BCE, and then, gradually, the remaining books. This Greek translation, known as the Septuagint, has survived from ancient times, since it soon became the official Bible of Greek-speaking Christians. From an early point, people were aware that the Greek version differed somewhat from the traditional Hebrew text of the Bible preserved by Jews. Mostly, the differences were a matter of a word or two, but sometimes they were much greater. In the case of the book of Jeremiah, the traditional Hebrew text is a full 12 percent longer than the Greek—a difference of some 2,700 words! What is more, the chapters are ordered differently: chapters 46–51 of the traditional Hebrew text are found in Greek following Jer. 25:13.[42]

What is one to make of such differences? For centuries, both Christians and Jews assumed that the Greek text, since it was a translation from the original Hebrew, had taken liberties here and there, skipping and adding and changing things around. The great champion of this view was Jerome, who was commissioned by Pope Damasus in 382–83 CE to produce a new Latin translation of the Bible. At first Jerome planned to use the Septuagint as the basis of his new version: he knew Greek well, so it would simply be a matter of turning the Greek text into polished, eloquent Latin (and Jerome was a great Latin stylist). But as he progressed he became convinced that only a direct translation from the Hebrew would do. Learning Hebrew was no easy task in those days—there were no textbooks or grammars or dictionaries. After a time Jerome went to Palestine itself, settling in Bethlehem in 386 and studying under one or more rabbinic teachers.[43]

He referred proudly to the translation he produced as the *Hebraica veritas,* the "Hebrew truth." His basic assumption—that the Hebrew text he had used was right and that the Septuagint was wrong—was shared by subsequent scholars for centuries and centuries. In the post-Reformation era, however, people began to question all sorts of assumptions about the Bible, including, prominently, the reliability of the traditional Hebrew text itself. Soon people were looking back to the Septuagint text, and the idea gradually sank in—though it was not widely understood, even among scholars, until the nineteenth century—that the Septuagint translators had not been overly free in their rendering. They simply had a different Hebrew original in front of them.

Sometimes, a difference of even a single letter can be crucial. Take, for example, the angel's words to Jacob after their night of fighting at the Jabbok ford:

"Your name will not be Jacob any longer, but Israel, since you have struggled with God and with men and have prevailed."

Gen. 32:38

What did the angel mean by saying, "You have struggled with God and with
men"? The "struggled with God" part is easy: it refers to Jacob's just concluded, night-long fight with the angel. (See above, chapter 7.) But what *men*
could the angel be referring to? Perhaps to himself. After all, he is identified
in the passage as a "man"; perhaps "with God and with men" was a kind of
combination phrase (hendiadys) summing up what the angel really was, a
divine humanoid, both God and man at the same time. If not, then perhaps
the angel was saying, "Jacob, you have had a hard life—you've had to leave
home, you've fought with your uncle Laban, and now you've fought all
night with me, and still you've always come out on top. Let your name
henceforth be Israel."

The Hebrew text underlying the Septuagint had one less letter, but this
changes the whole meaning. There, the angel's words are

"Your name will not be Jacob any longer, but Israel, since you have struggled with God, and with men you will prevail."

Gen. 32:38

The Hebrew text underlying the Septuagint lacked the letter *waw* (or *vav*) at
the start of the last Hebrew word. With it there, the verb is in the past tense,
"with men, and [you] have prevailed." Without it, the *and* disappears and the
verb is in the future, "with men you will prevail." If the latter is the right text,
then the "men" that the angel is talking about would seem to refer specifically
to Jacob's brother, Esau, who, Jacob had just heard the previous day, was
coming to meet him with a mini-army of four hundred men. What the angel
says to him is, in effect, "You've fought with me all night and won—why
should you be afraid of merely human opponents this afternoon?"

If one letter can make that kind of difference, what can one say about a
difference of 2,700 words? Is it even proper to say that the traditional
Hebrew version of Jeremiah is the same book as that underlying the Septuagint Jeremiah? And Jeremiah is not the only example, although it is the most
egregious. The Greek version of Job is also much shorter than the traditional
Hebrew version; chapters 4–6 of the book of Daniel are substantially different in the Septuagint; and the Septuagint version of the story of David and
Goliath (1 Samuel 17) is considerably shorter than the traditional Hebrew
version. In the last case it seems pretty clear that the Hebrew version was supplemented (rather than the Greek version having been condensed).

Since the discovery of the Dead Sea Scrolls in the late 1940s, scholars have
been able to compare the traditional Hebrew text preserved by Jews not only

with the Septuagint, but with the biblical manuscripts found among the scrolls. (Fragments from more than two hundred biblical manuscripts were found, although many of them consisted of only a few scraps or a fragmentary chapter or two.) The results have been surprising. In some respects, the traditional Hebrew text has proven to be remarkably similar to some of the Dead Sea Scrolls—virtually a word-for-word match. Equally surprising, however, was the discovery that some books—including Jeremiah—seem to have circulated in ancient times in two or more different "editions." Thus, one of the Dead Sea Scrolls manuscripts of Jeremiah is very close to the Septuagint Jeremiah, while at least two others substantially agree with the traditional Hebrew text. Did it bother people that there were two different versions in circulation? Apparently not, since both were found in the library of the same community. But *why* not? And how did the differences between the versions originate?

As biblical scholarship has developed over the past century, a small group of researchers has devoted itself to answering such questions; their field is known as the *textual criticism* of the Hebrew Bible. By comparing all the extant versions of the text—the best manuscript representatives of the traditional Hebrew text, numerous Septuagint manuscripts, the Dead Sea Scrolls biblical manuscripts, the ancient manuscript tradition of the Pentateuch preserved by the Samaritans, and yet others—they have tried to reconstruct, in verse after verse, how minute variants in wording might have come about. Sometimes, it turns out, a scribe simply omitted a word in the process of copying. This often happens when the scribe's eye accidentally jumps from the word or letter he was copying in one place to the same word or letter in another place. (By the same token, scribes sometimes accidentally copy the same word or letter twice, changing the meaning of the text.) But textual criticism has also revealed that the changes are not always accidental. Scribes sometimes deliberately inserted a letter, or a different word, or even a whole phrase, in order to alter the meaning.

In a case like that of the book of Jeremiah, scholars have built up a very complex picture of how the differences between the Greek and traditional Hebrew versions originated. Scribal errors account for some of the apparent omissions in the Greek text, while deliberate glosses and other expansions account for some of the Hebrew text's greater length. (For example: the scribe inserted a "thus says the LORD" here or there, or added the word "the prophet" to Jeremiah's name.)[44] Most scholars also agree that chapters 46–51 of the traditional Hebrew text had originally been located where they are in the Greek text, after Jer. 25:13. Apparently, then, it was a later Hebrew scribe or editor of the traditional Hebrew text who decided to move these "oracles against the nations" to the end of the book.

Such conclusions are particularly troubling to Christians who uphold the literal "inerrancy" of Scripture.[45] All the examples of scribal errors that scholars have assembled make it difficult to maintain that the Bible as we have it is absolutely error-free. More than that, however, textual scholarship has made some Christians ask why they should continue to give preference to the traditional Hebrew text. Just because Jerome thought it was a good idea? After all, if the first Christians mostly read and quoted the Bible in Greek, then shouldn't modern Christians be using a translation of the shorter, Septuagint Jeremiah—since that was the version found in the church's official Bible—rather than a translation based on the traditional Hebrew text? Or should we perhaps forget about both of these versions and try instead to restore the earliest form of Jeremiah that can be reconstructed from the various surviving versions—the putative ancestor of all the current Greek and Hebrew texts? Once again, the matter of "original meaning" raises its head. Which text is the right text—the one used now, the one used by the first Christians, the earliest putative form behind all attested texts, or perhaps only the *ipsissima verba* of the real Jeremiah?

32

Ezekiel

The Vision of Ezekiel by Raphael.

OTHERWORLDLINESS. "BLESSED FROM HIS PLACE."
FIGURES ON THE CHARIOTS. THE CALL OF EZEKIEL. THE LAWS
OF LEVITICUS. VICARIOUS PUNISHMENT. DRY BONES.
A DIFFERENT KIND OF PROPHECY.

Ezekiel saw the divine throne chariot as he stood among the Judean exiles in
Babylon. What was Israel's God doing there?

Ezekiel son of Buzi was a younger contemporary of Jeremiah and, like Jeremiah, a priest and prophet. But there the resemblance ends. What stands out
with Jeremiah is his human side; he is often passionate and always utterly
engaged with his fellow Judeans. "Hurry up," he tells them, "Change your
ways! Otherwise, all will be lost." Ezekiel is quite the opposite; otherworldly
and oddly detached, he is the recipient of strange visions and symbolic messages. His prophesying may have physically taken place in Babylon during the
exile, but the precise circumstances are often left vague. He seems to jump
inexplicably from place to place, and much of the time he appears to be
addressing no one in particular. True, his admonitions can be bitingly personal on occasion. But mostly, his gaze is turned upward, fixed on the divine
part of the divine-human axis. As for what people will do with his message,
he often sounds oddly indifferent: "I've done my part."

In Ezekiel's prophecies, two words in particular stand out. The first is *ben-*
adam, the term by which God most frequently addresses Ezekiel. Literally, it
means "son of man," but it might be better translated as "little man" or
"mere mortal."* No phrase could better bespeak an individual's smallness in
the presence of God's overwhelming and powerful being.[1] The other word,
less often noticed, is *ya'an*, "whereas" or "since"—usually followed by a
"therefore." Like any verbal tic, this one is significant. It is a formal-sound-
ing word (one might even say, a lawyer's kind of word). It seems to say that
everything is orderly and everything has an identifiable cause: even the chaos
of Jerusalem's collapse and the subsequent exile were not random events, but
the product of a single, powerful, divine will.

---

* The slight hint of condescension in these translations is meant to convey the tone
implied not only by the mere fact of a superhuman and immortal deity referring to His
addressee as a human or mortal, but moreover by the very form *ben-adam*. This sounds
like the standard patronymic or "last name" in Hebrew, "son-of-So-and-So." To call
someone by his patronymic alone—"son of Jesse," for example, instead of "David" or
"David son of Jesse"—was, as we have seen, a somewhat condescending, even insulting,
form of reference.

The Heavenly Throne

Ezekiel's most striking vision is also the first in the book.

In the thirtieth year, in the fourth month, on the fifth day of the month, as I was among the exiles by the river Chebar, the heavens opened and I saw visions of God. (On the fifth day of the month—it was the fifth year of the exile of King Jehoiachin—the word of the LORD came to the priest Ezekiel son of Buzi, in the land of the Chaldeans [Babylonians] by the river Chebar; and the hand of the LORD was on him there.)

I looked and saw a wind-storm coming in from the north: a huge cloud with flashing fire and a glow all around; and coming out of the fire, something that was the color of amber. And coming out of it [also] were the figures of four creatures. This is what they looked like: They seemed like humans, but each one had four faces; their legs went down straight, but their feet were calves' feet that sparkled like polished bronze. They had human arms under their wings on all four sides, and the wings and faces on the four sides were connected, one wing to the other, and they [the creatures] would not turn when they moved, but each could proceed in the direction of [any one of] its faces.

Their faces were like this: all four had a human face [in front] and a lion's face on the right side, and the face of an ox on the left side, and an eagle's face [in back]. Their faces and their wings were separated on top. Each [face] had the two connected wings and two [others] that covered their bodies; and each could proceed in the direction of [any one of] its faces, wherever the spirit might be to go, there they would go, and they would not turn when they moved . . .

As I was watching the creatures, I noticed that there was a wheel on the ground next to each of the four-faced creatures. The wheels seemed to be made out of something like beryl, and all four looked the same: they appeared to be made in such a way that there was one wheel within another. And when they moved, each could move in the direction of any of its four quadrants without having to be turned as they moved. Their rims were high and most frightening, since the rims of all four were covered over with eyes all around. When the creatures moved, the wheels would move along with them; and when the creatures were lifted up above the earth, the wheels would be lifted too. Wherever the spirit might be to go, there they would go, and the wheels would be lifted up next to them, since the creature's spirit was in the wheels. When they [the creatures] would move, [the wheels] would move too, and when these stopped, so would they; and when these were lifted above the earth, the wheels too would be lifted next to them, since the creature's spirit was in the wheels.

Above the heads of the creatures was some sort of an expanse, with the fearsome gleam of crystal stretching above their heads . . . And above the expanse over their heads was something like a throne, as if of sapphire; and seated above this likeness of a throne was what seemed to be a human form . . . There was a glow all around Him, like the look of a rainbow in a cloud on a rainy day; that was what the glow looked like all around; this was the appearance of the semblance of the LORD's glory. When I saw this, I fell on my face, and then I heard a voice speaking.

Ezek. 1:1–28

What did Ezekiel see? It seems to have been nothing less than God's own heavenly throne, the same throne that Isaiah had seen when God called him to be His messenger (Isaiah 6). But here the description is strikingly detailed: the throne depicted here was apparently movable, arriving in a cloud amidst a wind storm and supported by four creatures with wings and multiple faces, wheels and wheels-within-wheels—what did it all mean? From ancient times, readers have sensed a power, and a danger, in this passage. It has thus been, on the one hand, the point of departure for generations of mystics, who have scrutinized it in the hope of retracing Ezekiel's steps and finding their own path to the direct encounter with God's very being.[2] Precisely for that reason, however, Jewish law forbade the public teaching of Ezekiel's vision, and tradition even limited its study in private to the company of mature adults.[3] Its esoteric character notwithstanding, the passage has long been a central part of Ezekiel's image in popular culture. Many Americans remember the words of the old Negro spiritual:

> Ezekiel saw a wheel a-turning,
> Way in the middle of the air,
> A wheel within a wheel a-turning,
> Way in the middle of the air . . .

Having seen the very foundations of God's heavenly throne, Ezekiel is then formally commissioned as a prophet (Ezek. 1:28–3:11). At that point, his great vision ends—but with a sentence that proved as puzzling to ancient readers as all the rest:

> Then a spirit lifted me up and I heard behind me a great roaring sound, "Blessed is the LORD's glory from His place."

Ezek. 3:12

Who said these words that Ezekiel heard, and what for?

Even today, many of the details of Ezekiel's vision are as mysterious to interpreters as they were two and a half millennia ago. More than one modern reader has identified Ezekiel's vision as an encounter with aliens from outer space or a drug-induced hallucination, but the truth is that no one can say for sure what the prophet was describing or how his vision came about. This has not, however, stopped people from trying—starting with the Bible's most ancient interpreters.

Blessed from His Place

One important focus of interest for ancient interpreters was the last sentence cited, "Blessed is the LORD's glory from His (or its) place." Interpreters were drawn to it for the same reason that they were drawn to Isaiah's "Holy, holy, holy is the LORD of Hosts" (Isa. 6:3). They were eager to establish prayers and praises of God that would please Him, and they looked to the Bible for help in supplying just the right words. From the Isaiah passage it appeared that the angels—presumably on God's instructions—said "Holy, holy, holy" as they surrounded the divine throne; thus, one thing that humans could do was say these same words down here on earth, joining the angels, as it were, in God's favorite form of praise. By the same logic, "Blessed is the LORD's glory from His place" ought also to be said, since, according to Ezekiel, these words, too, were uttered around the divine throne. Indeed, these two biblical passages seemed to go together, since they both spoke specifically of God's "glory."[4]

It was not long, therefore, before ancient interpreters integrated the two into a single picture of the angels praising God in a kind of heavenly liturgy:

> Let us sanctify and praise You in keeping with the melodious song of the choir of heavenly seraphim, who triple their consecration to You, as was written through your prophet, "And each called to the other and said: Holy, holy, holy is the LORD of Hosts, the whole earth is full of His glory." Across from them they sing praises with the words, "Blessed is the LORD's glory from His place."
>
> *Kedushah* (Jewish daily prayer)

In reciting these two biblical verses together, in other words, human beings were simply repeating the two things that Scripture explicitly reported being said around God's heavenly throne. No less than "Holy, holy, holy," Ezekiel's "Blessed is the LORD's glory from His place" became a fixed part of Jewish prayers and has remained so to the present day.

But how exactly did the two verses fit together? As the above passage makes explicit (in the words "across from them"), it seemed to interpreters that there must have been two opposite choirs, one composed of seraphim in Isaiah 6, the other of the wheel angels (*ofanim*) described by Ezekiel. Not only were these two different groups, but they seemed to be praising in two quite different modes. In Isaiah, it will be recalled, the seraphim turn "one to the other," a gesture that suggested coordination and, hence, musical harmony. In Ezekiel, by contrast, the words come with "a great roaring sound." Interpreters thus saw these as contrasting sounds:

> They [the seraphim] lovingly give permission one to another to sanctify their Creator in *gentleness of spirit, in language pure and sacred melody,* all sing out in *harmonious* awe, "Holy, holy, holy is the LORD of Hosts, the whole earth is full of His glory."
>
> Thereupon, the wheel-angels and holy creatures *with a great roaring sound* lift themselves up across from the seraphim and say to them *in contrast*: "Blessed is the LORD's glory from His place."
>
> *Yotser 'Or* (Jewish morning prayer)

But what did the words "Blessed is the LORD's glory from His place" actually mean? This was far from clear. In the context of the above understanding it seemed to some as if this sentence might be some kind of a *response* to the preceding assertion of the seraphim, "the whole earth is full of His glory." That is, even if the whole world is full of God's glory, one might still think that there exists some specific place from which that glory emanates:

> And each called to the other and said: "Holy, holy, holy is the LORD of Hosts, the whole earth is full of His glory." [Indeed,] the world is full of His glory. [Still,] His servants [the angels] ask each other, "Where is the place [that is, the source] of His glory?" It is in response to these that they say the "Blessed" [part, namely]: "Blessed is the LORD's glory from His place."
>
> *Musaf Kedushah*

In this imagined context, "Blessed is the LORD's glory from His place" sounds a bit like a rebuke: the place of God's glory is His business alone—it is, after all, *His* place. If so, the implication would be that even inquiring angels are not to delve into such mysteries.[5]

A Movable Throne

In trying to understand the opening vision of the book of Ezekiel, modern scholars, as so often, seek to view things in terms of their historical setting—and, in this case, to connect that setting to the person of Ezekiel himself. Ezekiel was not just a priest, they point out, but most likely one of the elite

Zadokites. This priestly clan traced its lineage back to Zadok, whom Solomon had made his sole high priest after banishing Abiathar (1 Kings 2:27). Thereafter, it seems, the Zadokites ran the Jerusalem temple continuously, not just in Solomon's time, but for the next four hundred years, until the Babylonian exile. If Ezekiel was indeed a Zadokite, not only would that fit, scholars say, with what is known of his life history and with the closing vision of his book (chapters 40–48, focused on the Zadokites), but it would help explain his attitude toward the Jerusalem temple. Jeremiah may have seen the Babylonians' destruction of the temple as an event comparable to the earlier loss of the temple at Shiloh, but for Ezekiel, any such comparison was profoundly irrelevant and perhaps sacrilegious. The Jerusalem temple was, for Ezekiel, God's sole legitimate dwelling on earth; its destruction was thus nothing short of a cataclysm. How could He have allowed those blood-stained Babylonian boots to tramp unopposed in the very place of His earthly presence, the Holy of Holies?

Ezekiel's apparent answer is that God was no longer there at the time. He had left, ascending into the heavens on a movable throne chariot—the same chariot that Ezekiel sees in chapter 1—long before the actual Babylonian siege of Jerusalem began. (See also Ezekiel 10 and 11, which, in a flashback, describe God's departure from the temple.) That is why this God-bearing chariot could be seen by Ezekiel in Babylon, where he was "among the exiles by the river Chebar . . . in the fifth year of the exile of King Jehoiachin" (Ezek. 1:1–2), that is, in 593 BCE. Presumably, what happened was that Ezekiel, as a member of the elite, had been among the eight thousand Jews who were marched to Babylon by Nebuchadnezzar after his initial incursion into Jerusalem in 598 BCE. At some point thereafter, God abandoned His temple and ascended into heaven on His chariot, following this first wave of Jewish exiles to Babylon. Indeed, it seems likely to scholars that the wheels mentioned in Ezekiel's vision are precisely intended as an expression of mobility: God does not simply sit on a throne (as in Isaiah 6 and elsewhere), but on a throne *chariot,* one that moves through the air supported from underneath by four vaguely human-shaped, mythical beasts.

The Four Faces

Not long ago, archaeologists came upon an ancient pagan temple in 'Ein Dara', in modern Syria. The temple, which was perhaps built in the eighth century BCE, has shed some light on one aspect of Ezekiel's vision of God's throne chariot. In the excavated lower court, archaeologists unearthed the figures of a number of hybrid creatures—human bodies topped with the nonhuman heads of an eagle or a lion—plus an ox's head and body and a human figure with a human head.[6] These, it will be noticed, are precisely the same four creatures mentioned by Ezekiel in his vision, "all four had a *human* face [in front] and a *lion's* face on the right side, and the face of an *ox* on the left side, and an *eagle's* face [in back]." That these same four, and no others, should appear at 'Ein Dara' seems to scholars unlikely to be the product of coincidence. In addition, scholars have noted that these creatures all have upraised hands, as if they were supporting or carrying something—just as the four hybrid creatures in Ezekiel's vision were supporting God's throne chariot. How these similar elements might have entered into Ezekiel's vision is something of a mystery; as best anyone knows, he never was at 'Ein Dara', and in any case, the temple had been destroyed by the time of his birth. It was apparent—to these scholars, in any case—what Ezekiel *saw* was neither pure fancy nor extraterrestrial reality, but a vision rooted in a long-established ancient Near Eastern iconography (and not one exclusively associated with Israel's God!).

The words spoken at the end of Ezekiel's vision, "Blessed is the LORD's glory from His place," have also been investigated by modern scholars. In context, they seem somewhat problematic. To begin with, these words are not introduced as if they were a direct quote: Ezekiel does not say that someone *said* them, or even that they were said. On the contrary, the text simply says that he heard a "great roaring sound: 'Blessed is the LORD's glory from His place.'" This juxtaposition seems oddly abrupt.

Long ago it was remarked that the letters corresponding to our *K* and *M* are easily confused in the ancient (paleo-Hebrew) script of Ezekiel's time.

K, KH   ⤳

M   ⤳

Such a confusion, scholars say, is probably what gave rise to "Blessed is the LORD's glory from His place." For, if one replaces the *K* at the end of the first Hebrew word in this sentence with an *M*, it no longer means "blessed" (*barukh*) but "as it rose" (*berum*).[7] In context, this would seem to work much better. What Ezekiel now says is that, after having had this vision of the heavenly chariot, "a spirit lifted me up and I heard behind me a great roaring sound, *as the LORD's glory rose up from its place.*" What he heard was the roaring of the heavenly chariot as it departed; no words were spoken at all.

Thus, if scholars are right, then it would seem that the picture embodied in the Jewish prayers seen earlier—two choirs of angels, one singing, "Holy, holy, holy," the other intoning, "Blessed is the LORD's glory from His place"—really has nothing to do with Ezekiel's original vision. It derives from a scribe's confusion of two similarly shaped letters. Such a possibility raises yet another painful question for traditional faith, since these prayers are still said every day in synagogues around the world. But how can modern

Jews continue to praise God with these words if they are simply the result of an ancient copyist's error?

God's "Glory"

It should be clear, scholars also point out, that Ezekiel does not seem to share Deuteronomy's sense of God's remoteness and relative abstractness. For Ezekiel, as with the priestly texts of the Pentateuch, God has a definite, bodylike presence—precisely the sort of presence that would go with the whole idea of a temple, that is, a "house" in which a deity dwells. Thus, they say, Ezekiel would never ask the question posed by God in Deutero-Isaiah:

> The heavens are My throne, and the earth is but My little footstool.
> Where could you build a house for Me? In what place might My abode be?
>
> Isa. 66:1

The clear implication is: nowhere. God is much too huge to have any *true* abode on earth. (Similarly, as we have seen, in Deuteronomy the temple is the place where "I cause My name to dwell.") But for Ezekiel and the other priests, to say this was to deny the whole enterprise to which they devoted their lives, the serving of the actual being of God inside His holy temple through animal sacrifices, incense offerings, and other acts of devotion.

That is why, scholars say, Ezekiel speaks of God's *glory*. The word is somewhat misleading, since in English it often refers to visual phenomena. This sense is not entirely unknown in Hebrew either (see Isa. 60:1), but the Hebrew word *kabod* is most often associated with substance or weight (*kabed* means to "be heavy"). It is thus more appropriate to understand this word as designating some physical presence or manifestation of God—and so it is used, scholars say, specifically in priestly texts. Hence, Moses asks of God in Exod. 33:18 (a passage generally held to be of priestly origin), "Show me Your glory"—that is, let me actually catch sight of You. As was seen earlier, this is hardly a foreign way of conceiving of God in much of the biblical period, although it was eventually replaced by something closer to our current way of thinking of Him. Indeed, scholars note that Ezekiel's description is not fully anthropomorphic: on the throne chariot, for example, he sees only "what *seemed to be* a human form," and God's glory is hidden by a surrounding "glow." Still, this *glory* or physical presence moves from one place to another, from the Jerusalem temple into the skies over Babylon, and Ezekiel no doubt believed that, at some future point, the *glory* would return to Mount Zion.[8]

The Call of Ezekiel

Like other prophets, Ezekiel is summoned to act as God's messenger, but in this, too, there is something profoundly odd about what the Bible reports:

> He said to me: "Little man, stand up on your feet so I can speak to you. Then a spirit entered me while He was talking and stood me up on my feet, and I heard someone speaking to me, saying to me: Little man! I am sending you to the people of Israel, to the rebellious ones who have rebelled against Me; they and their fathers have disobeyed Me all along, to this very day. In fact, the sons—those to whom I am sending you—are impudent and stubborn-hearted. So say to them: 'Thus says the LORD God . . .' Then, whether they heed or refuse to heed (for they are a rebellious house), at least they will know that they had a prophet in their midst.
>
> "As for you, little man, do not be afraid of them, and do not be fearful of their words, though thistles and thorns surround you and you sit down among scorpions. Do not be afraid of their words, and do not lose your courage, for they are a rebellious house. But you will speak My words to them whether they heed or refuse to heed; for they are a rebellious house.
>
> "And you, little man, listen now to what I am telling you. Don't be rebellious like that rebellious house; open your mouth and eat what I am giving you."
>
> As I watched, a hand was stretched out to me holding a written scroll. He opened it in front of me; it was written on both the front side and on the back, and written on it were words of lamentation and mourning and woe.
>
> Then He said to me: "Little man, eat what is given to you; eat this scroll, and then go, speak to the house of Israel." So I opened my mouth, and He gave me the scroll to eat. He said to me: "Little man, eat this scroll that I give you and fill your stomach with it." So I ate it; and in my mouth it turned as sweet as honey.
>
> Ezek. 2:1–3:3

God's summons to Ezekiel is meant to sound a bit like that of a mother to her young son: "Be a good boy, eat this!" In this case, however, the one being so urged has cause for hesitation: the "food" in question looks doubly inedible. First of all, it consists of a rolled-up scroll, and if that isn't unappetizing enough, it is written on both sides with words of mourning and woe. Yet Ezekiel is quite the opposite of the rebellious Israelites to whom God is sending him. He obediently takes the scroll and starts to chew, and to his astonishment, it turns out to be as sweet as honey. The message embodied in this vision seems to be: although being My prophet does not look like it will be a happy mission, since what you will have to say is principally "lamentation and mourning and woe," try it nonetheless! Then you will see that, however sour the words you speak, being My emissary is indeed sweet.

In one respect, scholars say, this call narrative seems specifically crafted to evoke two others examined previously. Isaiah's *mouth* was touched by the burning coals, thereby becoming a worthy receptacle of God's words. Later, God actually put His words directly into Jeremiah's *mouth*. Now Ezekiel takes an entire scroll of God's words into his *mouth* and eats it. Indeed, for modern scholars, it seems as if the third prophet was quite consciously looking over his shoulder at the other two and, as it were, seeking to go them one better.[9] (In addition, scholars have noted that the central image in this passage seems likewise to evoke Jeremiah's previously cited assertion, "Your words were found *and I devoured them,*" Jer. 15:16). But altogether characteristic of Ezekiel is the striking "disconnect" here between God's message (sour words) and the messenger (to whom they taste sweet). What counts, Ezekiel says again and again in his book, is bringing God's words to the people; the fact that those words presage doom, or that the "rebellious house" to whom they are addressed will not care to heed them, seems to matter little or not at all to him. Elsewhere God tells him, "I have made you a sentinel for the house of Israel" (Ezek. 3:17). *Sentinel* is just right. His job is thus simply to report on what he sees, announcing the approaching doom like a city's watchman standing on the ramparts. Once he has discharged this duty, the sentinel is not to be responsible for what people do with his message: if they disobey, it is at their peril. And peril was indeed approaching: the Babylonians' military power seemed simply overwhelming. One way or another, it was simply a matter of time.

Ezekiel the Priest

As a member of the Zadokite clan of priests that ran the Jerusalem temple, Ezekiel naturally would have had a great interest in all the concerns that functioning priests had—ritual purity, maintenance of the temple, the correct offering of animal sacrifices, and so forth. But what has struck scholars is that these so-called ritual concerns are, in this prophet's world (as in some of the priestly parts of the Pentateuch), close neighbors of the most fundamental ethical norms. And so Ezekiel rebukes the people for their mistreatment of strangers or failure to honor their parents, but in the same breath he condemns them for ritual matters like not keeping the sabbath properly or contracting impurity through forbidden sexual unions. This might seem incongruous, but what strikes modern readers as the juxtaposition of two sets of quite different concerns was, for Ezekiel, the whole point. In the priestly world, a sin does not just go away or get forgotten.[10] It stuck to the sinner, who was condemned to carry it around everywhere until forgiveness could be obtained—just as cultic impurity was thought to cling to a person's body until he or she had undergone purification. Indeed, in its various aspects, guilt for wrongdoing is treated in priestly texts in a way altogether analogous to ritual impurity.[11]

Such a mingling of ritual and ethical prohibitions is a prominent feature, scholars have noted, of the Holiness Code of Leviticus 17–26. At times it seems as if Ezekiel is consciously thinking of sections of this code as he rebukes the people. Compare, for example:

> Father and mother are treated by you with contempt; among you, the stranger is oppressed, the widow and the orphan are taken advantage of. . . . One man commits abomination with his neighbor's wife, another man defiles his daughter-in-law with lewdness. . . .
>
> Ezek. 22:7, 11

> For every man who treats his father or his mother with contempt shall be put to death . . . A man who commits adultery with a married woman, with his neighbor's wife, shall be put to death—both the adulterer and the adulteress. . . . And a man who sleeps with his daughter-in-law, the two of them shall be put to death.
>
> Lev. 20:9–12

It is hardly surprising that Ezekiel should have known these prohibitions from the Holiness Code; he was, after all, a priest and these laws were the particular patrimony of the priesthood. Still, a further point has struck scholars with regard to Ezekiel 22 and similar passages. The prophet looks out at his contemporaries and sees . . . Scripture! That is, he rebukes his fellow citizens "by the book," echoing the exact language found in the Pentateuch. In this, some scholars say—as indeed in Ezekiel's account of his own call—we are witnessing the growing influence of an already established body of sacred *texts*. These texts, whenever they originated, were not understood to belong to some other age and circumstances. For Ezekiel and others, they were addressed to present reality, they told *us* what to do. Israel did not yet have a Bible as such, but at least for some Israelites, the holy words written down of old contained a message brimming with significance for their own day.

Deferred Punishment

Ezekiel's words of reproof were sometimes bitter: taking up an old image, he compared the people of Israel to a beautiful woman who had "played the harlot" (Ezek. 16:15), abandoning her true husband, God, to lie down with other gods. Had she forgotten all that He had done for her in the past? Israel's current punishment was thus deserved—and it was not, as some people maintained, a punishment incurred because of the sins of an earlier generation:

> The word of the LORD came to me: Why should you cite that [old] proverb in connection with the land of Israel, "When parents eat sour grapes, it's the children's teeth that hurt [that is, we all pay for our parents' sins]?" As I live, says the Lord GOD, this proverb shall no more be cited by you in Israel. The lives of everyone belong to Me, the parent's as much as the child's is mine: [therefore,] the one who sins is the one who will die. If a man is righteous and does what is right and just—if he does not eat upon the mountains or lift up his eyes to the idols of the house of Israel, does not defile his neighbor's wife or approach a woman during her menstrual period; if he does not oppress anyone, but restores to the debtor his pledge; if he has not acquired anything through theft, but gives his food to the hungry and covers the naked with a garment; if he does not take advance or accrued interest, abstains from wrongdoing [in court], dealing fairly [in disputes] between one man and another; [in short,] if he follows My statutes, and is careful to observe My ordinances, acting faithfully—then such a one is [judged] righteous; he shall surely live, says the Lord GOD.
>
> Ezek. 18:1–9

This passage is remarkable in part for the reason already seen: it is full of allusions to Scripture. Thus, eating "on the mountains" apparently refers to eating things sacrificed on the "high places," a practice forbidden in Deut. 12:2 and elsewhere; and lifting up one's eyes to idols is the omnipresent sin of idolatry. The other violations are mostly word-for-word quotations from Leviticus: see Lev. 18:19–20; 19:13, 15; 25:17, 36; 26:3. Beyond this point, however, is what this passage says about the idea of vicarious or deferred punishment, that is, the notion that people are sometimes punished for the sins of others, particularly their own forebears. This was a commonplace in the ancient Near East. How better to understand the suffering of apparently innocent people than to suppose that they were being punished for something that their parents, or grandparents, or still more remote ancestors, had done? It is apparently in this sense as well that God is described as "visiting the punishment of the parents on the children to the third and the fourth generation of those who reject Me" (Exod. 20:5). Indeed, the Deuteronomistic historian's idea that it was the "sin of Manasseh" (2 Kings 21:10–16), Josiah's *grandfather,* that caused the fall of Jerusalem in the generation after Josiah likewise presumes the idea of vicarious punishment (although Deut. 24:16 specifically rejected vicarious punishment, at least in human jurisprudence).

What Ezekiel asserts here is quite the opposite. It is not a matter of the parents "eating sour grapes," racking up a big tab of sins, and their sons paying the bill (see also Jer. 31:30).[12] God holds each person responsible for his or her own actions. Indeed, even the person who sins is not necessarily doomed:

> But if the wicked person turns away from all the sins he has committed and keeps all My statutes and does what is right and just, he will live; he will not die. None of the transgressions he has committed will be counted against him. By virtue of the righteousness that he has done, he will live. Do I take any pleasure in the death of the wicked? says the Lord GOD. Do I not instead [take pleasure] in his turning from his ways and living?
>
> Ezek. 18:21–23

Here truly was an important message of consolation for the exiled community—and a sharp break with an ancient conception of divine justice.

Dry Bones

The book of Ezekiel is set against the gloom of the Babylonian exile, yet it contains a dream: not only would the people one day return to Judah, but they would eventually be reunited with the long-lost northern tribes, exiled from Israel by the Assyrians some 150 years earlier. Reestablished in their ancient homeland, these tribes would join with Judah to resurrect the Davidic monarchy, and fortune would once again smile on Jacob's progeny. This dream was announced in different ways, but perhaps none so memorably as Ezekiel's vision of the valley of dry bones:

> The hand of the LORD came upon me, and He took me out by the spirit of the LORD and put me down in the midst of a valley that was full of bones. He led me all around them; there were a great many of them across the valley, and they were very dry. He said to me, "Little man, can these bones come back to life?" and I answered, "O Lord GOD, You are the one who knows." Then He said to me, "Prophesy over these bones, and say to them: O you dry bones, hear the word of the LORD. Thus says the Lord GOD to these bones: I will put breath into you so that you come back to life. Then I will put sinews on you and cover you over with flesh, and then spread skin all over you, and put breath inside of you, so that you come back to life. Then you will know that I am the LORD."
>
> I started prophesying as I had been told, but while I was prophesying, there was a sound, a whirring, and the bones came toward each other, one bone connecting another. Then I noticed that they had sinews on them, and flesh had formed on them, and skin spread over them; but there still was no breath inside them. Then He said to me, "Prophesy to the breath [or

wind].* Prophesy, little man, and say to the breath [wind]: Thus says the Lord GOD: From the four winds, O breath, come and breathe upon these, who were killed, so that they come back to life." I prophesied as He told me to do, and the breath went into them, and they came back to life and stood on their feet, a huge multitude.

Then He said to me, "Little man, these bones are the whole house of Israel. They are saying, 'Our bones are dried up, and our hope is lost; we are cut off completely.' So prophesy, and say to them: Thus says the Lord GOD: I will open your graves and lift you out of your graves, my people; and I will take you back to the land of Israel. And you will realize, my people, when I open your graves and lift you out of your graves, that I am the LORD. Then I will put My spirit inside you, and you will come back to life, and I will put you back on your own land. Then you will know that it is I, the LORD, who have spoken [that is, promised] and carried out," says the LORD.

Ezek. 37:1–14

When Ezekiel saw a valley full of bones, dried out by the sun and seeming beyond all hope of revivification, he understood the message: the bones represent the "whole house of Israel," those northern tribes that had been deported. They might appear dead now, and yet, God could and would bring them back to life.[13] North and south would once again be united, and a mighty empire would raise its head as in days of old. Indeed, it was not, Ezekiel said, just a matter of physical resuscitation, but of a changed spirit. Like the book of Jeremiah, Ezekiel said that God would make a new covenant with His people, and things would return to what they were before:

My servant David [that is, one of his descendants] will rule over them, and they will all have one shepherd. They will follow My rules and they will carefully carry out My laws. They will settle in the land that I gave to My servant Jacob, and in which your ancestors lived. They and their children and their children's children will live there forever, and My servant David will be their prince forever. Then I will make a covenant of peace with them. It will be an eternal covenant with them, and I will bless them and make them numerous, and I will set down My sanctuary in their midst forever. My dwelling place will be with theirs, and I will be their God, and they will be My people.

Ezek. 37:24–26

But it was never to be. Wherever the northern tribes had ended up, they never again returned to the Samarian hills. To this day, their fate is quite unknown.

---

* The same Hebrew word means "breath," "wind," and "spirit." All three meanings are evoked throughout this passage.

The Resurrection of the Dead

What happens to a person after death? The question has fascinated people from earliest times, and the peoples of the ancient Near East were no exception. The Egyptians had an elaborate picture of the realm of the dead, and, in a different way, so did the Mesopotamians. But ancient Israel, at least judging by the Hebrew Bible, had only a rather vague view of the subject. People were frequently said to "go down to Sheol," the underworld, but not much seems to have gone on once they got there. "The dead do not praise the LORD, none who go down to the Pit" (Ps. 115:17). Still, some biblical texts imply that the dead were not altogether dead. Saul summoned up Samuel from the grave, and biblical laws prohibiting the offering of sacrifices to or for the dead, necromancy, and similar practices all seem to indicate that a lively "cult of the dead" existed at times in Israel and environs. Archaeological evidence from the eastern Mediterranean has offered some confirmation for these conclusions.[14]

In late- and postbiblical times, the subject came to be discussed more openly, and in somewhat different terms. Both Judaism and Christianity came to affirm the belief in the resurrection of the dead, and, predictably, both turned to the Bible for confirmation. The Pentateuch, however, seemed to be silent on this matter—and its silence was, particularly for Jews, puzzling and disturbing. But if no programmatic statement could be found in that highly authoritative book, there was at least the evidence of Ezekiel. His vision of the valley of dry bones may have been, as we have seen, essentially concerned with the "resurrection" of the northern tribes and their eventual reunion with Judah. But for later readers, it acquired a quite different meaning. It was now a favorite example of the Hebrew Bible's doctrine of the resurrection of the dead:

> The mother of seven sons [said]: "[Your father] read to you about Abel slain by Cain, and Isaac who was offered as a burnt offering, and about Joseph in prison . . . He reminded you of the scripture of Isaiah, which says, 'Even though you go through the fire, the flame shall not consume you.' He sang to you songs of the psalmist David, who said, 'Many are the afflictions of the righteous.' He recounted to you Solomon's proverb, 'There is a tree of life for those who do his will.' *He confirmed the query of Ezekiel, 'Shall these dry bones live?'* For he did not forget to teach you the song that Moses taught, which says, 'I kill and I make alive: this is your life and the length of your days.' "[15]
>
> 4 Macc. 18:6–19

> Then the heavenly one will give souls and breath and voice to the dead,
> and bones fastened with all kinds of joinings . . . flesh and sinews
> and veins and skin about the flesh, and the former hairs.
> Bodies of humans, made solid in heavenly manner,
> breathing and set in motion, will be raised in a single day.
>
> *Sibylline Oracles* II 221–26

> For the prophets have foretold his two comings: one, which has already
> taken place, as a dishonored and suffering man; the second when, accord-
> ing to prophecy, he will raise the bodies of all men who have ever lived, and
> will clothe those among the worthy with immortality, and will send the
> wicked . . . into everlasting fire with evil devils. And we can demonstrate
> these things to come have likewise been foretold. This is what was spoken
> through Ezekiel the prophet: "Joint shall be joined to joint, and bone to
> bone, and flesh shall grow again" and "every knee shall bow to the LORD,
> and every tongue shall confess him" [Ezek. 37:7–8; Isa. 45:24]
>
> Justin Martyr, *First Apology* 52

Apart from its inherent interest, the transformation of Ezekiel's words
attested in these passages written by ancient interpreters is a good example of
how texts can change their meaning over time. Ezekiel was talking about a
fairly immediate and altogether political matter: can those northern tribes be
brought back to Israel and reestablish the mighty empire of David? But for
later ages, that question receded. Ezekiel's *new* message was that God could,
and would, resurrect the dead.

Ezekiel in Modern Scholarship

Modern scholars' questioning of the authorship of the book of Ezekiel has
not been as far-reaching or consequential as that of the book of Isaiah.[16]
Much of Ezekiel, they say, stems from a single period, the Babylonian exile,
indeed, from a single hand. This does not mean, however, that that hand was
Ezekiel's. As with Jeremiah, some scholars believe that the work of committing the original prophet's words to writing might well have been done by
someone else, a proposition supported here and there by passages that appear
to have been glossed or otherwise refashioned. So, while it is basically the
book *of* Ezekiel, it is the prophet's words as reported and, at times, reformulated and supplemented by someone else.[17]

The book as a whole shows clear signs of having been organized by topic.
Its first part opens with Ezekiel's vision of the throne chariot and his sum-
mons by God. Then we find him in the company of the Jewish exiles in the
Chebar valley, where he denounces the sins that will lead to destruction

(chapters 4–9); then he describes in detail the departure of God's glory from Jerusalem in the throne chariot (10–11), thus ending this first section through a reconnection to the opening chapter. The next section of the book, chapters 12–24, consists of divine condemnations of Judah, often in the form of vivid metaphorical depictions: Jerusalem is a faithless and ungrateful woman (chapter 16); two great eagles beset little Judah (chapter 17); a huge sword is whetted and readied for the slaughter (chapter 21); and so forth. Chapters 25–32 are condemnations of foreign nations, one by one (but mostly focusing on Tyre, the coastal city-kingdom to Israel's north), while chapters 33–39 are taken up with prophecies of Israel's restoration. The book's last chapters, 40–48, deal exclusively with the rebuilding of the Jerusalem temple and all that will go on there. Some scholars have expressed doubt that the restoration prophecies or the temple visions have any connection with the historic Ezekiel; perhaps, they say, these chapters are the work of a fellow Zadokite priest who wrote at the very end of the exile, or even after it was over.

Of particular interest in the latter part of the book is Ezekiel's vision of a certain foreign king named Gog and his kingdom, Magog (a name that seems to mean "Gog's place"). No such kingdom existed, and if there ever was a Gog, Ezekiel probably knew little more of him than his name. (A certain Gyges ruled the area that is today western Turkey about a century before Ezekiel's birth, and his name, scholars say, may have provided the inspiration for this vision.) What is striking about this vision is that it seems to contain elements characteristic of a kind of writing that was to flourish later on in the postexilic period, a kind referred to loosely as "apocalyptic." This sort of writing is not given to easy definition (in fact, some scholars have suggested retiring *apocalyptic* as a genre classification, since it seems too vague and covers too broad a range of texts). In general, however, "apocalyptic" has been used to describe revelations (in Greek, *apokalupsis*) of some future, climactic series of events that will set things aright again or bring history to some dramatic climax (sometimes referred to as the *eschaton* or "end-time").

Gog appears to be a kind of generalized, one-size-fits-all tyrant, perhaps connected with figures in earlier Israelite prophecies, since he is called the one "of whom I spoke earlier through my servants the prophets" (Ezek. 38:17). Gog will band together with Israel's hostile neighbors in a mythic battle, one that will end in Israel's triumph. "On that day, I will give Gog a burial place in Israel," God promises (Ezek. 39:11); he and all his army will be interred, a process that will take seven months to complete. Then the land will be purified, and "I will set My glory before the nations . . . and the house of Israel will know that I am the LORD their God, from that day on" (Ezek. 39:21–22).

Then I will restore Jacob to its place, and have mercy on the whole house of Israel; and I will act zealously for My holy name. They will forget their shame, and all the treachery they practiced against Me when they were dwelling securely in their own land, with no one to make them afraid. But when I bring them back from the peoples and gather them up from the lands of their enemies, then I will be sanctified by them in the sight of many nations. And they will realize that I am the LORD their God, both when I sent them into exile among the nations and when I gathered them back into their own land. I will leave none of them behind, and I will never again hide My face from them, for I will pour out My spirit upon the house of Israel, says the Lord GOD.

Ezek. 39:25–29

But this, too, was not to be. No Gog ever materialized, at least no great-but-defeated foe such as that described in Ezekiel. Instead, when the Babylonian domination ended, it did so because of another foreign power, the Persians, who overcame it. As for the Jews, they did indeed return to their homeland, but as a subject people once again. This only whetted their appetite for some dramatic conclusion to their confusing history.

33

Twelve Minor Prophets

Tempest: Jonah Cast Out
by Bernard (full name unknown).

Scrolls of rolled-up parchment or papyrus were the main form in which writings were preserved in Israel at the close of the biblical period.[1] As was already mentioned, this was fine for lengthy books like Isaiah or Jeremiah: they got to have their own private scrolls. But shorter compositions were usually combined with others to fill out a single large scroll. So it was that the writings of the prophets Hosea, Joel, Amos, and others came to be transmitted on a single roll of parchment, called "the Scroll of the Twelve [prophets]."

The order in which these prophetic mini-books are arranged may once have been someone's idea of their chronological order. Modern scholars generally agree, however, that this order does not really correspond to the history reflected in their contents. Both Hosea and Amos go back to the eighth century, for example (Amos actually being a bit older by most estimates), but Joel, currently located between them, seems to belong much later on—in the postexilic, Persian period. No matter; the twelve books in this scroll cover a large part of biblical history, from before the fall of the northern kingdom in the eighth century BCE to the fifth century or even later.

A Wife of Harlotry

The eighth-century prophet Hosea was a northerner and, as such, was caught up in the swirl of events that eventually led to his homeland's conquest by the Assyrian army. As a prophet, his job was to warn his countrymen to mend their ways. But God devised an unusual way for him to do so:

> The LORD said to Hosea:
> "Go, get yourself a prostitute wife and a prostitute's children.
> For the country has prostituted itself and stopped following the LORD."
> So he went and took Gomer, the daughter of Diblaim, and she conceived
> and bore him a son.
>
> Hos. 1:2–3

Readers of the Bible have long been puzzled by this summons. Did God really tell Hosea to marry a prostitute? Or was this just a pious man's way of explaining retroactively a marriage that went bad? Or was it perhaps all a visionary message, something that never occurred in fact?

The current consensus among scholars seems to be that Hosea must indeed have married such a woman, perhaps, as he says, after God told him to do so. After all, prophets were sometimes commanded to perform symbolic actions of one sort or another. The Bible reports that Isaiah was instructed to take off his clothes and walk around naked "as a sign and a portent," and he did so—for three years (Isa. 20:1–3)! God told Jeremiah to put an ox's yoke and thongs on his neck as a way of symbolizing Judah's required submission to Nebuchadnezzar (Jer. 27:2). At one point, He instructed Ezekiel to take a brick and use it to make a model of the coming siege of Jerusalem (Ezek. 4:1–3); afterward, He told him to lie on his left side for 390 days, symbolizing the 390 years of Israel's punishment (Ezek. 4:4–5). Still later, God told him to take two sticks and join them together, signifying the eventual reunion of Judah and Israel (Ezek. 36:15–23). Against such a background, it certainly would not be difficult to imagine that God had ordered Hosea to marry the notorious Gomer as a similarly symbolic message: stop whoring around with other gods! ("Whoring," it should be noted, was a standard metaphor for Israel's unfaithfulness to its God, one that is found in the writings of other prophets as well. It is predicated on the fundamental comparison of monolatry or monotheism to monogamy: stepping out on one's lawfully wedded deity was a horrible act of infidelity, one that could only be punished in the severest way.)

As for the children of this union, God instructed Hosea to give them names that would, like the marriage itself, symbolize something. The first son was thus named Jezreel, after the valley of Jezreel, where a bloody coup d'état took place (2 Kings 9–10). The second, a daughter, was given a still more symbolic name: Lo-ruhama, "Unloved"—"Because," God explains, "I will have no more love for the house of Israel and I will not forgive them" (Hos. 1:6). The third child, a son, was called Lo-'ammi, "For you are not My people, and I am not your God" (1:9). One could hardly imagine a more brutal manner for this prophet to have delivered his chilling message. "I am not just talking; these children of mine carry in their very names the bad news that I am bringing you."

It is against this background that one should read Hosea's first specific indictment of Israel's people, in which he calls on them to rebuke their "mother," the personified, whoring ex-wife of God:

> Blame your mother, blame *her*—for she is no longer my wife, and I am
>   not her husband—
> [Tell] her to put her prostitutions behind her and take her adulteries from
>   between her breasts.*
> Otherwise I will strip her naked, I will show her as bare as the day she
>   was born,

---

* The place where a lover might lean his head or where a woman might hang a little clasp of sweet-scented myrrh (for both: Song 1:13).

[that is,] I will make her like a desert, a parched land, so I can kill her off
    with thirst.
As for her children, I disown them, since they were born of adultery.
She was a whore; she conceived them in shamefulness.
She said: "I'll follow my lovers, who provide me with food and drink,
    wool and linen, oil and beverages."
... But though she chased after her lovers, she could never quite catch
    them; she went looking for them without ever finding.
[At last] she said, "I guess I'll go back to my first husband. I was better
    off then than now."
[But still] she never understood that *I* was the one who gave her the grain
    and the wine and the oil;
I gave her the silver, and the gold they gathered for Baal.
So now I'm taking back My grain as it ripens, and My new wine in its
    vintage,
and I will snatch up my wool and my linen, which would have covered
    her nakedness,
and I will uncover her shame right in front of her lovers, and no one will
    save her from Me.
                Hos. 2:2–10 (some translations, 2:4–12)

To understand this passage, it is necessary to think back to Elijah and his message to the same northern tribes on Mount Carmel: "The LORD is God [*or the gods*]; the LORD is God." In other words, you do not need any other deity; the LORD will take care of your agricultural needs, even though in the past you may have thought of Baal as the agricultural "specialist." That was back in the ninth century, and here we are in the eighth and the people of the north have apparently learned nothing. They are, according to Hosea's indictment, still whoring after Baal and the other deities.

The metaphor of adultery is particularly powerful here. "But they give me such nice presents!" Israel's metaphorical mother says of Baal and her other lovers, "all that wine and oil and grain—and those nice clothes Baal offers, the wool and flax that can be turned into beautiful garments!" So, as punishment for her infidelities, God promises to strip her bare. Such public shaming was indeed one way in which an adulteress was punished (see Num. 5:18[2] and Ezek. 16:37–39), but here the act acquires a frightening new meaning: the *land* of Israel is to be stripped bare, that is, the plants and crops that used to cover her are to be taken away and she is to be turned into a dry wasteland.

Research into Hosea has followed along the same lines seen earlier in conjunction with the book of Isaiah and other prophetic works, and for a time scholars were convinced that much of the book came from a later period. At present, the pendulum seems to have swung back in the other direction; while a few later additions or glosses are widely acknowledged, most of the book today is assigned to the eighth-century prophet.[3] One particularly significant element in the book, therefore, is the apparent theme of a great covenant between God and Israel. A passage seen earlier reads:

> Hear the word of the LORD, O people of Israel; for the LORD has a legal case against the inhabitants of the land.
> There is no **faithfulness or loyalty**, and no **obedience to God** in the land.
> **False swearing**, and **murder**, and **stealing**, and **adultery** break out; bloodshed follows bloodshed.
> Therefore the land mourns, and all who live in it languish . . .
>
> Hos. 4:1–3

This seems to be an allusion to the Ten Commandments, and if God speaks of the absence of "faithfulness" and "obedience to God," the point would seem to be that Israel is failing to live up to its end of an agreement—in other words, a covenant with God. Later on, Hosea says specifically that Israel has "transgressed My covenant [*běrit*] and sinned against My law [*torah*]."

It is, of course, hard to know how widespread this way of conceiving of things was in the eighth century. Perhaps, some scholars have suggested, it was at first a theme peculiar to the north. A number of striking resemblances exist between Hosea and Deuteronomy, another text believed to have northern connections, and one whose central theme is the covenant between God and Israel. Both books present the exodus from Egypt as a central, defining event in history (although Hosea makes no mention of Moses); both condemn worship at the "high places" (Hos. 10:8) and describe sinfulness as "forgetting God" (Hos. 2:13; 8:14; 13:6; Deut. 6:12; 8:14, 19; 32:18). Perhaps, some scholars say, the covenant theme became a major item in Judah's religious world only after the fall of the northern kingdom to Assyria in 722.

The Three Days

One particular verse in Hosea proved highly significant for later readers:

> Come, let us return to the LORD; for it is He who has torn, and He will heal us;
> He has struck down, and he will bind us up.
> After two days He will revive us; on the third day He will raise us up, and we will live before Him.
>
> Hos. 6:2

Suffering does not come from elsewhere, from other powers, Hosea says: *He is the one who has torn, but by the same token He has the power to fix what* is torn, to heal. The same God that strikes us down can bind us up. As such, this verse came to be considered an important affirmation of monotheism in Judaism and was incorporated in penitential prayers. Interestingly, however, it was also taken as another of the rare biblical assertions of the resurrection of the dead:

> Another explanation for "I kill and bring to life" [Deut. 32:39]: This is one of the four promises given to them [the Israelites] as a hint concerning the resurrection of the dead. "I kill and bring to life"; "Let my soul die the death of the righteous" [Num. 23:10]; "Let Reuben live and not die" [Deut. 33:6]; and "after two days he revives us" [Hos. 6:2].[4]
>
> Sifrei Deuteronomy 329

It was a curiosity in Hebrew grammar that made this same verse highly significant for Christians. The suffix *–ēnu,* "us" in the expressions "heal *us,*" "bind *us* up," and "raise *us* up," could also be read as *ennu,* "him." That would yield:

> Come, let us return to the LORD; for it is He who has torn, and He will
>   heal *him*;
> He has struck down, and he will bind *him* up.
> After two days He will revive *him*; on the third day He will raise *him* up,
>   and we will live before him.

For early Christians, the meaning was unmistakable:

> Then he [Jesus] said to them, "These are my words that I spoke to you while I was still with you—that everything written about me in the law of Moses, *the prophets,* and the psalms must be fulfilled." Then he opened their minds to understand the scriptures, and he said to them, "Thus it is written, that the Messiah is to suffer and to rise from the dead *on the third day.*"
>
> Luke 24:44–46

> For I handed on to you as of first importance what I in turn had received: that Christ died for our sins in accordance with the scriptures, and that he was buried, and that he was raised *on the third day in accordance with the scriptures* . . .
>
> 1 Cor. 15:3–4

There was one problem with this interpretation, however; it worked fine in Hebrew, but the standard Greek translation of the Hebrew Bible, the Septuagint, had translated all the "him"s as "us." For later Christians, who knew the Hebrew Bible only in Greek or Latin, it was therefore necessary to understand the "us" as some sort of figurative language:

> This prophet [Hosea] also announced the future resurrection of Christ on the third day, as it was fitting to be announced, *with prophetic loftiness,* when he said, "He will heal us after two days, and in the third day we shall rise again."
>
> Augustine, City of God 18:28

Nowadays, most scholars agree that "us" is indeed the right translation of the Hebrew: everywhere else in this passage, the prophet speaks in the first person plural, "Let *us* return . . . and *we* will live before Him" are quite unambiguous. Moreover, most commentators take the latter part of the verse not as a reference to resurrection at all, but as a metaphor taken from the recovery from serious illness: "After two days [of being near death], He will revive us; on the third day He will raise us up [completely], and we will live before Him."

A Prophet in Spite of Himself

Hosea's slightly older contemporary Amos of Tekoa was a blunt-spoken southerner who went north to prophesy the destruction of the Kingdom of Israel. "Your king Jeroboam," he told the northerners, "is going to be killed, and your land will be taken away from you and divided up among foreigners" (Amos 7:9, 17). This was not a message guaranteed to win him friends in the north, and indeed, it was not long before he was told by a local priest to go home. "Prophet, go back to the land of Judah and earn your living there. You may be a prophet there, but don't try prophesying any more in Bethel. This is the king's own sanctuary here, and the kingdom's temple" (7:12–13). Amos's answer was equally direct:

> "I am not a prophet and not the son of a prophet;
> I breed livestock and tend my fig-trees.
> But the LORD took me from following the flock, and the LORD said to me,
>   'Go, prophesy to My people Israel.'
> So now you can hear the word of the LORD.
>
> Amos 7:14–16

In so saying, Amos presented himself as a kind of prophet *malgré lui,* and this was very much his image among ancient interpreters. He was, Augustine said, a man from the country, unschooled in city manners and fancy rhetoric; it was God who turned him into a prophet.[5] Elsewhere, Amos stresses the fact that he, like any other prophet, simply had no choice when God called him:

Does a lion roar in the forest when it has no prey?
Does a beast cry out from its den if it hasn't caught something?
Does a bird fall to the ground if no trap was set?
Does a snare jump up from the ground if nothing's inside it?
When the signal-horn sounds in the city, don't people tremble?
And if ruin should strike that city, did not the LORD send it?

Surely the Lord GOD does nothing, without revealing His plans to His
     servants the prophets. [So:]
If a lion roars, who is not afraid? If the Lord GOD speaks, who will not
     prophesy?

Amos 3:4–6

Thus, Amos did not volunteer to be a prophet, and he did not go about the
job as if he were looking for anyone's approval. The straight-talking, no-non-
sense character of his words has remained quite unmistakable despite all the
intervening centuries. In particular, he did not shrink from denouncing what
he saw as the widespread corruption of northern society.[6]

"Right-thinking" people detest a rebuker, despise one who speaks the
     truth.
But since you crush the needy and tax them with levies of grain,
these villas you've built out of stone—you won't last in them,
and those charming vineyards you planted—you won't taste their wines.
I know all the crimes you commit. Your sins are unbounded.
Attacking the innocent, taking a bribe, swindling the poor in court—
whoever sees it keeps quiet, for "this is an evil time."

Pursue what is good and not evil, and you may yet get to live.
"May the LORD God of hosts be with you," as you like to say.
If you hate the evil and love the good, and establish justice in court,
perhaps the LORD God will have pity—on you, the remnant of Joseph
     [that is, the northern tribes].
But thus says the LORD, God of hosts and my Lord:
In all the squares will be cries of lament, and in all the streets, "Oh no!"

Amos 5:10–16

Amos may indeed have presented himself as an untutored rustic, but scholars
have their doubts. They have noted a certain rhetorical flair amidst his blunt-
ness. In particular, some have suggested that he must have been familiar with
the artful constructions of wisdom literature, since his way of speaking bears
some of its characteristics.[7] For example, the long list of rhetorical questions
cited earlier ("Does a lion roar in the forest . . . ?" and so forth) is certainly

reminiscent of the way sages instructed their charges, and its progression of images—the beasts of prey, the trapped animals, and then, dramatically, the city under attack—was clearly meant not only to support the idea that prophets have no choice in doing what *they* do, but in the process to give his listeners some sense of foreboding for their own future. This, when you think about it, was really a rather clever ploy. Indeed, this same passage's insistence on the cause-and-effect nature of divine justice is also somewhat reminiscent of the wisdom mentality. There are rules, Amos says: lions don't just start roaring and traps don't go off by themselves. Sometimes, the great divine plan is not immediately apparent, but "if ruin should strike that city, did not the LORD send it?"

One particularly rhetorical feature of wisdom literature has already been seen (above, chapter 23), the numerical saying:

> Three things are too wondrous for me, and four I do not know . . .
>
> Prov. 30:18

> For three things the earth groans, and for four it cannot endure . . .
>
> Prov. 30:21

This same construction appears time after time in the opening chapters of Amos:

> Thus says the LORD:
> For three transgressions of Damascus, indeed, for four, I will not revoke
> it [the punishment] . . .

> Thus says the LORD:
> For three transgressions of Gaza, indeed, for four, I will not revoke it . . .

> Thus says the LORD:
> For three transgressions of Tyre, indeed, for four, I will not revoke it . . .
>
> Amos 1:3, 6, 9

So: was Amos an untutored man of the country, or was he rather a student of wisdom? The two are perhaps not contradictory; particularly if he had extensive holdings, this rustic may also have had the leisure to learn the ways of ancient sages and, thus, to see what was in store for the immoral and corrupt society to his north.

In addition to his harangues against the corruption of the upper classes, Amos also indicted the sacrificial worship as practiced at Bethel and other sites. The two matters were actually related, by his account: the wealthy could keep on sinning, they thought, so long as they paid off God with their sacrificial animals. For that reason his sarcasm is particularly unsparing with regard to what went on at the northern temples:

> Oh come to Bethel for sins, to Gilgal for sins galore!
> But bring your offerings every morning, and a tithe every three days;
> send up a thanksgiving, yell "Voluntary sacrifice!"
> —let people know—for such is your devotion, Israel, says the LORD
>   God . . .

> I hate, I despise your festivals! Your assemblies give Me no pleasure.
> No matter how many your sacrifices, I will not be appeased.
> The fatlings you offer to please Me I will not even consider.
> Take away the din of your singers and the melody of your harps!
> But let justice roll down like waters, and righteousness like a mighty
>   stream.
>
> Amos 4:4–5; 5:21–24

Oracles Against the Nations

Modern sermons tend to highlight the biblical prophets' ethical teachings and their critique of their own societies. But one very common feature of prophetic speech is exemplified in the brief numerical sayings of Amos mentioned above ("For three transgressions of Damascus, indeed, for four . . ."). Prophets frequently turned their attention to the cities and kingdoms across Israel's borders in order to ritually denounce them, indeed, proclaim their coming downfall. This form of prophetic pronouncement—known to scholars as the "oracles against the nations" (OANs for short)—is not particularly appealing: such speeches are frequently full of venom and vituperation against foreigners. But they are prominently found in the books of Isaiah and Jeremiah and, as well, in the Scroll of the Twelve.

> The word of the LORD is against you, O Canaan, land of the
>   Philistines:
> "I will destroy you until no inhabitant is left."
> And you, O seacoast, will be pastureland, meadows for shepherds
> and folds for flocks.
> The seacoast will become the possession of the remnant of the house of
>   Judah, on which they will pasture.
> And in the houses of [Philistine] Ashkelon they [the Judahites] shall lie
>   down at evening.
> For the LORD their God will be mindful of them and restore their fortunes.

I have heard the taunts of Moab and the insults of the Ammonites,
how they have scorned My people and made boasts against their
    territory.
Therefore, as I live, says the LORD of hosts, the God of Israel,
Moab shall become like Sodom and the Ammonites like Gomorrah,
a land possessed by nettles and salt pits, and a waste forever.
The remnant of My people shall plunder them, and the survivors of My
    nation shall possess them . . .

You also, O Ethiopians, will be killed by His sword.
And He will stretch out His hand against the north, and destroy Assyria;
and He will make Nineveh a desolation, a dry waste like the desert.

Zeph. 2:1–13

Thus says the Lord GOD concerning Edom:
We have heard a report from the LORD, and a messenger has been sent
    among the nations:
"Rise up! Let us rise against it for battle!"
I will surely make you least among the nations; you shall be utterly
    despised.

Obad. 1:1–2

Nineveh is like a pool whose waters are rushing out.
"Stop them! Stop them!" [the Ninevites say]—but there is no one who
    can.
So plunder the silver, plunder the gold!
There's no end to the treasure, a hoard of expensive loot.
Rob and ransack and rout! [Their] courage melts and knees give way,
Bodies tremble and faces turn pale—
What now has become of the "lion's" den,* the cave of ferocious beasts?
Where has the lioness gone, and the lion's cubs—since no one's afraid?
[Where's] the lion that hunted for his cubs and cornered prey for his
    mates,
who filled his caverns with carrion and his den with pieces of flesh?
Now *I* am taking care of you, says the LORD of hosts:
I will burn your forest in smoke, and a sword will wipe out your cubs;
You'll have no more prey in the land, and the sound of your munching
    will be heard no more.

Nah. 2:8–13

---

* The lion as emblematic of Assyria is found as well in Assyrian literary sources,
though not in its plastic iconography.

Before the rise of modern scholarship, such passages tended to be passed over. People liked the idea of prophets criticizing their own people; cursing out foreigners seemed mean-spirited and xenophobic. But research has shown that OANs were no incidental part of the prophetic repertoire. Scholars are not sure why this was so. Some have suggested that these condemnations represent "one of the earliest, if not the earliest, form of Hebrew prophecy, and that the style and motifs were taken over from non-Israelite prototypes." [8] If so, they argue, then a professional curser like Balaam might actually represent an earlier stage of prophecy in the ancient Near East, indeed, might constitute the immediate ancestor of Israelite prophets like Amos and Isaiah. After a while, the prophet's repertoire expanded, but at the beginning, cursing other nations was much of what the biblical prophet was expected to do.

What Happens If a Prophet Succeeds Too Well?

The basic question addressed by the book of Jonah tends to be lost nowadays. The only thing most readers remember about this book is that Jonah was swallowed by a big fish at the beginning of the story as he tried to flee from God's summons to prophesy. (It was indeed a "big fish," by the way, and not a whale—that was Pinocchio.) But the big-fish incident is actually only an introduction to the main part of the book. The main part begins in chapter 3: God sends Jonah to far-off Nineveh to announce that the city is doomed: "Forty days from now and Nineveh will be overthrown!" (Jon. 3:4). Jonah walks the streets of the city shouting out this message, and, contrary to all expectation, he is taken seriously. The king and all his subjects at once put on sackcloth and ashes and fast in an attempt to stave off the divine decree. It works. God reverses His decision and the city is saved.

Is Jonah happy about all this? Not at all! He feels his reputation as a prophet has been ruined. After all, the most basic thing about prophecy is that God is supposed not to let the prophet's words "fall to the ground" (1 Sam. 3:19); in other words, everything a true prophet says must come to pass. Indeed, the very definition of a false prophet is one who announces something "but the thing does not take place or prove true" (Deut. 18:22). Jonah therefore feels betrayed: God ought to have destroyed the people of Nineveh just the way He said He would.

Jonah retires to a spot east of the city to see what will happen next. God prepares a fast-growing plant (a *qiqayon*—perhaps a castor bean plant, or, as some translations have it, a gourd)[9] to shelter Jonah from the beating sun. But the next day, God sends a worm to attack the bush and it withers. Jonah is so upset at this loss of shelter that he asks God to take his life, since now "it is better for me to die than to go on living" (4:8). Whereupon God announces the lesson of the story:

"You are upset about the *qiqayon* bush, for which you did not labor and which you did not grow; overnight it came into being and overnight it died. So should I not be concerned about Nineveh, that great city, in which there are more than a hundred and twenty thousand people who do not even know their right hand from their left, and also much cattle?"

Jon. 4:10–11

In other words, God says, it is indeed important for Me to be consistent and carry out what I said—but if the people have turned aside from their evil ways and are no longer deserving of punishment, their lives are more precious to Me than any divine consistency. (This message may seem obvious today, but it was hardly so in ancient times, where punishment was often collective and vicarious, and the pronouncement of Ezek. 18:21–23 was a relative novelty.)

The story was very popular with ancient Jews and Christians, but for different reasons. Jews prized it for its lesson about repentance. Indeed, on a public fast day, according to the Mishnah, the people were to gather in the public square and put ashes on their head as a sign of mourning:

Then a wise elder among them would address them with words of preaching: "Brethren, it is not said about the people of Nineveh that God 'saw their sackcloth and their fasting,' but that 'God saw their actions, how they had turned aside from their evil way' (Jonah 3:1)."

m. *Ta'anit* 2:1

The book's lesson, in other words, is that external signs of fasting and regret go only so far; what really counts is a sincere turning aside from one's previous misdeeds.

For Christians, by contrast, it was the story of the big fish that gained prime importance. The reason is that Jonah's three days in the fish's belly seemed to correspond typologically to the three days from the crucifixion to the resurrection. The big fish, in other words, was Christ's tomb, and Jonah's reemergence from its belly was a foreshadowing of what was told in the New Testament about the resurrection. Indeed, Jonah's whole adventure resonated with the (earlier) classical theme of the descent into the underworld (*descensus Averni* in Virgil), apparently related to the Christian theme, found in the Apostles' Creed and elsewhere, to the effect that Christ descended into hell before being resurrected. The depiction of Jonah first entering the fish and then being vomited out thus became a favorite of early Christian art, especially prized for ornamenting burial tombs. It is a remarkable feature of these illustrations that Jonah is usually represented as fully clothed on his way into the fish and stark naked on the way out—completely reborn, as it were, following physical death.

Jonah and Modern Scholarship

The story of Jonah really does not seem to fit with the other eleven books of the Scroll of the Twelve: they are all the putative words *of* different prophets, whereas Jonah is a story *about* a prophet (Jonah hardly speaks at all), or about prophecy. Why was it written? Presumably as a way of asserting what its author felt to be a great theological truth: God *can* change His mind; no divine decree is final. Moreover, it is significant that this parable involves the non-Israelite people of Nineveh: the point would seem to be that, if God's mercy was extended to this foreign people, indeed, to people who "do not even know their right hand from their left," how much more is He inclined to pardon Israel, if only it turns from evil with the same sincerity as the Ninevites.

Scholars are divided on the date of the book's composition, but its language seems to belong to the postexilic period. So too does Jonah's assertion that "I worship the LORD, the God of heaven, who made the sea and the dry land" (1:9) and the subsequent acceptance of that description by Jonah's shipmates. At the same time, the story may not all be of one piece. A certain "Jonah son of Amitai," a prophet in the northern kingdom, is mentioned in passing in 2 Kings 14:25. The author of the book of Jonah may simply have adopted the name to suit his tale, but it is also possible that the origins of his book go back to legendary material about this figure, material that was once so well known as to have its hero accorded a brief mention in 2 Kings. Scholars also point out that the book of Jonah itself is somewhat uneven, as if patched together from here and there. In particular, chapter 4 seems to be a composite, since Jonah first asks to die (4:3), then goes outside the city, sees the bush die, and again asks to die (4:8).

And then there is the matter of the first two chapters. One theory is that the original story began in chapter 3, then chapter 1 was added to demonstrate that Jonah was an unwilling—and, hence, sincere—prophet: God called him, and he immediately hopped a ship for Tarshish to escape the divine call. This would be another, if extreme, example of a true prophet's initial refusal of the divine summons (just as in the call narratives of Moses, Isaiah, and Jeremiah). So Jonah first flees God's mission, only to be cast overboard in a storm and thus forced to accept his mission, whereupon he arrives in Nineveh. But if that is the purpose of Jonah's flight, one must wonder why the book's author should have gone to such lengths. Surely Jonah could simply have turned down God's summons without actually trying to leave the country. And what sense did it make to have him swallowed by the big fish?

One theory is thus that the prayer that Jonah prays from the fish's belly in chapter 2 of the book may have actually played a role in shaping the preceding narrative. This prayer, it is not hard to see, is really no different from quite a few compositions in the book of Psalms—as a matter of fact, it is not a prayer but a hymn of thanksgiving, intended to be sung by or on behalf of someone who has recovered from serious illness or some other danger. Its language is thus intentionally vague and highly metaphorical:

> "I called to the LORD out of my distress, and He answered me;
> out of the belly of Sheol I cried, and You heard my voice.
> You cast me into the deep, into the heart of the seas, and the flood
>   surrounded me;
> all Your waves and Your billows passed over me.
> Then I said, 'I am driven away from Your sight.
> Will I ever look again upon Your holy temple?'
> The waters closed in over me; the deep surrounded me; weeds were
>   wrapped around my head.
> I sank to the roots of the mountains; earth's bars closed upon me
>   forever . . ."
>
> Jon. 2:3–7

The idea of drowning as an image of helplessness and desperation is a commonplace in the book of Psalms. Compare:

> Save me, O God, for the waters are rising up to my neck.
> I am drowning in the murky depths, with no place to stand;
> I am in deep water, and the flood sweeps over me.
>
> Ps. 69:1–2

> I call out to You . . .
> above the beat of your waters, as all Your waves and breakers sweep
>   over me . . .
>
> Ps. 42:6–8

> You have put me in the depths of the Pit, in the regions dark and deep.
> Your wrath lies heavy upon me, and You overwhelm me with all Your
>   waves.
>
> Ps. 88:6–7

It thus seems likely that Jonah's "prayer" in chapter 2 had been a psalm of thanksgiving long before it was part of the book of Jonah. Normally, according to scholars, what happens is that a later editor inserts such a preexisting hymn or psalm into a narrative. This is what scholars say about the songs found in Exodus 15, Deuteronomy 32, Judges 5, 1 Samuel 2, 2 Samuel 22, and elsewhere.[10] The fact that there is often a disagreement between the song and the surrounding narrative* supports the idea that these songs were originally quite independent compositions that were inserted only later on.

But in the case of Jonah's prayer things may have been a little different. Jonah's author, looking around for some dramatic way of having his hero refuse God's summons, thought of the words of a well-known hymn, in which the speaker says that God "cast me into the deep, into the heart of the seas." If he had Jonah flee God's call *by ship*, that would certainly be a dramatic way of refusing his mission; then Jonah could be cast overboard, saved by God, and subsequently speak the words of this well-known hymn, thereby "becoming" the hymn's original author. Suddenly, all its water imagery—somewhat excessive, even in terms of the biblical convention— would have a context.

Logically, Jonah could have uttered the words of the hymn once he had safely drifted back to shore. But the hymn's phrase "out of the belly of Sheol I cried" was too tempting. After all, how could a drowning man cry out if he were already underwater and in Sheol? So perhaps the "belly of Sheol" was a way of designating some actual belly, the belly of a great fish that swallowed Jonah in the midst of the sea. It thus seems possible that the whole motif of Jonah being swallowed up by the fish was generated by this unusual phrase. Little matter—the great fish soon became the story's most memorable detail and, for Christian readers of the Bible, yet another proof that "what is hidden in the Old is said openly in the New."

Prophecy Wanes

From a chronological standpoint, the earliest prophets in the Scroll of the Twelve are Amos and Hosea. Next is Micah, a slightly later contemporary who also witnessed the Assyrian threat firsthand. Nahum then celebrates the fall of Nineveh and Assyria's collapse. Zephaniah and Habakkuk belong to the same period, reflecting both the fall of Assyria and Babylon's mounting menace. (However, the third chapter of Habakkuk seems once to have been an independent composition, a psalm of perhaps considerably earlier date.) The book of Obadiah, only twenty-one verses long, was written just after Jerusalem's fall. It is a sustained screed against the Edomites, who may have helped the Babylonians in their destruction of the city or, more likely, who swept in afterward to grab what they could.

---

* For example, the disagreements discussed earlier between the Song of Deborah in Judges 5 and the narrative in Judges 4, or the fact that Hannah is not the "mother of seven" as her song maintains (1 Sam. 2:6), and that this song has, apart from that verse, no apparent connection with its alleged subject, the birth of a child.

The postexilic prophets are Joel (of uncertain date) and Haggai, Zechariah, and Malachi, all of whom belong early in the postexilic period. This in itself raises a question: why are there not prophets through the very end of the biblical period? Jewish tradition holds that the reason is that prophecy simply ceased. Thus the book of 1 Maccabees (late second or early first century BCE) speaks of "the time that prophets ceased to appear among them [the Jews]" (9:27, cf. 14:41), and the "Prayer of Azariah" (second century BCE) laments: "In our day we have no ruler or *prophet* or leader" (1:15). Similarly:

> Our fathers in earlier times and former generations had helpers, righteous prophets and holy men . . . But now the righteous have been gathered in and the prophets are dead. Also, we have left our land, and Zion has been taken away from us; so we have nothing now except the Mighty One and His Torah.
>
> 2 Baruch 85:1–3

> After the last prophets, Haggai, Zechariah, and Malachi, died, the spirit of prophecy [*ruaḥ ha-qodesh*] departed from Israel, though they still had recourse to the *bat qol* [a heavenly voice].
>
> b. *Yoma* 9b

The historical reality seems somewhat different from these descriptions, however. There certainly were people who presented themselves as prophets;[11] the problem with at least some was that they did not enjoy much popular recognition or support. Beyond this, many scholars have noted that the very idea of prophecy and the role of past prophets came to be reconfigured in postexilic times. Some of the evidence for this reconfiguration is to be found in the book of Chronicles.[12] There, for example, Isaiah's role is diminished, while the role of King Hezekiah is correspondingly augmented—so much so that the latter is somewhat prophetlike himself. Jeremiah's prophetic role is similarly underplayed in Chronicles.[13] Elsewhere, Chronicles suggests that Samuel, Nathan, Isaiah, and other prophets were the authors of otherwise unattested histories—again, a somewhat different role.[14] Indeed, the Chronicler seems bent on demoting some prophets, referring to them instead as "seers" and the like.[15] All this suggests that the author of Chronicles—perhaps reflecting a wider trend in early postexilic times—no longer saw the prophet as the vital figure he had once seemed, God's representative in Israel's midst.[16]

Many factors may have contributed to this changed reality,[17] but one of them may be adumbrated in the above assertion of 2 Baruch that "we have nothing now apart from the Mighty One and His Torah." As some scholars have suggested, the very existence of a great body of authoritative Scripture must have diminished the felt need for a "prophet in your midst" to tell people what God wanted of them. What God wanted was right there in the Torah and the other sacred books, if only one knew how to interpret them aright. In this sense, the interpreter was beginning to encroach on the territory that formerly belonged to the prophet—a process especially evident later on, in the writings of the Dead Sea Scrolls community.

Connected with this increasing recourse to the Torah and the prophetic books were other changes—the rise of wisdom and the sage in postexilic times, and along with that, the growing role of books and writing in the popular imagination. The prophets themselves bear witness to the beginnings of this change. When Jeremiah is summoned to prophesy, God *puts His words* in the prophet's *mouth* (an old expression meaning "tells him what to say").[18] In Ezekiel's call, as we have seen, this idiom is modified and concretized: God actually gives the prophet *a rolled-up scroll* to eat and digest. Prophecy was becoming a thing of written texts.[19] A still more vivid expression is found in Zechariah's vision of a huge, flying scroll:

> Again I looked up and saw a flying scroll. And he [the angel] said to me, "What do you see?" I answered, "I see a flying scroll; its length is twenty cubits, and its width ten cubits." Then he said to me, "This is the curse that goes out over the face of the whole land; for everyone who steals shall be cut off according to the writing on one side, and everyone who swears falsely shall be cut off according to the writing on the other side. I have sent it out, says the LORD of hosts, and it shall enter the house of the thief, and the house of anyone who swears falsely by My name; and it shall abide in that house and consume it, both timber and stones."
>
> Zech. 5:1–4

The huge scroll seems to be inscribed with (perhaps among other things) the Ten Commandments, which prominently prohibit stealing and false oaths. Here the scroll itself seems to be playing the role of God's own angels, entering the house of the thief or the person who swears falsely and imposing God's punishment. One could hardly ask for a more vivid illustration of the written word's increasing role—here, *sub specie divinitatis*! It was now Scripture itself that spoke to people, telling them what God wished of them and—in Zechariah's vision—entering their innermost chambers to punish them if they did not carry out Scripture's words.

34

Job and Postexilic Wisdom

THE BOOK OF JOB

Job and His Daughters by William Blake.

A SYMPTOM OF WISDOM'S NEW STANDING. PATIENCE AND PATIENTS.
CHALLENGE OF THE SATAN. REFUSING TO BE COMFORTED.
"BLESSED JOB."

Job was put to the test by God, at Satan's instigation. Did he pass the test, or
fail?

The broad characteristics of the wisdom movement have already been examined: its international character, its favorite literary form (the *mashal,* or
proverb), and its underlying ideology of self-restraint and moderation. When
did this way of thinking begin to leave its mark on the books that were to
make up the Hebrew Bible? Scholars have found traces of wisdom teachings
in a number of pre-exilic books and passages,[1] including chapters in the
books of Amos,[2] Hosea,[3] Isaiah,[4] as well as in some pre-exilic psalms,[5] parts
of Leviticus,[6] and in Deuteronomy.[7] Considered as a whole, however, the corpus of putatively pre-exilic writings does not indicate that wisdom was a particularly widespread pursuit. Rather, it was in the period after the return from
Babylonian exile that the wisdom ideology truly began to emerge as a dominant stream in biblical texts.[8]

Perhaps the Jews' half-century stay in Babylon had something to do with
this change. Babylon was certainly home to its own, centuries-old wisdom
traditions, and it had its own impressive cadre of professional sages and wisdom teachers. It is impossible to know if, and to what extent, the exiled Jews
came into direct contact with Babylonian wisdom, but its role in shaping the
overall cultural climate in which they lived can scarcely be doubted. What is
more, the very fact of their living in exile as a conquered people may have
drawn many Jews to question some of their old views—of themselves and of
their place in the grand scheme of things. Suddenly they were merely one very
small people in a world of mighty nations. It is easy to see how, under such
circumstances, the wisdom outlook might exercise a certain appeal: universal-
ist in character, it posited a great set of immutable rules underlying all of reality, whether that reality was west of the Jordan or east of the Euphrates.

Crucial as well were wisdom's views on the subject of reward and punishment. Wisdom's advocates posited an utterly just world, in which the righteous were ultimately rewarded and the wicked punished. But divine justice
often took years to work itself out. This certainly corresponded to at least one
explanation for the catastrophic fall of Jerusalem. The people had sinned and
broken their covenant with God; it took a while, but ultimately they were
punished, which was altogether right and proper. But by the same logic, the
wicked Babylonians ought not to be rewarded for their depredations. That,

too, took a while, but ultimately they were also punished, utterly routed by the Persian Empire. All this seemed to confirm the wisdom outlook.

And then there was the whole matter of patience. Since divine justice did take time, a crucial virtue in the world of wisdom was the ability to tough it out. "Just as the completion of a thing is better than its beginning, so is patience better than a haughty spirit" (Eccles. 7:8).[9] The way of wisdom was thus one of waiting for God's inevitable justice to work itself out. In Hebrew as in English, the idea of patience is related to suffering. (People in the doctor's waiting room are called *patients* not because they are waiting, but because they are suffering [Latin *patior*] from some medical problem.) The key to survival and ultimate triumph was often the ability to endure pain. This was another side of the wisdom outlook that must have appealed to the Jerusalem exiles in Babylon, many of them enduring present suffering in the hope that eventually things would change.

Perhaps for all these reasons, the people of Judah, reestablished in their ancient homeland after the edict of Cyrus (538 BCE), were more inclined to the wisdom outlook than before the exile. This is the period in which, scholars say, large chunks of the book of Proverbs, as well as the entire book of Ecclesiastes, were written; most of the Psalter's "wisdom psalms" are likewise dated to this period. Books like Tobit and the Wisdom of Ben Sira (Sirach) and the Wisdom of Solomon—all ultimately excluded from the Jewish canon but preserved by Christians—are also products of the postexilic age. Perhaps most significantly, this is the period when the sage interpreter of Scripture first emerged in full force and soon began to change utterly the way sacred texts from the ancient past would be read and understood.

Job's Protest

It would be wrong, however, to say that the Jews were entirely won over by the wisdom outlook. We have already seen that the book of Ecclesiastes is profoundly divided on the subject. On the one hand it endorses the wisdom way of life: "I saw that wisdom's advantage over folly is like that of light over darkness: the sage's eyes are in his head, but the fool walks about in the dark" (Eccles. 3:13–14). On the other hand, this author cannot help but tack onto the last sentence a further observation: "but I also realized that everyone meets the same end." No matter what the sages say, Ecclesiastes opines, the world really isn't fair: the righteous and wicked both die; indeed, "It happens that a righteous man perishes in his righteousness, while a wicked one lives on despite his wickedness" (Eccles. 7:15). This, and all the other injustices of the world, are *hebel*—elusive, baffling, and if you dare say it, perhaps just plain wrong.

The book of Job adopts a somewhat similar stance. Its opening scene takes place in Heaven. An accuser, the "Satan,"* comes before God and challenges Him concerning someone whom God considers to be an exemplary person, a sage of blameless virtue, Job:

> One day the sons of God [= angels, heavenly beings] came to stand before the LORD, and among them was the Satan [that is, the Accusing Angel]. The LORD said to the Satan, "Where are *you* coming from?" The Satan answered the LORD, "From wandering about the earth and walking all around it." The LORD said to the Satan, "Then you must have noticed my servant Job. Truly, there is no one like him on earth, so blameless and upright a man, who fears God and avoids any wrongdoing." The Satan answered the LORD, "Is Job God-fearing for no reason? Haven't You been protecting him and his house and everything that he possesses on all sides? You have blessed his holdings, and his earthly assets have only increased. But stretch out Your hand and hurt everything he has, and then see if he does not curse You to Your face." The LORD said to the Satan, "All right; whatever he owns is now in your power. Just make sure that you do not lay a hand on him!" So the Satan went out from the presence of the LORD.
>
> Job 1:7–12

The Satan sets to work at once, arranging for everything that is Job's—including even his children—to be destroyed. But Job, a champion of wisdom, takes it all with equanimity. What is wealth, or even family? "I was naked when I came out of my mother's womb," he says, "and naked will I return [that is, without any possessions or kin]. Whether the LORD gives or the LORD takes, blessed be the name of the LORD" (1:21).

Frustrated, the Satan returns to God and says that the test was not really fair: if Job himself were physically afflicted, then he surely would be a little less philosophical! God agrees to up the ante—"Just don't kill him!" He says (2:6). The Satan then arranges for Job's body to be afflicted "with loathsome sores from the soles of his feet to the top of his head" (2:7). But Job knows how to take it. "Should we accept only the good from God and not accept the bad?" he asks (2:10).

Refusing to Be Comforted

All this is the frame story that leads to the heart of the book, Job's discussions with his comforters. There was a certain ritual practiced in the ancient Near

---

* This is not yet the devil, the Satan of later Judaism and Christianity who is God's opponent and the embodiment of evil, but merely one of the heavenly attendants, the "sons of God." The Hebrew śāṭān means "accuser" or "adversary."

East by anyone who had endured a severe loss—for example, the death of a parent or other close relative. The person would be visited by friends and family, who would seek to reconcile him or her to what had happened. But the normal, expected posture of the sufferer in such circumstances was to "refuse to be comforted," at least for a time. This ritual of mourning called for sufferers to reject all such efforts for a while and remain plunged in grief, tearing their clothes, putting ashes on their heads, and wearing sackcloth (very scratchy and uncomfortable). So, for example, when Jacob's sons come to him with the (false, as it turned out) evidence that his son Joseph had been killed by a wild animal,

> He recognized it [Joseph's tunic], and said, "My son's robe! A wild animal must have eaten him; Joseph has been mauled to death!" Then Jacob tore his clothes and put on sackcloth and mourned for his son many days. All his sons and daughters tried to comfort him, *but he refused to be comforted.* "No," he said, "I will go down in mourning to my son in Sheol." Thus his father bewailed him.
>
> Gen. 37:34–35

The people who come to perform this ritual for Job are not, it turns out, family members but fellow sages—professors of wisdom, one might say. The heart of the book thus consists of a series of learned exchanges between these exponents of orthodox wisdom and Job, who, in "refusing to be comforted," ultimately calls into question the most hallowed doctrines of the wisdom outlook.

Their exchanges start off slowly. At first, Job simply bemoans his fate, and his colleagues politely suggest that he is not following the very dictates of wisdom that he has long taught. "Your words have saved many from falling; the weak-kneed you've kept on their feet. But now that it's *your* turn, you falter; when it comes to yourself, you give way" (4:4–5). But Job refuses to toe the wisdom line. "This can't be right!" he says again and again, and eventually he turns the argument to divine justice itself. God, he says, is supposed to reward the just and punish the wicked—but anyone with eyes to see knows that this is simply not the case.

> Why do the wicked live on? Growing older, they only get richer.
> They multiply, smile on descendants, while they themselves live
>   securely—no rod of God's ever strikes them.
> The bulls in their fields rut on demand and their cows give birth
>   without fail.
> Their offspring gambol like sheep, their children dance in a round,
> playing on harp and timbrel, singing to the sound of the pipe.
> They live out their days in comfort, then peacefully go to Sheol.

To God they say, "Let me be. I have no desire to revere You.
What is God, after all, that we serve Him? What good does it do to
     pray?"
Yet all that they have didn't come from themselves—the fate of the
     wicked is too much for me.

How often is *their* light snuffed out, as their downfall at last overtakes
     them?
Let God, in His anger, repay them! Send them off like straw in the wind,
     like the chaff that the storm bears away.
"God visits the sins on the children"? Let Him punish the sinner himself!
Let his own eyes behold his destruction! Let him taste the Almighty's dis-
     pleasure!
Will *he* see when his family is stricken, when their lives are severed in
     half?
Meanwhile, he seems to best God, as if *he* were the heavenly judge!

Oh, one man dies in perfect condition; how tranquil he was, at his ease.
His haunches were full and plump, his bone marrow rich and moist.
Another man dies with gullet unfilled—never once did he taste a good
     meal.
Now the two lie together in dirt, as the worms of the grave eat away.
Job 21:7–26

The conversation seesaws back and forth: at times it sounds as if the "wisdom side" has a point, but Job parries every argument. Finally comes the dramatic denouement, when God Himself intervenes, speaking to Job "out of a
whirlwind" (38:1). What He says, in effect, is: "Job, you don't begin to
understand. You have no real idea of the great rules underlying existence."

Where were *you* when I made earth's foundations? Tell me, if you are so
     smart.
Who fixed its size—you must know!—or measured its breadth with a
     cord?
In what were its bases contained, and who laid its cornerstone down,
as the morning stars droned in chorus, and the sons of God all gave
     voice? . . .
Have your eyes seen the gateway to Death, or gazed at the entrance to
     blackness?
Have you surveyed the earth as a whole? (Tell Me as soon as you have.)
How does one get to light's source? And where is the home of all
     darkness?
Can you take it back to its mountain, or follow the path to its house?

You were born back then—you must know! Your life has gone on for *so*
    long!

Job 38:4–7, 17–21

Confronted with this (rather cloyingly sarcastic) evidence of his own ignorance, Job crumbles. "I am too small to give answer. I cover my mouth with
my hands," he says (40:4). What else could he say? At this juncture, God
restores Job to his former state of well-being:

> The LORD blessed Job's latter years more than his beginning. He had four-
> teen thousand sheep, six thousand camels, a thousand yoke of oxen, and a
> thousand donkeys. He also had seven sons and three daughters . . . In the
> whole land, no women were as beautiful as Job's daughters; their father
> gave them an inheritance along with their brothers. Job went on to live [to
> the age of] one hundred and forty years, and saw his children, and his chil-
> dren's children, four generations. And Job died, old and full of days.

Job 42:12–17

Some scholars have questioned the significance of the book's ending, suggesting that it may ultimately be intended ironically, even comically—but that
hardly seems likely. The author's message is not so elusive. Job's questioning
of divine justice may not have conformed to the dictates of orthodox wisdom,
but that was precisely the author's point. Like Ecclesiastes, this writer could
not quite make his peace with what the "sages of the East" said about suffering. Sometimes, he says, suffering seems to be utterly undeserved and unjus-
tifiable; we accomplish nothing by pretending that it is otherwise. At the same
time, however, human knowledge *is* limited: we were not there when God
was setting up the rules of our game. In the end—as with many a book of dia-
logues—the author of Job is playing both sides with his whole heart. His
answer is neither Job's nor the comforters' nor, for that matter, even God's,
but all three together—which is to say, his answer is the back-and-forth of the
book itself.

No one knows for sure when the book of Job was written. Some modern
scholars have claimed on the basis of its language that it is a very ancient
work, indeed, one of non-Israelite origin, but there is little in the book itself
to support such a view. The language is, to put it impolitely, phony baloney,
a language no real person ever spoke. The reason is that, while the book is
written basically in Hebrew, the author has stuffed it with loan words from
Aramaic, Akkadian, and other foreign tongues. This was done in an attempt
to give the work a foreign flavor—rather the way Tolstoy liked to insert long
passages of French into his Russian novels so that readers would feel they
were peering into the aristocratic circles of the *dvorjanstvo*. The loan words
in Job are similarly meant to suggest the slightly foreign, highbrow world of

wisdom sages. For the same reason, neither Job nor any of the other characters is described as an Israelite: they are all from lands to the southeast of
Israel, in or near the region of northwest Arabia, a traditional home of
Semitic wisdom. But peering beyond this patina of foreignness, one can see
words or turns of phrase found elsewhere only in the book of Jeremiah or the
latter part of the book of Isaiah; that might suggest that the book's true genesis was in the time of the Babylonian exile or shortly thereafter. That was
also a period when, for the first time, a Jewish writer might expect his
learned readership to recognize many or all of the learned Aramaisms in his
composition. Such a date, scholars say, would also fit the content. It would
make the most sense for this book to have been composed at a time when the
wisdom philosophy was well known, and yet not quite acceptable to Judean
sensibilities. Both Job and Ecclesiastes attest to the growing power of wisdom
in postexilic times—and to the lovers' quarrel that the returning exiles had
with its view of divine justice and human suffering.

For some ancient interpreters, it is worth noting, the book of Job was a
problem—for precisely the same reason that biblical figures like Esau or
Balaam were a problem: "Is he good or bad?" There was one biblical suggestion that Job was altogether good: the prophet Ezekiel had mentioned a certain "Job," presumably the same one as in our book, who, along with Noah
and Dan[i]el, was distinguished by his righteousness (Ezek. 14:14, 20). But in
the book of Job itself, Job says some potentially blasphemous things, and he
ends up being reproved by God—certainly not a good sign. Once the Bible
had become a great book of lessons, the question "What am I to learn from
this?" had to have a straightforward answer: the sort of nuanced, highly
sophisticated, both-sides-against-the-middle stance of Job's author did not
provide one. Jewish interpreters were thus deeply divided, and the controversy surrounding him continued throughout the Middle Ages.[10]

For Christians, on the other hand, the matter was rather simple. To begin
with, the fact that Job was apparently not an Israelite but someone from "the
land of Uz" (1:1) might serve as proof that one did not have to be a genetic
Israelite in order to be altogether righteous and good—so Christian interpreters tended to highlight Job's virtue.[11] A New Testament epistle singles out
Job as the outstanding model of faithful endurance:

> As an example of suffering and patience, brothers, take the prophets who
> spoke in the name of the Lord. Indeed, we call blessed those who showed
> endurance. You have heard of the endurance of Job, and you have seen the
> purpose of the Lord, how the Lord is compassionate and merciful.
>
> Jas. 5:10–11

Job's fundamental righteousness continued to be a favorite Christian theme
thereafter:

Think again, I ask you, upon the holy Job. He was covered all over with sores, afflicted in all his limbs, and filled with pain over his entire body. [Yet] he was not swayed in his affliction, nor did he falter even in the mass of his own words, but "in all those things he did not sin with his lips" [Job 2:10], as Scripture testifies. Rather, he found strength in his affliction, through which he was strengthened in Christ.

Ambrose of Milan, *The Prayer of Job*[12]

As a result of the New Testament passage cited above, Job's standard epithet in Western Christianity became "the blessed Job" (*beatus Iob*). Along with his blessedness was the fact that Job's suffering seemed to have presaged that of Christ on the cross. Job could thus join other Old Testament figures (Adam, Abel, Enoch, and so forth) as a typological foreshadowing of Jesus. This approach found its most eloquent expression in Milton's minor epic, *Paradise Regained*.[13]

35

Daniel the Interpreter

The Book of Daniel and Ezra 9

and Nehemiah 8–9

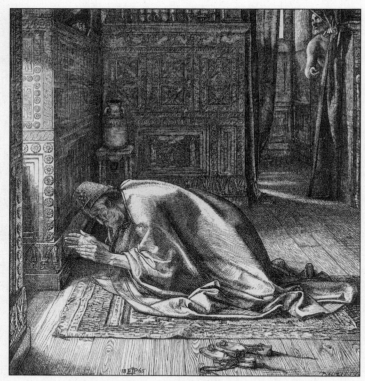

Daniel's Prayer by Sir Edward J. Poynter.

The Persian Empire. Esther. Ezra and the Torah.
The rise of the interpreter. Daniel and the four kingdoms.
The Nahum Pesher. Torah is wisdom.

As we have seen, Cyrus, king of the Medes and the Persians, toppled the Babylonian Empire, and all that was Babylon's became his. Part of this treasure was the territory beyond the Euphrates, including Yehud (Judah), the small but important stretch of land located between Egypt and the coastland north of it and, to the east, Persia itself.[1] In 538, Cyrus issued a decree allowing the Judean exiles still in Babylon to return to their home. That year some of them did; others returned in a second wave, in 520 BCE.[2] (Still others stayed in Babylon and established a Jewish community there, one that continued to exist under a succession of different caliphates and empires and states until 1951.) Thus, from the late sixth century BCE until Alexander's conquest of the ancient Near East two centuries later, Judah and the Jews were ruled by the Persian Empire. This was a significant time for the Hebrew Bible and for Judaism—a period when numerous biblical books were being edited and put into their final form, and when several of the most characteristic features of later Judaism were first taking shape.

As rulers, the Persians adopted a rather laissez-faire attitude toward their subject peoples. Their sprawling empire—stretching from Egypt and Turkey eastward to the borders of India—preserved the basic administrative framework set up by the Babylonians, and life went on pretty much as before. By the testimony of the book of Ecclesiastes, it was a government bureaucracy in which bribing judges and corrupt officials was the order of the day: "Don't be surprised when you see it," Kohelet says of the perversion of justice, "for one money-taker watches over another, with the higher-ups over them" (Eccles. 5:7).[3]

As far as the people of Yehud were concerned, the central Persian government was powerful but distant. The book of Esther contains a somewhat farcical, but probably not entirely fanciful, depiction of one Persian emperor, Ahasuerus (probably Xerxes I, 486–465 BCE). Ahasuerus is a pompous windbag, whose main concern in life is the endless stream of all-night drunken revels that he enjoys in the company of various members of his immense harem. When the DTs get so bad that he cannot fall asleep (Esth. 6:1), he has his servants read to him from the official records of his own court, since affairs of state are *so* boring that, even in his infirm condition, their recitation has at least the potential to put him back to sleep. Surrounded by scheming courtiers and officials cleverer (or at least more sober) than himself, Ahasuerus is easily manipulated and careens from one extreme to the next. In fact, it is thanks to this quality that Esther, hero of the book, is able to save the Jewish community from certain destruction at the hands of the archvillain Haman.

Besides books like Ecclesiastes and Esther, the Bible contains a number of works that belong to, and reflect on, the Persian period. Among the historical books are Ezra and Nehemiah (Chronicles, though it deals with earlier times, is also to be located in this period). A number of prophetic books were probably put into final form in this period, but two already mentioned, Haggai and Zechariah, are specifically connected to events that took place and figures who lived under Persian rule not long after the time of the return from exile. Although it lacks such a specific connection to the Persian period, Malachi probably belongs chronologically with these two.* There exists as well a body of Persian royal archives and other texts that can aid in reconstructing the history of the period. Nevertheless, the Persian period remains somewhat cloudier than earlier ages, and scholars still debate a number of basic issues. Part of the problem is that the sources contradict one another; several scholars have suggested that the biblical record is overlaid with ideological fabrications.

At the head of the second wave of returning exiles, in 520 BCE, was Zerubbabel, whom the new king, Darius, had chosen to be governor. Along with him was Jeshua, the high priest (Ezra 2:2; 3:2; etc.; Neh. 7:7). Zerubbabel may have been a descendant of David and a member of the royal family. If so, some of the Judean exiles probably hoped that he would eventually become a true king—that the Persian yoke would be shaken off and that Judah would become an independent power once again. But that did not happen, and Zerubbabel disappears mysteriously from the pages of history.[4]

Those who had come back with Zerubbabel did not find their homeland empty. A number of Judeans had never been deported by the Babylonians (they were probably mostly farmers from the countryside); in addition, Edomites and other foreigners had subsequently encroached onto Judah's territory and settled down. These "natives" may not have been particularly delighted by the arrival of the returning exiles—and vice versa, particularly since some of the returnees had their own, quite idealistic views about how things should work in their restored homeland. (Nor were the returnees all of one mind.) Their disagreements and struggles are reflected in the last parts of the book or Isaiah as well as in Haggai and Zechariah. Plans to rebuild the temple and refortify Jerusalem were eventually carried out, but not as quickly as people had hoped, nor to everyone's satisfaction (Ezra 3:12–13).

---

* "Malachi" may not be the prophet's name at all, but simply a reference to him (*mal'aki* means "my envoy"; the same word occurs in Zech. 1:9, 11 as a reference to the prophet). For this and other reasons, scholars connect the book of Malachi with that of Zechariah—either the two were at one point a single book that was divided to arrive at the round number of twelve books in the Scroll of the Twelve, or at some point "Malachi"— presumably a collection of anonymous oracles—was appended to make twelve.

At some later point (probably toward the middle of the fifth century BCE, although here the historical record is particularly confusing), Nehemiah, an advisor of the Persian king, seems to have been dispatched to Judah as governor, and at roughly the same time another figure, Ezra, arrived; he was a priest and a sage learned "in the commandments of the LORD and His laws for Israel" (Ezra 7:11).[5] Ezra, in particular, is presented as a significant religious figure. It was he who denounced his fellow Jews for having taken foreign wives (Ezra 9). In fact, he relates, he is so upset at the idea that

> When I heard this, I tore my clothes and my cloak and pulled out the hair of my head and beard, and sat dismayed . . . At the evening sacrifice I got up from my fasting, with my clothes and my cloak torn, and I fell on my knees, spread out my hands to the LORD my God, and said, "O my God, I am too ashamed and embarrassed to lift my face to You, my God, for our iniquities have risen higher than our heads, and our guilt has mounted up to the heavens . . . For we have forsaken Your commandments, which You commanded by Your servants the prophets, saying, 'The land that you are entering to possess is a land unclean with the pollutions of the peoples of the lands, with their abominations. They have filled it from end to end with their uncleanness. Therefore do not give your daughters to their sons, neither take their daughters for your sons, and never seek their peace or prosperity, so that you may be strong and eat the good of the land and leave it for an inheritance to your children forever.' "
>
> Ezra 9:3–12

One interesting thing about this passage is that the biblical quote at the end is a phony. The "prophets" never said this. The quote is actually a loose rewording of two parts of the Pentateuch, Lev. 18:24–30 and Deut. 7:3–4. It seems unlikely that Ezra (if these are his actual words) or some later editor could not have quoted the passages exactly. Apparently, however, exact quotation and attribution were simply not that important at this point—a religious leader like Ezra felt free to rework the inspired words of Scripture, just as the editors and interpolators of various prophetic books had. (Another matter of interest: scholars note that this conflation of a passage attributed to P with one from Deuteronomy may indicate that the completed Pentateuch was now *the* authoritative source, God's Torah.)

The Great Public Reading

The book of Nehemiah records another important event, a great public reading of the Torah, "the book of the law of Moses" (Neh. 8:1). The people tell Ezra to bring the book to a public square:

Accordingly, the priest Ezra brought the Torah before the assembly . . . He read from it facing the square before the Water Gate from early morning until midday, in the presence of the men and the women and those who could understand; and the ears of all the people were attentive to the book of the Torah. And Ezra opened the book in the sight of all the people, for he was standing above all the people; and when he opened it, all the people stood up. Then Ezra blessed the LORD, the great God, and all the people answered, "Amen, Amen," lifting up their hands. Then they bowed their heads and worshiped the LORD with their faces to the ground. Also Jeshua, Bani, Sherebiah, Jamin, Akkub, Shabbethai, Hodiah, Maaseiah, Kelita, Azariah, Jozabad, Hanan, Pelaiah, the Levites, helped the people to understand the law, while the people remained in their places. So they read from the book, from the law of God, with interpretation. They gave the sense, so that the people understood the reading.

Neh. 8:2–8

Scholars are not sure about the historicity of this passage, or even if it reflects attitudes in the time of Ezra himself or in some slightly later period. But it is certainly significant in any case for what it says about Scripture. The public reading is said to take place at the people's initiative, and they stand patiently—not just community leaders, but men and women and older children—for something like five or six hours to hear God's words. For such an account to be plausible, Scripture must have already acquired a central place in people's consciousness, and a central role in their lives. Interesting too is the fact that Ezra's listeners don't just listen to the words: the Levites are there to help them "understand the law," explaining what the words mean and "giving the sense" (perhaps, as one tradition has it, restating the text for them in Aramaic). The Age of Interpretation is here.

The same trend is reflected as well in the great public prayer that Ezra prays in the next chapter. Standing before the people, he says:

"You are the LORD, You alone; You have made heaven, the heaven of heavens, and all their host [= the stars], the earth and all that is on it, the seas and all that is in them. To all of them You give life, and the host of heaven worships You.

"You are the LORD, the God who chose Abram and brought him out of Ur of the Chaldeans and gave him the name Abraham; and You found his heart faithful before You, and made with him a covenant to give to his descendants the land of the Canaanite, the Hittite, the Amorite, the Perizzite, the Jebusite, and the Girgashite; and You fulfilled Your promise, for You are righteous.

"And You saw the oppression of our ancestors in Egypt and heard their cry at the Red Sea. You performed signs and wonders against Pharaoh and all his servants and all the people of his land, for You knew that they acted insolently against our ancestors. You made a name for Yourself, which remains to this day. And You divided the sea before them, so that they passed through the sea on dry land, but You threw their pursuers into the depths, like a stone into mighty waters. Moreover, You led them by day with a pillar of cloud, and by night with a pillar of fire, to give them light on the way in which they should go. You also came down upon Mount Sinai, and spoke with them from heaven, and gave them right ordinances and true laws, good statutes and commandments, and You made known Your holy sabbath to them and gave them commandments and statutes and a law through Your servant Moses. For their hunger You gave them bread from heaven, and for their thirst You brought water for them out of the rock, and You told them to go in to possess the land that You swore to give them . . . Forty years You sustained them in the wilderness so that they lacked nothing; their clothes did not wear out and their feet did not swell . . . You multiplied their descendants like the stars of heaven, and brought them into the land that You had told their ancestors to enter and possess.

Neh. 9:6–23

Again, scholars are not sure when precisely this passage was written, but the view of Scripture it represents is quite striking. Scripture is not *essentially* a recitation of past events, but one long series of lessons.[6] Each episode that Ezra evokes he sums up in a few words, and each one of them demonstrates some important truth. Thus, the account of the creation in Genesis 1 shows that "You are the LORD, You alone," since no other deity was involved. The stars, deemed in other religions to be the heavenly embodiment of various gods, bow down and worship You. As for Abraham, "You found his heart faithful before You" and *therefore* made a covenant with him, giving him the land of Canaan—faithfulness is indeed rewarded. What's more, "You fulfilled Your promise," because that is what You are like, "You are righteous." Scripture, in other words, is primarily a form of theological education.

Readers familiar with the Pentateuch will recognize that this passage is sown through and through with little snippets and quotes from it: "brought [him] out of Ur of the Chaldeans," "the Canaanite, the Hittite, the Amorite, the Perizzite, the Jebusite," "saw the oppression of [our ancestors] in Egypt and heard their cry," "like a stone into mighty waters," and many, many more—every sentence contains at least one quote, usually several. At the same time, however, the passage contains a good bit of what one might identify as ancient biblical interpretation. For example, the passage says that God "chose" Abraham and then took him out of Ur—as if his leaving was a result of that choice. But that is not what Genesis says. In Genesis Abraham leaves Ur because his father, Terah, "takes" him out (Gen. 11:31). It is only in the light of Gen. 15:7 (perhaps combined with Josh. 24:2–3) that one might conclude that Abraham's departure was the result of his prior "choice" by God. Sometimes, this passage does not so much interpret difficulties as merely acknowledge them. Thus, an apparent conflict in the biblical account of the Sinai revelation—Exod. 19:20 asserts that God actually descended onto Mount Sinai to speak with Moses, while elsewhere it is asserted that God spoke "from heaven" (Exod. 20:21; Deut. 4:36)[7]—is here resolved, at least in some fashion, by asserting that both things were simultaneously true: "You also came down upon Mount Sinai, and spoke with them from heaven." At other times, one half of the contradiction is simply silenced. Thus: was manna a good thing to eat, a marvelous "bread from heaven" (Exod. 16:4), or was it "this miserable food" (Num. 21:5)? There is not a hint of the latter here: "Forty years you sustained them in the wilderness so that they lacked nothing" (see Deut. 2:7).

In short, we are now in the world of Scripture. The writings of the past are full of lessons for the present, and actual interpreters—the Levites mentioned in Nehemiah 8 or Ezra himself here in Nehemiah 9—will tell you what the lessons are and what Scripture really means for you to think and do.

The Greeks Arrive

The Persians were eventually kicked out of Judah, but not by the Jews. Alexander of Macedonia, Greece's greatest military genius, managed to conquer most of the world known to him before his death in June of 323 BCE, just short of his thirty-third birthday. The vast territory he subdued stretched all the way from the Mediterranean to India. The land of Judah was thus still part of a huge empire, but this time it was one that spoke Greek and understood the world through Greek ideas.

After Alexander's death, his generals fell to feuding and eventually divided up the conquered lands among themselves. The Hellenistic rulers of Egypt, known as the Ptolemies (after the name of one of Alexander's generals and the founder of their dynasty, Ptolemaios), held sway over Judah for about a century, until 201 BCE, when they were ousted by the Seleucids, descended from another of Alexander's generals, Seleucus. The Seleucids ruled Syria and the lands to its east, and like the Ptolemies, they were thoroughly Greek in outlook and ideas.

Hellenistic rule saw the semiautonomous Greek city, or *polis,* with its standard institutions, as the ideal administrative unit. Each polis had an *ekklesia* or assembly of its citizens, which would meet from time to time; day-to-day affairs were entrusted to a city council. Theaters were an important feature of city life, providing not only entertainment but instruction in Greek culture. Similarly, the gymnasium, although its main function was providing a place for male athletes to train and work out, was also an instrument of culture; in it, young men might meet and discuss things, undergo some military training, and be further steeped in Greek literature and mythology. Both theaters and gymnasia were connected as well with Greek gods and goddesses, and the Greek cities of course also featured temples, which were attended as part of one's civic duties.

Many Jews no doubt welcomed the establishment of Hellenistic rule within their own borders and yearned to establish such cities in their own land. Greek culture seemed as pervasive and inevitable then as American culture seems today (and, perhaps, Chinese tomorrow). A few may denounce America as the Great Satan, but nowadays a surprisingly large part of the world's population nevertheless listens to the Great Satan's music, quaffs its noxious soft drinks, thrills to the pregnancies and extramarital affairs of its movie stars, and signals approval or assent by grunting the word "okay" in various odd accents. In the Hellenized eastern Mediterranean, Greek civilization was similarly pervasive—and it was good. The polis might, in some ways, be described as democratic, and it was in any case a relatively benign form of government. The Greeks themselves were far from jingoistic xenophobes; if you learned the Greek language and had a decent acquaintance with Homer and the classics, the whole world was open to you—it did not matter where you were from or whether or not you were of Greek descent. And Greek learning was extraordinarily impressive: in philosophy, mathematics, history, musical theory, rhetoric, and other domains, it really had no rival.

Nevertheless, some Judeans did not welcome the idea of full-scale Hellenization. As we have observed, sacred Scripture had, since the return from Babylonian exile, come to play an increasingly important part in people's lives. Why should Jews study Homer when they had the Torah? And, in view of the Torah's insistent propagandizing against worshiping "other gods" and its denunciation of making idols and statues, what was one to think of the Greek polis and temple and gymnasium? The last, in particular, offended religious sensibilities, since the male athletes were completely naked (*gumnos* in Greek); not only did such public nudity run counter to traditional Jewish modesty, but Jews who wished to join the gymnasium's adepts were sometimes ridiculed because their bodies had been mutilated by the strange practice of circumcision.

Judean society was thus divided, and the division became sharper after the Seleucids took over from the Ptolemies. For a time the country struggled on tolerably well, but when Antiochus IV ascended the Seleucid throne in 175 BCE, open conflict soon broke out. According to the account in 2 Maccabees, Jason became high priest in Jerusalem and set about turning the city into a bastion of Hellenism, seeking to establish a gymnasium in its midst and in other ways to make it fit the Greek model. It was not long before Antiochus joined in this effort, and a period of outright persecution of Judaism ensued. Copies of the Torah were confiscated and burned, people were forbidden to circumcise their sons, traditional worship was outlawed, and worst of all, an altar to Olympian Zeus was set up right in the Jerusalem temple.

The Book of Daniel

It is against this background, scholars say, that the biblical book of Daniel must be read. It is probably the latest book in the Hebrew Bible.* Although it is set in Babylon four centuries earlier, its last six chapters (7–12) seem to reflect directly the period of religious persecution under Antiochus IV. (The first six chapters are actually a collection of separate courtier tales about Daniel and his friends. Scholars believe that these tales must have circulated independently for a time, until an unknown Jewish author got the idea of making their hero, Daniel, the first-person narrator of a series of visions— the ones that make up chapters 7–12. This author therefore decided to append those visions to the existing Daniel tales to make one big book of Daniel.)[8]

The courtier tales begin with Daniel and his friends being inducted into Nebuchadnezzar's court. Though young, they are wise; indeed, the king finds them "ten times better than all the magicians and enchanters in his whole kingdom" (1:20). When the king has a dream that troubles him, he turns first to his own court sages, but none of them can be of help—so he summons Daniel. This is somewhat reminiscent of the story of Joseph, where Pharaoh had a troubling dream and none of his advisors could explain it until Joseph was called in. In this story, however, there is a significant difference. Nebuchadnezzar refuses to tell his wise men the nature of his dream—part of their job is to guess what he has dreamt, and only after that to interpret it. In other words, interpretation is not just figuring things out—it requires some kind of divine help for the interpreter to even know *what* he is supposed to interpret.

Daniel gets that help. God reveals the content of the king's dream to him in a night vision. The king, he learns, dreamt of a great statue made of metal. The head was made out of gold, the chest and arms of silver, the mid-section and thighs of bronze, and its legs of iron. The feet, however, were a mixture of iron and clay. (This is where the expression "feet of clay" comes from.) Daniel goes to court and tells the king his dream and then offers his interpretation: the golden head represents the king himself and his own kingdom. After him will rise another kingdom, inferior to his but still good— that is the silver—and after that another kingdom, represented by the bronze, "which shall rule over the whole earth" (Dan. 2:39). Then will come a

---

* According to the Jewish canon; the biblical apocrypha or deuterocanonical books of Christian Bibles contain some slightly later works.

fourth kingdom, "strong as iron; just as iron crushes and smashes everything, so it shall crush and shatter all these" (2:40). But it will not hold; the feet alloyed with clay will cause it to collapse, after which "the God of heaven will set up a kingdom that will never be destroyed" (2:44).[9]

The Writing on the Wall

A similar episode occurs in chapter 5. In the midst of a court party, the king and his guests are shocked to see a human hand appear and start writing on the wall of the palace. Enchanters and wise men are called in, but no one can even read the script that the hand used to write its message. At last, Daniel is called in, and he deciphers the message and explains it (Dan. 5:25). The words written are *mene, mene, teqel* and *parsin*. In Aramaic, these were the common terms for different weights: a *tekel* was one sixtieth of a *mene*, and *parsin* were twin spheres, each of which was half a *tekel*. But in the handwriting on the wall, these words are all intended as puns. *Mene* can also be a verb, "count," and *tekel* "weigh," while *parsin* suggests the Aramaic word for "split" or "break apart," *peras*. The message to the king is thus: "God has *counted* the days of your kingdom . . . you have been *weighed* on the scales and found wanting—your kingdom will be *split apart* and given to the Medes and the Persians" (5:26–28). So indeed it turns out: the king is killed that very night and his kingdom is given to "Darius the Mede."[10]

Chapters 7–12, as noted, were written in the time of Antiochus IV and reflect on the religious persecutions he introduced—but there are nevertheless continuities between these later chapters and the earlier ones. Chapter 7, for example, takes up again the four-kingdoms motif seen in chapter 2. Here, Daniel sees four beasts rising out of the sea—once again, the four kingdoms. But his attention soon focuses on the fourth, which "had great iron teeth and was devouring, breaking in pieces, and stamping what was left with its feet" (Dan. 7:7). The beast has ten horns, but as Daniel watches, an eleventh horn appears. Only later does the "Ancient of Days" (God) explain the meaning of this vision to Daniel. The fourth beast represents the empire of Alexander the Great, and the ten horns are ten Hellenistic kings who will arise from it. The eleventh horn is different from the others, however—it represents Antiochus:

> He will speak words against the Most High and will grind down the Most High's holy ones [that is, the Jews] and seek to change the law's sacred festivals. They will be given into his power for one time, two times, and half a time. But then sentence will be passed and his domination will be taken away, to be consumed and totally destroyed. Sovereignty and dominion and the greatness of the kingdoms under the whole heaven will be given to the

people of the holy ones of the Most High. Their kingdom will be an everlasting kingdom, and all [other] authorities shall serve and obey them.

Dan. 7:25–27

In other words, Antiochus will eventually be overthrown, and the Jews will
once again gain sovereignty over their own land.

The Messiness of History

That is, in fact, what happened: a group of Jewish rebels, led by a family of
rural priests—Mattathias and his five sons—fomented a full-scale guerrilla
war against Antiochus and his forces. When Mattathias died, his son Judah
took over; Judah's nickname was *"makkabi"* (meaning uncertain), so the
guerrilla war came to be known as the "revolt of the Maccabees." The
revolt started in 167 BCE, and within three years the rebels were in control of
Jerusalem. They purified and rededicated the Jerusalem temple, in commemoration of which the Jewish holiday of Hanukkah was established. Soon, the
Syrian troops of Antiochus were driven out of Judah entirely and a new
period of Jewish independence ensued.

No clear cultural divide separates the time of the Maccabees (when the last
words of the Jewish Bible were being penned in what might therefore be
called, from a Jewish standpoint, the "end of the biblical period")* from the
periods that preceded or followed them. The Maccabean rebels may have
burned with anti-Hellenizing fervor, but those of their descendants who succeeded them on the throne—referred to as the "Hasmoneans," after Mattathias's family's traditional last name, Hasmon—soon turned out to be as
Hellenizing as the people they overthrew. The Hasmoneans were priests and
thus controlled the temple, the central institution from which Judea was governed. But soon they proclaimed themselves actual kings, arousing the wrath
of their political opponents. Power seesawed back and forth in a series of
coups and countercoups. Judaism continued its path as before, but it was
now clearly divided into different schools and warring factions, Pharisees,
Sadducees, Essenes, and others. Soon, the growing Roman influence in the
area turned the rulers of Judea into virtual puppets, and Roman rule became
an established fact by the first century BCE.

This was just the latest installment in a series of puzzling events. Indeed,

---

* That is to say, the Hebrew Bible of Judaism. For Christians, the events of the New Testament are also in the "biblical period." Some Christian scholars therefore refer to the final
two centuries BCE as the "intertestamental period," the time between the completion of the
Old and the beginning of the New Testaments. But this name bespeaks a solely Christian
point of view, so today many scholars prefer to refer to this time as part of the "Second Temple period," that is, up until the destruction of the second temple by the Romans in 70 CE.

for Jews living throughout most of the postexilic period, history in general no longer seemed to make much sense.

Earlier, it had—at least according to what Scripture recounted. Abraham, Isaac, and Jacob had founded the nation. Israel was enslaved in Egypt for a time, but then—as He had announced to Abraham—God freed the people from slavery and gave them the land of Canaan. Soon David arose to rule them, and a brief golden age ensued. The northerners broke away and sinned, and as a consequence were conquered by the Assyrians. When the Kingdom of Judah also fell into sin, it too was conquered, but God quickly showed that the Babylonians were only the "stick of His wrath"—He made sure that they too were conquered in short order. Then the Persians let the Jews return to their homeland. Up until that point, the course of events had a definite logic to it.

But how was one to make sense of what followed? The Persians continued to rule Judah. No new David arose (as some had hoped), and the long-lost northern tribes did not return. The Persians were then succeeded by the Greeks, the Greeks by the Hasmoneans, the Hasmoneans by the Romans— what was going on? Had not the Jews already paid for their sins through the Babylonian exile? By all rights God ought to have restored them to their former glory just as soon as they returned to their homeland. Instead came a succession of foreign rulers who were neither awful nor great—and this, from a religious standpoint, was probably the worst of all possible worlds. The Jews were not being rewarded or punished, but seemed to be in some indeterminate state.[11]

Apocalyptic Writings

That is why, scholars say, the book of Daniel exhibits such interest in the great patterns of history—the succession of four empires represented by the four metals or four beasts. Describing everything that had happened since the Babylonian exile as part of some larger picture was a way of asserting that God had not lost control of history. He was still manipulating events—you just had to see the forest instead of the trees in order to make sense of it. And of course, included in the great plan was Israel's eventual triumph: the multi-metalled statue would collapse right on schedule, the eleventh horn of the fourth beast would be overthrown, and Israel would have dominion.

In this respect, Daniel is not alone. A whole body of literature grew up at this time among the Jews, known as *apocalyptic* writings. The book of Daniel is the only exemplar of this literary genre to be included in the Jewish Bible, but there were plenty of others written in the same period—the first and second books of Enoch, the fourth book of Ezra, the second and third books of Baruch, and many others. The New Testament book of Revelation is another example of this genre. Apocalyptic literature typically presents a visionary (sometimes a figure from the biblical past like Enoch or Ezra) who is given a glimpse of divine secrets—not only the great patterns of history, but sometimes also the way the world works, the location of the Garden of Eden, how the righteous are rewarded and the wicked punished, and so forth. Apocalypses also often disclose details about the great and imminent conclusion to which Israel's history is headed—the "end-time," sometimes know to scholars by the Greek word *eschaton* (the "last" or "ultimate").

Apocalyptic writings are in some sense a continuation of late biblical prophecy, but scholars also point out its affinities with wisdom writing.[12] It is certainly striking that the anonymous writers of apocalypses often choose not a prophet but an ancient sage or other worthy as the alleged author of their work: Enoch (described as the "scribe/sage of heaven"), Ezra, or Baruch (both sages). Like earlier wisdom writings, apocalyptic texts hold that there is a great, divine plan governing all of reality, a plan whose rules were established long ago.[13] And like wisdom writings, they hold that wisdom is basically hidden and requires deep contemplation in order to be revealed. Daniel and his fellow visionaries are thus *interpreters*. They interpret both dreams and texts (using, surprisingly, the same techniques for both).[14] Indeed, the book of Daniel refers often to books and writing, continuing the trend observed earlier in Zechariah. "The books were opened," Daniel says in one of his visions (Dan. 7:10), and the angel Michael tells him, "But you, Daniel, keep the words secret and the book sealed" (12:4).

Royal sages were always interpreters—witness Joseph in Genesis. But in apocalyptic writings, the sage's job is quite impossible without divine help. The common element joining chapters 2 and 5 of Daniel is that in both cases the sage must first provide the text itself—tell the king what he dreamt, decipher the undecipherable writing on the wall—before he can begin to say what the text means. This is no ordinary sort of interpretation. The whole mentality of this period is that something is happening, but it is not seen by the naked eye. Eloquent indeed are Daniel's words of thanks to God after He has revealed to him the king's dream:

"Blessed be the name of God from age to age, for wisdom and might are
  His.
He changes times and seasons, deposes kings and sets up kings;
He gives wisdom to the wise, and knowledge to those who have under-
  standing.
He reveals deep and hidden things; He knows what is in the darkness,
  and light dwells with Him."

Dan. 2:20–22

The great patterns of history are like the weather: God changes kings the way He replaces spring with summer and summer with fall. But what is really going on is not visible to all, precisely because the patterns are so big. It is only to the wise and "those who have understanding" that He reveals "deep and hidden things."

Hidden Interpretations

By the time the book of Daniel was being written, biblical interpretation had been around for a long while. The book of Chronicles, a subtle reinterpretation of the books of Samuel and Kings,[15] dates back to the beginning of the postexilic period; still earlier, scholars say, are the interpretation and reworkings of biblical laws, the glosses and interpolations of prophetic collections, and related phenomena. What was changing now, however, was the character of interpretation. In part because of the apocalyptic mentality, interpreting the Bible was becoming—especially in some circles—a matter of seeking out the *hidden* messages that God had intended for the sage to unravel. Thus, at one point the book of Daniel itself interprets earlier Scripture, namely, Jeremiah's prophecy that in "seventy years" after the Babylonian conquest, God would restore the Jewish people to their land and give them a "future with hope" (Jer. 25:11–12; 29:11–14):

> I, Daniel, considered in the [sacred] writings the number of years that—according to the word of the LORD that had come to the prophet Jeremiah—were to last for the devastation of Jerusalem, [namely,] seventy years. Then I turned my face to the Lord God, to seek an answer by prayer and supplication with fasting and sackcloth and ashes. I prayed to the LORD my God and made confession . . .
>
> While I was praying, the angel Gabriel, whom I had seen before in a vision, came to me in swift flight at the time of the evening sacrifice. He came and said to me, "Daniel, I have now come out to give you wisdom and understanding . . . Seventy groups of seven years have been decreed for your people and your holy city in order to obliterate the transgression and wipe out the sin and atone for the iniquity—to bring in eternal righteousness and seal the prophet and his vision and anoint the Holy of Holies."
>
> Dan. 9:2–4, 21–24

Jeremiah had plainly said that things would go back to the way they were in seventy years. But what he really meant, according to Daniel, was seventy *groups* of seven years apiece, in other words, 490 years. That would put the real fulfillment of Jeremiah's words sometime in the future (from the standpoint of Daniel's real author)—and it would explain, therefore, why Israel had not yet been restored to its full independent glory, why Babylonians had been succeeded by Persians and Persians by Hellenizing Ptolemies and Seleucids.[16]

But if Jeremiah meant to say 490 years, why didn't he just say that? This is not a question Daniel addresses—probably, it did not even occur to him. Scripture just *was* cryptic; this assumption was already well established. In keeping with it (and not long after Daniel), a member of the Dead Sea Scrolls community explained a certain passage from the seventh-century BCE prophet Nahum as referring to events in the interpeter's own time, five hundred years *after* Nahum:

> "Where the lion goes, and the lion's cubs, with no one to disturb them" [Nah. 2:11]. This refers to Demetrius, the Greek king, who wished to enter Jerusalem on the advice of "smooth-tongued interpreters." But he could not do so, for God did not give Jerusalem into the hands of the Greek kings, from the time of Antiochus on—until there arose the rulers of the Kittiyim [the Romans].
>
> 4Q169 frag. 3

According to this interpreter, the "lion" mentioned in chapter 2 of Nahum was "Demetrius the Greek king," apparently Demetrius III Eukairos (who ruled 95–88 BCE), the Hellenizing king of Seleucid Syria. Demetrius did seek to enter Jerusalem and conquer it, but he failed. The author of this text asserts that this attempted invasion took place at the advice of the "smooth-tongued interpreters" (*doreshei ḥalaqot*). This is an allusion to one of the religious rivals of the Dead Sea Scrolls Jews, the Pharisees. They were famous as interpreters of biblical law (*doreshei halakhot*)—the author is punning on this name by calling them "smooth-tongued." [17]

As for the Kittiyim, the name of this people, found several times in the Bible (Gen. 10:4; Num. 24:24; Isa. 23:1, etc.) was often used in the Dead Sea Scrolls to refer to the Romans (the same interpretation is found in later Jewish writings as well). [18] Thus, the author of this text is saying, the prophet Nahum predicted the attempted invasion of Jerusalem by Demetrius, but he also said that this invader and his allies would be frustrated as earlier invaders were, since God had decreed that Jerusalem would not fall into the hands of the "Greek" (Seleucid) kings but would remain undisturbed ("with no one to disturb them"). With the arrival of the "Kittiyim," however, all that would change.

How could this interpreter believe that Nahum was predicting things half a millennium into the future? Wasn't Nahum really talking about the events of his own day? No one can say for sure, but our interpreter probably would have answered such questions by saying that Nahum and his times were not necessarily relevant. Nahum's words were part of Scripture, and everyone knew that Scripture often contains hidden messages—hidden even from the prophet himself. After all, God gave Scripture to Israel to guide it in *every* generation, including the interpreter's. So why not?

The Predominance of Legal Interpretation

Not all interpretation in this period was concentrated on finding hints in Scripture of the Seleucids or the Romans. Those "smooth-tongued interpreters," the Pharisees, concerned themselves a great deal with the application and interpretation of biblical laws—as did, for that matter, the Dead Sea Scrolls community, the Sadducees, and Jesus. Indeed, understanding and explaining biblical laws was a concern that united *all* Jews in this period (though they disagreed, sometimes violently, in their conclusions). Perhaps one of the most striking testimonies to the enduring interest in this activity is Psalm 119, in which the Psalmist endlessly—for 176 verses—professes his allegiance to God's "statutes," "laws," "commandments," and so forth and seeks divine help (like Daniel) in understanding and interpreting them. Yet the most revealing verse in this psalm is not one of those requests for insight, but an offhand observation:

> Your laws have been songs for me in my dwelling-place.
>
> Ps. 119:54

Sitting about his house, this Psalmist says, what he hums to himself is not popular music or even the hymns and praises of God found in Scripture, but the *laws* of Exodus and Deuteronomy! This is to say how much biblical laws were on everybody's mind.

Despite this and a great deal of other biblical and extrabiblical evidence, many scholars have, for one reason or another, understated the importance of biblical law in surveying the whole of Scripture, as if it were a necessary but minor feature. That certainly was not the view in late biblical times, and the evidence of Scripture itself, from the Ten Commandments through the laws of the Covenant Code and Leviticus and Deuteronomy, suggests that the Bible's laws had not just recently come into focus. They had been a central concern from well before the Babylonian exile. One would have to be (to use an old word) purblind to miss this crucial point. And so, as biblical interpretation came to the fore as a major preoccupation, it is no wonder that legal interpretation was a large part of the whole.

The author of *Jubilees,* a contemporary of the author of Daniel, was a close interpreter of the stories of Genesis—but many of his interpretations of stories were aimed specifically at finding hints in them about the laws found later in the Bible. As noted, the Dead Sea Scrolls community was also interested in—one might say, without much exaggeration, obsessed with—the close interpretation of biblical laws, although this aspect of their writings has only recently begun to be explored.[19] One hardly would have expected Philo, the philosophical allegorist, or Josephus, whose stated goal was simply to set forth his people's history, to go on for pages and pages about biblical law, but both of them do. Neither even needed to make explicit the point that the Torah's laws were an overwhelmingly important part of Scripture.

I do not wish to overstate the case; there was a great deal more to ancient interpretation than the understanding and application of biblical laws. Ben Sira might serve as a model of the well-rounded interpreter. He certainly had a profound interest in the Bible's stories; in fact, the last six chapters of his book are a review of biblical heroes, each of whose narratives, he believed, carried a simple, easily summarized message:

> Abraham was the great father of a multitude of nations, and his glory
>   was unblemished.
> He kept the Most High's commandment, and made a covenant with
>   Him;
> He cut His covenant into his flesh, and when he was tested was found
>   faithful.
> Therefore He swore by oath to bless the nations with his seed.
> Sir. 44:19–20

Along with this, though, Ben Sira was also an interpreter of biblical laws—he discourses at length about the commandment to honor one's parents, for example, as well as on the "law of reproof" (Lev. 10:17)—since

> A wise man understands a commandment, and His Torah is reliable as
> prophecy.
> Sir. 33:3

Along with these expected interests, however, his book also includes—rather uncharacteristically—an apocalyptic glimpse of the future (36:1–22). In short, for him and his contemporaries, Scripture contained *everything*—it was nothing less than all of divine wisdom in book form. In a famous passage, he recounts how Wisdom, a female figure, is commanded by God to leave her post next to Him in highest heaven and pitch her tent amidst one people on earth, Israel. Ben Sira then explains who this female figure *really* is:

> All this is the book of the covenant of the Most High God, the law that
> Moses commanded us as an inheritance for the congregations of Jacob.
> Sir. 24:23

And so we have come full circle. The last of the Hebrew Bible's canonical books is about an ancient interpreter, Daniel. Ben Sira and the author of *Jubilees* were his close contemporaries (though you probably would not have found all three at the same lunch counter); their generation was followed by another, with its own interpreters, who passed on and expanded the interpretations they had received. Soon, these interpretations acquired canonical status: what the text meant is what the interpreters of old had always said it meant. Interpretations continued to multiply and solidify over the next three centuries, until the broad outlines of the Interpreted Bible were well established. It was this Interpreted Bible that both Judaism and Christianity gave to their followers, and it was to remain, quite simply, *the* Bible for centuries and centuries afterward. Only with the rise of modern scholarship did this Interpreted Bible begin to come apart, undone by the very different set of assumptions that scholars brought to the task of reading Scripture.

36

After Such Knowledge . . .

Viewed in its broad perspective, the modern study of the Bible must rightly appear to be an extraordinary intellectual achievement. Working at first with nothing but the biblical text itself, scholars were able to discover, through the most painstaking analysis, little clues that ultimately changed their whole conception of Scripture and how it had come to be. Thus, by studying the varying use of divine names in different parts of the Pentateuch, researchers gradually developed a theory of its composite authorship and the stages of its composition. Wellhausen's version of the Documentary Hypothesis and his analysis of its implications for the history of Israel's religion, while certainly not the last word, was nonetheless a model of analytical and synthetic creativity. His younger contemporary Hermann Gunkel was a scholar of no less impressive powers: in particular, Gunkel's whole approach to breaking down biblical texts into their smallest component parts and then exploring their common literary genres and their role in daily life led the way to an utterly new understanding of where the stories of Genesis came from and how the prayers and hymns of the book of Psalms came into existence.

Historians of the ancient Near East, using recently deciphered texts from Egypt, Mesopotamia, and elsewhere—texts whose decipherment was itself a most impressive accomplishment, the product of international teamwork carried out over several generations—were able to illuminate hundreds of previously misunderstood biblical words and phrases, as well as numerous elements in the Bible's narratives and prophecies and laws. Just as strikingly, they demonstrated that quite a few parts of the Bible, from the flood story to the laws of Exodus, the wise sayings of Proverbs, the Psalter's songs of praise, and the dirges of Lamentations, had striking parallels in the compositions of ancient Israel's neighbors. Indeed, some of the most basic elements of Israel's religion—its ways of conceiving of and describing God, as well as the sacrifices through which He was worshiped, the very construction of His temples, and the cycle of His holy days—were connected with institutions that existed earlier in Mesopotamia, Ugarit, and other ancient Near Eastern sites.

Every book of the Bible was put under the microscope, and here too, modern scholars' analytical skills proved little short of dazzling. The great history stretching from the death of Moses to the Babylonian exile (covering the books of Joshua, Judges, Samuel, and Kings) was, they argued, assembled by a group of historians late in pre-exilic times; these writers had gathered disparate legends, royal archives, and other material to compose a highly theological and idealistic retelling of Israel's past. Prophetic books were similarly scrutinized, as were the Psalms, Proverbs, and other works; in each case, painstaking attention to detail yielded insights that could hardly have been anticipated. The institutions of Israel's daily life, as well as of its religion, were also studied. Prophecy was examined phenomenologically and in a comparative perspective; still more recently, an examination of the priesthood and the priestly worldview have thrown new light on an altogether unique theology that existed in biblical times.

All these, and much more, are the accomplishments of modern biblical scholars. Their work has not been accorded the wide acclaim given to scholars in other fields, but this is hardly surprising. For one thing, biblical research has been of interest to only a relatively small circle of researchers, clergymen, and a few laymen, and while its conclusions have had far-reaching results, the study of the Bible's origins could never be as consequential as the drive to understand the secrets of the physical universe, or the development of life on earth, or the inner workings of the human mind. Still, if most people today know the names of Albert Einstein and Charles Darwin and Sigmund Freud, while they have never heard of Julius Wellhausen or Hermann Gunkel or W. F. Albright, I do not believe that, in terms of intellectual achievement and intellectual courage, especially in their willingness to challenge long-held beliefs and to try to rethink problems from the beginning, it would be entirely wrong to compare this group of scholars with that one. Over the course of little more than a hundred years, they succeeded in utterly transforming what had always been *the* central text of Western civilization, so that—at least to those familiar with their work—scarcely a sentence of the Hebrew Bible continues to mean what it meant before they came along.

A Misunderstanding

From the start, however, many of the greatest modern scholars suffered from a fundamental misunderstanding of what their discipline was about and where it would eventually lead. That misunderstanding was highlighted in a passage cited earlier from the writings of Charles Augustus Briggs at the start of the twentieth century:

> Holy Scripture, as given by divine inspiration to holy prophets, lies buried beneath the rubbish of centuries. It is covered over with the débris of the traditional interpretations of the multitudinous schools and sects . . . Historical criticism is digging through this mass of rubbish. Historical criticism is searching for the rock-bed of the Divine word, *in order to recover the real Bible.**

For Briggs and many others, the whole point of modern scholarship was to sweep aside everything people had always thought about the Bible—"the débris of the traditional interpretations of the multitudinous schools and sects"—in order to discover pure, unadulterated Scripture, the "real Bible."[1]

That is not how things have turned out. For the most part, modern scholarship has served only to undermine the very notion of a "Holy Scripture as given by divine inspiration to holy prophets." To begin with, the books attributed by Scripture to Moses or Isaiah or Jeremiah are largely not, in the current consensus, the words of those prophets, but the writings of anonymous figures, some of whom may have been prophets but others of whom seem more likely to have been editors or scribes. They inserted large chunks of their own or other people's thoughts into the text. To be sure, divine inspiration may guide the work of a scribe or interpolator as closely as it does that of a prophet—but the great mass of specific instances investigated by modern scholars has certainly seemed to point in quite the opposite direction. Why, one might rightly ask, would the same God have inspired the various authors of the text groups J, E, P, H, and D to set forth such different conceptions of proper and improper conduct, indeed, to take contrasting positions on the most basic theological issues, including the nature of God Himself? And why would the divine voice have inspired these authors to compose different accounts of the same event or contradictory versions of the same law? Time and again, scholarship has highlighted precisely the absence of agreement between one part of the Bible and another, and this in turn has necessarily undermined the notion of the common, divine origin of the whole.

Along with this, the resemblances between specific laws or proverbs or stories found in the Bible and similar ones discovered in Egypt or Mesopotamia have also worked against the idea of Scripture's divine origins: Did God also inspire Hammurabi and Amenemope and the authors of *Gilgamesh* and the Sargon legend—and if He didn't, why did He cause biblical prophets to copy the words of these human authors instead of giving them His own original laws and sayings and stories? What is more, the striking resemblances between various institutions described in the Bible and those discovered to have existed in ancient Babylon or Ugarit likewise have had a negative effect on the traditional understanding of divine inspiration. Why should the layout

---

* The italics are Briggs's.

of the temple that God commanded Solomon to build have been so much like that of the pagan temple unearthed in Syria at 'Ein Dara' (whose construction God presumably did not supervise)? Why should the sacrifices He commanded Israel to offer bear the same names and the same basic form as those of ancient Canaanite religion—a religion the Israelites were told to uproot utterly from their midst? Examples could be multiplied.

Beyond such specifics, moreover, was the whole approach to reading biblical texts adopted from the start by the modern scholarly movement. Divine inspiration notwithstanding, scholars asserted, the Bible is a collection of texts that were transmitted by human beings who lived in a certain time and a certain place. In seeking out its meaning, therefore, interpreters believed that they ought first to try to read it as if it were no different from any other human text. This postulate was inherent in Spinoza's program,[2] and it was accepted, with vague apologies, by Robert Lowth.[3] A few decades later it was stated in the plainest terms by J. G. Herder:

> One must read the Bible in human terms [*menschlich*], since it is a book written by humans and for humans. Human is the language, human the [physical] means by which it was written down and preserved; human finally is the sense in which it is to be understood, [indeed, human also must be] every aid that illuminates it, as well as the purpose and use to which it is to be applied.[4]

The Bible was to be read as any other human creation. So it was no accident that scholars began for the first time to highlight as such what they saw as the Bible's *flaws*—apparent contradictions and inconsistencies and duplications in the putative sources of the Pentateuch and the like. It is not that interpreters in an earlier day had been unaware of contradictions or illogical statements in the Bible, but (because of Assumption 3) they had reacted to them differently. These were, Augustine and others maintained, deliberate hints that some "mystery," a hidden teaching of some kind, was being imparted.[5] Now, on the contrary, they were just errors in the text. The implications of this stance for the Bible's divine origin are not particularly obscure. To err, after all, is human; error is not generally held to be characteristic of the divine. So what are all these inconsistencies, repetitions, and outright mistakes doing in a book attributed to God's authorship?

Along with its focus on the Bible's frailties, modern scholarship generally insisted that, wherever possible, the Bible's words were to be understood within their own historical context. Thus, when Isaiah spoke of a future ideal king, one ought first to try to understand his words as referring to someone born (or about to be born) in his own day, and not to someone whose birth was centuries away. Likewise, Psalm 137 probably ought not to be attributed to David's authorship, since it refers to the Babylonian exile, which occurred four hundred years after his time. Such an approach certainly had much to recommend it—for one thing, it corresponded to the way in which the world as we know it works. But to read in this manner was also to assert sub rosa that prophetic knowledge of future events, if not quite impossible, ought in any case to be the biblical interpreter's last resort in seeking to understand the meaning of a biblical passage. By the same token, the addressees of biblical prophets were assumed to be listeners or readers of the prophets in their own day. Thus, Deutero-Isaiah must certainly have been speaking to his own contemporaries about the return to Zion and not (as Jews and Christians had long assumed) about events in a much later day. The same has come to be accepted, reluctantly, about this prophet's "suffering servant."[6] Jeremiah's "evil from the north" referred to an immediate threat from biblical Babylon, not a distant one in the end of days. As for the many mysterious foreshadowings and cryptic references found by earlier readers of the Bible, modern scholars were agreed that these were largely illusory. The binding of Isaac was not a typological prefiguring of the crucifixion, but an etiological tale about human sacrifice; a law prohibiting Molech worship was not a cryptic reference to intermarriage, but a straightforward interdiction of a form of worship that existed early within the biblical period.

With the emphasis on reading the Bible in human terms and in its historical context also came a subtle shift in tone. As modern biblical scholarship gained momentum, studying the Bible itself was joined with, and eventually overshadowed by, studying the historical reality behind the text (including how the text itself came to be). In the process, learning *from* the Bible gradually turned to learning *about* it. Such a shift might seem slight at first, but ultimately it changed a great deal. The person who seeks to learn *from* the Bible is smaller than the text; he crouches at its feet, waiting for its instructions or insights. Learning *about* the text generates the opposite posture. The text moves from subject to object; it no longer speaks but is spoken about, analyzed, and acted upon. The insights are now all the reader's, not the text's, and anyone can see the results. This difference in tone, as much as any specific insight or theory, is what has created the great gap between the Bible of ancient interpreters and that of modern scholars.

As modern scholars learned more and more *about* biblical texts, what they often saw was the human side of the text at its worst. If they were right about the etiological purpose of ancient narratives, whereby eponymous ancestors (Cain, for example) were invented by a narrator in order to explain later reality (the cruelty of Cain's putative descendants, the Kenites), then the very existence and preservation of such tales seemed to bespeak an almost childlike simplemindedness. What did it say of ancient Israelites—readers and writers both—if they really believed that the in utero rivalry of two brothers, Jacob and Esau, could explain the later rivalry of two nations, Israel and Edom? Frequently, moreover, the Bible was found to distort the truth or lie outright.

Thus, scholars concluded, there really could have been no massive exodus from Egypt or any sweeping conquest of Canaan. The desert tabernacle was the later invention of a priestly writer. Royal propagandists disguised David's violent putsch (and perhaps his participation in Saul's murder) as his magnanimous accession to the northerners' desire to have him replace Saul on the throne. The canonical prophets did not really write much of the material the Bible attributed to them, nor did David or Solomon; but *someone* was responsible for these attributions, and that someone could not have been a very honest fellow.

Modern scholars' explanations have proven very persuasive—and that is just the problem, since, in approaching the text in the way they have, they seemed to have stripped the Bible of much of its special status. How is the Hebrew Bible any different now from the altogether human creations of ancient Near Eastern literature? Far from uncovering "Holy Scripture, as given by divine inspiration to holy prophets," as Briggs had thought, modern scholarship has actually accomplished exactly the opposite, reducing Scripture to the level of any ordinary, human composition—in fact, arguing that it was in some cases even worse: sloppy, inconsistent, sometimes cynical, and more than occasionally deceitful.

Ancient Interpreters

The next question ought logically to be: why did anyone ever think otherwise? What on earth could have ever made people suppose the story of Isaac was actually a foreshadowing of the crucifixion? Why should anyone have ever believed that Psalm 137 (a psalm that certainly does not present itself as a prophecy, but rather seems to have been written by someone looking *back* on the Babylonian exile after it was over) could possibly have been written by David, who therefore must have foreseen events that would not occur until four hundred years after his death? How did the worship of a god named Molech ever come to be understood as a reference to intermarriage? More generally, what could have led readers to suppose that, in an anthology of individual texts that were written over the course of more than a thousand years, the texts themselves would *not* disagree with one another on the most fundamental matters? And why should anyone have ever thought such a large and diverse collection of texts would not contain a single inconsistency, a factual error or scribal mistake, or the like? Even more strikingly, how did anyone ever arrive at the conclusion that texts composed hundreds and hundreds of years earlier were addressed to readers today?

The answer is that this whole way of approaching the Bible is the product of its ancient interpreters. There is little in the biblical texts themselves to suggest that they were intended to be read in this fashion. Nevertheless, that is how they came to be read, and it was this way of reading that made the Bible what it was for so many centuries, a divine guidebook full of instruction and wisdom, yea, the word of God—or, to cite again the words of the Geneva Bible,

> the light to our paths, the keye to the kingdome of heaven, our comfort in affliction, our shielde and sworde against Satan, the school of all wisdome, the glasse [mirror] wherein we behold God's face, the testimonie of his favour, and the only foode and nourishment of our soules.[7]

Disquieting as it may be, one is left with the conclusion that most of what makes the Bible *biblical* is not inherent in its texts, but emerges only when one reads them in a certain way, a way that came into full flower in the closing centuries BCE.

By all accounts this way of reading started slowly and only gradually gained momentum.[8] Its first stages are attested within the Bible itself—in the psalm headings that seek to connect individual psalms with events in David's life;[9] in the book of Chronicles and its recasting of the history related in the books of Samuel and Kings;[10] in the editorial rearranging and supplementation of prophetic collections; in the revision of earlier laws to harmonize conflicts or to accommodate them to changed circumstances or later practices. But it is really in the closing centuries BCE and the first century CE that Israel's sacred library underwent its most dramatic change. This is the period in which, in the interpretations found in the biblical apocrypha and pseudepigrapha, biblical texts are for the first time explicitly held to be replete with hidden meanings and subtle hints, so that when the Bible says X it often really means Y.[11] This is likewise the time when (as the Dead Sea Scrolls attest), prophecies from five or six centuries earlier are openly asserted to refer to events of Seleucid Syria or the Roman occupation of Palestine.[12] It is also the time when Ben Sira and 1 Baruch proclaim that the Torah is no other than the world's great book of divine wisdom, nay, personified divine Wisdom on earth,[13] and when, in *Jubilees* and other ancient texts, the *entire* text of the Pentateuch is attributed to the authorship of God.[14] What happened in these few centuries was nothing less than a radical refashioning of Israel's ancient library. The texts themselves were not changed, or at least not much. What changed—at first ever so slightly, but then more and more dramatically—was the set of assumptions that interpreters brought to the task of reading. Soon enough, those assumptions were generating a large body of actual interpretations, and each new interpretation only reinforced the overall approach that interpreters were taking.[15]

How It Happened

A number of specific instances mentioned in the preceding chapters offer a series of snapshots of *how* ancient interpreters came to change the whole character of Israel's ancient library of texts. It did not happen all at once.

In the area of biblical law, for example, apparent contradictions or conflicts between laws must have demanded the attention of interpreters from an early period. So, for example, Exod. 12:8 said that the Passover sacrifice had to be "roasted," but Deut. 16:7 said "boiled." What was a person supposed to do? We know that this contradiction must have bothered people from very early times, since a solution (of sorts) appears even within the Bible itself, in one of its later books. "They *boiled* the Passover lamb *in fire*," reports 2 Chron. 35:13, thereby implying that "boil" in Deuteronomy really meant "roast" (= boiling in fire) as stated in Exodus.

A somewhat more complicated instance was the biblical law of guardians (Exod. 22:6–14). This law seemed to contradict itself in the most flagrant manner, saying in one paragraph that a guardian who had been robbed could get off with a solemn oath, while in the very next paragraph asserting that a robbed guardian had to repay the value of the stolen goods. To ancient interpreters, it was simply axiomatic that the Bible *couldn't* contradict itself. The contradiction disappeared as soon as someone hit upon the solution that paragraph 1 was referring to an unpaid guardian, while paragraph 2 referred to a paid one. Once accepted, this interpretation surely became a prime example of the fact that the Bible does *not* contradict itself, even when at first it might seem to. Moreover, this interpretation proved that the Bible often does not say openly what it means but must be examined for any hidden implications—since, in this instance, the text had nowhere said that it was dealing with two different kinds of guardians.

Most scholars agree that at least some of Israel's ancient texts had been preserved *in writing* as early as the eighth, ninth, or even tenth centuries BCE. If so, this would indicate that way back then, these writings must have had some role in people's lives, some ongoing function. (Otherwise, why write them down and keep copying them, century after century?) This proposition seems most interesting in the case of prophetic texts. After all, there were good reasons for preserving other sorts of texts in precise, written form. One needed to know the exact language of laws; likewise, detailed records of events were certainly necessary for kings to preserve, for reasons of state; priests probably kept in writing the procedures of their profession in order to insure that they would be followed unchangingly from generation to generation. But why should the exact words of Isaiah or Amos have been written down and saved from the eighth century on? The most plausible explanation seems to be that, at a relatively early stage, the words of these prophets were considered precious and worthy of preservation.

Yet these prophetic texts also seem rather quickly to have changed their significance. They were apparently rearranged and supplemented by editors, and this has suggested to scholars that, once the immediate occasion of their being uttered faded into the past, prophetic sayings began to be reinterpreted. Eventually they came to be perceived as bits of timeless ethical instruction, or evidence of the divine plan for history or of the prophet's own foreknowledge of much later times.[16] The rise of apocalyptic writings toward the end of the biblical period probably also left its stamp on the prophetic utterances of an earlier age: a reference no longer understood (such as Ezekiel's Gog and Magog) or some ominous prediction ("I will make the sun go down at noon, and darken the earth at daylight," Amos 8:9) could surely have served the purposes of religious figures in a later age eager for the end-time: "What Amos predicted is about to happen now!"[17]

Other ways in which ancient texts changed their meanings have already been discussed. In the Psalter is evidence of the emergence of a new kind of psalm that had no connection with the original psalms' use in temple worship. The new psalms speak of praising God "in my house" or "continually," or, like Psalm 119, seem like an unending litany to be read through in private, ritual recitation. This shift must, in turn, have brought about the reinterpretation—and probably reappropriation—of the old cultic psalms. They too could be put to noncultic use, so long as "I come before You" was understood to refer to the now omnipresent deity, and the "offerings" proffered were offerings of the lips and of the heart. This might seem like a small change, but its reverberations were enormous: properly interpreted, the reading and studying of *any* part of Scripture could become a kind of offering. It is thus hardly surprising that a text from the Dead Sea Scrolls prescribes that "anywhere where there are ten people, let there not be lacking a man expounding the Torah day and night, continuously, concerning the right conduct of a man with his fellow. And let the [Assembly of the] Many see to it that in the community a third of every night of the year [is spent] in reading the Book and expounding the law and offering blessings together" (*Community Rule* 6:6–8).

The Song of Songs is another striking instance because its very inclusion in the biblical canon presumes that its words had, at some earlier point, undergone a radical reinterpretation. Someone must have said: "This song isn't really about love between a man and woman; it's about God and Israel." The fact that it is in the Bible may attest to the persuasive powers of this particular individual, but it seems as well to argue that, by that stage in the emergence of the biblical canon, all sorts of texts were being interpreted in a way quite out of keeping with their apparent meaning. It is not difficult to imagine that by then the stories of Genesis had acquired the character of moral instruction (indeed, they explicitly had done so by around 180 BCE, in the writings of Ben Sira, as well as in somewhat later compositions such as the *Testaments of the Twelve Patriarchs*), while the exodus narrative and subsequent wilderness wanderings had become, in some quarters, metaphors or timeless examples of the ways of God and men (in the Wisdom of Solomon and Philo's writings, in the first centuries BCE and CE). It was in these crucial centuries that the great literary heritage of the past was truly becoming Scripture.

The special role of wisdom writings and the wisdom mentality—in its ascendancy after the return from the Babylonian exile—deserves to be singled out. It is really the wisdom mind-set that made so many ancient texts into Scripture. Like wisdom writings, *all* of Israel's ancient library now became a series of eternally valid lessons, the wisdom of the ages. History, for example, was not history but instruction, and the people whose lives it charted thereby acquired a *representative* character: they all became the "righteous man" and the "wicked man" of the book of Proverbs, their lives exemplars of either all good or all bad. (This is how Cain and Abel, Jacob and Esau, and dozens of others were changed by ancient interpreters.) Along with this was the presumption that, no less than the gnomic proverbs of wisdom literature, the Bible's stories, prophecies, psalms, and songs were likely as well to have a concealed message: wisdom's full meaning was never immediately apparent. And just as even the most obvious contradiction in wisdom writings was *axiomatically* true and no contradiction at all ("Do not answer a fool according to his folly, lest you be a fool yourself. Answer a fool according to his folly, lest he be wise in his own eyes," Prov. 26:4–5),[18] so an apparent inconsistency or contradiction anywhere in Scripture must likewise simply be illusory. Finally, wisdom itself had no real author, so neither did Scripture: whoever its particular tradent might have been, Moses or Solomon or Isaiah, he was no more the real author than was the ancient Egyptian who wrote down the eternal wisdom contained in the *Instructions of Ptah-hotep*. Wisdom's true source was God. Not to put too fine a point on it, each of the wisdom traits just listed corresponds to one of the Four Assumptions.

In short, the wisdom mentality seems to have exercised a profound influence on how the Bible was perceived in late biblical times. Examined through the lens of wisdom writings, the original meaning and even the original genres of Israel's ancient texts were subtly modified, reconfigured by a whole new way of reading.[19] It was this way of reading, as much as the texts themselves, that Jews and Christians canonized as their Bible. Along with it came the great flood of interpretive motifs created by the ancient interpreters; in ten thousand particulars, these individual motifs changed the whole character of Israel's sacred library. It is this book of changed meanings that *was* the original Bible.

A Massive Rewriting

One would not be wrong to think of this transformation as, in effect, a kind of massive act of rewriting. The raw material that made up the Bible was *written anew* not by changing its words but by changing the way in which those words were approached and understood. This sounds like an exaggeration when stated so baldly, but I hope the previous chapters have offered proof that it is not. What we have observed all along are two very different sets of documents, the biblical texts in their original settings and meanings and what those texts were later made out to mean by Jewish and Christian authorities. The words of the two sets of documents are basically the same, but they nonetheless make up, side by side, two completely different books.[20]

Modern biblical scholarship began in the belief that the Bible's meaning was simply inherent in its words, indeed, that by throwing away the Four Assumptions of ancient readers and all the interpretations they had generated, the "real Bible" would emerge. This, as we have seen, did not happen. But now that the genie is out of the bottle and modern scholarship has discovered everything it has discovered about the text's original meaning, what is to become of the Bible?

The first step in formulating an answer to that question, it seems to me, is to understand that the answer must depend very much on who is doing the asking. I do not think it can ever be the same for both Christians and Jews, or for Catholics and Protestants, or even for Episcopalians and Southern Baptists. The historical reasons for these differences need not be treated here, but one or two observations about how some of these groups differ in their approach to the Bible may make things clearer.

Fundamentalism

The first observation concerns the whole phenomenon of Protestant fundamentalism.[21] Modern biblical scholarship started out as a largely Protestant movement; it did not, however, advance unopposed. Indeed, it has played a major role in dividing the Protestant world into its liberal and conservative camps, the latter including various groups usually described as fundamentalist or evangelical. This split is older than the twentieth century: we briefly glimpsed the opposing forces in the heresy trial of Charles Augustus Briggs at the end of the nineteenth century, and the tensions and controversies created by modern scholarship go back further than that. Nor would it be fair to pin everything on research into the Bible: the rise of science and rational thought had raised troubling questions about the Bible's veracity still earlier, and the weight to be given to arguments from reason as opposed to divine revelation is a debate that has been conducted from medieval times on.

Still, most studies of Christian fundamentalism point to the late nineteenth century as its time of origin, and the rise of modern biblical scholarship as the most important of its proximate causes. The term "fundamentalism" itself derives from a series of volumes called *The Fundamentals,* published between the years 1910 and 1915 and ultimately distributed in more than 3 million copies. The authors of the various essays in these books were, in large measure, scholars and ministers disturbed by German "higher criticism," which highlighted the human authorship (and human fallibility) of Scripture, as well as by scholarly inquiries into the "historical Jesus" that emphasized his humanity at the expense of his divinity. Something had to be done, the authors felt, to defend Holy Writ and the doctrine of divine inspiration.[22] Many liberal Protestants found this approach muddled and anti-intellectual; in fact, the word "fundamentalist" was originally a liberal's jibe aimed at anyone who subscribed to the basic approach advocated in *The Fundamentals.* But conservatives were heartened by these books and the approach they advocated, and their basic stance has not changed significantly since then.

It is, I think, simply in the nature of things that this state of affairs will continue; evangelical Christians and others of a conservative bent will continue to be wary of modern scholarship (although some thoughtful conservatives have, in different ways, sought to explore the extent to which such scholarship can coexist with their faith).[23] Beyond this obvious point, however, one might ask whether the preceding chapters can shed any light on the nature of this conservative stance. Fundamentalists/evangelicals would scarcely appreciate being told that they have inherited anything from the Bible's ancient interpreters. Their whole position is, on the contrary, that Scripture speaks directly and literally to us today, without any need for traditional interpretations or ideologically motivated expositors dragging the text hither and yon. But to someone looking from afar, it should be clear that the fundamentalist stance is in fact predicated on at least three of the Four Assumptions of ancient interpreters. Fundamentalists certainly hold that the Bible is perfectly consistent and free of error; that it is addressed to human beings today, speaking about our present and immediate future as well as teaching lessons necessary to salvation; and that it is, in the strictest terms, the word of God. In these respects, indeed, in their whole way of reading Scripture, fundamentalists have much more in common with those ancient Jewish and Christian interpreters than many would likely suspect.

In place of the fourth assumption, however—that the Bible speaks cryptically—fundamentalism asserts that almost everything Scripture says is literally true. It is this proposition that has created the greatest difficulties for fundamentalist hermeneutics—and, interestingly enough, it is one that would certainly have puzzled the ancient interpreters. On the one hand, they would have readily agreed that what the Bible reports did indeed happen—there were indeed real people named Abraham and Sarah, Jacob and Rachel and Rebekah; the Israelites did indeed cross the Red Sea on dry land, and so forth. On the other hand, they would have also dismissed such statements as obvious; Scripture's *important* message, they would say, is often hidden, so that only by going beyond the obvious can one arrive at its true meaning. It is precisely that message, they would tell fundamentalists, that you are missing.

It is certainly not my purpose here to take sides in Protestantism's liberal/conservative debate, but one basic irony underlying the above observations deserves to be spelled out. To liberals, fundamentalists and evangelicals often seem like naïve Bible thumpers. *Haven't they heard about modern science or biblical scholarship? Don't they care about the truth?* Yet, in the broad perspective, the fundamentalist stance—occasional anti-intellectualism and all—has succeeded in preserving much of what is most basic about the Bible, the ancient approach to reading it. By contrast, what now seems naïve is precisely the liberal faith that, despite their abandonment of a good bit of that approach, the Bible can somehow still go on being the Bible.

Related to this is another irony, though one that is less far-reaching in its implications. What liberals and conservatives generally share (although there are, of course, exceptions) is a profound discomfort with the actual interpretations that the ancients came up with—these have little or no place in the way Scripture is to be expounded today. Midrash, allegory, typology—what for? But the style of interpretation thus being rejected is precisely the one that characterizes the numerous interpretations of Old Testament texts by Jesus, Paul, and others in the New Testament, as well as by the succeeding generations of the founders of Christianity.[24]

A Liberal Approach to Scripture

The most sustained reckoning with the conclusions of modern scholarship has been in the "liberal" camp or, rather, camps (that is, not only liberal Protestants, but many liberal-minded Catholics and Jews as well). It would be quite impossible to survey here the many different ways in which nineteenth- and twentieth-century theologians have sought to deal with scholarship's sometimes disturbing conclusions, but certainly one overall trend has been to retreat from the idea of the Hebrew Bible as a factual recitation of past events[25] and to see it as something else: a proclamation of faith, a history with a theological message,[26] a text with a "fuller meaning" or "more than literal" sense,[27] and much more. In the process, theologians have frequently sought to distance themselves from the actual details of the text (many of which seem inappropriate to modern thinking) in order to focus on its "main ideas" or theological "center" or overall theme.[28] Anything unrelated to these,[29] including bloodthirsty oracles against neighboring peoples or divine calls for vengeance or the utter destruction of Israel's enemies, as well as accounts of miracles and other items that challenge modern science or common sense or our modern knowledge of ancient Near Eastern history and civilization, could be "demythologized" or simply ignored.[30]

This overall change in focus has been joined with the broader philosophical and literary-critical debate about hermeneutics, that is, the nature of a text's signification and meaning. In particular, the role of the reader and readerly assumptions in establishing meaning has been highlighted—not (as this subject has been evoked in the present study) as a way of understanding ancient biblical interpreters, but as a justification for reading the Bible today in ways that are at odds with the assumptions of modern scholars. Some theologians have thus highlighted the role of the "community of believers"— either today's church members or the original community of Christianity's founders—in establishing the norms by which Scripture is to be read. For others, a purely literary approach to the Bible has seemed to offer a way out of the straitjacket of original meaning. Just as readers of a novel do not need to concern themselves with the stages by which it was created or whether the events described really happened, so too with the Bible; and if the modern, literature-minded reader's approach is not freighted with the same assumptions and knowledge of a hardnosed biblical scholar, so what? "Postmodernism" has served as a rallying cry for a great many of these different approaches.[31]

Along with this has been a gradual shift in the idea of Scripture's divine inspiration. For centuries people were content to believe that God had simply whispered His words into the prophet's ear or otherwise inspired him in the most concrete manner: the prophet was, in one well-worn image, the pipe through which God's breath blew to make Scripture's wondrous music. More recently, however, various theologians have come up with a range of different understandings of inspiration, so that nowadays a person can choose "limited verbal inspiration" instead of "strict verbal inspiration" or else opt for "nontextual inspiration" or "content inspiration," all of which are yet different from "inspired experiences" or "social inspiration."[32] By the same token, Scriptural "infallibility" is distinguished from Scriptural "inerrancy," and both of these have been found to be different from the "essential truth" of Scripture, which emerges despite its human authors and their many errors.

It would be misleading, however, to characterize this liberal stance as fundamentally defensive—certainly that is not how its proponents would describe it. On the contrary, most would express relief at being rid of an earlier approach to the Bible that they feel to have been untrue—and untruthful. If it is possible to hold on to the general idea of divine inspiration without requiring people to believe in all sorts of unlikely attributions and improbable scenarios, then most would say: thank goodness! And such a stance will go far toward resolving honestly the theological problems of Scripture's many contradictions (with itself, with modern science, and with everything historians have discovered about the ancient Near East) and will likewise free the modern reader from having to give equal weight to everything found in the Old Testament—treating its teachings about *herem* and homosexuality, for example, with the same seriousness as its lessons about love of God and love of one's neighbor. Moreover, while few liberals even bother to contemplate seriously the ancient interpreters' way of reading the Bible, those who do usually express thanks that modern scholarship has also freed them from the grip of the Four Assumptions and the great body of interpretive motifs they generated. Surely we are immeasurably better off, they say, for having jettisoned this artificial way of reading; no serious person could ever advocate its readoption.

Still, an observer perched on a distant promontory might find this assessment of things somewhat rosier than the reality it seeks to describe. Ancient interpretive methods may sometimes appear artificial, but this hardly means that abandoning them guarantees unbiased interpretation. In fact, so much of what liberal theologians and commentators have to say is typically *not* all that modern scholarship has brought to light, but rather represents an attempt to find a compromise between that scholarship and what the commentators themselves would still like the Bible to be. Thus liberal commentators, in the face of all they know about etiological narratives and the like, often prefer to tell their readers about other things: Abraham's or Jacob's supposedly righteous behavior (despite appearances!), Rahab's proto-feminism, or the vast moral gulf separating the biblical flood narrative from its Mesopotamian counterparts. (I have, in an appendix to this volume, assembled some representative examples of this phenomenon; see "Apologetics and Biblical Criticism Lite" on the website www.jameskugel.com.) At times, their interpretations are scarcely less forced than those of ancient midrashists (and usually far less clever).

Looking beyond such specifics, our distant observer would no doubt also point out that the Bible of liberal theologians *has* changed. It simply is not what it was in the days of the Geneva Bible, or even a century or two ago: the *verbum Dei,* God's great book—open it to any page and His timeless guidance will tell you, *you* in particular, what to believe and think and do. Without any widespread acknowledgment of the fact, the Bible seems to have dropped down a peg. Sensible and sober, still containing uplifting words here and there, it is nevertheless more of a human document than ever before, which is to say that its power to command and even instruct has been diminished. "But is this such a bad thing?" liberals might respond. "Was it better to have an entire belief system built on sand?"

Today's liberal theologians are thus being pulled in two opposite directions. On the one hand, they want to be honest about what the Bible really says and really is—even if such honesty includes some of the painful discoveries of modern scholarship. Long live the truth! On the other hand, they are still wedded to the idea of the Bible continuing to play the role it always has played, as a divinely inspired (if only in some attenuated sense) guide and a source of still-relevant teachings—in short, the Good Book. These two aims are often at odds with one another. The attempt to reconcile them thus puts liberal scholars in the uncomfortable position of wanting to have their Bible and criticize it too.

Have their efforts at reconciliation succeeded? It seems to me that the jury is still out. Thirty or forty years ago, some of those familiar with the discoveries of recent scholarship were warning that biblical theology was "in crisis." [32] More recently, others have proclaimed the "death of Scripture" [33]—and it is not biblical scholars alone who are worried. When all is said and done, I think a great many ordinary people are dissatisfied with what Scripture has become. Their first question is: *Is the Bible true?*, and they are uncomfortable with the apologetic tone of the answers they get back, as well as with the invocation of modern hermeneutical theories about the reader's role in creating the text. Someone who sees the Bible primarily as an account of things that actually happened usually has a hard time continuing to honor it when archaeologists and biblical scholars deny the historicity of most of its stories.

Is this likely to change? Or perhaps I should say "change back," since, as we have seen, this was not primarily how the Bible's first readers read the text. Indeed, for most of the Bible's history, it was the words of Scripture and its "lessons" that were all-important; these words were the gateway to all the key teachings (and, often, hidden meanings) underneath the text. The historical reality of the events being described (what came to be called, in medieval Christianity, the text's *sensus litteralis* or *historicus*) was altogether secondary. Thus, Philo could remark that there was indeed an actual Abraham who once walked the globe, but the significant sense of his story was a representation of the human soul in search of God—anytime, anywhere. Similarly, Paul could say that the events that occurred during the Israelites' desert wanderings "happened to them as a warning, but they were written down for our instruction, upon whom the end of the ages has come" (1 Cor. 10:11). To put it differently: the events of the past are one thing, but the words of Scripture are quite another, and it is the words that count for us. In precisely this sense, another New Testament letter saw the importance of Scripture in its capacity "for teaching, for reproof, for correction, and for training in righteousness" (2 Tim. 3:16).

Scripture's Changed Meaning

In trying to coax modern readers back in this direction, some scholars have sought to build a bridge between the true, historical reality as they know it,

including the original meaning of various biblical texts, and the way of reading those same texts described in the preceding paragraph, reading the Bible
not as history but "for teaching, for reproof, for correction, and for training
in righteousness." These scholars therefore stress that the Bible itself offers
ample evidence that the original meaning of this or that text was drastically
altered even within the biblical period—by editors or perhaps by people
who were themselves prophets, who rearranged, supplemented, interpo-
lated, and otherwise put a very different spin on the original prophet's words.

From the standpoint of this book's overall concern with the role of ancient
interpreters, this might seem to be a step in the right direction. Nevertheless,
I think I would not be wrong to say that most liberal theologians still see the
border between the biblical and the postbiblical, between the prophet and the
interpreter, as absolute. Indeed, the further back one moves into biblical
territory, the safer one is. How else, for example, to understand Gerhard von
Rad's insistence that one must give equal attention to "each phase" leading
up to the biblical text's final form, rather than just reading the final form
itself? It was the latter, after all, that *was* the Bible, accepted by Christianity's
original community of believers;[34] what any earlier form of the text might
have been, and what it might have meant to which group, are a matter of
pure speculation. But if you believe that the biblical is good and the postbiblical is at least irrelevant and perhaps corrupting, then the form of the text
that sits on the border between the two cannot take precedence over earlier
forms.[35] That is why "each phase" leading up to the final text must be considered—to locate the beginnings of a changed way of reading safely within *sola
scriptura*-land. One scholar has even gone so far as to claim that the final,
canonized form of the text is actually to be considered inferior to those earlier forms, the precanonical editions and stages.[36]

As we have seen, however, it was not principally the rearranging and
interpolating done by editors that turned these ancient writings into Scripture,
but the whole tradition of interpretation that emerged toward the end of the
biblical period. This point, it seems to me, is most important even with
regard to those contemporary theologians who, at first glance, might seem to
have taken a step still closer to the argument of the present study—that is,
"canonical" critics who, in various shades and forms, assert the primacy of the
final, canonical form of the text over its earlier stages.[37] But any appearance
of closeness is an illusion. Faced with the theological problems posed by modern biblical scholarship, canonical critics correctly insist that a text's original
meaning is not necessarily its only meaning, indeed, that the original con-
stituents of the Bible necessarily took on a new meaning as soon as they began
to be supplemented and edited and ultimately placed in a larger environment
of texts, the biblical canon. But this apparently historical argument takes no
account of what those texts actually meant at the time of their canonization.
That is, canonical criticism draws the line at the canonical *text*. It does not

seem to realize that the earliest "community of believers" canonized not only the text but their own peculiar way of reading and interpreting it. There was nothing optional about the latter: it *was* what the text meant. Nor is there anything obscure about what that way of reading and interpreting was: it cries out from nearly every page of the New Testament and other early Christian writings, and has been documented in dozens of modern studies. I should make it clear that I am not saying that the only legitimate way now to read the Bible is the way Paul or Jerome read it, only that the canonical critics' appeal to the magical moment of canonization as decisive is, historically speaking, highly selective. It takes what it wants—the final, canonical shape of the text—and throws out the rest: the whole unwritten set of instructions as to *how* the text is to be read, along with the rich body of specific interpretations that accompanied it at that time. And it does this only the better to pursue the great Protestant enterprise of interpreting things afresh.

Moreover, from a historical standpoint, canonical criticism's location of the great change in the Bible's meaning within the Bible itself (in the psalm headings, for example, or the editorial shifts within prophetic books) is, as already indicated, quite misguided. These are indeed the signs of the *beginnings* of change, but they pale before the immense transformation introduced by interpreters in the third, second, and first centuries BCE. It was truly out of the work of these interpreters that the canonized Bible emerged, and without it, one might well doubt if the Bible ever could have come to occupy the central place that it did within Judaism and Christianity. Indeed, the very idea of the Bible—that God conceived everything within it in order to tell people what to think and do, and that, in keeping with this, its every word is significant and potentially full of hidden meaning as well as perfectly consistent with every other word—is the product of the interpretative revolution of these closing centuries BCE. If so, why should canonical critics devote so much attention to the scattered forerunners of this revolution found within the Bible itself while largely ignoring the fact that the great change came later and was the product of an anonymous group of Jewish interpreters? The answer, I have already suggested, lies in the historic Protestant allegiance to the Bible alone—*sola scriptura*. Nothing else can rival the Bible's authority.

Judaism and Modern Biblical Scholarship

The situation in Judaism is quite the opposite. The founders[38] of what was to become, after the first century CE, the dominant form of Judaism ("rabbinic Judaism") had always attributed great importance to the Torah's traditions of interpretation. In fact—for various reasons that need not detain us here[39]—those traditions were granted a special status in Judaism: they were referred to collectively as the Torah-that-was-transmitted-orally (or "Oral Torah" for short), and they were sometimes asserted to go back all the way to the time of Moses himself, who had received them at the same time that he received the written text of the Pentateuch.[40] If so, according to the exponents of rabbinic Judaism, then there were really *two* Torahs, the written Pentateuch and the traditions of its proper interpretation and application, which had been transmitted orally along with it.[41] In the terms that we have seen, this was a kind of canonization of the idea that Abraham was a monotheist who underwent ten tests; that Jacob was a learned student, while his brother Esau was a brutish lout; that the Israelites heard only the first two of the Ten Commandments directly from God; that in forbidding "work" on the sabbath, the Torah had in mind precisely thirty-nine different types of work; that the Torah's law of guardians distinguishes between a paid and an unpaid guardian; that a water-giving rock followed the Israelites in the desert; that the Shema is to be recited every morning and evening; and so on and so forth. All such traditions were held to be of equal authority with the written text, and this idea has remained a central tenet of Judaism to this day.

The "Oral Torah," it should be noted, consisted of more than biblical interpretation alone—it also contained rules governing a number of matters not covered in the Pentateuch (for example, prayers and blessings to be recited on various occasions; agricultural laws; some torts and other areas of civil law; matters connected with betrothal, marriage, and divorce; parts of criminal law and judicial procedure; a detailed description of temple rites, purity statutes, and so forth). It thus included a vast body of material, and even though it continued to be called the *"Oral* Torah," this material was eventually committed to writing—it became the Mishnah and Tosefta and the two Talmuds and various compilations of midrash in different genres. Thus, today, Judaism has essentially two canons, the biblical one and the great corpus of writings included under the Oral Torah.

Although these two bodies of writings were, and are, said to be of equal authority, in practice, the Oral Torah always wins. The written Torah may say "an eye for an eye," but what these words mean is what the Oral Torah says they mean, namely, monetary compensation for any such injury (*b. Baba Qamma* 83b–84a). The written Torah may say that Jacob went to his father "deceitfully," but the Oral Torah explains that he really didn't lie. And so on and so forth for every apparent problem, every inconsistency or contradiction or infelicity in the written text. The solutions produced by the Bible's ancient interpreters simply became what the text meant. So Judaism has at its heart a great secret. It endlessly lavishes praise on the written Torah, exalting its role as a divinely given guidebook and probing lovingly the tiniest details of its wording and even spelling. Every sabbath the Torah is, quite literally, held up above the heads of worshipers in synagogue, kissed and bowed to and touched in gestures of fealty and absolute submission, some of which may, incidentally, be traced all the way back to ancient Mesopotamia.[42] Yet upon inspection Judaism turns out to be quite the opposite of fundamental-ism. The written text alone is not all-powerful; in fact, it rarely stands on its own. Its true significance usually lies not in the plain sense of its words but in what the Oral Torah has made of those words; this is its definitive and final interpretation.[43]

As a result, the whole approach of modern biblical scholarship, which is predicated on disregarding the ancient interpretive traditions of Judaism (and, for that matter, Christianity) and rejecting the four fundamental assumptions that underlie them, must inevitably come into conflict with tra-ditional Jewish belief and practice. The modern program rules out of bounds precisely that which is, for traditional Jews, the Torah's ultimate signifi-cance and its definitive interpretation. To insist on taking the Torah's words at face value, without regard to what the Oral Torah says about them, is thus for a traditional Jew somewhat comparable to telling a Christian that he or she must take the laws of the Old Testament at face value, without regard for all that Paul has to say about them in the New Testament, as well as about the new covenant of Christianity that has come to take their place. I do not know any Christians who would accept such a proposition.

My own view, therefore—though others may disagree—is that modern biblical scholarship and traditional Judaism are and must always remain completely irreconcilable. Individual Jews may, for one reason or another, seek to speculate about how different parts of the Bible came to be written or about the historical circumstances and original purposes of its various com-ponents, but none of this speculation can have any part in traditional Jewish study or worship; indeed, the whole attitude underlying such speculation is altogether alien to the spirit of Judaism and the role of Scripture within it. Nothing in the present volume is intended to suggest otherwise.

But if this is so, does Judaism have any response to all that modern bibli-cal scholarship has discovered? This is a question with more than a century of answers to it, and one cannot rightly speak of a single answer or even a sin-gle direction.[44] Still, I do not think it would be wrong to characterize at least one major voice in this polyphony as basically following part of the argument about original meaning that we have been tracing throughout. What Scrip-ture means is not what today's ingenious scholars can discover about its orig-inal meaning (and certainly not about the events and persons it describes), but what the ancient interpreters have always held it to mean. A more theoretical version of this answer—and more in keeping with what we have seen in the previous chapters—might go like this: The texts that make up the Bible were originally composed under whatever circumstances they were com-posed. What made them the Bible, however, was their definitive reinterpreta-tion, along the lines of the Four Assumptions of the ancient interpreters—a way of reading that was established in Judaism in the form of the Oral Torah. Read the Bible in this way and you are reading it properly, that is, in keeping with the understanding of those who made and canonized the Bible. Read it any other way and you have drastically misconstrued the intentions of the Bible's framers. You are like someone who thinks Swift's satirical *Modest Proposal* was a serious program for ending the famine in Ireland—or perhaps a better example from our discussion of the Song of Songs: you are like someone who understands the words of "She'll Be Comin' Round the Mountain" like a twelve-year-old camper. No one has ever told you about its other meaning; that is to say, no one has explained to you why the adults are singing it with religious fervor. Don't tell me that original songwriter's inten-tion is everything:[45] when the grown-ups sing it, every word has the messianic meaning I described. Now if it doesn't for you (and if you're not a twelve-year-old camper), then why are you singing it at all? Similarly with the Song of Songs and with *all* of Scripture: its true meaning is not the original mean-ing of its constituent parts, but the meaning it had for the people who first saw it as the Bible, God's great book of instruction. If it doesn't have that meaning for you anymore—if all it is is etiological tales and priestly polemics and political speeches—then why are you singing it?

The Very Idea of the Bible

This seems to me a plausible position in the light of all we have seen about the emergence of the Bible. And yet, for someone who takes the Bible seriously, this stance alone hardly resolves the difficulties posed by the last century or so of biblical scholarship. For such a person, hearing or reading about the Doc-umentary Hypothesis for the first time—or any of the other basics of biblical criticism—can be devastating. Items such as the divine origin of the Torah and the role ascribed in it to Moses, as well as the historicity of the patriar-chal narratives, the exodus, and the conquest of Canaan, all play a crucial role in his or her faith. Yet all of these, as we have seen, have been cast into doubt by modern scholarship. In the face of such doubts, "Sorry, that isn't how *we* read the text" or even "That isn't how the Bible was first read when it became the Bible" may not be an adequate response.

Another sort of answer, it seems to me, has been lurking in the background of this book all along. It is probably not the sort of answer that will satisfy most traditional readers of the Bible, certainly not at the first shock of discov-ering modern scholarship. In the long run, however, it may at least suggest a somewhat different approach to thinking about Scripture and the problems raised by modern scholarship. It all has to do with the way in which God was apprehended in ancient Israel, and more particularly, with a significant change that took place in that way of apprehension.

When God first appeared to Abraham or Jacob, He was, by the Bible's own testimony, the God of Old: He stepped through the curtain that divides ordinary from extraordinary reality, spoke for a minute or two, and then disappeared. Such encounters are consistently represented in the Bible as frightening; the normal human reaction to His appearance was that of the Israelites at Sinai: "When the people saw, they trembled and stood at a distance" (Exod. 20:18). And yet, along with fear, there was, at least for some, the desire—or perhaps more correctly, the perceived need—to meet the deity, to somehow maintain the vital, if dangerous, connection with Him. This, after all, was the whole idea of the ancient Near Eastern temple, a safe and carefully controlled environment in which trained cultic personnel could stand up close (and not "at a distance") in order to seek the deity's favor.

Yet, at a certain point in this history (it is difficult to say precisely when), Israel began to conceive of a different sort of "standing up close," and the change proved revolutionary. It had to do with *serving* God. The idea of human beings as the gods' servants or slaves has an ancient pedigree in the Near East, but in Israel this commonplace came to define a relationship, first between God and specific individuals, then between Him and the whole people: "They are My servants, whom I brought out of the land of Egypt" (Lev. 25:42, 55). To be a servant or slave was to be in a state of humble subjection, ever eager to do the master's bidding; but it was also conceived to be a state of closeness, even familiarity. (This English word, it might be noted, is related to the Latin *familiaris,* the household slave who "belonged to the family.") To be God's servant was to be part of His household.[46]

But what exactly did God want *His* familiar servants to do? The laws of the Decalogue, according to some scholars, may have begun as the simple code of conduct among scattered tribes, binding them to their distant Suzerain and imposing on them minimal standards of decency in dealing with one another. But the idea of *divinely* given laws—the whole idea of the Decalogue—was a remarkable one, and soon a broad range of other laws and statutes (civil and criminal, cultic and ethical) were promulgated in this same God's name. This made for a unique legal system. Elsewhere, to violate the law was a crime; in Israel it was also, explicitly, a sin. By the same token, to keep the law scrupulously was not merely good citizenship; it was to do God's bidding. So it was that, with ever greater emphasis, serving God meant not only offering sacrifices in the temple, but carrying out His many statutes. This is, among other things, the central theme of the legal core of Deuteronomy. In these laws the temple is presented as distant, a place to which pilgrims repair periodically. It is thus far from most people's ordinary experience, whereas God's laws are ever-present, governing a person's everyday life and that of his neighbors and his village. Indeed, there were soon so many divine commandments it was difficult to remember them all; so, "I will put my Torah inside them, I will write it on their very hearts: I will be their God, and they will be my people. No longer will they need to teach one another or say one to the other, 'Be obedient to the LORD,' for they shall all be obedient to Me, from the least of them to the greatest, says the LORD" (Jer. 31:33–34).

True, the people of Israel were not always, and not uniformly, conceived as God's servants in the Bible. In much of it, those servants were individuals, notably "His servants the prophets" (Amos 3:7; 2 Kings 17:23; etc.). They, like the priests, were uniquely close to Him; their words expressed His judgments on Israel and on its neighbors. Yet as those words were preserved beyond their immediate time, they also changed. The divine intermediaries who uttered them and the specific situations that they addressed faded into the background. Instead, the prophets' utterances—now timeless and without precise context—became instructions to any who cared to know God's will and God's ways, "O you who tremble at His word" (Isa. 66:5).

The period following the return from Babylonian exile was one of renewed dedication to God's will. It is in this context that one should locate the seeds of the very idea of a Bible, a great, multifarious corpus of divinely given instruction. All those texts saved from the ancient past came, slowly but steadily, to be united behind a single purpose: to tell people what God wanted them to know and believe *and do,* to tell them how to be God's familiar servants.[47] Of course, the Pentateuch or Torah was foremost, as a glance at the great corpus of ancient interpretation will confirm (that is, the material found in the biblical apocrypha, the pseudepigrapha, the Dead Sea Scrolls, and the writings of Philo and Josephus). The first five books of the Bible were by far the most important ones to study and understand, because their laws, but also their stories, told you how to act and what to do. Indeed, the fact is that the Pentateuch *as a whole* came to be known as the *Torah,* a term that, while it might broadly be translated as "teaching," retained some of its earlier nuance of "law" or "legal procedure." (Hence the Greek translation of this title—in the Septuagint and Philo and the New Testament—as the *nomos,* the "law" or *regula vitae.*)

Yet here is a most interesting point: the words of that Torah were evidently not sacrosanct. On the contrary, as we have seen throughout this study, their apparent meaning was frequently modified or supplemented by ancient interpreters—sometimes expanded or limited in scope, very often concretized through specific applications or homey examples,[48] sometimes (as with "an eye for an eye") actually overthrown. An obvious question arises: if the laws and stories of the Pentateuch were deemed to come from God, how dare mere humans fiddle with them, adding to them, taking them out of context, changing their meaning, or even getting them to say the opposite of what they said?[49] Did not the Torah itself quite explicitly command: "You must neither add anything to what I command you nor take anything away from it" (Deut. 4:2)?

This is, I believe, *the* question to ask, since the answer reveals the very idea of Scripture at its essence. The answer is that there was something considered even more important, more powerful, than the words of the text themselves. That something was precisely the "standing up close" mentioned above: the supreme mission of serving God, of being God's familiar servants. Scripture was sacred, but more sacred still was the purpose underlying the very idea of Scripture. How else to explain that the Torah's laws could be treated as they were, modified even within the Bible itself, and then lavishly, unashamedly expanded and reinterpreted and applied to the concrete situations of daily life by the ancient interpreters? Indeed, this same tendency has carried through clearly even into modern times.[50]

Viewed from this perspective, the sometimes disturbing insights of modern scholarship must necessarily take on a different aspect. In Judaism, Scripture is ultimately valued not as history, nor as theology, nor even as *the* great, self-sufficient corpus of divine utterances—all that God had ever wished to say to man. Judaism is not fundamentalism, nor even Protestantism. What Scripture is, and always has been, in Judaism is the beginning of a manual entitled *To Serve God,* a manual whose trajectory has always led from the prophet to the interpreter and from the divine to the merely human. To put the matter in, I admit, rather shocking terms: since in Judaism it is not the words of Scripture themselves that are ultimately supreme, but the service of God (the "standing up close") that they enjoin, then to suggest that everything hangs on Scripture might well be described as a form of fetishism or idolatry, that is, a mistaking of the message for its Sender and the turning of its words into idols of wood or stone. Rabbinic Judaism's whole attitude toward the written text is quite the opposite of such fetishism. For Judaism, the crucial element in Scripture has always been the imperative that Scripture's very existence embodies (and the changed apprehension that underlies that imperative), the basic divine commandment reflected in Deuteronomy's exhortation "to serve the LORD your God with all your heart and all your soul" (Deut. 10:12) and similar pronouncements. To flesh out this commandment was the purpose of all of Scripture and all later interpretation. With such a purpose foremost, the Bible's original component texts easily lent themselves to flexible reinterpretation. As a matter of fact, a fossilized, petrified meaning would, soon enough, end up betraying this purpose of Scripture by making it outmoded and obsolete.[51]

In saying this, I may seem to have doubled back to an earlier theme, the importance of the ancient interpretations that have accompanied Scripture on its journey. But this time, the point I am seeking to make is slightly different. The very idea of Scripture, I wish to say, was at its origin an expression of a certain way of apprehending God—not the fleeting, frightening way in which the God of Old was encountered, but the way of coming before Him in constancy as His familiar servants. Seen in the broadest perspective, this is hardly the only way that human beings have sought to apprehend God (not even within the confines of ancient Israel). But it was the way that came to increasing prominence, especially after the Babylonian exile, and it left its mark most visibly in Hebrew Scripture. Scripture was the set of written instructions God had given to His familiar servants.

This character of Scripture subsequently underwent not one but three significant revisions, first with the rise of Christianity, later with the Protestant Reformation, and finally with the full flowering of modern scholarship. Early Christianity never abandoned the basic servants-of-God posture that underlay the religion of Israel in later times, even though at the heart of Paul's theology was the replacement of the old covenant of laws with a new one of grace. Belief and devotion are, after all, also a kind of service, even when disconnected from a specific menu of devotional acts. Thus *Quid agas*—"what you should do"—never ceased to be a major element in Christian teaching, and it was held to be one of the three spiritual senses of Scripture. But as a practical matter, "what you should do" was, in late antiquity and medieval times, no longer primarily located in Scripture: the laws of the Old Testament were now mediated by the New. Instead, the service of God was a matter of direct church teaching and of the creeds—some of it certainly based on Scripture, but interpreted by papal authority and hallowed tradition. As for the actual text of the Old Testament, it became, from the church's ascendancy through the Middle Ages and beyond, significant primarily for its connection to the New Testament, often as the foreshadowing and confirmation of the New, or the promise that was fulfilled in the events of the New.[52]

The new Protestant denominations ushered in a further change. With no pope and no authoritative traditions of interpretation, the words of Scripture now stood alone—*sola scriptura*. As such, Scripture was summoned to play a role it had never played before and for which, by the nature of things, it was rather ill-suited. How indeed was one to reconcile apparent contradictions, and what was one to do with teachings that no longer corresponded to anything in current reality? The latter was an especially pressing question for the new Protestant denominations, in which the doctrine of justification by faith alone—*sola fide*—had only widened the gap between Torah and Gospel. The answer proposed was twofold. On the one hand, Scripture soon became the raw material for theologians to use in formulating its important message or messages; troubling elements could simply be omitted. ("*Had* to be omitted," theologians now said, since if ancient Judaism's "apprehension of God" was different from that which preceded it, Christianity's was necessarily different from that of ancient Judaism.) On the other hand—and here we join the movement of modern biblical scholarship—it was the real events and real people about which Scripture reported that moved to the fore and began to be studied for their own sake. The imperfections of the text were simply that, imperfections; they mattered little if what counted was "what really happened" and its corollary, "what really was said."[53] C. A. Briggs and his generation had hoped that archaeology, ancient Near Eastern history, and philology would combine to restore the "real Bible." This has not happened.

And so, while the fundamentally changed apprehension of God that underlay the very idea of Scripture remains alive to some degree in *all* the biblical religions, its connection with Scripture is, for many readers, increasingly strained.

This, it seems to me, is the larger picture behind the story traced on these pages, and a deeper understanding of this sequence of events may help illuminate the nature of the Bible's current difficulties. I am certainly not saying that this evolution ought now to be reversed. But it is really only through an appreciation of the original idea of Scripture, and the apprehension of God that underlies it, that those difficulties can be put in proper perspective.

By the same logic, it seems to me that the whole matter of Scripture's inspiration can only be understood in connection with the overall change in Israel's apprehension of God described above. Divine inspiration is not, at bottom, a matter of conferring a seal of divine approval on this or that passage of Scripture, or even on Scripture as a whole. Precisely in the light of what was just seen about the flexible way in which Scripture's words were treated by the very people who maintained its uniformly divine character, such a conception of inspiration seems to make little sense. Rather, as some rabbinic texts themselves intimate,[54] it all has to do with the great, single revelation that inaugurated (and on which was predicated) Israel's changed apprehension of God. Scripture reflects the real moment in the history of the human apprehension of the divine that occurred back in biblical times and subsequently changed everything, first for Israel and then for much of humanity: the moment when Israel first stood before God as His familiar servants, eager to carry out His will in myriad particulars. The Bible, it seems to me, remains the most accessible avenue into the world of that change, setting out both what preceded it as well as what immediately followed, a basic program for the service of God in daily life.

Harvard Prof Says Bible Research a Mistake

I have, in some sense, been writing this last chapter for the past thirty years, and now that it is done, I still have the feeling that I have left too many things unsaid. In any case, as someone with some experience in such matters, I can readily imagine how this chapter may be misconstrued. The above is certainly an appealing headline, and I have some premonition that it will appear somewhere, the review underneath it conveniently skipping over the first thirty-five chapters of this book in order to concentrate on (and misrepresent) the thirty-sixth. In truth, however, my subject has been not the ruin of the Bible but the Bible itself—its highways and little byways, heroes, brigands, walk-ons, and also-rans, its mysteries and its ineffables, as well as its sometimes treacherous little details. Beyond all these, this book is about two extraordinary sets of interpreters, and I have made no effort to disguise my admiration for both. Their approaches, however, are quite irreconcilable—

this, if some headline is required, is the one I would prefer. Happy the reader who can open the Bible today and still understand it as it was understood by those who first proclaimed it the Bible. For anyone else, I hope that this book may at least offer some help in finding an escape from the box of original meaning and, perhaps as well, some greater appreciation of the way of reading championed by the Bible's first interpreters—those who turned the erotic Song of Songs into the allegorical one, the stories of Genesis or Judges into moral tales, and the temple-centered, cultic psalms into the timeless and placeless stirrings of every heart. No doubt, a bit of imaginative effort is demanded nowadays to enter into their frame of mind—to focus first on the text itself, on its very words, and then quite consciously to allow them to speak as best they can about God and man, heaven and earth, and how it is that these may meet. I certainly have nothing against exploring "what really happened" and how the Bible came to be written, but I would not mistake such things for what is foremost. They are rightly the province of specialists, people who (like me) got bitten by the bug. As for all I have omitted, it seems best to me simply to let this study sputter out with a few disjointed observations I have jotted down over the years.

Anyone who has studied different religions knows that the "ideas" part of them counts for relatively little. Someone rhythmically chanting "Hari Krishna" may, in some technical sense, be speaking words, but these phonemes are clearly only a kind of vehicle. So too for formulaic prayers and hymns, repeated week after week or day after day. There always has to be something to make the connection between human beings and God, and that something often consists of words (we humans are speakers and thinkers, after all)—words of prayers and, sometimes, even the words of theological doctrines and ideas. But those words are really the frail filament through which the electric current passes. Without them it would not pass at all, of course; but they are frail nonetheless. (I remember, with a smile but also some understanding, the woman who told her pastor that she "had found great support in that blessed word, Mesopotamia.") [55]

Scripture is, in one sense, the opposite of prayer (words from God rather than to God), but it makes this same connection. Scripture in different religious traditions always seems to have the remarkable ability to become the locus of people's deepest inner fumblings and mumblings: those words suddenly contain so much—their quality of Scripture gives them that right—and they fill up with all that is most important: they become the theater of the soul.

• • •

How can you distinguish the word of God from other, ordinary, human words in Scripture? I do not know of any litmus test that can be used. I suppose I have my suspicions about this verse or that one, but I really do not believe it is my business to try to second-guess the text's divine inspiration. And so, I like to think about Scripture in the same terms I think about the Temple Mount in Jerusalem. That little flat-topped, squared-off hill (a short walk from my house) was once the site of Solomon's temple, and then, after that temple was destroyed by the Babylonians, it soon became the site of the second temple, until it too was put to the torch, this time by the Romans. It lay in ruins for several centuries, until the Muslim conquest of Jerusalem, when the Dome of the Rock and the al-Aqsa mosque were built on it. Not immediately thereafter, but soon enough, custom and, eventually, rabbinical decree forbade pious Jews from ascending that hill and walking about, lest by accident their foot defile the place where once the Holy of Holies stood, the place of God's presence on earth (which could be entered only once a year, and only by one man, the high priest). This prohibition is in force to this day. So every day, pious Muslims and Christian pilgrims and Japanese tourists climb up the steps and walk all around the Temple Mount, but religious Jews do not. I do not.

Now, of course, I have my own ideas about where the Holy of Holies once stood. I think there is every reason to doubt that it stood, for example, in the extreme northeastern corner of the Temple Mount—why should anyone have built the temple way over there, and in such a way that the Holy of Holies stood precariously close to the flat hill's edge? In fact, I doubt that it was close to any of the edges of the current Temple Mount. So couldn't I just walk very carefully around on the outer perimeter and stand there, safe in the knowledge that I am not violating the space once occupied by God's presence? But of course I don't.

I like to think of Scripture as a similar sort of space. I certainly could not pinpoint Scripture's Holy of Holies, the very center from which the divine presence radiated outward. But I suppose I could try to put together my own collection of verses that might correspond to the extreme northeastern corner of the Temple Mount: could God truly have resided over here? Still, I am content to respect Scripture's current dimensions and its integrity. Even if I could somehow distinguish divinely inspired words from ordinary human ones, such an exercise would be pointless from the Bible's standpoint. We have seen that, since ancient times, the trajectory of being God's servants inevitably led from words of God to merely human words, and that the latter have had a great deal to do with the essence of the Bible, turning all of it into a manual of "what to do." So, while I could not be involved in a religion that was entirely a human artifact, it would, in theory at least, be enough for me if God said what He is reported to have said in Exodus and Deuteronomy: "Do you want to come close to Me? Then do My bidding, become My employees." The fleshing out of that primal commandment takes place in Scripture and outside of Scripture, and it is all one sacred precinct; indeed, the divine presence suffuses every part of it.

PICTURE CREDITS

A NOTE TO THE READER

For the following:

1. Appendix 1: "Apologetics and Biblical Criticism Lite"
2. Bibliography—A List of Works Cited in the Notes
3. A Guide to Ancient Biblical Interpreters Cited in This Book
4. Questions and Reactions from Readers (and send in your own!)
5. Calendar of Upcoming Talks and Other Information Relevant to This Book
6. A Reply to My Critics

PLEASE GO TO THE WEB SITE: www.jameskugel.com

NOTES

Citations here refer to author, date of publication, and, where relevant, page numbers within the cited work. For complete bibliographic information, please see www.jameskugel.com.

1. The Rise of Modern Biblical Scholarship

1. An important, and not unrelated, heresy trial had taken place in the previous decade, when the biblical scholar W. Robertson Smith was tried by the Scottish Free Church. For an account of his work and the trial, see Beidleman (1974). Worthy of mention also is the less well known case of Bishop J. W. Colenso of Natal in southern Africa, whose study, *The Pentateuch and Book of Joshua Critically Examined* (7 vols., 1862–79) was among the things that caused him to be accused of heresy by his superior, Bishop Robert Gray of Cape Town, in 1863. He was convicted the next year but was subsequently acquitted on a jurisdictional ruling. This notwithstanding, the English bishops voted to depose him in 1869; he continued to minister to a dwindling band of followers until his death in 1883. Indeed, Colenso had been mired in controversy in South Africa and England since 1861, not only because of his views about the Bible, but also because of his criticism of British colonial policies with regard to the Zulus, to whom he ministered.

   Colenso's masterwork is well surveyed in Rogerson (1984: 220–37), who calls the book "the most remarkable achievement by a British scholar in the field of Old Testament criticism in the nineteenth century" (232). Colenso's critique of traditional ideas was based in part on his reading of the work of earlier German and British scholars, and in part on his own careful analysis and original formulations. His seriousness of purpose did not prevent him from adopting at times a somewhat flippant approach to obvious problems in the text. See below, chapter 13, note 6.

2. Much of Briggs's biography I owe to Massa (1990: 24–52), as well as to Hatch (1969: 21–65) and Ludlow (1891: 7–12). I have also consulted: Smith (1913: 497–508); Waugh (2004: 401–11), and Fogarty (1989: 140–70). My thanks to Professor Gary Anderson for this last reference.

3. Cited in Massa (1990: 28).

4. Ludlow (1891: 11).

5. Briggs (1891: 31; 34–35).

6. Ibid., p. 33.

7. Ibid., p. 37–38.

8. Ibid., p. 38.

9. Reported in the *New York Tribune*, Nov. 10, 1892; cited in Massa (1990: 104).

10. Many Christian Bibles include a group of biblical "apocrypha" or "deutero-canonical" works, and these include some further representatives of wisdom writing, such as The Wisdom of Ben Sirach and the Wisdom of Solomon.

11. I have explained at greater length some of the factors leading up to the rise of these ancient interpreters in Kugel and Greer (1986: 27–51).

12. See on this, Japhet (1989: 395–504).

13. It used to be argued that the Persians initiated their rule of Judea and other captured provinces by demanding a version of local laws, which might then be integrated with elements of Persian law as the province's legal foundation; this, many scholars argued, might have served as a spur to the final editing of the Pentateuch, Judea's local "law-code." See Ezra 7:21, 25–26; E. Bickerman (1988), and Kugel (1998: 8–9). Lately, this line of argument has been contested (Watts, 2001). See below, chapter 21, note 35.

14. For a fuller answer, readers are referred to the introduction to my *Traditions of the Bible* (henceforth: Kugel 1998), pp. 1–41. The same introduction appears in the shorter version, *The Bible As It Was* (Cambridge: Harvard University Press, 1997), 1–49.

15. See Kugel (2001: 1–26).

16. In this connection: the Book of Ben Sira (Sirach), 38:24—30:11.

17. See Nahum 2:12 as explained in the Dead Sea Scrolls text 4Q169 Nahum Pesher.

18. See on this: Simon (1982); Kugel (1990: 45–55).

19. See Kugel and Greer (1986: 27–39); and Kugel (2001).

20. Contrast this with Philo's explanation in *On the Virtues*, 156–158, which presents no allegorical reading.

21. This is one reason why, in geographic terms, the allegorical approach was thus primarily associated with the city of Alexandria. As we have already glimpsed, Philo's method of reading was picked up by Clement of Alexandria and other early Christians. See on this van den Hoek (1988). For the example of Clement's use of Lev. 19:23 with regard to the development of faith, see pp. 99–100. Alexandrian Christians transmitted a number of Philo's allegorical interpretations largely unchanged to later interpreters, including the influential Origen (ca. 185–254 CE). For the Alexandrian Christians overall, Scripture was thus a highly symbolic world, a pageant of spiritual and philosophical truths moving along, as it were, in the form of human beings and historical events.

22. If the city of Alexandria was associated with the allegorical approach to Scripture, its opposite number was another center of Christian learning, the city of Antioch (in northern Syria). The interpreters of Antioch are often said to have championed a more literal or historical approach to Scripture, and this is true; but along with this came a certain friendliness to the typological approach. Typology, as generally conceived, stays on the same level of human history; it simply seeks to find in the events described in the Old Testament hints to later historical events or teachings, things that belong to the time of the New. Christian typologists used various terms to describe these Old Testament hints: they were called shadows or pictures or types or figures of their New Testament counterparts—hence our use of words like foreshadowing or prefiguring or typology. *How to Read the Bible* was not an undisputed subject even in those days, and the fights over interpretive methods were sometimes bitter; in the end, however, both allegory and typology found a place in the Christian interpretative handbook. Indeed, although nowadays we clearly differentiate these two methods—allegory reads concrete things as if they represent abstract ones, while typology reads earlier things as foreshadowing later ones—this distinction was not always clear to early Christians; in fact, both approaches were sometimes simply called "allegory," or else typology was called "prophetic allegory." What was important was that both were nonliteral ways of reading, both part of Scripture's *sensus spiritualis*. See on this Young (1997: 152–54, 165–85). Young also points out that, while describing typology (as I have) as acting on the "horizontal" axis of history has helped scholars focus on its most characteristic feature, there is more to typology than that. Types can have symbolic quality and "become windows through bearing the 'impress' of eternal truth" (p. 156). What *was* common to all Christian exegetes was the attempt to go beyond the *sensus litteralis* to some deeper truth. Note also the classic study of Preus (1969).

23. Eberling (1970: 98–109).

24. On the history of this little poem, written around 1260 by one Augustine of Dacia, and similar compositions, see de Lubac (1998: 1–14).

25. Dante's ideas about allegory, and specifically his distinction in the *Convivio* between the three-

fold "allegory of the poets" and the fourfold "allegory of the theologians," has been extensively studied by Singleton (1954) and Hollander (1969). See also Cecchini (2000: 340–78).

26. "The Letter to Can Grande," in Haller (1973: 99).

27. The story of medieval Christian interpretation and the rise of scholasticism has been frequently treated, that of medieval Jewish exegesis somewhat less. In good conscience, therefore, I should at least name some of what is being omitted on the Jewish side—the initial persistence of midrashic interpretation, then the difficulties with it raised by both Arabic philosophy and the rise of Karaism; the response of Se'adya Gaon and, shortly afterward, the pursuit of biblical exegesis in medieval Spain, spurred on by the above-named forces as well as the development of a far more accurate understanding of Hebrew grammar and biblical lexicography. (Crucial here is the work of the eleventh-century grammarians Jonah ibn Janah, Judah Hayyuj, Dunash ben Labrat, and the lexicographer Meanhem b. Saruq.) In northern France in the eleventh and twelfth centuries there arose a new center of Jewish exegetes, centering around Rashi and his school, some of whose members had direct contact with, and some influence on, the Christian exegetes of the Abbey of Saint Victor in Paris. These contacts—now studied in numerous articles and monographs following Beryl Smalley's pioneering work, *The Study of the Bible in the Middle Ages* (1964)—served to arouse new interest among Christians in the *sensus litteralis* after centuries of relative neglect. Important along the same lines were the *Postillae* of Nicholas de Lyra (1270–1340), studied by Halperin (1963). Two important synthesists among Jewish interpreters were the Provençal (France) commentator David Kimhi (1160–1235, called in Hebrew RaDaK) and his slightly later contemporary in Catalonia (Spain), Moses Nahmanides (1194–ca.1270, RaMBaN). Both succeeded in fusing traditional Jewish learning with the new philology and other exegetical trends; noteworthy as well are the later medieval commentaries of Joseph ibn Kaspi (1279–1340), Levi b. Gerson (1288–1344; RaLBaG, Gersonides), as well as the commentaries of Isaac Abrabanel (ca. 1437–1508).

28. On Renaissance "humanists"—classical scholars—and their role in this sea change, see the studies of Kristeller (1974; 1979).

29. Conrad Pellican's *De modo legendi et intelligendi hebraeum* appeared in 1504, soon followed by J. Reuchlin's more influential Hebrew grammar (1506); before both a Hebrew grammar had been written by Aldo Manuzio ca. 1500, and other, somewhat sketchier works apparently go back to the end of the fifteenth century. See Weil (1963: 249–52).

30. On the gradual overthrow of Jerome's ideas about biblical poetry, see Kugel (1982: 218–64). The challenge to Jerome's *auctoritas* as a translator began somewhat earlier, perhaps as early as the twelfth century in some quarters, but was not widespread; see Grabois (1975: 613–34).

31. One useful survey is Obermann (1966). See also Kugel (1990b: 146–48).

32. It should be noted that this slogan, or complex of slogans, was not, however, the invention of the Reformers, nor ought the authority that they attributed to Scripture be thought of as a wholly new departure. See Eberling (1970: 96–97); Pfürtner (1977).

33. Luther (1897: 96).

34. Quoted in Eberling (1970: 107).

35. Geneva Bible (1560: iiii).

36. Martin Bucer, "allegedly the most tolerant reformer in the most tolerant Protestant city of the time," unsuccessfully argued that adulterers in Strasbourg ought to be punished by stoning. Ozment (1980: 367–68).

37. Bredvold (1933: 210).

38. The story of modern biblical scholarship is thus basically a Protestant tale. Individual Roman Catholics had contributed arguments that ultimately supported the Documentary Hypothesis, for example, but they did so principally as a way of undercutting the Protestant reliance on Scripture alone; see below. Catholic scholars felt free to join the historical-critical approach to Scripture only after Pope Pius XII issued his encyclical *Divino Afflante Spiritu* in 1943, which encouraged Catholics to enter the field (and even then, their entry was not altogether smooth): see Robinson (1988); also Brown (1990: xix). Indeed, after this pope's death, a countermovement was launched; some bishops even refused to teach the encyclical, and a few did not believe it authentic, preferring to think it a Fascist forgery.

Jews were, until recently, also a very small part of this scholarly movement. Although the modern, scholarly approach had met with some initial approval in liberal Jewish circles in the nineteenth century, support for it soon waned, in part because of its sometimes undisguisedly anti-Jewish character. See Ran Ha-Cohen, "The Encounter of *Wissenschaft des Judentums* in Germany with Nineteenth-Century Biblical Criticism" (Ph.D. dissertation, Tel Aviv University, 2003). Thus it was that the Jewish scholar Solomon Schechter observed that the "Higher Criticism" (that is, biblical source criticism and the like) was really the "higher anti-Semitism." See Schreiner (2003: 140–71). Schreiner concludes, "To this day, Christian and Jewish Bible studies have existed to a large extent on parallel lines." See also Sperling (1992). Only after the middle of the twentieth century did Jews begin to enter the mainstream of biblical scholarship in any significant measure.

39. To these two names ought to be added a third, that of the French Protestant scholar Isaac LaPeyrère. Now largely forgotten, LaPeyrère published his *Prae-Adamitae* in 1655. In this study he sought to prove that Adam was actually not the first human being created (a matter that was important to him because it would force a reinterpretation of the Christian doctrine of original sin). This led him to suggest, in Book 4, that the story of Adam and Eve was not the work of the divinely inspired Moses but of later writers (who may have used, he said, Moses' "notes"). La Peyrère knew Hobbes and may have shown him the manuscript of *Prae-Adamitae* before Hobbes wrote *Leviathan*. As for Spinoza, his *Tractatus* was published only in 1670, but his questioning of traditional attributions of biblical authorship may go back to the 1650, when he was essentially excommunicated by the Amsterdam Jewish community. Spinoza had a copy of La Peyrère's book in his library—it is not clear when he might have read it. He probably had also read *Leviathan* by the time he wrote the *Tractatus*, since he uses proofs and even wording similar to that of Hobbes. For a fine attempt at unraveling the interrelationship of the three men and their works, see Malcolm (2002: 383–431).

40. See ibn Ezra *ad* Deut. 1:2. Other problematic verses mentioned there are the "twelve," namely, the last twelve verses of Deuteronomy, which recount in the third-person Moses' death and burial; Deut. 31:22, which speaks of Moses writing down the song "on that day," as if it were some time before the writing of the rest; and Deut. 3:11, which asserts that the giant Og's bed is to be found in the city of Rabbat-Ammon (presumably, it could have been moved from Og's homeland of Bashan only long after the death of Moses).

41. These and other examples from medieval Jewish exegetes were discussed by Sarna (1983: 22–24); Jon Levenson (1993: 62–81) more correctly assesses their significance in his essay "The Eighth Principle of Judaism and the Simultaneity of Scripture." See also chapter 36.

42. Among the many biblical scholars involved, mention should be made of the fifteenth-century Spanish Jesuit Tostatus (Tostado), who not only added further examples to those of ibn Ezra's list but also suggested that the Babylonians had actually destroyed Moses' Torah and that Ezra rewrote it. Another Roman Catholic, the Flemish priest Andreas Masius, published his commentary on the book of Joshua in 1574. There he suggested that Ezra was the author of the Pentateuch, having collected material from various sources (including the Book of the Wars of the LORD); Ezra edited and rewrote some of this material. (For example, Masius wrote, Hebron is not the old name of the city, but Kiryat Arba.) The Spanish Jesuit Bento Pereira claimed during his lectures in the 1580s that the diaries and annals of Moses were put into shape long after his time by some other hand(s). For all these, see Malcolm (2002: 383–431).

43. Hobbes (1968: 418).

44. See the brief remarks of Finkelstein (1990: 73–77).

45. Spinoza (1998: 90). Hobbes similarly asserted: "The light that must guide us in this question [of the Pentateuch] must be that which is held out to us from the Bookes themselves" (Hobbes 1968: 417).

46. For Spinoza (1998: 90), this language was Hebrew even for the New Testament writers, "since all the writers of both the Old and the New Testament were Hebrews."

47. Ibid., p. 91

48. "Therefore, the question as to whether Moses did or did not believe that God is fire must in no wise be decided by the rationality or irrationality of this belief, but solely from the other pronouncements of Moses," Ibid., p. 91.

49. Ibid., 92.

50. Ibid., 93.
51. "We may also discover whether or not it [Scripture] may have been contaminated by spurious insertions, whether errors have crept in, and whether these have been corrected by experienced and trustworthy scholars," Ibid., p. 92.
52. He deals with prophecy principally in the first two chapters of the *Tractatus*.
53. Ibid., 13–14.
54. Ibid., 22.
55. Ibid., 24.
56. Feldman, S. (1998: vii).
57. Mention here should be made of Richard Simon, the Catholic author of the *Histoire critique du Vieux Testament* (1678); he is often cited alongside of Spinoza as one of the seventeenth-century founders of modern scholarship. Simon was indeed a sophisticated Hebraist who put forward a number of arguments against the Mosaic authorship of the Pentateuch; in particular, he highlighted internal contradictions within the text (Genesis 1 vs. Genesis 2), unnecessary repetitions, and inconsistencies of style. All this led him to suggest that the Pentateuch was actually a compilation of different sources—a striking anticipation of later theories. At the same time, his stance must be understood in the context of Catholic-Protestant polemics of the seventeenth century; see Malcolm, N. (2002: 414–24); also below, note 60. Somewhat different is the case of another early contributor to the Documentary Hypothesis, Johannes Clericus (Jean Le Clerc, 1657–1736). Clericus was a Huguenot and thus found himself on the opposite side of the Catholic-Protestant divide. A critic of Simon's book, he nevertheless went on to argue that the Pentateuch had been composed sometime after the Assyrian conquest of Israel in the eighth century. On his life and his somewhat odd theories about biblical poetry, see further in Kugel (1982: 247–51).
58. Hume (1966: 144–45).
59. On Voltaire and the other *encyclopédistes* vis-à-vis the Bible, see the essays by Schwarzbach and Cotoni in Belavel and Bourel (1986: 759–803).
60. Throughout this period, Protestant scholars were pitted against Catholics in a rather unanticipated way. On the face of things, Protestants ought to have been at the forefront of questioning the tradition of Mosaic authorship of the Pentateuch. After all, their whole movement derived from the questioning of such received traditions. Nowhere in the Pentateuch itself does it clearly say that Moses was the author of these five books, although that is what traditional Jewish and Christian interpretation had long inferred. Deut. 31:9 says: "Then Moses wrote down *this law* and gave it to the priests, the sons of Levi . . . and to all the elders of Israel" (see also Deut. 31:24). The phrase *this law* (*ha-torah hazzot*) is ambiguous; it might refer to the legal corpus of Deuteronomy (frequently referred to as "this law" within that book), or it might refer to the entire Pentateuch, which itself came to be known as the *Torah*. True, numerous later books refer to the Torah of Moses, though again, the referent is not absolutely clear (Josh. 8:31, 23:6, 24:26, 1 Kings 2:3, 2 Kings 14:6, 23:25, Mal. 3:22, Neh. 8:7, Dan. 9:11, 13; Ezra 3:2, 7:6, 2 Chr. 23:18, 30:16).

Since the Protestant movement was predicated on the overthrow of the Church's *auctoritas*, the Mosaic authorship should have been among the first things cast into doubt. But the only Protestant alternative to the Catholic Church's authority was Scripture itself: by Scripture alone would all matters be determined. In order for that to work, Scriptural authority had to be rock-solid—every word had to be the inspired word of God, the *verbum Dei*. That meant not only that Moses must have authored every word, but that he must also have communicated the Torah in such a way that all the potential ambiguities of the Hebrew writing system had been resolved by him. In practice, this meant that not only was every letter exactly what Moses had been given, but even the little vowel-points that accompanied the text would have to be authentically Mosaic. See Kugel (1982: 258–64).

Catholics had no such problem—on the contrary, precisely because they held by Church traditions and the *auctoritas* of earlier figures, they declared (at the Fourth Tridentine Council) that Jerome's translation, the Vulgate, was the text for Catholics, more reliable than the Jews' then-current Hebrew text, which, they said, had undergone corruption and whose vowel-points were a later innovation. In this, they were aided by the research of Jewish scholars such as ibn Ezra and Elias Levita, who asserted (in 1538) that the vowel-points

were a later invention. See Weil (1963: 315). Some Catholics claimed that Ezra had completely rewritten Moses' Torah—and that the Protestants were therefore fools to rely on it.
Less radical Catholics, such as Cardinal Roberto Bellarmino (1542—1621), maintained that
the Hebrew Scriptures, while they contained errors, had not been deliberately tampered with
or rewritten—after all, he observed, the Jews did not take out the Old Testament references
to Jesus! While the Vulgate was thus the best text, one still needed Church doctrine to complete what Scripture left out or left unexplained.

61. Armogathe (1986: 431–39).
62. Again, see Weil (1963).
63. Mention here should be made of the proposal by F. Masclef in his *Grammaire hébraique*
(1716) that Hebrew consonants be vocalized according to the first vowel in the name of the
letter in question: thus, when the letter *bet* occurred in a word, it was normally to be vocalized as *be*, while a *gimel* should be vocalized as *gi* and a *dalet* as *da*. Thus the word consisting of the letters *dalet, bet,* and *resh* should be vocalized as *daber*. In addition, the letters
alef, waw, heh, heth, yod and *'ayin* also sometimes functioned as vowel signs, representing,
respectively, the vowels *a, e, i, u, ai,* and *â*. The name of Moses, written with the letters *mem,
waw, shin,* and *heh,* should thus be pronounced: Meshi. This nutty system actually won
other adherents, including, prominently, Charles F. Hioubigant (1686–1784). See on him,
J. W. Rogerson (forthcoming).
64. Since the rise of Christianity, Jews had maintained that *'almah* means only "young woman."
For a reflection of the debate, see Justin Martyr, *Dialogue with Trypho* 84; Hirschman
(1996: 31–41, 55–66).
65. J. L. Isenbiehl, cited in Armogathe (1986: 432).
66. Barr (1983: 48) has suggested that such an approach is effectively dyed in the wool in Christianity, a consequence of the very nature of that faith: "Romans is authoritative because St.
Paul is authoritative, and still more the Gospels have authority because of Jesus Christ, the
person and his life, of which they tell. *Christianity as a faith is not directed in the first place
towards a book, but towards the persons within and behind that book* and the life of the
ancient community which was their context and in which they made themselves known"
(italics mine). This statement would be true if, in place of "Christianity," one were to substitute the words "Liberal Protestantism." Certainly Scripture in early and medieval Christianity (as well as in Roman Catholicism and some Protestant denominations on into far
later periods) was predicated on an undifferentiated faith in Scripture and the events it
related. It was only with the rise of modern biblical scholarship that a dissonance developed
between what Scripture said and the real-life happenings that might presumably stand
behind Scripture's words. It may indeed be (as Barr's observation suggests) that it was in
confronting such a dissonance in the Gospels in particular that many Protestants felt com-
pelled to distance themselves from Scripture in favor of a more credible account of "what
really happened." The Gospels were indeed the make-or-break case; as Barr later observes:
"It is the Gospels that are the supreme source and the supreme problem area for historical
revelation. It is in them that something is narrated of which one may say that, broadly
speaking, if this did not happen, then there is no salvation and faith is vain" (p. 99). Thus,
"something" basic referred to in the Gospel narrative had to be maintained as true, even if
the narration of that "something" could be shown to have been amplified by human hands
and frequently flawed, contradictory, or even unreasonable. It is easy to see how such an
approach then came to characterize their reading of the Old Testament as well. For such
Protestants, it was no longer the biblical *story* of Abraham, but the real person Abraham
summoned to Canaan, and the reconstruction of the historical circumstances in which his
"call" took place, that became the new Scripture. See also chapter 36.
67. This evolution has been explored in detail in Frei (1974).
68. Mention here should be made of the earlier scholars J. D. Michaelis (1717–1791), Johannn
Semler (1725–1791), and J. G. Eichhorn (1752–1827) all of whom contributed mightily to
the scientific study of the Bible's history of composition and the attempt to understand it in
its historical context; their work helped set the stage for nineteenth-century German scholarship. There were, of course, modern biblical scholars outside of Germany in the nineteenth
century. On S. R. Driver, see Emerton (2002: 123–38).

69. This was first recognized by K. D. Ilgen in 1798; see Seidel (1933), but later rediscovered and popularized in Germany by Hupfeld (1853).

70. At first scholars had conceived of two E-writers, designated E¹ and E². This was Hupfeld's designation, for example (previous note). It was K. H. Graf who came to identify the author of the priestly laws and other passages such as a Genesis 1 (designated by Hupfeld as E¹) as a priestly writer, P, who lived *after* D, not before. That would explain, he said, why D appears unaware of the priestly laws in Exodus-Numbers. (Lately, this conclusion has come under attack; see chapter 19.) There are many summaries of the development of the Documentary Hypothesis; among the best: Hayes (1979: 115–20); Eissfeldt (1965: 158–70); Nicholson (1998: 3–28); and Römer (2006: 9–27).

71. Wellhausen first published this work under the title *Geschichte Israels, 1* (Berlin, 1878); he renamed it *Prolegomena zur Geschichte Israels* for the second (Berlin, 1883) and subsequent editions. Citations herein are from the translation by W. Robertson Smith (= Wellhausen, 1957).

72. On this: Miller, (1982: 61–73).

73. Wellhausen, *Prolegomena,* 361.

74. See Brisman (1978).

75. Used in the philosophical sense of ontological simplicity, as discussed in Quine (1981).

76. The Wellhausen four-source approach to the Pentateuch survived long into the twentieth century, but its details have frequently been the subject of controversy. From the beginning, some scholars had found it necessary to hypothesize additional sources or editors to account for J's complexity: in truth, they said, there are not four major sources but at least five or six. Wellhausen himself had suggested that his J actually represented a complex of different editions (J¹, J², and J³) and the same for E (E¹, E², and E³). Karl Budde similarly distinguished two different authors, J¹ and J²: *Die biblische Urgeschichte* (Giessen, 1883). Rudolf Smend similarly saw two J sources; *Die Erzählung des Hexateuch auf ihre Quellen untersucht* (Berlin, 1912). For all these see de Pury and Römer (1989: 24–30). Discontent with the unity of J was certainly fueled by the popularity of Gunkel's ideas, on which see next note and chapter 3. Smend's J¹ became L (for "Lay Source") in Otto Eissfeldt's terminology (1965: 194–99) and N (for "nomadic source") in Fohrer and Sellin (1965: 173–79). See Nicholson (1998: 43–44); Ska (2000). Nor has the multiplication of sources been limited to J and E; again, see below. This complexity has not gone away; on the contrary, it has only been compounded by more recent research. A second priestly source, H (long acknowledged but once considered minor), has been argued by some to have had a major role in the Pentateuch's final form; on the work of Israel Knohl, Jacob Milgrom, Baruch Schwartz, and others, see chapter 19. Meanwhile other scholars have questioned the very existence of any continuous text by a J or an E, as well as their subsequent combination into a history (JE). Instead, attention has focused on the role of D as a potential editor of disparate materials whose origins and earlier form are basically unknowable. Thus, speaking of J as a source is, these scholars say, an illusion, since the letter J actually stands for a congeries of traditions and texts stretching over a broad chronological range. The latter approach—in some ways descended from Gunkel's—has been championed in particular by the German scholar Rolf Rendtorff (1977) and his student Erhard Blum (1985; 1990). Despite some similarities in their conclusions, a profound methodological difference separates teacher from student. In particular, Blum has sought to argue, through detailed analysis of different passages, that major elements of the Bible's first four books are simply a reflection of parts of Deuteronomy and that these follow, rather than precede, Deuteronomy's composition; they therefore belong to the exilic or postexilic period. Blum had his predecessors; see Van Seters (1979: 663–73). If so, how can one talk about J's "theology," as, for example, Gerhard von Rad did? See Rendtorff's dispute with von Rad and others (1975: 158–66). One refinement of this argument holds that behind the Pentateuch's history ultimately stand two "rival myths" of Israel's origins, the first focusing on the stories of Israel's remote ancestors, the patriarchs, the second on the tradition of the Exodus from Egypt as Israel's founding event. See Schmid (1999) and Dozeman and Schmid (2006), with essays by Dozeman and Schmid, as well as E. Blum, A. de Pury, T. C. Römer, and others. See also next note, as well as chapter 6, notes 17, 18, and 19. At the same time, numerous scholars have risen to the defense of

(more or less) the traditional source-critical view. See in particular the balanced study of Nicholson (1998) as well as Friedman (1998: 350–78).

77. Wellhausen's ideas were disturbing to traditional belief, but in his view at least some parts of the Pentateuch were fairly old; his younger contemporary Hermann Gunkel (again, see chapter 3) posited an early stage of orally transmitted tales, some presumably going back to the period before David and the United Monarchy (tenth century BCE). In recent years, however, a school of "minimalist" historians has arisen, some of whose members seek to claim that the entire Bible was written during a century or two of the post-exilic period. Thus, the stories of Abraham and Jacob, Moses and the Exodus, and the Sinai covenant—long felt to reflect an early period in Israel's history (even if they were not written precisely in the period in which these people lived)—are now viewed by members of this school as having been written only in the period of the Babylonian exile (sixth century BCE), or even later, to the period of Persian domination of Israel's homeland. Two important works in opening this line of inquiry were: Thompson (1974) and Van Seters (1975); see also Van Seters (1994 and 1999). These authors' first works more or less coincided with the dissertation of Schmid (1976). A similar line is followed by Levin (1993), who argues that J's depiction of the patriarchs building altars around the countryside is essentially a polemic directed against the centralization of cultic worship advocated by D. On other aspects of the minimalist approach, see below, as well as chapter 6, notes 17 through 19.

Their arguments have not necessarily prevailed—a great many scholars still feel such a late dating is untenable—but they have introduced a new element of uncertainty in a major area of biblical scholarship. "It is doubtful . . . that any theory of the composition of the Pentateuch will again command the kind of consensus enjoyed by the documentary hypothesis in the past" (J. J. Collins (1999: 460) [review of Nicholson]). Note also the recent review of things by R. Rendtorff (2006). About the only thing that scholars are still prepared to agree on is that the traditional view of the Pentateuch's origin—as the inspired word of God given to Moses after the Exodus—cannot possibly be true and that the text of the Pentateuch is a composite of different sources.

78. Cited in Massa (1990: 37).

79. The formulation goes back to the German historian Leopold von Ranke. Ranke's historical ideas played a crucial role in the emergence of biblical scholarship in nineteenth century Germany as well as in the "spiritual crisis of the Gilded Age," as noted by Massa (1990: 3–21).

80. Cited in Hatch (1969: 116).

81. Briggs (1891: 67).

82. Ibid.

2. The Creation of the World—and of Adam and Eve

1. For a longer account, see Kugel (1998: 94–144); Anderson (2001).

2. It is actually quite surprising how many modern scholars persist in referring to this episode as the "Fall of Man" as if that were the plain sense of the text. One rare exception is Westermann (2004: 28): "However else [the idea of the "Fall of Man"] may be supported . . . it is not an exposition of Genesis 2–3. The Primal History portrays human existence as created existence in a sequential narrative that attempts to explain the juxtaposition of positive and negative in humanity, the potential and limitations of creatureliness. It does not speak of 'Fall.' Neither, in the Bible, is sin something that can be inherited. The real tragedy in associating Genesis 2–3 with a doctrine of fall or original sin is that once we grasp this doctrine, we think we grasp the narrative or what it intends to convey; we no longer need to hear it."

3. Of course, all this could be considered a flashback, a more detailed account of the creation of humanity that was mentioned in passing in chapter 1. But if so, a lot of things had to happen on that sixth day—Adam had to be created (Gen. 2:7), then the Garden of Eden had to be planted and its trees grow and bear fruit (Gen. 2:9), then the animals had to be created and named by Adam (Gen. 2:19–20), and, finally, Eve had to be created (Gen. 2:21–22). Not only is this a lot for one day—unless one follows the "thousand-year day" interpretation— but, as will be seen, it contradicts the order of the creation of things set out in Genesis 1.

4. This observation goes back to the very beginnings of biblical scholarship; Wellhausen

(1883: 387–90) picked it up to argue on linguistic grounds that Genesis 1 was the product of a priestly writer.

5. Emerton (1988) offers an important examination as well as references to some earlier writings on this specific question. For scholarship on various other aspects of P, see the notes to chapters 18 and 19 below.

6. Although, in the case of Genesis, the priestly author was found to allow a bit more leeway than in later books; see Knohl (1995: 125–26).

7. Von Rad (1963: 47)

8. On the specific lexical resemblances between God's completion of the world in Gen. 2:1–3 and the sabbath law in Exod. 31:14–17, see Rofe (1999: 36).

9. For some time, scholars sought to connect the creation account presented in Genesis 1 with a Babylonian and Assyrian work known as *Enuma Elish* ("When, on high . . ."), sometimes referred to as the "Babylonian Genesis." For a brief description of the discovery of this text and its contents: Heidel (1955: 1–17). The notion that this text was in some way the Mesopotamian equivalent of Genesis 1 was frequently asserted following the publication of George Smith's pioneering *The Chaldean Account of Genesis* in 1876. After almost a century, however, scholars began to reject this description; though there certainly are common elements, the equation of the two texts, and even the title "Babylonian Genesis," are now recognized as misleading. See Michalowski (1990: 381–96). With regard to the end of the priestly creation story, namely, Gen. 2:1–3, it has recently been suggested that verses 2 and 3 are to be attributed to the Pentateuchal source H, since they contain "basic H terms." See Milgrom (2000: 1344). This may well be so, but it is difficult to imagine that any pre-H form of the text recounted the six days of creation without any mention of the seventh day, the sabbath. Perhaps H rephrased an earlier conclusion which did not speak of God "resting" (too anthropomorphic for P!) but simply of all work ceasing before the seventh day.

10. Nevertheless, some scholars have been reluctant to date this account to *any* pre-exilic source because, they claim, the representation of YHWH as creator of the world is a strictly postexilic theme: see Vorländer (1978: 267–71). This argument has been aptly rebutted by Emerton (2004: 107–30). Emerton points to the presence of this theme in such pre-exilic psalms as Psalms 89, 93 and 96. Vorländer later suggests that the association of YHWH with creation is dependent on the existence of some sort of monotheism, hence postexilic; but as Emerton notes, creator deities (including El) abound elsewhere in the ancient Near East without being bound to anything resembling monotheism.

11. This is currently a somewhat freighted topic, since the study of these societies has often been marred by cultural and ideological biases of the most blatant sort. One older example is Morgan (1877). More recently, anthropologists have been zealous in their attempts to reexamine hunter-gatherers in more sophisticated and culturally specific terms. On the possibility of understanding past interaction of hunter-gatherers with agriculturalists on the basis of present data, see Spielmann and Elder (1994: 303–23), esp. 315–18. Note also the telling critique of R. B. Lee and others in Shapiro (1998: 489–510); he ends by expressing the hope that hunter-gatherer studies are moving away from "Edenic paradigms" (503). This, however, should not be confused with the opposite operation, understanding Eden via hunter-gatherer paradigms.

12. On the importance of this discovery in the expansion of human populations, with particular reference to the ancient Near East, see Cavalli-Sforza (2000: 92–113).

13. An extensive anthropological literature exists on this subject, written throughout the twentieth century, much of it in reaction to the writings of B. Malinowski (see, inter alia, 1932): see Hartland (1909); Jones (1924: 109–30); Austin (1934: 102–18); Montagu (1939). Read (1918: 146–54) expressed early misgivings about Malinowski's attribution of ignorance of physiology to the Trobrianders; later, Riesenfeld (1949: 145–55) suggested that the doctrine of asexual reproduction in Melanesia actually reflects motifs brought there by megalithic outsiders. As he and others have argued, such ideas do not necessarily stem from an ignorance of physiology. They may reflect a particular ideology or existing social organization; thus also Merlan (1986: 471–93), Levine and Silk (1997: 375–98). See also the articles on "Theology and Physical Paternity" collected in *Man* 1938–39; Leach (1966: 39–50); Spiro (1968: 243–61), and the remarks of Powell, Leach, et al. (1968). With regard to Genesis 2–3, one

ought to distinguish between the imputation of ignorance and the fact of ignorance; it is really the former that seems to underlie the narrative. As for actual ignorance, however, it must be conceded that a knowledge of the physiology of paternity is hardly an inborn human trait, nor is it a necessity for sexual reproduction to take place; thus, it seems quite impossible that, at some point in the prehistory of all societies, an ignorance of paternity did not exist in fact.

14. As will be seen later, some modern scholars associate the emergence of Israel in Canaan with a change in lifestyle, namely, the "sedentarization" of formerly nomadic shepherds and their adoption of agriculture as a means of living. That change may also have contributed to this story's speculative reconstruction of humanity's distant past.

15. Snakes were widely worshipped in the ancient Near East, indeed, apparently in biblical Israel itself; Moses is said to have created the image of a bronze/copper snake for healing purposes (Num. 21:9, 2 Kings 18:4). A copper snake was found at the twelfth-century BCE shrine at Timnah, north of Eilat, and snake images have also been unearthed at Megiddo (Late Bronze IIB), Hazor (Late Bronze IIA and IIB), Gezer (Middle Bronze and Late Bronze IIA) and Tel Meborak (LB IIA). An altar with an engraved serpent was discovered at Beer Sheba (800–700 BCE). See, inter alia, W. Dever, "The Contribution of Archaeology to the Study of Canaanite and Early Israelite Religion," in Miller et al. (1987: 209–47). Note also R. Steiner's recent report of an ancient Semitic text, dated to the 25th to 30th centuries BCE, which speaks of a "mother snake." (Scientific publication of the text has not yet occurred.)

16. Honeyman (1952); cf. Massart (1956).

3. Cain and Abel

1. Note that in this version of things, the phrase "angel of the LORD" refers to the newborn Cain and not his progenitor, but this appears to be a later modification of the original motif. See Kugel (1998: 147, 169).

2. Apparently in the sense of the "book of the beginning," that is, Genesis.

3. This, of course, did not answer all the questions raised by the Genesis account: Who did Cain marry? Why did Cain visit his anger against God on Abel, who was an innocent bystander? For the answers given by ancient interpreters to these and other questions: Kugel (1998: 146–69).

4. Here we will be concerned with Gunkel's work on the stories of Genesis (1895); for his form-critical work on the Psalms, see chapter 26. On Gunkel and his influence: Klatt (1969), which contains a detailed bibliography (pp. 272–74). Hempel (1923: 214–25); see also von Rabenau (1970: 433–44). An excellent analysis of Gunkel's concept of *Sitz im Leben* in its historical context (including his probable debt to the sociologist and philosopher Georg Simmel, who taught in Berlin during the period of Gunkel's stay there): Buss (1999: 234–44; and 2002).

5. Buss is probably right in connecting Gunkel's insight into the etiological character of many biblical stories to his interest in Germanics, but it may well be that his enthusiasm for the classics—as Buss also documents—was more relevant here; Buss (1999: 228–32). Gunkel was not quite the first to connect the concept of etiological narratives to the Bible, but he was the one who argued it most extensively and persuasively.

6. Gunkel himself did not treat the story of Cain and Abel in connection with the Kenites; indeed, many contemporary treatments still mistakenly seek to connect Cain's name with the profession of [metal-]smith, although this has absolutely no basis in the narrative. Similarly misguided are the many attempts to see in the brothers' rivalry a prototype of the range wars that supposedly have always existed between shepherds and farmers (perhaps true in Wyoming, but quite out of place in the ancient Near East). The analysis of the story presented here is an elaboration of Kugel (1989: 167–90). In general, I refer in the body of this book to "modern scholars" in the plural, mentioning individuals by name only when they have played a particularly significant role in the development of modern scholarship. I have nevertheless tried to acknowledge in footnotes some, if not all, of the scholars who have contributed to the development of a particular explanation or line of thought. Ideas that, as best I know, have not been advanced elsewhere I have tried to tag throughout this work with the words "theory" or "theorize."

7. See Num. 35:19; the victim's family would provide a "redeemer of [the victim's] blood," who would inflict a compensatory loss on the kinship group of the murderer. It was of course desirable that the victim's blood be redeemed through the death of the murderer himself, but—especially in early times—this may not have been a requirement: anyone from the same clan or family might do. Note that Lamech boasts that he will kill "a boy" to avenge a bruise; it seems quite unlikely that he means that the boy in question will himself have inflicted the bruise. He will just be a victim—a poor innocent!—of Lamech's lopsided revenge.

8. On the "Kenite hypothesis," see chapter 24.

9. Its precise purpose was simply to explain the otherwise unexplained name "Cain" (*qayin*). Since this name appears to be related to the Hebrew root *qnh*—which can mean both "acquire" and "create"—Eve appropriately names Cain by saying that she has [be]*gotten* him. She likely referred to him as an *'ish* in the same sentence because, as Eve's firstborn, Cain was the first *begotten* human being in history—she herself, along with Adam, had been created by God alone, and not "with the LORD" as Cain was. But it should be stressed that this opening sentence is quite foreign to the original story. The related names *Cain* and *Kenan* were clearly connected by ancient tradition with an antediluvian figure (see following note); Gen. 4:1 sought to account for this name by focusing on the theme of human "begetting," an appropriate subject of wonderment in humanity's first generation.

10. Scholars point to the similarity of the name Cain to that of Kenan in Gen. 5:9–14 (in Hebrew, the latter name is identical to the former save for the addition of another "n" at the end). Kenan is not the son of Adam and Eve, but of Enosh and his wife. It thus may be that the placement of the etiological story of the Kenites' founder came to be relocated at the start of human history because of the similarity or the two names.

11. More literally, it says: "And the LORD set a sign for Cain . . ." and as such the text still makes sense. But it has seemed more probable to some scholars that a scribe at some point may have mistaken the last consonants in the word "set it" (*wysym[y]hw*) for the name "the LORD." (Just this scribal mistake is attested more than once in the Dead Sea Scrolls.) If so, the original text would have simply read: "And He set it as a sign for Cain."

4. The Great Flood

1. This initiative came to be credited to the antediluvian Enosh, mentioned in that verse. As S. Fraade (1984) has shown, two quite contrary interpretations arose. The first held that Enosh was an altogether righteous figure, one who called on the name of the LORD as an act of piety. But that would hardly help to explain the advent of the flood! Therefore there arose another tradition that he was the first polytheist, that is, he "began to call by the name of the LORD" the sun, the moon, the stars and other objects of pagan worship. Actually, the verse in question may have nothing to do with any of this. See below.

2. A modern scholar would probably say that all but the last two sentences cited above originally had no connection with the flood story—the preceding sentences concern a race of super-heroes who existed long ago and whose mention has been appended to the great genealogical list of Genesis chapter 5. See Gruppe (1889: 135–55). (The chapter divisions, incidentally, are a medieval innovation; the original text contained only paragraph breaks within each book.) That is, having listed the descendants of Adam and Eve, the text then adds that there were other creatures on earth besides these humans—divine-human hybrids that had special powers and so became great heroes. Why are such super-humans no longer around? Because, as the passage reports, God at one point decided to put an end to such creatures: "My spirit shall not abide in humanity forever, for they are flesh." From now on He would only allow ordinary human beings, with a normal lifespan of one hundred twenty years, to be created. End of genealogical chapter. The flood story proper really ought to begin only with the next words, "The Lord saw that the wickedness of humankind was great on the earth."

3. Angels were sometimes called *'irin* in Aramaic (Dan. 4:10, 14, 20, as well as in the Enoch passage cited and frequently elsewhere). The origin of this word is obscure, but at least at one point it was connected to the Aramaic *'ir*, "awake," and understood as reflecting the fact

that the tireless angels never sleep: see Sokolow (2002: 860) and the incantation bowl text cited there, "angels that do not sleep." Cf. Sir. 16:28 and Kugel (1998: 76–77). In an earlier phase of English, the word "watch" was used to mean "stay awake" (it is actually from the same root as "wake")—as in "[night] watchman," a sailor's "watch" (that is, nighttime duty), and so forth. Thus, these 'irin came to be known as the "Watchers" in English.

4. Translation: Foster (2001: 85–90). For the somewhat longer Atrahasis version, on which the above-cited text of Gilgamesh, Tablet XI, is apparently based, see Foster (1993: 160–203).

5. Despite these arguments, some modern scholars have attempted to argue the original unity of the biblical flood story on the basis of its alleged use of chiasmus. These have been refuted by Emerton (1987: 401–20 and 1988: 1–21).

6. In addition to the matter of seven pairs of clean animals vs. one pair, note the length of the flood as specified in 7:4–12 as opposed to 7:24 (not necessarily a contradiction, but certainly a contrasting statement) and the two accounts of Noah's entrance into the ark with his family (7:7 and 7:13).

5. The Tower of Babel

1. See on this: Kugel (2003: 86–89; 1998: 228–42). Current interpretations of this narrative are still quite varied. See, among others, those of von Rad (1949: 147–52); Cassuto (1964: 229); C. Westermann, *Genesis* (1987: 79–83); Sarna (1966: 63–77); Di Vito (1992: 39–56); Uehlinger, (1990); Anderson (1994: 165–78); van Wolde (1994: 84–109); Hebert (2007: 29–58). Hebert aptly analyzes contemporary misgivings about the traditional "pride and punishment" reading of the story. In its place, some scholars have proposed a "critique of empire" theme—not exactly the same as that presented here, but one directed against "the imperial suppression of local languages and cultures . . . God's punishment brings down the empire with its monolithic aims, setting free the local languages and cultures to flourish" (30). Hebert rightly rejects this interpretation, but his own underplays, I think, the rather local nature of this narrative and its fundamental independence from the chapters that precede it. Thus, it is not about "all the earth" in the sense of all of humanity, but all the inhabitants of a specific region, Babel; and what it seeks to do is not to account for the "extravagant array of the world's cultures" so much as to denounce Mesopotamian urban civilization, including its complicated religious practices.

2. To be sure, even the derivation of "Babel" from bab 'ilu is now largely discounted by scholars.

3. Gunkel championed the idea of two originally separate narratives, but this suggestion has not been widely adopted; see Westermann (1987: 80–81).

4. See Kugel (1998: 235–37).

5. The expression "the holy tongue" appears for the first time in the Dead Sea Scrolls, 4Q464 Apocryphon[b]; see Stone and Eshel (1993: 169–78).

6. See Finch (2000: 60).

7. Hebrew of course developed its own th-sound, an allophone of t, but it is quite unrelated to Proto-Semitic th-.

8. This subject has become one of great significance with regard to the school of "minimalist" historians of the biblical period, some of whom seek to claim that the entire Bible was written during a century or two of the post-exilic period. See, inter alia, Davies (1992); Blenkinsopp (1996: 495–518). Such a claim, however, will not square any better with the linguistic evidence than the traditional attribution of the Pentateuch to Moses; see the detailed evidence amassed by, inter alia, the "Jerusalem School" of A. Hurvitz, M. Weinfeld, M. Haran, S. Japhet, and others. To counter this evidence, some minimalists have argued that the linguistic differences actually reflect two distinct, contemporaneous dialects rather than a long process of linguistic change—but this will not accommodate the ample evidence of gradual shifts: see, inter alia, Hurvitz (1997: 301–15). This is especially demonstrable in the realm of syntax. Note the recent paper of Joosten (2005). See also chapter 19, esp. the section "Whence P and H" and the notes thereto.

9. The term "Israelian" goes back to H. L. Ginsberg and has been popularized by Rendsburg (1990 and 2002).

6. The Call of Abraham

1. Strictly speaking, many interpreters held him to be the *rediscoverer* of monotheism, since Adam and Eve obviously must have known God face to face, but that knowledge was lost, interpreters held, after the time of Enosh: Kugel (1998: 266–67).
2. The Qur'an proclaims Abraham, because of his beliefs, "the first Muslim" (*awwal al-mus-limīn* 3:60). On the Muslim tradition and some of its pre-Qur'anic roots: Athamina (2004: 184–205).
3. The theme of Abraham going through a series of false gods is found in earlier sources, Apocalypse of Abraham 7: 1–9 and Genesis Rabba 38:13; see on this Kugel (1998: 296–326).
4. The excavation of Ur was jointly conducted by the British Museum and the University of Pennsylvania and led by the British archeologist Sir Leonard Woolley (1880–1960). For his own account: Woolley (1965).
5. For a recent critical assessment of this school: Long (1997); Davis (2004); note also the recent collection of essays in Hoffmeier and Millard (2004).
6. Albright (1963: 1–2).
7. A problem was that the city was called "Ur of the Chaldeans" in Gen. 11:31 and elsewhere; at the reputed time of Abraham, the Chaldeans were still centuries away from ruling the area. Still, this could be explained as a later writer's/editor's gloss of the name Ur.
8. Albright (1968: 57–58).
9. Roth (1989: 245–60). Level-headed summary of some of the pitfalls of using Mesopotamian sources: Selman (1977: 9–16).
10. Abiram appears later as the name of a leader in Korah's rebellion (Num. 16:1), as well as of another figure in 1 Kings 16:34. See on this Thompson (1974: 22–36).
11. Wright (1962: 40). This was the view imparted to the next generation of biblical scholars. Let the testimony of one speak for many: "When I was in graduate school at Harvard years ago, we studied the patriarchs, who were said to have originated in Ur of the Chaldees, come down from Syria to Canaan and Egypt, and ultimately returned to Palestine, to Canaan. We were taught that this happened ca. 2000 BCE, during the "Age of the the Patriarchs" or MB I period . . . In those days, not only were the patriarchs set in real time, but the focus of much of our graduate work was to study the languages and cultures of Israel's neighbors in the second millennium in Egypt and Mesopotamia"—Myers (2006: 256–64).
12. Among other points, scholars have noted that the Philistines of Genesis differed from the later Philistines geographically: the later ones live along the coastal plain, whereas in Genesis they are inland, in the area between Beer Sheba and the Egyptian border. Moreover, the city of Gerar, a Philistine stronghold in Genesis, is never mentioned among the cities held by the later Philistines. The later Philistines are warriors hostile to Israel, whereas the former are basically friendly shepherds. For all these reasons, it has been suggested that the people called Philistines in later times were distinct from the original Philistines; perhaps the old name came to be applied to the later invaders. See Kitchen (1966: 80); Grintz (1969: 99–129); Harrison (1988: 11–19); Hamilton (1990: 94); Drews (1998: 39–61).
13. This is especially true of what was once thought to be the specifically Hurrian character of the laws of Nuzi. See Eichler (1989: 107–19).
14. In fact, the theory of wife-sister marriage cannot be supported on either the Nuzi or the biblical evidence offered by Speiser. See Weir (1967: 14–25); Thompson (1974: 234–48); Van Seters (1975: 71–76).
15. Niditch (1987: 23–69).
16. See Van Seters (1975).
17. See chapter 1, notes 76 and 77. As mentioned there, two important works in the development of this movement were that of Van Seters (previous note) and Thompson (1974). Out of this approach developed the much farther-reaching revisionist (or "minimalist" proper) movement among some historians: See also: Davies (1992); Whitelam (1996); Grabbe (1997); Van Seters (1994; and 1999); Thompson (1999).

    Most of the claims of the minimalist school remain highly controversial. Indeed, I think it would be fair to say that the minimalist position is, despite the prolific output (and occasional vehemence) of its supporters, rejected in part or in toto by many, perhaps most, contemporary scholars. See, in addition to the works mentioned throughout this book, the responses of Halpern (1995: 25–47); Dever (1995: 61–80); Japhet (1998); Levine and Mazar (2001); and Day (2004). Specifically in regard to the patriarchal narratives: Frymer-Kensky (1981: 209–14); Emerton (1982: 14–32); Friedman (1998: 350–78); McCarter and Hendel (1999: 1–31).

18. It was Rolf Rendtorff—certainly no minimalist—who opened the way to this analysis by highlighting some of the inconsistencies in the Documentary Hypothesis: Rendtorff (1977). Rendtorff denied that there ever were two lengthy sources, J and E, that were combined into a single work, J-E: the units were shorter, independent, and often contradicted one another even within a single "source" tradition. Important as well was another work from the same time, H. H. Schmid (1976). See also Vorländer (1978). Rendtorff's student, Erhard Blum (1984 and 1990), subsequently offered a fully developed scheme rejecting the old Documentary Hypothesis. In its place, Blum proposes two basic documents, the "D Composition" (dating from the early postexilic period) and the "P Composition," from a still later period, which edited and changed elements in the D Composition. He allows that the D Composition had some earlier source material—a patriarchal history corresponding to Genesis 12–50, dating to the Babylonian exile or just before, and a history of Moses and his times, composed shortly after the fall of the Northern Kingdom to Assyria. The history of Israel's earliest ancestors (Genesis 1–11) was added by the author of the Priestly Composition, although he too relied on some earlier traditions. An excellent overview of Blum's and other theories against the background of classical Wellhausian source criticism can be found in Nicholson (1998). Note also the review of scholarship in de Pury (1989: 1–80) and Davies (1996: 71–86), and, most recently, the essays collected in Dozeman and Schmid (2006).

19. Thus, it is hard to understand why a later writer would have depicted Abraham as offering sacrifices in ways that violate priestly laws and offering them in places that violate the laws of Deuteronomy, if his stories were composed *after* these laws were in place—indeed, if they were composed (or even heavily edited) by one of the writers/editors of Deuteronomy and/or the priestly parts of the Pentateuch. And, for the same reason, would not Abraham also have been depicted as keeping the sabbath and observing other ritual practices if these were crucial items for the writers/editors involved? One might of course counter that, by the Torah's own account, such laws were not promulgated until the time of Moses, generations *after* Abraham. Still, why should a later writer/editor go out of his way to depict the spiritual founder of Israel (whose God was the "God of *Abraham*, Isaac, and Jacob") doing things that that God would later outlaw? The most obvious answer is that such a writer/editor had no choice: the stories themselves were not vague traditions but actual texts (oral or written) well known by ordinary people. Beyond these matters, many scholars have pointed to other ancient features of the Genesis narratives—see, for example, Grintz (1983) (somewhat outdated but still valuable). From a linguistic standpoint, too, most of the patriarchal narratives seem to represent a far earlier stage of Hebrew than the books that exponents of this line claim preceded them. In addition is the striking fact that *none* of the people mentioned in the stories of Abraham, Isaac, or Jacob has a name formed from the name of Israel's national deity, YHWH. A few such names appear in narratives relating to the time of Moses and afterwards (Joshua, Jochebed), but even these are somewhat questionable (see chapter 24, subsection "Named for God"); it is really in the time of David that such names become common. This has suggested to many scholars that these Genesis stories— or at least the traditions on which they are based—must go back to a time before, or not long after, this deity had become prominent in Israel. That might point to a date before the tenth century BCE. See McCarter's treatment of this argument (1999: 19–20). McCarter points out that the absence of YHWH names in texts attributed to E and P would be consistent with their position that the name YHWH was only first communicated to Moses. However, the fact that such names are also absent in J texts—although these texts maintain that the name YHWH was in use throughout the patriarchal period—considerably strengthens the claim that these stories as a whole go back to a pre-YHWH time. Finally, the depiction of God found in the stories of J and E is far more anthropomorphic than in other sources; that too would suggest that they are earlier.

20. Most scholars would probably now agree that assigning a particular date to the material attributed to J and E is simply impossible. To begin with, they say, these never were unified compositions, so there really was no *author* corresponding to J or E. Indeed, this was the view of Wellhausen, who subdivided J into different constituent sources or editions, (J¹, J², and J³) and did the same for E (E¹, E², and E³); the same was true of Budde, Smend and others. See above, chapter 1, note 76.

21. Indeed, in Genesis 14 Abraham meets King Melchizedek of Salem, who is also a "priest of El Elyon" (El Elyon, scholars now know, was the head of the Canaanite pantheon). In their conversation, Abraham seems to identify his own God, YHWH, with this Canaanite deity, telling Melchizedek, "I have sworn to the LORD [i.e., YHWH], El Elyon, maker of heaven and earth . . ." (Gen. 14:22). A bit later on, Abraham plants a tamarisk tree in Beer Sheba, "and he called there on the name of the LORD, El Olam"—the latter being another name for the same Canaanite deity. These texts seem out to tell us that, although these sites are traditionally associated with the "Canaanite" god (though how exclusively Canaanite he was, and when, are, as we shall see, not questions with simple answers), they actually all go back to the time of our ancestor Abraham, who worshiped YHWH but sometimes called Him by these Canaanite names. On the phenomenon of religious syncretism, see chapter 29.

22. On the contrary, what many modern scholars would say is rather the opposite—that the God who would become Israel's in later times, known by the letters Y-H-W-H, is out of place in these stories—that there is no indication anywhere that such a deity was worshiped during the time when Abraham would have lived. Moreover, as we shall see, a modern scholar's account of the emergence of Israel's religion would be far more complex, and evolutionary, than anything that could be attached to the person of Abraham as depicted in Genesis.

23. Thus at Mari, "to kill a donkey foal" (Akk *ḥāyaram qatālum*) was a technical term for covenant-making; Held (1970: 33, 34, n. 11); also McCarthy (1978).

24. Hillers (1969: 41).

25. Cited in Weinfeld (1972: 103).

26. On this and on covenant in general, see also Tadmor (1982: 127–52). Note that priestly texts refer to "establishing" covenants; Day (2003). Note that "cutting" an agreement also exists in classical Greek, *horkia pista tamein*.

27. This verse is usually mistranslated, "I am your shield; your reward shall be very great." The idea of God as a shield is hardly foreign to the biblical idiom, and might seem only appropriate after "Do not be afraid." But the connection between that and getting a great reward is tenuous; it therefore seems more appropriate to read the Hebrew consonants *mgn* as coming from a verb meaning "grant" rather than the noun for shield. Cf. Cross (1973: 4n). On the time of composition of this pericope there is still some disagreement; while most scholars seem to date it relatively early, see Kaiser (1958: 107–26); Perlitt (1969: 68–77).

28. Scholars have noted the similar act of ratification mentioned in the book of Jeremiah: "And I will give over [to their enemies] the men who have transgressed My covenant, who have not carried out the words of the covenant which they had made before Me, when they cut the calf in two, and then passed between its parts" (Jer. 34:18).

7. Two Models of God and the "God of Old"

1. The text reads "rides in the desert regions," *rkb b'rbwt*, but this seems to be a deliberate alteration of *rkb 'rpwt*, "rides on the clouds," an epithet of Baal known from the writings of Ugarit.

2. As medieval Jewish thinkers liked to say (enlisting a phrase from the Talmud), "The Torah speaks in the language of human beings." Note that this phrase was originally used in a very limited sense to explain apparent repetitions and pleonasms in the biblical text; it was only in the Middle Ages that it came to be used to explain biblical anthropomorphisms. On this see Harris (1995: 33–43, 109–10).

3. "Penman" reflects the language of the conservative Protestant "Chicago Statement on Biblical Inerrancy"; see Achtemeier (1999: 38).

4. A nazirite was a type of ascetic in ancient Israel, one who abstained from wine and haircuts and other earthly comforts; see Numbers 6 and 1 Samuel 1.

5. To be clear, I am not assuming that this story, like the previous one, presumes that angels do not eat. I only mean that his generosity ought not to be interpreted as a sign that he has understood who his visitors' really were—the point, on the contrary, seems to be that he was gratuitously generous.

6. One such interpreter was the New Testament author of the Letter to the Hebrews, who draws the following lesson from Abraham's behavior: "And remember always to welcome strangers, for by doing this, some people have entertained angels without knowing it" (Heb. 13:2).

7. For Balaam's moment of confusion, see Kugel (2003: 25–27).

8. For several decades, brain scientists have been struggling to understand what might be called the brain physiology of religious experience. As might be expected, the results are often highly speculative and sometimes reveal a certain ideological bias, either pro- or antireligious, on the part of the author. Nevertheless, this is an increasingly popular and promising field of study. (One landmark work, interesting but ultimately unpersuasive, was Jaynes 1976.) An excellent introduction to the field is Peterson (2003); note also the collection of essays edited by Block, Flanagan, et al. (1997).

9. For these and other examples, Kugel (1998: 127–28, 153–54).

8. The Trials of Abraham

1. In citing Gen. 15:6, Paul may have been seeking to make a more precise point. As scholars have shown, the word "righteousness" was used by Jews in Paul's time as a kind of shorthand way of saying "keeping the commandments of the Torah." Paul's message was that what counts in the new covenant of Christianity is not keeping the commandments so much as belief in God. Therefore, a verse that said, "Abraham believed in God, and it was reckoned to him as righteousness" could be interpreted as: "Abraham believed God, and God considered this as good as keeping the commandments." See further, Kugel (1998: 310–11).

2. The only potential candidate was Samson, who pulls the temple of Dagon down on himself and the Philistine merrymakers (Jud. 16:23–30). But this was hardly an act of martyrdom; Samson himself calls it an act of "revenge" (16:28), and it is done at his personal initiative and not as a religious necessity. Nadab and Abihu (Leviticus 10) were sometimes said to be martyrs; see Kugel (1998: 745–46, 760)—but they too apparently knew nothing of their fate before their death.

3. Interpreters sometimes stated Isaac's age as 26 or 37, but there is no solid evidence from the text as to how old he was. See Kugel (1998: 320).

4. On this passage see further Kugel (1998: 323).

5. Indeed, a modern scholar would see multiple sources behind the existence of narrative doublets in Abraham's saga. Thus, the fact that Abraham concludes two covenants with God, one in chapter 15 and the other in chapter 17, is accounted for in the Documentary Hypothesis by the attributing the first to J and the second to P. Likewise, the banishing of Hagar and Ishmael seems to occur twice, first in chapter 16, then again in chapter 21—here too, critics say, is the same story recounted by two different sources. There are two accounts of Sarah being taken for Abraham's sister and not his wife—in Genesis 12 and in Genesis 20, attributed to J and E respectively. And so forth.

6. This is certainly implied by the sentence "He dealt generously with Abraham because of her, and he had sheep, oxen . . . ," etc. Some commentators, however, took a different tack and argued that this sentence actually meant that Pharaoh dealt generously with him although Abraham already possessed numerous sheep, oxen, and so forth. This is a possible, but unlikely, reading of the Hebrew; in either case, Sarah's contretemps with Pharaoh led to a major increase in Abraham's wealth.

7. The Hebrew word 'am later came to mean, more generally, "kinsman" (Lev. 21:1, etc.), but in early texts it seems to mean specifically "father." Thus, "to be gathered to one's 'ammim" and "to sleep with one's fathers" are parallel euphemisms meaning "to die," and the Hebrew onomasticon is dotted with names containing the particle 'am and, in parallel forms,

'ab ("father"). Note also that the Arabic *'am* means, specifically, paternal uncle. The understanding of "kinsman" here goes back to the Septuagint; see Porter (1978: 140, n.5).

8. See further such passages as Jud. 11:29–40, 2 Kgs 3:26–27, Jer. 19:5, Ezek. 20:25–26, Micah 6:7 and the enlightening discussion of all these in Levenson (1993). On Molech worship and passing offspring through fire, see also Heider (1985); Day (1989) and sources cited there.

9. In the aforementioned study, Levenson (as others earlier) have adduced evidence that some Israelites at some point did indeed subscribe to the practice of child sacrifice—but this hardly disproves the etiological character of the story of Abraham and Isaac. At most it proves that its message had not always been the norm in Israel, or that it was not universally accepted until later times. Beyond this is the basic fact that substitution for child sacrifice is reflected elsewhere in the Bible (specifically, in Exod. 34:20). I am among those who find it improbable that Exod. 22:28 was ever understood to enjoin the actual sacrifice of the firstborn—but again, even if that were so, it hardly undermines the etiological message embedded in Genesis 22. See also Milgrom (2000: 1587–91).

9. Jacob and Esau

1. There is a vast literature on this subject, going back to the Russian Formalists and the Prague Linguistic Circle, on which see Erlich (1955). Particularly significant are the writings on genre by M. M. Bakhtin (1981, 1986, and 1990), and Pam Morris (1994). Note also: Lodge (1987); Holquist (1990); Morson and Emerson (1990), and Morson (1991: 1071–92). The continuation of this critical movement among Western European and American critics is a well-known story. Among significant contributions: Barthes, ([1953=] 1967 and 1957); Riffaterre (1970: 188–230); Culler (1975); Eco (1976 and 1981); Derrida (1974 and 1978); Fish (1980); Todorov (2000: 193–209). The application of these insights to biblical interpretation has also been discussed by numerous scholars. On the matter of "literary competence" (as in Culler, 1975: 113–14) see in particular Barton (1984: 8–19); also Kugel (1981: 217–36).

2. A modern scholar's answer would be that Jacob here is an etiological figure for all of Israel—Jacob dwells in tents in the plural because the people of Israel do. Cf. chapter 3, where God's decree, "All who kill Cain . . ." envisages a plurality of killers because Cain, too, is not one man but the embodiment of an entire tribe.

3. Most translations read "he maintained his anger perpetually" or the like, and that may well be the safest translation. *Perpetually* is certainly one sense of *le'ad* in Hebrew, and there is no doubt this meaning was intended to resound in the listeners' ears with the synonym "forever" at the end of the sentence. But it seems there may be a play on words here, with the other sense of *'ad*, namely, "prey" or "game." Such a meaning would work well with a verb like *tarap*, usually used of a wild beast ripping apart its captured prey. (The *le-* part of *le'ad* is sometimes the marker of the direct object in Hebrew, as in Aramaic.) Job 16:9 seems to use the same expression, with "anger" again as the subject, not the object. Note also that, in this understanding, both "anger" and "wrath" stand at the head of their clauses and are syntactically parallel.

4. Both this passage from Obadiah and the earlier ones from Amos and Malachi are, in context, talking about the later Edomites, not Esau himself. But this did not stop ancient interpreters from reading these national references as if they referred to a particular individual, Jacob's brother.

5. In saying this, I realize that I am contradicting what was said above about biblical figures no longer representing later nations in the interpretations of the ancient interpreters. That was generally true—ancient interpreters simply did not think in terms of etiology. But here, for various reasons, the identification of Esau as Rome was nonetheless a rabbinic commonplace. For some possible historical considerations: Kugel (1998: 366–67).

6. I should make clear that my discussion of the etiological side of this story deals with the biblical text as we have it, in which Esau is identified as the founder of Edom. Gunkel, Noth, and some more recent scholars have supposed that the present text is actually a reworking of an old tradition, in which Esau represented either some unknown and unrecoverable ethnic group or is simply "a type of the huntsman in contrast to Jacob who represents the

herdsman"—Noth (1972: 96–97). This approach seems to me highly problematic. To begin with, nowhere in the three stories in question (the birth of Jacob and Esau; the birthright sale; the stolen blessing) is Jacob presented as a herdsman; indeed, his father's blessing specifies that he is to receive "the dew of the heavens and the bounty of the earth, with much grain and wine" (Gen. 27:28). This sounds like the blessing of a farmer, not of a herdsman *or* a hunter. What is more, it seems most unlikely that, even embedded in Israel's deepest historic memories, there could have been the recollection of a time when "the hunter" was an actual socioeconomic antitype of the herdsman. Esau's hunting is part of an overall characterization of him as a somewhat rugged, unreflective outdoorsman. He is certainly not meant to represent hunting as a profession—there was no such thing at that time. But by far the most problematic element in this approach is its systematic ignoring of the central theme of these three Jacob-Esau narratives, which, as will be seen presently, is that of an actual, historic *displacement*. At one time Esau was superior, these stories say, but "now" he has just been displaced by his previously weaker younger sibling. Noth, no slouch for details, was obviously troubled by the prominence of this theme throughout the stories. At one point he therefore argued that the original version of the oracle in Gen. 25:23 could not have said that the "elder will serve the younger," since that would indeed be appropriate to the founders of two peoples but not to two types such as he proposed; he therefore suggested that in the original version "the twins were designated differently in the divine oracle, perhaps as 'the hairy one' and 'the smooth one'" (Ibid.). But even that would not solve his problem, since "hairy" (*sa'ir*) is clearly an allusion to a particular place, Mt. Seir in Edom, which would again point to these two as ancestor-figures, not types.

It thus seems more likely that the present series of stories is not terribly different, if different at all, from their earliest hypothetical form. Esau (a name of uncertain origin) may at first have been associated with only one of the peoples settled in the region of Mt. Seir who came to constitute the nation of Edom, but at a certain point he evidently began to be thought of as the forefather of all Edomites. (Thus, just as with the name "Jacob," "Esau" became the founder of a nation whose name was different from his own.) It is in this sense that Esau appears in these three, brief etiological tales. As for the time of their creation, as we shall see, they give every sign of having been composed shortly after David's rise and the conquest of Edom by little Jacob's descendants. (On the multiethnic composition of Edom, see next note as well as chapter 9, subsection "The Change of Names.")

Part of Noth's line of argument has been taken up and modified somewhat by Hendel (1987). Hendel endorsed the Gunkel-Noth claim that the stories of Jacob and Esau could not have originally stood for relations between Israel and Edom. Instead, Hendel saw the Jacob cycle as a congeries of folkloric motifs paralleled elsewhere in the Bible as well as in the literature of Ugarit and Mesopotamia. Of late, however, Hendel has sought to sharpen his position and distinguish it from that of Gunkel, suggesting that Jacob and Esau are not socioeconomic types but representatives of the conflict between civilization and nature (or barbarism). This is a correct characterization: the two sets of contrasting traits in these two figures are indeed projections of Israel's self-image (clever, sometimes tricky) and the counterimage it seeks to associate with the Edomites ("dumb jocks")—but this contrast is hardly the point of the stories. The point is that, thanks to this difference, the originally smaller and weaker Jacob was able to overcome and dominate his older brother. See McCarter and Hendel (1999: 27).

Finally, it should be noted that the encounter between Jacob and Esau in Genesis 33 is altogether separate from these three Jacob-Esau narratives. It is clearly different in style and language, and the utterly changed Jacob who appears in it (pious and altogether deferential toward Esau) attests to its lack of connection with the etiological tales in Genesis 25–27. Genesis 33 is in fact a quite later composition intended to rehabilitate relations between Esau and Jacob in view of the rivalry attributed to them in the original three Jacob-Esau tales. This is another way of saying that Genesis 33 is directly related to Deut. 23:7: The Edomites are now *not* to be hated—"because they are your kinsman." Thus, in the story, Jacob is wary of his brother because of what happened in the past, but then it turns out that Esau bears no grudge and there is no bad blood between them—nor, the story is meant to say, should there be any between Israel and Edom now. Indeed, the only reason Edomites and Israelites do not dwell together is that Jacob, still a bit nervous, was reluctant to follow his brother to Mt. Seir and settled instead in the central highlands.

7. No doubt because of the reddish color of the sandstone in that region.

8. Some modern scholars have questioned the historicity of this reference: the genealogical table of Genesis 36 seems to be patched together from originally separate lists, and the archaeological evidence does not seem to support the picture of a unified Edomite kingdom at an early stage. Still, that hardly rules out the possibility of an ancient kingdom in Edom. See Bartlett (1965: 315–27, 1977: 2–27, and 1989). It should also be noted that Edom is mentioned as an enemy in what most modern scholars consider a very early text, Exod. 15:15, and the whole etiological message of the Jacob-Esau cycle is undeniably one in which Edom was perceived as the originally more powerful—though certainly not hated—rival who was ultimately overcome by an upstart Israel. Israel's self-perception as (1) having started out as Edom's kid brother and (2) now having overtaken Edom could hardly fit anywhere other than the tenth century BCE. (Israel was hardly the "kid brother," for example, in the time of Jehoshaphat or Jehoram.) See also next note.

9. Again, it is doubtful that the stories (I am not speaking necessarily of the present *texts*, but the Jacob-Esau tales as they must have first circulated) could belong to any later period of Judahite dominion over Edom, such as in the reign of Jehoshaphat, since at that point "Jacob" was certainly no younger brother at all but a former ruler of Edom. The Jacob-Esau stories in Genesis are all focused on the moment of transition from younger brother to first-born, that is, on the moment when Israel first overcame what was perceived as an earlier, more powerful Esau/Edom. That the basic elements of the story of Jacob's youth were well known in the eighth century is demonstrated by Hosea's reference to them in Hosea 12. These are clearly allusions to existing material and not new creations, although scholars are divided as to the extent to which the material in Genesis might have existed in anything like their present form at that time. See, inter alia, Weisman (1985: 1–13); Whitt (1991: 18–43).

10. The point has been made eloquently by Propp (1968), as well as by such modern literary theorists as M. Bakhtin, Roland Barthes, Stanley Fish, J. Derrida, and T. Todorov. In particular, some contemporary scholars have highlighted the genre conventions of nonliterary genres, for example: Jefferson (1978: 219–48); Walter (1988); and Eggins et al. (1997). One of the most frequently cited essays on the "Bible as literature" is Erich Auerbach's chapter on the story of Abraham and Isaac in his *Mimesis* (Auerbach, 1953) The rest of this book—not nearly so often read by biblical scholars—is quite wonderful, but this chapter stumbles on precisely the point we have been making. Abraham and the other figures in the tale are not, as Auerbach claims, "fraught with background"; there is no background! There is only the schematic foreground, in which Abraham's only "trait" is his willingness to kill his son, and in which Isaac barely exists as a human being at all; he is a mere prop. Indeed, Auerbach's essay is a fine example of what happens when someone trained as a literary critic tries to read a text that is fundamentally not literature. See further the remarks of Brettler (1995: 14–20), as well as this book's Appendix 1, "Apologetics and Biblical Criticism Lite," available on the Web site: jameskugel.com.

11. Note again, in this connection, the contrast suggested by Deut. 23:3–7: "No Ammonite or Moabite shall be admitted to the assembly of the LORD . . . You shall not abhor any of the Edomites, for they are your kin."

12. Some scholars have suggested, on the basis of Akkadian *simmiltu*, that *sullam* (a *hapax* in biblical Hebrew) is to be translated "staircase" rather than "ladder." Note, however, that Mishnaic Hebrew *sullam* is used consistently in the sense of "ladder" (see, e.g., j. Mo ʿed Q. 1 (end).

13. Kugel (1998: 362–64, 373–76 and 2006: 9–35).

14. Some have argued that this narrative goes back only to Jeroboam's choice of Bethel as one of his state's two official cultic sites (1 Kings 12:29); see Blum (1984). This seems unlikely. Jereboam chose Bethel precisely because it was already a well established cultic center (cf. Noth, 1972: 80). Long before that time—going back to the period when emergent Israel was eager to distinguish itself and its origins from "the Canaanites"—this story was created to say that Luz/Bethel had no association with any deity until Jacob happened to spend the night there. See below.

15. Or indeed, perhaps for Israel's own ancestors.

16. Otto Eissfeldt, W. F. Albright, J. P. Hyatt, and others have all pointed to the existence of a Northwest Semitic deity named Bethel and have sought to connect this deity to Genesis 28 or other biblical mentions, but these efforts are strained and unconvincing. See the brief review of scholarship in E. Dalglish's entry "Bethel (Deity)" in Freedman (1992).

17. Josh. 16:2 implies that Luz and Bethel were separate locations, which would only strengthen the hypothesis that the real "former name" of Bethel was . . . Bethel! That is, it had always been called Bethel, but this account (along with its twin, Gen. 35:5–8) was out to assert that the name Bethel went back to Jacob, not the Canaanites.

10. Jacob and the Angel

1. Kugel (1998: 382–83).

2. Here too, a modern scholar would recognize an etiological theme: the site is called Gilead because of the "pile of witness" (gal 'ed) they heaped up there, and the maṣṣebah that marks the spot is, once again, utterly disconnected from its Canaanite worship function. Some modern scholars have attempted to date the composition of the Jacob-Laban encounter to some specific period in history, for example, the defeat of the Arameans in 2 Sam. 8:3–8. This seems most unlikely; Laban is a national stereotype, a family member, but not a particularly beloved one. Such a characterization might fit in almost any age except one of out-and-out hostility and warfare.

3. Some of these matters were explored by Johnson (1969); Malamat (1973: 126–36), and more fully in Wilson (1977). Sasson (1978: 171–85) argued that genealogies are sometimes artificially constructed to place the significant or positive figure in the seventh (or, sometimes, fifth) position.

4. Most translations harmonize this with the name "Jethro," but it is distinct in the Masoretic text as well as in the Septuagint.

5. This goes back to Noth (1971). The name Jacob-El (that is, y'qb 'el) or variations thereon also appears at Ugarit as well as in Egypt during the period of Hyksos rule (1675–1552 BCE). One of the Hyksos kings was named "Y'qb-HR," (apparently the Egyptian form of Ya'aqub-Haddu). In 1969, a scarab inscribed with the name Y'qb-HR in hieroglyphics was found at the site of present-day Shiqmona, near Haifa, Israel; the scarab has been dated back to the eighteenth century BCE—before the time of the Hyksos king in question. Another scarab, also inscribed with the name Y'qb-HR and almost identical to the first, had been published in 1930 by Martin Pieper. See the discussion of these items in Kempinski (1988: 42–47, and 1985: 129–37). (I owe the latter reference to McCarter and Hendel (1999).) Kempinski asserts that the two scarabs were almost certainly produced by the same artisan. They thus seem to indicate that someone named Ya'aqub-Haddu ruled some part of Canaan in the eighteenth century BCE. About a hundred years later, someone with the same name, quite possibly a direct descendant, was one of the Hyksos kings of Egypt. Interestingly, Jacob-El is also known as a toponym (place name), occurring in the list of conquests of Thuthmosis III (ca. 1479–1425 BCE) and other kings. The toponym Y-['-]-ku-b-r(w) appears on a list of Ramses II: see Weill (1918: vol. 1, 188–91). It may well be that the toponym derives from the name of some real or legendary founder of a city or tribe, perhaps even the Ya'aqub-Haddu mentioned on the scarabs. This is certainly a matter of great speculation, but one could not rule out the possibility that this same Ya'aqub-Haddu later came to be thought of as the founder of part of what would eventually be the people of Israel. See also T. Thompson (1974: 45–48), McCarter and Hendel, (1999: 26).

6. Interestingly, although the Bible itself derives the name Israel from a rare word meaning "struggle" or "fight," ancient interpreters sought to find another meaning in the name. Various translations rendered the angel's explanation of Jacob's new name as "you have been great" or "you have been strong" with God. More significantly, Philo explained that the name Israel means a "man seeing God" or "the mind that contemplates God and the world," an understanding that was adopted by early Greek-speaking Christians. This interpretation was certainly significant in early Christianity's identification of itself as the "new Israel" (novus Israel), for if one understands Israel to refer to the contemplation of

God, then it can readily apply to any human being and not just to members of one particular people. Kugel (1998: 387–88, 396–97).

7. Freud (1980: 311–85).

11. Dinah

1. The text here follows the Septuagint translation of this verse, which, instead of rendering literally the Hebrew "It shall not be done thus," reads "It shall not be thus."

2. On the issue of intermarriage in Ezra and later times there is a vast literature; see Kugel (1998: 419–27) and notes there. Eskenazi and Judd (1994) seek to explain Ezra's ban in terms of the sociology of religion (with analogies to modern-day Israel, based on the studies of S. N. Eisenstadt). For later developments: Hayes (1999: 3–36); Himmelfarb (1999: 1–24).

3. Here, a modern interpreter would surely object: after all, the story itself says nothing against intermarriage per se. The brothers are upset because their sister has been raped—it did not much matter by whom; in all the discussion that follows, the issue of intermarriage is never evoked. Their proposal of a mass circumcision is, as we have seen, a trick, a way of incapacitating the people of Shechem; it really has nothing to do with the fitness or unfitness of Shechem to marry Dinah. If, however, one is looking for some lesson in a story that does not appear to have one—and if one happens to be the author of the book of Jubilees, who believed in nothing so much as the utter separateness of Jews as a people, and consequently, in the absolute horror that intermarriage represented—then the tale of Dinah takes on an entirely new coloring.

4. See Kugel (1998: 408–9; 420–22). This interpretation made great sense, for, after all, if all the brothers had proposed circumcision as a trick, then why did only two of them, Simeon and Levi, end up attacking the city? If everyone was in on it, everyone should have participated. If, however, there was a disagreement among the brothers, then the story makes perfect sense.

5. Numerous studies have dealt with this question. See recently: Sternberg (1973: 193–201 and 1992); cf. Fewell and Gunn (1991: 193–211); Lehming (1978: 228–50); Laffey (1988: 43–44); Geller (1990: 1–15); Exum (1990: 7:45); Keefe, (1993: 79–97); Bechtel (1994: 16–36); Perry (2000); Fleischman (2000: 101–16); and Van Seters (2001: 239–47).

6. What follows is a brief summary of a paper I presented twice in the spring of 1992, first at the Eastern Great Lakes Society of Biblical Literature convention and then at the departmental seminar of the Bible Department, Hebrew University of Jerusalem. I am grateful to both groups for their suggestions.

7. Cf. Van Seters (2001: 239–47).

8. See: S. Lehming (1958). His suggestion that the original story involved the sons of Jacob located at the central amphictyony at Shechem is best abandoned, but he did correctly see this chapter as a historical explanation for Jacob's cursing of the two brothers in Gen. 49:5–7.

9. It should be noted that the name form "Hamor father of Shechem" does not mean what it might first appear. Elsewhere in the Bible, there is a set pattern for certain names, "X, the father of Y," where Y is the name of a particular place and no person at all. For example: "Machir, the father of Gilead" (Josh. 17:1, 1 Chr. 2:21, 23); "Shobal, the father of Kiryath Yearim" (1 Chr. 2:50); "Asshur, the father of Tekoa" (1 Chr. 2:24, 4:5); "Salma, the father of Bethelehem" (1 Chr. 2:51). (My thanks to Sara Japhet for this point.) "Hamor, the father of Shechem" fits the same pattern. Indeed, the chapter that just precedes the Dinah story says, "And from the sons of Hamor the father of Shechem he [Jacob] bought the plot of land on which he had pitched his tent . . ." (Gen. 33:19). Why does it not say "And from Shechem and the other sons of Hamor"? And why should he be buying the land from the sons and not the father? Obviously, "Hamor the father of the Shechem" is a formulaic way to refer to the leading clan of Shechem, whichever particular Hamorites happened to be in office at the time. If so, even though it cannot be proven, it seems likely that the original story involved some "Hamor the father of Shechem," and that this phrase itself gave rise (perhaps in the original story, perhaps not) to the notion that a certain Hamor had a son

named Shechem. It may well be that the original story was set in the period of the Judges: the lack of social order would fit well with the original portrayal of that period, and the mention of "the men of Hamor father of Shechem" in Judg. 9:28 might solidify this connection. Beyond that, one might guess (though it is only a guess) that the original story had some etiological connection with circumcision: perhaps its original purpose had been to explain why the Shechemites, while not Israelites, nevertheless practice circumcision. The whole thing was the result of a trick played on them by a bunch of Israelites long ago. In this case, not all the Shechemites would have been killed, but only the rapist, or the rapist and his father. In truth, that would explain another inconsistency in the present story, the mention of the killing of Shechem and Hamor after the text had already asserted that all the males in the town had been killed (Gen. 34:25–26); the latter should have been said after, not before, the mention of Shechem and Hamor.

10. Another remnant of the original form of stories is found in the fact that the deceptive proposal that the Shechemites be circumcised was made by "the sons of Jacob" (Gen. 34:13), presumably all of them. But if so, then why is it that, later on, Simeon and Levi alone attack the city? If all the sons had planned the deception, then why did they not all carry it out? The answer is that, in the original story, a bunch of "us" did indeed all go and attack Shechem together. But in seeking a good reason for Jacob's condemnation of (only) Simeon and Levi in Gen. 49:5–7, the editor had to make these two alone, quite improbably, the sole perpetrators of the massacre.

12. Joseph and His Brothers

1. For this as a parade example of "full repentance," see Maimonides, *Mishneh Torah*, Sefer ha-Madda', Laws of Repentance 2:1.
2. On this passage see Kugel (1990: 94–96).
3. To counter any possible double-entendre, the *Onqelos* targum translates "to do his work" as "to check the account books."
4. The idea that it was a sudden vision of his father's face that saved Joseph from sinning was itself a clever bit of exegesis of Gen. 49:24. See Kugel (1998: 448).
5. Kugel (1990: 98–105).
6. Scholars have long noted the resemblance between the incident with Potiphar's wife and an episode in the ancient "Story of the Two Brothers" (*ANET* 23–25), in which the older brother's wife first seeks to seduce the younger brother and then wrongfully accuses him. But this is indeed a universal theme; see Yohannan (1968).
7. This thesis was advanced by D. Redford (1970), and has been taken up by later scholars. See recently the review of scholarship by J. Van Seters, "The Joseph Story: Some Basic Observations" in Knoppers (2004).
8. One might argue that the story is describing how things were before Benjamin's birth, and that is certainly possible; still, since notice of his birth precedes this story in Genesis, one would expect some formulation other than "more than any of his other children."
9. Scholars used to attribute this inconsistency to multiple authorship—it was at one point judged to be a combination of two versions, those of J and E. This thesis has largely been abandoned (and, indeed, Redford's thesis makes it quite unnecessary). See Coats (1976).
10. This aspect of the story was first highlighted by G. von Rad in his "Josephsgeschichte und ältere Chokhma," reprinted in von Rad (1965: see esp. 292–300), as well as in von Rad (1972; see 199–200). See also Fox (2001: 26–41), which seeks to distinguish the story's wisdom from that of the book of Proverbs.
11. Our knowledge of the Hyksos mostly derives from the brief account of Manetho's Egyptian history contained in the writings of Josephus (*Against Apion,* 73–105, 227–287) and the attempts of scholars to correlate it with Egyptian records and realia. See Van Seters (1966). Since Van Seters' study, new information has emerged from excavations at Tell ed-Dab'a (now definitively identified as the Hyksos city of Avaris) and Tell Mas uta. See Redford (1986: 276–96); Kempinski (1985: 129–37). Assmann (1997: 28–44) reviews the Hyksos material and concludes that some historical memory of this period may underlie the Exodus narrative.

12. Redford (1986: 241–42).
13. Why is an interesting question. Borrowing an idea from scholarship of ancient Greece (and from the writings of his predecessor, Albrecht Alt), M. Noth (1930) popularized the notion that Israel had existed as an amphictyony, with each of twelve tribes taking charge of a central shrine for one month out of the year; hence, the number twelve was unchangeable. More recent scholarship has not been kind to the amphictyony idea: to begin with, there was no central shrine for these tribes to take care of during the period of the Judges, when it was supposed to have existed. For various reasons (including the number of months in a lunar year) the number twelve came to be a conventional unit in Israel and elsewhere; that is probably sufficient to explain its fixity.
14. Many names of people in the Hebrew Bible sound, by their form, more like names of places (toponyms); this would certainly include the name Ephraim (or, for that matter, Judah). Manasseh, on the other hand, seems to be a personal name.
15. For a more detailed treatment of the exegetical history of this incident: Kugel (1995: 525–54).
16. A modern scholar might note that the phrase is a simply a euphemism for a son sleeping with his father's wife or concubine—but ancient interpreters chose to understand it as a literal description of what happened.
17. Unlike Hebrew, English has no one-word synonyms for "lion," so I have substituted this common kenning. Similarly, "your brothers" two lines above has been substituted for "your father's sons."
18. See Kugel (1998: 371, 497).
19. Moses' blessing of Reuben (another ancient text) begins, "Let Reuben live and not die . . ." (Deut. 33:6); these words in themselves seem to provide an ancient indication that the tribe had been severely diminished in number. In David's census, Joab passes through the area previously occupied by the Reubenites, but only the tribe of Gad is mentioned (2 Sam. 24:5). This may be a clue that, by that time, Reuben had been effectively absorbed into Gad and had ceased to exist.
20. Kugel (1995: 525–54). Note that, while it is "Jacob" who is referred to in the sentences preceding and following the insertion, the insertion itself calls him "Israel"—another indication that it is, indeed, an afterthought.

13. Moses in Egypt

1. Tigay (1978) argues, on the basis of Akkadian parallels to these Hebrew expressions, that Moses did indeed suffer from a physical ailment that impeded his speech, as suggested by ancient interpreters (Kugel 1998: 510–11). However, the absence of any confirming specifics in the narrative, the precise wording of Exod. 4:10, and the improbability that a heroic narrative would so portray Israel's great hero, make all this most unlikely. As the overall narrative of chapters 3 and 4 makes clear, Moses is casting about for an excuse not to go. Having tried "I don't know Your name" and "They won't listen to me anyway," he then says, "Besides, I'm not a good speaker." Had he said that he had an actual physical impairment, the matter could clearly have been investigated and Moses revealed to be a liar.
2. See on this Iversen (1961).
3. See below, however, as well as Montet (1981); Redford (1987); Halpern (1992 and 1993); the various articles collected in Frerichs and Lesko (1994); Hoffmeier (1997) (an attempted defense of the general historicity of the biblical account, but one that is honest about the problems and lack of archaeological evidence); Redmount (1998); Davies (2004).
4. *Against Apion,* 1:223, 229–250.
5. See Gager (1972).
6. See Dever (1994), Weinstein (1994). Even before archaeologists expressed their reservations, scholars sometimes appealed to mathematics to cast doubt on the biblical account of the Exodus and the Israelites' prolonged stay in the wilderness. For example, Hermann Samuel Reimarus (1694–1768) observed that if the figures for the total number of Israelite adult males at the time of the Exodus is used as a base, then "[m]arching ten abreast, such a number would have formed a column 180 miles long and have required nine days as a minimum to

march through the parted Red Sea" (cited in Hayes 1979: 115). Similarly, Rogerson (1984) reports about Bishop Colenso's *The Pentateuch and Book of Joshua Critically Examined* (seven volumes, 1862–79): "Perhaps the most amusing parts of Colenso's first volume are those dealing with the sacrifices, and worship. He pointed out that there were apparently only *three* priests in the wilderness: Aaron and his two sons Eleazar and Ithamar. These three would have had to perform the following tasks. First, on the assumption that two million people would produce 250 births each day, the two prescribed offerings (Lev. 12:6–8) would amount to 500 sacrifices, which, on the assumption of five minutes for each [sacrifice], would involve nearly 42 hours [of work] a day for the three priests. At the Passover, following the Deuteronomic regulations, it would have been necessary for the blood of some 120,000 lambs (one to every 15 to 20 persons) to be sprinkled, probably in the space of two hours; that is, the lambs would have been killed at the rate of 100 a minute by the three priests" (222).

7. Finkelstein and Silberman (2001: 63). Note also the withering analysis of the Egyptologist D. B. Redford (1992), esp. 257–64; he finds no support for the historicity of the Exodus in Egyptological data (though the last phrase is indeed an important qualification).

8. Dever (1994: 67).

9. Redford (1992: 417); Assmann (1997: 253, n. 20).

10. It must be admitted that this is more an argument from silence than from science: no plausible Hebrew, or even Semitic, etymology has been offered for either name, so perhaps an Egyptian origin, now distorted, is to be conjectured. Of more certain Egyptian origin is "Hophni," paired with another Phinehas in 1 Sam. 1:3, both of them the sons of Eli, the priest at Shiloh. See on these: Redford (1992: 417–19).

11. The old identification of Per-Atum with Heliopolis/On has been largely rejected. Some archaeologists now suggest that it should be identified with Tell el-Maskhuta or Tell el-Retabeh; see Bleiberg (1992). This identification has been questioned on the grounds that neither site fits with the conventional dating of the Exodus to the late thirteenth century BCE; see Dever (2003: 14); note, nevertheless, the discussion in Davies (2004: 28–30), and the sources cited there. Scholars have also observed that *P(r) R'mss*, "House of Rameses," ceased to be an important site after the mid-eleventh century, suggesting that the reference to it in the Exodus account must be of ancient vintage; see Davies (2004: 28).

12. A somewhat mythic figure by the time of Diodorus, but in some ways perhaps to be identified with Rameses II.

13. Diodorus of Sicily, *History* 1.56.2.

14. The use of Pharaoh in this sense "does not occur until the Eighteenth Dynasty, sometime before the reign of Thutmose III (1449–1425 BC) . . . From its inception until the tenth century, the term 'Pharaoh' stood alone, without juxtaposed personal name. In subsequent periods, the name of the monarch was generally added on. This precise practice is found in the Old Testament; in the period covered from Genesis and Exodus to Solomon and Rehoboam, the term 'Pharaoh' occurs alone, while after Shishak (ca. 925 BC) the title and name appear together (e.g., Pharaoh Neco, Pharaoh Hophra)" Hoffmeier (1997: 87).

15. See on this Hoffmeier (1997: 114) and references cited there. Papyrus Leiden 349 similarly refers to *'Apiru* engaged in state service.

16. The *'apiru/ḫabiru* connection with "Hebrew" has been studied by numerous scholars, including Oswald Loretz (1984), who saw *'ibri* in connection with the Bible's Egyptian narratives as a way of later writers to indicate Israel's ancestors *avant la lettre*. Somewhat similar is the position of N. Na'aman, who argues that the biblical term *'ibri* itself underwent a shift in meaning, from its original "uprooted people living on the margins of society"—a usage found in the Mari texts, El Amarna usage, and other ancient Near Eastern references and found in the Bible in reference to certain elements within the future society of ancient Israel—to being a "social ethnonym" used in various stories to apply to Israelites outside of their homeland, and finally a "synonym of the ethnicon 'Israelite'" in post-biblical writers such as Philo and Josephus: Na'aman (1986: 285–86). See also Na'aman (2000: 621–24). One weakness in this hypothesis is precisely the absence of the term *'ibri* in those passages in Judges and 1 Samuel that depict the *'apiru*-like elements in early Israel; see also below.

17. This is the thesis of M. Greenberg (1955); see also Buccellati (1977) and Bottéro (1980).

18. It may also be, as Na'aman suggests, that in later times "Hebrew" had simply become, for Israelite historians, a contemptuous name to put in the mouth of any foreigner talking about the Israelites, as indeed is the case with Philistines: (1 Sam. 4:6, 9; 13:19; 14:11, 21; 29:3). However, it is to be noted that this does not characterize the way all, or even most, disdainful foreigners refer to Israelites. Thus Balak does not call them Hebrews (Num. 22:5), nor do the ancient oracles of Balaam (Numbers 23 and 24), nor the Ammonite king who opposed Jephthah (Judges 11), and so on. The name is associated principally with pre-Israelite Egyptians and with the Philistines.

19. Note in this connection A. D. Smith (2004), although he misses this aspect of the Exodus story; and the related B. Anderson (1991).

20. See sources cited above, note 3; also K. A. Kitchen (1998). J. C. de Moor (1990) and A. Malamat (1997) have sought to connect other Egyptian evidence with elements of the Exodus tradition, but the argument, like so many on the subject, remains only suggestive; see the treatment in Davies (2004: 34–36). Ron Hendel has cogently suggested that the Israelite "memory" of the period of Egyptian slavery and subsequent liberation may indeed have arisen from the experience of individuals. The Amarna letters give evidence of Canaanites being sent to Egypt as slaves, as well as the Egyptian deportation of Canaanites back to their homeland. See Hendel (2001); also Loprieno (1997). If so, the biblical account's failure to mention a specific pharaoh may derive, Hendel argues, from the collective nature of this collective memory: no one particular pharaoh was involved.

21. From Foster (1993: 819–20). See also B. Lewis (1980), who argues that the birth legend originated in the time of a much later namesake of the king, Sargon II of the neo-Assyrian empire (721–705 BCE); its purpose would have been "to glorify Sargon II by showing that he was a worthy successor of Sargon of Akkad" (97). Compare Longman (1991: 53–60).

22. Traditionally, the burning plant has been identified as a bush, but the Hebrew *eneh* might just as easily designate a larger plant, perhaps even a tree. J. D. Levenson has suggested that it might have been an emblem of the God of Israel; note that He is designated as "the one who dwells in the *śeneh*" in Deut. 33:16. See Levenson (1985: 20–21), who further suggests a iconographic connection of this deity with the "arborescent lampstand"—complete with branches, almond-shaped cups, calyces, and petals (Exod. 25:31–39)—found in the tabernacle and the temple (1 Kings 7:49). See also C. L. Meyers (1976).

23. In the passage, I have translated Exod. 3:12 as having God say to Moses, "I will be with you; and *this is the guarantee* that I am the one who is sending you: after you have brought the people out of Egypt, you will worship God on this mountain." "Guarantee" is not a very biblical-sounding word, but the usual translation, "this is the sign that it is I who sent you" misses the point entirely. As was pointed out in chapter 3, an '*ot* in biblical Hebrew can be a sign, as in "signs and wonders," but in the case of the '*ot* given to Cain or the '*ot* given to Moses here (and to Ahaz in Isa. 7:14), it is more of a verbal undertaking that such-and-such will happen in the future. "I will be with you," God says to Moses, "and the proof that I am sending you and that you will in fact successfully complete your mission is My guarantee that, after it is all over, you will be back at this same mountain offering sacrifices to Me." But Moses is not reassured.

24. A confused or dissatisfied silence was indicated by a subtle convention of biblical and Mishnaic Hebrew: the words "he said . . ." were followed by "he said" a second time, when the speaker of both "he said's" was the same. See Septimus (2004).

25. Modern scholars would point out that the author of this passage (attributed to E) is not the same as that of Exod. 7:7 (attributed to P), which says Moses was fully eighty years old when he appeared before Pharaoh. P's concern for the overall chronology of the Exodus period caused him to make Moses an old man, since he was only the great-grandson of one of the original Israelite immigrants (Levi); even with the extraordinary longevity of biblical figures, three generations were scarcely enough to justify P's assertion that the total length of the Israelites' stay in Egypt was 430 years (Exod. 12:40). For ancient interpreters' solution to this problem, Kugel (1998: 570–74).

26. Modern scholarly speculation on this question is voluminous; some of it is surveyed in R. Mayer (1958: 26–53) and Cross (1973: 60 n. 60–75 and 61). For the evolution of one par-

ticular school on this question: Haupt (1909), Albright (1925) and (1948), Cross (1962), and Freedman (1960).

27. One side-point of interest: unlike many ancient Near Eastern deities, YHWH does not seem to have been widely known elsewhere in the ancient Near East. He does not appear on various lists of gods found that were compiled in ancient times, although the name is attested in the Mesha Stone (see chapter 29) and in an ostracon from Kuntillet 'Ajrud (eighth century) to be discussed later. Still, the relative lack of reference to Him is somewhat surprising, and scholars do not quite know what to make of it. G. Pettinato (1980) claimed that the name YHWH was found in apocopated form at Ebla, but see H-P. Mueller (1981). More recently, S. Dalley (1990) has advanced a similar case for Syria; see van der Toorn (1992).

14. The Exodus

1. Kugel (1998: 518–19, 538–41).
2. On this passage there is a vast scholarly literature, most of it more diverting than enlightening. See the bibliography assembled by Childs (1974: 90). Nevertheless see, inter alia: Wellhausen (1957: 340); Smith, H. P. (1906: 14–24); Kosmala (1962: 14–28); Morgenstern (1963: 35–70); Houtman (1983: 81–105). The theory presented herein was previously presented in brief in Kugel (1998: 517, n.12).
3. Either verb form, qatal or yiqtol, may be used after 'az; the meaning "that was when" occurs with both. Thus, I cannot accept the argument of Rabinowitz (1984).
4. For this interpretation to work, one would have to suppose that the biblical text underwent a slight change in the course of transmission. The present text reads: "that was when people began to call on the name of the LORD." But "to call" can just as easily be read as "to be called" (involving no change in the consonantal text, just a different vocalization of the letters), and "the name of the LORD" might be understood as "that name," that is, hhw' in place of yhwh. The confusion of these two vocables is attested, inter alia, in the Dead Sea Scrolls. Read in this way, the text indeed would be saying that after Enosh's birth, "that was when it [humanity] began to be called by this name [Enosh]." Otherwise, modern scholars say, the verse seems quite incomprehensible in context.
5. In Islamic tradition, a wide range of ages for circumcision is attested. See Wensick (1979).
6. Note that adult circumcision occurs in Gen. 17:23–24, 34:24, and Josh. 5:1–12, albeit under special circumstances. More relevant here is Ishmael, eponym of the Ishmaelites, who is circumcised at age thirteen (Gen. 17:25); the Ishmaelites were geographically and in other ways close to the Midianites, with whom they are apparently synonymous (or confused) in Gen. 37:25–28. They were also intermarried with the Edomites (Gen. 36:3). It would not be surprising, then, if one or more of these peoples (Ishmaelites, Edomites, and Midianites) circumcised their sons as a rite of puberty, calling them "bridegrooms of blood" on the occasion.
7. Humphreys (2004): For a discussions of potential natural causes in the crossing of the Red Sea, see Segert (1994).
8. See recently: Nof and Paldor (1992).
9. The problem has been poignantly stated—particular with reference to the miracles of the Exodus—in a famous essay of Langdon Gilkey (1961): "When we are asked about what actually happened [at the Exodus] and how revelation actually occurred, all we can say [if we accept the 'naturalistic' approach to miracles] is that in the continuum of the natural order, an unusual event rescued the Hebrews from a sad fate; from this they concluded that there must be somewhere a great God who loved them; thus they interpreted their own past in terms of his dealings with them and created all the other familiar characteristics of Hebrew religion: covenant, law, and prophecy. This understanding of Hebrew religion is strictly 'liberal'; it pictures reality as a consistent world order, and religious truth as a human interpretation based on religious experience. And yet at the same time, having castigated the liberals, who at least knew what their fundamental theological principles were, we proclaim that our real categories are orthodox: God acts, God speaks, God reveals."

10. Scholars have thus sought to differentiate the account attributed to J, which tends toward scientific "realism," from that of P. See Noth (1959: 82–83), Childs (1974: 221–22).

11. On this passage: P. Enns (1997: esp. 56–66).

12. *Mekhilta deR. Yishma'el* (*Beshallah* 4) (Horowitz-Rabin ed. 1970: 100); cf. m *Abot* 5:4.

13. Kugel (1998: 588–90).

14. Some scholars have suggested that the Exodus narrative may also contain a historical reminiscence of a (bubonic?) plague that struck the region of Egypt and Canaan during the era of Hyksos rule. Assmann (1997: 27) cites Tutankhamun's Restoration Stela—"The land was in grave disease; the gods have forsaken this land"—and explains: "According to my theory, the trauma resulting from the events of the Amarna period reflected both the experience of religious otherness and intolerance and suffering caused by a terrible epidemic. Indeed, the Egyptian name for this epidemic was 'the Asiatic illness.'" See also: Redford (1970). Hendel (2001) assembles impressive evidence of pestilence in Canaan during the Amarna period.

15. For those who fancy this sort of explanation, there is plenty more where these came from—the same approach seeks to explain the destruction of Sodom and Gomorrah as a seismic event, the Sinai revelation as a volcanic eruption, and Ezekiel's vision of the divine chariot as a sighting of flying saucers.

16. Kugel (1998: 562–63).

17. On this whole theme: Loewenstamm (1965). For a close analysis of the compositional history of the plagues narrative in Exodus: Propp (1999: 286–354).

18. On the identity of the Red/Reed Sea, see Hoffmeier (1997: 199–215); the Hebrew *yam sup* may have been the equivalent of the proper name *p3twfy,* "a marshy region in the eastern Delta."

19. Support for this theory was found in the fact that the song begins in the first person singular, "*I* will sing," rather than "Let us sing" or "Sing [plural imperative] . . ." (Both of these exist, however, as textual variants, the first in the Septuagint and various targums, the second in the Samaritan Pentateuch; Kugel (1998: 595). A second argument in favor of this scenario was the fact that the introductory sentence, "that was when Moses and the Israelites sang . . ." uses the singular form of the verb "sang," as if to imply that there was only one singer at first.

20. If so, that unison would likewise explain the singular form of the verb "sang" (see previous note): they all sang as one man.

21. Cf. Song 5:16.

22. See Kugel (1998: 610).

23. See in this connection Lambdin (1971).

24. Some readers of biblical Hebrew may object that the definite article is found in its elided form in the song, that is, following prepositions, such as *bayyam* in Exod. 15:1. But it should be recalled that the vocalization (vowel-points) is a later addition; the consonantal text could be equally understood as indicating *beyam.* That this is actually more likely is suggested by the absence of the definitive article where one would expect it, for example, *mayim* (and not *hammayaim*) in Exod. 15:8, *'oyeb* (and not *ha'oyeb*) or *shalal* (and not *hashalal*) in the next line, and so forth.

25. Cross and Freedman (1955) and Cross (1974: 112–44). Cross and Freedman's analysis, based on their joint doctoral dissertation and earlier work by W. F. Albright and others, has been accepted by most modern scholars; see, however, G. Ahlstrom (1986: 46–55) and Brenner (1991).

26. Cross and Freedman (1955: 238–39). Cross later elaborated on the idea in Cross, (1974: 112–44). See also: Wolters (1990).

27. Wolters (ibid.) suggests that "stood up" ought to be read as the *niphal* of the root *ṣ-b-h* "swell," and that *nd* be understood (in keeping with the targum tradition) as *no'd,* "wineskin," which swells up when filled with liquid—both suggestions in support of the Cross-Freedman reading.

28. Cross (1974: 134).

29. The whole phenomenon of inserted songs is studied in Weitzman (1997).

30. A somewhat different theory: Mark Smith (2001).

31. Many scholars have suggested that the narratives of the Pentateuch represent the transformation of now lost hymnic or epic literature into prose narratives, for example: Cassuto (1975: 1:7–16) and (2:69–109); Albright, (1968: 66–68); and in general, Cross (1973: 166–70); Kselman (1978); Conroy (1980). Methodologically, some of these studies are open to criticism; see Kugel (1981: 85–87). Still, the idea of a prose reworking is not to be rejected. This scenario will not, however, easily account for the inconsistencies contemporary scholars have observed *within* the J and E collections of texts: they seem clearly not to have stemmed from a single recasting of poetic texts into prose. See above, chapter 1, note 76, and chapter 6, note 18.

32. Still, as scholars have observed, the Exodus seems to have remained a favorite theme of, specifically, the northern tribes for some time. See Davies (2004: 26). Thus, most pre-exilic references to the Exodus are concentrated in compositions with northern connections, such as the prophecies of Amos and Hosea and the book of Deuteronomy, as well as psalms of reputedly northern origin such as Pss. 77, 80, and 81. On their northernness, see Nasuti (1988: 78–93 and 97–102) and Rendsburg (1990: 73–81). True, Jeremiah, who frequently invoked the Exodus tradition, lived just outside of Jerusalem; even he, however, had northern connections (see chapter 31). On the other hand, as Davies observes, Ps. 114 is clearly a psalm from Judah in which the Exodus theme is prominent; it may well be preexilic. The last verses of Psalm 78, 56–72, criticize the north and exalt David and Judah, but this may not mean, as Davies argues, that the psalm is of southern origin; see Nasuti (1988: 93). If Exodus 15 was connected to a southern sanctuary, then it, too, would give evidence of a very early southern adoption of this theme.

15. A Covenant with God

1. If so, it may also have something to do with the word "throne" that appears in the curious last two verses of this episode (not cited above): "And Moses built an altar and called it 'The LORD is my sign.' He said: A hand upon the throne [*kes*] of the LORD! The LORD will have war with Amalek from generation to generation" (Exod. 17:15–16). But the word *kes* is otherwise unattested in biblical Hebrew, and in any case, many scholars believe that, in its present form, this verse makes little sense: why would the altar be called 'the LORD is my sign' [*nes*] if the next verse, apparently explaining this name, refers to God's throne [*kes*]? Perhaps this *kes* is to be amended to *nes*, as was suggested as early as Samuel David Luzzatto (1800–1865). If so, then the verse might be understood as: " . . . and called it 'The LORD is my sign.' He said: For it will be known as a sign of the LORD. The LORD's war against Amalek [will continue] from generation to generation" (*k[y] ywdʿ lns yh mlḥmh lyhwh bʿmlq mdr dr*).

2. See Kugel (1998: 616–20, 630–31) for various ancient interpretations of manna; also Borgen (1981).

3. Indeed, some scholars have suggested that P's version is a deliberate recasting of E's story. The latter presents Moses in an altogether positive light: he performs a miracle that gives the people water while at the same time proving to them that their lack of faith is unjustified. In P's version, Moses does something wrong—it is not clear what—that makes God reprove him and Aaron for a lack of faith: "you did not trust Me enough to affirm my sanctity in the sight of the Israelites" (Num. 20:12). Whether or not the two versions were once independent accounts based on a common tradition or the later is a deliberate recasting of the first, scholars say that it is no accident that E's exalts Moses and the miraculous while P's does the opposite; these tendencies are altogether characteristic of the two sources in question. See Friedman (1987: 197–201).

4. The two names are associated by scholars with different sources, Horeb with E and D, Sinai with J and P. Some scholars have questioned whether these two names refer to the same geographic location; see the discussion in Levenson (1985: 16–17). Scholarly literature on the various aspects of the narrative in Exod. 19–20 is understandably enormous. Particularly of interest has been the source-critical analysis. Some important recent works: Zenger (1971); Toeg (1977: 144–59); Mowberly, (1983); Dozeman (1989); B. Schwartz (1996). With regard to Sinai, this last article asserts (among other important points) that for P "Mount

Sinai is not the place of lawgiving. It is merely the place where the [glory] of God rested before the lawgiving commenced. The laws were given in[side] the tabernacle [there]; Sinai is simply the site where the tabernacle was first erected" (123).

5. Scholars have argued back and forth about the antiquity of this passage, as well as about the various hands visible in the shaping of the entire Sinai pericope. Many scholars, it would be fair to say, probably still agree with Gressmann's assessment that in its present form this section presents "an apparently irresolvable tangle" ("einen scheinbar unheilbaren Wirrwarr"—Gressman 1913: 181). Of late, however, and in keeping with his "minimalist" approach (chapter 1, notes 76 and 77), John Van Seters has argued on the contrary that the Sinai pericope and the Covenant Code that follows it actually constitute a single unified composition of J—for Van Seters, J is an exilic author—with only a few priestly touches added later on. See Van Seters (2003). It is difficult, however, to reconcile such a view with the evidence. Scholars over the past century have identified so many internal contradictions, repetitions, and gaps in the Sinai pericope itself (leaving aside for the moment its connection with the Covenant Code) that the assertion that it is nonetheless a single compositional unit has seemed to most rather unlikely. For a review: Levinson 2004: 280–81 and notes there. On the other hand, both B. Schwartz and M. Haran, while rejecting the view of a single author, nevertheless see here "three distinct, readable, consistent and continuous strands" (Schwartz) that can be disentangled in the pericope.

As to Exod. 19:5–6 in particular, some have returned to the suggestion that these words are indeed quite ancient; see in this connection: Cross (1998: 33). To be sure, other scholars have argued that the whole idea of a great covenant between God and Israel is relatively late; see below, note 12. They thus argue that Exodus 19:1–6, since it speaks of a covenant with God (among other reasons), must belong to the time of Deuteronomy or later: Perlitt (1969: 271–75); cf. Zenger (1971: 167–68); H. H. Schmid (1976: 98, 117); Van Seters, (1994: 270–80); Nicholson (1986: 166–67 and 1998: 189–91). For all its recent popularity, the overall line of argument of these studies is still open to criticism. In addition to the source-critical and form-critical arguments that have been adduced (see below), the pan-hieratic nation envisaged in "a kingdom of priests" seems to bespeak an early period before the existence of an official, hereditary priesthood; such a conception would hardly sit well with the assignment of this passage to D, for example. Nor would this passage seem to suit P: "The occasional suggestion that Exod. 19:3–8 (with its reference to a 'kingdom of priests and holy nation' in v. 6) betrays Priestly authorship is rightly dismissed; nothing could be less Priestly than the notion that all Israel is as sacred as a priesthood, even if intended as a rhetorical figure and not as an actual viewpoint"—Schwartz, Baruch (1996: 112). See also: R. Coggins (1995: 135–48); Schearing and McKenzie (1999).

6. Note that the portrait of Hammurabi on his famous law stele shows the god Shamash giving him a scepter and ring, the conventional symbols of justice; the implication is that Shamash has granted the king the right to promulgate the laws on the stele. Still, this is only a granting of authority—the right and duty to create a legal system. This is still significantly different from the claim of divine authorship of laws.

7. This is in fact the first commandment according to the reckoning of most Christians; Jewish tradition sees the first-person statement about God in Exod. 20:2 ("I am the LORD your God, who brought you out of the land of Egypt, out of the house of bondage") as the first commandment—a commandment to recognize the existence of God and His role in history. See Kugel (1998: 642–43, 683).

8. Early treatments of the subject include: Mendenhall (1954), who based himself principally on the monograph of Korosec (1931), followed by Baltzer (1960); McCarthy (1963); Hillers (1964); Tucker (1965), Beyerlin (1965); Hillers (1969). For subsequent scholarship, see below.

9. Note in this connection: Altman (2004).

10. Two years after Mendenhall's ground-breaking article (previous note), D. J. Wiseman (1958) argued on the basis of the recently discovered vassal treaties of Esarhaddon that the basic forms of state treaties attested in the Hittite finds continued to be used, with minor modifications, from the time of the Hittite Empire to the end of the neo-Assyrian empire.

11. As Weinfeld (1972: 67–68) noted, the evidence for this is spotty: of the five Assyrio-

Aramean treaties of the first millennium, the opening section (exactly where the historical prologue should be found) is incomplete or missing in three of them; an historical prologue might have been inappropriate with the Esarhaddon treaty, since it is concerned with continuance of the vassal relationship and not its establishment; it is not even clear if the fifth example, the Aramaic Sefire treaties, belong to the vassal treaty type.

12. Some have argued that the very idea of a covenant cannot be dated earlier than Deuteronomy; see the extended discussion in Perlitt (1969); also E. W. Nicholson (1986). Others have rejected this line of argument, for example, Mendenhall (1973: 1–31). Patrick Miller has put it well: "There does not seem to have been any period in Israel's religious history when the specific recognition of the relation of the deity and tribe or people was not expressed in such a pact, though it took different forms prior to the monarchy and during it, and may have been understood or formulated differently in the North and in the South" (2000: 5). See also Weinfeld (1972: 59–157), and above, note 5.

13. This view actually goes back to Wellhausen, whose evolutionary picture of Israel's religion precluded anything like a legal, covenant-based connection between God and the people at an early stage. "The relation of Jehovah to Israel was in its nature and origin a natural one, there was no interval between Him and His people to call for thought or question. Only when the existence of Israel had come to be threatened by the Syrians and the Assyrians did such prophets as Elijah and Amos raise the Deity high above the people, sever the natural bond between them, and put in its place a relation depending on conditions, conditions of a moral character"—Wellhausen (1957: 417). See on this P. D. Miller (1982: 61–73).

14. Some scholars seek to date the Decalogue pericopes in Exodus and Deuteronomy (sometimes along with the rest of that book) in the exilic or post-exilic period. See the recent review in Aaron (2006).

15. Even an Israelite from the time of the monarchy who recognized that there had been no actual king at the supposed time of this covenant would certainly have attributed the king's treaty-making powers to Moses rather than creating this odd, unmediated agreement between the divine suzerain and all the people collectively.

16. There seems little reason to doubt that traditions of ancient treaty conventions exemplified in the Hittite models could have been preserved and passed on in some form long after the Hittite empire had passed from the scene. Indeed, the fullest example of an elaborate historical prologue (held to be a Hittite—as opposed to neo-Assyrian—feature) is found in the book of Deuteronomy. In the end, then, a rigid reliance on the presence or absence of one or another feature does not appear to be a decisive factor in dating the covenant tradition. Indeed, some such features might be expected in any official agreement of this sort. Thus, the Magna Carta (which was produced in four different editions, 1215, 1216, 1217, 1225) contains elements corresponding to some of those in the ancient Hittite treaties, for example: self-presentation of the suzerain (first sentence of the Preamble); brief historical prologue (Preamble); treaty stipulations (articles 1–61); disposition of the "letters testimonial patent" with the archbishops (article 62); oaths (article 63); invocation of God and (human) divines acting as witnesses (Preamble, article 1). I do not think anyone has argued that the Englishmen in thirteenth-century Runnymede were basing the document on Hittite treaty models. To be sure, this list of resemblances is only partial and the order of items is different—still, the resemblances are all the more striking in that this is *not* a suzerain-type treaty at all.

17. Perlitt (1969) and above notes 5 and 12.

18. Note also the connection of the Ten Commandments with Amos 3:1–2 proposed by Weiss (1985: 67–82).

16. The Ten Commandments

1. Kugel (1998: 638–40). See also Schwartz (1994).

2. Kugel (1998: 636–38, 677); and Schwartz (1994).

3. It is certainly true that "murder" is a bit too narrow to translate the Hebrew root *rṣḥ*, as was recently argued by Bailey (2005). I am disturbed, however, that *kill* errs on the other side. It certainly includes all manner of permitted acts in biblical law, from the slaughter of

animals to warfare and capital punishment. On balance, "murder" is still the better translation.

4. Kugel (1998: 638–40).

5. The question of the antiquity of the prohibition of images was first raised by Mowinckel (1930); for the actual text of the Decalogue and this question, see Zimmerli, (1950: 550–63), and more recently, Dohmen (1985). See also Kugel (2003: 71–107) and notes.

6. A small bronze statue of a bull was found at a twelfth-century BCE site, apparently (though this is not certain) in what has been identified as a cultic site; see Mazar (1982 and 1990: 350–51). It is, however, far from clear what deity was thereby represented. See the discussion in Zevit (2001: 176–79, 448–57) and sources cited there. Some scholars have also seen in the various biblical references to seeing God's "face" in such verses as Exod. 23:15, 34:23–24, Ps. 42:3, and so forth allusions to an actual statue or other plastic representation of Israel's God that may at one time have been a standard feature in one or more ancient temples. This is a tantalizing proposal, but difficult to accept without further proof. There is hardly another Hebrew word with so many idiomatic and figurative meanings as *panim*: seeing God's face could certainly mean coming into His presence or receiving his favor, just as "seeking His face" meant to earnestly request something from Him. Considering the many texts (some of them indisputably early) that speak of God "appearing" (see Kugel, 2003: 99–107) to people, and in light of any archaeological evidence to the contrary, it would seem that—as with some other ancient Near Eastern peoples—the tradition of aniconic worship of Israel's God goes back very far. At the same time, many scholars distinguish between what they see as the "official" cult in any given period or locale and popular piety as it may have existed in the same place and time. Archaeologists have turned up a profusion of figurines in Judah that apparently represent the goddess Asherah and other deities and date to the eighth and seventh centuries; these include hundreds and hundreds of statues that were discovered in the very shadow of the Jerusalem temple. Such evidence may not be conclusive (see Kugel, 2003: 218–19), but it suggests that, whatever the practices followed within the temple itself, ordinary people continued to worship other gods—and worshiped them through little figurines and statues.

17. A Religion of Laws

1. Some translations read, "draw near to the judges," and understanding the word *'elohim* as "judges" would indeed suit a phrase in the last sentence of this passage, "the one whom *'elohim* finds guilty," that is, "the one whom *the judges* find guilty." Still, the usual meaning of *'elohim* is "God" or "the gods." See below.

2. Readers familiar with the Revised Standard Version and similar translations will note that their version of this law differs somewhat from my more literal rendering—for reasons to be made clear presently. Note the somewhat more accurate translation of the Jewish Publication Society (1985: 119).

3. Scholars have speculated about the basis for the Septuagint translation, but in the end it appears to be essentially an attempt to make sense of an otherwise puzzling law. It may indeed be connected with an Aristotelian distinction between the initial period after conception, during which the fetus is not yet "animated," and later stages—as suggested by Lafont 1994. But such a connection would hardly explain the same view of the fetus being adopted by the Qumran community (see Kugel 1998: 695–98, and notes there). The suggestion that Hebrew *'ason* was identified with Greek *asoma* (bodiless, hence, unformed) is ingenious but flawed. To begin with, would not the Septuagint translators have used this very word if that was the basis for their translation? Moreover, since for the case in which the punishment is merely a fine, the Hebrew reads *'im lo' yihyeh 'ason*, whereas the condition for imposing the death penalty is *we'im 'ason yihyeh*, the word *'ason* cannot be understood to mean "unformed"; if it were, the penalty for causing the death of an unformed fetus is death, whereas the penalty for causing the death of a fully formed fetus is a fine. (One might, of course argue that in the case of the fully formed fetus, the fetus is viable and therefore is presumed to live—but that would still fail to explain why the death penalty is imposed on one who caused an unformed fetus to perish. This certainly goes

against the Aristotelian distinction invoked by Lafont, as well as against Philo's interpretation of the Septuagint text and, for that matter, all documented understanding of this law from Qumran to rabbinic exegesis. See also next note. Equally unconvincing, I am afraid, is the attempt by Westbrook (1986) to distinguish the two cases mentioned in this law as referring to instances in which the perpetrator is known or unknown.

4. It might be asked why such a person was subject to the death penalty when in other cases of accidental death the person responsible was not (see Exod. 21:13, Deut. 19:4–7). The difference, according to rabbinic interpreters, was the matter of intention. In the case described, the man certainly did *intend* to do harm—he picked up a two-by-four, say, and swung it at the person he was fighting with, hitting the woman by mistake. Without some intent to harm, the accident would never have occurred; his level of guilt is therefore greater than in any accident in which no harm was intended by anyone. To put it in more modern terms, someone who shoots a gun at X and hits Y instead is not found innocent because he missed his intended victim.

5. It should be stated that, although both Roman Catholics and Orthodox Jews interpret the biblical passage in the manner of interpretation #2, neither group has concluded therefore that abortion under any circumstances is permissible; nor do they hold, for that matter, that the whole question of terminating a pregnancy is to be decided solely on the basis of the biblical passage cited.

6. See Kugel (1998: 695–98).

7. It is unlikely that size itself is intended here, but rather strength of vision; that is, removing an eye that is weak or virtually blind (not an uncommon situation in ancient times) would not be a sufficiently severe punishment for the perpetrator; whereas removing his other (good) eye in such a case would be too severe, leaving the person virtually blind.

8. This was done by the Elamite ruler Shutruk-Nahhunte I in the twelfth century BCE; see Roth (1998: 73).

9. It appeared in Scheil (1902).

10. See on this Greenberg (1976).

11. Listed in Levinson (2004: 290).

12. All translations from Roth (1998).

13. Note that both LE ¶37 and LH ¶125 stipulate that the guardian's house must also have been burglarized for his oath to be credible. This was first hypothesized by P. Koschaker (1917: 26–33); see Greengus (1994).

14. Above, note 1.

15. The other possibility is that this is a frozen expression, "draw near to the gods," passed on literally from a polytheistic environment and, eventually, no longer understood by Israelites, who may therefore have explained its meaning as "judges" from a relatively early period.

16. See on this Isser (1990).

17. "The significance of this phrase has been much debated. I favor the view that the person is entitled to . . . recover damages from the estate of the perpetrator" (note of H. A. Hoffner, Jr., in Roth, 1998: 238).

18. In the present ordering of the text, it would seem to imply that the Israelites heard all of the Decalogue directly from God, and then Moses received the entirety of "Book of the Covenant" after having entered the "thick darkness" (Exod. 20:21). He then related its contents to the people (Exod. 24:3, 7). At the same time, some scholars find the present account somewhat confusing and suggest it results from the combination of different accounts. Again, see Levinson (2004: 280–81).

19. For the opposite view, proposed by Van Seters: above, chapter 15, note 5.

20. In support of this hypothesis, scholars have pointed to formal differences between the Ten Commandments and these other laws. Thus, while the prohibitions of the Decalogue are relatively straightforward—"Do this," "Don't do that"—the laws of the Covenant Code often describe complicated situations, "If so and so should happen and such and such be the case, then . . ." The distinction was first highlighted by Albrecht Alt, who referred to the Decalogue's simple kind of statute as "apodictic" law and the other laws as "casuistic." See Alt (1966: 79–132). Scholars have subsequently expressed doubts about the absoluteness of Alt's distinction; note especially Gerstenberger (1965).

21. On the text's own distinction between the "words" of the Decalogue and the "ordinances" of the Covenant Code, see Levinson (2004: 281–83).
22. Indeed, even the old model of the Covenant Code's derivation from "orally transmitted legal traditions" that made their way from second-millennium Babylon to first-millennium Israel has not survived recent scrutiny. Van Seters and others have argued that the resemblances between the two codes are just too close to make this plausible: far more likely is some sort of direct copying from a Mesopotamian text or texts. Van Seters (2003) locates that act of copying in Babylon during the time of the exile; Levinson (2004) argues on the contrary that the period of neo-Assyrian domination is the most likely time for its adoption.
23. Johns (1917: 62).
24. The circumstances and extent of this issue's emergence is still a matter of debate; see my brief discussion and the sources cited in Kugel (2005: 77–80 and notes).
25. Kugel (1998: 425–27). On Molech worship see Weinfeld (1972), Heider (1985) Day (1989).
26. See Najman (2003) as well as the essays collected in Poffet (2002).
27. Here, the scholarly literature is so vast that citing one or two works would only mislead. See, however, some of the sources cited in Kugel (1998: 704–10)
28. Lull (1986).
29. On which in general: Preus (1969).
30. Kugel (1998: 558–59).
31. Ibid., 841–42.

18. Worship on the Road

1. Possibly, they approach Hur with their request because he is the grandfather of Bezalel, the man who would fashion the desert tabernacle and its appurtenances (Exod. 31:2). If Bezalel possessed the metalworking skills necessary to accomplish that task, it seemed reasonable that he had learned those skills from his own father, and his father from Hur (since, in traditional societies, professions were generally passed on from father to son). Thus, if Hur was murdered by the mob, perhaps the reason was not only that he had been opposed to the idea of making a golden calf, but that he, the master craftsman, had actually refused to lend his knowledge of metal-making to aid in the project's realization.
2. Kugel (1998: 719–21, 732–35).
3. On the later elaboration of this passage within the Bible and thereafter: Kugel (1998: 721–27).
4. Kugel: (2003: 71–107, 217–34 and sources cited there).
5. See the brief survey in Milgrom (1991: 440–43 and 2001: 2439). In addition to the reasons cited above, Milgrom also mentions that of the shared meal with the god or goddess, designed to "effect unity with the deity." (On this see next note.) As he notes, however, these explanations are not, for the most part, those most often put forward by biblical texts. Thus, E. Regev (2004) has surveyed the various references to cultic sacrifice within the book of Psalms. Among the reasons given in the Psalms themselves for temple worship and sacrificing are: (1) recognition of the deity's greatness; (2) payment of a vow; (3) as an expression of the feeling of righteousness and trust in God; (4) as an expression of faith and obedience; (5) sacrifice as a form of prayer; (6) sacrifice as an embodiment of closeness to the deity; and yet others. Among all these, Regev notes, the Psalms contain no explicit mention of the idea that sacrifices are intended for the deity's well-being or as food, or as expiation for the sacrificer's sins or as a means to preserving his own life or even as a way of making the animal's flesh fit for human consumption—all arguments that have been put forward in the past.
6. Particularly important to the modern discussion has been the contribution of structural anthropologists, starting with Lévi-Strauss (1966: especially 225–28); Leach (1976: 81–93). See also Burkert (1983) and Hendel (1989).
7. This argument is associated in particular with the writings of René Girard, especially (1977) and (1986); Girard's claims have been cogently disputed in the biblical sphere by Klawans (next note).
8. See Klawans (2003); for the argument in full, see Klawans (2005).

9. This famous remark was reported in one of O'Connor's private letters; on its relation to her fiction, J. Andreas (1989).

10. I owe this citation to Jonathan Klawans.

11. On this see Monson (2000).

12. F. M. Cross (1961); (1974: 36, n. 144; 72, n. 112); and (1998: 84–95), as well as Clifford (1971); Friedman (1980).

13. Haran (1962) and (1978: 199–204); Y. Aharoni (1973); Friedman (1987: 174–87).

14. See the discussion in Milgrom (1991: 600–606).

15. These interpretations are reflected in various retellings of the story by the Bible's ancient interpreters; see Kugel (1998: 744–45, 760–62).

16. The term first appeared in German ("Das Heiligkeitsgesetz"); see Klöstermann (1877: 401–5).

17. On biblical holiness there is a vast literature. One excellent recent treatment is Jenson (1992: esp. 40–55). See also: Milgrom (1976) and (2000: 1397–1400; B. Schwartz (1999); Knohl (1995: 180–86).

18. This is true, more specifically, of chapter 19 of Leviticus, which scholars since at least the 1930s have identified as a kind of reformulation of the Decalogue: Mowinckel (1937). Moshe Weinfeld (1990), among others, has suggested that, indeed, the Decalogue is the cause of this chapter's unusual character within the corpus of priestly writings: "A list of commands similar to those laid down in the Decalogue is found in Leviticus chapter 19. This is the only place in the Priestly Code where we encounter an intermingling of cultic and ethical laws, such as we find in the Ten Commandments . . . Leviticus does begin with the Fifth, Fourth, and Second Commandments of the Decalogue." See further Milgrom (2000), 1600–1602. It would be inexact, however, to suggest that ethical legislation is absent from H apart from this chapter—that is far from the truth.

19. See Kugel (1999: 255–57).

20. My translation departs somewhat from the extant Greek text (the original Hebrew of this section is missing); the latter reads, "Reprove a friend—perhaps he did not do it." It seems likely, however, that reproving before and after the fact is Ben Sira's way of reckoning with the "doubled verb" in Lev. 19:17, hokeah tokiah (that is, the combination of the infinitive absolute with a finite form of the same verb). Though this is simply idiomatic in Standard Biblical Hebrew, by Second Temple times such doubling was seen as carrying extra significance, and was therefore regularly represented in the Septuagint translation ("reprove with a reproval," in this case). See on this: Lee (1983: 17). Ben Sira's before-and-after approach thus seems to be one way to account for two verb forms that, morphologically, might be connected respective with past and future events. See further: Kugel (1998: 752–55, 766–68).

21. Kugel (1998: 756–59, 768–70).

22. Here it is clear that the text presents an integrated interpretation of Lev. 19: 17–18. Hatred is altogether forbidden; an offender should be reproached, and if he does not respond positively, he should be "prayed for" but must never be the object of revenge or grudge bearing. One who is, on the contrary, a true friend or neighbor deserves to be loved more than oneself.

23. This is of course somewhat different from the interpretation in Didache 2:7 cited earlier. It may well be that the words "and whatever you do not want to be done to you, you shall not do to anyone else" are a standard gloss, as suggested by Targum Pseudo-Jonathan.

24. Just as another law, Deut. 6:4, was deemed to sum up the "vertical" dimension: "You shall love the LORD your God with all your heart and all your soul and all your might." Both commandments began with "You shall love" and were apparently paired from an early period. See Sir. 17:14, 18:13; Rom. 13:8–9. Also Flusser (1990) and Kugel (1998: 768–69).

19. P and D

1. Wellhausen and others believed it was composed only a short while before it was "discovered" in the Jerusalem temple. He dated it even a bit later: "About the origin of Deuteronomy there is even less dispute: in all circles where appreciation of scientific results can be

looked for at all, it is recognized that it was composed in the same age as that in which it was discovered," that is, in the age of Josiah at the end of the seventh century.

2. Inter alia multa, see. Weinfeld (1961); Mettinger (1982: 38–79; 123–32). Note also Zakovitch (1972: 338–40. On the Akkadian roots of this expression see Richter (2002). Richter's thesis is that the "name theology" attributed to Deuteronomy by modern scholars is the result of a great misunderstanding: the biblical phrase "to cause My name to dwell" is essentially a cognate translation of the Akkadian expression *šuma šakānu,* which refers to the erection of a "display monument" marking a victory and a claim to the land where the monument is erected. Despite this erudite argument—elements of which are noted in Weinfeld (1972: 193–34)—her critics have rightly countered that Deuteronomy itself offers ample evidence of its far more abstract concept of deity than that of earlier writers. As Richter herself notes (60–88), Deuteronomy and the Deuteronomistic history contain, beside the Hebrew cognate of this phrase, other noncognate expressions, "to build a house for the name" of God, to "offer praise to the name," and so forth. These would suggest that, whatever the origin of "to cause My name to dwell," the idea of God's "name" as a kind of a divine hypostasis is reflected in these other uses; "name" had·been freed from its specific meaning in the original Akkadian idiom. Indeed, her overall argument appears to be based on a misconception, that because a word or phrase meant X in its original language, it will also mean X when borrowed by another language. Reality is full of examples of precisely the opposite. Thus, the French loan-word *outrage* suggests to most speakers of English an element of anger that is quite lacking in French. The reason is that English speakers unconsciously analyze the word as a combination of *out + rage,* whereas French speakers, having no morphological *out,* do not isolate the element *rage* (indeed, most native speakers will correctly perceive -age as the nominalizing suffix of *outre,* "beyond" [Latin *ultra*]). The legal phrase *corpus delicti* originally meant "the body of the offense," that is, "the actual facts that prove that a crime or offense against the law has been committed." But many people (including some lawyers) with a poor grasp of Latin understand *corpus* in the specific sense of a "(dead) body," corpse. It is true that in a murder trial, the corpse does constitute the *corpus delicti,* but the phrase of course has much wider applicability—it can mean the stolen bicycle or the broken storefront window as well. Nevertheless, *corpus delicti* has actually developed in English the secondary meaning of a dead body—even in some dictionaries. Other examples could be given. Thus, the fact that *šuma šakānu* had the meaning it had in Akkadian does not guarantee that it *ever* had the same meaning in Hebrew. (To quote Weinfeld, who notes its use in Amarna Akkadian, the original phrase "had nothing to do with an abstract notion of God; it was the Deuteronomic school that endowed it with a specific theological meaning," 193.) Indeed, it is not hard to imagine the learned Deuteronomist borrowing this foreign idiom with the specific intention of creating an authoritative-sounding equivalent that would support his new theology. That is, he consciously took over *šuma šakānu* to help legitimate the idea that God had merely caused His "name," but not Himself, to dwell in the earthly temple devoted to Him.

3. Cross's observation (1998: 15) is apposite: "For Wellhausen, the relationship between God and Israel in premonarchical times and in early prophecy was 'natural,' spontaneous, free, interior (individualistic). Such language is his inheritance from a philosophic milieu created by idealism and romanticism, borrowed immediately from Vatke, and congruent with Protestant antinomianism."

4. See further: Weinfeld (1980).

5. The big change of late (as we have already glimpsed) has been the minimalist challenge to the early dating of these sources, especially J and E, and, along with this, the refusal to see in the various narratives attributed to J and E the work of individual authors. Some scholars have, however, sought virtually to eliminate J and E as sources altogether. Again, chapter 1, notes 76 and 77.

6. An apologetic answer is frequently supplied here, the argument of "accommodation": at first the people of Israel were not ready for such an abstract deity, they needed to be led to it gradually, and/or they needed to be weaned from polytheistic notions. This sort of argument is at least as old as Pauline Christianity; "accommodation" itself is an Augustinian term, and, interestingly, the same argument was taken up (apparently, quite independently) by Maimonides. Despite its distinguished pedigree, exponents of this argument with regard

to Israel's God have always failed to address its main weakness: why? What would have been so hard about Israel accepting a brand new notion of divinity, and how would two or three centuries of divinely given contradictory information improve the situation when the change-over was finally made? See Benin (1993).

7. The complete letter is in M. Ernst (1956: vol. 2, pp. 47 ff.)
8. Hertz (1952: vii).
9. For the dimensions of P and a survey of some recent scholarship: Jenson (1992: 15–26), and the specific references to works by Haran, Knohl, Milgrom, B. Schwartz, and others cited below.
10. Modern scholars are quite divided on the question of whether the P material was ever an actual, independent work or simply a series of editorial insertions in an existing text. See Cross (1973: 294–319); Noth (1972: 234–47) and (1987: 107–47); Cross (1973: 301–25); Rendtorff (1977); Koch (1987: 446–56); Vervenne (1990). More recent theories are mentioned below.
11. This phrase actually means "And God was pleased." See Kugel (1980).
12. McEvenue (1971: 138–39).
13. On these and other lexical traits: M. Paran (1989: 243–72). For *kabod*, see below, chapter 32.
14. Some of these are traced in McEvenue (1971), others in Paran (1989).
15. Kaufmann (1937: 113–42); see also Kaufmann (1972: 175–200).
16. For a summary of this school's arguments, see Krapf (1992: 3–66); Weinfeld (2004).
17. On the antiquity of some of these (based on ancient Near Eastern parallels): Weinfeld (1983).
18. Hurvitz (1974), (1982), and (1988); note also Zevit (1982). Jacob Milgrom (1991: 3–35) summarizes some of the arguments of Hurvitz and others. He notes that Hurvitz point to some ten typical terms of P that are not found in Ezekiel "in contexts in which one would expect to find them"—terms such as *reaḥ niḥoaḥ* (and *heriah*), *'amit, ledoroteikhem*, and so forth. More important, there are certain standard replacements of P's terminology found in Ezekiel, in which the Ezekiel substitute is a word or form widely attested in post-exilic Hebrew. Thus: P says *'amatayim*, while Ezekiel says *šetei 'amot*; P says *heqim* while Ezekiel says *qiyyem*; P says *tabnit*, Ezekiel says *ṣurah*; and so forth. Finally, Hurvitz documents the disappearance of some of Ezekiel's vocabulary in post-exilic books such as Chronicles, Ezra, and Nehemiah.
19. See Milgrom (1991: 3–35).
20. It is true that Moses objects to their taking the adult Midianite women after they had been instrumental and leading the Israelites astray (Num. 31:15–16), but there was no problem with taking innocent young girls (31:18), presumably for purposes of cohabitation. See Milgrom (1990: xxxiv). Milgrom has assembled other arguments for P's pre-exilic dating as well, starting on xxxiii; see above, note 18; also, Milgrom (2000: 1361–64).
21. On D's possible reuse of P, see Moran (1966); Milgrom (1976: 9–12); Japhet (1978). On the other hand, D apparently knows nothing of Korah's role in the revolt of Dathan and Abiram; see as well next note.
22. More recently, the debate seems to have turned in the opposite direction; see the recent review of scholarship and new proposal Levinson (2006). On the general topic, inter alia: Milgrom (1991: 9–13); Perlitt (1988: 65–88); Joosten (1996).
23. Van Seters (1999: 80), an opponent of this view, rejects it as ideologically based: "The problem with this kind of argument is that its primary motivation is ideological, no less so for the Israeli scholars than for those they accuse of anti-Judaism bias [that is, "Wellhausen and his contemporaries"]." But surely sticking the label "ideological" on an argument (a label that in some measure fits a great many arguments in modern biblical scholarship) without addressing any of its specific claims cannot be considered a serious rebuttal. While his is a somewhat slim volume, I nonetheless find it odd that Van Seters fails to cite a single article or book by any of the post-Kaufmann scholars who have elaborated the view he opposes—nothing by Hurvitz, Zevit, Haran, Milgrom, Knohl—nor does he demonstrate much awareness of the actual arguments, linguistic and others, advanced by these and numerous other scholars (Weinfeld, S. Japhet, W. Moran, J. Joosten, et al.).

24. Knohl claims that the H school "originated in the period in the latter part of the eighth century BCE, in the period from the rule of Ahaz to that of his successor Hezekiah; the material in P must go back still earlier, "sometime during the two hundred year period between the construction of Solomon's Temple and the reign of Ahaz-Hezekiah. This time period also accounts for the many strata in P, which indicate a compilation made over a long period of time" (1995: 220). It was the school of H that, centuries later, undertook "the gigantic task of editing the Pentateuch, which consisted primarily of combining Priestly and popular material" (224). Although he is cautious about stipulating a date for this editing, he points to the early post-exilic period as the appropriate time, both on linguistic grounds (see 103, n. 152) and on the basis of content (p. 202). Milgrom's dating (2001: 2440–46) is similar, but he is unwilling to date *any* of H later than the Babylonian exile: "I cannot find any statement by H that postdates the exile . . . [T]he very last layer of the H school, namely, the framework of Leviticus 23, has to be set in the exilic period."

25. Knohl's striking demonstration that H came *after* P is only part of the last half-century's revolutionary reevaluation of the priestly strata of the Pentateuch. In addition to Knohl's own teachers—in particular, Menaham Haran and Moshe Greenberg (and, *par personne interposée*, Y. Kaufmann)—mention must be made in this context of the numerous contributions of Baruch Levine, Jacob Milgrom, Baruch Schwartz, and others. (While acknowledging Knohl's contributions, Milgrom has also clarified some of their disagreements—see in particular *Leviticus 1–16*, 13–63; *Leviticus 17–22*, 1328–44; and *Leviticus 23–27*, 2440–46.)

26. Knohl (1995: 6–7, 44).

27. Ibid., 3.

28. Ibid., 180.

29. Milgrom (1991: 16) thus scarcely exaggerates when he speaks of the "gaping ideological chasm that divides P from H," in particular with regard to their very conceptions of God; see below. A similar point against the old, evolutionary view of things is made with regard to D by Levinson (1997: 54–56): "It has long been held that the festival calendar of Deut. 16:1–8 involves 'a process of growth . . . in the course of which two separate festivals, Passover and Unleavened Bread (Mazzot), have been combined' [cited from Mayes (1959: 254)]. According to this approach, the text achieves its form as the result of prior cultic or tradition history, which it reflects. Allegedly, the gradual shift from nomadic to settled life leads to the obsolescence of such ancient nomadic customs as the paschal slaughter, and the festival calendar thus mirrors already achieved, de facto, empirical development. Despite its popularity, that hypothesis has no real supporting evidence . . . What is prior is neither Passover nor Unleavened Bread in itself, but rather the innovation of centralization and the historical program of Deuteronomy's authors. In Deut. 16:1–8, the authors of Deuteronomy construct and sanction an entirely new observance that supplants both the original Passover and the original Unleavened Bread and that is now consistent with the Deuteronomic program."

30. The point is somewhat obscured in Milgrom's (1991: 19) rebuttal of Knohl. It is not that such singing did not exist in the pre-Hezekian rite of the Jerusalem temple, but that the P school did not want to acknowledge it, since it did not conform to their own theology.

31. These observations follow Knohl (1995; on prayer see p. 149), although, as Knohl acknowledges, many of them go back to Kaufmann (1937). Thus Kaufmann: "Those acts performed in the temple itself—on the altar, in the sanctuary, and in the Holy of Holies—were all oriented toward one idea: sanctification of the place of God's name and the symbol of His Word, purification of all who approach Him, expression of the awe of the holy; not material requital nor even supplication for kind gifts—just awe of the holy" (1972: 476). On Milgrom's reservations about Knohl's view, see above, note 25. This is not the place to rehash their disagreements; I must observe, however, that some of Milgrom's objections are unconvincing. On the issue at hand, for example, he writes: "While it is true that there is no *explicit* statement in the P corpus concerning the hope for 'blessing and salvation,' there is scarcely a rite that does not take it for granted" p. 18 (emphasis his). It seems to me that "explicit" is precisely the issue: the reality of the sacrificial cult (the "rites") existed long before P; the question is rather what P chooses to make of it. That nothing explicit is said about the hoped-for benefits of the rites is a statement in itself. The same is true of the Priestly Blessing (Num. 6:22–24); it now seems clear that this blessing is quite ancient, going

back at least to the ninth century. (See on this Yardeni, 1991.) What is crucial is what P chooses to make of it, namely, nothing at all (Lev. 9:23). It was H who inserted the polemical note of Num. 6:27: "They [the priests] shall place My name on the Israelites, but I will be the one who actually blesses them." This assertion promised that the blessings in this ancient formula would indeed be carried out, and it also displaced the power to carry them out from the priesthood to God.

32. The term *bamah* ("high place") does not actually occur in Deuteronomy itself, which refers instead to "altars." As M. Haran points out (1978:20), "in the Pentateuch the word [*bamah*] occurs quite rarely with this meaning and then only in the Holiness Code (Lev. 26:30, Num. 33:52). He further observes that the term appears in "pre-Deuteronomistic sources" without negative connotations: it is only in the Deuteronomistic redaction of the book of Kings that the "*bamah* features more prominently and is considered an absolutely illegitimate, detestable object." As to the precise physical form of the *bamah*, scholars continue to disagree. To this day not a single "high place" has been identified with certainty, although the excavations at Megiddo have produced one likely candidate. See Epstein (1965), Finkelstein and Silberman, (2001: 241–42).

33. Wellhausen (1957: 76).

34. Rofe (1985) suggests that Deut. 4:32–40 was originally a short "sermon." When a historical prologue (Deut. 4:1–31) was added to the original core of Deuteronomy (Deut. 4:44—26:19, and chapter 28), Rofe argues, the interpolator decided to end this historical review with the short sermon. He further suggests that the Masoretic text shows signs of later, tendentious editing when compared to the Samaritan Pentateuch and the Septuagint: in the MT, the Israelites are all virtually prophets. On the date of Deuteronomy and various scholarly arguments connected thereto: Nicholson (1967), who favors a seventh-century dating.

35. Contrast Deut. 18:6–8 with 2 Kings 23:9; Josiah deposed the idolatrous priests, killing them and defiling the altars with their bones (2 Kings 23:5, 20); Deuteronomy provides no justification for this, having prescribed only a procedure for dealing with apostate prophets. See Tigay (1996: xx).

36. See on this Cogan (1974).

37. Kugel (1989).

38. Weinfeld (1972: 244–81).

39. Ibid., 333, 336–37.

40. Ibid., esp. 179–90. "Before us, then, are two theological schools, one of which is characterized by its theocentric and the other by its anthropocentric approach. The humanistic vein distinguishing the book of Deuteronomy has its roots . . . in wisdom teaching, which embodied the humanistic thought of the ancient Near East" (189).

41. See above, note 2.

42. See von Rad (1953: 37–44); Weinfeld (1962).

43. This is the theme of Weinfeld (1995). Note also Levinson (2002).

44. My thanks to my student Baruch Alster for this point.

45. See Cross (1973: 198–99).

46. All well catalogued in Schwartz (1996, esp. 123–30).

20. On the Way to Canaan

1. The child's mention of the different categories of laws, "the decrees and the statutes and the ordinances," indicates that this is a wise offspring.

2. There is some confusion in the sources, since, although the synoptic gospels seem to connect the Last Supper with Passover, John states that it occurred prior to Passover (John 19:14, 42). This may be a different tradition or an act of deliberate dissociation. See Bokser (1984: 25–26).

3. See further Kugel (1998: 750–52, 764–65).

4. Wellhausen (1957: 76).

5. A general reflection of some current thinking about the festivals: Soggin (2001).

6. Haran (1978: 320–21) and brief review of scholarship there.

7. Ibid. For an account of the transformation of this holiday from its earlier stages to its rad-

ical revision in Deuteronomy: Levinson (1997: 53–97), building on earlier scholarship; see Loewenstamm (1965, esp. 84–88).

8. Some scholars have asserted that the word p-s-ḥ represents two originally distinct roots that became homonymous, the first meaning to "hop" or "limp," the second "to protect." See Otto (1988: 31–35), and the discussion in Levinson (1997: 58), as well as Milgrom (2001: 1970–71). The only evidence for the existence of the second root in Hebrew is the somewhat ambiguous Isa. 31:5. In fact, Exod. 12:13 makes good sense if pasaḥti means "I will hop over": God will pass through Egypt striking every house (verse 12), but seeing the blood on the lintel, He will jump over the houses of the Israelites; the same understanding is reflected in Exod. 12:27. On the other hand, the presence of ḥiṣṣil in both the latter verse and Isa. 31:5 may support the "protect" thesis.

9. Two verses later, however, the text adds: "You shall not offer the blood of My sacrifice with leaven, and the sacrifice of the festival of the Passover shall not be left until the morning (Exod. 34:25). Scholars thus see 34:18–25 as the combination of different sources.

10. On this passage and its radical refashioning of these holidays—necessitated by the Josianic requirement of the centralization of worship at the Jerusalem temple—see Levinson (1997: 53–97).

11. The connection with booths may derive from the little shelters (sukkot) that farmers customarily built in their fields spring and fall, both as a place to store their harvested crop safely and so as to enable them to do the maximum amount of harvesting before dark (since farmers often lived at some distance from their fields); they could sleep in the booths during the hottest part of the day and again at night and thus not lose time going back and forth to their homes. This may be why dwelling in booths came to be a stipulation of the holiday: "You shall dwell in booths for seven days" (Lev. 23:42). Tur-Sinai and some later writers have argued against this explanation on the grounds that Deut. 16:13 associates the Festival of Booths with the grain and grape harvests; but the grain harvest actually begins in the spring, as we have seen—long before this festival. What is more, this verse seems to be speaking not of harvesting produce, but of processing it once it has been harvested, since it speaks of gathering in from the "threshing floor" and the "vat," not the field and the vineyard. Thus, the booths that gave this holiday its name cannot have been harvest booths. See Milgrom, (2001: 2048–49); the idea of building booths would instead have developed from the fact that the pilgrims who went to Jerusalem for this festival had to make booths for themselves as temporary dwellings; see Neh. 8:14–16. By contrast, Tigay, while admitting that Deut. 16:13 refers to the processing of earlier crops, has urged that the dwelling in booths is nevertheless connected to the harvest since it "symbolizes the harvest season just completed" (1996: 538).

12. Wellhausen (1957: 92).

13. See Kugel (1998: 667–68).

14. Cited at greater length in Milgrom (1991: 1068). See as well Milgrom's earlier work on this subject, especially (1983) and (1986).

15. Knohl (1995: 27–34).

16. Milgrom (1991: 628).

17. Here I have simply elaborated on a suggestion of Milgrom (1991: 1061) although he ultimately sees a different purpose in the narrative (pp. 628–33).

18. Ibid., 1011.

19. If so, then Lev. 16:2 may not have been part of the original instructions about purifying the sanctuary but a later addition inspired by the opening words of the procedure itself, "Thus shall Aaron come into the holy place."

20. Kugel (1998: 524–26).

21. See Heinemann (1970: 142); Kugel (1998: 789–90).

22. These were analyzed by Liver (1961).

23. See Cross (1998: 53–70).

21. Moses' Last Words

1. See the discussion Hackett (1980), Hoftijzer and G. Van der Kooij (1991); M. Dijkstra (1995); Nuilleumeier (1996).

2. Hackett (1980: 29).

3. Of course the answer was: not necessarily. Scholars were quick to point out that the mention of Balaam's name at Deir 'Alla did not prove that there ever was a "real" Balaam, and even if there was, that his name had not simply been taken over by the biblical writer for an utterly fictional tale. See recently, R. P. Carroll (1997: 91–93).

4. Rofe (1979) (Hebrew) reviews previous scholarship and offers its own assessment; see also Moore (1990).

5. Rofe (*ibid.*) observed that the blessings mention "the LORD" only once, in a stock phrase (24:6), preferring otherwise to speak of divinity in general terms, whereas the prose narrative is all about the dominion of Israel's particular God. This indicates, he says, that the source of the blessings was different from that of the prose (27–28).

6. Albright (1944).

7. Even if the introductory lines are original, they seem to highlight the disjunction between the blessings in chapter 24 and those of chapter 23: Balaam introduces himself as if he were an unknown quantity. Rofe (1999: 589).

8. Contrast this with Deuteronomy's account of the incident, where Balaam seems to take a turn for the worse: "No Ammonite or Moabite shall be admitted to the assembly of the Lord. Even to the tenth generation, none of their descendants shall be admitted to the assembly of the Lord, because they did not meet you with food and water on your journey out of Egypt, and because they hired against you Balaam son of Beor, from Pethor of Mesopotamia, to curse you. (Yet the Lord your God refused to heed Balaam; the Lord your God turned the curse into a blessing for you, because the Lord your God loved you)" (Deut. 23:3–5). Unfortunately, this passage is hard to date, scholars say: the parenthetical remark may be an editorial gloss of much later vintage.

9. See on this Vermes (1973: 127–77); Kugel (1998: 799–810; 818–23).

10. "All your heart" was taken by rabbinic interpreters to mean with both the heart's inclination to good (*yeṣer ha-ṭob*) and its inclination to evil (*yeṣer ha-ra'*)—see the passage Sifrei Deuteronomy 32 cited next. As for "with all your soul," this might mean "even at the cost of your soul," that is, even if you have to give up your life for the love of God. See Kugel (1998: 868–70). That left "with all your might." The word *me'od* is rightly translated nowadays as "strength" or "might," a translation that corresponds to the root meaning of *m'd* as reflected in Akkadian and Ugaritic. But in biblical Hebrew, *me'od* is usually an adverb meaning "very much." Its precise meaning as a noun was thus less obvicus to ancient interpreters than might appear nowadays. It is noteworthy while most ancient versions (Septuagint, Vulgate, Samaritan Pentateuch, etc.) render the word as "strength," the New Testament citations (Mark 12:28, etc.—see below) render it as *dianoia* ("mind"). Still more striking is the version of Onqelos, which translates it as "wealth"; the same understanding is found in tannaitic commentaries. "Wealth" seems to parallel a secondary meaning of the Greek *dunamis* (the word used by the Septuagint and rendered in English as "might"); while this word primarily designates strength, it could also mean "wealth" in Hellenistic times. See Bauer (1979: 208). The same understanding is explicitly espoused in the *Didascalia Apostolorum*; see Kugel (1998: 868–70). It may be that this concrete meaning, "wealth," was preferred precisely because it was able to be carried out (whereas loving God "with all your strength" seemed an odd assignment): should your love of God require you to sacrifice all your wealth, this interpretation held, then you must do it. (Cf. Song of Songs, 8:7, a rhetorical question.) Indeed, such an understanding would match that of "all your soul" in rabbinic sources as meaning "even if He should require to take your soul [= life]."

11. This is a well-known *topos* from rabbinic literature, but it is found earlier as well: See Murphy (1958); Seitz (1960); Wernberg-Moller (1961–62); Charlesworth (1972: 76–89); as well as Kugel (1998: 850–52, 880–81).

12. The weakening of *aleph* to phonetic zero in late and post-biblical Hebrew is well attested; it turned *me'od* into *mod*. M. Bar Asher (2000) has suggested that this is the reason for the rise of adverbial *moda* (= *me'od*) in Qumran Hebrew. Given this reduction of *aleph,* R. Akiba's reading of Deut. 6:5 seems, more precisely, to have divided the verse in two: you shall love the LORD your God with all your heart and all your soul; and in all things [say: "I] give thanks to You," that is, *ubakkol ['ani] modekka.*

13. Note that this does not necessarily mean that "these words" should be recited, but simply some part of the divine legislation; the same is true of the next two passages. Rabbinic texts are unanimous that the Shema was recited in the Jerusalem temple; it is certainly possible that these writers are being intentionally vague.

14. These *tefillin* are actually of different types, suggesting they may have belonged to two different halakhic schools, each of which, however, accepted the basic idea that attaching "these words" to the body was precisely what Scripture meant. See Tov (1997).

15. A thorough exploration of the transformation of the Exodus Covenant Code in the laws of Deuteronomy: Levinson (1997).

16. See Greenberg, "Decalogue Tradition Critically Examined," 109–10 and references there.

17. See on this S. Japhet (1978), 158–63.

18. Wiseman (1958: 1–99); cited in Weinfeld (1972: 117).

19. From the bilingual inscription of Tell Fakhariyeh. See J. Greenfield and A. Schaffer (1983) and Greenfield (1985).

20. For that reason, Deuteronomy asserts that the only thing that was revealed to Israel at Mount Sinai were the "ten words" of the Decalogue. After having repeated them, Deuteronomy adds: "These are the words the LORD spoke to your whole assembly . . . in a loud voice, *and He added no more.* Then He wrote them upon two stone tablets and gave them to Me" (Deut. 5:22). By the indicated words, "this text's Deuteronomistic author seeks to displace the divine speech of the Covenant Code and leave room for the Mosaic mediation of divine speech in the legal corpus of Deuteronomy. Deuteronomy's polemic rewrites literary history"—B. Levinson (2004: 284).

21. These first words of the sentence are missing in the traditional Hebrew text but are preserved in the Old Greek (Septuagint) translation.

22. See on this my essay on "starkness" in the Bible in Kugel (2003: 137–68).

23. Moran (1963).

24. Later, he moved to Harvard University as a professor of Assyriology. A gentle soul and a lover of the ancient world, he is sorely missed.

25. Moran (1963: 87).

26. The very fact that Moses had to be told so many times gave rise to the interpretive motif of Moses' refusal to die; Kugel (1998: 856–59, 885–87).

27. The traditional Hebrew text reads "according to the number of the Israelites," but this hardly makes sense in context; a manuscript from the Dead Sea Scrolls as well as the Septuagint tradition offer a variant reading, "according to the number of the sons of God/El," that is, lesser divine beings. Alexander (1972); Kugel (1998: 701–3).

28. Nicol (1980: 536–39); Cogan (1979: 37–39); Cross (1999: 53–54).

29. Cross, Ibid., 54.

30. An apparent reference to the water-from-a-rock incident narrated in both Exodus 17 and Numbers 20—though here the incident is presented as a "test" of the whole tribe.

31. Some scholars have expressed doubt about the historicity of this number and the overall picture of the Levites' holdings, though not of the underlying geopolitics. See among others, M. Haran (1985: 112–31); Barmash (2004).

32. Scholars further note the lavish blessing accorded to Joseph (vv. 13–17), the progenitor of the northern tribes of Ephraim and Manasseh. Joseph's blessing is longer and considerably more generous than that accorded to Judah (v. 7), a fact which has led many to hypothesize a northern provenance for this entire chapter. Despite the claims of some, it clearly belongs to the period preceding the Assyrian conquest of the north in 722.

33. On this passage in its broader setting: Rhu (1990).

34. Indeed, some contemporary scholars see in the Pentateuch two originally quite distinct "foundation myths"—the first presenting Israel as the descendents of a set of beloved ancestors to whom God promised the land of Canaan, the second depicting them as an enslaved people in Egypt chosen by God to enter a land to which they had no prior claim. It was only later that these two "foundation myths" would be combined. In regard to the call of Moses in Exodus 3–4, Rolf Rendtorff observed: "The land is introduced here as an unknown land . . . there is not a word which mentions that the patriarchs have already lived a long time in this land and that God has promised it to them and their descendants as a per-

manent possession . . ."—cited in Römer (2006: 19). This subject is explored in depth in K. Schmid (1999).

35. As noted earlier, some scholars have argued that it was Persian imperial policy to use local laws in combination with Persian statutes for governing the different populations they ruled—and to demand, therefore, an official copy of those local laws. Thus, in the year 518 BCE, Darius I wrote to his satrap in Egypt to send him Egyptian scholars who might write down "the former law of Egypt." See Bickerman (1988: 30). It has thus seemed likely to these scholars that something similar happened with the Jews; the Pentateuch was presented to the Persian emperor as the "former law of the Jews," and thereafter it acquired the full authority and backing of the Persians. The Bible actually says as much, quoting the Persian emperor Artaxerxes I (who ruled from 465 or 464 to 424 BCE) as ordering Ezra to implement "the laws of your God" as the civil and criminal code of the Persian province of Judah (Ezra 7:25–26). Some scholars have therefore supposed that the final redaction of the Pentateuch may have been made specifically in preparation for this official presentation of Israel's law code to the Persian emperor. This line of argument has been contested in Watts (2001). Most of the essays in this collection successfully highlight the lack of supporting evidence for this contention, which, incidentally, had been vigorously endorsed and promoted by Peter Frei. (Frei has reiterated his position in the essay that opens this collection.) It may well be that the other essayists are right in suggesting a more complex, and more purely infra-Judean, process: the Persians really did not care that much about the internal legal systems of their satrapies, and the Torah's final editing may not have coincided with the start of Persian rule. Even if the details cannot be filled in by the current historical data, however, the imposition of the laws of the Pentateuch and the intense scrutiny of the Torah as a whole certainly seem to belong to the beginning of this period rather than later on; perhaps that is the most that can be said at present. It should be noted that the argument for a late, and gradual, final editing of the Torah dovetails somewhat with the "minimalist" approach to its composition as a whole; see on this P. Davies (1998). For a telling critique: Leiman (2000).

36. Kugel (1998: 11–14, 22); also, Kugel (2001a).

37. Thus, the wisdom tendency to divide all of humanity into the righteous and the wicked found expression in the interpretive recasting of different biblical figures as altogether good (sometimes despite the evidence: Abraham, Jacob) or altogether bad (ditto: Esau, Balaam). Ancient wisdom had no real author, since wisdom itself was of divine origin, part of the great plan by which the world operated. Similarly, the Pentateuch now had no author other than God, who had entrusted His supernal wisdom to a single tradent, Moses. See Kugel (2001a).

22. Joshua and the Conquest of Canaan

1. Joshua's words came to be called the "song of Joshua," listed among the ten canticles sung by heroes of the Hebrew Bible. See Kugel (1982). Scholars point out, however, that the city of Gibeon does not seem to have existed at the time of Joshua. Excavations there led by James Pritchard turned up some items from the Late Bronze Age in reused tombs, but they uncovered no evidence of the existence of a city during that period. What place could Joshua have been referring to when he said, "O sun, stand still at Gibeon"? See Pritchard (1962).

2. Her standing as a prophet was proven by the fact that she said, "I know that the LORD is giving you this land." How could she *know* (rather than merely think or fear or suspect) unless God Himself had informed her?

3. See Kugel (1998: 415–17).

4. See the thorough inventory of characteristic phrases in Weinfeld (1972: 320–65).

5. Kaufmann's *History of the Israelite Faith* was printed in Hebrew in four separate volumes (in the years 1937, 1938, 1947, and 1956), but the English abridgment appeared only decades later (Kaufmann 1972). A number of scholars have written on the specific matter of the brief summations of kings' reigns cited above (called "regnal formulae" or "judgment formulae" by scholars); the variations among these formulae have been used as a basis for distinguishing different editions of the Deuteronomistic history. See Weippert (1972); Halpern and Vanderhooft (1991); Knoppers (1993).

6. M. Noth (1943).

7. Today's scholars would define the original core somewhat differently: above, chapter 19, note 31, and following note.

8. Noth actually distinguished between two authors, that of the central law code of Deuteronomy (D), comprising Deut. 4:44—30:20, whom he referred to as the *Deuteronomic* writer, and the author/redactor of the other parts of Deuteronomy as well as of the long history of Israel stretching from Joshua–2 Kings; he called the latter writer the *Deuteronomistic* historian. Subsequent scholars have proposed various editions of this history, and the distinction Deuteronomic/Deuteronomistic has become rather muddled. Some scholars have therefore abandoned the term "Deuteronomistic" and the now too-simple distinction it implies. See the essays in L. S. Schearing and S. L. McKenzie (1999); also Person (2002: 4–7). Nevertheless, I have preferred the term "Deuteronomistic" since it more clearly designates someone or some group who are "Deuteronomy-like."

9. As mentioned, numerous scholars have suggested that a plurality of historians is involved— perhaps a school, perhaps simply a succession of editors. See below.

10. A compendium of recent views: T. Römer (2000). For what seems a well-balanced assessment of the arguments, see G. Knoppers (1999 and 2000).

11. Among other studies touching on this question: Nicholson (1967); Cross (1973: 274–89); Levenson (1975); Friedman (1981); Nelson (1981); Weinfeld (1992), Knoppers, (1993–1994); Halpern (1996).

12. See Cross (1968 and 1973: 274–89). His approach contrasts with that of the "Göttingen School" represented by Rudolph Smend, Walter Dietrich, and others. See Person (2002: 2–4); note also the new study of Römer (2006), which sees three separate editions of this literary work, the first dating back to the time of Josiah (Cross's proposal), the second located in the period of neo-Babylonian ascendancy and the exile, and the third in the time of the return from exile under Persian rule.

13. Some have questioned the etiological understanding of this narrative on the grounds that there are no other biblical references to any Rahab entity in Canaan; this is certainly troubling, but hardly decisive. The descendants of other eponymous figures among Israel's neighbors (Esau, Lot) had long since disappeared in later biblical times or been merged with other entities; were it not for extra-biblical evidence, the eponymous character of such names as Terah or Serug would probably not be recognized today. Note that the etiological reading of this story is followed by Tucker and Muller (1973: 29–30).

14. This does not, on the face of it, even sound like a woman's name in Hebrew.

15. No doubt the inspiration for Woody Allen, "The Whore of Mensa," in Allen (1975).

16. Kenyon nevertheless sought to defend the historicity of Joshua 5–6; see her article in Avi-Yonah (1975: vol. 2, 563–64). Subsequent analysis has, however, only tended to strengthen the case against the accuracy of the biblical account. "[T]he only evidence of any occupation from the closing centuries of the Late Bronze Age is the remnant of one corner of a small mudbrick house, built on top of the ruins of the city destroyed in about 1560 BCE. A juglet found on the packed earth floor of the 3-foot-square remnant can be dated to about 1325 BCE. The location of the hut on the mound's eastern slope suggests that squatters lived on top of the ruins of the ancient city"—Calloway and Miller (1999: 66).

17. On the similarity of this conquest account to others from the ancient Near East: Younger (1990).

18. On this vast subject see the recent surveys of scholarship in Weippert (1971); W. Dever (1991 and 1995); also N. Naaman (1994), Callaway and Miller (1999), and works referred to below.

19. Following John Garstang's excavations at Ai (1928) and those of Judith Marquet-Krause (1933–35), Joseph Callaway excavated Ai from 1964 to 1976. See Callaway (1976). Confirming the conclusions of Marquet-Krause, Callaway asserted that there was no walled city at Ai after 2400 BCE; the only evidence of occupation of the site thereafter was a small, unfortified village built over the earlier ruins. The village was constructed around 1200 BCE and survived until around 1050 BCE, after which it was abandoned and never rebuilt; see Josh. 8:28. Ai was apparently closely connected with Bethel, about two miles away; perhaps this unfortified town was part of the city-state of Bethel during the Late Bronze age and con-

tinued to be associated with it in later times (see Josh. 8:17; also Neh. 7:32, Ezra 2:28). More recently, Zevit (1984) has sought to reconstruct a series of stages through which the biblical account might have been created. See also below, note 23.

20. Moreover, the destruction of even these two seems to be out of sync with each other: see Callaway and Miller (1999: 68–69. Bethel is not mentioned as a conquered city in the book of Joshua.

21. Noted by Wright (1946). Note further 1 Kings 9:20–21, which, reporting on the period of Solomon's rule, mentions "all the people who were left of the Amorites, the Hittites, the Perizzites, the Hivites, and the Jebusites, who were not of the people of Israel—their descendants who were still in the land, whom the Israelites were unable to destroy completely—these Solomon conscripted for slave labor, and so they are to this day."

22. The inhabitants of Shechem were reported to have been killed by Simeon and Levi in revenge for the rape of Dinah (Gen. 34); Jacob likewise speaks of having captured Shechem "with my sword and bow" (Gen. 48:22). One might thus claim that there was no need for Shechem to be captured by Joshua—the city had been destroyed long before. But archaeologists find it difficult to support such a claim, and, even if Shechem had been attacked and briefly subdued in patriarchal times, there is nothing to support the notion that Shechem remained a ghost-town thereafter until the arrival of Joshua—this is in fact quite counter to the archaeological evidence as well as the testimony of the Amarna letters (see below). On the other hand, there was also no conquest of Shechem in the time of Joshua: there is no evidence of destruction there in the Late Bronze age; its temple, defensive walls, and city gate provide evidence of continued, peaceful occupation. L. E. Toombs, "Shechem," in Freedman (1992).

23. Gottwald (1979: 153).

24. See M. Noth (1972: 175–77).

25. Indeed, there are some who suggest a true history of ancient Israel can never be written, or should never be written (though most scholars reject such an extreme position). Note the essays in Grabbe (1997); also chapter 1, note 76.

26. Bethel is, somewhat surprisingly, not mentioned among the cities conquered by Joshua. However, since modern Beitin, identified as the site of ancient Bethel, is only two miles from modern et-Tell, identified as the site of Ai, and since the people of Bethel are said to have joined with inhabitants of Ai in opposing the Israelites (Josh. 8:12–17), Albright suggested that it was the conquest of Bethel, and not Ai, to which the narrative in Joshua refers.

27. See the discussion to follow; note also Cross (1999: 50–70); Zevit (2001: 84–121).

28. On these, see below.

29. Numerous scholars have studied the linguistic side of the El Amarna letters and their implications for Hebrew; see briefly Kutcher (1982: 77–79) and the more detailed treatments by W. L. Moran, his (1965) and (1975); also Rainey (1973) and (1975). The situation is summarized in Moran (1992: "Introduction").

30. The capital city of the writer, Rib-Addi.

31. First advanced by an Albright student, George Mendenhall (1961; see also his 1973). A similar approach, but with a somewhat different coloring, was adopted; Gottwald (1979: esp. 210–19). Critics often connect Gottwald's account with his own Marxist sympathies, openly announced in that book. Personally, I find this regrettable. I doubt that Gottwald's ideology has been any more decisive in the formation of his scholarship than, say, Lutheranism has been in shaping the ideas of a number of other scholars mentioned in this book (nor, I might add, than Judaism has been in shaping my own outlook). Indeed, ideological or confessional influences tend to be invoked only in the case of people perceived as outsiders; such influences are least likely to be recognized when they are shared by a majority of scholars in the field—but this, of course, is where recognition is most crucial.

32. Gottwald (1985: 272).

33. On this stele see recently L. Stager (1985), Singer (1988) Görg (1997: 58–63); Lemche (1998: 35–38).

34. Much has been made of the fact that the name "Israel" on this stele is preceded not with a locative marker (name of a foreign place) but with one designating a foreign people. However, as Ahlstrom has stressed, the Egyptian use of determinatives is inconsistent; it would be

unwise to build on this one detail any larger hypothesis of what "Israel" might have referred to at the time. See the discussion in Lemche (1998: 35–38). Moreover, although Merenptah came be known as the "subduer of Gezer," there is no indication that his forces actually came into contact with Israel on the occasion commemorated by this stele. Perhaps Israel (again: whatever Israel was at the time) was simply included to round out a list of names representative of the inhabitants of the land. See also Stager (1985); Redford (1992).

35. The change was apparently instituted by the Persian ambassador to Germany, at the encouragement of the Nazis; *Iran*, cognate with *Aryan*, was a way of signaling the country's superior racial makeup as well as its clean break with the colonial past. See Yarshater (1989).

36. On the reinterpretation of this evidence: A. Mazar (1985); Finkelstein (1988: 280–85); W. Dever (1991 and 2003: 124–25).

37. See on this Finkelstein (1988: 237–59); Giv'on (1995); Dever (2003: 76–78, 102–103).

38. Callaway (1984); D. Hopkins (1985); Ahlstrom (1992: 334–70).

39. More bluntly: how could a bunch of seminomads be responsible precisely for those features held to be characteristic of the earliest proto-Israelite settlements, the four-room house, the collared-rim jar, and terrace farming (on this, see below)? N. P. Lemche (1998: 72) has put the case well: "What scholars ask early Israelite ingenuity to have produced is simply amazing: first of all they [despite their] being nomads, should have introduced a new style of [permanent] housing. Second, they should have started producing rather cumbersome types of pottery such as the collared-rim jars, quite unsuitable for nomads on the move; and, finally, they should almost at once have become engaged in technical highland agriculture."

40. This widely held view comes in various formulations: see inter alia Fritz (1981 and 1987); Finkelstein and Na'aman (1994: 150–78); Albertz (1994); and the voluminous writings of W. G. Dever, most recently (as of this writing) (2003); as well as other works cited below. See also note 21 above.

41. The pattern of building in these new settlements and its correlation with Judges 5 (Song of Deborah) and other biblical texts was first explored by Stager (1985).

42. Gonen (1984) estimates that the urban population of Canaan at this time declined by more than 50 percent. Also: Finkelstein and Silberman (2001: 86–90, 118). Scholars have noted a general depopulation of cities throughout the eastern Mediterranean in the Late Bronze period—possibly connected to outbreaks of plague in urban centers; see Mendenhall (1973: 106–7).

43. See previous notes; also, Coote and Whitelam (1986). Note that Whitelam's position has subsequently been modified somewhat—see his (1996); note also Lemche (1988 and 1998).

44. Lemche has proposed an opposite scenario: the late thirteenth century was a time when Egypt tightened its grip over the area. The Egyptians themselves, or the new domestic regime that their strengthened presence created, would therefore have controlled trade more tightly and imposed heavier taxation, leading to worsening economic conditions inside the cities; the Egyptians may also have regularly deported parts of the urban population of Canaan. (On this: Ahituv (1978); Na'aman (1981); Redford, (1992: 207–14.) Certainly policies such as these might have encouraged large numbers of former city-dwellers to head for the hills and settle in little, isolated, unprotected villages. See Lemche (1998: 76–77).

45. Stager (1985: 5–9).

46. Ibid., 9–11.

47. The "fringe-area pastoralists" explanation is basically Israel Finkelstein's position: see, inter alia, his (1988); Finkelstein and Na'aman (1994: 150–78); Finkelstein and Silberman (2001: 106–18). For a partial critique of this position: Dever (2003: 153–66). Cross, relying more on the biblical evidence, sees an entrance of pastoral nomads from the southeast: (1999: 51–52, 68–70). As various scholars have argued, while the pottery associated with these sites is similar to Canaanite pottery, it is not identical; see most recently Killebrew (2005: esp. 110–35, 177–80).

48. Finkelstein and Silberman (2001: 119–20).

49. Some have expressed reservations about the ethnic explanation: See Hesse and Wapnish (1997).

50. A. Zertal (1991 and 1994: 53–100); also, Finkelstein (1998: 185–200).

51. In this connection, scholars have noted that, when Israel's eighth-century prophets intoned against those who worshiped Baal or other foreign deities, they *never* accused the guilty parties of being non-Israelites, "sojourners," or resident Canaanites who worshiped other gods; they did not even speak of them as peoples who were at one point joined to Israel but who had subsequently reverted to their old faith. Nor, for that matter, did Deuteronomy or the historical books that follow it ever present worshiping other gods as some sort of reversion to a faith once espoused by elements of Israel. This is certainly strange, since "Blame the foreigners" is a universal reflex, and, by the Bible's own account, a "mixed rabble" of foreigners (Exod. 12:38, Num. 11:4) had indeed accompanied the Israelites out of Egypt, and after the conquest, some Canaanites and others nonetheless remained in Israel's midst. The absence of any hint that foreigners were to blame for Israel's religious lapses might thus suggest that, from a relatively early period, the memory that any part of Israel had once belonged to the peoples of Canaan had been programmatically purged from Israelite consciousness. Apparently, any hint of this idea was simply *verboten* for quite some time. (True, Ezekiel could say of Jerusalem, "Your mother was a Hittite" [Ezek. 16:3], but that was in another century, and besides, the wench was dead.) This in turn might lead one to believe (though it may seem paradoxical at first) that the number of Canaanites involved was not negligible. After all, a small number could be countenanced, admitted, reckoned with. But if nearly all of Israel came from Canaanite stock, then nothing but an absolute denial of history, repeated by common accord for generations and centuries, would erase this embarrassing truth. See on this Zevit (2001: 120).

23. Judges and Chiefs

1. Weber borrowed the term from Rudolf Sohm, but it ultimately goes back to early Christian literature; for Weber, it refers to "a certain quality of an individual personality by virtue of which he is set apart from ordinary men and treated as endowed with supernatural, superhuman, or at least specifically exceptional powers or qualities," Weber (1964: 363). See on this Blenkinsopp (1977: 148–51). For Weber's application of this approach to the Hebrew Bible: Weber (1952: 11, 97–98). On the question of Weber's anti-Semitic sentiments and such role as they may have had in his scholarship, see H. Gerth and D. Martindale, "Preface" in Weber (1952: esp. xiv–xxvii).

2. Thus, the *moreh* of the "oak tree of Moreh" (Gen. 12:6, cf. Deut. 11:30) may mean "[divinely guided] teacher"; note as well the "oak tree of the diviners" (*'elon me'onenim*) in Jud. 9:37. W. Richter (1963) argued that Deborah's "palm-tree" was originally not a palm at all but, like these others, an oak tree. In fact, it was none other than the oak tree mentioned in Gen. 35:8, not specifically called there the "oak of Deborah" but suspiciously linked with the cameo appearance of an otherwise unknown nurse of Rebekah's, Deborah. Richter also identified this tree with the "oak of Tabor" in 1 Sam. 10:3, "Tabor" being an error for "Deborah." Oddly, he did not go one step further: the "Deborah" associated with this tree is neither Rebekah's nurse nor Barak's comrade in arms, but the generic word *daborah*, "[female] speaker" or "prophetess." (Such *qatol* active agentives are relatively rare in biblical Hebrew, but they certainly exist; see GKC 84[a], k [= p. 231]. Indeed, the traditional vocalization of *shadud* in this same song (Jud. 5:27), along with the same word in its feminine form *shadudah* in Ps. 137:8, should both be repointed to the *qatol* form to reflect their active meaning of "despoiler." That the vocalization *daborah* is correct might seem to be supported by its confusion with "Tabor" in 1 Sam. 10:3.) The person named "Deborah" is thus actually a creation of the Deuteronomistic historian, who misunderstood "Up, up, O *daborah*, up, up, sing a song!" (Jud. 5:12) as containing a proper noun, "Deborah." Actually, the prophetess in the song is quite anonymous; indeed, even this anonymous but specific prophetess may herself be a back-formation from the "oak of the prophetess," originally quite unconnected to the battle of Barak against Sisera. At a certain point, however, the popular imagination, or perhaps theology, demanded that Barak's victory be somehow connected to a divine oracle: a *daborah* was invented, or rather, imported from the "oak of the *daborah*." Note further that most modern scholars parse Jud. 5:7 as a second person verb, in which case it would be addressed to the anonymous prophetess, "Until

you arose, O *daborah*"—that is, until you could deliver the crucial divine oracle, things were going sour in Israel. This is altogether possible, but it also may have been an archaic third-person or may have been changed to conform with the second-person address that appears later in the song, "Up, up, *daborah*, up, up, sing a song!" Further: Kugel (1999: 133–46).

3. This point, like many to follow, is made explicitly in B. Halpern's treatment (1983) of the Song of Deborah, reprinted in Halpern (1996; see p. 78). On this song see also (inter alia multa) Globe (1975); Coogan (1978); Stager (1988); Schloen (1993: 18–38).

4. This was asserted even by Wellhausen (1957: 241), who concluded that chapter 4 was therefore altogether dependent on the song in chapter 5. However, as subsequent scholars have pointed out, the two chapters differ on a number of other details (precise location of the battle, participating tribes, numbers of troops, and so forth). Apparently, while the line "She put her hand to a stick, [and] her right hand to a workman's club" may have been the same, the song known to the prose author was, according to many scholars, slightly different. Halpern (1996: 95) however, seeks to argue through clever exegesis that "virtually every element of the prose account stems directly, or by a dialectical process, indirectly, from the Song of Deborah."

5. Iron, Lemche argued, began to be used in the Iron Age not because it was previously unknown, but because the tin needed to make bronze, which is not found in any abundance in the region, became difficult to import in the political chaos of the Late Bronze Age. Iron "is in fact a metal found all over the place [and] was known already before the coming of the Iron Age. It was, however, not used to produce weapons and utensils for the simple reason that it was brittle and not in any way comparable to weapons and utensils made of bronze, not, at least, before smiths learned to produce steel. That hardly happened before the beginning of the first millennium BCE. Iron was in fact inferior to bronze before steel was invented"—Lemche (1998: 66–67). See also Negbi (1974: 159–72), and Fritz (1996: 101–2). (References are from Lemche 1998.)

6. A vast scholarly literature surrounds the identity of the Sea Peoples. See recently: Niemeyer (1998) as well as material cited below. As to the name itself, "Sea Peoples" is now widely conceded to be somewhat inaccurate; the ancient Egyptian sources that refer to them actually depict them moving both overland and by sea. On this point: Mendenhall (1973: 142).

7. On this: A. Mazar (1980); Dothan (1982: and 1982a: 33).

8. Here I am paraphrasing a conversation with Frank Cross some years ago.

9. There are two apparent exceptions to this generalization, but they both turn out badly. The first is David, whose lust for Bathsheba leads him to have Uriah killed; he gets the girl but is then punished by God—nothing celebratory here. On Amnon and Tamar, see below, chapter 28.

10. Halpern (1996: 125).

11. For a different explanation: Greenstein (1981).

12. On the territories occupied by Dan in biblical times: A. Demsky (2004: 284). Indeed, the name of this Israelite tribe has been connected with that of the Danuna, who were themselves one of the Aegean Sea Peoples that settled along the eastern Mediterranean coast. See Yadin (1965). If so, then Samson might be an altogether Aegean hero.

13. Note, however, the clear assertion of *Leviticus Rabba* 1:2–3 that such a change of names is unnecessary, since, from God's standpoint, "the [original] names of converts are as pleasing to Me as libation wine [intended for pagan ceremonies] that is offered instead on My altar."

14. This feature is highlighted in Ackerman (1998).

15. To be sure, the issue had been raised earlier, particularly in the classic of late nineteenth-century feminism, Elizabeth Cady Stanton's *The Woman's Bible* (reprinted Stanton, 1986). Stanton's famous conclusion was that "the Bible in its teachings degrades Women from Genesis to Revelation."

16. Reuther (1974); Wegner (1988).

17. On the phenomenon of anonymity in general: Reinhartz (1992). For a catalogue of unnamed female figures: C. Meyers (2000: 145–475).

18. Plaskow (1989).

19. Among many: Fuchs (2000).

20. Frymer-Kensky (1992). On Asherah, see below, chapter 24, note 9.

21. Keel and Uehlinger (1998: 19–48, 397).
22. C. Myers (1978: 98–103).
23. Ibid.
24. C. Myers (1988: 190).
25. Trible (1976: 965).
26. Schüssler-Fiorenza (1983); also Brooten (1982). Note, however, Peleg (2002).
27. Kugel (1999: 129–58).
28. From the bilingual (Phoenician and Luwian) Karatepe inscription, column 2, 4–5. A similar boast is found in a bilingual tablet of royal correspondence unearthed at Susa, "A man walks wherever his heart desires, and [even] a woman with her spindle and distaff." The closeness of the two formulations may indicate that this was the somewhat standardized boast of a monarch, a boast whose actual relation to reality remains to be otherwise attested.
29. Trible (1984: 87).
30. The period of the judges ought to have lasted about 200 years—from the first, identifiably "Israelite" settlements to the beginning of David's reign, that is, from roughly 1200 to 1000 BCE. "When, however, the periods of time given for each episode in the book of Judges are added together, the total far exceeds 200 years. It even exceeds the 480 years the Bible says elapsed between the Exodus and the founding of Solomon's temple (1 Kings 6:1). This is because the episodes are not to be joined as consecutive events; some undoubtedly occurred simultaneously" (Callaway and Miller 1999: 88). Another explanation might be that much of the material is legendary, indeed, going back even before the existence of any distinctly Israelite settlements.
31. Scholars have backed off some of Frankfort's writings about Egyptian kings as divine beings; see Silverman (1995).
32. Wellhausen and his followers were initially skeptical about the authenticity of this anti-monarchic theme, dating it to the time of the Babylonian exile and the disenchantment with dynastic rule; others connected it to the time of Hosea and the Assyrian conquest of the northern kingdom. Subsequently, many scholars have come to accept the antiquity of this antimonarchic material and the political reality that lay behind it. See briefly M. Weinfeld in Friedman (1983: 86–87).
33. Frankfort (1948: 3).
34. Of course the connection between the gods and the king's authority to rule is found throughout the ancient Near East; the god is sometimes conceived elsewhere as the image of the earthly king, or the earthly king as an embodiment of the god's rule. But such notions are quite different from the Israelite idea of divine kingship. See on this point Weinfeld (1972: 82–83), Halpern (1981: 71). Indeed, "divine kingship" itself is a somewhat ambiguous item in scholarship, referring both to God's enthronement in heaven above all other divine beings and, at the same time, to the theme examined here. See M. Brettler (1989).
35. On this commandment, see above, chapter 15.
36. Whether they did—or even, whether this commandment was actually intended to be enforced as monolatry—is an entirely different question; see below.
37. The received text says *šebeṭ*, "tribe," and such a reading would only strengthen this argument; however, it should be noted that *šebeṭ* often meant "leader"—indeed, sometimes it was confused with *šofeṭ*. See Falk (1966).
38. Hebrew *'am*, usually "people," sometimes has the more specific meaning of "army," Num. 20: 20; 31:32; Josh. 8:1, 3, 11; 10:7; 11:7; Jud. 5:8; 1 Sam. 11:11, etc. The JPS translation of this verse thus reads: "army."
39. Heb. *mippenei,* that is, "confronted by."
40. The history of research into this subject is long and complicated. For a good summary: Longman and Reid (1995: 19–26). Among many works see especially P. D. Miller (1973).
41. "Arise Barak . . ." is the oracle that the *daborah* produces after having been ordered to "awake, awake."
42. See Judges 20–21. Not only (as already mentioned) does the Song of Deborah fail even to mention any tribe south of Benjamin—as if Judah were simply out of consideration, off the

map—but the book of Judges as a whole pays relatively little attention to Judah. What is more, the fact that the "Benjaminites" (a term that can mean simply "southerners") are sometimes presented in a negative light may reinforce the impression that this is basically a collection of northern tales.

43. Cross tried to reckon with this (1999: 55n), somewhat unconvincingly.

24. The Other Gods of Canaan

1. This follows the classic formulation of St. Anselm (1033–1109). A later try: "A working definition of God will help to focus both the claims of theologians and the problems of establishing the existence of this God: God is an omnipotent, omniscient, and eternal person who is pure spirit. He is both transcendent and immanent. He created the universe and human beings are his special creation. He loves them, interacts with them, and desires their love"—Diamond (1974: 4). By citing this I do not mean to imply that this definition would meet with universal approval nowadays; many contemporary theologians would object to the use of the male pronoun, others to His being described as a "person," interacting with or reacting to humans, still others to humans being thought of as His "special creation." (A reasonable person might be forgiven for asking at this point, "What's left?" But that is not our concern here.)

2. One such attempted reconstruction is Jacobsen (1976), but see the reservations of Oppenheim (1964); Bottéro (1993 and 1998).

3. This was the starting point of Albrecht Alt's seminal essay, "Der Gott der Väter" (Alt 1929). See below.

4. That is how, in texts attributed to E, God is referred to before the time of Moses—and in fact 'elohim occurs elsewhere, either alone or in combination (the "'elohim of Abraham, Isaac and Jacob"). The precise relationship of 'elohim to 'el remains a matter of speculation. It is certainly significant that peripheral Akkadian construes ilānū ([the] gods) as a singular noun, since this would seem to be an evident precedent for the biblical usage. See Burnett (1999: 7–24). Note also: Pagolu (1998: 185) and references there.

5. Note the entry El Elyon in Hastings, ed. (1903: vol. 2, 682): "It is probably a proper name, the appellation of a Canaanite deity."

6. Alt (1929). The bulk of Alt's essay was not, however, devoted to this subject but to the deity or deities called the "God of Abraham (perhaps also the "shield [or "benefactor"] of Abraham"; this name is deduced from Gen. 15:1; see Dahood (1966: 16–17), the "Fear [or possibly "kinsman"] of Isaac" (Gen. 31:42, 53) and the "Mighty One of Jacob" (Gen. 49:24, etc.). What was striking about them to Alt was that the epithet of the deity was connected with a particular person or tribal founder. The deity himself had no name, nor any connection with a cultic site; his identity was essentially that of the divinity associated with a particular group. In fact, Alt suggested that these gods of Abraham, Isaac, and Jacob were originally distinct clan deities that were ultimately merged into a single God, "the God of your fathers, the God of Abraham, the God of Isaac, and the God of Jacob" (Exod. 3:14); they became one God and, as a result, these three founders were (artificially, said Alt and others) linked as grandfather, father, and son. Finally, what struck Alt as particularly significant about the form of reference "god of PN" was that, since such a deity was not attached to a particular local shrine (like the Canaanite numina) but to a person or clan, such a deity would be by definition mobile. A seminomad—like those that Alt felt had first begun to frequent the rugged Canaanite hilltops—might indeed worship such a deity, traveling with him wherever he went. Then, once settled in Canaan, those who worshiped the previously nameless "God[s] of the Fathers," might ultimately have unified them, emerging finally as devotees of YHWH.

7. The only exception was the glottal stop corresponding to Hebrew aleph, which was represented in three distinct configurations to indicate the vowel accompanying it.

8. On Psalm 29 see chapter 29.

9. See the recent summary of the discussion by Mastin (2004); also Kugel (2003: 232–34) and sources cited there. Note that mention of Kuntillet 'Ajrud was mistakenly omitted from my book, p. 232, line 23; reference also should have been made there to the article of P. Xella

(2000) that argues for the use of pronominal suffixes with proper names at Ugarit. Given the great distance in time and space between Ugarit (not to speak of Ebla) and Kuntillet 'Ajrud, however, this argument on its own strikes me as less than overwhelming, though in combination with the (admittedly ambiguous) painting found at the site, the claim must be considered seriously. On both see S. H. Horn and P. K. McCarter in Shanks (1999: esp. 157–58). Whatever one concludes about these inscriptions, many recent scholars have suggested that the worship of Asherah continued long into monarchic times: Dever (1982); McCarter (1987); P. D. Miller (1986 and 2000: 35–40); Olyan (1988); Ackerman (1992).

10. Moses' in-laws are identified as Kenites, not Midianites, in Judg. 1:16 and 4:11 (cf. 5:24). The Kenites were of course from the same general region as the Midianites.

11. The Amalekites are usually depicted as Israel's blood enemies, save in what may be the very earliest reference to Amalek in the Hebrew Bible, "From Ephraim [came] those whose roots are in Amalek" (Judg. 5:14). This positive note commends itself precisely because of its uniqueness. See Coogan (1978: 49) and M. Smith (2001: 145).

12. On these see also de Vaux (1969) and Schloen (1993).

13. Rowley (1950: 149–56.

14. M. Weippert (1971: 105–6); Cross (1999: 97); L. Stager (1998). See also van der Toorn (1993).

15. M. Weippert (1974); Astour (1979); Ahituv (1984: 169).

16. On this Levenson (1985: 19–23, 89–93).

17. See in this connection: Schloen (1993).

18. This is the view adopted by Fritz (1987: 84–100 and 1981: 61–73); Mettinger (1988: 78–79) and (1990), as well the various works cited in Mettinger (1995: 168, n. 138); Albertz (1994: esp. 87–94). Scholars have sometimes claimed that the name YHWH is attested elsewhere, but this claim has not been widely accepted. G. Pettinato (1980) claimed that the name was found in apocopated form at Ebla, but see H-P. Mueller (1981). More recently, S. Dalley (1990) has advanced a similar case for Syria; see van der Toorn (1992).

19. An apparent exception is Joshua, to be dealt with presently, and Jochebed (Exod. 6:20, Num. 26:59).

20. In both these examples, the name YHWH has been abbreviated to YW; these are referred to as hypocoristic names. See in general: Tigay (1986); Pike (1989).

21. On the apparent exception 'nnyh in Neh. 11:32, see Z. Zevit (2001: 594).

22. Ibid, 592–94.

23. Kugel (2003: 96); see also Dearman (1993).

24. Influential in this approach was Ahlstrom (1963: 9–88); see also Lemche (1985: 209–57); Mark Smith (1990); P. D. Miller (2000: 57–62). The term *syncretism* has sometimes been criticized by scholars as implying the existence of a "pure" form of the religion that was then corrupted by syncretists—a notion judged to be particularly inappropriate for the Bible. But the term itself (originally coined, incidentally, to describe an alliance of different inhabitants of Crete against a common foe) need not imply any process of corruption of an earlier, purer state of things; certainly the examples cited above do not.

25. On the much discussed Khirbet el-Qom and Kuntillet 'Ajrud inscriptions, see above, note 9. To repeat an observation from there: Whatever one concludes about these inscriptions, many recent scholars have suggested that the worship of Asherah continued long into monarchic times: Dever (1982: 37–43); McCarter (1987); P. D. Miller (1986 and 2000: 35–40); S Olyan (1988); Ackerman (1992).

26. This seems to be the case of the twelfth-century temple at Shechem that was in use from the Late Bronze age on; it may be true as well of later examples, such as the Arad sanctuary (tenth or ninth century), the Dan temple complex (tenth-ninth century), and others. On the latter: Biran (1994); note also the discussion in Zevit (2001: 156–70; 181–96).

27. Many scholars have contributed to this subject since the pioneering work of Morton Smith, especially (1952) and (1971). Among others: Albrektson (1967: 1–122); Roberts (1976: 181–90); Lang (1983: 13–56); Albertz (1994).

28. Keel and Uehlinger (1998) and the discussion and other works cited in Kugel (2003: 217–234).

29. Albertz (1994: 146–56). On the cult of Asherah, see three notes above, note 9.

30. See in general the arguments for an early, exclusive devotion to the God of Israel in P. Miller (2000: esp. pp. 40–45); the opposite claim is surveyed in Zevit (2001).

31. For Morton Smith and others, above n. 27. Also Lang (1983).

32. Indeed, the written records of a community of Jewish soldiers stationed at a military colony at Elephantine (in Egypt) seem to indicate that they were still polytheistic in the fifth century BCE—long after the laws of Deuteronomy had been adopted and the "strict monotheism" of the latter part of the book of Isaiah had been preached and accepted. On the Elephantine colony in general: G. R. Driver (1965). On the complicated problem of the religious beliefs reflected in the Elephantine documents: Porten (1969) and (1974); van der Toorn (1986); Dalglish (1992).

33. Here I am relying principally on Stager (1985).

34. Ibid., 18–23; also King and Stager (2001:) 12–15.

35. Stager (1985: 22).

36. Ibid., 6–9.

37. Stager (1985: 25–28).

38. Stager (1985: 9).

39. Albright (1943).

40. See on this Mazar (1982). The identification of this as an Israelite site has been questioned: Coogan (1987); see also Zevit (2001: 176–80), King and Stager (2001: 322–23).

41. See above, chapter 16, note 5.

42. Kugel (2003: 71–107, 217–34) and sources cited.

43. That is, Alt's classic distinction between apodictic and casuistic laws.

44. This of course runs counter to the claim of minimalist historians and even more "mainstream" views; Albertz (1994), for example, prefers to see in these narratives a reflection of rural, "popular" religiosity, as opposed to the urban way of life and its "official" forms of worship. Still, such an approach fails to account for some of the major singularities in the patriarchal narratives that set them off from later practice; see the arguments in Grintz (1983).

25. Samuel and Saul

1. The distinction between northern and southern prophets was highlighted in R. R. Wilson (1980) and D. Peterson (1981). See also chapter 29.

2. Alternately "word [dbr] of the LORD," "utterance [n'm] of the LORD" see Westermann (1967).

3. This point was stressed by Gunkel in his form-critical analysis of prophecy, as well as by his student Sigmund Mowinckel; see Blenkinsopp (1983: 30–31).

4. On this pattern in the utterances of prophets from the eighth to the sixth century BCE: P. D. Miller (1982a).

5. Biblical prophecy is explored in this broad (and comparative) context by Grabbe (1995: 85–118). See also Wilson (1980: 21–88).

6. Within the Mari corpus have been found two ritual texts, twelve economic documents, and approximately fifty letters, all of which describe or allude to prophetlike figures. The subject of Mesopotamian parallels to biblical prophecy has been studied by a number of scholars, particularly by H. Huffmon in a series of works stretching back to the 1960s. See his recent assessment, Huffmon (2000); also, the brief treatment and bibliography in Grabbe (1995: 87–91).

7. For these, S. Parpola (1999).

8. The first two figures are known from Mari; the latter two (with the variant spelling maḫḫu/maḫḫutu) from Assyria. The two forms indicated are masculine and feminine. Again, see Huffmon (2000: 49–57).

9. The term nabi' seems to have been favored especially in northern texts; see Wilson (1980: 136, 256). Scholars have argued that the Hebrew term designates one who "calls out" or, alternately, one who has been "called." See Fleming (1993); Huehnergard (1999).

10. See on this Wilson (1980); J. R. Porter (1982). I find it difficult to accept Grabbe's assertion that "[t]here is no qualitative distinction between OT prophets and those known in Mesopotamia or other pre-modern cultures" (1995: 117).

11. Cross (1973: 223).

12. The Bible is somewhat inconsistent about Saul's actual title; sometimes he is being made king (*melekh*) (1 Sam. 8:5–6, 10:19, 25), while at other times he is referred to as *nagid* (9:16, 10:1, 123:14). The inconsistency derives from the combination of different sources (see below). Scholars are still divided about the precise nuance of the term *nagid*; for a time, exegetes saw this as a military post, perhaps "commander-in-chief." That theory has now been largely rejected. The term may mean something like "king designate," or it may be a more general term for a kinglike leader (governor, ruler) perhaps used of Saul to classify him as a forerunner of what the Deuteronomistic History considered the "true" kingship given to Israel, namely, the house of David. On other ideas: Halpern (1981: 1–11). (It is noteworthy that, starting in 1027 CE, the governor of Spain's semiautonomous Jewish community was called the *nagid*: see, for example, Cole, 1996: xvii.)

13. Literally, the text reads, "Is it not so that . . . ?" But this is how courtiers typically addressed the king (since court etiquette dictated that the courtier pretend that the king already knows whatever it is that the courtier wishes to tell him). "Your Majesty" is thus really the most accurate English equivalent of this phrase in context.

14. For a review, Halpern (1996: 186–94) and at greater length (1981: 149–74).

15. Halpern (1996: 194).

16. Ibid., 183–86.

17. See F. M. Cross (1983).

18. B. M. Levinson in M. D. Coogan, ed. (2001: 256n; ad Deut. 7:1). On the biblical institution of *ḥerem* see: Gottwald, *The Tribes of YHWH* (1979); von Rad (1991: 49–51; P. D. Stern (1991); Niditch (1993: 28–77). *Ḥerem* could be commanded by God or could be taken on as a vowed obligation—the latter seems to be the priestly idea of this institution (Love: 27:21, 28; Num. 18:14; Ezek. 44:29).

19. Many scholars have written about the extraordinarily moving presentation of Saul's fall from grace. See inter alia: Gunn (1980); Humphreys (1982: 95–116); Edelman (1991).

20. Commentators often point out that being a shepherd of sheep is, in the biblical world, preparation for being a shepherd of men—hence, Moses, David, and others are presented as shepherds. This is certainly true, but it is well not to lose sight of the fact that caring for the sheep was (and is) often an occupation given to fairly young children, boys or girls (so long as they did not need to be absent from home overnight).

21. Scholars have long noted the heavy Deuteronomistic hand in this story, as well as the significant differences between the version preserved in the traditional Hebrew text (MT) and the Septuagint version; the latter is held by Tov and others to represent an earlier stage in the redaction of the Deuteronomistic history. See Tov, "The Composition of 1 Samuel 16–18," in J. Tigay (1985: 97–130) and (1986); Rofé (1987: 117–51). (Note also: McCarter (1980: 306–7); Lust (1986). These studies in turn suggest that a final (post-exilic?) editor of the Deuteronomistic history produced the MT text of 1 Samuel 16–18 by combining two separate David and Goliath narratives. But Baruch Halpern may be right in suggesting the opposite: "The omissions in the Greek contain all the verses suggesting that David was unknown to Saul when the confrontation with Goliath took place. So it looks as though the Greek text was harmonizing contradictions" (2001: 7).

22. See Knoppers (1995).

23. See the excellent summary article of V. H. Matthews s.v. "Perfumes and Spices" in Freedman (1992).

24. The interdiction found in the Aramaic floor inscription of the Ein Gedi synagogue, calling on worshipers not to reveal "the secret of the city" (*raza' di qarta'*) may thus refer to the manufacturing process used for the manufacture of storax (*s ori*), since tanks for its production appear to have been hidden in some structures that have been excavated uphill from the synagogue.

25. See, for example, 2 Sam. 14:2. Anointing is thus forbidden on the Day of Atonement in rabbinic practice, and this association with mourning goes back at least as far as the Elephantine papyri: the Jewish soldiers garrisoned there report that their mourning for a destroyed temple included "wearing sackcloth and fasting, making our wives as widows, *not anointing ourselves with oil* or drinking wine"; Cowley (1923), no. 30.

26. Scholars used to argue that the anointing of high priests is a late element in the Hebrew Bible. For example, Noth (1967: 237–38) claimed that the anointing of priests is an entirely postexilic phenomenon, taken over by analogy from the anointing kings, and this argument has been followed by many subsequent scholars. See, however, Fleming (1998), which offers a plausible refutation of this argument.

27. Often mistranslated as if a noun, "light," but this is the adjectival form, like 'orah in the next sentence.

28. I have discussed this in greater detail in Kugel (1990c).

29. Literally, "I can say to you confidently," that is, without fear of contradiction.

30. *Anastasis* here probably means "rise" and not "resurrection," unless it refers to *David's* resurrection in the coming of Jesus.

31. It seems possible that Peter's original point may have gotten a bit garbled in transmission. The intended sense may have been this: Although we all know that David lies dead and buried, we also know that he said in Psalm 15, "You will not abandon my soul in Hades, nor will You let my flesh experience corruption" (a paraphrase of the biblical verse). But how can this be true if David indeed is dead and buried? David was not talking literally about himself, but about the coming of the messiah, in whom his soul and his flesh will come back to life.

26. *The Psalms of David*

1. On this phenomenon see the essay by W. Holladay, "How the Twenty-Third Psalm Became an American Secular Icon" in Holladay (1993: 359–71).

2. Davidic authorship of the psalms is admirably surveyed in Cooper (1983).

3. Kugel (1998: 366–67).

4. On the history of this psalm's interpretation: Kugel (1990: 173–213).

5. This hypothesis was adopted by Mowinckel (1962: 77).

6. Cooper (1983: 129).

7. The role of such headings has been studied in a comparative context: Driver (1926); Sawyer (1967–68); Lambert (1957) and (1962); Gevaryahu (1975); see also Childs (1971).

8. By 1900, the Davidic authorship position was in full retreat. In that year, for example, Alexander Wright (1900) sought to prove that "it is reasonable to suppose that David at least wrote certain of the psalms to which his name as author is prefixed."

9. See Childs (1971).

10. See on this the *Oxford English Dictionary* (Murray, 1970: 1300). Apparently *tornado* was originally a mariner's term for a circular sea storm on the Atlantic (including, but not limited to, hurricanes); gradually the word came to be applied to various sorts of land-storms as well. W. S. Gilbert pulled it out of his back pocket to rhyme with "mikado," but earlier in the nineteenth century the word *cyclone* had been created, presumably as a more scientific-sounding general term for any circular storm of atmospheric disturbance. As such it certainly appealed to *Oz*'s creator, L. Frank Baum, as well as others, although eventually the swarthy, eye-patched *tornado* returned.

11. Note that this verse is thus mistranslated in both the NRSV and JPS versions.

12. See on this G. Rendsburg (1990: 51–53, 59n).

13. It disturbed scholars that Pentateuch itself had made no mention of such hymns in describing worship in the tabernacle; to some this suggested that temple hymnody was a postexilic innovation. See Kugel (1986).

14. See P. D. Miller (1983: 34).

15. As Claus Westermann correctly observed, Gunkel was hardly the first to set himself to classifying different types of psalms; rather, his *Introduction* stands at the "end" of a long process carried out largely by German scholars: Westermann (1981: 16).

16. First argued by R. Smend (1888).

17. See in general, Westermann (1981).

18. See on this: Kugel (2003: 109–36). In addition to the psalms, the book of Job also describes suffering in great detail—but its exception to the rule of silence is certainly a product of the book's unique theme.

19. Often translated as "my blood," "my death," and so forth, because the Masoretic text has been mis-pointed. The whole point is "my silence," that is, my not being able to praise.

20. For example, Westermann (1981: 75).

21. For the psalm as a whole: Kugel (2003: 121–24, 235–37) and sources cited there.

22. These have been studied in detail by, among others, M. Dahood (1972), (1975), and (1981); note also Gevirtz (1973) and Avishur (1984). However, as I argued some time ago (and others more recently) there is really nothing surprising in this apparent overlap of Ugaritic and biblical poetry, nor is there any indication that it derives from Semitic "poet-performers" having memorized lists of standard pairs of words as ancient Greek or more recent south Slavic bards memorized their standard formulae. These "fixed pairs" are simply part of the normal competence of any native speaker: Kugel (1981: 33–34).

23. This same meaning of *rain* appears in Jer. 17:6 ("They shall be like a shrub in the desert and shall not see when the rain comes"), Amos 4:7, and other texts. See the discussion in Dahood (1965: 25–26).

24. Morton Smith (1984); Sarna (1979).

25. See Kugel (1999: 250–70).

26. See Holladay (1993: 359–61), who locates this relatively late, at least in America.

27. Scholars have known for some time the Akkadian root *ṣalāmu,* "be dark," as well as the Arabic and Ethiopic cognates with the same meaning. It thus seems most likely that the original text had a single word, *ṣalmut* or *ṣalmot* ("darkness, obscurity"), which was subsequently divided—by mistake or perhaps on purpose—into two words, *ṣal mawet* ("shadow of death"). (Cf. Ps. 48:15, which appears in the MT as two words, *'l mwt* ["over death'], but was doubtless a single word, *'lmwt,* "forever," as in the LXX version.) Among the problems associated with this two-word compound is the fact that a "shade" or "shadow" in the world of the ancient Near East usually represents protection from the burning sun, hence more generally "shelter," though shadows also are metaphorically fleeting; neither meaning, however, could be appropriately combined with "death." Some modern scholars have sought nevertheless to salvage the old understanding, without, however, convincing many of their colleagues. An excellent summary: Chaim Cohen (1996).

28. Technically, *šbty* should be "return" rather than "stay" *[yšbty]*, but this may be a copyist's error, since in Hebrew as in English, one does not return "in" but "to." What is more, the sentiment here parallels Ps. 27:4; remaining in the temple was a figure of being blessed. Alternately, the text might mean: "And I will return in [= to] the house of the LORD *after* a length of days."

29. In a delightful essay, W. L. Holladay shows how the meaning of this psalm (assuming heuristically that it does go back to David's times) would have changed its meaning several times even within the biblical period. After a while, "The LORD is my shepherd" would no longer appear to be singling out the God of Israel among other possible divine shepherds, although that is probably how the verse would have been understood in the tenth century BCE. Later on, the *shepherd* certainly changed for Christians in the light of John 10:11 ("I am the good shepherd") and other verses. The "house of the LORD" would have changed its sense several times depending on whether there was only one such house and whether it was standing at the time; the "table" spread before the psalmist's enemies was, for later Christians, the Eucharist, the still waters represented baptism, and so forth. Holladay's concluding question is worth citing: "As we survey the journey of the Twenty-third Psalm from then to now, it is clear that some of its original implications are lost on us and that it has taken on the baggage of later implications. How much of this loss and gain is legitimate, to be encouraged? How much of it is illegitimate, to be fought against? To put it in the strongest terms: Is it possible that the Holy Spirit urged on the original poet, in pre-exilic Israel, words whose true import is only to be understood in later centuries, in the light of further revelation?" Holiday (1993: 13).

30. See Kugel (1983).

31. My thanks to Professor Carol Newsom for this point.

27. David the King

1. This is a very rich topic, which extends from the earliest patristic writings through Cassiodorus and Augustine's *De Doctrina Christiana* and on into later medieval sources. I have dealt with some of them in Kugel (1981, esp. 135–70). See also: Roger (1938); McKitterick (1992). Note that a number of apologetic arguments were marshaled in favor of the classics: they presented a somewhat garbled form of Christian teaching since their authors had borrowed ideas liberally from the ancient Hebrews; they too contained hidden teachings of which their authors were unaware; they aided in education and so helped prepare Christians for sacred study. (On the latter two arguments, see next note and below.)

2. For Virgil in particular, a mitigating circumstance was often invoked: he was, like the Greek Sibyl, a pagan prophet who had foreseen the coming of the Messiah. See Clausen (1990: 65–74).

3. Kugel (1981: 164–67).

4. This is a much studied topic, and the situation varied widely from place to place and from century to century. It would seem foolish even to try to generalize about it in a paragraph, but omitting all mention of Jewish education would certainly be worse. On various aspects, see Goitein (1972: 173–90); Kanarfogel (1992); de Lange (1994: 115–28).

5. An important instance is the introduction by Profiar Duran (1350–1414) to his *Ma'aseh Efod*, where he outlines a curriculum for the broader study of biblical texts by his contemporaries. On the Talmudic complaint and this work, see Leslie (1993: 212).

6. Scholars in general have their doubts about the story of David's ascension to power as presented in 1 and 2 Samuel. Some see in it a largely apologetic account (written, perhaps, shortly after the monarchy split apart) designed to legitimate David and whitewash him of any role in the defeat or death of Saul and, in particular, any role in the defeat or death of Saul, as well as in the death of Abner and Ishboshet. On this: McCarter (1980: 439–504 and 1981: 355–67); Whitelam (1984: 61–87); and Ishida (1999: 159–61)—he rejects, however, the characterization of the Abner account as apologetic. See also: Campbell (2003: 310–11 and references there); Brettler (1998: 91–111). Two recent book-length studies of David are particularly important, and persuasive, in their depiction of David as a tyrannical and ruthless leader: MacKenzie (2000) and Halpern (2001). In contrast to these scholars, those adopting the "minimalist" approach tend to see the entire Davidic empire, along with David himself, as a later fiction; see below. For a decent attempt at defending the historical David against the suspicions of modern historians: Bosworth (2006: 191–210).

7. On this chapter as well as the biblical prohibition of necromancy and other aspects of the world of the dead, see Kugel (2000: 169–200) and the sources cited 247–51.

8. For the complete text and commentary, Kugel (1999: 98–104).

9. See note 6.

10. See VanderKam (1980: 521–39).

11. See on this: Na'aman (1996: 17–27 and 1998: 42–44).

12. R. Shapira, "A Debate of Biblical Proportions," *Haaretz,* August 5, 2005. Cf. E. Mazar (1997: 50–57 and 2006: 16–27; 70).

13. See the judicious review of the evidence by Knoppers (1997: 19–44). He concludes: "Revisionist treatments have been more successful in attacking the case for a Davidic-Solomonic empire than they have been in justifying the nihilist position on the existence of Solomon and the united kingdom. My own position . . . is to accept David and Solomon as historical figures and to acknowledge the domains they governed as 'states,' rather than as chiefdoms.'" (p. 42).

14. The literature on, and controversy surrounding, this inscription is quite extensive; scholars have disputed the dating of the inscription[s], the sense of *bytdwd*, as well as the unity of the two fragments found. See Biran and Naveh (1993: 81–98 and 1995: 1–18); Tropper (1993: 395–406); Cryer (1994: 3–19). B. Halpern (1994: 63–80) provided a careful analysis of the *editio princeps*, suggesting that the inscription belongs to the end, rather than the beginning, of the ninth century. Note also: Demsky (1995: 29–35); Lemche and Thompson, (1994: 3–22); Sasson (1995: 11–30); Knoppers (1997: 36–40 and the further bibliography there);

also, Lemche (1998: 38–43 and *passim*). On the absence of a word divider in *byt dwd,* hold to be crucial: Ben Zvi (1994: 29–32); Rendsburg (1995: 22–25); and Athas (2002).

15. Lemaire (1994: 30–34).

16. See on this Noth (1960: 189–91); Kenyon (1971: 12); Hermann (1981: 154–57).

17. That David surrounded himself by "a foreign bodyguard with no loyalties but to David" was observed by Cross (1973: 230). It is certainly possible that Jebusites were incorporated into David's army or personal guard, perhaps those identified elsewhere as Hittites; see on this Licht (1958). On the reaction of David's wife Michal to his behavior in transferring the Ark, David Wright (2002: 201–25) has suggested that this element may be a later addition to the narrative intended to underscore her family's opposition to David's rule.

18. See Weinfeld (1983: esp. 104–14).

19. On the text of this passage, see McCarter (1984). Many scholars date the passage quite early. For example, Cross (1973: 255): "There is no reason to doubt, in view of the antitemple sentiment of the old oracle, that in poetic form it goes back to Davidic times"; see also Schniedewind (1999), who dates the original oracle to the time of David. One argument for the antiquity of the passage cited (apart from some archaic features of its language) is that it seems to take no cognizance of the coming split between north and south; were its author aware of the split, would he not have included some allusion to it in formulating God's promise? But such an argument from silence is relatively weak. One might equally claim that, by the time these words were written, the split (and perhaps even the northern kingdom's fall) were such an established fact that they were, as it were, "off the radar" of the writer; his whole concern was to account for the Davidic dynasty's legitimacy and longevity. As for its "antitemple sentiment" (Cross), this may be less a sentiment against the institution of the temple than a straightforward attempt to reconcile the divine choice of David with the (by then) widespread attribution of the Jerusalem temple's founding to David's son Solomon; cf. that other attempt, 1 Chronicles 22–29. But the whole question must be considered in light of the various other references to this same promise, some of which present it rather differently (inter alia: I Kings 2:3–4; 8:25; 9:2–9; 2 Kings 21:7–8; and Psalm 132). See among many others the discussion in McCarter (1984) as well as R. E. Friedman (1981: 10–13); Halpern (1996: 144–80); Levenson (1984: 353–61).

Scholars have long identified in the Davidic covenant a central theme in the Deuteronomistic history and other parts of the Hebrew Bible, one with great resonance for later, messianic themes, See, inter alia, Mowinckel (1955), Mettinger (1976); and the recent essays in Day (1998). The promise of Davidic rule "forever" is not conditional on the people's obedience to divine law, or anything else, for that matter; in keeping with this, scholars have contrasted two "covenant" types in the Bible, "conditional" and "unconditional." Weinfeld (1970: 184–203 and 1972: 73–81) explored ancient Near Eastern parallels to the two sorts of agreements. Actually, the distinction between "conditional" and "unconditional" covenants goes back at least to Mendenhall (1954: 50–76), who, in this seminal article, contrasted the Mosaic covenant with the covenants of Abraham in Genesis 15 and 17: "It is not often enough seen that no obligations are imposed on Abraham. Circumcision is not originally an obligation, but a *sign* of the covenant, like the rainbow in Gen. 9 . . . The covenant of Moses, on the other hand, is almost the exact opposite. It imposes specific obligations" (p. 62). In what follows, Mendenhall goes on to elaborate the connection of the (unconditional) Davidic covenant with Christianity. Two brief passages are worth quoting: "[D]uring the monarchy and according to every indication we have in the time of David, the tradition of the covenant with Abraham became the pattern of the covenant between YHWH and David . . . The covenant with Abraham was the 'prophecy' and that with David the 'fulfillment.' . . . It is likewise not surprising that *J* does not seem to emphasize the Mosaic covenant—the important one was that which YHWH gave to Abraham. *The Mosaic legal tradition could hardly have been more attractive to Solomon than it was to Paul.* [p. 72] . . . The New Covenant of Christianity obviously continued the Abraham-Davidic covenant with its emphasis on the Messiah, Son of David. . . . The new stipulations of the covenant are not a system of law to define in detail every obligation in every conceivable circumstance, but the *law of love*" (75–76, italics mine). As some later scholars have suggested, the distinction has probably been drawn too sharply, perhaps for apologetic purposes. Nevertheless, many writers have seen a conflict between the account of a great covenant of laws at Sinai—upon which Israel's connection with its God and, consequently, its continued presence in its land, is conditioned—and a divine promise to David that he and his descendants will rule Israel forever.

In place of "conditional" and "unconditional" covenants, Jon Levenson (1975: 203–33, esp. 225–27) proposed to substitute "contemporary" vs. "ancestral" covenants. This article's argument is, however, far broader: Levenson suggests that the original Deuteronomistic history did not include the legal core, since that history's covenant was the divine grant of kingship to David and his descendants, a covenant that precluded any conditional grant of the land based on the people's adherence to the laws given at Sinai (and reiterated and elaborated in the legal core of Deuteronomy). (Levenson cites M. Tsevat: "If the existence of the confederacy, which is conditional, is the body, then kingship, which is an organ, cannot be unconditional," p. 227). Levenson later elaborated this theme (1985). In his view, the "subordination of the Davidic covenant to the Sinaitic in I Kings 8:25 . . . must be seen as a reinterpretation of the pristine Davidic covenant material, a reinterpretation that reflects the growing canonical status of the Sinaitic traditions that will become the Pentateuch. I Kings 8:25 is the vengeance of Moses upon David, of the 'kingdom of priests' upon the hubris of the political state, for it resolves the clash between the two covenants in favor of the Mosaic one." Levenson (1985: 211).

20. One scholar has recently argued the opposite, claiming that the books of Samuel and Chronicles draw on a common source, and that the Bathsheba incident was inserted into the former as a bit of antimonarchic propaganda: Auld (1994).

21. On this psalm: Kugel (1999: 147–58).

22. This approach was first put forward in Rost (1926). Gunn's study (1978) actually argued against Rost, suggesting that what Rost had identified as an isolatable literary unit was merely part of a larger composition. See below.

23. This was the theme of von Rad's famous essay, "The Beginnings of History-Writing in Ancient Israel" (1965: 166–204). Lately, this idea has been strongly challenged. See, for example, the essays by Erhard Blum, John Van Seters and others in de Pury and Römer (2000); also Gunn (1978). From a rather different angle, Friedman (1998) has also argued against the "Succession Narrative" thesis. Without adopting Rost's (or von Rad's) thesis, John Barton (2004: 95–106) has, I believe, presented a series of strong arguments against those who would date the David narratives to post-exilic times and see in them a work of pure fiction.

24. See note 23.

28. Solomon's Wisdom

1. Thus many commentators and historians take its account at face value; as noted earlier, von Rad (1965) even distinguished the "Succession Narrative" from earlier sagas and stories of heroes, calling it the "oldest specimen of ancient Israelite historical writing" (176); see above, chapter 27, note 23. See also Hermann (1982: 145–73).

2. Whybray (1968: 10); although he, like Hermisson (1971: 136–54) and others, finds traces of the "wisdom ideology" in this narrative.

3. On David's last words and similar biblical scenes: Kugel (1999: 176–79).

4. See Weinfeld (1972: 246), for the obvious bits of Deuteronomic wording. Some scholars, including Weinfeld (1972: 248–51), have argued that this is a reworking of an "ancient and genuine" tradition; see also Hermann (1953–54: 51ff) (reference from Weinfeld). Note also Halpern (1996: *First Historians*, 146, 176 notes 6 and 8).

5. G. von Rad (1984: 203) connected the rise of wisdom in Israel with the time of Solomon himself, a period when the "blossoming of economic life was naturally followed close behind by an intensive interchange of spiritual ideas . . . In short, the time of Solomon was a period of 'enlightenment,' of a sharp break with the ancient patriarchal code of living." A similar line was followed by Heaton (1974). See also Lemaire (1995: 106–18). This argument, theoretically plausible, has been challenged by many scholars, including Weeks (1994: 110–31). It is obviously rejected as well as by those who deny the historicity of

Solomon's great empire or wide-ranging commercial contacts—all a much later pipe-dream, according to revisionist historians. On the latter phenomenon: Knoppers (1997). Thus, the jury is still out.

6. Weinfeld (1972: 254–557) judges it "pre-Deuteronomic"; see also Halpern (1996: 147 and n.).

7. Particularly problematic was Solomon's imposition of the *mas,* or conscription of forced labor; see 1 Kings 5:13 (some texts: 5:27).

8. Above, note 5. In any case, M. K. Fox's study (196: 239) of the social environment reflected in the book of Proverbs points (as earlier studies had) to the court as the apparent location of Israelite wisdom. "The generations of readers who interpreted Proverbs as the wisdom of one man, Solomon, went too far, but they were going in the right direction."

9. This principle is attested in the Mishnaic law in Baba Metzi'a 1:1, but it is doubtless considerably older.

10. On ancient Near Eastern wisdom: Kugel (1999: 107–28).

11. Indeed, the whole concept of wisdom as described in the foregoing owes much to the ancient Egyptian *ma'at,* justice and the divine order; See Volten (1963: 72–102); Wuertwein (1976: 113–33). This international effort is extremely ancient. From Old Kingdom Egypt (third millennium BCE) comes such collections as the "Instructions of Ptah-hotep" and the "Instructions from Kagemni"; see Faulkner (1972). Old Sumerian proverbs survive from early in the second millennium BCE: Kramer (1959: 119–26).

12. On the *mashal:* Kugel (1999: 159–80).

13. This section's structure has been much discussed: P. Skehan (1971: 9–45); Kayatz (1966): Lang (1972).

14. The Egyptian origin of Proverbs 22:17—23:11 (or possibly up to 24:22) was first argued by Erman (1924: 241–52); see also Romheld (1989); see also Shupak (1993).

15. See Kugel (2004: 32–52).

16. It has been argued that this is a uniquely *Israelite* feature; see van der Toorn (1985: 100–13); on the phenomenon in Ecclesiastes, see also Loader (1979).

17. For a fuller description of this book: Kugel (1999: 305–23).

18. See below, chapter 34, as well as Kugel (1999: 105–28).

19. Whitley (1979) presents a careful linguistic analysis of key verses; still better: Davila (1990: 69–87).

20. Ullendorff (1962: 215).

21. Ancient interpreters associated the root of this name with another meaning of *qhl,* "assemble" or "gather"; perhaps, they thought, he referred to himself that way because he had "assembled gatherings" of sages. As a result, when the book was translated into Greek it was called *ekklesiastes,* the "man of the assembly." Still later, when *ekklesia* came to refer specifically to the Christian churches (cf. Latin *ecclesia,* French *église,* etc.), *ekklesiastes* became "the preacher," as the book is still known in some vernaculars.

22. Again, sec Kugel (1999: 307–23).

23. The opening word of this line, *yašqeni* ("Let him cause me to drink") has long been mispointed as *yešaqqeni,* hence the tautological mistranslation, "Let him kiss me with the kisses of his mouth." On the contrary, drinking is the common element joining parts A and B; it is the whole point of the *mashal.*

24. The rustic figures of this song are reminiscent of those in classical Greek and Roman pastoral; this is not to argue any direct influence, but to suggest that the impulse of urban poets to glorify the simple life of the country and all that goes on there may arise in more than one setting.

25. See Tosefta *Sanhedrin,* 12:10.

26. Marvin Pope (1978) sought to associate the song with funeral rites in the *beit marzeah,* but this suggestion has attracted few adherents. His commentary remains an outstanding (and exhaustive) contribution to scholarship.

27. It is strikingly symptomatic of modern scholarship's romance with original meaning that some scholars have in fact sought to suggest that the Song of Songs might have become part of Israel's sacred library *before* it was ever understood as a divine allegory: it was a liturgy for the mourning revel, it was Solomonic propaganda, and so forth. I do not find the slightest merit in any of these arguments, most of which are contradicted by the text of the Song itself.

28. That is, the *shekhinah* or divine presence, whose female-ness was lovingly elaborated by Jewish mystics throughout the ages.
29. Ginzbcrg (1998: 43–47, esp. notes 127, 129, 136); Hollander (1993: 218–19).
30. M. *Yadayim* 3:5; see on this Lieberman (1965: 118–26). On Akiba's role see Kugel (1999: 276–78).

29. North and South

1. On this see Monson (2000: 20–35).
2. See 1 Kings 22:10.
3. See on this m. *Baba Batra*, 2:8; note also Hosea 13:3, Jer. 51:33.
4. Rupprecht (1977).
5. On this translation see Weinfeld (1982: 27–53).
6. On Shoshenq and the Karnak inscription: Kitchen (1973: 293–300). Scholars disagree on the question of whether there may be a direct, literary relationship between the inscription and the biblical account: Na'aman (1999: 13–17); Parker (2000: 357–78).
7. See the discussion in Cross (1973: 198–99); for the bronze statue of a bull at a twelfth-century BCE site, see above, chapter 16, note 9. The cherubim iconography is attested, for example, in the Ahiram sarcophagus from Byblos (Pritchard, 1975: vol. 1, illustration 126), where the king is represented sitting on a cherub throne before an offering table.
8. Geneva Bible (1560), iiii.
9. Ahab and his wife Jezebel are the conventional "bad monarchs" and seem to have been framed so as to conform to an existing type; they stand in contrast to the strictly moral, unbending prophet (in their case, Elijah). The Ahab-Elijah story shows many parallels to the Saul-Samuel narrative; see Campbell (1986).
10. If the onomasticon is any guide, Ahab was certainly not an opponent of the worship of YHWH: the names of his sons Y[eh]oram and Ahaziyah[u] would seem to indicate his allegiance. But if the narrative has any historical reality, he seems not to have backed the monolatrous devotion to this deity—that, for Elijah, was his crime. The eighth-century Samarian ostraca (discovered in 1910 in the capital of the Northern Kingdom), document a host of personal names, some constructed with the divine name Baal and some with YHWH; this too might seem to indicate a somewhat syncretistic society, but see above, chapter 24, "Named for God."
11. See Pritchard (1969a: plate 490).
12. Thus the Jewish Publication Society (1985) version, "The LORD alone is God."
13. For this translation: Kugel (1999: 69); Burnett (2001: 118).
14. Most translations read, "The voice of the LORD . . ."; Hebrew *qol* can indeed mean both "listen" (as an imperative) and the noun "voice." In the case of this psalm, the "voice of the LORD" would presumably be a reference to the thunder accompanying the storm. But if so, then the "voice of the LORD" ends up doing a lot of things one would not normally expect voices, even divine voices, to do, such as shattering trees and shooting forth sparks. "Listen!" thus seems a better translation.
15. Ginsberg (1935: 472–76 and 1936: 129–35); Gaster (1946–47: 55–65); Cross (1950: 19–21 and 1973: 151–52 and n. 23); Day (1979: 143–51). Some have dissented: Margulis (1970: 332–48); Craigie (1972: 143–51); Loretz (1984); see the latter for further bibliography.
16. See Gaster (1946–47: 58).
17. Herdner (1963: 1.4 v 6–7; vii 27–35).
18. Music by Ben Weisman, with lyrics by Al Stillman.
19. See on this Wuerthwein (1993: 152–66).
20. In this connection: Cross (1973: 194); Miller (1986: 239–48).
21. This is not a strictly northern feature, of course. Still, it does seem more characteristic of prophets in the north than in the south: Miller (1986a: 82–95).
22. Wilson (1980: 135–251).
23. For Elisha's secret, see Graves (1925).
24. On Jesus as miracle-worker, see the pioneering work of Morton Smith (1998, originally published 1978), followed by Vermes (1982: 20–22, 182, 239–44) and Meier (1994: 535–50).

25. Note the description of Elijah in Blenkinsopp (1983: 71–72).
26. On the reading "Israel" see Ben-Hayyim (1973: 60); Skehan and Di Lella (1987: 531).
27. This is true of the Masoretic text; the Septuagint reports Phinehas's death at Josh. 24:33.
28. Further: Kugel (1998: 811–14, 824–25).
29. Levenson (1993: 179–80) surveys the extensive biblical and extra-biblical evidence for the institution child sacrifice in the ancient Near East. In connection with the Mesha Stone, see also Horn (1986: 62–63).
30. Some light was shed on the missing part of this name by the discovery of a ninth-century inscription at Kerak (Jordan) that referred to a certain [K]mšyt. See Reed and Winnett (1963: 1–9). They analyze the name as kmš + šyt, that is, "Chemosh has established (him over the land)" (7).
31. As appropriate for such a long and detailed inscription, a large scholarly literature has grown up around the Mesha Stone. One recent collection of essays: Dearman (1989).

30. *The Book of Isaiah(s)*

1. Haran (1982: 163 and 1985: 1–11).
2. The chronology is not quite certain; some scholars have suggested the lower date of 733. Starting with Kaplan's article (1926: 251–59), scholars have expressed skepticism about Isa. 6:1–8 being Isaiah's "call," in part because of its placement in the book: if it were really his first summons to prophecy, why is it not at the head of the book? In addition, there is the striking resemblance between Isa. 6:1–8 and the prophet Micaiah's account of a certain vision of his, "I saw the LORD sitting on his throne, with all the host of heaven standing beside him to the right and to the left of him. And the LORD said, 'Who will entice Ahab, so that he may go up and fall at Ramoth-gilead?' Then one said one thing, and another said another, until a spirit came forward and stood before the LORD, saying, 'I will entice him.'" (1 Kings 22:19–21). Since this vision does *not* announce Micaiah's inauguration as a prophet, why should the similar vision in Isaiah 6 be taken as his inauguration? On such grounds, J. Blenkinsopp (2000: 223) and earlier scholars have suggested that the passage represents Isaiah's "commissioning for a special political mission in connection with the threat of a Syrian Samarian invasion in or about the year 734." This argument seems ill-conceived. On form-critical grounds, there is no reason not to see the fundamental similarity of Isaiah 6 to other call narratives; indeed, Jeremiah seems to have seen it as such since he echoes its principal gesture, the seraphim touching the prophet's lips, in his own call narrative (Jer. 1:9). Did the authors of these narratives all misunderstand the original function of the Isaiah passage? Moreover, there is the *mīs-pî* connection, on which see below and note 10. As for the literary resemblance between Isaiah's vision and Micaiah's, it is certainly remarkable, but it hardly sheds light on the significance of Isaiah's vision: its connection to the latter can only be addressed once the literary-critical problem of their common material has been resolved. Finally, some scholars have suggested that the whole passage is post-exilic: Kaiser (1983); Gosse (1992: 340–49). However, the arguments have hardly been accepted as persuasive; see Williamson (1994); Barthel (1997: 79–82).
3. This might be suggested by his presence in the "temple" in the passage cited below. Some have seized on this detail to suggest that the vision was brought on by a temple incubation (the practice of sleeping in a temple or other sacred site for oracular purposes: cf. 1 Samuel 3). For a review of the evidence see Wildberger (1972: 230–45).
4. Greenfield (1985: 193–98) adduced comparative evidence to suggest that the reference to the throne's height as well as the deity's stature—His train filling the temple—derive from the iconography of the enthroned Baal as well as Marduk iconography. R. Knierim (1968: 47–68) had earlier pointed to the dependence of this throne image on the Baal iconography.
5. On this there is a vast bibliography; note inter alia Aptowitzer (1931: 137–53, 257–87); for Qumran, Strugnell (1960: 318–45), and Newsom, (1985: 39–58, 79–80); and Kugel (1998: 54, 58–59, 713–15, 730–31 and the bibliography cited there).
6. On the appearance of this motif in the *Apostolic Constitutions*, see Newman (2004). Direct citation of Isa. 6:3 is puzzlingly absent in the Dead Sea Scrolls (as is that of Ezek. 3:12). though allusions to both have been found. See Chazon (2003: 35–47).

7. Note the slight changes: "triumphal song" (it is hardly so described in Isaiah); "never-silent" (this is the theme of *laus perpetua*, part of the larger angelic topos of "Tireless Angels," Kugel (1998: 76–77); and *"the heaven* and the earth are full of Your glory"—since, if God is omnipresent, then surely that includes heaven as well.

8. On this psalm, see Kugel (2003: 120–25). On the divine council: Mullen (1980); De Moor (1970: 195–220); Miller (2000); Handy (1994); Mark Smith (2001: 41–53).

9. My student S. Z. Aster argues in a forthcoming article that the six-winged creatures in Isaiah's vision are paralleled by multiwinged creatures in Assyrian iconography who guard the entrance to the king's throne-room. Note that the Ahiram sarcophagus from Byblos represents the king seated on his throne and flanked by cherubim.

10. The connection of Isaiah 6 with *mīs-pî* was first suggested by Egnell (1949: 40–41). The matter is treated fully in Hurowitz (1989: 39–89).

11. For Assurnasirpal II's account: Pritchard (1969: 275–76); also Grayson (1972–76, vol. 2: 153–56).

12. See, briefly, Lambert (2004: 352–65).

13. On the image of Assyria in biblical sources from this time, see Machinist (1983: 719–37), who shows the sometimes striking resemblance between Isaiah's descriptions and those found in neo-Assyrian propaganda, for example, Isa. 37:24 (2 Kings 19:23) and the royal boasts of Shalmaneser III and Sennacherib.

14. On the actual fate of the deportees: Zadok (1979 and 2003), Na'aman (2000).

15. On some of the problems arising from the usual explanation of the Syro-Ephraimite war, see Cazelles (1978: 70–78); and Cazelles in Garrone (1991: 31–48); also Tomes (1993: 55–71) and Barthel (1997).

16. Scholars are divided about the references in chapter 7 and their connection to Isaiah's *ipsissima verba*. See, for example, Clements (1980: 78–103). Some scholars view the material in 7:1—8:18 (or, according to others, 9:7) as a "memoir" detailing the prophet's role in advising the king and penned by Isaiah himself or his followers; to such an account chapter 6 was, they argue, appended as a kind of introduction and then the whole complex inserted into the larger bloc of material extending from 5:1 through 12:6.

17. This is described in the text as an *'ot*, usually translated as a "sign," but as we have seen earlier in the cases of Cain and Moses, the word *'ot* sometimes means a solemn promise or pledge. It does here as well. See above, chapter 13, note 23.

18. The next verse, "The LORD will bring on you and on your people and on your ancestral house such days as have not come since the day that Ephraim departed from Judah—the king of Assyria," seems to be a non sequitur and has long troubled scholars. Perhaps Isaiah is quoting an earlier oracle given to or about the Kingdom of Israel (Ephraim)—you are about to undergo the worst event in your history.

19. In so saying, Ahaz was proposing a formal suzerainty treaty (or perhaps invoking one that was already in existence) between Assyria and Judah. As Judah's suzerain, Assyria would be obliged to come to its vassal's aid. On the formula "servant [or "vassal"] and son," see Loewenstamm (1969: 148).

20. On his return to Jerusalem, Ahaz is said to have replaced the altar in the Jerusalem temple and introduced other changes (2 Kings 16:7–18). The reason for these changes is not explicit in the biblical text, but earlier scholars suggested that this as well was some sort of kowtowing to Assyria; see, for example, Gray (1963: 576). Cogan (1974: 73–77), however, argued that imposing syncretistic worship was not a characteristic of Assyrian policy. He therefore endorsed the suggestion that the model for the altar was Syrian, not Assyrian, and that the change was prompted by "aesthetic reasons"; the new altar "served only a legitimate YHWH cult," in keeping with 2 Kings 16:15.

21. "Samuel took *the* [not mentioned previously] cruse of oil . . ." [1 Sam. 10:1]; "This lowly man called out and the LORD heard him . . ." (Ps. 34:7).

22. On this topic there is, understandably, an enormous scholarly literature; most recent surveys, citing (inter alia) the use of the Ugaritic cognate *ģlmt*, suggest that the term does not reflect virginity or the absence thereof. On the other hand, in this particular semantic field changeability seems to be the rule: Ugaritic *btlt* does not necessarily mean *virgin*, although the cognate in Hebrew did acquire that meaning; French *pucelle* moved in the same direc-

tion, while English *maid*, which used to imply virginity, now designates a domestic helper. See also chapter 1, note 64.

23. A more extended treatment of this passage: Kugel (1999: 181–91).

24. Allen (1983).

25. Some scholars have suggested that the Deuteronomistic history was originally created in the time of Hezekiah and then revised and expanded in Josiah's time; that might account for the attention lavished on Hezekiah. See Peckham (1985); Halpern (1996: 111–17).

26. See further: Pritchard (1969: 287–88), as well as the more recent translation and discussion of Fuchs (1998).

27. Tadmor (1985: 74–78). Note also Ben Zvi (2003: 73–105).

28. Scholars have long been troubled by what appears to be chronological incompatibility in the dates contained in the biblical account (see 2 Kings 18:13—19:37 [= Isaiah 36–37] and 2 Chr. 32:1–23) with the Assyrian record. Some have sought to reconcile the dates by positing two separate campaigns of Sennacherib, others have rejected this approach. For the latter see Cogan and Tadmor (1988: 246–51) and Gallagher (1999). Scholars have also debated the relationship between Isaiah 36–27 and 2 Kings 18:13—19:37; see Williamson (2004: 184–86).

29. Paying such tribute might seem to be inconsistent with the report of Hezekiah's successfully resisting a siege; this has led some scholars to suggest that there were in fact two invasions of Judah. Such a conclusion hardly imposes itself, however.

30. These include all the direct citations, but certainly other passages—for example, Mark 9:12, 15:28 and 1 Cor. 15:3; 1 Pet. 2:21–25—have also been included. Further: Zimmerli and Jeremias (1965: 88–106).

31. The questioning began with the rise of modern biblical scholarship and was debated for some time. Most modern scholars today reject the identification of the "servant" with Jesus and even the isolation of the "servant songs" as such: see in particular the brief monograph of Mettinger (1983) and the extensive bibliography there (pp. 48–50); see also this volume's Appendix 1, "Apologetics and Biblical Criticism Lite," on the Web site jameskugel.com.

32. For a brief history of the research into such oracles: Mettinger (1983: 2–9), as well as chapter 33. For Isaiah, see also Miller (1982a: 37–59).

33. This passage has been much discussed by commentators, who disagree as to who the "voice" belongs to and whether "Humanity is only grass . . ." is the prophet's response to the summons to speak or (as I once preferred) the message that the prophet is to deliver, followed by his own response. Cross (1953: 274–77) saw in chapter 40 a recrudescence of the divine council motif: the plural imperatives "Comfort . . . speak . . ." in 40:1–2 are directed to the members of the council, and the voice that speaks in 40:3 and 6 belongs to one of these members. This has seemed convincing to many.

34. More on this theme: Kugel (1999: 288–304).

35. Note the excellent history of scholarship in Seitz (1996).

36. One particularly important recent study is Sommer (1998), which carefully examines allusions to earlier Scripture in these chapters. The author demonstrates that the form of allusion and its overall style is rather uniform throughout chapters 40–66, supporting the idea that they are the work of a single author. See in particular his review of scholarship on the question of Trito-Isaiah (187–95). Sommer also shows that, quite surprisingly, the clearest allusions in chapters 40–66 (along with Isaiah 35) are to passages from Jeremiah, which might imply (*contra* several other recent studies) that chapters 40–66 were not originally intended to supplement "First Isaiah."

37. For the characteristics of the call narrative: Habel (1965: 297–323). Habel suggests that the genre may have originated in imitation of a diplomat presenting his credentials. Also: Long (1977).

38. Von Rad (1972: 27). Von Rad's focus on the Hexateuch (rather than the Pentateuch) was both historical and theological; it was the book of Joshua, he argued, that originally closed the circle of the promises made to Israel's ancestors in Genesis. But if so, scholars properly asked, then why had the final form been the Pentateuch rather than the Hexateuch? What sense did it make for the Pentateuch to end with the death of Moses, instead of ending with the book of Joshua and Israel's triumphal entrance into the land? And, for that matter, who

juxtaposed one thing to another within the Pentateuch—why were laws mixed in with historical records, in fact, what were all these priestly laws doing in a book apparently intended for a much wider audience than the priests? It might well be argued that the present form of the Pentateuch was simply a matter of happenstance—bits and pieces had been added to an original text in haphazard fashion. (See, in a broader context, Haran: 1996–2003.) But the apparent disorder might also be the result of conscious design: an editor may have purposely decided to separate the era of Moses from everything that followed. It was thus that tradition history and redaction criticism ultimately led to canonical criticism and the focus on the text's final, canonical form. "None of the ancient witnesses within the Bible itself . . . provide the slightest hint that the Torah story in any form ever ended where the Pentateuch ends . . . When one fully understands that it was the Torah story which gave divine authority to the various customs and laws which are included in the Pentateuch—i.e., that Judaism's authentic laws were understood to derive their authority from the fact that they were inherited from the Torah story period, or as we later came to say, from Sinai—then one understands why, in its final form, all laws had to be read back into that period" (Sanders (1972: 25–26)—a most important point, to which 1 return in chapter 36. Sanders and other canonical critics have likewise highlighted the fact (also seen herein) that some of the laws in Exodus or Leviticus seem to be contradicted by laws on the same subjects in Deuteronomy. If these contradictions were left to stand, it was not because some later editor had failed to notice them. Rather, the present form of the Pentateuch argues that these laws were given in a certain sequence: some were first promulgated at Mount Sinai, others thereafter, and then, forty years later, Moses "expounded" the Torah in the plains of Moab just before his own death (Deut. 1:1–5), introducing some new statutes and revising some of the old ones in the process. This sequence, scholars now said, was quite purposely created to account for the contradictions in what were originally separate law codes. For this same reason Deuteronomy had been connected to the books that preceded it and separated off from the book of Joshua that followed it, since this made the resultant Pentateuch into what is was for later Jews, the one, single corpus of divine law.

39. An important first step was Mowinckel (1933: 267–92), followed by Scott (1950: 175–86); Jones (1955: 226–46) and subsequent works; see below.

40. See his compendium (1979: 330–33).

41. Milgrom (1964: 164–82) answered the question of his title with a yes; he finds the historical background, pattern of repentance proffered and refused, along with what he sees in 2:10 ff. as an eyewitness description of the earthquake that took place in Uzziah's time and which was mentioned also in Amos 1:1 and Zech. 14:4. If so, then at least some of the material in chapters 1–5 might indeed precede chapter 6 chronologically; but the argument is weak.

42. Scholars have long been aware of the parallel to Isaiah 6 in 1 Kings 22: 19–21. See above, chapter 30, note 2.

43. Clements (1982: 117–29 and 1985: 95–113); Rendtorff (1984: 295–320); Sweeney (1988); Seitz (1991); and Carr (1993). See, however, Sommer (1998) and note 35 above.

44. Childs' position has been attacked on such grounds by several scholars, and this is not the place to review the arguments; see, inter alia, Barr (1983) and the sources cited in chapter 36.

45. See the discussion in Barr (1983: 23–26).

46. Moreover, it is often unclear what an editor intended us to understand. Levenson (1993: 62–81) has made this point well with regard to the Pentateuch. As is well known, the laws for the release of slaves are significantly different in different parts of the Pentateuch. Thus, in Exod. 21:20–26, release is quite unconnected to the sabbatical year: "six years shall he serve, and in the seventh year he shall go free." The same "seventh year" provision appears in Deut. 15: 12, but its juxtaposition to the law of remission of debts in the seventh year (Deut. 15:1–11) suggests that here the old law's phrase "seventh year" has been reinterpreted as the sabbatical year, no matter how long the slave has served. Meanwhile, in the Leviticus law of slaves (Lev. 25:8–17, 29–34) release is said to come in the jubilee year. There are other differences as well. Leviticus has no provision for a slave opting to stay with his master in perpetuity, while Exodus and Deuteronomy do. Exodus specifies that manumis-

sion of female slaves is to be different from that of males, while Deuteronomy explicitly denies this. So what was an ancient Israelite to do? Some scholars have argued that Deuteronomy's position at the end of the Pentateuch was meant to suggest that its position on manumission and other matters was to be regarded as God's "last word." But how is one to know? Perhaps an editor's inclusion of these discordant laws in the final version of the Pentateuch represents his unwillingness (or political inability) to give preference to one version over the others. Or may it perhaps indicate that, even at that relatively early stage, some sort of harmonistic exegesis was already being practiced? Such harmonizing was, in any case, practiced later on. Rabbinic exegesis—in keeping with the Four Assumptions—seeks to wrest a single meaning from these disparate passages, but in so doing, as Levenson points out, "the rabbis produce a law for which *no* one passage in the Torah provides no evidence."

47. Hobbes (1968: 453 = p. 223 of 1651 edition).

48. Hobbes (1968: 425 = p. 205 of 1651 edition). See the discussion in Malcolm (2002: 423–25).

49. Barton (1986). To begin with, Barton notes, prophecy itself was generally understood as applying to *distant* or even eschatological times rather than the immediate future (which, by their time, was long past; see esp. pp. 179–213). Nor was prophecy limited to that which is identified as such in the text: psalms, songs, laws, and other genres might be equally prophetic. Hence, a New Testament writer "could say in a vague, summarizing way that 'God spoke of old to our fathers by the prophets' (Hebrews 1:1) and then go on to quote verses from the prophets, the psalms, the Pentateuch even, without any sense of incongruity" (95). What is more, prophetic texts were held to contain all sorts of teachings quite apart from the announcement of God's judgments or imminent interventions: prophets were conceived to teach about matters of *halakhah* or ethical instruction, or to transmit information about God's very nature or the ways of heaven. His conclusions accord altogether with those bits of ancient biblical interpretation examined in this and the preceding chapters.

50. Kugel (1999: 288–304).

51. Nor, for Christians, does the matter end there. The first Christians who adopted and accepted Isaiah as Scripture not only thought of it as one single book à la today's canonical criticism. They also thought that the "servant of the LORD" passages, along with Isaiah's references to the coming offspring "from the tree trunk of Jesse" and the little baby "born to us" were all about Jesus—indeed, such passages had not a little to do with Christianity's whole acceptance of Jewish Scripture as their own. If the authority of Scripture derives from the community that accepted it as such, then can this aspect of Christian Scripture's meaning really be shrugged off? Are Christians not bound by what the Bible was thought to mean in the decisive moment in which it was accepted? B. Childs (2004) has himself wrestled with this question in a recent work.

31. Jeremiah

1. An important body of evidence was amassed by Herbert Huffmon; see his summary in Freedman (1992: 5:477–82; also Barstad (1993: 39–60); Weippert (1997: 196–230); van der Toorn (1998: 55–70); Nissinen (1998: 4–9).

2. This may be connected with the absence of lengthy written records of prophetic speeches, and what that may (or may not) reflect about their standing in society. See on this the essays by van der Toorn and Nissinen (2000: 234–77).

3. Overholt (1989); Wilson (1980); see also Grabbe (1995).

4. Huehnergard (1999: 88–93).

5. Poignantly described by one great initiate: "Poet appointed dare not decline/ to walk among the bogus, nothing to authenticate/ the mission imposed, despised by toadies, confidence men, kept boys." Bunting (1966).

6. Some of these issues are discussed in the various essays in Kugel (1990).

7. See on this Kugel (1981: 140–48 and 1990: 1–25).

8. This feature he described as *parallelismus membrorum*, "the parallelism of the clauses." but his—and even more, later scholars'—focus on *paralleling* as the generative feature of Hebrew verse was a mistake. See O'Connor (1980), Kugel (1981: 1–58).

9. Lowth (1829: 176).

10. Some uncertainties persist in the precise dating of this and related events, although they are minor compared to other problems in biblical and ancient Near Eastern chronology. In general: Hughes (1990).

11. The subsequent Babylonian attempt to invade Egypt, in 601 BCE, was, however, frustrated; see below, note 25.

12. On this passage, as with the call of Isaiah, there is a vast scholarly literature. For an interesting analysis and review of recent scholarship: Sharp (2000: 421–43). One treatment of Jeremiah's call suggesting that the passage is a secondary addition is that of Nicholson (1970: 114–15). Note also: Berquist (1989: 129–33). In general, scholars going back to Duhm have been quite reluctant to attribute much of the book of Jeremiah to the prophet himself (see next note), and this tendency has continued, with some modifications, into today's commentaries and monographs. In particular, Carroll (1986) expressed profound doubts about the authenticity of much of the material contained in the book, and even about the figure of Jeremiah himself (largely the creation of Deuteronomic historians, he said); his work has been highly influential on subsequent criticism. For a recent reassessment: Reimer (2004: 207–24).

13. Mowinckel, Gunkel's student, adopted Duhm's overall approach in his own study of Jeremiah (Mowinckel, 1914). He held that the first-person sermons were composed by Deuteronomic editors no earlier than 400 BCE. Some subsequent critics have retreated from this late dating as well as the disconnection of these sermons from *some* things the prophet himself might have said. See inter alia: Bright (1951: 15–35) and Weinfeld (1972: 27–32), as well as the more recent commentaries and monographs cited below.

14. On the contrary, this style seems to be a stylistic development that emerges precisely in Jeremiah's time: see Kugel (1981: 59–95 and with regard to Jeremiah, esp. 77–80). Note in this connection Weippert (1973), who, however, sees this "artistic prose" as a recasting of Jeremiah's original poetic oracles.

15. Lundbom (1999: 252) notes that "most translators omit" the word *lakh*. This is true, but Lundbom's own translation, "I remember about you your bridal devotion" only makes things worse. The idiom *zkr l-* is found as well in the positive sense of "remember to X's credit" in Lev. 26:45 and Ps. 132:1. and in the negative sense in Pss. 79:8 and 137:7.

16. Vocalizing *hēnnāh*, cf. Gen. 21:23.

17. On this: S-M. Kang (1996: 157). On this and the other Deuteronomic stereotypical expressions cited, see also Weippert (1973: 42, 215–22).

18. R. E. Friedman (1987) argued that Jeremiah himself was the Deuteronomistic historian (145–48), but this claim has not met with wide approval. On the other hand, the Deuteronomistic authorship of Jeremiah's "prose sermons" has also been sharply questioned. Blenkinsopp (1977: 35–39) has noted some obvious instances of dissonance between Jeremiah's preaching and Deuteronomy's laws. Moreover, the language and characteristic expressions of Jeremiah, while similar to those of Deuteronomy, are in some ways distinct: Holladay (1984: 213–28). On this question see also Carroll (1986a: 38–50); Nicholson (1970: 1–138). On the specific matter of the "Temple sermon," Reimer (2004: 215) argues persuasively that, precisely because of the changed status of the Jerusalem temple in post-exilic times, the "sermon" underlying both Jeremiah 7 and 26 "demands a pre-exilic setting, even if it was subsequently elaborated in different ways."

19. The scholarly search for Jeremiah's *ipsissima verba* was not exactly carried out in a vacuum. The same Protestant scholars who pursued this quest were well aware of a similar search for the *ipsissima verba* of Jesus in the New Testament. This was, of course, a much older undertaking—and for Christians, a far more consequential one. Four canonical gospels purport to set forth the very words that Jesus spoke, and, especially in the first three, there is a great deal of overlap. For centuries the slight differences between one gospel and the next were actually comforting. After all, four witnesses to the same events had reported substantially the same message, with slight variations; was this not proof of the fundamental veracity of all four? As New Testament scholarship advanced, however, a different explanation emerged, especially for the overlap of the first three gospels: Matthew and Luke had in fact copied a good deal of what they said from the gospel of Mark, supplementing it with their own additions, while the other common material shared by Matthew and Luke had come

from a now-lost source, Q. In either case, the overlap proved nothing about the authenticity of what was being reported, only about the *in*authenticity of their additions. So what had Jesus actually said? The last century of New Testament scholarship has gradually whittled away all or part of a great many of the sayings attributed to Jesus in the gospels. Some things have been clearly identified as later inventions, and internal contradictions and doctrinal inconsistencies in others have suggested that they too may not even be close to the *ipsissima verba* of Christianity's founder. These researches, along with many others (too numerous to mention here), have raised the most troubling questions for devout Christians: To what extent can Christian teaching be identified with the things actually taught by Jesus of Nazareth? What is the historical reality that stands behind the things recounted in the New Testament? Where does the religion of Christianity come from, and what is it really? This in turn has served to shift the focus from the Scripture's words to the real-life events that stand behind them. See above, chapter 1, note 65, as well as chapter 36.

20. Again, see Carroll (1986).
21. See the discussion in Holt (1986: 73–87); and Sharp (2003: 44–62). In general, opinion is still divided on Duhm's basic attribution of the book to different sources, some scholars still maintaining a strict separation between the third-person biographical passages and the so-called prose sermons, others rejecting it. See, inter alia, the recent commentaries by Weippert (1973); Thiel (1973); Carroll (1981).
22. As many scholars suggest, the "enemy from the North" may have long before acquired a stereotypical character. On the passage, see also Harris (1983).
23. Jeremiah's confessions continue to be extensively studied, from the standpoint of their authorship, genre, and relationship to the rest of the book. Generally included in the confessions are Jer. 11:18—12:6; 15:10–21; 17:14–18; 18:18–23; 20:7–13. Their Jeremianic authorship has been maintained by, for example, O'Connor (1988); contrast Pohlmann (1989). See also Diamond (1987) and Smith (1990, esp. 12–14, 24–28) for an analysis of the two passages cited.
24. See Nelson (1983: 177–89).
25. Egypt always had the tactical advantage of the Sinai desert: any invader seeking to cross the desert and enter Egypt would need fresh water for the troops—no minor concern in those days. Moreover, even after managing the crossing, the invader would be running a considerable risk: if he was defeated in battle, his army faced total annihilation, since any tactical retreat was blocked off by the same desert. See Eph'al (1993: 180–83).
26. Published by Wiseman (1956); see also Grayson (1975) and Glassner (2004).
27. Translation from: Glassner (2004: 228–29).
28. Ibid.
29. An alternate theory is that these ostraca were actually drafts of letters to be sent from Lachish to elsewhere—possibly Jerusalem—in which case Yaush would have been the commander there. See Yadin (1984: 179–86).
30. Others have suggested that this letter actually contradicts the biblical account, since the verse cited says that Azekah had not yet fallen, or that the letter originated in a different locale; most likely, however, the letter and the biblical verse represent two different moments in the deteriorating situation. See Begin (2002: 166–74).
31. A synthetic overview of warfare in biblical times: King and Stager (2001: 223–58).
32. Jerusalem's two walls are apparently referred to in Isa. 26:1 and Lam. 2:8; cf. Ps. 48:14.
33. See further: Kugel (1999: 221–32).
34. A description of the site and the bullae: Shiloh and Tarler (1986: 196–209).
35. See Avigad (1986). The text reads: *lbrkyhw bn nryhw hspr* ("To Berekhyahu son of Neriyahu the scribe"); Berekhyahu, a common name in biblical times, might have been a more official form of Baruch's name. The problem, however, is that this bulla was not found in situ and might thus be a forgery (many scholars have so concluded). Incidentally, Avigad questioned Shiloh's identification of the Germaryahu bulla (which *was* found in situ) with the scribe mentioned by Jeremiah since the seal contained no mention of his title (Avigad 1986: 129). This, however, may not be sufficient ground for rejecting the identification.
36. 2 Kings 24:6 implies that Jehoiakim actually died a natural death: "So Jehoiakim slept with his fathers; then his son Jehoiachin succeeded him." That this description is apparently at

odds with Jer. 22:13–10 would seem to argue that this passage was written before Jehoiakim's actual death, since there would be no point in having Jeremiah "predict" after the fact a dishonorable death that did not take place. See Reimer (2004: 217).

37. Note also that its placement makes a significant difference. In the shorter version of the book of Jeremiah found in the Septuagint text (on which see below), this prediction precedes the oracles against foreign nations, including those against Babylon, which do not appear in the traditional Hebrew text until chapters 50–51.

38. Luckernbill (1927, vol. 2: 243). See on this: Holladay (1986, vol. 1: 668–69); note also Zech. 1:12, 2 Chron. 36:21, and Dan. 9:2, 24–27. Professor Israel Eph'al suggested to me orally that this typological number influenced subsequent events, dictating the start of the rebuilding of the Jerusalem temple; see Israel Eph'al (forthcoming).

39. Like so many things, the historicity of this edict has at times been questioned, but a surviving cylinder inscription of Cyrus reports of the cities west of Mesopotamia, "I gathered all their [former] inhabitants and returned [them to] their habitations," Pritchard (1969: 316). See on this I. Eph'al (1984) and Berquist (1995: 24–26).

40. This passage, taken from the section of Jeremiah known as the "Book of Consolation" (chapters 30–33), touches on a theme witnessed elsewhere as well in this section, the idea that Israel, Judah's erstwhile northern neighbor, will also be restored to its ancient homeland. (Thus, "when I will make a new covenant with the *house of Israel* and the house of Judah . . .") Of course, Israel's restoration never took place. An earlier generation of scholars held that such references tell us nothing about when the passage was composed. After all, even Ben Sira in the second century BCE still hoped for Israel's restoration: Elijah, he wrote, waits in heaven for the time "to calm the divine wrath before it bursts forth, to turn the hearts of the fathers to the children, and to *restore the tribes of Jacob*" (Sir. 48:10; fragmentary Hebrew text of MS.B completed on the basis of the Greek). Many scholars have, accordingly, dated this passage (or at least the "new covenant" part) to a period somewhat later that of the historical Jeremiah; see, for example, Levin (1985). Still, of late some researchers have maintained that the fact that this is another unfulfilled prophecy suggests that it may indeed go back to Jeremiah's own time. W. Rudolph (1968: 189) actually dated this passage to the period preceding Josiah's death. Marvin Sweeney (1996: 569–83) similarly finds some references to Israel's eventual restoration reflective of Josiah's program, hence early, although the above-cited passage has, according to his analysis, redactional formulae indicating that it is later than the passages that immediately precede and follow it.

41. The "newness" question has been much debated: Swetnam (1974); Potter (1983: 347–57).

42. Tov (1972: 189–99 and 1984: 211–37) pioneered the thesis that the shorter version of the book of Jeremiah in the Old Greek translation preserves an earlier form of the text than that of the traditional Hebrew text.

43. On this subject see the recent dissertation of Hillel Newman (1997).

44. See J. R. Lundbom, s.v. "Jeremiah, book of," in Freedman (1992).

45. On this idea and its relation to "strict verbal inspiration," Gnuse (1985: 24).

32. Ezekiel

1. The term appears some 93 times in Ezekiel and nowhere else in the Hebrew Bible except for Dan. 8:17. The New Testament usage seems to be a modest form of self-reference.

2. See the various treatments of Gershom Scholem (1960: 42–67 and 1990: 20–21).

3. See Mishnah *Hagigah* 2:1, Tosefta *Hagigah* 2:1, Bab. *Hagigah* 13a; on the age limits imposed, see Scholem (1960: 42 and 1965: 36–42).

4. See Elbogen (1972: 49).

5. Alternately, the vague reference "from its/His place" might be taken as implying that the exact place is unknown. In one form or another, this reading seems to underlie b. *Hagigah* 13b, where this verse is adduced to support the contention that "there is no one who knows it," that is, the place of God's glory. It is even grammatically possible that the verse was read as a comparative: "More blessed is His glory than its source," that is, do not concern yourselves with the place of the glory's emanation. Indeed, understanding the verse in this comparative sense might illuminate the targum's rendering, *m'tr byt škntyh*. This phrase

might be taken as a reference to the temple, making the meaning of the two-verse sequence: God's glory is everywhere (Isa. 6:3), indeed, His glory is more blessed than the [now destroyed] place of His dwelling (Ezek. 3:12).

6. Horowitz (2005).

7. This was first noted independently by two scholars, F. Hitzig in 1874 and S. D. Luzzatto in 1876. See Greenberg (1983: 70); cf. Ezek. 10:7.

8. See on this: Zimmerli (1979, vol. 1: 106); Greenberg (1983: 39–125, esp. 94). Uffenheimer (1995: 32). Odell (1998: 229–48) offers a somewhat different interpretation: He suggests that the eating is a kind of ordeal of prophetic initiation, whereby the prophet takes on (by internalizing, eating) the fate of his people.

9. On this, see Milgrom (1971): sin is a "miasma" that gathers in the sanctuary and must be purged; also, Schwartz (1995: 3–21).

10. Schwartz (1995: 4–5). Much has been written of late about the apparent distinction between ritual and moral impurity, starting with the study of Klawans (2000). My own feeling is that this distinction was not as sharp as Klawans and others have maintained, but in the present context, the precise degree of distinctness is immaterial: the main point is the fundamental analogy between the two in the priestly world.

11. The similar messages of Jer. 31:29–30 and Ezekiel 18 have been studied by numerous scholars. Particularly suggestive is the recent discussion by Kaminsky (1995: 139–78), which also surveys previous scholarship (155, n. 40). Kaminsky, who holds that Ezekiel 18 probably preceded the Jeremiah passage (159), sees the Ezekiel material in explicit dialogue with Deut. 24:16 ("Let not fathers be put to death for the children, and the children not for their fathers, but let each person be executed [only] for his own sin"): "Ezekiel creates a hypothetical drama to explore the theology found in the first two clauses of Deut. 24:16 . . . by constructing a tri-generational scheme with a wicked middle generation. Although he speaks about the first generation, his interest is not at all focused on the question of a vertical transference of sin from the wicked middle generation back to the father. In fact, nowhere in the Hebrew Bible is there an instance in which guilt works backward" (164–65). As for the apparently individual language of verses 1–20, Kaminsky suggests that this too may be a reflection of the precise formulation of the Deuteronomy passage; in Ezekiel 18, "the focus all along is on generations of people, not on individuals." It thus has little to do with the "emergence of the concept of the individual" or other such themes often associated with it. Instead, its message is a rejection of "the notion of trans-generational retribution when the current generation is innocent: it abolishes the idea that a generation could live off its previous merits, or is completely doomed because of its earlier misdeeds" (177).

12. In a sense, Ezekiel's vision of the dry bones plays on one of the most ancient observations— and hopes—of humanity. Human beings, everyone knew, arc formed in their mothers' wombs, but exactly how they come alive was something of a mystery: "Just as you do not know how the spirit gets into the bones inside a pregnant woman's belly," says Koheleth. "so you do not understand [any of] God's deeds, the creator of all" (Eccles. 11:5). Still more mysterious was the end of life. People stop breathing—the spirit departs—and soon all their flesh rots and melts away. But the bones stay on. Why would God have arranged things like that, instead of having the last traces of each person disappear? From very ancient times, people came to believe that the physical survival of bones might betoken some future purpose or use: presumably that is one reason why people treated the bones of their long-departed relatives with such care. On other aspects of this matter: Kugel (2003: 169–79) and the sources cited there (pp. 247–53).

13. Ibid. See also Greenspoon in Halpern and Levenson (1981: 247–321).

14. All of the texts cited are being presented as examples of the Bible's support of martyrdom and the related belief in resurrection. Thus, Abel was a martyr killed by his wicked brother (yet even after his death, his blood could still "cry out" from the ground): on the death and resurrection of Isaac, see Spiegel (1979: 28–37); Joseph's going down into the pit (of prison) could be taken as a figure of death, followed by his resurrection; Isaiah's verse is being interpreted as a reference to human survival through the "flame" of death; the continuation of the psalmist's verse (Ps 34:20) is "and the LORD will save him from all of them," presumably after death; Solomon's "tree of life" is the Torah (so called, apparently, because

through it one gains eternal life); Moses' citation of God's words "I kill and bring to life" [Deut. 32:39] seemed to imply, by reversing the natural order, that God brings people to life *after* their death; while the phrase "life and length of days" (Deut. 30:20), if not pleonastic, must refer to two things, life on earth and length of days in the world to come.

15. See three excellent commentaries: Zimmerli (1979: 3–9); also Greenberg (1983): and in Hebrew, Kasher (2004).
16. On this whole phenomenon: Fishbane (1985), esp 458–99.

33. Twelve Minor Prophets

1. See above, chapter 20, n. 1.
2. About this the Mishnah notes: "She uncovered herself for purposes of sinning, God uncovered her [as a fitting punishment]" (m. Sotah 1:7).
3. See the discussion in Wolff (1974: xxi–xxix). Interestingly, Wolff's analysis of the book of Amos (1977) still seeks to separate a basic "core" (attributable to the prophet himself) from a wealth of later accretions, whereas the more recent commentary of Paul (1991) holds that the great bulk of the book can be traced back to the prophet's own speech.
4. Because of the unusual order, "I kill and [then] bring to life" seemed to imply resurrection: the rest of Balaam's verse is "Let my soul die the death of the righteous and let my *aḥarit* be like him," where *aḥarit* is being understood not as "progeny" (which is certainly what it means here) but "afterlife"; when Moses uttered "Let Reuben live," the individual named Reuben had been long dead.
5. *De Doctrina Christiana.* 4:7.15–16.
6. On Israelite society at the time, as reflected in archaeological evidence: Barkay (1992: 302–73); also Dever (1995: 416–31). Particularly eloquent is the cache of elaborate ivory carvings and what they say about social stratification; see Dever, loc. cit. Some have nevertheless expressed skepticism about using Amos's words as any indication of the true state of northern society: see Grabbe (1995: 103).
7. Terrien (1962: 108–15); Wolff (1973); Crenshaw (1967: 42–53); Soggin (1994: 119–23). See also: Dell (1997: 135–51).
8. Gottwald (1964: 49); cited in Christensen (1975: 5–6).
9. The former, presently the common understanding, goes back to rabbinic sources (on which Jerome apparently drew in his commentaries, but not in the Vulgate, which translated this word as "ivy" [*hedera*]). The Septuagint rendered the word as *kolokunthē* ("gourd"), an understanding reflected in other translations. Aquila, Theodotion, and Targum Pseudo-Jonathan give up and simply transliterate. See Zohari (1976: 176).
10. Weitzman (1997).
11. Wisd. 7:27; Philo, *Quis Haeris*, 259; 1 Cor. 12:7–10, 14:4–5; Josephus, *Jewish Antiquiries* 13:311–13, 20:97, 169, etc. Also: Blenkinsopp (1974: 239–63); Aune (1983); Horsely (1985: 135–63); Feldman (1990: 402–11).
12. Van Rooy (1994: 163–79).
13. Begg (1988: 100–107).
14. Blenkinsopp (1983: 255). This tradition, as Blenkinsopp notes, may be reflected in Josephus' famous characterization of Israel's historians as being exclusively prophets in *Against Apion* 1:37.
15. Van Rooy (1994: 175).
16. Van Rooy (1994).
17. On this: Urbach (1946: 1–27); Vermes (1973: 69–82); Greenspahn (1989: 37–49); Milikowsky (1994: 83–94).
18. Exod. 4:15; Num. 23:5, 16, etc.
19. See on this Davis (1989). Note also Kugel and Greer (1986: 19).

34. Job and Postexilic Wisdom

1. See in general the recent survey by Dell (2004: 251–71). Note also Whybray (1982: 181–99).

2. See above, chapter 33, note 6.
3. Macintosh (1994: 124–32).
4. McKane (1965); Whedbee (1971); Fichtner (1976: 429–38)
5. Perdue (1977).
6. Kugel (1987: 43–61, esp. 43–47 and n. 10).
7. Weinfeld (1972).
8. Gese (1984: 190–99).
9. Kugel (1999: 123–24).
10. But the matter was far from clear, see m. Sota. 5:5, b. *Baba Batra* 15b. On this: Glatzer (1966: 197–220).
11. As Glatzer (1996) points out, this line really begins with the apocryphal *Testament of Job* (first century BCE?), wherein Job/Jobab, king of Edom, incurs Satan's wrath by destroying a precious idol people are worshiping. He is thus saintly from the start, and his sufferings derive not from any satanic challenge to God, but as Satan's revenge for his anti-idolatry campaign.
12. In McHugh (1972: 374).
13. Lewalski (1966).

35. Daniel the Interpreter

1. The actual geographic dimensions of this province are nowhere delineated, and the population figures given for it in the Bible are somewhat at odds with the archeological evidence; see Carter (1994: 106–45). Carter estimates the population at approximately 11,000 in the late sixth and early fifth centuries, moving to a high of 17,000 in the late fifth and early fourth centuries. This is far lower than the biblical traditions of Ezra 2 and Nehemiah 7, both of which record approximately 42,000 exiles leaving Babylon for Yehud.
2. On the historical background of Cyrus' decree and the subsequent waves of emigration, see Berquist (1995: esp. 24–29).
3. On this translation: Kugel (1989: 38).
4. Japhet (1982: 89–105 and 1989: 395–504).
5. The chronological difficulties within Ezra-Nehemiah as well as between these books and extra-biblical sources are notorious. With regard to Ezra himself, he is said to come to Jerusalem "in the seventh year of Artaxerxes" (Ezra 7:1–7), while Nehemiah is said to have arrived in the twentieth years of Artaxerxes (Neh. 2:1), putting the Nehemiah's arrival *after* that of Ezra. There were, however, three Persian kings named Artaxerxes: Artaxerxes I (465–424 BCE), Artaxerxes 11 (405/404–359/358 BCE), and Artaxerxes III (359/8–338 BCE), and, while Nehemiah's connection with Artaxerxes I seems certain, it may be that Ezra's arrival is to be dated in the period of Ataxerxes II. On this: Williamson (1985). Note also Japhet (1994: 189–216).
6. An equally interesting phenomenon is that this collection of Scriptural allusions is actually a prayer, since prayers now regularly involve elements from Scripture. See Newman (1999), esp. 65–95; also Kugel (ed.), (2006a).
7. Kugel (1998: 634–36).
8. Chapters 1–6 are written in the third person, whereas 7–12 are in the first person; while the foreign court is a potentially dangerous place in 1–6, a wise courtier can make out well there; in 7–12, by contrast, foreign rule is hostile, even demonic. Many scholars have discussed these differences; see Collins (1993); Wills (1990).
9. Many scholars have observed that the Four Kingdoms motif was apparently borrowed from earlier models. The sequence of four metals appears earlier in Hesiod (ca. 700 BCE) as well as in a late Persian text, the Bahman Yasht. The latter may be based on much earlier tradition and hence indirectly related to Daniel; see Collins (1993: 30). Note also Hadas-Lebel (1986: 297–312); Flusser (1988: 317–44); Lucas (1988: 185–202).
10. Of course there was no Darius the Mede; Darius (ruled from 522–486 BCE) was a Persian: see on this Berquist (1995; 51–53). This is one of many indications that the courtier tales are not contemporaneous with the events described.
11. It was to explain this odd situation that the author of *Jubilees*—a contemporary of the

author/redactor of Daniel—wrote chapter 23 of his book. See Kugel (1994: 322–37).

12. Again, the scholarly literature on the affinities of apocalyptic is quite extensive. Two classical studies: Hanson (1975) and Collins (1984). Note also: Peterson (1977: 1–54); Gruenwald (1979: 89–118); Knibb (1982: 155–80).

13. Note in this connection von Rad (1972: 263–83).

14. On this: Finkel (1963/64: 357–70).

15. Studied in detail by Japhet (1989).

16. See on this: Hartmann and Di Lella (1978); Collins (1995: 352–55).

17. The specific historical event being alluded to here is described by Josephus (*Jewish Antiquities* 13:372–83; *Jewish War* 1:90–98). He reports that, during the reign of Alexander Yannai, the Jewish king who ruled in Judah 103–76 BCE, a civil war broke out that pitted Alexander against a rebel faction supported by the Pharisees. This war continued from 93 to 88 BCE. Then, in the year 88, the desperate rebels appealed to the Syrian king Demetrius for help, and he responded by invading and defeating the forces of Alexander Yannai at Shechem. However, Demetrius and his army did not go on to enter Jerusalem—apparently his Jewish allies went over to the other side to prevent him from doing so, and he went back to Syria. The civil war was not over, however; Alexander continued to battle the rebels and, in the end, killed a great many of them. In fact, some eight hundred Jews who had been taken prisoner, Josephus says, were subsequently crucified by the cruel king.

18. See Kugel (1998: 366–67).

19. Particularly important has been the work of two scholars who have worked extensively on the subject, L. Schiffman and J. Baumgarten. On the general neglect of the subject early on: Schiffman (1994).

36. After Such Knowledge

1. Considered at a distance, Briggs's view of the Bible sounds somewhat similar to the sixteenth-century Reformers' view of Christianity—first there was something pristine, then it became corrupted, now we have to go about restoring it. Beyond this rather obvious point, however, lies a somewhat subtler one. The whole attempt to free the Bible of its traditional interpretations also carries with it the privileging of the *unmediated encounter* which is also prominent in early Protestant thought. That is to say, between God and the individual human will stand no intercessory saints, no pardoners or confession-hearing clergy—in the view of some, no other person whatsoever. Similarly, between God's word and the individual human reader will stand no authorized interpreter or church official, not even the most hallowed exegetical tradition from the past, since nothing should be allowed to intercede in the flush encounter between the book and the reader. As Luther was cited earlier (chapter 1), "Scripture is to be interpreted only by the Spirit through which Scripture was written, because the Spirit is never to be found more present and lively than in the sacred writings themselves." Of course, such a stance was in danger of leading to the chaos Dryden described, "The spirit gave the doctoral degree" and so forth (also chapter 1); soon, this unmediated encounter had to be tempered. Nor, more broadly, do I wish to imply that Reformation thought alone was responsible for the making of modern biblical scholarship—the Enlightenment was certainly not a Protestant plot, nor was the scientific revolution. Still, it seems to me that both of these connections between Protestantism and modern scholarship were not a negligible factor in the latter's unfolding: certainly no one would deny that specifically Protestant theological faculties and other institutions were the ones that fostered the rise of modern biblical scholarship and that have been, right up to the present, its principal sponsors (while Catholic and Jewish institutions have been, until recently, indifferent or openly hostile to it). Was it not because, until recently, there was every reason to hope that, with Scripture as earlier with Christianity itself, sweeping away the accumulated corruption of centuries and eliminating the popish intermediaries would indeed yield something purer and truer, "the real Bible"?

2. Above, chapter 1.

3. Ibid.

4. Herder (1877–1913, vol. 10: p. 7); see on this passage Frei (1974: 184).

5. Indeed, Augustine himself went further: "Whatever in the [biblical] text has nothing to do with right conduct or questions of faith . . . must be understood figuratively," *De Doctrina Christiana* 3.10; 14. See Marrou (1938: 478). This is an extension of the earlier doctrine, "Whatever *contradicts* right conduct . . ."

6. See on this Appendix 1, "Apologetics and Biblical Scholarship Lite."

7. Geneva Bible (1560): iiii.

8. On the change in the way in which Scripture came to be perceived there is an extensive literature, part of it seeking to document that change through what is called "inner-biblical exegesis" (later parts of the Bible that interpret earlier parts). Much of this work has centered on the book of Chronicles; see, inter alia: Willi (1972); Seligmann (1979–80: 14–32); Japhet (1989); Williamson (1982). In addition, a considerable body of research has emerged on the subject of legal reinterpretation within the Bible; see Levinson (1988), whose central claim is that Deuteronomy "represents a radical revision of the Covenant Code." On the editing and reshaping of prophetic collections see below, and on the change in the entire perception of prophecy see in particular Barton (1986). Y. Zakovitch (1993) has published a great number of studies (mostly in modern Hebrew) of inner-biblical exegesis, particularly in biblical narrative. A much-cited work on the entire phenomenon of inner-biblical interpretation is Fishbane (1985). (I expressed my admiration for, but also some misgivings about this book in a review [1987]). More generally, however, a difficult matter, but an important one for our discussion, is the extent to which the recasting or reinterpretation of earlier material in the later parts of the Bible can be informative about a change in *attitude* about the biblical texts. To put it another way, "inner-biblical exegesis" ought not to be automatically equated with the appearance of a new set of conventions about *how* to read Scripture, nor is it, often, *exegesis* at all. If the laws of Deuteronomy recast those of the Covenant Code, for example, this may tell us that the Covenant Code was perceived as an authoritative document at the time, so that its laws could not simply be abrogated; as Levinson puts it, Deuteronomy represents "the deliberate attempt to rework prestigious texts in light of the innovation of centralization [of worship at a single sanctuary]" (p. 6). But this does not derive from a *change in attitude* about how to read Scripture, nor even from a new *understanding* of what the Covenant Code means. It derives instead from the desire to create a fundamentally new set of laws (centralization of worship was only one issue) while seeking wherever possible to respect the "prestigious" text of the Covenant Code and so act as if the Deuteronomy laws were really not innovations (or at least not significantly different). Similarly, the Chronicler's recasting of material from Samuel and Kings reflects (as Japhet and others have shown) the definite theological and political program of the Chronicler; it does not, however, *necessarily* reflect a change in the way Scripture (that is, Samuel and Kings) was approached or understood at the time. Such a change is indeed reflected here and there in the Bible (including in the books of Chronicles), but these cases are relatively minor and often ambiguous. The great change in attitude is witnessed extensively only outside of the Bible, in Jewish writings from the third century BCE on.

9. This would seem to indicate that the Psalm heading *le-dawid* was an attribution of authorship; see above, chapter 26.

10. The omission of the Bathsheba incident and, more generally, the pervasive idealization of David might (but only might) indicate the belief that the history of David's life should embody moral lessons for the reader thereof; on the other hand, it might simply be propaganda for the reestablishment of the Davidic monarchy.

11. On this phenomenon in general, Kugel (1998). As noted above, this assumption is occasionally witnessed within the canon of the Hebrew Bible: on Daniel, see chapter 35.

12. The case of the Nahum Pesher has been extensively studied; see the recent edition, commentary, and bibliography by Doudna (2001).

13. See chapter 34.

14. See on "And thus it shall not be done" in chapter 11, "God Was in Favor."

15. As an aside, it might be worthwhile to summarize here what this great body of interpretations ultimately led to. What did the Interpreted Bible of Judaism and Christianity consist of—from the first century CE to, almost, the twentieth?

    To put it in a phrase, the Hebrew Bible was the great and infinitely subtle story of God's ways with Israel and all of humanity, which brought with it His detailed instructions for everyone to follow. This story began in the Garden of Eden, with the Fall of Man and the loss of immortality. From there, humankind began its steady decline, with the diabolical Cain, the world's first murderer, and his offspring leading inevitably to the great Flood, whose proximate cause was, however, the mating of lustful angels with earthly women and the generation of divine-human hybrids thus produced. Noah, preacher of righteousness, survived the Flood, and from his descendants at last arose Abraham, the iconoclast astronomer from Ur. God loved Abraham for his rejection of idolatry and his belief in the one, true God—a devotion that was rewarded with the grant of the land of Canaan to him and his children. Though sorely tried by life, Abraham never lost his faith, and he in turn was blessed with virtuous offspring—Isaac, a volunteer for martyrdom, and Jacob, a model of scholarly virtue who overcame his wicked brother. From this man and his equally virtuous wives would spring the people of Israel. Cast into slavery and subjection in Egypt, the Israelites were freed by the efforts of the world's greatest prophet, Moses, a Godlike man who led them to Mount Sinai to receive God's laws. God spoke the first two of His commandments directly to the people; then Moses ascended into heaven on the mountain's peak to receive the rest, which he duly delivered to his countrymen. Ever afterwards, these laws—supplemented by the additional information passed on to the prophet—have guided Israel on the proper path.

Arrived at the edge of the Promised Land, Moses passed the leadership to his protégé, Joshua, who led the people into battle with the Canaanites, ultimately securing the entire territory for God's chosen people. Things were not always smooth, but eventually David was selected as king and founder of the royal dynasty. A sweet psalmist and prophet-king, David was also a valiant warrior who overcame Israel's enemies and brought peace and prosperity to the land. His son Solomon became, thanks to his pious prayer, the wisest of men and the author of three great books of wisdom: Proverbs, Ecclesiastes, and the Song of Songs. When the northern tribes split off and rejected the Davidic line, they survived for a time, thanks to the ministrations of the immortal Elijah (Phinehas *redivivus*) and his successor, Elisha. But ultimately the sin of Jeroboam was punished with conquest and exile, and all that remained was the Kingdom of Judah. The prophet Isaiah was sent to guide them during this difficult time; he ascended to the heavenly sanctuary and heard the exquisite harmony of the seraphim singing "Holy, holy, holy." Back on earth, he tried to guide Judah's kings along the proper path; he was followed by other prophets, notably Jeremiah, but human weakness eventually overcame the best of divine guidance. Despite Jeremiah's warnings, the people continued to sin and were punished for their apostasy—Jeremiah himself composed five mournful lamentations for the fallen city before his own death. Seventy years later, God punished the Babylonians for their conquest of Jerusalem, and Israel joyfully returned to its homeland, just as Isaiah and David had foreseen centuries earlier. Reestablished in Judah, they fervently observed God's laws and waited for the fulfillment of biblical prophecy and the arrival of the Messiah.

This overview—which has given no more than the broadest glimpse of the Interpreted Bible—may serve to illustrate some of the great gap that separates the Bible as it existed for twenty centuries from the Bible as it looks to scholars nowadays. But it fails, I am afraid, to capture much of the *flavor* that the Bible had for different religious communities over all those years. What is missing, for Christians, is the basic secret of the Old Testament—its hidden lessons and its teachings about the path to salvation—and in particular all its detailed allusions to the founding events and doctrines of Christianity: the "first Adam" whose fall was healed by the crucifixion and resurrection of the second Adam; the three-personed God who visited Abraham's tent and shared in the Eucharist there with him; the aged Jacob, who foretold the Messiah's triumph; the Old Testament Jesus (that is, Joshua) who defeated the devil while his teacher and predecessor, Moses, stood on the sidelines and made the sign of the cross; the prophet Isaiah, who heard the Trinity preached by the seraphim in God's heavenly temple; and so on and so forth, including Abel and Isaac and Jacob and Moses and Joshua and all the other foreshadowings of Christ. For Jews what is missing is the whole, detailed exegetical process (whose retracing was and is itself the stuff of Jewish study and piety) and its results: the great body of midrash that offered detailed insights into biblical figures and their stories—pointing up crucial aspects only hinted at in the Bible's own words—as well, of course, as the exposition of the 613 commandments which were at the very heart of the Torah, from the laws of reading the Shema morning and night to the detailed instructions concerning the keeping of the sabbath and laws of repentance and cooking on festivals and what to do with lost objects found in the street, along with the blessings recited before and after the meal and the rules of kosher food and getting rid of leaven on Passover and on and on, a whole, detailed way of life rooted in the subtlest hints and turns of phrase found in Scripture.

This was the Bible for twenty centuries. In hundreds of ways, little and great, its original meaning was transformed by ancient interpreters. It became a different book. Then, along came modern scholarship with its own (I say this with no intended irony) altogether laudable agenda: to get rid of stale doctrines that strained credibility, to throw out the traditional ways of interpreting and all the specific interpretations that went with them, getting down to the "real Bible." This was hardly an evil program—on the contrary! But where it would lead was not visible at first; its results have worked themselves out slowly, and it is really only now that they have come into focus. Gradually, the Bible has ceased—at least for those who know modern scholarship and reckon honestly with its findings—to be the great divine guidebook it once was. Instead, it has come to look more and more like any other human work, indeed, another piece of ancient Near Eastern literature, or rather, a hundred pieces often quite unrelated to each other. In place of the seamless and perfect, often cryptic word of God, scholars have shown the Bible to be the sometimes seamy and all-too-imperfect, usually obvious words of men from different periods and social strata and ideological affiliations.

16. Again, see on all these Barton (1986).
17. See the nuanced discussion of the relation between apocalyptic and such verses in Barton (1986: 202–10).
18. To this might be added the many contradictory statements in Ecclesiastes, on which Kugel (1999: 305–23).
19. For a longer account, see Kugel (2001: 1–26).
20. But if a text's meaning change, can it change only once? The very point I am making, it seems, can now be turned against me. "True, that *was* the Bible, but it no longer is. Now that we know everything that modern scholars have discovered, the text has changed again, whether you like it or not. It's gone back to what it originally meant." Indeed. To this observation, however, should be added another: in historical terms, this Bible of modern scholarship is not so much the Bible as the pre-Bible, the material out of which the first Bible was fashioned. So if indeed the Bible has changed again, it has actually turned into something that never was the Bible. People nowadays may still call this book the Bible, and they may, by various apologetic strategies, still try to have it play the role it always used to play; things change slowly, after all, especially things connected with religion. But as the lessons of modern biblical scholarship sink in and become more widely known, people will, I think, inevitably find it more and more difficult to talk and think about the Bible as they have in the past.
21. Of the many treatments of this subject, I have in mind here James Barr's *Fundamentalism* (1977), to which these brief observations are intended as a supplement of somewhat different orientation.
22. In fact, even before *The Fundamentals* were issued, a group of conservative biblical scholars had gathered at Niagara-on-the-Lake. Ontario, starting in 1883, and ended up hammering out a statement of basic principles similar to *The Fundamentals*. The very first article the *Niagara Bible Conference Creed* asserted: "We believe 'that all Scripture is given by inspiration of God' [2 Tim. 3:16], by which we understand the whole of the book called the Bible; nor do we take the statement in the sense in which it is sometimes foolishly said that works of human genius are inspired, but in the sense that the Holy Ghost gave the very words of the sacred writings to holy men of old; and that His Divine inspiration is not in different degrees, but extends equally and fully to all parts of these writings, historical, poetical, doctrinal, and prophetical and to the smallest word, and inflection of a word, provided such word is found in the original manuscripts."

For liberals, statements like this one and, more generally, the conservative refusal to countenance everything modern scholars have discovered about the Bible seem, at bottom, profoundly anti-intellectual. *Blind faith* is not a happy posture for anyone who believes in the human capacity to figure things out. For that reason, liberals have been eager to redefine the inspiration of Scripture and the extent and basis of its authority in such a way as to accommodate everything scholars have discovered about the origin and development of biblical texts. (The issues are laid out clearly in Achtemeier, 1999.) Often, of course, such accommodation leads to the "Yes, but still . . ." sort of biblical commentaries, on which see Appendix 1, "Apologetics and Biblical Criticism Lite" on the Web site: jameskugel.com.

23. See, recently: Enns (2005).

24. On this: Enns (2005: 132–63). One example of the transmission of midrashic traditions in New Testament texts is Stephen's speech in Acts 7; see Kugel (2004: 206–18).

25. The early stages of this retreat are charted in Frei (1974).

26. The roots of what was to become a major theme in twentieth-century Protestant neo-orthodoxy, the Bible as *Heilsgeschichte* or a "history of salvation," can be traced back to the seventeenth century; again, see Frei (1974: 46–47, 173–82). In its later manifestation, however, it has introduced a fundamental theological contradiction: see Langdon Gilkey's essay on the theological assumptions of G. Ernest Wright and other exponents of the "mighty acts of God": Gilkey (1961: 194–205), and chapter 14, note 9. See also Gnuse (1989 and 1994: 893–918).

27. Brown (1955 and 1981).

28. The notion of such a "center" (*Mitte*) was made explicit in W. Eichrodt's promotion of covenant as the central concept of the Old Testament, but its roots are deeper, identifiable even in Spinoza's assertion that it was only the items of which all biblical books agree, such as monotheism or ideas about governance, that had prescriptive value today. See Hasel (1972: 77–103). About this assumption Gerhard von Rad wrote: "What's it all about with this almost *unisono*-asked question about the 'unity,' the 'center' of the Old Testament? Is it something so self-evident [that] its proof belongs, so to speak, as a *conditio sine qua non* to an orderly Old Testament theology?" (cited in Collins (2005: 135)]. The answer is that it is all about getting the Bible to continue having some theologically valid teachings to offer despite its many now-unacceptable particulars.

29. Monotheism as part of Scripture's central messager (previous note) was stressed in Spinoza's *Tracratus* (along with the Bible's teachings on government); the theme of Israel's rigorous monotheism was taken up again by the Israeli theologian Yehezkel Kaufman—not particularly convincingly, as it turned out.

30. See in greater detail Appendix 1 to this volume, located on the Web site: jameskugel.com.

31. See Appendix 1.

32. See the useful short survey by Gnuse (1985: 14–65). Among other treatments: Achtemeier (1999: 28–63). For a thoughtful evangelical perspective on the question of inspiration: Enns (2005).

33. Childs (1970).

34. Morgan (1988: 44–61); cited in Collins (2005: 6).

35. Suspending, for the sake of argument, the text-critical question of *which* final form is intended.

36. "This is the chief practical danger that the rise of canonical criticism has brought about: it has been quick to produce a strong zealotic legalism of the final text, that insists; you *must must must* work from the final form of the text. I think this is completely wrong, and that the preacher is perfectly free to work with a portion representing an earlier stage of the text. He is free to expound the creation story of Genesis 1 without tying it by links of meaning to the quite different story of chapter 2; he is free to expound the pericopes that represent Amos's original message without being forced to integrate them with the quite different message of the book's conclusion . . . This is not because what is early and original is authentic and therefore authoritative. What is earlier *was* the text at one time, it was thus 'canonical,' if we must call it so, in the biblical period itself" [Barr (1983: 92–3)]. But *was* it canonical, and what exactly, in that case, does *canonical* mean? There is no indication that Genesis 1 *ever* existed apart from Genesis 2, but even if Barr were to reverse the example and assert that Genesis 2 was 'canonical' before Genesis 1 was appended to it, he would be on very

shaky grounds. Perhaps the story of Ådam and Eve was preserved for centuries only because it was an entertaining folktale, like *Goldilocks and the Three Bears*. It may have begun to be read *as Scripture* only after it had been included in the book of Genesis, indeed, only after the book of Genesis and the rest of the Bible had begun to be read in accordance with the Four Assumptions of ancient interpreters. The position that Barr is arguing against (that of Brevard Childs) is thus quite correct, even if (as I shall argue presently) Childs does not go far enough: Barr's belief that there was something "canonical" about anything before the final form lacks any supporting evidence other than the somewhat ambiguous fact that the ancient texts themselves survived. They *were* preserved, but by whom, and for what purpose, and *how* they were read are all a matter of speculation. (I find odd, to say the least, Barr's use of the phrase "strong zealotic legalism" in the above-cited passage, and odder still the fact that it was actually cited with favor by Nicholson [1998: 267]. What exactly is it supposed to suggest?)

37. This is the position of De Vries (1995). De Vries criticizes Childs, Sanders, and others precisely for favoring the final form of the text, which he actually sees as a degenerate stage, the moment when, at last, prophecy had ceased to be an active force in Israel. "Among contemporary scholars, Brevard S. Childs has been the most effective champion of the view that the ultimate 'canonical' message of a particular biblical book might possess greater importance than the ideas coming to expression at individual stages in the growth of the book," De Vries writes; but he himself rejects this position: "To be sure, canonization might have been inevitable in the sense that what is dynamically expanding [that is, biblical prophecy] will, in the end, need to be closed off, once the forces empowering it have faded away." And why did prophecy "fade away"? Because "it had become more a threat than a help to the increasingly institutionalized, that is, nomistic, community." He adds: "To equate inner-scriptural and extra-scriptural development confuses a process of unrestrained creativity with a subsequent process of institutionally bound rationalizing," the latter certainly including the exegetical traditions that accompanied Scripture at the moment of its canonization and thereafter. (All De Vries quotes are from 1995: 266–67). Actually, most of this argument had been refuted before it was made, principally by the Dead Sea Scrolls and other Second Temple texts, which well illustrate that creative exegesis was not a *post*-biblical phenomenon but was already in full flower by the third century BCE; indeed, its beginnings go back at least to the start of the post-exilic period, if not earlier (Fishbane. 1985). Moreover, as many scholars have argued, it was the dynamism of post-exilic exegesis, and not any petering out of prophecy itself, that allowed the former to displace the latter in that period. Far from being institutionally bound, nomistic, or any of the other things that De Vries calls it, biblical exegesis became, in the closing centuries before the common era, a force infinitely more daring and dynamic than anything the glossators, scribal annotators, and chapter-rearrangers he champions could have dreamt of. A far more level-headed view of the ancient interpreters' role in canonization and thereafter is that of John Barton (1986).

38. The leading exponent of this school (though he does not particularly identify with its name or some of the claims made for it) has been Brevard Childs of Yale. It is no pleasure for me to have to disagree on this point with Childs, whose analysis of the theological problems posed by the attempted synthesis of modern scholarship and theological concerns was set out systematically in his landmark study, Childs (1970). The application of a new way of talking about biblical texts was exposed a few years later in his commentary Exodus (1974), and then in a major synthetic work, his *Introduction to the Old Testament as Scripture* (1979). His views have often been attacked and sometimes distorted by various writers, including some of those cited in this chapter. A somewhat dissenting but more balanced account is to be found in Barton (1984: 77–103, 208–11 and *passim*).

39. These were at first known by various names: the "sages" or "bookmen" [*soferim*], the "Pharisees," but then, starting in the first century CE, the "rabbis." On these names and the beginnings of these traditions: Urbach (1984: 7–10, 35–45).

40. On the various ways that authority was claimed by different groups in this period: Najman (2003).

41. For the forerunners of this stance, Najman (2003: 108–37). This position was not without its problems; see below, note 50.

42. "It happened that some stood before Shammai and said to him: 'Rabbi, how many *torahs* do you have?' He said: 'Two, one that is written and one that is oral'" (*Abut deR. Natan* [A] 15). On this theme Kugel (1998: 657–60, 700–701).

43. See van der Toorn (1997: 229–48).

44. It is of course true that the rabbinic corpus of interpretation was not the end of Jewish biblical interpretation; one might point to the rise of *peshat* exegesis in the Middle Ages, or, for that matter, the emergence of Kabbalistic and philosophical exegesis in this same period. But these and similar instances actually support rather than undermine my generalization, since what is remarkable about all these later forms of interpretation is the extent to which they adhere to the Four Assumptions and extend their basic approach. Several scholars have thus aptly criticized the contention of Nahum Sarna that Abraham ibn Ezra and some of those who followed him were modern biblical scholars in medieval dress. See: Levenson (1993: 62–81 and passim); also, Simon (1985: 257–71); M. Haran (1985); Hoffman (1997). On the contrary, the noteworthy thing in these medieval commentators is not the "modern" insight they occasionally present, "but the way in which that dangerous foreign body was then instantly sealed off by the commentator's own efficient immune system," Kugel (1990b: 151). The deference of ibn Ezra, Rashbam, and others to the Oral Law in matters of *halakhah* is well known. Noteworthy as well is their deference to the *textus receptus*, including vocalization and accents. Even a commentator who saw himself as offering a radically different reading of the text—such as Yosef ibn 'Aqnin in his commentary on the Song of Songs, which, he claims to have discovered, is really about the union of the human soul with the Active Intellect (see Halkin 1964)—was consistently deferential to the established tradition of interpretation, in this case, the *targum* of Song of Songs, which explains the song as an allegory of God and Israel in various periods of history.

45. Numerous writers in the past have considered this question. For Orthodox Judaism, see the survey by Rosenberg (1979). Among contemporary scholars, note in particular Lamm (1971), the writings in Hebrew by Breuer (esp. 1999), as well as the thoughtful essays in Jon Levenson (1993). The other articles in the Simon volume are likewise of interest in this connection, as are those in a more recent collection, Carmy (1996), especially the contributions of B. Eichler and S. Z. Leiman (181–87).

46. Scholars are uncertain as to what that intention was. The song goes back to nineteenth century Appalachia, and was later popular among work gangs building the railroad network in the American midwest. Some have ventured that the "she" is none other than "Mother Jones," the famous union organizer who sought to unionize the Appalachian mine workers, while others suppose the "she" might simply be a train coming down the tracks. But my putative adults singing it with religious fervor may actually have returned to the song's original source of inspiration, since according to musicologists "She'll Be Coming 'Round the Mountain" is loosely based on the Negro spiritual "When the Chariot Comes," which describes a series of events leading up to the *eschaton*.

47. This sense, incidentally, is often missed in translations of the famous description of Moses in Num. 12:7: he is the *ne'eman bayit*, the trusted slave who is, therefore, allowed to go into any room of the divine house.

48. I fear that, at this point, some of my learned readers may object that my description is one-sided. Surely there was more to Judaism in this period than seeking to do God's will. What, for example, of the whole period's apocalyptic temper and its yearning for the restoration of Israel's fortunes, a yearning that blossomed into the fervent messianism of later times and, with it, the rise of Christianity? With such observations I have no argument whatsoever. My point is not about Judaism but about Scripture, and here I think there is good reason to be fairly one-sided. It is true that the Dead Sea covenanters, for example, sometimes sought to read biblical prophecies, psalms, and even passages of the Pentateuch (the "Song of the Well" in Num. 21:17–18) as references to themselves and the events of their own day (the same is true of the first Christians). But I am quite sure that members of the Dead Sea Scrolls community would nonetheless have asserted that the primary purpose of Scripture was to tell people what God wished them to do: indeed, this community's overriding concern with legal exegesis hardly needs glossing. (Among many discussions: Sussman 1994: 179–200). The same is true of their rivals, the interpreters of *halakhot/halaqot* who led eventually to

rabbinic Judaism. Even Philo of Alexandria, whose main interest was in the allegorical interpretation of Scripture, devoted a hefty portion of his exposition to the practical application of the Pentateuch's laws. Josephus, although he alleges his purpose in writing the *Antiquiries* was to relate the Jewish nation's past, similarly could not refrain from giving Scripture's laws a lengthy and detailed exposition. More generally—for him as for Philo and *all* the interpreters mentioned—even the recounting of history or lofty ideas was closely tied to Scripture's essential part, its laws: "The main lesson to be learned from this history by any who care to peruse it," writes Josephus, "is that men who conform to the will of God, and do not venture to transgress laws that have been excellently laid down, prosper in all things beyond belief and are granted happiness by God as their reward" (*Ant.* 1:14). Beyond this point, however, I should make it clear that I am *not* claiming that carrying out God's laws is in fact the great, central theme of Scripture. Rather, it was the great, central theme that the ancient interpreters found in it. (Actually, Scripture is full of all sorts of things besides what-to-do—indeed, the apprehension of God underlying this view is hardly the only one found in Scripture.) Thus, the ancient interpreters were the first people to be guilty of searching for Scripture's *Mitte,* and this search was prompted by the specific apprehension of God that they had inherited from their forebears.

49. In so doing, interpreters were in a sense (though certainly not knowingly) following the same fast-and-loose approach to sacred utterances (not just the Pentateuch, but prophetic and historical writings as well) that had been followed by earlier editors and glossators and interpolators. This approach, in other words, has deep biblical roots. See Fishbane (1985:19).

50. True, one response to this question has been to assert that these changes were not the work of "mere humans" at all—that they were given by God to Moses on Mount Sinai, or (a somewhat different answer) that later, historical figures, from Ràshi to the late Rabbi Moshe Feinstein z"l, were guided by divine inspiration. The former position has not been without its problems: was Moses truly given the laws governing the holiday of Purim contained in the Mishnaic tractate *Megillah*, even though the events that were to inspire that holiday did not occur until centuries after Moses' death? And if they were given to him at that time, why was there no hint of them in the written text of the Torah, which otherwise does contain allusions to events far in the future as well as laws that could not be carried out at the time of their transmission? Moreover, while the Babylonian Talmud and other rabbinic texts sometimes assert that the Oral Torah goes back to Moses and is thus *not* interpretation but an independent body of teachings, this assertion is gainsaid on nearly every page of the Talmud by the question "Whence do we know this?"—that is, what is the verse in Scripture from which such-and-such a rabbinic teaching is derived? Such a question clearly implies the priority of Scripture as well as the derivative nature of the *halakhah* in question. The history of this assertion has been aptly explored in J. Harris (1995). As for the second response—that later interpreters were themselves divinely inspired—it may well be so; see below, note 54. However, numerous rabbinic texts specifically gainsay this approach, from the ancient interpretation of Deut. 30:11–14 ("It is not in heaven . . .")—on which see Kugel (1998: 846–48)—to the famous story of the oven of Achnai, whereby a heavenly voice is not permitted to overrule the decision of human authorities (b. *Baba Metzi'a* 59b).

51. In fact, a great deal of what constitutes God's service in Judaism today will be found to have little or nothing to do with Scripture. Religious Jews get up in the morning and recite obligatory prayers never mentioned in the Torah; they obey dietary laws strikingly different from the ones listed in Scripture; they wash their hands and recite blessings before eating, but this is not commanded in Scripture. Many Jews today attend *yeshivot* or other institutions of Jewish higher learning in which, as a matter of fact, not Scripture, but the Babylonian Talmud, is the main text studied. On Passover, although Scripture has unambiguously told them to rid their houses of any leaven or leavened product, a great many observant Jews spend the holiday—thanks to a post-biblical legal procedure that need not be detailed here—in the intimate company of significant quantities of such leaven. In all these ways and many more, it is possible to glimpse the "deep structure" (I know the metaphorical use of this term has become somewhat hackneyed nowadays, but here I mean it very much as Noam Chomsky first used it) underlying the surface expression of the Jewish allegiance to Torah. It is ulti-

mately not the words of Scripture themselves that are foremost in Judaism, but the idea that underlies them, namely, the service of God.

52. See on this Levinson (2005) as well as Kugel (2002: 139–51). I admit that the comparison is imperfect, but one might compare this circumstance to that of a foundational legal document of human origin, such as, for example, the U.S. constitution. New situations or particular cases soon arise that require the foundational document's lofty and revered words to become subject to the generally less lofty and revered interpretations and applications of subsequent generations. The fact that they are *not* the words of the Original Framer can hardly invalidate them; on the contrary, they are deemed to be the natural and necessary continuation of the trajectory establish by the original document, even when, as sometimes is the case, they go well beyond, or even contradict, what might be identified by others as the document's original intent.

53. See chapter 17, "Christianity and the Laws of the Bible": also Preus (1969).

54. See chapter 1, note 66.

55. "And God spoke *all* the[ese] words, saying 'I am the LORD your God . . . '" [Exod. 20:1]. Said Rabbi Isaac: "Even the things that the prophets were later to prophesy were likewise given to them at Mount Sinai. Whence do we know this? [From what God said later about His covenant with Israel,] 'Not with you alone do I conclude this covenant, but both with those who are standing here with us today [and with those who are not with us today]'" (Deut. 29:14–15). Someone who has already been created is someone who already exists in the world. But "those who are not" refers to those who are yet to be created, and thus are "not with us today." . . . Not only were the prophets [present at the covenant, although they were not yet born], but also all the sages who were yet to be [born were also present then]. Thus it says, "The LORD spoke all these words to your assembly with a mighty voice, and said no more [*we lo' yasap*]" (Deut. 5:19) [*Midrash Tanhuma, Yitro* 11]. God "said no more," this exegete claims, because there was essentially only one, great revelation in all of human history. The essential content of all the prophetic writings, and all the Oral Law, right down to yesterday's ruling by a Talmudic sage in Jerusalem or Monsey or Gateshead, was contained in the one great revelation at Mount Sinai. See, in somewhat the same spirit (and with a decidedly Conservative Jewish coloring), Milgrom (2000: 1368–71).

56. Cited in Hallo (1980: 1).

SUBJECT INDEX

Page numbers in *italics* refer to maps.

Aaron, *64n*, 224, 238, 246, 314, 331
  death of sons of, 289–90, 326–28
  Golden Calf incident and, 281–83,
    315, 525
  Korah's jealousy of, 329
  meaning of name of, 205
  in Rephidim battle, 234, 236
Aaronide priesthood, *64n*, 289–90,
  313–14, 314, 315
  Korah's revolt and, 330, 334
Abel, as foreshadowing of Jesus, 21,
  127, 643
  see also Cain and Abel narrative
Abiathar, 500, 575, 604
Abigail, 501
Abihu, 246, 289–90, 326–28
Abijah, 327–28
Abimelech, 62, 103, 375, 460
Abiram, 101, 330, 331, 333–34
Abishag the Shunammite, 499–501,
  518
Abner, 452, 482, 483, 484
abortion, 266–69
m. *Abot*, 275, 283, 352
Abot deR. Natan, 277, 338, 544
Abraham, 11–22, 25, 62, 90–106, 210,
  216, 242, 298, 356, 358, 360,
  361, 563, 655, 660, 676, 682
  ancient interpreters and, 11–17,
    90–95, 120–21, 122, 124–25,
    490, 518
  and binding of Isaac, 11–14, 20–21,
    109, 121–28, 361
  circumcision covenant, 146, 301,
    649

covenant made with God, 39
David compared with, 501
departure from Mesopotamia of,
  18–19, 30, 90–92, 96, 100, 101,
  102, 113–14, 120, 648, 649–50
early Christian interpretation of
  binding of Isaac, 17, 20, 21, 37,
  126–28
in Egypt, 120, 128–29, 132, 184
in encounters with angels, 110,
  113–14
faithfulness of, 20, 121–23, 128, 649
as first monotheist, 17, 90, 92–96,
  103, 121, 148, 518, 680
foreshadowed events of New Testament and, 20, 21, 37, 126–28,
  278
genealogy of, 158
God's call to, 90–92, 94, 649–50
grant of land to, 103–6
Hagar expelled by, 120, 121, 407
historicity of, 96–101, 377
Jacob loved by, 138
largely absent from prophetic writings, 102
modern biblical scholars and,
  96–103, 128–29
name change of, 101, 159
and search for wife for Isaac, 97,
  153–54, 166
ten trials of, 11–13, 100, 119–32
wealth of, 129, 132
  see also Sarah
Abraham and offering of Isaac, 11–16,
  109, 121–28, 361

773

VERSES CITED